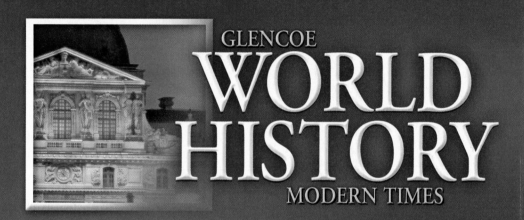

GLENCOE
WORLD HISTORY
MODERN TIMES

JACKSON J. SPIELVOGEL, PH.D.

NATIONAL GEOGRAPHIC

Glencoe

New York, New York   Columbus, Ohio   Chicago, Illinois   Woodland Hills, California

ABOUT THE COVER

Main image: Pyramid entrance to the Louvre in France
Top images (left to right): Luisa Diogo, Mozambique's prime minister; Napoleon Bonaparte; Anwar el-Sadat, former Egyptian president; Mao Zedong; Eva Perón, former first lady of Argentina

The McGraw·Hill Companies

 Glencoe

Copyright © 2008 by The McGraw-Hill Companies, Inc. All rights reserved. Except as permitted under the United States Copyright Act, no part of this publication may be reproduced or distributed in any form or by any means, or stored in a database or retrieval system, without prior permission of the publisher.

The name "National Geographic Society" and the Yellow Border Rectangle are trademarks of the National Geographic Society and their use, without prior written permission, is strictly prohibited.

TIME Notebook © TIME Inc. Prepared by TIME Learning Ventures in collaboration with Glencoe/McGraw-Hill. TIME and the red border design are trademarks of TIME Inc., and used under license.

Send all inquiries to:
Glencoe/McGraw-Hill
8787 Orion Place
Columbus, OH 43240-4027

ISBN: 978-0-07-874527-0
MHID: 0-07-874527-6

Printed in the United States of America.

1 2 3 4 5 6 7 8 9 10 071/055 12 11 10 09 08 07

AUTHORS

JACKSON J. SPIELVOGEL

Jackson J. Spielvogel is associate professor emeritus of history at The Pennsylvania State University. He received his Ph.D. from The Ohio State University, where he specialized in Reformation history under Harold J. Grimm. His articles and reviews have appeared in such journals as *Moreana, Journal of General Education, Archiv für Reformationsgeschichte,* and *American Historical Review.* He has also contributed chapters or articles to *The Social History of the Reformation, The Holy Roman Empire: A Dictionary Handbook, Simon Wiesenthal Center Annual of Holocaust Studies,* and *Utopian Studies.* His book *Hitler and Nazi Germany* was published in 1987 (fifth edition, 2005). His book *Western Civilization* was published in 1991 (sixth edition, 2006). He is the co-author (with William Duiker) of *World History,* published in 1994 (fifth edition, 2007). Professor Spielvogel has won five major university-wide teaching awards, and in 1997, he became the first winner of the Schreyer Institute's Student Choice Award for innovative and inspiring teaching.

NATIONAL GEOGRAPHIC

The National Geographic Society, founded in 1888 for the increase and diffusion of geographic knowledge, is the world's largest nonprofit scientific and educational organization. Since its earliest days, the Society has used sophisticated communication technologies, from color photography to holography, to convey geographic knowledge to a worldwide membership. The School Publishing Division supports the Society's mission by developing innovative educational programs—ranging from traditional print materials to multimedia programs including CD-ROMs, videos, and software.

CONTRIBUTING AUTHOR

Dinah Zike, M.Ed., is an award-winning author, educator, and inventor known for designing three-dimensional hands-on manipulatives and graphic organizers known as Foldables™. Foldables are used nationally and internationally by teachers, parents, and educational publishing companies. Dinah has developed over 150 supplemental educational books and materials. She is the author of *The Big Book of Books and Activities,* which was awarded Learning Magazine's Teachers' Choice Award. In 2004 Dinah was honored with the CESI Science Advocacy Award. Dinah received her M.Ed. from Texas A&M, College Station, Texas.

CONSULTANTS & REVIEWERS

Academic Consultants

Jeremy Baskes, Ph.D.
Associate Professor
Department of History
Ohio Wesleyan University
Delaware, Ohio

David Berger, Ph.D.
Broeklundian Professor of History
Brooklyn College and the
   Graduate Center
City University of New York
Brooklyn, New York

Stephen F. Dale, Ph.D.
Professor
Department of History
The Ohio State University
Columbus, Ohio

Steven Gish, Ph.D.
Distinguished Research Professor
Department of History
Auburn University Montgomery
Montgomery, Alabama

Richard Golden, Ph.D.
Professor of History and Director,
   Jewish Studies Program
University of North Texas
Denton, Texas

Lyman Johnson, Ph.D.
Professor
Department of History
The University of North Carolina
   at Charlotte
Charlotte, North Carolina

Lisa Lindsay, Ph.D.
Associate Professor
Department of History
The University of North Carolina
   at Chapel Hill
Chapel Hill, North Carolina

Farid Mahdavi, Ph.D.
Lecturer
Department of History
San Diego State University
San Diego, California

Guy Welbon, Ph.D.
Emeritus Associate Professor
Department of South Asia Studies
Universtiy of Pennsylvania
Philadelphia, Pennsylvania

Teacher Reviews

Maggie Favretti
Scarsdale High School
Scarsdale, New York

Jane McGrigor Forde
Needham B. Broughton High School
Raleigh, North Carolina

Carl Hansen
Hilton High School
Hilton, New York

Lee Holder
North Lenoir High School
LaGrange, North Carolina

Thomas J. Lawson
McCluer High School
Florissant, Missouri

Laura Delmore Lay
James River High School
Midlothian, Virginia

Christopher M. Lee
West Memphis High School
West Memphis, Arkansas

Rosanne Lichatin
West Morris Central High School
Chester, New Jersey

Donald V. Morabito
Great Valley High School
Malvern, Pennsylvania

Donald Perreault
Valley Regional High School
Deep River, Connecticut

Richard J. Shaw
Cleveland High School
Cleveland, Tennessee

Christina M. Smith
Algonquin Regional High School
Northborough, Massachusetts

Kathleen H. Stokes
Cherokee High School
Marlton, New Jersey

Denise Tanner
Friendswood High School
Friendswood, Texas

Michele Roussel Wasson
North Little Rock High School,
   East Campus
North Little Rock, Arkansas

CONTENTS

Understanding the Big Ideas	xx
Scavenger Hunt	xxii

NATIONAL GEOGRAPHIC

REFERENCE ATLAS — A1

World: Political	A2
World: Physical	A4
North America: Political	A6
North America: Physical	A7
South America: Political	A8
South America: Physical	A9
Europe: Political	A10
Europe: Physical	A12
Africa: Political	A14
Africa: Physical	A15
Asia: Political	A16
Asia: Physical	A18
Pacific Rim: Physical/Political	A20
World's People	A22
World Population Cartogram	A24
Geographic Dictionary	A26

THEMES AND ELEMENTS — GH1
GEOGRAPHIC SKILLS HANDBOOK — GH2

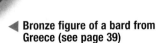
◀ Bronze figure of a bard from Greece (see page 39)

THE WORLD BEFORE MODERN TIMES,
Prehistory–A.D. 500 — **1**

CHAPTER 1
The First Civilizations and Empires, Prehistory–A.D. 500 — **2**

1	The First Humans	4
2	Western Asia and Egypt	10
3	India and China	22

CHAPTER 2
Ancient Greece and Rome, 1900 B.C.–A.D. 500 — **36**

1	Ancient Greece	38
2	Rome and the Rise of Christianity	48

CHAPTER 3
Regional Civilizations, 400–1500 — **88**

1	The World of Islam	90
2	Early African Civilizations	98
3	The Asian World	106
4	Europe and the Byzantine Empire	118

CHAPTER 4
Toward a New World, 800–1500 — **130**

1	Europe in the Middle Ages	132
2	The Americas	144

UNIT 2

THE EARLY MODERN WORLD, *1350–1815*　**158**

CHAPTER 5
Renaissance and Reformation, 1350–1600　**160**
1 The Renaissance	162
2 Ideas and Art of the Renaissance	170
3 The Protestant Reformation	176
4 The Spread of Protestantism	182

CHAPTER 6
The Age of Exploration, 1500–1800　**192**
1 Exploration and Expansion	194
2 The Atlantic Slave Trade	204
3 Colonial Latin America	208

CHAPTER 7
Crisis and Absolutism in Europe, 1550–1715　**216**
1 Europe in Crisis: The Wars of Religion	218
2 Social Crises, War, and Revolution	222
3 Response to Crisis: Absolutism	228
4 The World of European Culture	236

CHAPTER 8
The Muslim Empires, 1450–1800　**246**
1 The Ottoman Empire	248
2 The Rule of the Ṣafavids	256
3 The Grandeur of the Moguls	262

CHAPTER 9
The East Asian World, 1400–1800　**272**
1 China at Its Height	274
2 Chinese Society and Culture	280
3 Tokugawa Japan and Korea	284
4 Spice Trade in Southeast Asia	290

CHAPTER 10
Revolution and Enlightenment, 1550–1800　**300**
1 The Scientific Revolution	302
2 The Enlightenment	310
3 The Impact of the Enlightenment	318
4 The American Revolution	330

CHAPTER 11
The French Revolution and Napoleon, 1789–1815　**338**
1 The French Revolution Begins	340
2 Radical Revolution and Reaction	350
3 The Age of Napoleon	360

◀ Catherine II (Catherine the Great) ruled Russia from 1762 to 1796 (see page 321)

CONTENTS

UNIT 3

AN ERA OF EUROPEAN IMPERIALISM, *1800–1914* — 374

CHAPTER 12
Industrialization and Nationalism, 1800–1870 — *376*
- 1 The Industrial Revolution — 378
- 2 Reaction and Revolution — 388
- 3 National Unification and Nationalism — 394
- 4 Romanticism and Realism — 402

CHAPTER 13
Mass Society and Democracy, 1870–1914 — *414*
- 1 The Growth of Industrial Prosperity — 416
- 2 The Emergence of Mass Society — 422
- 3 The National State and Democracy — 430
- 4 Toward the Modern Consciousness — 438

CHAPTER 14
The Height of Imperialism, 1800–1914 — *448*
- 1 Colonial Rule in Southeast Asia — 450
- 2 Empire Building in Africa — 456
- 3 British Rule in India — 466
- 4 Nation Building in Latin America — 472

CHAPTER 15
East Asia Under Challenge, 1800–1914 — *486*
- 1 The Decline of the Qing Dynasty — 488
- 2 Revolution in China — 496
- 3 Rise of Modern Japan — 502

UNIT 4

THE TWENTIETH-CENTURY CRISIS, *1914–1945* — **518**

CHAPTER 16
War and Revolution, 1914–1919 — *520*
- 1 The Road to World War I — 522
- 2 World War I — 526
- 3 The Russian Revolution — 536
- 4 End of World War I — 542

CHAPTER 17
The West Between the Wars, 1919–1939 — *552*
- 1 The Futile Search for Stability — 554
- 2 The Rise of Dictatorial Regimes — 560
- 3 Hitler and Nazi Germany — 568
- 4 Cultural and Intellectual Trends — 576

CHAPTER 18
Nationalism Around the World, 1914–1939 — *584*
- 1 Nationalism in the Middle East — 586
- 2 Nationalism in Africa and Asia — 592
- 3 Revolutionary Chaos in China — 600
- 4 Nationalism in Latin America — 608

CHAPTER 19
World War II, 1939–1945 — *618*
- 1 Paths to War — 620
- 2 The Course of World War II — 628
- 3 The New Order and the Holocaust — 638
- 4 Home Front and Aftermath of War — 644

UNIT 5

TOWARD A GLOBAL CIVILIZATION,
1945–Present   **660**

CHAPTER 20
Cold War and Postwar Changes, 1945–1970   **662**
1 Development of the Cold War   664
2 The Soviet Union and Eastern Europe   674
3 Western Europe and North America   678

CHAPTER 21
The Contemporary Western World, 1970–Present   **692**
1 Decline of the Soviet Union   694
2 Eastern Europe   700
3 Europe and North America   704
4 Western Society and Culture   710

CHAPTER 22
Latin America, 1945–Present   **722**
1 General Trends in Latin America   724
2 Mexico, Cuba, and Central America   730
3 The Nations of South America   736

CHAPTER 23
Africa and the Middle East, 1945–Present   **748**
1 Independence in Africa   750
2 Conflict in the Middle East   760

CHAPTER 24
Asia and the Pacific, 1945–Present   **774**
1 Communist China   776
2 Independent States in Asia   782
3 Japan and the Pacific   788

CHAPTER 25
Changing Global Patterns   **800**
1 Challenges of a New Century   802
2 New Global Communities   812

REFERENCE SECTION

Mini Almanac   R1
Foldables   R6
Skills Handbook   R12
Primary Sources and Literature Library   R32
English and Spanish Glossary   R58
Index   R83
Acknowledgements and Photo Credits   R104

◀ The Mothers of the Plaza de Mayo demonstrate in Buenos Aires, Argentina (see page 738).

FEATURES

ANALYZING PRIMARY SOURCES

What was the Role of Religion in Aztec Society?	150
Who Should Be a Citizen?	358
Describing the Lives of Workers in The Early 1800s	386
What Were the Causes of World War II?	626
What Challenges did Apartheid Create for South Africans	768

PEOPLE in HISTORY

Socrates	45
Plato	45
Julius Ceasar	51
Augustus	51
Hildegard of Bingen	137
St. Francis of Assisi	137
Leonardo da Vinci	174
Michelangelo	174
Erasmus	178
Martin Luther	178
Henry VIII	184
Sir Thomas More	184
King Alfonso I	206
Charles I	226
Oliver Cromwell	226
Süleyman the Magnificent	252
Voltaire	313
Adam Smith	313
Frederick II (Frederick the Great)	320
Maria Theresa	320
Catherine II (Catherine the Great)	321
Denis Diderot	321
Jean-Paul Marat	352
Maximillien Robespierre	352
Otto von Bismarck	398
Giuseppe Garibaldi	398
Queen Liliuokalani	435
Herbert Spencer	442
Theodor Herzl	442
Saya San	454
Cecil Rhodes	460
Shaka Zulu	460
Mohandas K. "Mahatma" Gandhi	470
Rabindranath Tagore	470
José de San Martín	474
Simón Bolívar	474
Guang Xu	492
Ci Xi	492
Sun Yat-sen	498
General Yuan Shigai	498
Georges Clemenceau	545
John Maynard Keynes	558
Nikita Krushchev	675
Jomo Kenyatta	752
Kwame Nkrumah	752
Indira Gandhi	784
Mother Teresa of Kolkata	784

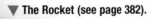

▼ The Rocket (see page 382).

NATIONAL GEOGRAPHIC GEOGRAPHY & HISTORY

The Indian Ocean Trade	104
Ottoman Empire in the 1450s	254
Africa on the Eve of Colonialism	464
Normandy Invasion, June 6, 1944	636
Germany, 1950–1961	672

CONNECTING TO THE UNITED STATES

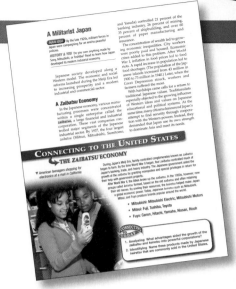

Jewish Traditions 18
Migration and Diversity 198
The Rights of the People 240
Civil Liberties and Social Justice 258
The Martial Arts 288
Guaranteed Freedoms 332
Revolutionary Ideas 342
Louisiana Purchase 362
Nursing and Public Health 400
Women's Rights 425
Made in Japan 505
The Influenza Epidemic of 1918 532
Mass Culture Then and Now 578
The *Zaibatsu* Economy 598
The U.S. Holocaust Memorial Museum 642
The American Women's Movement 684
A Growing Hispanic American Population 728

Terrorism in the U.S. 766
Japanese Anime in the U.S. 791
Homeland Security 810

TIME NOTEBOOK

Unit 1   The First Civilizations and Empires 66
Unit 1   New Patterns of Civilization 156
Unit 2   The Early Modern World 372
Unit 3   An Era of European Imperialism 516
Unit 4   The Twentieth-Century Crisis 658
Unit 5   Toward a Global Civilization 822

SCIENCE, TECHNOLOGY, & SOCIETY

Gutenberg's Press 166
Technology and Exploration 197
The Scientific Method 308
The Power of Steam 382
The Automobile: Technology that Changed the Global Landscape 418
The New Technology of World War I 528
Satellite Communications 803

POLITICAL CARTOONS   PRIMARY SOURCE

The Seven Years' War in North America 324
France's Three Estates 341
Evaluating the Terror 356
The Estates-General forging a new constitution 371
The Irish Potato Famine 384
Political Reform in Great Britain 398
William II Fires Bismarck 436
Women's Suffrage 447
The New Imperialism 453
The Clemency of Canning 467

The Monroe Doctrine and Roosevelt Corollary 477
Open Door Policy 494
Before the Russo-Japanese War 515
Let Sam Do It 527
Chamberlain and Mussolini 583
John Bull hated to drop his bundle 617
The Nazi-Soviet Nonaggression Pact 623
The Cuban Missile Crisis 670
Global Warming 821

Social History

Early Housing 8
Games of Death in Ancient Rome 60
Life in Genghis Khan's Army 116
The Black Death 142
Renaissance Society 168
Is it New World or Old World 202
A Palace Fit for the Sun King 234
The Safavids: At the Crossroads of Trade
   and of History 260
Kabuki: A New World of Entertainment 294
The 18th Century Salon 328
A Revolution in Clothing 348
A Showcase for Industry and Progress 408
At Home in London, 1890 430
Indochina: French Colonialism in Vietnam 480
Sumo Wresting: The Sport of Giants 510
Technology and Trench Life Define Total War 534
Hitler Youth: The Future of a Doomed State 574
The Two Chinas of the 1930s 606

The Blitz: London's Finest Hour 652
Popular Culture of the 50s and 60s 686
Rock and Roll Around the World 716
Teenage Life in Argentina 742
Teenagers in Nigeria 758
Teenagers in Tokyo Today 794

HISTORY & ARTS   PRIMARY SOURCE

The Standard of Ur 12
Hieroglyphics 17
Stupas Show Spread of Buddhism 25
Art in the Dark Ages 39
Polis: The Center of Greek Life 40
Roman Life 52
The Great Mosque of Sāmarrā' 96
Hindu Temple at Khajuraho 112
Gothic Architecture 138
Patronage of the Medici Family 165
Dante's Divine Comedy 171
Differences in Renaissance Art 172
Louis XIV and Absolutism 229
St. Peter's Basilica 237
Topkapi Palace 251
The Rule of Akbar 264
Ming Porcelain 282
Japanese and European Feudalism 286
The Dutch at Batavia 292
Rococo Style 326
Tennis Court Oath 343

The King Concedes 344
The Fate of the King 351
The Coronation of the Emperor Napoleon I 361
The Overthrow of King Louis Philippe 391
Romanticism: The Prisoner of Chillon 403
A Romantic Response to Industrialization 404
Realism in the Visual Arts 406
Marx and the Class Struggle 420
Leisure 428
Impressionists and Postimpressionists 439
The Opium War 491
China's Changing Culture 500
The Westernization of Japan 506
Assassination of Francis Ferdinand 524
The Treaty of Versailles 546
The Destruction of Guernica 566
Nazi Propaganda Film 577
The Armenian Genocide 588
The Political Art of Diego Rivera 612
The Final Solution at Auschwitz 641

TURNING POINT

Neolithic Revolution 6
The Rule of Merit 30
Pericles Expands Athenian Democracy 42
The Spread of Christianity in the Roman Empire 57
The Battle of Tours 95
The Bantus Spread Ironworking 102
Japanese Isolation 111
The Magna Carta 121
Luther's Ninety-five Theses 180
The Columbian Exchange and International Trade 200
Defeat of the Spanish Armada 219
The British Gain Control of India 266
The Isolation of China 278
The Scientific Revolution 306

Spreading the Principles of the Revolution 364
Industrialization Transforms Society 381
Freud: In Search of the Unconscious 441
Japan Becomes an Imperial Power 508
The Russian Revolution 539
Political Effects of the Great Depression 557
Gandhi and Nonviolence 597
Hiroshima, Nagasaki, and the Nuclear Age 649
The Spread of the Cold War 668
The Collapse of the Soviet Union 697
The Panama Canal Treaty 734
The End of Apartheid in South Africa 755
The Vietnam War 786

INFOGRAPHIC

Change comes to India's Civilization 23
Dynastic Cycles and the Mandate of Heaven 28
The Great Wall of China in History and Legend 29
Roman Law 54
The Justinian Code 123
Organization of a Manor 133
Hundred Years' War 140
The Pyramid of Kukulcan 146
The Encomienda System 210
Witchcraft Hysteria 223
The Globe Theatre 239
Economic Changes in China 281
Laissez-Faire Economics 314
John Wesley Brings a New Message of Salvation 316
Britain's Suffragists 427
The Suez Canal Opens for Business 458
The Great Rebellion in India 467
The Mexican Revolution 478
The Sinking of the Lusitania 530
Communism in Russia 540
Fascism in Italy 553
The Message of Nazism 569
Himmler and the SS 571
Kristallnacht or "Night of Shattered Glass" 572
The Balfour Declaration 590
Ho Chi Minh: Vietnam's Communist Leader 595
The Long March: Mao Zedong's Rise to Power 602
China's New Life Movement 604

Selected Nationalist Movements in the
 Early Twentieth Century 610
D-Day: June 6, 1944 634
The Home Front in World War II 645
Japanese Internment in the United States 646
The Berlin Airlift 667
A Comparison of Market and Command Economies 675
Political Change in Postwar Germany 680
The Civil Rights Act of 1964 and the Voting Rights Acts 683
Challenges for the New Russia 698
The Fall of the Berlin Wall 702
North African Immigration to France 706
The United States at War 708
Technology and the Environment 711
Women in the Workforce 712
Fidel Castro's Cuban Revolution 732
The Mothers of the Plaza de Mayo 738
Liberation Theology: A New Role for
 the Catholic Church 740
Africa's Colonial Legacy 756
Peacemakers in the Middle East 764
Communism Under Deng Xiaoping 779
The Continuing Role of the United Nations in Korea 792
The Global AIDS Epidemic 805
Destruction of Tropical Rain Forests 807
Women Entrepreneurs of the Developing World 808
UNESCO and World Literacy 813
Economic Interdependence 815
The UN Millennium Development Goals 816

PRIMARY SOURCE
QUOTES

UNIT 1
The World Before Modern Times

Chapter 1 The First Civilizations and Empires
Isaiah 2:4   19
Isaiah 3:14–17, 24–26   19
King Ashurbanipal, on his treatment of prisoners   20
Confucius, on importance of the family   31

Chapter 2 Ancient Greece and Rome
Plato, *The Republic, Book II*   44
Mark 12:30–31   55

Chapter 3 Regional Civilizations
Marco Polo, on conditions in China   108
Magna Carta   121
Excerpts from *The Body of Civil Law*   123

Chapter 4 Toward a New World
Saint Bernard of Clairvaux, on Cistercian monasticism   136
Observer describing reaction to the Black Death   139
Prayer to Aztec god   150
Hernán Cortés, description of Aztec temple   150

UNIT 2
The Early Modern World

Chapter 5 Renaissance and Reformation
Baldassare Castiglione, from *The Book of the Courtier*   166
A Venice Merchant, on the poor   167
Dante Alighieri, on not writing in Latin   171
Christine de Pizan, on the nature of women   172
Vittorino de Feltre, on intellectual pursuits   173
Martin Luther's Ninety-five Theses   180
Niccolò Machiavelli, from *The Prince*   191

Chapter 6 The Age of Exploration
Dutch trader, on the slave trade   207
Bartolomé de las Casas, *A Brief Account of the Destruction of the Indies*   210
German Tourist, on the effects of missionaries in Latin America   211
Christopher Columbus, reporting on his first journey   215

Chapter 7 Crisis and Absolutism in Europe
Excerpts on Witchcraft, *Malleus Maleficarum*   223
Jaques-Benigne Bossuet, on the divine right of kings   229
Louis XIV of France, on his own absolute power   229
William Shakespeare, from *As You Like It*   239
Queen Elizabeth I, The Golden Speech   245

Chapter 8 The Muslim Empires
Akbar the Great, on conquest   264
Traveler, on the lives of Indian people of the Mogul Empire   271

Chapter 9 The East Asian World
Ferdinand Verbiest, on Chinese Emperor Kangxi   278
Emperor Qianlong, on China's "closed country" policy   278
Chinese Woman, on the status of women in China   282
Lord Tokitaka, on how to use a firearm   285
King George III, letter to the Chinese Emperor   299

Chapter 10 Revolution and Enlightenment
Cardinal Bellarmine, on Holy Scripture   305
Galileo Galilei, on scientific truths   305
Margaret Cavendish, on the idea of humans as the masters of nature   307
Gottfried Kirch, on his wife Maria Winklemann's discovery of a comet   307
René Descartes, *Discourse on Method*   308
Francis Bacon, on the scientific method   308
John Locke, *Essay Concerning Human Understanding*   310
George Washington, diary excerpt on the precursor to the French and Indian War   314

Chapter 11 The French Revolution and Napoleon
An English Traveler, on the misery of French peasants   338
Olympe de Gouges, from *Declaration of the Rights of Women and the Female Citizen*   345
An observer, on the beginning of the war with Austria   347
Philipe Pinel, describing the execution of Louis XVI in a letter   351
Henri de Firmont, describing the execution of Louis XVI   352
A German Observer, on the French Revolution   353
Maximillien Robespierre, on virtue and terror   353
Committee of Public Safety, mobilization decree   355
William Wordsworth, from *The Prelude, Book X, Residence in France*   356

Maximillien Robespierre, on Citizenship 358
Etta Palm d'Aelders, from "The Injustices of the
    Laws and Favor of Men at the Expense of Women" 358
Napoleon Bonaparte, on spreading the principles of
    the French Revolution 364
Napoleon Bonaparte, advising his brother Jerome,
    the new King of Westphalia 371

UNIT 3
An Era of European Imperialism

Chapter 12 Industrialization and Nationalism
British Parliamentary Report on Child Labor 380
Miner Betty Harris on British mining conditions 386
Friedrich Engels on industrial Manchester 386
"Carding, Drawing, and Roving" by Edward Baines 387
Mary Shelley, about her monster in Frankenstein 404
William Wordsworth, from "The Tables Turned," 405

Chapter 13 Mass Society and Democracy
Guglielmo Marconi, reporting discovery of radio waves 417
Karl Marx and Friedrich Engels. The Communist
    Manifesto 420
Alfred Lord Tennyson, on the Marriage Ideal
    in The Princess 426
Emmeline Pankhurst, on efforts of women to vote 427
Description of massacre of petitioners of
    Czar Nicholas II 447

Chapter 14 The Height of Imperialism
Senator Albert Beveridge, on U.S. colonialism in Asia 453
Rudyard Kipling, from The White Man's Burden 462
Edward Morel, from The Black Man's Burden 462
King Lobengula, letter to Queen Victoria 463
Thomas Macaulay, on the English language 468
Rabindranath Tagore, on India 471
Miguel Hidalgo, on Independence in Mexico 473

Chapter 15 East Asia Under Challenge
Zhang Zhidong, arguing against political reforms 488
Lin Zexu, from a Letter to Queen Victoria 490
Emperor William II of Germany, on the Boxer Rebellion 495
Ba Jin, on Writing 501

UNIT 4
The Twentieth-Century Crisis

Chapter 16 War and Revolution
German Ambassador at Vienna, on the Assassination
    of Francis Ferdinand 524
H.G. Wells, on War Technology 528
"War Girls," poem, on jobs for women 533
V.I. Lenin, on the goals of the Bolsheviks 539
V.I. Lenin, remarks to the Congress of Soviets, 1920 540
Erich Ludendorff, on the Second Battle of the Somme 543
Alfred von Wegerer, on the Treaty of Versailles 546
British Ambassador to Vienna, on the
    potential for war 551

Chapter 17 The West Between the Wars
Benito Mussolini, "The Doctrine of Fascism" 562
Francisco Franco declares an end to
    the Spanish Civil War 567
Excerpt from a Hitler Youth Handbook 569
Adolf Hitler, demanding allegiance of
    all Germans 570
Heinrich Himmler, "Lecture on the Nature and
    Tasks of the SS" 571
SS Officer Reinhard Heydrich, Kristallnacht Directive 572
Adolf Hitler, on power 583

Chapter 18 Nationalism around the World
Eyewitness account of the Armenian Deportation 588
Enver Pasha, on the Young Turks campaign
    against Armenians 588
Harry Thuku, on European authority in Kenya 594
Jomo Kenyatta, on the struggle for African Culture 594
Ho Chi Minh, from The Path which led me
    to Leninism 595
Mohandas K. Gandhi, Non-Violence (Satyagraha) 597
Mao Zedong, on the Long March 602
Participant Li Xiannian on the Long March 603
Sun Yat-sen, on China's transition 603
Madame Chiang Kai-Shek, on China's New Life
    Movement 604
Sun Fo, expressing disapproval of the Nanjing
    Government 605
Gunther Gerzso on his Art 613
Mao Zedong, calling for massive peasant revolt 617

Chapter 19 *World War II*

Dr. G.P. Gooch on the Threat of War 626
Victor Klemperer, diary excerpts on German Power 626
English Skipper Len Deighton, on the
   Evacuation of Dunkirk 629
Adolf Hitler, on the war with the Soviet Union 633
Death squad leader, on the Einsatzgruppen 640
Filip Müller, Auschwitz prisoner 641
California Governor Culbert Olson,
   on Japanese Internment 646
Rudolf Höss, on the experience of Jews at Auschwitz 657

UNIT 5
Toward a Global Civilization

Chapter 20 *Cold War and Postwar Changes*

Dean Acheson, on the Cold War 666
Adviser to President Kennedy on the
   Bay of Pigs Invasion 670
Nikita Khrushchev, on the Cuban Missile Crisis 670
President Dwight Eisenhower, on Postwar Politics 681
Bob Dylan, "The Times They Are A-Changin'," 691

Chapter 21 *The Contemporary Western World*

Boris Yeltsin, on the challenges of the New Russia 698
Economist E.F. Schumacher, on evolving lifestyle 721

Chapter 22 *Latin America*

Architect Oscar Niemeyer, describing his work
   in Brasília 729
An observer's account of the U.S. invasion of Panama 747

Chapter 23 *Africa and the Middle East*

Nelson Mandela, opening statement at the
   Rivonia Trial 755
Tunde Obadina, on industrialization in Africa 756
King Hussein of Jordan, on making peace with Israel 764
Humphrey Taylor, on massacre of demonstrators
   in South Africa 773

Chapter 24 *Asia and the Pacific*

Wei Jingsheng, "The Fifth Modernization" 779
Japanese Women, 1955 799

Chapter 25 *Challenges and Hopes*

The United Nations, from the Universal
   Declaration of Human Rights 809
Domitila Barrios de Chungara, on Equality
   for women in Bolivia 809
Kofi Annan, on the UN Millennium Development Goals 816
Hazel Henderson, on Grassroots Organizations 817
Rachel Carson, on use of pesticides, from
   Silent Spring 821

PRIMARY SOURCE LIBRARY

An Egyptian Father's Advice to His Son R34
The Burning of Books R35
Plague in Athens R35
From The Illiad R36
Muhammad's Wife Remembers the Prophet R38
A Woman May Need to Have the Heart of a Man R39
The Buddha's Sermon R39
Five Poems R40
A Reformation Debate R42
The Silk Industry in China R43
Declaration of the Rights of Women and the
   Female Citizen R43
From Candide R44
Imperial Decree to Free the Serfs R46
The Unfortunate Situation of Working Women R47
The Impact of British Rule in India R47
From Shooting an Elephant R48
Over the Top—World War I R50
Gandhi Takes the Path of Civil Disobedience R51
The Holocaust—The Camp Victims R51
From A Room of One's Own R52
Progress Never Stops R54
An Ideal for Which I am Prepared to Die R55
China's Gilded Age R55
Civil Peace, from Girls at War and Other Stories R56

Charts, Graphs, & Tables

UNIT 1

The Four Noble Truths	25
The Eightfold Path	25
Early Dynasties of China	28
Dynastic Cycle	28
Twelve Tables of Rome, 449 B.C.	54
Constantine's Contribution to the Spread of Christianity	57
The Five Pillars of Islam	92
Two Centers of Trade in Africa	99
The Body of Civil Law (The Justinian Code)	123

UNIT 2

Roman Catholic, Lutheran, Calvinist, and Anglican Beliefs	186
Top Ten Organized Religions of the World (2004 estimates)	191
Native American Population	209
Ethnic Groups of Mexico, 2007	215
Changes Made by Peter the Great	245
Expansion of the Ottoman Empire, 1451–1566	271
Chinese Population Growth	281
Comparing Feudalism	286
Major Explorers	299
Views of Astronomy	306
Three Estates in Pre-Revolutionary France	341
Percentage of Victims of the Terror by Class	356
Napoleon's Family & his Empire (1799–1812)	364
Napoleon's 1812 Russian Campaign	366

UNIT 3

Estimated Population of England, 1750–1851	379
American Civil War Casualties (1861–1865)	412
Nineteenth-Century Urban Dwellers	446
Major Regions of European Control	453
Troops Employed in British India, 1857	467
Height of European Imperialism	485
Opium Imported into China	491
Japan's Foreign Trade, 1878–1917	503
Significance of the Russo-Japanese War of 1904–1905	508

UNIT 4

Estimated Army Size, 1914	523
United States War Casualties	551
Unemployment, 1928–1938	557
Soviet Industry	565
Great Depression in Latin America	609
Jewish Population in Europe before and after World War II	639
Mobilization for War	645
U.S. Unemployment Rates	657

UNIT 5

Major Developments in the Cold War, 1947–1973	668
Comparison of Market and Command Economies	675
Marshall Plan Aid, 1948–1951	679
Percentage of People Without Health Insurance (United States, 2006)	691
The Former Soviet Republics	697
Key Events in the European Union	705
Percentage of Women in the Workforce	712
U.S. Government Budget Deficit	721
Population of Latin America, 1950–2020	725
Gross Domestic Product per Capita	725
Growing Hispanic Population in the United States, 1990–2050	728
U.S. Agricultural Trade with NAFTA Partners, 1989–2002	747
Arab-Israeli Relations	761
Religion in India, 2001	783
Foundations of Postwar Japan	789
Projection of World Population (based on 1995–2000 levels)	799

MINI ALMANAC

World Population, A.D. 1–2001	R2
Population by Continent, 2005	R2
Life Expectancy	R2
Infant Mortality	R2
Most Populous Countries	R2
World's Richest Countries	R3
World's Poorest Countries	R3
Highest Inflation Rates	R3
Lowest Inflation Rates	R3
World's Ten Largest Companies, 2000	R3
Most Livable Countries	R4
Highest Adult Literacy Rates	R4
Lowest Adult Literacy Rates	R4
Lowest Inflation Rates	R4
Years, by Country, in Which Women Gained the Right to Vote	R4
Highest Military Expenditures	R5
Nuclear Weapons Capability	R5
Communication Around the World	R5

MAPS

NATIONAL GEOGRAPHIC

REFERENCE ATLAS

World: Political	A2
World: Physical	A4
North America: Political	A6
North America: Physical	A7
South America: Political	A8
South America: Physical	A9
Europe: Political	A10
Europe: Physical	A12
Africa: Political	A14
Africa: Physical	A15
Asia: Political	A16
Asia: Physical	A18
Pacific Rim: Physical/Political	A20
World's People	A22
World Population Cartogram	A24
Geographic Dictionary	A26

UNIT 1

Evidence of Early Humans	**5**
Spread of Farming	6
Ancient Mesopotamia	**11**
"City of Ur"	11
The Geography of Ancient Egypt	15
The Persian Empire, 500 B.C.	20
Trade Routes of the Ancient World	26
Building the Great Wall	**29**
The Empire of Alexander the Great, 323 B.C.	46
Punic Wars, 264–146	49
End of the Roman Empire, A.D. 200–500	58
Southwest Asia in Muhammad's Time, c. 600	91
Spread of Islam, 632–750	**94**
Arab Campaigns into France	95
The Kingdoms of Kush and Axum	99
Trade in West Africa, 800–1500	**100**
Indian Ocean Trade	104
Mongol Empire, 1294	109
Southeast Asia, 1200	114
New Germanic Kingdoms, A.D. 500	119
The Crusades	124
Medieval Trade Routes	134
Hundred Years' War	140
Cultures of Mesoamerica, 900 B.C.–A.D. 1500	145
Cultures of South America, A.D. 700–1500	148

UNIT 2

Renaissance Italy, 1500	**163**
Europe after the Peace of Augsburg, 1555	177
European Religions, 1600	183
Holy Roman Empire, 1400	190
European Voyages of Discovery	195
Atlantic Slave Trade, 1500s–1600s	205
Colonial Latin America to 1750	209
Routes of Cortés, 1519–1525	215
Height of Spanish Power under Philip II, c. 1560	219
Route of the Spanish Fleet, 1588	**220**
Europe after the Peace of Westphalia	224
Expansion of Prussia and Austria to 1720	**231**
Expansion of Russia, 1505–1725	**232**
Thirty Years' War, 1618–1648	244
Expansion of the Ottoman Empire to 1699	**249**
Ottoman Empire in the 1450s	254
Şafavid Empire, 1501–1722	**257**
Expansion of the Mogul Empire 1530–1707	**263**
The British in India	270
China Under the Ming and Qing Dynasties, 1368–1911	**275**
Voyages of Zheng He, 1405–1433	277
Japan and Korea, 1560–1600	**285**
Religions and Cultures of Southeast Asia, 1500	291
Southeast Asia, 1700	298
Intellectuals of the Scientific Revolution	**303**
Europe and the Age of Enlightenment	311
Enlightened Absolutism	**319**
The Seven Years' War, 1756–1763	323
The French and Indian War, 1754–1763	324
Land Claims After the American Revolution, 1783	331
Seven Years' War in the West Indies	337
Napoleonic Europe, 1799–1812	**364**
Disaster in Russia	366
Reign of Terror	370

UNIT 3

Industry in Great Britain by 1850	**379**
Europe after the Congress of Vienna, 1815	389
Nationalities in Austria-Hungary, mid-1800s	392
Unification of Italy and Germany	**395**
Revolutions in Europe, 1848–1849	413
Industrialization of Europe by 1914	**417**
European Population Growth and Relocation, 1820–1900	**423**
Europe, 1871	433
Imperialism in Southeast Asia, 1900	451
Imperialism in Africa, 1880–1914	**457**
Africa on the Eve of Colonialism	464
British Possessions in India, 1858–1914	**469**
European Colonies in Latin America	**473**
Travel Distance (and the Panama Canal)	484
Spheres of Influence in China, 1900	489
Fall of the Qing Empire	**497**
Japanese Expansion, 1870–1918	**503**
Japanese Expansion, 1873–1910	514

UNIT 4

Alliances in Europe, 1914	523
World War I in Europe, 1914–1918	**527**
Russian Revolution and Civil War, 1917–1922	537
Europe and the Middle East after World War I	543
Middle East in World War I, 1914–1918	550
Europe, 1923	555
Politics in Europe, 1930's	**561**
Soviet Union by 1939	565
Spanish Civil War, 1936–1939	582
Middle East, 1919–1935	**587**
Africa, 1919–1939	**593**
China, 1926–1937	601
Latin America, 1939	609
Japanese Expansion, 1910–1933	616
German and Italian Expansion, 1935–1939	**621**
Japanese Expansion, 1933–1941	**624**
World War II in Europe and North Africa, 1939–1941	**629**
World War II in Europe and North Africa, 1941–1945	630
World War II in Asia and the Pacific, 1941–1945	**632**
D-Day: The Five Beaches	634
Normandy Invasion, June 6, 1944	636
Major Nazi Death Camps	639
Japan, 1945	649
Europe after World War II	650
German-Controlled Territory, 1943	656

UNIT 5

Balance of Power after World War II	**665**
Divided Germany and the Berlin Airlift	667
Germany, 1950–1961	672
European Economic Community, 1957	679
Cuban Missile Crisis, 1962	690
Breakup of the Soviet Union, 1991	**695**
Eastern Europe: The Transition from Communism	701
Expansion of the European Union, 1957–2007	705
Regional Identity in Western Europe	714
Former Yugoslavia, 1991–1999	720
Main Latin American Exports in the 1990s	725
Major Developments in Latin America since 1945	727
Hispanic Population by State, 2000	728
Political Events in Mexico, Central America, and the Caribbean	731
The Panama Canal	734
Political Events in South America	**737**
Population of Latin America, 2000	746
Independent Africa	751
Arab-Israeli Disputes	**761**
Modern Middle East	762
Israel and Israeli-Occupied Territory	772
China Since 1945	777
Korean War, 1950–1953	**780**
Partition of India, 1947	**783**
Vietnam War, 1968–1975	**786**
Modern Japan	789
Indochina, 1946–1954	798
People Living with HIV, 2006	805
Percentage of Population That Is Literate	813
Radioactive Fallout from Chernobyl, 1986	820

Maps In Motion See *StudentWorks*™ *Plus* or glencoe.com.

Maps labeled with the In Motion icon have been specially enhanced on the StudentWorks™ Plus CD-ROM and on glencoe.com. These In Motion maps allows you to interact with layers of displayed data and to listen to audio components.

Entries in blue indicate In Motion maps.

UNDERSTANDING THE BIG IDEAS

World history is the story of the human community—how people lived on a daily basis, how they shared ideas, how they ruled and were ruled, and how they fought. As you read, you will see a number of "big ideas" or broad themes behind world history events. These big ideas are described below.

▶ Order and Security
Throughout history, people and governments have tried to resolve conflicts and establish order and security.
People have sought ways to protect themselves from danger and uncertainty. To provide for their security, people have created communities, nations, and organizations. To help provide order, people have created laws and economic systems.

▶ Ideas, Beliefs, and Values
Ideas, beliefs, and values have resulted in distinct societies and political systems.
Throughout history, people have sought to find a deeper meaning to human life. Religion, cultural values, and codes of ethics have always influenced social customs, laws, and forms of government.

▶ Physical Geography
Physical geography influences the development of culture and trade.
People and societies have been affected by the physical world in which they exist. In turn, human activities have had a profound impact on the world.

▶ Self-Determination
The quest for national self-determination is universal.
Free will is the cornerstone of humanity. People unite as a nation because they believe that independence is essential to freedom—and that freedom is essential to leading a full life.

▶ Struggle for Rights
Throughout history, people have struggled for rights.

The struggle for rights has been reflected in struggles for the vote, for economic freedom, for personal liberties, and for national independence. There are few nations in the world whose history has not been marked by a struggle for rights among its people.

▶ New Technologies
New technologies bring changes that can be both positive and negative for societies.

For thousands of years, people have made scientific discoveries and technological innovations that have changed the world. New discoveries can bring benefits, or pose new dangers, to the world.

▶ Devastation of War
War causes immeasurable devastation.

Wars have always meant destruction and disruption to some level. In the modern period, wars usually have brought greater devastation than in earlier epochs. Genocide and ethnic cleansing have also characterized the wars of the twentieth century. Recovering from such losses is costly, and the desire for revenge or triumph can color the attitudes of an entire generation.

▶ Competition Among Countries
Countries compete for natural resources and strategic advantages over other countries.

Competition among nations has led to the development of stable economies in some cases, but also to the depletion of economies in others. Strong economies tend to mean stronger governments, and this provides a sense of safety for citizens.

▶ Human Rights
A totalitarian system violates human rights in pursuit of power.

By definition, the totalitarian state smothers the individuality of its citizens. This system seeks to control political, economic, social, intellectual, and cultural areas of life and does so through propaganda and through force.

Using the BIG IDEAS

You will find BIG IDEAS listed at the beginning of each section in the text. Use these clues to help you preview the material you are about to read. You can also use the BIG IDEAS to compare and contrast how different peoples and societies dealt with similar issues.

SCAVENGER HUNT

Glencoe World History contains a wealth of information. The trick is to know where to look to access all the information in the book. If you run through this scavenger hunt exercise with your teachers or parents, you will see how the textbook is organized, and how to get the most out of your reading and study time. Let's get started!

1 How many chapters and how many units are in the book?

2 What time period does Unit 2 cover?

3 On what pages is the time line for Chapter 24?

4 In what two places can you find the Content Vocabulary for Section 2 of Chapter 6?

5 Where can you find a map on imperialism in Africa?

6 How are the Academic Vocabulary words for Section 3 of Chapter 12 indicated in the narrative?

7 The Web site has six activities for each chapter. The first previews the chapter. The second has activities. The third has quizzes. What do the others do?

8 Where do you look if you want to quickly find all the maps in the book?

9 Most sections of a chapter include primary sources from the time in the narrative. Where else can you find extended primary sources in the textbook?

10 Where can you learn the definition of a physical map, a political map, and a thematic map?

REFERENCE ATLAS

NATIONAL GEOGRAPHIC

World: Political	A2	Africa: Political	A14
World: Physical	A4	Africa: Physical	A15
North America: Political	A6	Asia: Political	A16
North America: Physical	A7	Asia: Physical	A18
South America: Political	A8	Pacific Rim: Physical/Political	A20
South America: Physical	A9	World's People	A22
Europe: Political	A10	World: Population Cartogram	A24
Europe: Physical	A12	Geographic Dictionary	A26

ATLAS KEY

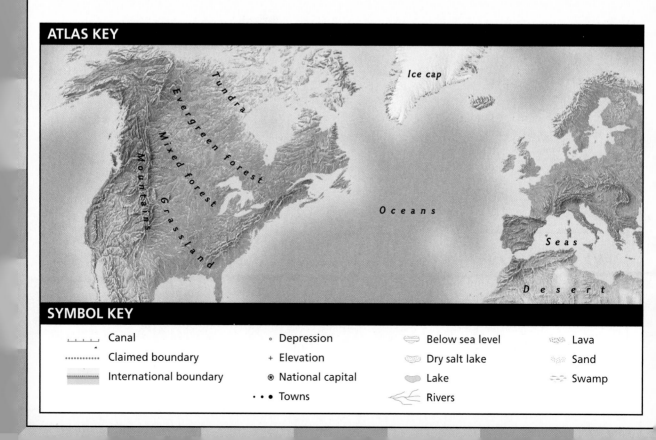

SYMBOL KEY

Canal	∘ Depression	Below sea level	Lava
Claimed boundary	+ Elevation	Dry salt lake	Sand
International boundary	⊛ National capital	Lake	Swamp
	• • Towns	Rivers	

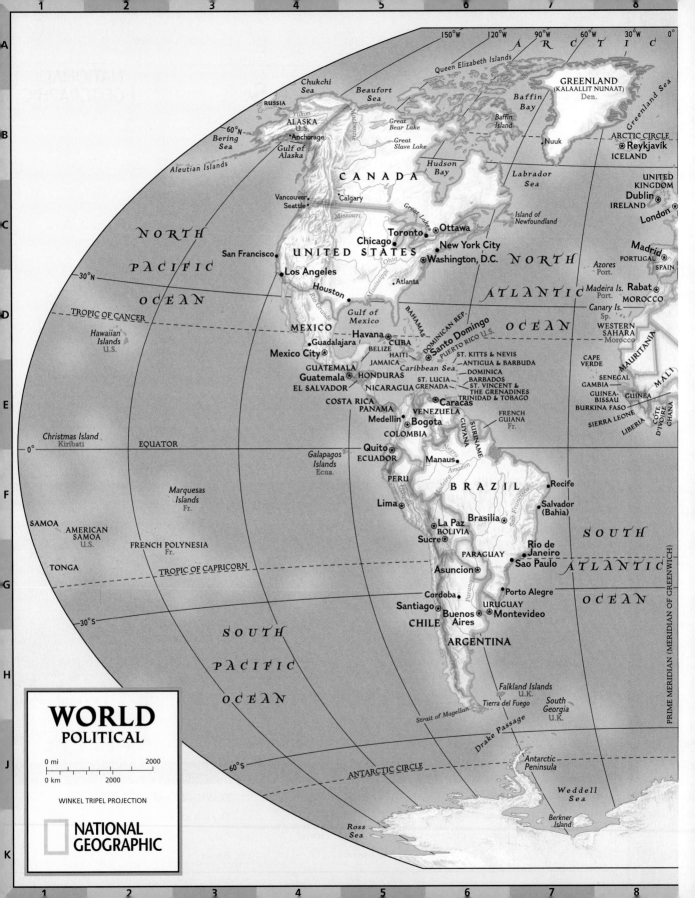

WORLD
POLITICAL

0 mi ———————— 2000
0 km ———————— 2000

WINKEL TRIPEL PROJECTION

NATIONAL
GEOGRAPHIC

ARCTIC

Queen Elizabeth Islands

GREENLAND
(KALAALLIT NUNAAT)
Den.

Chukchi Sea

Beaufort Sea

RUSSIA

Yukon

ALASKA
U.S.

Anchorage

60°N

Bering Sea

Gulf of Alaska

Aleutian Islands

Mackenzie

Great Bear Lake

Great Slave Lake

Baffin Bay

Baffin Island

Nuuk

Greenland Sea

ARCTIC CIRCLE

Reykjavík
ICELAND

Hudson Bay

Labrador Sea

UNITED KINGDOM

Dublin
IRELAND

London

CANADA

Island of Newfoundland

Vancouver
Seattle

Calgary

Great Lakes

Missouri

Toronto
Ottawa

Chicago

New York City
Washington, D.C.

NORTH

Madrid
PORTUGAL
SPAIN

Azores
Port.

NORTH

San Francisco

UNITED STATES

Ohio

Los Angeles

30°N

Houston

Atlanta

Mississippi

ATLANTIC

Madeira Is.
Port.

Rabat
MOROCCO

PACIFIC

Rio Grande

Gulf of Mexico

Canary Is.
Sp.

WESTERN
SAHARA
Morocco

TROPIC OF CANCER

Hawaiian Islands
U.S.

OCEAN

MEXICO

Havana

CUBA

BAHAMAS

DOMINICAN REP.

Santo Domingo

PUERTO RICO
U.S.

OCEAN

CAPE
VERDE

MAURITANIA

MALI

Guadalajara

Mexico City

HAITI

JAMAICA

ST. KITTS & NEVIS

ANTIGUA & BARBUDA

SENEGAL

GAMBIA

GUINEA-
BISSAU

GUINEA

BELIZE

GUATEMALA

Guatemala
HONDURAS

EL SALVADOR
NICARAGUA

Caribbean Sea

DOMINICA

ST. LUCIA
BARBADOS
ST. VINCENT &
GRENADA THE GRENADINES

TRINIDAD & TOBAGO

BURKINA FASO

SIERRA LEONE

LIBERIA

CÔTE
D'IVOIRE

GHANA

COSTA RICA
PANAMA

Caracas

Medellin

VENEZUELA

Bogota

COLOMBIA

GUYANA

SURINAME

FRENCH
GUIANA
Fr.

NORTH

0°

EQUATOR

Christmas Island
Kiribati

Galapagos Islands
Ecua.

Quito
ECUADOR

Manaus

Negro

Amazon

Madeira

PERU

B R A Z I L

Recife

São Francisco

Marquesas Islands
Fr.

SAMOA

AMERICAN
SAMOA
U.S.

Lima

La Paz
BOLIVIA

Sucre

Brasilia

Salvador
(Bahia)

SOUTH

FRENCH POLYNESIA
Fr.

TONGA

TROPIC OF CAPRICORN

PARAGUAY

Rio de
Janeiro

Sao Paulo

ATLANTIC

Asuncion

Porto Alegre

Parana

30°S

Cordoba

Santiago

SOUTH

URUGUAY

Buenos
Aires

Montevideo

OCEAN

CHILE

ARGENTINA

PACIFIC

Falkland Islands
U.K.

Tierra del Fuego

South Georgia
U.K.

OCEAN

Strait of Magellan

Drake Passage

60°S

ANTARCTIC CIRCLE

Antarctic
Peninsula

Weddell Sea

Berkner Island

Ross Sea

150°W 120°W 90°W 60°W 30°W 0°

PRIME MERIDIAN (MERIDIAN OF GREENWICH)

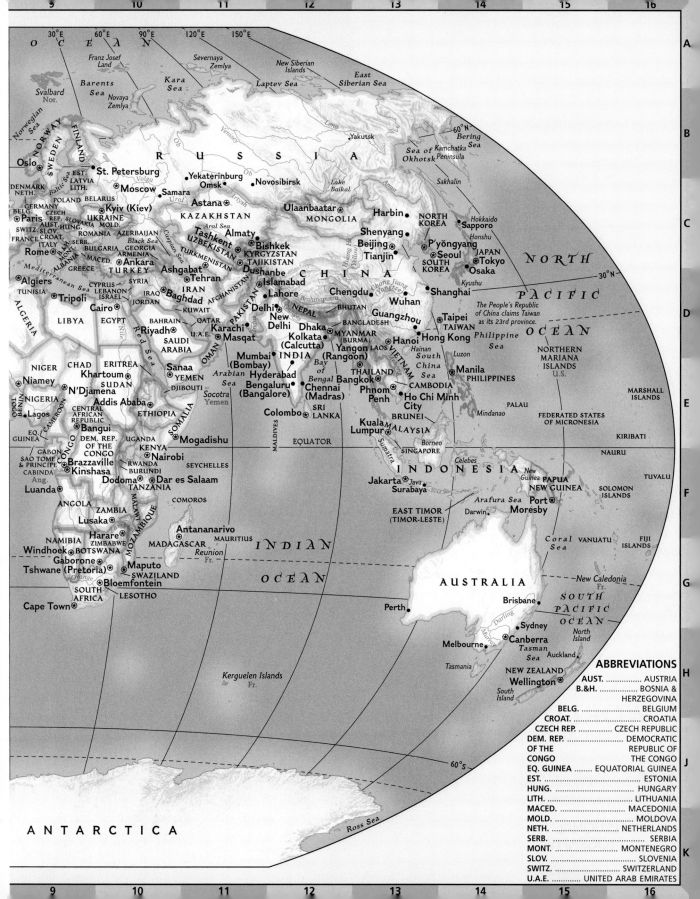

9   **10**   **11**   **12**   **13**   **14**   **15**   **16**

30°E   60°E   90°E   120°E   150°E

O C E A N

Franz Josef Land

Barents Sea

Svalbard Nor.

Novaya Zemlya

Severnaya Zemlya

Kara Sea

New Siberian Islands

Laptev Sea

East Siberian Sea

60°N

Bering Sea

Kamchatka Peninsula

Norwegian Sea

Lena

Yakutsk

NORWAY

SWEDEN

FINLAND

Oslo

Baltic Sea

R U S S I A

Sea of Okhotsk

Sakhalin

St. Petersburg

Volga

Ob

Yekaterinburg

Omsk

Novosibirsk

Ob

Irtysh

Hokkaido

Sapporo

Moscow

Samara

Ural

Astana

Ulaanbaatar

Harbin

NORTH KOREA

Honshu

DENMARK

NETH.

GERMANY

BELG.

Paris

CZECH REP.

SWITZ.

FRANCE

ITALY

Rome

POLAND BELARUS

Kyiv (Kiev)

UKRAINE

SLOVAKIA HUNG.

AUST.

SLOV.

CROAT.

B.H. SERB.

MONT.

ALBANIA MACED.

GREECE

ROMANIA

BULGARIA

MOLD.

KAZAKHSTAN

Aral Sea

Tashkent

Almaty

Bishkek

MONGOLIA

Shenyang

Beijing

Tianjin

P'yŏngyang

Seoul

SOUTH KOREA

JAPAN

Tokyo

Osaka

Kyushu

N O R T H

P A C I F I C

30°N

Mediterranean Sea

Algiers

TUNISIA

Tripoli

Black Sea

GEORGIA

ARMENIA

AZERBAIJAN

Ankara

TURKEY

CYPRUS

LEBANON

ISRAEL

SYRIA

IRAQ

Baghdad

JORDAN

Caspian Sea

UZBEKISTAN

TURKMENISTAN

Ashgabat

Tehran

IRAN

KYRGYZSTAN

TAJIKISTAN

Dushanbe

Islamabad

AFGHANISTAN

Lahore

PAKISTAN

C H I N A

Huang He Yellow

Chengdu

Chang Jiang Yangtze

Wuhan

Guangzhou

Shanghai

Taipei

TAIWAN

Hong Kong

O C E A N

The People's Republic of China claims Taiwan as its 23rd province.

ALGERIA

LIBYA

EGYPT

Cairo

Nile

Red Sea

BAHRAIN

QATAR

U.A.E.

Riyadh

SAUDI ARABIA

KUWAIT

OMAN

Karachi

Masqat

Delhi

New Delhi

NEPAL

Brahmaputra

BHUTAN

BANGLADESH

Dhaka

Kolkata (Calcutta)

MYANMAR (BURMA)

Yangon (Rangoon)

Hanoi

LAOS

Hainan

South China Sea

Luzon

Manila

PHILIPPINES

NORTHERN MARIANA ISLANDS U.S.

Philippine Sea

MARSHALL ISLANDS

NIGER

CHAD

SUDAN

ERITREA

Khartoum

N'Djamena

YEMEN

Sanaa

DJIBOUTI

Socotra Yemen

Arabian Sea

Mumbai (Bombay)

Hyderabad

I N D I A

Bengaluru (Bangalore)

Chennai (Madras)

Bay of Bengal

Bangkok

THAILAND

VIETNAM

Phnom Penh

CAMBODIA

Ho Chi Minh City

PALAU

Mindanao

FEDERATED STATES OF MICRONESIA

KIRIBATI

NIGER

BENIN

NIGERIA

Lagos

CAMEROON

CENTRAL AFRICAN REPUBLIC

Bangui

EQ. GUINEA

GABON

SAO TOME & PRINCIPE

CABINDA Ang.

Addis Ababa

ETHIOPIA

SOMALIA

Mogadishu

UGANDA

KENYA

Nairobi

RWANDA

BURUNDI

Colombo

SRI LANKA

MALDIVES

EQUATOR

Kuala Lumpur

MALAYSIA

BRUNEI

SINGAPORE

Borneo

NAURU

TUVALU

Luanda

ANGOLA

Congo

DEM. REP. OF THE CONGO

Brazzaville

Kinshasa

TANZANIA

Dodoma

Dar es Salaam

SEYCHELLES

COMOROS

I N D O N E S I A

Jakarta

Java

Surabaya

Celebes

Sumatra

Arafura Sea

Darwin

New Guinea

PAPUA NEW GUINEA

Port Moresby

SOLOMON ISLANDS

ZAMBIA

Lusaka

Harare

ZIMBABWE

NAMIBIA

BOTSWANA

Windhoek

Gaborone

Tshwane (Pretoria)

MADAGASCAR

Antananarivo

MAURITIUS

Reunion Fr.

I N D I A N

O C E A N

EAST TIMOR (TIMOR-LESTE)

Coral Sea

VANUATU

New Caledonia Fr.

FIJI ISLANDS

MALAWI

MOZAMBIQUE

Orange

SWAZILAND

Maputo

SOUTH AFRICA

LESOTHO

Bloemfontein

Cape Town

A U S T R A L I A

Perth

Darling

Murray

Brisbane

Sydney

S O U T H

P A C I F I C

O C E A N

North Island

Melbourne

Canberra

Tasman Sea

Auckland

NEW ZEALAND

Wellington

South Island

Tasmania

Kerguelen Islands Fr.

60°S

A N T A R C T I C A

Ross Sea

ABBREVIATIONS

AUST.	AUSTRIA
B.&H.	BOSNIA & HERZEGOVINA
BELG.	BELGIUM
CROAT.	CROATIA
CZECH REP.	CZECH REPUBLIC
DEM. REP. OF THE CONGO	DEMOCRATIC REPUBLIC OF THE CONGO
EQ. GUINEA	EQUATORIAL GUINEA
EST.	ESTONIA
HUNG.	HUNGARY
LITH.	LITHUANIA
MACED.	MACEDONIA
MOLD.	MOLDOVA
NETH.	NETHERLANDS
SERB.	SERBIA
MONT.	MONTENEGRO
SLOV.	SLOVENIA
SWITZ.	SWITZERLAND
U.A.E.	UNITED ARAB EMIRATES

9   **10**   **11**   **12**   **13**   **14**   **15**   **16**

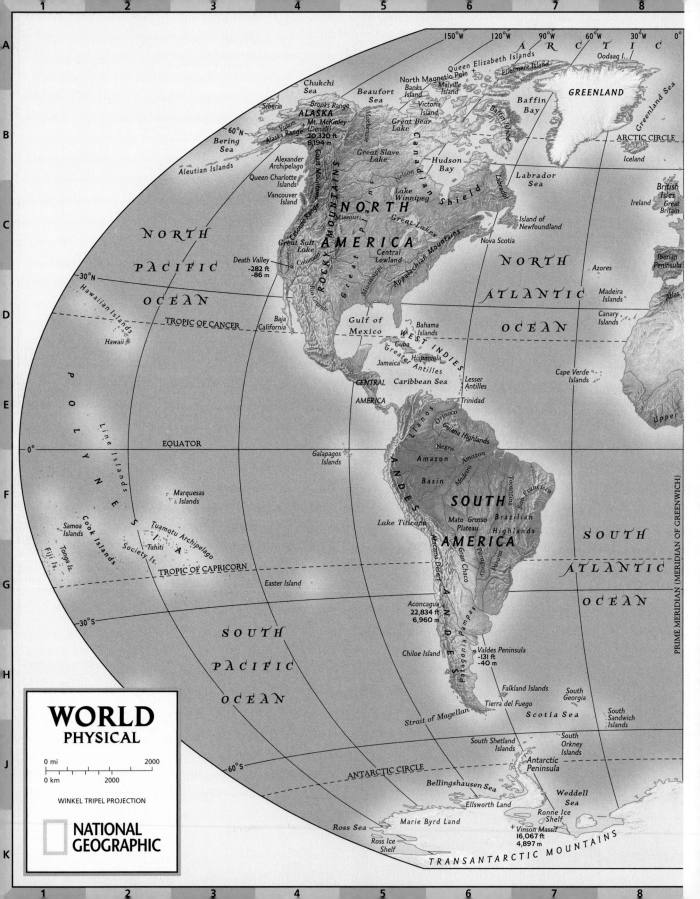

WORLD
PHYSICAL

0 mi ————————— 2000
0 km ————————— 2000

WINKEL TRIPEL PROJECTION

NATIONAL
GEOGRAPHIC

NORTH PACIFIC OCEAN

NORTH AMERICA

SOUTH AMERICA

SOUTH PACIFIC OCEAN

NORTH ATLANTIC OCEAN

SOUTH ATLANTIC OCEAN

ARCTIC

GREENLAND

POLYNESIA

ARCTIC CIRCLE

30°N

TROPIC OF CANCER

EQUATOR

TROPIC OF CAPRICORN

30°S

ANTARCTIC CIRCLE

60°S

60°N

0°

150°W · 120°W · 90°W · 60°W · 30°W · 0°

PRIME MERIDIAN (MERIDIAN OF GREENWICH)

Chukchi Sea
Siberia
Bering Sea
ALASKA
Brooks Range
Yukon
Alaska Range
Mt. McKinley (Denali) 20,320 ft 6,194 m
Aleutian Islands
Alexander Archipelago
Queen Charlotte Islands
Vancouver Island
Coast Mountains
Cascade Range
ROCKY MOUNTAINS
Great Salt Lake
Colorado
Great Basin
Death Valley -282 ft -86 m
Rio Grande
Baja California
Gulf of Mexico
CENTRAL AMERICA
Great Plains
Missouri
Central Lowland
Mississippi
Appalachian Mountains
Beaufort Sea
Mackenzie
Great Bear Lake
Great Slave Lake
Lake Winnipeg
Nelson
Canadian Shield
Hudson Bay
Great Lakes
Labrador
North Magnetic Pole
Banks Island
Victoria Island
Melville Island
Baffin Island
Queen Elizabeth Islands
Ellesmere Island
Oodaaq I.
Baffin Bay
Labrador Sea
Island of Newfoundland
Nova Scotia
Greenland Sea
ARCTIC CIRCLE
Iceland
British Isles
Ireland
Great Britain
Iberian Peninsula
Azores
Madeira Islands
Atlas
Canary Islands
Cape Verde Islands
Upper
WEST INDIES
Bahama Islands
Cuba
Jamaica
Hispaniola
Greater Antilles
Lesser Antilles
Caribbean Sea
Trinidad
Hawaiian Islands
Hawaii
Line Islands
Marquesas Islands
Samoa Islands
Cook Islands
Tonga Is.
Fiji Is.
Society Is.
Tahiti
Tuamotu Archipelago
Easter Island
Galapagos Islands
ANDES
Llanos
Orinoco
Guiana Highlands
Negro
Amazon
Amazon Basin
Madeira
Tocantins
São Francisco
Mato Grosso Plateau
Brazilian Highlands
Lake Titicaca
Atacama Desert
Gran Chaco
Paraguay
Paraná
Pampas
Patagonia
Aconcagua 22,834 ft 6,960 m
Chiloe Island
Valdes Peninsula -131 ft -40 m
Strait of Magellan
Tierra del Fuego
Falkland Islands
South Georgia
Scotia Sea
South Sandwich Islands
South Orkney Islands
South Shetland Islands
Antarctic Peninsula
Bellingshausen Sea
Ellsworth Land
Marie Byrd Land
Ross Sea
Ross Ice Shelf
Weddell Sea
Ronne Ice Shelf
Vinson Massif 16,067 ft 4,897 m
TRANSANTARCTIC MOUNTAINS

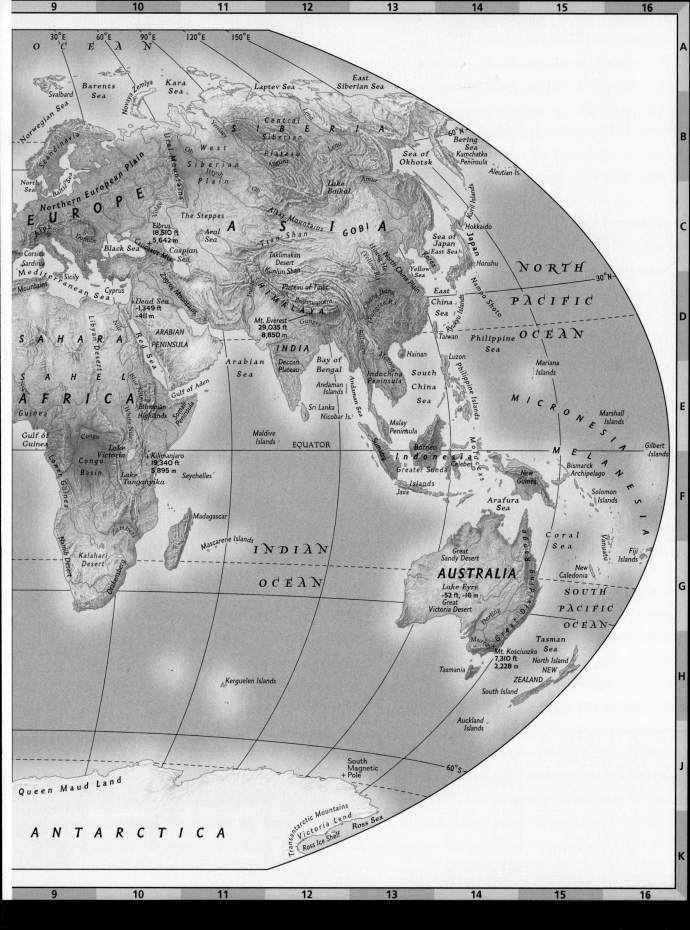

O C E A N
30°E 60°E 90°E 120°E 150°E

Svalbard
Barents
Sea
Novaya Zemlya
Kara
Sea
Laptev Sea
East
Siberian Sea

Norwegian Sea
Scandinavia
Yenisey
C e n t r a l
S i b e r i a n
P l a t e a u
60°N
Bering
Sea
Kamchatka
Peninsula
Aleutian Is.

North
Sea
Baltic Sea
Northern European Plain
Ural Mountains
Ob
W e s t
S i b e r i a n
P l a i n
Irtysh
Lena
Angara
Amur
Sea of
Okhotsk
Kuril Islands

E U R O P E
Volga
A S I A
The Steppes
Ob
Lake
Baikal
Hokkaido

Alps
Corsica
Sardinia
Danube
Elbrus
18,510 ft
5,642 m
Aral
Sea
Caspian
Sea
Altay Mountains
Tian Shan
G O B I
Sea of
Japan
(East Sea)
Japan
Honshu
30°N

Mediterranean Sea
Sicily
Black Sea
Caucasus Mts.
Zagros Mountains
Taklimakan
Desert
Kunlun Shan
Huang He (Yellow R.)
North China Plain
Korea
Yellow
Sea
North
Pacific

Mountains
Cyprus
Dead Sea
-1,349 ft
-411 m
ARABIAN
PENINSULA
Indus
H I M A L A Y A
Plateau of Tibet
Brahmaputra
Chang Jiang
(Yangtze R.)
East
China
Sea
Ryukyu Islands
Nampo Shoto
30°N

S A H A R A
Libyan Desert
Red Sea
Nile
Arabian
Sea
Deccan
Plateau
Ganges
Mt. Everest
29,035 ft
8,850 m
I N D I A
Salween
Taiwan
Philippine
Sea
P A C I F I C

S A H E L
Blue Nile
White Nile
Ethiopian
Highlands
Gulf of Aden
Somali Peninsula
Maldive
Islands
Bay of
Bengal
Andaman
Islands
Hainan
Luzon
Mariana
Islands
O C E A N

A F R I C A
Guinea
Niger
Sri Lanka
Nicobar Is.
Andaman Sea
Indochina
Peninsula
South
China
Sea
Mekong
Philippine Islands
M I C R O N E S I A
Marshall
Islands

Gulf of
Guinea
Congo
Lower Guinea
Congo
Basin
Lake
Victoria
Kilimanjaro
19,340 ft
5,895 m
Seychelles
Malay
Peninsula
Sumatra
EQUATOR
Borneo
Indonesia
Celebes
Moluccas
New
Guinea
Bismarck
Archipelago
M E L A N E S I A
Gilbert
Islands

Lake
Tanganyika
Greater Sunda
Islands
Java
Arafura
Sea
Solomon
Islands

Zambezi
Madagascar
Mascarene Islands
I N D I A N
Coral
Sea
Vanuatu
Fiji
Islands

Namib Desert
Kalahari
Desert
Drakensberg
O C E A N
Great
Sandy Desert
AUSTRALIA
Lake Eyre
-52 ft, -16 m
Great
Victoria Desert
Great Dividing Range
New
Caledonia
S O U T H

P A C I F I C

O C E A N

Darling
Murray
Mt. Kosciuszko
7,310 ft
2,228 m
Tasman
Sea
North Island
NEW

Kerguelen Islands
Tasmania
ZEALAND
South Island

Auckland
Islands

60°S
South
Magnetic
Pole

Queen Maud Land
Transantarctic Mountains
Victoria Land
Ross Ice Shelf
Ross Sea

A N T A R C T I C A

A B C D E F G H J K

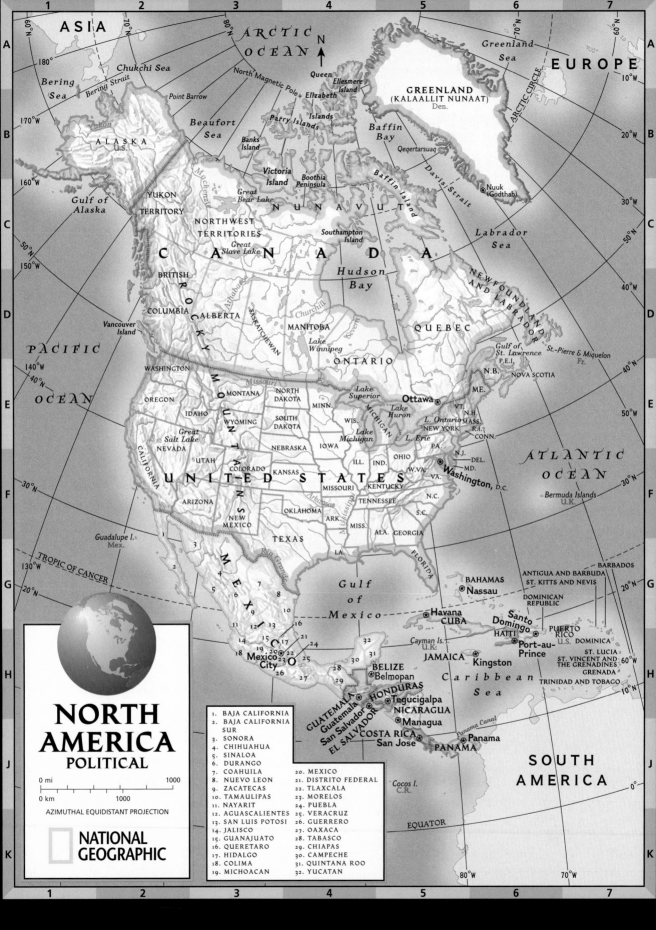

NORTH AMERICA
POLITICAL

0 mi   1000

0 km   1000

AZIMUTHAL EQUIDISTANT PROJECTION

NATIONAL GEOGRAPHIC

1. BAJA CALIFORNIA
2. BAJA CALIFORNIA SUR
3. SONORA
4. CHIHUAHUA
5. SINALOA
6. DURANGO
7. COAHUILA
8. NUEVO LEON
9. ZACATECAS
10. TAMAULIPAS
11. NAYARIT
12. AGUASCALIENTES
13. SAN LUIS POTOSI
14. JALISCO
15. GUANAJUATO
16. QUERETARO
17. HIDALGO
18. COLIMA
19. MICHOACAN
20. MEXICO
21. DISTRITO FEDERAL
22. TLAXCALA
23. MORELOS
24. PUEBLA
25. VERACRUZ
26. GUERRERO
27. OAXACA
28. TABASCO
29. CHIAPAS
30. CAMPECHE
31. QUINTANA ROO
32. YUCATAN

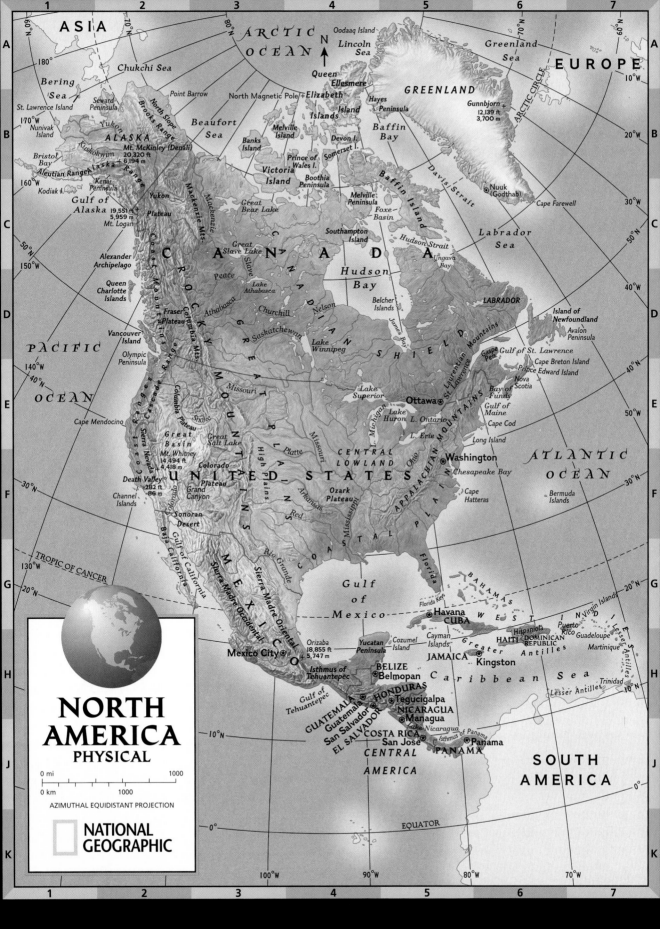

NORTH AMERICA
PHYSICAL

0 mi   1000

0 km   1000

AZIMUTHAL EQUIDISTANT PROJECTION

NATIONAL GEOGRAPHIC

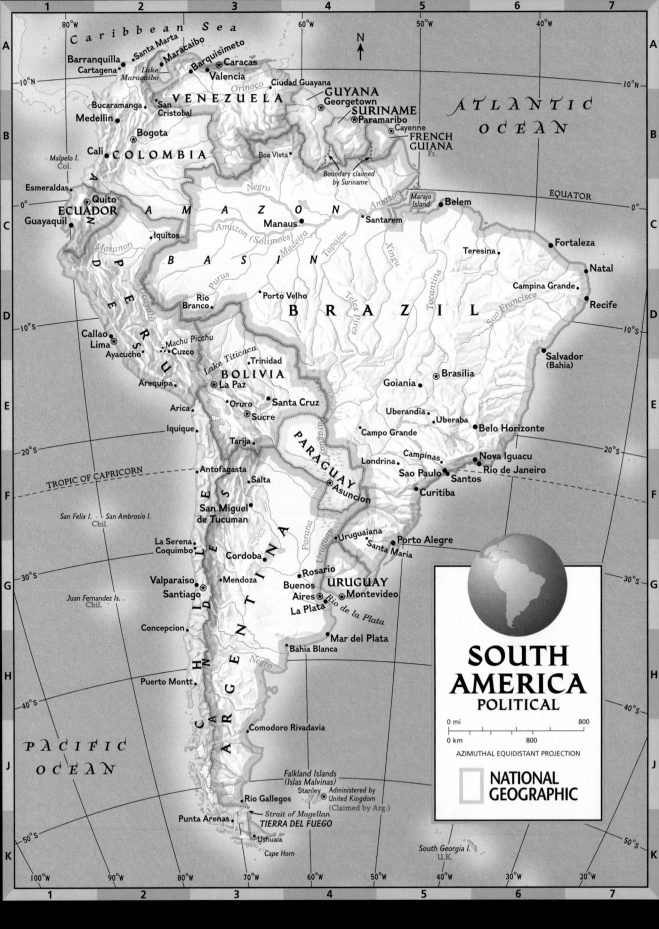

SOUTH AMERICA POLITICAL

0 mi   800

0 km   800

AZIMUTHAL EQUIDISTANT PROJECTION

NATIONAL GEOGRAPHIC

SOUTH AMERICA

PHYSICAL

0 mi   800
0 km   800

AZIMUTHAL EQUIDISTANT PROJECTION

NATIONAL GEOGRAPHIC

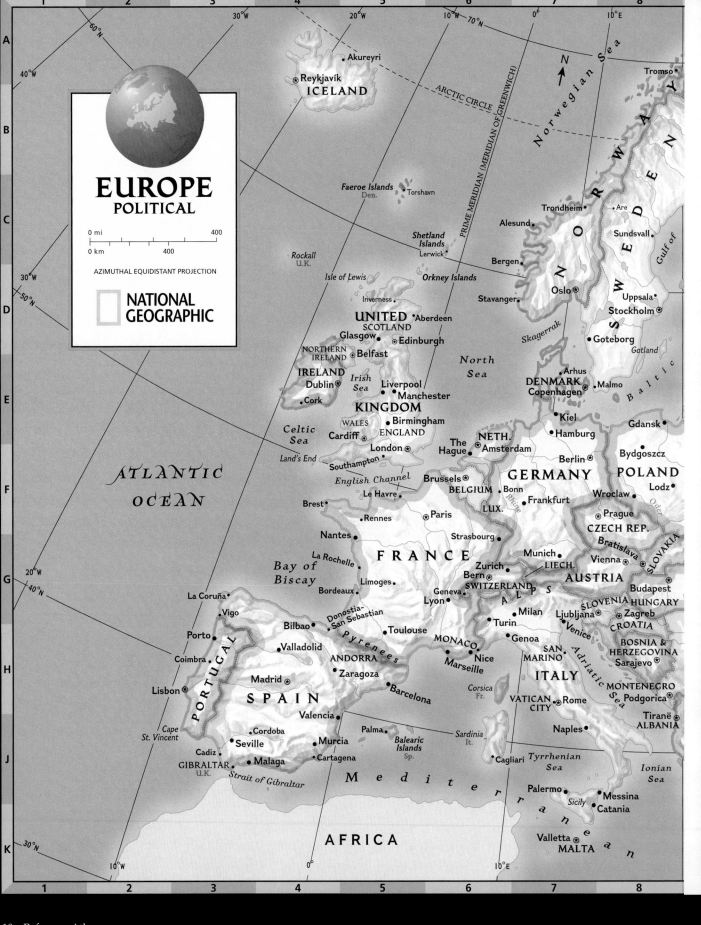

EUROPE
POLITICAL

0 mi   400
0 km   400

AZIMUTHAL EQUIDISTANT PROJECTION

NATIONAL GEOGRAPHIC

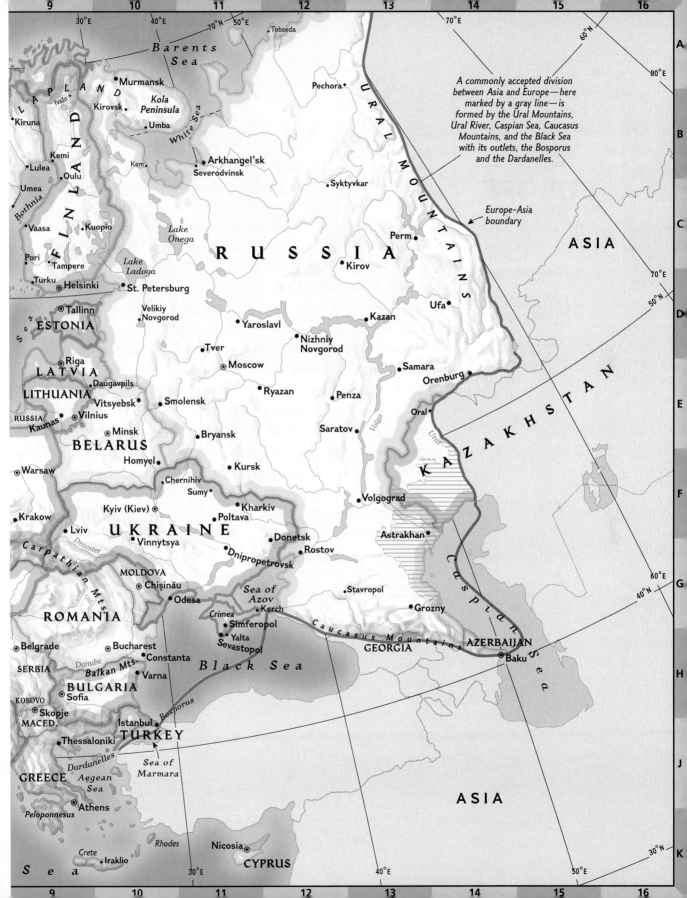

A commonly accepted division between Asia and Europe—here marked by a gray line—is formed by the Ural Mountains, Ural River, Caspian Sea, Caucasus Mountains, and the Black Sea with its outlets, the Bosporus and the Dardanelles.

Europe–Asia boundary

Barents Sea

LAPLAND

Tobseda

Murmansk
Kirovsk
Kola Peninsula
Kiruna
Ivalo
Umba
Kemi
White Sea
Lulea
Oulu
Kem
Arkhangel'sk
Severodvinsk
Umea
Bothnia
FINLAND
Pechora
URAL MOUNTAINS
Vaasa
Pori
Tampere
Turku
Helsinki
Lake Onega
Syktyvkar
Lake Ladoga
St. Petersburg
Tallinn
Sea
ESTONIA
Velikiy Novgorod
RUSSIA
Perm
ASIA
Kirov
Ufa
Riga
Yaroslavl
Kazan
LATVIA
Tver
Nizhniy Novgorod
LITHUANIA
Daugavpils
Moscow
Vitsyebsk
Smolensk
Samara
Orenburg
RUSSIA
Vilnius
Ryazan
Penza
Oral
Kaunas
Minsk
Volga
Saratov
KAZAKHSTAN
BELARUS
Bryansk
Warsaw
Homyel
Kursk
Chernihiv
Volgograd
Krakow
Sumy
Kyiv (Kiev)
Kharkiv
Lviv
Poltava
Astrakhan
UKRAINE
Dniester
Vinnytsya
Donetsk
Dnipropetrovsk
Rostov
Caspian Sea
MOLDOVA
Chișinău
Stavropol
Odesa
Sea of Azov
Kerch
Crimea
Grozny
ROMANIA
Simferopol
GEORGIA
Caucasus Mountains
AZERBAIJAN
Belgrade
Bucharest
Yalta
Sevastopol
Baku
Danube
Constanta
SERBIA
Balkan Mts.
Varna
BULGARIA
Black Sea
Sofia
KOSOVO
Skopje
MACED.
Bosporus
Istanbul
Thessaloniki
TURKEY
Dardanelles
GREECE
Aegean Sea
Sea of Marmara
Peloponnesus
Athens
ASIA
Rhodes
Nicosia
Crete
Iraklio
CYPRUS
Sea

EUROPE
PHYSICAL

0 mi   400
0 km   400

AZIMUTHEL EQUIDISTANT PROJECTION

NATIONAL GEOGRAPHIC

Reykjavik ⊛
ICELAND

ARCTIC CIRCLE

PRIME MERIDIAN (MERIDIAN OF GREENWICH)

Faeroe
Islands

Shetland
Islands

Orkney
Islands

Outer Hebrides

Highlands

British
Isles

Edinburgh ⊛

Belfast ⊛

UNITED

IRELAND
Dublin ⊛

Irish
Sea

Great
Britain

KINGDOM

Cardiff ⊛

London ⊛

North
Sea

Jutland

DENMARK
Copenhagen ⊛
Zealand

Oslo ⊛

Stockholm ⊛

Gulf of

S C A N D I N A V I A

N O R W A Y

S W E D E N

Baltic

Amsterdam ⊛
NETH.

Berlin ⊛

N O R T

POLAND

BELGIUM
Brussels ⊛
LUX.

GERMANY

Rhine

Elbe

Oder

Prague ⊛
CZECH REP.

Bratislava ⊛

Vienna ⊛

SLOVAKIA

English Channel

Seine

Paris ⊛

Brittany

Loire

FRANCE

Danube

LIECH.

AUSTRIA

Budapest ⊛

HUNGARY

ATLANTIC
OCEAN

Bay of
Biscay

Mont Blanc
15,771 ft
4,807 m

Bern ⊛
SWITZ.

A L P S

SLOVENIA
Ljubljana ⊛

Zagreb ⊛
CROATIA

Drava

Danube

Massif
Central

Rhône

MONACO

Po

Sava

BOSNIA &
Sarajevo ⊛
HERZEGOVINA

Cantabrian Mountains

Pyrenees

Riviera

SAN MARINO

A p e n n i n e s

Adriatic
Sea

Douro

Ebro

ANDORRA

Corsica

ITALY

VATICAN
CITY

Rome ⊛

MONTENEGRO

Tiranë ⊛
ALBANIA

I B E R I A N

Madrid ⊛

Lisbon ⊛

Tagus

SPAIN

P O R T U G A L

PENINSULA

Baetic Mountains

Sardinia

Tyrrhenian
Sea

Ionian
Sea

GIBRALTAR
Strait of Gibraltar

Balearic Islands

M e d i t e r r a n e a n

Sicily ✛ Etna
10,902 ft
3,323 m

Valletta ⊛
MALTA

AFRICA

Norwegian Sea

N

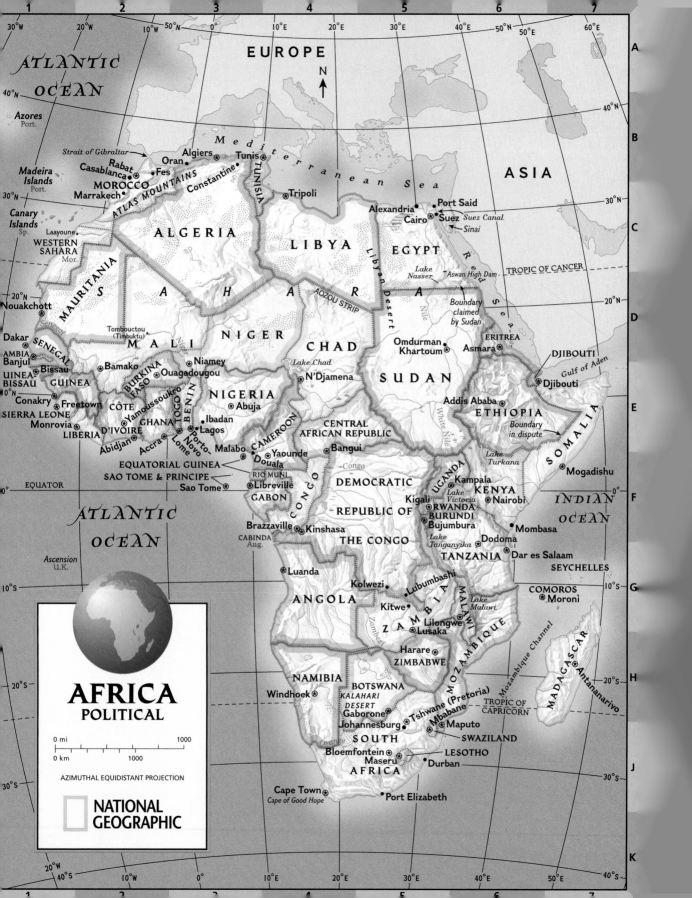

AFRICA
POLITICAL

0 mi   1000

0 km   1000

AZIMUTHAL EQUIDISTANT PROJECTION

NATIONAL GEOGRAPHIC

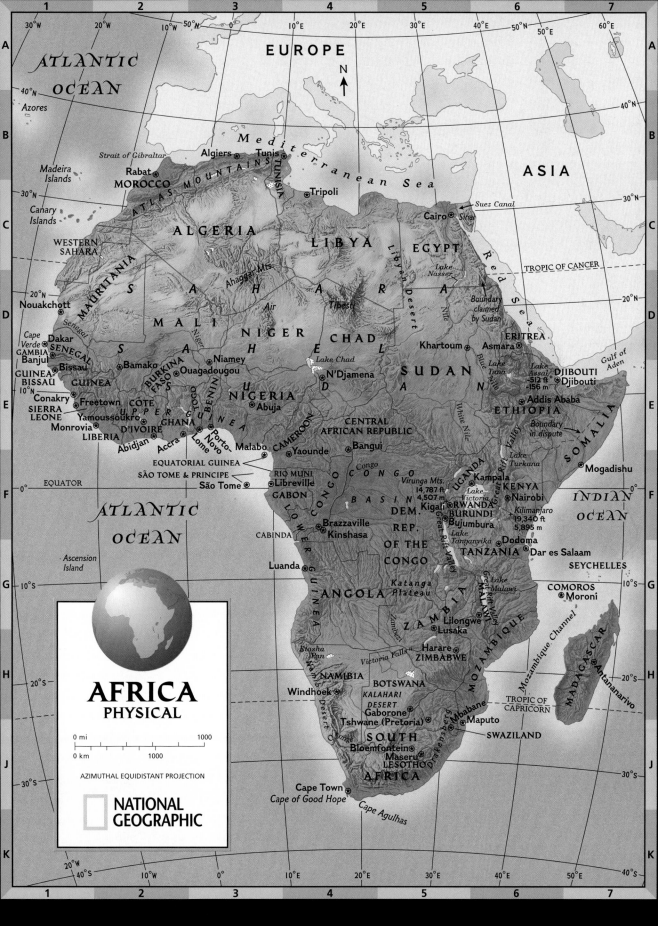

AFRICA
PHYSICAL

0 mi 1000
0 km 1000

AZIMUTHAL EQUIDISTANT PROJECTION

NATIONAL
GEOGRAPHIC

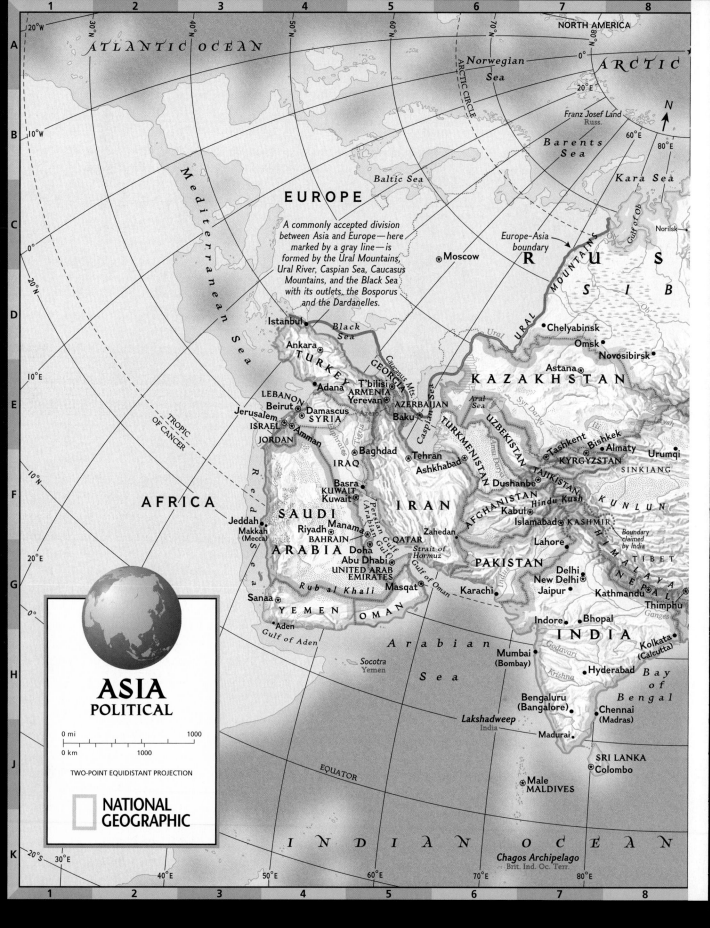

ASIA POLITICAL

A commonly accepted division between Asia and Europe—here marked by a gray line—is formed by the Ural Mountains, Ural River, Caspian Sea, Caucasus Mountains, and the Black Sea with its outlets, the Bosporus and the Dardanelles.

ATLANTIC OCEAN

NORTH AMERICA

ARCTIC

Norwegian Sea

Franz Josef Land
Russ.

Barents Sea

Kara Sea

EUROPE

Baltic Sea

Moscow

RUSSIA

SIB

Norilsk

Europe-Asia boundary

Gulf of Ob

Ob

Chelyabinsk

Omsk

Novosibirsk

Istanbul

Black Sea

Ankara

TURKEY

GEORGIA

Caucasus Mts.

T'bilisi

ARMENIA

Adana

Yerevan

AZERBAIJAN

Aral Sea

Astana

KAZAKHSTAN

Syr Darya

Ili

Urumqi

LEBANON

Beirut

Damascus

SYRIA

Azer.

Baku

Caspian Sea

TURKMENISTAN

UZBEKISTAN

Tashkent

Bishkek

Almaty

KYRGYZSTAN

SINKIANG

Jerusalem

ISRAEL

Amman

JORDAN

Tigris

Euphrates

Baghdad

IRAQ

Tehran

Ashkhabad

Amu Darya

Dushanbe

TAJIKISTAN

KUNLUN

Mediterranean Sea

Basra

KUWAIT

Kuwait

IRAN

AFGHANISTAN

Kabul

Hindu Kush

Islamabad

KASHMIR

Boundary claimed by India

TIBET

AFRICA

Red Sea

Jeddah

Makkah
(Mecca)

SAUDI

Riyadh

Manama

BAHRAIN

Persian (Arabian) Gulf

Doha

QATAR

Zahedan

Lahore

New Delhi

Delhi

HIMALAYA

Jaipur

NEPAL

Kathmandu

Thimphu

Ganges

ARABIA

Abu Dhabi

UNITED ARAB
EMIRATES

Strait of Hormuz

PAKISTAN

Indus

Karachi

Indore

Bhopal

INDIA

Kolkata
(Calcutta)

Sanaa

YEMEN

Rub al Khali

OMAN

Masqat

Gulf of Oman

Godavari

Mumbai
(Bombay)

Krishna

Bay of Bengal

Aden

Gulf of Aden

Arabian Sea

Hyderabad

Socotra
Yemen

Bengaluru
(Bangalore)

Chennai
(Madras)

Lakshadweep
India

Madurai

SRI LANKA

Colombo

Male

MALDIVES

EQUATOR

INDIAN OCEAN

Chagos Archipelago
Brit. Ind. Oc. Terr.

TROPIC OF CANCER

0 mi 1000
0 km 1000

TWO-POINT EQUIDISTANT PROJECTION

NATIONAL GEOGRAPHIC

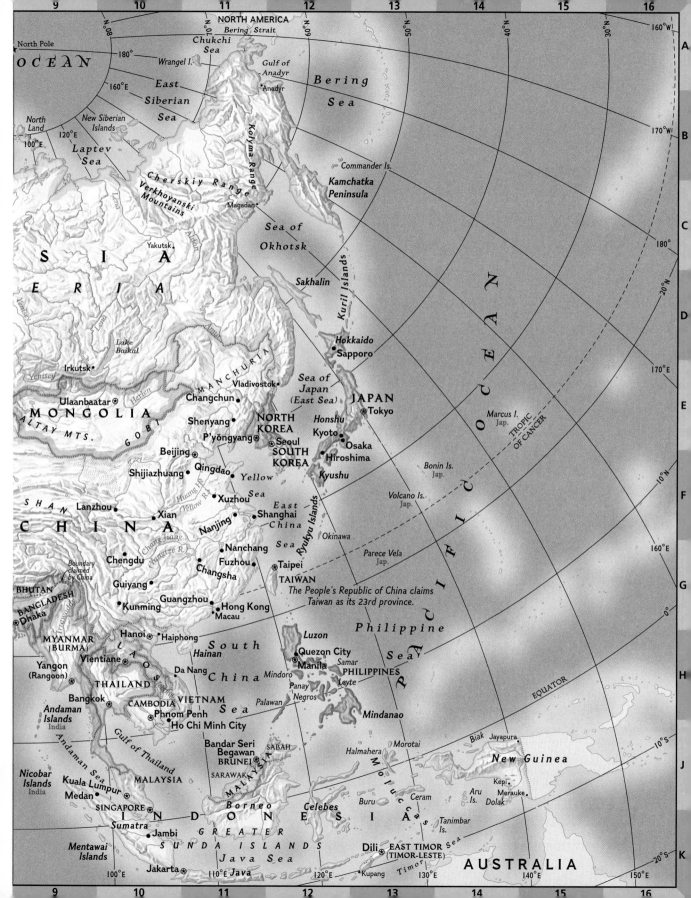

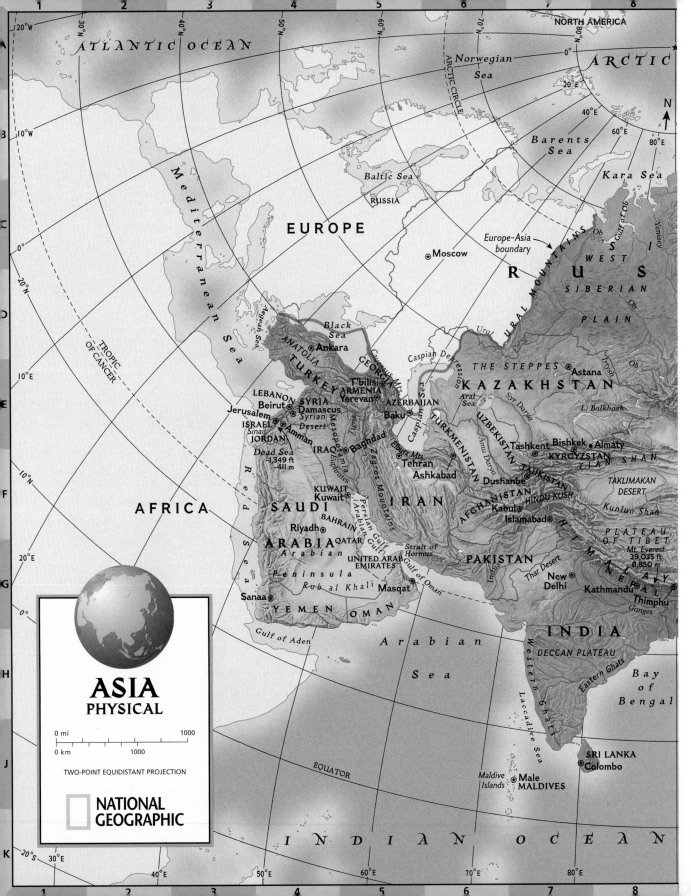

ATLANTIC OCEAN

NORTH AMERICA

ARCTIC

Norwegian
Sea

ARCTIC CIRCLE

Barents
Sea

Baltic Sea

RUSSIA

Kara Sea

EUROPE

⊛ Moscow

Europe-Asia
boundary

R U S S I A

WEST
SIBERIAN
PLAIN

Mediterranean Sea

Aegean Sea

Black Sea

ANATOLIA

⊛ Ankara

TURKEY

GEORGIA

T'bilisi ⊛
ARMENIA
Yerevan ⊛

Caucasus Mts.

Caspian Depression

THE STEPPES

⊛ Astana

KAZAKHSTAN

Ural

TROPIC
OF CANCER

LEBANON
Beirut ⊛
Jerusalem
ISRAEL ⊛
JORDAN

SYRIA
Damascus ⊛

Syrian
Desert

Amman ⊛

Sinai

Dead Sea
-1,349 ft
-411 m

AZERBAIJAN
Baku ⊛

Caspian Sea

TURKMENISTAN

Aral
Sea

UZBEKISTAN

Syr Darya

L. Balkhash

Tashkent ⊛
Bishkek ⊛ ⊛ Almaty
KYRGYZSTAN
TIAN SHAN

Amu Darya

IRAQ ⊛
Baghdad ⊛

Euphrates
Mesopotamia
Tigris

Zagros Mountains
Elburz Mts.

Tehran ⊛
Ashkabad ⊛

Dushanbe ⊛
TAJIKISTAN

TAKLIMAKAN
DESERT

AFRICA

SAUDI

KUWAIT
Kuwait ⊛

BAHRAIN

Riyadh ⊛

QATAR

IRAN

Persian Gulf
(Arabian Gulf)

AFGHANISTAN

Kabul ⊛
Islamabad ⊛

HINDU KUSH

Kunlun Shan

PLATEAU
OF TIBET
Mt. Everest
29,035 ft
8,850 m

HIMALAYA

ARABIA

Arabian

Peninsula

Rub al Khali

Strait of
Hormuz

UNITED ARAB
EMIRATES

Gulf of Oman

Masqat ⊛

PAKISTAN

Thar Desert

New ⊛
Delhi

Kathmandu ⊛
NEPAL
Thimphu ⊛

Indus

Ganges

Sanaa ⊛

YEMEN

OMAN

Gulf of Aden

Red Sea

Arabian

Sea

INDIA

DECCAN PLATEAU

Western Ghats

Eastern Ghats

Bay
of
Bengal

ASIA
PHYSICAL

0 mi   1000

0 km   1000

TWO-POINT EQUIDISTANT PROJECTION

NATIONAL
GEOGRAPHIC

EQUATOR

Laccadive Sea

SRI LANKA
⊛ Colombo

Maldive
Islands
⊛ Male
MALDIVES

I N D I A N   O C E A N

N

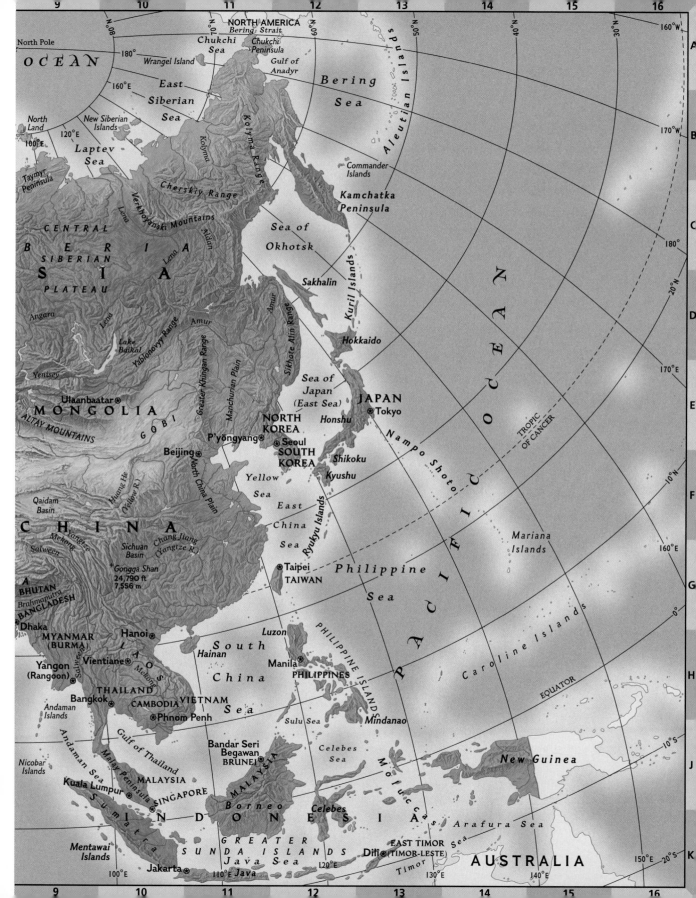

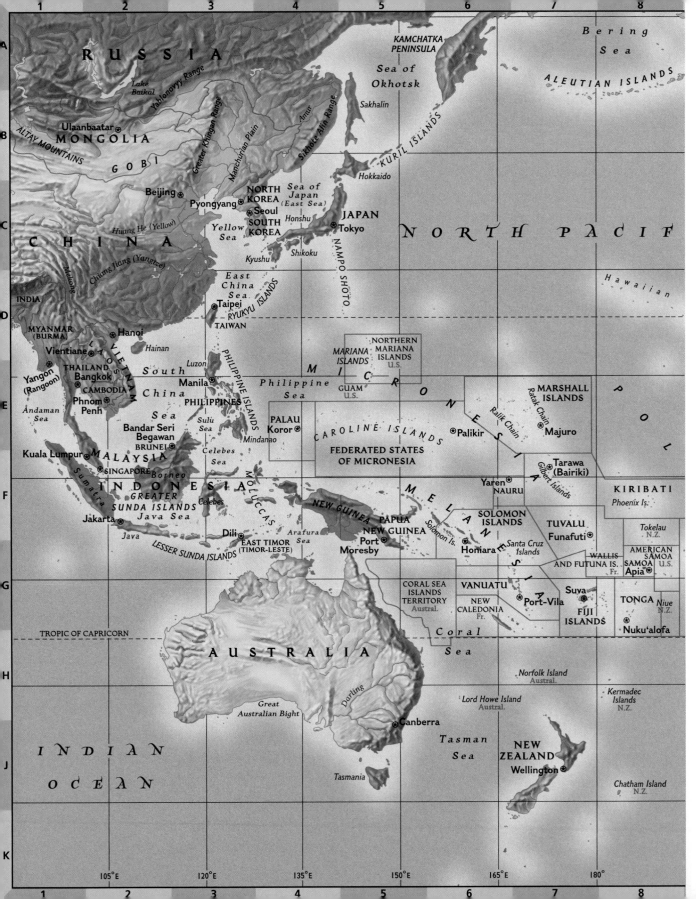

PACIFIC RIM
PHYSICAL/POLITICAL

0 mi   1500
0 km   1500

MILLER CYLINDRICAL PROJECTION

NATIONAL GEOGRAPHIC

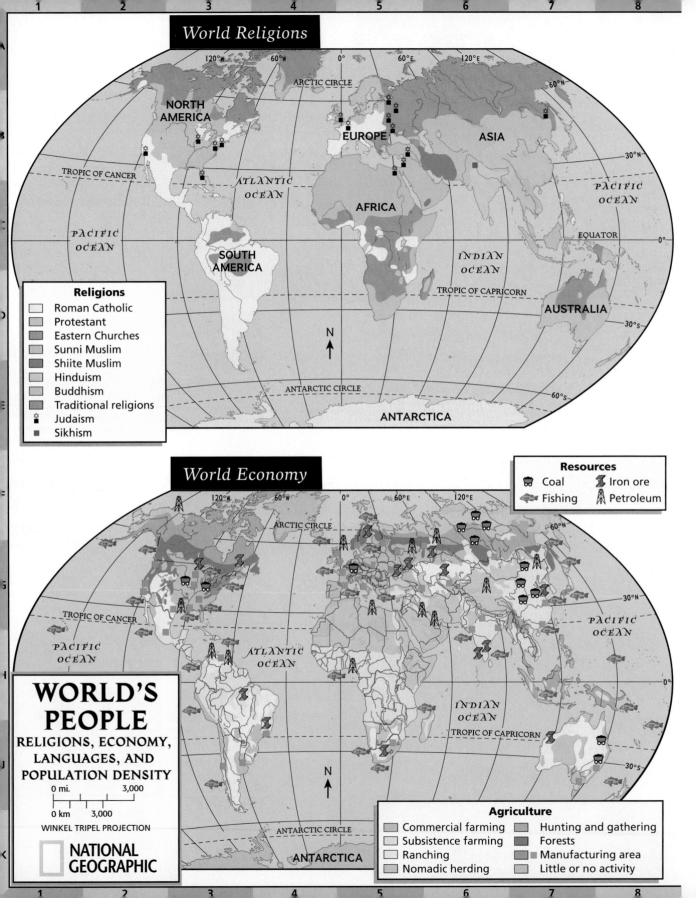

World Religions

Religions
- Roman Catholic
- Protestant
- Eastern Churches
- Sunni Muslim
- Shiite Muslim
- Hinduism
- Buddhism
- Traditional religions
- ✡ Judaism
- ■ Sikhism

NORTH AMERICA

EUROPE

ASIA

AFRICA

SOUTH AMERICA

INDIAN OCEAN

AUSTRALIA

ANTARCTICA

ATLANTIC OCEAN

PACIFIC OCEAN

PACIFIC OCEAN

ARCTIC CIRCLE
TROPIC OF CANCER
EQUATOR
TROPIC OF CAPRICORN
ANTARCTIC CIRCLE

120°W   60°W   0°   60°E   120°E
60°N   30°N   0°   30°S   60°S

N

World Economy

Resources
- 🛒 Coal
- 🐟 Fishing
- Iron ore
- Petroleum

ATLANTIC OCEAN

PACIFIC OCEAN

PACIFIC OCEAN

INDIAN OCEAN

ARCTIC CIRCLE
TROPIC OF CANCER
TROPIC OF CAPRICORN
ANTARCTIC CIRCLE
ANTARCTICA

120°W   60°W   0°   60°E   120°E
60°N   30°N   0°   30°S

N

WORLD'S PEOPLE
RELIGIONS, ECONOMY, LANGUAGES, AND POPULATION DENSITY

0 mi.   3,000

0 km   3,000

WINKEL TRIPEL PROJECTION

NATIONAL GEOGRAPHIC

Agriculture
- Commercial farming
- Subsistence farming
- Ranching
- Nomadic herding
- Hunting and gathering
- Forests
- Manufacturing area
- Little or no activity

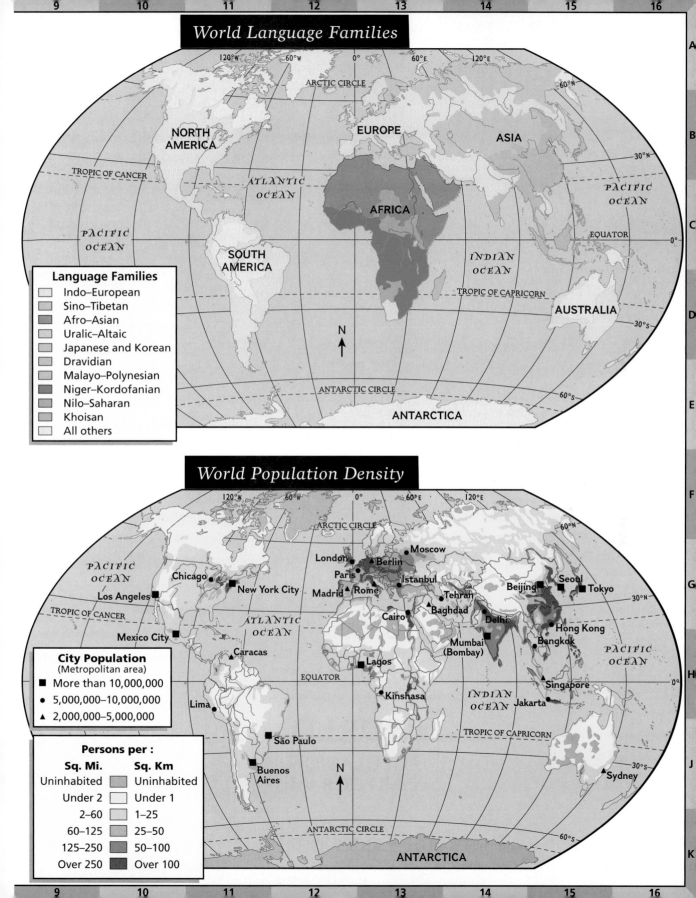

World Language Families

NORTH AMERICA

EUROPE

ASIA

AFRICA

SOUTH AMERICA

AUSTRALIA

ANTARCTICA

ARCTIC CIRCLE

TROPIC OF CANCER

ATLANTIC OCEAN

PACIFIC OCEAN

PACIFIC OCEAN

INDIAN OCEAN

EQUATOR

TROPIC OF CAPRICORN

ANTARCTIC CIRCLE

120°W 60°W 0° 60°E 120°E

60°N 30°N 0° 30°S 60°S

N

Language Families

- Indo–European
- Sino–Tibetan
- Afro–Asian
- Uralic–Altaic
- Japanese and Korean
- Dravidian
- Malayo–Polynesian
- Niger–Kordofanian
- Nilo–Saharan
- Khoisan
- All others

World Population Density

PACIFIC OCEAN

ARCTIC CIRCLE

TROPIC OF CANCER

ATLANTIC OCEAN

EQUATOR

INDIAN OCEAN

PACIFIC OCEAN

TROPIC OF CAPRICORN

ANTARCTIC CIRCLE

ANTARCTICA

120°W 60°W 0° 60°E 120°E

60°N 30°N 0° 30°S 60°S

N

Chicago
Los Angeles
New York City
Mexico City
Caracas
Lima
São Paulo
Buenos Aires
London
Paris
Madrid
Berlin
Rome
Moscow
Istanbul
Cairo
Tehran
Baghdad
Lagos
Kinshasa
Beijing
Delhi
Mumbai (Bombay)
Bangkok
Seoul
Tokyo
Hong Kong
Singapore
Jakarta
Sydney

City Population
(Metropolitan area)

- ■ More than 10,000,000
- ● 5,000,000–10,000,000
- ▲ 2,000,000–5,000,000

Persons per :

Sq. Mi.	Sq. Km
Uninhabited	Uninhabited
Under 2	Under 1
2–60	1–25
60–125	25–50
125–250	50–100
Over 250	Over 100

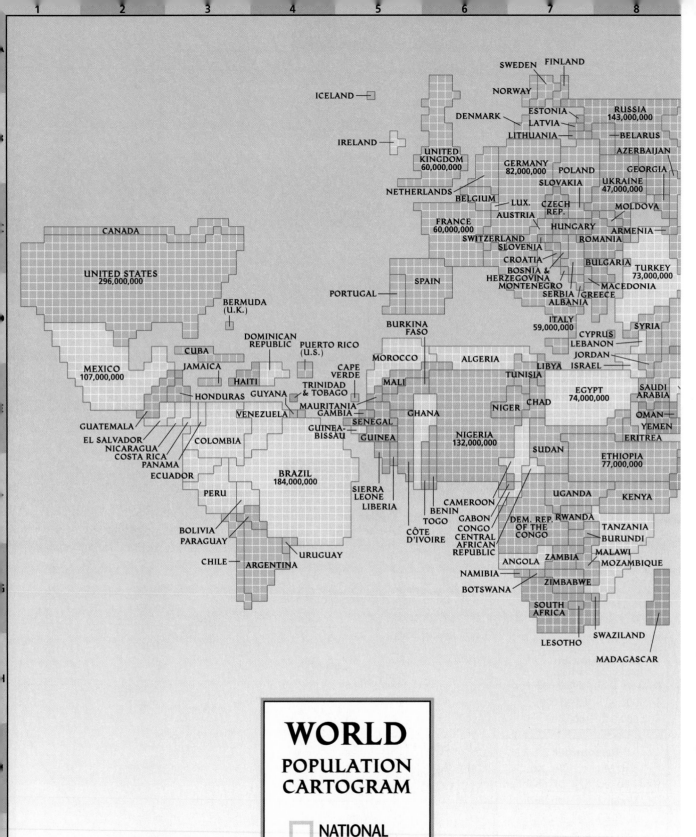

WORLD
POPULATION CARTOGRAM

NATIONAL GEOGRAPHIC

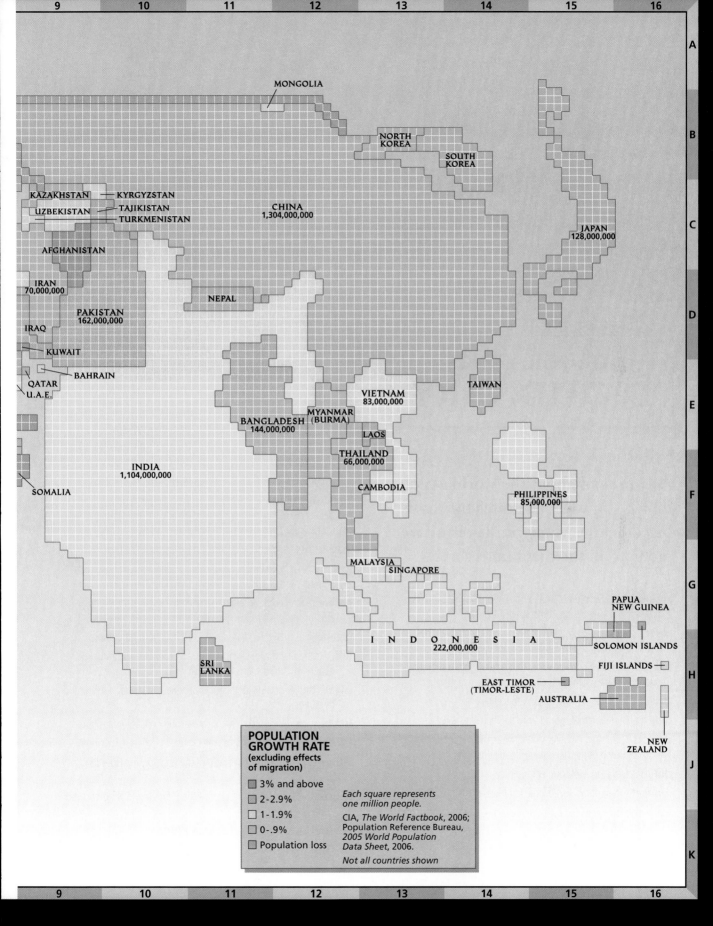

POPULATION
GROWTH RATE
(excluding effects
of migration)

■ 3% and above
□ 2-2.9%
□ 1-1.9%
□ 0-.9%
■ Population loss

Each square represents
one million people.

CIA, *The World Factbook*, 2006;
Population Reference Bureau,
*2005 World Population
Data Sheet*, 2006.

Not all countries shown

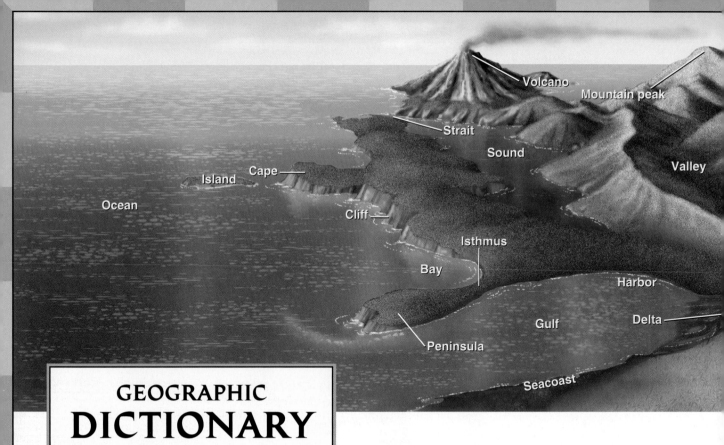

Volcano
Mountain peak
Strait
Sound
Valley
Island   Cape
Ocean   Cliff
Isthmus
Bay
Harbor
Peninsula
Gulf   Delta
Seacoast

GEOGRAPHIC DICTIONARY

As you read about the world's geography, you will encounter the terms listed below. Many of the terms are pictured in the diagram.

absolute location exact location of a place on the Earth described by global coordinates

basin area of land drained by a given river and its branches; area of land surrounded by lands of higher elevations

bay part of a large body of water that extends into a shoreline, generally smaller than a gulf

canyon deep and narrow valley with steep walls

cape point of land that extends into a river, lake, or ocean

channel wide strait or waterway between two landmasses that lie close to each other; deep part of a river or other waterway

cliff steep, high wall of rock, earth, or ice

continent one of the seven large landmasses on the Earth

delta flat, low-lying land built up from soil carried downstream by a river and deposited at its mouth

divide stretch of high land that separates river systems

downstream direction in which a river or stream flows from its source to its mouth

elevation height of land above sea level

Equator imaginary line that runs around the Earth halfway between the North and South Poles; used as the starting point to measure degrees of north and south latitude

glacier large, thick body of slowly moving ice

gulf part of a large body of water that extends into a shoreline, generally larger and more deeply indented than a bay

harbor a sheltered place along a shoreline where ships can anchor safely

highland elevated land area such as a hill, mountain, or plateau

hill elevated land with sloping sides and rounded summit; generally smaller than a mountain

island land area, smaller than a continent, completely surrounded by water

isthmus narrow stretch of land connecting two larger land areas

lake a sizable inland body of water

latitude distance north or south of the Equator, measured in degrees

longitude distance east or west of the Prime Meridian, measured in degrees

lowland land, usually level, at a low elevation

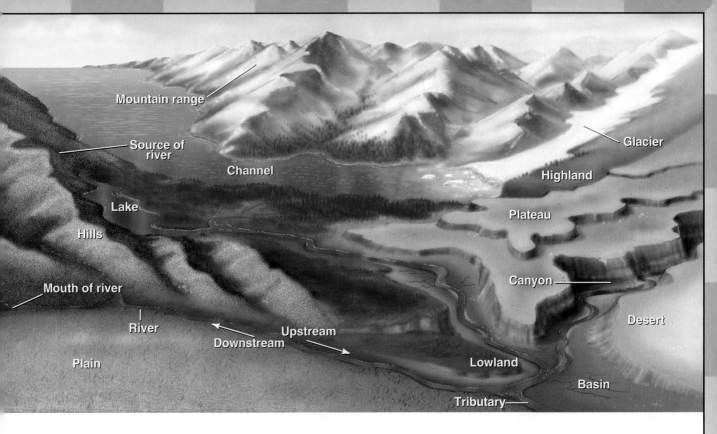

Mountain range
Source of river
Channel
Glacier
Highland
Lake
Plateau
Hills
Canyon
Desert
Mouth of river
River
Upstream
Downstream
Plain
Lowland
Basin
Tributary

map drawing of the Earth shown on a flat surface

meridian one of many lines on the global grid running from the North Pole to the South Pole; used to measure degrees of longitude

mesa broad, flat-topped landform with steep sides; smaller than a plateau

mountain land with steep sides that rises sharply (1,000 feet or more) from surrounding land; generally larger and more rugged than a hill

mountain peak pointed top of a mountain

mountain range a series of connected mountains

mouth (of a river) place where a stream or river flows into a larger body of water

ocean one of the four major bodies of salt water that surround the continents

ocean current stream of either cold or warm water that moves in a definite direction through an ocean

parallel one of many lines on the global grid that circles the Earth north or south of the Equator; used to measure degrees of latitude

peninsula body of land jutting into a lake or ocean, surrounded on three sides by water

physical feature characteristic of a place occurring naturally, such as a landform, body of water, climate pattern, or resource

plain area of level land, usually at low elevation and often covered with grasses

plateau area of flat or rolling land at a high elevation, about 300 to 3,000 feet (90 to 900 m) high

Prime Meridian line of the global grid running from the North Pole to the South Pole at Greenwich, England; starting point for measuring degrees of east and west longitude

relief changes in elevation over a given area of land

river large natural stream of water that runs through the land

sea large body of water completely or partly surrounded by land

seacoast land lying next to a sea or an ocean

sound broad inland body of water, often between a coastline and one or more islands off the coast

source (of a river) place where a river or stream begins, often in highlands

strait narrow stretch of water joining two larger bodies of water

tributary small river or stream that flows into a large river or stream; a branch of the river

upstream direction opposite the flow of a river; toward the source of a river or stream

valley area of low land usually between hills or mountains

volcano mountain or hill created as liquid rock and ash erupt from inside the Earth

THEMES AND ELEMENTS

How Do I Study Geography?

Geographers have tried to understand the best way to teach and learn about geography, so they created the *Five Themes of Geography*. The themes acted as a guide for teaching the basic ideas about geography to students. However, many thought that the Five Themes were too broad. In 1994, geographers created 18 national geography standards. These standards were more detailed about what should be taught and learned. The Six Essential Elements act as a bridge connecting the Five Themes with the standards.

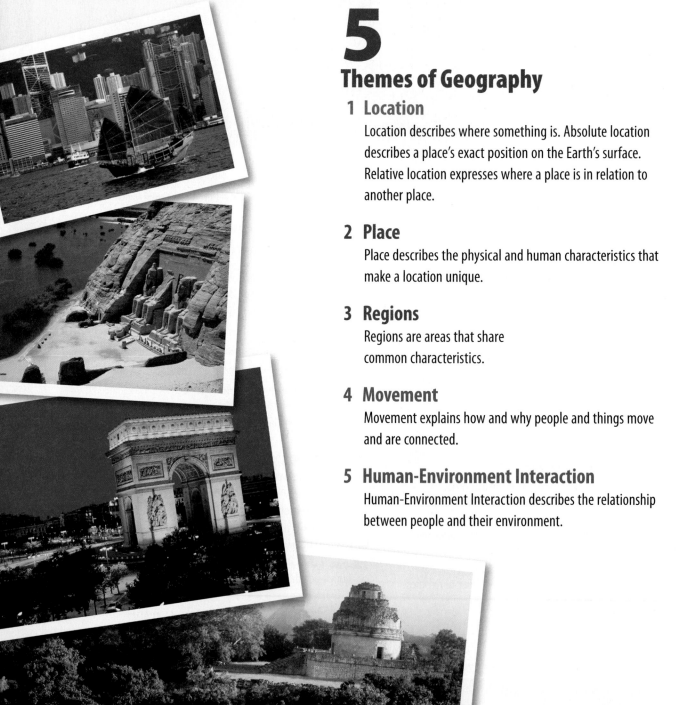

5
Themes of Geography

1 Location
Location describes where something is. Absolute location describes a place's exact position on the Earth's surface. Relative location expresses where a place is in relation to another place.

2 Place
Place describes the physical and human characteristics that make a location unique.

3 Regions
Regions are areas that share common characteristics.

4 Movement
Movement explains how and why people and things move and are connected.

5 Human-Environment Interaction
Human-Environment Interaction describes the relationship between people and their environment.

6 Essential Elements

I. The World in Spatial Terms
Geographers look to see where a place is located. Location acts as a starting point to answer "Where Is It?" The location of a place helps you orient yourself as to where you are.

II. Places and Regions
Place describes physical characteristics such as landforms, climate, and plant or animal life. It might also describe human characteristics, including language and way of life. Places can also be organized into regions. **Regions** are places united by one or more characteristics.

III. Physical Systems
Geographers study how physical systems, such as hurricanes, volcanoes, and glaciers, shape the surface of the Earth. They also look at how plants and animals depend upon one another and their surroundings for their survival.

IV. Human Systems
People shape the world in which they live. They settle in certain places but not in others. An ongoing theme in geography is the movement of people, ideas, and goods.

V. Environment and Society
How does the relationship between people and their natural surroundings influence the way people live? Geographers study how people use the environment and how their actions affect the environment.

VI. The Uses of Geography
Knowledge of geography helps us understand the relationships among people, places, and environments over time. Applying geographic skills helps you understand the past and prepare for the future.

18 Geography Standards

1 How to use maps and other tools

2 How to use mental maps to organize information

3 How to analyze the spatial organization of people, places, and environments

4 The physical and human characteristics of places

5 How people create regions to interpret Earth's complexity

6 How culture and experience influence people's perceptions of places and regions

7 The physical processes that shape Earth's surface

8 The distribution of ecosystems on Earth's surface

9 The characteristics, distribution, and migration of human populations

10 The complexity of Earth's cultural mosaics

11 The patterns and networks of economic interdependence

12 The patterns of human settlement

13 The forces of cooperation and conflict

14 How human actions modify the physical environment

15 How physical systems affect human systems

16 The meaning, use, and distribution of resources

17 How to apply geography to interpret the past

18 How to apply geography to interpret the present and plan for the future

GEOGRAPHY SKILLS HANDBOOK

CONTENTS

Globes and Maps
- From 3-D to 2-D
- Great Circle Routes

Projections
- Planar Projection
- Cylindrical Projection
- Conic Projection
- Common Map Projections

Determining Location
- Latitude
- Longitude
- The Global Grid
- Northern and Southern Hemispheres
- Eastern and Western Hemispheres

Reading a Map
- Using Scale
- Absolute and Relative Location

Physical Maps

Political Maps

Thematic Maps
- Qualitative Maps
- Flow-Line Maps

Geographic Information Systems

Throughout this text, you will discover how geography has shaped the course of events in world history. Landforms, waterways, climate, and natural resources all have helped or hindered human activities. Usually people have learned either to adapt to their environments or to transform it to meet their needs. The resources in this Geography Skills Handbook will help you get the most out of your textbook—and provide you with skills you will use for the rest of your life.

Geographers use a wide array of tools to collect and analyze information to help them understand the Earth. The study of geography is more than knowing a lot of facts about places. Rather, it has more to do with asking questions about the Earth, pursuing their answers, and solving problems. Thus, one of the most important geographic tools is inside your head: the ability to think geographically.

Globes and Maps

A **globe** is a scale model of the Earth. Because Earth is round, a globe presents the most accurate depiction of geographic information such as area, distance, and direction. However, globes show little close-up detail. A printed **map** is a symbolic representation of all or part of the planet. Unlike globes, maps can show small areas in great detail.

From 3-D to 2-D

Think about the surface of the Earth as the peel of an orange. To flatten the peel, you have to cut it like the globe shown here. To create maps that are not interrupted, mapmakers, or **cartographers,** use mathematical formulas to transfer information from the three-dimensional globe to the two-dimensional map. However, when the curves of a globe become straight lines on a map, distortion of size, shape, distance, or area occurs.

Great Circle Routes

A straight line of true direction—one that runs directly from west to east, for example—is not always the shortest distance between two points. This is due to the curvature of the Earth. To find the shortest distance, stretch a piece of string around a globe from one point to the other. The string will form part of a *great circle,* an imaginary line that follows the curve of the Earth. Ship captains and airline pilots use these **great circle routes** to reduce travel time and conserve fuel.

The idea of a great circle route is an important difference between globes and maps. A round globe accurately shows a great circle route, as indicated on the map below. However, as shown on the flat

map, the great circle distance (dotted line) between Tokyo and Los Angeles appears to be far longer than the true direction distance (solid line). In fact, the great circle distance is 345 miles (555 km) shorter.

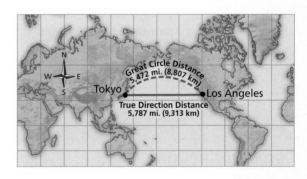

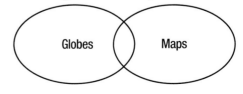

PRACTICING THE SKILL

1. **Explain** the significance of: globe, map, cartographer, great circle route.

2. **Describe** the problems that arise when the curves of a globe become straight lines on a map.

3. **Use** a Venn diagram like the one below to identify the similarities and differences between globes and maps.

Globes   Maps

Projections

To create maps, cartographers project the round Earth onto a flat surface—making a **map projection.** Distance, shape, direction, or size may be distorted by a projection. As a result, the purpose of the map usually dictates which projection is used. There are many kinds of map projections, some with general names and some named for the cartographers who developed them. Three basic categories of map projections are shown here: **planar, cylindrical,** and **conic.**

Planar Projection

A planar projection shows the Earth centered in such as way that a straight line coming from the center to any other point represents the shortest distance. Also known as an azimuthal projection, it is most accurate at its center. As a result, it is often used for maps of the Poles.

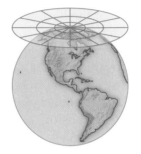

Cylindrical Projection

A cylindrical projection is based on the projection of the globe onto a cylinder. This projection is most accurate near the Equator, but shapes and distances are distorted near the Poles.

Conic Projection

A conic projection comes from placing a cone over part of a globe. Conic projections are best suited for showing limited east-west areas that are not too far from the Equator. For these uses, a conic projection can indicate distances and directions fairly accurately.

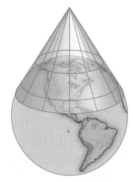

Common Map Projections

Each type of map projection has advantages and some degree of inaccuracy. Four of the most common projections are shown here.

Winkel Tripel Projection

Most general reference world maps are the Winkel Tripel projection. It provides a good balance between the size and shape of land areas as they are shown on the map. Even the polar areas are depicted with little distortion of size and shape.

Robinson Projection

The Robinson projection has minor distortions. The sizes and shapes near the eastern and western edges of the map are accurate, and outlines of the continents appear much as they do on the globe. However, the polar areas are flattened.

Goode's Interrupted Equal-Area Projection

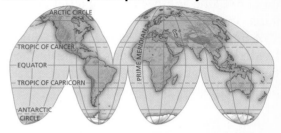

An **interrupted projection** looks something like a globe that has been cut apart and laid flat. Goode's Interrupted Equal-Area projection shows the true size and shape of Earth's landmasses, but distances are generally distorted.

Mercator Projection

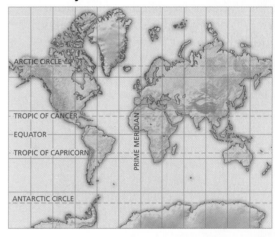

The Mercator projection increasingly distorts size and distance as it moves away from the Equator. However, Mercator projections do accurately show true directions and the shapes of landmasses, making these maps useful for sea travel.

PRACTICING THE SKILL

1. **Explain** the significance of: map projection, planar, cylindrical, conic, interrupted projection.
2. **How** does a cartographer determine which map projection to use?
3. **How** is Goode's Interrupted Equal-Area projection different from the Mercator projection?
4. **Which** of the four common projections described above is the best one to use when showing the entire world? Why?
5. **Use** a Venn diagram like the one below to identify the similarities and differences between the Winkel Tripel and Mercator projections.

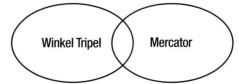

Winkel Tripel   Mercator

Determining Location

Geography is often said to begin with the question: *Where?* The basic tool for answering the question is **location.** Lines on globes and maps provide information that can help you locate places. These lines cross one another forming a pattern called a **grid system,** which helps you find exact places on the Earth's surface.

A **hemisphere** is one of the halves into which the Earth is divided. Geographers divide the Earth into hemispheres to help them classify and describe places on Earth. Most places are located in two of the four hemispheres.

Latitude

Lines of **latitude,** or parallels, circle the Earth parallel to the Equator and measure the distance north or south of the Equator in degrees. The Equator is measured at 0° latitude, while the Poles lie at latitudes 90°N (north) and 90°S (south). Parallels north of the Equator are called north latitude. Parallels south of the Equator are called south latitude.

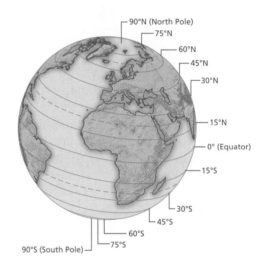

Longitude

Lines of **longitude,** or meridians, circle the Earth from Pole to Pole. These lines measure distance east or west of the **Prime Meridian** at 0° longitude. Meridians east of the Prime Meridian are known as east longitude. Meridians west of the Prime Meridian are known as west longitude. The 180° meridian on the opposite side of the Earth is called the International Date Line.

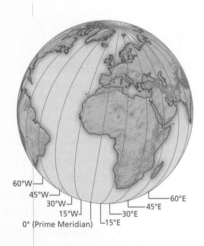

The Global Grid

Every place has a global address, or **absolute location.** You can identify the absolute location of a place by naming the latitude and longitude lines that cross exactly at that place. For example, Tokyo, Japan, is located at 36°N latitude and 140°E longitude. For more precise readings, each degree is further divided into 60 units called minutes.

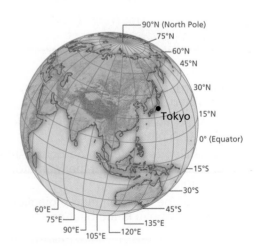

Northern and Southern Hemispheres

The diagram below shows that the Equator divides the Earth into the Northern and Southern Hemispheres. Everything north of the Equator is in the **Northern Hemisphere.** Everything south of the Equator is in the **Southern Hemisphere.**

Northern Hemisphere

Southern Hemisphere

Eastern and Western Hemispheres

The Prime Meridian and the International Date Line divide the Earth into the Eastern and Western Hemispheres. Everything east of the Prime Meridian for 180° is in the **Eastern Hemisphere.** Everything west of the Prime Meridian for 180° is in the **Western Hemisphere.**

Eastern Hemisphere

Western Hemisphere

PRACTICING THE SKILL

1. **Explain** the significance of: location, grid system, hemisphere, Northern Hemisphere, Southern Hemisphere, Eastern Hemisphere, Western Hemisphere, latitude, longitude, Prime Meridian, absolute location.

2. **Why** do all maps label the Equator 0° latitude and the Prime Meridian 0° longitude?

3. **Which** lines of latitude and longitude divide the Earth into hemispheres?

4. **Using** the Reference Atlas maps, fill in a chart like the one below by writing the latitude and longitude of three world cities. Have a partner try to identify the cities.

5. **Use** a chart like the one below to identify the continents in each hemisphere. Some may be in more than one hemisphere.

Hemisphere	Continents
Northern	
Southern	
Eastern	
Western	

Reading a Map

In addition to latitude and longitude, maps feature other important tools to help you interpret the information they contain. Learning to use these map tools will help you read the symbolic language of maps more easily.

Key
The key lists and explains the symbols, colors, and lines used on the map. The key is sometimes called a legend.

Title
The title tells you what kind of information the map is showing.

Scale Bar
The scale bar shows the relationship between map measurements and actual distances on the Earth. By laying a ruler along the scale bar, you can calculate how many miles or kilometers are represented per inch or centimeter. The map projection used to create the map is often listed near the scale bar.

Compass Rose
The compass rose indicates directions. The four cardinal directions—north, south, east, and west—are usually indicated with arrows or the points of a star. The intermediate directions—northeast, northwest, southeast, and southwest—may also be shown.

Cities
Cities are represented by a dot. Sometimes the relative sizes of cities are shown using dots of different sizes.

Capitals
National capitals are often represented by a star within a circle.

Boundary Lines
On political maps of large areas, boundary lines highlight the borders between different countries or states.

Using Scale

All maps are drawn to a certain scale. **Scale** is a consistent, proportional relationship between the measurements shown on the map and the measurement of the Earth's surface.

Small-Scale Maps A small-scale map, like this political map of France, can show a large area but little detail. Note that the scale bar on this map indicates that about 1 inch is equal to 200 miles.

Large-Scale Maps A large-scale map, like this map of Paris, can show a small area with a great amount of detail. Study the scale bar. Note that the map measurements correspond to much smaller distances than on the map of France.

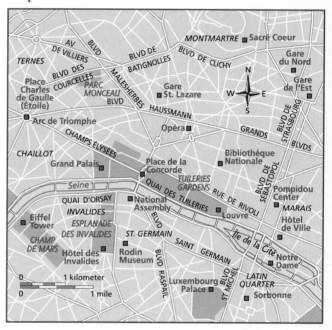

Absolute and Relative Location

As you learned on page GH6, absolute location is the exact point where a line of latitude crosses a line of longitude. Another way to indicate location is by **relative location,** or the location of one place in relation to another. To find relative location, find a reference point—a location you already know—on a map. Then look in the appropriate direction for the new location. For example, locate Paris (your reference point) on the map of France above. The relative location of Lyon can be described as southeast of Paris.

PRACTICING THE SKILL

1. **Explain** the significance of: key, compass rose, cardinal directions, intermediate directions, scale bar, scale, relative location.

2. **Describe** the elements of a map that help you interpret the information displayed on the map.

3. **How** does the scale bar help you determine distances on the Earth's surface?

4. **Describe** the relative location of your school in two different ways.

5. **Use** a Venn diagram to identify the similarities and differences of small-scale maps and large-scale maps.

Small-scale maps   Large-scale maps

Physical Maps

A **physical map** shows the location and the **topography**, or shape of the Earth's physical features. A study of a country's physical features often helps to explain the historical development of the country. For example, mountains may be barriers to transportation and rivers and streams can provide access into the interior of a country.

Relief
Physical maps use shading and texture to show general relief—the differences in elevation, or height, of landforms.

Landforms
Physical maps may show landforms such as mountains, plains, plateaus, and valleys.

Water Features
Physical maps show rivers, streams, lakes, and other water features.

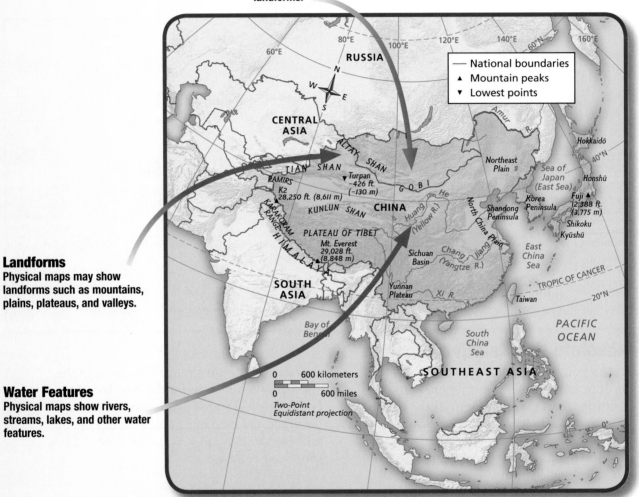

PRACTICING THE SKILL

1. **Explain** the significance of: physical map, topography, relief, elevation.
2. **Complete** a table like the one right to explain what you can learn from the map about each of the physical features listed.

Physical Feature	What You Can Learn From the Map
Tian Shan	
Chang Jiang	
Northeast Plain	

Political Maps

A **political map** shows the boundaries and locations of political units such as countries, states, counties, cities, and towns. Many features depicted on a political map are **human-made,** or determined by humans rather than by nature. Political maps can show the networks and links that exist within and between political units.

Human-Made Features
Political maps show human-made features such as boundaries, capitals, cities, roads, highways, and railroads.

Nonsubject Area
Areas surrounding the subject area of a map are usually a different color to set them apart. They are labeled to give you a context for the area you are studying.

Physical Features
Political maps may show some physical features such as relief, rivers, and mountains.

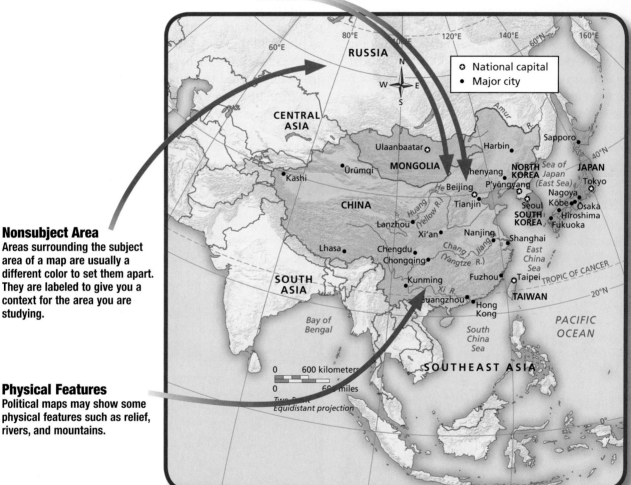

PRACTICING THE SKILL

1. **Explain** the significance of: political map, human-made.

2. **What** types of information would you find on a political map that would not appear on a physical map?

3. **Complete** a table like the one below to explain what you can learn from the map about each of the human-made features listed.

Human-Made Feature	What You Can Learn From the Map
Seoul	
Tokyo	
North Korea/South Korea boundary	

Thematic Maps

Maps that emphasize a single idea or a particular kind of information about an area are called **thematic maps**. There are many kinds of thematic maps, each designed to serve a different need. This textbook includes thematic maps that show ancient civilizations, the spread of religious ideas, exploration and trade, and war and political conflicts.

Qualitative Maps

Maps that use colors, symbols, lines, or dots to show information related to a specific idea are called **qualitative maps**. Such maps are often used to depict historical information. For example, the qualitative map below shows the spread of farming in Latin America over time.

Flow-Line Maps

Maps that illustrate the movement of people, animals, goods, and ideas, as well as physical processes like hurricanes and glaciers, are called **flow-line maps**. Arrows are usually used to represent the flow and direction of movement. The flow-line map below shows the movement of Slavic peoples throughout Europe.

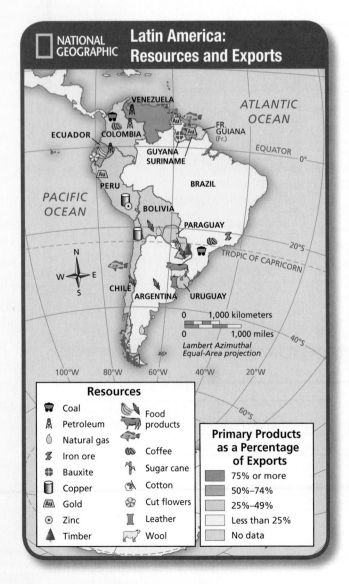

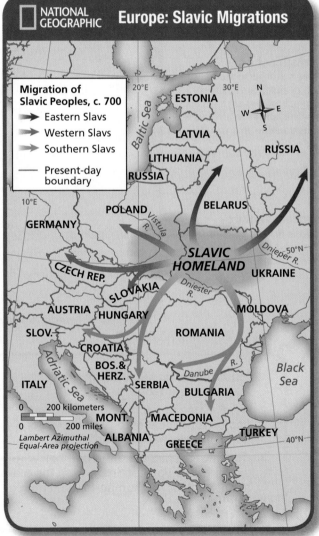

Geographic Information Systems

Modern technology has changed the way maps are made. Most cartographers use computers with software programs called **geographic information systems (GIS)**. A GIS is designed to accept data from different sources—maps, satellite images, printed text, and statistics. The GIS converts the data into a digital code, which arranges it in a database. Cartographers then program the GIS to process the data and produce maps. With GIS, each kind of information on a map is saved as a separate electronic layer.

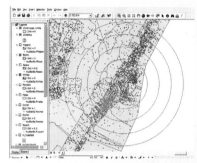

The first layer of information in a GIS pinpoints the area of interest. This allows the user to see, in detail, the area he or she needs to study. In this case, the area of study is a 5 mile (8 km) radius around Christ Hospital in Jersey City, New Jersey.

Additional layers of information are added based on the problem or issue being studied. In this case, hospital administrators want to find out about the population living in neighborhoods near the hospital so they can offer the community what it needs. A second layer showing African Americans who live within the 5 mile (8 km) radius has been added to the GIS.

Complex information can be presented using more than one layer. For example, the hospital's surrounding neighborhoods include other groups in addition to African Americans. A third layer showing whites who live within the 5 mile (8 km) radius has been added to the GIS. Administrators can now use this information to help them make decisions about staffing and services associated with the hospital.

PRACTICING THE SKILL

1. **Explain** the significance of: thematic maps, qualitative maps, flow-line maps.

2. **Which** type of thematic map would best show the spread of Islam during Muhammad's time?

3. **Which** type of thematic map would best show average income per capita in the United States?

4. **How** does GIS allow cartographers to create maps and make changes to maps quickly and easily?

5. **Complete** a chart like the one below by identifying three examples of each type of thematic map found in this textbook. Note the page numbers of each.

Qualitative Maps	Flow-Line Maps

The World Before Modern Times

Prehistory–A.D. 1500

▶ Why It Matters

For thousands of years, human beings survived by hunting, fishing, and gathering food. In the space of a few thousand years, humans began to master the art of growing food crops. As more food was produced, the population grew, and people began to live in cities, form governments, and develop writing and art. This was the beginning of civilization. As civilizations emerged in different parts of the world, new political systems, religions, arts, and sciences developed. These developments continue to influence the modern world.

CHAPTER 1   THE FIRST CIVILIZATIONS AND EMPIRES, *PREHISTORY–A.D. 500*

CHAPTER 2   ANCIENT GREECE AND ROME, *1900 B.C.–A.D. 500*

CHAPTER 3   REGIONAL CIVILIZATIONS, *400–1500*

CHAPTER 4   TOWARD A NEW WORLD, *800–1500*

The "Maiden Porch" of the Erechtheion, overlooking the city of Athens, Greece, is an example of Greek architecture from the fifth century B.C.

The First Civilizations and Empires, Prehistory–A.D. 500

Section 1 The First Humans

Section 2 Western Asia and Egypt

Section 3 India and China

MAKING CONNECTIONS

How does geography influence civilization?

The first civilizations developed near rivers. Rivers provided water for irrigation and rich soil to sustain successful agriculture needed to feed growing populations. Egyptian civilization developed along the Nile. Remnants of this early civilization, such as Ramses II's temple Abu Simbel, can still be seen today.

- Why did ancient civilizations develop near rivers?
- What geographical features led to the settlement of your city or state?

THE WORLD ▶

c. 8000 B.C.
Systematic agriculture develops

c. 3000 B.C.
Cities built in Indus River valley

| 2,500,000 B.C. | 8500 B.C. | 3500 B.C. |

c. 2,500,000 B.C.
Paleolithic humans carve with stone tools

c. 1792 B.C.
Hammurabi
comes to power
in Babylon

c. 200 B.C.
Travel on the Silk
Road begins

1500 B.C.

A.D. 200

c. 521 B.C.
Darius I begins
expanding
Persian Empire

A.D. 220
Han dynasty ends

FOLDABLES™
Study Organizer

Organizing Create a
Four-Tab Book to record
What, Where, When, and
Why/How facts while
you read about the
Great Wall of China or
the Silk Road.

What
Where
When
Why/How

History ONLINE

Chapter Overview—Visit glencoe.com to preview Chapter 1.

The First Humans

Scientists study the evidence left by prehistoric people to better understand them. The transition from nomadic hunters to city dwellers was a major turning point in history and is part of the Neolithic Revolution.

GUIDE TO READING

The BIG Idea
Physical Geography After *Homo sapiens sapiens* spread throughout the world, the development of systematic agriculture led to the rise of early civilizations.

Content Vocabulary
• hominid *(p. 4)*
• Neolithic Revolution *(p. 7)*
• systematic agriculture *(p. 7)*
• civilization *(p. 7)*

Academic Vocabulary
• survive *(p. 5)*
• revolution *(p. 7)*

People and Places
• *Africa (p. 4)*
• *Homo sapiens (p. 4)*
• *Neanderthals (p. 4)*
• *Homo sapiens sapiens (p. 4)*

Reading Strategy
Summarizing Information As you read, create a chart like the one below listing six characteristics of a civilization.

1.	4.
2.	5.
3.	6.

Before History

MAIN IDEA Scientists use fossils and artifacts as clues to how early humans lived.

HISTORY & YOU How do you meet your needs for food, shelter, and clothing? Read how early humans met their needs.

Historians rely mostly on documents, or written records, to create their pictures of the past. However, no written records exist for the prehistory of humankind. In fact, *prehistory* means the time before writing was developed. The story of prehistoric humans depends on archaeological and, more recently, biological evidence. Scientists use this information to develop theories about our early past. Archaeologists dig up and examine artifacts such as tools, weapons, art, and even buildings made by early humans. Anthropologists use artifacts and human fossils to create a picture of people's everyday lives. One of the most important and difficult jobs of both archaeologists and anthropologists is dating their finds. Dating human fossils and artifacts helps scientists understand when and where the first humans lived.

What is a **hominid**? A hominid was a humanlike creature that walked upright. The earliest hominids lived in **Africa** four million years ago. For decades scientists assumed these earliest of upright walking creatures must also have used tools. The discovery of a common ancestor, *Australopithecus,* or "southern ape," who flourished in eastern and southern Africa challenged this theory. Another hominid, *Homo erectus,* or "upright human," existed from 1.8 million to 100,000 years ago. *Homo erectus* had arms and legs in proportion to modern humans and was probably the first hominid to leave Africa.

Around 200,000 years ago, *Homo sapiens,* "wise human," emerged. Two kinds of early humans descended from ***Homo sapiens***: **Neanderthals** and ***Homo sapiens sapiens***. The earliest remains of Neanderthals, or Neandertals, were first found in the Neanderthal, a valley in Germany. They probably lived between 100,000 B.C. and 30,000 B.C. and have been found in Europe and Turkey. Besides using many kinds of stone tools, Neanderthals seem to be the first early people to bury their dead.

The second group descended from *Homo sapiens* is *Homo sapiens sapiens,* meaning "wise, wise human." These are the first hominids

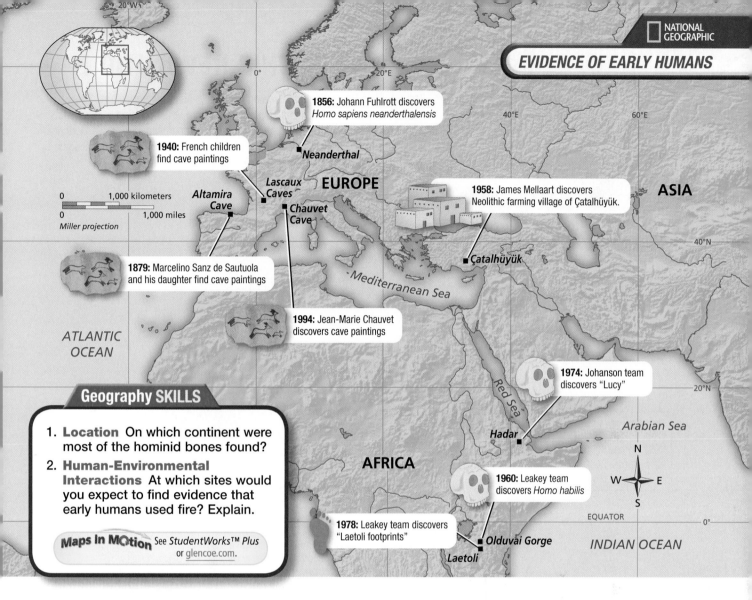

EVIDENCE OF EARLY HUMANS

20°W

0°

20°E

40°E

60°E

1856: Johann Fuhlrott discovers *Homo sapiens neanderthalensis*

1940: French children find cave paintings

Neanderthal

Lascaux Caves

EUROPE

1958: James Mellaart discovers Neolithic farming village of Çatalhüyük.

ASIA

0   1,000 kilometers

0   1,000 miles

Miller projection

Altamira Cave

Chauvet Cave

40°N

Çatalhüyük

1879: Marcelino Sanz de Sautuola and his daughter find cave paintings

Mediterranean Sea

1994: Jean-Marie Chauvet discovers cave paintings

ATLANTIC OCEAN

1974: Johanson team discovers "Lucy"

20°N

Red Sea

Arabian Sea

Hadar

N

Geography SKILLS

AFRICA

W   E

S

1. **Location** On which continent were most of the hominid bones found?

2. **Human-Environmental Interactions** At which sites would you expect to find evidence that early humans used fire? Explain.

1960: Leakey team discovers *Homo habilis*

EQUATOR

0°

Maps in MOtion See *StudentWorks™ Plus* or glencoe.com.

1978: Leakey team discovers "Laetoli footprints"

Olduvai Gorge

INDIAN OCEAN

Laetoli

to have an anatomy similar to that of people today.

Homo sapiens sapiens appeared in Africa between 150,000 and 200,000 years ago. They probably spread out of Africa 100,000 years ago. By 30,000 B.C., *Homo sapiens sapiens* had replaced the Neanderthals, who had died out, possibly as a result of conflicts between them.

Over many thousands of years *Homo sapiens sapiens* spread over the globe as they searched for food and new hunting grounds. Over hundreds of thousands of years, they moved enough to populate the world. Today, all humans, whether they are Europeans, Asians, Aborigines, or Africans, belong to the same subgroup of human beings.

One of the basic distinguishing features of the human species is the ability to make tools. The term *Paleolithic Age* (approximately 2,500,000 B.C. to 10,000 B.C.), is used to designate the period of human history in which humans used simple stone tools. Paleolithic is Greek for "old stone" and the Paleolithic Age is sometimes called the Old Stone Age.

For hundreds of thousands of years, humans relied on hunting and gathering for their daily food. These Paleolithic humans were nomads—people who moved from place to place to **survive.** Archaeologists and anthropologists think these nomads probably lived in small groups of twenty or thirty. Over the years, they developed better tools to aid in hunting and daily tasks. The systematic use of fire made it possible to provide a source of both light and heat within both caves and handmade structures in which they lived.

✓ **Reading Check** **Summarizing** Describe the stages of early human development.

—NEOLITHIC REVOLUTION—

The Neolithic Revolution was the beginning of systematic agriculture. This revolution was marked by the establishment and growth of farming villages such as Jericho. Located near a spring, which made the land especially fertile, Jericho was established by 8000 B.C. It was one of the largest Neolithic farming villages, with an estimated population over 1,000.

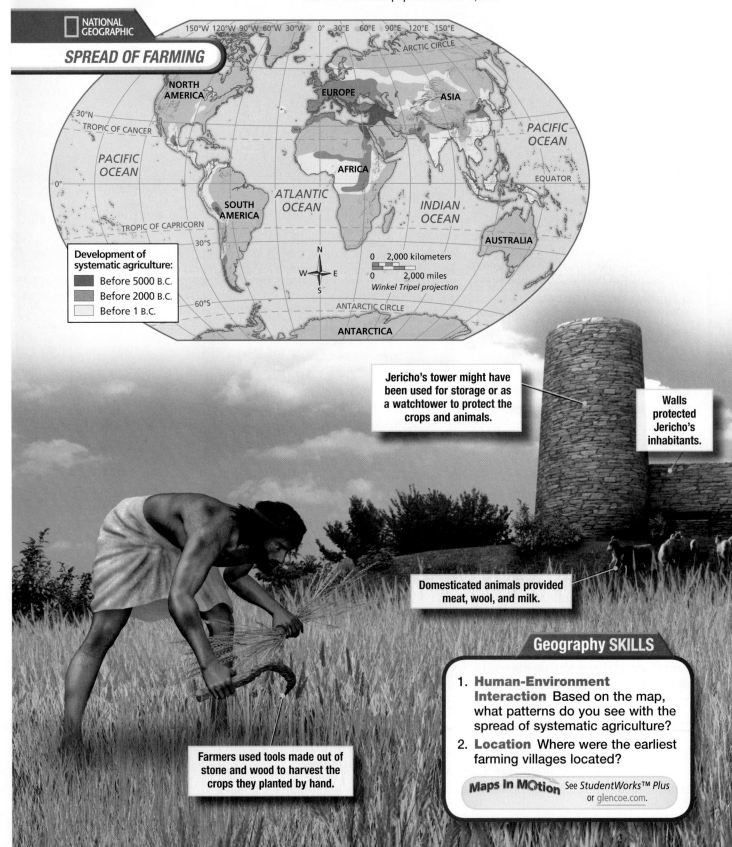

NATIONAL GEOGRAPHIC

SPREAD OF FARMING

Development of systematic agriculture:
- Before 5000 B.C.
- Before 2000 B.C.
- Before 1 B.C.

0   2,000 kilometers
0   2,000 miles
Winkel Tripel projection

Jericho's tower might have been used for storage or as a watchtower to protect the crops and animals.

Walls protected Jericho's inhabitants.

Domesticated animals provided meat, wool, and milk.

Farmers used tools made out of stone and wood to harvest the crops they planted by hand.

Geography SKILLS

1. **Human-Environment Interaction** Based on the map, what patterns do you see with the spread of systematic agriculture?

2. **Location** Where were the earliest farming villages located?

Maps In Motion See *StudentWorks™ Plus* or glencoe.com.

The Neolithic Revolution

MAIN IDEA Civilization developed from the agricultural revolution of the Neolithic Age.

HISTORY & YOU Do more people live on farms or in cities today? Read how efficient farming led to the rise of cities.

The last ice age was followed by what is called the **Neolithic Revolution**—that is, the **revolution** that occurred in the Neolithic Age, the period of human history from around 8000 B.C. to 4000 B.C. The word *Neolithic* is Greek for "new stone," but the term *New Stone Age* is misleading. The real change in the Neolithic Revolution was the shift from the hunting of animals and the gathering of food to the keeping of animals and the growing of food on a regular basis—what we call **systematic agriculture.**

The planting of grains and vegetables provided a regular supply of food. The domestication of animals, adapting them for human use, added a reliable source of meat, milk, and wool. Animals could also be used to do work. Growing crops and taming food-producing animals caused an agricultural revolution. Because there was enough food, humans had more control over their lives. It also meant they could give up their nomadic ways of life and begin to live in settled communities. Some historians believe this revolution was the most important development in human history.

The Neolithic Age set the stage for major changes to come. As people mastered farming, some villages developed more complex and wealthier societies. As their wealth increased, these societies began to create armies and to build walled cities. Gradually, more complex cultures developed into a new form of human society called civilization.

A **civilization** is a complex culture in which large numbers of human beings share a number of common elements. Historians have identified the basic characteristics of civilizations. Six of the most important are: cities, government, religion, social structure, writing, and art. The first civilizations developed in river valleys where people could carry on the large-scale farming needed to feed a large population. As farming became abundant, more people lived in cities. Growing numbers of people and the need for defense soon led to the growth of governments. A new social structure based on economic power arose and was dominated by rulers and the upper class. Important religious developments, writing, and significant artistic activity, such as architecture, also characterized these new urban civilizations. These civilizations constituted nothing less than a revolutionary stage in the growth of human society.

✓ Reading Check **Describing** Describe the relationship between an increase in food production and the rise of cities.

SECTION 1 REVIEW

Vocabulary
1. **Explain** the significance of: hominid, Africa, *Homo sapiens*, Neanderthal, *Homo sapiens sapiens*, survive, Neolithic Revolution, revolution, systematic agriculture, civilization.

Main Ideas
2. **Contrast** the evidence that archaeologists and anthropologists use to understand the past to that used by historians.

3. **List** the species that emerged during the early stages of human development.

4. **Explain** How did settled farming make it possible for cities to develop?

Critical Thinking
5. **The BIG Idea** **Analyzing** Does the development of systematic agriculture by Neolithic peoples after the end of the last Ice Age deserve to be called a revolution? Why was the shift to systematic agriculture important to the development of civilization?

6. **Sequencing Information** Create a diagram like the one below to show how changes during the Neolithic Revolution led to the emergence of civilization.

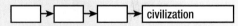

7. **Analyzing Visuals** Examine the art on page 6. List six items that are results of the Neolithic Revolution.

Writing About History
8. **Expository Writing** Conduct research on Çatalhüyük, Jericho, or another early site of the Neolithic period. Then write a short essay explaining how people may have lived in that city in its early period.

History ONLINE

For help with the concepts in this section of *Glencoe World History—Modern Times*, go to glencoe.com and click Study Central.

Social History

Early Housing

What a house looks like has much to do with where it is located, when it was built, and what materials were available. Zhoukoudianzhen Cave, in China, shows evidence of use from around 700,000 to around 200,000 years ago. Pincevent, in modern-day France, shows how early humans lived in northern Europe at the end of the Ice Age, around 13,000 years ago. And Çatalhüyük, in modern-day Turkey, was an early farming village from 6700 B.C. to 5700 B.C.

Zhoukoudianzhen Cave

The remains of 40 *Homo erectus* men, women, and children were found here.

They probably ate nuts, berries, insects, reptiles, rats, birds, eggs, and large mammals.

The first evidence of the use of fire was 20 feet of ash from c. 500,000 years ago.

These *Homo erectus* used wood, bamboo, and stone tools to scrape, chop, and cut.

Pincevent Site

Pincevent was a summer camp near water and food sources, such as reindeer and horses.

These early humans lived in round tents made of animal skins held up by wooden poles.

Rings of stone were used to hold the tent edges down. Hearthstones, animal bones, and flint tools show where the tents were located.

Temporary Settlements

Before around 8000 B.C., early humans were nomads who lived in temporary settlements. They moved every season, migrating with the animals they hunted. Early humans used caves for shelter. If they lived in a place without rock outcroppings, they made their homes out of available materials. Tents made of animal bones or wood were covered with animal hides or turf.

ÇATALHÜYÜK

The villagers buried their dead beneath platforms in their houses.

Some houses had yards—probably for domesticated animals like cattle and dogs.

Because there were no streets and the houses were connected, people used ladders to enter their homes from the rooftops. This construction style made the village easier to defend.

When the mud-brick homes were damaged, villagers knocked them down and rebuilt on top. The layers of homes created a mound, or *hüyük*.

Map locations: Pincevent (EUROPE), Zhoukoudianzhen (ASIA), Çatalhüyük; AFRICA, ATLANTIC OCEAN, INDIAN OCEAN, PACIFIC OCEAN, AUSTRALIA

PERMANENT SETTLEMENTS

After 8000 B.C., people began settling in one place, planting crops and raising livestock. These farming settlements began in river valleys in the Fertile Crescent and in Turkey. Rivers provided water for irrigation and transportation. Permanent walls provided protection from the weather, as well as from other humans—many of whom were still nomads—and animals.

ANALYZING VISUALS

1. **Comparing** Why are there similarities between the homes despite the differences in era and location?

2. **Analyzing** What are three major differences between temporary and permanent settlements?

Western Asia and Egypt

GUIDE TO READING

The BIG Idea
Ideas, Beliefs, and Values Ancient civilizations rose along rivers in Western Asia and Egypt and gave humankind new technologies and belief systems.

Content Vocabulary
- city-state *(p. 10)*
- empire *(p. 11)*
- dynasty *(p. 14)*
- Judaism *(p. 18)*
- monotheistic *(p. 19)*

Academic Vocabulary
- innovations *(p. 13)*
- transport *(p. 13)*

People and Places
- Tigris River *(p. 10)*
- Euphrates River *(p. 10)*
- Fertile Crescent *(p. 10)*
- Sargon *(p. 11)*
- Hammurabi *(p. 11)*
- Nile River *(p. 14)*
- Lower Egypt *(p. 14)*
- Upper Egypt *(p. 14)*
- Menes *(p. 14)*
- King Solomon *(p. 18)*
- Jerusalem *(p. 18)*
- Cyrus *(p. 21)*
- Royal Road *(p. 21)*

Reading Strategy
Categorizing Information As you read, complete a chart like the one below listing the geographic locations of the civilizations of western Asia and Europe.

Western Asia	Egypt

The societies of western Asia and Egypt contributed innovations in language, science, and religion, which continue to influence societies worldwide. Codified laws and organized class structures set the foundation for the development of future empires.

Ancient Mesopotamia

MAIN IDEA City-states were the basic units within the earliest civilizations in Mesopotamia.

HISTORY & YOU How do Americans define a city or a state? Read how the city-states functioned in ancient Mesopotamia.

The ancient Greeks spoke of the valley between the **Tigris** and **Euphrates Rivers** as Mesopotamia, the land "between the rivers." Mesopotamia was at the eastern end of an area known as the **Fertile Crescent,** an arc of land from the Mediterranean Sea to the Persian Gulf. Rich soil and abundant crops allowed the land to sustain an early civilization.

People in the valley could not tell exactly when the rivers would flood or how much they would flood. Therefore, people in ancient Mesopotamia learned to control the flow of the rivers. By using irrigation and drainage ditches, farmers were able to grow crops regularly. An abundance of food allowed many people to live together in cities, and civilization emerged.

City-States and Empires

The origins of the Sumerian people remain a mystery. By 3000 B.C., they had established a number of independent cities in southern Mesopotamia, including Eridu, Ur, and Uruk. As the cities expanded, they gained political and economic control over the surrounding countryside. They formed **city-states,** the basic units of Sumerian civilization.

The most prominent building in a Sumerian city was the temple dedicated to the chief god or goddess of the city. This temple was often built atop a massive stepped tower called a ziggurat. The Sumerians believed that gods and goddesses owned the cities. The people devoted much of their wealth to building temples, as well as elaborate houses for the priests and priestesses who served the gods. The temples and related buildings served as the center of the city physically, economically, and even politically. Priests and priestesses, who supervised the temples and their property, had a great deal of power.

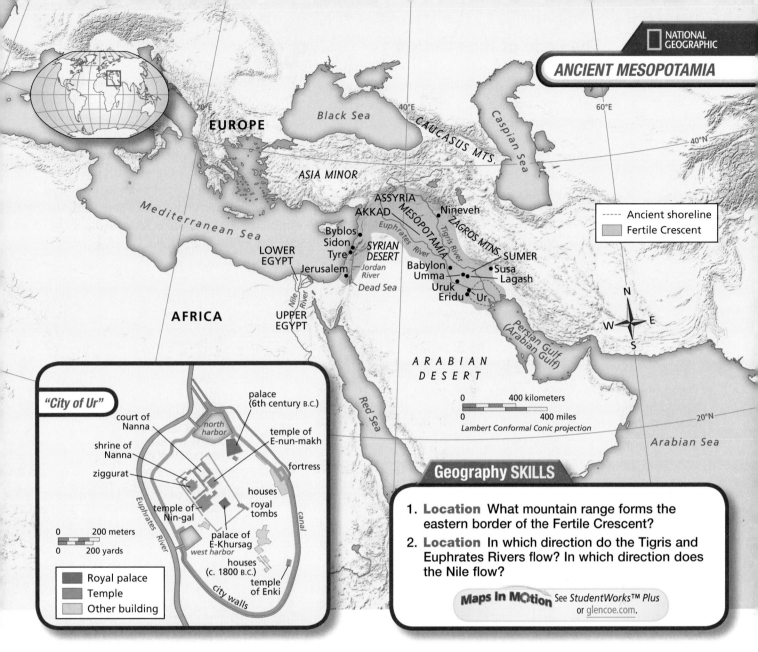

EUROPE

Black Sea

CAUCASUS MTS.

Caspian Sea

ASIA MINOR

Mediterranean Sea

ASSYRIA

AKKAD

MESOPOTAMIA

Nineveh

Euphrates River

Tigris River

ZAGROS MTS.

Byblos
Sidon
Tyre

SYRIAN DESERT

SUMER

LOWER EGYPT

Jerusalem

Jordan River

Dead Sea

Babylon
Umma
Uruk
Eridu

Susa
Lagash

Ur

AFRICA

Nile River

UPPER EGYPT

Red Sea

ARABIAN DESERT

Persian Gulf (Arabian Gulf)

- - - - Ancient shoreline

Fertile Crescent

Arabian Sea

```
0          400 kilometers
0          400 miles
```
Lambert Conformal Conic projection

"City of Ur"

court of Nanna

shrine of Nanna

ziggurat

north harbor

palace (6th century B.C.)

temple of E-nun-makh

fortress

houses

royal tombs

temple of Nin-gal

palace of E-Khursag
west harbor

houses (c. 1800 B.C.)

canal

city walls

temple of Enki

Euphrates River

```
0     200 meters
0     200 yards
```

■ Royal palace
■ Temple
□ Other building

Geography SKILLS

1. **Location** What mountain range forms the eastern border of the Fertile Crescent?
2. **Location** In which direction do the Tigris and Euphrates Rivers flow? In which direction does the Nile flow?

Maps In Motion See *StudentWorks™ Plus* or glencoe.com.

The Sumerians believed that the gods ruled the cities, making the state a theocracy—a government by divine authority. Even when power passed into the hands of kings, Sumerians believed that these rulers derived their power from the gods and were agents of the gods. Kings led armies and organized workers for the irrigation projects on which farming depended.

As the number of Sumerian city-states grew and the city-states expanded, new conflicts arose. City-state fought city-state for control of land and water. Located on the flat land of Mesopotamia, the Sumerian city-states were also open to invasion by other groups. To the north of the Sumerian city-states were the Akkadians (uh•KAY•dee•uhnz).

Around 2340 B.C., **Sargon,** leader of the Akkadians, overran the Sumerian city-states and set up the first **empire** in world history. An empire is a large political unit or state, usually under a single leader, that controls many territories. Empires are often difficult to maintain. The rise and fall of empires is an important part of history.

Attacks from neighbors caused the Akkadian Empire to fall by 2100 B.C. Wars between city-states lasted until 1792 B.C. In Babylon, a city-state south of Akkad, **Hammurabi** (HA•muh•RAH•bee) came to power. He gained control of Sumer and Akkad, creating a new Mesopotamian kingdom. After his death in 1750 B.C., a series of weak kings was unable to keep the empire united, and it finally fell to new invaders.

The Code of Hammurabi

Hammurabi is remembered for his law code. For centuries in Mesopotamia, laws had regulated people's relationships with one another. Hammurabi's collection of laws provides great insight into social conditions there. The Code of Hammurabi was based on a system of strict justice. Penalties for criminal offenses were severe, and they varied according to the social class of the victim. A crime against a noble by a commoner was punished more severely than the same offense against a member of the lower class.

Moreover, the principle of retaliation ("an eye for an eye, tooth for a tooth") was a fundamental part of this system of justice.

Hammurabi's code took seriously the duties of public officials. Officials who failed to solve crimes had to make personal restitution to the victims or their families. Judges could be penalized for ruling incorrectly on a case.

HISTORY & ARTS   PRIMARY SOURCE
The Standard of Ur

The Standard of Ur was found in a grave in the Royal Cemetery at Ur. The Standard has two main panels titled "War" and "Peace." The "War" panel, shown here, depicts a Sumerian army. It should be read from the bottom up, and left to right.

The top panel shows the king receiving prisoners and other spoils of war.

Sumerian soldiers use spears to drive their prisoners forward, in the middle panel.

It is believed that the middle panel depicts men carrying tribute to their conquerors.

A king figure in the bottom left-hand corner drives a chariot, which crushes enemies under its wheels.

DOCUMENT-BASED QUESTIONS

1. **Describing** What events are depicted in these panels?
2. **Interpreting** What does the "War" panel reveal about Sumerian society?

The law code also included what we would call consumer protection laws. Builders were held responsible for the buildings they constructed. If a house collapsed and caused the death of the owner, the builder was put to death.

The largest category of laws in the Code of Hammurabi focused on marriage and the family. Parents arranged marriages for their children. After marriage, the two parties signed a marriage contract that made the marriage legal.

Mesopotamian society was patriarchal—that is, men dominated the society. Hammurabi's code shows that women had far fewer rights in marriage than did men.

A woman's place was in the home. A husband could divorce his wife if she failed to fulfill her duties, was unable to bear children, or tried to leave home to engage in business. Even harsher, a wife who neglected her home or humiliated her husband could be drowned.

Fathers ruled their children as well as their wives. Obedience was expected: "If a son has struck his father, he shall cut off his hand." If a son committed a serious enough offense, his father could disinherit him. Obviously, Hammurabi's law code covered almost every aspect of people's lives.

Sumerian Creativity

The Sumerians invented the oldest writing system. Historians also credit them with many other technological **innovations.**

Around 3000 B.C., the Sumerians created a cuneiform ("wedge-shaped") system of writing. Using a reed stylus (a tool for writing), they made wedge-shaped impressions on clay tablets, which were then baked or dried in the sun. Once dried, these tablets lasted a very long time. Several hundred thousand tablets have been found. They have been a valuable source of information for modern scholars.

Mesopotamian peoples used writing primarily for record keeping. Cuneiform texts, however, were also used in schools to train scribes, members of the learned class who served as copyists, teachers, and jurists.

For boys of the upper class in Mesopotamia, becoming a scribe was the key to a successful career. Men who began their careers as scribes became the leaders of their cities, temples, and armies. Scribes came to hold the most important positions in Sumerian society.

To become scribes, boys from wealthy families, many of them the sons of scribes, attended the new schools that were in operation by 2500 B.C. Young boys seeking to become scribes began school when they were small children and trained until they were young men. School days began at sunrise and ended at sunset. Discipline was harsh.

Scribal students spent most of their school days following the same routine. They copied and recopied standard works on clay tablets and then recited from them. Although boring, this was probably the scribe's only way of learning how to form the cuneiform writing signs neatly and correctly.

Writing was important because it allowed a society to keep records and to pass along knowledge from person to person and generation to generation. Writing also made it possible for people to communicate ideas in new ways. This is especially evident in *The Epic of Gilgamesh*, a Mesopotamian epic poem that records the exploits of a legendary king named Gilgamesh.

The Sumerians also invented several tools and devices that made daily life easier and more productive. They developed the wagon wheel, for example, to help **transport** people and goods from place to place.

The potter's wheel to shape containers, the sundial to keep time, and the arch used in construction are other examples of Sumerian technology. The Sumerians were the first to make bronze out of copper and tin, creating finely crafted metalwork.

The Sumerians also made outstanding achievements in mathematics and astronomy. In math, they devised a number system based on 60. Geometry was used to measure fields and to erect buildings. In astronomy, the Sumerians charted the heavenly constellations. A quick glance at your watch and its division of an hour into 60 minutes should remind you of our debt to the Sumerians.

✓ **Reading Check** **Identifying** Identify five features of Mesopotamian society as revealed by the Code of Hammurabi.

Ancient Egypt

MAIN IDEA Located along the Nile, Egyptian society thrived during three major historical periods called kingdoms.

HISTORY & YOU Why might periods of political stability also be times of cultural achievement? Learn about Egypt's accomplishments.

The **Nile River** begins in the heart of Africa and courses northward for more than 4,000 miles (6,436 km). It is the longest river in the world. The Nile splits into two major branches before it empties into the Mediterranean. This split forms a triangular territory called a delta. The Nile Delta is called **Lower Egypt;** the land upstream, to the south, is called **Upper Egypt.** Egypt's important cities developed at the tip of the delta, the point at which the Nile divides.

Scholars divide Egyptian history into three major periods: the Old Kingdom, the Middle Kingdom, and the New Kingdom. These were periods of long-term stability marked by strong leadership, freedom from invasion, great building projects, and considerable intellectual and cultural activity. Between the periods of stability were ages of political disorder and invasion.

Egypt's history begins around 3100 B.C., when King **Menes** (MEE•NEEZ) united Upper and Lower Egypt into a single kingdom and created the first royal **dynasty.** A dynasty is a family of rulers whose right to rule is passed on within the family.

The Old Kingdom

The Old Kingdom, from around 2700 B.C. to 2200 B.C., was an age of prosperity and splendor. Like the kings of the Sumerian city-states, the monarchs of the Old Kingdom were powerful rulers over a unified state. Among the various titles of Egyptian monarchs, that of *pharaoh*—originally meaning "great house" or "palace"—eventually became the most common. Kingship was a divine institution in ancient Egypt and formed part of a universal cosmic order. In obeying their pharaoh, subjects believed they were helping to maintain a stable world order.

The Pyramids

One of the great achievements of Egyptian civilization, the building of pyramids, occurred in the time of the Old Kingdom. Pyramids were built as part of a larger complex of buildings dedicated to the dead—in effect, a city of the dead. The area included: a large pyramid for the pharaoh's burial; smaller pyramids for his family; and several mastabas, rectangular structures with flat roofs used as tombs for the pharaoh's officials. The tombs contained rooms stocked with chairs, weapons, games, and a variety of food. If the physical body was preserved and provided with earthly comforts, then the spirit could return to it.

To preserve the physical body after death, the Egyptians practiced mummification, a process of slowly drying a dead body to prevent it from rotting. This process took place in workshops run by priests, primarily for the wealthy families who could afford it. Workers first removed the liver, lungs, stomach, and intestines and placed them in four special jars that were put in the tomb with the mummy. The priests also removed the brain by extracting it through the nose. They then covered the corpse with a natural salt that absorbed the body's water. Later, they filled the body with spices and wrapped it with layers of linen soaked in resin. At the end of the process, which took about 70 days, a lifelike mask was placed over the head and shoulders of the mummy. The mummy was then sealed in a case and placed in its tomb.

Pyramids were tombs for pharaohs and their families. The largest and most magnificent of all the pyramids was built under King Khufu (KOO•FOO). Constructed at Giza around 2540 B.C., the Great Pyramid of King Khufu covers 13 acres (5.3 ha), measures 756 feet (230 m) at each side of its base, and stands 481 feet (147 m) high.

Guarding the Great Pyramid at Giza is a huge figure carved from rock, known as the Great Sphinx. This colossal statue is 240 feet (73 m) long and 66 feet (20 m) high. It has the body of a lion and a human head. The head is believed by many to be a likeness of Khufu's son Khafre, who ordered the statue's construction.

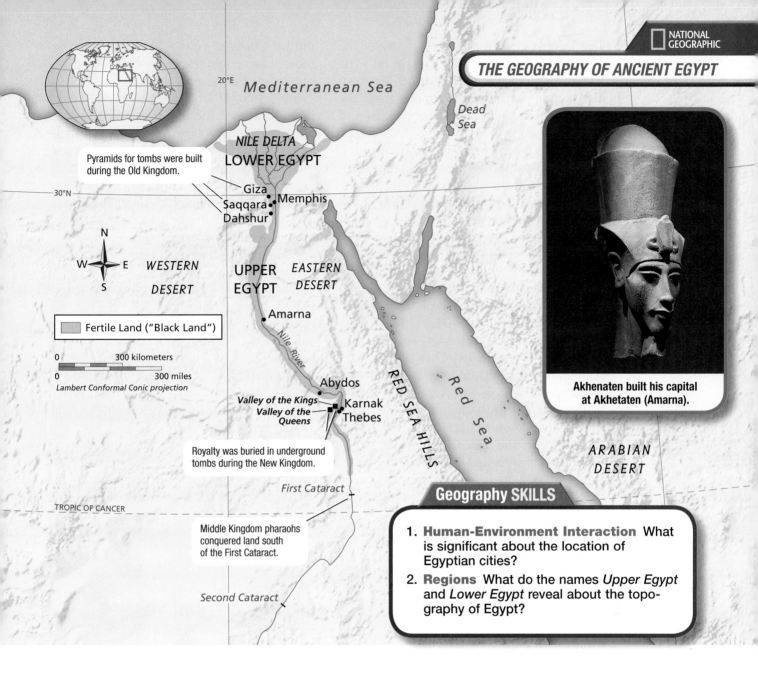

20°E *Mediterranean Sea*

Dead Sea

NILE DELTA
LOWER EGYPT

Pyramids for tombs were built during the Old Kingdom.

30°N

Giza • Memphis
Saqqara •
Dahshur •

N
W—E
S

WESTERN DESERT

UPPER EGYPT

EASTERN DESERT

• Amarna

☐ Fertile Land ("Black Land")

0   300 kilometers
0   300 miles
Lambert Conformal Conic projection

Nile River

• Abydos

Valley of the Kings
Valley of the Queens

■ Karnak
Thebes

RED SEA HILLS

Red Sea

Royalty was buried in underground tombs during the New Kingdom.

First Cataract

TROPIC OF CANCER

Middle Kingdom pharaohs conquered land south of the First Cataract.

Second Cataract

ARABIAN DESERT

Akhenaten built his capital at Akhetaten (Amarna).

Geography SKILLS

1. **Human-Environment Interaction** What is significant about the location of Egyptian cities?
2. **Regions** What do the names *Upper Egypt* and *Lower Egypt* reveal about the topography of Egypt?

Middle Kingdom

The Old Kingdom eventually collapsed, followed by a period of disorder that lasted about 150 years. Finally, a new royal dynasty gained control of all Egypt and began the Middle Kingdom, a period of stability lasting from about 2055 B.C. to 1650 B.C. Egyptians later portrayed the Middle Kingdom as a golden age of stability.

One feature of the Middle Kingdom was a new concern of the pharaohs for the people. Pharaohs of the Middle Kingdom undertook a number of helpful projects. The draining of swampland provided thousands of acres of new farmland. The digging of a canal from the Nile to the Red Sea aided trade.

New Kingdom

The Middle Kingdom came to an end around 1650 B.C. with the invasion of Egypt by a group of people from western Asia known as the Hyksos (HIK•SAHS). The Hyksos used horse-drawn war chariots to overwhelm the Egyptian soldiers, who fought from donkey carts. For almost a hundred years, the Hyksos ruled much of Egypt. The conquered Egyptians learned a great deal from their conquerors. From the Hyksos, the Egyptians learned to use bronze to make tools and weapons.

The Egyptians also mastered many of the military skills of the Hyksos, especially the use of horse-drawn war chariots. Eventually, a new dynasty of pharaohs used the new weapons to drive out the Hyksos and reunite Egypt.

The New Kingdom lasted from approximately 1550 B.C. to 1070 B.C. This reunification launched the Egyptians onto a new militaristic path. During this period, Egypt created an empire and became the most powerful state in Southwest Asia.

Massive wealth boosted the power of the pharaohs, and they showed their wealth by building new temples. Hatshepsut—one of the first women to become pharaoh—built a great temple at Deir el-Bahri.

The New Kingdom was not without troubles, however. One pharaoh, Akhenaten, introduced monotheism—the worship of one god—which caused unrest in Egypt. New invasions in the 1200s B.C. by the "Sea Peoples," as Egyptians called them, drove the Egyptians back within their old frontiers and ended the Egyptian Empire. The New Kingdom itself collapsed in 1070 B.C.

For the next thousand years, Egypt was dominated by Libyans, Nubians, Persians, and, finally, Macedonians after the conquest of Alexander the Great (see Chapter 2). In the first century B.C., the pharaoh Cleopatra VII tried to reestablish Egypt's independence. However, her involvement with Rome led to her defeat and suicide, and Egypt became a province in Rome's mighty empire.

Egyptian Society

See page R34 to read excerpts from Vizier Ptah-hotep's *An Egyptian Father's Advice to His Son* in the **Primary Sources and Literature Library**.

Egyptian society maintained a simple structure. It was organized like a pyramid, with the god-king at the top. The pharaoh was surrounded by an upper class of nobles and priests, who joined in the elaborate rituals of the pharaoh's life. The members of this ruling class ran the government and managed landed estates. Below the upper class were merchants, artisans, scribes, and tax collectors. Merchants traded up and down the Nile, as well as in local markets. Egyptian artisans made a huge variety of well-built, beautiful goods: stone dishes; wooden furniture; painted boxes; gold, silver, and copper tools and containers; paper and rope made of papyrus; and linen clothes.

Most people in Egypt worked on the land. In theory, the pharaoh owned all the land but granted portions of it to his subjects. Most of the lower classes were peasants who farmed on estates. They paid taxes in the form of crops to the pharaoh, nobles, and priests; lived in small villages; and provided military service and forced labor for building projects.

Ancient Egyptians had a positive attitude toward daily life on Earth. They married young (girls at 12 and boys at 14) and established homes and families. Monogamy (marriage to one person) was the general rule, but a husband could have additional wives if his first wife was childless.

The husband was master in the house, but wives were very well respected. Wives were in charge of the household and the education of the children.

Women's property and inheritance stayed in their hands, even in marriage. Most careers and public offices were closed to women, but some women did operate businesses. Peasant women worked in the fields and in the home. Upper-class women could become priestesses, and four queens became pharaohs.

Writing, Art, and Science

One system of writing in Egypt emerged around 3000 B.C. The Greeks later called this earliest Egyptian writing **hieroglyphics**, meaning "priest-carvings" or "sacred writings." The complex hieroglyphic system used both pictures and more abstract forms. Learning it took much time and skill. Hieroglyphic script was used for writing on temple walls and in tombs. A highly simplified version of hieroglyphics, known as hieratic script, came into being. It used the same principles as hieroglyphic writing, but the drawings were simplified by using dashes, strokes, and curves to represent them. Hieratic script was used for business transactions, record keeping, and the needs of daily life. Egyptian hieroglyphs were at first carved in stone. Later, hieratic script was written on papyrus, a paper made from reeds that grew along the Nile.

Pyramids, temples, and other monuments bear witness to the architectural and artistic achievements of the Egyptians. Artists and sculptors followed a particular style. This gave Egyptian art a distinctive look. For example, the human body was often portrayed as a combination of profile, semiprofile, and frontal view to accurately represent each part.

Egyptians also made advances in mathematics and science. Math helped them build their massive monuments. They calculated area and volume and used geometry to survey flooded land. They developed an accurate 365-day calendar by basing their year on the movements of the moon and the bright star Sirius. Egyptians also had medical expertise. Archaeologists have recovered directions from Egyptian doctors for treating wounds and diseases. Other ancient civilizations acquired medical knowledge from the Egyptians.

✓ Reading Check **Contrasting** What were the major differences between the Old Kingdom, the Middle Kingdom, and the New Kingdom?

HISTORY & ARTS — PRIMARY SOURCE

Hieroglyphics

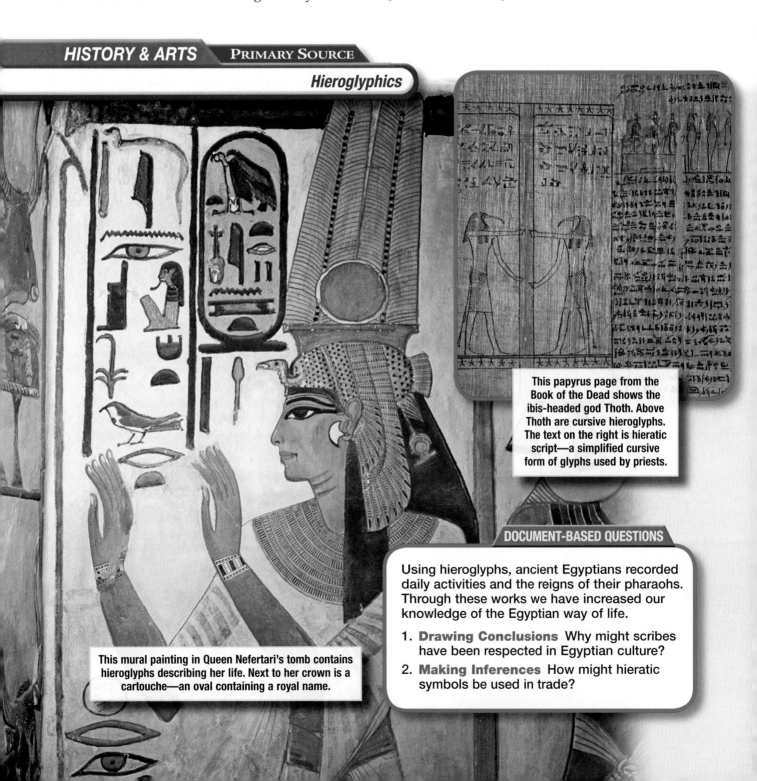

This papyrus page from the Book of the Dead shows the ibis-headed god Thoth. Above Thoth are cursive hieroglyphs. The text on the right is hieratic script—a simplified cursive form of glyphs used by priests.

This mural painting in Queen Nefertari's tomb contains hieroglyphs describing her life. Next to her crown is a cartouche—an oval containing a royal name.

DOCUMENT-BASED QUESTIONS

Using hieroglyphs, ancient Egyptians recorded daily activities and the reigns of their pharaohs. Through these works we have increased our knowledge of the Egyptian way of life.

1. **Drawing Conclusions** Why might scribes have been respected in Egyptian culture?
2. **Making Inferences** How might hieratic symbols be used in trade?

The Israelites

MAIN IDEA Israelites are remembered for establishing new religious ideas.

HISTORY & YOU How do religious beliefs affect daily life? Read about early Israel.

By 1200 B.C. the decline of Mesopotamia and Egypt allowed a number of small states to emerge and flourish. Though the Israelites were a minor factor in the politics of the region, their religion—known today as **Judaism**—flourished and later influenced the religions of Christianity and Islam.

"Children of Israel"

The Israelites were a group of Semitic-speaking people. Much of their history and religious beliefs was eventually recorded in the Hebrew Bible, which is known to Christians as the Old Testament.

According to Israelite tradition, they are descendants of the patriarch Abraham. Their ancestors migrated from Mesopotamia to Canaan. Their lifestyle was based on grazing animals rather than on farming. Then, because of drought, the Israelites moved to Egypt, where they were enslaved until Moses led them out of Egypt. They wandered for many years in the desert until they returned to Canaan.

Some interpretations of recent archaeological evidence contradict the details of the biblical account. It is generally agreed, however, that between 1200 B.C. and 1000 B.C., the Israelites organized in tribes, and established a united kingdom known as Israel.

By the time of **King Solomon,** who ruled from about 970 B.C. to 930 B.C., the Israelites had established control over all of the land that came to be called Israel and made **Jerusalem** its capital. Solomon expanded the government and army of ancient Israel and also encouraged trade. Solomon is best known for building a temple in the city of Jerusalem. The Israelites started to view the temple as the symbolic center of

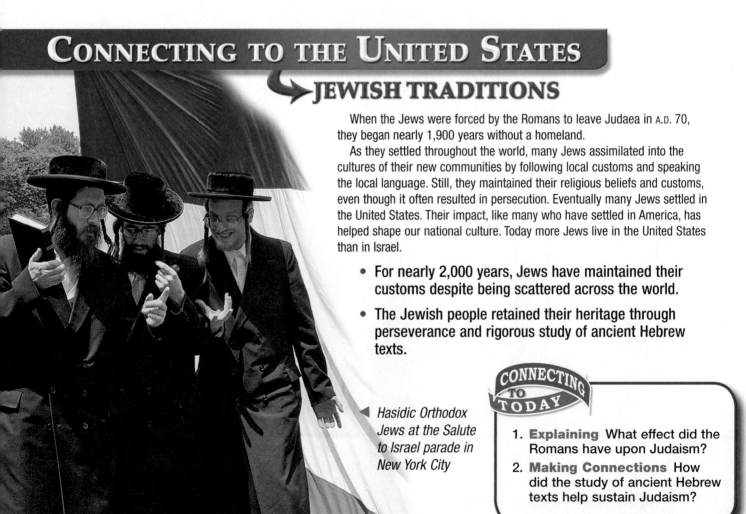

CONNECTING TO THE UNITED STATES
JEWISH TRADITIONS

When the Jews were forced by the Romans to leave Judaea in A.D. 70, they began nearly 1,900 years without a homeland.

As they settled throughout the world, many Jews assimilated into the cultures of their new communities by following local customs and speaking the local language. Still, they maintained their religious beliefs and customs, even though it often resulted in persecution. Eventually many Jews settled in the United States. Their impact, like many who have settled in America, has helped shape our national culture. Today more Jews live in the United States than in Israel.

- For nearly 2,000 years, Jews have maintained their customs despite being scattered across the world.

- The Jewish people retained their heritage through perseverance and rigorous study of ancient Hebrew texts.

Hasidic Orthodox Jews at the Salute to Israel parade in New York City

CONNECTING TO TODAY

1. **Explaining** What effect did the Romans have upon Judaism?
2. **Making Connections** How did the study of ancient Hebrew texts help sustain Judaism?

their religion and of the Israelite kingdom itself. Under King Solomon, ancient Israel reached the height of its power.

After Solomon's death, tension among the tribes within Israel led to the creation of two separate kingdoms. The Kingdom of Israel was composed of the ten northern tribes and had its capital at Samaria. To the south, the Kingdom of Judah consisted of two tribes and had its capital at Jerusalem. The Assyrians overran the Kingdom of Israel. The Kingdom of Judah retained its independence for a while but was conquered by the Chaldeans. The people of Judah survived, eventually becoming known as the Jews and giving their name to Judaism.

Religion in Israel

The Jews were **monotheistic;** they believed in one God called Yahweh (YAH•WAY), the Creator of the world and everything in it. In the Jewish view, God ruled the world; all peoples were his servants, whether they knew it or not. God had created nature but was not in nature. The sun, the wind, and other natural phenomena were not gods, but God's creations to be admired but not worshiped.

This powerful creator was not removed from the life he had created. God was just and good, and he expected goodness from his people. If they did not obey his will, they would be punished. However, he was also "compassionate, slow to anger, and rich in love." Each person could have a personal relationship with this being.

The covenant, law, and prophets were three aspects of the Jewish religious tradition. The Jews believed that during the exodus from Egypt, when Moses led his people out of bondage, God made a covenant, or contract, with them. Yahweh promised to guide them if they obeyed the law of God as expressed most prominently in the Ten Commandments. According to the Bible, Yahweh gave these laws to Moses on Mount Sinai.

The Jews believed that God sent certain religious teachers, or prophets, to serve as his voice to his people. The age of prophecy lasted from the 1000s B.C. to the 400s B.C., a time when the people were threatened or conquered by powerful neighbors. The prophets declared that faithlessness to God would bring catastrophe, but that turning from evil would bring God's mercy. Later prophets embraced a concern for all humanity. All nations would come to the God of Israel and find peace.

PRIMARY SOURCE

"Nation will not take up sword against nation, nor will they train for war anymore."
—Isaiah 2:4

The prophets also cried out against social injustice. They condemned the rich for causing the poor to suffer. They denounced luxuries, and they threatened Israel with prophecies of dire punishments for these sins. They said that God's command was to live justly, share with others, and care for the poor and the unfortunate. These words became a source for the ideals of social justice. This selection shows the prophets' belief that unjust actions would bring God's punishment.

PRIMARY SOURCE

"The Lord enters into judgment against the elders and leaders of his people: 'It is you who have ruined my vineyard; the plunder from the poor is in your houses. What do you mean by crushing my people and grinding the faces of the poor?' . . . Your men will fall by the sword, your warriors in battle. The gates of Zion will lament and mourn. . . ."
—Isaiah 3:14–17; 24–26

The religion of Israel was unique among the religions of western Asia and Egypt. The biggest difference was its belief in one God (monotheism). In other ancient religions, only priests (and some rulers) had access to the gods. In the Jewish tradition, God's wishes, though communicated to the people through prophets, had been written down. No leader of Israel could claim that he alone knew God's will. This knowledge was available to anyone who could read the Hebrew Bible.

✓ Reading Check **Identifying** Which aspect of the Israelite culture had the greatest impact on Western civilization?

New Empires

MAIN IDEA The Assyrian and the Persian Empires increased trade throughout the region.

HISTORY & YOU How is communication different for you than it was for your parents? Read about communication in the empires.

After the decline of Egypt, new empires arose that conquered vast stretches of the ancient world. The first of the new empires was formed in Assyria, located on the upper Tigris River. Later, the Persians controlled land from Egypt to India.

Assyrian Empire

The Assyrians were a Semitic-speaking people who exploited the use of iron weapons to establish an empire by 700 B.C. The Assyrian Empire included Mesopota-mia, parts of the Plateau of Iran, sections of Asia Minor along the Mediterranean coast, and Egypt to Thebes. In less than a hundred years, however, internal strife and resentment of Assyrian rule began to tear the Assyrian Empire apart. In 612 B.C., the empire fell to a coalition of Chaldeans and Medes (people who lived in the East) and was divided between those powers.

The Assyrians used terror as an instrument of warfare. They regularly laid waste to the land in which they were fighting. They smashed dams; looted and destroyed towns; set crops on fire; and cut down trees, particularly fruit trees. The Assyrians were especially known for committing atrocities on their captives. King Ashurbanipal recorded this account of his treatment of prisoners: "3,000 of their combat troops I felled . . . Many I took alive; from some of these I cut off their hands to the

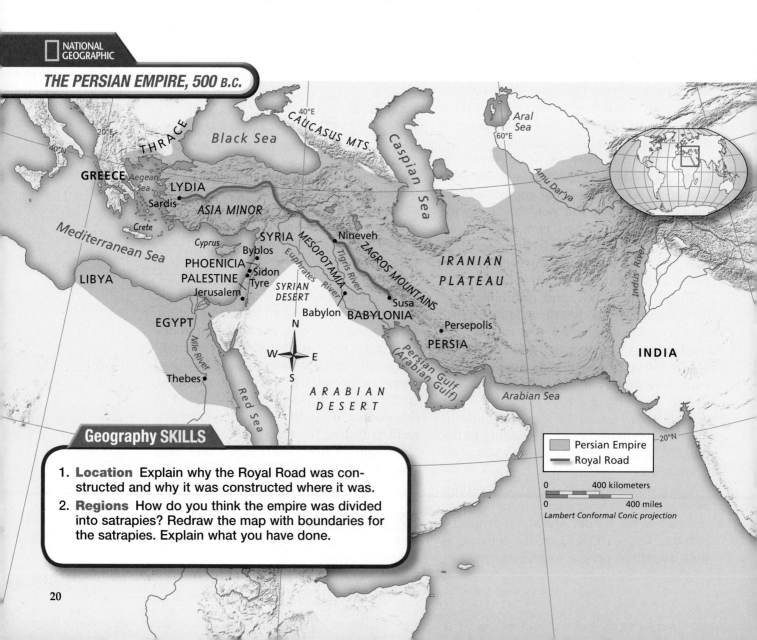

NATIONAL GEOGRAPHIC

THE PERSIAN EMPIRE, 500 B.C.

Aral Sea

Black Sea

CAUCASUS MTS.

Caspian Sea

THRACE

GREECE

Aegean Sea

LYDIA

Sardis

ASIA MINOR

Crete

Mediterranean Sea

Cyprus

SYRIA

Byblos

PHOENICIA

Sidon

PALESTINE

Tyre

Jerusalem

SYRIAN DESERT

LIBYA

Euphrates River

MESOPOTAMIA

Nineveh

Tigris River

ZAGROS MOUNTAINS

IRANIAN PLATEAU

Amu Darya

Indus River

Babylon

BABYLONIA

Susa

Persepolis

PERSIA

EGYPT

Nile River

Thebes

ARABIAN DESERT

Red Sea

Persian Gulf (Arabian Gulf)

Arabian Sea

INDIA

Persian Empire
Royal Road

0   400 kilometers
0   400 miles
Lambert Conformal Conic projection

Geography SKILLS

1. **Location** Explain why the Royal Road was constructed and why it was constructed where it was.
2. **Regions** How do you think the empire was divided into satrapies? Redraw the map with boundaries for the satrapies. Explain what you have done.

wrist, from others I cut off their noses, ears, and fingers; I put out the eyes of many of the soldiers. . . . I burned their young men and women to death."

After the collapse of the Assyrian Empire, the Chaldean king Nebuchadnezzar (NEH•byuh•kuhd•NEH•zuhr) II made Babylonia the leading state in western Asia. He rebuilt Babylon as the center of his empire and gave it a reputation as one of the great cities of the ancient world, but Babylon fell to the Persians in 539 B.C.

Persian Empire

The Persians were an Indo-European people who lived in what is today southwestern Iran. Primarily nomadic, the Persians were eventually unified by one family. One member of this family, **Cyrus,** created a powerful Persian state that stretched from Asia Minor to India.

Cyrus ruled from 559 B.C. to 530 B.C. In 539 B.C., he captured Babylon. His treatment of Babylonia showed remarkable restraint and wisdom. Cyrus also allowed the Jews, who had been held there as captives, to return to Israel.

The people of his time called Cyrus "the Great." He demonstrated wisdom and compassion in the conquest and organization of his empire. Unlike the Assyrian rulers, Cyrus had a reputation for mercy. Cyrus had a genuine respect for other civilizations. For example, he used Assyrian, Babylonian, and Egyptian designs for building his palaces.

Cyrus's successors sought to extend the territory of the Persian Empire. His son Cambyses (kam•BY•SEEZ) successfully invaded Egypt. Darius, who ruled from 521 B.C. to 486 B.C., added a new Persian province in western India. He then conquered Thrace in Europe and created the world's largest empire to that time. Darius divided the empire into 20 provinces, called satrapies (SAY•truh•pees). A governor, or satrap, ruled each province, collected taxes, provided justice, and recruited soldiers.

An efficient communication system sustained the Persian Empire. Officials easily traveled through the empire on well-maintained roads dotted with way stations that provided food, shelter, and fresh horses. The **Royal Road** stretched from Lydia to Susa, the empire's chief capital.

After Darius, the Persian kings became more and more isolated at their courts, surrounded by luxuries. As the Persian kings increased taxes, loyalty to the empire declined. Struggles over the throne weakened the monarchy (rule by a king or queen). Over a period of time, this bloody struggle for the throne weakened the empire and led to its conquest by the Greek ruler Alexander the Great during the 330s B.C.

✓ Reading Check **Examining** What caused the Persian Empire to decline after the death of Darius?

SECTION 2 REVIEW

Vocabulary
1. **Explain** the significance of: Tigris River, Euphrates River, Fertile Crescent, city-state, Sargon, empire, Hammurabi, innovations, transport, Nile River, Lower Egypt, Upper Egypt, Menes, dynasty, Judaism, King Solomon, Jerusalem, monotheistic, Cyrus, Royal Road.

Main Ideas
2. **Describing** What were the common features of each ancient society? How were they different?

3. **Listing** Tell which rivers fostered the development of ancient civilizations and what society goes with each.

4. **Creating** Make a chart like the one below to show the dates and achievements of each period in Egyptian history.

	Dates	Achievements
Old Kingdom		
Middle Kingdom		
New Kingdom		

Critical Thinking
5. **BIG Idea** **Contrasting** What features were distinctive about the beliefs of the Israelites compared to other ancient civilizations?

6. **Evaluating** Explain why Hammurabi's code was a significant development.

7. **Analyzing Visuals** Examine the image on page 17. How did ancient Egyptians paint the human form?

Writing About History
8. **Informative Writing** Research the modern Middle East. Prepare a brief research report summarizing what you have learned about today's cultures.

History ONLINE
For help with the concepts in this section of *Glencoe World History—Modern Times*, go to glencoe.com and click Study Central.

India and China

The ancient societies of India and China were defined by imperial and dynastic rule with rigid social structures. Their historical legacies include Hinduism, Buddhism, and Confucianism, which continue to have major influences on the lives of millions of people today.

GUIDE TO READING

The BIG Idea
Ideas, Beliefs, and Values
Civilizations in India and China developed unique philosophies, religions, and societal ideas.

Content Vocabulary
• varna *(p. 23)*
• caste system *(p. 23)*
• Hinduism *(p. 24)*
• Buddhism *(p. 24)*
• Mandate of Heaven *(p. 27)*
• Dao *(p. 27)*
• Confucianism *(p. 31)*

Academic Vocabulary
• conversion *(p. 26)*
• cycle *(p. 27)*

People and Places
• India *(p. 22)*
• Indus River *(p. 22)*
• Aryans *(p. 22)*
• Hindu Kush *(p. 22)*
• Deccan Plateau *(p. 23)*
• Siddhãrtha Gautama *(p. 24)*
• Aśoka *(p. 26)*
• China *(p. 27)*
• Qin Shihuangdi *(p. 27)*
• Gobi *(p. 27)*
• Confucius *(p. 31)*

Reading Strategy
Compare and Contrast As you read this section, prepare a Venn diagram like the one below to show the similarities and differences between Hinduism and Buddhism.

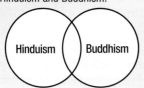

Hinduism   Buddhism

Early Civilization in India

MAIN IDEA The culture of India was influenced by the environment, migration, and religion.

HISTORY & YOU What factors have influenced your community's culture? Learn about factors that affected India's culture.

India is a land of diversity. Today, about 18 languages and hundreds of dialects—varieties of language—are spoken in India. Diversity is also apparent in India's geography. The Indian subcontinent, shaped like a triangle hanging from the southern ridge of Asia, is composed of mountain ranges, river valleys, a dry interior plateau, and fertile coastal plains.

Indus Valley Civilization and Aryan Influence

As in Mesopotamia and Egypt, early civilizations in India emerged in river valleys. Between 3000 B.C. and 1500 B.C., the valleys of the **Indus River** supported a flourishing civilization. It extended hundreds of miles from the Himalaya, the highest mountains in the world, to the coast of the Arabian Sea. Archaeologists have found the remains of more than a thousand settlements in this region. Two of the ruins, about 400 miles (644 km) apart, were sites of what once were the cities of Harappa (huh•RA•puh) and Mohenjo Daro (moh•HEHN•joh DAHR•oh). An advanced civilization—known as Harappan or Indus civilization—flourished in these cities for hundreds of years. Eventually, floods, an earthquake, changes in climate, and even a change in the course of the Indus River weakened the once-flourishing civilization in the Indus River valley. The final blow to the cities may have been an influx of new peoples.

Around 2000 B.C. a group of Indo-European-speaking nomadic peoples began to move out of the steppes of Asia. Indo-Europeans all spoke similar languages. Some migrated west to Europe. Others moved south to Iran and later to the Indus Valley. One group, known as the **Aryans**, moved south across the **Hindu Kush** mountain range into the plains of northern India. Historians know little about the origins and early culture of the Aryans.

Change Comes to India's Civilization

The Indus Valley civilization began a gradual decline around 2000 B.C., and its cities became deserted. By 1500 B.C., major changes had taken place in India's written language, religion, and social order. Today there is still debate among scholars surrounding the reasons for these changes.

Changes in India's Civilization

Social Changes
- Caste system develops into four *varnas*, or groups
- *Varnas* compare society to parts of a body, all parts working together

Economic Changes
- Shift to farming and away from trade
- Settle in small and more pastoral villages

Cultural Changes
- Arts—change in pottery and materials
- Hinduism—dominant religion by 1500 B.C.
- Sanskrit—language of the Four Vedas

Varnas	Jobs	Body Parts	Functions
Brahmans	priests, teachers	mouth	teach, advise
Kshatriyas	warriors, police	arms	defend, protect
Vaisyas	merchants, farmers	legs	supply needs
Sudras	peasants, servants	feet	support society

▲ Sample of Sanskrit writing from the Four Vedas

Mohenjo Daro, shown in this photo, was abandoned around 1500 B.C.

Analyzing VISUALS

1. **Identifying** What are the roles of each *varna*?
2. **Drawing Conclusions** How did India's civilization change?

From around 1500 B.C. to 1000 B.C., the Aryan peoples gradually advanced eastward from the Indus Valley, across the fertile plain of the Ganges, and later southward into the **Deccan Plateau.** Eventually they extended their political control throughout all of India. The ongoing migrations and interaction between the Aryans and the Dravidians—descendents of the Indus Valley people—resulted in a new and unique culture.

The social structure of ancient India reflected Aryan ideas of the ideal society.

The Aryans believed that society was divided into four *varnas,* or social groups. At the top were the Brahmins, the priestly class. The Kshatriyas (KSHA•tree•uhz), or warriors, were next in importance. The Vaisyas (VYSH•yuhz), commoners, were merchants and farmers. The lowest varna were the Sudras, peasants or servants. They made up most of the population.

Over the centuries, a rigid social structure—the **caste system**—drew on the ideas of the Aryans. In this system, every person in India was born into a caste.

A caste is a social group defined by occupation and family lineage. Caste determined what job people could have, whom they could marry, and what groups they could socialize with. *Caste* is a word Portuguese traders used. The Indian word for *caste* is *jati*. One reason it was difficult to escape one's *jati* is that caste is based on beliefs about religious purity—higher castes had greater religious purity, while bottom castes were seen as impure.

The lowest level of Indian society were the Untouchables, people who were viewed as so impure that they were outside the caste system completely. The Untouchables were given menial tasks, such as collecting trash and handling dead bodies. Untouchables made up about 5 percent of the ancient Indian population.

Hinduism

Hinduism had its origins in the religious beliefs of the Aryan peoples who settled in India. Evidence about these religious beliefs comes from the Vedas, collections of hymns and religious ceremonies that were passed down orally by Aryan priests and then eventually written down.

Early Hindus believed in the existence of a single force in the universe, a form of ultimate reality or God, called *Brahman*. It was the duty of the individual self—called the *atman*—to seek to know this ultimate reality. By doing so, the self would merge with Brahman after death.

Hindus developed the practice of yoga, a method of training designed to achieve oneness with God. The goal of yoga, which means "union," is to leave behind earthly life and join Brahman in a kind of dreamless sleep. Most ordinary Indians, however, could not easily relate to this ideal and needed a more concrete form of heavenly salvation. It was probably for this reason that Hinduism came to have a number of humanlike gods and goddesses. The three chief gods are Brahma the Creator, Vishnu the Preserver, and Shiva (SHIH•vuh) the Destroyer. Many Hindus regard these gods as simply different expressions of the one ultimate reality, Brahman. However, the various gods and goddesses give ordinary Indians a way to express their religious

See page R39 to read excerpts from the Buddha's sermon in the **Primary Sources and Literature Library.**

feelings. Hinduism is the religion of the vast majority of the Indian people.

By the sixth century B.C., the idea of reincarnation had appeared in Hinduism. Reincarnation is the belief that the individual soul is reborn in a different form after death. After a number of existences in the earthly world, the soul reaches its final goal in a union with Brahman. Important to this process is the idea of karma, the force generated by a person's actions that determines how the person will be reborn in the next life. According to this idea, what people do in their current lives determines what they will be in their next lives. In the same way, a person's current status is not simply an accident. It is a result of the person's actions in a past existence.

The system of reincarnation provided a religious basis for the rigid class divisions in Indian society. It justified the privileges of those on the higher end of the scale. After all, they would not have these privileges if they did not deserve them. The concept of reincarnation also gave hope to the poor. For example, if they behaved properly in this life, they hoped to improve their condition in the next.

Buddhism

In the sixth century B.C., a new doctrine, called **Buddhism,** appeared in northern India. This doctrine soon became a rival of Hinduism.

Buddhism was the product of one man, **Siddhārtha Gautama** (sih•DAHR•tuh GOW•tuh•muh). Born around 563 B.C., Siddhārtha Gautama is better known as the Buddha, or "Enlightened One." Siddhārtha gained thousands of devoted followers. The religion of Buddhism began with a man who claimed that he had awakened and seen the world in a new way.

Siddhārtha believed the physical surroundings of humans were simply illusions. The pain, poverty, and sorrow that afflict human beings are caused by their attachment to worldly things. Once people let go of their worldly cares, pain and sorrow can be forgotten. Then comes *bodhi*, or wisdom, which is the root of the word Buddhism and of Siddhārtha's usual name—Gautama Buddha.

Achieving wisdom is key to achieving nirvana—ultimate reality—the end of the self and a reunion with the Great World Soul. Siddhārtha taught that all human beings, without division into caste, could reach nirvana as a result of their behavior in this life. He preached his simple message based on the Four Noble Truths:

FOUR NOBLE TRUTHS	
1.	Ordinary life is full of suffering.
2.	This suffering is caused by our desire to satisfy ourselves.
3.	The way to end suffering is to end desire for selfish goals and to see others as extensions of ourselves.
4.	The way to end desire is to follow the Middle Path.

This Middle Path is also known as the Eightfold Path, because it consists of eight steps:

THE EIGHTFOLD PATH	
1.	*Right view* We need to know the Four Noble Truths.
2.	*Right intention* We need to decide what we really want.
3.	*Right speech* We must seek to speak truth and to speak well of others.
4.	*Right action* The Buddha gave five precepts: "Do not kill. Do not steal. Do not lie. Do not be unchaste. Do not take drugs or drink alcohol."
5.	*Right livelihood* We must do work that uplifts our being.
6.	*Right effort* The Buddha said, "Those who follow the Way might well follow the example of an ox that arches through the deep mud carrying a heavy load. He is tired, but his steady, forward-looking gaze will not relax until he comes out of the mud."
7.	*Right mindfulness* We must keep our minds in control of our senses: "All we are is the result of what we have thought."
8.	*Right concentration* We must meditate to see the world in a new way.

History ONLINE

Student Web Activity—
Visit glencoe.com and complete the activity on Buddhism.

HISTORY & ARTS

Stupas Show Spread of Buddhism

Evolution of Buddhist Architecture
a. third to first century B.C. Indian stupa
b. second century A.D. Indian stupa
c. fifth to seventh century A.D. Chinese pagoda
d. seventh century A.D. Japanese pagoda

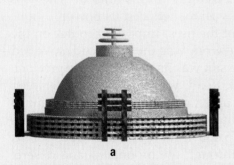

a

b

c

d

According to legend, the Buddha told his followers to place his relics at four sites: at his birthplace, at the bodhi tree, at the place where he preached his first sermon, and at the place where he died. Then he folded his robe into a cube and placed his begging bowl upside down on top to indicate the shape of the monuments. Over centuries in different countries, stupas changed, but five basic components remained: a square base, a dome, a spire, a crescent moon, and a circular disc; symbolizing earth, water, fire, air, and space.

CRITICAL THINKING SKILLS

1. **Identifying** What is another name for a Buddhist stupa?
2. **Drawing Conclusions** Why did the shape and name for stupas change?

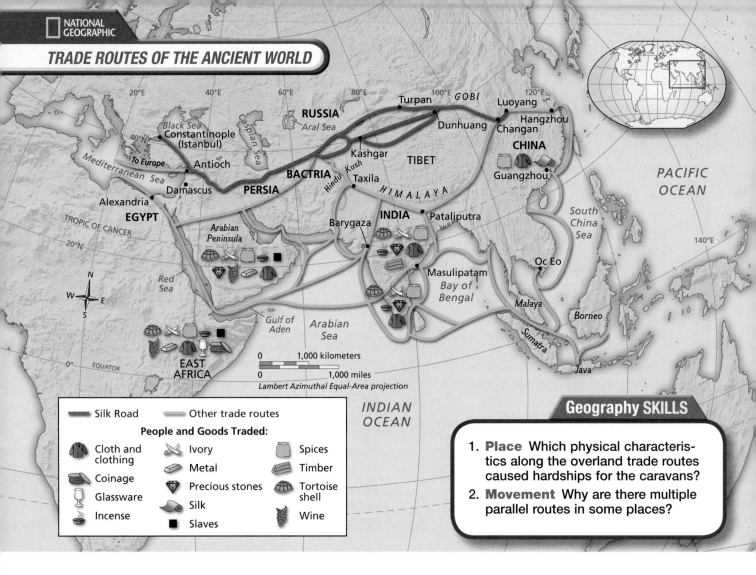

Silk Road — **Other trade routes**

People and Goods Traded:

Cloth and clothing | Ivory | Spices
Coinage | Metal | Timber
Glassware | Precious stones | Tortoise shell
Incense | Silk | Wine
Slaves

Geography SKILLS

1. **Place** Which physical characteristics along the overland trade routes caused hardships for the caravans?
2. **Movement** Why are there multiple parallel routes in some places?

Early Empires in India

For most of the time between 325 B.C. and A.D. 500, India was a land of many different states. Two major empires, however, were able to create unified Indian states.

The first of these empires, the Mauryan Empire in northern India, lasted from 324 B.C. to 183 B.C. The Mauryan Empire flourished during the reign of **Aśoka** (uh•SHOH•kuh), who ruled from 269 B.C. until 232 B.C. Aśoka is considered to be the greatest ruler in the history of India.

After his **conversion** to Buddhism, Aśoka used Buddhist ideals to guide his rule. He set up hospitals for both people and animals. He ordered that trees and shelters be placed along the road to provide shade and rest for weary travelers.

Aśoka's kingdom also prospered as India became a major crossroads in a vast trade network. After Aśoka's death in 232 B.C., the Mauryan Empire began to decline, and in 183 B.C., it collapsed. India then fell back into disunity until a new empire arose. This new empire, the Gupta Empire, flourished from A.D. 320 until the late 400s when invasions reduced its power.

One of the most important routes on the trade network was the Silk Road, so called because silk was its most valuable product. The Silk Road, which had arisen between 200 B.C. and A.D. 100, reached from China to Mesopotamia, a distance of about 4,000 miles (6,436 km). Caravans transported goods through the mountains and deserts to Antioch, a port on the eastern Mediterranean Sea. At Antioch, goods from the West were traded for goods from the East. Only luxury goods were carried on the Silk Road because camel caravans were difficult, dangerous, and thus expensive.

✓ **Reading Check** **Evaluating** Why was Aśoka considered a great ruler?

Early Chinese Civilizations

MAIN IDEA Much of Chinese history was defined by dynastic cycles, the Mandate of Heaven, and Confucianism.

HISTORY & YOU What gives someone the right to rule a country? Read about the Mandate of Heaven.

Of the great civilizations discussed so far, **China** was the last to come into full flower. By the time the first Chinese dynasty began to emerge as an organized state, the societies in Mesopotamia, Egypt, and India had already reached an advanced level of civilization. One likely reason was China's isolation from the emerging centers of culture elsewhere in the world.

Shang Dynasty

The Shang dynasty, about 1750 B.C. to 1045 B.C., created the first flourishing Chinese civilization. Under the Shang, China developed organized government, a system of writing, and advanced bronze-making skills.

The Chinese believed they could communicate with supernatural forces to obtain help in worldly affairs. To do so, they made use of oracle bones. These were bones on which priests scratched questions asked by the rulers, such as: Will the king be victorious in battle? Will the king recover from his illness? Heated metal rods were then stuck into the bones, causing them to crack. The priests interpreted the shapes of the cracks as answers from the gods. The priests recorded the answers and stored the bones. The inscriptions on the bones are a valuable source of information about the Shang period.

Zhou Dynasty

The Zhou dynasty, the longest-running dynasty in Chinese history, ruled for almost eight hundred years (1045 B.C. to 256 B.C.). The Zhou dynasty claimed that it ruled China because it possessed the **Mandate of Heaven.** It was believed that Heaven— an impersonal law of nature—kept order in the universe through the Zhou king.

The Mandate of Heaven, however, was double-edged. The king, who was chosen to rule because of his talent and virtue, was then responsible for ruling the people with goodness and efficiency. The king was expected to rule according to the proper "Way," called the **Dao** (DOW). It was his duty to keep the gods pleased in order to protect the people from natural disaster or a bad harvest. If the king failed to rule effectively, he could be overthrown and replaced by a new ruler.

The Mandate of Heaven was closely tied to the pattern of dynastic **cycles.** From the beginning of Chinese history to A.D. 1912, China was ruled by a series of dynasties. The Zhou dynasty lasted for almost eight hundred years. Others did not last as long, but the king of each dynasty ruled with the Mandate of Heaven.

No matter how long the dynasties lasted, all went through a cycle of change. A new dynasty established its power, ruled successfully for many years, and then began to decline. The power of the central government would begin to collapse, giving rise to rebellions or invasion. Finally, the dynasty collapsed and a new dynasty took over, beginning another dynastic cycle.

See page R35 to read an excerpt from *The Burning of Books* by Li Su in the **Primary Sources and Literature Library.**

Qin Dynasty

The collapse of the Zhou dynasty was followed by two hundred years of civil war. A new dynasty, known as the Qin, then created an era of Chinese unity. The Qin dynasty was founded by **Qin Shihuangdi** (CHIHN SHUR•HWONG•DEE), meaning "the First Qin Emperor."

Qin Shihuangdi, a person of much ambition, unified the Chinese world through methods like establishing a single monetary system and building a system of roads throughout the entire empire. His major foreign concern, however, was in the north. Near the **Gobi** resided a nomadic people, organized loosely into tribes, known to the Chinese as the Xiongnu (SYEN•NOO). They often raided Chinese territory. Qin Shihuangdi's answer to this problem was to strengthen the existing system of walls to keep the nomads out. Today we know this project as the Great Wall of China.

The Great Wall that we know today from films and photographs was built 1,500 years after the rule of Qin Shihuangdi. Some of the walls built by Qin Shihuangdi remain, but most of them were constructed of loose stone, sand, or piled rubble, and disappeared long ago.

This is not to say that the wall was not a massive project. It required the efforts of thousands of laborers. Many of them died while working on the wall and, according to legend, are now buried within the wall. With his wall, the First Qin Emperor had some success in fighting off nomads, but the victory was only temporary. Over the next two thousand years, China's northern frontier became one of the great areas of conflict in Asia.

Han Dynasty

Qin Shihuangdi was to be the Qin dynasty's only ruler. A new dynasty—the Han—then established an empire that lasted over four hundred years (202 B.C. to A.D. 220).

China under the Han dynasty was a vast empire. The population increased rapidly. The large population created a growing need for a bigger and more efficient bureaucracy to keep the state in proper working order. During the Han dynasty, China extended the boundaries of its empire far into the sands of central Asia and southward along the coast of the South China Sea into what is modern-day Vietnam. Chinese cultural, scientific, and technological achievements were unsurpassed.

INFOGRAPHICS

Dynastic Cycles and the Mandate of Heaven

When the Zhou overthrew the Shang dynasty, they explained their right to rule as a Mandate of Heaven. Dynasties that abused their power lost the Mandate of Heaven. The Mandate passed to another family who overthrew the old dynasty and established a new one.

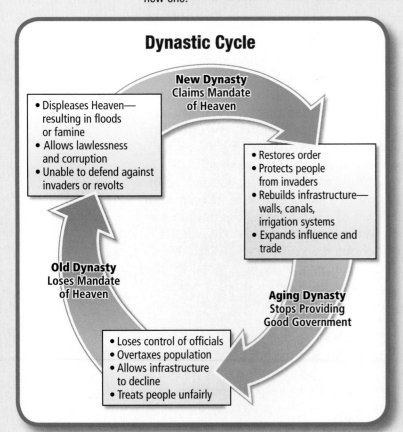

Dynastic Cycle

New Dynasty
Claims Mandate of Heaven

- Displeases Heaven—resulting in floods or famine
- Allows lawlessness and corruption
- Unable to defend against invaders or revolts

- Restores order
- Protects people from invaders
- Rebuilds infrastructure—walls, canals, irrigation systems
- Expands influence and trade

Old Dynasty
Loses Mandate of Heaven

Aging Dynasty
Stops Providing Good Government

- Loses control of officials
- Overtaxes population
- Allows infrastructure to decline
- Treats people unfairly

Early Dynasties of China

DYNASTY	DATES	ACCOMPLISHMENTS
Shang	1750–1045 B.C.	First dynasty, writing, ancestor worship, bronze
Zhou	1045–256 B.C.	Classical arts, silk discovered, Daoism and Confucianism
Qin	221–206 B.C.	China united, measurements and writing standardized
Han	202 B.C.–A.D. 220	Silk Road, civil service, paper invented, Buddhism

Analyzing VISUALS

1. **Recognizing Bias** Why did the Zhou dynasty develop the concept of the Mandate of Heaven?
2. **Theorizing** Why do you think each of the dynasties came to an end?

The Great Wall of China: In History and Legend

The Great Wall winds across China's landscape and through its history. Over 2,000 years, piled stone gave way to elaborate watchtowers and forts. In the seventeenth century, visiting Europeans mistakenly assumed the wall was one continuous structure and called it "The Great Wall of China." Besides guarding trade routes, the wall became the source of legends.

The Legend of Meng Jiangnu Whose Wails Split the Wall

Near Shanhaiguan Pass is a temple to Meng Jiangnu. Fan, Meng's husband, was one of thousands forced to work on the wall. With winter coming, Meng carried warm clothes to Fan. When Meng reached the place where her husband had been working, she learned that Fan had died from overwork and been buried in the wall. Hearing this awful news, Meng wept so loudly that miles of wall collapsed, exposing the bodies of laborers.

Geography SKILLS

1. **Location** Compare the location of the Great Wall with the Silk Road and other trade routes shown on the map on page 26.
2. **Human-Environment Interaction** What physical features of the environment made it difficult to build the Great Wall?

Maps In Motion See *StudentWorks™ Plus* or glencoe.com.

NATIONAL GEOGRAPHIC

BUILDING THE GREAT WALL

ALTAY SHAN
MONGOLIA
GOBI
DA HINGGAN LING
Mu Us
Huang He (Yellow R.)
Wei He
Beijing
Bo Hai
KOREA
QINLING SHANDI
Xi'an
Luoyang
Yellow Sea
JAPAN
CHINA
Chang Jiang (Yangtze R.)
Hangzhou
East China Sea

50°N
90°E 100°E 110°E 120°E 130°E
40°N
30°N

Great Wall
— Warring States Period (403–221 B.C.)
— Qin Dynasty (221 B.C.–206 B.C.)
— Han Dynasty (ca. 202 B.C.– A.D. 220)
— Ming Dynasty (1368–1644)
— Present-day China

0   400 kilometers
0   400 miles
Two-point Equidistant projection

The Family in Ancient China

As in most agricultural societies, the family served as the basic economic and social unit. However, the Chinese family took on an almost sacred quality as a symbol of the entire social order.

What explains the importance of the family in ancient China? The need to work together on the land was a significant factor. In ancient times, farming required the work of many people. Children were essential to the family because they worked in the fields. Later, sons were expected to take over the physical labor on the family plots and provide for their parents.

Central to the concept of family in China was the idea of filial piety. It refers to the duty of members of the family to subordinate their needs and desires to those of the male head of the family. The term describes a system in which every family member had his or her place.

Male supremacy was a key element in the social system of ancient China, as it was in the other civilizations that we have examined. Men worked in the fields and provided food for their families. They also governed society and were the warriors, scholars, and government ministers. Women raised the children and worked in the home.

TURNING POINT — THE RULE OF MERIT

Confucius equated education with public service and virtue. He taught that rulers should be devoted to the welfare of the people and that government officials should earn their positions through education and talent—merit. Merit-based civil service became official during the Qin dynasty and later included written examinations. Although there were periods of corruption in the 1300-year history of the exams, testing made it possible for any male adult, regardless of social status or wealth, to become a high-ranking public official. Eventually, the Chinese civil service influenced the development of European and American systems.

Civil service exam under Emperor Jen-Tsung

A young woman applies for a civil service position.

CRITICAL THINKING SKILLS

1. **Making Inferences** What are some differences between ancient and modern civil service exams?

2. **Drawing Conclusions** Is the civil service still important in China today?

The Importance of Confucius

The civilization of China is closely tied to **Confucius,** who was known to the Chinese as the First Teacher. *Confucius* is the westernized form of Kongfuzi (KUNG•FOO•DZUH), meaning "Master Kung," as he was called by his followers. Confucius was born in 551 B.C. He hoped to get a job as a political adviser, but he had little success in finding a patron. Instead he became a teacher to a faithful band of followers who revered him as a great teacher and recorded his sayings. Until the twentieth century, almost every Chinese pupil studied his sayings, making **Confucianism,** or the system of Confucian ideas, an important part of Chinese culture.

Confucius believed that the universe was made in such a way that if humans would act in harmony with its purposes, their own affairs would prosper. Much of his concern was with human behavior. The key to proper behavior was to behave in accordance with the Dao (Way).

Two elements stand out in the Confucian view of the Dao: duty and humanity. The concept of duty meant that all people had to subordinate their own interests to the broader needs of the family and the community. Everyone should be governed by the Five Constant Relationships: parent and child, husband and wife, older sibling and younger sibling, older friend and younger friend, and ruler and subject. Each person in the relationship had a duty to the other. Parents should be loving, and children should revere their parents. Husbands should fulfill their duties, and wives should be obedient. The elder sibling should be kind, and the younger sibling respectful. The older friend should be considerate, and the younger friend deferential. Rulers should be benevolent, and subjects loyal. Showing the importance of family, Confucius said: "The duty of children to their parents is the foundation from which all virtues spring."

The Confucian concept of duty is often expressed in the form of a "work ethic." If each individual worked hard to fulfill his or her duties, then the affairs of society as a whole would prosper as well.

Above all, the ruler must set a good example. If the king followed the path of goodness, then subjects would respect him, and society would prosper.

The second key element in the Confucian view of the Dao is the idea of humanity. This consists of a sense of compassion and empathy for others. Confucius said, "Do not do unto others what you would not wish done to yourself." Confucius urged people to "measure the feelings of others by one's own," for "within the four seas all men are brothers." After his death in 479 B.C., Confucius's message spread widely throughout China.

✓ **Reading Check** **Describing** Describe the meaning of duty and humanity in the Confucian view of the Dao.

SECTION 3 REVIEW

Vocabulary

1. **Explain** the significance of: India, Indus River, Aryans, Hindu Kush, Deccan Plateau, *varnas,* caste system, Hinduism, Buddhism, Siddhārtha Gautama, Aśoka, China, Mandate of Heaven, Dao, cycle, Qin Shihuangdi, Gobi, Confucius, Confucianism.

Main Ideas

2. **Describe** the four *varnas* in Indian society. Name the group that is not part of the caste system.

3. **List** the Four Noble Truths.

4. **Summarize** the relationship between the dynastic cycle and the Mandate of Heaven.

Critical Thinking

5. **BIG Idea** **Contrasting** How do Chinese philosophies differ from Buddhism and Hinduism?

6. **Taking Notes** Use an outline format. Describe the Confucian Five Constant Relationships.

```
I.  The Five Constant Relationships
    A.  Parent and Child
        1.
    B.
    C.  Older Sibling and Younger Sibling
    D.
    E.  Ruler and Subject
        1.
```

7. **Analyzing Visuals** Examine the painting on page 30. How can you tell who is the highest ranking person in the picture? What does the painting show about taking exams?

Writing About History

8. **Expository Writing** Write a paper about the philosophical traditions of Confucianism. Research to find examples of how this philosophy influenced historic and contemporary world events.

History ONLINE

For help with the concepts in this section of *Glencoe World History—Modern Times,* go to glencoe.com and click Study Central.

STUDY TO GO You can study anywhere, anytime by downloading quizzes and flash cards to your PDA from glencoe.com.

EARLY CIVILIZATIONS DEVELOPED IN RIVER VALLEYS

Recreation of Çatalhüyük, an early farming settlement

THE FIRST HUMANS

- Early humans used technological innovations, including stone tools, to change their physical environment.
- The Neolithic Revolution was the beginning of systematic agriculture—the keeping of animals and the growing of food on a regular basis.
- Civilizations began to develop in river valleys in Mesopotamia, Egypt, India, and China.

SUMERIAN WRITING FROM 2360 B.C.

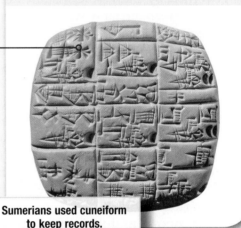

Sumerians used cuneiform to keep records.

WESTERN ASIA AND EGYPT

- Hammurabi's code influenced law codes in later civilizations.
- The Sumerians invented the oldest writing system, cuneiform, which dates from about 3000 B.C.
- The Israelites did not create an empire, but their religion, Judaism, flourished and later influenced Christianity and Islam.
- New empires that arose in Assyria and Persia conquered vast stretches of the ancient world.

CONFUCIUS

Japanese woodcut of Confucius

INDIA AND CHINA

- Two of the world's major religions, Hinduism and Buddhism, began in India.
- From China across central Asia to Mesopotamia, the Silk Road connected the ancient world through trade.
- Confucius believed that government officials should earn their jobs through education and talent.
- The Mandate of Heaven explained the cycle of dynasties.

STANDARDIZED TEST PRACTICE

TEST-TAKING

When a question asks for an answer related to a specific topic, such as geography, eliminate any choices that do not mention anything about that topic. Then choose the best answer from the choices that remain.

Reviewing Vocabulary

Directions: Choose the word or words that best complete the sentence.

1. The keeping of animals and the growing of food on a regular basis is known as _____.

   A systematic agriculture

   B domesticated agriculture

   C Neolithic agriculture

   D Paleolithic agriculture

2. A _____ is a Sumerian stepped tower.

   A ziggurat

   B pyramid

   C stylus

   D papyrus

3. In Buddhism, reaching _____, or ultimate reality, is the end of the self and a reunion with the Great World Soul.

   A reincarnation

   B kharma

   C nirvana

   D ascetic

4. _____ is belief in one god rather than many gods.

   A Polytheism

   B Monotheism

   C Theocracy

   D Monarchy

Reviewing Main Ideas

Directions: Choose the best answers to the following questions.

Section 1 *(pp. 4–7)*

5. Which type of scientist uses fossils and artifacts to study early humans?

   A Chemists

   B Physicists

   C Anthropologists

   D Geologists

6. Which hominids do scientists believe were probably the first to leave Africa?

   A *Homo erectus*

   B *Australopithecus*

   C *Homo sapiens sapiens*

   D Neanderthals

7. During which age did the agricultural revolution lead to the development of civilization?

   A Paleolithic

   B Ice

   C Neolithic

   D Bronze

Section 2 *(pp. 10–21)*

8. What was the most important Sumerian invention?

   A Alphabet

   B Writing

   C Bronze

   D Number system

Need Extra Help?								
If You Missed Questions . . .	1	2	3	4	5	6	7	8
Go to Page . . .	7	10	25	19	4	4	7	13

9. During whose reign was the Great Pyramid at Giza built?

   A Khufu

   B Hatshepsut

   C Khafre

   D Menes

10. Which Persian ruler was known for his wisdom and compassion?

   A Ashurbanipal

   B Cyrus

   C Darius

   D Solomon

Section 3 (pp. 22–31)

11. Which of the following is a true statement about Buddhists?

   A They are the majority in India.

   B They try to follow the Middle Path.

   C They believe in a rigid caste system.

   D They worship the Buddha as a god.

12. Out of what did the caste system grow?

   A Rajas

   B Aryans

   C Vedas

   D *Varnas*

13. The Mandate of Heaven refers to whose responsibilities?

   A Parent to child

   B Children to parents

   C Husbands and wives to each other

   D Rulers to provide good government

Critical Thinking

Directions: Choose the best answers to the following questions.

14. According to the Mandate of Heaven, what happened to a bad ruler?

   A He continued to rule.

   B He ruled jointly with another ruler.

   C He was overthrown.

   D He selected a new king.

Base your answer to questions 15 and 16 on the map below.

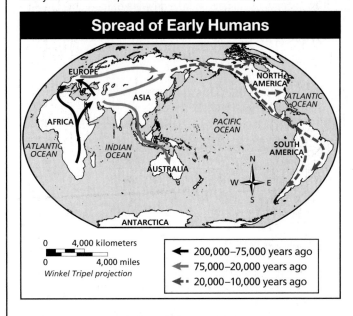

Spread of Early Humans

0   4,000 kilometers
0   4,000 miles
Winkel Tripel projection

← 200,000–75,000 years ago
← 75,000–20,000 years ago
← 20,000–10,000 years ago

15. In which areas of Africa did human life begin?

   A Eastern and southern

   B Eastern and northern

   C Western and southern

   D Western and northern

16. Into which areas did early humans spread most recently?

   A Asia

   B Europe

   C Australia

   D North and South America

Need Extra Help?								
If You Missed Questions . . .	9	10	11	12	13	14	15	16
Go to Page . . .	14	21	25	23	27	27	34	34

17. Which statement best reflects the principles in the Code of Hammurabi?

   A Women and men are equal.

   B Demand an eye for an eye.

   C Let the buyer beware.

   D Judges are above the law.

Analyze the chart and answer question 18. Base your answer on the chart and on your knowledge of world history.

Comparing Life in Mesopotamia and Egypt		
	Mesopotamia	**Egypt**
Natural Barriers	Flat plains	Deserts, seas, cataracts
Government	City-states ruled by divinely selected kings	Rural villages ruled by dynastic god-kings
Social Structure	Nobles; commoners; slaves	Nobles and priests; merchants, scribes, artisans and tax collectors; farmers

18. How was life in Mesopotamia and Egypt similar?

   A They were both extremely hierarchical.

   B They both were made up of rural villages.

   C Egypt's kings were treated as gods, while Mesopotamia's kings were men who were divinely selected.

   D Commoners had no rights in either society.

19. How did the system of reincarnation justify the class divisions in Indian society?

   A It left society divisions up to fate.

   B It justified the privileges of those higher in society.

   C It discouraged the poor.

   D It encouraged social mobility in life.

Document-Based Questions

Directions: Analyze the document and answer the short-answer questions that follow the document.

Read the following Mesopotamian poem.

> *"The rampant flood which no man can oppose,*
> *Which shakes the heavens and causes earth to tremble,*
> *In an appalling blanket folds mother and child,*
> *And drowns the harvest in its time of ripeness."*

20. How does this poem represent the Mesopotamians' attitude toward nature?

21. Explain the meaning of the line: "Which shakes the heavens and causes earth to tremble."

Extended Response

22. Literature often reflects a people's worldview. How does this poem represent the importance of the physical environment and religion in the lives of the Mesopotamians?

History ONLINE

For additional test practice, use Self-Check Quizzes—Chapter 1 at **glencoe.com**.

Need Extra Help?						
If You Missed Questions . . .	17	18	19	20	21	22
Go to Page . . .	12	35	24	35	35	35

CHAPTER 2

Ancient Greece and Rome 1900 B.C.–A.D. 500

Section 1 Ancient Greece

Section 2 Rome and the Rise of Christianity

MAKING CONNECTIONS

How did the Greeks and Romans shape our culture?

Today we still see Greek and Roman contributions in Western civilization. The Greeks gave us the foundations for democracy, art, philosophy, and drama. The Romans provided a pattern for representative government and city building. They were also practical civil engineers, building multipurpose structures like the Pont du Gard, a bridge to move trade and troops and an aqueduct that carried water.

- What influences of the Greeks and Romans impact your life?
- What types of cultural influences do you find in your own community?

THE WORLD ▶

c. 1100 B.C.
Dark Age begins

509 B.C.
Start of
Roman Republic

323 B.C.
Death of
Alexander
the Great

| 1350 B.C. | 500 B.C. | 300 B.C. |

c. 1360 B.C.
Height of Mycenaean
civilization

500 B.C.
Height of
classical Greece

A.D. 313
Constantine
legalizes
Christianity

A.D. 100

A.D. 500

27 B.C.
Augustus becomes
Roman emperor

A.D. 476
Fall of the Western
Roman Empire

FOLDABLES™
Study Organizer

Analyzing Create a Four-
Door Book to analyze the
impact of geography on
the rise of Rome. On the
inside of the book, write
descriptive phrases
explaining the geographic
importance of Rome, Sicily, Carthage
and the Alps to Rome's rise.

Rome | Sicily

Carthage | Alps

History ONLINE

Chapter Overview—Visit glencoe.com to preview Chapter 2.

Ancient Greece

While China, India, Egypt, and Mesopotamia had large empires, the geography of ancient Greece favored the rise of separate city-states with local governments and cultures. Their differences led to conflict between the Greek cities and conquest by other societies. Ancient Greece laid the foundations for Western philosophy, epic poetry, drama, and democracy.

GUIDE TO READING

The BIG Idea

Ideas, Beliefs, and Values For a long time, Greek life was centered around the polis, but Alexander the Great's conquests spread Greek culture.

Content Vocabulary

- epic poem *(p. 39)*
- polis *(p. 40)*
- acropolis *(p. 40)*
- democracy *(p. 41)*
- oligarchy *(p. 41)*
- direct democracy *(p. 43)*

Academic Vocabulary

- classical *(p. 43)*
- ethics *(p. 45)*

People and Places

- Mycenae *(p. 38)*
- Homer *(p. 39)*
- Sparta *(p. 41)*
- Athens *(p. 41)*
- Pericles *(p. 43)*
- Socrates *(p. 44)*
- Plato *(p. 44)*
- Aristotle *(p. 45)*
- Alexander the Great *(p. 46)*

Reading Strategy

Organizing Information Use a concept map like the one below to show the elements that contributed to the classical age of Greece.

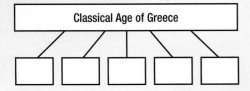

Classical Age of Greece

Early Greek Civilization

MAIN IDEA Homer's epic poems provided the foundation for classical Greek education. Athens and Sparta were both influenced by this tradition.

HISTORY & YOU What stories do we use to help tell about history? Read about Homer's *Iliad*.

Geography played an important role in the development of Greek civilization. Compared with Mesopotamia and Egypt, Greece occupies a small area. It consists of a mountainous peninsula and numerous islands and is about the size of the state of Louisiana. Much of Greece consists of small plains and river valleys surrounded by high mountain ranges. The mountains isolated Greeks from one another, causing different Greek communities to develop their own ways of life.

The sea also influenced the evolution of Greek society. Greece has a long seacoast dotted by bays and inlets that provided many harbors. The Greeks lived on a number of islands to the west, south, and east of the Greek mainland. It was no accident that the Greeks became seafarers.

The First Greek State: Mycenae

Mycenae (my•SEE•nee) was a fortified site on the Greek mainland that was first discovered by the German archaeologist Heinrich Schliemann. Mycenae was one of a number of centers in an early Greek civilization that flourished between 1600 B.C. and 1100 B.C.

The Mycenaean Greeks were part of the Indo-European family of peoples who spread into Europe and Asia. One of these groups entered Greece around 1900 B.C. Over a period of time, this group managed to gain control of the Greek mainland.

Mycenaean civilization, which reached its high point between 1400 B.C. and 1200 B.C., was made up of powerful monarchies. Each resided in a fortified palace center. Like Mycenae, these centers were built on hills and surrounded by gigantic stone walls.

Art in the Dark Age

This statue shows a traveling musician and storyteller, or bard, like Homer.

In the seventh century B.C., art began to take on a more Eastern appearance as the Greeks made contact with civilizations in Asia. The griffin's head design on pottery was found in Greece as well as throughout Southwest Asia.

From 1100-700 B.C., geometric patterns were typical of Greek pottery. This amphora, or two-handled jar, decorated graves near the Dipylon gate in Athens.

DOCUMENT-BASED QUESTIONS

Some art from the Dark Age has survived, giving a hint of life during that period.

1. **Making Inferences** Study these art objects. What conclusion might you draw about life during the Dark Age?
2. **Drawing Conclusions** What practical purpose do you think the object with the griffin's head served?

Archaeological evidence indicates that the Mycenaean monarchies developed an extensive commercial network. Some historians believe that the Mycenaeans also spread outward militarily, conquering Crete and making it part of the Mycenaean world. The most famous of all their supposed military adventures is recounted in the poetry of **Homer.**

The Dark Age and Homer

After the collapse of Mycenaean civilization around 1100 B.C., Greece entered a difficult period in which the population declined and food production dropped. Historians call the period from approximately 1100 B.C. to 750 B.C. the Dark Age, because few records of what happened exist. At the same time, the basis for a new Greece was forming. Near the very end of the Dark Age, the work of Homer appeared.

The *Iliad* and the *Odyssey* were the first great epic poems of early Greece. An **epic poem** is a long poem that tells the deeds of a great hero. The *Iliad* and the *Odyssey* were based on stories that had been passed down from generation to generation.

Specifically, Homer used stories of the Trojan War to compose his epic poems. The war is caused by Paris, a prince of Troy. By kidnapping Helen, the wife of the king of the Greek state of Sparta, Paris outrages all the Greeks. Under the leadership of the Spartan king's brother, King Agamemnon, the Greeks attack Troy. The *Iliad* is not so much the story of the war itself, however, as it is the tale of the Greek hero Achilles (uh•KIH•leez) and how the anger of Achilles led to disaster.

The *Odyssey* recounts the journeys of one of the Greek heroes, Odysseus, after the fall of Troy, and his ultimate return to his wife. The *Odyssey* has long been considered Homer's other masterpiece.

Homer did not so much record history; he created it. The Greeks looked on the *Iliad* and the *Odyssey* as true history and as the works of one poet, Homer. These masterpieces gave the Greeks an ideal past with a cast of heroes. The epics were used as texts for the education of Greek males.

See page R36 to read excerpts from *Iliad* in the **Primary Sources and Literature Library.**

In his epic poems, Homer gave to later generations of Greek males a model of heroism and honor. The *Iliad* taught students to be proud of their Greek heritage and their heroic ancestors.

The Polis: Center of Greek Life

By 750 B.C., the city-state—what the Greeks called a **polis**—became the central focus of Greek life. Our word *politics* is derived from the Greek word *polis*. The polis was a town, city, or even a village, along with its surrounding countryside. The polis served as the central meeting place for political, social, or religious activities.

The main gathering place in the polis was usually a hill. At the top of the hill was a fortified area called an **acropolis**. The acropolis served as a place of refuge and sometimes a religious center on which temples and public buildings were built. Below the acropolis was an agora, an open area that served as a place where people assembled and as a market.

City-states varied in size and population. Athens had more than 300,000 people by the fifth century B.C., but most city-states were much smaller, consisting of only a few hundred to several thousand people. The polis was, above all, a group of people who shared a common identity and common goals. The community consisted of citizens with political rights (adult males), citizens without political rights (women and children), and noncitizens (including agricultural laborers, slaves, and resident aliens). A citizen's rights were coupled with responsibilities. The Greek

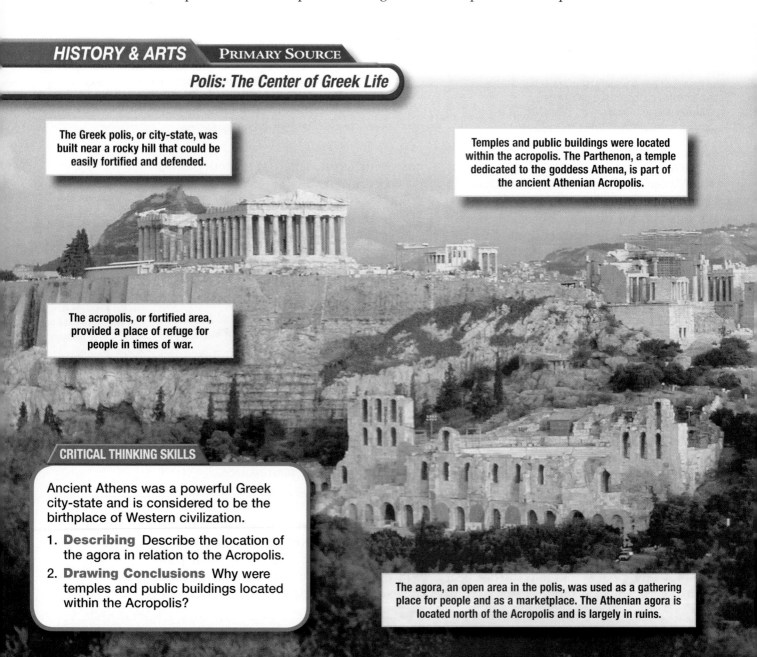

HISTORY & ARTS **PRIMARY SOURCE**

Polis: The Center of Greek Life

The Greek polis, or city-state, was built near a rocky hill that could be easily fortified and defended.

Temples and public buildings were located within the acropolis. The Parthenon, a temple dedicated to the goddess Athena, is part of the ancient Athenian Acropolis.

The acropolis, or fortified area, provided a place of refuge for people in times of war.

CRITICAL THINKING SKILLS

Ancient Athens was a powerful Greek city-state and is considered to be the birthplace of Western civilization.

1. **Describing** Describe the location of the agora in relation to the Acropolis.
2. **Drawing Conclusions** Why were temples and public buildings located within the Acropolis?

The agora, an open area in the polis, was used as a gathering place for people and as a marketplace. The Athenian agora is located north of the Acropolis and is largely in ruins.

philosopher Aristotle argued that a citizen did not belong just to himself or herself: "We must rather regard every citizen as belonging to the state."

Greek states had different forms of government. In some Greek city-states, there emerged **democracy,** which is government by the people or rule of the many. Other city-states remained committed to government by an **oligarchy,** rule by the few. The differences in the Greek city-states can be understood by examining the two most famous and powerful city-states, **Sparta** and **Athens.**

Sparta

Between 800 B.C. and 600 B.C., the lives of Spartans were rigidly organized and tightly controlled—hence our word *spartan,* meaning "highly self-disciplined." Males spent their childhood learning military discipline. Then they enrolled in the army for regular military service at age 20. Although allowed to marry, they continued to live in the military barracks until age 30. At 30, Spartan males were allowed to vote in the assembly and live at home, but they stayed in the army until the age of 60.

While their husbands lived in the barracks, Spartan women lived at home. Because of this separation, Spartan women had greater freedom of movement and greater power in the household than elsewhere in Greece. Many Spartan women upheld strict Spartan values, expecting their husbands and sons to be brave in war. The story is told of a Spartan mother who, as she handed her son his shield, told him to come back carrying his shield or being carried on it.

Sparta was an oligarchy headed by two kings who led the army on its campaigns. A group of five men, known as the ephors (EH•fuhrs), were elected each year and were responsible for the education of youth and the conduct of all citizens. A council of elders, composed of the two kings and 28 citizens over the age of 60, decided any issues presented to an assembly made up of male citizens. This assembly did not debate; it only voted on the issues.

To make their military state secure, the Spartans turned their backs on the outside world. Foreigners were discouraged from visiting. Except for military reasons, Spartans were not allowed to travel abroad, where they might encounter ideas dangerous to the stability of the state. Likewise, Spartan citizens were discouraged from studying philosophy, literature, or the arts. The art of war was the Spartan ideal. All other arts were frowned upon.

Athens

By 700 B.C., Athens had become a unified polis on the peninsula of Attica. Early Athens was ruled by a king. By the seventh century B.C., however, Athens had become an oligarchy under the control of its aristocrats. These aristocrats owned the best land and controlled politics. The assembly of all the citizens had few powers.

Near the end of the seventh century B.C., Athens faced turmoil because of serious economic problems. Many Athenian farmers were sold into slavery when they were unable to repay their debts. There were cries to cancel debts and give land to the poor. Civil war seemed likely.

The ruling Athenian aristocrats gave full power to Solon, a reform-minded aristocrat, in 594 B.C. Solon canceled all land debts and freed people who had fallen into slavery for debts. He refused, however, to take land from the rich and give it to the poor.

Solon's reforms, though popular, did not solve the problems of Athens. Aristocrats were still powerful, and poor peasants could not obtain land. It was not until 508 B.C. that Cleisthenes (KLYS•thuh•NEEZ), another reformer, gained the upper hand.

Cleisthenes created a council of five hundred that supervised foreign affairs, oversaw the treasury, and proposed the laws that would be voted on by the assembly. The Athenian assembly, composed of male citizens, was given final authority to pass laws after free and open debate. Because the assembly of citizens now had the central role in the Athenian political system, the reforms of Cleisthenes created the foundations for Athenian democracy.

✓ Reading Check **Identifying** Who had political rights in a Greek polis? Who did not?

PERICLES EXPANDS ATHENIAN DEMOCRACY

Pericles was a prominent political leader in Athens from 461 B.C. to 429 B.C. During this time, he expanded Athenian democracy to enable all citizens to play a role in government. In his famous speech, the Funeral Oration, given to honor those who perished in Athens's war with Sparta, Pericles describes the Greek ideal of democracy:

"Our constitution does not copy the laws of neighboring states; we are rather a pattern to others than imitators ourselves. Its administration favors the many instead of the few; this is why it is called a democracy. If we look to the laws, they afford equal justice to all in their private differences; if no social standing, advancement in public life falls to reputation for capacity, class considerations not being allowed to interfere with merit; nor again does poverty bar the way. . . . The freedom which we enjoy in our government extends also to our ordinary life. . . . [W]e do not feel called upon to be angry with our neighbor for doing what he likes. . . . But all this ease in our private relations does not make us lawless as citizens. Against this fear is our chief safeguard, teaching us to obey the magistrates and the laws. . . .

—Pericles, as quoted in *History of the Peloponnesian War,* Book 2, Thucydides

Pericles, here giving his famous Funeral Oration, encouraged all citizens to participate in the government of Athens.

COMPARING DEMOCRATIC SYSTEMS

	ATHENIAN DEMOCRACY	MODERN U.S. DEMOCRACY
Scale	• Athenian population = 300,000 • Number of adult males eligible to vote = 43,000	• U.S. population = 300,000,000 • Number of adult citizens eligible to vote = 203,000,000
Participation	Direct—all men voted on all issues of government	Representative—officials are elected to speak for the people
Eligibility	Only adult male citizens of Athens were eligible to participate.	All adult male and female citizens of the United States are eligible to vote.

DOCUMENT-BASED QUESTIONS

The Greeks laid the political foundations of Western civilization through their democratic ideals.

1. **Analyzing** According to Pericles, how does one advance in public life?

2. **Comparing** How do participation and eligibility in Athenian democracy differ from participation and eligibility in modern U.S. democracy?

Classical Greece

MAIN IDEA Classical Greek ideas about government, philosophy, and the arts created the foundation of Western society.

HISTORY & YOU What government leaders are important to you or to your family? Read about Pericles' political legacy.

Classical Greece is the name given to the period of Greek history from around 500 B.C. to the conquest of Greece in 338 B.C. This period was marked by two wars. In the first one, fought between 499 B.C. and 479 B.C., the Greeks worked together to defeat two invasions by the Persians.

The Age of Pericles

After the defeat of the Persians, Athens took over the leadership of the Greek world. Under **Pericles,** who was a dominant figure in Athenian politics between 461 B.C. and 429 B.C., Athens expanded its new empire abroad. At the same time, democracy flourished at home. This period of classical Athenian and Greek history, which historians have called the Age of Pericles, saw the height of Athenian power and brilliance.

In the Age of Pericles, the Athenians became deeply attached to their democratic system, which was a **direct democracy**. In a direct democracy, every male citizen participates directly in government decision making through mass meetings. In Athens, every male citizen participated in the governing assembly and voted on all major issues. By making lower-class male citizens eligible for public office and by paying office-holders, all citizens could take part in and be proud of their democracy.

The Great Peloponnesian War

The Greek world came to be divided into two major camps after the defeat of the Persians: the Athenian Empire and Sparta and its supporters. Athens and Sparta had built two very different kinds of societies, and neither state was able to tolerate the other's system. Sparta and its allies feared the growing Athenian Empire, and a series of disputes finally led to the outbreak of the Great Peloponnesian War in 431 B.C.

A crushing blow to the Athenians came in 405 B.C., when their fleet was destroyed at Aegospotami (EE•guh•SPAH•tuh•MY) on the Hellespont. Within the next year, Athens surrendered. Its walls were torn down, the navy was disbanded, and the Athenian Empire was destroyed.

The Great Peloponnesian War weakened the major Greek states and ruined any possibility of cooperation among them. During the next 67 years, Sparta, Athens, and Thebes (a new Greek power) struggled to dominate Greek affairs. In continuing their petty wars, the Greeks ignored the growing power of Macedonia to their north.

Classical Greek Arts

Classical Greece, especially Athens under Pericles, witnessed a period of remarkable intellectual and cultural growth. The developments of this period became the main source of Western culture.

The arts of the Western world have been largely dominated by the standards set by the Greeks of the classical period. Classical Greek art was concerned with expressing eternal ideals—reason, moderation, balance, and harmony in all things. The subject matter of this art was the human being, presented as an object of great beauty. The classic style was meant to civilize the emotions.

In architecture, the most important form was the temple, dedicated to a god or goddess. At the center of Greek temples were walled rooms that housed both the statues of deities and treasuries in which gifts to the gods and goddesses were safeguarded. These central rooms were surrounded by a screen of columns that made Greek temples open structures rather than closed ones.

Some of the finest examples of Greek classical architecture were built in Athens in the fifth century B.C. The Parthenon is regarded as the greatest example of the classical Greek temple. It was built between 447 B.C. and 432 B.C. Dedicated not only to Athena, the patron goddess of Athens, but also to the glory of Athens and the Athenians, the Parthenon was an expression of Athenians' great pride in their city-state.

See page R35 to read about a plague in Athens in 430 B.C. in the **Primary Sources and Literature Library.**

The Parthenon shows the principles of classical architecture, which are: the search for calmness, clarity, and freedom from unnecessary detail.

Greek sculpture also developed a classical style. Lifelike statues of the male nude, the favorite subject of Greek sculptors, showed relaxed attitudes. Their faces were self-assured; their bodies smooth and muscled. Greek sculptors sought to achieve an ideal beauty rather than realism.

Greek Drama

Drama as we know it in Western culture was created by the Greeks. Plays were presented in outdoor theaters as part of religious festivals. The first Greek dramas were tragedies, which were presented in a trilogy—a set of three plays—built around a common theme. The only complete trilogy we possess today, called the *Oresteia*, was composed by Aeschylus. This set of three plays relates the fate of Agamemnon, a hero in the Trojan War, and his family after his return from the war. In the plays, evil acts breed evil acts and suffering. In the end reason triumphs over evil.

Greek tragedies dealt with universal themes still relevant today. They examined such problems as the nature of good and evil, the rights of the individual, the nature of divine forces, and the nature of human beings. In the world of the Greek tragedies, striving to do the best thing may not always lead to success, but the attempt is a worthy endeavor. Greek pride in accomplishment and independence was real. As the chorus chanted in Sophocles' *Antigone*, "Is there anything more wonderful on earth, our marvelous planet, than the miracle of man?"

Greek Philosophy

Philosophy refers to an organized system of thought. The term comes from a Greek word that means "love of wisdom." Early Greek philosophers were concerned with the development of critical or rational thought about the nature of the universe. In the fifth and fourth centuries B.C., Socrates, Plato, and Aristotle raised basic questions that have been debated for two thousand years.

Socrates was a stonemason, but his true love was philosophy. Because he left no writings, we know about him from the writings of his pupils, such as Plato. He taught many pupils, but he accepted no pay. He believed that the goal of education was to improve the individual.

Socrates used a teaching method that is still known by his name. The Socratic method of teaching uses a question-and-answer format to lead pupils to see things for themselves by using their own reason. Socrates believed that all real knowledge is already present within each person. Only critical examination is needed to call it forth. This is the real task of philosophy, because, as Socrates said, "The unexamined life is not worth living." This belief in the individual's ability to reason was an important contribution of the Greeks.

One of Socrates' students was **Plato,** considered by many to be the greatest philosopher of Western civilization. Unlike his teacher Socrates, who did not write down his thoughts, Plato wrote a great deal. He was particularly fascinated with the question of reality: How do we know what is real?

Plato explained his ideas about government in a work entitled *The Republic*. Based on his experiences in Athens, Plato had come to distrust the workings of democracy. To him, individuals could not achieve a good life without living in a just and rational state.

Plato's search for the just state led him to construct an ideal state in which people were divided into three basic groups. At the top was an upper class of philosopher-kings. Plato argued that "unless . . . political power and philosophy meet together . . . there can be no rest from troubles . . . for states, nor for all mankind." The second group in Plato's ideal state consisted of warriors who protected society. The third group contained all the rest, the masses, people driven not by wisdom or courage but by desire. They were society's producers—artisans, tradespeople, and farmers. Contrary to Greek custom, Plato also believed that men and women should have the same education and equal access to all positions.

Plato established a school at Athens that was known as the Academy. His most famous pupil was **Aristotle,** who studied there for 20 years. Aristotle's many interests lay in analyzing and classifying things based on observation and investigation. He wrote about many subjects, including **ethics,** logic, politics, poetry, astronomy, geology, biology, and physics.

Like Plato, Aristotle wanted an effective form of government that would rationally direct human affairs. Unlike Plato, he did not seek an ideal state but tried to find the best form of government by analyzing existing governments. For his *Politics,* Aristotle looked at the constitutions of 158 states and found three good forms of government: monarchy, aristocracy, and constitutional government. He favored constitutional government as the best form for most people.

✓ **Reading Check** **Summarizing** What ideals do classical Greek art, architecture, and drama express?

Alexander and the Hellenistic Era

MAIN IDEA Alexander the Great spread Greek culture across Southwest Asia, into Egypt, and to India.

HISTORY & YOU How are you influenced by other cultures? Read about the Hellenistic Era.

The Greeks viewed their northern neighbors, the Macedonians, as barbarians, but in 359 B.C., Philip II came to the Macedonian throne. A great admirer of Greek culture, he longed to unite all of Greece under Macedonia. He finally did so in 338 B.C. at the Battle of Chaeronea (KEHR•uh•NEE•uh), near Thebes. The Macedonian army crushed the Greeks.

Philip insisted that the Greek states form a league and then cooperate with him in a war against Persia. Before Philip could undertake his invasion of Asia, however, he was assassinated, leaving the task to his son Alexander.

PEOPLE *in* HISTORY

Socrates
c. 470 B.C.–c. 399 B.C. Greek philosopher

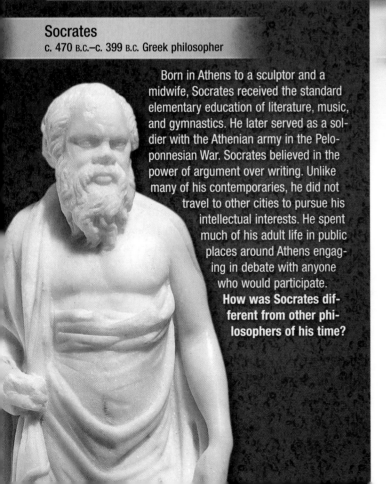

Born in Athens to a sculptor and a midwife, Socrates received the standard elementary education of literature, music, and gymnastics. He later served as a soldier with the Athenian army in the Peloponnesian War. Socrates believed in the power of argument over writing. Unlike many of his contemporaries, he did not travel to other cities to pursue his intellectual interests. He spent much of his adult life in public places around Athens engaging in debate with anyone who would participate.
How was Socrates different from other philosophers of his time?

Plato
c. 428 B.C.–c. 347 B.C. Greek philosopher

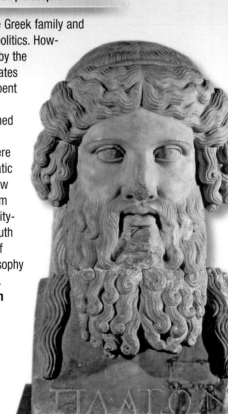

Plato was from a noble Greek family and had planned a career in politics. However, he was so horrified by the death of his teacher Socrates that he left politics and spent many years traveling and writing. When Plato returned to Athens in 387 B.C., he founded an academy where he taught using the Socratic method. His academy drew bright young students from Athens and other Greek city-states. Plato looked for truth beyond the appearance of everyday objects, a philosophy reflected in his teachings.
How did Socrates' death impact Plato?

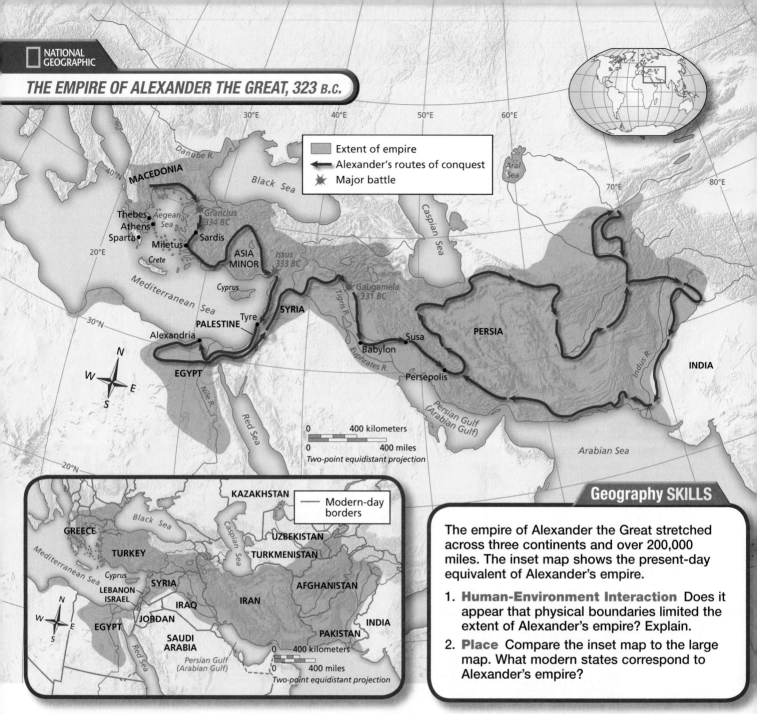

Extent of empire
Alexander's routes of conquest
Major battle

MACEDONIA
Thebes
Athens
Sparta
Miletus
Crete
Sardis
ASIA MINOR
Granicus 334 BC
Black Sea
Aegean Sea
Cyprus
Mediterranean Sea
Issus 333 BC
Tyre
PALESTINE
SYRIA
Alexandria
EGYPT
Nile R.
Red Sea
Tigris R.
Euphrates R.
Gaugamela 331 BC
Babylon
Susa
Persepolis
PERSIA
Persian Gulf (Arabian Gulf)
Caspian Sea
Aral Sea
Indus R.
INDIA
Arabian Sea

Danube R.

0   400 kilometers
0   400 miles
Two-point equidistant projection

N W E S

Modern-day borders

KAZAKHSTAN
GREECE
TURKEY
Cyprus
LEBANON
ISRAEL
SYRIA
IRAQ
JORDAN
EGYPT
SAUDI ARABIA
Black Sea
Mediterranean Sea
Caspian Sea
UZBEKISTAN
TURKMENISTAN
AFGHANISTAN
IRAN
PAKISTAN
INDIA
Persian Gulf (Arabian Gulf)
Red Sea

N W E S

0   400 kilometers
0   400 miles
Two-point equidistant projection

Geography SKILLS

The empire of Alexander the Great stretched across three continents and over 200,000 miles. The inset map shows the present-day equivalent of Alexander's empire.

1. **Human-Environment Interaction** Does it appear that physical boundaries limited the extent of Alexander's empire? Explain.

2. **Place** Compare the inset map to the large map. What modern states correspond to Alexander's empire?

History ONLINE

Student Web Activity—

Visit glencoe.com to learn more about Alexander the Great and his conquests.

Alexander the Great

Alexander the Great was only 20 when he became king of Macedonia. Philip had carefully prepared his son for kingship by taking Alexander along with him on military campaigns. Philip taught Alexander the basics of military leadership. After his father's death, Alexander moved quickly to fulfill his father's dream—the invasion of the Persian Empire. He was motivated by the desire for glory and empire but also by the desire to avenge the Persian burning of Athens in 480 B.C. In the spring of

334 B.C., Alexander entered Asia Minor with an army of some 37,000 men, both Macedonians and Greeks. By 331 B.C., Alexander had taken possession of the Persian Empire, but he was not content.

Over the next three years, Alexander moved as far east as modern-day Pakistan. In 326 B.C., he crossed the Indus River and entered India, where he experienced a number of difficult campaigns. Weary of fighting year after year, his soldiers refused to go farther.

Alexander returned to Babylon, planning more conquests. In June 323 B.C., exhausted from wounds, fever, and too much alcohol, he died. He was 32 years old.

The Hellenistic Era

Alexander created a new age, the Hellenistic Era. The word *Hellenistic* comes from a Greek word meaning, "to imitate Greeks." It is an appropriate way to describe an age that saw the expansion of the Greek language and ideas to Southwest Asia and beyond.

The united empire that Alexander created by his conquests fell apart soon after his death as the most important Macedonian generals engaged in a struggle for power. By 300 B.C., any hope of unity was dead. Eventually, four Hellenistic kingdoms emerged as the successors to Alexander: Macedonia, Syria in the east, the kingdom of Pergamum in western Asia Minor, and Egypt. All were eventually conquered by the Romans.

Hellenistic rulers encouraged a spread of Greek colonists to Southwest Asia. Greeks (and Macedonians) provided not only new recruits for the army but also a pool of civilian administrators and workers. Architects, engineers, dramatists, and actors were all in demand in the new Greek cities. The Greek cities of the Hellenistic Era spread Greek culture to Southwest and Central Asia.

The Hellenistic Era was a period of considerable cultural accomplishment in many areas. These achievements occurred throughout the Hellenistic world. Certain centers—especially the great Hellenistic city of Alexandria—stood out. Alexandria became home to poets, writers, philosophers, and scientists—scholars of all kinds.

After one of Alexander's generals, Ptolemy, became ruler of Egypt, he began construction on the famous lighthouse at Alexandria, which served as a landmark until damaged by earthquakes in the A.D. 1300s. The library in Alexandria became the largest in ancient times, with more than 500,000 scrolls. The library encouraged the careful study of literature and language. There was also a museum that welcomed scholarly research.

Pergamum, the most important city in Asia Minor, also became a leading cultural center. As a result, Pergamum also attracted both scholars and artists. The library at Pergamum was second only to Alexandria's library.

The founding of new cities and the rebuilding of old ones presented opportunities for Greek architects and sculptors. Both Hellenistic kings and rich citizens patronized sculptors. Thousands of statues were erected in towns and cities all over the Hellenistic world. Hellenistic sculptors maintained the technical skill of the classical period, but they moved away from idealism to a more emotional and realistic art.

✓ Reading Check **Identifying** Which four Hellenistic kingdoms emerged following Alexander's death?

SECTION 1 REVIEW

Vocabulary
1. **Explain** the significance of: Mycenae, Homer, epic poem, polis, acropolis, democracy, oligarchy, Sparta, Athens, classical, Pericles, direct democracy, Socrates, Plato, Aristotle, ethics, Alexander the Great.

Main Ideas
2. **Explaining** How did the *Iliad* and the *Odyssey* influence different parts of Greek culture?

3. **Identify** which Greek states struggled for power after the Great Peloponnesian War.

4. **Creating** Using a table like the one below, identify the reforms that led to democracy in Athens and the leaders who initiated them.

Leader	Reforms
Solon	
Cleisthenes	
Pericles	

Critical Thinking
5. **The BIG Idea Analyzing** How were the governments favored by Plato and Aristotle different? Which view makes more sense to you? Why?

6. **Evaluating** What effect did Alexander the Great have on the spread of Greek culture?

7. **Analyzing Visuals** Examine the photo of the Parthenon shown on page 40. To whom was it dedicated? What does its placement demonstrate about the role of religion in city life?

Writing About History
8. **Descriptive Writing** Imagine that you are a 25-year-old male living in Sparta in 700 B.C. Create a diary in which you record your activities for one week. Write one diary page for each day.

History ONLINE

For help with the concepts in this section of *Glencoe World History—Modern Times*, go to glencoe.com and click Study Central.

Rome and the Rise of Christianity

GUIDE TO READING

The BIG Idea

Order and Security The Romans created a large and successful empire that spread Greco-Roman culture and later Christianity.

Content Vocabulary
- republic *(p. 49)*
- patrician *(p. 49)*
- plebeian *(p. 49)*
- imperator *(p. 50)*
- Christianity *(p. 56)*

Academic Vocabulary
- virtually *(p. 48)*
- transformation *(p. 55)*

People and Places
- Rome *(p. 48)*
- Carthage *(p. 48)*
- Hannibal *(p. 49)*
- Julius Caesar *(p. 50)*
- Augustus *(p. 50)*
- Pax Romana *(p. 51)*
- Jesus *(p. 55)*
- Constantine *(p. 57)*

Reading Strategy
Categorizing Information As you read this section, complete a chart like the one shown below listing the government officials and the legislative bodies of the Roman Republic.

Officials	Legislative Bodies

Roman history begins with the conquest of Italy and eventually the entire Mediterranean world. The Romans spread their forms of government and Greco-Roman culture throughout their empire and eventually adopted Christianity. Evidence of the Roman Empire can be found in many countries today.

The Rise of Rome

MAIN IDEA The Romans were able to use their political and military skills to create a large and successful empire.

HISTORY & YOU Is the United States a republic? Learn how the Romans governed.

Indo-European peoples moved into Italy from about 1500 B.C. to 1000 B.C. We know little about them, but we do know that one group called the Romans lived in the region of Latium. These people spoke Latin, which, like Greek, is an Indo-European language. The Romans were herders and farmers who lived in settlements consisting of huts on the tops of Italy's hills. After 800 B.C., other people also began settling in Italy—most notably, the Greeks and the Etruscans. The Greeks came to Italy in large numbers during the age of Greek colonization (750 B.C. to 550 B.C.). It was the Etruscans, however, who most influenced the early development of Rome. They found **Rome** a village and turned it into a city. In 509 B.C., the Romans overthrew the last Etruscan king and began a new era in Rome's history: the Roman Republic.

Rome Conquers the Mediterranean

At the beginning of the republic, Rome was surrounded by enemies. For the next two hundred years, the city was engaged in almost continuous warfare. By 264 B.C., the Romans had overcome the Greeks and completed their conquest of southern Italy. After defeating the remaining Etruscan states to the north, Rome had conquered **virtually** all of Italy.

To rule Italy, the Romans devised the Roman Confederation. Under this system, Rome allowed some peoples—especially Latins—to have full Roman citizenship. Most of the remaining communities were made allies. They remained free to run their own local affairs but were required to provide soldiers for Rome. The Romans made it clear that loyal allies could improve their status and become Roman citizens. The Romans made the conquered peoples feel they had a real stake in Rome's success. After their conquest of Italy, the Romans found themselves face-to-face with a strong power in the Mediterranean—the state of **Carthage.**

Hannibal's army

Geography SKILLS

From 264 B.C. to 146 B.C. the Romans fought the Carthaginians in the Punic Wars.

1. **Human-Environment Interaction** What natural barriers did the Romans and Carthaginians have to cross to fight in these wars?

2. **Movement** Why did Hannibal choose to cross the Alps to get to Rome?

Map labels: ATLANTIC OCEAN · GAUL · Trebia 218 B.C. · ALPS · PYRENEES · SPAIN · Metaurus 207 B.C. · Lake Trasimene 217 B.C. · Corsica · Rome · Saguntum 219 B.C. · Balearic Islands · Sardinia · Cannae 216 B.C. · Mediterranean Sea · Sicily · Carthage · Zama 202 B.C. · AFRICA

Legend: Roman territory · Carthaginian territory · Scipio's routes · Hannibal's routes · Roman victory · Carthaginian victory

0 400 kilometers · 0 400 miles · Lambert Azimuthal Equal-Area projection

---

Carthage was founded around 800 B.C. on the coast of North Africa and created a large trading empire in the western Mediterranean. By the third century B.C., the Carthaginian Empire included northern Africa, southern Spain, Sardinia, Corsica, and western Sicily.

The presence of the Carthaginians in Sicily, an island close to the Italian coast, made the Romans fearful. The Romans fought three wars with Carthage, beginning in 264 B.C. During the second war, Rome came close to disaster as a result of the victories of **Hannibal,** Carthage's greatest general. Despite their losses, the Romans refused to give up and created new armies and a navy to carry on the struggle. In 202 B.C., the Romans crushed Hannibal's forces, ending the second war. Carthage lost Spain, which became a Roman province. Rome had become the dominant power in the western Mediterranean. Fifty years later, the Romans fought their third and final war with Carthage, completely destroying Carthage in 146 B.C.

During its struggle with Carthage, Rome also battled the Hellenistic states in the eastern Mediterranean. By 133 B.C., Macedonia, Greece, and Pergamum were under Roman control. Rome was now master of the Mediterranean Sea.

Roman Republic

In 509 B.C., the Romans established a **republic.** In a republic, the leader is not a monarch and some citizens have the right to vote. This was a beginning of a new era in Rome's history.

Early Rome was divided into two groups or orders—the patricians and the plebeians (plih•BEE•uhnz). The **patricians** were wealthy landowners, who became Rome's ruling class. Less wealthy landowners, small farmers, craftspeople, and merchants were part of a larger group called **plebeians.**

Men in both groups were citizens and could vote, but only the patricians could be elected to governmental offices.

The chief executive officers of the Roman Republic were the consuls and praetors (PREE•tuhrz). Two consuls, chosen every year, ran the government and led the Roman army into battle. The praetor was in charge of civil law—laws that applied to Roman citizens. As Roman territory expanded, another praetor was added to judge cases involving noncitizens. The Romans also had a number of officials who had special duties, such as supervising the treasury.

The Roman Senate came to hold an especially important position in the Roman Republic. It was a select group of about three hundred patricians who served for life. At first, the Senate's only role was to advise government officials. However, the advice of the Senate carried a great deal of weight. By the third century B.C., it had the force of law.

The Roman Republic had several people's assemblies in addition to the Senate. By far the most important of these was the centuriate assembly. The centuriate assembly elected the chief officials, such as consuls and praetors, and passed laws. Because it was organized by classes based on wealth, the wealthiest citizens always had a majority. The council of the plebs was the assembly for plebeians only, and it came into being as a result of the struggle between the two social orders in Rome.

There was often conflict between the patricians and the plebeians in the early Roman Republic. Children of patricians and plebeians were forbidden to marry each other. Plebeians resented this situation, especially since they served in the Roman army that protected the republic. They thought that they deserved both political and social equality with the patricians.

The struggle between the patricians and plebeians dragged on for hundreds of years. Ultimately, it led to success for the plebeians. The council of the plebs, an assembly for plebeians only, began to gain more power. New officials, known as tribunes of the plebs, were given the power to protect the plebeians. Plebeians were permitted to marry patricians and to become consuls in the fourth century B.C.

Finally, in 287 B.C., the council of the plebs received the right to pass laws for all Romans. Thus, all male Roman citizens were now supposedly equal under the law. In reality, however, a few wealthy patrician and plebeian families formed a new senatorial ruling class. The Roman Republic had not become a democracy.

From Republic to Empire

Between 509 B.C. and 264 B.C., most of what is modern-day Italy was unified under Rome's control. Even more dramatic is that by 133 B.C., Rome stood supreme over the Mediterranean Sea.

Rome's republican institutions, however, proved inadequate for ruling an empire. By the second century B.C., the Senate had become the real governing body of the Roman state. Within the Senate, rival factions of wealthy families began to compete for power, creating disorder.

In addition, in the first century B.C., Roman leaders began to recruit armies that swore an oath of loyalty to the general, not to the Roman state. For the next 50 years (82 B.C.–31 B.C.), Roman history was characterized by civil wars as a number of individuals competed for power. In one of these struggles, **Julius Caesar** defeated the forces led by Pompey. Caesar was officially made dictator, or absolute ruler, in 45 B.C. After Caesar was assassinated in 44 B.C., Octavian, Caesar's heir and grandnephew, defeated Mark Antony and took control of the Roman world. After the collapse of Rome's republican institutions and a series of brutal civil wars, Augustus created a new order that began the Roman Empire.

The period beginning in 31 B.C. and lasting until A.D. 14 came to be known as the Age of Augustus. In 27 B.C., the Senate had awarded Octavian the title of **Augustus**— the revered one. Augustus proved to be highly popular, but his continuing control of the army was the chief source of his power. The Senate gave Augustus the title **imperator**, or commander in chief. The English word *emperor* comes from *imperator*. Augustus thus became the first emperor of the Roman Empire.

The Early Empire

Beginning in A.D. 14, a series of new emperors ruled Rome. This period, ending in A.D. 180, is called the Early Empire.

The first four emperors after Augustus grew increasingly more powerful and corrupt. At the beginning of the second century, a series of five so-called good emperors—Nerva, Trajan, Hadrian, Antoninus Pius, and Marcus Aurelius— came to power. These rulers treated the ruling classes with respect, ended arbitrary executions, maintained peace in the empire, and supported domestic policies that were generally helpful to the empire. These emperors were part of a period known as the **Pax Romana**—the Roman Peace. The *Pax Romana* lasted for about 200 years (27 B.C.–A.D. 180).

Under the five good emperors, the powers of the emperor continued to expand at the expense of the Senate. Officials who were appointed and directed by the emperor took over the running of the government.

The good emperors also created new programs to help the people. Trajan, for example, created a program that provided state funds to assist poor parents in the raising and education of their children. The good emperors were widely praised for their building programs. Trajan and Hadrian were especially active in building public works—aqueducts, bridges, roads, and harbor facilities—throughout the provinces and in Rome.

At its height in the second century A.D., the Roman Empire was one of the greatest states the world had ever seen. It covered about 3.5 million square miles (about 9.1 million square km) and had a population that has been estimated at more than 50 million.

The Early Empire was also a period of much prosperity, with internal peace leading to high levels of trade. Merchants from all over the empire came to the chief Italian ports of Puteoli (pyu•TEE•uh•LY) on the Bay of Naples and Ostia at the mouth of the Tiber River.

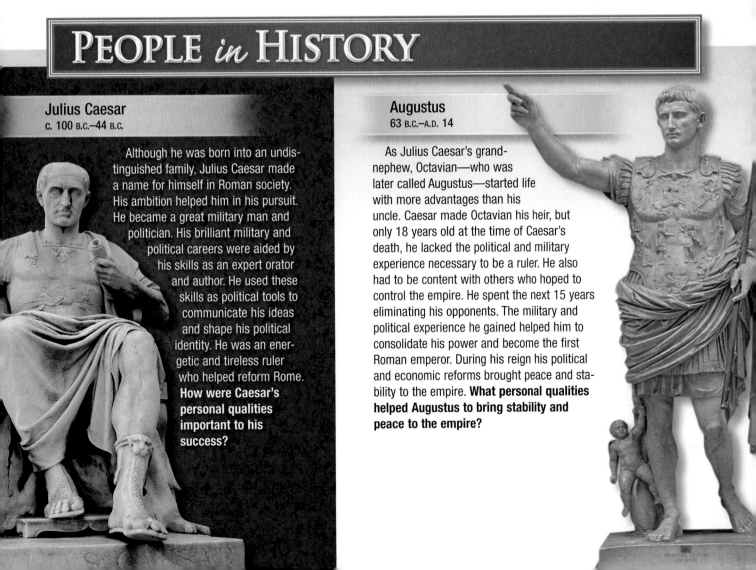

PEOPLE *in* HISTORY

Julius Caesar
c. 100 B.C.–44 B.C.

Although he was born into an undistinguished family, Julius Caesar made a name for himself in Roman society. His ambition helped him in his pursuit. He became a great military man and politician. His brilliant military and political careers were aided by his skills as an expert orator and author. He used these skills as political tools to communicate his ideas and shape his political identity. He was an energetic and tireless ruler who helped reform Rome. **How were Caesar's personal qualities important to his success?**

Augustus
63 B.C.–A.D. 14

As Julius Caesar's grand-nephew, Octavian—who was later called Augustus—started life with more advantages than his uncle. Caesar made Octavian his heir, but only 18 years old at the time of Caesar's death, he lacked the political and military experience necessary to be a ruler. He also had to be content with others who hoped to control the empire. He spent the next 15 years eliminating his opponents. The military and political experience he gained helped him to consolidate his power and become the first Roman emperor. During his reign his political and economic reforms brought peace and stability to the empire. **What personal qualities helped Augustus to bring stability and peace to the empire?**

Trade went beyond the Roman frontiers and even included Chinese silk goods. Large quantities of grain were imported, especially from Egypt, to feed the people of Rome. Luxury items poured in to satisfy the wealthy upper classes. Despite the active trade and commerce, however, farming remained the chief occupation of most people and the underlying basis of Roman prosperity.

✓ **Reading Check** **Summarizing** What events made Rome the master of the Mediterranean Sea by 129 B.C.?

The Roman Empire

MAIN IDEA The Romans spread Greco-Roman arts and culture throughout the empire.

HISTORY & YOU What cultures have had a major impact on the United States? Learn how Rome borrowed from Greece.

After conquering Greece, the Romans adopted many aspects of Greek culture and society. The Romans spread Greco-Roman civilization throughout their empire.

HISTORY & ARTS   PRIMARY SOURCE

Roman Life

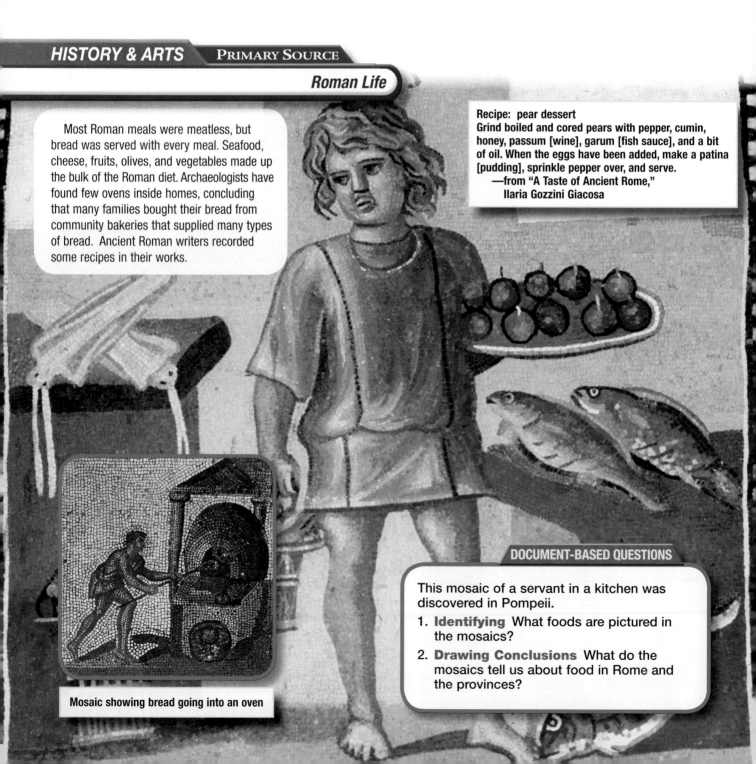

Most Roman meals were meatless, but bread was served with every meal. Seafood, cheese, fruits, olives, and vegetables made up the bulk of the Roman diet. Archaeologists have found few ovens inside homes, concluding that many families bought their bread from community bakeries that supplied many types of bread. Ancient Roman writers recorded some recipes in their works.

Recipe: pear dessert
Grind boiled and cored pears with pepper, cumin, honey, passum [wine], garum [fish sauce], and a bit of oil. When the eggs have been added, make a patina [pudding], sprinkle pepper over, and serve.
—from "A Taste of Ancient Rome,"
Ilaria Gozzini Giacosa

DOCUMENT-BASED QUESTIONS

This mosaic of a servant in a kitchen was discovered in Pompeii.

1. **Identifying** What foods are pictured in the mosaics?

2. **Drawing Conclusions** What do the mosaics tell us about food in Rome and the provinces?

Mosaic showing bread going into an oven

The Arts

During the third and second centuries B.C., the Romans adopted many features of the Greek style of art. They developed a taste for Greek statues, which they placed not only in public buildings but also in their private houses. Reproductions of Greek statues became popular once the supply of original works ran low. While Greek sculptors aimed for an ideal appearance in their figures, Roman sculptors produced more realistic statues that included even unattractive physical details.

The Romans excelled in architecture, a highly practical art. Although they continued to use Greek styles such as colonnades and rectangular buildings, the Romans also used curved forms: the arch, the vault, and the dome. The Romans were the first people in antiquity to use concrete on a massive scale. Using concrete along with the new architectural forms made it possible for the Romans to construct huge buildings undreamed of by the Greeks.

The Romans were superb builders. Their remarkable engineering skills were put to use constructing bridges, aqueducts, and roads such as the Appian Way. The Romans built a network of some 50,000 miles (80,450 km) of roads throughout the empire. In Rome, almost a dozen aqueducts kept a population of one million supplied with water.

Although there were many talented writers, the high point of Latin literature was reached in the Age of Augustus. Indeed, the Augustan Age has been called the golden age of Latin literature.

The most distinguished poet of the Augustan Age was Virgil. The son of a small landholder in northern Italy near Mantua, he welcomed the rule of Augustus and wrote his greatest work, the *Aeneid* (ih•NEE•uhd), in honor of Rome. Virgil's epic poem was meant to rival the work of Homer. In the poem, the character of Aeneas is the ideal Roman whose virtues are duty, piety, and faithfulness. Aeneas fulfilled his purpose by establishing the Romans in Italy and starting Rome on its mission to rule the world. The poem was also meant to express that Rome's gift was the art of ruling.

The most famous Latin prose work of the golden age was written by the historian Livy. Livy saw history in terms of moral lessons. His stories revealed the character of the chief figures and demonstrated the virtues that made Rome great.

Slavery in Ancient Rome

Slavery was common throughout the ancient world, but no people had more slaves or relied so much on slave labor as the Romans did. Before the third century B.C., slaves used in Rome were usually from parts of Italy and were often regarded as part of the family household.

The Roman conquest of the Mediterranean brought a drastic change in the use of slaves. Large numbers of foreign peoples who had been captured in wars were brought back to Italy as slaves. Greek slaves were in much demand as tutors, musicians, doctors, and artists. Roman businessmen would employ them as shop assistants or craftspeople. Slaves of all nationalities were used as household workers, such as cooks, valets, waiters, cleaners, and gardeners.

Slaves built roads and public buildings, and farmed the large estates of the wealthy. The conditions under which these slaves lived were often pitiful. One Roman writer argued that it was cheaper to work slaves to death and then replace them than to treat them well.

Some slaves revolted against their owners and even murdered them. The most famous slave revolt in Italy occurred in 73 B.C. Led by the gladiator Spartacus, the revolt broke out in southern Italy and involved 70,000 slaves. Spartacus managed to defeat several Roman armies before being trapped and killed in 71 B.C. The Romans crucified (put to death by nailing to a cross) 6,000 of Spartacus's followers.

Living in Rome

At the center of the colossal Roman Empire was the ancient city of Rome. Truly a capital city, Rome had the largest population of any city in the empire—close to one million by the time of Augustus. For anyone with ambitions, Rome was the place to be. People from all over the empire lived there.

Rome was an overcrowded and noisy city. Because of the congestion, cart and wagon traffic was banned from the streets during the day, making the streets noisy at night.

Rome boasted public buildings unequaled anywhere in the empire. Its temples, markets, baths, theaters, governmental buildings, and amphitheaters gave parts of the city an appearance of grandeur and magnificence.

Despite this grandeur, an enormous gulf existed between rich and poor. The rich had comfortable villas, while the poor lived in apartment blocks called *insulae*, which could be six stories high. Constructed of concrete walls with wooden beam floors, these buildings were poorly built and often collapsed.

Fire was a constant threat in the *insulae* because stoves, torches, candles, and lamps were used for heat and light. Once started, fires were extremely difficult to put out. In A.D. 64, Nero was falsely accused of starting a fire that destroyed a large part of the city.

High rents forced entire families to live in one room. There was no plumbing or central heating. As a result, many poor Romans spent most of their time outdoors in the streets.

INFOGRAPHICS

Roman Law

The Twelve Tables were the first written set of laws that were publicly displayed in Rome. Prior to the Twelve Tables the patricians, who both made the laws and served as judges, had clear advantages over plebeians in Roman society. Having the Twelve Tables established and protected certain rights for both patricians and plebeians in the Roman Republic. The original tablets that contained the laws were destroyed when Rome fell, but the idea of establishing rights and procedures in legal systems was adopted by later cultures. The influence of the Twelve Tables can still be seen in legal systems today.

Twelve Tables of Rome, 449 B.C.

Table I: Proceedings Preliminary to Trial
9. If both parties are present, sunset shall be the time limit of the proceedings.

Table II: Trial

Table III: Execution of Judgment
1. Thirty days shall be allowed by law for payment of confessed debt and for settlement of matters adjudged in court.

Table IV: Paternal Power

Table V: Inheritance and Guardianship

Table VI: Ownership and Possession

Table VII: Real Property

Table VIII: Torts or Delicts

Table IX: Public Law
6. For anyone whomsoever to be put to death without a trial and unconvicted . . . is forbidden.

Table X: Sacred Law

Table XI: Supplementary Laws

Table XII: Supplementary Laws
5. Whatever the people ordain last shall be legally valid.

CRITICAL THINKING SKILLS

1. **Evaluating** Why would it be important to record and display the laws for citizens to see?
2. **Comparing** Explain how the laws in the Twelve Tables are similar to laws in the United States.

Although it was the center of a great empire, Rome had serious problems. Beginning with Augustus, emperors provided the poor with food. Even so, conditions remained grim for the poor.

Entertainment was provided on a grand scale for the inhabitants of Rome. Public spectacles were provided by the emperor as part of the great religious festivals celebrated by the state. The festivals included three major types of entertainment. At the Circus Maximus, horse and chariot races attracted hundreds of thousands. Dramatic performances were held in theaters. The most famous of all the public spectacles, however, were the gladiatorial shows held in the Colosseum.

Roman Law

One of Rome's chief gifts to the Mediterranean world of its day and to later generations was its system of law. Rome's first code of laws was the Twelve Tables, adopted in 450 B.C. This code was a product of a simple farming society and proved inadequate for later Roman needs.

From the Twelve Tables, the Romans developed a more sophisticated system of civil law. This system applied only to Roman citizens, however, and as Rome expanded, legal questions arose that involved both Romans and non-Romans. The Romans found that although some of their rules of civil law could be used in these cases, special rules were often needed. These rules gave rise to a body of law known as the Law of Nations. The Romans came to identify the Law of Nations with natural law, or universal law based on reason. This enabled them to establish standards of justice that applied to all people.

These standards of justice included principles still recognized today. A person was regarded as innocent until proved otherwise. People accused of wrongdoing were allowed to defend themselves before a judge. A judge, in turn, was expected to weigh evidence carefully before arriving at a decision. These principles lived on long after the fall of the Roman Empire.

✓ Reading Check **Summarizing** What problems did people face in the ancient city of Rome?

The Rise of Christianity

MAIN IDEA Although Christians were initially persecuted, Christianity gained acceptance and spread through the empire.

HISTORY & YOU What other groups have been persecuted for their beliefs? Read how the Roman Empire spread Christianity.

In Hellenistic times, the Jewish people had been given considerable independence. By A.D. 6, however, Judaea, which embraced the lands of the old Jewish kingdom of Judah, had been made a Roman province placed under the direction of a Roman official called a procurator. Unrest was widespread in Judaea, but the Jews differed among themselves about Roman rule. A Jewish revolt began in A.D. 66 but was crushed four years later.

The Teachings of Jesus

Decades before the revolt, a Jewish prophet named **Jesus** preached throughout Judaea and neighboring Galilee. Jesus believed his mission was to complete the salvation that God had promised to Israel. He stated: "Do not think that I have come to abolish the Law or the Prophets; I have not come to abolish them but to fulfill them." According to Jesus, what was important was not strict adherence to the letter of the law but the **transformation** of the inner person: "So in everything, do to others what you would have them do to you, for this sums up the Law and the Prophets."

God's command was to love God and one another. Jesus said, "Love the Lord your God with all your heart and with all your soul and with all your mind and with all your strength. This is the first commandment. The second is this: Love your neighbor as yourself." Jesus voiced the ethical concepts—humility, charity, and love toward others—that would later shape the value system of Western civilization.

Jesus' preaching eventually stirred controversy. Some people saw Jesus as a potential revolutionary who might lead a revolt against Rome. Jesus' opponents finally turned him over to the Roman authorities.

The procurator Pontius Pilate ordered Jesus' crucifixion.

After the death of Jesus, his followers proclaimed he had risen from death and had appeared to them. They believed Jesus to be the Messiah (anointed one), the long-expected deliverer who would save Israel from its foes and bring peace and prosperity.

The Spread of Christianity

Christianity began as a religious movement within Judaism. The Christian movement won followers in Jerusalem and throughout Judaea and Galilee.

Prominent apostles, or leaders, arose in early Christianity. One was Simon Peter, a Jewish fisherman who had become a follower of Jesus during Jesus' lifetime. Peter was recognized as the leader of the apostles. Another major apostle was Paul, a highly educated Jewish Roman citizen who joined the movement later. Paul took the message of Jesus to Gentiles—non-Jews—as well as to Jews. He founded Christian communities throughout Asia Minor and along the shores of the Aegean Sea.

At the center of Paul's message was the belief that Jesus was the Savior, the Son of God who had come to Earth to save humanity. Paul taught that Jesus' death made up for the sins of all humans. By accepting Jesus as Christ (from *Christos,* the Greek term for Messiah) and Savior, people could be saved from sin and reconciled to God.

The teachings of early Christianity at first were passed on orally. Written materials, in the form of letters written by Paul and other followers of Jesus, outlined Christian beliefs for communities they helped found. Some also may have preserved some of the sayings of Jesus in writing. Later, between A.D. 70 and 100, these accounts became the basis of the written Gospels—the "good news" concerning Jesus. These writings give a record of Jesus' life and teachings, and they form the core of the New Testament, the second part of the Christian Bible.

By 100, Christian churches had been established in most of the major cities of the eastern empire and in some places in the western part of the empire. Most early Christians came from the Jews and the Greek-speaking populations of the east. In the second and third centuries, however, an increasing number of followers were Latin-speaking people.

Many Romans came to view Christians as harmful to the Roman state because Christians refused to worship the state gods and emperors. The Romans saw the Christians' refusal to do so as an act of treason, punishable by death. The Christians, like the Jews, believed there was only one God. To them, the worship of state gods and the emperors meant worshiping false gods and endangering their own salvation.

The Roman government began persecuting (harassing to cause suffering) Christians during the reign of Nero (A.D. 54–68). The emperor blamed the Christians for the fire that destroyed much of Rome and subjected them to cruel deaths. In contrast, in the second century, persecution of Christians diminished. By the end of the reigns of the five good emperors, Christians still represented a small minority, though it was one of considerable strength.

Roman Empire Adopts Christianity

Although Christians were persecuted in the first and second centuries, this did nothing to stop the growth of Christianity. In fact, it strengthened Christianity in the second and third centuries by forcing it to become more organized.

Crucial to this change was the emerging role of the bishops, who assumed more control over church communities. The Christian Church was creating a new structure in which the clergy, or the church leaders, had distinct functions separate from the laity, or the regular church members.

Christianity grew quickly in the first century, took root in the second, and by the third had spread widely. Why was Christianity able to attract so many followers?

First, the Christian message had much to offer the Roman world. Christianity was personal and offered salvation and eternal life to individuals. Christianity gave meaning and purpose to life.

Christianity also fulfilled the human need to belong. Christians formed communities where people could express their love by helping one another and offering assistance to the poor and the sick. Christianity satisfied the need to belong in a way that the huge Roman Empire could not.

Christianity was attractive to all classes, but especially to the poor and powerless. Eternal life was promised to all—rich, poor, aristocrats, slaves, men, and women. Christianity stressed a sense of spiritual equality for all people.

In the fourth century, Christianity prospered when **Constantine** became the first Christian emperor. Although he was not baptized until the end of his life, in 313 Constantine issued the Edict of Milan, proclaiming official tolerance of Christianity. Under Theodosius the Great, who ruled from 378 to 395, the Romans adopted Christianity as the empire's official religion.

✓ Reading Check **Explaining** What effect did persecution have on the Christian Church in the second and third centuries?

TURNING POINT

THE SPREAD OF CHRISTIANITY — IN THE ROMAN EMPIRE

The conversion of Emperor Constantine aided in the spread of Christianity. Although he did not make Christianity the official religion of the empire, he took an active role in protecting Christians and in shaping the religion. With the Edict of Milan and later edicts, Constantine made Christianity a "permitted" religion and gave Christians back confiscated property. He also convened the Council of Nicaea to organize and unify Christianity. Constantine also ordered the construction of churches. In A.D. 380 Emperor Theodosius I made Christianity the official religion of the empire.

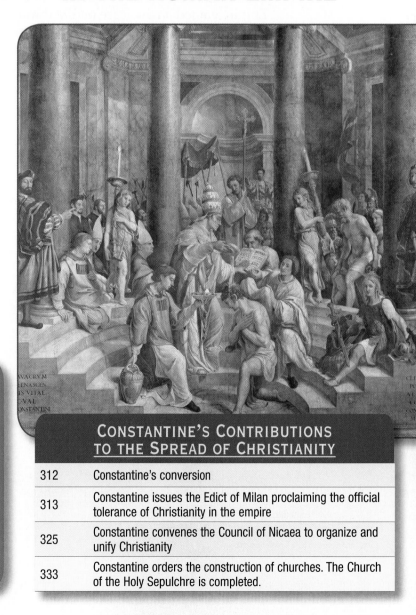

DOCUMENT-BASED QUESTIONS

This fresco shows Constantine being baptized, an event which may not have occurred. The work is in the Pope's apartments in Rome and was completed by Raphael's students after the painter died in 1520. The painting illustrates the significance of Constantine's role in the spread and legitimization of Christianity.

1. **Summarizing** How did Constantine support the Christian movement?

2. **Speculating** What do you think might have happened to Christianity if it had not been officially recognized before the Roman Empire fell?

CONSTANTINE'S CONTRIBUTIONS TO THE SPREAD OF CHRISTIANITY

312	Constantine's conversion
313	Constantine issues the Edict of Milan proclaiming the official tolerance of Christianity in the empire
325	Constantine convenes the Council of Nicaea to organize and unify Christianity
333	Constantine orders the construction of churches. The Church of the Holy Sepulchre is completed.

End of the Empire

MAIN IDEA Although emperors used control and coercion to keep the empire functioning, migrating Germanic tribes took control of the Western Roman Empire.

HISTORY & YOU What problems are there in running a large organization? Read how the Romans tried to solve these problems.

Marcus Aurelius, the last of the five good emperors, died in A.D. 180. For the next hundred years a period of civil wars, political disorder, and economic decline almost brought the Roman Empire to an end.

The Decline

At the end of the third century and the beginning of the fourth century, the Roman Empire gained a new lease on life through the efforts of two emperors, Diocletian and Constantine. The empire was changed into a new state: the Late Roman Empire, which included a new governmental structure, a rigid economic and social system, and a new state religion—Christianity. Believing that the empire had grown too large for a single ruler, Diocletian, who ruled from 284 to 305, divided it into four units, each with its own ruler. Diocletian's military power still enabled him to hold the ultimate authority.

Constantine, who ruled from 306 to 337, continued and expanded the policies of Diocletian. By 324, Constantine had emerged as the sole ruler of the empire. Constantine's biggest project was the construction of a new capital city in the east, on the site of the Greek city of Byzantium on the shores of the Bosporus. The city, eventually renamed Constantinople (now İstanbul, Turkey), was developed for defensive reasons because of its strategic location. Called the "New Rome," Constantinople became the center of the Eastern Roman Empire and one of the greatest cities of the world.

Both rulers greatly strengthened and enlarged the administrative bureaucracies

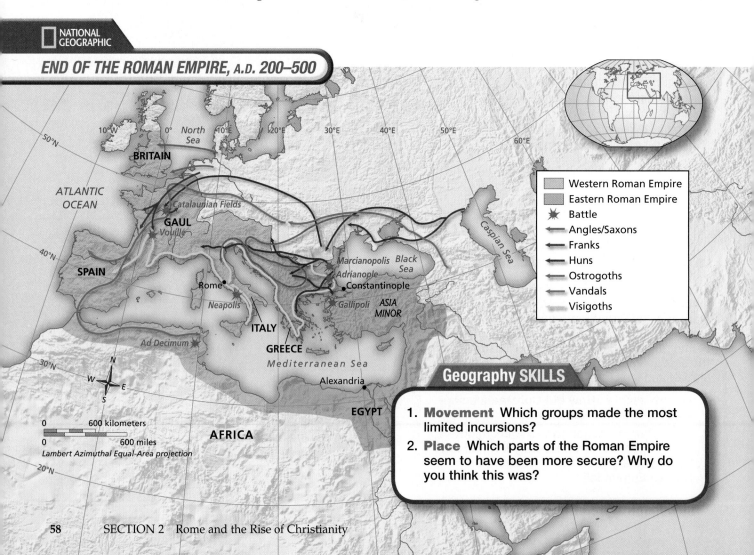

NATIONAL GEOGRAPHIC

END OF THE ROMAN EMPIRE, A.D. 200–500

Legend:
- Western Roman Empire
- Eastern Roman Empire
- Battle
- Angles/Saxons
- Franks
- Huns
- Ostrogoths
- Vandals
- Visigoths

Geography SKILLS

1. **Movement** Which groups made the most limited incursions?
2. **Place** Which parts of the Roman Empire seem to have been more secure? Why do you think this was?

of the Roman Empire. A hierarchy of officials exercised control at the various levels of government. The army was enlarged to 500,000 men, including Germanic troops.

Diocletian's and Constantine's political and military reforms enlarged two institutions—the army and the civil service—which drained most of the public funds. The population was not growing, so the tax base could not be increased to pay for the army and the bureaucracy.

To ensure the tax base and keep the empire going despite the labor shortage, the emperors issued edicts forcing workers to remain in their designated vocations. Hence, jobs, such as bakers and shippers, became hereditary. The fortunes of free tenant farmers also declined.

In general, the economic and social policies of Diocletian and Constantine were based on control and coercion. Although temporarily successful, such policies in the long run stifled the very vitality the Late Empire needed to revive its sagging fortunes.

The Fall

The restored empire of Diocletian and Constantine limped along for more than a century. After Constantine, the empire continued to be divided into western and eastern parts. The capital of the Western Roman Empire remained in Rome. Constantinople remained the capital of the Eastern Roman Empire.

The Western Roman Empire came under increasing pressure from migrating Germanic tribes. The major breakthrough of Germanic tribes into the west came in the second half of the fourth century. The Huns, who came from Asia, moved into eastern Europe and put pressure on the Germanic Visigoths. The Visigoths, in turn, moved south and west, crossed the Danube River into Roman territory, and settled down as Roman allies until they revolted. The Romans attempted to stop the revolt at Adrianople in 378, but the Visigoths defeated them.

Increasing numbers of Germanic groups now crossed the frontiers. In 410, the Visigoths sacked Rome. Another group, the Vandals, poured into southern Spain and Africa. They crossed into Italy from northern Africa and, in 455, they too sacked Rome. The words *vandal* and *vandalize* come from this ruthless tribe.

In 476, the western emperor, Romulus Augustulus, was deposed by the Germanic head of the army. This is usually taken as the date of the fall of the Western Roman Empire. As we shall see in Chapter 3, a series of Germanic kingdoms replaced the Western Roman Empire. The Eastern Roman Empire, or the Byzantine Empire, however, continued to thrive with its center at Constantinople.

✓ Reading Check **Identifying** Which groups moved into the Western Roman Empire?

Vocabulary
1. **Explain** the significance of: Rome, virtually, Carthage, Hannibal, republic, patrician, plebeian, Julius Caesar, Augustus, imperator, *Pax Romana*, Jesus, transformation, Christianity, Constantine.

Main Ideas
2. **Contrast** the Roman Republic and the Roman Empire.

3. **List** the ethical concepts voiced by Jesus.

4. **Describe** the economic and military problems that contributed to the decline of the Roman Empire.

Critical Thinking
5. **The Big Idea** **Explaining** Explain why Romans began to accept Christianity and why it took so long for it to be accepted by the state.

6. **Summarizing Information** Create a table like the one below describing the contributions of the Greeks and the contributions of the Romans to Western civilization.

Greek Contributions	Roman Contributions

7. **Analyzing Visuals** Examine the mosaic on page 52. How is the servant portrayed? Can you identify the servant's age or gender?

Writing About History
8. **Expository Writing** Use the Internet or library sources to research the theories about why the Roman Empire fell. Summarize the theories in a brief essay and explain why some theories seem more convincing than others.

History ONLINE

For help with the concepts in this section of *Glencoe World History—Modern Times*, go to glencoe.com and click Study Central.

Social History

Games of Death in Ancient Rome

Public spectacles have always been a part of civilization. The earliest city-states held ceremonies where the punishment of criminals, the awarding of honors, and parades of soldiers were conducted for all to see. Such events reinforced cultural values and the existing social order. In ancient Rome, the most mesmerizing public spectacles were of gladiators fighting to the death. They embodied the Roman virtues of bravery, honor, and glory in a world that was cruel and unpredictable.

THE ARENA

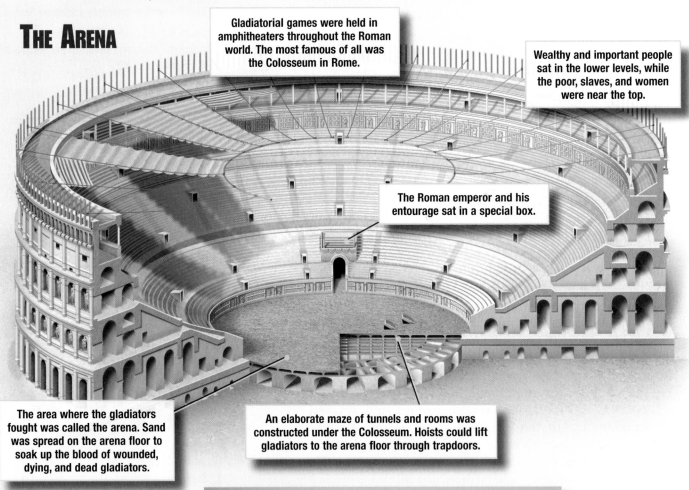

Gladiatorial games were held in amphitheaters throughout the Roman world. The most famous of all was the Colosseum in Rome.

Wealthy and important people sat in the lower levels, while the poor, slaves, and women were near the top.

The Roman emperor and his entourage sat in a special box.

The area where the gladiators fought was called the arena. Sand was spread on the arena floor to soak up the blood of wounded, dying, and dead gladiators.

An elaborate maze of tunnels and rooms was constructed under the Colosseum. Hoists could lift gladiators to the arena floor through trapdoors.

GLADIATORS IN ROMAN SOCIETY

Gladiatorial combat began as funerary rites and evolved into spectacles sponsored by the wealthy to gain prestige. The fights were wildly popular, and so were taken over by the government and later by the emperor himself. The Roman view of gladiatorial combat was complex. Men who ran training schools for gladiators were wealthy but were looked down upon socially. The gladiators were admired as kinds of heroes, but most of them were slaves, prisoners of war, or criminals.

THE COMBATANTS

A fighting net is used to tangle up his opponent. It has weights so it will travel farther when thrown.

A large, curved shield protects the *secutor* from his opponent's trident.

A RETIARIUS ("NET-MAN")

His strategy is to keep his distance, strike with the trident when he can, capture his opponent with the net, and then finish him off with the dagger. His lack of armor is both an advantage—he is mobile—and a disadvantage—he is vulnerable.

A SECUTOR ("PURSUER")

He plans to pursue his opponent and strike him down with the sword. His equipment provides protection, but he must come in close to attack, making him vulnerable to the reach of his opponent's trident and net.

GLADIATORIAL STYLES

The *secutor* and the *retiarius* were but two of many types of gladiators. Each type was equipped with unique equipment for different fighting styles. Many of the gladiatorial types were supposed to emulate Rome's enemies. The *Thraex* type, for example, represented the fighting man of Thrace. Arguments about the advantages and disadvantages of each gladiator type added to the sheer spectacle of the bloody duels.

ANALYZING VISUALS

1. **Contrasting** What modern events are comparable to gladiatorial combat? How are they similar to and different from the Roman practice?

2. **Making Judgments** How might you explain the existence of gladiatorial combat in the highly developed Roman civilization?

STUDY TO GO You can study anywhere, anytime by downloading quizzes and flash cards to your PDA from <u>glencoe.com</u>.

HELLENISTIC MASTERPIECE

Winged Victory from Hellenistic Era

ANCIENT GREECE

- The polis, or city-state, was the center of Greek political and economic life.
- Sparta and Athens followed very different ideals.
- Pericles expanded Athenian democracy to enable more citizens to participate in the government.
- Greeks wrote the first analytical history, staged dramas, developed philosophy, and created art and architecture known for balance and harmony.
- Alexander the Great created an empire that spread Greek (Hellenistic) culture throughout Southwest Asia.

ARCH OF CONSTANTINE IN ROME

Monuments told stories to the public about rulers.

ROME & THE RISE OF CHRISTIANITY

- After the collapse of Rome's Republic, Augustus created a new order that began the Roman Empire.
- Public works, a shared culture, and architecture unified Rome's far-flung cities.
- The Roman Empire adopted Christianity as its official religion after Christianity spread through the empire.
- Outside threats, civil strife, and economic woes weakened the empire.
- In 476, the Western Roman Empire ended, but the Eastern Roman Empire continued to thrive.

STANDARDIZED TEST PRACTICE

TEST-TAKING TIP

Look for key words such as *best, always,* and *never* in questions and answer choices.

Reviewing Vocabulary

Directions: Choose the word or words that best complete the sentence.

1. The term _____ comes from the Greek word that means "love of wisdom."

   A literature

   B theater

   C philosophy

   D mathematics

2. A/an _____ tells the deeds of a great hero.

   A epic poem

   B oracle

   C philosopher

   D artist

3. Judaea became a Roman province under the direction of an official called a/an _____.

   A dictator

   B praetor

   C procurator

   D imperator

4. The writings that record Jesus' life and teachings form the core of the _____.

   A Old Testament

   B New Testament

   C laity

   D Twelve Tables

Reviewing Main Ideas

Directions: Choose the best answers to the following questions.

Section 1 *(pp. 38–47)*

5. Which of the following best describes Sparta?

   A A city-state that valued alliances with other cultures

   B A Macedonian democracy

   C A strict society run by helots

   D A military state focused on the art of war

6. How did Cleisthenes create the foundation for democracy in Athens?

   A By declaring war on Sparta

   B By creating an Athenian assembly

   C By giving aristocrats' land to the poor

   D By discouraging the study of the arts

7. What do Aeschylus and Sophocles have in common?

   A They developed mathematical proofs.

   B They studied under Plato.

   C They wrote tragedies.

   D They were gifted historians.

8. How did Alexander's father prepare him for kingship?

   A By having him brought up in Athens

   B By bringing him on military campaigns

   C By enlisting him in the Spartan army

   D By sending for Socrates to tutor him

Need Extra Help?								
If You Missed Questions . . .	1	2	3	4	5	6	7	8
Go to Page . . .	44	39	55	56	41	41	44	46

 GO ON

9. Who benefited from the power struggles of Athens, Sparta, and Thebes?

   A Philip II of Macedonia

   B The Delian League

   C Women in all three societies

   D Pericles of Athens

Section 2 *(pp. 48–59)*

10. What is the Law of Nations primarily based on?

   A Sacrifice

   B Civil law

   C Reason

   D Democracy

11. Who became the first Roman emperor known as Augustus?

   A Crassus

   B Julius Caesar

   C Antony

   D Octavian

12. What culture influenced Roman art and architecture?

   A American

   B Etruscan

   C Egyptian

   D Greek

13. Who wrote the *Aeneid*?

   A Virgil

   B Horace

   C Livy

   D Plato

14. What caused the fall of the Roman Empire?

   A Migration of Germanic tribes

   B An increase in taxes

   C The rise of the Christian religion

   D Death of Constantine

Critical Thinking

Directions: Choose the best answers to the following questions.

15. What event blinded the major Greek states to the threat from Macedonia?

   A The Age of Pericles

   B The establishment of Sparta

   C The Great Peloponnesian War

   D The end of the Persian Empire

Analyze the map and answer the question that follows. Base your answer on the map.

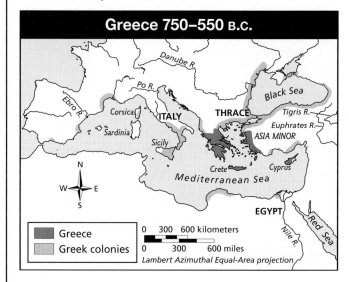

16. Based on the map, which of the following is most likely true?

   A The Greeks relied heavily on their navy.

   B The Greeks planned to conquer all of Western Europe.

   C Greeks had little interest in colonization.

   D Greece was the largest colony in the empire.

17. On which group of people were Romans dependent for manual labor on farms and to help build roads and buildings?

   A Women

   B Greeks

   C Slaves

   D Children

Need Extra Help?									
If You Missed Questions . . .	9	10	11	12	13	14	15	16	17
Go to Page . . .	43	55	50	53	53	59	43	38	50

Use the time line to answer question 18.

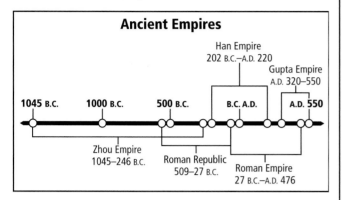

Ancient Empires

Han Empire
202 B.C.–A.D. 220

Gupta Empire
A.D. 320–550

1045 B.C.   **1000 B.C.**   **500 B.C.**   **B.C. A.D.**   **A.D. 550**

Zhou Empire
1045–246 B.C.

Roman Republic
509–27 B.C.

Roman Empire
27 B.C.–A.D. 476

18. How long did the Roman civilization last?

A Almost 1,000 years

B 2,000 years

C 50 years

D About 500 years

19. What concepts did Jesus preach that shaped the value system of Western civilization?

A Humility, charity, and love

B Reason and logic

C Wisdom and self-sacrifice

D Duty and hard work

20. Plato's ideal state was divided into three groups, made up of _____.

A philosopher-kings, priests, and peasants

B philosopher-kings, warriors, and the masses

C aristocrats, teachers, and farmers

D aristocrats, merchants, and slaves

21. Which Roman emperor helped spread Christianity?

A Crassus

B Constantine

C Antony

D Octavian

Document-Based Questions

Directions: Analyze the document and answer the short-answer questions that follow the document. Base your answers on the document and on your knowledge of world history.

While Athens was at war with Sparta, Pericles spoke at a public funeral to honor those who had died in combat. He spoke of the greatness of Athens and the strength of its political system. Read the following excerpt.

> *"Our Constitution is called a democracy because the power is in the hands not of a minority but of the whole people. When it is a question of settling private disputes, everyone is equal before the law. Just as our political life is free and open, so is our day-to-day life in our relations with each other. . . . Here each individual is interested not only in his own affairs but in the affairs of the state as well."*

22. According to Pericles, what is the relationship between the individual and the state in a democracy?

23. What is the historical significance of this speech in Pericles' own day and now?

Extended Response

24. Select a particular piece of Roman architecture. Discuss how it demonstrates Roman culture, including potential influence from other cultures. In what ways do archaeologists and anthropologists analyze Roman culture, based on the limited remains of architecture and artifacts? Support your answer with outside research.

History ONLINE

For additional test practice, use Self-Check Quizzes—Chapter 2 at **glencoe.com**.

Need Extra Help?

If You Missed Questions . . .	18	19	20	21	22	23	24
Go to Page . . .	49	55	44	57	43	43	50

STOP

MARY EVANS PICTURE LIBRARY/ALAMY

What a Blast!

In A.D. 79 **PLINY THE YOUNGER,** *an 18-year-old Roman, was vacationing in southern Italy when a nearby volcano, Vesuvius, erupted. It eventually buried the cities of Herculaneum and Pompeii. Pliny described the event in letters to the historian Tacitus. Here is a terrifying excerpt.*

"Being at a convenient distance from the houses, we stood still, in the midst of a most dangerous and dreadful scene. . . . The sea seemed to roll back upon itself, and to be driven from its banks by the convulsive motion of the earth. . . . On the other side, a black and dreadful cloud . . . revealed behind it various shaped masses of flame. . . .

"The ashes now began to fall upon us. . . . I looked back: a dense dark mist seemed to be following us, spreading itself over the country like a cloud. . . . The night came upon us, [like] that of a room when it is shut up, and all the lights put out. You might hear the shrieks of women, the screams of children, and the shouts of men. . . . [A] heavy shower of ashes rained upon us, which we were obliged to stand up to shake off, otherwise we should have been crushed and buried in the heap."

VERBATIM

" The truth is always the strongest argument. **"**

SOPHOCLES,
*Greek playwright,
in his tragedy* Phaedra

" To everything there is a season, a time for every purpose under the sun. **"**

BOOK OF ECCLESIASTES

" A man should practice what he preaches but should also preach what he practices. **"**

CONFUCIUS,
*Chinese philosopher
and founder of Confucianism*

" Where there's life, there's hope. **"**
CICERO,
Roman senator and famed orator

" You are young again. You live again. . . . Forever. **"**

BOOK OF THE DEAD,
*a series of prayers written
on the walls of Egyptian tombs*

SCALA/ART RESOURCE

Athenian thinkers Aristotle and Plato

ATHENS VS. SPARTA

ROLF RICHARDSON/ALAMY

Everyone knows that the Greek city-states of Athens and Sparta are as alike as, well, oil and water. Athens is known as a city of culture, Sparta as a burg that likes to battle. This chart describes some differences between the two places. Which town would you prefer to call home?

Spartan
warrior
Leonidas

Sparta	Athens
Trains boys to become soldiers from age 7	Trains boys in the arts and sciences from age 7
Allows women to move about the city	Forces women to stay at home
Values physical superiority	Values intellectual superiority
Builds mostly military barracks	Builds beautiful buildings
Produces good warriors	Produces good citizens

BASS MUSEUM OF ART/CORBIS

All Wrapped Up

To Egyptians, death is the final frontier. They believe that a dead person can live on in the afterworld—but only if that person's body is well preserved, through embalming. Special priests are in charge of the process of mummification, which takes 70 days. Below we've scrambled the steps it takes to make a mummy. Can you put them in the right order?

1. Innards are dried out, wrapped in linen, and placed in containers called canopic jars to be preserved forever.

2. The body is wrapped in linen bandages and placed in a coffin called a sarcophagus.

3. All the inner organs, except the heart, are removed through a slit in the abdomen.

4. The body is covered inside and out with a kind of salt called natron. It dries out the body.

5. A small hook draws out the brain through the nose.

6. The body is covered with myrrh and other fragrant spices.

Answers: 5, 3, 1, 4, 6, 2

Milestones

HELD. FIRST OLYMPIC GAMES, in 776 B.C., in the city of Olympia. Male athletes competed in events that included boxing, wrestling, and chariot racing. Winners received a crown of olive leaves. Koroibos of Elis won the first prize at these games, which are scheduled to take place every four years.

CONQUERED. By ALEXANDER THE GREAT, most of the known world. A legend in his own time, Alexander had defeated Persia, Egypt, India, and other empires before his untimely death in 323 B.C. at age 32.

ASSASSINATED. CALIGULA, unpopular Roman emperor, in A.D. 41 by members of his security force. Caligula's strange behavior and cruelty were factors in his murder. The final straw came when he declared himself a god. In a move that surprised political observers, Claudius was named the new emperor.

DIED. ZHANG HENG, an engineer, mathematician, inventor, artist, and scholar in the Eastern Han Dynasty, in A.D. 139. Among his innovations were a more accurate calendar and the world's first seismograph, to measure the force of earthquakes.

INVENTED. THE WHEEL, by potters in the Mesopotamian city of Ur, around 3500 B.C. This flat, circular piece of wood sits atop a wooden stick called an axle. As the axle spins, so does the wheel, allowing very uniform pots to be made more quickly. Experts speculate that the wheel may have many potential uses.

BY THE NUMBERS

50,000 Number of people who can fit into the Roman Colosseum

25,000 Approximate number of laborers who worked on the Great Pyramid of Giza

450 Height in feet of the lighthouse built in the harbor of Alexandria, Egypt

VISUAL ARTS LIBRARY (LONDON)/ALAMY

12 Number of years it takes for a Sumerian student of cuneiform to become a scribe

7 Number of "Wonders of the Ancient World," which include the Great Pyramid of Giza, the Hanging Gardens of Babylon, the Statue of Zeus at Olympia, the Temple of Artemis at Ephesus, the Mausoleum at Halicarnassus, the Colossus at Rhodes, and the Lighthouse of Alexandria

CRITICAL THINKING

1. **Comparing and Contrasting** What are the differences between living in Athens and living in Sparta?

2. **Drawing Conclusions** What is causing the darkness that Pliny the Younger describes?

World Religions

A *religion* is a set of beliefs in an ultimate reality and a set of practices used to express those beliefs. Religion is a key component of culture.

Each religion has its own special celebrations and worship styles. Most religions also have their own sacred texts, symbols, and sites. All of these aspects of religion help to unite followers regardless of where in the world they live.

TERMS

animism—belief that spirits inhabit natural objects and forces of nature

atheism—disbelief in the existence of any god

monotheism—belief in one god

polytheism—belief in more than one god

secularism—belief that life's questions can be answered apart from religious belief

sect—a subdivision within a religion that has its own distinctive beliefs and/or practices

NATIONAL GEOGRAPHIC   World Religions Today

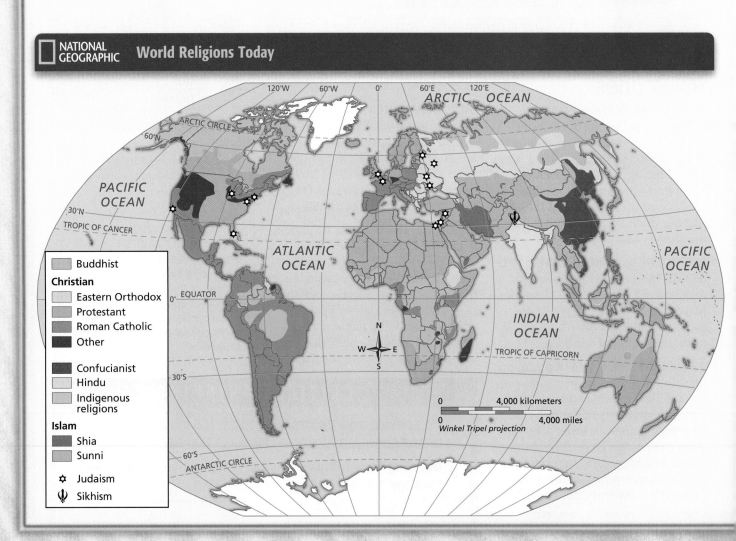

Legend:
- Buddhist
- **Christian**
  - Eastern Orthodox
  - Protestant
  - Roman Catholic
  - Other
- Confucianist
- Hindu
- Indigenous religions
- **Islam**
  - Shia
  - Sunni
- ✡ Judaism
- ☬ Sikhism

Winkel Tripel projection

0   4,000 kilometers
0   4,000 miles

We study religion because it is an important component of civilization, shaping how people interact with one another, dress, and eat. Religion is at the core of the belief system of a civilization.

The diffusion of religion throughout the world has been caused by a variety of factors including migration, missionary work, trade, and war. Buddhism, Christianity, and Islam are the three major religions that spread their religion through missionary activities. Religions such as Hinduism, Sikhism, and Judaism are associated with a particular culture group. Followers are usually born into these religions. Sometimes close contact and differences in beliefs have resulted in conflict between religious groups.

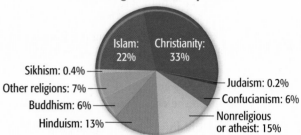

Percentage of World Population

Note: Total exceeds 100% because numbers were rounded.
Sources: www.cia.gov, The World Factbook 2006; www.adherents.com.

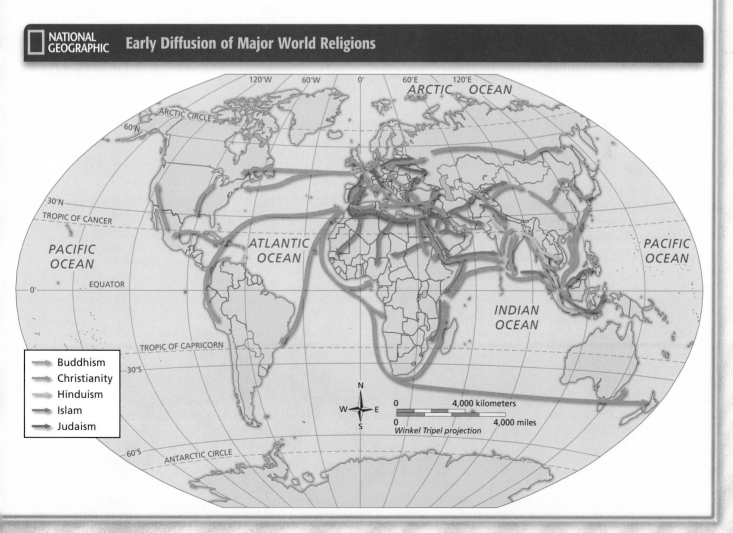

NATIONAL GEOGRAPHIC   **Early Diffusion of Major World Religions**

Buddhism
Christianity
Hinduism
Islam
Judaism

0   4,000 kilometers
0   4,000 miles
Winkel Tripel projection

BUDDHISM

Siddhārtha Gautama, known as the Buddha ("the Awakened") after his enlightenment at the age of 35, was born some 2,500 years ago in what is now Nepal. The Buddha's followers adhere to his teachings (dharma, meaning "divine law"), which aim to end suffering in the world. Buddhists call this goal Nirvana; and they believe that it can be achieved only by understanding the Four Noble Truths and by following the 4th Truth, which says that freedom from suffering is possible by practicing the Eightfold Path. Through the Buddha's teachings, his followers come to know the impermanence of all things and reach the end of ignorance and unhappiness.

Over time, as Buddhism spread throughout Asia, several branches emerged. The largest of these are Theravada Buddhism, the monk-centered Buddhism that is dominant in Sri Lanka, Burma, Thailand, Laos, and Cambodia; and Mahayana, a complex, more liberal variety of Buddhism that has traditionally been dominant in Tibet, Central Asia, Korea, China, and Japan.

▲ Statue of the Buddha, Kamakura, Japan

Sacred Text For centuries the Buddha's teachings were transmitted orally. For Theravada Buddhists, the authoritative collection of Buddhist texts is the Tripitaka ("three baskets"). These texts were first written on palm leaves in a language called Pali. This excerpt from the *Dhammapada*, a famous text within the Tripitaka, urges responding to hatred with love:

Sacred Symbol The *dharmachakra* ("wheel of the law") is a major Buddhist symbol. Among other things, it signifies the overcoming of obstacles. The eight spokes represent the Eightfold Path—right view, right intention, right speech, right action, right livelihood, right effort, right mindfulness, right concentration—that is central for all Buddhists.

> ❝ Never in this world is hate
> Appeased by hatred.
> It is only appeased by love—
> This is an eternal law. ❞
>
> —Dhammapada I.5

Sacred Site Buddhists believe that Siddhārtha Gautama achieved enlightenment beneath the Bodhi Tree in Bodh Gayā, India. Today, Buddhists from around the world flock to Bodh Gayā in search of their own spiritual awakening.

Worship and Celebration The ultimate goal of Buddhists is to achieve Nirvana, the enlightened state in which individuals are free from ignorance, greed, and suffering. Theravada Buddhists believe that monks are most likely to reach Nirvana because of their lifestyle of renunciation, moral virtue, study, and meditation.

Christianity

Christianity claims more members than any of the other world religions. It dates its beginning to the death of Jesus in A.D. 33 in what is now Israel. It is based on the belief in one god and on the life and teachings of Jesus Christ. Christians believe that Jesus, who was born a Jew, is the son of God and is fully divine and human. Christians regard Jesus as the savior who died for humanity's sins. Christians feel that people are saved and achieve eternal life by faith in Jesus Christ.

The major forms of Christianity are Roman Catholicism, Eastern Orthodoxy, and Protestantism. All three are united in their belief in Jesus Christ as savior, but have developed their own individual theologies.

Sacred Text The Bible is the spiritual text for all Christians and is considered to be inspired by God. This excerpt, from Matthew 5:3-12, is from Christ's Sermon on the Mount.

Stained glass window depicting Jesus Christ

> " *Blessed are the poor in spirit, for theirs is the kingdom of heaven.*
> *Blessed are those who mourn, for they shall be comforted.*
> *Blessed are the meek, for they shall inherit the earth.*
> *Blessed are those who hunger and thirst for righteousness, for they shall be satisfied.*
> *Blessed are the merciful, for they shall obtain mercy.*
> *Blessed are the pure in heart, for they shall see God.*
> *Blessed are the peacemakers, for they shall be called sons of God.*
> *Blessed are those who are persecuted for righteousness' sake, for theirs is the kingdom of heaven.*
> *Blessed are you when men revile you and persecute you and utter all kinds of evil against you falsely on my account.*
> *Rejoice and be glad, for your reward is great in heaven, for so men persecuted the prophets who were before you.* "

Sacred Symbol Christians believe that Jesus Christ died for their sins. His death redeemed those who follow his teachings. The statue *Christ the Redeemer,* located in Rio de Janeiro, Brazil, symbolizes this fundamental belief.

Sacred Site Bethlehem was the birthplace of Jesus Christ and holds great importance to Christians. The Church of the Nativity is located in the heart of Bethlehem. It houses the spot where Christians believe Jesus was born.

Worship and Celebration Christians celebrate many events commemorating the life and death of Jesus. Among the most widely known and observed are Christmas, Good Friday, and Easter. Christmas is often commemorated by attending church services to celebrate the birth of Jesus. As part of the celebration, followers often light candles.

CONFUCIANISM

Confucianism began oven 2,500 years ago in China. Although considered a religion, it is actually a philosophy. It is based upon the teachings of Confucius, which are grounded in ethical behavior and good government.

The teachings of Confucius focused on three areas: social philosophy, political philosophy, and education. Confucius taught that relationships are based on rank. Persons of higher rank are responsible for caring for those of lower rank. Those of lower rank should respect and obey those of higher rank. Eventually his teachings spread from China to other East Asian societies.

▲ *Students studying Confucianism, Chunghak-dong, South Korea*

▲ *The* Analects

Sacred Text Confucius was famous for his sayings and proverbs. These teachings were gathered into a book called the *Analects* after Confucius's death. Below is an example of Confucius's teachings.

Confucius said:

> ❝ *To learn and to practice what is learned time and again is pleasure, is it not? To have friends come from afar is happiness, is it not? To be unperturbed when not appreciated by others is gentlemanly, is it not?* ❞
>
> —*The* Analects

Sacred Symbol The symbol of Confucianism, yin-yang, symbolizes the harmony the philosophy offers. The white is *yin*, the light, bright, cheerful, playful aspect of life. The black is *yang*, the dark, mysterious, serious part of life. The two act together to balance one another.

Sacred Site The temple at Qufu is a group of buildings dedicated to Confucius. It is located on Confucius's ancestral land. It is one of the largest ancient architectural complexes in China. Every year followers gather at Qufu to celebrate the birthday of Confucius.

Worship and Celebration Confucianism does not have a god or clergy, but there are temples dedicated to Confucius, the spiritual leader. Those who follow his teachings see Confucianism as a way of life and a guide to ethical behavior and good government.

HINDUISM

Hinduism is the oldest of the world's major living religions. It developed among the cultures in India as they spread out over the plains and forests of the subcontinent. It has no single founder or founding date. Hinduism is complex: it has numerous sects and many different divinities are honored. Among the more famous Hindu gods are Brahma, Vishnu, and Shiva, who represent respectively the creative, sustaining, and destructive forces in the universe. Major Hindu beliefs are reincarnation, karma, and dharma.

Hindus believe the universe contains several heavens and hells. According to the concept of rebirth or reincarnation, which is central to their beliefs, souls are continually reborn. In what form one is reborn is determined by the good and evil actions performed in his or her past lives. Those acts are karma. A soul continues in the cycle of rebirth until release is achieved.

Sacred Text The Vedas consist of hymns, prayers, and speculations composed in ancient Sanskrit. They are the oldest religious texts in an Indo-European language. The Rig Veda, Sama Veda, Yajur Veda, and Atharva Veda are the four great Vedic collections. Together, they make up one of the most significant and authoritative Hindu religious texts.

▲ Statue of Vishnu

> **❝** Now, whether they perform a cremation for
>   such a person or not,
> people like him pass into the flame,
> from the flame into the day,
> from the day into the fortnight of the waxing moon
> from the fortnight of the waxing moon into the six
>   months when the sun moves north,
> from these months into the year,
>   from the year into the sun,
> from the sun into the moon, and from
>   the moon into the lightning.
> Then a person who is not human—
>   he leads them to Brahman.
> This is the path to the gods, the path to Brahman.
> Those who proceed along this path do not
> return to this human condition. **❞**
>
> —The Chandogya Upanishad 4:15.5

▲

Sacred Symbol One important symbol of Hinduism is actually a symbol for a sound. "Om" is a sound that Hindus often chant during prayer, mantras, and rituals.

Sacred Site Hindus believe that when a person dies his or her soul is reborn. This is known as reincarnation. Many Hindus bathe in the Ganges and other sacred rivers to purify their soul and to be released from rebirth.

Worship and Celebration Holi is a significant North Indian Hindu festival celebrating the triumph of good over evil. As part of the celebration, men, women, and children splash colored powders and water on each other. In addition to its religious significance, Holi also celebrates the beginning of spring.

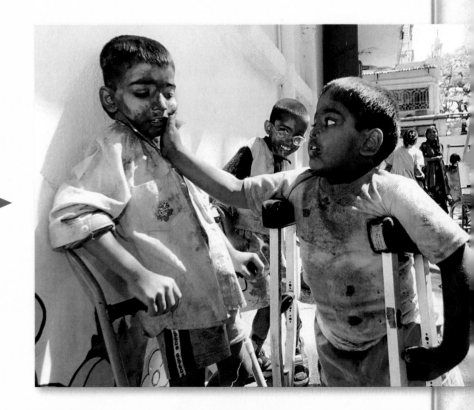

Islam

Followers of Islam, known as Muslims, believe in one God, whom they call Allah. The word *Allah* is Arabic for "the god." The spiritual founder of Islam, Muhammad, began his teachings in Makkah (Mecca) in A.D. 610. Eventually the religion spread throughout much of Asia, including parts of India to the borders of China, and a substantial portion of Africa. According to Muslims, the Quran, their holy book, contains the direct word of God, revealed to the Prophet Muhammad sometime between A.D. 610 and A.D. 632. Muslims believe that God created nature and without his intervention, there would be nothingness. God serves four functions: creation, sustenance, guidance, and judgment.

Central to Islamic beliefs are the Five Pillars. These are affirmation of the belief in Allah and his prophet Muhammad; group prayer; tithing, or the giving of money to charity; fasting during Ramadan; and a pilgrimage to Makkah once in a lifetime if physically and financially able. Within Islam, there are two main branches, the Sunni and the Shia. The differences between the two are based on the history of the Muslim state. The Shia believed that the rulers should descend from Muhammad. The Sunni believed that the rulers need only be followers of Muhammad. Most Muslims are Sunni.

Sacred Text The sacred text of Islam is the Quran. Preferably, it is written and read only in Arabic, but translations have been made into many languages. The excerpt below is a verse repeated by all Muslims during their five daily prayers.

The Dome of the Rock, Jerusalem

The Quran ▼

> In the Name of Allah, the Compassionate,
>   the Merciful,
>   Praise be to Allah, the Lord of the World,
>   The Compassionate, the Merciful,
>   Master of the Day of Judgment,
>   Only You do we worship, and only You
>   Do we implore for help.
>   Lead us to the right path,
>   The path of those you have favored
>   Not those who have incurred
>   Your wrath or
>   Have gone astray.
>
> —The Quran

Sacred Symbol Islam is often symbolized by the crescent moon. It is an important part of Muslim rituals, which are based on the lunar calendar.

Sacred Site Makkah is a sacred site for all Muslims. One of the Five Pillars of Islam states that all those who are physically and financially able must make a hajj, or pilgrimage, to the holy city once in their life. Practicing Muslims are also required to pray facing Makkah five times a day.

Worship and Celebration Ramadan is a month-long celebration commemorating the time during which Muhammad received the Quran from Allah. It is customary for Muslims to fast from dawn until sunset all month long. Muslims believe that fasting helps followers focus on spiritual rather than bodily matters and creates empathy for one's fellow men and women. Ramadan ends with a feast known as Eid-al-Fitr, or Feast of the Fast.

Judaism

Judaism is a monotheistic religion. In fact, Judaism was the first major religion to believe in one god. Jews trace their national and religious origins back to God's call to Abraham. Jews have a covenant with God. They believe God will someday send a messiah who will redeem them from exile and usher in an era of world peace.

Over time Judaism has separated into branches, including Orthodox, Reform, Conservative, and Reconstructionist. Orthodox Jews are the most traditional of all the branches.

Sacred Text The Torah is the five books of Moses, which tell the story of the origins of the Jews and explain Jewish laws. The remainder of the Hebrew Bible contains the writings of the prophets, Psalms, and ethical and historical works.

▲ El Ghriba Synagogue, Jerba, Tunisia

> ❝ I am the Lord your God, who brought you out of the land of Egypt, out of the house of slavery; you shall have no other gods before me. ❞
>
> —Exodus 20:2

Sacred Symbol ▶ The menorah is used in the celebration of Hanukkah, commemorating the rededication of the Temple of Jerusalem following the Maccabees' victory over the Syrians.

◀ The Torah scroll

Sacred Site The Western Wall is what remains of the structure surrounding the Second Jerusalem Temple, built after the Jews' return from the Babylonian captivity. It is considered a sacred spot in Jewish religious tradition. Prayers are offered at the wall three times a day—morning, afternoon, and evening.

Worship and Celebration The day-long Yom Kippur service ends with the blowing of the ram's horn (shofar). Yom Kippur is the holiest day in the Jewish calendar. During Yom Kippur, Jews do not eat or drink for 25 hours. The purpose is to reflect on the past year and gain forgiveness from God for one's sins. It falls in September or October, ten days after Rosh Hashanah, the Jewish New Year.

Sikhism

Sikhism emerged in the mid-1500s in the Punjab, in northwest India, rising from the religious experience and teachings of Gurū Nānak. The religion exhibits influences from Islam and Hinduism, but it is distinct from both. Sikh traditions teach that Nānak encountered God directly and was commissioned by Him to be His servant.

Sikhs ("students, disciples") believe in one almighty god who is formless and without qualities (*nirguna*) but can be known through meditation and heard directly. Sikhism forbids discrimination on the basis of class, color, religion, caste, or gender. While 80 percent of the world's 20 million Sikhs live in the Punjab, Sikhism has spread widely as many Sikhs have migrated to new homes around the world.

▲ *Sikh man, Chapeltown, England*

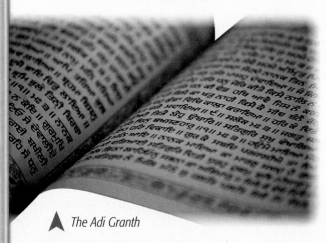

▲ *The Adi Granth*

Sacred Text The great authoritative sacred text for Sikhs is the Adi Granth ("Principal Book," also known as the Guru Granth Sahib). Compiled from the mid-1500s through the 1600s, it includes contributions from Sikh gurus and also from some persons also claimed as saints by Hindus and Muslims, such as Namdev, Ravidas, and Kabir.

> ❝Enshrine the Lord's Name within your heart. The Word of the Guru's Bani prevails throughout the world, through this Bani, the Lord's Name is obtained. ❞
>
> —*Gurū Amar Dās, page 1066*

▲

Sacred Symbol The sacred symbol of the Sikhs is the *khanda.* It is composed of four traditional Sikh weapons: the *khanda* or double-edged sword (in the center), from which the symbol takes its name; the *cakkar* (disk), and two curved daggers (*kirpan*) representing temporal and spiritual power, respectively Piri and Miri.

Sacred Sites Amritsar is the spiritual capital of Sikhism. The Golden Temple (*Harimandir Sahib*) in Amritsar is the most sacred of Sikh shrines.

Worship and Celebration Vaisakhi is a significant Punjabi and Sikh festival in April celebrating the new year and the beginning of the harvest season. Celebrations often take place along riverbanks with participants dancing and wearing brightly colored clothes.

Indigenous Religions

There are many varieties of religious belief that are limited to particular ethnic groups. These local religions are found in Africa as well as isolated parts of Japan, Australia, and the Americas.

Most local religions reflect a close relationship with the environment. Some groups teach that people are a part of nature, not separate from it. Animism is characteristic of many indigenous religions. Natural features are sacred, and stories about how nature came to be are an important part of religious heritage. Although many of these stories have been written down in modern times, they were originally transmitted orally.

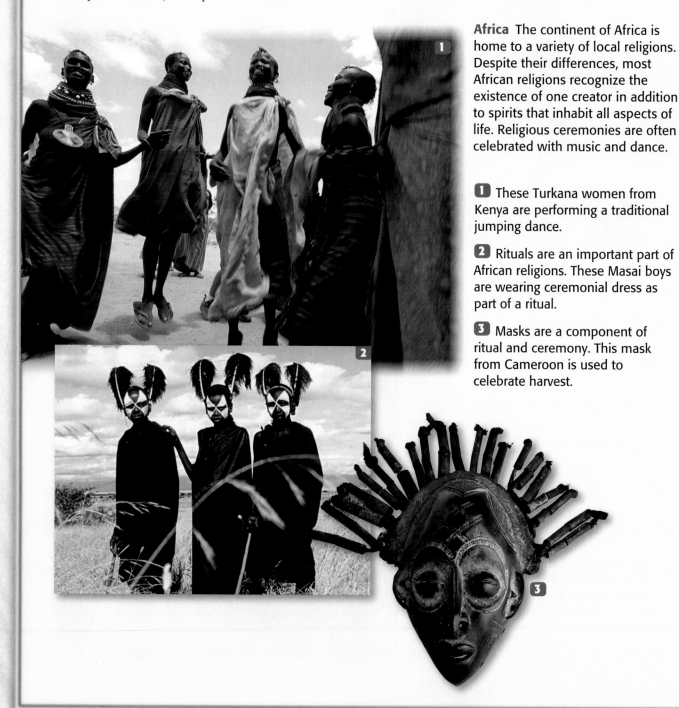

Africa The continent of Africa is home to a variety of local religions. Despite their differences, most African religions recognize the existence of one creator in addition to spirits that inhabit all aspects of life. Religious ceremonies are often celebrated with music and dance.

1 These Turkana women from Kenya are performing a traditional jumping dance.

2 Rituals are an important part of African religions. These Masai boys are wearing ceremonial dress as part of a ritual.

3 Masks are a component of ritual and ceremony. This mask from Cameroon is used to celebrate harvest.

Japan Shinto, founded in Japan, is the largest indigenous religion. It dates back to prehistoric times and has no formal doctrine. The gods are known as kami. Ancestors are also revered and worshiped. Its four million followers often practice Buddhism in addition to practicing Shinto.

4 This Shinto priest is presiding over a ritual at a Japanese temple. These priests often live on shrine grounds.

5 Shinto shrines, like this one, are usually built in places of great natural beauty to emphasize the relationship between people and nature.

Australia The Australian Aboriginal religion has no deities. It is based upon a belief known as the Dreaming, or Dreamtime. Followers believe that ancestors sprang from the Earth and created all people, plant, and animal life. They also believe that these ancestors continue to control the natural world.

6 These Aborigine women are blessing a newborn with smoke during a traditional ritual intended to ensure the child's health and good fortune.

7 Aborigines, like these young girls, often paint their faces with the symbols of their clan or family group.

Indigenous Religions

Native Americans The beliefs of most Native Americans center on the spirit world; however, the rituals and practices of individual groups vary. Most Native Americans believe in a Great Spirit who, along with other spirits, influences all aspects of life. These spirits make their presence known primarily through acts of nature.

The rituals, prayers, and ceremonies of Native Americans are often centered on health and good harvest and hunting. Rituals used to mark the passage through stages of life, including birth, adulthood, and death, are passed down as tribal traditions. Religious ceremonies often focus on important points in the agricultural and hunting seasons. Prayers, which are offered in song and dance, also concentrate on agriculture and hunting themes as well as health and well-being.

1 Rituals are passed down from generation to generation. These Native Americans are performing a ritual dance in Utah.

2 There are many different Native American groups throughout the United States and Canada. This Pawnee is wearing traditional dress during a celebration in Oklahoma.

3 Totem poles, like this one in Alaska, were popular among the Native American peoples of the Northwest Coast. They were often decorated with mythical beings, family crests, or other figures. They were placed outside homes.

Assessment

Reviewing Vocabulary

Match the following terms with their definition.

1. sect
2. monotheism
3. polytheism
4. animism
5. atheism

a. belief that spirits inhabit natural objects and forces of nature
b. belief in one god
c. a subdivision within a religion that has its own distinctive belief and/or practices
d. belief in more than one god
e. disbelief in the existence of any god

Reviewing the Main Ideas

World Religions (pp. 68–69)

6. Which religion has the most followers worldwide? Which has the fewest?

7. Analyzing Visuals Compare the maps at the bottom of pages 68 and 69. Which religions have spread throughout the world? What factors may have contributed to this spread?

8. On a separate sheet of paper, make a table of the major world religions. Use the chart below to get you started.

Name	Founder	Geographic distribution	Sacred sites
Buddhism			
Christianity			
Confucianism			
Hinduism			
Islam			
Judaism			
Sikhism			
Indigenous			

Buddhism (pp. 70–71)

9. According to Buddhism, how can the end of suffering in the world be achieved?

10. What is Nirvana? According to Buddhists, who is most likely to achieve Nirvana and why?

Christianity (pp. 72–73)

11. In what religion was Jesus raised?

12. Why do Christians regard Jesus as their savior?

Confucianism (pp. 74–75)

13. What is Confucianism based on? Why might some not consider it a religion?

14. What does yin-yang symbolize?

Hinduism (pp. 76–77)

15. What type of religion is Hinduism? Where did it develop?

16. Describe reincarnation. What role do Hindus believe karma plays in this process?

Islam (pp. 78–79)

17. What are the two branches of Islam? What is the main difference between the two groups?

18. What role does Makkah play in the Islamic faith?

Judaism (pp. 80–81)

19. What is the Torah?

20. What is the purpose of Yom Kippur?

Sikhism (pp. 82–83)

21. Where do most Sikhs live? Why?

22. What other religions have contributed to the Adi Granth?

Indigenous Religions (pp. 84–85)

23. Many of the sacred stories in local religions explain the creation of people, animals, and plant life. Why would religions feature such stories?

24. Which of the indigenous religions has the largest membership?

Critical Thinking

25. Drawing Conclusions How are major religions similar? How are they different?

26. Analyzing Information How do people's religious beliefs affect what people eat and how they dress?

27. Making Inferences How do religious beliefs influence a society's laws?

Writing About History

28. Expository Writing Select one of the religions profiled and write an essay on how that religion has affected the history of a particular country.

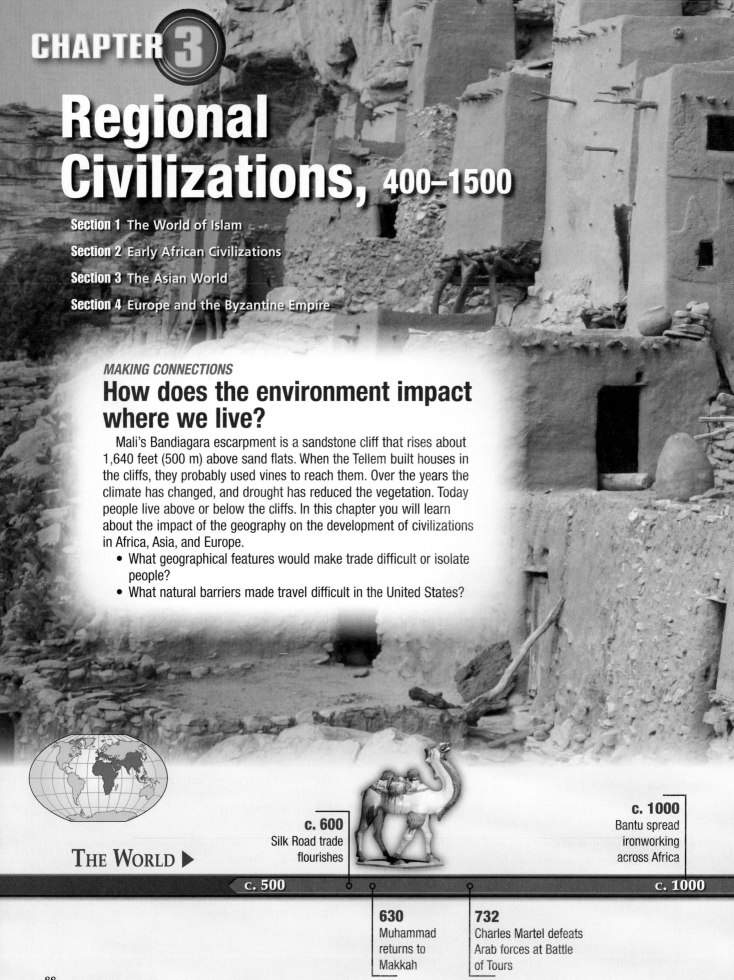

CHAPTER 3

Regional Civilizations, 400–1500

Section 1 The World of Islam

Section 2 Early African Civilizations

Section 3 The Asian World

Section 4 Europe and the Byzantine Empire

MAKING CONNECTIONS

How does the environment impact where we live?

Mali's Bandiagara escarpment is a sandstone cliff that rises about 1,640 feet (500 m) above sand flats. When the Tellem built houses in the cliffs, they probably used vines to reach them. Over the years the climate has changed, and drought has reduced the vegetation. Today people live above or below the cliffs. In this chapter you will learn about the impact of the geography on the development of civilizations in Africa, Asia, and Europe.

- What geographical features would make trade difficult or isolate people?
- What natural barriers made travel difficult in the United States?

THE WORLD ▶

c. 600
Silk Road trade
flourishes

c. 1000
Bantu spread
ironworking
across Africa

c. 500   c. 1000

630
Muhammad
returns to
Makkah

732
Charles Martel defeats
Arab forces at Battle
of Tours

1192
Minamoto
Yoritomo
establishes
Kamakura
shogunate

c. 1300
Yorubas produce
metal and
terra-cotta
sculptures

1215
King John
signs Magna Carta

c. 1300

c. 1500

FOLDABLES™
Study Organizer

Identifying Create a
Four-Tab Book to record
Who, What, When, and
Where facts while you
read about Kublai Khan
or Genghis Khan.

Who | What
When | Where

History ONLINE
Chapter Overview—Visit glencoe.com to preview Chapter 3.

The World of Islam

GUIDE TO READING

The BIG Idea
Ideas, Beliefs, and Values In the 600s, the Arabian prophet Muhammad created the religion of Islam, which led to great changes in the social and political systems of Southwest Asia.

Content Vocabulary
• Islam (p. 91)
• caliph (p. 92)
• sultan (p. 94)

Academic Vocabulary
• revelation (p. 90)
• submission (p. 91)

People and Places
• Arabian Peninsula (p. 90)
• Makkah (p. 90)
• Muhammad (p. 90)
• Madinah (p. 91)
• Abū Bakr (p. 92)
• Damascus (p. 93)
• Baghdad (p. 93)
• Ibn Sīnā (p. 97)

Reading Strategy
Summarizing Information Use a chart like the one below to identify the achievements of Islamic civilization.

Achievements of Islam

Early Arabs were nomads who believed in many gods. In the seventh century, the Arabian prophet Muhammad founded the Islamic religion. Today, more than one billion people around the world are Muslims. Islamic cultural, artistic, and scientific contributions and achievements continue to enrich our lives.

The Rise of Islam

MAIN IDEA The Arabian Peninsula was the birthplace of Muhammad and Islam.

HISTORY & YOU How does a leader's life reflect his or her birthplace? Read about Muhammad's life and teachings.

Like the Israelites and the Assyrians, the Arabs were a Semitic-speaking people who lived in the **Arabian Peninsula,** a desert land sorely lacking in rivers and lakes. The Arabs were nomads who, because of their hostile surroundings, moved constantly to find water and food for their animals. Survival in such a harsh environment was not easy, and the Arabs organized into tribes to help one another.

The Arabs lived on the oases and rain-fed areas of the Arabian Peninsula. After the camel was domesticated in the first millennium B.C., the Arabs populated more of the desert and expanded the caravan trade. Towns developed along the routes as the Arabs became major carriers of goods between the Indian Ocean and the Mediterranean, where the Silk Road ended.

Arabs trace their ancestors to Abraham and his son Ishmael, who were believed to have built a house of worship called the Kaaba (KAH•buh) at **Makkah** (Mecca). A sacred stone, called the Black Stone, is the cornerstone of the Kaaba. The Arabs recognized a supreme god named Allah (*Allah* is Arabic for "God"), but they also believed in other tribal gods.

The Life of Muhammad

Born in Makkah to a merchant family, **Muhammad** grew up to become a caravan manager and married a rich widow named Khadījah. Troubled by the growing gap between the generosity of most Makkans and the greediness of the wealthy elite, he visited the nearby hills to meditate. During one of these visits, Muslims believe, Muhammad received **revelations** from God. According to Islamic teachings, the messages were given by the angel Gabriel. Muhammad came to believe that Allah had already revealed himself in part through Moses and Jesus—and thus through the Hebrew and Christian traditions.

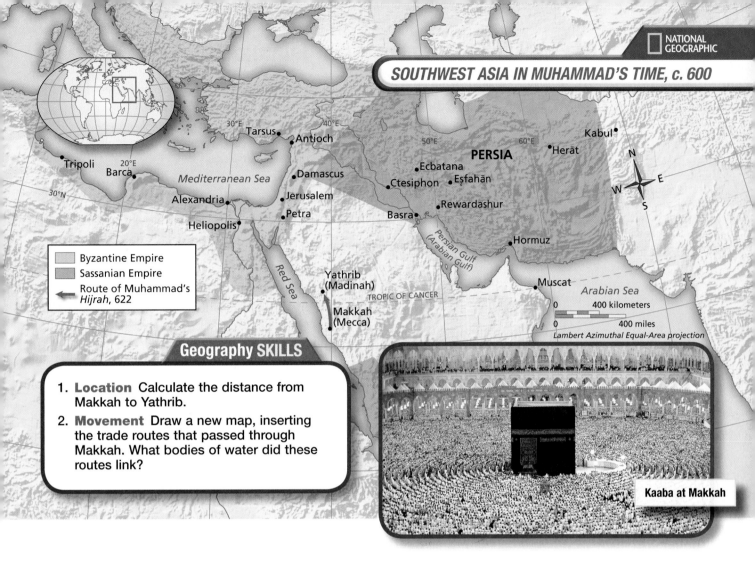

SOUTHWEST ASIA IN MUHAMMAD'S TIME, c. 600

NATIONAL GEOGRAPHIC

Tripoli · Barca · Tarsus · Antioch · Damascus · Jerusalem · Petra · Alexandria · Heliopolis

Mediterranean Sea · Red Sea

PERSIA · Kabul · Herāt · Ecbatana · Ctesiphon · Eşfahān · Rewardashur · Basra · Hormuz

Persian Gulf (Arabian Gulf)

Muscat · Arabian Sea

Yathrib (Madinah) · Makkah (Mecca) · TROPIC OF CANCER

Byzantine Empire
Sassanian Empire
Route of Muhammad's *Hijrah*, 622

0   400 kilometers
0   400 miles
Lambert Azimuthal Equal-Area projection

Geography SKILLS

1. **Location** Calculate the distance from Makkah to Yathrib.
2. **Movement** Draw a new map, inserting the trade routes that passed through Makkah. What bodies of water did these routes link?

Kaaba at Makkah

He believed, however, that the final revelations of Allah were now being given to him. Out of these revelations, which were eventually written down, came the Quran, the holy book of the religion of **Islam**. The word *Islam* means "peace through **submission** to the will of Allah." The Quran contains the ethical guidelines and laws by which the followers of Allah are to live. Those who practice Islam are called Muslims. Islam has only one God, Allah, and Muhammad is God's prophet.

After receiving the revelations, Muhammad set out to convince the people of Makkah of the truth of his revelations. After three years of preaching, he had only 30 followers. Muhammad became discouraged by persecution of his followers, as well as by the failure of the Makkans to accept his message.

In 622, the year 1 of the Islamic calendar, he and some of his closest supporters left Makkah and moved north to Yathrib, later renamed **Madinah** (Medina; "city of the prophet"). The journey of Muhammad and his followers to Madinah is known as the Hijrah (HIH•jruh).

Muhammad soon began to win support from people in Madinah, as well as from Arabs in the desert, known as bedouin. From these groups, he formed the first community of practicing Muslims.

Muhammad soon became both a religious and a political leader. His political and military skills enabled him to put together a reliable military force to defend himself and his followers.

In 630, Muhammad returned to Makkah with a force of 10,000 men. After the city surrendered and most of the people converted to Islam, Muhammad declared the Kaaba a sacred shrine of Islam. Two years after his triumphal return to Makkah, just as Islam was beginning to spread throughout the Arabian Peninsula, Muhammad died.

The Teachings of Muhammad

Like Judaism and Christianity, Islam is a monotheistic religion. Allah is the all-powerful being who created the universe and everything in it. Islam emphasizes salvation and offers the hope of an afterlife.

See page R38 to read *Muhammad's Wife Remembers the Prophet* in the **Primary Sources and Literature Library.**

Unlike Christianity, Islam does not believe that its first preacher was divine. Muhammad is considered a prophet, similar to Moses, but he was also a man like other men. Muslims believe that because human beings rejected Allah's earlier messengers, Allah sent his final revelation through Muhammad.

Islam is a direct and simple faith, stressing the need to obey the will of Allah. This means practicing the Five Pillars of Islam: belief, prayer, charity, fasting, and pilgrimage. Muslims believe there is but One God, and Muhammad is his messenger (belief). They pray five times a day (prayer) and give to the poor (charity). During Ramadan, Muslims do not eat or drink from dawn to sunset (fasting). Finally, believers are expected to make a pilgrimage to Makkah, known as the hajj (HAJ), at least once in their lifetime (pilgrimage). The faithful who follow the law go to an eternal paradise.

✓ **Reading Check** **Comparing** How is Islam similar to Judaism and Christianity?

Islamic Empires

MAIN IDEA As the Arab Empire expanded, the influence of Islam grew and trade flourished.

HISTORY & YOU What cultural and economic influences affect your community? Learn about the impact of Islamic expansion.

Muhammad had been accepted as both the political and religious leader of the Islamic community. The death of Muhammad left his followers with a problem: Muhammad had never named a successor. Shortly after Muhammad's death, some of his closest followers chose **Abū Bakr** (uh•BOO BA•kuhr), a wealthy merchant and Muhammad's father-in-law, to be their leader. He was named **caliph** (KAY•luhf)—successor to Muhammad.

The Arab Empire

Under Abū Bakr's leadership, the Islamic movement began to grow. As the Romans had slowly conquered Italy, so also the Muslims expanded over Arabia, and beyond.

At Yarmūk in 636, the Arabs, unified under Abū Bakr, defeated the Byzantine army in the midst of a dust storm that enabled the Arabs to take their enemy by surprise. Later, they took control of the

The Five Pillars of Islam

Belief (Shahaadatayn)
Believing there is no deity but the One God, and Muhammad is his messenger

Prayer (Salaah)
Performing the prescribed prayers five times a day

Charity (Zakaah)
Giving part of one's wealth to the poor ("giving alms")

Fasting (Siyamm)
Refraining from food and drink from dawn to sunset through the month of Ramadan

Pilgrimage (Hajj)
Making a pilgrimage to Makkah once in a lifetime

Quran

Chart SKILLS

Muslims practice acts of worship called the Five Pillars of Islam.

1. **Describing** What behaviors are encouraged by the Five Pillars of Islam?

Byzantine province of Syria. By 642, Egypt and other areas of northern Africa had been added to the new Arab Empire. To the east, the Arabs had conquered the entire Persian Empire by 650.

The Arabs, led by a series of brilliant generals, created a large, dedicated army. The courage of the Arab soldiers was enhanced by the belief that Muslim warriors were assured a place in Paradise if they died in battle. After Abū Bakr died, problems arose over who should become the next caliph. There were no clear successors to Abū Bakr.

Overall, the period of the Arab Empire was prosperous. The Arabs carried on extensive trade, not only within the Islamic world, but also with China, the Byzantine Empire, India, and Southeast Asia. Trade was carried by ship and by camel caravans, which traveled from Morocco in the west to the countries beyond the Caspian Sea.

The Umayyads

In 661, Mu'āwiyah (mu•AH•wee•ya), the governor of Syria, became caliph. Mu'āwiyah made the office of caliph, called the caliphate, hereditary in his own family. In doing this, he established the Umayyad (um•Y•yuhd) dynasty. He then moved the capital of the Arab Empire from Madinah to **Damascus,** in Syria.

At the beginning of the 700s, Arab armies conquered and converted the Berbers, a pastoral people living along the Mediterranean coast of North Africa. Around 710, combined Berber and Arab forces crossed the Strait of Gibraltar and occupied southern Spain. By 725, most of Spain had become a Muslim state with its center at Córdoba. In 732, Arab forces were defeated at the Battle of Tours in Gaul (now France). Arab expansion in Europe came to a halt.

In 717, another Muslim force had launched an attack on Constantinople with the hope of defeating the Byzantine Empire. The Byzantines survived, however, by destroying the Muslim fleet. By 750, the Arab advance ended, but not before the southern and eastern Mediterranean parts of the old Roman Empire had been conquered. Arab power also extended to the east in Mesopotamia and Persia and northward into central Asia.

The Abbasid Dynasty

Abū al-'Abbās, a descendant of Muhammad's uncle, overthrew the Umayyad dynasty in 750 and set up the Abbasid (uh•BA•suhd) dynasty, which lasted until 1258.

In 762, the Abbasids built a new capital city at **Baghdad,** on the Tigris River, far to the east of the Umayyad capital at Damascus. Baghdad's location took advantage of river traffic in the Persian Gulf and the caravan route from the Mediterranean to central Asia.

Best known of the caliphs of the time was Hārūn ar-Rashīd (huh•ROON ahr•ruh• SHEED), whose reign is often described as the golden age of the Abbasid caliphate. Hārūn ar-Rashīd was known for his charity, and he lavished support on artists and writers.

This was also a period of growing prosperity. The Arabs had conquered many of the richest provinces of the Roman Empire, and they now controlled the trade routes to the East. Baghdad became the center of an enormous trade empire that extended into Asia, Africa, and Europe, adding to the riches of the Islamic world.

Starting around 750, trade flourished under the Abbasid dynasty. From south of the Sahara came gold and salt; from China, silk and porcelain; from eastern Africa, gold and ivory; and from the lands of Southeast Asia and India, sandalwood and spices. Within the empire, Egypt contributed grain; Iraq provided linens, dates, and precious stones; and western India supplied textiles.

Eventually, rulers of the provinces of the Abbasid Empire began to break away from the central authority and establish independent dynasties. A new dynasty under the Fatimids was established in Egypt, with its capital at Cairo, in 973.

The Seljuk Turks

The Fatimid dynasty soon became the dynamic center of Islamic civilization. The Fatimids played a major role in the trade from the Mediterranean to the Red Sea. They created a strong army by hiring nonnative soldiers. One such group was the Seljuk (SEHL•JOOK) Turks.

The Seljuk Turks were a nomadic people from central Asia. They had converted to Islam and prospered as soldiers for the Abbasid caliphate. As the Abbasids grew weaker, the Seljuk Turks grew stronger, moving gradually into Iran and Armenia. By the eleventh century, they had taken over the eastern provinces of the Abbasid Empire.

In 1055, a Turkish leader captured Baghdad and took command of the empire. His title was **sultan**—or "holder of power." The Abbasid caliph was still the chief religious authority, but, after they captured Baghdad, the Seljuk Turks held the real military and political power of the state.

The Mongols

The Mongols were a pastoral, horse-riding people who swept out of the Gobi in the early thirteenth century to seize control over much of the known world (see Chapter 3, Section 3).

Beginning with the advances led by Genghis Khan in North China, Mongol armies spread across central Asia. In 1258, under the leadership of Hülegü (hoo•LAY•GOO), brother of the more famous Kublai (KOO•BLUH) Khan, the Mongols seized Persia and Mesopotamia. The Abbasid caliphate at Baghdad ended. Hülegü had a strong hatred of Islam. After his forces captured Baghdad in 1258, he decided to destroy the city.

Over time, the Mongol rulers converted to Islam, intermarried with local peoples, and rebuilt the cities. By the 1300s, the Mongol Empire had begun to split into separate kingdoms. The old Islamic Empire established by the Arabs had come to an end. The new center of Islamic civilization now became Cairo, Egypt.

✓ **Reading Check** **Describing** How did the Mongols bring about the end of the old Islamic Empire?

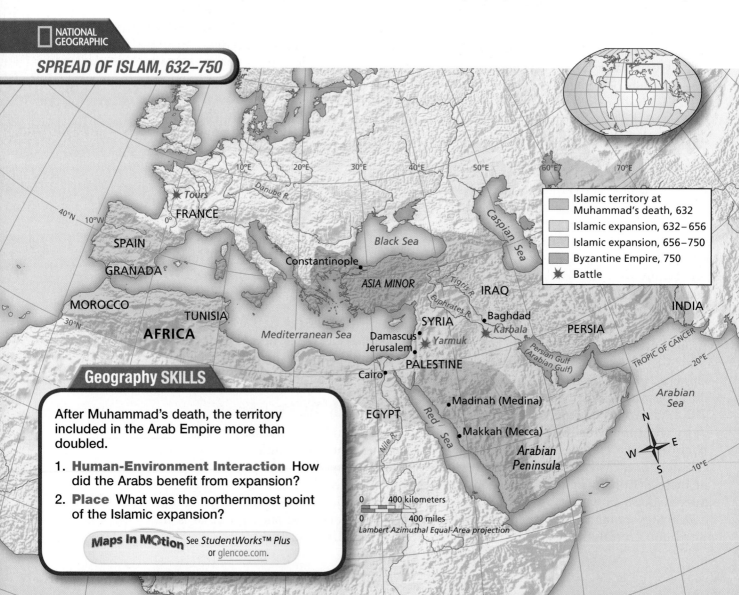

NATIONAL GEOGRAPHIC

SPREAD OF ISLAM, 632–750

Islamic territory at Muhammad's death, 632
Islamic expansion, 632–656
Islamic expansion, 656–750
Byzantine Empire, 750
Battle

Geography SKILLS

After Muhammad's death, the territory included in the Arab Empire more than doubled.

1. **Human-Environment Interaction** How did the Arabs benefit from expansion?

2. **Place** What was the northernmost point of the Islamic expansion?

Maps In Motion See StudentWorks™ Plus or glencoe.com.

0   400 kilometers
0   400 miles
Lambert Azimuthal Equal-Area projection

THE BATTLE OF TOURS

Encouraged by their success in Spain, Arab armies crossed the Pyrenees and marched northward into southern France. The forces led by 'Abd a-Raḥmān easily captured Bordeaux in Aquitania, and then continued north toward Poitiers and Tours.

The defeated Duke of Aquitaine called on Charles Martel, the Frankish mayor of Austrasia, to help stop the Arab advance. In October 732, Charles's army met 'Abd a-Raḥmān's forces on the road between Poitiers and Tours. The Franks killed 'Abd a-Raḥmān and routed the Arabs, who fled south. The Franks' defeat of Arab forces at the Battle of Tours ended Arab expansion in Europe.

'Abd a-Raḥmān is shown using an Arab scimitar, or long sword with a curved blade.

Charles Martel (mounted), also called "Charles the Hammer" for the hammer-like shape of his weapon and his victory at Tours.

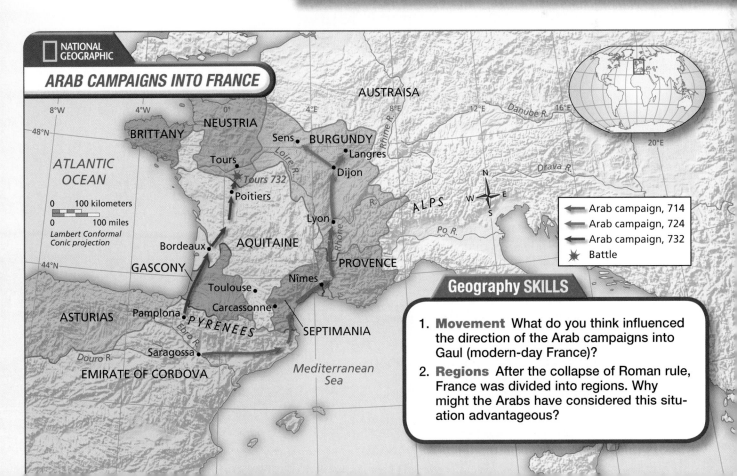

NATIONAL GEOGRAPHIC

ARAB CAMPAIGNS INTO FRANCE

ATLANTIC OCEAN

0   100 kilometers
0   100 miles
Lambert Conformal Conic projection

BRITTANY
NEUSTRIA
Sens
BURGUNDY
AUSTRAISA
Langres
Tours
Tours 732
Dijon
Poitiers
Loire R.
Rhine R.
Danube R.
Drava R.
ALPS
Lyon
Rhône
Po R.
Bordeaux
AQUITAINE
PROVENCE
GASCONY
Nîmes
Toulouse
Carcassonne
Pamplona
PYRENEES
SEPTIMANIA
ASTURIAS
Ebro R.
Saragossa
Douro R.
EMIRATE OF CORDOVA
Mediterranean Sea

Arab campaign, 714
Arab campaign, 724
Arab campaign, 732
★ Battle

Geography SKILLS

1. **Movement** What do you think influenced the direction of the Arab campaigns into Gaul (modern-day France)?

2. **Regions** After the collapse of Roman rule, France was divided into regions. Why might the Arabs have considered this situation advantageous?

Islamic Culture

MAIN IDEA Islamic culture made advancements in philosophy, science, and history.

HISTORY & YOU How have the achievements of others helped you learn new things? Learn how Islamic achievements contributed to civilization.

To be a Muslim is not simply to worship Allah but also to live one's life according to Allah's teachings as revealed in the Quran. Questions concerning politics, economics, and social life are answered by following Islamic teachings.

Islamic Society

According to Islam, all people are equal in the eyes of Allah. In reality, however, this was not strictly the case in the Arab Empire. There was a fairly well-defined upper class that consisted of ruling families, senior officials, nomadic elites, and the wealthiest merchants. Even ordinary merchants, however, enjoyed a degree of respect that merchants did not receive in Europe, China, or India.

The Quran granted women spiritual and social equality with men. Women had the right to the fruits of their work and to own and inherit property. Islamic teachings did account for differences between men and women in the family and social order. Both had duties and responsibilities. As in most societies of the time, however, men were dominant in Muslim society.

Philosophy and Science

During the first few centuries of the Arab Empire, the ancient Greek philosophers were largely unknown in Europe. The Arabs, however, were not only aware of Greek philosophy, they were translating works by Plato and Aristotle into Arabic.

The process of translating works and making them available to scholars was aided by the making of paper, which was introduced from China in the eighth century. It was through the Muslim world that Europeans recovered the works of Aristotle and other Greek philosophers.

In the twelfth century, the Arabic translations were in turn translated into Latin, making them available to the West. The

HISTORY & ARTS   PRIMARY SOURCE

The Great Mosque of Sāmarrā'

The Great Mosque of Sāmarrā' was built by Caliph al-Mutawakkil of the Abbasid dynasty. Constructed of baked brick, it was the largest mosque of its time. Today the mosque is mostly a ruin. A walled area on three sides provided for additional worshippers at Friday prayers. The entire mosque complex was enclosed by an outer wall.

The muezzin climbed the spiral minaret to call the people to prayer.

DOCUMENT-BASED QUESTIONS

1. **Drawing Conclusions** Why do you think the Abbasid dynasty built this mosque?
2. **Making Inferences** Minarets originally served as watchtowers illuminated by torches. What other feature probably aided with the defense of the mosque and city?

brilliant Islamic civilization contributed more than translations, however. When Aristotle's works arrived in Europe, they were accompanied by commentaries written by Arabic philosophers. One such philosopher was Ibn-Rushd (IH•buhn-RUSHT). He wrote a commentary on virtually all of Aristotle's surviving works.

Islamic scholars also made contributions to mathematics and the natural sciences. The Muslims adopted and passed on the numerical system of India, including the use of the zero. In Europe, it became known as the "Arabic" system. A ninth-century Arab mathematician developed the mathematical discipline of algebra.

In astronomy, Muslims set up an observatory at Baghdad to study the position of the stars. They were aware that Earth was round, and they named many stars. They also perfected an instrument called the astrolabe, used by sailors to determine their location by observing the positions of heavenly bodies. The astrolabe enabled Europeans to sail to the Americas.

Muslim scholars developed medicine as a field of scientific study. Especially well-known was the philosopher and scientist **Ibn Sīnā** (IH•buhn SEE•nah). He wrote a medical encyclopedia that, among other things, stressed the contagious nature of certain diseases. Ibn Sīnā showed how diseases could be spread by contaminated water supplies. After it was translated into Latin, Ibn Sīnā's work became a basic medical textbook for university students in medieval Europe.

Literature, Art, and Architecture

Islam brought major changes to the culture of Southwest Asia, including its literature. One of the most familiar works of Middle Eastern literature is the *Rubaiyat* (ROO•bee•AHT) of Omar Khayyám. Another is *The 1001 Nights* (also called *The Arabian Nights*).

Islamic art is a blend of Arab, Turkish, and Persian traditions. The best expression of Islamic art is found in the way magnificent Muslim mosques (houses of worship) represent the spirit of Islam. The Great Mosque of Sāmarrā' in present-day Iraq was the world's largest mosque at the time it was built (848 to 852), covering 10 acres (more than 40,000 square m). The most famous section of the Sāmarrā' mosque, its minaret, is nearly 90 feet (27 m) tall and has an unusual outside spiral staircase. The muezzin (moo•EH•zuhn), or crier, calls the faithful to prayer five times a day from the minaret. The famous ninth-century mosque at Córdoba in southern Spain is still in remarkable condition today. Its hundreds of columns, which support double-horseshoe arches, transform this building into a unique "forest of trees."

✓ **Reading Check** **Identifying** Name two cultural achievements of the Arab Empire after 700.

Vocabulary

1. **Explain** the significance of: Arabian Peninsula, Makkah, Muhammad, revelation, Islam, submission, Madinah, Abū Bakr, caliph, Damascus, Baghdad, sultan, Ibn Sīnā.

Main Ideas

2. **List** the Five Pillars of Islam.

3. **Describe** how the Arabs created a trade empire. Identify the items traded in the empire and where they came from.

4. **Explain** how Muslim contributions to mathematics were spread throughout the world.

Critical Thinking

5. **The Big Idea Explaining** How did Islam affect the social and political systems of Southwest Asia?

6. **Summarizing Information** Create a diagram to list the main characteristics of the Islamic religion. Your diagram can list more characteristics than this example.

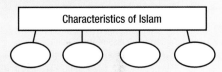

Characteristics of Islam

7. **Analyzing Visuals** Examine the photograph on page 96. What architectural element is characteristic of mosques?

Writing About History

8. **Descriptive Writing** Imagine that you are a young Muslim Arab corresponding with a European friend. In one or two brief paragraphs, describe Islamic accomplishments in philosophy, mathematics, science, medicine, art, and architecture to your friend.

History ONLINE

For help with the concepts in this section of *Glencoe World History— Modern Times*, go to glencoe.com and click Study Central.

Early African Civilizations

GUIDE TO READING

The BIG Idea
Physical Geography The expansion of trade led to migration and the growth of new African kingdoms and societies.

Content Vocabulary
- Bantu (p. 101)
- lineage group (p. 103)

Academic Vocabulary
- culture (p. 99)
- military (p. 101)

People and Places
- Sahara (p. 98)
- King 'Ezānā (p. 99)
- Ghana (p. 100)
- Mali (p. 100)
- Sundiata Keita (p. 100)
- Mansa Mūsā (p. 101)
- Songhai (p. 101)
- Sunni Ali (p. 101)
- Muhammad Ture (p. 101)

Reading Strategy
Locating Using a chart like the one below, list the African kingdoms discussed in this chapter and whether they were in north, south, east, or west Africa.

Kingdom	Location

As African civilizations developed, great trading states arose. Traveling across the desert and over the wide Indian Ocean, traders from these states helped make their people rich and powerful. Trade resulted not only in a transfer of ivory, gold, and other valuable merchandise, but also in a transfer of cultures, spreading religion, languages, and new ideas.

The Emergence of African Civilizations

MAIN IDEA Kush and Axum arose as strong early civilizations. Later, Islam would influence Africa.

HISTORY & YOU How do people in your region benefit from local natural resources? Read how the early Africans used the resources in their environment.

After Asia, Africa is the largest of the continents. It stretches nearly 5,000 miles (around 8,000 km) from the Mediterranean Sea in the north to the Cape of Good Hope in the south and is almost completely surrounded by two oceans and two seas.

Africa includes four distinct climate zones: a mild zone across the northern coast and southern tip; deserts in the north (the **Sahara**) and south (the Kalahari); the rain forest along the equator; and savannas (broad grasslands) that stretch across Africa both north and south of the rain forest. These four climate zones have affected the way the peoples of Africa live.

The mastery of farming, called the Agricultural Revolution, gave rise to the first civilizations in Africa: Egypt (discussed in Chapter 1), Kush, and Axum. Much later, Islam became an important factor in the development of African empires.

Kush

By 2000 B.C., a busy trade had arisen between Egypt and the area to the south known as Nubia. Although Nubia was subject to Egyptian control for many centuries, it freed itself around 1000 B.C. and became the independent state of Kush.

The economy of Kush was at first based on farming, but soon emerged as one of the major trading states in the region. Kush provided iron products, ivory, gold, ebony, and slaves from central and eastern Africa to the Roman Empire, the Arabian Peninsula, and India. In return, the Kushites received luxury goods from India and the Arabian Peninsula. Kush flourished from about 250 B.C. to about A.D. 150 but declined because of the rise of a new power in the region known as Axum.

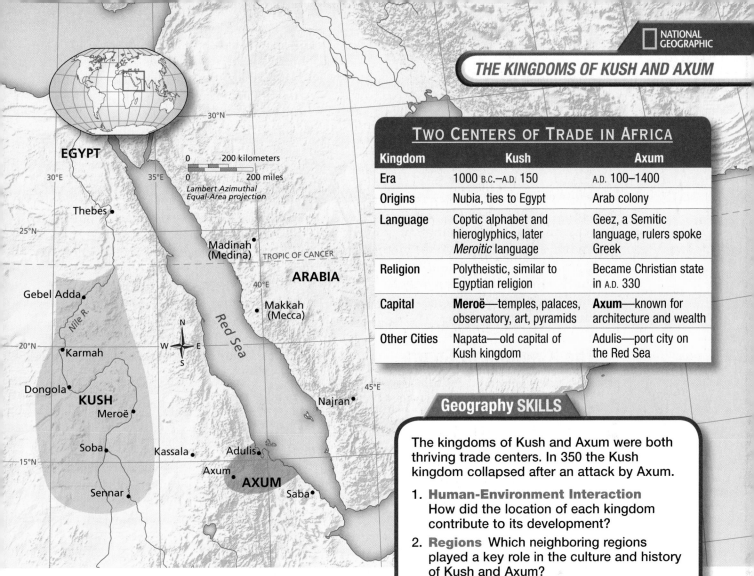

TWO CENTERS OF TRADE IN AFRICA

Kingdom	Kush	Axum
Era	1000 B.C.–A.D. 150	A.D. 100–1400
Origins	Nubia, ties to Egypt	Arab colony
Language	Coptic alphabet and hieroglyphics, later *Meroitic* language	Geez, a Semitic language, rulers spoke Greek
Religion	Polytheistic, similar to Egyptian religion	Became Christian state in A.D. 330
Capital	**Meroë**—temples, palaces, observatory, art, pyramids	**Axum**—known for architecture and wealth
Other Cities	Napata—old capital of Kush kingdom	Adulis—port city on the Red Sea

Geography SKILLS

The kingdoms of Kush and Axum were both thriving trade centers. In 350 the Kush kingdom collapsed after an attack by Axum.

1. **Human-Environment Interaction** How did the location of each kingdom contribute to its development?

2. **Regions** Which neighboring regions played a key role in the culture and history of Kush and Axum?

Axum

Axum was located in what is now Ethiopia. It was founded by Arabs and combined Arab and African **cultures.**

Axum owed much of its prosperity to its location along the Red Sea, on a trade route between India and the Mediterranean. Axum exported ivory, frankincense, myrrh, and slaves. It imported textiles, metal goods, wine, and olive oil. For a time, Axum competed with the neighboring state of Kush for control of the ivory trade. Probably as a result of this competition for ivory, in the fourth century A.D., **King 'Ezānā,** the Axumite ruler, invaded and conquered Kush. Perhaps the most distinctive feature of Axumite civilization was its religion.

About A.D. 330, King 'Ezānā converted to Christianity and made it the official religion of Axum. Within a few centuries, a new religion—Islam—brought profound challenges to the kingdom. Islam rose from the Arabian Peninsula and then spread across the region. In 641, Arab forces took control of Egypt. By the early 700s, Arabs ruled North Africa's coast west to the Strait of Gibraltar. Several Muslim states also occupied lands along the Red Sea. The relationship between the Muslims and Christian Axum was relatively peaceful. Beginning in the 1100s, Muslim states moved inland to gain control over the trade in slaves and ivory. Axum fought back.

✓**Reading Check** **Identifying** What were the first three civilizations in Africa?

Kingdoms in West Africa

MAIN IDEA The expansion of trade enabled the kingdoms and states of Africa to protect their people and to prosper.

HISTORY & YOU Why do some empires and countries expand more easily than others? Read how West African rulers were able to expand their empires.

During the eighth century, a number of trading states emerged in the area south of the Sahara in West Africa. Eventually, these states—Ghana, Mali, and Songhai—made the Sahara into a leading avenue of world trade.

The Kingdom of Ghana

Ghana, the first great trading state in West Africa, emerged as early as A.D. 500 in the upper Niger River valley. (The modern state of Ghana takes its name from this early state but is located in the forest region to the south.)

The kings of Ghana were strong rulers who governed without any laws. Their wealth was vast. To protect their kingdom and enforce their wishes, Ghanaian kings relied on a well-trained regular army of thousands of men.

Ghana had an abundance of gold. The heartland of the state was located near one of the richest gold-producing areas in all of Africa. Ghana's gold made it the center of an enormous trade empire.

Ghanaians traded their abundant gold for products brought from North Africa. Muslim merchants from North Africa exchanged metal goods, textiles, horses, and salt with the Ghanaians. Salt, a highly desired item, was used to preserve food. It was also important because people needed extra salt to replace what their bodies lost in the hot climate.

Much of the trade across the desert was carried by the Berbers, nomadic peoples whose camel caravans became known as the "fleets of the desert." Camels became a crucial factor in trade across the Sahara, since they were well adapted to desert conditions.

The Kingdom of Mali

The state of Ghana flourished for several hundred years. Eventually weakened by wars, it collapsed around 1200. In its place rose new trading states in West Africa. The greatest of these states was **Mali**, established in the mid-thirteenth century by **Sundiata Keita.** He is considered the founder of his nation. In 1240, he defeated

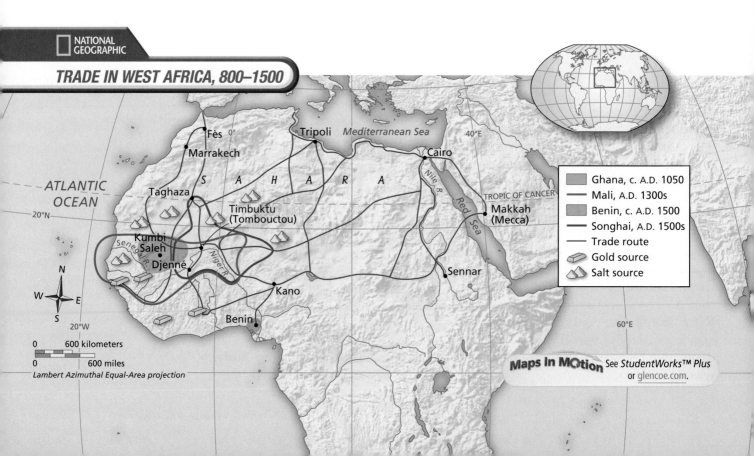

NATIONAL GEOGRAPHIC

TRADE IN WEST AFRICA, 800–1500

Legend:
- Ghana, c. A.D. 1050
- Mali, A.D. 1300s
- Benin, c. A.D. 1500
- Songhai, A.D. 1500s
- Trade route
- Gold source
- Salt source

Lambert Azimuthal Equal-Area projection

Maps In MOtion See StudentWorks™ Plus or glencoe.com.

the Ghanaians and captured their capital. He united the people of Mali and created a strong government. Mali built its wealth and power on the gold and salt trade. Most of its people, however, were farmers who grew sorghum, millet, and rice.

One of the richest and most powerful kings was **Mansa Mūsā,** who ruled from 1312 to 1337 (mansa means "king"). Mansa Mūsā doubled the size of the kingdom of Mali. He created a strong central government and divided the kingdom into provinces. Once he felt secure, Mansa Mūsā decided—as a devout Muslim—to make a pilgrimage to Makkah.

A king, of course, was no ordinary pilgrim. He was joined on his journey by thousands of servants and soldiers and hundreds of camels carrying gold, as well as food, clothing, and other supplies. Mansa Mūsā's pilgrimage demonstrated his wealth and power. His journey had another legacy. It inspired him to make Timbuktu a center of Islamic leaning and culture. In Timbuktu, he built mosques and libraries. He brought scholars to the city to study the Quran.

The Kingdom of Songhai

By the fifteenth century, a new kingdom—**Songhai**—was beginning to surpass Mali. Under the leadership of **Sunni Ali,** who created the Sunni dynasty in 1464, Songhai began to expand. Sunni Ali spent much of his reign on horseback and on the march as he led his army in one **military** campaign after another. His conquests gave Songhai control of the trading empire—especially trade in salt and gold—that had made Ghana and Mali so prosperous.

The Songhai Empire reached the height of its power during the reign of **Muhammad Ture.** He continued Sunni Ali's policy of expansion, creating an empire that stretched a thousand miles along the Niger River. The chief cities of the empire prospered as never before from the salt and gold trade until the end of the sixteenth century.

✔**Reading Check** Summarizing What were Mansa Mūsā's accomplishments?

Societies in East and South Africa

MAIN IDEA Migration and trade influenced the societies of East and South Africa.

HISTORY & YOU Why do people migrate to new regions? Read how the Bantus spread their culture.

In eastern Africa, a variety of states and small societies took root. Islam strongly influenced many of them. Some became extremely wealthy as a result of trade.

Beginning in the first millennium B.C., farming peoples who spoke dialects of the **Bantu** (BAN•TOO) family of languages began to move from the region of the Niger River into East Africa and the Congo River basin. They moved slowly, not as invading hordes but as small communities. The Bantus spread iron-smelting techniques and high-yield crop farming across Africa.

On the eastern fringe of the continent, the Bantu-speaking peoples gradually began to take part in the regional trade that moved by sea up and down the East African coast. Beginning in the eighth century, Muslims from the Arabian Peninsula and the Persian Gulf began to settle at ports along the coast. The result was a string of trading ports that included Mogadishu (MAH•guh•DIH•shoo), Mombasa, and Kilwa in the south.

In the southern half of the African continent, states formed more slowly than in the north. From about 1300 to about 1450, Zimbabwe (zihm•BAH•bwee) was the wealthiest and most powerful state in the region. It prospered from the gold trade with the trading communities on the eastern coast of the continent. The ruins of Zimbabwe's capital, known as Great Zimbabwe, illustrate the kingdom's power and influence. The town sits on a hill overlooking the Zambezi River and is surrounded by stone walls. The local people stacked granite blocks together without mortar to build the massive walls. Up to 10,000 people would have been able to live in the area enclosed by the walls.

✔**Reading Check** Evaluating What do the walled enclosures tell us about Great Zimbabwe?

THE BANTUS SPREAD —
—— IRONWORKING

Through migration, the Bantus spread ironworking through eastern and southern Africa. Early uses for iron likely included small personal items like razors, needles, and knives. Advances in iron smelting eventually led to the development of agricultural implements such as axes and hoes. Africans replaced their stone and wooden tools with these more effective, iron versions that aided in agricultural advances and the rise of village life. Ironworking was the key component in the rise of many African kingdoms.

Bantu migration → **Transfer of ironworking technology** → **Development of better tools** → **Growth of agriculture** → **Growth of villages**

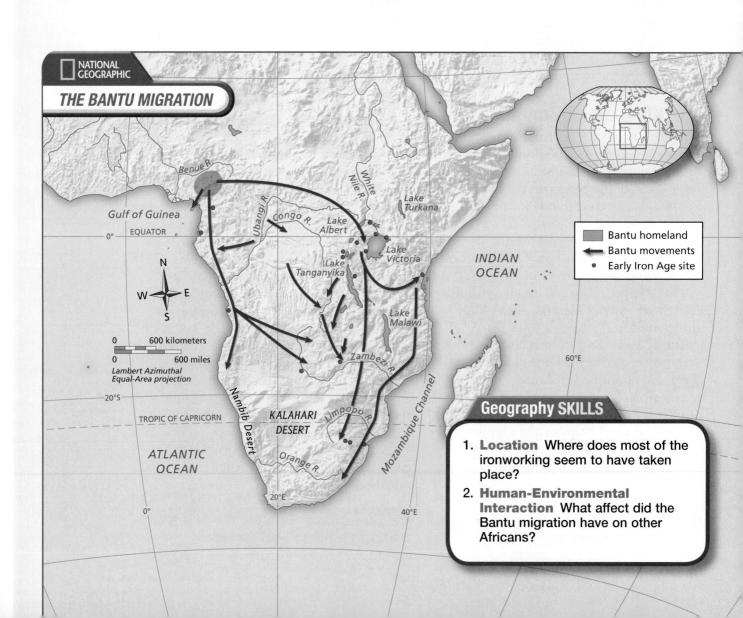

NATIONAL GEOGRAPHIC

THE BANTU MIGRATION

Legend:
- Bantu homeland
- ← Bantu movements
- • Early Iron Age site

0 600 kilometers
0 600 miles
Lambert Azimuthal Equal-Area projection

Geography SKILLS

1. **Location** Where does most of the ironworking seem to have taken place?

2. **Human-Environmental Interaction** What affect did the Bantu migration have on other Africans?

African Society and Culture

MAIN IDEA African society was strongly influenced by values and customs, such as the importance of the family and common ancestors.

HISTORY & YOU What role do family and ancestors play in your community? Read about the role they played in African society.

The relationship between king and subjects was often less rigid in African society than in other civilizations. Frequently, the ruler would allow people to voice their complaints to him. Still, the king was held in a position high above all others.

Few Africans, of course, ever met with their kings. Most people lived in small villages. Their sense of identity was determined by their membership in an extended family and a lineage group.

At the basic level was the extended family, made up of parents, children, grandparents, and other family dependents. **Lineage groups,** which were communities of extended family units, were the basis of African society. All members of a lineage group could claim to be descended from a real or legendary common ancestor. A lineage group provided support for all its members, and members were expected to care for one another.

Early African religious beliefs varied from place to place. Most African societies shared some common religious ideas. These ideas included belief in various gods, the power of diviners (people who believe they can foretell events), and the importance of ancestors. Ritual ceremonies were dedicated to ancestors because the ancestors were believed to be closer to the gods. They had the power to influence the lives of their descendants.

In early Africa, as in much of the rest of the world at the time, the arts—whether painting, literature, or music—were a means of serving religion. A work of art was meant to express religious conviction. The earliest forms in Africa were rock paintings.

Wood-carvers throughout Africa made remarkable masks and statues. The carvings often represented gods, spirits, or ancestral figures and were believed to embody the spiritual powers of the subjects.

In the thirteenth and fourteenth centuries, metalworkers at Ife (EE•feh), in what is now southern Nigeria, produced handsome bronze and iron statues. The Ife sculptures may have influenced artists in Benin in West Africa, who produced equally impressive works in bronze during the same period. The Benin sculptures include bronze heads, many of kings, and figures of various types of animals.

✓ Reading Check **Summarizing** Describe the role of lineage groups on African society.

SECTION 2 REVIEW

Vocabulary
1. **Explain** the significance of: Sahara, culture, King ´Ezānā, Ghana, Mali, Sundiata Keita, Mansa Mūsā, Songhai, Sunni Ali, military, Muhammad Ture, Bantu, lineage group.

Main Ideas
2. **Describe** the most distinctive feature of Axumite civilization. How did this affect Axum's relations with its neighbors?

3. **List** the trading commodities that made the African kingdoms wealthy. How were camels a crucial factor in African trade?

4. **Describe** what motivated the people of Africa to trade.

5. **Explain** the importance of honoring ancestors in traditional African religious practices.

Critical Thinking
6. **The Big Idea** **Making Connections** How did trade help facilitate the spread of Islam across Africa?

7. **Sequencing Information** Using a diagram like the one below, put the royal kingdoms of West Africa in chronological order (include dates) along the top row of boxes. In the second row, add details about the accomplishments of each kingdom.

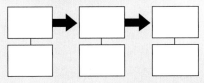

8. **Analyzing Visuals** Examine the map on page 100. Which kingdoms had gold mines?

Writing About History
9. **Expository Writing** Music, dance, and storytelling do not leave a physical record in the same way as buildings or roads. Describe the significance of the performing arts in African society.

History ONLINE

For help with the concepts in this section of *Glencoe World History— Modern Times*, go to glencoe.com and click Study Central.

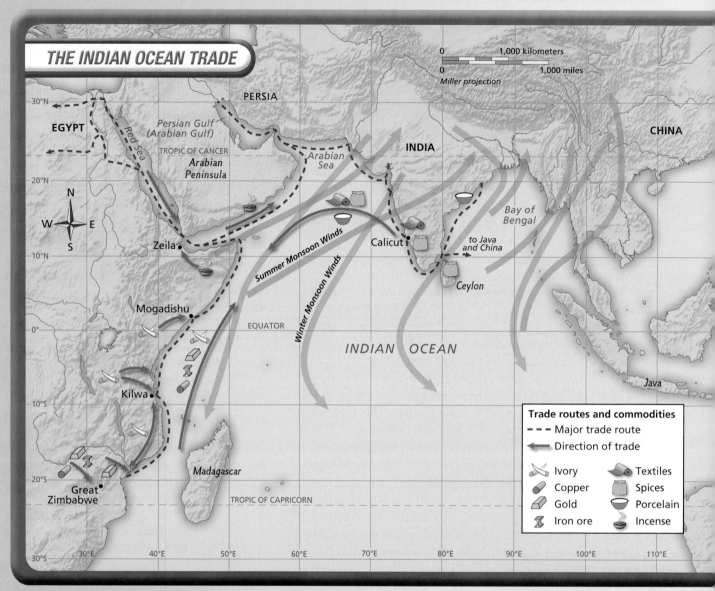

THE INDIAN OCEAN TRADE

0   1,000 kilometers
0   1,000 miles
Miller projection

PERSIA

EGYPT

30°N

Red Sea

Persian Gulf
(Arabian Gulf)

TROPIC OF CANCER

Arabian
Peninsula

Arabian
Sea

INDIA

CHINA

20°N

N
W   E
S

Zeila

10°N

Summer Monsoon Winds

Calicut

Bay of
Bengal

to Java
and China

Winter Monsoon Winds

Ceylon

Mogadishu

0°
EQUATOR

INDIAN   OCEAN

Kilwa

10°S

Java

Madagascar

Great
Zimbabwe

20°S

TROPIC OF CAPRICORN

Trade routes and commodities

- - - Major trade route
←   Direction of trade

Ivory   Textiles
Copper   Spices
Gold   Porcelain
Iron ore   Incense

30°S   30°E   40°E   50°E   60°E   70°E   80°E   90°E   100°E   110°E

◄ The Great Mosque of
Kilwa, built of coral
limestone from the
Indian Ocean, dates
from the 11–13th
centuries.

Trading made Great
Zimbabwe the wealthy
capital of an inland African
society around 1290.   ►

Early version of lateen, or triangular sail

Hull made of planks of teak or coconut palm wood, stitched together with twine

▲ Manuscript showing 13th-century sailing ship, called a dhow, used by Arab traders to travel the Indian Ocean trade routes.

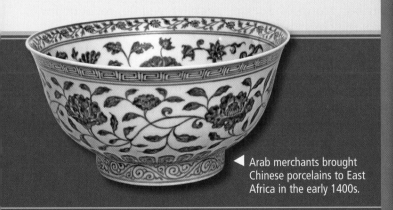

◄ Arab merchants brought Chinese porcelains to East Africa in the early 1400s.

TRADE NETWORKS FROM EAST AFRICA TO ASIA

Crossing the Indian Ocean For over one thousand years Arab traders controlled the sea routes from East Africa to Asia. They began to sail these routes as early as A.D. 500 and kept their hold on the valuable Indian Ocean trade until 1500.

As they sailed back and forth across the Indian Ocean, Arab traders and sailors took advantage of the seasonal Indian Ocean wind patterns known as the monsoons. Formed as a result of air warming or cooling over the Asian continent, these winds blow in a northeasterly direction in the spring and summer and in a southwesterly direction in the fall and winter. Traders relied on the seasonal monsoon winds to help them cross the Indian Ocean to Asia in the late spring and summer and return speedily to East Africa in the late fall or winter.

Inland Networks Swahili traders built regional trade links between inland African kingdoms and states and coastal cities to obtain local trade goods for trade with Asia. These goods included natural resources such as ivory, copper, and iron, as well as rhinoceros horn. Gold came to Sofalo from the area near Great Zimbabwe.

Portuguese Take Control In the early 1500s, Arab traders lost control of trade with Asia. In 1498 Portuguese explorer Vasco da Gama established a sea route to Asia across the Indian Ocean. The Portuguese moved quickly to take control of trading at the East African ports. Lacking large armies, weapons, or forts for protection, the traders were no match for their Portuguese attackers. The disruption of the long-established networks ended East African trading.

Geography SKILLS

1. **Place** How did the location of the East African cities contribute to their success as trading ports?

2. **Movement** How did the movement of goods along the Indian Ocean trade networks contribute to the spread of ideas?

The Asian World

GUIDE TO READING

The BIG Idea
Physical Geography The diverse landforms of Asia influenced the development of distinct cultures.

Content Vocabulary
- samurai *(p. 110)*
- Bushido *(p. 110)*
- shogun *(p. 110)*
- Shinto *(p. 112)*

Academic Vocabulary
- complexity *(p. 107)*
- traditional *(p. 109)*

People and Places
- Tibet *(p. 106)*
- Mongolia *(p. 108)*
- Beijing *(p. 108)*
- Nara *(p. 110)*
- Kyōto *(p. 110)*
- Angkor Thom *(p. 115)*
- Malay Peninsula *(p. 115)*

Reading Strategy
Identify Using a diagram like the one below, identify all the civilizations that were affected by Mongol expansion.

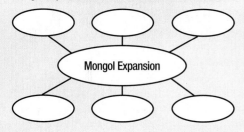

The societies of the Asian world developed their own distinct cultures. Geography played a significant role in how these individual societies developed.

China Reunified

MAIN IDEA The Sui, Tang, and Song dynasties restored peace to China in between periods of chaos, civil war, and disorder.

HISTORY & YOU Can you name other countries that have had civil wars? Read how China was reunified after years of chaos.

In 581, a new Chinese dynasty, known as the Sui (SWAY), was established. The Sui (581–618) did not last long, but it managed to unify China once again under the emperor's authority.

The Tang Dynasty
A new dynasty, the Tang (TAHNG), soon emerged. It would last for nearly 300 years, from 618 until 907. The early Tang rulers began their reigns by instituting reforms, as rulers often did in the early days of new dynasties. They also tried to create a more stable economy by giving land to the peasants and breaking up the power of the owners of large estates. They restored the civil service examination from earlier times to serve as the chief method of recruiting officials for the civilian bureaucracy.

Tang rulers worked hard to restore the power of China in East Asia. They brought peace to northwestern China and expanded their control to the borders of **Tibet,** an area north of the Himalaya. China claimed to be the greatest power in East Asia.

During the eighth century, the Tang dynasty weakened and became prey to rebellions. Tang rulers hired Uighurs (WEE•GURZ), a northern tribal group of Turkic-speaking people, to fight for them. Instead, they overthrew the Tang ruler in 907.

The Song Dynasty
In 960, a new dynasty known as the Song (SUNG) rose to power. The Song ruled during a period of economic prosperity and cultural achievement, from 960 to 1279. From the start, however, the Song also experienced problems, especially from northern neighbors. Song rulers were forced to move the imperial court farther south to Hangzhou (HAHNG•JOH), on the coast just south of the Chang Jiang river delta. The Song dynasty could never overcome the challenge from the north. Within 70 years, the Mongols overthrew the Song and created a new dynasty in China.

The Role of Women in the Tang and Song Dynasties

One of the most famous women of the Tang dynasty is Empress Wu. Born Wu Zhao, she became mistress to the emperor in 649. She so longed for power that she accused the empress of a crime. The emperor deposed his wife and chose Wu Zhao as his new empress. After his death she gained supreme power.

Known for her ruthlessness, she was also a strong leader. She was the first ruler to give graduates of the civil service examinations the highest government positions. She also formed an alliance with Korea and lowered taxes.

Most women, however, had few rights and privileges during the Tang dynasty. Women were allowed to join in sports such as horseback riding and polo, and activities such as dancing and playing music. Most marriages were arranged, and a woman was permitted to marry only once in her lifetime.

During the Song dynasty, the practice of foot binding became popular among upper-class women. Foot binding, which made feet unnaturally small, permanently deformed women's feet, caused great pain, and often made women unable to stand or walk without assistance. A woman's willingness to bind her feet was considered a sign of her virtue. On the other hand, two-thirds of aristocratic women in the Song dynasty were literate and well-educated. Some women benefited from new inheritance rights. If there was no male heir, the estate could pass to a woman in the family.

During the Tang dynasty, Wu Zhao began as the emperor's concubine and became Empress Wu, ruling in her own right after 690.

DOCUMENT-BASED QUESTIONS

1. **Making Generalizations** How did the roles of women compare to the roles of men during the Tang and Song dynasties in China?
2. **Drawing Conclusions** How did foot binding affect women's roles in society?

Politics, Economy, and Society

The era from the beginning of the Sui dynasty to the end of the Song dynasty lasted nearly seven hundred years. During that period, a mature political system, based on principles first put into practice during the Qin and Han dynasties, gradually emerged in China. As in the Han Era, China was a monarchy with a large bureaucracy. Confucian ideals were still the cement that held the system together.

During the period between the Sui and Song dynasties, the Chinese economy grew in size and **complexity.** Agriculture flourished, and manufacturing and trade grew.

In Chinese cities, technological developments added new products and stimulated trade. During the Tang dynasty, for example, the Chinese began to make steel for swords and sickles and invented gunpowder, used for explosives.

Long-distance trade had declined between the fourth and sixth centuries as a result of the collapse of both the Han dynasty and the Roman Empire. Trade began to revive under the Tang dynasty. The Silk Road was renewed and thrived as caravans carried goods between China and the countries of Southwest and South Asia.

Economic changes had an impact on Chinese society. For wealthier city dwellers, the Tang and Song eras were an age of prosperity. There was probably no better example than the Song capital of Hangzhou. In the late thirteenth century the Italian merchant Marco Polo described the city to European readers as one of the largest and wealthiest cities on Earth. He said, "So many pleasures may be found that one fancies himself to be in Paradise."

The vast majority of the Chinese people still lived off the land in villages. Most peasants never left their villages except for an occasional visit to a nearby market town. Changes were taking place in the countryside, however. Before, there had been a great gulf between wealthy landowners and poor peasants. A more complex mixture of landowners, free peasants, sharecroppers, and landless laborers now emerged.

The Mongol Empire

The Mongols were a pastoral people from the region of modern-day Mongolia who were organized loosely into clans. Temüjin (TEHM•yuh•juhn), born during the 1160s, gradually unified the Mongols. In 1206, he was elected Genghis Khan ("strong ruler") at a massive meeting somewhere in the Gobi. From that time on, he devoted himself to conquest.

The Mongols brought much of the Eurasian landmass under a single rule, creating the largest land empire in history. To rule the new Mongol Empire, Genghis Khan set up a capital city at Karakorum. Mongol armies traveled west and east. Some went as far as central Europe.

After the death of Genghis Khan in 1227, the empire began to change. Following Mongol custom, upon the death of the ruling khan, his heirs divided the territory. The once-united empire of Genghis Khan split into several separate territories called khanates, each under the rule of one of his sons.

In 1231, the Mongols attacked Persia and then defeated the Abbasids at Baghdad in 1258. Mongol forces attacked the Song dynasty in China in the 1260s. In their attack on the Chinese, the Mongols faced the use of gunpowder. By the 1300s, foreigners employed by the Mongol rulers introduced gunpowder into Europe.

The Mongol Dynasty in China

In 1279 one of Genghis Khan's grandsons, named Kublai Khan (KOO•BLUH KAHN), completed the conquest of the Song and established a new Chinese dynasty, the Yuan (YWAN). Kublai Khan, who ruled China until his death in 1294, established his capital at Khanbalik—the city of the Khan—later known by the Chinese name Beijing.

Under the leadership of the talented Kublai Khan, the Yuan dynasty continued to expand the empire. Mongol armies advanced into Vietnam, and Mongol fleets were launched against Java and Sumatra and twice against the islands of Japan. Only Vietnam was conquered and then only for a while.

The Mongols had more success in ruling China. Mongol rulers adapted to the Chinese political system. Over time, the Mongol dynasty won the support of many Chinese people. Some came to respect the stability and economic prosperity that the Mongols at first brought to China. The capital at Khanbalik reflected Mongol prosperity. It was a magnificent city, and foreign visitors were impressed by its splendor.

The Mongol dynasty eventually fell victim to the same problems that plagued other dynasties. In 1368, Zhu Yuanzhang (JOO YWAHN•JAHNG), the son of a peasant, raised an army, ended the Mongol dynasty, and set up a new dynasty, the Ming dynasty.

Religion

By the time the Mongols established their dynasty in China, religious preferences in the Chinese court had undergone a number of changes. Confucian principles became the basis for Chinese government during the Han dynasty. By the time of the Sui and Tang dynasties, Buddhism and Daoism rivaled the influence of Confucianism. During the Song dynasty, however, Confucianism became dominant at court, a position it retained until the early twentieth century.

A Golden Age in the Arts

The period between the Tang and Ming dynasties was in many ways the great age of Chinese art and literature. During the Song and Mongol dynasties, landscape painting reached its high point. Influenced by Daoism, Chinese artists went into the mountains to find the Dao, or Way, in nature. This practice explains in part the emphasis on nature in **traditional** Chinese painting. The word for landscape in Chinese means "mountain-water" and reflects the Daoist search for balance between the earth and water.

Chinese artists tried to reveal the hidden forms of the landscape. Rather than depicting the realistic shape of a specific mountain, for example, they tried to portray the idea of "mountain." Empty spaces were left in the paintings because in the Daoist vision, one cannot know the whole truth.

The invention of printing during the Tang dynasty helped to make literature more readily available and more popular. It was in poetry, above all, that the Chinese of this time best expressed their literary talents. The Tang dynasty is viewed as the great age of Chinese poetry. At least 48,000 poems were written by 2,200 authors. These poems celebrated the beauty of nature, the changes of the seasons, and the joys of friendship. They expressed sadness at the shortness of life and the necessity of parting.

Li Bo (LEE BWAW) was one of the most popular poets during the Tang Era. Li Bo was a free spirit whose writing often centered on nature. Probably the best-known poem in China, "Quiet Night Thoughts," has been memorized by schoolchildren for centuries.

See page R40 to read five poems by Li Bo in the **Primary Sources and Literature Library**.

✓ **Reading Check** **Summarizing** What invention helped make literature more available?

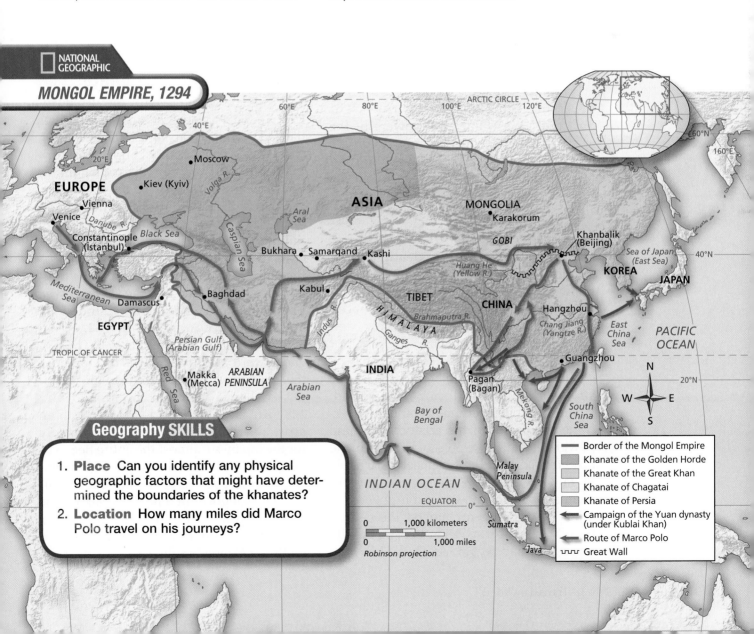

NATIONAL GEOGRAPHIC

MONGOL EMPIRE, 1294

Geography SKILLS

1. **Place** Can you identify any physical geographic factors that might have determined the boundaries of the khanates?
2. **Location** How many miles did Marco Polo travel on his journeys?

Legend:
- Border of the Mongol Empire
- Khanate of the Golden Horde
- Khanate of the Great Khan
- Khanate of Chagatai
- Khanate of Persia
- Campaign of the Yuan dynasty (under Kublai Khan)
- Route of Marco Polo
- Great Wall

0   1,000 kilometers
0   1,000 miles
Robinson projection

Emergence of Japan

MAIN IDEA Early Japan was unified by emperors and then military leaders.

HISTORY & YOU Have you ever visited an island? Read how Japan's geography isolated it from others.

Chinese and Japanese societies have historically been very different. One of the reasons for these differences is geography. Whereas China is located on a vast continent, Japan is a chain of many islands. The population is concentrated on four main islands: Hokkaidō, the main island of Honshū, and the two smaller islands of Kyūshū and Shikoku. Japan's total land area is approximately 146,000 square miles (378,000 sq km).

In the early seventh century, Shōtoku Taishi, a prince of the Yamato clan, tried to unify the various clans so that the Japanese could more effectively resist an invasion by the Chinese. He then began to create a new centralized system of government in Japan, based on the Chinese model.

Prince Shōtoku wanted a centralized government under a supreme ruler. His objective was to limit the powers of the aristocrats and enhance the Yamato ruler's (his own) authority. As a result, the ruler was portrayed as a divine figure and the symbol of the nation.

The Nara and Heian Periods

After Shōtoku Taishi's death in 622, political power fell into the hands of the Fujiwara clan. A Yamato ruler was still emperor, but he was strongly influenced by the Fujiwara family. In 710 a new capital was established at **Nara.** The emperor began to use the title "Son of Heaven."

Though the reforms begun by Prince Shōtoku continued during this period, Japan's central government could not overcome the power of the aristocrats. These powerful families were able to keep the taxes from the lands for themselves. Unable to gain tax revenues, the central government steadily lost power and influence.

In 794 the emperor moved the capital from Nara to nearby Heian-kyo, on the site of present-day **Kyōto.** At Heian-kyo, the emperor continued to rule in name, but actual power remained in the hands of the Fujiwara clan.

In fact, the government was returning to the decentralized system that had existed before the time of Shōtoku Taishi. Powerful families whose wealth was based on the ownership of tax-exempt farmland dominated the rural areas. With the decline of central power, local aristocrats took justice into their own hands. They turned to military force, and a new class of military servants emerged whose purpose was to protect the security and property of their employers. Called the **samurai** ("those who serve"), these warriors resembled the knights of medieval Europe. The samurai fought on horseback, clad in helmet and armor, and carried a sword and a bow and arrow. Like knights, the samurai were supposed to live by a strict warrior code, known in Japan as **Bushido** ("the way of the warrior"). The samurai's code was based on loyalty to his lord.

The Kamakura Shogunate

By the end of the twelfth century, rivalries among Japanese aristocratic families had led to almost constant civil war. Finally, a powerful noble named Minamoto Yoritomo defeated several rivals and set up his power near the modern city of Tokyo.

To strengthen the state, he created a more centralized government under a powerful military leader known as the **shogun** (general). In this new system—the shogunate—the emperor remained ruler in name only, and the shogun exercised the actual power. The Kamakura shogunate, founded by Yoritomo, lasted from 1192 to 1333.

At first the system worked well. The Japanese were fortunate that it did, because the government soon faced its most serious challenge yet from the Mongols. In 1281 Kublai Khan invaded Japan with an army nearly 150,000 strong. Fortunately for the Japanese, almost the entire fleet was destroyed by a massive typhoon (violent storm) before the forces could land. Fighting the Mongols put a heavy strain on the political system. In 1333 the Kamakura shogunate was overthrown by a group led by the Ashikaga family.

Mongol emperor Kublai Khan expected an easy victory when he attacked Japan in 1272. Strengthened with Korean and Chinese troops, the Mongols seized the beach at Hakata when a huge storm sank 200 of his ships, drowning about 13,000 men.

In 1281, Kublai Khan attacked with a larger fleet, but most of the ships were destroyed by a typhoon. The Japanese called the storms *kamikaze*, or "divine wind." They took this as a sign that they were invincible because they were protected by divine powers. After defeating the Mongol invaders, Japan isolated itself from foreign influence until 1945.

Japanese samurai attacking a Mongol ship

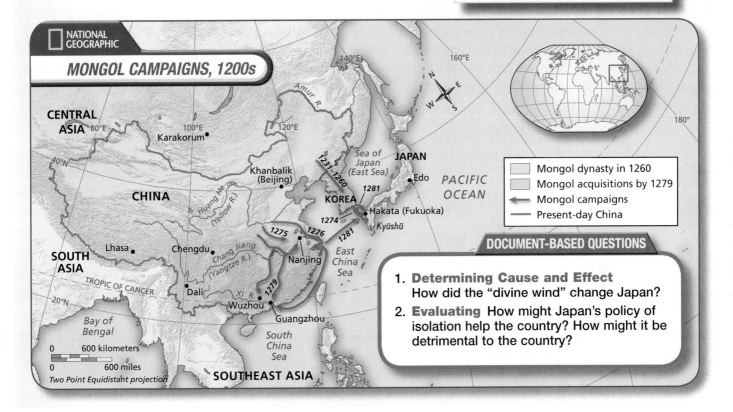

NATIONAL GEOGRAPHIC

MONGOL CAMPAIGNS, 1200s

- Mongol dynasty in 1260
- Mongol acquisitions by 1279
- Mongol campaigns
- Present-day China

DOCUMENT-BASED QUESTIONS

1. **Determining Cause and Effect**
   How did the "divine wind" change Japan?

2. **Evaluating** How might Japan's policy of isolation help the country? How might it be detrimental to the country?

The power of the local aristocrats grew during the fourteenth and fifteenth centuries. Heads of noble families, now called daimyo (DY•mee•oh), "great names," controlled vast landed estates that owed no taxes to the government. By 1500, Japan was close to chaos. A disastrous civil war, known as the Onin War, which lasted from 1467 to 1477, led to the virtual destruction of the capital city of Kyōto. Armies passed through the city, burning temples and palaces. Central authority disappeared.

Life and Culture in Early Japan

Early Japan was mostly a farming society. Its people took advantage of the limited amount of farmland and abundant rainfall to grow wet rice (rice grown in flooded fields).

Trade and manufacturing developed during the Kamakura period. Markets appeared in the larger towns, and papermaking and porcelain industries and iron casting emerged. Foreign trade, mainly with Korea and China, began in the eleventh century.

Japan exported raw materials, paintings, swords, and other manufactured items.

Early Japanese people worshiped spirits, called *kami*, who the Japanese believed resided in trees, rivers, streams, and mountains. The Japanese also believed that the spirits of their ancestors were present in the air around them. In Japan, these beliefs evolved into a religion called **Shinto** ("the Sacred Way" or "the Way of the Gods"), which is still practiced today.

Shinto, however, did not satisfy the spiritual needs of all the Japanese people. Some turned to Buddhism, which Buddhist monks from China brought to Japan during the sixth century A.D.

In Japanese art and architecture, landscape serves as an important means of expression. The landscape surrounding the Golden Pavilion in Kyōto displays a harmony of garden, water, and architecture that makes it one of the treasures of the world.

✓**Reading Check** **Describing** What difficulties did Japanese rulers encounter in establishing a strong central government?

India After the Guptas

MAIN IDEA Muslim conquerors took control of most of the Indian subcontinent.

HISTORY & YOU What causes conflicts between people of different backgrounds? Read about the tensions in India.

In the early eighth century, Islam became popular in the northwestern part of the Indian subcontinent and had a major impact on Indian civilization. This impact is still evident today in the division of the Indian subcontinent into mostly Hindu India and two Islamic states, Bangladesh and Pakistan.

One reason for Islam's success was the state of political disunity in India when it arrived. The Gupta Empire had collapsed, and no central authority had replaced it. India was divided into about seventy states, which fought each other constantly.

When the Arab armies reached India in the early eighth century, they did little more than move into the frontier regions. At the

HISTORY & ARTS
Hindu Temple at Khajuraho

The *sikhara*, the tallest tower of the temple, sits above the sanctuary.

Exterior and interior walls have relief sculpture.

The temple's position on a high base emphasizes that it is a holy place.

end of the tenth century, however a new phase of Islamic expansion took place when a group of rebellious Turkish slaves founded a new Islamic state called Ghazna (Ghaznī), located in present-day Afghanistan.

When the founder of the new state died in 997, his son, Maḥmūd of Ghazna, succeeded him. Maḥmūd, an ambitious man, began to attack neighboring Hindu kingdoms to the southeast. Before his death in 1030, he was able to extend his rule throughout the upper Indus Valley and as far south as the Indian Ocean.

Resistance against the advances of Maḥmūd and his successors into northern India was led by the Rajputs, who were Hindu warriors. They fought bravely, but their military tactics, based on infantry supported by elephants, were no match for the cavalry of the invaders. Maḥmūd's cavalry was able to strike with great speed, and his successors continued their advances. By 1200, Muslim power had reached over the entire plain of northern India, creating a new Muslim state known as the sultanate of Delhi. In the 1300s, this state extended its power into the Deccan Plateau.

The Impact of Timur Lenk

During the late 1300s, the sultanate of Delhi began to decline and a new military force crossed the Indus River from the northwest. The invader raided the capital of Delhi and then withdrew. As many as 100,000 Hindu prisoners were massacred before the gates of the city. It was India's first meeting with Timur Lenk.

Timur Lenk was the ruler of a Mongol state based in Samarqand, to the north of the Pamirs. Born sometime during the 1330s, Timur Lenk seized power in 1369 and immediately launched a program of conquest. During the 1380s, he placed the entire region east of the Caspian Sea under his authority and then occupied Mesopotamia. After his brief foray into northern India, he turned to the west. He died in 1405 in the midst of a military campaign.

The death of Timur Lenk removed a menace from the various states of the Indian subcontinent, but the calm did not last long. By the early 1500s, two new challenges had appeared. One came from the north in the form of the Moguls, a newly emerging nomadic power. The other came from Europe, from Portuguese traders in search of gold and spices.

Islam and Indian Society

The Muslim rulers in India viewed themselves as foreign conquerors. They tried to maintain a strict separation between the Muslim ruling class and the Hindu population.

Many Muslim rulers in India were tolerant of other faiths. They generally used peaceful means to encourage people to convert to Islam. Most Muslim rulers realized that there were too many Hindus to convert them all and accepted the need to tolerate religious differences. However, they did impose many Islamic customs on Hindu society. Overall, the relationship between Muslims and Hindus was that of conqueror and conquered, a relationship marked by suspicion and dislike rather than friendship and understanding.

✓ **Reading Check** **Evaluating** What was the relationship between the Muslims and Hindus in India?

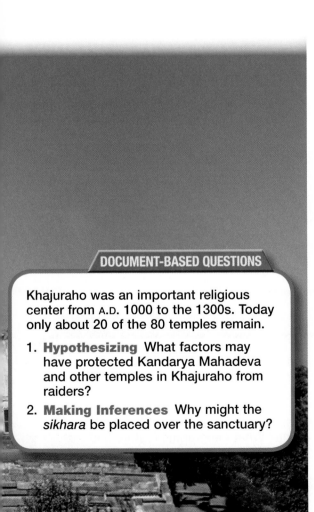

DOCUMENT-BASED QUESTIONS

Khajuraho was an important religious center from A.D. 1000 to the 1300s. Today only about 20 of the 80 temples remain.

1. **Hypothesizing** What factors may have protected Kandarya Mahadeva and other temples in Khajuraho from raiders?

2. **Making Inferences** Why might the *sikhara* be placed over the sanctuary?

Civilization in Southeast Asia

MAIN IDEA Southeast Asia was never unified under a single empire or kingdom.

HISTORY & YOU Can you think of ways geography has divided people? Read about the development of Southeast Asia.

Between China and India lies the region that today is called Southeast Asia. It has two major parts. One is the mainland region, extending southward from the Chinese border down to the tip of the Malay Peninsula. The other is an extensive archipelago, or chain of islands, most of which is part of present-day Indonesia and the Philippines. Located between India and China—two highly advanced and densely populated regions of the world—Southeast Asia contains a vast mixture of races, cultures, and religions.

The Formation of States

Between 500 and 1500, a number of organized states developed throughout Southeast Asia. When the peoples of the region began to form states, they used models from China and India. At the same time, they adapted these models to their own needs and created their own unique states.

After over a hundred years of warfare, the Chinese conquered Vietnam in 111 B.C., but the Vietnamese overthrew Chinese rule in the tenth century. Chinese influence remained, however. Vietnamese rulers realized the advantages of taking over the Chinese model of centralized government. Following the Chinese model, the rulers called themselves emperors and adopted Chinese court rituals. The new Vietnamese state, which called itself Dai Viet—Great Viet—also adopted state Confucianism.

In the ninth century, the kingdom of Angkor arose in the region that is now called Cambodia. A powerful figure named

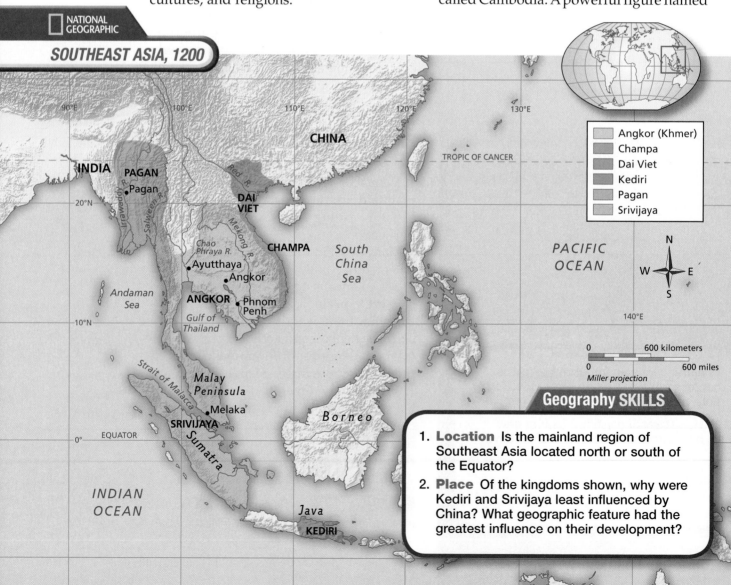

NATIONAL GEOGRAPHIC

SOUTHEAST ASIA, 1200

Legend:
- Angkor (Khmer)
- Champa
- Dai Viet
- Kediri
- Pagan
- Srivijaya

TROPIC OF CANCER

CHINA

INDIA

PAGAN • Pagan

DAI VIET

CHAMPA

Chao Phraya R. • Ayutthaya • Angkor

Andaman Sea

ANGKOR • Phnom Penh

Gulf of Thailand

South China Sea

PACIFIC OCEAN

Strait of Malacca

Malay Peninsula • Melaka

SRIVIJAYA Sumatra

Borneo

INDIAN OCEAN

Java

KEDIRI

EQUATOR

0   600 kilometers
0   600 miles
Miller projection

Geography SKILLS

1. **Location** Is the mainland region of Southeast Asia located north or south of the Equator?
2. **Place** Of the kingdoms shown, why were Kediri and Srivijaya least influenced by China? What geographic feature had the greatest influence on their development?

Jayavarman united the Khmer (kuh•MEHR) people and established a capital at **Angkor Thom.** For several hundred years, Angkor—or the Khmer Empire—was the most powerful state in mainland Southeast Asia.

In 1432 the Thai—a migrating people from the north—destroyed the Angkor capital. The Thai set up their own capital at Ayutthaya (AH•yoo•TY•uh) on the Chao Phraya River, where they remained as a major force in the region for the next 400 years.

The Thai were threatened from the west by the Burmese peoples, who had formed their own society along the Salween and Irrawaddy Rivers. In the eleventh century, they founded the first great Burmese state, the kingdom of Pagan. Like the Thai, they adopted Indian political institutions and culture.

In the **Malay Peninsula** and the Indonesian archipelago, a different pattern emerged. For centuries, this area had been tied to the trade that passed from East Asia into the Indian Ocean. The area had never been united under a single state, however. The vast majority of the people of the region were of Malay background, but the peoples were divided into numerous separate communities. Two organized states eventually emerged: Srivijaya (SREE•wih•JAW•yuh) and Saliendra. Both were influenced by Indian culture.

Society and Culture

At the top of the social ladder in most Southeast Asian societies were the hereditary aristocrats. They held both political power and economic wealth. Most aristocrats lived in the major cities. Angkor Thom, for example, was a city with royal palaces and parks, a massive parade ground, reservoirs, and numerous temples.

Beyond the major cities lived the rest of the population, which consisted of farmers, fishers, artisans, and merchants. In most Southeast Asian societies, the majority of people were probably rice farmers who lived at a bare level of subsistence and paid heavy rents or taxes to a landlord or local ruler.

Chinese culture made an impact on Vietnam. In many other areas of Southeast Asia, Indian cultural influence prevailed. The most visible example of this influence was in architecture. Of all the existing structures at Angkor Thom, the temple of Angkor Wat is the most famous and most beautiful. It combines Indian architectural techniques with native inspiration in a structure of impressive grace. The construction of Angkor Wat, which took 40 years to complete, required an enormous quantity of stone—as much as it took to build Egypt's Great Pyramid.

✓ Reading Check **Contrasting** How did the development of the Malay Peninsula and the Indonesian archipelago differ from development elsewhere in Southeast Asia?

Vocabulary

1. **Explain** the significance of: Tibet, complexity, Mongolia, Beijing, traditional, Nara, Kyōto, samurai, Bushido, shogun, Shinto, Angkor Thom, Malay Peninsula.

Main Ideas

2. **Describe** why the Tang rulers reinstituted civil service examinations.

3. **Describe** Shōtoku Taishi's vision for Japan.

4. **Summarize** the impact of the introduction of Islam into the Indian culture.

5. **Explain** how the development of the Malay Peninsula and the Indonesian archipelago differed from the development of Southeast Asia.

Critical Thinking

6. **The BIG Idea** **Explaining** How did geography impact the development of culture in Asia?

7. **Organizing Information** Use a table like the one below to list the achievements of the Sui, Tang, Song, and Mongol dynasties.

Dynasty	Achievements
Sui	
Tang	
Song	
Mongol	

8. **Analyzing Visuals** Examine the painting of Wu Zhao on page 107. What indicates her status in Chinese society?

Writing About History

9. **Descriptive Writing** Imagine that you are a samurai living in Japan during the fourteenth century. Describe your role and your daily duties.

History ONLINE

For help with the concepts in this section of *Glencoe World History— Modern Times,* go to glencoe.com and click Study Central.

Life in Genghis Khan's Army

Most states that have disappeared into history met their demise in the same way: they were conquered by a foreign army. There have always been outsiders who threaten force to take territories and goods away from other groups. One of the most feared of these outside forces was the army of the Mongol ruler Genghis Khan. It was an army and state in one—and it could move. What was it like to march with him on his conquests that built the largest empire in history?

75,000 oxen and camels carried the Mongols' felt tents, called *ger,* as well as supplies and gear.

A Mongol tumen moved very slowly. The procession could be 50 miles long and move only 5 miles a day.

Each cavalry rider had two to four remounts to keep his horse fresh for and during battle.

THE MONGOLS ON THE MOVE

The Mongol army was a highly disciplined fighting force. A group of ten 1,000-man units formed the 10,000-man Mongol fighting unit called the *tumen.* Tumens traveled separately from one another, but could converge rapidly on horseback to form an intimidating 100,000-man army. When battle was anticipated, horse soldiers left the women, children, and animals behind and became a highly mobile fighting force.

Women were in charge of tending animals and domestic duties. During battle they collected arrows and killed wounded enemy soldiers.

100,000 sheep and 10,000 goats kept a tumen supplied with milk, meat, and wool.

Men were expected to be expert horsemen, archers, and fighters.

Children were taught how to fight or cook, depending on gender. Younger children collected animal dung, the Mongols' primary fuel source.

Cavalry members were equipped with bows and arrows, a dagger, a lance, and a saber. Their light leather armor offered protection and mobility.

MONGOL MEALS

"An army," Napoleon Bonaparte was believed to have said, "marches on its stomach." Genghis Khan knew as much 500 years earlier. Not surprisingly, meat and dairy products formed the basis of the marching Mongols' diet. They cooked mutton and lamb on and over rocks heated by dung fires. Milk tea and fermented mare's milk were common drinks.

ANALYZING VISUALS

1. **Evaluating** What do you think the tumen's main strengths were? Its greatest weaknesses?

2. **Comparing and Contrasting** How was life for Mongol children similar to and different from the life of children in other cultures you have read about?

Europe and the Byzantine Empire

A new European civilization came into being in western Europe after the collapse of the Western Roman Empire. This new civilization was formed from three major elements: the Germanic peoples who had settled the Western Roman Empire, the legacy of the Romans, and the Christian Church. The Eastern Roman Empire became the Byzantine Empire, which was an important center of learning and of trade until 1453.

GUIDE TO READING

The BIG Idea

Order and Security The western European states were formed by the Germanic peoples, the legacy of the Romans, and the Christian Church. Byzantine rulers continued an empire in the East.

Content Vocabulary
- feudalism *(p. 120)*
- vassal *(p. 120)*
- Magna Carta *(p. 121)*
- Crusades *(p. 125)*

Academic Vocabulary
- document *(p. 120)*
- revenue *(p. 122)*

People and Places
- England *(p. 120)*
- Runnymede *(p. 120)*
- Holy Roman Empire *(p. 122)*
- Kiev *(p. 122)*
- Jerusalem *(p. 125)*

Reading Strategy

Contrasting Information Use a table like the one below to list the differences between the systems of feudalism and kingdoms.

Feudalism	Kingdoms

European Kingdoms and Feudalism

MAIN IDEA Germanic states emerged in the former Western Roman Empire and created a new European civilization.

HISTORY & YOU What groups keep order in your town? Read how the Church and monarchs brought order to Europe.

A new European civilization emerged and developed during a period called the Middle Ages or the medieval period, which lasted from about 500 to 1500. To historians who first used the title, the Middle Ages was a middle period between the ancient world and the modern world. By 500, the Western Roman Empire had been replaced by a number of states ruled by German kings. Only one of the German states on the European continent proved long lasting—the kingdom of the Franks. The Frankish kingdom was established by Clovis, a strong military leader who around 500 became the first Germanic ruler to convert to Christianity. By 510, Clovis had established a powerful Frankish kingdom that stretched from the Pyrenees in the southwest to German lands in the east (modern-day France and western Germany).

The Role of the Church

By the end of the fourth century, Christianity had become the supreme religion of the Roman Empire. As the official Roman state fell apart, the Christian Church played an increasingly important role in the growth of the new European civilization.

By the fourth century, the Christian Church had developed a system of organization. Local Christian communities called parishes were led by priests. A group of parishes was headed by a bishop, whose area of authority was known as a bishopric, or diocese.

Over time, one bishop—the Bishop of Rome—began to claim that he was the leader of what was now called the Roman Catholic Church. Later bishops of Rome came to be known as popes

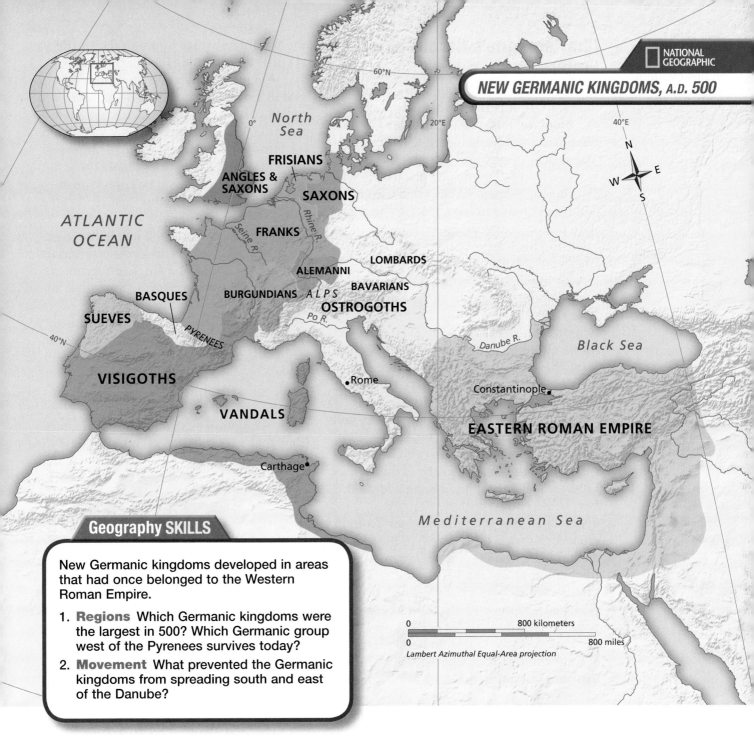

North Sea

60°N

20°E

40°E

FRISIANS

ANGLES & SAXONS

SAXONS

ATLANTIC OCEAN

FRANKS

Rhine R.

Seine R.

LOMBARDS

ALEMANNI

BASQUES

BURGUNDIANS

ALPS

BAVARIANS

OSTROGOTHS

SUEVES

PYRENEES

Po R.

Danube R.

Black Sea

40°N

VISIGOTHS

Rome

Constantinople

VANDALS

EASTERN ROMAN EMPIRE

Carthage

Mediterranean Sea

Geography SKILLS

New Germanic kingdoms developed in areas that had once belonged to the Western Roman Empire.

1. **Regions** Which Germanic kingdoms were the largest in 500? Which Germanic group west of the Pyrenees survives today?

2. **Movement** What prevented the Germanic kingdoms from spreading south and east of the Danube?

0   800 kilometers
0   800 miles
Lambert Azimuthal Equal-Area projection

(from the Latin word *papa*, "father") of the Catholic Church.

The Catholic Church developed a body of doctrine. The Church council, a meeting of representatives from the entire Christian community, was very important. Church councils defined Church teachings.

Also important to the early Christian Church was the role of monks. A monk is a man who separates himself from ordinary society to dedicate himself to God.

The practice of living the life of a monk is known as monasticism. In the sixth century, Saint Benedict wrote a set of rules to guide a community of monks he founded. The Benedictine rule came to be used by other monastic groups. Monks were the social workers of their communities, providing schools for the young, hospitals for the sick, and hospitality for travelers. They became the new heroes of Christian civilization.

History ONLINE

Student Web Activity—
Visit glencoe.com and complete the activity on Medieval Europe.

Charlemagne's Carolingian Empire

In 768, a new ruler came to the throne of the Frankish kingdom. This new king was the dynamic and powerful ruler Charles the Great, or Charlemagne. Charlemagne was a determined and decisive man who was highly intelligent and curious. He was a strong statesman and a pious Christian. Although unable to read or write, he was a wise patron—supporter—of learning.

During his lengthy rule from 768 to 814, Charlemagne greatly expanded the territory of the Frankish kingdom and created what came to be known as the Carolingian (KAR•uh•LIN•jee•uhn) Empire. At its height, Charlemagne's empire covered much of western and central Europe. Not until the time of Napoleon Bonaparte in the nineteenth century would an empire its size be seen again in Europe.

As Charlemagne's power grew, so too did his prestige as the most powerful Christian ruler. One monk even described Charlemagne's empire as the "kingdom of Europe." In 800, Charlemagne acquired a new title—emperor of the Romans.

Charlemagne's coronation as Roman emperor showed the strength of the idea of an enduring Roman Empire. It symbolized the joining of Roman, Christian, and Germanic elements. A Germanic king had been crowned emperor of the Romans by the pope, the spiritual leader of Western Christendom. A new civilization had emerged.

After the death of Charlemagne in 814, the Carolingian Empire that he had established began to fall apart. Rulers found it more and more difficult to defend their subjects from invaders such as the Vikings, a Germanic people from Scandinavia. Thus, people began to turn to local landed aristocrats, or nobles, to protect them. It became important to find a powerful lord who could offer protection in return for service. This led to a new political and social order known as **feudalism.**

Feudalism

At the heart of feudalism was the idea of vassalage. In Germanic society, warriors swore an oath of loyalty to their leaders and fought in battles for them. The leaders, in turn, took care of the warriors' needs. By the eighth century, a man who served a lord in a military capacity was known as a **vassal.** The lords granted each vassal a piece of land that supported the vassal and his family. Land was the most important gift a lord could give to a vassal. The grant of land made to a vassal became known as a fief (FEEF). Vassals who held fiefs came to hold political authority within them. As the Carolingian world fell apart, the number of separate, powerful lords and vassals increased. Instead of a single government, many people were now responsible for keeping order.

The feudal system put power into the hands of many lords. Gradually, however, kings began to extend their own powers. Their actions laid the foundations for the European kingdoms that have dominated Europe ever since. One of these kingdoms—**England**—created political institutions that later influenced the formation of the democratic political system of the United States.

England

On October 14, 1066, an army of heavily armed knights under William of Normandy landed on the coast of England and defeated King Harold and his soldiers at the Battle of Hastings. William became king of England and began combining Anglo-Saxon and Norman institutions to create a new England.

The power of the English monarchy was enlarged during the reign of Henry II, from 1154 to 1189. Henry moved a number of criminal and property cases from local courts to the royal courts. By expanding the royal courts, Henry expanded the power of the king. In addition, because the royal courts were now found throughout England, a body of common law—law that was common to the whole kingdom—began to replace law codes that varied from place to place.

Many English nobles resented the ongoing growth of the king's power and rose in rebellion during the reign of King John. At **Runnymede** in 1215, John was forced by the nobles to put his seal on a **document** of rights called the **Magna Carta,** or the Great Charter.

Feudal custom had always recognized that the relationship between king and vassals was based on mutual rights and obligations. The Magna Carta gave written recognition to that fact and was used in later years to strengthen the idea that a monarch's power was limited, not absolute.

During the reign of Edward I, in the thirteenth century, an important institution in the development of representative government—the English Parliament—also emerged. The Parliament of Edward I granted taxes, discussed politics, and passed laws. Parliament was composed of two knights from every county, two people from every town, and all the nobles and bishops throughout England. Eventually, nobles and Church leaders formed the House of Lords; knights and townspeople composed the House of Commons.

TURNING POINT — THE MAGNA CARTA —

▲ *A depiction of John of England signing the Magna Carta from* Cassell's History of England—Century Edition

In the Magna Carta's 63 clauses, King John vowed that the church would remain free, listed rights due to landholders, said he would dismiss his mercenaries from foreign countries, and gave a council of 25 barons the right to go to war with him if he did not honor the Magna Carta. John was not the first king to make promises to his barons. However, previous monarchs had made general promises and granted them freely, while King John's barons demanded very specific promises from him. By recognizing the rights of nobles, the Magna Carta limited the power of English monarchs.

39. No freeman shall be . . . imprisoned . . . except by the lawful judgment of his peers or by the law of the land.
40. To no one will we sell, to no one will we refuse or delay, right or justice.
51. As soon as peace is restored, we will banish from the kingdom all foreign-born knights, cross-bowmen, serjeants, and mercenary soldiers . . .
52. If anyone has been dispossessed or removed by us, without the legal judgment of his peers, from his lands, castles, franchises, or from his right, we will immediately restore them to him . . .
55. All fines made with us unjustly and against the law of the land, and all amercements[1] imposed unjustly and against the law of the land, shall be entirely remitted . . .

—from the *Magna Carta*

---

[1] **amercements:** punishments by fine

DOCUMENT-BASED QUESTIONS

1. **Making Inferences** Why might the nobles have insisted that King John send away his foreign army?
2. **Summarizing** What permanent effects did the Magna Carta have on the English monarchy?

The French Kingdom

In 843, the Carolingian Empire was divided into three sections. One of them, the west Frankish lands, formed the core of what would become the kingdom of France.

In 987, after the death of the last Carolingian king, the west Frankish nobles made Hugh Capet their new king, establishing the Capetian (kuh•PEE•shuhn) dynasty of French kings. The Capetians had little power and controlled only the area around Paris. The reign of King Philip II Augustus, from 1180 to 1223, was a turning point in the French monarchy, expanding its income and power. Philip waged wars against the rulers of England to take control of the French territories of Normandy, Maine, Anjou, and Aquitaine. By 1300, France was the largest state in Europe.

The Holy Roman Empire

In the tenth century, the powerful dukes of the Saxons became kings of the eastern Frankish kingdom, which came to be known as Germany. The best-known Saxon king of Germany was Otto I. In return for protecting the pope, Otto I was crowned emperor of the Romans in 962.

As leaders of a new Roman Empire, the German kings attempted to rule both German and Italian lands. Kings Frederick I and Frederick II, instead of building a strong German kingdom, tried to create a new kind of empire. Frederick I planned to get his chief **revenues** from Italy. He considered Italy the center of a "holy empire"—hence the name **Holy Roman Empire.** Frederick's attempt to conquer northern Italy was opposed by the pope and the cities of northern Italy. The main goal of Frederick II was to establish a centralized state in Italy. However, he also became involved in a losing struggle with the popes and the northern Italian cities.

While fighting in Italy, the German emperors left Germany in the hands of German lords. These nobles ignored the emperor and created their own independent kingdoms. This made the monarchy weak and incapable of maintaining a strong monarchical state. As a result, the German Holy Roman Emperor had no real power over either Germany or Italy.

Central and Eastern Europe

The Slavic peoples were originally a single people in central Europe. Gradually, they divided into three major groups: the western, southern, and eastern Slavs.

The western Slavs eventually formed the Polish and Bohemian kingdoms. The Poles and Czechs, along with the non-Slavic Hungarians (Magyars), accepted Western Christianity and became part of the Roman Catholic Church and its Latin culture.

The southern Slavic peoples, which included the Croats, the Serbs, and the Bulgarians, and the eastern Slavic peoples of Morovia took a different path. Most of them embraced Eastern Orthodoxy. The Croats came to accept the Roman Catholic Church. The acceptance of Eastern Orthodoxy by many southern and eastern Slavic peoples linked their cultural life to the Byzantine state.

Eastern Slavic peoples had also settled in the present-day Ukraine and Russia. There, beginning in the late eighth century, they began to encounter Swedish Vikings. The Vikings eventually came to dominate the native peoples. The native peoples called the Viking rulers the Rus, the source of the name Russia.

One Viking leader, Oleg, settled in **Kiev** (present-day Kyiv) at the beginning of the tenth century and created the Rus state known as the principality of Kiev. His successors extended their control over the eastern Slavs and expanded Kiev until it included land between the Baltic and Black Seas and the Danube and Volga Rivers.

Civil wars and invasions brought an end to the first Russian state in 1169. In the 1200s, the Mongols conquered Russia. They occupied Russian lands and required tribute from Russian princes.

One prince emerged as more powerful than the others—Alexander Nevsky, prince of Novgorod. The khan, leader of the western Mongol Empire, awarded Nevsky the title of grand-prince. Nevsky's descendants became princes of Moscow and eventually leaders of all Russia.

✓ **Reading Check** **Analyzing** Why is 1066 considered an important date in history?

Byzantine Empire and Crusades

MAIN IDEA The Crusades had a significant effect on medieval society in both the East and the West.

HISTORY & YOU Have you ever tried to help someone and ended up in trouble? Read about the effect of the crusades on the Byzantine Empire.

During the fifth century, Germanic tribes moved into the western part of the Roman Empire and established their states. In contrast, the Roman Empire in the East, centered in Constantinople, continued to exist, although pressured by powerful Islamic forces.

When Justinian became emperor of the Eastern Roman Empire in 527, he was determined to reestablish the Roman Empire in the entire Mediterranean world. By 552, he appeared to have achieved his goals. However, only three years after Justinian's death in 565, the Lombards had conquered much of Italy, and other areas were soon lost.

Justinian's most important contribution was his codification of Roman law. He was able to simplify a vast quantity of legal materials, resulting in *The Body of Civil Law.*

INFOGRAPHICS — PRIMARY SOURCE

The Justinian Code

Soon after assuming the throne, Emperor Justinian appointed several commissions to collect and organize the complicated body of Roman laws. The result, *The Body of Civil Law* (or the Justinian Code), stands as one of the great accomplishments of the Middle Ages. Much of the modern world, including Scotland, Quebec, Louisiana, and most of mainland Europe, is governed by systems of justice that descend from the code.

On law: "The precepts of the law are these: to live honestly, to injure no one, and to give every man his due."

On property: "By the law of nature these things are common to mankind—the air, running water, the sea, and consequently the shores of the sea."

On theft: "The penalty for manifest theft is quadruple the value of the thing stolen, whether the thief be a slave or a freeman."

On marriage: "We have enacted that puberty in males should be considered to commence immediately on the completion of their fourteenth year; while, as to females . . . they are esteemed fit for marriage on the completion of their twelfth year."

Emperor Justinian

The Body of Civil Law (The Justinian Code)

Codex Constitutionem	A collection of all known ordinances issued by previous emperors. Redundant and obsolete material was left out. Published in 10 books.
Digest	A selection of the most valuable writings of Roman jurists. Any statement not selected for the Digest was considered invalid. Published in 50 books.
Institutes	An elementary law textbook for use by first-year law students. Extracts from the Codex and Digest were included.
Novels	Several collections of new ordinances passed by Justinian himself after the publication of the Codex.

DOCUMENT-BASED QUESTIONS

1. **Contrasting** Study the excerpts from the Justinian Code. How do these laws differ from modern American law?

2. **Making Inferences** Why were the Novels published years after the rest of the Code?

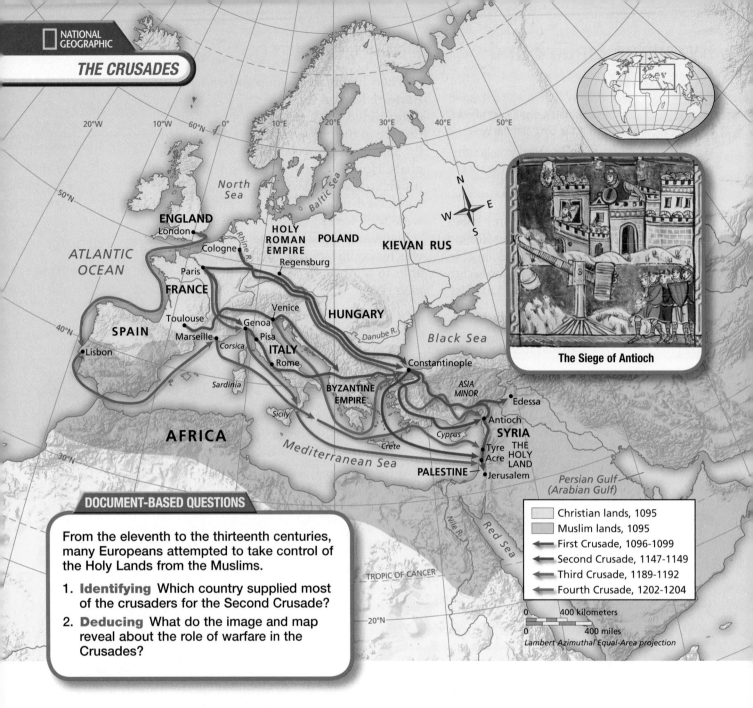

The Siege of Antioch

DOCUMENT-BASED QUESTIONS

From the eleventh to the thirteenth centuries, many Europeans attempted to take control of the Holy Lands from the Muslims.

1. **Identifying** Which country supplied most of the crusaders for the Second Crusade?

2. **Deducing** What do the image and map reveal about the role of warfare in the Crusades?

Christian lands, 1095
Muslim lands, 1095
First Crusade, 1096-1099
Second Crusade, 1147-1149
Third Crusade, 1189-1192
Fourth Crusade, 1202-1204

0   400 kilometers
0   400 miles
Lambert Azimuthal Equal-Area projection

This code of Roman laws was the basis of imperial law in the Eastern Roman Empire until its end in 1453. In addition, it became the basis for most legal systems in Europe.

A serious challenge to the Eastern Roman Empire came from the rise of Islam, which unified Arab groups and created a powerful new force that swept through the Eastern Roman Empire. Islamic forces defeated an army of the Eastern Roman Empire at Yarmūk in 636. Problems arose along the northern frontier as well, especially in the Balkans.

By the beginning of the 700s, the Eastern Roman Empire was much smaller, consisting only of the eastern Balkans and Asia Minor. Historians call this smaller Eastern Roman Empire the Byzantine Empire, a unique civilization that lasted until 1453.

The Byzantine Empire was both a Greek and a Christian state. Greek, the common language, replaced Latin as the official language of the empire. At the same time, the empire was built on a Christian faith that was shared by many of its citizens. The Christian church of the Byzantine Empire came to be known as the Eastern Orthodox Church.

The Byzantine Empire recovered and even expanded, due to the efforts of a new dynasty of emperors known as the Macedonians, who ruled from 867 to 1081. By 1025, the Byzantine Empire was the largest it had been since the seventh century.

The Byzantine Empire continued to face threats from abroad, however. The greatest challenge came from the Seljuk Turks—in Asia Minor—the empire's main source of food and workers. In 1071, a Turkish army defeated Byzantine forces at Manzikert. Lacking the resources to undertake new campaigns against the Turks, Emperor Alexius I turned to Europe for military aid.

The Crusades

From the eleventh to the thirteenth centuries, European Christians carried out a series of military expeditions to regain the Holy Land from the Muslims. These expeditions are known as the **Crusades.** The push for the Crusades came when the Byzantine emperor Alexius I asked the Europeans for help against the Seljuk Turks, who were Muslims. Pope Urban II, who responded to the request, saw an opportunity to provide papal leadership for a great cause. That cause was rallying the warriors of Europe to free **Jerusalem** and the Holy Land (Palestine) from the infidels or unbelievers—the Muslims.

The First Crusade was the only successful one. The crusaders captured Jerusalem in June 1099. After further conquests, the crusaders organized four Latin crusader states. Surrounded by Muslims, these crusader kingdoms depended on Italian cities for supplies.

It was not easy for the crusader kingdoms to maintain themselves. By the 1140s, the Muslims had begun to strike back. In 1187, the Holy City of Jerusalem fell to Muslim forces under Saladin. During the Fourth Crusade, the Venetian leaders of the crusade used the fight over the Byzantine throne to weaken their main trade competitor, the Byzantine Empire. In 1204, the crusaders sacked Constantinople.

Did the Crusades have much effect on European civilization? Historians disagree. The Crusades certainly benefited some Italian port cities, especially Genoa, Pisa, and Venice. Even without the Crusades, Italian merchants would have increased trade with the Eastern world.

Perhaps the greatest impact of the Crusades was political. They eventually helped weaken feudalism. As kings levied taxes and raised armies, nobles joining the Crusades sold their lands and freed their serfs. As nobles lost power, the kings created stronger central governments. Taxing trade with the East also provided kings with new wealth. This paved the way for the development of true nation-states. By the mid-1400s, three strong nation-states—Spain, England, and France—emerged in Europe.

✓ Reading Check **Evaluating** How did the rise of Islam affect the Eastern Roman Empire?

Vocabulary
1. **Explain** the significance of: feudalism, vassal, England, Runnymede, document, Magna Carta, revenue, Holy Roman Empire, Kiev, Crusades, Jerusalem.

Main Ideas
2. **Describe** the role of monks in the Christian Church.

3. **Explain** the effect the Crusades had upon the economy of Italian cities such as Venice.

Critical Thinking
4. **The BIG Idea** **Explaining** What significance did Charlemagne's coronation as Roman emperor have to the development of European civilization.

5. **Organizing Information** Use a chart to identify key achievements of monarchs in England and France.

Monarch/Country	Achievements

6. **Analyzing Visuals** Analyze the image of King John on page 121. What mood is being conveyed between the king and the nobles?

Writing About History
7. **Informative Writing** Imagine that you are a journalist attending a meeting of the first English Parliament. What questions would you ask? Write a newsletter for people of your town explaining what happened.

History ONLINE

For help with the concepts in this section of *Glencoe World History—Modern Times*, go to glencoe.com and click Study Central.

You can study anywhere, anytime by downloading quizzes and flash cards to your PDA from <u>glencoe.com</u>.

ARAB WORLD AND AFRICA

- The Islamic religion arose in the Arabian Peninsula during the 600s and quickly spread throughout Southwest Asia and to parts of Africa and Europe.
- Extensive trade helped bring prosperity to the Arab Empire.
- The earliest African states, Kush and Axum, thrived on farming and trade, while the later kingdoms of Ghana, Mali, and Songhai in western Africa carried out the trade of gold and salt.
- The Bantu spread ironworking through eastern and southern Africa.

THE SELJUK TURKS BUILD AN EMPIRE

The Seljuk Turks defeated the Byzantine army.

CONWY CASTLE, WALES, BUILT IN 1283

Castles provided protection during the Middle Ages.

EUROPE AND THE BYZANTINE EMPIRE

- A new European civilization emerged in the Middle Ages.
- By recognizing the rights of nobles, the Magna Carta limited the power of the English monarchs.
- The Byzantine Empire created its own unique civilization in the eastern Mediterranean.

THE ASIAN WORLD

- The Sui, Tang, and Song dynasties brought peace and prosperity to China, but in 1279 the Mongols conquered the Song dynasty and made China part of their vast empire.
- State power was centralized in Japan in a new system called the shogunate.
- Chinese and Indian examples of government and religion influenced new states in Southeast Asia.

SAMURAI BATTLE IN 1159

Sanjo Palace in Kyōto was burned during the Kamakura period.

STANDARDIZED TEST PRACTICE

TEST-TAKING

When a question asks for an answer that is supported by information presented in a table, find the answer choice that is *proven true* by the information in the table.

Reviewing Vocabulary

Directions: Choose the word or words that best complete the sentence.

1. What is the term for a Muslim house of worship?

  A Hajj

  B Mosque

  C Madinah

  D Allah

2. What are the broad grasslands that run both north and south of Africa's rain forest?

  A Savannas

  B Plateaus

  C Lowlands

  D Highlands

3. What was the name for the strict code of behavior followed by the warrior class of early Japan?

  A Bushido

  B Shogunate

  C Daimyo

  D Mahayana

4. What was the grant of land from the lord to a vassal in return for military service called?

  A Feudal contract

  B Schism

  C Wergild

  D Fief

Reviewing Main Ideas

Directions: Choose the best answers to the following questions.

Section 1 *(pp. 90–97)*

5. Who established the Umayyad dynasty?

  A Abū Bakr

  B Abū al-'Abbās

  C Mu'āwiyah

  D Hārūn ar-Rashīd

6. What are some examples of Islamic achievements?

  A Translations of Aristotle's works, paper, and the use of zero

  B Commentaries on Aristotle's works, the astrolabe, and algebra

  C Paper, silk, and algebra

  D Medicine, the astrolabe, and the telescope

Section 2 *(pp. 98–103)*

7. Which was the first great trading state to emerge in West Africa?

  A Kush

  B Ghana

  C Mali

  D Ethiopia

8. Under whose reign did the Songhai Empire reach the height of its power?

  A Muhammad Ture

  B Sunni Ali

  C Mansa Mūsā

  D Sundiata Keita

Need Extra Help?								
If You Missed Questions . . .	1	2	3	4	5	6	7	8
Go to Page . . .	97	98	110	120	93	97	100	101

Section 3 *(pp. 106–115)*

9. Which of the following best describes the Mongol Empire?

A Militarily powerful, but poor

B The largest land empire in history

C The last government to control China

D An Islamic state

10. Who were the Hindu warriors who led the resistance against the advances of Maḥmūd and his successors into northern India?

A Moguls

B Samurai

C Uighurs

D Rajputs

11. Who founded the kingdom of Angkor?

A Jayavarman

B Dai Viet

C Maḥmūd

D Dandin

Section 4 *(pp. 118–125)*

12. What was the most important gift a lord could give a vassal?

A Gold

B Arms and armor

C Serfs

D Land

13. What important English political institution emerged during the reign of Edward I?

A House of Lords

B Anglican Church

C Parliament

D Royal courts

Critical Thinking

Directions: Choose the best answers to the following questions.

Use the following table to answer question 14.

Muslim Conquests and Defeats

YEAR	PLACE	VICTOR
636	Yarmūk	Muslim
640	Syria	Muslim
650	Persian Empire	Muslim
710	Southern Spain	Muslim
717	Constantinople	Byzantine

14. Which of the following statements is supported by the information in the table?

A In 717, the Byzantines forced the Muslims to give up all their territories.

B By 710, the Arab Empire had conquered all of Spain.

C After conquering Syria, Muslim rulers forced their people to study Islamic law.

D In less than 100 years, the Muslim Empire had conquered all the territories it invaded.

15. Why were Sunni Ali's conquests in Mali and Ghana especially important?

A They were vital port cities.

B They ensured that his son would rule after him.

C They gave his empire control of the trade in salt and gold.

D They gave his empire control of the trade in ivory and iron ore.

16. What was the purpose of the samurai in Japan?

A Creating laws

B Leading religious ceremonies

C Conducting trade

D Protecting property and providing security

Need Extra Help?							
If You Missed Questions . . .	9	10	11	12	13	14	15	16
Go to Page . . .	108	113	115	120	121	92	101	110

Analyze the map and answer the question that follows. Base your answer on the map.

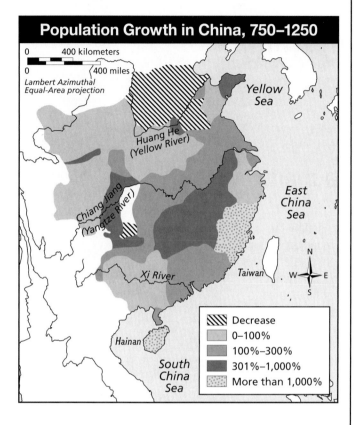

Population Growth in China, 750–1250

0   400 kilometers
0   400 miles
Lambert Azimuthal
Equal-Area projection

Yellow Sea

Huang He (Yellow River)

Chiang Jiang (Yangtze River)

East China Sea

Xi River

Taiwan

N W E S

Hainan

South China Sea

Decrease
0–100%
100%–300%
301%–1,000%
More than 1,000%

17. In what geographic direction did the population shift during this period?

  A To the northeast

  B To the northwest

  C To the southeast

  D To the southwest

18. Why was Justinian's codification of laws so significant?

  A The Eastern Roman Empire never adopted them.

  B The Eastern Roman Empire based its laws on them until the fifteenth century.

  C The rest of Europe ignored the laws.

  D They actually were collected by the Lombards.

19. Why was the reign of King Philip II Augustus a turning point for the French monarchy?

  A His wars gained France territories from England.

  B Ruling power was distributed among aristocrats.

  C The kingdom was conquered by the Holy Roman Empire.

  D Territory was lost to England.

Document-Based Questions

Directions: Analyze the document and answer the short-answer questions that follow the document. Base your answers on the document and on your knowledge of world history.

Known in the West as Avicenna, Ibn Sīnā was an eleventh-century Islamic scholar. In his *Autobiography,* he described his early training. Read the following excerpt.

> "By the time I was [10] I had mastered the Quran and a great deal of literature. There followed training in philosophy . . . then I took to reading texts by myself . . . mastering logic, geometry and astronomy. I now occupied myself with mastering the various texts and commentaries on natural science and metaphysics, until all the gates of knowledge were open to me. Next I desired to study medicine, and proceeded to read all the books that have been written on this subject. At the same time I continued to study and dispute on law, being now sixteen years of age."

20. What can you infer about Ibn Sīnā from this passage?

21. How might Ibn Sīnā's *Autobiography* have helped people to understand and value his other writings?

Extended Response

22. Through trade, many civilizations came into contact with each other. What civilizations outside of Africa did African kingdoms and states contact? How did these civilizations influence each other?

History ONLINE

For additional test practice, use Self-Check Quizzes—Chapter 3 on **glencoe.com**.

Need Extra Help?						
If You Missed Questions . . .	17	18	19	20	21	22
Go to Page . . .	107	123	122	97	97	98

STOP

CHAPTER 4

Toward a New World, 300–1500

Section 1 Europe in the Middle Ages

Section 2 Early American Civilizations

What advancements will be made in your lifetime?

El Caracol at Chichén Itzá, shown in this photo, was used by the Maya and the Toltec to measure the movement of the moon, stars, and planets. Built without metal tools, the windows of the observatory were placed at precise points in relation to the planets. In this chapter you will learn how people on different continents at different times tried to understand their place in the universe through science and religion.

- Why do you think studying the moon, stars, and planets was important to the Maya and the Toltec?
- How do people today try to understand the universe?

EUROPE & THE AMERICAS ▶

c. 300
Maya civilization begins to flourish

c. 800
Teotihuacán collapses

c. 1088
University of Bologna founded

A.D. 300   A.D. 1000

THE WORLD ▶

852
Great Mosque of Sāmarrā' finished

c. 1000
Bantu spread ironworking across Africa

1347
Plague spreads to Italy and France

1430
English capture Joan of Arc during Hundred Years' War

1440
Inca leader Pachacuti launches campaign of conquest

A.D. 1300   A.D. 1500

1279
Kublai Khan establishes the Yuan dynasty in China

1492
Christopher Columbus reaches the Americas

FOLDABLES™
Study Organizer

The Inca
Political Structure
Social Structure
Building and Culture

Organizing Create a Layered-Look Book to organize facts about the Maya, Inca, or Aztec civilizations. Read the related text and conduct research to learn more about the political structure, social structure, and buildings and culture of the civilization.

History ONLINE

Chapter Overview—Visit glencoe.com to preview Chapter 4.

Europe in the Middle Ages

GUIDE TO READING

The BIG Idea
New Technologies New farming practices led to population growth, and architectural innovation made Gothic cathedrals possible.

Content Vocabulary
- manor *(p. 133)*
- serf *(p. 133)*
- money economy *(p. 134)*
- commercial capitalism *(p. 134)*
- Inquisition *(p. 136)*
- new monarchies *(p. 141)*

Academic Vocabulary
- technology *(p. 132)*
- corporation *(p. 139)*

People and Places
- Venice *(p. 134)*
- Papal States *(p. 135)*
- Pope Gregory VII *(p. 135)*
- Henry IV *(p. 135)*
- Hildegard of Bingen *(p. 136)*
- Saint Francis of Assisi *(p. 136)*
- Rome *(p. 137)*
- Avignon *(p. 140)*

Reading Strategy
Cause and Effect Use a chart like the one below to show the effects of the growth of towns on medieval European society.

Cause	Effects	Growth of Towns

During the High Middle Ages, new farming methods led to an increase in Europe's population. Cities flourished, universities were founded, and trade expanded. The Catholic Church had become a dominant and forceful presence in European society. In the 1300s, war, religious differences, and the plague created new crises for Europeans.

Peasants, Trade, and Cities

MAIN IDEA New innovations in farming and more stability led to the increase in trade and the rise of cities.

HISTORY & YOU What technologies help modern farmers produce more food? Read how medieval farming methods improved.

In the Early Middle Ages, Europe had a relatively small population. In the High Middle Ages (1000–1300), however, population increased dramatically. The number of people almost doubled, from 38 million to 74 million. What caused this huge increase in population? For one thing, conditions in Europe were more settled and peaceful after the invasions of the Early Middle Ages had stopped. This increased peace and stability also led to a dramatic expansion in food production after 1000.

The New Agriculture
In part, food production increased because of a climate change during the High Middle Ages that improved growing conditions. In addition, peasants cultivated more land when they cut down trees and drained swamps during the 1000s and 1100s. Changes in **technology** also aided the development of farming. The Middle Ages witnessed an explosion of labor-saving devices. For example, the people of the Middle Ages harnessed water and wind power to do jobs once done by humans or animal power.

Many new devices were made from iron, which was mined in various areas of Europe. Iron was used to make scythes, axes, and hoes for use on farms. Iron was crucial in making the *carruca,* a heavy, wheeled plow with an iron plowshare. Unlike earlier plows, this plow could easily turn over heavy clay soils.

The shift from a two-field to a three-field system of crop rotation also added to the increase in food production. In the Early Middle Ages, peasants divided their land into two fields. One field was planted, while the other was allowed to lie fallow, or remain unplanted, to regain its fertility. Now lands were divided into three parts.

Organization of a Manor

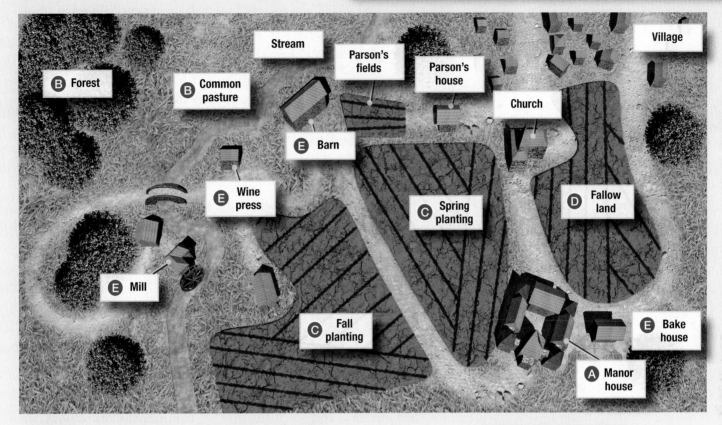

A **Manor house** Home to the lord and his family and refuge for the peasants during an attack

B **Common lands** Shared areas such as pasture where peasants could graze animals or forest where peasants could hunt, fish, and gather firewood

C **Cultivated land** Spring and fall plantings laid out in long strips to minimize the number of turns required while plowing

D **Fallow land** During crop rotation, land left unplanted to allow it to recover

E **Common workshops** Shared work areas such as a mill to grind grain; bake house to bake bread; wine press to make wine; or barn to shelter and care for animals

CRITICAL THINKING SKILLS

The medieval manor was a mostly self-sustaining community.

1. **Explaining** How did the heavy plows of the time influence the layout of the fields?

2. **Making Inferences** In what ways did the manorial system promote group cooperation?

Peasants planted one field in the fall that they harvested in summer. They planted the second field in the spring to harvest in the fall. They allowed the third field to lie fallow. This way, only one-third, rather than one-half, of the land lay fallow at any time. Rotating crops kept the soil fertile, while allowing people to grow more crops.

The Manorial System

Landholding nobles were a military elite that depended on having the leisure time to pursue the arts of war. Landed estates, worked by peasants, provided the economic support that made this way of life possible.

A **manor** was an agricultural estate run by a lord and worked by peasants. Although free peasants continued to exist, increasing numbers of free peasants became **serfs,** or peasants legally bound to the land. Serfs had to provide labor services, pay rents, and be subject to the lord's control. By 800, probably 60 percent of the people of western Europe were serfs.

The life of peasants in Europe was simple. Their thatch-roofed cottages had wood frames filled with rubble and plastered over with clay. The houses of poorer peasants consisted of a single room. There was little privacy in a medieval peasant household.

The position of peasant women in manorial society was both important and difficult. They were expected to work in the fields, to manage the household, and to bear children. Their ability to manage the household might determine whether their family would starve or survive in difficult times.

The seasons of the year largely determined peasant activities. Each season brought a new round of tasks. Harvest time in August and September was especially hectic. A good harvest of grains for making bread was crucial to survival in the winter months. A new cycle of labor began in October, when peasants worked the ground for the planting of winter crops. In November came the slaughter of excess livestock. The meat would be salted to preserve it for winter use. In February and March, the land was plowed for the spring planting—oats, barley, peas, and beans.

See page R39 to read excerpts from Christine de Pizan's *A Woman May Need to Have the Heart of a Man* in the **Primary Sources and Literature Library**.

The Revival of Trade

Medieval Europe was an agricultural society in which most people lived in small villages. In the eleventh and twelfth centuries, a revival of trade and an associated growth of cities changed the economic foundation of European civilization.

Cities in Italy took the lead in the revival of trade. **Venice** developed a mercantile fleet—a fleet of trading ships—and by the end of the 900s had become a major trading center in the Mediterranean. The towns in Flanders, areas of present-day Belgium, Netherlands, and France, were an ideal location for northern European traders.

By 1100, a regular exchange of goods had developed between Flanders and Italy. As trade increased, demand for gold and silver coins arose at fairs and trading markets. Slowly, a **money economy**—an economic system based on money, rather than barter—began to emerge. New trading companies and banking firms were set up to manage the exchange and sale of goods. All of these new practices were part of the rise of **commercial capitalism,** an economic system in which people invested in trade and goods to make profits. Some

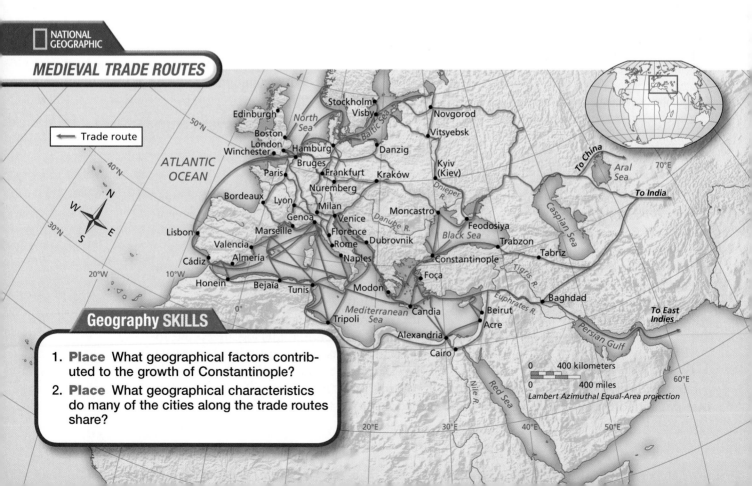

NATIONAL GEOGRAPHIC

MEDIEVAL TRADE ROUTES

← Trade route

Geography SKILLS

1. **Place** What geographical factors contributed to the growth of Constantinople?

2. **Place** What geographical characteristics do many of the cities along the trade routes share?

historians have called this the beginnings of a Commercial Revolution.

The Growth of Cities

Towns had greatly declined in the Early Middle Ages, especially in Europe north of the Alps. Old Roman cities had continued to exist, but they had dwindled in size and population. The revival of trade led to a revival of cities. Merchants, followed by craftspeople or artisans, began to settle in the old Roman cities. In the 1000s and 1100s, the old Roman cities came alive with new populations and growth.

Many new cities or towns were also founded, especially in northern Europe. Usually, a group of merchants built a settlement along a trade route and near a castle. If the settlement prospered, new walls were built to protect it. The merchants and artisans of these cities came to be called *burghers* or bourgeoisie, from the German word *burg*, meaning "a walled enclosure."

Medieval cities were surrounded by stone walls. Walls were expensive to build, so the space within was precious and tightly filled. The streets were narrow and winding. Houses were crowded together, with their second and third stories built over the streets. Dwellings were mostly made of wood, and candles and wood fires were used for light and heat. The danger of fire was great. Often dirty, cities smelled from animal and human waste. Air pollution was a fact of life from the ever-present wood fires.

The revival of trade enabled cities and towns to become important centers for manufacturing. A host of craft activities were carried on in houses located in the narrow streets of the medieval cities. From the 1000s on, craftspeople began to organize themselves into guilds, or business associations. Guilds played a leading role in the economic life of the cities. By the 1200s, there were guilds for tanners, carpenters, bakers, and artisans of almost every other craft. There were also separate guilds for specialized groups of merchants, such as dealers in silk or money (banking).

✓**Reading Check** **Identifying** List three physical characteristics of medieval cities.

Medieval Christianity and Culture

MAIN IDEA The Catholic Church had political as well as religious power.

HISTORY & YOU What conflicts could you predict between kings and popes? Read about the power of the medieval Church.

Since the fifth century, the popes of the Catholic Church had claimed supremacy over the affairs of the Church. They had also gained control of territories in central Italy that came to be known as the **Papal States.** This control kept the popes involved in political matters, often at the expense of their spiritual duties.

The Papal Monarchy

During the Early Middle Ages, the Church became increasingly involved in the feudal system. Chief officials of the Church, such as bishops and abbots, came to hold their offices as grants from nobles. As vassals, they were obligated to carry out feudal services, including military duties. Lords often chose their vassals from other noble families for political reasons.

By the eleventh century, Church leaders realized the need to be free from the interference of lords in the appointment of Church officials. **Pope Gregory VII** decided to fight this interference. Elected pope in 1073, he was convinced that he had been chosen by God to reform the Church. To pursue this aim, Gregory claimed that he—the pope—was truly God's "vicar on earth" and that the pope's authority extended over all the Christian world, including its rulers. He also asserted the right of the Church to appoint clergy and run its own affairs. If rulers did not accept this, the pope would remove them.

Gregory VII and **Henry IV,** the king of Germany, disagreed about these claims. For many years, German kings had appointed high-ranking clerics, especially bishops, as their vassals in order to use them as administrators. Without them, the king could not hope to maintain power over the powerful German nobles.

In 1075, Pope Gregory issued a decree forbidding high-ranking clerics from receiving their offices from lay (secular) leaders. Although Henry IV opposed the pope's actions, the new papal policy ultimately won out.

The popes of the twelfth century did not give up the reform ideals of Pope Gregory VII, and they were even more inclined to strengthen papal power and build a strong administrative system. During the papacy of Pope Innocent III in the thirteenth century, the Catholic Church reached the height of its political power. Innocent III's actions were those of a man who believed that he, the pope, was the supreme judge of European affairs. For example, he forced the king of France, Philip Augustus, to take back his wife and queen after Philip had tried to have his marriage annulled.

New Religious Orders

In the second half of the 1000s and the first half of the 1100s, a wave of religious enthusiasm seized Europe. This movement led to a rise in the number of monasteries and the emergence of new monastic orders. Both men and women joined religious orders in increasing numbers.

In the 1000s, an important new order was the Cistercian order. It was founded in 1098 by a group of monks who were unhappy with the lack of discipline at their own Benedictine monastery. Cistercian monastacism spread rapidly from southern France into the rest of Europe.

The Cistercians played a major role in developing a new, activistic spiritual model for twelfth-century Europe. While Benedictine monks spent hours inside the monastery in personal prayer, the Cistercians took their religion to the people outside the monastery. Saint Bernard of Clairvaux embodied the new spiritual ideal of Cistercian monasticism: "Arise, soldier of Christ, arise! Get up off the ground and return to the battle from which you have fled! Fight more boldly after your flight, and triumph in glory!"

Women were also actively involved in the spiritual movements of the age. The number of women joining religious houses grew dramatically. In the High Middle Ages, most nuns were from the ranks of the landed aristocracy. Female intellectuals found convents a haven for their activities. Most of the learned women of the Middle Ages, especially in Germany, were nuns. This was true of **Hildegard of Bingen,** who became abbess of a religious house for females in western Germany.

In the 1200s two new religious orders emerged. The Franciscans and the Dominicans had a strong impact on the lives of ordinary people.

The Franciscans were founded by **Saint Francis of Assisi.** Francis was born to a wealthy Italian merchant family in Assisi. After having been captured and imprisoned during a local war, he had a series of dramatic spiritual experiences. These experiences led him to abandon all worldly goods and material pursuits and to live and preach in poverty, working and begging for his food. His simplicity, joyful nature, and love for others soon attracted a band of followers.

The Franciscans became very popular. They lived among the people, preaching repentance and aiding the poor. They also undertook missionary work in all parts of Europe and even in the Muslim world.

The Dominican order was founded by a Spanish priest, Dominic de Guzmán. Dominic wanted to defend Church teachings from heresy—the denial of basic Church doctrines. Heretical movements became especially widespread in southern France. Dominic believed that a new religious order of men who lived lives of poverty and were capable of preaching effectively would best be able to attack heresy.

The Church's desire to have a method of discovering and dealing with heretics led to the creation of a court called the **Inquisition,** or Holy Office. This court developed a regular procedure to find and try heretics. The Dominicans became especially well known for their roles as examiners of people suspected of heresy.

Popular Religion

The Church of the High Middle Ages was a crucial part of ordinary people's lives from birth to death. The sacraments, such as baptism, marriage, and the Eucharist (Communion), were seen as means for receiving God's grace and were necessary for salvation. Since only the clergy could administer the rites, people depended on them to achieve this goal.

Other Church practices were also important to ordinary people. One practice involved the veneration of saints. Saints were men and women who were considered especially holy and who had achieved a special position in Heaven. Saints were able to ask for favors for people who prayed to them, and they were very popular with all Christians.

Jesus Christ's apostles, of course, were recognized throughout Europe as saints. There were also numerous local saints who were of special significance to a single area. The Italians, for example, had Saint Nicholas, the patron saint of children, who is known today as Santa Claus.

Medieval Christians also believed that a pilgrimage to a holy shrine produced a spiritual benefit. The greatest shrine and the most difficult to reach was Jerusalem.

In Europe, two pilgrim centers were especially popular in the High Middle Ages: **Rome,** which contained the relics of Saints Peter and Paul, and the town of Santiago de Compostela, supposedly the site of the tomb of the apostle James. Local attractions, such as shrines dedicated to the Blessed Virgin Mary, also became pilgrimage centers.

Architecture

Pilgrimages and the influence of the Church led to an explosion of church building in medieval Europe. In the late Roman Empire, churches were built in the basilica style—a rectangular building with a flat ceiling and a wooden roof.

By the eleventh and twelfth centuries churches were built in the Romanesque style. Romanesque style used stone arched roofs called barrel vaults. Because stone roofs were heavy, massive pillars and walls were required to support them.

This left little space for windows, so Romanesque churches were dark.

PEOPLE *in* HISTORY

Hildegard of Bingen
1098–1179 Medieval Abbess

Hildegard was a weak and sickly child. From an early age, she received mystical vision: "I saw much, and related some of the things seen to others, who would inquire with astonishment, whence such things might come. . . . I would relate future things, which I saw as if present." When she was 43, the Church confirmed the authenticity of her visions. With Church approval, she recorded 26 prophecies in her work *Scivias* (Know the Way). Powerful men, including kings and popes, sought her advice. About 1147 Hildegard founded a new convent, where she continued to record her visions and write on many topics. She also composed lyric poems and music. Although never formally canonized, she is considered a saint by the Catholic Church. **Why did powerful men seek Hildegard's advice?**

St. Francis of Assisi
1182–1226 Medieval Monk

Although Francis of Assisi is associated with a life of poverty, humility, and devotion to the example of Jesus, he did not start out that way. As a youth he was handsome and fun-loving with a fondness for fancy clothes and popular songs. He even fought bravely in a war before being captured and imprisoned. However, his sympathies were always with the poor. On one occasion he embraced a poor, disfigured leper and gave him all the money he had. On a pilgrimage to Rome he emptied his money pouch at the tomb of St. Peter, giving it all to the poor and exchanging his fancy clothes with those of a beggar. His humility and generosity have made him one of the Catholic Church's most beloved saints. **With whom did Francis of Assisi sympathize?**

Gothic Architecture

▼ St. Vitus Cathedral, Prague

A Gothic vault, or arched ceiling, uses diagonal, pointed ribs to hold the masonry.

Decorative pinnacles

Stained glass windows provide a play of light and color throughout the day. Pointed arches draw worshipers' eyes upward, toward God.

Flying buttresses support the heavy vaulted ceiling, allowing for a higher ceiling and more windows to bring natural light into the expansive interior.

St. Etienne Cathedral, Bourges, France ▲

DOCUMENT-BASED QUESTIONS

1. **Locating** Where are flying buttresses located?
2. **Making Inferences** What role might stained glass windows play in addition to providing light and color in the cathedral?

A new style, called Gothic, appeared in the 1100s and was brought to perfection in the 1200s. The Gothic cathedral remains one of the greatest artistic triumphs of the High Middle Ages. Two basic innovations made Gothic cathedrals possible.

One innovation was the replacement of the round barrel vault of Romanesque churches with a combination of ribbed vaults and pointed arches. This change enabled builders to make Gothic churches higher than Romanesque churches.

Another technical innovation was the flying buttress—a heavy, arched support of stone built onto the outside of the walls. Flying buttresses made it possible to distribute the weight of a church's vaulted ceilings outward and down. This eliminated the heavy walls needed in Romanesque churches. Gothic cathedrals were built, then, with relatively thin walls, which could be filled with magnificent stained glass windows. These windows depict both religious scenes and scenes from daily life. Light coming through the windows was a symbol of the divine light of God.

Universities

The university of today is a product of the High Middle Ages. The word *university* comes from the Latin word *universitas*, meaning **"corporation"** or "guild." Medieval universities were educational guilds that produced educated individuals. Kings, popes, and princes thought it honorable to found new universities. By 1500, Europe had 80 universities.

The first European university appeared in Bologna (buh•LOH•nyuh), Italy. The first university in northern Europe was the University of Paris. In the second half of the 1100s, a number of students and masters (teachers) left Paris and started their own university at Oxford, England.

Students began their studies with the traditional liberal arts curriculum, or course of study, consisting of grammar, rhetoric, logic, arithmetic, geometry, music, and astronomy. Teaching was done by a lecture method. The word *lecture* is derived from Latin and means "to read." Before the development of the printing press in the 1400s, books were so expensive that few students could afford them. Teachers read from a basic text, adding their own explanations.

After completing the liberal arts curriculum, a student could study law, medicine, or theology. Theology—the study of religion and God—was the most highly regarded subject of the medieval university.

Vernacular Literature

Used in the Church and schools, Latin was the universal language of medieval Europe. However, in the 1100s, new literature was being written in the vernacular—the language of everyday speech in a particular region, such as Spanish, French, English, and German.

Perhaps the most popular vernacular literature of the 1100s was troubadour poetry. Another type of vernacular literature was the *chanson de geste,* or heroic epic. The finest example was the *Song of Roland,* which was written in French around 1100.

✓**Reading Check** **Explaining** Why were most university courses taught as lecture classes?

The Late Middle Ages

MAIN IDEA Wars, disease, and turmoil in the Church brought changes in the 1300s.

HISTORY & YOU How do you react to setbacks? Read about the Late Middle Ages.

The Middle Ages in Europe had reached a high point in the thirteenth century. In the fourteenth century, some disastrous changes took place. Especially catastrophic was the Black Death, the most devastating natural disaster in European history.

The Black Death

Bubonic plague was the most common form of the Black Death. It was spread by black rats infested with fleas carrying a deadly bacterium. Italian merchants brought the plague with them from Kaffa, on the Black Sea, to the island of Sicily in October 1347. The plague had spread to parts of southern Italy and southern France by the end of 1347.

Usually, the path of the Black Death followed trade routes. In 1348 and 1349, the plague spread through France, the Low Countries (modern Belgium, Luxembourg, and the Netherlands), and Germany. It ravaged England in 1349 and expanded to northern Europe and Scandinavia. Eastern Europe and Russia were affected by 1351.

Out of a total European population of 75 million, possibly as many as 38 million people died of the plague between 1347 and 1351. Especially hard hit were Italy's crowded cities, where 50 to 60 percent of the people died. In England and Germany, entire villages disappeared.

One observer wrote that "father abandoned child, wife [abandoned] husband, one brother [abandoned] another, for the plague seemed to strike through breath and sight. And so they died. And no one could be found to bury the dead, for money, or friendship."

The death of so many people in the 1300s had severe economic consequences. Trade declined, and a shortage of workers caused a dramatic rise in the price of labor. At the same time, the decline in the number of people lowered the demand for food.

This resulted in falling prices. Landlords were now paying more for labor while their incomes from rents were declining. Some peasants bargained with their lords to pay rent instead of owing services. This change freed them from serfdom, an institution that had been declining throughout the High Middle Ages.

The Decline of Church Power

The popes of the Roman Catholic Church reached the height of their power in the 1200s. Then, in the 1300s, a series of problems led to a decline in the Church's political and spiritual position.

By the end of the 1200s, European kings had grown unwilling to accept papal claims of supremacy. The struggle between Pope Boniface VIII and King Philip IV of France had serious consequences for the papacy.

After the pope's death, Philip engineered the election of a French pope in 1305, who took up residence in **Avignon** (a•veen•YOHN), in southern France.

From 1305 to 1377, the popes lived in Avignon. Sentiments against the papacy grew during this time. The pope was the bishop of Rome, and it seemed improper that he should reside in Avignon, not Rome. Perceiving the decline in papal prestige, Pope Gregory XI returned to Rome in 1377 but soon died. After his death, a group of Italian cardinals elected an Italian pope, while a group of French cardinals elected a French pope.

The existence of two popes caused the Great Schism, which lasted from 1378 to 1417. It divided Europe. France and its allies supported the French pope in Avignon. England and England's allies supported the pope in Rome.

INFOGRAPHICS

Hundred Years' War

Joan of Arc announcing her mission to Charles VII

Joan of Arc's claims to mysterious visions led to her greatest successes. She predicted that the French army would suffer a major defeat. When that happened, officials began to take her seriously. She was taken to King Charles VII, who disguised himself to test her. She had never seen him before, yet she picked him out of a group without hesitation. When the king offered her a sword, she said she wanted the sword that mysterious voices told her was buried behind the altar of a nearby church. It was found exactly where she said it would be. However, after her capture by the English, Joan's claims of visions worked against her. Many people believed that only witches had visions, and witches were heretics. Her pious conduct at the stake moved witnesses to tears. Few doubted that she died a faithful Christian.

DOCUMENT-BASED QUESTIONS

1. **Identifying** What did Joan of Arc envision buried behind an altar?
2. **Drawing Conclusions** Based on the map, when did the tide begin to turn in favor of the French during the Hundred Years' War?

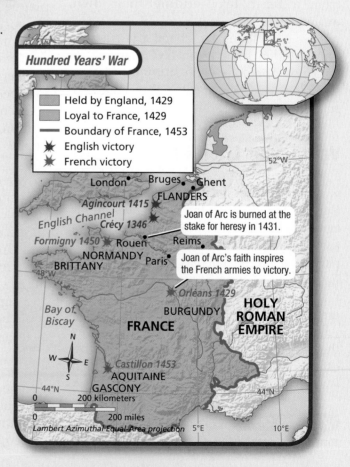

Hundred Years' War

- Held by England, 1429
- Loyal to France, 1429
- Boundary of France, 1453
- ✸ English victory
- ✸ French victory

London • Bruges • Ghent
FLANDERS
Agincourt 1415
English Channel   Crécy 1346
Formigny 1450 ✸ Rouen   Reims •
NORMANDY   Paris •
BRITTANY
52°W
48°W

Joan of Arc is burned at the stake for heresy in 1431.

Joan of Arc's faith inspires the French armies to victory.

✸ Orléans 1429

Bay of Biscay
BURGUNDY
FRANCE
HOLY ROMAN EMPIRE

✸ Castillon 1453
AQUITAINE
44°N   GASCONY   44°N

0   200 kilometers
0   200 miles
Lambert Azimuthal Equal-Area projection   5°E   10°E

The pope was widely believed to be the true leader of Christendom. When each line of popes denounced the other as the Antichrist (one who opposes Christ), people's faith in both the papacy and the Church was undermined. Although the schism was finally ended in 1417, the Church had lost much of its political and spiritual authority.

Political Crisis and Recovery

Plague, economic crisis, and the decline of the Catholic Church were not the only problems of the Late Middle Ages. War and political instability must also be added to the list. The Hundred Years' War between England and France, which lasted from 1337 to 1453, was the most violent struggle during this period. It also proved to be an important turning point in the nature of warfare. France's heavily armed noble cavalrymen, or knights, viewed foot soldiers as social inferiors. Although the English relied heavily on armed cavalry too, they also relied more on foot soldiers. English soldiers were armed, not only with pikes, but with longbows. The longbow had greater striking power, longer range, and more rapid firing speed than the crossbow—formerly the weapon of choice. At the battles of Crécy and Agincourt, the English longbows struck down the French knights. It took the efforts of a simple peasant girl, Joan of Arc, to help the French armies and finally bring an end to the war.

In the fourteenth century, France, England, and other European states faced serious problems. In the fifteenth century, recovery set in as new rulers in Europe attempted to reestablish the centralized power of monarchies. Some historians have spoken of these reestablished states as the **new monarchies.** This term applies especially to the monarchies of France, England, and Spain at the end of the 1400s. For example, the armies of Ferdinand and Isabella recaptured southern Spain from the Moors in 1492. This made Spain a strong monarchial state and an important power in European affairs.

Unlike France, England, and Spain, the Holy Roman Empire did not develop a strong monarchical authority. The failures of German emperors in the 1200s had made Germany a land of hundreds of independent states.

In Eastern Europe, rulers also found it difficult to centralize their states. Religious differences troubled the area as Roman Catholics, Eastern Orthodox Christians, and other groups confronted one another. Since the thirteenth century, Russia had been under the domination of the Mongols. Gradually, the princes of Moscow rose to prominence. Under the great prince Ivan III, a new Russian state was born.

✓ Reading Check **Explaining** Why were popes criticized for living in Avignon?

Vocabulary

1. **Explain** the significance of: technology, manor, serf, Venice, money economy, commercial capitalism, Papal States, Pope Gregory VII, Henry IV, Hildegard of Bingen, Francis of Assisi, Inquisition, Rome, corporation, Avignon, new monarchies.

Main Ideas

2. **Explain** how the new crop rotation increased food production.

3. **Describe** the new religious orders created during the Middle Ages.

4. **List** the economic and social effects of the Black Death.

Critical Thinking

5. **The BIG Idea** **Determining Cause and Effect** What were some major results of farming improvements and the revival of trade in the Middle Ages?

6. **Compare and Contrast** Use a table like the one below to note the differences between the Romanesque and Gothic styles of church architecture.

Romanesque	Gothic

7. **Analyzing Visuals** Imagine yourself standing inside the Gothic cathedral shown on page 138. How would you describe the look and feel of the interior?

Writing About History

8. **Persuasive Writing** Imagine you are a trader doing business at the beginning of the money economy. Write a letter addressed to other traders convincing them to convert to a money system from bartering.

History ONLINE

For help with the concepts in this section of *Glencoe World History—Modern Times,* go to glencoe.com and click Study Central.

The Black Death

The Black Death spread throughout Europe from 1347 to 1351. The disease wiped out nearly half of Europe's population. Many towns and villages lost most of their population, and some completely disappeared. There were three versions of the disease that infected the population, the most well-known of these being the bubonic plague. Flea-infested rats aboard trading ships carried the disease along trade routes and throughout the continent. As the fleas jumped to humans, the pandemic began.

The bubonic plague hit urban areas hardest, where crowded conditions and poor sanitation helped spread disease.

Disposal of bodies became a nightmarish problem. Communal graves became common, as was disposal in rivers.

There was no garbage collection or sanitation. All forms of refuse were simply thrown into the street, aiding the breeding of disease.

ESCAPING DEATH

Many people believed the impure air carried the disease. Those who could afford it escaped to the countryside. They boarded up their homes and either left their sick loved ones in the care of servants, or just left them inside. Still others isolated themselves in their homes in hopes of avoiding infection. The poor had no means of escape. They lived with and cared for their sick. Because they were in close quarters, the poor often fell victim to the disease themselves.

The plague terrified people. It was not uncommon for families to abandon the sick, including husbands, wives, and children, in an attempt to save themselves.

The bubonic plague was transmitted from rats to humans by fleas.

There was no running water. People seldom bathed, so it was common for them to have lice and fleas.

Inflamed lymph node (bubo)

A Terrible Death

The Black Death was so named because of the black color of the swollen lymph nodes, called buboes, its victims experienced. They appeared in the neck, armpits, legs, and groin. Other symptoms were severe head and body aches, high fever, rapid pulse, general weakness, and vomiting of blood. Symptoms appeared within a few days of exposure; the bursting of the buboes and death followed in just a few days more.

ANALYZING VISUALS

1. **Cause and Effect** What effects of the Black Death do you think had the greatest impact on European history? Why?

2. **Comparing** How is the response to pandemics today different from the ones of the Middle Ages? Are there any similarities?

Early American Civilizations

GUIDE TO READING

The BIG Idea
Order and Security The Maya, Aztec, and Inca developed sophisticated civilizations in Mesoamerica and South America.

Content Vocabulary
• tribute (p. 147)
• quipu (p. 149)

Academic Vocabulary
• major (p. 144)
• region (p. 146)

People and Places
• Mesoamerica (p. 144)
• Tenochtitlán (p. 147)
• Yucatán Peninsula (p. 144)
• Inca (p. 148)
• Pachacuti (p. 148)
• Maya (p. 144)
• Ecuador (p. 148)
• Toltec (p. 146)
• Cuzco (p. 149)
• Aztec (p. 147)
• Machu Picchu (p. 149)

Reading Strategy
Summarizing Information As you read, create a separate chart, like the one shown here, for each of the cultures discussed in this section.

People	
Location	
Religion	
Architecture	
Year/Reason Declined	

Archaeology tells us about the ancient societies that once existed in Mesoamerica and South America. In Mesoamerica, first came the Olmec and then the Maya, who developed a sophisticated civilization. They were followed by the Toltec and the Aztec. In South America, after many early civilizations, the Inca Empire became a spectacular and well-organized empire.

Early Civilizations in Mesoamerica

MAIN IDEA The Maya and the Toltec ruled Mesoamerica for nearly nine centuries.

HISTORY & YOU How would dividing each year into 18 months affect you? Read to learn about the Maya calendar.

The Americas make up an enormous land area, stretching about 9,000 miles (more than 14,000 km) from the Arctic Ocean in the north to Cape Horn at the tip of South America. Over this vast area are many different landscapes: ice-covered lands, dense forests, fertile river valleys ideal for hunting and farming, coastlines for fishing, lush tropical forests, and hot deserts. The peoples of both North and South America created a remarkable number of different cultures. In North America, the Inuit, Mound Builders, Anasazi, Plains Indians, and Iroquois all developed flourishing societies that responded in their own unique ways to the environmental conditions that they faced. The same holds true for the inhabitants of Mesoamerica.

The Maya and the Toltec

Signs of civilization in **Mesoamerica**—a name we use for areas of Mexico and Central America that were civilized before the Spaniards arrived—appeared around 1200 B.C. with the Olmec. Located in the hot and swampy lowlands along the coast of the Gulf of Mexico south of Veracruz, the Olmec peoples farmed along the muddy riverbanks in the area. The Olmec had large cities that were centers for their religious rituals. Around 400 B.C., the Olmec civilization declined and eventually collapsed.

Later, on the **Yucatán Peninsula**, a **major** civilization arose— that of the **Maya,** which flourished between A.D. 300 and 900. It was one of the most sophisticated civilizations in the Americas. The Maya built splendid temples and pyramids and developed a complicated calendar. Maya civilization came to include much of Central America and southern Mexico.

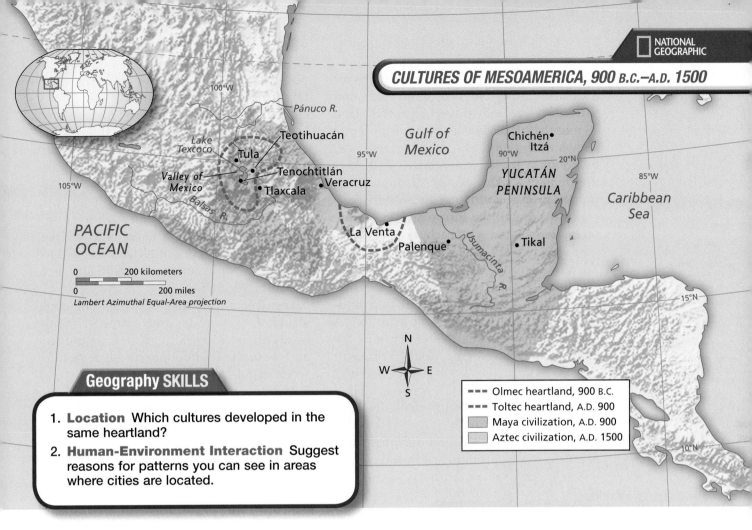

CULTURES OF MESOAMERICA, 900 B.C.–A.D. 1500

PACIFIC OCEAN

Gulf of Mexico

Caribbean Sea

YUCATÁN PENINSULA

Pánuco R.

Lake Texcoco

Teotihuacán
Tula
Tenochtitlán
Valley of Mexico
Tlaxcala
Veracruz

La Venta
Palenque
Tikal

Chichén Itzá

Usumacinta R.

Balsas R.

100°W
105°W
95°W
90°W
85°W
20°N
15°N
10°N

0   200 kilometers
0   200 miles
Lambert Azimuthal Equal-Area projection

N
W   E
S

- - - Olmec heartland, 900 B.C.
- - - Toltec heartland, A.D. 900
⬛ Maya civilization, A.D. 900
⬜ Aztec civilization, A.D. 1500

Geography SKILLS

1. **Location** Which cultures developed in the same heartland?
2. **Human-Environment Interaction** Suggest reasons for patterns you can see in areas where cities are located.

Maya cities were built around a central pyramid topped by a shrine to the gods. Nearby were other temples, palaces, and a sacred ball court. Some scholars believe that urban centers such as Tikal (in present-day Guatemala) may have had as many as 100,000 inhabitants.

Maya civilization was composed of city-states, each governed by a hereditary ruling class. These Maya city-states were often at war with each other. Ordinary soldiers who were captured in battle became slaves. Captured nobles and war leaders were used for human sacrifice.

Rulers of the Maya city-states claimed to be descended from the gods. The Maya rulers were helped by nobles and a class of scribes who may also have been priests. Maya society also included townspeople who were skilled artisans, officials, and merchants. Most of the Maya people were peasant farmers.

Crucial to Maya civilization was its belief that all of life was in the hands of the divine powers. The name of their supreme god was Itzamna (eet•SAWM•nuh) or "Lizard House." Gods were ranked in order of importance. Some, like the jaguar god of night, were evil rather than good.

Like other ancient civilizations in Meso-america, the Maya practiced human sacrifice as a way to appease the gods. Human sacrifices were also used for special ceremonial occasions. When a male heir was presented to the throne, war captives were tortured and then beheaded. In A.D. 790, one Maya ruler took his troops into battle to gain prisoners for a celebration honoring his son.

The Maya created a sophisticated writing system based on hieroglyphs, or pictures. Maya hieroglyphs remained a mystery to scholars for centuries. Then, modern investigators discovered that many passages contained symbols that recorded dates in the Maya calendar known as the Long Count. This calendar was based on a belief in cycles of creation and destruction. According to the Maya, our present world was created in 3114 B.C.

History ONLINE

Student Web Activity— Visit glencoe.com and complete the activity about early civilizations in the Americas.

The world is scheduled to complete its downward cycle on December 23, 2012.

The Maya used two different systems for measuring time. One was based on a solar calendar of 365 days, divided into 18 months of 20 days each, with an extra 5 days at the end. The other system was based on a sacred calendar of 260 days divided into 13 weeks of 20 days. Only trained priests could read and use this calendar to foretell the future and know the omens associated with each day.

The Maya civilization in the central Yucatán Peninsula eventually began to decline. Explanations for the decline include invasion, internal revolt, or a natural disaster such as a volcanic eruption. A more recent theory is that overuse of the land led to reduced crop yields. Whatever the case, Maya cities were abandoned and covered by dense jungle growth. They were not rediscovered until the nineteenth and twentieth centuries.

As the Maya civilization declined, new peoples rose to prominence in the central

part of Mexico. Most significant were the **Toltec.** The Toltec Empire reached its high point between A.D. 950 and 1150. The capital of the Toltec Empire was at Tula, built on a high ridge northwest of present-day Mexico City. The Toltec had a flourishing agriculture, which enabled Tula to support a population of between 40,000 to 60,000 people. Another 60,000 people lived in the surrounding territory. The city itself was between 5 and 6 square miles (13 to 16 sq. km). The Toltec were a fierce and warlike people who extended their conquests into the Maya lands of Guatemala and the northern Yucatán.

The Toltec were also builders who constructed pyramids and palaces. They brought metalworking to Mesoamerica and were the first people in the **region** to work in gold, silver, and copper.

They controlled the upper Yucatán Peninsula from another capital at Chichén Itzá for several centuries, beginning around A.D. 900. The Toltec Empire began to decline around A.D. 1125 as a result of fighting

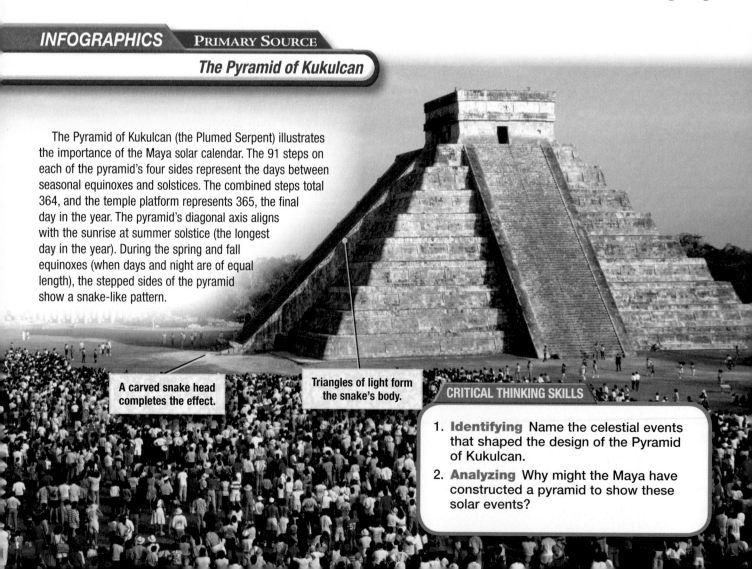

The Pyramid of Kukulcan

The Pyramid of Kukulcan (the Plumed Serpent) illustrates the importance of the Maya solar calendar. The 91 steps on each of the pyramid's four sides represent the days between seasonal equinoxes and solstices. The combined steps total 364, and the temple platform represents 365, the final day in the year. The pyramid's diagonal axis aligns with the sunrise at summer solstice (the longest day in the year). During the spring and fall equinoxes (when days and night are of equal length), the stepped sides of the pyramid show a snake-like pattern.

A carved snake head completes the effect.

Triangles of light form the snake's body.

CRITICAL THINKING SKILLS

1. **Identifying** Name the celestial events that shaped the design of the Pyramid of Kukulcan.

2. **Analyzing** Why might the Maya have constructed a pyramid to show these solar events?

among different groups in Tula. Around 1170, the city was sacked and much of it burned. There was no single ruling group for nearly 200 years. The Aztec Empire then gained control and carried on many Toltec traditions.

The Aztec

The origins of the **Aztec** are uncertain. Sometime during the 1100s, however, they began a long migration that brought them to the Valley of Mexico. They eventually established their capital, beginning in 1325, at **Tenochtitlán** (tay•NAWCH•teet•LAHN), on an island in the middle of Lake Texcoco, now the location of Mexico City.

For the next 100 years, the Aztec built their city. They constructed temples, other public buildings, and houses. They built roadways of stone across Lake Texcoco to the north, south, and west, linking the many islands to the mainland. While they were building their capital city, the Aztec consolidated their rule over much of what is modern Mexico. The new kingdom was not a centralized state but a collection of semi-independent territories that local lords governed. The Aztec ruler supported these rulers in return for **tribute,** goods or money paid by conquered peoples to their conquerors.

By 1500, as many as 4 million Aztec lived in the Valley of Mexico and the surrounding valleys. Power in the Aztec state was vested in the hands of the monarch, who claimed to be descended from the gods. A council of lords and government officials assisted the Aztec ruler.

The nobility, the elite of society, held positions in the government. Male children in noble families were sent to temple schools, which stressed military training. Once they became adults, males selected a career in the military service, the government bureaucracy, or the priesthood. As a reward for their services, nobles received large estates from the government.

The rest of the population consisted of commoners, indentured workers, and slaves. Indentured workers were landless laborers who contracted to work on the nobles' estates. Slaves worked in the households of the wealthy. Male and female slaves were sold in the markets.

Most people were commoners, and many commoners were farmers. Farmers built *chinampas.* These were swampy islands crisscrossed by canals that provided water for their crops. The canals also provided easy travel to local markets. Aztec merchants were also active traders. Merchants exported and traded goods made by Aztec craftspeople from imported raw materials. In exchange for their goods, the traders obtained tropical feathers, cacao beans, animal skins, and gold.

Though considered not equal to men, Aztec women could own and inherit property and enter into contracts, something not often allowed in other world cultures at the time. Women were expected to work in the home, weave textiles, and raise children. However, some were also trained to become priestesses.

Like other peoples in the Americas and around the world, the Aztec believed in many gods. Aztec religion was based on a belief in an unending struggle between the forces of good and evil. This struggle had created and destroyed four worlds, or suns. People believed they were now living in the time of the fifth sun. This world, too, was destined to end with the destruction of Earth by earthquakes. To postpone the day of reckoning, the Aztec practiced human sacrifice. They believed they could delay the final destruction of their world by appeasing the sun god Huitzilopochtli with sacrifices.

Aztec religion had a significant influence on their art and architecture. At the center of Tenochtitlán was the sacred district, dominated by a massive pyramid dedicated to Huitzilopochtli. At the top was a platform containing shrines to the gods and an altar for performing human sacrifices.

With the help of two other city-states, Tenochtitlán formed a Triple Alliance. This alliance enabled the Aztec to dominate an empire that included much of today's Mexico, from the Atlantic to the Pacific and as far south as the Guatemalan border.

✓ **Reading Check** **Describing** How did the Maya measure time?

South American Civilizations

MAIN IDEA The Inca civilization dominated South America.

HISTORY & YOU How do you keep records? Read about the Inca's record-keeping system.

As in Mesoamerica, great civilizations flourished in early South America. The people of the Chavin, Nazca, and Moche cultures lived before the Inca gained power in South America. The cities, buildings, and artifacts these peoples left behind provide clues about their cultures.

In the fifteenth century, another remarkable civilization—that of the **Inca**—flourished in South America. In the 1440s, under the leadership of the powerful ruler **Pachacuti,** the Inca launched a campaign of conquest that eventually brought the entire region under their control.

Pachacuti and his immediate successors, Topa Inca and Huayna Inca (the word *Inca* means "ruler"), extended the boundaries of the Inca Empire as far as **Ecuador,** central Chile, and the edge of the Amazon basin. The empire included perhaps 12 million people. At the top was the emperor, who was believed to be descended from Inti, the sun god.

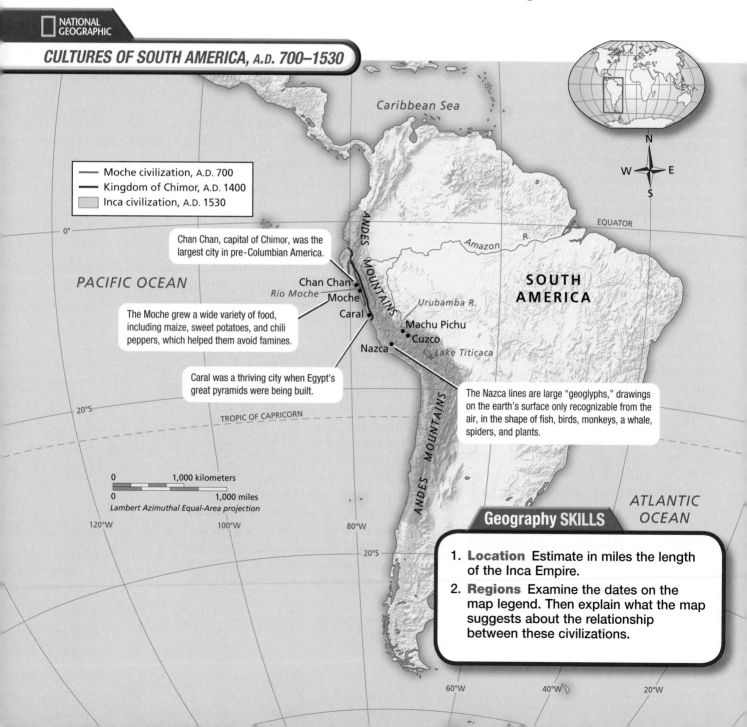

NATIONAL GEOGRAPHIC

CULTURES OF SOUTH AMERICA, A.D. 700–1530

— Moche civilization, A.D. 700
— Kingdom of Chimor, A.D. 1400
▢ Inca civilization, A.D. 1530

Chan Chan, capital of Chimor, was the largest city in pre-Columbian America.

The Moche grew a wide variety of food, including maize, sweet potatoes, and chili peppers, which helped them avoid famines.

Caral was a thriving city when Egypt's great pyramids were being built.

The Nazca lines are large "geoglyphs," drawings on the earth's surface only recognizable from the air, in the shape of fish, birds, monkeys, a whale, spiders, and plants.

Caribbean Sea

PACIFIC OCEAN

SOUTH AMERICA

ANDES MOUNTAINS

Amazon R.

Urubamba R.

Chan Chan
Río Moche
Moche
Caral
Machu Pichu
Cuzco
Nazca
Lake Titicaca

EQUATOR
0°
20°S
TROPIC OF CAPRICORN
20°S

ATLANTIC OCEAN

0   1,000 kilometers
0   1,000 miles
Lambert Azimuthal Equal-Area projection

120°W   100°W   80°W   60°W   40°W   20°W

Geography SKILLS

1. **Location** Estimate in miles the length of the Inca Empire.
2. **Regions** Examine the dates on the map legend. Then explain what the map suggests about the relationship between these civilizations.

The Inca state was built on war, so all young men were required to serve in the Inca army. With some 200,000 members, the army was the largest and best armed in the region. Once an area was under Inca control, the local inhabitants were instructed in the Quechua (KEH•chuh•wuh) language. Control of new territories was carefully regulated. A noble of high rank was sent out to govern the new region. Local leaders could keep their posts as long as they were loyal to the Inca ruler.

Forced labor was an important feature of the state. All Inca subjects were responsible for labor service, usually for several weeks each year. Laborers, often with their entire communities, were moved according to need from one part of the country to another to take part in building projects.

One such project was a system of some 24,800 miles (around 40,000 km) of roads extending from the border of modern-day Colombia to a point south of modern-day Santiago, Chile. Two major roadways extended in a north-south direction, one through the Andes and the other along the coast, with connecting routes between them.

Inca society was highly regimented. So, too, were marriage and the lives of women. Men and women were required to select a marriage partner from within their own social groups. After marriage, women were expected to care for the children and to weave cloth. For women, there was only one alternative to a life of working in the home. Some young girls were chosen to serve as priestesses in temples.

In rural areas, the people lived chiefly by farming. In the mountains, they used terraced farms, watered by irrigation systems that carried precise amounts of water into the fields. These were planted with corn, potatoes, and other crops. The farmers' houses, built of stone or adobe with thatched roofs, were located near the fields.

The Inca were great builders. The buildings and monuments of the capital city of **Cuzco** were the wonder of early European visitors. These structures were built of close-fitting stones without mortar—the better to withstand the frequent earthquakes in the area. This technique can be seen at the ruins of the abandoned city of **Machu Picchu** (MAH•CHOO PEE•CHOO). Machu Picchu, elevation 8,000 feet (2,400 m), was built on a lofty hilltop surrounded by mountain peaks far above the Urubamba River. It contained only about 200 buildings.

The Inca had no writing system. Instead, they kept records using a system of knotted strings called the **quipu**. The lack of a fully developed writing system, however, did not prevent the Inca from attaining a high level of cultural achievement.

✓**Reading Check** **Describing** What technology helped the Inca farm in the mountains?

SECTION 2 REVIEW

Vocabulary
1. **Explain** the significance of: Mesoamerica, Yucatán Peninsula, major, Maya, Toltec, region, Aztec, Tenochtitlán, tribute, Inca, Pachacuti, Ecuador, Cuzco, Machu Picchu, quipu.

Main Ideas
2. **List** some accomplishments of the Maya. Use a chart like the one below to make your list.

Maya Accomplishments
1.
2.
3.

3. **Summarize** the role of women in the Aztec Empire.

4. **Summarize** the different roles in Inca society.

Critical Thinking
5. **The BIG Idea** **Evaluating** Why was trade important to early Mesoamerican civilizations?

6. **Assessing** How did Pachacuti's system of political organization contribute to the success of the Inca Empire?

7. **Analyzing Visuals** Examine the pyramid on page 146. What about it indicates the presence of a sophisticated civilization?

Writing About History
8. **Expository Writing** Write an essay about how Pachacuti ruled the Inca Empire. You may use outside sources for research. Your essay should describe Pachacuti's achievements as well as his failures.

History ONLINE

For help with the concepts in this section of *Glencoe World History—Modern Times*, go to glencoe.com and click Study Central.

What Was the Role of Religion in Aztec Society?

How did the Aztec worship their gods? Religion was an important feature of Aztec life. Prayers, legends, and ceremonies at great temples were all part of Aztec religious practice.

How did outsiders view Aztec religion? After their arrival in Mexico in 1519, the Spanish were shocked by the Aztec religious rituals. The Spaniards immediately worked to convert the Aztec to Christianity.

The Aztec and the Spanish had extremely different viewpoints about Aztec religion. Read the passages and study the illustration to learn more about the role religion played in Aztec society.

SOURCE 1

The Aztec king Ahuizotl, who ruled from 1486 to 1502, offered the following prayer to the god Huitzilopochtli while celebrating a successful military campaign.

O almighty, powerful lord of All Created
   Things,
You who give us life, and whose **vassals**[1] and
   slaves we are,
Lord of the Day and of the Night, of the Wind
   and the Water,
Whose strength keeps us alive! I give you
   infinite thanks
For having brought me back to your city of
   Mexico
With the victory which you granted me.
   I have returned. . . .
Since you did not frown upon my extreme
   youth
Or my lack of strength or the weakness of
   my chest,
You have subjected those remote and
   barbarous nations
To my power. You did all of these things!
   All is yours!
All was won to give you honor and praise!
Therefore, O powerful and heroic
   Huitzilopochtli,
You have brought us back to this place which
   was only water
Before, which was enclosed by our ancestors,
And where they built our city.

SOURCE 2

Spanish conquistador Hernán Cortés wrote the following description of a temple in the Aztec capital in a 1520 letter to the Spanish king, Charles V.

Three halls are in this grand temple, which contain the principal idols; these are of wonderful extent and height, and admirable workmanship, adorned with figures sculptured in stone and wood; leading from the halls are chapels with very small doors . . . In these chapels are the images of idols, although, as I have before said, many of them are also found on the outside; the principal ones, in which the people have greatest faith and confidence, I **precipitated**[2] from their pedestals, and cast them down the steps of the temple, purifying the chapels in which they had stood, as they were all polluted with human blood, shed ill the sacrifices. In the place of these I put images of Our Lady and the Saints, which excited not a little feeling in **Moctezuma**[3] and the inhabitants, who at first **remonstrated**[4], declaring that if my proceedings were known throughout the country, the people would rise against me; for they believed that their idols bestowed on them all **temporal**[5] good, and if they permitted them to be ill-treated, they would be angry and without their gifts, and by this means the people would be deprived of the fruits of the earth and perish with famine. . . .

---

[1] **vassals:** people in a subordinate position
[2] **precipitated:** threw down

[3] **Moctezuma:** the Aztec king in 1520
[4] **remonstrated:** vocally protested

▲ Tenochtitlán priests sacrifice warriors to the sun god in this Aztec drawing dated after 1519.

Human sacrifice was a central part of Aztec religion. The Aztec believed their deities, such as the war god Huitzilopochtli, demanded a steady supply of human sacrifices. At the dedication of the great pyramid of Tenochtitlán, for example, Aztec priests sacrificed more than 20,000 people. Most of the Aztec's sacrifice victims were prisoners captured from enemy tribes. For this purpose, Aztec warriors were trained to capture, rather than kill, their enemies in battle.

The above image is an Aztec drawing of a sacrifice ritual. During these ceremonies, priests cut out the victim's heart and held it up to the sun as an offering. As shown in the image, the victim's body was then thrown down the steps of the pyramid temple.

[5] **temporal:** relating to earthly life

DOCUMENT-BASED QUESTIONS

1. **Explaining** Why did King Ahuizotl pray to the god Huitzilopochtli?

2. **Identifying Points of View** How did Cortés's background influence his actions in the Aztec temple?

3. **Drawing Conclusions** What does this image reveal about the Aztec's relationship with their gods?

4. **Contrasting** How would Ahuizotl's description of the scene in the above image have contrasted from Cortés's description of the same image?

5. **Synthesizing** On what points do Ahuizotl and Cortés agree in their description of Aztec religious beliefs?

6. **Recognizing Bias** Consider the question "What was the role of religion in Aztec society?" How would an Aztec have answered that question differently than a Spaniard? Which answer do you think would have been most similar to your own answer to the question?

You can study anywhere, anytime by downloading quizzes and flash cards to your PDA from glencoe.com.

EUROPE in the Middle Ages

- Farming inventions and efficient use of land contributed to population growth.
- As trade grew, cities expanded and became manufacturing and trade centers.
- The Catholic Church played a dominant role in the lives of people during the Middle Ages.
- New technological innovations during the High Middle Ages led to the building of Gothic cathedrals, one of the period's great artistic triumphs.
- The Black Death caused major economic and social changes in the Late Middle Ages.

TRADE EXPANDED IN EUROPE

Merchants in a covered market in the 1400s

THE INCA CITY OF MACHU PICCHU

No mortar was used to build the walls at Machu Picchu.

THE AMERICAS

- Unique civilizations developed as people spread through North and South America.
- Because of the variety of climate and geographic features, many different cultures emerged in the Americas.
- In Mesoamerica, the Olmec, Maya, Toltec, and Aztec developed influential civilizations.
- In South America, the Inca established a sophisticated civilization, with sharp social and political divisions.

STANDARDIZED TEST PRACTICE

TEST-TAKING **TIP**

Some answer choices are better than others. Be sure you have read **all** the choices carefully before you pick your answer.

Reviewing Vocabulary

Directions: Choose the word or words that best complete the sentence.

1. A _____ was an agricultural estate that a lord ran and peasants worked.

   A castle

   B guild

   C *carruca*

   D manor

2. The term for the language of a particular region is _____.

   A vernacular

   B *chanson de geste*

   C secular

   D scholasticism

3. The Maya writing system was based on _____.

   A alphanumerics

   B hieroglyphs

   C *chinampas*

   D knotted strings

4. _____ was goods or money paid by conquered peoples to their conquerors.

   A Tribute

   B Penance

   C Tithe

   D Sacrifice

Reviewing Main Ideas

Directions: Choose the best answers to the following questions.

Section 1 *(pp. 132–141)*

5. Approximately what portion of western Europeans were serfs by 800?

   A 80 percent

   B 40 percent

   C 20 percent

   D 60 percent

6. What economic system arose during the High Middle Ages?

   A Subsistence agriculture

   B The barter system

   C Commercial capitalism

   D Mercantilism

7. Who founded the Franciscans?

   A Saint Francis of Assisi

   B Dominic de Guzmán

   C Pope Innocent III

   D Hildegard of Bingen

8. What new architectural style appeared in the twelfth century?

   A Neoclassic

   B Romanesque

   C Baroque

   D Gothic

Need Extra Help?								
If You Missed Questions . . .	1	2	3	4	5	6	7	8
Go to Page . . .	133	139	145	147	133	134	136	138

GO ON

Section 2 *(pp. 144–149)*

9. How did the Maya appease their gods?

  A Parades

  B Penance

  C Fasting

  D Human sacrifice

10. Which two cities were capitals of the Toltec Empire?

  A Tula and Chichén Itzá

  B Tikal and Tenochtitlán

  C Cuzco and Tula

  D Chichén Itzá and Tenochtitlán

11. According to Aztec religion, how many worlds had been created and destroyed?

  A 2

  B 3

  C 4

  D 5

12. What was the name of the Inca language used for instruction?

  A *Chinampas*

  B Quechua

  C Inti

  D Quipu

13. Where can Inca building techniques best be seen?

  A The Yucatán Peninsula

  B Lake Texcoco

  C Tenochtitlán

  D Machu Picchu

Critical Thinking

Directions: Choose the best answers to the following questions.

Use the following map to answer question 14.

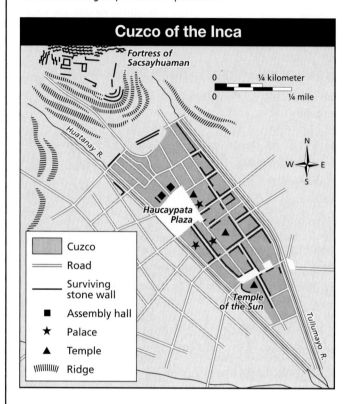

14. What do you notice about the roads leading out of Cuzco?

  A Lead out to the east only

  B Lead out in all directions

  C Lead out to the west only

  D Do not intersect at any point

15. What is one reason for the growth of medieval cities?

  A The spread of the Black Death

  B The decline of the manorial system

  C The revival of trade

  D The decline of feudalism

Need Extra Help?							
If You Missed Questions . . .	9	10	11	12	13	14	15
Go to Page . . .	145	146	147	149	149	149	134

GO ON

16. With which group did signs of civilization first appear in Mesoamerica?

   A The Olmec

   B The Maya

   C The Toltec

   D The Inca

Base your answer to question 17 on the following illustration and on your knowledge of world history.

17. What structural innovation of the Middle Ages does this drawing illustrate?

   A Barrel vaults

   B Cross vaults

   C Flying buttresses

   D Basilicas

Document-Based Questions

Directions: Analyze the document and answer the short-answer questions that follow the document. Base your answers on the document and on your knowledge of world history.

A medieval father wrote a letter to his son, who was away at university:

> *"I have recently discovered that you live dissolutely and slothfully, preferring license to restraint and play to work and strumming a guitar while the others are at their studies, whence it happens that you have read but one volume of law while your more industrious companions have read several. Wherefore I have decided to exhort you to repent utterly of your dissolute and careless ways, that you may no longer be called a waster and your shame may be turned to good repute."*

18. What are the concerns of the father?

19. What methods does the father use to motivate his son?

Extended Response

20. Throughout time people have had to adapt to their environment in order to survive. What was the relationship between the early peoples of Mesoamerica and South America and their environment?

History ONLINE

For additional test practice, use Self-Check Quizzes—Chapter 4 at **glencoe.com**.

Need Extra Help?					
If You Missed Questions . . .	16	17	18	19	20
Go to Page . . .	144	139	144	139	139

ROGER-VIOLLET/TOPHAM/THE IMAGE WORKS

SCOTT MACNEILL

Profile

Ibn Battuta: The Ultimate Road Trip

Ibn Battuta makes Marco Polo seem like a couch potato. The Arab explorer has journeyed just about everywhere in the world, covering nearly 70,000 miles over 30 years.

Battuta's first trip was a pilgrimage to Makkah from his hometown of Tangier, Morocco, in 1325. From there, he just kept going and going. First stop was Mesopotamia, and then he continued along the Silk Road in central Asia. Next was a voyage along the coast of East Africa, where he visited Ethiopia and Zanzibar. After a quick trip home to refresh himself, Battuta left to explore Constantinople, headed into Afghanistan and India, and later made the trek to China. He also explored Europe, North Africa, and finally, the kingdom of Mali.

In his journeys, Battuta didn't always travel first class. He was attacked by pirates and thieves, nearly drowned in storms at sea, kidnapped, and avoided the Black Death like, well, the plague. Battuta promises to write down the story of his epic adventures. No doubt it will be a very thick book.

VERBATIM

" Blood was pooled and the skulls of the people of the central place of Tikal were piled up. "

WORDS ON A STAIRCASE
of a 7th century pyramid in Guatemala, describing the fate of the enemies of a ruler of the Maya city of Dos Pilas

" Solomon, I have outdone thee. "

JUSTINIAN THE GREAT,
in 537, head of Byzantine Empire, comparing the magnificent church Hagia Sophia, in Constantinople, to the ancient Temple of Solomon in Israel

" Teach your tongue to say 'I do not know' and you will progress. "

MOSES MAIMONIDES,
rabbi and philosopher born in Muslim Spain in 1135

" To no man will we sell, or deny, or delay, right or justice. "

THE MAGNA CARTA,
On the powers of the English king, 1215

" Fireworks crackle, the year ends/ Spring wind wafts, and I downed cups of wine/Early New Year morning, as sun shines bright/Every household is busy replacing old with new. "

WANG ANSHI,
politician and poet, who as a minister of the Song dynasty in 11th century China, has reformed the government and created policies to help the poor

THE SOFTER SIDE OF THE VIKINGS

They loot. They pillage. And occasionally they loot *and* pillage. That's the impression most people have about Vikings. But Europe's bad boys do have their good points. Although *Viking* is the name given to those Norse who go on raids, most Norse are farmers and herders. The Norse have composed epic poems, play chess, make iron tools, and craft jewelry. They also build the greatest ships in the world. Of course, complaints about the Vikings' rude behavior are justified. After all, they have been stealing stuff from the coasts of England and Ireland for a couple of hundred years. With the Norse, it seems that you have to take the bad with the good.

THE PRINT COLLECTOR/ALAMY

Annals of Medicine

Getting sick in medieval Europe is no picnic. Here are some standard medical treatments—along with a fake one. Can you find it?

1. Herbal treatments are recommended for anything from the Black Death to insomnia. Ingredients may include urine, ground-up worms, and roasted snake skin.

2. Want relief from smallpox? Hang colored cloth around your bed.

3. Diseases, say experts, are caused by a buildup of bodily fluids (called "humors"), such as blood. Having a barber open a vein to rid you of some blood should balance the humors and bring good health.

4. Many doctors diagnose problems by a patient's astrological sign. For example, a person with a certain sign might be prone to colds or sadness.

5. To treat a cough and other lung problems, patients should set moldy chestnuts on fire and breathe in the smoke.

6. Some physicians believe physical sickness is caused by sin. Their prescription? Go on a pilgrimage and/or pray.

7. Here's an effective way to clean your teeth: Simply rub them with powder made from crushed seashells.

Answer: 5

VISUAL ARTS LIBRARY (LONDON)/ALAMY

BY THE NUMBERS

0 The number of times that rules for the use of the number zero in mathematical calculations appeared before Indian mathematician Brahmagupta put them to paper in 628 in a book called *Brahmasputha Siddhanta*

275 million The approximate world population in the year 1000

33 The average life expectancy of an English person during the Middle Ages

68.27 The average height in inches of a European during the eleventh century

MARY EVANS PICTURE LIBRARY/THE IMAGE WORKS

33 The percent of the total population of the Muslim world killed by the Black Death by the year 1349

Milestones

PUBLISHED. *THE TALE OF GENJI* in the year 1000, by Murasaki Shikibu, a Japanese noblewoman. It is the story of the son of the emperor and his romantic adventures in the royal court. Because of its length and insight into the characters, many scholars are claiming that this is the world's first novel.

BUILT. A major urban project called **MACHU PICCHU,** by Inca architects for the emperor Pachacuti, completed around 1470. Located 8,000 feet high in the Andes, it consists of about 200 buildings. About 1,200 people are expected to move into this city in the sky, many of them members of the royal family. Most impressive are the spectacular views. Location, as they say, is everything.

SUCCEEDED. SUNNI ALI by his son Sunni Baru, as emperor of the kingdom of Songhai. Through military might, Sunni Ali managed to turn that backwater nation into a vast empire. After taking power in 1464, Sunni Ali built up a powerful army and navy. When he died in 1492, he controlled much of the territory belonging to the Mali Empire. Pundits believe that Askia Muhammad Toure already has designs on Baru's office.

CRITICAL THINKING

1. **Identifying Points of View** What does the writer think about the Vikings? Explain the reasons for your answer.

2. **Speculating** Why do you think Ibn Battuta traveled so widely and for so many years?

UNIT 2

The Early Modern World 1350–1815

► Why It Matters

The modern world began during this period. Asian empires and European countries expanded their influence through exploration, which led to colonialism, trade, and conflict. By the eighteenth century, political and social revolutions resulted in new democratic nations.

CHAPTER 5 RENAISSANCE AND REFORMATION
1350–1600

CHAPTER 6 THE AGE OF EXPLORATION
1500–1800

CHAPTER 7 CRISIS AND ABSOLUTISM IN EUROPE
1550–1715

CHAPTER 8 THE MUSLIM EMPIRES
1450–1800

CHAPTER 9 THE EAST ASIAN WORLD
1400–1800

CHAPTER 10 REVOLUTION AND ENLIGHTENMENT
1550–1800

CHAPTER 11 THE FRENCH REVOLUTION
1789–1815

The Blue Mosque dominates the skyline of old İstanbul, which is located strategically on the peninsula where Europe and Asia meet.

159

CHAPTER 5

Renaissance and Reformation 1350–1600

Section 1 The Renaissance

Section 2 Ideas and Art of the Renaissance

Section 3 The Protestant Reformation

Section 4 The Spread of Protestantism

MAKING CONNECTIONS

How was architecture influenced by the Renaissance?

Tremendous advances in architecture took place during the Italian Renaissance. Among the great masterpieces was the dome of St. Peter's Basilica shown in the photo. Architect Donato Bramante began this project for Pope Julius II; however, Michelangelo completed the design of this structure. In this chapter you will learn about social, political, economic, and cultural effects of the Renaissance.

- What are some other accomplishments for which Michelangelo is famous?
- Compare and contrast the design of the dome of St. Peter's Basilica to that of more modern domes such as the U.S. Capitol.

EUROPE ▶

1350
Italian Renaissance begins

1434
Cosimo de' Medici takes control of Florence

1517
Martin Luther presents his Ninety-five Theses

1350 — 1500

THE WORLD ▶

1405
Zheng He of China begins first voyage of exploration

1518
Spanish ship carries first enslaved Africans to the Americas

1534
Henry VIII initiates
creation of Church
of England

1555
Peace of Augsburg
divides Christianity
in Germany

1600

1535
Francisco Pizarro
conquers the Inca Empire

FOLDABLES™
Study Organizer

Analyzing Analyze
how the Renaissance
and Reformation
affected various parts
of Europe. Record
your findings in a layered-look book.
Make sure you label each effect as
Renaissance or *Reformation*.

Renaissance &
Reformation

Italian States: Milan, Venice, Florence

Germany

Switzerland

Flanders

England

Italy

History ONLINE

Chapter Overview—Visit glencoe.com to preview Chapter 5.

The Renaissance

Beginning in Italy and spanning two centuries, the Renaissance emphasized secularism, awareness of ties to the ancient Greek and Roman worlds, and the ability of the individual. City-states became centers of political, economic, and social life. Machiavelli influenced political thought, and Castiglione defined what made a perfect Renaissance noble. The Renaissance affected everyone, from noble to peasant.

GUIDE TO READING

The BIG Idea

Ideas, Beliefs, and Values Between 1350 and 1550, Italian intellectuals believed they had entered a new age of human achievement.

Content Vocabulary

- urban society (p. 162)
- mercenaries (p. 164)
- secular (p. 162)
- dowry (p. 167)

Academic Vocabulary

- instability (p. 162)
- decline (p. 162)

People, Places, and Events

- Italian Renaissance (p. 162)
- Cosimo de´ Medici (p. 164)
- Leonardo da Vinci (p. 162)
- Lorenzo de´ Medici (p. 164)
- Milan (p. 163)
- Rome (p. 164)
- Venice (p. 163)
- Niccolò Machiavelli (p. 165)
- Florence (p. 163)
- Francesco Sforza (p. 164)

Reading Strategy

Categorizing Information As you read, use a web diagram like the one below to identify the major principles of Machiavelli's work *The Prince*.

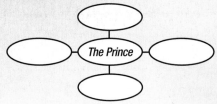

The Italian Renaissance

MAIN IDEA As the Renaissance began, three Italian city-states were the centers of Italian political, economic, and social life.

HISTORY & YOU Do you excel at more than one skill, for example, math and art? Read to learn about the Renaissance belief in individual ability.

The word *renaissance* means "rebirth." A number of people who lived in Italy between 1350 and 1550 believed that they had witnessed a rebirth of the ancient Greek and Roman worlds. To them, this rebirth marked a new age. Historians later called this period the Renaissance, or **Italian Renaissance**—a period of European history that began in Italy and spread to the rest of Europe. What are the most important characteristics of the Renaissance?

First, Renaissance Italy was largely an **urban society.** As the Middle Ages progressed, powerful city-states became the centers of Italian political, economic, and social life. Within this growing urban society, a **secular,** or worldly, viewpoint emerged as increasing wealth created new enjoyment of material things.

Second, the Renaissance was an age of recovery from the disasters of the fourteenth century—the plague, political **instability,** and a **decline** of Church power. Recovery went hand in hand with a rebirth of interest in ancient culture. Italian thinkers became aware of their own Roman past—the remains of which were to be seen all around them. They also became intensely interested in the culture that had dominated the ancient Mediterranean world. This revival affected both politics and art.

Third, a new view of human beings emerged as people in the Italian Renaissance emphasized individual ability. As Leon Battista Alberti, a fifteenth-century Italian, said, "Men can do all things if they will." A high regard for human worth and a realization of what individuals could achieve created a new social ideal. The well-rounded, universal person could achieve much in many areas. **Leonardo da Vinci** (VIHN•chee), for example, was a painter, sculptor, architect, inventor, and mathematician.

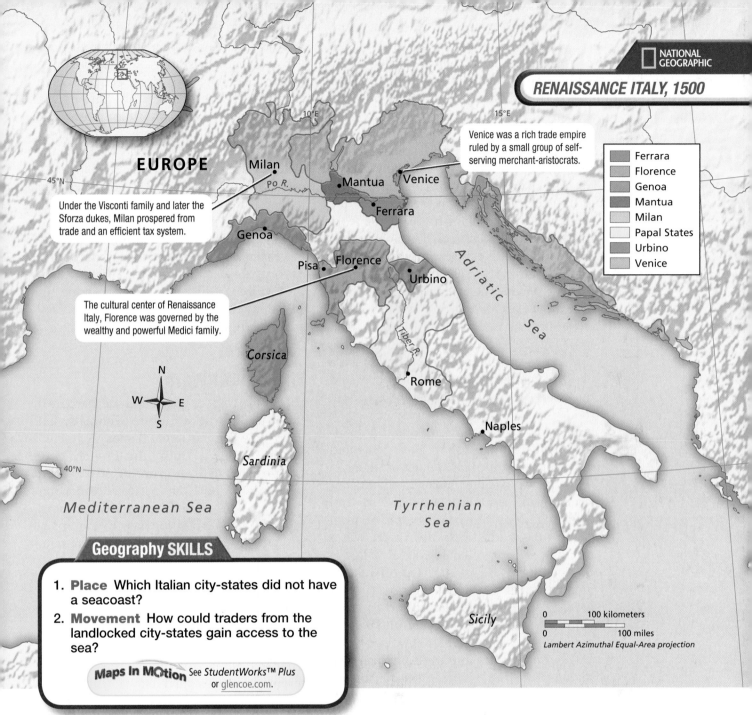

EUROPE

Venice was a rich trade empire ruled by a small group of self-serving merchant-aristocrats.

Under the Visconti family and later the Sforza dukes, Milan prospered from trade and an efficient tax system.

The cultural center of Renaissance Italy, Florence was governed by the wealthy and powerful Medici family.

Milan

Mantua

Venice

Po R.

Ferrara

Genoa

Pisa

Florence

Urbino

Adriatic Sea

Tiber R.

Corsica

Rome

Naples

Sardinia

Mediterranean Sea

Tyrrhenian Sea

Sicily

| Ferrara |
| Florence |
| Genoa |
| Mantua |
| Milan |
| Papal States |
| Urbino |
| Venice |

N
W   E
S

0   100 kilometers
0   100 miles
Lambert Azimuthal Equal-Area projection

Geography SKILLS

1. **Place** Which Italian city-states did not have a seacoast?
2. **Movement** How could traders from the landlocked city-states gain access to the sea?

Maps In Motion See *StudentWorks™ Plus* or glencoe.com.

Of course, not all parts of Italian society were directly affected by these three general characteristics of the Italian Renaissance. The wealthy upper classes, who made up a small percentage of the total population, more actively embraced the new ideas and activities. Indirectly, however, the Italian Renaissance did have some impact on ordinary people. Especially in the cities, many of the intellectual and artistic achievements of the period were highly visible and difficult to ignore. The churches, wealthy homes, and public buildings were decorated with art that celebrated religious and secular themes, the human body, and an appreciation of classical antiquity.

The Italian States

During the Middle Ages, Italy had failed to develop a centralized monarchical state. The lack of a single strong ruler made it possible for a number of city-states in northern and central Italy to remain independent. Three of them—**Milan, Venice,** and **Florence**—expanded and played crucial roles in Italian politics.

The Italian city-states prospered from a flourishing trade that had expanded in the Middle Ages. Italian merchants had profited from the Crusades as well and were able to set up new trading centers in eastern ports. There, the Italian merchants obtained silks, sugar, and spices, which they carried back to Italy and the West.

Milan was one of the richest city-states in Italy. It was located in the north, at the crossroads of the main trade routes from Italian coastal cities to the Alpine passes. In the fourteenth century, members of the Visconti family established themselves as dukes of Milan. They extended their power over all of Lombardy.

The last Visconti ruler of Milan died in 1447. **Francesco Sforza** then conquered the city and became its new duke. Sforza led a band of **mercenaries**—soldiers who sold their services to the highest bidder. Both the Visconti and Sforza rulers worked to build a strong centralized state. By creating an efficient tax system, they generated enormous revenues for the government.

Venice was another major northern Italian city-state. As a link between Asia and Western Europe, the city drew traders from all over the world. Officially Venice was a republic with an elected leader called a doge. In reality, a small group of wealthy merchant-aristocrats ran the government of Venice for their benefit. Venice's trade empire was tremendously profitable and made Venice an international power.

The republic of Florence dominated the region of Tuscany. During the fourteenth century, a small but wealthy group of merchants established control of the Florentine government. They waged a series of successful wars against their neighbors and established Florence as a major city-state.

In 1434, **Cosimo de' Medici** (MEH•duh•chee) took control of the city. The wealthy Medici family ran the government from behind the scenes. Using their wealth and personal influence, Cosimo, and later **Lorenzo de' Medici,** his grandson, dominated the city when Florence was the cultural center of Italy.

During the late 1400s, Florence experienced an economic decline. Most of its economy was based on the manufacturing of cloth. Increased competition from English and Flemish cloth makers drove down profits. During this time a Dominican preacher named Girolamo Savonarola began condemning the corruption and excesses of the Medici family. Citizens, tired of Medici rule and frustrated by economic events, turned to Savonarola. So many people followed him that the Medici family turned Florence over to his followers.

Eventually people tired of Savonarola's strict regulations on gambling, horseracing, swearing, painting, music, and books. Savonarola also attacked the corruption of the Church, which angered the pope. In 1498, Savonarola was accused of heresy and sentenced to death. The Medici family returned to power.

The Italian Wars

The growth of powerful monarchical states in the rest of Europe eventually led to trouble for the Italian states. Attracted by the riches of Italy, the French king Charles VIII led an army of 30,000 men into Italy in 1494. He occupied the kingdom of Naples in southern Italy. Northern Italian states turned for help to the Spanish, who gladly agreed to send soldiers to Italy. For the next 30 years, the French and the Spanish battled in Italy as they fought to dominate the country.

A decisive turning point in their war came in 1527. On May 5, thousands of troops belonging to the Spanish king Charles I, along with mercenaries from different countries, arrived at the city of **Rome.** They had not been paid for months. When they yelled, "Money! Money!" their leader responded, "If you have ever dreamed of pillaging a town and laying hold of its treasures, here now is one, the richest of them all, queen of the world."

The next day the invading forces smashed the gates and pushed into the city. The troops went berserk in a frenzy of bloodshed and looting. The terrible sack of Rome in 1527 by the armies of the Spanish king Charles I ended the Italian wars and left the Spanish a dominant force in Italy.

✓ **Reading Check** **Explaining** What attracted the French king Charles VIII to Italy?

Machiavelli on Power

MAIN IDEA Machiavelli's *The Prince* has profoundly influenced political leaders.

HISTORY & YOU Do you believe that morality has a place in politics? Read to learn about Machiavelli's views on political power.

No one gave better expression to the Italians' love affair with political power than **Niccolò Machiavelli** (MA•kee•uh•VEH•lee). His book *The Prince* is one of the most influential works on political power in the Western world.

Machiavelli's central thesis in *The Prince* concerns how to acquire—and keep—political power. In the Middle Ages, many writers on political power had stressed the moral side of a prince's activity—how a ruler ought to behave based on Christian principles. Machiavelli rejected this popular approach. He believed that morality had little to do with politics.

From Machiavelli's point of view, a prince's attitude toward power must be based on an understanding of human nature, which he believed was basically self-centered. Political activity, therefore, should not be restricted by moral principles. A prince acts on behalf of the state. According to Machiavelli, then, for the state's sake, a prince must be willing to let his conscience sleep.

Machiavelli was among the first to abandon morality as the basis for analyzing political activity. His views have had a profound influence on political leaders who followed.

✓ Reading Check **Identifying** What was Machiavelli's central thesis in *The Prince*?

HISTORY & ARTS — PRIMARY SOURCE
Patronage of the Medici Family

Under the rule of the wealthy Medici family, Florence became the cultural center of Europe. Their patronage supported many artists, including Brunelleschi, Donatello, and Michelangelo.

Piero de' Medici hired Benozzo Gozzoli in 1459 to paint frescoes in the chapel at the Medici Palace. Frescoes on three walls depict the biblical stories about the processions of the three Magi to Bethlehem. The wall with the youngest king (shown here) is the most lavish. The artist included portraits of Piero and his father, Cosimo, as well as a self-portrait. The young king is a portrait of Piero's son Lorenzo, who was then only ten years old, but would come to be known as Lorenzo the Magnificent.

CRITICAL THINKING SKILLS

1. **Explaining** How did the Medici influence the Renaissance in Florence?
2. **Making Inferences** Why do you think Gozzoli included portraits of several members of the Medici family in his fresco depicting a biblical scene?

Renaissance Society

MAIN IDEA Changes in the social classes occurred during the Renaissance.

HISTORY & YOU Should your parents choose your future spouse? Read to learn about the marriage customs during the Renaissance.

In the Middle Ages, society was divided into three estates, or social classes (see Chapter 3). Although this social order continued into the Renaissance, some changes became evident.

The Nobility

Although many European nobles faced declining incomes prior to the Renaissance, many had retained their lands and titles. By 1500, nobles, old and new, again dominated society. Making up only 2 to 3 percent of the population in most countries, nobles held important political posts and served as advisers to the king.

Nobles, or aristocrats, were expected to fulfill certain ideals. The characteristics of a perfect Renaissance noble were expressed in *The Book of the Courtier*, written by Baldassare Castiglione (KAHS•teel•YOH•NAY), an Italian, in 1528. First, a noble was born, not made. He must have character, grace, and talent. Second, the noble had to be a warrior, but also needed a classical education and interest in the arts. Third, the noble had to follow a certain standard of conduct. What was the purpose of these standards?

PRIMARY SOURCE

"[T]he aim of the perfect Courtier is so to win . . . the favor and mind of the prince whom he serves that he may be able to tell him . . . the truth about everything he needs to know . . . and that when he sees the mind of his prince inclined to a wrong action, he may dare to oppose him . . . so as to dissuade him of every evil intent and bring him to the path of virtue."

—Baldassare Castiglione, *The Book of the Courtier*, 1528

SCIENCE, TECHNOLOGY, & SOCIETY

Gutenberg's Press

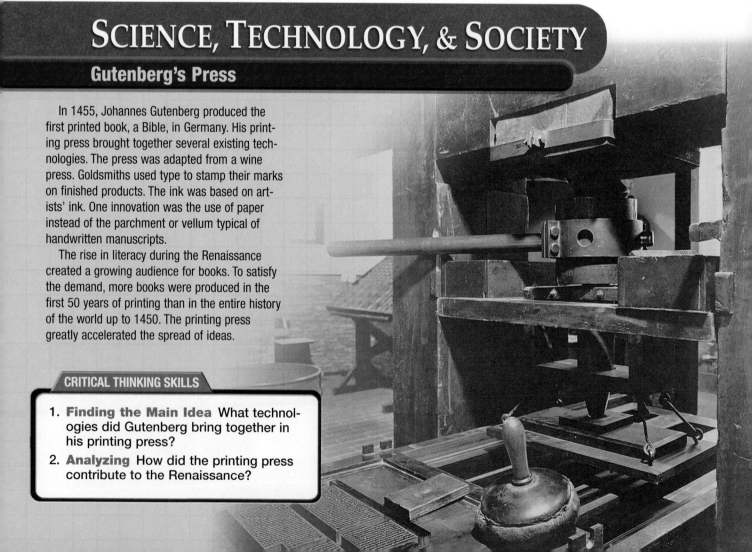

In 1455, Johannes Gutenberg produced the first printed book, a Bible, in Germany. His printing press brought together several existing technologies. The press was adapted from a wine press. Goldsmiths used type to stamp their marks on finished products. The ink was based on artists' ink. One innovation was the use of paper instead of the parchment or vellum typical of handwritten manuscripts.

The rise in literacy during the Renaissance created a growing audience for books. To satisfy the demand, more books were produced in the first 50 years of printing than in the entire history of the world up to 1450. The printing press greatly accelerated the spread of ideas.

CRITICAL THINKING SKILLS

1. **Finding the Main Idea** What technologies did Gutenberg bring together in his printing press?

2. **Analyzing** How did the printing press contribute to the Renaissance?

The aim of the perfect noble was to serve his prince in an effective and honest way. Nobles would adhere to Castiglione's principles for hundreds of years while they continued to dominate European social and political life.

Peasants and Townspeople

In the Renaissance, peasants still constituted 85 to 90 percent of the total European population. Serfdom continued to decrease with the decline of the manorial system. By 1500, especially in western Europe, more and more peasants became legally free.

Townspeople made up the rest of the third estate. At the top of urban society were the patricians. With their wealth from trade, industry, and banking, they dominated their communities. Below them were the burghers—the shopkeepers, artisans, guild masters, and guild members. Below the burghers were the workers, who earned pitiful wages, and the unemployed. Both groups lived miserable lives. These people made up perhaps 30 or 40 percent of the urban population.

During the late 1300s and the 1400s, urban poverty increased dramatically throughout Europe. One rich merchant, who had little sympathy for the poor, wrote:

PRIMARY SOURCE

"Those that are lazy in a way that does harm to the city, and who can offer no just reason for their condition, should either be forced to work or expelled from the city. The city would thus rid itself of that most harmful part of the poorest class."

—fifteenth-century Florence merchant

Family and Marriage

The family bond was a source of great security. Parents carefully arranged marriages to strengthen business or family ties. Often they worked out the details when their children were only two or three years old. The marriage contract included a **dowry,** a sum of money that the wife's family gave to the husband upon marriage.

The father-husband was the center of the Italian family. He managed all finances (his wife had no share in his wealth) and made the decisions that determined his children's lives. The mother's chief role was to supervise the household. A father had absolute authority over his children until he died or formally freed them. In Renaissance Italy, children did not become adults at a certain age. Instead, they became adults when their fathers went before a judge to free them. Adulthood age varied from the early teens to the late twenties.

✓ **Reading Check** **Contrasting** How was the Renaissance noble different from the medieval knight?

SECTION 1 REVIEW

Vocabulary
1. **Explain** the significance of: Italian Renaissance, urban society, secular, instability, decline, Leonardo da Vinci, Milan, Venice, Florence, Francesco Sforza, mercenaries, Cosimo de' Medici, Lorenzo de' Medici, Rome, Niccolò Machiavelli, dowry.

Main Ideas
2. **Explain** why the Italian city-states were so prosperous.
3. **Summarize** Machiavelli's view of human nature.
4. **Contrast** the social structure of the Middle Ages and the Renaissance.

	Middle Ages	Renaissance
Nobility		
Peasants		
Townspeople		

Critical Thinking
5. **The BIG Idea** **Evaluating** Why has Leonardo da Vinci been viewed as a model Renaissance man?
6. **Making Inferences** What would families of Renaissance Italy consider to be a good marriage for their child?
7. **Analyzing Visuals** Examine the image on page 165. What feeling do you get from this painting? What details in the painting create this feeling?

Writing About History
8. **Expository Writing** Read a few passages from *The Prince.* Write a brief essay explaining why you agree or do not agree with Machiavelli's theory of politics.

History ONLINE
For help with the concepts in this section of *Glencoe World History— Modern Times,* go to glencoe.com and click Study Central.

Renaissance Society

As Europe entered the Renaissance, it was a highly structured society. Its class system had changed during the Middle Ages. Serfs became peasants in the countryside. A middle class was developing in the towns and its merchants began to create wealth from trade. They were a distinct class, separate from the land-owning nobles.

> In theory, nobles personified European ideas of honor and prestige.

> Only nobles were allowed some luxuries, such as purple silk.

> Titles of nobility were passed down generation to generation.

> Noble women were responsible for training girls of high birth, in courtly manners and household administration.

> Fashion became important to nobles and well-off townsfolk during the Renaissance. Clothing styles changed faster than before.

NOBLE MEN AND WOMEN

During the Middle Ages, nobles held vital roles in government. As top advisors and military leaders, they guarded the power of monarchs. In return, the nobles governed the manors and received wealth from the control of the land. The nobility was protected as a class through passing its titles and offices to the next generations. The income of the nobility was not protected; however, as Renaissance towns came to control the agricultural countryside.

Urban trade brought new emphasis on using cash for payment, instead of barter. Checks became a common way of transferring money among merchants. Banks developed to back and cash them.

Imported fabrics brought vibrant fashions to successful town-dwellers as well as nobles.

Peasants brought goods from the countryside to sell in town markets.

Over time, some successful merchants bought their way into the nobility.

PEASANTS AND THE MIDDLE CLASS

Wealthy merchants rivaled the nobles in luxurious clothing. The peasants and the poor laborers and beggars of the towns lived outside this world of fashion. Material for clothing and other goods could be obtained by urban dwellers in the town market. As commercial capitalism started in the Middle Ages, economic power began to disperse among merchants, financiers, and other middle-class figures.

ANALYZING VISUALS

1. **Describing** What do the nobles' clothes tell you about their station in life?

2. **Assessing** What role did peasants play in the economies of towns?

Ideas and Art of the Renaissance

GUIDE TO READING

The BIG Idea
Ideas, Beliefs, and Values
Humanism was an important intellectual movement of the Renaissance and was reflected in the works of Renaissance artists.

Content Vocabulary
- humanism *(p. 170)*
- vernacular *(p. 171)*
- fresco *(p. 173)*

Academic Vocabulary
- attain *(p. 172)*
- style *(p. 173)*

People and Places
- Petrarch *(p. 170)*
- Dante *(p. 171)*
- Chaucer *(p. 171)*
- Canterbury *(p. 171)*
- Christine de Pizan *(p. 172)*
- Raphael *(p. 174)*
- Michelangelo *(p. 174)*
- Flanders *(p. 175)*
- Jan van Eyck *(p. 175)*
- Albrecht Dürer *(p. 175)*

Reading Strategy
Summarizing Information As you read, use a chart like the one below to describe the three pieces of literature written by Dante, Chaucer, and de Pizan. What was the primary importance of each of these works?

Divine Comedy	The Canterbury Tales	The Book of the City of Ladies

During the Renaissance, humanism revived interest in the literary works of ancient Greece and Rome and in classical Latin. While many scholars used classical Latin, writers such as Dante and Chaucer made literature written in regional languages more popular. Humanism also became an educational curriculum, and at the core of humanist schools were the liberal studies. The art, sculpture, and architecture of the Renaissance reflected a realistic, human-centered world.

Italian Renaissance Humanism

MAIN IDEA Humanism, based on study of the classics, revived an interest in ancient Latin; but many authors wrote great works in the vernacular.

HISTORY & YOU Do you use a different style of language with your friends than with adults? Read about languages used in Renaissance literature.

Secularism and an emphasis on the individual characterized the Renaissance. These characteristics are most noticeable in the intellectual and artistic accomplishments of the period. A key intellectual movement of the Renaissance was humanism.

Development of Humanism

Humanism was based on the study of the classics, the literary works of ancient Greece and Rome. Humanists studied grammar, rhetoric, poetry, moral philosophy, and history. Today these subjects are called the humanities.

Petrarch (PEE•TRAHRK), who often has been called the father of Italian Renaissance humanism, did more than any other individual in the fourteenth century to foster the development of humanism. Petrarch looked for forgotten Latin manuscripts and set in motion a search for similar manuscripts in monastic libraries throughout Europe. He also began the humanist emphasis on using pure classical Latin (Latin as used by the ancient Romans, as opposed to medieval Latin). Humanists used the works of Cicero as a model for prose and those of Virgil for poetry.

Fourteenth-century humanists like Petrarch had described the intellectual life as one of solitude. They rejected family and a life of action in the community. In contrast, humanists in the early 1400s took a new interest in civic life. They believed that intellectuals had a duty to live an active civic life and to put their study of the humanities to the state's service. It is no accident that they served as secretaries in the Italian city-states and to princes or popes.

Dante's Divine Comedy

When Dante Alighieri wrote the *Divine Comedy* in the early fourteenth century, he chose the ancient Roman poet Virgil as his "guide" for the soul's journey to Paradise. By doing so, Dante hoped to lend legitimacy to a work written in the dialect of Florence. Dante later defended his use of the vernacular in a treatise he wrote in Latin, the language of literature at the time, because he wanted it to be taken seriously.

Dante called his masterpiece *Comedy.* The adjective *Divine* was added later, partly because of the poem's religious subject and partly in recognition of its greatness. It soon became a classic, helping to make the Florentine dialect the literary language of the entire Italian Peninsula.

Heaven

Purgatory

Hell

Dante holds a copy of the *Divine Comedy.*

The artist depicted the walls and buildings of Florence as they appeared in 1465, rather than during Dante's lifetime.

QVI COELVM CECINIT MEDIVMQVE IMVMQVE TRIBVNAL   LVSTRAVITQVE ANIMO CVNCTA POETA SVO   DOCTI SENSIT CONSILIIS AC PIETATE PATREM   NIL POTVIT TANTO MORS SAEVA NOCERE POETAE   QVEM VIVVM VIRTI

"The Latin could only have explained them [the poetry of the *Divine Comedy*] to scholars; for the rest would have not understood it. Therefore, as among those who desire to understand them there are many more illiterate than learned, it follows that the Latin would not have fulfilled this behest as well as the vulgar tongue, which is understood both by the learned and the unlearned."

—Dante Alighieri, *De vulgari eloquentia* ("Of Literature in the Vernacular"), 1304–1306

DOCUMENT-BASED QUESTIONS

This painting by Domenico di Michelino shows parts of Dante's famous poem.

1. **Explaining** Why did Dante choose not to write his *Divine Comedy* in Latin?
2. **Making Connections** Why would the use of Virgil make Dante's poem seem more legitimate to Renaissance scholars?

Vernacular Literature

The humanist emphasis on classical Latin led to its widespread use in the writings of scholars, lawyers, and theologians. However, some writers wrote in the **vernacular** (the language spoken in their own regions, such as Italian, French, or German). In the fourteenth century, the literary works of the Italian author **Dante** (DAHN•tay) and the English author Geoffrey **Chaucer** helped make vernacular literature more popular.

Dante's masterpiece in the Italian vernacular is the *Divine Comedy.* It is the story of the soul's journey to salvation. The lengthy poem has three major sections: Hell, Purgatory, and Heaven, or Paradise. Dante is led on an imaginary journey through these three realms until he reaches Paradise, where he beholds God.

Chaucer used the English vernacular in his famous work *The Canterbury Tales.* His beauty of expression and clear language were important in making his dialect the chief ancestor of the modern English language. *The Canterbury Tales* consists of a collection of stories told by a group of 29 pilgrims journeying to the tomb of Saint Thomas à Becket at **Canterbury**, England.

This format gave Chaucer the chance to portray an entire range of English society.

Another writer who used the vernacular was **Christine de Pizan,** a Frenchwoman who is best known for her works written in defense of women. In *The Book of the City of Ladies,* written in 1404, she denounced the many male writers who had argued that women, by their very nature, are unable to learn. Women, de Pizan argued, could learn as well as men if they could attend the same schools:

PRIMARY SOURCE

"Should I also tell you whether a woman's nature is clever and quick enough to learn speculative sciences as well as to discover them, and likewise the manual arts. I assure you that women are equally well-suited and skilled to carry them out and to put them to sophisticated use once they have learned them."

—Christine de Pizan

✓ **Reading Check** **Explaining** What literary format does Chaucer use to portray English society?

Renaissance Education

MAIN IDEA Education during the Renaissance focused on the liberal studies.

HISTORY & YOU What is your favorite subject? Read to learn about the subjects of study during the Renaissance.

The humanist movement had a profound effect on education in the 1300s and 1400s. Renaissance humanists believed that education could dramatically change human beings. They wrote books on education and opened schools based on their ideas.

At the core of humanist schools were the liberal studies. Humanists believed that liberal studies (or, today, liberal arts) enabled individuals to reach their full potential. One humanist wrote: "We call those studies liberal by which we **attain** and practice virtue and wisdom; which calls forth and develops those highest gifts of body and mind which ennoble men."

HISTORY & ARTS   PRIMARY SOURCE

Differences in Renaissance Art

Marriage of the Virgin by Raphael (1504) ▼

◀ Central panel of *Mérode Altarpiece* by Robert Campin (c. 1425–28)

Flemish artists typically placed their subjects among everyday objects. The space depicted was tight and boxlike.

DOCUMENT-BASED QUESTIONS

Artists of the Northern Renaissance placed their works in everyday settings, while Italian Renaissance artists were influenced by classical styles and geometric precision. Religious themes were a common subject matter.

1. **Contrasting** How did the Renaissance style in Northern Europe differ from that of Italy?

2. **Interpreting** How might the settings of each painting reveal differences in religious ideals between Northern Europe and Italy?

Raphael used the technique of perspective to give the illusion of scale, distance, and three dimensions on a two-dimensional surface.

What, then, were the liberal studies? According to the humanists, students should study history, moral philosophy, eloquence (or rhetoric), letters (grammar and logic), poetry, mathematics, astronomy, and music. In short, the purpose of a liberal education (and thus the reason for studying the liberal arts) was to produce individuals who follow a path of virtue and wisdom. These individuals should also possess rhetorical skills so they can persuade others to take this same path of virtue and wisdom.

PRIMARY SOURCE

"Not everyone is called to be a physician, a lawyer . . . nor has everyone outstanding gifts of natural capacity, but all of us . . . are responsible for the personal influence that goes forth from us."

—Vittorino da Feltre (1373–1446)
humanist educator, Mantua, Italy

Following the Greek ideal of a sound mind in a sound body, humanist educators also emphasized physical education. Students learned the skills of javelin throwing, archery, and dancing. They ran, wrestled, hunted, and swam.

Humanist educators thought that a humanist education was a practical preparation for life. Its aim was not to create great scholars but complete citizens. Humanist education was also considered necessary for preparing the sons of aristocrats for leadership roles. Humanist schools were the model for the education of Europe's ruling classes until the twentieth century.

Females were largely absent from these schools. The few female students who did attend humanist schools studied the classics and were encouraged to know some history as well as how to ride, dance, sing, play the lute (a stringed instrument), and appreciate poetry. They were told not to learn mathematics or rhetoric. It was thought that religion and morals should be foremost in the education of "Christian ladies" so that they could become good wives and mothers.

✓ **Reading Check** **Explaining** How did a humanist education prepare a student for life?

Italian Renaissance Art

MAIN IDEA The Renaissance produced great artists and sculptors such as Michelangelo, Raphael, and Leonardo da Vinci.

HISTORY & YOU Do you recall the features of Gothic style? Read to learn how Renaissance architects diverged from Gothic style.

Renaissance artists sought to imitate nature. They wanted viewers to see the reality in their subjects. At the same time, these artists were developing a new, human-focused worldview. As one artist proclaimed, human beings were the "center and measure of all things."

New Techniques in Painting

Frescoes by Masaccio (muh•ZAH•chee•oh) are the first masterpieces of Early Renaissance (1400–1490) art. A **fresco** is a painting done on fresh, wet plaster with water-based paints. Human figures in medieval paintings look flat, but Masaccio's figures have depth and come alive. By mastering the laws of perspective, Masaccio could create the illusion of three dimensions, leading to a new, realistic **style.**

Other fifteenth-century Florentine painters used and modified this new, or Renaissance, style. Especially important were two major developments. One development stressed the technical side of painting—understanding the laws of perspective and the organization of outdoor space and light through geometry. The second development was the investigation of movement and human anatomy. The realistic portrayal of the individual, especially the human nude, became one of the chief aims of Italian Renaissance art.

Sculpture and Architecture

The Renaissance produced equally stunning advances in sculpture and architecture. The sculptor Donatello studied the statues of the Greeks and Romans. His works included a realistic, free-standing figure of Saint George.

The work of architect Filippo Brunelleschi (BROO•nuhl•EHS•kee) was inspired by the buildings of classical Rome.

His design of the church of San Lorenzo in Florence reflects this. The classical columns and rounded arches in the church's design create an environment that does not overwhelm the worshiper, as Gothic cathedrals might. The church creates a space to fit human, and not divine, needs. Like painters and sculptors, Renaissance architects sought to reflect a human-centered world.

High Renaissance Masters

The final stage of Italian Renaissance painting flourished between 1490 and 1520. Called the High Renaissance, the period is associated with Leonardo da Vinci, Raphael, and Michelangelo.

Leonardo mastered the art of realistic painting and even dissected human bodies to better see how nature worked. However, he wanted to advance beyond such realism to create idealized forms that captured the perfection of nature and the individual—perfection that could not be expressed fully by a realistic style.

At age 25, **Raphael** was already one of Italy's best painters. He was admired for his numerous madonnas (paintings of the Virgin Mary). In these, he achieved an ideal of beauty far surpassing human standards. Raphael is also well known for his frescoes in the Vatican Palace. His *School of Athens* reveals a world of balance, harmony, and order—the underlying principles of classical Greek and Roman art.

Michelangelo, an accomplished painter, sculptor, and architect, was another master of the High Renaissance. Fiercely driven by his desire to create, he worked with great passion and energy on a remarkable number of projects. Michelangelo's figures on the ceiling of the Sistine Chapel in Rome depict an ideal type of human being with perfect proportions. The beauty of this idealized human being is meant to be a reflection of divine beauty. The more beautiful the body, the more godlike the figure.

✓ **Reading Check** **Identifying** Name three Italian artists of the High Renaissance.

PEOPLE in HISTORY

Leonardo da Vinci
1452–1519 Italian Artist and Scientist

Leonardo da Vinci was the model "Renaissance man." He was an artist, scientist, inventor, and visionary. In 1503, the government of Florence sought his genius on a military matter. With the help of Niccolò Machiavelli, Leonardo da Vinci devised a plan to help Florence defeat the city of Pisa in a war. The plan was to divert the Arno River away from Pisa to cut Pisa off from the sea. However, the engineer hired to dig a diversion canal did not follow Leonardo's instructions, and the canal walls collapsed. Although the plan failed, the maps Leonardo drew up were so detailed that they were used long afterward. He also envisioned an industrial corridor along the river that eventually came to pass after his death. **What famous person helped Leonardo with his plan?**

Michelangelo
1475–1564 Italian Artist

Michelangelo Buonarroti was a man of many talents. A painter, sculptor, poet, architect, and literary scholar, there was little he could not do once he set his mind to it. When Pope Julius II asked him to paint the ceiling of the Sistine Chapel in 1508, Michelangelo protested that "painting is not my art." Despite his protests, the work that emerged four years later ranks among the greatest masterpieces of all time.

For his sculptures, Michelangelo would sometimes spend months in a marble quarry personally selecting the ideal block from which to carve his works of art. Some of his contemporaries believed that "he could see the figure imprisoned in it." Creative to the end of his long life, he famously lamented that "art and death do not go well together." **Where do some of Michelangelo's most famous paintings appear?**

The Northern Artistic Renaissance

MAIN IDEA Northern European artists, especially those in the Low Countries, portrayed their world realistically but in a different way than did the Italian artists.

HISTORY & YOU Have you ever used a varnish to seal woodwork? Read to learn about a new medium the Flemish artist Jan van Eyck used.

Like the artists of Italy, the artists of northern Europe became interested in portraying their world realistically. However, their approach was different from that of the Italians. This was particularly true of the artists of the Low Countries (present-day Belgium, Luxembourg, and the Netherlands).

Circumstance played a role in the differences. The large wall spaces of Italian churches had given rise to the art of fresco painting. Italian artists used these spaces to master the technical skills that allowed them to portray humans in realistic settings. In the north, the Gothic cathedrals with their stained glass windows did not allow enough space for frescoes. Thus, northern European artists painted illustrations for books and wooden panels for altarpieces. Great care was needed to depict each object on a small scale.

The most important northern school of art in the 1400s was in **Flanders,** one of the Low Countries. The Flemish painter **Jan van Eyck** (EYEK) was among the first to use and perfect the technique of oil painting. He used a varnish made of linseed oil and nut oils mixed with resins. This medium enabled van Eyck to use a wide variety of brilliant, translucent colors. With his oil paints, he could create striking realism in fine details as in his painting *Giovanni Arnolfini and His Bride.* Like other Northern Renaissance artists, however, van Eyck imitated nature not by using perspective, as the Italians did, but by simply observing reality and portraying details as best he could.

By 1500, artists from the north had begun to study in Italy and to be influenced by what artists were doing there. One German artist who was greatly affected by the Italians was **Albrecht Dürer.** He made two trips to Italy and absorbed most of what the Italians could teach on the laws of perspective.

As can be seen in his famous *Adoration of the Magi,* Dürer did not reject the use of minute details characteristic of northern artists. He did try, however, to fit those details more harmoniously into his works in accordance with Italian artistic theories. Like the Italian artists of the High Renaissance, Dürer tried to achieve a standard of ideal beauty that was based on a careful examination of the human form.

✓ Reading Check **Examining** Why was Jan van Eyck's use of oil paint significant?

SECTION 2 REVIEW

Vocabulary
1. **Explain** the significance of: humanism, Petrarch, vernacular, Dante, Chaucer, Canterbury, Christine de Pizan, attain, fresco, style, Raphael, Michelangelo, Flanders, Jan van Eyck, Albrecht Dürer.

Main Ideas
2. **Describe** Petrarch's contributions to the development of humanism.

3. **Identify** Christine de Pizan's main argument in *The Book of the City of Ladies.*

4. **Summarize** the accomplishments of Leonardo da Vinci, Raphael, and Michelangelo. Use a chart like the one below to make your summary.

Leonardo da Vinci	Raphael	Michelangelo

Critical Thinking
5. **The BIG Idea** **Identifying Central Issues** How was humanism reflected in the works of Renaissance artists?

6. **Contrasting** How did the education of females differ from that of males in humanist schools?

7. **Analyzing Visuals** Examine the painting on page 171. What can you infer about Purgatory based on its location in this painting?

Writing About History
8. **Expository Writing** Assume the role of an art docent (a person who guides people through museums). Prepare a lecture to be given to a group of students on the works of Jan van Eyck and how they differ from Italian Renaissance paintings.

History ONLINE

For help with the concepts in this section of *Glencoe World History—Modern Times*, go to glencoe.com and click Study Central.

The Protestant Reformation

During the second half of the fifteenth century, Christian humanist Desiderius Erasmus paved the way for Martin Luther's reform movement. Political instability in the Holy Roman Empire allowed Lutheranism, the first Protestant faith, to spread. The Peace of Augsburg formally accepted the division of Christianity in Germany—Lutheranism and Catholicism.

GUIDE TO READING

The BIG Idea
Ideas, Beliefs, and Values In northern Europe, Christian humanists sought to reform the Catholic Church, and Protestantism emerged.

Content Vocabulary
- Christian humanism *(p. 176)*
- salvation *(p. 178)*
- indulgence *(p. 178)*
- Lutheranism *(p. 180)*

Academic Vocabulary
- precise *(p. 177)*
- ignorant *(p. 178)*

People, Places, and Events
- Martin Luther *(p. 176)*
- Desiderius Erasmus *(p. 176)*
- Wittenberg *(p. 179)*
- Ninety-five Theses *(p. 179)*
- Edict of Worms *(p. 179)*
- Charles V *(p. 181)*
- Bohemia *(p. 181)*
- Hungary *(p. 181)*
- Peace of Augsburg *(p. 181)*

Reading Strategy
Determining Cause and Effect As you read, use a diagram like the one below to identify steps that led to the Reformation.

```
┌─────────────────┐
│ Steps Leading to │ ⇐
│ the Reformation  │
└─────────────────┘
```

Prelude to Reformation

MAIN IDEA Christian humanism and Desiderius Erasmus paved the way for the Protestant Reformation.

HISTORY & YOU Is there a school policy or rule that you would like to change? Read how Erasmus pointed out the need for Church reform.

The Protestant Reformation is the name given to the religious reform movement that divided the western Church into Catholic and Protestant groups. Although **Martin Luther** began the Reformation in the early 1500s, earlier developments set the stage for religious change.

Christian Humanism

One such development grew from widespread changes in intellectual thought. During the second half of the fifteenth century, the new classical learning that was part of Italian Renaissance humanism spread to northern Europe. From that came a movement called **Christian humanism**, or Northern Renaissance humanism. The major goal of this movement was the reform of the Catholic Church.

The Christian humanists believed in the ability of human beings to reason and improve themselves. They thought that if people read the classics, and especially the basic works of Christianity, they would become more pious. This inner piety, or inward religious feeling, would bring about a reform of the Church and society. Christian humanists believed that in order to change society, they would first have to change human beings.

The best-known Christian humanist was **Desiderius Erasmus** (ih•RAZ•muhs). He called his view of religion "the philosophy of Christ." By this, he meant that Christianity should show people how to live good lives on a daily basis, not just provide beliefs for them to be saved. Stressing the inwardness of religious feeling, Erasmus thought the external forms of medieval religion (pilgrimages, fasts, relics) were not all that important.

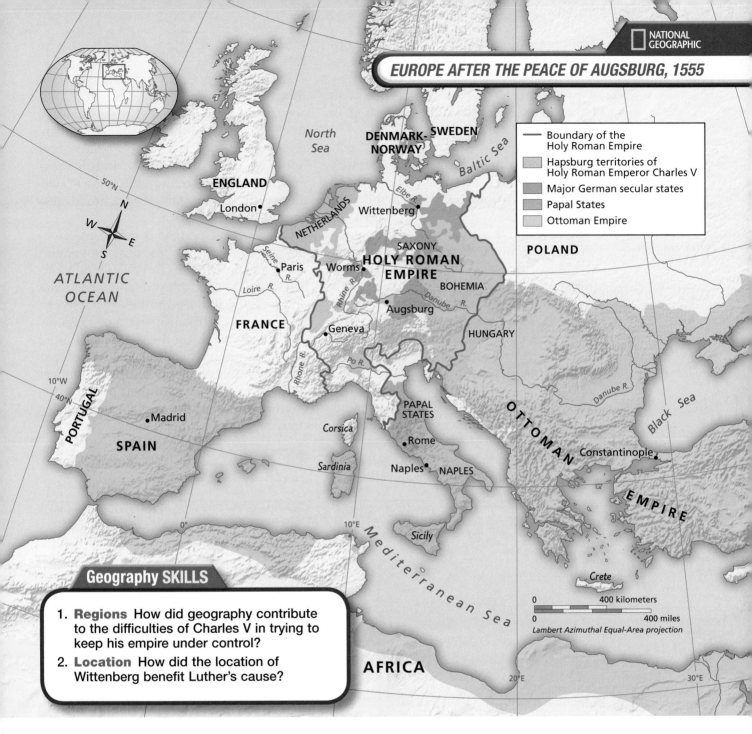

EUROPE AFTER THE PEACE OF AUGSBURG, 1555

North Sea

DENMARK-NORWAY SWEDEN

Baltic Sea

ENGLAND

London

NETHERLANDS

Wittenberg

Elbe R.

SAXONY

POLAND

HOLY ROMAN EMPIRE

Worms

Paris

Seine R.

Loire R.

Rhine R.

BOHEMIA

Danube R.

Augsburg

ATLANTIC OCEAN

FRANCE

Geneva

Rhone R.

Po R.

HUNGARY

50°N

10°W

40°N

PORTUGAL

Madrid

SPAIN

Corsica

Sardinia

PAPAL STATES

Rome

Naples NAPLES

OTTOMAN

Danube R.

EMPIRE

Constantinople

Black Sea

0°

10°E

Sicily

Mediterranean Sea

Crete

AFRICA

20°E

30°E

Legend:
- —— Boundary of the Holy Roman Empire
- Hapsburg territories of Holy Roman Emperor Charles V
- Major German secular states
- Papal States
- Ottoman Empire

0   400 kilometers
0   400 miles
Lambert Azimuthal Equal-Area projection

Geography SKILLS

1. **Regions** How did geography contribute to the difficulties of Charles V in trying to keep his empire under control?

2. **Location** How did the location of Wittenberg benefit Luther's cause?

To reform the Church, Erasmus wanted to spread the philosophy of Christ, provide education in the works of Christianity, and criticize the abuses in the Church. In his work *The Praise of Folly*, written in 1509, Erasmus humorously criticized aspects of his society that he believed were most in need of reform. He singled out the monks for special treatment. Monks, he said, "insist that everything be done in **precise** detail. . . . Just so many knots must be on each shoe and the shoelace must be of only one color."

Erasmus sought reform within the Catholic Church. He did not wish to break away from it. His ideas, however, did prepare the way for the Reformation. As people of his day said, "Erasmus laid the egg that Luther hatched."

Need for Reform

Why the call for reform? Corruption was one reason. From 1450 to 1520, a series of popes—known as the Renaissance popes—failed to meet the Church's spiritual needs.

The popes were supposed to be the spiritual leaders of the Catholic Church. As leaders of the Papal States, however, they were all too often more concerned with Italian politics and worldly interests than with spiritual matters.

Julius II, the fiery "warrior-pope," personally led armies against his enemies. This disgusted Christians who viewed the pope as a spiritual, not a military, leader.

Many Church officials used their church offices to advance their careers and their wealth. At the same time, many ordinary parish priests seemed **ignorant** of their spiritual duties. People wanted to know how to save their souls, and many parish priests were unwilling or unable to offer them advice or instruction.

While the leaders of the Church were failing to meet their responsibilities, ordinary people desired meaningful religious expression and assurance of their **salvation,** or acceptance into Heaven. As a result, for some, the process of obtaining salvation became almost mechanical. Collections of relics grew more popular as a means to salvation.

According to Church practice at that time, through veneration of a relic, a person could gain an **indulgence**—release from all or part of the punishment for sin. Frederick the Wise, Luther's prince, had amassed over 5,000 relics. Indulgences attached to them could reduce time in purgatory by 1,443 years. The Church also sold indulgences.

Other people sought certainty of salvation in the popular mystical movement known as the Modern Devotion. The Modern Devotion downplayed religious dogma and stressed the need to follow the teachings of Jesus. This deepening of religious life was done within the Catholic Church. However, many people soon found that the worldly-wise clergy had little interest in the spiritual needs of their people. This environment helps to explain the tremendous impact of Luther's ideas.

✓ Reading Check　**Explaining** How did Erasmus pave the way for the Reformation?

PEOPLE *in* HISTORY

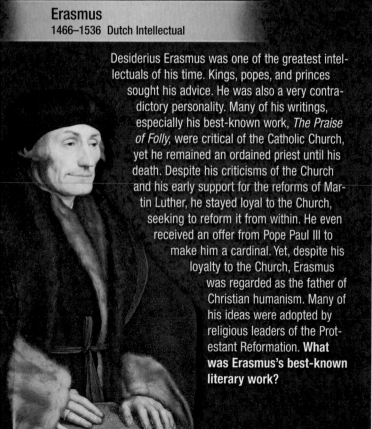

Erasmus
1466–1536　Dutch Intellectual

Desiderius Erasmus was one of the greatest intellectuals of his time. Kings, popes, and princes sought his advice. He was also a very contradictory personality. Many of his writings, especially his best-known work, *The Praise of Folly*, were critical of the Catholic Church, yet he remained an ordained priest until his death. Despite his criticisms of the Church and his early support for the reforms of Martin Luther, he stayed loyal to the Church, seeking to reform it from within. He even received an offer from Pope Paul III to make him a cardinal. Yet, despite his loyalty to the Church, Erasmus was regarded as the father of Christian humanism. Many of his ideas were adopted by religious leaders of the Protestant Reformation. **What was Erasmus's best-known literary work?**

Martin Luther
1483–1546　Church Reform Leader

As Martin Luther returned to his village on a stormy night, a lightning bolt threw him off his horse. "St. Anne, help me, and I will become a monk!" Luther's cry reflected his intense fear of death and of what lay beyond. Like most people of his time, he believed the medieval view of a wrathful God, granting salvation to the righteous few and eternal fire to the rest.

Luther feared he could never do enough to win salvation. Pondering the words of the apostle Paul about the "righteousness of God," Luther arrived at a new insight. What Paul meant, he decided, was not that people can earn righteousness by good works, but that God grants the righteousness needed for salvation. All people need is faith. "From that moment, the whole face of Scripture appeared to me in a different light." **What insight did Luther gain from Paul's words?**

Martin Luther

MAIN IDEA Believing in his new doctrine of salvation, Martin Luther broke from the Catholic Church and established Lutheranism.

HISTORY & YOU Did you ever speak up for something you strongly believed, despite the disapproval of your friends? Read about Martin Luther's split with the Catholic Church.

Martin Luther was a monk and a professor at the University of **Wittenberg,** in Germany, where he lectured on the Bible. Through his study of the Bible, Luther arrived at an answer to a problem—the certainty of salvation—that had bothered him since he had become a monk.

Catholic teaching had stressed that both faith and good works were needed to gain personal salvation. In Luther's opinion, human beings were powerless in the sight of an almighty God and could never do enough good works to earn salvation.

Through his study of the Bible, Luther came to believe that humans are not saved through their good works but through their faith in God. This idea, called justification by faith alone, became the chief teaching of the Protestant Reformation.

Because Luther had arrived at his understanding of salvation by studying the Bible, the Bible became for Luther, as for all other Protestants, the only source of religious truth.

The Ninety-five Theses

Luther did not see himself as a rebel, but he was greatly upset by the widespread selling of indulgences. Especially offensive in his eyes was the monk Johann Tetzel, who sold indulgences with the slogan: "As soon as the coin in the coffer [money box] rings, the soul from purgatory springs." People, Luther believed, were simply harming their chances for salvation by buying these pieces of paper.

On October 31, 1517, Luther, who was greatly angered by the Church's practices, sent a list of **Ninety-five Theses** to his church superiors, especially the local bishop. The theses were a stunning attack on abuses in the sale of indulgences.

Thousands of copies of the Ninety-five Theses were printed and spread to all parts of Germany.

Pope Leo X did not take the issue seriously, however. He said that Luther was simply "some drunken German who will amend his ways when he sobers up."

A Break With the Church

By 1520, Luther had begun to move toward a more definite break with the Catholic Church. He called on the German princes to overthrow the papacy in Germany and establish a reformed German church. Luther also attacked the Church's system of sacraments. In his view, they were the means by which the pope and the Church had destroyed the real meaning of the gospel for a thousand years. He kept only two sacraments—baptism and the Eucharist (also known as Communion). Luther also called for the clergy to marry. This went against the long-standing Catholic requirement that the clergy remain celibate, or unmarried.

Through all these calls for change, Luther continued to emphasize his new doctrine of salvation. It is faith alone, he said, and not good works, that justifies and brings salvation through Christ.

Unable to accept Luther's ideas, the Church excommunicated him in January 1521. He was also summoned to appear before the imperial diet—or legislative assembly—of the Holy Roman Empire, which was called into session at the city of Worms by the newly elected emperor Charles V. The emperor believed he could convince Luther to change his ideas. However, Luther refused.

The young emperor was outraged. "A single friar who goes counter to all Christianity for a thousand years," he declared, "must be wrong!" By the **Edict of Worms,** Martin Luther was made an outlaw within the empire. His works were to be burned and Luther himself captured and delivered to the emperor. However, Luther's ruler, Frederick, the elector of Saxony, was unwilling to see his famous professor killed. He sent Luther into hiding and then protected him when Luther returned to Wittenberg at the beginning of 1522.

The Rise of Lutheranism

Luther's religious movement soon became a revolution. Many German rulers who supported Luther took control of the Catholic churches in their territories, forming state churches supervised by the government. As part of the development of these state-dominated churches, Luther also set up new religious services to replace the Catholic mass. These services consisted of Bible readings, preaching of the word of God, and song. Luther's doctrine soon became known as **Lutheranism** and the churches as Lutheran churches. Lutheranism was the first Protestant faith.

In June 1524, Luther faced a political crisis. German peasants revolted against their lords and looked to Luther to support their cause. Luther instead supported the lords. To him, the state and its rulers were called by God to maintain the peace necessary to spread the Gospel. It was the duty of princes to stop all revolt. By the following spring, the German princes had crushed the peasant revolts. Luther found himself even more dependent on state authorities for the growth of his church.

✓ **Reading Check** **Contrasting** How did Luther and the Church differ on achieving salvation?

TURNING POINT — LUTHER'S NINETY-FIVE THESES —

Martin Luther's Introduction to his Ninety-five Theses, 1517

Out of love for the truth and the desire to bring it to light, the following propositions will be discussed at Wittenberg, under the presidency of the Reverend Father Martin Luther, Master of Arts and of Sacred Theology, and Lecturer in Ordinary on the same at that place. Wherefore he requests that those who are unable to be present and debate orally with us, may do so by letter.

Martin Luther's protest of indulgences began the Protestant Reformation. The Catholic Church had authorized Johann Tetzel to sell indulgences to raise money to build St. Peter's Basilica in Rome. Tetzel told the faithful that their purchases would free the souls of their loved ones from Purgatory. This enraged Luther, who believed that indulgences only soothed the conscience. They did not forgive sins.

When Luther wrote his Ninety-five Theses, his intention was to open a dialogue on abuses in the Catholic Church. Instead, his words sparked a revolutionary firestorm. Aided by the newly invented printing press, his words soon spread across Europe.

Luther's attempts to reform the Catholic Church led to a new form of Christianity—Protestantism—and the birth of a new church. It also ignited decades of bloody religious conflict, ending a thousand years of domination by the Catholic Church.

This image shows Martin Luther posting his Ninety-five Theses on the door of the Castle Church in Wittenberg, Germany, in 1517.

DOCUMENT-BASED QUESTIONS

1. **Finding the Main Idea** In his introduction to the Ninety-five Theses, what did Luther invite people to do?

2. **Analyzing** In what ways did the Ninety-five Theses represent a turning point in history?

Politics in the German Reformation

MAIN IDEA Political and religious problems forced the emperor of the Holy Roman Empire to seek peace with the Lutheran princes.

HISTORY & YOU Have you ever met so much opposition from all sides that you just had to give in? Read to learn why Charles V had to seek peace with the Lutheran princes of his empire.

From its very beginning, the fate of Luther's movement was tied closely to political affairs. **Charles V,** the Holy Roman emperor (who was also Charles I, the king of Spain), ruled an immense empire consisting of Spain and its colonies, the Austrian lands, **Bohemia, Hungary,** the Low Countries, the duchy of Milan in northern Italy, and the kingdom of Naples in southern Italy.

Politically, Charles wanted to keep this enormous empire under the control of his dynasty—the Hapsburgs. Religiously, he hoped to preserve the unity of his empire by keeping it Catholic. However, a number of problems kept him busy and cost him both his dream and his health. These same problems helped Lutheranism survive by giving Lutherans time to organize before having to face the Catholic forces.

The chief political concern of Charles V was his rivalry with the king of France, Francis I. Their conflict over disputed territories in a number of areas led to a series of wars that lasted more than 20 years. At the same time, Charles faced opposition from Pope Clement VII. Guided by political considerations, the pope had joined the side of the French king. The invasion of Ottoman Turks into the eastern part of the empire forced Charles to send forces there as well.

Finally, the internal political situation in the Holy Roman Empire was not in Charles's favor. Germany was a land of several hundred territorial states. Although all owed loyalty to the emperor, many individual rulers of the German states supported Luther as a way to assert their own local authority. By the time Charles V brought military forces to Germany, the Lutheran princes were well organized. Unable to defeat them, Charles was forced to seek peace.

An end to religious warfare in Germany came in 1555 with the **Peace of Augsburg.** This agreement formally accepted the division of Christianity in Germany. The German states were now free to choose between Catholicism and Lutheranism. Lutheran states were to have the same legal rights as Catholic states. However, the right of each German ruler to determine the religion of his subjects was accepted, but not the right of the subjects to choose their own religion.

✓ Reading Check **Evaluating** How did the Peace of Augsburg influence the political and religious development of Germany?

Vocabulary

1. **Explain** the significance of: Martin Luther, Christian humanism, Desiderius Erasmus, precise, ignorant, salvation, indulgence, Wittenberg, Ninety-five Theses, Edict of Worms, Lutheranism, Charles V, Bohemia, Hungary, Peace of Augsburg.

Main Ideas

2. **Sequence** the actions of Luther that led to the emergence of Protestantism using a diagram like the one below.

Luther's Actions

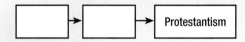
Protestantism

3. **Discuss** the impact of the Edict of Worms.

4. **Explain** why many German princes supported Luther.

Critical Thinking

5. **The BIG Idea** **Analyzing** How did Martin Luther's religious reform lead to conflict? To what extent were these conflicts resolved?

6. **Contrasting** How did the views of Erasmus and the Church differ on the topic of religious relics?

7. **Analyzing Visuals** Examine the map on page 177. Identify three cities where important events occurred in the rise of Lutheranism and explain their significance.

Writing About History

8. **Persuasive Writing** Martin Luther's father wanted him to become a lawyer. Write a letter in which Martin Luther tries to convince his father that the path he chose was better.

History ONLINE

For help with the concepts in this section of *Glencoe World History— Modern Times,* go to glencoe.com and click Study Central.

The Spread of Protestantism

GUIDE TO READING

The BIG Idea
Ideas, Beliefs, and Values Different forms of Protestantism emerged in Europe as the Reformation spread, and the Catholic Church underwent a religious rebirth.

Content Vocabulary
• predestination *(p. 183)* • annul *(p. 184)*

Academic Vocabulary
• published *(p. 182)* • justification *(p. 183)*

People and Places
• Ulrich Zwingli *(p. 182)*
• Zürich *(p. 182)*
• John Calvin *(p. 182)*
• Geneva *(p. 184)*
• King Henry VIII *(p. 184)*
• Ignatius of Loyola *(p. 187)*
• Trent *(p. 187)*

Reading Strategy
Determining Cause and Effect As you read, use a diagram like the one below to list some of the reforms proposed by the Council of Trent. Beside each, give the Protestant viewpoint to which it responded.

Council of Trent		Protestant Viewpoint
	←	
	←	
	←	

As the Reformation spread, different forms of Protestantism emerged in Europe. Calvinism replaced Lutheranism as the most important and dynamic form of Protestantism. In England, King Henry VIII created a national church, the Church of England. The Anabaptists believed in a complete separation of church and state. The Catholic Church underwent a revitalization under the direction of Pope Paul III.

Divisions in Protestantism

MAIN IDEA By the mid-sixteenth century, Calvinism replaced Lutheranism as the most important and dynamic form of Protestantism.

HISTORY & YOU Can you imagine life in a society where dancing is a crime? Read to learn about the Calvinist teachings.

The Peace of Augsburg meant that Christian unity was forever lost. Even before the peace, however, division had appeared in Protestantism. One of these new groups appeared in Switzerland.

Zwinglian Reformation

Ulrich Zwingli was a priest in **Zürich**. The city council of Zürich, strongly influenced by Zwingli, began to introduce religious reforms. Relics and images were abolished. All paintings and decorations were removed from the churches and replaced by whitewashed walls. A new church service consisting of Scripture reading, prayer, and sermons replaced the Catholic mass.

As his movement began to spread to other cities in Switzerland, Zwingli sought an alliance with Martin Luther and the German reformers. Both the German and Swiss reformers realized the need for unity to defend themselves against Catholic authorities, but they were unable to agree on certain Christian rites.

In October 1531 war broke out between the Protestant and Catholic states in Switzerland. Zürich's army was routed, and Zwingli was found wounded on the battlefield. His enemies killed him, cut up his body, and burned the pieces, scattering the ashes. The leadership of Protestantism in Switzerland now passed to John Calvin.

Calvin and Calvinism

John Calvin was educated in his native France. After his conversion to Protestantism, however, he was forced to flee Catholic France for the safety of Switzerland. In 1536 he **published** the

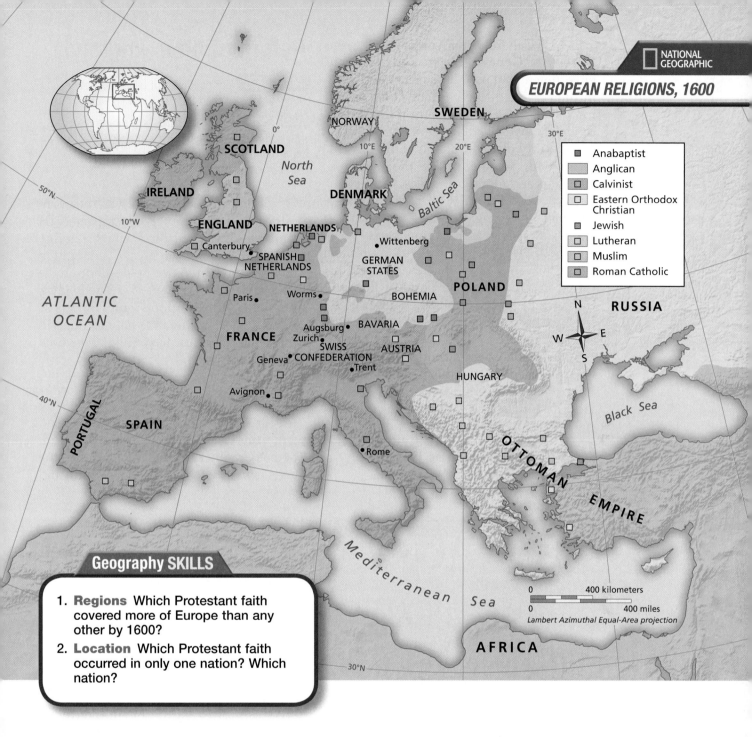

EUROPEAN RELIGIONS, 1600

Legend:
- Anabaptist
- Anglican
- Calvinist
- Eastern Orthodox Christian
- Jewish
- Lutheran
- Muslim
- Roman Catholic

Geography SKILLS

1. **Regions** Which Protestant faith covered more of Europe than any other by 1600?
2. **Location** Which Protestant faith occurred in only one nation? Which nation?

Institutes of the Christian Religion, a summary of Protestant thought. This work, which eventually became known as his masterpiece, immediately gave Calvin a reputation as one of the new leaders of Protestantism.

On most important doctrines, Calvin stood very close to Luther. He, too, believed in the doctrine of **justification** by faith alone to explain how humans achieved salvation. However, Calvin also placed much emphasis on the all-powerful nature of God—what Calvin called the "power, grace, and glory of God."

Calvin's emphasis on the all-powerful nature of God led him to other ideas. One of these ideas was **predestination.** This "eternal decree," as Calvin called it, meant that God had determined in advance who would be saved and who would be damned.

The belief in predestination gave later Calvinists the firm conviction that they were doing God's work on Earth. This conviction, in turn, made them determined to spread their faith to other people. Calvinism became a dynamic and activist faith.

In 1536 Calvin began working to reform the city of **Geneva.** He created a church government that used both clergy and laity in the service of the church. The Consistory, a special court for enforcing moral discipline, oversaw the moral life and doctrinal purity of Genevans. It could punish those who deviated from the church's teachings and moral principles. Citizens in Geneva were punished for such "crimes" as dancing, singing obscene songs, drunkenness, swearing, and playing cards.

Geneva became a powerful center of Protestantism. Missionaries trained in Geneva were sent to all parts of Europe. Calvinism became established in France, the Netherlands, Scotland, and central and eastern Europe.

By the mid-sixteenth century, Calvinism had replaced Lutheranism as the most important and dynamic form of Protestantism. Calvin's Geneva stood as the fortress of the Protestant Reformation.

✓ **Reading Check** **Explaining** How did the Consistory enforce moral discipline in Geneva?

Reformation in England

MAIN IDEA For political, not religious, reasons, Henry VIII established the Church of England.

HISTORY & YOU As a child, how did you react when someone told you no? Read about how Henry VIII reacted after the pope said no.

The English Reformation was rooted in politics, not religion. **King Henry VIII** wanted to divorce his first wife, Catherine of Aragon, with whom he had a daughter, Mary, but no son. Since he needed a male heir, Henry wanted to marry Anne Boleyn. Impatient with the pope's unwillingness to **annul** (declare invalid) his marriage to Catherine, Henry turned to England's own church courts.

The Break from Rome

As the archbishop of Canterbury, head of the highest church court in England, Thomas Cranmer ruled in May 1533 that the king's marriage to Catherine was "null and

PEOPLE *in* HISTORY

Henry VIII
1491–1547 King of England

Historians have found it ironic that Henry VIII, who led the break between England and the Roman Catholic Church, was proclaimed "Defender of the Faith" by the head of the church he left. However, that is how Pope Leo X praised him after Henry's attack on Martin Luther in 1521. In *Assertio Septem Sacramentorum* (Declaration of the Seven Sacraments), Henry upheld Church doctrines that Luther and his followers were trying to discredit. To this day, all British coins carry the initials F.D. after the reigning monarch's name. They refer to the Latin words *Fidei Defensor* or "Defender of the Faith," a hereditary title for all British monarchs since Henry VIII. **Who was Henry VIII attacking in his book?**

Sir Thomas More
1478–1535 British Author and Theologian

A Man for All Seasons—that was the title of a twentieth-century movie about Thomas More. He was a trusted adviser to Henry VIII and the author of the book *Utopia*, which means a perfectly harmonious society. Published in 1516, the book is a work of fiction about an ideal state. More describes how goods are produced and shared equally among the Utopians. *Utopia* became a model for Utopian Socialists, who in the 1800s attempted to set up communities based on the socialistic principles described in the book. More was later beheaded under orders from Henry VIII for not supporting England's break with the Church of Rome. In 1935, More was made a saint. **For what group did More's book become an inspiration?**

absolutely void." At the beginning of June, Anne was crowned queen. Three months later a child was born. Much to the king's disappointment, the baby was a girl. She would later become Queen Elizabeth I.

In 1534, at Henry's request, Parliament moved to finalize the break of the Catholic Church in England with the pope in Rome. The Act of Supremacy of 1534 declared that the king was "the only supreme head on earth of the [new] Church of England." This position gave the king control over religious doctrine, clerical appointments, and discipline. Thomas More, a Christian humanist and devout Catholic, opposed the king's action and was beheaded.

Henry used his new powers to dissolve the monasteries and sell their land and possessions to wealthy landowners and merchants. The king received a great boost to his treasury and a group of supporters who now had a stake in the new order. In matters of doctrine, however, Henry remained close to Catholic teachings.

When Henry died in 1547, he was succeeded by Edward VI, his nine-year-old son by his third wife. During Edward's reign, church officials who favored Protestant doctrines moved the Church of England, or the Anglican Church, in a Protestant direction. New acts of Parliament gave the clergy the right to marry and created a new Protestant church service. Before he turned 16, Edward died of tuberculosis.

"Bloody Mary"

The rapid changes during Edward's reign aroused opposition. When Mary, Henry's daughter by Catherine of Aragon, came to the throne in 1553, England was ready for a reaction. Mary was a Catholic who wanted to restore England to Roman Catholicism. However, her efforts had the opposite effect. Among other actions, she had more than 300 Protestants burned as heretics, earning her the nickname "Bloody Mary." As a result of her policies, England was even more Protestant by the end of Mary's reign than it had been at the beginning.

✓ **Reading Check** **Examining** What were the results of Bloody Mary's religious policies?

Anabaptists

MAIN IDEA For believing in the complete separation of church and state, Anabaptists were viewed as dangerous radicals.

HISTORY & YOU Would you consider someone who refuses to kill to be a "dangerous radical"? Read to learn about the Anabaptists.

Reformers such as Luther had allowed the state to play an important, if not dominant, role in church affairs. However, some people strongly disliked giving such power to the state. These were radicals known as the Anabaptists.

To Anabaptists, the true Christian church was a voluntary community of adult believers who had undergone spiritual rebirth and had then been baptized. This belief in adult baptism separated Anabaptists from Catholics and Protestants, who baptized infants.

Anabaptists also believed in following the practices and the spirit of early Christianity. They considered all believers to be equal, a belief they based on the accounts of early Christian communities in the New Testament. Each Anabaptist church chose its own minister, or spiritual leader. Because all Christians were considered priests, any member of the community was eligible to be a minister (though women were often excluded).

Finally, most Anabaptists believed in the complete separation of church and state. Not only was government to be kept out of the realm of religion, it was not even supposed to have any political authority over real Christians. Anabaptists refused to hold political office or bear arms, because many took literally the biblical commandment "Thou shall not kill."

Their political beliefs, as much as their religious beliefs, caused the Anabaptists to be regarded as dangerous radicals who threatened the very fabric of sixteenth-century society. Indeed, the chief thing other Protestants and Catholics could agree on was the need to persecute Anabaptists.

✓ **Reading Check** **Describing** Why were the Anabaptists considered to be dangerous political radicals?

Reformation and Society

MAIN IDEA Although the family became the center of life during the Reformation, the lives of most women and Jews did not improve.

HISTORY & YOU Should anyone be an "obedient servant" to another person? Read to learn about women's roles during the Reformation.

During the political and religious turmoil of the Reformation, the lives of most women and Jewish people did not improve. Women were still subservient, and anti-Semitism continued.

Women and Family

The Protestants developed a new view of the family. Both monasticism and the requirement of celibacy for the clergy had been abolished. The family could now be placed at the center of life, and the "mutual love between man and wife" could be extolled.

Were idea and reality the same, however? More often, reality reflected the traditional roles of husband as the ruler and wife as the obedient servant. Luther stated it clearly: "The rule remains with the husband, and the wife is compelled to obey him by God's command."

Obedience was not a woman's only role. Her other important duty was to bear children, which both Calvin and Luther saw as part of the divine plan.

Anti-Semitism

During the Reformation, anti-Semitism remained common in northern Europe. Martin Luther expected Jews to convert to Lutheranism. When they resisted, Luther wrote that Jewish synagogues and houses should be destroyed. In the Papal States, Jews who would not convert to Christianity were segregated into ghettos.

✓**Reading Check** **Evaluating** What impact did the Protestant Reformation have on women?

Roman Catholic, Lutheran, Calvinist, and Anglican Beliefs

	CATHOLIC	LUTHERAN	CALVINIST	ANGLICAN
Church Hierarchy	Pope, bishops, priests	Ministers lead congregations.	Council of elders for each church; ministers	Monarch, bishops, priests
Salvation	Salvation requires faith and good works.	Salvation requires faith alone.	Salvation requires faith alone.	Salvation requires faith alone.
Importance of the Bible	The Bible and Church traditions are both sources of truth.	The Bible is the only source of truth.	The Bible is the only source of truth.	The Bible is the only source of truth.
Interpretation of Beliefs	Priests interpret the Bible and Church teachings for believers.	Believers interpret the Bible themselves.	Believers interpret the Bible themselves.	Believers interpret the Bible themselves.
Worship	Services based on rituals and devotional practices	Services based on preaching with some rituals	Services based on preaching	Services based on preaching and rituals
Sacraments	Seven sacraments: baptism, confession, communion, confirmation, marriage, ordination, anointing the sick	Baptism, communion	Baptism, communion	Baptism, communion

Chart SKILLS

1. **Describing** In what way were Anglicans more similar to Catholics than to either Lutherans or Calvinists?
2. **Making Inferences** Why do you think the Protestant churches eliminated most of the seven sacraments?

Catholic Reformation

MAIN IDEA Perceiving a need for a change, Pope Paul III steered the Catholic Church toward a reformation in the 1500s.

HISTORY & YOU When a task doesn't turn out as well as you had hoped, do you look for ways to do it better next time? Read to learn how the Catholic Church determined what it needed to change.

The Catholic Church also had a revitalization in the sixteenth century, giving it new strength and enabling it to regain much that it had lost to the Protestant Reformation. Three chief pillars—the Jesuits, reform of the papacy, and the Council of Trent—supported the Catholic Reformation.

A Spanish nobleman, **Ignatius of Loyola,** founded the Society of Jesus, known as the Jesuits. Loyola's small group of followers was recognized as a religious order by Pope Paul III in 1540. All Jesuits took a special vow of absolute obedience to the pope, making them an important instrument for papal policy. Jesuits used education to spread their message. Jesuit missionaries were very successful in restoring Catholicism to parts of Germany and eastern Europe and in spreading it to other parts of the world.

Reform of the papacy was another important factor in the Catholic Reformation. Participating in dubious financial transactions and Italian political and military affairs, the Renaissance popes had created many sources of corruption. It took the jolt of the Protestant Reformation to bring about serious reform.

Pope Paul III perceived the need for change. He took the bold step of appointing a Reform Commission in 1537 to determine the Church's ills. The commission blamed the Church's problems on the popes' corrupt policies. Paul III also began the Council of Trent, another pillar of the Catholic Reformation. Beginning in March 1545, a group of cardinals, archbishops, bishops, abbots, and theologians met off and on for 18 years in the city of **Trent,** on the border between Germany and Italy.

The final decrees of the Council of Trent reaffirmed traditional Catholic teachings in opposition to Protestant beliefs. Both faith and good works were declared necessary for salvation. The seven sacraments, the Catholic view of the Eucharist, and clerical celibacy were all upheld. Belief in purgatory and in the use of indulgences was strengthened, although the selling of indulgences was forbidden. The Roman Catholic Church now possessed a clear body of doctrine and was unified under the pope's supreme leadership. Catholics were as well prepared as Calvinists to do battle for their faith.

✓ **Reading Check** **Describing** What was the relationship between the Jesuits and the pope?

Vocabulary

1. **Explain** the significance of: Ulrich Zwingli, Zürich, John Calvin, published, justification, predestination, Geneva, King Henry VIII, annul, Ignatius of Loyola, Trent.

Main Ideas

2. **Describe** how Calvin reformed the city of Geneva.

3. **Explain** why Henry VIII formed the Church of England.

4. **Contrast** how the Calvinists and the Anabaptists differed in their attitudes toward church members participating in government activities.

Calvinists		Anabaptists
___		___
___	Church Participation in Government	___
___		___
___		___

Critical Thinking

5. **The BIG Idea** **Assessing** How effective was the Catholic Church's response to the Protestant Reformation?

6. **Determining Cause and Effect** How did "Bloody Mary's" actions affect the religious makeup of England by the end of her reign?

7. **Analyzing Visuals** Compare the chart on page 186 to the map on page 183. Name one country in which the dominant Christian faith included the seven sacraments.

Writing About History

8. **Expository Writing** Research the treatment of the Jewish people during the Reformation. Then write a short essay analyzing why they were segregated to ghettos.

History ONLINE

For help with the concepts in this section of *Glencoe World History—Modern Times*, go to glencoe.com and click Study Central.

You can study anywhere, anytime by downloading quizzes and flash cards to your PDA from glencoe.com.

THE RENAISSANCE in Italy and Northern Europe

- Milan, Venice, and Florence became centers of Renaissance learning and culture.
- Machiavelli's views on gaining and holding power influenced political leaders.
- Humanist education focused on liberal studies.
- Artists sought to portray the world realistically.

DETAIL OF SISTINE CHAPEL CEILING, BY MICHELANGELO

Michelangelo painted people with perfect proportions as a reflection of divine beauty.

MARTIN LUTHER PUBLICLY BURNS HIS EXCOMMUNICATION DOCUMENTS

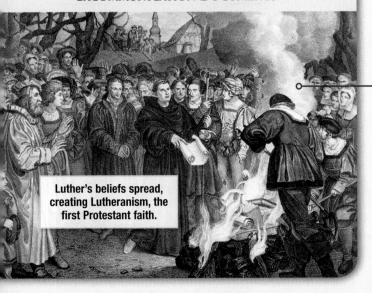

Luther's beliefs spread, creating Lutheranism, the first Protestant faith.

THE REFORMATION Begins

- Erasmus and other Christian humanists paved the way for the Protestant Reformation.
- Catholic teaching stressed faith and good works, but Luther believed that faith alone was sufficient for salvation.
- The Peace of Augsburg ended the religious wars and allowed German states to choose between Catholicism and Lutheranism.

PERSECUTION OF AN ANABAPTIST

Anabaptists were viewed as dangerous radicals.

THE REFORMATION Spreads

- Calvinism replaced Lutheranism as the most important form of Protestantism.
- Henry VIII established the Church of England for political rather than religious reasons.
- Anabaptists believed in the total separation of church and state.
- Pope Paul III took steps to reform the Catholic Church.

STANDARDIZED TEST PRACTICE

TEST-TAKING TIP

If a question asks you to read a quote, look for clues that reveal its historical context—the title, the date, the quote itself. Determining the historical context will help you determine the quote's historical significance. It will also help you determine the correct answer.

Reviewing Vocabulary

Directions: Choose the word or words that best complete the sentence.

1. Theologians of the Reformation disagreed about how people could achieve _____, or acceptance into Heaven.

   A indulgence

   B predestination

   C annulment

   D salvation

2. The money and goods given by the wife's family to the husband at the time of marriage is called a _____.

   A settlement

   B dowry

   C tithe

   D taille

3. John Calvin emphasized _____, the belief that God determined in advance who would be saved and who would be damned.

   A predisposition

   B salvation

   C predestination

   D humanism

4. An image painted on fresh, wet plaster is called a _____.

   A ceramic

   B flying buttress

   C fresco

   D relic

Reviewing Main Ideas

Directions: Choose the best answers to the following questions.

Section 1 *(pp. 162–167)*

5. Which of the following was a characteristic of the Renaissance?

   A Rejection of the classical learning of ancient Greece and Rome

   B Renewed emphasis on an all-powerful God

   C Emergence of a more secular worldview

   D Reawakening of feudalism

6. Who helped to make Florence the cultural center of Europe during the Renaissance?

   A Francesco Sforza

   B Lorenzo de' Medici

   C Niccolò Machiavelli

   D Girolamo Savonarola

Section 2 *(pp. 170–175)*

7. Who has been called the father of Italian Renaissance humanism?

   A Petrarch

   B Leonardo da Vinci

   C Dante

   D Albrecht Dürer

8. What was the *Divine Comedy*?

   A A collection of stories told by a group of pilgrims on a journey

   B A defense of women

   C An ancient Roman poem by Virgil

   D A poem about a soul's journey to Heaven

Need Extra Help?								
If You Missed Questions . . .	1	2	3	4	5	6	7	8
Go to Page . . .	178	167	183	173	162	164	170	171

 GO ON

9. Which artist painted figures on the ceilings of the Sistine Chapel in Rome?

   A Leonardo da Vinci

   B Michelangelo

   C Raphael

   D Jan van Eyck

Section 3 (pp. 176–181)

10. What was the major goal of Christian humanism?

    A To create a new form of Christian faith

    B To preserve religious unity in the Holy Roman Empire

    C To promote external forms of religion, such as pilgrimages and relics

    D To reform the Catholic Church

11. What agreement ended the religious warfare in Germany in 1555?

    A Ninety-five Theses

    B Edict of Worms

    C Peace of Augsburg

    D Great Schism

Section 4 (pp. 182–187)

12. Why did King Henry VIII break with Rome and establish the Church of England?

    A To marry Anne Boleyn

    B To promote his religious views

    C To force the Catholic Church to reform

    D To separate church and state

13. Who founded the Jesuits?

    A John Calvin

    B Ignatius of Loyola

    C Martin Luther

    D Pope Paul III

Critical Thinking

Directions: Choose the best answers to the following questions.

Use the following map to answer question 14.

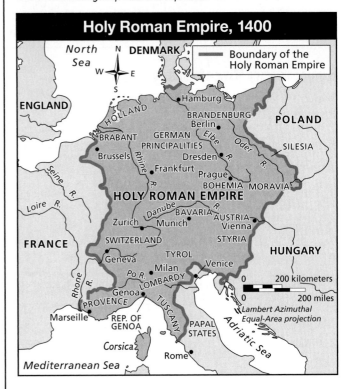

14. Which of the following is a true statement about the Holy Roman Empire in 1400?

    A It had no access to the Mediterranean Sea.

    B It did not include parts of Italy.

    C Rome was not a part of the Empire.

    D Denmark was part of the Empire.

15. How did fifteenth-century humanists differ from those in the fourteenth century?

    A They preferred to live in solitude.

    B They believed in service to the state.

    C Most moved to the country.

    D They emphasized classical Latin.

Need Extra Help?							
If You Missed Questions . . .	9	10	11	12	13	14	15
Go to Page . . .	174	176	181	184	187	164	170

16. Why were liberal studies at the core of a humanist curriculum?

   A To create great scholars

   B To promote advances in science

   C To enable more people to read Latin

   D To provide practical preparation for life

17. In his Ninety-five Theses, Martin Luther wrote: "Christians are to be taught that he who gives to the poor or lends to the needy does a better work than buying pardons." To what is Luther objecting in this statement?

   A The doctrine of predestination

   B The lack of concern for the poor

   C The sale of indulgences

   D The spread of secular humanism

Base your answer to question 18 on the following table.

Top Ten Organized Religions of the World (2004 estimates)

Religion	Number of Members	Percentage
Christianity	2.1 billion	33.0%
Islam	1.3 billion	20.1%
Hinduism	851 million	13.3%
Buddhism	375 million	5.9%
Sikhism	25 million	0.4%
Judaism	15 million	0.2%
Baha'ism	7.5 million	0.1%
Confucianism	6.4 million	0.1%
Jainism	4.5 million	0.1%
Shintoism	2.8 million	0.0%

Source: *Encyclopedia Britannica*

18. Which of the following is a true statement about the world's top 10 organized religions?

   A Hindus exceed Buddhists by more than double.

   B There are more Muslims than Christians.

   C Jews far outnumber Buddhists.

   D Christianity is the most organized religion in the world.

Document-Based Questions

Directions: Analyze the document and answer the short-answer questions that follow the document. Base your answers on the document and on your knowledge of world history.

Niccolò Machiavelli wrote:

> *"Everyone realizes how praiseworthy it is for a prince to honor his word and to be straightforward rather than crafty in his dealings; nonetheless experience shows that princes who have achieved great things have been those who have given their word lightly, who have known how to trick men with their cunning, and who, in the end, have overcome those abiding by honest principles. . . . A prince, therefore, need not necessarily have all the good qualities I mentioned above, but he should certainly appear to have them. . . . He should not deviate from what is good, if that is possible, but he should know how to do evil, if that is necessary."*
>
> —Niccolò Machiavelli, *The Prince*, George Bull, trans., 1981

19. According to Machiavelli, what kinds of princes have achieved great things?

20. According to Machiavelli, what role does evil play in governance?

Extended Response

21. Analyze how the Reformation shaped the political and religious life of Europe. Be sure to identify the historical effects of the Reformation.

History ONLINE

For additional test practice, use Self-Check Quizzes—Chapter 5 at glencoe.com.

Need Extra Help?						
If You Missed Questions . . .	16	17	18	19	20	21
Go to Page . . .	172	165	165	165	181	182

STOP

CHAPTER **6**

The Age of Exploration 1500–1800

Section 1 Exploration and Expansion

Section 2 The Atlantic Slave Trade

Section 3 Colonial Latin America

MAKING CONNECTIONS
How are the Americas linked to Africa?

The demand for enslaved Africans increased dramatically after Europeans began to settle in the Americas. The Cape Coast Castle in Ghana, shown in this photo, is one of the forts where enslaved Africans were held until ships arrived to take them to the Americas. This fort could hold about 1,500 slaves usually locked in dark, crowded dungeons for many weeks. Today, the Cape Coast Castle contains a museum that allows people to learn about slavery. In this chapter you will learn about the exploration of new lands and its global impact.

- Why might people want to visit the Cape Coast Castle?
- Does slavery occur in any parts of the world today?

EUROPE AND
THE AMERICAS ▶

1500
Pedro Cabral lands in South America

1520
Ferdinand Magellan sails into the Pacific Ocean

1500   **1600**

THE WORLD ▶

1568
Japan's unification begins

1632
Building of Taj Mahal begins

1663
Canada becomes
a French colony

1787
Northwest Ordinance bans
slavery in the Northwest
Territory of the United States

1794
Congress bans
slave trade
between U.S. and
foreign countries

1700

1800

1722
Rule of Emperor Kangxi
of China ends

FOLDABLES™
Study Organizer

Describing As you
read, take notes on
exploration, slave
trade, and colonial Latin America on
quarter sheets of paper. Organize your
notes in a three-pocket book.

Exploration *Slave Trade* *Colonial Latin America*

History ONLINE

Chapter Overview—Visit **glencoe.com** to preview Chapter 6.

Exploration and Expansion

On a quest for "God, glory, and gold," the Portuguese and Spanish led the way in exploring new worlds. Setting sail to the east, the Portuguese eventually gained control of the Spice Islands. In the west, Portugal and Spain each claimed new lands in the Americas. By the end of the sixteenth century, however, the Dutch, French, and English began competing with the Portuguese and Spanish for these new lands and the riches they held.

GUIDE TO READING

The BIG Idea
Competition Among Countries
Europeans began exploring the world in the 1400s, and several nations experienced economic heights through worldwide trade.

Content Vocabulary
- conquistadors *(p. 198)*
- *encomienda (p. 199)*
- Columbian Exchange *(p. 200)*

Academic Vocabulary
- overseas *(p. 194)*
- percent *(p. 196)*

People and Places
- Hernán Cortés *(p. 195)*
- Portugal *(p. 196)*
- Vasco da Gama *(p. 196)*
- Melaka *(p. 196)*
- Christopher Columbus *(p. 196)*
- Cuba *(p. 196)*
- Ferdinand Magellan *(p. 196)*
- John Cabot *(p. 197)*
- Amerigo Vespucci *(p. 197)*
- Montezuma *(p. 198)*
- Francisco Pizarro *(p. 199)*

Reading Strategy
Organizing Information As you read, use a chart like the one below to list the explorers and lands explored by each European nation.

	Explorers	Lands Explored
Portugal		
Spain		
England		
France		
Netherlands		

Motives and Means

MAIN IDEA Europeans began to explore distant lands, motivated by religious zeal and the promise of gold and glory.

HISTORY & YOU Recall that Isabella and Ferdinand of Spain sought religious unity for their country. Read to learn how religious zeal also played a part in the European quest for riches in other lands.

The dynamic energy of Western civilization between 1500 and 1800 was most apparent when Europeans began to expand into the rest of the world. First Portugal and Spain, then later the Netherlands, England, and France, all rose to new economic heights through their worldwide trading activity.

For almost a thousand years, Europeans had mostly remained in one area of the world. At the end of the fifteenth century, however, they set out on a remarkable series of **overseas** journeys. What caused them to undertake such dangerous voyages to the ends of the Earth?

Europeans had long been attracted to Asia. In the late thirteenth century, Marco Polo had traveled with his father and uncle to the Chinese court of the great Mongol ruler Kublai Khan. He had written an account of his experiences, known as *The Travels*. Many, including Christopher Columbus, read the book and were fascinated by the exotic East. In the fourteenth century, conquests by the Ottoman Turks reduced the ability of westerners to travel by land to the East. People then spoke of gaining access to Asia by sea.

Economic motives loom large in European expansion. Merchants, adventurers, and state officials had high hopes of expanding trade, especially for the spices of the East. The spices, which were needed to preserve and flavor food, were very expensive after Arab middlemen shipped them to Europe. Europeans also had hopes of finding precious metals. One Spanish adventurer wrote that he went to the Americas to "to give light to those who were in darkness, and to grow rich, as all men desire to do."

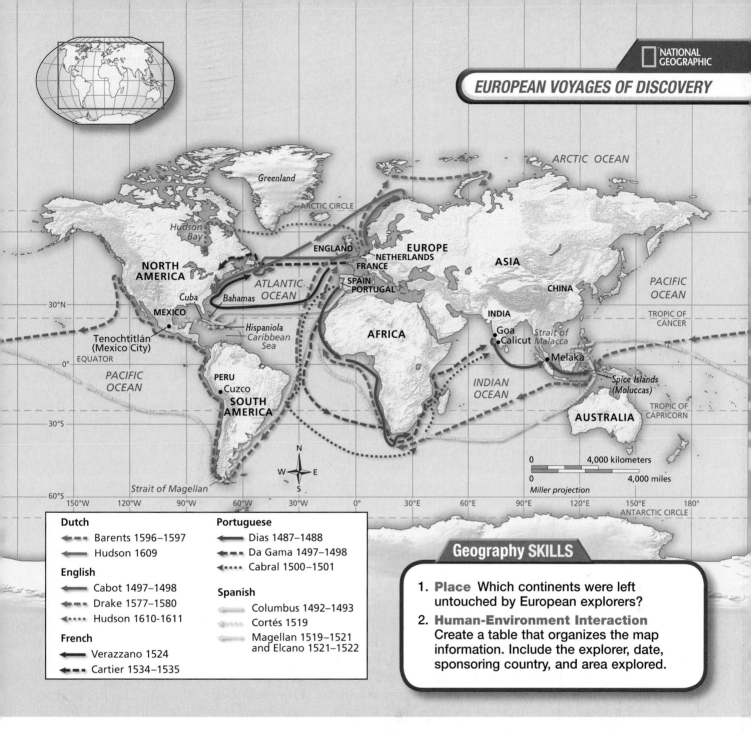

EUROPEAN VOYAGES OF DISCOVERY

ARCTIC OCEAN

Greenland

ARCTIC CIRCLE

Hudson Bay

ENGLAND
EUROPE
NETHERLANDS
FRANCE
SPAIN
PORTUGAL

ASIA

NORTH AMERICA

ATLANTIC OCEAN

CHINA

PACIFIC OCEAN

TROPIC OF CANCER

30°N

Cuba
Bahamas

MEXICO

INDIA

Goa
Calicut

Strait of Malacca

Tenochtitlán (Mexico City)

Hispaniola
Caribbean Sea

AFRICA

Melaka

0°
EQUATOR

PACIFIC OCEAN

PERU
Cuzco

SOUTH AMERICA

INDIAN OCEAN

Spice Islands (Moluccas)

TROPIC OF CAPRICORN

30°S

AUSTRALIA

Strait of Magellan

N
W E
S

0   4,000 kilometers
0   4,000 miles
Miller projection

60°S
150°W   120°W   90°W   60°W   30°W   0°   30°E   60°E   90°E   120°E   150°E   180°
ANTARCTIC CIRCLE

Dutch
- ◄- - Barents 1596–1597
- ◄— Hudson 1609

English
- ◄— Cabot 1497–1498
- ◄- - Drake 1577–1580
- ◄···· Hudson 1610-1611

French
- ◄— Verazzano 1524
- ◄- - Cartier 1534–1535

Portuguese
- ◄— Dias 1487–1488
- ◄- - Da Gama 1497–1498
- ◄···· Cabral 1500–1501

Spanish
- ◄— Columbus 1492–1493
- ◄— Cortés 1519
- ◄— Magellan 1519–1521 and Elcano 1521–1522

Geography SKILLS

1. **Place** Which continents were left untouched by European explorers?
2. **Human-Environment Interaction** Create a table that organizes the map information. Include the explorer, date, sponsoring country, and area explored.

This statement suggests another reason for the overseas voyages: religious zeal. Many people shared the belief of **Hernán Cortés,** the Spanish conqueror of Mexico, that they must ensure that the natives were "introduced into the holy Catholic faith."

There was a third motive as well. Spiritual and secular affairs were connected in the sixteenth century. People like Cortés wanted to convert the natives to Christianity; but grandeur, glory, and a spirit of adventure also played a major role in European expansion.

"God, glory, and gold," then, were the chief motives for European expansion, but what made the voyages possible? By the mid-1400s, European monarchies had increased their power and their resources and could focus beyond their borders. Europeans had also reached a level of technology that enabled them to make regular voyages beyond Europe. A new global age was about to begin.

✓**Reading Check** **Explaining** What does the phrase "God, glory, and gold" mean?

A Race for Riches

MAIN IDEA Portuguese and Spanish explorers took the lead in discovering new lands.

HISTORY & YOU Does your vehicle have a navigational system? Read to learn how the early explorers found new lands.

At the end of the 1400s, Europeans sailed out into the world in new directions. Portuguese ships took the lead when they sailed southward along the West African coast. Spain soon followed with the dramatic voyages of Christopher Columbus to the Americas.

Portuguese Explorers

Portugal took the lead in European exploration. Beginning in 1520, under the sponsorship of Prince Henry the Navigator, Portuguese fleets began probing southward along the western coast of Africa. There, they discovered a new source of gold. The southern coast of West Africa thus became known to Europeans as the Gold Coast.

Portuguese sea captains heard reports of a route to India around the southern tip of Africa. In 1488 Bartholomeu Dias rounded the tip, called the Cape of Good Hope. Later, **Vasco da Gama** went around the cape and cut across the Indian Ocean to the coast of India. In May of 1498, he arrived off the port of Calicut. There he took on a cargo of spices. After returning to Portugal, da Gama made a profit of several thousand **percent.** Is it surprising that da Gama's voyage was the first of many along this route?

Portuguese fleets returned to the area to take control of the spice trade from the Muslims. In 1509 Portuguese warships defeated a combined fleet of Turkish and Indian ships off the coast of India. A year later, Admiral Afonso de Albuquerque (AL-buh-KUR-kee) set up a port at Goa, on the western coast of India.

The Portuguese then began to range more widely for the source of the spice trade. Soon, Albuquerque sailed into **Melaka**, a thriving spice trade port, on the Malay Peninsula. Having Melaka would destroy Arab control of the spice trade and provide the Portuguese with a way station on the route to the Moluccas, then known as the Spice Islands.

From Melaka, the Portuguese launched expeditions to China and the Spice Islands. There they signed a treaty with a local ruler for the purchase and export of cloves to the European market. This treaty established Portuguese control of the spice trade. However, the Portuguese had a limited empire of trading posts on the coasts of India and China. The Portuguese had neither the power, the people, nor the desire to colonize the Asian regions.

Guns and seamanship made the Portuguese the first successful European explorers. Heavily armed, their fleets were able to defeat local naval and land forces. Later, however, the Portuguese would be no match for other European forces—the English, Dutch, and French.

Spanish Explorers

Educated Europeans knew the world was round but had no idea of its circumference, the size of the Asian continent, or that another continent lay to the west between Europe and Asia. While the Portuguese sailed eastward through the Indian Ocean, the Spanish sailed westward across the Atlantic Ocean to find the route to Asia.

Convinced that the Earth's circumference was not as great as others thought, **Christopher Columbus** believed he could reach Asia by sailing west instead of east around Africa. Columbus persuaded Queen Isabella of Spain to finance an exploratory expedition. In October 1492 he reached the Americas, where he explored the coastline of **Cuba** and the island of Hispaniola.

Columbus believed he had reached Asia. After three voyages, he had still not found a route through the outer islands to the Asian mainland. In his four voyages, Columbus reached all the major Caribbean islands and Honduras in Central America—all of which he called the Indies.

Another important explorer to Spain was **Ferdinand Magellan.** Magellan persuaded the king of Spain to finance his voyage to Asia through the Western

Hemisphere. He set sail in September 1519 down the coast of South America in search of a sea passage through America. In October 1520 Magellan passed through a waterway (later called the Strait of Magellan) into the Pacific Ocean. The fleet reached the Philippines, but Magellan was killed by the native peoples there. Although only one of his ships returned to Spain, Magellan is still remembered as the first person to circumnavigate the globe.

New Lands to Explore

The voyages of the Portuguese and Spanish had opened up new lands to exploration. Both Spain and Portugal feared that the other might claim some of its newly discovered territories. They resolved their concerns with the Treaty of Tordesillas, signed in 1494. The treaty called for a line of demarcation extending from north to south through the Atlantic Ocean and the easternmost part of the South American continent. Unexplored territories east of the line would be controlled by Portugal, and those west of the line by Spain. This treaty gave Portugal control over its route around Africa, and it gave Spain rights to almost all of the Americas.

Soon, government-sponsored explorers from many countries joined the race to the Americas. A Venetian seaman, **John Cabot,** explored the New England coastline of the Americas for England. The Portuguese sea captain Pedro Cabral landed in South America in 1500. **Amerigo Vespucci** (veh•SPOO•chee), a Florentine, went along on several voyages. His letters describing the lands he saw led to the use of the name America (after Amerigo) for the new lands.

Europeans called these lands the New World although they already had flourishing civilizations made up of millions of people when the Europeans arrived. The Americas were, of course, new to the Europeans, who quickly saw opportunities for conquest and exploitation.

✓ **Reading Check** **Explaining** Why did the Spanish and Portuguese sign the Treaty of Tordesillas?

SCIENCE, TECHNOLOGY, & SOCIETY

Technology and Exploration

How did early European explorers make their way across the Atlantic Ocean in the 1400s and 1500s? They relied upon several new and improved inventions, as well as technology borrowed from other cultures.

The caravel was a faster ship design invented by the Portuguese, which made long voyages of exploration possible. Its triangular (lateen) sails allowed explorers to sail against the wind. Europeans learned to use lateen sails from the Arabs. The caravel design included a large cargo hold.

At the same time, cartography (the art and science of mapmaking) had advanced to the point where Europeans had fairly accurate maps. European sailors used the astrolabe, an invention of Greek astronomers, to plot their latitude using the sun or stars. The magnetic compass, invented in China, also helped sailors to chart a course across the ocean.

CRITICAL THINKING SKILLS

1. **Analyzing Visuals** How did the caravel's design help European explorers?
2. **Synthesizing** What were the sources of the technology used by early European explorers?

The caravel was well suited for long voyages of exploration.

Explorer Amerigo Vespucci using an astrolabe, a Greek invention that was improved by the Arabs

The Spanish Empire

MAIN IDEA The great Aztec and Inca civilizations succumbed to the Spanish.

HISTORY & YOU How did the Romans treat their conquered peoples? Read how the Spanish conquered the Aztec and Inca.

The Spanish conquerors of the Americas—known as **conquistadors**—were individuals whose firearms, organizational skills, and determination brought them incredible success. With their people and resources, the Spanish established an overseas empire quite different from the Portuguese trading posts.

Aztec Civilization Destroyed

For a century, the Aztec ruled much of central Mexico from the Gulf of Mexico to the Pacific coasts. Most local officials accepted the authority of the Aztec king in Tenochtitlán. In the region of Tlaxcala to the east, however, the local lords wanted greater independence. Areas that had never been conquered wanted to remain free of the Aztec.

In 1519, a Spanish force under the command of Hernán Cortés landed at Veracruz, on the Gulf of Mexico. Cortés marched to Tenochtitlán with a small body of troops (550 soldiers and 16 horses). As he went, he made alliances with city-states that had tired of the oppressive rule of the Aztec. Particularly important was the alliance with Tlaxcala.

In November, Cortés arrived at Tenochtitlán and was welcomed by the Aztec monarch **Montezuma** (also spelled Moctezuma). The Aztec were astounded to see the unfamiliar sight of men on horseback and firearms, cannon, and steel swords. These weapons gave the Spanish a great advantage in fighting the Aztec.

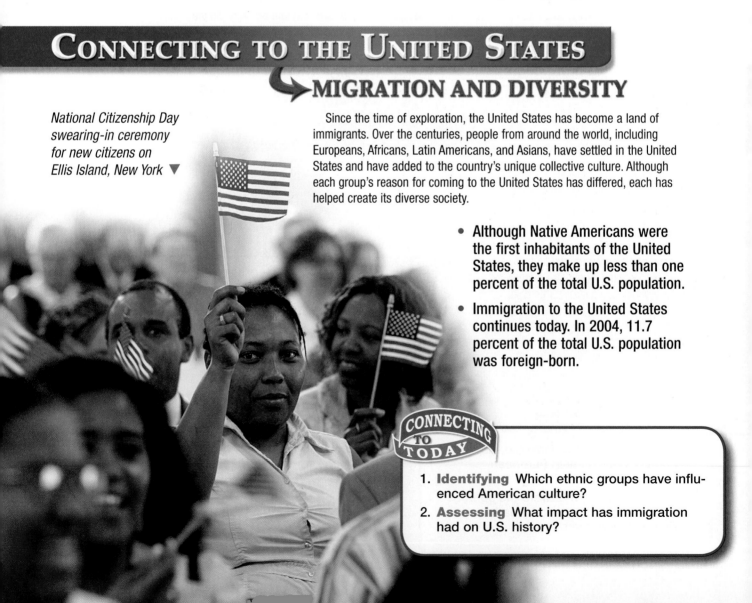

CONNECTING TO THE UNITED STATES

MIGRATION AND DIVERSITY

National Citizenship Day swearing-in ceremony for new citizens on Ellis Island, New York ▼

Since the time of exploration, the United States has become a land of immigrants. Over the centuries, people from around the world, including Europeans, Africans, Latin Americans, and Asians, have settled in the United States and have added to the country's unique collective culture. Although each group's reason for coming to the United States has differed, each has helped create its diverse society.

- **Although Native Americans were the first inhabitants of the United States, they make up less than one percent of the total U.S. population.**

- **Immigration to the United States continues today. In 2004, 11.7 percent of the total U.S. population was foreign-born.**

CONNECTING TO TODAY

1. **Identifying** Which ethnic groups have influenced American culture?
2. **Assessing** What impact has immigration had on U.S. history?

Eventually, tensions arose between the Spaniards and the Aztec. The Spanish took Montezuma hostage and began to pillage the city. In the fall of 1520, one year after Cortés had first arrived, the local population revolted and drove the invaders from the city. Many of the Spanish were killed.

The Aztec soon experienced new disasters, however. As one Aztec related, "But at about the time that the Spaniards had fled from Mexico, there came a great sickness, a pestilence, the smallpox." With no natural immunity to European diseases, many Aztec fell sick and died. Meanwhile, Cortés received fresh soldiers from his new allies; the state of Tlaxcala alone provided 50,000 warriors. After four months, the city surrendered.

The forces of Cortés leveled pyramids, temples, and palaces and used the stones to build government buildings and churches for the Spanish. The rivers and canals were filled in. The magnificent city of Tenochtitlán was no more. During the next 30 years, the Spanish expanded their control to all of Mexico.

Conquest of the Inca

The Inca Empire was still flourishing when the first Spanish expeditions arrived in the central Andes. In December 1530, **Francisco Pizarro** landed on the Pacific coast of South America with only a small band of about 180 men. However, like Cortés, Pizarro brought steel weapons, gunpowder, and horses. The Inca had seen none of these.

The Inca Empire also experienced an epidemic of smallpox. Like the Aztec, the Inca had no immunities to European diseases. Smallpox soon devastated entire villages. Even the Inca emperor was a victim.

When the emperor died, his two sons each claimed the throne. This led to a civil war. Atahuallpa, one of the sons, defeated his brother's forces. Taking advantage of the situation, Pizarro captured Atahuallpa. With their stones, arrows, and light spears, Inca warriors provided little challenge to the charging Spanish horses, guns, and cannons.

After executing Atahuallpa, Pizarro and his soldiers, aided by their Inca allies, marched on Cuzco and captured the Inca capital. By 1535, Pizarro had established a new capital at Lima for a new colony of the Spanish Empire.

The Columbian Exchange

By 1550, much territory in Mexico, Central America, and South America had been brought under Spanish control. (The Portuguese took over Brazil, which fell on their side of the line of demarcation.) Already by 1535, the Spanish had created a system of colonial administration in their new American empire.

Queen Isabella declared Native Americans (then called Indians, after the Spanish word *Indios*, "inhabitants of the Indies") to be her subjects. She granted to Spanish settlers in the Americas the *encomienda*. This was the right of landowners to use Native Americans as laborers.

The holders of an *encomienda* were supposed to protect the Native Americans, but Spanish settlers were far from Spain and largely ignored their government. Native Americans were put to work on sugar plantations and in the gold and silver mines. Few Spanish settlers worried about protecting them.

Forced labor, starvation, and especially disease took a fearful toll on Native American lives. With little natural resistance to European diseases, the native peoples were ravaged by smallpox, measles, and typhus. Many of them died. Hispaniola, for example, had a population of 250,000 when Columbus arrived. By 1538, only 500 Native Americans had survived. In Mexico, the population dropped from 25 million in 1500 to 1 million in 1630.

In the early years of the conquest, Catholic monks converted and baptized hundreds of thousands of Native Americans. With the arrival of the missionaries came parishes, schools, and hospitals—all the trappings of a European society. Native American social and political structures were torn apart and replaced by European systems of religion, language, culture, and government.

As the Spanish and Native Americans married and had families, they created a new people with roots in both cultures.

TURNING POINT

THE COLUMBIAN EXCHANGE AND INTERNATIONAL TRADE

One of the major goals of European exploration and expansion was to gain wealth. Following the ideas of mercantilism (see Section 2), European nations sought to build wealth by increasing their exports of goods and their imports of precious metals and raw materials. When Columbus landed in the Americas and established a colony for Spain, he took the first step in creating an immense trade network. Ultimately international trade in the 1500s and 1600s opened the door to a world economy.

The exchange of plants and animals between Europe and the Americas—known as the Columbian Exchange—had far-reaching effects on the world's cultures. Diseases brought by Europeans killed a large number of Native Americans. Elsewhere in the world, new food crops from the Americas supported population growth, changed tastes, and created new markets.

A ship departs from the port of Lisbon, Portugal, for Brazil in 1562. Trade between European nations and their colonies in the New World had profound effects on the entire world.

Spanish explorer Hernán Cortés meets with the Aztec monarch Montezuma. Native Americans had never seen horses before meeting the Spanish. The Spanish likewise learned about many native plants and animals from the Aztec.

CRITICAL THINKING SKILLS

1. **Identifying** How did mercantilism relate to European exploration?
2. **Synthesizing** In what ways did the voyages of Columbus mark a turning point in world history?

Some aspects of the indigenous culture survive. In Mexico, the Nahua Indians, descendants of the Aztec, weave on the same kind of loom used by the Aztec.

Spanish conquests in the Americas affected not only the conquered but also the conquerors. Colonists established plantations and ranches to raise sugar, cotton, vanilla, livestock, and other products introduced to the Americas for export to Europe. While Europeans were bringing horses, cattle, and wheat to the Americas, agricultural products native to the Americas, such as potatoes, cocoa, corn, tomatoes, and tobacco, were shipped to Europe. The exchange of plants and animals between Europe and the Americas—known as the **Columbian Exchange**—transformed economic activity in both worlds. Potatoes, for example, became a basic dietary staple in some areas of Europe. By enabling more people to survive on smaller plots of land, a rapid increase in population was made possible.

✓ Reading Check **Identifying** What products were sent from the Americas to Europe?

European Rivals

MAIN IDEA The Portuguese and Spanish found new rivals in the Dutch, French, and English for trading rights and for new lands.

HISTORY & YOU What if someone set up and operated a concession stand just beyond your school's property during a championship basketball game? Read to learn how European countries competed for trading rights and for new lands.

By the end of the sixteenth century, several new European rivals had begun to challenge the Portuguese and Spanish. At the beginning of the seventeenth century, an English fleet landed on the northwestern coast of India and established trade relations with the people there. The first Dutch fleet arrived in India in 1595. Shortly after, the Dutch formed the East India Company and began competing with both the English and the Portuguese for Indian Ocean trade.

The Dutch also formed their own West India Company to compete with the Spanish and Portuguese in the Americas. Although it made some inroads in Portuguese Brazil and the Caribbean, the company's profits were less than its expenditures.

In the early seventeenth century Dutch settlements were established on the North American continent. The colony of New Netherland stretched from the mouth of the Hudson River as far north as Albany, New York. Modern names such as Staten Island, Harlem, and the Catskill Mountains remind us that it was the Dutch who initially settled the Hudson River valley.

During the seventeenth century, the French colonized parts of what is now Canada and Louisiana. In 1608 Samuel de Champlain founded Quebec, the first permanent French settlement in the Americas. Meanwhile, English settlers were founding Virginia and the Massachusetts Bay Colony.

After 1660, however, rivalry with the English and the French (who had also become active in North America) brought the fall of the Dutch commercial empire in the Americas. In 1664 the English seized the colony of New Netherland from the Dutch and renamed it New York. The Dutch West India Company soon went bankrupt.

By the end of the seventeenth century, the English had established control over most of the eastern seaboard of North America. They had also set up sugar plantations on several Caribbean islands. Nevertheless, compared to the enormous empire of the Spanish in Latin America, the North American colonies still remained of minor importance to the English economy.

✓ Reading Check **Identifying** Which century marked the beginning of English rivalry with Spain and Portugal for trading rights in India?

Vocabulary

1. **Explain** the significance of: overseas, Hernán Cortés, Portugal, Vasco da Gama, percent, Melaka, Christopher Columbus, Cuba, Ferdinand Magellan, John Cabot, Amerigo Vespucci, conquistadors, Montezuma, Francisco Pizarro, *encomienda*, Columbian Exchange.

Main Ideas

2. **Identify** the motives for European exploration. Use a web diagram like the one below to list the motives.

Motives for Exploration

3. **Explain** why the Portuguese were the first successful European explorers.

4. **Define** the *encomienda* system. What effect did this system have on the Native American populations?

Critical Thinking

5. **The BIG Idea** **Making Generalizations** What forces came together in the mid-1400s that made the European age of exploration possible?

6. **Evaluating** What impact did European technology, food, and disease have on the Americas? How did the Columbian Exchange affect the Americas and Europe?

7. **Analyzing Visuals** Why do you think there is a cross on the table in the portrait of Amerigo Vespucci on page 197?

Writing About History

8. **Descriptive Writing** Imagine you are an Aztec residing in Tenochtitlán when Cortés arrives. Write a journal entry describing the Spanish—their clothing, weapons and horses.

History ONLINE

For help with the concepts in this section of *Glencoe World History— Modern Times*, go to **glencoe.com** and click Study Central.

Is It New World or Old World?

The ingredients in foods enjoyed today come from all over the world. The geographic origins of these foods, however, might come as a surprise. For example, tomatoes, which are associated with Italian cuisine, originated in the Americas. Food crops and animals native to one part of the world rarely existed in another part of the world until the voyages of Christopher Columbus. His voyages triggered one of the most significant events in world history—the Columbian Exchange—an extensive exchange of plants and animals between the Old and New Worlds.

NEW WORLD

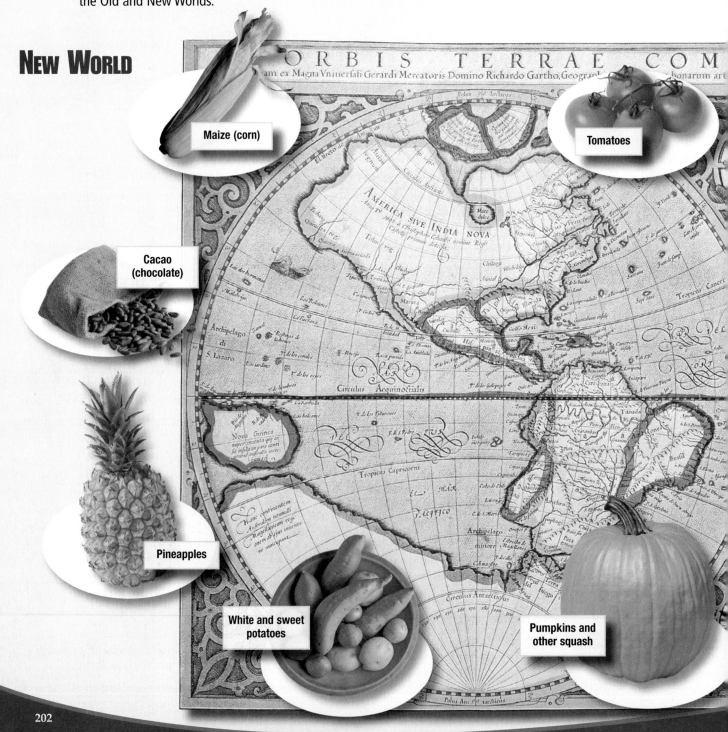

Maize (corn)

Tomatoes

Cacao (chocolate)

Pineapples

White and sweet potatoes

Pumpkins and other squash

Cattle

Horses

OLD WORLD

Peaches and pears

DESCRIPTIO
familiaritatis memoriã Rumoldus Mercator fieri curabat A'. M.D.Lxxxvii.

Lettuce

Wheat, barley, oats, rye, and rice

Sugar

DISEASES

Plants and animals were not the only things that were exchanged between Europe, Africa, Asia, and the Americas. People traveling from the Old World to the New World also brought with them many infectious diseases. These diseases included chicken pox, measles, smallpox, malaria, flu, and the common cold. Because people in the New World had not had previous exposure to these diseases, they were not immune to their devastating effects.

ANALYZING VISUALS

1. **Inferring** What do you think it might have been like to see for the first time a completely unfamiliar animal, such as a horse or cow?

2. **Comparing** What infectious diseases are people worried about being exposed to today? What are the geographic origins of these diseases?

The Atlantic Slave Trade

As the number of European colonies increased, so did the volume and area of European trade. An Atlantic slave trade also began. Altogether, as many as 10 million enslaved Africans were brought to the Americas between the early 1500s and the late 1800s. Not until the late 1700s did European feeling against slavery begin to grow.

GUIDE TO READING

The BIG Idea

Human Rights European expansion affected Africa with the dramatic increase of the slave trade.

Content Vocabulary

- colony *(p. 204)*
- mercantilism *(p. 204)*
- balance of trade *(p. 204)*
- subsidies *(p. 204)*
- plantations *(p. 205)*
- triangular trade *(p. 206)*
- Middle Passage *(p. 206)*

Academic Vocabulary

- transportation *(p. 204)*
- primary *(p. 205)*

People and Places

- King Afonso *(p. 206)*
- Benin *(p. 207)*

Reading Strategy

Determining Cause and Effect As you read, use a table like the one below to identify economic and political factors that caused the slave trade to be profitable. List the economic and political effects of the trade.

Economic/Political Factors	Economic/Political Effects

Trade, Colonies, and Mercantilism

MAIN IDEA The slave trade increased as enslaved Africans were brought to the Americas.

HISTORY & YOU Have you seen movies about slavery? Read to learn how the slave trade became part of the triangular trade pattern.

In less than 300 years, the European age of exploration changed the world. In some areas, such as the Americas and the Spice Islands, it led to the destruction of local civilizations and the establishment of European colonies. In others, such as Africa and mainland Southeast Asia, it left native regimes intact but had a strong impact on local societies and regional trade patterns. European expansion affected Africa with the dramatic increase of the slave trade, which played an important part in European trade.

The increase in the volume and area of European trade as a result of European expansion was a crucial factor in producing a new age of commercial capitalism. This is one of the first steps in the development of the world economy. The nations of Europe were creating trading empires.

Led by Portugal and Spain, European nations established many trading posts and colonies in the Americas and the East. A **colony** is a settlement of people living in a new territory, linked with the parent country by trade and direct government control.

Colonies played a role in the theory of **mercantilism,** a set of principles that dominated economic thought in the seventeenth century. According to mercantilists, the prosperity of a nation depended on a large supply of bullion, or gold and silver. To bring in gold and silver payments, nations tried to have a favorable **balance of trade.** The balance of trade is the difference in value between what a nation imports and what it exports over time. When the balance is favorable, the goods exported are of greater value than those imported.

To encourage exports, governments stimulated industries and trade. They granted **subsidies,** or payments, to new industries and improved **transportation** systems by building roads, bridges,

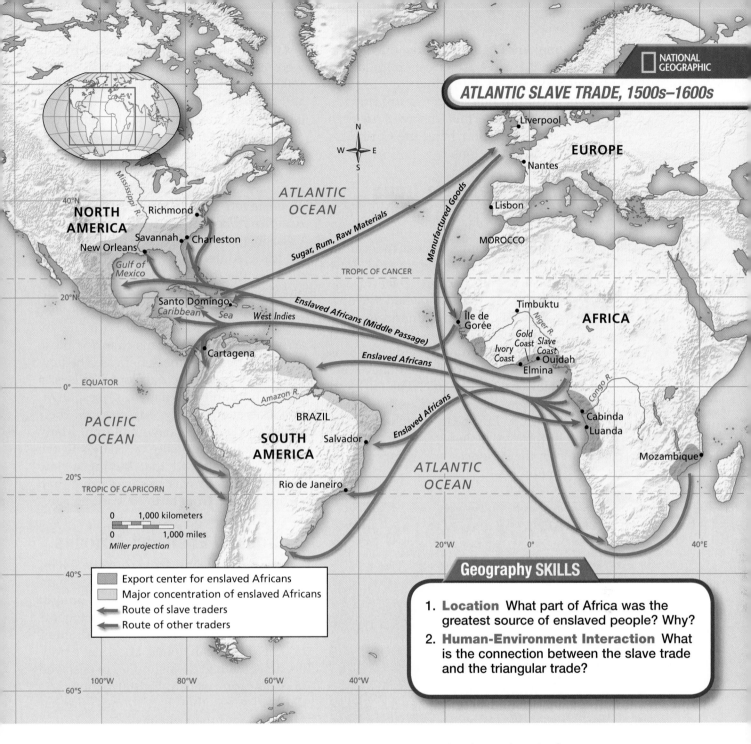

ATLANTIC SLAVE TRADE, 1500s–1600s

Liverpool

EUROPE

Nantes

Lisbon

MOROCCO

Manufactured Goods

ATLANTIC OCEAN

NORTH AMERICA

Richmond

Savannah • Charleston

New Orleans

Gulf of Mexico

Mississippi R.

Sugar, Rum, Raw Materials

TROPIC OF CANCER

Santo Domingo
Caribbean Sea West Indies

Enslaved Africans (Middle Passage)

Île de Gorée

Timbuktu

AFRICA

Niger R.

Gold Coast
Ivory Coast
Slave Coast
Ouidah
Elmina

Enslaved Africans

Cartagena

EQUATOR

Amazon R.

PACIFIC OCEAN

BRAZIL

SOUTH AMERICA

Salvador

Enslaved Africans

Congo R.

Cabinda
Luanda

Mozambique

ATLANTIC OCEAN

TROPIC OF CAPRICORN

Rio de Janeiro

0   1,000 kilometers
0   1,000 miles
Miller projection

Export center for enslaved Africans
Major concentration of enslaved Africans
Route of slave traders
Route of other traders

100°W   80°W   60°W   40°W   20°W   0°   40°E

Geography SKILLS

1. **Location** What part of Africa was the greatest source of enslaved people? Why?
2. **Human-Environment Interaction** What is the connection between the slave trade and the triangular trade?

and canals. They placed high tariffs, or taxes, on foreign goods to keep them out of their own countries. Colonies were considered important both as sources of raw materials and markets for finished goods.

The Slave Trade

Traffic in enslaved people was not new. As in other areas of the world, slavery had been practiced in Africa since ancient times. In the 1400s, it continued at a fairly steady level.

The **primary** market for enslaved Africans was Southwest Asia where most served as domestic servants as in some European countries like Portugal. The demand for enslaved Africans changed dramatically with the discovery of the Americas in the 1490s and the planting of sugarcane there.

Cane sugar was introduced to Europe from Southwest Asia during the Crusades of the Middle Ages. **Plantations,** or large agricultural estates, were established in the 1500s along the coast of Brazil and on Caribbean islands to grow sugarcane.

Growing cane sugar demands much labor. The small Native American population, much of which had died of diseases imported from Europe, could not provide the labor needed. Thus, enslaved Africans were shipped to Brazil and the Caribbean to work on plantations.

Growth of the Slave Trade

In 1518 a Spanish ship carried the first enslaved Africans directly from Africa to the Americas. During the next two centuries, the trade in enslaved people grew dramatically and became part of the **triangular trade** that connected Europe, Africa and Asia, and the American continents. European merchant ships carried European manufactured goods, such as guns and cloth, to Africa where they were traded for enslaved people. The enslaved Africans were then shipped to the Americas and sold. European merchants then bought tobacco, molasses, sugar, and raw cotton in the Americas and shipped them back to Europe.

History ONLINE
Student Web Activity—
Visit glencoe.com and complete the activity about the Age of Exploration.

An estimated 275,000 enslaved Africans were exported during the 1500s. In the 1600s, the total climbed to over 1 million and jumped to 6 million in the 1700s. Altogether, as many as 10 million enslaved Africans were brought to the Americas between the early 1500s and the late 1800s.

One reason for these astonishing numbers was the high death rate. The journey of enslaved people from Africa to the Americas became known as the **Middle Passage,** the middle portion of the triangular trade route. Many enslaved Africans died on the journey. Those who arrived often died from diseases to which they had little or no immunity.

Death rates were higher for newly arrived enslaved Africans than for those born and raised in the Americas. The new generation gradually developed at least a partial immunity to many diseases. Owners, however, rarely encouraged their enslaved people to have children. Many slave owners, especially on islands in the Caribbean, believed that buying a new enslaved person was less expensive than raising a child from birth to working age.

Sources of Enslaved Africans

Before Europeans arrived in the 1400s, most enslaved persons in Africa were prisoners of war. Europeans first bought enslaved people from African merchants at slave markets in return for gold, guns, or other European goods. Local slave traders first obtained their supplies of enslaved persons from nearby coastal regions. As demand grew, they had to move farther inland to find their victims.

Local rulers became concerned about the impact of the slave trade on their societies. In a letter to the king of Portugal in 1526, **King Afonso** of Congo (Bakongo) said, "so great is the corruption that our country is being completely depopulated."

Europeans and other Africans, however, generally ignored such protests. Local rulers who traded in enslaved people viewed the slave trade as a source of income. Many sent raiders into defenseless villages.

✓ **Reading Check** **Describing** Describe the purpose and path of the triangular trade.

PEOPLE in HISTORY

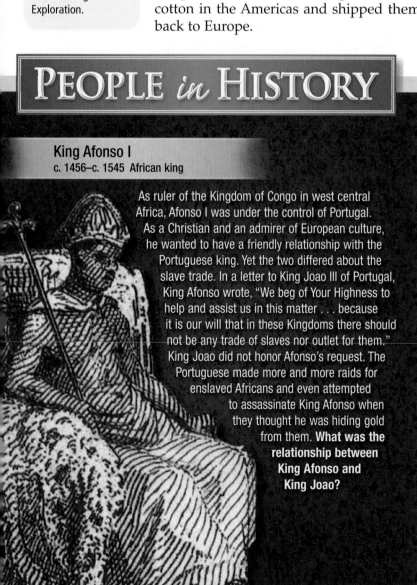

King Afonso I
c. 1456–c. 1545 African king

As ruler of the Kingdom of Congo in west central Africa, Afonso I was under the control of Portugal. As a Christian and an admirer of European culture, he wanted to have a friendly relationship with the Portuguese king. Yet the two differed about the slave trade. In a letter to King Joao III of Portugal, King Afonso wrote, "We beg of Your Highness to help and assist us in this matter . . . because it is our will that in these Kingdoms there should not be any trade of slaves nor outlet for them." King Joao did not honor Afonso's request. The Portuguese made more and more raids for enslaved Africans and even attempted to assassinate King Afonso when they thought he was hiding gold from them. **What was the relationship between King Afonso and King Joao?**

Effects of the Slave Trade

MAIN IDEA The slave trade led to depopulation, increased warfare, and devastation for many African states.

HISTORY & YOU Have you seen the TV miniseries *Roots?* Read to learn about the devastating effect of the slave trade on Benin.

The effects of the slave trade varied from area to area. Of course, it always had tragic effects on the lives of individual victims and their families. The slave trade led to the depopulation of some areas, and it deprived many African communities of their youngest and strongest men and women.

The desire of slave traders to provide a constant supply of enslaved persons led to increased warfare in Africa. Coastal or near-coastal African chiefs and their followers, armed with guns acquired from the trade in enslaved people, increased their raids and wars on neighboring peoples.

Only a few Europeans lamented what they were doing to traditional African societies. One Dutch slave trader remarked:

PRIMARY SOURCE

"From us they have learned strife, quarrelling, drunkenness, trickery, theft, unbridled desire for what is not one's own, misdeeds unknown to them before, and the accursed lust for gold."

—*Africa in History: Themes and Outlines* rev. ed., Basil Davidson, 1991

The slave trade had a devastating effect on some African states. The case of **Benin** (buh•NEEN) in West Africa is a good example. A brilliant and creative society in the 1500s, Benin was pulled into the slave trade.

As the population declined and warfare increased, the people of Benin lost faith in their gods, their art deteriorated, and human sacrifice became more common. When the British arrived there at the end of the 1800s, they found a corrupt and brutal place. It took years to discover the brilliance of the earlier culture destroyed by slavery.

The use of enslaved Africans remained largely acceptable to European society. Europeans continued to view Africans as inferior beings fit chiefly for slave labor. Not until the Society of Friends, known as the Quakers, began to condemn slavery in the 1770s did European feeling against slavery begin to build. Even then, it was not until the French Revolution in the 1790s that the French abolished slavery. The British did the same in 1807. Nevertheless, slavery continued in the newly formed United States until the Civil War of the 1860s.

✓ **Reading Check** **Describing** What effect did the slave trade have on Benin?

SECTION 2 REVIEW

Vocabulary

1. **Explain** the significance of: colony, mercantilism, balance of trade, subsidies, transportation, primary, plantations, triangular trade, Middle Passage, King Afonso, Benin.

Main Ideas

2. **Explain** why a nation would want a favorable balance of trade.

3. **Illustrate** the triangular trade pattern using the graph below. Indicate what goods were shipped among the points of trade.

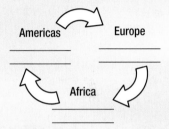

4. **Identify** the effects of the slave trade on the culture of Benin.

Critical Thinking

5. **The BIG Idea Evaluating** What impact did the slave trade have on the populations in Africa and the Americas?

6. **Analyzing** Why did some Africans engage in the slave trade? Did they have a choice?

7. **Analyzing Visuals** Examine the portrait of King Afonso on page 206. How can you tell he is a king?

Writing About History

8. **Persuasive Writing** Does the fact that Africans participated in enslaving other Africans make the European involvement in the slave trade any less wrong? Write an editorial supporting your position.

History ONLINE

For help with the concepts in this section of *Glencoe World History—Modern Times,* go to glencoe.com and click Study Central.

Colonial Latin America

GUIDE TO READING

The BIG Idea
Competition Among Countries
Portugal and Spain reaped profits from the natural resources and products of their Latin American colonies.

Content Vocabulary
- *peninsulares (p. 208)*
- *creoles (p. 208)*
- *mestizos (p. 208)*
- *mulattoes (p. 208)*
- *mita (p. 210)*

Academic Vocabulary
- *labor (p. 208)*
- *draft (p. 210)*

People and Places
- Brazil *(p. 208)*
- Juana Inés de la Cruz *(p. 211)*

Reading Strategy
Organizing Information As you read, create a diagram like the one below to summarize the political, social, and economic characteristics of colonial Latin America.

Colonial Latin America

Rich in natural resources, the Latin American colonies proved very profitable for Portugal and Spain. The interactions of native peoples, enslaved Africans, and Spanish colonists caused new social classes to form in Latin America. To convert Native Americans to Christianity, the Catholic Church set up missions throughout Latin America.

Colonial Empires in Latin America

MAIN IDEA The Portuguese and Spanish built colonial empires in Latin America and profited from the resources and trade of their colonies.

HISTORY & YOU Does your family own property outside of your home state or outside of the country? Read to learn why Spanish and Portuguese monarchs relied on officials to administer their colonies in Latin America.

In the 1500s, Portugal came to dominate **Brazil.** At the same time, Spain established an enormous colonial empire that included parts of North America, Central America, and most of South America. Within the lands of Central America and South America, a new civilization arose, which we call Latin America.

Social Classes

Colonial Latin America was divided by social classes that were based on privilege. At the top were *peninsulares.* These were Spanish and Portuguese officials who had been born in Europe and held all important government positions. Below the *peninsulares* were the **creoles.** Descendants of Europeans born in Latin America, creoles controlled land and business. They deeply resented the *peninsulares,* who regarded the creoles as second-class citizens. (See Chapter 14.)

Beneath the *peninsulares* and creoles were numerous multiracial groups. The Spanish and Portuguese who moved into Latin America lived with both Native Americans and African people brought in for **labor.** Spanish rulers permitted intermarriage between Europeans and Native Americans. Their offspring became known as the **mestizos.** In addition, over a period of three centuries, possibly as many as 8 million enslaved Africans were brought to Spanish and Portuguese America to work on the plantations. **Mulattoes**—the offspring of Africans and Europeans—became another social group. Other groups emerged as a result of unions between mestizos and mulattoes and between Native Americans and Africans. The coexistence of these various groups produced a unique multiracial society in Latin America.

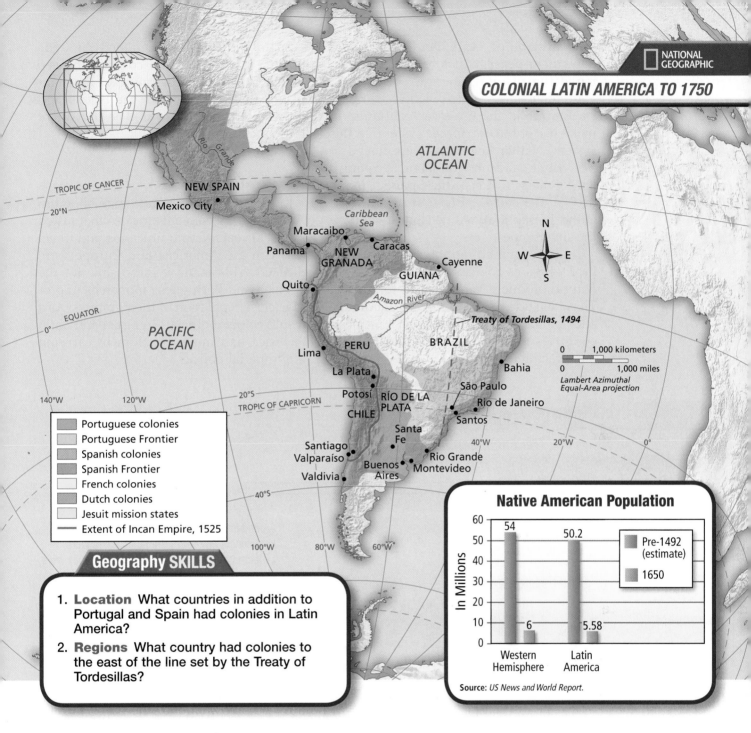

ATLANTIC OCEAN

TROPIC OF CANCER

20°N

NEW SPAIN

Mexico City

Caribbean Sea

Maracaibo

Panama

Caracas

NEW GRANADA

Cayenne

GUIANA

Quito

Amazon River

EQUATOR

0°

PACIFIC OCEAN

Treaty of Tordesillas, 1494

PERU

BRAZIL

Lima

La Plata

Bahia

140°W   120°W

20°S

TROPIC OF CAPRICORN

Potosí

RÍO DE LA PLATA

CHILE

São Paulo

Rio de Janeiro

Santos

Santa Fe

40°W   20°W   0°

Santiago

Valparaíso

Buenos Aires

Rio Grande

Montevideo

Valdivia

40°S

N
W   E
S

0   1,000 kilometers
0   1,000 miles
Lambert Azimuthal Equal-Area projection

Legend
- Portuguese colonies
- Portuguese Frontier
- Spanish colonies
- Spanish Frontier
- French colonies
- Dutch colonies
- Jesuit mission states
- Extent of Incan Empire, 1525

Rio Grande

100°W   80°W   60°W

Geography SKILLS

1. **Location** What countries in addition to Portugal and Spain had colonies in Latin America?

2. **Regions** What country had colonies to the east of the line set by the Treaty of Tordesillas?

Native American Population

In Millions

60
54
50 — 50.2
40
30
20
10 — 6   5.58
0

Western Hemisphere   Latin America

Pre-1492 (estimate)
1650

Source: *US News and World Report.*

All of these multiethnic groups were considered socially inferior by the *peninsulares* and creoles. However, over a period of time, mestizos grew in importance due to their increasing numbers. Some mestizos became artisans and small merchants in cities, while others became small-scale farmers or ranchers. Mestizos eventually came to be seen as socially superior to other multiracial groups. The groups at the very bottom of the social scale were imported enslaved persons and conquered Native Americans.

Economic Foundations

Both the Portuguese and the Spanish sought ways to profit from their colonies in Latin America. One source of wealth came from abundant supplies of gold and silver that were sent to Europe. Farming, however, became a more long-lasting and rewarding source of prosperity for Latin America. Spanish and Portuguese landowners created immense estates. Native Americans worked on the estates or worked as poor farmers on marginal lands.

This system of large landowners and dependent peasants has remained a lasting feature of Latin American society.

To maintain a supply of labor, the Spanish Empire in the Americas continued to make use of the *encomienda* system. In this system, Native Americans were forced to pay tribute and provide labor to Spanish landowners. In Peru, the Spanish made use of the *mita*. This system allowed authorities to **draft** native labor to work in the silver mines.

Trade provided another avenue for profit. Besides gold and silver, many other natural products were shipped to Europe. These included sugar, tobacco, diamonds, and animal hides. In turn, the European countries supplied their colonists with manufactured goods.

Spain and Portugal regulated the trade of their Latin American colonies to keep others out. By the beginning of the eighteenth century, however, the British and French were too powerful to be kept out of these lucrative markets.

State and Church

Portuguese Brazil and Spanish Latin America were colonial empires that lasted over 300 years. Communication and travel between the Americas and Europe were difficult. This made it impossible for the Spanish and Portuguese monarchs to provide close regulation of their empires. As a result, colonial officials in Brazil and Latin America had much freedom in carrying out imperial policies.

INFOGRAPHICS　PRIMARY SOURCE
The Encomienda System

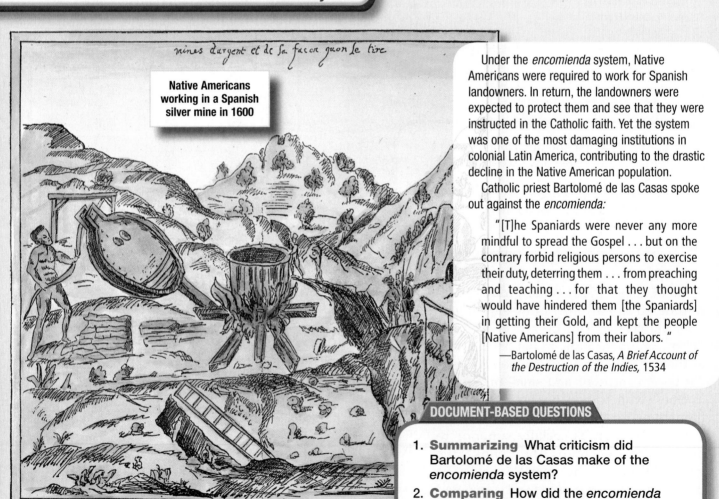

Native Americans working in a Spanish silver mine in 1600

Under the *encomienda* system, Native Americans were required to work for Spanish landowners. In return, the landowners were expected to protect them and see that they were instructed in the Catholic faith. Yet the system was one of the most damaging institutions in colonial Latin America, contributing to the drastic decline in the Native American population.

Catholic priest Bartolomé de las Casas spoke out against the *encomienda*:

"[T]he Spaniards were never any more mindful to spread the Gospel . . . but on the contrary forbid religious persons to exercise their duty, deterring them . . . from preaching and teaching . . . for that they thought would have hindered them [the Spaniards] in getting their Gold, and kept the people [Native Americans] from their labors."

—Bartolomé de las Casas, *A Brief Account of the Destruction of the Indies*, 1534

DOCUMENT-BASED QUESTIONS

1. **Summarizing** What criticism did Bartolomé de las Casas make of the *encomienda* system?

2. **Comparing** How did the *encomienda* system resemble feudalism?

Beginning in the mid-sixteenth century, the Portuguese monarchy began to assert its control over Brazil by creating the position of governor-general. The governor-general (later called a viceroy) developed a bureaucracy. At best the govenor-general had only loose control over the officials below him who governed the districts into which Brazil was divided.

To rule his American empire, the Spanish king also appointed viceroys. The first was established for New Spain (Mexico) in 1535. Another viceroy was appointed for Peru in 1543. In the 1700s, two additional viceroyalties were added. Spaniards held all major government positions.

From the beginning of their conquest of the New World, Spanish and Portuguese rulers were determined to Christianize the native peoples. This policy gave the Catholic Church a powerful role to play in the Americas.

Catholic missionaries—especially the Dominicans, Franciscans, and Jesuits—fanned out to different parts of the Spanish Empire. To make their efforts easier, the missionaries brought Native Americans together into villages, or missions. There, the natives could be converted, taught trades, and encouraged to grow crops. A German tourist in the 1700s said:

PRIMARY SOURCE

"The road leads through plantations of sugar, indigo, cotton, and coffee. The regularity which we observed in the construction of the villages reminded us that they all owe their origin to monks and missions. The streets are straight and parallel; they cross each other at right angles; and the church is erected in the great square situated in the center."

—*Latin America: A Concise Interpretative History,* 4th ed., E. Bradford Burns, 1986

The Jesuits established more than 30 missions in the region of Paraguay. Well organized, the Jesuits made their missions into profitable business activities. Missions enabled missionaries to control the lives of the Native Americans and make them docile members of the empire.

Along with the missions, the Catholic Church also built cathedrals, hospitals, orphanages, and schools in the colonies. The schools taught Native American students the basics of reading, writing, and arithmetic.

The Catholic Church provided an outlet other than marriage for women. They could enter convents and become nuns. Women in religious orders, however—many of them of aristocratic background—often lived well. Many nuns worked outside their convents by running schools and hospitals. Indeed, one of these nuns, **Juana Inés de la Cruz** (KWAHN•ah ee•NAYS de la KROOS) wrote poetry and prose and urged that women be educated.

✓ **Reading Check** **Explaining** How did the Portuguese and the Spanish profit from their colonies in Latin America?

SECTION 3 REVIEW

Vocabulary
1. **Explain** the significance of: Brazil, *peninsulares*, creoles, labor, mestizos, mulattoes, *mita*, draft, Juana Inés de la Cruz.

Main Ideas
2. **List** in order the social classes in colonial Latin America. Use a chart like the one below to make your list.

Social Classes in Colonial Latin America
1.
2.
3.

3. **Explain** how the Spanish Empire maintained a supply of labor in the Latin American colonies.

4. **Identify** the actions of the Catholic Church in colonial Latin America.

Critical Thinking
5. **The BIG Idea** **Evaluating** In return for natural resources and products, a parent country provided its colony with manufactured products. How could this affect the colony's economy after it became an independent state?

6. **Determining Cause and Effect** How did expansion of the Spanish Empire affect demographics in Latin America?

7. **Analyzing Visuals** Examine the illustration on page 210. What does it tell you about Native American laborers in the *encomienda* system?

Writing About History
8. **Descriptive Writing** Suppose that you are a native laborer on one of the large Latin American sugarcane plantations. Write two to three paragraphs describing your typical workday—what you do, what hours you work, what you have to eat, and with whom you work.

History ONLINE

For help with the concepts in this section of *Glencoe World History— Modern Times,* go to glencoe.com and click Study Central.

STUDY TO GO You can study anywhere, anytime by downloading quizzes and flash cards to your PDA from glencoe.com.

CHRISTOPHER COLUMBUS ARRIVES IN THE AMERICAS

The Spanish brought Christianity with them.

EARLY EXPLORATION of West Africa, India, and the Americas

- Motivated by religious zeal, gold, and glory, Europeans began to explore distant lands.
- The Portuguese sailed east around Africa to India.
- Spanish ships sailed west to the Americas.
- Spanish conquistadors seized lands ruled by the Aztec and Inca.
- Diseases introduced by Spanish explorers killed much of the Native American population.
- By the late 1600s, the Dutch, French, and English entered the rivalry for new lands and trade.

ENSLAVED AFRICANS WORKING ON A SUGARCANE PLANTATION

Europeans established sugar plantations in the Americas, creating a demand for slave laborers.

AFRICAN SLAVE TRADE of Europe, Asia, and the Americas

- Before the new exploration, the primary market for enslaved Africans had been Southwest Asia.
- The demand for plantation laborers in the Americas greatly increased slave trade.
- Enslaved Africans were part of the triangular trade between Europe, Africa and Asia, and the Americas.
- In Africa, the slave trade led to increased warfare, depopulation, and the deterioration of society.

SILVER MINES IN BRAZIL

Silver was a natural resource that attracted European colonizers.

Native Americans were forced to work in silver mines.

COLONIAL EMPIRES of Latin America

- The Portuguese and Spanish profited from their colonial empires in Latin America.
- *Peninsulares* were the top social class, followed by creoles, mestizos and mulattoes, and finally enslaved Africans and Native Americans.
- Catholic missionaries spread across the Americas to try to Christianize Native Americans.

STANDARDIZED TEST PRACTICE

TEST-TAKING

If a test question involves reading a map, make sure you read the title of the map and look at the map carefully for information before you try to answer the question

Reviewing Vocabulary

Directions: Choose the word or words that best complete the sentence.

1. _____ were the offspring of Africans and Europeans.

   A Creoles

   B *Peninsulares*

   C Mestizos

   D Mulattoes

2. Spanish conquerors of the Americas were known as _____.

   A viceroys

   B conquistadors

   C *peninsulares*

   D governor-generals

3. The _____ is a trading route that connected Europe, Africa and Asia, and the Americas.

   A triangular trade

   B Bermuda Triangle

   C Middle Passage

   D circular trade

4. The _____ system allowed authorities to draft natives to work in silver mines.

   A *encomienda*

   B feudal

   C *mita*

   D tithe

Reviewing Main Ideas

Directions: Choose the best answers to the following questions.

Section 1 *(pp. 194–201)*

5. What were the chief motives for European expansion?

   A Adventure, travel, and war

   B Politics, taxes, and war

   C God, glory, and gold

   D Oil, gold, and coal

6. Which country took the lead in European exploration?

   A Portugal

   B The Netherlands

   C England

   D France

7. Who was the first explorer to circumnavigate the world?

   A Bartholomeu Dias

   B Christopher Columbus

   C Ferdinand Magellan

   D Vasco da Gama

8. Which ruler granted *encomienda* to the Spanish settlers in the Americas?

   A Louis XII

   B Isabella

   C Ferdinand

   D Henry VI

Need Extra Help?								
If You Missed Questions . . .	1	2	3	4	5	6	7	8
Go to Page . . .	208	198	206	210	195	196	197	199

9. Which nation controlled most of the eastern seaboard of North America by the end of the 1600s?

A France

B Spain

C England

D The Netherlands

Section 2 (pp. 204–207)

10. What set of principles dominated economic thought in the seventeenth century?

A Mercantilism

B Capitalism

C Secularism

D Socialism

11. In what year did the first enslaved Africans arrive in the Americas?

A 1560

B 1492

C 1518

D 1430

Section 3 (pp. 208–211)

12. Which of the following is a true statement about colonial Latin American society?

A It had no class system.

B It was largely Protestant.

C It had few peasants.

D It was multiracial.

13. Who worked on the immense estates or worked as farmers on marginal lands in Latin America?

A Creoles

B Native Americans

C Conquistadors

D *Peninsulares*

Critical Thinking

Directions: Choose the best answers to the following questions.

Use the following map to answer question 14.

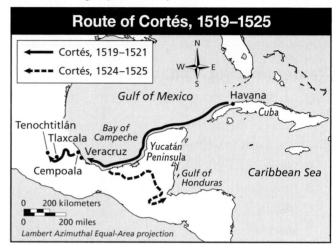

Route of Cortés, 1519–1525

14. Which of the following best describes the route of Cortés during the years 1519–1521?

A He traveled from Havana to Tenochtitlán.

B He traveled from Veracruz to the Gulf of Honduras.

C He traveled from Tlaxcala to Veracruz.

D He traveled from the Gulf of Honduras to Tenochtitlán.

15. What caused the most deaths in the Aztec and Inca populations?

A Combat with the Europeans

B Human sacrifice

C European diseases

D Combat with rival cities

16. Why did some slave owners believe that buying a new enslaved person was cheaper than raising a child to working age?

A New enslaved people had immunity to diseases.

B Providing food and shelter until the child was of working age cost more than a new enslaved person.

C Slave traders gave slave owners discounts on new enslaved people.

D A child took longer to train how to work.

Need Extra Help?								
If You Missed Questions . . .	9	10	11	12	13	14	15	16
Go to Page . . .	201	204	206	208	209	195	199	206

17. What impact did European mercantilism have on colonies in the Americas?

  A Latin American colonies became industrialized.

  B Mercantilism promoted export of manufactured goods.

  C Mercantilism promoted freedom of the indigenous peoples of the colonies.

  D Latin American colonies depended on cash crops for export.

Base your answer to question 18 on the graph below and on your knowledge of world history.

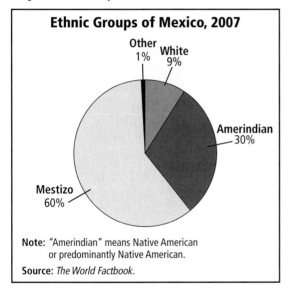

Ethnic Groups of Mexico, 2007

Other 1%
White 9%
Amerindian 30%
Mestizo 60%

Note: "Amerindian" means Native American or predominantly Native American.

Source: *The World Factbook.*

18. What can be said about the ethnic groups of Mexico?

  A Most Mexicans are descendants of Spanish and Native American peoples.

  B Native American people out number mestizos in Mexico.

  C There are four times as many Native Americans as there are whites in Mexico.

  D Mestizos are a minority ethnic group in Mexico.

Document-Based Questions

Directions: Analyze the document and answer the short-answer questions that follow the document. Base your answers on the document and on your knowledge of world history.

In a letter to the treasurer of the king and queen of Spain, Christopher Columbus reported on his first journey:

> "Believing that you will rejoice at the glorious success that our Lord has granted me in my voyage, I write this to tell you how in thirty-three days I reached the Indies with the first fleet which the most illustrious King and Queen, our Sovereigns, gave me, where I discovered a great many thickly-populated islands. Without meeting resistance, I have taken possession of them all for their Highnesses. . . . When I reached [Cuba], I followed its coast to the westward, and found it so large that I thought it must be the mainland—the province of [China], but I found neither towns nor villages on the seacoast, save for a few hamlets."
>
> —*Letters from the First Voyage*, edited 1847

19. What continent did Columbus believe he had reached?

20. How long did it take Columbus to reach his destination?

Extended Response

21. Analyze the reasons why Native Americans might be offended by the term New World. What does the use of the term suggest about European attitudes toward the rest of the world?

History ONLINE

For additional test practice, use Self-Check Quizzes— Chapter 6 at glencoe.com.

Need Extra Help?					
If You Missed Questions . . .	17	18	19	20	21
Go to Page . . .	210	208	196	196	197

STOP

CHAPTER 7

Crisis and Absolutism in Europe 1550–1715

Section 1 Europe in Crisis: The Wars of Religion

Section 2 Social Crises, War, and Revolution

Section 3 Response to Crisis: Absolutism

Section 4 The World of European Culture

MAKING CONNECTIONS

How does architecture reflect history?

The palace at Versailles, shown in this photo, was home to the kings of France from 1682 until 1790. In seventeenth century Europe, Versailles was a symbol of Louis XIV's absolute rule. In this chapter, you will learn about crises throughout Europe and the rulers who sought stability through absolute rule.

- What are some famous government buildings that are tourist attractions in the United States? What do they symbolize?
- Compare the symbolism of the palace at Versailles with the symbolism of St. Peter's Basilica in Rome shown on page 237.

EUROPE ▶

1562
French Wars of Religion begin

1588
England defeats the Spanish Armada

1618
Start of the Thirty Years' War

1550 ・・・・・・・・・・・・・・ 1600 ・・・・・・・・・・・・・・

THE WORLD ▶

1568
Oda Nobunaga seizes Kyōto, Japan

1605
Akbar expands Mogul rule in India

1630
English found Massachusetts Bay Colony

1661
Louis XIV begins
absolute rule
of France

1690
John Locke writes
*Two Treatises of
Government*

1715

1689
England's House of Parliament
enacts the Bill of Rights

1689
Peter the Great becomes
czar of Russia

FOLDABLES™
Study Organizer

Organizing Make a
Three-Pocket Book
to organize informa-
tion about Europe in
the sixteenth, seventeenth, and early
eighteenth centuries. Store your notes
in the appropriate pocket.

Europe 16th Century | Europe 17th Century | Europe Early 18th Century

History ONLINE

Chapter Overview—Visit glencoe.com to preview Chapter 7.

Europe in Crisis: The Wars of Religion

GUIDE TO READING

The BIG Idea
Competition Among Countries
Religious and political conflicts erupted between Protestants and Catholics in many European nations.

Content Vocabulary
• militant *(p. 218)*   • armada *(p. 220)*

Academic Vocabulary
• conflict *(p. 218)*   • policy *(p. 219)*

People, Places, and Events
• King Philip II *(p. 218)*   • Ireland *(p. 220)*
• Netherlands *(p. 218)*   • Huguenots *(p. 221)*
• William the Silent *(p. 219)*   • Henry of Navarre *(p. 221)*
• Elizabeth Tudor *(p. 219)*   • Edict of Nantes *(p. 221)*
• Scotland *(p. 220)*

Reading Strategy
Comparing and Contrasting
As you read, complete a chart like the one below comparing the characteristics of Spain, England, and France.

	Spain	England	France
Government			
Religion			
Conflicts			

During the sixteenth and seventeenth centuries, conflicts between Protestants and Catholics in many European nations resulted in wars for religious and political control.

Spain's Conflicts

MAIN IDEA King Philip II championed Catholic causes throughout his lands, while England became the leader of Protestant nations of Europe.

HISTORY & YOU Suppose you won an arm-wrestling contest against someone who seemed much bigger and stronger? Learn how England defeated Spain at sea.

By 1560, Calvinism and Catholicism had become highly **militant** (combative) religions. They were aggressive in winning converts and in eliminating each other's authority. Their struggle was the chief cause of the religious wars that plagued Europe in the sixteenth century. However, economic, social, and political forces also played an important role in these **conflicts**.

Spain's Militant Catholicism

The greatest supporter of militant Catholicism in the second half of the sixteenth century was **King Philip II** of Spain, the son and heir of Charles V. King Philip II, whose reign extended from 1556 to 1598, ushered in an age of Spanish greatness.

Philip's first major goal was to consolidate the lands inherited from his father. These included Spain, the **Netherlands,** and possessions in Italy and the Americas. To strengthen his control, Philip insisted on strict conformity to Catholicism and strong monarchical authority.

During the late Middle Ages, Catholic kingdoms in Spain had reconquered Muslim areas there and expelled the Spanish Jews. Driven by this heritage, Spain saw itself as a nation of people chosen by God to save Catholic Christianity from Protestant heretics.

The "Most Catholic King," Philip II championed Catholic causes. His actions led to spectacular victories and defeats. Spain's leadership in a Holy League against the Turks, for example, resulted in a stunning victory over the Turkish fleet in the Battle of Lepanto in 1571. Philip was not so fortunate in his other conflicts.

Resistance from the Netherlands

One of the richest parts of Philip's empire, the Spanish Netherlands, consisted of 17 provinces (modern Netherlands and Belgium). Philip's attempts to strengthen his control in this region caused resentment and opposition from the nobles of the

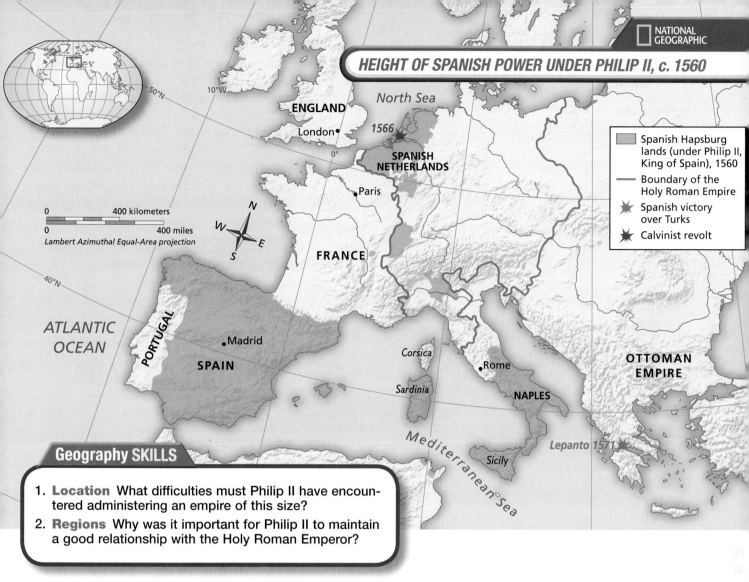

HEIGHT OF SPANISH POWER UNDER PHILIP II, c. 1560

North Sea

ENGLAND

London•

1566

SPANISH NETHERLANDS

•Paris

FRANCE

	Spanish Hapsburg lands (under Philip II, King of Spain), 1560
	Boundary of the Holy Roman Empire
✸	Spanish victory over Turks
✸	Calvinist revolt

0   400 kilometers
0   400 miles
Lambert Azimuthal Equal-Area projection

N W E S

50°N
10°W
0°
40°N

ATLANTIC OCEAN

PORTUGAL

•Madrid

SPAIN

Corsica

Sardinia

•Rome

NAPLES

OTTOMAN EMPIRE

Mediterranean Sea

Sicily

Lepanto 1571 ✸

Geography SKILLS

1. **Location** What difficulties must Philip II have encountered administering an empire of this size?
2. **Regions** Why was it important for Philip II to maintain a good relationship with the Holy Roman Emperor?

Netherlands. Philip also tried to crush Calvinism in the Netherlands. Violence erupted in 1566. Philip sent ten thousand troops to crush the rebellion.

Philip faced growing resistance from the Dutch in the northern provinces led by **William the Silent,** the prince of Orange. The struggle dragged on until 1609 when a 12-year truce finally ended the war. The northern provinces began to call themselves the United Provinces of the Netherlands and became the core of the modern Dutch state. In fact, the seventeenth century has often been called the golden age of the Dutch Republic because the United Provinces held center stage as one of Europe's great powers.

Protestantism in England

Elizabeth Tudor ascended the English throne in 1558. During her reign, the small island kingdom became the leader of the Protestant nations of Europe and laid the foundations for a world empire.

Intelligent, careful, and self-confident, Elizabeth moved quickly to solve the difficult religious problem she inherited from her Catholic half-sister, Queen Mary Tudor. Elizabeth repealed the laws favoring Catholics. A new Act of Supremacy named Elizabeth as "the only supreme governor" of both church and state. The Church of England under Queen Elizabeth followed a moderate Protestantism that kept most people satisfied.

Elizabeth was also moderate in her foreign **policy.** She tried to keep Spain and France from becoming too powerful by balancing power. If one nation seemed to be gaining in power, England would support the weaker nation. The queen feared that war would be disastrous for England and for her own rule; however, she could not escape a conflict with Spain.

Defeat of the Spanish Armada

In 1588, Philip II made preparations to send an **armada**—a fleet of warships—to invade England. A successful invasion of England would mean the overthrow of Protestantism. The fleet that set sail had neither the ships nor the manpower that Philip had planned to send.

The hoped-for victory never came. The armada was battered by the faster English ships and sailed back to Spain by a northern route around **Scotland** and **Ireland** where it was pounded by storms.

By the end of Philip's reign in 1598, Spain was not the great power that it appeared to be. Spain was the most populous empire in the world, but it was bankrupt. Philip II had spent too much on war. His successor spent too much on his court. The armed forces were out of date, and the government was inefficient. Spain continued to play the role of a great power, but the real power in Europe had shifted to England and France.

✓ **Reading Check** **Explaining** What did Philip II hope to accomplish by invading England?

TURNING POINT

In the mid-1500s, the English supported the Protestant side in religious wars between Protestants and Catholics within France and the Netherlands. Resenting this, Philip II of Spain decided to invade England to overthrow Protestantism and establish Catholic rule there.

The English fleet had clear superiority in gunnery and naval tactics. It dealt the Spanish Armada a terrible blow in the English Channel. The Spanish retreated on a northward route around Scotland without charts or a pilot. There the fleet was battered by storms. Half of the Spanish fleet and three-quarters of the men were lost. After defeating the Spanish Armada, England remained Protestant and began to create a world empire.

The defeat of the Spanish Armada:

- **Guaranteed that England would remain a Protestant country**

- **Signaled a gradual shift in power from Spain to England and France**

Geography SKILLS

1. **Location** Use the map to estimate the distance covered by the Spanish retreat.
2. **Region** Why was the defeat of the Spanish Armada a turning point?

Maps in MOtion See *StudentWorks™ Plus* or glencoe.com.

DEFEAT OF THE SPANISH ARMADA

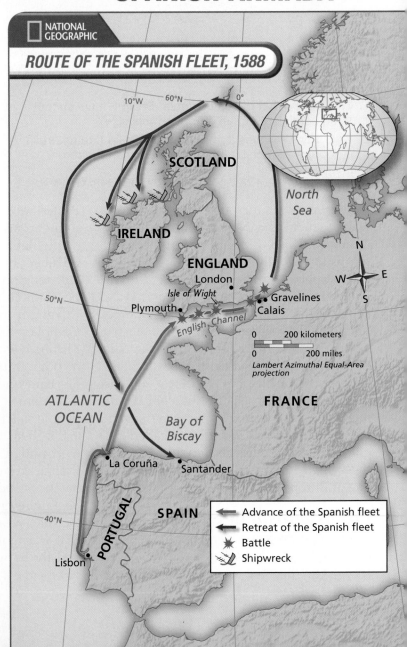

NATIONAL GEOGRAPHIC

ROUTE OF THE SPANISH FLEET, 1588

SCOTLAND

North Sea

IRELAND

ENGLAND
London
Isle of Wight
Plymouth
Gravelines
Calais
English Channel

ATLANTIC OCEAN

Bay of Biscay

La Coruña
Santander

PORTUGAL SPAIN

FRANCE

Lisbon

0   200 kilometers
0   200 miles
Lambert Azimuthal Equal-Area projection

→ Advance of the Spanish fleet
← Retreat of the Spanish fleet
✳ Battle
Shipwreck

The French Wars of Religion

MAIN IDEA Conflict between Catholics and Protestants was at the heart of the French Wars of Religion.

HISTORY & YOU What would you do if some classmates started a trend that you didn't like? Learn how Catholic leaders in France protested the spread of Protestantism.

Of the sixteenth-century religious wars, none was more shattering than the French civil wars known as the French Wars of Religion (1562–1598). Religious conflict was at the center of these wars. The French kings persecuted Protestants, but the persecution did little to stop the spread of Protestantism.

Huguenots

Huguenots (HYOO•guh•NAWTS) were French Protestants influenced by John Calvin. They made up only about 7 percent of the total French population, but 40 to 50 percent of the nobility became Huguenots. This made the Huguenots a powerful political threat to the Crown.

An extreme Catholic party—known as the ultra-Catholics—strongly opposed the Huguenots. Having the loyalty of parts of northern and northwestern France, they could pay for and recruit large armies.

Religion was the most important issue, but other factors played a role in the French civil wars. Towns and provinces were willing to assist the nobles in weakening the growing power of the French monarchy.

Henry IV and the Edict of Nantes

For 30 years, battles raged in France between the Catholics and Huguenots. Finally, in 1589, **Henry of Navarre,** the Huguenot political leader, succeeded to the throne as Henry IV. He realized that as a Protestant he would never be accepted by Catholic France. Therefore, he converted to Catholicism. When Henry IV was crowned king in 1594, the fighting in France finally came to an end.

To solve the religious problem, Henry IV issued the **Edict of Nantes** in 1598. The edict recognized Catholicism as the official religion of France. It also gave the Huguenots the right to worship and to enjoy all political privileges such as holding public offices.

✓Reading Check **Identifying** List the sequence of events that led to the Edict of Nantes.

Vocabulary
1. **Explain** the significance of: militant, conflict, King Philip II, Netherlands, William the Silent, Elizabeth Tudor, policy, armada, Scotland, Ireland, Huguenots, Henry of Navarre, Edict of Nantes.

Main Ideas
2. **Explain** how Philip II championed Catholic causes throughout his lands.

3. **Create** a Venn diagram like the one shown below to compare and contrast the reigns of Philip II, Elizabeth Tudor, and Henry of Navarre.

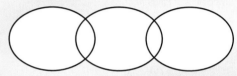

4. **Describe** how the Edict of Nantes appeased both Catholics and Huguenots.

Critical Thinking
5. **The BIG Idea** **Analyzing** Analyze which of the major three nations—Spain, England, or France—lost the most power and standing during their religious and political conflicts.

6. **Drawing Conclusions** What did Elizabeth hope to achieve—or to avoid—with her moderate foreign policy of balancing power between France and Spain?

7. **Analyzing Visuals** Examine the maps on pages 219 and 220. How do you think the defeat of the Spanish Armada might have affected Philip's ability to rule the Spanish empire? Explain your answer.

Writing About History
8. **Persuasive Writing** Write a persuasive essay arguing whether it was a good idea for Philip II to sail against England. Identify the main reason the king of Spain decided to invade.

History **ONLINE**

For help with the concepts in this section of *Glencoe World History— Modern Times,* go to **glencoe.com** and click Study Central.

Social Crises, War, and Revolution

GUIDE TO READING

The BIG Idea
Order and Security Social, economic, and religious conflicts challenged the established political order throughout Europe.

Content Vocabulary
• inflation *(p. 222)*
• witchcraft *(p. 222)*
• divine right of kings *(p. 225)*
• commonwealth *(p. 225)*

Academic Vocabulary
• restoration *(p. 226)*   • convert *(p. 226)*

People and Places
• Holy Roman Empire *(p. 224)*
• Bohemia *(p. 224)*
• James I *(p. 225)*
• Puritans *(p. 225)*
• Charles I *(p. 225)*
• Cavaliers *(p. 225)*
• Roundheads *(p. 225)*
• Oliver Cromwell *(p. 225)*
• James II *(p. 226)*

Reading Strategy
Summarizing Information As you read, use a chart like the one below to identify which conflicts were prompted by religious concerns.

Religious Conflicts

Severe economic and social crises plagued Europe in the sixteenth and seventeenth centuries. The Holy Roman Empire was devastated, and France emerged as the dominant nation in Europe. Conflicts between the kings of England and its parliament led to a civil war, an execution of a king, and a revolution. From such crises, constitutional monarchy emerged.

Crises in Europe

MAIN IDEA Population decline in Europe and the hysteria of witchcraft trials contributed to economic and social problems in seventeenth-century Europe.

HISTORY & YOU What if the number of students in your school declined by half this year? Learn how Europeans responded to economic and social problems.

From 1560 to 1650, Europe witnessed severe economic and social crises. One major economic problem was **inflation,** or rising prices. A growing population in the sixteenth century increased the demand for land and food and drove up prices for both.

Economic and Social Crises

By 1600, an economic slowdown had begun in parts of Europe. Spain's economy, grown dependent on imported silver, was failing by the 1640s. The mines were producing less silver. Fleets were subject to pirate attacks. Also, the loss of Muslim and Jewish artisans and merchants hurt the economy. Italy, the financial center of Europe in the Renaissance, was also declining economically.

Population figures in the sixteenth and seventeenth centuries reveal Europe's worsening conditions. Population grew in the sixteenth century. The number of people probably increased from 60 million in 1500 to 85 million by 1600. By 1620, the population had leveled off. It had begun to decline by 1650, especially in central and southern Europe. Warfare, plague, and famine all contributed to the population decline and to the creation of social tensions.

The Witchcraft Trials

A belief in **witchcraft,** or magic, had been part of traditional village culture for centuries. The religious zeal that led to the Inquisition and the hunt for heretics was extended to concern about witchcraft. During the sixteenth and seventeenth centuries, an intense hysteria affected the lives of many Europeans. Perhaps more than a hundred thousand people were charged with witchcraft. As more and more people were brought to trial, the fear of witches

The *Malleus Maleficarum*, or the Hammer of the Witches, of 1486 was a guide for prosecuting witches during the Inquisition. It influenced witch trials in Europe for more than 200 years. Here are some excerpts:

On the classification of witches:
"The category in which women of this sort are to be ranked is called the category of Pythons, persons in or by whom the devil either speaks or performs some astonishing operation. . . ."

On extracting a confession:
"The method of beginning an examination by torture is as follows: The jailers . . . strip the prisoner. This stripping is lest some means of witchcraft may have been sewed into the clothing—such as often, taught by the Devil, they prepare from the bodies of unbaptized [murdered] infants . . . the judge . . . tries to persuade the prisoner to confess the truth freely; but, if [the witch] will not confess, he bids attendants make the prisoner fast to . . . some . . . implement of torture."

Witches were thought to enjoy casting their spells on the weak and vulnerable, such as infants.

DOCUMENT-BASED QUESTIONS

This painting is entitled *Witches' Sabbath: The Conjurers* by Goya (1746–1828).

1. **Describing** According to the excerpts, who do witches serve?
2. **Comparing** Describe similarities between witchcraft trials and the Inquisition.

grew, as did the fear of being accused of witchcraft.

Common people—usually the poor and those without property—were the ones most often accused of witchcraft. More than 75 percent of those accused were women. Most of them were single or widowed and over 50 years old.

Under intense torture, accused witches usually confessed to a number of practices. For instance, many said that they had sworn allegiance to the devil and attended sabbats, nightly gatherings where they feasted and danced. Then others admitted to casting evil spells.

By 1650, the witchcraft hysteria had begun to lessen. As governments grew stronger, fewer officials were willing to disrupt their societies with trials of witches. In addition, attitudes were changing. People found it unreasonable to believe in the old view of a world haunted by evil spirits.

✓ **Reading Check** **Explaining** What caused a decline in witchcraft trials?

The Thirty Years' War

> **MAIN IDEA** Started over religious conflicts, the Thirty Years' War was sustained by political conflicts.
>
> **HISTORY & YOU** What if fierce arguments destroyed your best friendship? Learn what caused thirty years of warfare.

Religious disputes continued in Germany after the Peace of Augsburg in 1555. One reason for the disputes was that the peace settlement had not recognized Calvinism. By the 1600s, Calvinism had spread through Europe.

Causes of the War

Religion played an important role in the outbreak of the Thirty Years' War, called the "last of the religious wars." However, political and territorial motives were also evident. Beginning in 1618 in the **Holy Roman Empire,** the war first involved the struggle between Catholic forces, led by the Hapsburg Holy Roman emperors, and Protestant (primarily Calvinist) nobles in **Bohemia.** As Denmark, Sweden, France, and Spain entered the war, the conflict became more political. Especially important was the struggle between France and Spain and the Holy Roman Empire for European leadership.

Effects of the War

All major European powers except England became involved in the Thirty Years' War. For 30 years Germany was plundered and destroyed. The Peace of Westphalia officially ended the war in Germany in 1648.

The Peace of Westphalia divided the more than three hundred states of the Holy Roman Empire into independent states and gave them power to determine their own religion and to conduct their own foreign policy. This brought an end to the Holy Roman Empire as a political entity. Germany would not be united for another two hundred years.

✓ **Reading Check** **Summarizing** What three major powers struggled for European leadership during the Thirty Years' War?

NATIONAL GEOGRAPHIC

EUROPE AFTER THE PEACE OF WESTPHALIA

Boundary of the Holy Roman Empire

SCOTLAND
North Sea
SWEDEN
IRELAND
ENGLAND
DENMARK
Baltic Sea
ATLANTIC OCEAN
London
UNITED PROVINCES
PRUSSIA
Berlin
POLAND
RUSSIA
SPANISH NETHERLANDS
GERMAN STATES
Warsaw
Paris
Prague
Nantes
Vienna
Augsburg
FRANCE
SWITZERLAND
ITALIAN STATES
OTTOMAN EMPIRE
PORTUGAL
Lisbon
Madrid
SPAIN
Corsica
PAPAL STATES
Rome
Sardinia
THE TWO SICILIES
Mediterranean Sea

0   400 kilometers
0   400 miles
Lambert Azimuthal Equal-Area projection

Geography SKILLS

1. **Regions** Compare this map to the map on page 177. Describe the effects of the Thirty Years' War on the Holy Roman Empire?

2. **Movement** Research what led France to become involved in the Thirty Years' War.

Revolutions in England

MAIN IDEA Civil war raged over what roles the king and Parliament should have in governing England.

HISTORY & YOU What if your class had to decide who should be the leader of an important school project? Learn how the struggle for power in England was resolved.

In addition to the Thirty Years' War, a series of rebellions and civil wars rocked Europe in the seventeenth century. By far the most famous struggle was the civil war in England known as the English Revolution. At its core was a struggle between king and Parliament to determine what role each should play in governing England. It would take another revolution later in the century to finally resolve this struggle.

The Stuarts and Divine Right

With the death of Queen Elizabeth I in 1603, the Tudor dynasty came to an end. The Stuart line of rulers began with the accession to the throne of Elizabeth's cousin, the king of Scotland, who became **James I** of England.

James believed that he received his power from God and was responsible only to God. This is called the **divine right of Kings**. Parliament did not think much of the divine right of kings. It had come to assume that the king or queen and Parliament ruled England together.

Religion was an issue as well. The **Puritans** (Protestants in England inspired by Calvinist ideas) did not like the king's strong defense of the Church of England. While members of the Church of England, the Puritans wished to make the church more Protestant. Many of England's gentry, mostly well-to-do landowners, had become Puritans. The Puritan gentry formed an important part of the House of Commons, the lower house of Parliament. It was not wise to alienate them.

The conflict that began during the reign of James came to a head during the reign of his son, **Charles I.** Charles also believed in the divine right of kings. In 1628, Parliament passed a petition that prohibited the passing of any taxes without Parliament's consent. Although Charles I initially accepted this petition, he later changed his mind. Charles realized that the petition would put limits on the king's power.

Charles also tried to impose more ritual on the Church of England. When he tried to force Puritans to accept this policy, thousands chose to go to America. Thus the religious struggles of the Reformation in England influenced American history.

Civil War and Commonwealth

Complaints grew until England slipped into a civil war in 1642 between the supporters of the king (the **Cavaliers** or Royalists) and the parliamentary forces (called the **Roundheads** because of their short hair). Parliament proved victorious, due largely to the New Model Army of **Oliver Cromwell,** a military genius.

The New Model Army was made up chiefly of more extreme Puritans, known as the Independents. These men believed they were doing battle for God. As Cromwell wrote, "This is none other but the hand of God; and to Him alone belongs the glory." Some credit is due to Cromwell. His soldiers were well disciplined and trained in the new military tactics of the seventeenth century.

The victorious New Model Army lost no time in taking control. Cromwell purged Parliament of any members who had not supported him. What was left—the so-called Rump Parliament—had Charles I executed on January 30, 1649. The execution of the king horrified much of Europe. Parliament next abolished the monarchy and the House of Lords and declared England a republic, or **commonwealth.**

Cromwell found it difficult to work with the Rump Parliament and finally dispersed it by force. As the members of Parliament departed, he shouted, "It is you that have forced me to do this, for I have sought the Lord night and day that He would slay me rather than put upon me the doing of this work." After destroying the roles of both king and Parliament, Cromwell set up a military dictatorship.

The Restoration

Cromwell ruled until his death in 1658. George Monk, one of Cromwell's leading generals, realized that under any of Cromwell's successors the country would be torn apart. With his army, Monk created a situation favorable to restoring the monarchy in the person of Charles II, the son of Charles I. Charles II had lived years of exile during Cromwell's rule. With the return of the monarchy in 1660, England's time of troubles seemed at an end.

After the **restoration** of the Stuart monarchy, known as the Restoration period, Parliament kept much of the power it had gained earlier and continued to play an important role. One of its actions was to pass laws restoring the Church of England as the state religion and restricting some rights of Catholics and Puritans.

Resisting attempts by his mother and sister to **convert** to Catholicism, Charles II remained openly loyal to the Protestant faith. He was, however, sympathetic to Catholicism. Parliament was suspicious about his Catholic leanings, especially when Charles suspended the laws that Parliament had passed against Catholics and Puritans. Parliament forced the king to back down on his action.

Charles's brother James did not hide the fact that he was a Catholic. Complying with his brother's wishes, James agreed to raise his two daughters in the Protestant faith. Rather than take an anti-Catholic oath, James resigned from all of his offices. His second marriage to a Catholic gave Parliament even more concern.

When Charles died, leaving no heirs to the throne, **James II** became king in 1685. James was an open and devout Catholic. Religion was once more a cause of conflict between king and Parliament. James named Catholics to high positions in the government, army, navy, and universities.

Parliament objected to James's policies but stopped short of rebellion. Members knew that James was an old man. His Protestant daughters Mary and Anne, born to his first wife, would succeed him.

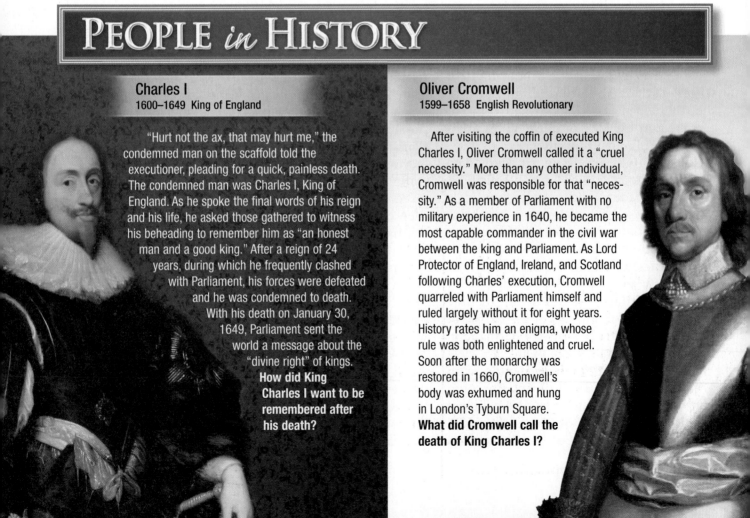

PEOPLE in HISTORY

Charles I
1600–1649 King of England

"Hurt not the ax, that may hurt me," the condemned man on the scaffold told the executioner, pleading for a quick, painless death. The condemned man was Charles I, King of England. As he spoke the final words of his reign and his life, he asked those gathered to witness his beheading to remember him as "an honest man and a good king." After a reign of 24 years, during which he frequently clashed with Parliament, his forces were defeated and he was condemned to death. With his death on January 30, 1649, Parliament sent the world a message about the "divine right" of kings.

How did King Charles I want to be remembered after his death?

Oliver Cromwell
1599–1658 English Revolutionary

After visiting the coffin of executed King Charles I, Oliver Cromwell called it a "cruel necessity." More than any other individual, Cromwell was responsible for that "necessity." As a member of Parliament with no military experience in 1640, he became the most capable commander in the civil war between the king and Parliament. As Lord Protector of England, Ireland, and Scotland following Charles' execution, Cromwell quarreled with Parliament himself and ruled largely without it for eight years. History rates him an enigma, whose rule was both enlightened and cruel. Soon after the monarchy was restored in 1660, Cromwell's body was exhumed and hung in London's Tyburn Square.

What did Cromwell call the death of King Charles I?

However, in 1688, James and his second wife, a Catholic, had a son. Now, the possibility of a Catholic monarchy loomed large.

A Glorious Revolution

A group of English nobles invited the Dutch leader, William of Orange, to invade England. In their invitation, the nobles informed William that most people throughout the kingdom wanted a change. The invitation put William and his wife Mary, the daughter of James II, in a difficult position. Based on Mary's relationship to James, it would be appalling to rise up against her father, the king of England. However, William, a foe of France's Catholic king Louis XIV, welcomed this opportunity to fight France with England's resources.

William began making preparations to invade England in early 1688. He made his plans as secretly as possible and thus kept them largely hidden from James. Not until early October did James realize William's intentions. In November 1688, William's forces landed at Torbay and began their march toward London. James responded by sending forward his army. Following the desertion of many of his soldiers and the defection of his daughter Anne and her husband, James retreated to London. There he made plans for his wife and son to flee to France where James later joined them.

With almost no bloodshed, England had undergone a "Glorious Revolution." The issue was not if there would be a monarchy but who would be monarch.

In January 1689, Parliament offered the throne to William and Mary. They accepted it, along with a Bill of Rights. The Bill of Rights set forth Parliament's right to make laws and to levy taxes. It also stated that standing armies could be raised only with Parliament's consent. Under the Bill of Rights, it was impossible for kings to oppose or to do without Parliament. The rights of citizens to keep arms and have a jury trial were also confirmed. The Bill of Rights helped create a system of government based on the rule of law and a freely elected Parliament. This bill laid the foundation for a limited, or constitutional, monarchy.

Another important action of Parliament was the Toleration Act of 1689. This act granted Puritans, but not Catholics, the right of free public worship. Few English citizens, however, would ever again be persecuted for religion.

By deposing one king and establishing another, Parliament had destroyed the divine-right theory of kingship. William was, after all, king by the grace of Parliament, not by the grace of God. Parliament had asserted its right to be part of the English government.

✔ **Reading Check** **Describing** Trace the sequence of events that led to the English Bill of Rights.

SECTION 2 REVIEW

Vocabulary
1. **Explain** the significance of: inflation, witchcraft, Holy Roman Empire, Bohemia, James I, divine right of kings, Puritans, Charles I, Cavaliers, Roundheads, Oliver Cromwell, commonwealth, restoration, convert, James II.

Main Ideas
2. **Explain** what contributed to the economic and social problems of sixteenth-century Europe.

3. **Illustrate** the causes and effects of the Thirty Years' War by using a chart like the one below.

Thirty Years' War	
Cause	Effect

4. **Explain** why Oliver Cromwell first purged Parliament and then declared a military dictatorship.

Critical Thinking
5. **The BIG Idea** **Drawing Conclusions** Which nation emerged stronger after the Thirty Years' War? Did 30 years of fighting accomplish any of the original motives for waging the war?

6. **Distinguishing** What are the differences, if any, between a military dictatorship and a king ruling by "divine right"?

7. **Analyzing Visuals** Examine the painting on page 223. How does Goya portray the witches? What details in the painting indicate that witches were feared?

Writing About History
8. **Expository Writing** Write an essay on why population increased and decreased in sixteenth- and seventeenth-century England. Include a population graph.

History ONLINE

For help with the concepts in this section of *Glencoe World History— Modern Times*, go to glencoe.com and click Study Central.

Response to Crisis: Absolutism

GUIDE TO READING

The BIG Idea
Competition Among Countries
France became the greatest power of the seventeenth century. Prussia, Austria, and Russia also emerged as great European powers.

Content Vocabulary
• absolutism *(p. 228)*   • czar *(p. 232)*
• boyars *(p. 232)*

Academic Vocabulary
• stability *(p. 228)*   • authority *(p. 228)*

People and Places
• Louis XIV *(p. 228)*
• Cardinal Richelieu *(p. 228)*
• Prussia *(p. 231)*
• Austria *(p. 231)*
• Frederick William the Great Elector *(p. 231)*
• Ivan IV *(p. 232)*
• Michael Romanov *(p. 232)*
• Peter the Great *(p. 233)*
• St. Petersburg *(p. 233)*

Reading Strategy
Summarizing Information As you read, complete a chart like the one below summarizing the accomplishments of Peter the Great.

Reforms	Government	Wars

Absolute monarchs reigned in several European nations during the seventeenth century. Louis XIV, considered the best example of absolute monarchy, ruled France with an extravagant lifestyle and waged many military campaigns. Meanwhile, Prussia, Austria, and Russia emerged as great European powers under their monarchs' leadership.

France under Louis XIV

MAIN IDEA Louis XIV was an absolute monarch whose rule was admired and imitated throughout Europe.

HISTORY & YOU What would happen if you used all the money in your family's bank account to throw a party? Learn how King Louis XIV spent his country's wealth.

One response to the crises of the seventeenth century was to seek more **stability** by increasing the power of the monarch. The result was what historians have called absolutism.

Absolutism is a system in which a ruler holds total power. In seventeenth-century Europe, absolutism was tied to the idea of the divine right of kings. This means that rulers received their power from God and were responsible to no one except God. They had the ability to make laws, levy taxes, administer justice, control officials, and determine foreign policy.

The reign of **Louis XIV** has long been regarded as the best example of absolutism in the seventeenth century. French culture, language, and manners reached into all levels of European society. French diplomacy and wars dominated the political affairs of Europe. The court of Louis XIV was imitated throughout Europe.

Richelieu and Mazarin

French history for the 50 years before Louis was a period of struggle as governments fought to avoid the breakdown of the state. Louis XIII and Louis XIV were only boys when they came to the throne. The government was left in the hands of royal ministers. In France, two ministers played important roles in preserving the **authority** of the monarchy.

Cardinal Richelieu (RIH•shuh•LOO), Louis XIII's chief minister, strengthened the monarchy's power. Because the Huguenots were seen as a threat to the king, Richelieu took away their political and military rights. He did preserve their religious rights. Richelieu also set up a network of spies to uncover plots by nobles. He then crushed the conspiracies and executed the conspirators.

Louis XIV and Absolutism

In his Political Treatise, *Jacques-Benigne Bossuet, popular orator during the time of Louis XIV, explained his perception of the divine right of kings:*

"Rulers . . . act as the ministers of God and as his lieutenants on earth. It is through them that God exercises his empire.

But kings, although their power comes from on high . . . should not regard themselves as masters of that power to use it at their pleasure . . . they must employ it with fear and self-restraint, as a thing coming from God and of which God will demand an account.

The royal power is absolute . . . Without this absolute authority the king could neither do good nor repress evil. It is necessary that his power be such that no one can hope to escape him, and, finally, the only protection of individuals against the public authority should be their innocence."

Louis XIV appears in the chariot of Apollo, the Greek god of light, surrounded by the rays of the sun.

Louis XIV is led by Aurora, Greek goddess of the dawn.

Emblem of Louis XIV, the Sun King.

DOCUMENT-BASED QUESTIONS

The painting by Joseph Werner II (1637–1710) depicts Louis XIV as Apollo, the Greek god of light.

1. **Explaining** Why did Louis XIV wish to be viewed as the mythological god Apollo?

2. **Speculating** Based on his rule, how might Louis XIV's views of absolutism have differed from those of Jacques-Benigne Bossuet?

Louis XIV came to the throne in 1643 at the age of four. Due to the king's young age, Cardinal Mazarin, the chief minister, took control of the government. Mazarin crushed a revolt led by nobles. Many French people concluded that the best hope for stability in the future lay with a strong monarch.

Louis Comes to Power

When Mazarin died in 1661, Louis XIV took over supreme power. The day after Cardinal Mazarin's death, the new king, at the age of 23, stated his desire to be a real king and the sole ruler of France:

PRIMARY SOURCE

"Up to this moment I have been pleased to entrust the government of my affairs to the late Cardinal. It is now time that I govern them myself. You [secretaries and ministers of state] will assist me with your counsels when I ask for them. I request and order you to seal no orders except by my command. I order you not to sign anything, not even a passport without my command; to render account to me personally each day and to favor no one."

Well aware of her son's love of fun and games and his affairs with the maids, Louis's mother laughed at these words. Louis was serious, however. He established and kept to a strict routine. He also fostered the myth of himself as the Sun King—the source of light for all of his people.

Government and Religion

One key to Louis's power was his control of the central policy-making machinery of government. The royal court that Louis established at Versailles (VUHR•SY) served three purposes. It was the personal household of the king. In addition, the chief offices of the state were located there. Finally, Versailles was the place where powerful subjects came to find favors and offices for themselves.

The greatest danger to Louis's rule came from very high nobles and royal princes. They believed they should play a role in the government. Instead, Louis removed them from the royal council. It was the king's chief administrative body, which supervised the government. At the same time, Louis enticed the nobles and royal princes to come to his court, where he kept them busy with court life and out of politics.

Louis's government ministers were to obey his every wish. Said Louis, "I had no intention of sharing my authority with them." Thus, Louis had complete authority over the traditional areas of royal power: foreign policy, the church, and taxes.

Although Louis had absolute power over nationwide policy making, his power was limited at the local level. Nobles, local officials, and town councils had more influence than the king in the daily operation of local governments. As a result, the king bribed important people in the provinces to see that his policies were carried out.

Desiring to maintain religious harmony as part of the monarchical power in France, Louis pursued an anti-Protestant policy aimed at converting the Huguenots to Catholicism. Early in his reign, Louis ordered the destruction of Huguenot churches and the closing of their schools. As many as two hundred thousand Huguenots fled to England, the United Provinces, and the German states.

The Economy and War

The cost of building palaces, maintaining his court, and pursuing his wars made finances a crucial issue for Louis XIV. He was most fortunate in having the services of Jean-Baptiste Colbert (kohl•BEHR) as controller-general of finances.

Colbert sought to increase France's wealth and power by following mercantilism. To decrease imports and increase exports, he granted subsidies to new industries. To improve communications and the transportation of goods within France, he built roads and canals. To decrease imports directly, Colbert raised tariffs on foreign goods and created a merchant marine to carry French goods.

To increase his royal power, Louis developed a standing army numbering four hundred thousand in time of war. He wished to achieve the military glory befitting the Sun King and ensure that his Bourbon dynasty dominated Europe.

To achieve his goals, Louis waged four wars between 1667 and 1713. Many nations formed coalitions to prevent him from dominating Europe. Through his wars, Louis added some territory and set up a member of his own dynasty on the throne of Spain.

Legacy of Louis XIV

In 1715, the Sun King died. He left France with great debts and surrounded by enemies.

On his deathbed, the 76-year-old monarch seemed remorseful when he told his successor (his great-grandson), "Soon you will be King of a great kingdom. . . . Try to remain at peace with your neighbors. I loved war too much. Do not follow me in that or in overspending. . . . Lighten your people's burden as soon as possible, and do what I have had the misfortune not to do myself."

Did Louis mean it? We do not know. In any event, his successor probably did not remember this advice; Louis's great-grandson was only five years old.

✓ **Reading Check** **Describing** How did Louis XIV maintain absolute power?

Absolutism in Central and Eastern Europe

MAIN IDEA Prussia and Austria emerged as great European powers in the seventeenth and eighteenth centuries.

HISTORY & YOU What if your neighborhood had its own government? Learn about the emergence of two new states in Europe.

After the Thirty Years' War, there were over three hundred German states. Of these, **Prussia** and **Austria** emerged in the seventeenth and eighteenth centuries as two great European powers.

The Emergence of Prussia

Frederick William the Great Elector laid the foundation for the Prussian state. Realizing that Prussia was a small, open territory with no natural frontiers for defense, Frederick William built a large and efficient standing army. He had a force of forty thousand men, which made the Prussian army the fourth-largest in Europe.

To maintain the army and his own power, Frederick William set up the General War Commissariat to levy taxes for the army and oversee its growth. The Commissariat soon became an agency for civil government as well. The new bureaucratic machine became the elector's chief instrument to govern the state. Many of its officials were members of the Prussian landed aristocracy, or the Junkers, who also served as officers in the army.

In 1701, Frederick William's son Frederick officially gained the title of king. Elector Frederick III became King Frederick I.

The New Austrian Empire

The Austrian Hapsburgs had long played a significant role in European politics as emperors in the Holy Roman Empire. By the end of the Thirty Years' War, their hopes of creating an empire in Germany had been dashed. The Hapsburgs made a difficult transition in the seventeenth century. They had lost the German Empire, but now they created a new empire in eastern and southeastern Europe.

NATIONAL GEOGRAPHIC

EXPANSION OF PRUSSIA AND AUSTRIA TO 1720

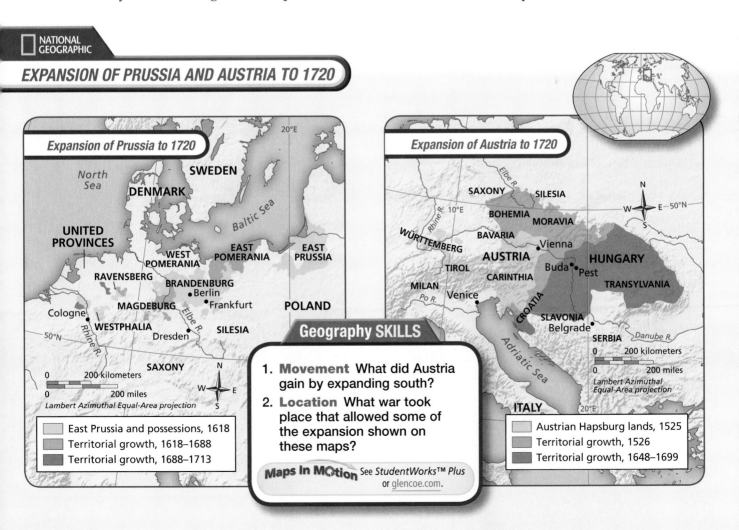

Expansion of Prussia to 1720

North Sea · SWEDEN · DENMARK · Baltic Sea · UNITED PROVINCES · WEST POMERANIA · EAST POMERANIA · EAST PRUSSIA · RAVENSBERG · BRANDENBURG · Berlin · Frankfurt · POLAND · Cologne · MAGDEBURG · Elbe R. · WESTPHALIA · Dresden · SILESIA · Rhine R. · 50°N · SAXONY · 20°E

0 — 200 kilometers
0 — 200 miles
Lambert Azimuthal Equal-Area projection

East Prussia and possessions, 1618
Territorial growth, 1618–1688
Territorial growth, 1688–1713

Expansion of Austria to 1720

Elbe R. · SAXONY · SILESIA · BOHEMIA · MORAVIA · Rhine R. · 10°E · WÜRTTEMBERG · BAVARIA · Vienna · AUSTRIA · TIROL · Buda · Pest · HUNGARY · MILAN · CARINTHIA · TRANSYLVANIA · Po R. · Venice · CROATIA · SLAVONIA · Belgrade · SERBIA · Danube R. · Adriatic Sea · ITALY · 20°E · N W E S · 50°N

0 — 200 kilometers
0 — 200 miles
Lambert Azimuthal Equal-Area projection

Austrian Hapsburg lands, 1525
Territorial growth, 1526
Territorial growth, 1648–1699

Geography SKILLS

1. **Movement** What did Austria gain by expanding south?
2. **Location** What war took place that allowed some of the expansion shown on these maps?

Maps In Motion See *StudentWorks™ Plus* or glencoe.com.

The core of the new Austrian Empire was the traditional Austrian lands in present-day Austria, the Czech Republic, and Hungary. After the defeat of the Turks at Vienna in 1683 (see Chapter 8), Austria took control of all of Hungary, Transylvania, Croatia, and Slavonia as well. By the beginning of the eighteenth century, the Austrian Hapsburgs had gained a new empire of considerable size.

The Austrian monarchy, however, never became a highly centralized, absolutist state, chiefly because it was made up of so many different national groups. The Austrian Empire remained a collection of territories held together by the Hapsburg emperor, who was archduke of Austria, king of Bohemia, and king of Hungary. Each of these areas had its own laws and political life. No common sentiment tied the regions together other than the ideal of service to the Hapsburgs, held by military officers and government officials.

✓**Reading Check** **Examining** Why was the Austrian monarchy unable to create a highly centralized, absolutist state?

Peter The Great

MAIN IDEA Russia emerged as a great power under Peter the Great.

HISTORY & YOU What if you discovered a great new way to save energy? Learn about the modernization of Russia.

A new Russian state emerged in the fifteenth century under the principality of Muscovy and its grand dukes. In the sixteenth century, **Ivan IV** became the first ruler to take the title of **czar,** the Russian word for *caesar.*

Ivan expanded the territories of Russia eastward. He also crushed the power of the Russian nobility, or **boyars.** He was known as Ivan the Terrible because of his ruthless deeds, among them stabbing his own son to death in a heated argument.

When Ivan's dynasty ended in 1598, a period of anarchy known as the Time of Troubles followed. This period ended when the *zemsky sobor,* or national assembly, chose **Michael Romanov** as the new czar in 1613.

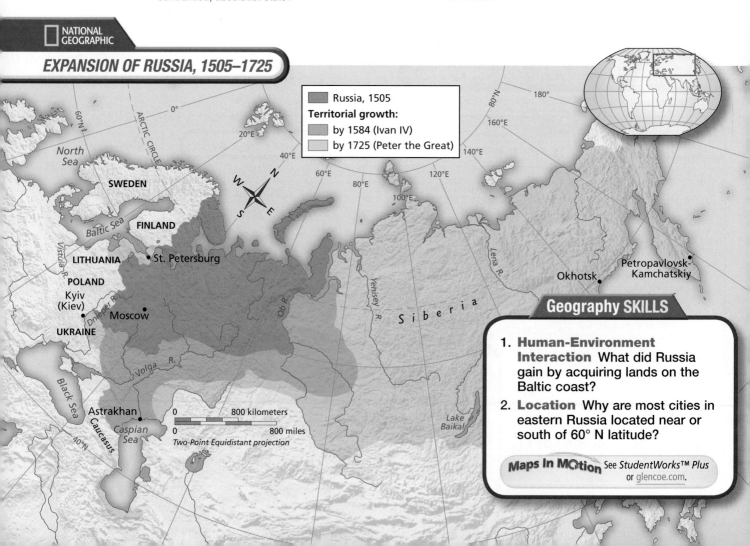

NATIONAL GEOGRAPHIC

EXPANSION OF RUSSIA, 1505–1725

Russia, 1505
Territorial growth:
by 1584 (Ivan IV)
by 1725 (Peter the Great)

Two-Point Equidistant projection

0   800 kilometers
0   800 miles

Geography SKILLS

1. **Human-Environment Interaction** What did Russia gain by acquiring lands on the Baltic coast?

2. **Location** Why are most cities in eastern Russia located near or south of 60° N latitude?

Maps In Motion See *StudentWorks™ Plus* or glencoe.com.

The Romanov dynasty lasted until 1917. One of its most prominent members was **Peter the Great**, who became czar in 1689. Like other Romanov czars who preceded him, Peter was an absolutist monarch who claimed the divine right to rule.

After becoming czar, Peter visited the West. Determined to westernize, or Europeanize, Russia, he was especially eager to borrow European technology. Only this kind of modernization could turn the army and navy into what he needed to make Russia a great power. By Peter's death in 1725, Russia was a great military power and an important European state.

Military and Governmental Changes

One of Peter's first goals was to reorganize the army. He employed both Russians and Europeans as officers. He drafted peasants for 25-year stints of service to build a standing army of 210,000 soldiers. Peter also formed the first Russian navy.

To impose the rule of the central government more effectively, Peter divided Russia into provinces. He hoped to create a "police state," a well-ordered community governed by law. However, few bureaucrats shared his concept of honest service and duty to the state. Peter's personality created an atmosphere of fear instead of a sense of civic duty. He wrote to one administrator, "According to these orders act, act, act. I won't write more, but you will pay with your head if you interpret orders again." Peter wanted the impossible—that his administrators be slaves and free persons at the same time.

Cultural Changes and a New Capital

After visiting the West, Peter began to introduce Western customs, practices, and manners into Russia. He ordered the preparation of the first Russian book of etiquette to teach Western manners. He insisted that Russian men shave their beards and shorten their coats. Upper-class women could remove their traditional face-covering veils and move out into society. Both sexes could mix for conversation and dancing at gatherings.

The object of Peter's domestic reforms was to make Russia into a great state and military power and to "open a window to the West," meaning a port with ready access to Europe. This could be achieved only on the Baltic Sea, which Sweden, the most important power in northern Europe, controlled. Peter acquired the lands he sought after a long war with Sweden. On the Baltic in 1703, Peter began construction of a new city, **St. Petersburg,** his window to the West. Finished during Peter's lifetime, St. Petersburg remained the Russian capital until 1918.

✓ **Reading Check** **Evaluating** Why was it so important that Peter the Great have a seaport on the Baltic?

Vocabulary

1. **Explain** the significance of: stability, absolutism, Louis XIV, authority, Cardinal Richelieu, Prussia, Austria, Frederick William the Great Elector, Ivan IV, czar, boyars, Michael Romanov, Peter the Great, St. Petersburg.

Main Ideas

2. **Summarize** the reign of Louis XIV of France using a chart like the one below.

Government	Wars	Economics	Religion

3. **Explain** why Frederick the Great Elector of Prussia thought it was so important to build a large and efficient standing army.

4. **Describe** the Western customs and practices that Peter the Great introduced to Russia.

Critical Thinking

5. **The BIG Idea** **Comparing and Contrasting** Compare and contrast the absolutist leadership styles of Louis XIV, Frederick William the Great Elector, and Peter the Great.

6. **Making Connections** Explain why building roads and canals and constructing a seaport would increase a nation's wealth and power.

7. **Analyzing Visuals** Examine the painting of Louis XIV on page 229. In what ways does this painting emphasize the absolute power of Louis XIV?

Writing About History

8. **Expository Writing** Historians have long considered the reign of Louis XIV to be the best example of the practice of absolute monarchy in the seventeenth century. Do you believe the statement is true? Why or why not? Write an essay supporting your opinion.

History ONLINE

For help with the concepts in this section of *Glencoe World History— Modern Times*, go to glencoe.com and click Study Central.

A Palace Fit for the Sun King

Versailles was at the center of court life during the reign of Louis XIV. Versailles was transformed from a hunting lodge by the finest architects and artists of the seventeenth century. Its extensive grounds became a showcase of the French court's splendor and wealth—with every detail in the immense and opulent palace a reflection of the Sun King's absolute power.

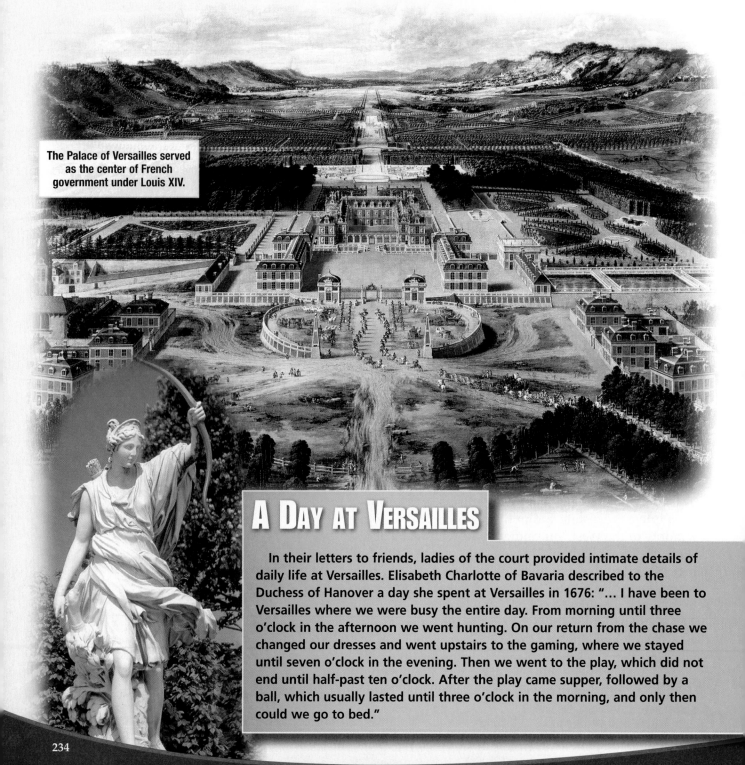

The Palace of Versailles served as the center of French government under Louis XIV.

A DAY AT VERSAILLES

In their letters to friends, ladies of the court provided intimate details of daily life at Versailles. Elisabeth Charlotte of Bavaria described to the Duchess of Hanover a day she spent at Versailles in 1676: "… I have been to Versailles where we were busy the entire day. From morning until three o'clock in the afternoon we went hunting. On our return from the chase we changed our dresses and went upstairs to the gaming, where we stayed until seven o'clock in the evening. Then we went to the play, which did not end until half-past ten o'clock. After the play came supper, followed by a ball, which usually lasted until three o'clock in the morning, and only then could we go to bed."

Dazzling seventeenth-century visitors, the Hall of Mirrors communicated the king's glory through the sparkling reflections of hundreds of mirrors.

With every leaf, branch, and flower precisely organized into formal patterns, the gardens reflected the seventeenth-century theme of man's triumph over nature.

Water pumped from the Seine River flowed through the 1,400 fountains in the gardens.

EARNING THE KING'S FAVOR

Hoping to obtain an office, title, or pension from Louis XIV, thousands of people—as many as 5,000 in winter—lived at Versailles. They took part in the strict daily routines of court life, all of which revolved around the king, from the time he woke in the morning to the time he went to bed at night. To leave Versailles, people had to ask the king's permission, which he did not like to grant. For many, the expense of life at Versailles led to debt and ruin. People risked such ruin, however, to earn the king's attention and favor. One of the highest honors anyone could hope for at Versailles was to hold the candle while the king's hair was combed at night before bed.

ANALYZING VISUALS

1. **Comparing** How did people gain political influence in seventeenth-century France? How about today?

2. **Predicting** How do you think people today would respond to government spending of large sums of money on elaborate building projects or entertainments? Why?

The World of European Culture

GUIDE TO READING

The BIG Idea
Ideas, Beliefs, and Values Art and literature reflected people's spiritual perceptions and the human condition.

Content Vocabulary
• Mannerism *(p. 236)*   • baroque *(p. 237)*
• natural rights *(p. 241)*

Academic Vocabulary
• drama *(p. 238)*   • creative *(p. 239)*

People and Places
• El Greco *(p. 236)*   • William Shakespeare
• Prague *(p. 237)*   *(p. 238)*
• Vienna *(p. 237)*   • Miguel de Cervantes
• Brussels *(p. 237)*   *(p. 239)*
• Gian Lorenzo Bernini   • Lope de Vega *(p. 240)*
  (p. 237)   • Thomas Hobbes
• Madrid *(p. 237)*   *(p. 240)*
                         • John Locke *(p. 241)*

Reading Strategy
Summarizing Information As you read, complete a chart like the one below summarizing the political thoughts of Thomas Hobbes and John Locke.

Thomas Hobbes	John Locke

The religious and political conflicts of seventeenth-century Europe were reflected in the art, literature, and political thought of the time. Art produced during the movements of Mannerism and the baroque aroused the emotions, and the literature spoke of the human condition. Political thinkers debated concerns about power and order in their works.

Art after the Renaissance

MAIN IDEA The artistic movements of Mannerism and the baroque began in Italy and reflected the spiritual perceptions of the time.

HISTORY & YOU What art form would you use to create something that reflects the mood of the current decade? Learn how Mannerism depicted the tensions in society after the Renaissance.

Mannerism and the baroque movement began in Italy and spread through Europe. The art produced during these movements reflected the tension of religious upheaval and the spirituality of religious revival.

Mannerism

The artistic Renaissance came to an end when a new movement, called **Mannerism**, emerged in Italy in the 1520s and 1530s. The Reformation's revival of religious values brought much political turmoil. Especially in Italy, the worldly enthusiasm of the Renaissance declined as people grew more anxious and uncertain and wished for spiritual experience.

Mannerism in art reflected this new environment by deliberately breaking down the High Renaissance principles of balance, harmony, and moderation. The rules of proportion were deliberately ignored as elongated figures were used to show suffering, heightened emotions, and religious ecstasy.

Mannerism spread from Italy to other parts of Europe and perhaps reached its high point in the work of **El Greco**, "the Greek." El Greco studied the elements of Renaissance painting in Venice. He also wrote many works on painting. From Venice, El Greco moved to Rome. His career as a painter stalled there possibly because he had criticized Michelangelo's abilities as a painter. When he moved to Spain, El Greco met with success.

In El Greco's paintings, the figures are elongated or contorted and he sometimes used unusual shades of yellow and green against an eerie background of stormy grays. The mood of his works reflects well the tensions created by the religious upheavals of the Reformation.

St. Peter's Basilica

Saint Peter's Basilica in Vatican City, Rome is designed in the shape of a Latin cross with a dome at the crossing, directly above the altar. The dome, designed by Michelangelo, covers the shrine of St. Peter the Apostle, a follower of Jesus. St. Peter's Basilica is the church of the popes and a major pilgrimage site.

The interior of Saint Peter's is filled with many masterpieces of Baroque art, including Bernini's baldachin, or architectural canopy, over the main altar (below). Its shape is meant to draw the worshipper's eyes upward as if to reach God. Bernini's *Throne of St. Peter* can be seen through the baldachin.

St. Peter's Basilica in Rome

Bernini's baldachin and Throne of St. Peter

Bernini described the two great colonnades he added to St. Peter's as reaching around the open piazza "like the motherly arms of the Church."

DOCUMENT-BASED QUESTIONS

The baldachin and *Throne of St. Peter* were works of Gian Lorenzo Bernini (1598–1680), built for St. Peter's Basilica, Vatican City, Rome.

1. **Describing** What aspects of St. Peter's Basilica make it an example of baroque architecture?
2. **Analyzing** In what ways did Bernini design the basilica as a Christian monument?

The Baroque Period

Mannerism was eventually replaced by a new movement—the **baroque.** This movement began in Italy at the end of the sixteenth century and eventually spread to the rest of Europe and Latin America. It was eagerly adopted by the Catholic reform movement as shown in the richly detailed buildings at Catholic courts, especially those of the Hapsburgs in **Madrid, Prague, Vienna,** and **Brussels.**

Baroque artists tried to bring together the classical ideals of Renaissance art and the spiritual feelings of the sixteenth-century religious revival. In large part, though, baroque art and architecture reflected a search for power. Baroque churches and palaces were magnificent and richly detailed. Kings and princes wanted others to be in awe of their power.

Perhaps the greatest figure of the baroque period was the Italian architect and sculptor **Gian Lorenzo Bernini,** who completed Saint Peter's Basilica in Rome. Action, exuberance, and dramatic effects mark the work of Bernini in the interior of Saint Peter's.

Bernini's *Throne of Saint Peter* is a highly decorated cover for the pope's medieval wooden throne. It is considered by many to be Bernini's crowning achievement in Saint Peter's Basilica. The throne seems to hover in midair, held by the hands of the four great theologians of the early Catholic Church. Above the chair, rays of heavenly light drive a mass of clouds and angels down and toward the spectator.

The baroque painting style was known for its use of dramatic effects to arouse the emotions as shown in the work of another important Italian artist of the baroque period, Caravaggio. Similar to other baroque painters, Caravaggio used dramatic lighting to heighten emotions, to focus details, and to isolate the figures in his paintings. His work placed an emphasis on everyday experience. He shocked some of his patrons by depicting religious figures as common people in everyday settings.

Artemisia Gentileschi is less well-known than the male artists who dominated the seventeenth-century art world in Italy but prominent in her own right. Born in Rome, she studied painting with her father. In 1616, she moved to Florence and began a successful career as a painter. At the age of 23, she became the first woman to be elected to the Florentine Academy of Design. She was known internationally in her day as a portrait painter, but her fame now rests on a series of pictures of Old Testament heroines.

The baroque style of art did not just flourish in Italy. Peter Paul Rubens embodies the baroque movement in Flanders (the Spanish Netherlands), where he worked most of his life. A scholar and diplomat as well as an artist, Rubens used his classical education and connections with noble patrons in Italy, Spain, England, France, and Flanders to paint a variety of genres. He is best known for his depictions of the human form in action. These images are lavish and extravagant, much like the court life he experienced during the baroque period.

History ONLINE

Student Web Activity—
Visit glencoe.com and complete the activity on William Shakespeare.

✓ **Reading Check** **Describing** What did the mood of El Greco's paintings reflect?

Golden Age of Literature

MAIN IDEA Shakespeare and Lope de Vega were prolific writers of dramas and comedies that reflected the human condition.

HISTORY & YOU Are there any contemporary artists or entertainers who could compare to William Shakespeare? Learn about the great writers in England and Spain.

In both England and Spain, writing for the theater reached new heights between 1580 and 1640. Other forms of literature flourished as well.

England's Shakespeare

A cultural flowering took place in England in the late sixteenth and early seventeenth centuries. The period is often called the Elizabethan Era, because so much of it fell within the reign of Queen Elizabeth. Of all the forms of Elizabethan literature, none expressed the energy of the era better than **drama**. Of all the dramatists, none is more famous than **William Shakespeare.**

When Shakespeare appeared in London in 1592, Elizabethans already enjoyed the stage. Elizabethan theater was a very successful business. London theaters ranged from the Globe, a circular, unroofed structure holding three thousand people, to the Blackfriars, a roofed structure that held only five hundred.

The Globe's admission charge of one or two pennies enabled even the lower classes to attend. The higher prices of the Blackfriars brought an audience of the well-to-do. Because Elizabethan audiences varied greatly, playwrights wrote works that pleased nobles, lawyers, merchants, and vagabonds alike.

William Shakespeare was a "complete man of the theater." Although best known for writing plays, he was also an actor and shareholder in the chief theater company of the time, the Lord Chamberlain's Men.

Shakespeare has long been viewed as a universal genius. A master of the English language, he also had a keen insight into human psychology. In his tragedies and his comedies, Shakespeare showed a remarkable understanding of the human condition.

Spain's Cervantes and Vega

One of the crowning achievements of the golden age of Spanish literature was the work of **Miguel de Cervantes** (suhr•VAN•TEEZ). His novel *Don Quixote* has been hailed as one of the greatest literary works of all time.

In the two main characters of this famous work, Cervantes presented the dual nature of the Spanish character. The knight, Don Quixote from La Mancha, is the visionary so involved in his lofty ideals that he does not see the hard realities around him. To him, for example, windmills appear to be four-armed giants. In contrast, the knight's fat and earthy squire, Sancho Panza, is a realist. Each of these characters finally comes to see the value of the other's perspective. The readers of *Don Quixote* are left with the conviction that both visionary dreams and the hard work of reality are necessary to the human condition.

The theater was one of the most **creative** forms of expression during Spain's golden century as well. The first professional theaters, created in Seville and Madrid,

Queen Elizabeth's interest in Renaissance playwrights led to a golden age for English theater. All social classes could attend the theater. The poor, called "groundlings," paid a small sum to stand in the open area near the stage. Those who could pay more sat in the galleries.

DOCUMENT-BASED QUESTIONS

Queen Elizabeth Watching The Merry Wives of Windsor at The Globe Theatre, by David Scott (1806–1849), depicts an audience enjoying Shakespeare's play.

1. **Summarizing** What classes of people attended Shakespeare's plays?

2. **Analyzing** How does Shakespeare relate art to life in the excerpt from *As You Like It*?

"All the world's a stage,
And all the men and women merely players;
They have their exits and their entrances;
And one man in his time plays many parts . . . "

—Philosophy of the character Jaques from *As You Like It*, Act 2, Scene 7, by William Shakespeare

were run by actors' companies, as they were in England. Soon, every large town had a public playhouse, including Mexico City in the New World. Touring companies brought the latest and most current Spanish plays to all parts of the Spanish Empire.

Beginning in the 1580s, the standard for playwrights was set by **Lope de Vega.** He wrote an extraordinary number of plays, perhaps 1,500 in all. Almost 500 of them survive to this day. Vega's plays are thought to be witty, charming, action-packed, and realistic.

Lope de Vega made no apologies for the fact that he wrote his plays to please his audiences and satisfy public demand. He remarked once that if anyone thought he had written his plays for the sake of fame, "undeceive him and tell him that I wrote them for money."

✓ **Reading Check** **Describing** When was the "golden age" of Spanish literature? Who set the standard for playwrights?

Political Thought

MAIN IDEA Hobbes and Locke wrote very different books about political thought in response to the English revolutions.

HISTORY & YOU What if you were asked to debate whether or not to wear school uniforms? Learn about England's influential political thinkers.

The seventeenth-century concerns with order and power were reflected in the political thought of the time. The English revolutions of the seventeenth century prompted very different responses from two English political thinkers, Thomas Hobbes and John Locke.

Hobbes

Thomas Hobbes was alarmed by the revolutionary upheavals in England. He wrote *Leviathan*, a work on political thought, to try to deal with the problem of disorder. *Leviathan* was published in 1651.

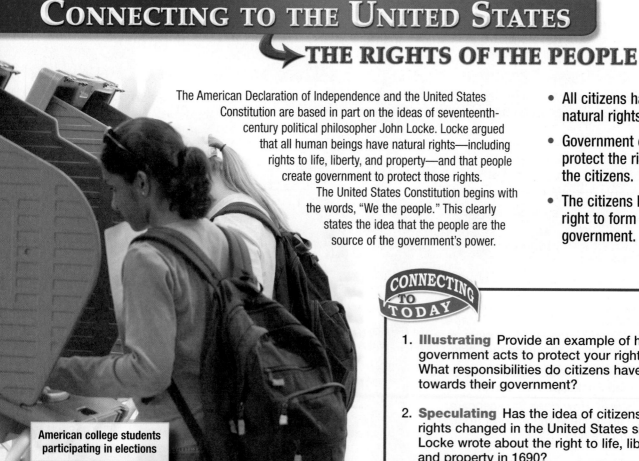

CONNECTING TO THE UNITED STATES
THE RIGHTS OF THE PEOPLE

The American Declaration of Independence and the United States Constitution are based in part on the ideas of seventeenth-century political philosopher John Locke. Locke argued that all human beings have natural rights—including rights to life, liberty, and property—and that people create government to protect those rights.

The United States Constitution begins with the words, "We the people." This clearly states the idea that the people are the source of the government's power.

- All citizens have natural rights.

- Government exists to protect the rights of the citizens.

- The citizens have the right to form a new government.

American college students participating in elections

1. **Illustrating** Provide an example of how government acts to protect your rights. What responsibilities do citizens have towards their government?

2. **Speculating** Has the idea of citizens' rights changed in the United States since Locke wrote about the right to life, liberty, and property in 1690?

Hobbes claimed that before society was organized, human life was "solitary, poor, nasty, brutish, and short." Humans were guided not by reason and moral ideals but by a ruthless struggle for self-preservation.

To save themselves from destroying one another, people made a social contract and agreed to form a state. Hobbes called the state "that great Leviathan to which we owe our peace and defense." People in the state agreed to be governed by an absolute ruler who possessed unlimited power. Rebellion must be suppressed. To Hobbes, such absolute power was needed to preserve order in society.

Locke

John Locke viewed the exercise of political power quite differently. His *Two Treatises on Government*, written in 1679 and 1680 but too radical and too dangerous to be published then, first appeared in 1690. In his treatises, especially the second one, Locke argued against the absolute rule of one person. He described how governments are formed and what justifies them.

Unlike Hobbes, Locke believed that before society was organized, humans lived in a state of equality and freedom rather than in a state of war. In this state of nature, no one was necessarily sovereign over anyone else. Locke believed that all humans had certain **natural rights**—rights with which they were born. These included rights to life, liberty, and property.

Like Hobbes, however, Locke believed that problems existed in the state of nature. People found it difficult to protect their natural rights. For that reason, they agreed to establish a government to ensure the protection of their rights and to judge those who violated them.

The contract between people and government involved mutual obligations. Government would protect the rights of the people, and the people would act reasonably toward government. However, if a government broke the contract—for example, if a monarch failed to protect citizens' natural rights—the people would be within their rights to remove or alter the government since it betrayed their trust. If the people chose to remove the government, then they could form a new one.

To Locke, "people" meant the landholding aristocracy, not landless masses. Locke was not an advocate of democracy, but his ideas proved important to both the Americans and the French in the eighteenth century. These ideas were used to support demands for constitutional government, the rule of law, and the protection of rights. Locke's ideas can be found in both the American Declaration of Independence and the United States Constitution.

✓ Reading Check **Explaining** According to Hobbes, why was absolute power needed?

Vocabulary

1. **Explain** the significance of: Mannerism, El Greco, baroque, Madrid, Prague, Vienna, Brussels, Gian Lorenzo Bernini, drama, William Shakespeare, Miguel de Cervantes, creative, Lope de Vega, Thomas Hobbes, John Locke, natural rights.

Main Ideas

2. **Label and identify** Mannerism and baroque art using a Venn diagram like the one below.

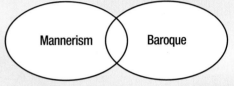

3. **Describe** what *Don Quixote* reveals about the nature of Spanish character.

4. **Summarize** the mutual obligations between people and government as expressed by Locke.

Critical Thinking

5. **The BIG Idea** **Analyzing** How did the Elizabethan theater experience provide a reflection of English society?

6. **Assessing** Assess how or if John Locke's *Two Treatises on Government* would justify the Glorious Revolution.

7. **Analyzing Visuals** Examine the painting on page 239. When did the artist live? Does this change the way you view his painting? Explain your answer.

Writing About History

8. **Persuasive Writing** In an essay, argue whether Shakespeare's quotation from *As You Like It* on page 239 is correct. Support your position with examples of historical figures from the chapter.

History ONLINE

For help with the concepts in this section of *Glencoe World History—Modern Times*, go to glencoe.com and click Study Central.

STUDY TO GO You can study anywhere, anytime by downloading quizzes and flash cards to your PDA from glencoe.com.

THE BATTLE OF IVRY (1590) DURING THE FRENCH WARS OF RELIGION

Henry of Navarre, later Henry IV, led the Huguenots to victory over Catholic forces to win the French throne.

RELIGIOUS CONFLICTS in Europe

- Religious conflicts between Protestants and Catholics were widespread.
- French kings persecuted Protestants.
- Philip II of Spain tried to crush Calvinism.
- The Thirty Years' War was triggered by religious and political conflicts.

POLITICAL, ECONOMIC, AND SOCIAL CRISES in Europe

- Civil war arose in England from power struggles between King Charles I and Parliament.
- English Protestant forces triumphed in the civil war and tried and executed King Charles I.
- Population growth, famine, and plague contributed to social tensions throughout Europe.
- The conflicts in seventeenth-century Europe were reflected in art, literature, and political works.

THE EXECUTION OF KING CHARLES I OF ENGLAND IN 1649

After the execution of Charles I, England became a commonwealth until the monarchy returned to power in 1660.

THE SIGNING OF THE PEACE TREATY OF NIJMEGEN REPRESENTED THE HIGH POINT OF LOUIS XIV'S REIGN

Many European monarchs tried to achieve the level of absolute power that Louis XIV enjoyed.

ABSOLUTISM as a Response to Crises

- Frederick William of Prussia used the General War Commissariat to maintain his power.
- The Austrian monarchy tried but failed to achieve a centralized, absolutist state.
- The absolute rule of Louis XIV of France influenced monarchs throughout Europe.
- Russia emerged as a great power under the absolute rule of Peter the Great.

STANDARDIZED TEST PRACTICE

TEST-TAKING TIP

If you do not know the answer to a question, eliminate any answer choices that you know are incorrect. Then choose the best answer from the remaining choices.

Reviewing Vocabulary

Directions: Choose the word or words that best complete the sentence.

1. The Stuart rulers of England believed in the _____ right of kings.

   A social

   B divine

   C supreme

   D property

2. John Locke called the rights to life, liberty, and property _____ rights.

   A inalienable

   B universal

   C rational

   D natural

3. Philip II of Spain sent a fleet of warships, or _____, to invade England.

   A armada

   B brigade

   C regiment

   D battalion

4. The term _____ is another name for a republic.

   A nation

   B democracy

   C commonwealth

   D monarchy

Reviewing Main Ideas

Directions: Choose the best answers to the following questions.

Section 1 *(pp. 222–225)*

5. Which monarch was called the "Most Catholic King?"

   A Louis XIV

   B Philip II

   C Elizabeth Tudor

   D James I

6. Who were the French Protestants influenced by John Calvin?

   A Philosophes

   B Methodists

   C Puritans

   D Huguenots

Section 2 *(pp. 226–231)*

7. Which act brought an end to the Holy Roman Empire as a political entity?

   A the Edict of Nantes

   B the Peace of Westphalia

   C the Treaty of Versailles

   D the Toleration Act

8. What did the struggle between King Charles I and Parliament to govern England result in?

   A the English Revolution

   B the American Revolution

   C the Thirty Years' War

   D the Seven Years' War

Need Extra Help?								
If You Missed Questions . . .	1	2	3	4	5	6	7	8
Go to Page . . .	225	241	220	225	218	221	224	225

9. In 1689, what laid the foundation for a limited, or constitutional, monarchy in England?

  A the Edict of Nantes

  B the Toleration Act

  C the Bill of Rights

  D the Stamp Act

Section 3 (pp. 232–237)

10. In which system does a ruler hold total power?

  A absolutism

  B republicanism

  C enlightened absolutism

  D deism

11. Who was one of the most prominent Russian rulers in the Romanov dynasty?

  A Frederick William the Great Elector

  B Philip II

  C Ivan IV

  D Peter the Great

Section 4 (pp. 240–245)

12. Which movement replaced the artistic Renaissance?

  A baroque

  B Puritanism

  C Mannerism

  D rococo

13. Elizabethan playwrights such as William Shakespeare generally wrote their plays for what social group?

  A nobles

  B all classes

  C merchants

  D lower classes

Critical Thinking

Directions: Choose the best answers to the following questions.

14. How did Louis XIV control the nobles and princes?

  A He kept them busy with court life.

  B He shared his power with them.

  C He imprisoned them.

  D He made them join his military.

Base your answer to questions 15 and 16 on the map below.

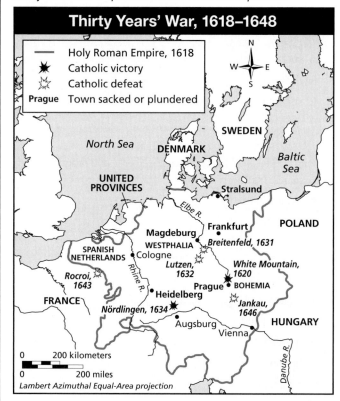

15. Which river flows nearest to Vienna?

  A Baltic

  B Elbe

  C Rhine

  D Danube

Need Extra Help?							
If You Missed Questions . . .	9	10	11	12	13	14	15
Go to Page . . .	227	228	233	236	238	230	224

16. What does the map tell you about the location of towns that were sacked or plundered?

  A They were located near rivers.

  B They were located in the northern and central parts of the Holy Roman Empire.

  C They were located west of the Elbe River.

  D They were located in the southern part of the Holy Roman Empire.

17. Which of the following was an important development in sixteenth-century European culture?

  A Mannerism replaced the baroque movement.

  B El Greco completed St. Peter's Basilica.

  C Miguel de Cervantes wrote *Don Quixote*.

  D Lope de Vega wrote *Leviathan*.

Analyze the chart and answer the question that follows. Base your answer on the chart and on your knowledge of world history.

Following Ivan IV's death, Russia experienced a period of anarchy. The troubles ended when the Romanov dynasty began its rule. Among the Romanov rulers was Peter the Great, who made several changes in his country.

Changes Made by Peter the Great

Military and Government	Cultural
Reorganized army	Prepared first Russian book of etiquette to teach Western manners
Formed the first Russian navy	?
Divided Russia into provinces for a more effective central government	Allowed upper-class women to remove their veils and move out into society

18. What other cultural change should be added to the chart?

  A commissioned a painting from El Greco

  B insisted that men shave their beards

  C prohibited Western customs

  D allowed all women to remove their veils

Document-Based Questions

Directions: Analyze the document and answer the short answer questions that follow the document.

Near the end of her life, Elizabeth Tudor gave her Golden Speech to Parliament. Following is an excerpt from that speech.

> "I do assure you there is no prince that loves his subjects better, or whose love can contradict our love. There is no jewel, be it of never so rich a price, which I set before this jewel; I mean your love. For I do esteem it more than any treasure or riches. …
>
> Of myself I say this: I never was any greedy, scraping grasper, nor a strait, fast-holding Prince, nor yet a waster. My heart was never set on any worldly goods, but only for my subjects' good. What you bestow on me, I will not hoard it up, but receive it to bestow on you again. Yea, mine own properties I account yours, to be expended for your good. … "

19. To whom does Elizabeth feel accountable?

20. Explain how Louis XIV of France might have disagreed with Elizabeth about expending properties for the good of her subjects.

Extended Response

21. During their rule, monarchs can either strengthen or weaken their countries. Which monarch described in this chapter do you most and least admire for how he or she governed? Support your answer with examples of actions taken by each monarch.

History ONLINE

For additional test practice, use Self-Check Quizzes—Chapter 7 at **glencoe.com**.

CHAPTER 8

The Muslim Empires 1450–1800

Section 1 The Ottoman Empire

Section 2 The Rule of the Ṣafavids

Section 3 The Grandeur of the Moguls

MAKING CONNECTIONS

How do Muslims celebrate their beliefs?

Jama Masjid, the largest mosque in India, was built during the Mogul Empire. The Muslims shown here are offering prayers during the celebration known as Eid-Al-Fitr, or the Celebration of Breaking the Fast. In this chapter, you will learn more about the history and culture of Muslims.

- What are the most widely practiced religions in the United States?
- How do other religious groups practice their beliefs?

MUSLIM
EMPIRES ▶

1453
Ottomans, led by Mehmed II, lay siege to Constantinople

1529
Ottomans are defeated at Vienna

1588
Rule of Shāh ʿAbbās begins, leading to peak of the Ṣafavid dynasty

1450   1500   1600

THE WORLD ▶

1464
The Sunni dynasty in Africa begins

1534
Henry VIII creates the Church of England

1598
Japanese unification begins

1739
Delhi is destroyed
by Persians

1757
British forces, led
by Sir Robert Clive,
defeat the Moguls

1700

1800

1776
Thomas Jefferson writes the
Declaration of Independence

FOLDABLES™
Study Organizer

Muslim Empires	Key Events and Rulers	Religion and Art	Society and Culture
Ottoman Empire			
Safavid Empire			
Mogul Empire			

Categorizing
Create a Folded
Table to categorize
information about
the Ottoman, Ṣafavid, and Mogul
Empires. Information should include key
events and rulers, religion and art, and
society and culture.

History ONLINE

Chapter Overview—Visit glencoe.com to preview Chapter 8.

The Ottoman Empire

GUIDE TO READING

The BIG Idea
Competition Among Countries
The Ottoman Empire grew strong as it expanded its borders.

Content Vocabulary
- janissaries (p. 248)
- pashas (p. 250)
- gunpowder empire (p. 250)
- sultan (p. 250)
- harem (p. 250)
- grand vizier (p. 251)
- ulema (p. 251)

Academic Vocabulary
- expand (p. 248)
- domain (p. 250)

People and Places
- Anatolian Peninsula (p. 248)
- Bosporus (p. 248)
- Dardanelles (p. 248)
- Sea of Marmara (p. 248)
- Mehmed II (p. 249)
- Constantiople (p. 249)
- Sultan Selim I (p. 249)
- Jerusalem (p. 249)
- Makkah (p. 249)
- Madinah (p. 250)
- Sinan (p. 252)

Reading Strategy
Organizing Information Create a chart to show the structure of the Ottoman society. List groups in order of importance.

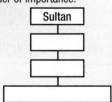

At its high point under Süleyman the Magnificent, the Ottoman Empire consisted of lands in western Asia, North Africa, and Europe. The Ottomans contributed a unique architectural design to world art, as seen in their magnificent mosques. They also practiced religious tolerance, which allowed subjects to follow their own religion.

Rise of the Ottoman Turks

MAIN IDEA Over a span of three hundred years, the Ottomans conquered the Byzantine Empire and expanded into western Asia, Africa, and Europe to create the Ottoman Empire.

HISTORY & YOU What would you do if you were asked to defend your city or hometown against invaders that had more advanced weapons? Learn how the Ottomans laid siege to the city of Constantinople.

In the late thirteenth century, a new group of Turks under their leader Osman began to build power in the northwest corner of the **Anatolian Peninsula.** In the early fourteenth century, the Osman Turks began to **expand** and began the Ottoman dynasty.

Expansion of the Empire

The Ottomans expanded westward and eventually controlled the **Bosporus** and the **Dardanelles.** These two straits (narrow passageways), separated by the **Sea of Marmara,** connect the Black Sea and the Aegean Sea, which leads to the Mediterranean. The Byzantine Empire had controlled this area for centuries.

In the fourteenth century, the Ottoman Turks expanded into the Balkans. The Ottoman rulers built a strong military by developing an elite guard called **janissaries.** Recruited from the local Christian population, the janissaries were converted to Islam. Trained as foot soldiers or administrators, they served the sultan.

As knowledge of firearms spread in the late fourteenth century, the Ottomans began to master the new technology. The janissaries, trained as a well-armed infantry, were able to spread Ottoman control in the Balkans. With their new forces, the Ottomans defeated the Serbs at the Battle of Kosovo in 1389. During the 1390s, they advanced northward and annexed Bulgaria.

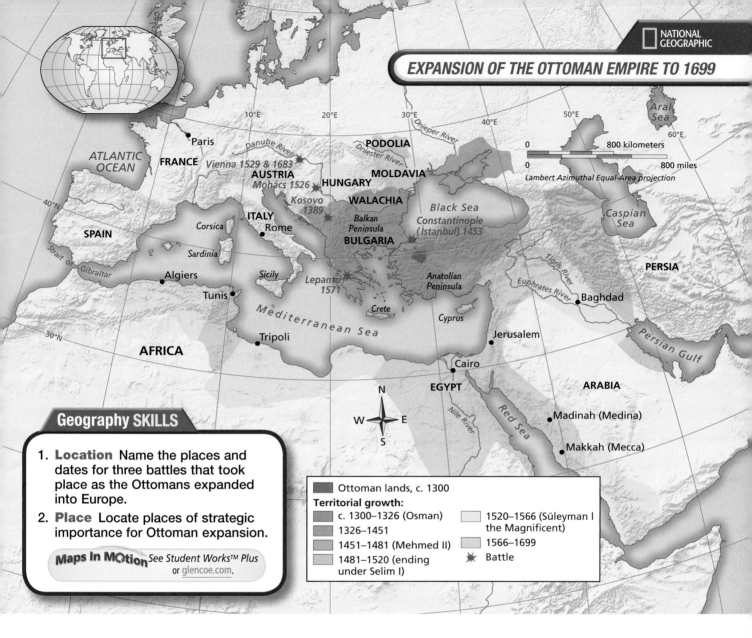

EXPANSION OF THE OTTOMAN EMPIRE TO 1699

800 kilometers

800 miles

Lambert Azimuthal Equal-Area projection

Geography SKILLS

1. **Location** Name the places and dates for three battles that took place as the Ottomans expanded into Europe.

2. **Place** Locate places of strategic importance for Ottoman expansion.

Maps In MOtion *See Student Works™ Plus or glencoe.com.*

Ottoman lands, c. 1300
Territorial growth:
c. 1300–1326 (Osman)
1326–1451
1451–1481 (Mehmed II)
1481–1520 (ending under Selim I)
1520–1566 (Süleyman I the Magnificent)
1566–1699
✴ Battle

The Byzantine Empire

Over the next three hundred years, Ottoman rule expanded to areas in western Asia, North Africa, and Europe.

Under the leadership of **Mehmed II,** the Ottomans moved to end the Byzantine Empire. With eighty thousand troops ranged against only seven thousand defenders, Mehmed laid siege to Constantinople.

The attack began on April 6, 1453, as the Ottomans bombarded the city with massive cannons hurling stone balls weighing up to 1,200 pounds (545 kg) each. The Byzantines took their final stand behind the walls along the western edge of the city. They fought desperately for almost two months to save their city. Finally, on May 29, the walls were breached, and Ottoman soldiers poured into the city.

The Byzantine emperor died in the final battle, and a great three-day sack of the city began. When Mehmed II saw the ruin and destruction, he lamented, "What a city we have given over to plunder and destruction."

Western Asia and Africa

With their new capital at **Constantinople** (later renamed İstanbul), the Ottoman Turks dominated the Balkans and the Anatolian Peninsula. From 1514 to 1517, **Sultan Selim I** took control of Mesopotamia, Egypt, and Arabia—the original heartland of Islam. Through these conquests, Selim I was now in control of several of Islam's holy cities.

These cities included **Jerusalem, Makkah** (Mecca), and **Madinah** (Medina). Selim declared himself the new caliph. That is, he was the defender of the faith and the successor to Muhammad. After their victories in the east, Ottoman forces spent the next few years advancing westward along the African coast almost to the Strait of Gibraltar.

The Ottomans were Muslims. Where possible, they administered their conquered regions through local rulers. The central government appointed officials, or **pashas,** who collected taxes, maintained law and order, and were directly responsible to the sultan's court in Constantinople.

Expansion into Europe

After capturing Constantinople in 1453, the Ottoman Turks tried to complete their conquest of the Balkans. They took the Romanian territory of Walachia, but the Hungarians stopped their advance up the Danube Valley.

Under Süleyman I, whose reign began in 1520, the Ottomans advanced anew up the Danube, seized Belgrade, and won a major victory over the Hungarians in 1526 at the Battle of Mohács (MOH•hach) on the Danube. They then conquered most of Hungary and moved into Austria. They advanced to Vienna, where they were defeated in 1529. At the same time, they advanced into the western Mediterranean until the Spanish destroyed a large Ottoman fleet at Lepanto in 1571 (see Chapter 7).

During the first half of the seventeenth century, the Ottoman Empire in eastern Europe remained a "sleeping giant." Occupied with internal problems, the Ottomans kept the status quo in eastern Europe. However, in the second half of the seventeenth century, they again went on the offensive.

By mid-1683, the Ottomans had laid siege to Vienna. Repulsed by a European army, the Ottomans retreated and were pushed out of Hungary. Although they retained the core of their empire, the Ottoman Turks would never again be a threat to central Europe.

✓ **Reading Check** **Identifying** What was the capital of the new Ottoman Empire?

History ONLINE

Student Web Activity— Visit glencoe.com and complete the activity on the Ottoman Empire.

The Ottoman World

MAIN IDEA The Ottomans created a strong empire with religious tolerance and artistic achievements.

HISTORY & YOU What jobs do people have in your city or county government? Learn how the Ottomans trained bureaucrats in a palace school.

Under the rule of the sultans, the Ottoman Empire grew strong. Religious tolerance and unique architectural designs, as seen in the mosques, were among the Ottoman Empire's strengths and contributions.

The Nature of Ottoman Rule

Like the other Muslim empires in Persia and India, the Ottoman Empire is often labeled a "**gunpowder empire.**" Gunpowder empires were formed by outside conquerors who unified the regions that they conquered. As the name suggests, such an empire's success was largely based on its mastery of the technology of firearms.

At the head of the Ottoman system was the **sultan,** who was the supreme authority in both a political and a military sense. The position of the sultan was hereditary. A son, although not necessarily the eldest, always succeeded the father. This practice led to struggles over succession upon the death of individual sultans. The losers in these struggles were often executed.

The Imperial Sultans

As the empire expanded, the status and prestige of the sultan increased. The position took on the trappings of imperial rule. A centralized administrative system was adopted, and the sultan became increasingly isolated from his people.

The private **domain** of the sultan was called the **harem** ("sacred place"). Here, the sultan and his wives resided. Often a sultan chose four wives as his favorites.

When a son became a sultan, his mother became known as the queen mother and acted as a major adviser to the throne. This tradition often gave considerable power to the queen mother in the affairs of state.

Topkapi Palace

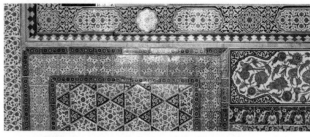

Islam forbids the depiction of human figures because of a belief that it might encourage idolatry. Thus geometric designs decorate the painted tiles in the Topkapi Palace.

The Topkapi Palace overlooks the Bosporus and Sea of Marmara, part of an essential trade route connecting the Aegean and Black Seas.

DOCUMENT-BASED QUESTIONS

The Topkapi Palace, the administrative center of the Ottoman Empire for almost 400 years, was begun soon after Constantinople was conquered.

1. **Describing** Describe the link between faith and art in the tile work of the Topkapi Palace.

2. **Theorizing** What was the symbolic importance of where the Topkapi Palace was located?

The sultan controlled his bureaucracy through an imperial council that met four days a week. The **grand vizier,** a chief minister who carried the main burdens of the state, led the meetings of the council. During the council meetings, the sultan sat behind a screen, overhearing the proceedings, and then privately indicated his desires to the grand vizier.

The empire was divided into provinces and districts, each governed by officials. They were assisted by bureaucrats who had been trained in a palace school for officials in İstanbul. The sultan gave land to the senior officials. They were then responsible for collecting taxes and supplying armies for the empire from this landed area.

The Topkapi ("iron gate") Palace in İstanbul, the new name for Constantinople, was the center of the sultan's power. The palace was built in the fifteenth century by Mehmed II. Like Versailles in France, it had an administrative purpose and served as the private residence of the ruler and his family.

Religion in the Ottoman World

Like most Turkic-speaking peoples in the Anatolian Peninsula and throughout western Asia, the Ottomans were Sunni Muslims (see Chapter 3). Ottoman sultans had claimed the title of caliph since the early sixteenth century. In theory, they were responsible for guiding the flock and maintaining Islamic law. In practice, the sultans gave their religious duties to a group of religious advisers known as the **ulema.** This group administered the legal system and schools for educating Muslims. Islamic law and customs were applied to all Muslims in the empire.

The Ottoman system was generally tolerant of non-Muslims, who made up a significant minority within the empire. Non-Muslims paid a tax, but they were allowed to practice their religion or to convert to Islam. Most people in the European areas of the empire remained Christian. In some areas, however, such as present-day Bosnia, large numbers of non-Muslims converted to the Islamic faith.

Architecture and the Arts

The Ottoman sultans were enthusiastic patrons of the arts. The period from Mehmed II to the early eighteenth century witnessed a flourishing production of pottery; rugs, silk, and other textiles; jewelry; and arms and armor. All of these adorned the palaces of the rulers. Artists came from all over the world to compete for the sultans' generous rewards.

By far the greatest contribution of the Ottoman Empire to world art was in architecture, especially the magnificent mosques of the last half of the sixteenth century. The Ottoman Turks modeled their mosques on the open floor plan of Constantinople's Byzantine church of Hagia Sophia, creating a prayer hall with an open central area under one large dome.

In the mid-sixteenth century, the greatest of all Ottoman architects, **Sinan,** began building the first of his 81 mosques. One of Sinan's masterpieces was the Suleymaniye Mosque in İstanbul. Each of his mosques was topped by an imposing dome, and often the entire building was framed with four towers, or minarets.

The sixteenth century also witnessed the flourishing of textiles and rugs. The Byzantine emperor Justinian had introduced silk cultivation to the West in the sixth century. Under the Ottomans, the silk industry resurfaced. Factories produced silks for wall hangings, sofa covers, and especially court costumes. Rugs were a peasant industry. The rugs were made of wool and cotton in villages from different regions. Each village boasted its own distinctive designs and color schemes.

Society and the Role of Women

The subjects of the Ottoman Empire were divided by occupation. In addition to the ruling class, there were four main occupational groups: peasants, artisans, merchants, and pastoral peoples—nomadic herders. Peasants farmed land that the state leased to them.

Ultimate ownership of all land resided with the sultan. Artisans were organized according to craft guilds. Each guild provided financial services, social security, and training to its members. Outside the ruling elite, merchants were the most privileged class in Ottoman society. They were largely exempt from government regulations and taxes and were able, in many cases, to amass large fortunes. Pastoral peoples were placed in a separate group with their own regulations and laws.

Technically, women in the Ottoman Empire were subject to the same restrictions as women in other Muslim societies. However, their position was somewhat better. As applied in the Ottoman Empire, Islamic law was more tolerant in defining the legal position of women. This relatively tolerant attitude was probably due to Turkish traditions that regarded women as almost equal to men. For instance, women were allowed to own and inherit property. They could not be forced into marriage and, in certain cases, were permitted to seek divorce. Women often gained considerable power within the palace. In a few instances, women even served as senior officials, such as governors of provinces.

PEOPLE in HISTORY

Süleyman the Magnificent
1495–1566 Ottoman Ruler

The Ottoman ruler Süleyman held absolute power and the right of life or death over his subjects. Yet he was known as *Kanuni*, the Lawgiver, who protected the powerless among his people. Upon visiting his empire, a Venetian ambassador reported, "I know of no State which is happier than this one. It is furnished with all God's gifts. . . ." Süleyman was skilled in crafts as well as in government and war. He supported the arts and built public baths, bridges, and grand mosque complexes. However, this educated man would be forced to kill two of his sons and even his grandsons to avoid civil war and preserve the throne for his son Selim II. His choice could have been better. Known as the Drunkard, Selim II left the running of the state to his advisers, and many date the slow decline of the empire to his reign. **How did Süleyman's choice of a successor affect the Ottoman Empire?**

✓ **Reading Check** **Identifying** What did the Ottomans contribute to world art?

Problems in the Ottoman Empire

MAIN IDEA After reaching its high point under Süleyman the Magnificent, the Ottoman Empire began to disintegrate.

HISTORY & YOU Have you heard a parent or teacher voice disapproval of a trend they felt was bad? Learn how some sultans tried to counter trends they believed were harmful to their country.

The Ottoman Empire reached its high point under Süleyman I. (He was called "the Magnificent" by Europeans who both feared and admired him.) It may also have been during Süleyman's rule (1520–1566) that problems began to occur, however. Having executed his two most able sons on suspicion of treason, Süleyman was succeeded by his only surviving son, Selim II.

The problems of the Ottoman Empire did not become visible until 1699. This is when the empire began to lose some of its territory. However, signs of internal disintegration had already appeared at the beginning of the 1600s.

Changes in Government

After the death of Süleyman, sultans became less involved in government. They allowed their ministers to exercise more power. The training of officials declined, and senior positions were increasingly assigned to the sons or daughters of elites. Members of the elite soon formed a privileged group seeking wealth and power. The central bureaucracy lost its links with rural areas. Local officials grew corrupt, and taxes rose. Constant wars depleted the imperial treasury. Corruption and palace intrigue grew.

Cultural Changes

Another sign of change within the empire was the exchange of Western and Ottoman ideas and customs. Officials and merchants began to imitate the habits and lifestyles of Europeans. They wore European clothes and bought Western furniture and art objects. Europeans borrowed Ottoman military technology and decorated their homes with tiles, tulips, pottery, and rugs. During the sixteenth and seventeenth centuries, coffee was introduced to Ottoman society and spread to Europe.

Some sultans attempted to counter this exchange. One sultan in the early seventeenth century issued a decree outlawing both coffee and tobacco. He even began to patrol the streets of İstanbul at night. If he caught any of his subjects in immoral or illegal acts, he had them immediately executed.

✓ Reading Check **Summarizing** What changes ultimately led to the disintegration of the Ottoman Empire?

SECTION 1 REVIEW

Vocabulary

1. **Explain** the significance of: Anatolian Peninsula, expand, Bosporus, Dardanelles, Sea of Marmara, Mehmed II, janissaries, Constantinople, Sultan Selim I, Jerusalem, Makkah, Madinah, pashas, gunpowder empire, sultan, domain, harem, grand vizier, ulema, Sinan.

Main Ideas

2. **Discuss** how superior weaponry aided the Ottoman siege of Constantinople.

3. **Identify** the four main occupational groups in the Ottoman Empire.

4. **Summarize** the contributions of Mehmed II, Selim I, and Süleyman I to the Ottoman Empire, using a chart like the one below.

Ruler	Contributions	Effect on Empire
Mehmed II		
Selim I		
Süleyman I		

Critical Thinking

5. **The BIG Idea** **Drawing Inferences** Describe the organization of Ottoman government and explain why it was effective.

6. **Evaluating** Evaluate how the problems in the Ottoman Empire may have begun during the reign of Süleyman the Magnificent.

7. **Analyzing Visuals** Examine the image of Topkapi Palace on page 251. What typical feature of the architect Sinan do you see?

Writing About History

8. **Expository Writing** Write a letter to a local university professor specializing in this period in history, inviting him or her to your class to discuss the expansion of the Ottoman Empire. Be sure to explain which factors are the most important to discuss.

History ONLINE

For help with the concepts in this section of *Glencoe World History— Modern Times*, go to glencoe.com and click Study Central.

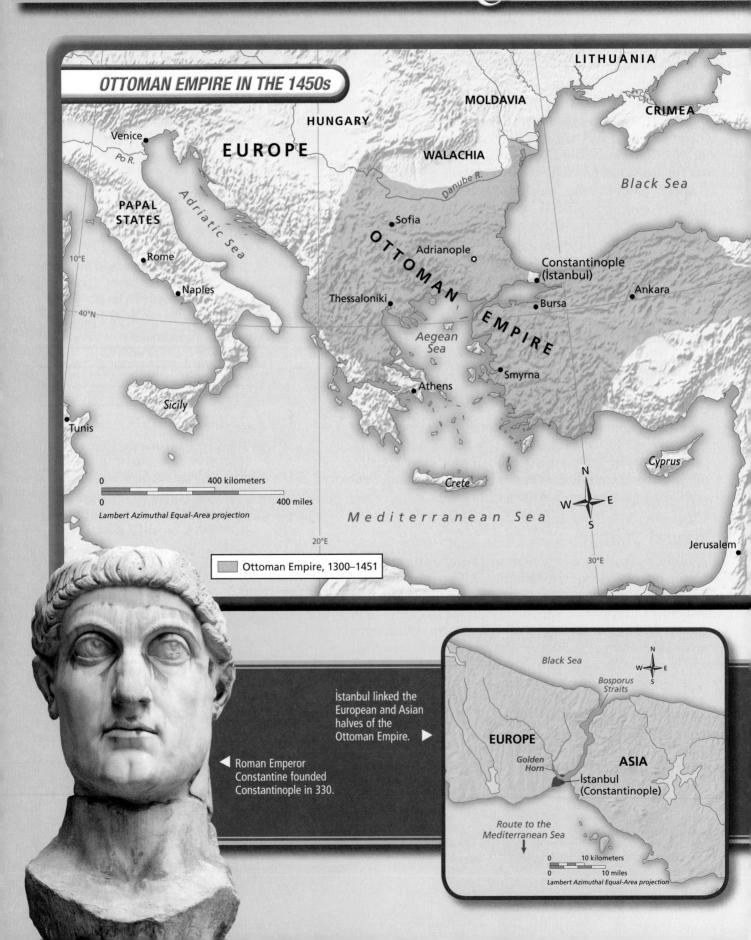

OTTOMAN EMPIRE IN THE 1450s

LITHUANIA

MOLDAVIA

CRIMEA

HUNGARY

EUROPE

WALACHIA

Venice

Po R.

Danube R.

Black Sea

PAPAL STATES

Adriatic Sea

Sofia

OTTOMAN

Adrianople

Constantinople (İstanbul)

10°E

Rome

Ankara

40°N

Naples

Thessaloníki

Bursa

EMPIRE

Aegean Sea

Smyrna

Sicily

Athens

Tunis

Crete

Cyprus

N

W   E

S

Mediterranean Sea

Jerusalem

0   400 kilometers

0   400 miles

Lambert Azimuthal Equal-Area projection

20°E

30°E

Ottoman Empire, 1300–1451

◀ Roman Emperor Constantine founded Constantinople in 330.

İstanbul linked the European and Asian halves of the Ottoman Empire. ▶

Black Sea

N

W   E

S

Bosporus Straits

EUROPE

ASIA

Golden Horn

İstanbul (Constantinople)

Route to the Mediterranean Sea

↓

0   10 kilometers

0   10 miles

Lambert Azimuthal Equal-Area projection

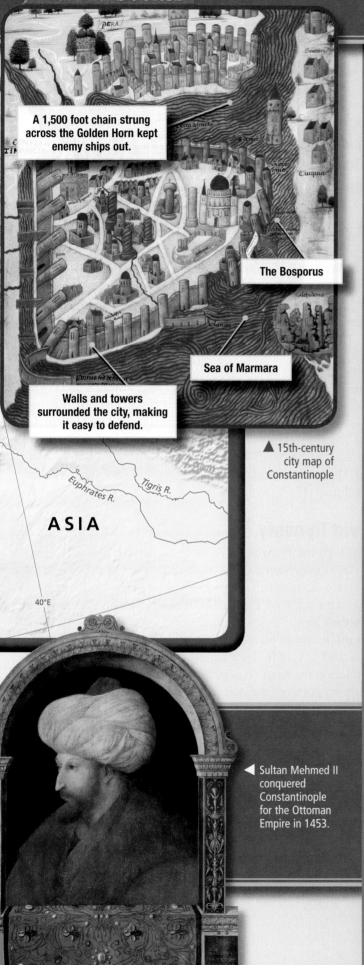

PRIMARY SOURCE

A 1,500 foot chain strung across the Golden Horn kept enemy ships out.

The Bosporus

Sea of Marmara

Walls and towers surrounded the city, making it easy to defend.

▲ 15th-century city map of Constantinople

ASIA

40°E

◄ Sultan Mehmed II conquered Constantinople for the Ottoman Empire in 1453.

The Fall of Constantinople

Crossroads of Europe and Asia For centuries, empires fought over the site of Constantinople because of its strategic location. Constantinople was located between Asia and Europe. The city controlled a choke point, or narrow passageway, where overland trade routes crossed the peninsula. Dominating the crossroads between continents, it became a wealthy trading city.

The Bosporus, a strait, divides the peninsula and links the Black Sea with the Mediterranean. Constantinople was surrounded by water—The Golden Horn, the Bosporus, and the Sea of Marmara—making it easy to defend and giving it control of this important passage between the Black Sea and the Mediterranean.

New Rome In the fourth century, Emperor Constantine, recognizing its strategic importance, built a new capital for the Roman Empire on the site. The new Rome was named Constantinople—Constantine's City. When the Roman Empire split in A.D. 395, Constantinople was the capital of the eastern half, which became the Byzantine Empire.

A Turning Point in History By the time Mehmed II laid siege to Constantinople, the city was all that remained of the once powerful Byzantine Empire. On May 29, 1453, the Turks took the city and linked the European and Asian parts of the Ottoman Empire. Mehmed II renamed the city İstanbul. With the Ottoman Empire in control of this important crossroads, Europeans looked to the seas for trading routes to Asia. These explorations lead Europeans to Africa and the Americas.

Geography SKILLS

1. **Location** What about İstanbul's location made it an important trading center?
2. **Place** Examine the fifteenth century map of Constantinople. Why would you expect the city to control travel on the waterways surrounding it?

The Rule of the Ṣafavids

The shortest-lived of the three Muslim empires, the Ṣafavid Empire was nonetheless influential. The Shia faith, declared as the state religion, unified the empire. The empire reached its high point under the reign of Shāh 'Abbās.

GUIDE TO READING

The BIG Idea
Ideas, Beliefs, and Values The Ṣafavids used their faith as a unifying force.

Content Vocabulary
• shah *(p. 256)*
• orthodoxy *(p. 258)*
• anarchy *(p. 258)*

Academic Vocabulary
• administrator *(p. 258)* • successor *(p. 258)*

People and Events
• Ṣafavids *(p. 256)*
• Shāh Esmā'īl *(p. 256)*
• Azerbaijan *(p. 256)*
• Caspian Sea *(p. 256)*
• Tabrīz *(p. 256)*
• Eṣfahān *(p. 257)*
• Riza-i-Abbasi *(p. 259)*

Reading Strategy
Comparing and Contrasting
As you read this section, use a Venn diagram like the one below to compare and contrast the Ottoman and Ṣafavid Empires.

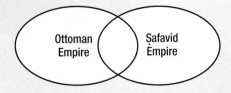

Ottoman Empire | Ṣafavid Empire

The Ṣafavid Empire

MAIN IDEA Unified as a Shia nation, the Ṣafavid Empire reached its height under Shāh 'Abbās.

HISTORY & YOU You and your friends probably have a bond because you believe in the same things. Learn how the Ṣafavids unified their empire.

After the empire of Timur Lenk (Tamerlane) collapsed in the early fifteenth century, the area extending from Persia into central Asia fell into anarchy. At the beginning of the sixteenth century, however, a new dynasty known as the **Ṣafavids** (sah•FAH•weedz) took control. Unlike many of their Isamic neighbors who were Sunni Muslims, the Ṣafavids became ardent Shias. (As discussed in Chapter 3, the Sunnis and Shias were the two major groups in the Islamic religion.)

The Ṣafavid Dynasty

The Ṣafavid dynasty was founded by **Shāh Esmā'īl** (ihs•MAH•EEL), the descendant of Ṣafī od-Dīn (thus the name *Ṣafavid*). In the early fourteenth century, Ṣafī od-Dīn had been the leader of a community of Turkish ethnic groups in **Azerbaijan,** near the **Caspian Sea.**

In 1501, Esmā'īl, in his teens at the time, used his forces to seize much of Iran and Iraq. He then called himself the **shah,** or king, of a new Persian state. Esmā'īl sent Shia preachers into the Anatolian Peninsula to convert members of Turkish tribes in the Ottoman Empire. The Ottoman sultan tried to halt this activity, but Esmā'īl refused to stop. Esmā'īl also ordered the massacre of Sunni Muslims when he conquered Baghdad in 1508.

Alarmed by these activities, the Ottoman sultan, Selim I, advanced against the Ṣafavids in Persia. With their muskets and artillery, the Ottomans won a major battle near **Tabrīz.** However, Selim could not maintain control of the area. A few years later, Esmā'īl regained Tabrīz.

During the following decades, the Ṣafavids tried to consolidate their rule throughout Persia and in areas to the west. The Ṣafavids were faced with the problem of integrating various Turkish peoples with the settled Persian-speaking population of the urban

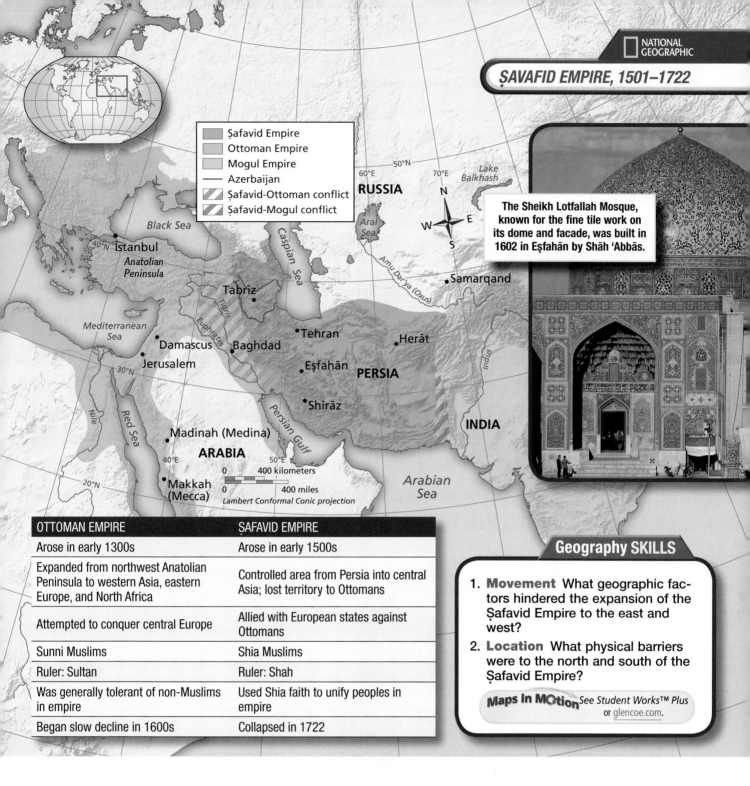

ṢAVAFID EMPIRE, 1501–1722

▓	Ṣafavid Empire
▓	Ottoman Empire
▓	Mogul Empire
—	Azerbaijan
▨	Ṣafavid-Ottoman conflict
▨	Ṣafavid-Mogul conflict

RUSSIA

Black Sea

İstanbul
Anatolian
Peninsula

Tabrīz

Caspian Sea

Aral Sea

Lake Balkhash

Amu Darya (Oxus)

Samarqand

The Sheikh Lotfallah Mosque, known for the fine tile work on its dome and facade, was built in 1602 in Eṣfahān by Shāh 'Abbās.

Tigris

Euphrates

Mediterranean Sea

Damascus

Baghdad

Tehran

Herāt

Jerusalem

Eṣfahān

PERSIA

Indus

Shīrāz

INDIA

Nile

Red Sea

Madinah (Medina)

Persian Gulf

ARABIA

Makkah (Mecca)

Arabian Sea

0   400 kilometers
0   400 miles
Lambert Conformal Conic projection

OTTOMAN EMPIRE	ṢAFAVID EMPIRE
Arose in early 1300s	Arose in early 1500s
Expanded from northwest Anatolian Peninsula to western Asia, eastern Europe, and North Africa	Controlled area from Persia into central Asia; lost territory to Ottomans
Attempted to conquer central Europe	Allied with European states against Ottomans
Sunni Muslims	Shia Muslims
Ruler: Sultan	Ruler: Shah
Was generally tolerant of non-Muslims in empire	Used Shia faith to unify peoples in empire
Began slow decline in 1600s	Collapsed in 1722

Geography SKILLS

1. **Movement** What geographic factors hindered the expansion of the Ṣafavid Empire to the east and west?

2. **Location** What physical barriers were to the north and south of the Ṣafavid Empire?

Maps In MOtion See Student Works™ Plus or glencoe.com.

areas. The Shia faith was used as a unifying force. Esmā'īl made conversion to the Shia faith mandatory for the largely Sunni population. Many Sunnis were either killed or exiled. Like the Ottoman sultan, the shah himself claimed to be the spiritual leader of all Islam.

In the 1580s, the Ottomans went on the attack. They placed Azerbaijan under Ottoman rule and controlled the Caspian Sea with their fleet. This forced the new Ṣafavid shah, 'Abbās, to sign a peace treaty in which he lost much territory in the northwest. The capital of the Ṣafavids was moved from the northwestern city of Tabrīz to the more centrally located city of **Eṣfahān.** 'Abbās adorned his new capital city with the latest Persian architecture. Eṣfahān became one of the world's largest cities with a population of one million.

Glory and Decline

Under Shāh 'Abbās, who ruled from 1588 to 1629, the Ṣafavids reached the high point of their glory. Similar to the Ottoman Empire, **administrators** were trained to run the kingdom. Shāh 'Abbās also strengthened his army, which he armed with the latest weapons.

In the early seventeenth century, Shāh 'Abbās moved against the Ottomans to regain lost territories. Several European states aided 'Abbās. The Ṣafavids had some initial success, but they could not hold all their territorial gains against the Ottoman armies. Nevertheless, in 1612, a peace treaty was signed that returned Azerbaijan to the Ṣafavids.

After the death of Shāh 'Abbās in 1629, the Ṣafavid dynasty gradually lost its vigor. Most of 'Abbās's **successors** lacked his talent and political skills. Eventually, the power of Shia religious elements began to increase at court and in Ṣafavid society at large.

Intellectual freedom marked the height of the empire. However, the pressure to conform to traditional religious beliefs, called religious **orthodoxy,** increased. For example, Persian women had considerable freedom during the early empire. Now they were forced into seclusion and required to adopt the wearing of the veil.

In the early eighteenth century, during the reign of Shah Hussein, Afghan peoples invaded and seized the capital of Eṣfahān. The remnants of the Ṣafavid ruling family were forced to retreat to Azerbaijan, their original homeland. The Turks took advantage of the situation to seize territories along the western border. Persia sank into a long period of political and social **anarchy** (lawlessness and disorder).

✓ **Reading Check**   **Identifying** What led to the fighting between Ottomans and Ṣafavids?

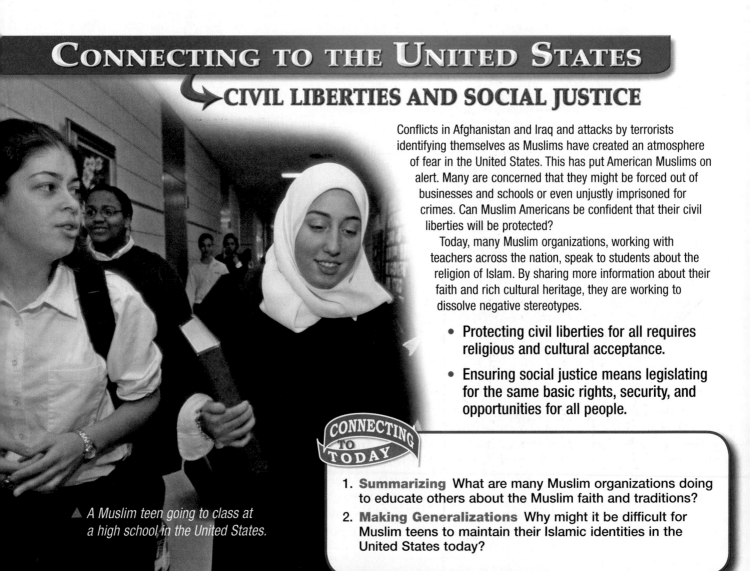

CONNECTING TO THE UNITED STATES
CIVIL LIBERTIES AND SOCIAL JUSTICE

Conflicts in Afghanistan and Iraq and attacks by terrorists identifying themselves as Muslims have created an atmosphere of fear in the United States. This has put American Muslims on alert. Many are concerned that they might be forced out of businesses and schools or even unjustly imprisoned for crimes. Can Muslim Americans be confident that their civil liberties will be protected?

Today, many Muslim organizations, working with teachers across the nation, speak to students about the religion of Islam. By sharing more information about their faith and rich cultural heritage, they are working to dissolve negative stereotypes.

- **Protecting civil liberties for all requires religious and cultural acceptance.**

- **Ensuring social justice means legislating for the same basic rights, security, and opportunities for all people.**

▲ *A Muslim teen going to class at a high school in the United States.*

CONNECTING TO TODAY

1. **Summarizing** What are many Muslim organizations doing to educate others about the Muslim faith and traditions?
2. **Making Generalizations** Why might it be difficult for Muslim teens to maintain their Islamic identities in the United States today?

Life under the Ṣafavids

MAIN IDEA The Ṣafavid shahs played an active role in government and trade, and they patronized the arts.

HISTORY & YOU Have you ever had to compete for a place on a team, show, or leadership position? Learn how the Ṣafavid shahs appointed their top administrators.

Persia under the Ṣafavids was a mixed society. The combination of Turkish and Persian elements affected virtually all aspects of Ṣafavid society.

Role of the Shah

The Ṣafavid rulers were eagerly supported by Shias. In return, the shahs declared Shia Islam to be the state religion. Shahs were more available to their subjects than were rulers elsewhere. "They show great familiarity to strangers," remarked one visitor, "and even to their own subjects, eating and drinking with them pretty freely."

Strong-minded shahs firmly controlled the power of the landed aristocracy. In addition, appointment to senior positions in the bureaucracy was based on merit rather than birth. For example, Shāh 'Abbās hired a number of foreigners from neighboring countries for positions in his government.

Economy and Trade

The Ṣafavid shahs played an active part in trade and manufacturing activity. Most goods in the empire traveled by horse or camel caravans, and the roads were kept fairly clear of thieves and bandits.

Ṣafavid Persia was probably not as prosperous as its neighbors to the east and west—the Moguls and the Ottomans. Hemmed in by the sea power of the Europeans to the south and the land power of the Ottomans to the west, the Ṣafavids found trade with Europe difficult.

Ṣafavid Culture

Knowledge of science, medicine, and mathematics under the Ṣafavids was equal to that of other societies in the region. Persia also witnessed an extraordinary flowering of the arts during the reign of Shāh 'Abbās. Silk weaving and carpet weaving flourished, stimulated by the great demand for Persian carpets in the West. Persian painting enjoyed a long tradition. **Riza-i-Abbasi,** the most famous artist of this period, created exquisite works. Soft colors and flowing movement dominated the features of Ṣafavid painting.

✓ Reading Check **Explaining** On what basis were appointments to senior bureaucratic positions made?

Vocabulary

1. **Explain** the significance of: Ṣafavids, Shāh Esmā'īl, Azerbaijan, Caspian Sea, shah, Tabrīz, Eṣfahān, administrator, successor, orthodoxy, anarchy, Riza-i-Abbasi.

Main Ideas

2. **Describe** how the Ṣafavids tried to bring the various Turkish and Persian peoples together.

3. **Summarize** the significant events that occurred during each shah's reign by using a chart like the one below.

Shah	Significant Events

4. **Explain** why the Ṣafavids may have found trade with Europe difficult.

Critical Thinking

5. **The BIG Idea** **Explaining** What was the shah's role in Ṣafavid society and government?

6. **Evaluating** What was the advantage in moving the Ṣafavid capital city from Tabrīz to Eṣfahān?

7. **Analyzing Visuals** Examine the map on page 257. Approximately how much territory did the Ṣafavids gain between 1501 and the height of the empire?

Writing About History

8. **Expository Writing** Analyze the impact of the Ṣafavid Empire's geographical location on its economy (what goods could be traded, trading partners, goods in high demand). Compare the Ṣafavid economy with that of another country.

History ONLINE

For help with the concepts in this section of *Glencoe World History—Modern Times*, go to **glencoe.com** and click Study Central.

Social History

The Ṣafavids: At the Crossroads of Trade and of History

The nation known today as Iran has been at the center of world commerce for centuries. From 1501 to 1722, the Ṣafavid Empire unified Iran and added parts of Turkey, Iraq, and Central Asia under their control. Trade with Europe was challenging for the Ṣafavids, but Iran (or Persia) was a vital connection between Asia and Europe throughout several dynasties. The bazaar at Eṣfahān, capitol under Shāh 'Abbās, was the center of Ṣafavid economic power. Across the empire, bazaars in regional capitols provided citizens with access to a variety of goods and merchandise.

A timce is a covered courtyard that houses a few shops selling the same special product. This one, the Timce Malek, is famous for carpets.

The bazaar sold household goods, tools, and other general merchandise besides luxury items. Barter was a common means of exchange.

Ṣafavid woven textiles were an essential item in the bazaar, and a vital part of overseas trade.

A PLACE FOR EVERYTHING, EVERYTHING IN ITS PLACE

Merchants came from across Central Asia to trade in the Ṣafavid region. The bazaar was the heart of their commerce. Many bazaars were enclosed and had high vaulted ceilings that covered narrow rows of stalls. Specific sections that housed similar types of goods for shoppers' convenience. Spaces for manufacturing, storage, and merchants' offices stood alongside shops. Caravansaries attached to the bazaar received trains of camels or mules loaded with goods. In the caravansary, newly arrived trade goods were sold wholesale. In the bazaar, they were sold retail.

Caravansaries were vital stops on the Silk Road, a trade route that stretched from China to Europe.

The caravansary also served as lodging for visiting traders and their animals. Its buildings formed a square with a garden or well in its center.

Merchants from as far away as China conducted business with the powerful Ṣafavid merchant class in the empire's bazaars.

Long on Trade, Short on Coins

The Ṣafavids had a chronic shortage of coins in circulation. Silver coins, like those above were used by the government to pay administrative costs, by merchants to pay for goods purchased in large trade deals and by some to pay taxes. Soldiers and the urban lower class used copper coins. Their value changed from year to year and could only be traded for silver coins in large sums. Rural people bartered for goods and services, and rarely saw coins. The empire's elite hoarded its small number of gold coins.

ANALYZING VISUALS

1. What role did currency play in Ṣafavid trade?
2. How might buyers have reacted to shopping for an item in a timce? How might merchants have felt about being organized this way?

261

The Grandeur of the Moguls

Although they were not natives of India, the Moguls established a new dynasty by uniting the country under a single government with a common culture. The Mogul Empire reached its high point under the reign of Shah Akbar. The Taj Mahal, built by Shāh Jahān, is a fine example of the blending of Persian and Indian influences in the Mogul Empire.

GUIDE TO READING

The BIG Idea
Ideas, Beliefs, and Values
A country's society and its culture reflect the shared heritage of its people.

Content Vocabulary
- zamindars *(p. 263)*
- suttee *(p. 265)*

Academic Vocabulary
- intelligent *(p. 262)*
- principle *(p. 265)*

People and Events
- Bābur *(p. 262)*
- Khyber Pass *(p. 262)*
- Delhi *(p. 262)*
- Akbar *(p. 262)*
- Shāh Jahān *(p. 264)*
- Deccan Plateau *(p. 264)*
- Aurangzeb *(p. 265)*
- Taj Mahal *(p. 265)*
- Agra *(p. 265)*
- Kolkata *(p. 267)*
- Chennai *(p. 267)*

Reading Strategy
Summarizing Information As you read this section, create a chart listing the accomplishments and weaknesses of the Mogul rulers.

Ruler	Accomplishments	Weaknesses

The Mogul Dynasty

MAIN IDEA Uniting India under a single government, the Moguls established a new dynasty but eventually lost their empire.

HISTORY & YOU What would you do if you owed $500 in taxes but had only $150? Learn how Akbar suspended the payment of taxes in hard times.

In 1500, the Indian subcontinent was still divided into a number of Hindu and Muslim kingdoms. However, the Moguls established a new dynasty and brought a new era of unity to the region.

Rise of the Moguls

The Moguls were not natives of India. They came from the mountainous region north of the Indus River valley. The founder of the Mogul dynasty was **Bābur**. His father was descended from the great Asian conqueror Timur Lenk; his mother, from the Mongol conqueror Genghis Khan. Bābur had inherited a part of Timur Lenk's empire in an upland river valley of the Syr Dar'ya. As a youth, he led a group of warriors who seized Kabul in 1504. Thirteen years later, Bābur's forces crossed the **Khyber Pass** into India.

Bābur's forces were far smaller than those of his enemies. However, they had advanced weapons, including artillery, and used them to great effect. Bābur captured **Delhi** and established his power in the plains of North India. He continued his conquests in North India until his death in 1530 at the age of 47.

The Reign of Akbar

Bābur's grandson **Akbar** was only 14 when he took the throne. **Intelligent** and industrious, Akbar set out to extend his domain. By 1605, he had brought Mogul rule to most of India.

How was Akbar able to place almost all of India under his rule? By using heavy artillery, Akbar's armies were able to overpower the stone fortresses of their rivals. The Moguls were also successful negotiators. Akbar's conquests created the greatest Indian empire since the Mauryan dynasty. The empire appeared highly centralized

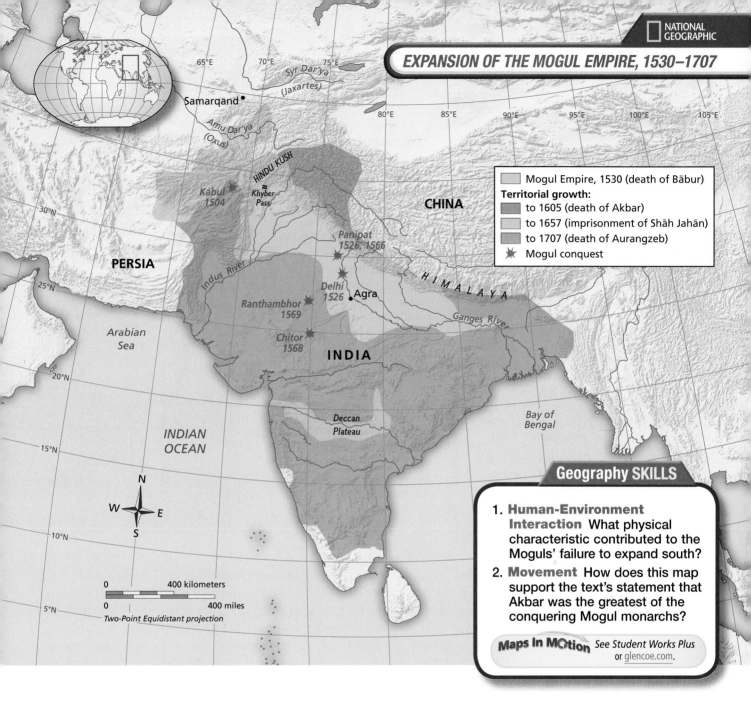

EXPANSION OF THE MOGUL EMPIRE, 1530–1707

Samarqand

Syr Dar'ya (Jaxartes)

Amu Dar'ya (Oxus)

HINDU KUSH

Kabul 1504

Khyber Pass

CHINA

PERSIA

Indus River

Panipat 1526, 1566

H I M A L A Y A

Delhi 1526

Agra

Ranthambhor 1569

Ganges River

Arabian Sea

Chitor 1568

INDIA

Deccan Plateau

Bay of Bengal

INDIAN OCEAN

N
W E
S

0 400 kilometers

0 400 miles

Two-Point Equidistant projection

	Mogul Empire, 1530 (death of Bābur)

Territorial growth:
- to 1605 (death of Akbar)
- to 1657 (imprisonment of Shāh Jahān)
- to 1707 (death of Aurangzeb)
- ✳ Mogul conquest

Geography SKILLS

1. **Human-Environment Interaction** What physical characteristic contributed to the Moguls' failure to expand south?

2. **Movement** How does this map support the text's statement that Akbar was the greatest of the conquering Mogul monarchs?

Maps In Motion See Student Works Plus or glencoe.com.

but was actually a collection of semi-independent states held together by the power of the emperor.

Akbar was probably the greatest of the conquering Mogul monarchs, but he is best known for the humane character of his rule. Like all Mogul rulers, Akbar was born a Muslim, but he adopted a policy of religious tolerance. As emperor, he showed a keen interest in other religions and tolerated Hindu practices. He even welcomed the expression of Christian views by his Jesuit advisers at court. By taking a Hindu princess as one of his wives, Akbar put his policy of religious tolerance into practice.

Akbar was also tolerant in his administration of the government. The upper ranks of the government bureaucracy were filled with nonnative Muslims, but many of the lower-ranking officials were Hindus.

It became common practice to give the lower-ranking officials plots of farmland for their temporary use. These local officials, known as **zamindars,** kept a portion of the taxes paid by the peasants in lieu of a salary. They were then expected to forward the rest of the taxes from the lands under their control to the central government. Zamindars came to exercise considerable power and authority in their local districts.

The Rule of Akbar

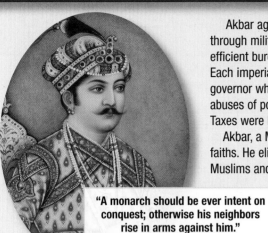

> "A monarch should be ever intent on conquest; otherwise his neighbors rise in arms against him."
> —Akbar the Great

Akbar aggressively expanded his empire through military conquest. He created an efficient bureaucracy to administer his empire. Each imperial province was ruled by a military governor who was held responsible for any abuses of power, helping to ensure fair rule. Taxes were levied equally.

Akbar, a Muslim, was accepting of other faiths. He eliminated a special tax on non-Muslims and included many Hindus in his bureaucracy. He granted a degree of autonomy to Hindu regions, allowing Hindus to keep their own laws. These actions helped to win over many Hindus to Mogul rule.

Akbar saw himself as a philosopher-king who was responsible for guiding his people spiritually. Though he believed in tolerance, he developed a new religion called "The Religion of God" for which he sought willing followers.

DOCUMENT-BASED QUESTIONS

The illustration at right from the *Akbarnama (History of Akbar)* shows officials paying homage to Akbar in central India about 1560.

1. **Explaining** Explain Akbar's attitude toward military conquest.
2. **Analyzing** What was the key to Akbar's successful rule?

Overall, the Akbar era was a time of progress, at least by the standards of the day. All Indian peasants were required to pay about one-third of their annual harvest to the state, but the system was applied justly. When bad weather struck in the 1590s, taxes were reduced or suspended altogether. Thanks to a long period of peace and political stability, trade and manufacturing flourished.

The era was an especially prosperous one in the area of foreign trade. Indian goods, notably textiles, tropical food products and spices, and precious stones, were exported in exchange for gold and silver. Arab traders handled much of the foreign trade because the Indians, like their Mogul rulers, did not care for travel by sea.

Decline of the Moguls

Akbar died in 1605 and was succeeded by his son Jahāngīr (juh•HAHN•GIHR).

Jahāngīr was able and ambitious. During the early years of his reign, he continued to strengthen the central government's control over his vast empire.

Eventually, however, his grip began to weaken when he fell under the influence of one of his wives, Persian-born Nūr Jahān. As Jahāngīr slowly lost interest in governing, he gave more authority to Nūr Jahān. The empress used her position to enrich her own family. She arranged the marriage of her niece to her husband's third son and successor, **Shāh Jahān.**

During his reign from 1628 to 1658, Shāh Jahān maintained the political system established by earlier Mogul rulers. He also expanded the boundaries of the empire through successful campaigns in the **Deccan Plateau** and against the city of Samarqand, north of the Hindu Kush.

Shāh Jahān's rule was marred by his failure to deal with growing domestic problems, however. He had inherited a nearly empty treasury. His military campaigns and expensive building projects put a heavy strain on the imperial finances and compelled him to raise taxes. The peasants were even more deprived as a result of these taxes. The majority of Jahān's subjects lived in poverty.

Shāh Jahān's troubles worsened with his illness in the mid-1650s. It was widely reported that he had died. Such news led to a struggle for power among his sons. Battles were fought; alliances and defections were made. The victorious son, **Aurangzeb,** had his brother put to death and imprisoned his father. Aurangzeb then had himself crowned emperor in 1658.

Aurangzeb is one of the most controversial rulers in the history of India. During his reign, the empire reached its greatest physical size. Constant warfare and religious intolerance, however, made his subjects resentful.

As man of high **principle**, Aurangzeb attempted to eliminate many of what he considered to be India's social evils. He forbade the Hindu custom of suttee (cremating a widow on her husband's funeral pyre), and he put a stop to the levying of illegal taxes. He tried to forbid gambling and drinking as well.

Aurangzeb was a devout Muslim and adopted a number of measures that reversed the Mogul policies of religious tolerance. For instance, he imposed a tax on non-Muslims. Also, he prohibited the building of new Hindu temples, and he forced Hindus to convert to Islam.

Aurangzeb's policies led to Hindu outcries and domestic unrest. He even received criticism from Shias. In addition, a number of revolts against imperial authority broke out in provinces throughout the empire. Rebellious groups threatened the power of the emperor.

After Aurangzeb's death in 1707, there were many contenders for the throne. Their reigns were short-lived. India was increasingly divided and vulnerable to attack from abroad. In 1739, Delhi was sacked by the Persians, who left it in ashes.

✓ **Reading Check** **Explaining** How did Akbar's religious policy affect his government?

Life in Mogul India

MAIN IDEA The Mogul society and its culture were both Muslim and Hindu.

HISTORY & YOU Do you know someone from a family with more than one religion? Learn how Indian society and culture reflected a shared heritage.

The Moguls were foreigners in India. In addition, they were Muslims ruling a largely Hindu population. The resulting blend of influences on the lives of ordinary Indians could be complicated. The treatment of women serves as a good example.

Society and the Role of Women

Women had long played an active role in Mogul tribal society. Mogul rulers often relied on female relatives for political advice. To a degree, these Mogul attitudes toward women affected Indian society. Women from aristocratic families frequently received salaries and were allowed to own land.

At the same time, the Moguls placed certain restrictions on women under their interpretations of Islamic law. These practices generally were adopted by Hindus. The practice of isolating women, for example, was followed by many upper-class Hindus.

In other ways, however, Hindu practices remained unchanged by Mogul rule. The custom of suttee continued in spite of efforts by the Moguls to abolish it. Child marriage also remained common.

The Mogul era saw the emergence of a wealthy nobility and a prosperous merchant class. During the late eighteenth century, this prosperity was shaken by the decline of the Moguls and the coming of the British. However, many prominent Indians established trading ties with foreigners.

Mogul Culture

The Moguls brought together Persian and Indian influences in a new and beautiful architectural style. This style is best symbolized by the **Taj Mahal,** which Shāh Jahān built in **Agra** in the mid-seventeenth century. The project lasted more than twenty years. To finance it, the government raised land taxes, driving many Indian peasants into complete poverty.

TURNING POINT — THE BRITISH GAIN CONTROL OF INDIA

The British East India Company faced challenges in its efforts to gain control of Indian trade. By the mid-1700s, the power of the French East India Company rivaled that of the British. In southern India, the French and British fought a series of wars in the region near Chennai (Madras). In 1751, Sir Robert Clive won an important victory there for the British East India Company against the French and their Indian allies.

In the north, Clive defeated a Mogul-led army at the Battle of Plassey near Fort William (Kolkata) in Bengal in 1757. The balance of power shifted to the British. After defeating the French and the Moguls, the British became the dominant power in India until after World War II. For much of that time, the British East India Company had all the sovereign powers of a government in ruling much of India.

Robert Clive and Mir Jaffier after the Battle of Plassey, 1757 by Francis Hayman depicts a meeting of Clive and a defecting Indian leader, Mir Jaffier, after the battle.

DOCUMENT-BASED QUESTIONS

In the mid-1700s, the British East India Company began to consolidate its control of India's commerce.

1. **Summarizing** How did the actions of Robert Clive affect English trade with India?
2. **Predicting** What problems do you foresee in allowing a private trading company to assume the powers of a government?

The Taj Mahal is widely considered to be the most beautiful building in India, if not in the entire world. The building seems to have monumental size, nearly blinding brilliance, and delicate lightness.

Another major artistic achievement of the Mogul period was in painting. Like architecture, painting in Mogul India resulted from the blending of two cultures: Persian and Indian. Akbar established a state workshop for artists, mostly Hindus, who worked under the guidance of Persian masters to create the Mogul school of painting. The "Akbar style" combined Persian with Indian motifs. It included the portrayal of humans in action, for example—a characteristic not usually seen in Persian art. Akbar also encouraged his artists to imitate European art forms, including the use of perspective and life-like portraits.

✓ **Reading Check** **Describing** What was significant about the "Akbar style" of art?

Europeans Come to India

MAIN IDEA Foreigners seeking trade opportunities in India hastened the decline of the Mogul Empire.

HISTORY & YOU What would you do if someone set up a concession stand opposite the one you have operated successfully for years? Learn how the British and French competed for trade in India.

The arrival of the British hastened the decline of the Mogul Empire. By 1650, British trading forts had been established at Surat, Fort William (which was renamed Calcutta and is now the city of **Kolkata**), and Madras (**Chennai**). British ships carried Indian-made cotton goods to the East Indies, where they were traded for spices.

British success in India attracted rivals, especially the French. The French established their own forts. For a brief period, the French went on the offensive, even capturing the British fort at Chennai.

The British were saved by the military genius of Sir Robert Clive, an aggressive British empire builder. Clive served as the chief representative in India of the East India Company, a private company that acted on behalf of the British Crown. Fighting any force that threatened the Company's power in India, Clive ultimately restricted the French to the fort at Pondicherry and a few small territories on the southeastern coast.

While fighting the French, Clive was also consolidating British control in Bengal. The Indian ruler of Bengal had attacked Fort William in 1756. He had imprisoned the British garrison in the "Black Hole of Calcutta," an underground prison. Due to the intense heat in the crowded space, only 23 people (out of 146) survived.

In 1757, Clive led a small British force of about three thousand to victory over a Mogul-led army more than ten times its size in the Battle of Plassey in Bengal. As part of the spoils of victory, the failing Mogul court gave the East India Company the power to collect taxes from lands in the area around Calcutta.

Britain's rise to power in India, however, was not a story of constant success. Many East India Company officials combined arrogance with incompetence. They offended both their Indian allies and the local population, who were taxed heavily to meet the Company's growing expenses.

In the late eighteenth century, the East India Company moved inland from the great coastal cities. British expansion brought great riches to individual British merchants and to British officials who found they could obtain money from local rulers by selling trade privileges. The British were in India to stay.

✓ Reading Check **Examining** How did Robert Clive save the British in India?

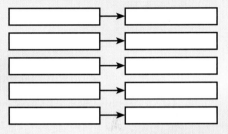

Vocabulary

1. **Explain** the significance of: Bābur, Khyber Pass, Delhi, Akbar, intelligent, zamindars, Shāh Jahān, Deccan Plateau, Aurangzeb, principle, suttee, Taj Mahal, Agra, Kolkata, Chennai.

Main Ideas

2. **List** and explain the events that led to the decline of the Mogul Empire using a chart like the one below.

3. **Explain** why the British and French built forts in India.

4. **Describe** the Taj Mahal. Who built it? Why is it considered the most beautiful building in India?

Critical Thinking

5. **The BIG Idea** **Analyzing** Analyze the impact of the Moguls on the Hindu and Muslim peoples of the Indian subcontinent.

6. **Evaluating** Evaluate how Akbar's reign reflected his humane character.

7. **Analyzing Visuals** Examine the illustration from *Akbarnama (History of Akbar)* on page 264. What details indicate that the officials are paying homage to Akbar?

Writing About History

8. **Descriptive Writing** Imagine that you are a British diplomat in India after the Battle of Plassey. Write a letter to the British government proposing ways to avoid future conflicts between British and Indian forces.

History ONLINE

For help with the concepts in this section of *Glencoe World History—Modern Times*, go to glencoe.com and click Study Central.

You can study anywhere, anytime by downloading quizzes and flash cards to your PDA from glencoe.com.

THE OTTOMAN EMPIRE
History & Culture

- Ottomans conquered the Byzantine Empire and expanded into the Balkans.
- Most Ottomans were Sunni Muslims and were tolerant of other religions.
- Ottoman sultans were enthusiastic patrons of the arts.
- After reaching its peak under Süleyman I, the Ottoman Empire began to decline.

THE TURKISH SULTAN REVIEWING HIS JANISSARIES

The sultan, the supreme government authority, built a strong military of janissaries.

DEMAND FOR PERSIAN CARPETS STIMULATED MANUFACTURING

Carpets made by the Safavids often incorporated animal motifs.

THE ṢAFAVIDS History & Culture

- To unify the Ṣafavid Empire, Shah Esmāʿīl forced Sunni Muslims to convert to the Shia faith.
- Under Shah ʿAbbās, the Ṣafavids reached the high point of their glory.
- The shahs played an active role in government, trade, and manufacturing activities.
- The empire's decline began after the death of Shah ʿAbbās.

THE MOGULS History & Culture

- The Moguls united India under a single government with a common culture.
- The Mogul ruler Akbar was Muslim, but he exercised tolerance toward Hindu practices.
- Persian and Indian cultures blended to create beautiful paintings and architecture.
- British forces defeated the Moguls at the Battle of Plassey. The British eventually ruled most of India.

TAJ MAHAL

The Taj Mahal is the most famous example of Mogul architecture.

STANDARDIZED TEST PRACTICE

TEST-TAKING TIP

Do not pick an answer just because it sounds good. Sometimes a choice is deliberately meant to sound correct but is not. Read all the answer choices carefully before you select the best one, and avoid making hasty decisions.

Reviewing Vocabulary

Directions: Choose the word or words that best complete the sentence.

1. The Hindu custom of cremating a widow on her husband's funeral pyre is known as _____.

A ulema

B suttee

C harem

D sultan

2. The _____ was the sultan's chief minister.

A grand vizier

B marshal

C shah

D pasha

3. What is another word for *lawlessness and disorder*?

A Rebellion

B Orthodoxy

C Revolt

D Anarchy

4. The private domain of a sultan was called the _____.

A sanctuary

B mosque

C harem

D zamindar

Reviewing Main Ideas

Directions: Choose the best answers to the following questions.

Section 1 *(pp. 248–253)*

5. Who were the janissaries?

A Pashas

B Bureaucrats

C Religious leaders

D An elite guard

6. The Ottomans ended the Byzantine Empire by laying siege to which city?

A Constantinople

B Lepanto

C Mohács

D Topkapi

7. The success of which type of empire was largely based on its mastery of firearms?

A Bourgeois

B Gunpowder

C Blackfriar

D Pastoral

8. Under which ruler did the Ottoman Empire reach its high point?

A Selim I

B Selim II

C Mehmed II

D Süleyman I

Need Extra Help?								
If You Missed Questions . . .	1	2	3	4	5	6	7	8
Go to Page . . .	265	251	258	250	248	249	250	253

CHAPTER 8   The Muslim Empires   **269**

Section 2 (pp. 256–259)

9. What did the Ṣafavids use as a unifying force?

   A Shia faith

   B Sunni faith

   C Grand vizier

   D Persians

10. Shāh 'Abbās moved the capital city of the Ṣafavids from Tabrīz to which city?

   A Azerbaijan

   B İstanbul

   C Eṣfahān

   D Riza-i-Abbasi

11. Ṣafavid society was a combination of Turkish and what kind of elements?

   A Mogul

   B Persian

   C Ottoman

   D French

Section 3 (pp. 262–267)

12. What was the "Black Hole of Calcutta"?

   A An oil spill

   B A great whirlpool

   C Ornamental art

   D An underground prison

13. Which building is widely considered the most beautiful in India, if not in the entire world?

   A Akbar Castle

   B Chennai Station

   C Taj Mahal

   D Bengal Mahal

Critical Thinking

Directions: Choose the best answers to the following questions.

14. How was the Ottoman Empire characterized in the first half of the seventeenth century?

   A The empire was preoccupied with internal problems.

   B The bureaucracy slowed down the government.

   C The queen mother was waiting to assume power.

   D The empire was preoccupied with the arts.

Base your answer to questions 15 and 16 on the map below and on your knowledge of world history.

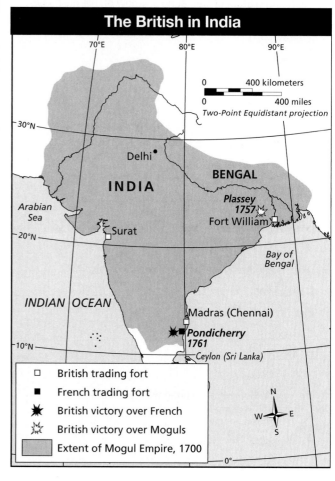

The British in India

15. At what location did the British defeat the French?

   A Fort William

   B Plassey

   C Pondicherry

   D Sri Lanka

Need Extra Help?							
If You Missed Questions . . .	9	10	11	12	13	14	15
Go to Page . . .	257	257	259	267	265	250	267

16. In what area of India did the British fight a Mogul army in 1757 for control of Indian trade?

  A Sri Lanka

  B Bengal

  C Delhi

  D Arabian Sea

17. Which of the following took place in the Ṣafavid Empire after the death of Shāh 'Abbās?

  A Women no longer wore the veil.

  B Women were forced from seclusion.

  C The power of religious elements declined.

  D Religious orthodoxy increased.

Analyze the chart and answer the question that follows. Base your answer on the chart and on your knowledge of world history.

Over a span of 300 years, the Ottomans conquered the Byzantine Empire and expanded into western Asia, Africa, and Europe to create the Ottoman Empire. The chart shows Ottoman expansion over a 115-year period.

Expansion of the Ottoman Empire, 1451–1566

Sultan	Dates	Conquered Territory
Mehmed II	1451–1481	Anatolian Peninsula Balkans Constantinople
Selim I	1512–1520	Arabia Egypt Mesopotamia
Süleyman I	1520–1566	Hungary Libya

18. Name the ruler and the area conquered that ensured Ottoman control of the Bosporus.

  A Selim I, Mesopotamia

  B Mehmed II, Constantinople

  C Süleyman I, Libya

  D Selim I, Arabia

Document-Based Questions

Directions: Analyze the document and answer the short-answer questions that follow the document.

Much of what is known about the life of ordinary Indians comes from the observations of foreign visitors. Following is an excerpt from one such description.

> "Their houses are built of mud with thatched roofs. Furniture there is little or none except some earthenware pots to hold water and for cooking and two beds, one for the man, the other for his wife; their bed cloths are scanty, merely a sheet or perhaps two, serving as under- and over-sheet. This is sufficient for the hot weather, but the bitter cold nights are miserable indeed, and they try to keep warm over little cow-dung fires."

19. What type of furnishings did this Indian family have?

20. From reading this passage, what can you conclude about the lives of Indian people during the Mogul Empire?

Extended Response

21. Compare and contrast the rule of Akbar with Louis XIV of France (see Chapter 7).

History ONLINE

For additional test practice, use Self-Check Quizzes—Chapter 8 at glencoe.com.

Need Extra Help?						
If You Missed Questions . . .	16	17	18	19	20	21
Go to Page . . .	267	258	249	265	265	262

CHAPTER **9**

The East Asian World 1400–1800

Section 1 China at Its Height

Section 2 Chinese Society and Culture

Section 3 Tokugawa Japan and Korea

Section 4 Spice Trade in Southeast Asia

MAKING CONNECTIONS

Can a palace reflect the philosophy of its rulers?

The Imperial City in Beijing represents one of the grand artistic accomplishments of the Ming and Qing dynasties. Originally the home of the emperors, the city was illegal to enter without permission and became known as the Forbidden City. In this chapter, you will learn more about the Ming and Qing emperors.

- How is the Imperial City similar to the Versailles palace in France?
- How did the Forbidden City symbolize the power of the emperor?

EAST ASIA ▶

1406 Construction of the Imperial City in China begins

1498 Portuguese explorer Vasco da Gama lands in Calicut in search of spices

1603 Tokugawa Ieyasu takes the title of shogun in Japan

1400   1500   1600

THE WORLD ▶

1440 Inca ruler Pachacuti builds an empire in South America

272

1644
China's Ming dynasty is overthrown; Qing dynasty begins

1793
Lord Macartney leads British trade mission to China

1700

1800

1633
The Church condemns teachings of Galileo

1791
In France, Olympe de Gouges writes declaration of rights for women

FOLDABLES™
Study Organizer

China's Contact | Japan's Contact

Portuguese

Comparing and Contrasting Use a Two-Tab Book to explore the experiences of the Chinese and Japanese as they came into contact with the Portuguese.

History ONLINE

Chapter Overview—Visit glencoe.com to preview Chapter 9.

China at Its Height

GUIDE TO READING

The BIG Idea
Ideas, Beliefs, and Values China preferred to keep its culture free of European influences.

Content Vocabulary
- queue *(p. 277)*
- banners *(p. 277)*

Academic Vocabulary
- series *(p. 275)*
- perspective *(p. 276)*

People and Places
- Ming *(p. 274)*
- Beijing *(p. 274)*
- Zheng He *(p. 275)*
- Guangzhou *(p. 276)*
- Manchus *(p. 276)*
- Manchuria *(p. 276)*
- Qing *(p. 276)*
- Taiwan *(p. 277)*
- Kangxi *(p. 278)*
- Qianlong *(p. 279)*

Reading Strategy
Comparing and Contrasting
As you read, complete a diagram like the one below to compare and contrast the achievements of the Ming and Qing dynasties.

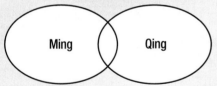

Under Ming rule, China extended the territory under its control. The Ming set up an efficient government bureaucracy and school system, and trade and manufacturing flourished. China enjoyed a cultural exchange with the West. The Ming dynasty eventually declined due to internal conflict and government corruption.

The Ming Dynasty

MAIN IDEA China flourished politically and culturally during the reign of the Ming Dynasty.

HISTORY & YOU What if Chinese explorers had reached the Americas before European explorers? Read to learn about the voyages of Zheng He.

The Mongol dynasty in China was overthrown in 1368. The founder of the new dynasty took the title of Ming Hong Wu (the Ming Martial Emperor). This was the beginning of the **Ming** dynasty, which lasted until 1644.

Under Ming emperors, China extended its rule into Mongolia and central Asia and briefly reconquered Vietnam. Along the northern frontier, the Chinese strengthened the Great Wall and made peace with the nomadic tribes that had troubled them for many centuries.

At home, Ming rulers ran an effective government using a centralized bureaucracy staffed with officials chosen by the civil service examination system. They set up a nationwide school system. Manufactured goods were produced in workshops and factories in vastly higher numbers. New crops were introduced, which greatly increased food production. The Ming rulers also renovated the Grand Canal, making it possible to ship grain and other goods from southern to northern China. The Ming dynasty truly began a new era of greatness in Chinese history.

The Voyages of Zheng He

Ming Hong Wu, founder of the dynasty, ruled from 1368 until 1398. After his death, his son Yong Le became emperor. This was after a four-year campaign to defeat the rightful heir. To establish the legitimacy of his rule, Yong Le built large monuments, strengthened the Great Wall, and restored Chinese rule and provincial authority over Vietnam.

In 1406 Yong Le began construction of the Imperial City in **Beijing** (BAY•JIHNG). In 1421, after construction was sufficiently far along, he moved the capital from Nanjing to Beijing. The

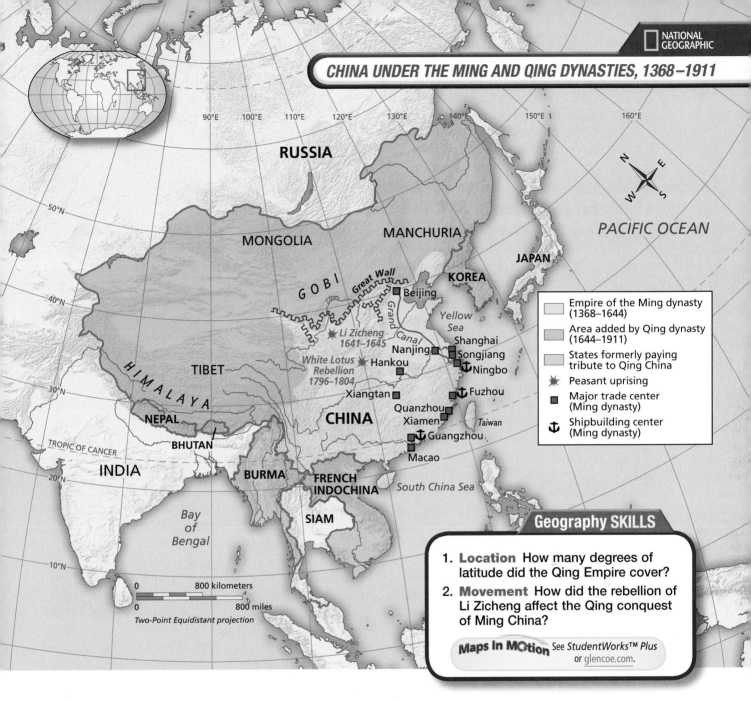

CHINA UNDER THE MING AND QING DYNASTIES, 1368–1911

90°E 100°E 110°E 120°E 130°E 140°E 150°E 160°E

RUSSIA

50°N

MONGOLIA

MANCHURIA

PACIFIC OCEAN

JAPAN

G O B I

Great Wall

40°N

KOREA

Beijing

Yellow Sea

Li Zicheng 1641–1645

Grand Canal

Nanjing

Shanghai

Songjiang

White Lotus Rebellion 1796–1804

Hankou

Ningbo

TIBET

30°N

Xiangtan

Fuzhou

CHINA

Quanzhou

Xiamen

Taiwan

H I M A L A Y A

NEPAL

Guangzhou

TROPIC OF CANCER

BHUTAN

Macao

20°N

INDIA

BURMA

FRENCH INDOCHINA

South China Sea

Bay of Bengal

SIAM

10°N

☐ Empire of the Ming dynasty (1368–1644)

☐ Area added by Qing dynasty (1644–1911)

☐ States formerly paying tribute to Qing China

✳ Peasant uprising

■ Major trade center (Ming dynasty)

⚓ Shipbuilding center (Ming dynasty)

0   800 kilometers
0   800 miles

Two-Point Equidistant projection

Geography SKILLS

1. **Location** How many degrees of latitude did the Qing Empire cover?

2. **Movement** How did the rebellion of Li Zicheng affect the Qing conquest of Ming China?

Maps In MOtion See *StudentWorks™ Plus* or glencoe.com.

Imperial City (known today as the Forbidden City) was created to convey power and prestige. For nearly five hundred years the Imperial City was home to China's emperors. Yong Le died in 1424 and was buried with his wife and 16 concubines in a new cemetery for emperors outside of Beijing.

During his reign, Yong Le also sent a **series** of naval voyages into the Indian Ocean that sailed as far west as the eastern coast of Africa. Led by the court official **Zheng He** (JUHNG•HUH), seven voyages of exploration were made between 1405 and 1433. On the first voyage, nearly 28,000

men embarked on 62 ships. The largest ship was over 440 feet (134.1 m) long. (Columbus's *Santa Maria* was only 75 feet [22.9 m] long.) The fleet passed through Southeast Asia and visited the western coast of India and the city-states of East Africa. It returned with items unknown in China and with information about the outside world. The emperor was especially fascinated by the giraffes from Africa, and he placed them in the imperial zoo.

The seven voyages by Zheng He led to enormous profits, which alarmed traditionalists within the bureaucracy.

Some of them held the Confucian view that trading activities were unworthy and that being a merchant was an inferior occupation. Shortly after Yong Le's death, the voyages were halted, never to be revived. One can only guess what a difference it would have made if Zheng He's fleet had reached the Americas before Columbus did.

First Contacts with the West

In 1514 a Portuguese fleet arrived off the coast of China. It was the first direct contact between the Chinese Empire and Europe since the journeys of Marco Polo.

At the time, the Ming government thought little of the arrival of the Portuguese. China was at the height of its power as the most magnificent civilization on Earth. From the **perspective** of the emperor, the Europeans were only an unusual form of barbarian. To the Chinese ruler, the rulers of all other countries were simply "younger brothers" of the Chinese emperor, who was seen as the Son of Heaven.

The Portuguese soon outraged Chinese officials with their behavior. They were expelled from **Guangzhou** (Canton) but were allowed to occupy Macao, a port on the southeastern coast of China.

At first, the Portuguese had little impact on Chinese society. Portuguese ships did carry goods between China and Japan, but direct trade between Europe and China remained limited. Perhaps more important than trade, however, was the exchange of ideas.

Christian missionaries had also made the long voyage to China on European merchant ships. The Jesuits, a Catholic order that focused on education and establishing missions, were among the most active. Many of them were highly educated men who brought along instruments, such as clocks, that impressed Chinese officials and made them more receptive to Western ideas.

Both sides benefited from this early cultural exchange. Chinese scholars marveled at their ability to read better with European eyeglasses. Christian missionaries were impressed with many aspects of Chinese civilization, such as the teachings of Confucius, the printing and availability of books, and Chinese architecture. When the Jesuits' reports began to circulate back home, Europeans became even more curious about this great civilization on the other side of the world.

Fall of the Ming Dynasty

After a period of prosperity and growth, the Ming dynasty gradually began to decline. During the late sixteenth century, internal power struggles developed. Groups worked to gain sole power and to place one of their leaders as emperor. Their efforts resulted in a series of weak rulers who were overpowered. Children, who had no control over their empire, were sometimes placed on the throne. Such internal power struggles led to a period of government corruption. High taxes, caused in part by this corruption, led to peasant unrest. Crop yields declined because of harsh weather.

In the 1630s, a major epidemic greatly reduced the population in many areas. One observer in a major city wrote, "There were few signs of human life in the streets and all that was heard was the buzzing of flies."

The suffering caused by the epidemic helped spark a peasant revolt led by Li Zicheng (LEE DZUH•CHUHNG). The revolt began in central China and then spread to the rest of the country. In 1644 Li and his forces occupied the capital of Beijing. When the capital fell, the last Ming emperor committed suicide by hanging himself from a tree in the palace gardens. Many officials took their own lives as well.

The overthrow of the Ming dynasty created an opportunity for the **Manchus.** They were a farming and hunting people who lived northeast of the Great Wall in the area known today as **Manchuria,** which is in the extreme northeast portion of China. The forces of the Manchus conquered Beijing, and Li Zicheng's army fell. The victorious Manchus then declared the creation of a new dynasty called the **Qing** (CHIHNG), meaning "pure." This expansive dynasty, created in 1644, remained in power until 1911.

✓ **Reading Check** **Describing** What were the achievements of the Ming dynasty?

The Qing Dynasty

MAIN IDEA Seeing how Western ideas were affecting its culture, China closed its doors to Europeans.

HISTORY & YOU What if trade with China were stopped today? Learn why China rejected foreign trade.

When some Chinese resisted their new rulers and seized the island of **Taiwan,** the Manchu government prepared to attack them. To identify the rebels, the government ordered all males to adopt Manchu dress and hairstyles. They had to shave their foreheads and braid their hair into a pigtail called a **queue.** Those who refused were assumed to be rebels and were executed: "Lose your hair or lose your head."

The Manchus were gradually accepted as legitimate rulers. The Qing flourished under a series of strong early rulers. The emperors pacified the country, corrected serious social and economic ills, and restored peace and prosperity.

Qing Adaptations

The Qing maintained the Ming political system but faced one major problem: the Manchus were ethnically and culturally different from their subject population. The Qing rulers dealt with this reality in two ways.

First, the Qing tried to preserve their distinct identity within Chinese society. The Manchus, who made up only 2 percent of the population, were defined legally as distinct from everyone else in China. The Manchu nobility maintained large landholdings and received revenues from the state treasury. Other Manchus were organized into separate military units, called **banners.** The "bannermen" were the chief fighting force of the empire.

Second, the Qing dealt with the problem of ethnic differences by bringing Chinese into the imperial administration. Chinese held more than 80 percent of lower posts, but they held a much smaller share of the top positions. Sharing of power won many Chinese supporters for the Manchus.

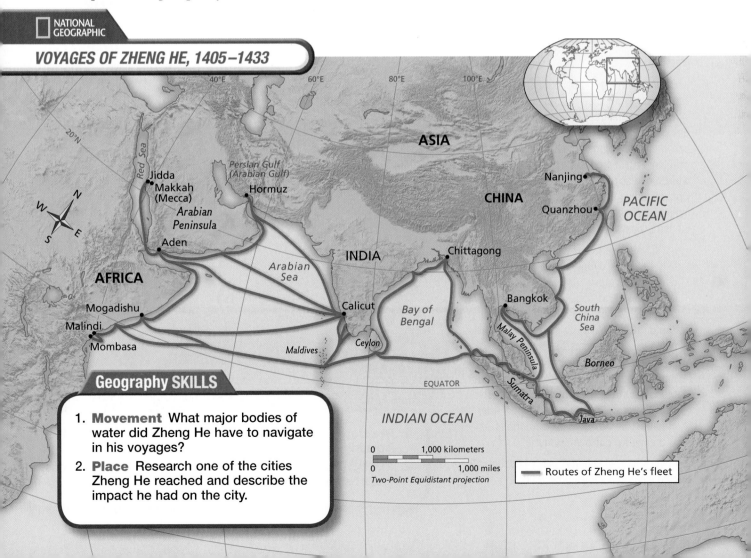

NATIONAL GEOGRAPHIC

VOYAGES OF ZHENG HE, 1405–1433

Geography SKILLS

1. **Movement** What major bodies of water did Zheng He have to navigate in his voyages?

2. **Place** Research one of the cities Zheng He reached and describe the impact he had on the city.

0 — 1,000 kilometers
0 — 1,000 miles
Two-Point Equidistant projection

Routes of Zheng He's fleet

Reign of Kangxi

Kangxi (KAHNG•SHEE), who ruled from 1661 to 1722, was perhaps the greatest of the many strong emperors who ruled China during the Ming and Qing dynasties. A person with political skill and a strong character, Kangxi took charge of the government while still in his teens and reigned for 61 years.

Kangxi rose at dawn and worked until late at night. He wrote: "One act of negligence may cause sorrow all through the country, and one moment of negligence may result in trouble for thousands of generations." Kangxi calmed the unrest along the northern and western frontiers by force. As a patron of the arts and letters, he gained the support of scholars throughout the country.

During Kangxi's reign, the efforts of Christian missionaries reached their height.

The emperor was quite tolerant of the Christians. One European missionary, Ferdinand Verbiest, made this report on his experience with the Chinese emperor:

PRIMARY SOURCE

"This emperor [punishes] offenders of the highest as well as the lowest class with marvelous impartiality, according to their misdeeds, depriving them of rank and dignity. . . . On this account men of all ranks and dignities whatsoever, even the nearest to him in blood, stand in his presence with the deepest awe, and recognize him as sole ruler. . . . He even ordered us sometimes to be entertained in his own tent."

—Ferdinand Verbiest

Several hundred officials became Catholics, as did an estimated 300,000 ordinary Chinese. The Christian effort was

TURNING POINT — THE ISOLATION OF CHINA

Beginning in the 1400s, both China and Japan isolated themselves from global influence for hundreds of years. In 1793 Lord George Macartney led a trade mission on behalf of King George III to China. He carried with him British products that he thought would impress the Chinese so much that they would open up their country to trade and cultural exchange with Great Britain. However, Emperor Qianlong was not impressed:

"If you assert that your reverence for Our Celestial dynasty fills you with a desire to acquire our civilisation, our ceremonies and code of laws differ so completely from your own that ... you could not possibly transplant our manners and customs to your alien soil. ... Our Celestial Empire possesses all things in prolific abundance and lacks no product within its own borders. There was therefore no need to import the manufactures of outside barbarians in exchange for our own produce."

China's "closed country" policy kept out foreign ideas and values until 1800.

Chinese emperor Qianlong

Lord Macartney's mission brought pottery, clocks, and scientific instruments to China.

DOCUMENT-BASED QUESTIONS

1. **Predicting** What long-term effects would you expect the isolation of China from the West to have on China?
2. **Recognizing Bias** As compared to the British, how does the artist depict the Chinese?

undermined by squabbling among the Western religious orders. Although Kangxi tried to resolve the problem, no solution was reached. After the death of Kangxi, however, his successor began to suppress Christian activities.

Europeans in China

Qianlong (CHEE•UHN•LUNG), who ruled from 1736 to 1795, was another outstanding Qing ruler. He expanded China to its greatest physical size. Qianlong's reign was also at the time of greatest prosperity during the Qing dynasty. It was during this great reign, however, that the first signs of decay appeared. Why did this happen?

As the emperor grew older, he fell under the influence of destructive elements at court. Corrupt officials and higher taxes led to unrest in rural areas. Population growth also exerted pressure on the land and led to economic hardship. In central China, unhappy peasants launched a revolt, the White Lotus Rebellion (1796–1804). The revolt was suppressed, but the expenses of fighting the rebels weakened the Qing dynasty.

Unfortunately for China, the Qing dynasty was declining just as Europe was seeking more trade. At first, the Qing government sold trade privileges to the Europeans. However, to limit contacts between Europeans and Chinese, the Qing confined all European traders to a small island just outside Guangzhou. The traders could reside there only from October through March and could deal only with a limited number of Chinese firms licensed by the government.

For a while, the British accepted this system. By the end of the eighteenth century, however, some British traders had begun to demand access to additional cities. At the same time, the Chinese government was under pressure from its own merchants to open China to British manufactured goods.

Britain had an unfavorable, or negative, trade balance with China. That is, Britain imported more goods from China than it exported to the country. For years, Britain had imported tea, silk, and porcelain from the Chinese. To pay for these imports, Britain had sent Indian cotton to China. The cotton, however, did not cover the entire debt, and the British had to pay for their imports with silver. The British sent ever-increasing quantities of silver to China, especially in exchange for tea, which was in great demand by the British.

In 1793 a British mission led by Lord George Macartney visited Beijing to seek more liberal trade policies. However, Emperor Qianlong responded that China had no need of "your country's manufactures." The Chinese would later pay for their rejection of the British request.

✓ **Reading Check** **Explaining** Who were the "bannermen"?

Vocabulary
1. **Explain** the significance of: Ming, Beijing, series, Zheng He, perspective, Guangzhou, Manchus, Manchuria, Qing, Taiwan, queue, banners, Kangxi, Qianlong.

Main Ideas
2. **Summarize** how both the Europeans and Chinese benefited from their early cultural exchange by using a chart like the one below.

European Benefits	Chinese Benefits

3. **List** the ways the Ming and Qing dynasties tried to limit contacts between Europeans and the Chinese people. Why did the British initially accept the restrictions?

4. **Explain** how the pigtail (queue) became a political symbol under the Qing dynasty.

Critical Thinking
5. **The BIG Idea** **Making Generalizations** What was the general attitude of the Chinese regarding trade with the Western world? Give examples from the text to support your answer.

6. **Making Connections** Why is it so important to have a balance of trade between a country and its trading partner?

7. **Analyzing Visuals** After examining the cartoon in the Turning Point feature on page 278, what conclusions can you draw about the mood of the participants in this meeting?

Writing About History
8. **Expository Writing** Using the Internet or print resources, research the voyages of Zheng He and Columbus. Write an essay comparing the technology, equipment, purpose, and results of their explorations.

History ONLINE
For help with the concepts in this section of *Glencoe World History— Modern Times*, go to glencoe.com and click Study Central.

Chinese Society and Culture

GUIDE TO READING

The BIG Idea
Ideas, Beliefs, and Values Chinese society was organized around the family.

Content Vocabulary
• commercial capitalism *(p. 280)*
• clan *(p. 281)*
• porcelain *(p. 283)*

Academic Vocabulary
• benefit *(p. 281)*
• incentive *(p. 282)*

People and Places
• Cao Xuein *(p. 283)*
• Imperial City *(p. 283)*
• Emperor Yong Le *(p. 283)*

Reading Strategy
Organizing Information As you read, show the organization of the Chinese family by using a concentric circle diagram like the one below.

Husband, Wife, and Family

During the Ming and Qing dynasties, China's population increased significantly and manufacturing grew. Organized around the family, Chinese society revered its elderly but restricted the role of its women. Meanwhile, the arts and architecture flourished.

Economy and Daily Life

MAIN IDEA China's agriculture-based economy changed as a rapid increase in population led to rural land shortages.

HISTORY & YOU What if you knew you would pay less tax if you decided to become a farmer and more tax if you decided to open a factory? Learn about changes to China's economy.

Between 1500 and 1800, China remained a mostly agricultural society. Nearly 85 percent of the people were small farmers. Nevertheless, the Chinese economy was changing.

Economic Changes
The first change for China involved an increase in population, from less than 80 million in 1390 to more than 300 million at the end of the 1700s. The increase had several causes. These included a long period of peace and stability under the early Qing dynasty and improvements in the food supply due to a faster growing species of rice from Southeast Asia.

The population increase meant that less land was available for each family. The imperial court tried to make more land available by limiting the amount wealthy landowners could hold. By the eighteenth century, however, almost all the land that could be farmed was already being farmed. Shortages of land in rural areas led to unrest and revolts.

Another change in this period was a steady growth in manufacturing and increased trade between provinces. Taking advantage of the long era of peace and prosperity, merchants and manufacturers expanded their trade in silk, porcelain, cotton goods, and other products.

Despite the growth in trade and manufacturing, China did not develop the kind of **commercial capitalism**—private business based on profit—that was emerging in Europe. Some key differences between China and Europe explain this fact.

In the first place, middle-class merchants and manufacturers in China were not as independent as those in Europe. Trade and manufacturing remained under the firm control of the government.

Economic Changes in China

Improvements in agriculture during the Ming dynasty caused great changes in Chinese society. As Ming traders ventured into Southeast Asia, they acquired rice that produced much larger harvests. In the 1500s, American foods were introduced to China, including the peanut, the sweet potato, and maize (corn).

The increase in rice production brought many changes. With a better food supply, peasants were now able to grow cash crops—crops produced for profit—like cotton and indigo. As a result, manufacturing and commerce increased. Chinese silk, cotton, tea, and porcelain were in demand around the world, especially in Europe and America.

The greater food supply also allowed for increases in population. Under Ming rule the population had doubled. During the Qing dynasty population grew dramatically.

Chinese farmers in a rice paddy

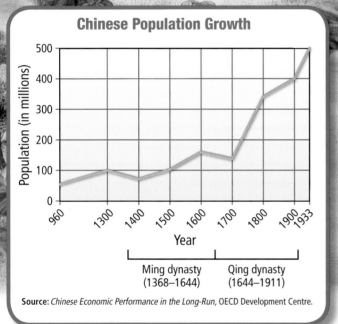

Chinese Population Growth

Population (in millions) vs. Year

Ming dynasty (1368–1644)
Qing dynasty (1644–1911)

Source: *Chinese Economic Performance in the Long-Run,* OECD Development Centre.

DOCUMENT-BASED QUESTIONS

1. **Describing** How did changes in agriculture affect the growth of China's population?
2. **Predicting** What does the population graph suggest about Chinese population during the Ming dynasty?

Many Chinese looked down on trade and manufacturing as inferior to farming. The state reflected this attitude by levying heavy taxes on manufacturing and trade and low taxes on farming.

Society and the Role of Women

Chinese society was organized around the family. The family was expected to provide for its members' needs, including the education of children, support of unmarried daughters, and care of the elderly. At the same time, all family members were expected to sacrifice their individual needs to **benefit** the family as a whole. This expectation was based on Confucian ideals.

The ideal family unit in Qing China was the extended family, in which as many as three or four generations lived under the same roof. When sons married, they brought their wives to live with them in the family home. Unmarried daughters also remained in the house, as did parents and grandparents. Chinese society held the elderly in high regard. Aging parents knew they would be cared for in their home by their children.

Beyond the extended family was the **clan,** which consisted of dozens, or even hundreds, of related families. These families were linked by a clan council of elders and common social and religious activities such as Buddhism and Confucianism.

See page R43 to read excerpts from Sung Ying-Hsing's *The Silk Industry in China* in the **Primary Sources and Literature Library.**

The clan system made it possible for wealthier families to help poorer relatives.

Women were considered inferior to men in Chinese society. One Chinese woman lamented her status in a poem:

<u>**PRIMARY SOURCE**</u>

"How sad it is to be a woman!!
Nothing on earth is held so cheap. . . .
No one is glad when a girl is born:
By *her* the family sets no store."
—a Chinese woman

Only males could have a formal education and pursue a career in government or scholarship. Within the family, capable women often played strong roles. Nevertheless, the wife was clearly subordinate to the husband. Legally, she could not divorce her husband or inherit property. The husband, in contrast, could divorce his wife if she did not produce sons. He could also take a second wife. Husbands were expected to provide support for their wives and children. In many cases, the head of the family would also be responsible for providing for more than just his own wife and children.

A feature of Chinese society that restricted the mobility of women was the practice of footbinding. The origins of footbinding are not clear. Scholars believe it began among the wealthiest class of women and was later adopted by all classes. Bound feet were a status symbol. Women who had bound feet were more marriageable than those who did not; thus, there was a status **incentive** as well as an economic incentive. An estimated one-half to two-thirds of the women in China bound their feet.

The process, begun in childhood, was very painful. Women who had their feet bound could not walk; they were carried. Not all clans looked favorably on footbinding. Women who worked in the fields or in occupations that required mobility did not bind their feet.

✓ **Reading Check** **Describing** Describe the role of women in China.

HISTORY & ARTS   PRIMARY SOURCE

Ming Porcelain

Ming porcelain artists studied nature to perfect their skill in painting traditional scenes. Blue-and-white porcelain pieces were created by artists who specialized in each step of the painting, glazing, and firing process.

Jingdezhen is known as the porcelain capital of the world. Porcelain was made there as early as about 200 B.C. during the Han dynasty. When the Ming Dynasty was close to collapse, there was less domestic demand for porcelain; so Jingdezhen potters increased shipments to foreign markets such as Japan and Europe. Soon Chinese porcelain was in worldwide demand.

DOCUMENT-BASED QUESTIONS

This blue-and-white porcelain vase is an example of the fine decorative arts that flourished during the Ming and Qing dynasties.

1. **Describing** What traditional Chinese images are painted on the vase?

2. **Making Connections** What does the growing demand for Ming porcelain tell you about changes taking place in the Chinese economy?

Chinese Art and Literature

MAIN IDEA Architecture, decorative arts, and literature flourished during the Ming and Qing dynasties.

HISTORY & YOU Under what conditions have art and literature flourished in your society? Learn about the artistic accomplishments of the Ming and Qing dynasties.

During the late Ming and the early Qing dynasties, traditional culture in China reached new heights.

The Chinese Novel

The Ming economic expansion increased standards of living, providing many Chinese with money to purchase books. Also, new innovations in paper manufacturing encouraged the growth of printing throughout China.

During the Ming dynasty, a new form of literature arose that evolved into the modern Chinese novel. Works in this literary form were quite popular, especially among well-to-do urban dwellers.

One Chinese novel, *The Golden Lotus*, is considered by many to be the first realistic social novel. *The Golden Lotus* depicts the corrupt life of a wealthy landlord in the late Ming period who cruelly manipulates those around him for sex, money, and power.

The Dream of the Red Chamber, by **Cao Xuein,** is generally considered even today to be China's most distinguished popular novel. Published in 1791, it tells of the tragic love between two young people caught in the financial and moral disintegration of a powerful Chinese clan.

Ming and Qing Art

During the Ming and the early Qing dynasties, China experienced an outpouring of artistic brilliance. In architecture, the most outstanding example is the **Imperial City** in Beijing. **Emperor Yong Le** began construction of the Imperial City—a complex of palaces and temples—in 1406. Succeeding emperors continued to add to the palace.

The Imperial City is an immense compound surrounded by six and one-half miles (10.5 km) of walls. It includes a maze of private apartments and offices, as well as stately halls for imperial audiences and banquets and spacious gardens. Because it was off-limits to commoners, the compound was known as the Forbidden City.

The decorative arts also flourished in this period. Perhaps the most famous of all the arts of the Ming Era was blue-and-white **porcelain.** Europeans admired the beauty of this porcelain and collected it in great quantities. Different styles of porcelain were produced during the reign of individual emperors.

✓ Reading Check **Describing** Describe the artistic accomplishments of the Ming and Qing dynasties.

Vocabulary

1. **Explain** the significance of: commercial capitalism, benefit, clan, incentive, Cao Xuein, Imperial City, Emperor Yong Le, porcelain.

Main Ideas

2. **Identify** the economic changes in China from 1500 to 1800 by using a diagram like the one below.

Economic Change

3. **Describe** the significance of the Chinese extended family.

4. **Explain** why the Imperial City was also known as the Forbidden City.

Critical Thinking

5. **The BIG Idea** **Drawing Conclusions** Although women were considered inferior to men, they filled important roles in peasant society. What were they?

6. **Comparing** Identify the similarities in plot between Cao Xuein's *The Dream of the Red Chamber* and William Shakespeare's *Romeo and Juliet.*

7. **Analyzing Visuals** Examine the picture of Chinese farmers on page 281. What do you see in the picture that teaches you about rice cultivation?

Writing About History

8. **Persuasive Writing** Imagine you are a Chinese mother talking to your daughter in 1700. Using research or your own ideas, convince her that footbinding is necessary and beneficial.

History ONLINE

For help with the concepts in this section of *Glencoe World History— Modern Times,* go to glencoe.com and click Study Central.

Tokugawa Japan and Korea

GUIDE TO READING

The BIG Idea
Order and Security Political unification often results in warfare and difficult economic and social changes.

Content Vocabulary
- daimyo *(p. 284)*
- hans *(p. 286)*
- hostage system *(p. 286)*
- eta *(p. 287)*

Academic Vocabulary
- process *(p. 284)*
- community *(p. 286)*

People and Places
- Oda Nobunaga *(p. 284)*
- Kyōto *(p. 284)*
- Toyotomi Hideyoshi *(p. 284)*
- Ōsaka *(p. 284)*
- Tokugawa Ieyasu *(p. 284)*
- Edo *(p. 284)*
- Matsuo Basho *(p. 288)*
- Korea *(p. 289)*

Reading Strategy
Categorizing Information As you read, categorize the different elements of Japanese culture using a diagram like the one below.

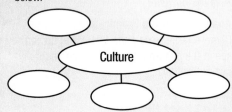

Culture

From the sixteenth century to the eighteenth century, Japan and Korea were unified through efforts of powerful leaders. Both nations imposed restrictive social systems and enforced cultural isolation. While trade and industry increased, the arts flourished in Japan's and Korea's distinctive cultures.

Political Changes in Japan

MAIN IDEA Japan's policies removed European influence and allowed Japan to remain in isolation for centuries.

HISTORY & YOU What if your family refused to allow people from outside your neighborhood to come into your home? Learn how European access to Japan was restricted during Tokugawa rule.

At the end of the fifteenth century, Japan was in chaos. The centralized power of the shogunate had collapsed. **Daimyo,** heads of noble families, controlled their own lands and warred with their neighbors. Soon, however, a dramatic reversal would unify Japan.

The Three Great Unifiers

The **process** of unification began in the late sixteenth century with three powerful political figures. The first was **Oda Nobunaga** (oh•dah noh•boo•nah•gah). Nobunaga seized the imperial capital of **Kyōto** and placed the reigning shogun under his control.

Nobunaga was succeeded by **Toyotomi Hideyoshi** (toh•yoh•toh•mee hee•day•yoh•shee), a farmer's son who had become a military commander. Hideyoshi located his capital at **Ōsaka**. By 1590, he had persuaded most of the daimyo on the Japanese islands to accept his authority.

After Hideyoshi's death in 1598, **Tokugawa Ieyasu** (toh•kuh•gah•wah ee•yah•soo), the powerful daimyo of **Edo** (modern-day Tokyo), took control of Japan. Ieyasu took the title of shogun in 1603. The Tokugawa rulers completed the restoration of central authority begun by Nobunaga and Hideyoshi. Tokugawa shoguns remained in power at their capital at Edo until 1868, a long period that became known as the "Great Peace."

Europeans in Japan

As the three great commanders were unifying Japan, the first Europeans began to arrive. Portuguese traders landed on the islands in 1543. In a few years, Portuguese ships began stopping regularly at Japanese ports to take part in the regional trade between Japan, China, and Southeast Asia.

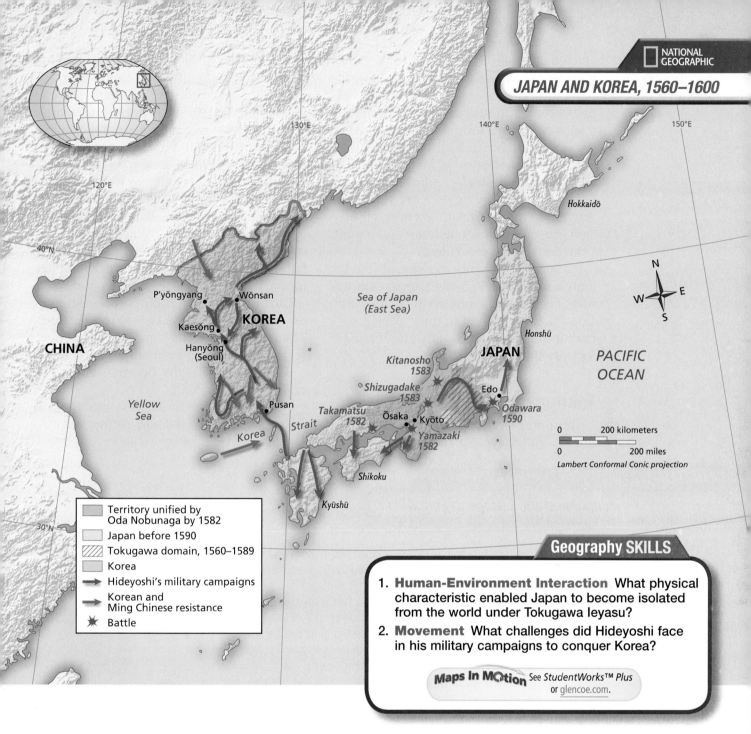

JAPAN AND KOREA, 1560–1600

Hokkaidō

130°E   140°E   150°E

120°E

40°N

P'yŏngyang   Wŏnsan

KOREA

Sea of Japan
(East Sea)

Kaesŏng

CHINA

Hanyŏng
(Seoul)

Honshū

*Kitanosho
1583*

JAPAN

Edo

Yellow
Sea

*Shizugadake
1583*

Pusan

Takamatsu
1582

Ōsaka   Kyōto

*Odawara
1590*

PACIFIC
OCEAN

Korea

Strait

*Yamazaki
1582*

N

W   E

S

Shikoku

0   200 kilometers

Kyūshū

0   200 miles

Lambert Conformal Conic projection

30°N

Map Legend

- Territory unified by Oda Nobunaga by 1582
- Japan before 1590
- Tokugawa domain, 1560–1589
- Korea
- → Hideyoshi's military campaigns
- → Korean and Ming Chinese resistance
- ✹ Battle

Geography SKILLS

1. **Human-Environment Interaction** What physical characteristic enabled Japan to become isolated from the world under Tokugawa Ieyasu?

2. **Movement** What challenges did Hideyoshi face in his military campaigns to conquer Korea?

Maps In MOtion See StudentWorks™ Plus or glencoe.com.

At first, the visitors were welcomed. The Japanese were fascinated by tobacco, clocks, eyeglasses, and other European goods. Nobunaga and Hideyoshi especially found the new firearms helpful in defeating their enemies and unifying the islands under their rule.

A local daimyo, Lord Tokitaka, acquired firearms from the Portuguese almost immediately after their landing in 1543. Within a few years, they were being mass-produced in Japan. Lord Tokitaka was in awe of the new weapons:

PRIMARY SOURCE

"To use it, fill it with powder and small lead pellets. Set up a small target on a bank. Grip the object in your hand, compose your body, and closing one eye, apply fire to the opening. Then the pellet hits the target squarely. The explosion is like lightning and the report like thunder. . . . This thing with one blow can smash a mountain of silver and a wall of iron. If one sought to do mischief in another man's domain, and he was touched by it, he would lose his life instantly. . . ."

—Lord Tokitaka

History ONLINE
Student Web Activity—
Visit glencoe.com and complete the activity on the role of the shogun in Japan.

The first Jesuit missionary, Francis Xavier, arrived in 1549. The Jesuits converted a number of local daimyo. By the end of the sixteenth century, thousands of Japanese had become Christians. However, after the Jesuits destroyed local shrines, Hideyoshi issued an edict in 1587 prohibiting Christian activities within his lands. The edict was at first not strictly enforced, and the Jesuits were allowed to continue their activities. Under Ieyasu, however, all missionaries were expelled, and Japanese Christians were persecuted.

European merchants were the next to go. Only a small Dutch (Netherlands) **community** was allowed to remain in Japan. Dutch ships were permitted to dock at Nagasaki harbor only once a year and could remain for only two to three months.

Tokugawa Rule

The Tokugawa rulers established control of the feudal system that had governed Japan for over 300 years. As before, the state was divided into about 250 separate territories called **hans,** or domains. Each was ruled by a daimyo. In theory, the daimyo were independent because they were able to support themselves from taxes on their lands. In actuality, the shogunate controlled the daimyo by a **hostage system.**

In this system, the daimyo were required to maintain two residences—one in their own lands and one in Edo, where the shogun's court was located. When the daimyo was absent from his residence in Edo, his family was forced to stay home as insurance for the daimyo's loyalty to the shogun.

During this long period of peace—known as the "Great Peace"—brought by Tokugawa rule, the samurai who had served the daimyo gradually ceased to be a warrior class. Many became managers on the daimyo's lands.

✓ **Reading Check** **Identifying** Sequence the events that led to the unification of Japan.

Japanese and European Feudalism

Feudalism in both Europe and Japan was a social and political system that developed to provide protection. European feudalism developed between 800 and 900 in response to weak central governments that could no longer protect their subjects. Within the European system, lords granted lands to vassals. In return, a vassal made an oath of loyalty to his lord and provided military support. Codes of conduct governed the relationship and obligations of lords and vassals to each other. Knights in armor dominated warfare in Europe for almost five hundred years.

Japanese feudalism developed between 800 and 1500. The emperor and shogun held the most power. Powerful nobles, called daimyo, gave only loose loyalty to the emperor and competed with each other for power. The shogun granted lands to the daimyo who, in turn, granted lands to their warriors, called samurai. The daimyo depended on their samurai who fought clad in armor like European knights.

Sixteenth-century German armor

Eighteenth-century Japanese armor

COMPARING FEUDALISM		
HIERARCHY	EUROPE	JAPAN
Top Level	king	emperor and shogun
Middle Level	lords or nobles	daimyo
Bottom Level	knights	samurai
Code of Conduct	chivalry	bushido

DOCUMENT-BASED QUESTIONS

1. **Comparing** How are the European and Japanese feudal systems similar?
2. **Analyzing** Why would a code of conduct be important under a feudal system?

The Tokugawa Era

MAIN IDEA Trade, industry, and arts flourished under the Tokugawa, even while the social system became restrictive.

HISTORY & YOU What if your parents selected the person you could date or marry? Learn how Japan established its strict social class distinctions.

A major economic change took place under the Tokugawa. Since the fourteenth century, many upper-class Japanese, influenced by Confucianism, had considered trade and industry beneath them. Under the Tokugawa rulers, however, trade and industry began to flourish as never before, especially in the growing cities of Edo, Kyōto, and Ōsaka.

Economic and Social Changes

By 1750, Edo had a population of over a million and was one of the largest cities in the world. Banking flourished, and paper money became the normal medium of exchange in business transactions. A Japanese merchant class emerged and began to play a significant role in the life of the Japanese nation.

What effect did these economic changes have on Japanese peasants who made up most of the population? Some farm families benefited by exploiting the growing demand for cash crops (crops grown for sale). Most peasants, however, experienced both declining profits and rising costs and taxes. Many were forced to become tenants or to work as hired help. When rural conditions became desperate, some peasants revolted. Almost seven thousand peasant revolts and demonstrations against high taxes took place during the Tokugawa Era.

Social changes also marked the Tokugawa Era. These changes affected the class system and the role of women. During this era, Japan's class system became rigid. Rulers established strict legal distinctions among the four main classes: warriors, peasants, artisans, and merchants. Intermarriage between classes was forbidden.

The emperor and imperial court families were at the very top of the political and social structure. Next came the warrior class—the shogun, daimyo, samurai, and *ronin*. The shogun was supreme ruler below the emperor and distributor of the national rice crop. The local daimyo received land and rice from the shogun in exchange for military service. Samurai received rice from the daimyo in exchange for their services as advisers, castle guards, and government officials. Finally, the *ronin* were warriors who had no masters and who traveled the countryside seeking jobs.

Below the warriors were the farmers (peasants). Farmers produced rice and held a privileged position in society but were often poor. The artisan class included craftspeople such as swordmakers and carpenters. Finally, the merchant class distributed food and essential goods. This class was at the bottom of the social hierarchy because they profited from the labor of others.

Below these classes were Japan's outcasts, the **eta**. The Tokugawa enacted severe laws to regulate the places of residence, the dress, and even the hairstyles of the *eta*.

Society and the Role of Women

Especially in the samurai class where Confucian values were highly prized, the rights of females were restricted. Male heads of households had broad authority over property, marriage, and divorce.

Among the common people, women were also restricted. Parents arranged marriages, and a wife had to move in with her husband's family. A wife who did not meet the expectations of her husband or his family was likely to be divorced. Still, women were generally valued for their roles as childbearers and homemakers among the common people. Women worked the fields as well, although men typically did the heavier labor.

Literature and Arts

In the Tokugawa Era, a new set of cultural values began to appear, especially in the cities. It included the rise of popular literature written by and for the people.

The best examples of the new urban fiction are from Ihara Saikaku, considered one of Japan's greatest writers. Saikaku's greatest novel, *Five Women Who Loved Love*, tells of a search for love by five women.

These five women of the merchant class are willing to die for love—and all but one eventually do.

Much popular literature of the Tokugawa Era was lighthearted and intended to please its audiences. Poetry remained a more serious form of literary expression. **Matsuo Basho,** the greatest Japanese poet, wrote exquisite poetry about nature in the seventeenth century.

A new world of entertainment in the cities gave rise in the theater to Kabuki, which emphasized action, music, and dramatic gestures to entertain its viewers. Early Kabuki dramas dealt with the world of teahouses and dance halls in the cities. Government officials feared that exposure to these subjects onstage might corrupt the moral standards of its people. They therefore forbade women to appear on stage. The result was that a new profession was created—male actors who portrayed female characters on stage.

Art also reflected the changes in Japanese culture under the Tokugawa Era. The shogun's order that all daimyo and their families have residences in Edo sparked an increase in building. Nobles competed to erect the most magnificent mansions with lavish and beautiful furnishings. The abundant use of gold foil on walls and ceilings reflected the light in dark castle rooms, where windows were often small.

Japanese art was enriched by ideas from other cultures. Japanese pottery makers borrowed techniques and designs from Korea to create handsome ceramic pieces. The Japanese studied Western medicine, astronomy, languages, and even painting styles. In turn, Europeans wanted Japanese ceramics, which were prized as highly as the ceramics of the Chinese.

✓**Reading Check** **Explaining** In what ways were the rights of women of the common class restricted?

CONNECTING TO THE UNITED STATES

⤷ THE MARTIAL ARTS

The martial arts are the arts of combat and self-defense that developed in Asian cultures over many centuries. Practice of the martial arts promotes not only physical fitness but also a philosophy or way of life.

In recent years, the martial arts have become part of Western culture. In the United States, one can learn Chinese kung fu and tai chi, Japanese karate and judo, and Korean tae kwon do. Judo and tae kwon do are Olympic sports.

- Training in martial arts develops self-discipline and strength.
- The practice of martial arts promotes better health through self-awareness.
- Competitive sports can bridge cultural differences.

CONNECTING TO TODAY

1. **Naming** Name a martial arts sport that originated in Korea.
2. **Summarizing** What are some of the benefits of practicing the martial arts?

Korea: The Hermit Kingdom

MAIN IDEA Due to its isolationist practices, Korea earned the name "the Hermit Kingdom."

HISTORY & YOU Did you and your best friend ever use a secret code to communicate? Learn about Korea's development of a distinctive alphabet.

The Yi dynasty in **Korea** began in 1392 when Yi Song-gye (YEE•sung•jay), a renowned military strategist, ascended the throne by overthrowing the Koryo dynasty. Lasting for five centuries, the Yi dynasty was one of the world's longest-lasting monarchies.

Distinctive Culture

From their capital at Hanseong (modern-day Seoul), Yi rulers consolidated their rule of Korea. They patterned their society after that of the Chinese to the north but maintained their distinctive identity.

Perhaps the single most distinctive characteristic of the Korean culture was development of a unique alphabet, Hangul. Unlike Japanese or Chinese, which uses thousands of characters or symbols, Hangul is a phonetically based writing system. That is, it uses one letter for each sound, similar to the English alphabet. Hangul is still largely the standard writing system in present-day Korea.

Cultural Isolation

The Yi dynasty was not to last forever. The dynasty was severely weakened during the late sixteenth and early seventeenth centuries. There were disruptive divisions within its elite classes. Both Japanese and Chinese invasions devastated Korea.

A Japanese force under Toyotomi Hideyoshi invaded Korea in the late sixteenth century. Hideyoshi wanted to use Korea as the transit route for his conquest of China. The Japanese invaders were defeated, but victory came at a high price. Korean farmlands were devastated, and villages and towns were burned. Skilled workers were also either killed or kidnapped by the Japanese.

In response to these events, the Korean rulers sought to limit contact with foreign countries and tried to keep the country isolated from the outside world. The country remained largely untouched by European merchants and Christian missionaries. Due to its isolationist practices, Korea earned the name "the Hermit Kingdom."

Korea was still recovering from the Japanese invasions when the Manchus attacked in the early seventeenth century. Korea surrendered, and the Yi dynasty became subject to China.

✓ **Reading Check** **Summarizing** Why was Korea called "the Hermit Kingdom"?

SECTION 3 REVIEW

Vocabulary
1. **Explain** the significance of: daimyo, process, Oda Nobunaga, Kyōto, Toyotomi Hideyoshi, Ōsaka, Tokugawa Ieyasu, Edo, community, hans, hostage system, *eta*, Matsuo Basho, Korea.

Main Ideas
2. **List** the three great Japanese unifiers and their capital cities.

3. **Illustrate** the four main social classes that existed during the Tokugawa Era using a diagram like the one below. Place the highest-ranking social class at the top of the pyramid.

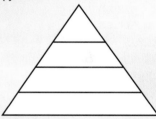

4. **Describe** the single most distinctive characteristic of the Korean culture.

Critical Thinking
5. **The BIG Idea** **Evaluating** What events led to Japan and Korea practicing cultural isolation?

6. **Drawing Inferences** How were most peasants affected by the economic changes in Japan?

7. **Analyzing Visuals** Examine the photographs of armor worn by knights and samurai on page 286. How does each suit of armor compare to and contrast with the other, and what does that reveal about warriors in each society?

Writing About History
8. **Descriptive Writing** Imagine that you are the literate wife of a samurai. Write a journal entry that describes your relationship to your husband, your children, and your mother-in-law.

History ONLINE

For help with the concepts in this section of *Glencoe World History—Modern Times*, go to glencoe.com and click Study Central.

Spice Trade in Southeast Asia

Attracted to the growing spice trade, Muslim merchants established a trade network along the Malay Peninsula and the Indonesian archipelago. In the sixteenth century, the Portuguese seized control of the spice trade, eventually attracting English and Dutch competition.

GUIDE TO READING

The BIG Idea
Competition Among Countries
Europeans struggled to control the profitable spice trade in Southeast Asia.

Content Vocabulary
• bureaucracy *(p. 292)*
• mainland states *(p. 293)*

Academic Vocabulary
• network *(p. 290)*
• impose *(p. 293)*

People and Places
• Khmer *(p. 290)*
• Philippines *(p. 291)*
• Moluccas *(p. 293)*
• Dutch *(p. 293)*
• Sumatra *(p. 293)*
• Java *(p. 293)*

Reading Strategy
Summarizing Information As you read, use a chart like the one below to list reasons why the destructive effects of European contact in Southeast Asia were only gradually felt.

European Contact in Southeast Asia

Emerging Mainland States

MAIN IDEA The spice trade influenced the politics, religion, and economy of the Malay Peninsula and the Indonesian archipelago.

HISTORY & YOU What if one student had a monopoly on providing music to your school? Learn what effect the arrival of spice traders had on Southeast Asia.

In 1500, mainland Southeast Asia was a relatively stable region. Throughout mainland Southeast Asia, from Burma in the west to Vietnam in the east, kingdoms with their own ethnic, linguistic, and cultural characteristics were being formed.

Conflicts in Southeast Asia

Conflicts erupted among the emerging states on the Southeast Asian mainland. Conflict over territory between the Thai and the Burmese was bitter until a Burmese army sacked the Thai capital in 1767. The Thai then created a new capital at Bangkok, farther to the south.

Across the mountains to the east, the Vietnamese had begun their "March to the South." By the end of the fifteenth century, they had subdued the rival state of Champa on the central coast. The Vietnamese then gradually took control of the Mekong Delta from the **Khmer**. By 1800, the Khmer monarchy (the successor of the old Angkor kingdom—see Chapter 3) had virtually disappeared.

Islamic Trade Network

The situation was different in the Malay Peninsula and the Indonesian archipelago. Muslim merchants were attracted to the growing spice trade. They gradually entered the area. The creation of an Islamic trade **network** had political results as new Islamic states arose along the spice route. The major impact of this trade network, however, came in the fifteenth century with the new Muslim sultanate at Melaka. Melaka owed its new power to its strategic location on the Strait of Malacca and to the rapid growth of the spice trade itself. Within a few years, Melaka had become the leading power in the region.

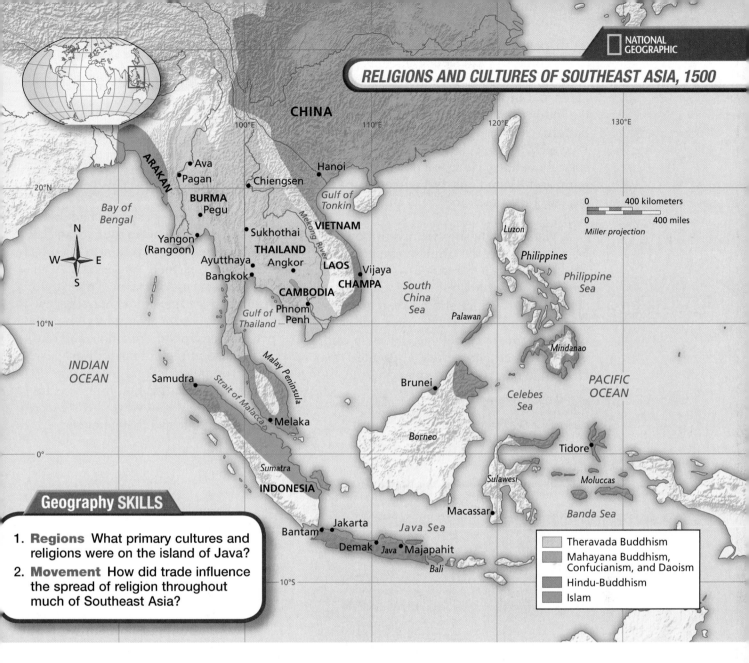

RELIGIONS AND CULTURES OF SOUTHEAST ASIA, 1500

Geography SKILLS

1. **Regions** What primary cultures and religions were on the island of Java?
2. **Movement** How did trade influence the spread of religion throughout much of Southeast Asia?

Legend:
- Theravada Buddhism
- Mahayana Buddhism, Confucianism, and Daoism
- Hindu-Buddhism
- Islam

Religious and Political Systems

Religious beliefs changed in Southeast Asia during the period from 1500 to 1800. Particularly in the non-mainland states and the **Philippines,** Islam and Christianity began to attract converts. Buddhism advanced on the mainland, becoming dominant from Burma to Vietnam. Traditional beliefs, however, survived and influenced the new religions.

The political systems in Southeast Asian states evolved into four styles of monarchy. Buddhist kings, Javanese kings, Islamic sultans, and Vietnamese emperors all adapted foreign models of government to suit their local circumstances.

The Buddhist style of kingship became the chief form of government in the mainland states of Burma, Thailand, Laos, and Cambodia. In the Buddhist model, the king was considered superior to other human beings and served as the link between human society and the universe.

The Javanese style of kingship was rooted in the political traditions of India and shared many characteristics of the Buddhist system. Like Buddhist rulers, Javanese kings were believed to have a sacred quality. They maintained the balance between the sacred world and the material world. The royal palace was designed to represent the center of the universe.

Its shape was like rays spreading outward to the corners of the Javanese realm.

Islamic sultans ruled on the Malay Peninsula and in the small coastal states of the Indonesian archipelago. In the Islamic pattern, the head of state was a sultan. Viewed as a mortal, he still possessed some special qualities. He was a defender of the faith and staffed his **bureaucracy** (nonelected government officials) mainly with aristocrats.

In Vietnam, kingship followed the Chinese model. Like the Chinese emperor, the Vietnamese emperor ruled according to the teachings of Confucius. Confucius believed that a ruler should treat subjects with love and respect. The ruler was seen as an intermediary between Heaven and Earth. The emperor was appointed by Heaven to rule by his talent and virtue.

 **Reading Check** **Listing** List the four styles of monarchy in Southeast Asia.

The Arrival of Europeans

MAIN IDEA Europeans struggled to control the profitable spice trade in the Malay Peninsula and the Indonesian archipelago.

HISTORY & YOU What if you controlled all of the money of your household? Learn about the shift in power in Southeast Asia.

Since ancient times, spices had been highly valued. Spices were more than flavorings for food. They were also used as medicines and as food preservers. After bad harvests and in winter, meat preserved with salt and pepper kept many people from starving. There was never enough pepper. Ginger, cloves, cinnamon, and nutmeg were also in high demand. European countries competed to find a sea route to the Indies. In particular, that hunt was for Melaka, the fabled gateway to the Spice Islands. Portugal found that gateway.

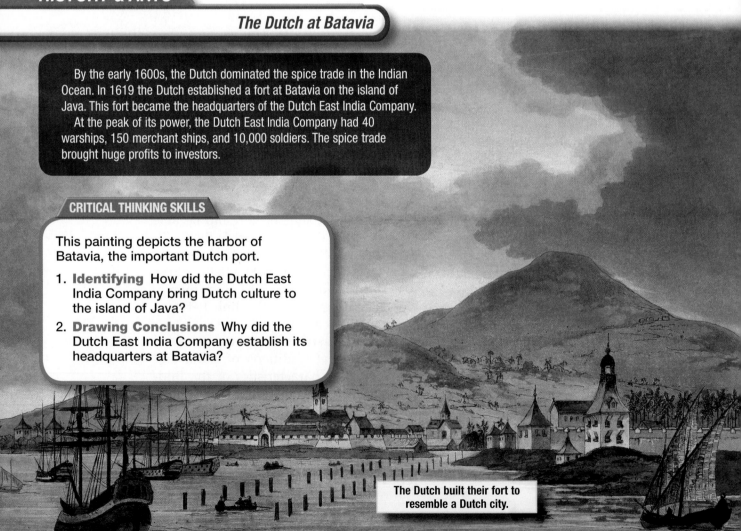

HISTORY & ARTS

The Dutch at Batavia

By the early 1600s, the Dutch dominated the spice trade in the Indian Ocean. In 1619 the Dutch established a fort at Batavia on the island of Java. This fort became the headquarters of the Dutch East India Company.

At the peak of its power, the Dutch East India Company had 40 warships, 150 merchant ships, and 10,000 soldiers. The spice trade brought huge profits to investors.

CRITICAL THINKING SKILLS

This painting depicts the harbor of Batavia, the important Dutch port.

1. **Identifying** How did the Dutch East India Company bring Dutch culture to the island of Java?
2. **Drawing Conclusions** Why did the Dutch East India Company establish its headquarters at Batavia?

The Dutch built their fort to resemble a Dutch city.

When Vasco da Gama and his crew came ashore at Calicut in 1498, they shouted, "For Christ and spices!" The voyage's purpose was twofold: conversion and trade. More important were the spices. In 1511, the Portuguese seized Melaka and soon occupied the **Moluccas.** Known to Europeans as the Spice Islands, the Moluccas were the main source of spices that first attracted the Portuguese to the Indian Ocean.

The Portuguese lacked the military and financial resources to **impose** their authority over broad areas. They set up small settlements along the coast and used them as trading posts during travel to and from the Spice Islands.

A Shift in Power

The situation changed with the arrival of the English and **Dutch** (Netherlands) traders, who were better financed than the Portuguese. The shift in power began in the early 1600s when the Dutch seized a Portuguese fort in the Moluccas and gradually pushed the Portuguese out of the spice trade.

During the next 50 years, the Dutch occupied most Portuguese coastal forts along the trade routes throughout the Indian Ocean. They drove the English traders out of the spice market. England was left with a single port on the southern coast of **Sumatra.**

The Dutch also began to consolidate their political and military control over the entire area. They established a fort on the island of **Java** at Batavia in 1619 to protect their possessions. Gradually the Dutch brought the entire island under their control and closed access to the Spice Islands.

Impact on the Mainland

By the early seventeenth century, other European nations had begun to compete actively for trade and missionary privileges in Southeast Asia. The arrival of the Europeans had less impact on mainland Southeast Asia. In general, the **mainland states** (part of the continent, as distinguished from peninsulas or offshore islands) were able to unite and drive the Europeans out.

Why were the mainland states better able to resist the European challenge than were the states in the Malay Peninsula and the Indonesian archipelago? The mainland states of Burma, Thailand, and Vietnam had begun to define themselves as distinct political entities. They had strong monarchies that resisted foreign intrusion.

In the non-mainland states, there was less political unity. Moreover, these states were victims of their own resources. The spice trade there was enormously profitable. European merchants and rulers were determined to gain control of the sources of the spices.

✓ **Reading Check** **Evaluating** Why were Europeans so interested in Southeast Asia?

Vocabulary
1. **Explain** the significance of: Khmer, network, Philippines, bureaucracy, Moluccas, impose, Dutch, Sumatra, Java, mainland states.

Main Ideas
2. **Explain** how the sultanate at Melaka impacted the Malay Peninsula and the Indonesian archipelago.

3. **Describe** the four types of political systems that developed in Southeast Asia by using a chart like the one below.

Region	Political System

4. **Specify** why the mainland states were better able than the non-mainland states to resist the Europeans.

Critical Thinking
5. **The BIG Idea** **Evaluating** What advantages did Dutch traders have in the struggle to control the spice trade?

6. **Comparing** From a religious point of view, how were the rulers under the four styles of monarchy seen by their subjects?

7. **Analyzing Visuals** Examine the painting on page 292. How does the artist capture the Dutch influence on the island of Java? What elements can you identify that are Javanese?

Writing About History
8. **Expository Writing** Suppose that you are a Portuguese merchant trying to establish trade relations with Southeast Asia. Write a letter to the authorities in Portugal explaining the particular difficulties you are encountering in Southeast Asia.

History ONLINE

For help with the concepts in this section of *Glencoe World History—Modern Times*, go to glencoe.com and click Study Central.

Kabuki: A New World of Entertainment

Kabuki, the Japanese theatrical art form that combines drama, dance, and music, has been popular since its beginning in 1603. Its unconventional and exciting style offered a welcome diversion from the worries and confusion brought about by changes to Japanese culture and society during the early years of the Tokugawa Era. An established art form by the 1700s, Kabuki and its professional class of male actors performed historical and contemporary plays, entertaining all members of society—from common townspeople to high-ranking nobles.

Throughout the history of Kabuki, families of male actors have become famous for performing specific male and female roles, passing on their acting traditions from one generation to the next.

Kabuki actors enter and exit the stage on the *hanamichi*, a raised path that extends from the back of the theater, through the audience, and to the left-hand side of the stage. In one type of stylized movement, called *roppō*, the actor exits the stage in a series of leaps.

COSTUMES AND MAKEUP

Among Kabuki's many unique elements are magnificent costumes, striking makeup, and a remarkable variety of wigs. The colors of face makeup and differences in wig styles are used to symbolize characters' traits. For example, bold red lines express a character's positive traits, such as strength or virtue. The color blue expresses negative traits, such as jealousy or wickedness. A wig styled so that the hair stands on end expresses a character's feelings of rage.

One of the most important dance poses occurs at a climactic moment, when the action of the play stops, and the leading actor strikes a fixed pose—called *mie*.

Behind a screen, musicians play instruments to create melodies and sound effects, such as wind or falling snow. A three-stringed instrument called a *shamisen* creates the music most associated with Kabuki.

The seats on the right-hand side of the stage are reserved for audience members of high rank. This is the reason why actors make their entrances by the *hanamichi* from the left-hand side of the stage.

In the Tokugawa Era, Kabuki performances stretched from dawn to dusk. The audience bustled with spectators coming and going and the serving of meals.

A FAMOUS HISTORICAL PLAY

One of the most famous Kabuki historical plays is *Kanadehon Chūshingura,* which was first performed on stage in 1748. The subject of the play centers on an actual incident—an act of revenge taken by a group of samurai warriors—that occurred in the early 1700s. Government officials in the Tokugawa Era, however, forbid the dramatization of real events that involved the upper classes or military. To avoid censorship, the events of the play were set in an earlier time.

ANALYZING VISUALS

1. **Comparing** How are costumes, makeup, and music used in today's plays and movies to communicate mood or give clues about a character's nature? Give examples.

2. **Analyzing** How do today's dramatic art forms comment on political or social events in contemporary society?

STUDY TO GO You can study anywhere, anytime by downloading quizzes and flash cards to your PDA from glencoe.com.

CHINESE WORKERS PACKING TEA

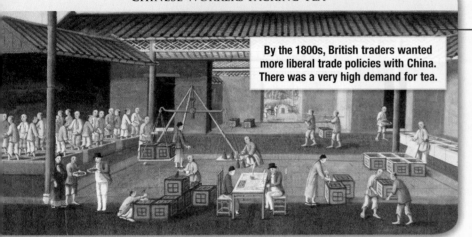

By the 1800s, British traders wanted more liberal trade policies with China. There was a very high demand for tea.

CHINA

- During the Ming dynasty, China sponsored voyages of exploration and made contact with the West.
- Qing rulers restricted trade with Europeans.
- By the late 1700s, China experienced growth in trade and manufacturing.
- Arts, architecture, and literature flourished during the Ming and Qing dynasties.

JAPAN AND KOREA

- Three powerful leaders unified Japan.
- At first Japan welcomed European traders, but later forced them to leave.
- Under Tokugawa rule, the Japanese class system became rigid while trade, industry, and the arts flourished.
- Korea tried to remain isolated, yet eventually became subject to China.

INSIDE A KABUKI THEATER

The theater and other arts grew very popular during Tokugawa rule in Japan.

THE SPICE TRADE IN THE MOLUCCAS

Spices were highly valued as flavorings, medicines, and preservatives.

SOUTHEAST ASIA
Trade in the Spice Era

- Seeking spices, Muslim merchants entered the Malay Peninsula and Indonesia.
- The religion, politics, and economics of the region were affected by the spice trade.
- European countries competed to control the spice trade.
- The Netherlands eventually gained control and closed access to the Moluccas (Spice Islands).

STANDARDIZED TEST PRACTICE

TEST-TAKING **TIP**

If a test question presents a map, make sure you carefully look at the map for information before you try to answer the question.

Reviewing Vocabulary

Directions: Choose the word or words that best complete the sentence.

1. Commercial capitalism refers to _____.
   A a nonprofit governmental agency
   B real estate that is used for business purposes
   C a private business that is based on profit
   D a nonprofit private business

2. The Tokugawa shogun controlled a daimyo by a _____ system.
   A social contract
   B democratic
   C serf
   D hostage

3. What was the Manchu pigtail called?
   A A barb
   B A queue
   C A braid
   D A kimono

4. A bureaucracy is _____.
   A a body of nonelected government officials
   B a piece of furniture with drawers for storage
   C an agency of private business individuals
   D a body of elected government officials

Reviewing Main Ideas

Directions: Choose the best answers to the following questions.

Section 1 *(pp. 274–279)*

5. The voyages of Zheng He took place under which dynasty?
   A Zicheng
   B Han
   C Ming
   D Qing

6. During whose reign did the efforts of Christian missionaries reach their height?
   A Qianlong
   B Ming Hong Wu
   C Yong Le
   D Kangxi

7. According to Emperor Qianlong, China did not have a need for what product(s) from England?
   A Manufactured goods
   B Diplomats
   C Tea
   D Porcelain

Section 2 *(pp. 280–283)*

8. Which of the following is a true statement about society in Qing China?
   A Women could legally inherit property.
   B The family was more important than the individual.
   C Aging parents had to support themselves.
   D Women often pursued government jobs.

Need Extra Help?								
If You Missed Questions . . .	1	2	3	4	5	6	7	8
Go to Page . . .	280	286	277	292	274	278	279	281

 GO ON

9. Which novel is considered by many to be the first realistic social novel?

  A *The Dream of the Red Chamber*

  B *The Imperial City*

  C *The Golden Lotus*

  D *The Imperial Chamber*

Section 3 *(pp. 284–289)*

10. Who was the first great unifier of sixteenth-century Japan?

  A Oda Nobunaga

  B Oda Osaka

  C Toyotomi Hideyoshi

  D Tokugawa Ieyasu

11. In the Japanese social hierarchy, which group was above the warrior class?

  A *Ronin*

  B Artisan class

  C *Eta*

  D Imperial families

Section 4 *(pp. 290–293)*

12. By which name did Europeans know the Moluccas?

  A Porcelain Islands

  B Spice Islands

  C Hawaiian Islands

  D Enchanted Islands

13. Which style of kingship was rooted in the political traditions of India?

  A Christian

  B Islamic

  C Javanese

  D Vietnamese

Critical Thinking

Directions: Choose the best answers to the following questions.

14. Why did the Tokugawa shogunate require the families of the daimyo to live in Edo?

  A To ensure the daimyo's loyalty to the shogun

  B To increase the members of the warrior class

  C To encourage trade in the city

  D To discourage peasant revolts

Base your answer to question 15 on the map below and on your knowledge of world history.

15. Where did the Dutch establish a fort in 1619 to help them control the spice trade?

  A Melaka

  B Batavia

  C Manila

  D Bangkok

16. How did Qing rulers win support from the Chinese?

  A Allowed the Chinese to adopt Qing dress and hairstyles

  B Formed the Chinese into military units called "banners"

  C Provided the Chinese with large landholdings

  D Brought the Chinese into the imperial administration

Need Extra Help?								
If You Missed Questions . . .	9	10	11	12	13	14	15	16
Go to Page . . .	283	284	287	293	291	286	293	277

17. What was a distinctive characteristic of Korean culture that developed under the Yi dynasty?

A Kabuki

B The extended family

C Hangul

D Urban fiction

Analyze the chart and answer the question that follows. Base your answer on the chart and on your knowledge of world history.

Major Explorers

Explorer	Date of Exploration	Territories Visited
Marco Polo	Late 1200s	Asia
Zheng He	1405–1433	Southeast Asia, west coast of India, East Africa
Bartholomeu Dias	1488	Cape of Good Hope
Christopher Columbus	1492	Bahamas, Cuba, Hispaniola
Vasco da Gama	1498	India
John Cabot	1497	New England coastline
Amerigo Vespucci	1499	South American coast
Pedro Cabral	1500	Brazil
Afonso de Albuquerque	1511	Melaka

18. Which explorer may have been the first to visit the region where the Spice Islands (Moluccas) are located?

A Afonso de Albuquerque

B Zheng He

C Vasco da Gama

D Bartholomeu Dias

Document-Based Questions

Directions: Analyze the document and answer the short-answer questions that follow the document.

In 1793 Lord George Macartney led a British mission to Beijing seeking to increase trade between his country and China. Macartney expected to impress the emperor with the Western trade goods he brought with him.

> *King George III wrote the following in a letter to the Chinese emperor:*
> *"… No doubt the exchange of goods between nations far apart tends to their mutual convenience, industry, and wealth."*
>
> *After the meeting, Emperor Qianlong wrote the following to King George III:*
> *"… there is nothing we lack. We have never set much store on strange or ingenious objects, nor do we need any more of your country's manufactures."*

19. Compare the attitudes of the British and Chinese toward trade between their countries.

20. Explain how the economies of China and Britain developed differently due to their attitudes toward trade with other countries.

Extended Response

21. Describe the isolationist periods of China, Japan, and Korea. Discuss their reasons for isolation.

History ONLINE

For additional test practice, use Self-Check Quizzes— Chapter 9 at glencoe.com.

Need Extra Help?					
If You Missed Questions . . .	17	18	19	20	21
Go to Page . . .	289	275	279	279	279

STOP

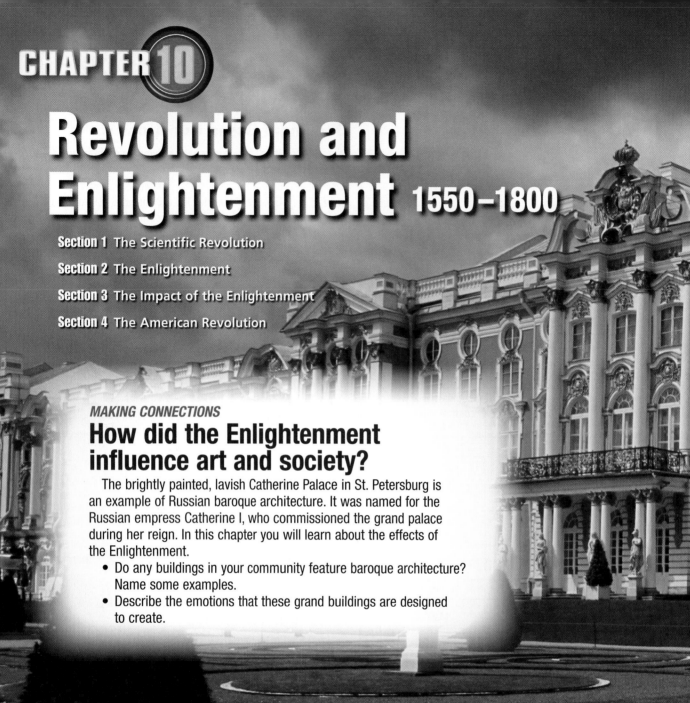

CHAPTER 10

Revolution and Enlightenment 1550–1800

Section 1 The Scientific Revolution

Section 2 The Enlightenment

Section 3 The Impact of the Enlightenment

Section 4 The American Revolution

MAKING CONNECTIONS

How did the Enlightenment influence art and society?

The brightly painted, lavish Catherine Palace in St. Petersburg is an example of Russian baroque architecture. It was named for the Russian empress Catherine I, who commissioned the grand palace during her reign. In this chapter you will learn about the effects of the Enlightenment.

- Do any buildings in your community feature baroque architecture? Name some examples.
- Describe the emotions that these grand buildings are designed to create.

EUROPE,
NORTH AMERICA,
AND INDIA ▶

1543
Copernicus publishes his proposal of a sun-centered universe

1633
Galileo's teachings are condemned by the Church

1550   1600   1650

THE WORLD ▶

1566
Süleyman I dies

1636
Manchus invade Korea

1702
First daily
newspaper
is printed
in London

1756
The Seven
Years' War
begins

1776
American colonies declare
independence from Britain

1700　　　　**1750**　　　　**1800**

1795
Rule of Emperor
Qianlong ends

FOLDABLES™
Study Organizer

Organizing Make a
Four-Door Book to orga-
nize significant facts on
astronomy, medicine and
chemistry, Descartes,
and the scientific method
during the Scientific
Revolution.

Revolution in Astronomy

Breakthroughs in Medicine and Chemistry

Descartes and Reason

The Scientific Method

History ONLINE
Chapter Overview—Visit <u>glencoe.com</u> to preview Chapter 10.

The Scientific Revolution

GUIDE TO READING

The BIG Idea
New Technologies The Scientific Revolution gave Europeans a new way to view humankind's place in the universe.

Content Vocabulary
- geocentric *(p. 304)*
- heliocentric *(p. 304)*
- universal law of gravitation *(p. 305)*
- rationalism *(p. 309)*
- scientific method *(p. 309)*
- inductive reasoning *(p. 309)*

Academic Vocabulary
- philosopher *(p. 302)*
- sphere *(p. 304)*

People and Places
- Nicolaus Copernicus *(p. 304)*
- Johannes Kepler *(p. 304)*
- Galileo Galilei *(p. 304)*
- Isaac Newton *(p. 305)*
- Margaret Cavendish *(p. 307)*
- Maria Winkelmann *(p. 307)*
- René Descartes *(p. 308)*
- Francis Bacon *(p. 309)*

Reading Strategy
Summarizing Information As you read, use a table like the one below to chart the contributions of Copernicus, Kepler, Galileo, and Newton to a new concept of the universe.

| Copernicus | |
| Kepler | |

Of all the changes that swept Europe in the sixteenth and seventeenth centuries, the most widely influential was the Scientific Revolution. We often associate this revolution with the various scientific and technological changes made during this time. However, the Scientific Revolution was also about the changes in the way Europeans looked at themselves and their world.

Causes of the Scientific Revolution

MAIN IDEA The development of new technology and scientific theories became the foundation of the Scientific Revolution.

HISTORY & YOU How would you feel if you had to share the school's only textbook with everyone in your school? Learn how new tools such as the printing press contributed to scientific knowledge.

In the Middle Ages, many educated Europeans took great interest in the world around them. However, these "natural **philosophers,**" as medieval scientists were known, did not make observations of the natural world. Instead they relied on a few ancient authorities—especially Aristotle—for their scientific knowledge. During the fifteenth and sixteenth centuries, a number of changes occurred that caused the natural philosophers to abandon their old views and to develop new ones.

Impact of the Renaissance

Renaissance humanists had mastered Greek as well as Latin. These language skills gave them access to newly discovered works by Ptolemy (TAH•luh•mee), Archimedes, and Plato. These writings made it obvious that some ancient thinkers had disagreed with Aristotle and other accepted authorities of the Middle Ages.

New Technology and Mathematics

Other developments also encouraged new ways of thinking. Technical problems that required careful observation and accurate measurements, such as calculating the amount of weight that ships could hold, served to stimulate scientific activity. Then, too, the invention of new instruments, such as the telescope and microscope, made fresh scientific discoveries possible. Above all, the printing press helped spread new ideas quickly and easily.

Mathematics played a key role in the scientific achievements of the sixteenth and seventeenth centuries. François Viète, a French

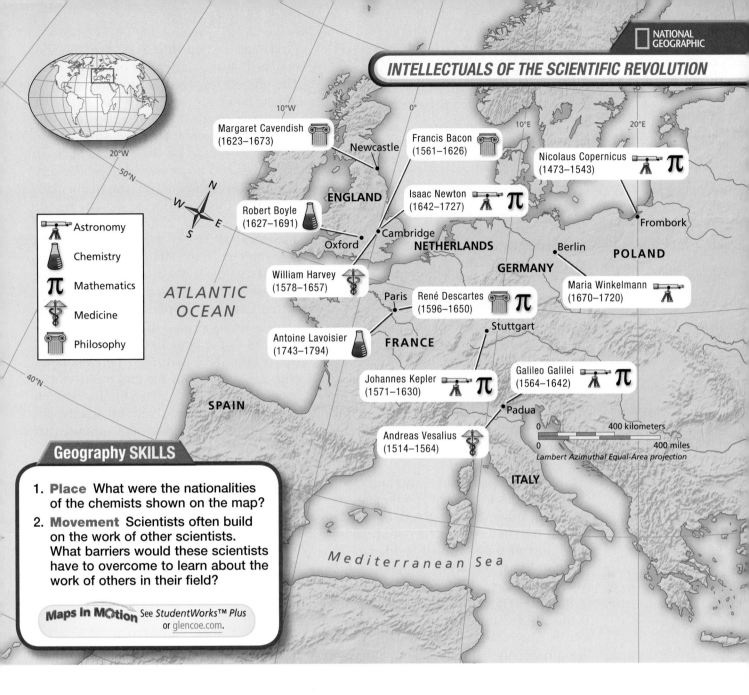

INTELLECTUALS OF THE SCIENTIFIC REVOLUTION

Margaret Cavendish
(1623–1673)

Francis Bacon
(1561–1626)

Nicolaus Copernicus
(1473–1543)

Newcastle

ENGLAND

Isaac Newton
(1642–1727)

Frombork

Robert Boyle
(1627–1691)

Cambridge

Oxford

NETHERLANDS

Berlin

POLAND

GERMANY

William Harvey
(1578–1657)

Paris

René Descartes
(1596–1650)

Maria Winkelmann
(1670–1720)

ATLANTIC
OCEAN

Antoine Lavoisier
(1743–1794)

Stuttgart

FRANCE

Johannes Kepler
(1571–1630)

Galileo Galilei
(1564–1642)

SPAIN

Padua

400 kilometers

400 miles

Lambert Azimuthal Equal-Area projection

Andreas Vesalius
(1514–1564)

ITALY

Mediterranean Sea

Legend

- Astronomy
- Chemistry
- π Mathematics
- Medicine
- Philosophy

Geography SKILLS

1. **Place** What were the nationalities of the chemists shown on the map?
2. **Movement** Scientists often build on the work of other scientists. What barriers would these scientists have to overcome to learn about the work of others in their field?

Maps In MOtion See *StudentWorks™ Plus* or glencoe.com.

lawyer, was among the first to use letters to represent unknown quantities. He applied this algebraic method to geometry and laid the foundation for the invention of trigonometry. Simon Stevin, a Flemish engineer, introduced the decimal system. John Napier of Scotland invented a table of logarithms. The work of both Stevin and Napier made it much easier to make the calculations critical to math problems.

The study of mathematics was promoted in the Renaissance by the rediscovery of the works of ancient mathematicians. Nicolaus Copernicus, Johannes Kepler, Galileo Galilei, and Isaac Newton were all great mathematicians who believed that the secrets of nature were written in the language of mathematics. After studying, and sometimes discarding, the ideas of the ancient mathematicians, these intellectuals developed new theories that became the foundation of the Scientific Revolution. With the advance of mathematics—what we now know as algebra, trigonometry, and geometry—it became much easier for scientists to demonstrate the proof of abstract theories with clear, logical evidence.

✓ Reading Check **Evaluating** What role did mathematics play in the Scientific Revolution?

Scientific Breakthroughs

MAIN IDEA Scientific discoveries expanded knowledge about the universe and the human body.

HISTORY & YOU What if you discovered another planet just like Earth? Learn about the stunning discoveries scientists made about the universe.

During the Scientific Revolution, discoveries in astronomy led to a new conception of the universe. Breakthroughs advanced medical knowledge and launched the field of chemistry as well.

The Ptolemaic System

Ptolemy, who lived in the A.D. 100s, was the greatest astronomer of antiquity. Using Ptolemy's ideas, as well as those of Aristotle and of Christianity, philosophers of the Middle Ages constructed a model of the universe known later as the Ptolemaic (TAH•luh•MAY•ihk) system. This system is **geocentric** because it places Earth at the center of the universe.

In the Ptolemaic system, the universe is seen as a series of concentric **spheres**—one inside the other. Earth is fixed, or motionless, at the center. The heavenly bodies—pure orbs of light—are embedded in the crystal-like, transparent spheres, which rotate about Earth. The moon is embedded in the first sphere, Mercury in the second, Venus in the third, and the sun in the fourth. The rotation of the spheres makes these heavenly bodies rotate about Earth and move in relation to one another.

The tenth sphere in the Ptolemaic system is the "prime mover." This sphere moves itself and gives motion to the other spheres. Beyond the tenth sphere is Heaven, where God resides. God was at one end of the universe, then, and humans were at the center.

Copernicus and Kepler

In May 1543, **Nicolaus Copernicus,** a native of Poland, published his famous book, *On the Revolutions of the Heavenly Spheres.* Copernicus, a mathematician, thought that his **heliocentric,** or sun-centered, conception of the universe offered a more accurate explanation than did the Ptolemaic system. In his system, the sun, not Earth, was at the center of the universe. The planets revolved around the sun. The moon, however, revolved around Earth. Moreover, according to Copernicus, the apparent movement of the sun around Earth was caused by the rotation of Earth on its axis and its journey around the sun.

Johannes Kepler, a German mathematician, took the next step in destroying the Ptolemaic system. Kepler used detailed astronomical data to arrive at his laws of planetary motion. His observations confirmed that the sun was at the center of the universe and also added new information. In his first law, Kepler showed that the planets' orbits around the sun were not circular, as Copernicus had thought. Rather, the orbits were elliptical (egg-shaped), with the sun toward the end of the ellipse instead of at the center. This finding, known as Kepler's First Law, contradicted the circular orbits and crystal-like spheres that were central to the Ptolemaic system.

Galileo's Discoveries

Scientists could now think in terms of planets revolving around the sun in elliptical orbits. Important questions remained unanswered, however. What are the planets made of? How does one explain motion in the universe? An Italian scientist answered the first question.

Galileo Galilei taught mathematics. He was the first European to make regular observations of the heavens using a telescope. With this tool, Galileo made a remarkable series of discoveries: mountains on Earth's moon, four moons revolving around Jupiter, and sunspots.

Galileo's observations seemed to destroy yet another aspect of the Ptolemaic conception. Heavenly bodies had been seen as pure orbs of light. They now appeared to be composed of material substance, just as Earth was.

Galileo's discoveries, published in *The Starry Messenger* in 1610, did more to make Europeans aware of the new view of the universe than did the works of Copernicus and Kepler. But in the midst of his newfound fame, Galileo found himself under suspicion by the Catholic Church.

The Church ordered Galileo to abandon the Copernican idea, which threatened the Church's entire conception of the universe. In the Copernican view, humans were no longer at the center of the universe; God was no longer in a specific place.

In spite of the Church's position, by the 1630s and 1640s, most astronomers had accepted the heliocentric conception of the universe. However, motion in the universe had not been explained. The ideas of Copernicus, Kepler, and Galileo had yet to be tied together. An Englishman—Isaac Newton— would make this connection; he is considered the greatest genius of the Scientific Revolution.

Newton's View of the Universe

Born in 1642, Isaac Newton showed few signs of brilliance until he attended Cambridge University. Later, he became a professor of mathematics at the university and wrote his major work, *Mathematical Principles of Natural Philosophy.* This work is known simply as the *Principia,* from a shortened form of its Latin title.

In the *Principia,* Newton defined the three laws of motion that govern the planetary bodies, as well as objects on Earth. Crucial to his whole argument was the **universal law of gravitation.** This law explains why the planetary bodies continue their elliptical orbits about the sun. The law states, in mathematical terms, that every object in the universe is attracted to every other object by a force called gravity. This one universal law, mathematically proved, could explain all motion in the universe.

At the same time, Newton's ideas created a new picture of the universe. It was now seen as one huge, regulated, uniform machine that worked according to natural laws. Newton's world-machine concept dominated the modern worldview until the twentieth century. Albert Einstein's concept of relativity would give a new picture of the universe.

OPPOSING VIEWPOINTS

Faith vs. Science

PRIMARY SOURCE 1

Cardinal Bellarmine argues that truth lies in the Holy Scriptures.

… But to want to affirm that the sun really is fixed in the center of the heavens and only revolves around itself … and that the earth … revolves … around the sun, is a very dangerous thing … by injuring our holy faith and rendering the Holy Scriptures false.

… [T]he holy Fathers … all agree in explaining literally that the sun is in the heavens and moves swiftly around the earth. . . . Now consider whether … the Church could encourage giving to Scripture a sense contrary to the holy Fathers. . . .

—**Cardinal Bellarmine, a leader of the Roman Catholic Church, April 12, 1615**

PRIMARY SOURCE 2

Galileo argues that the Church should reinterpret Scriptural truths if they conflict with scientific truths.

… I hold the sun to be situated motionless in the center of the revolution of the celestial orbs while the earth revolves about the sun. . . . [T]hese men [opponents] have resolved to fabricate [construct] a shield for their fallacies [mistakes] out of . . . . the authority of the Bible. These they apply with little judgment to the refutation [disproving] of arguments that they do not understand and have not even listened to. . . . [B]efore a physical proposition is condemned it must be shown to be . . . . false.

—**Galileo Galilei, scientist and mathematician, 1615**

DOCUMENT-BASED QUESTIONS

1. **Drawing Conclusions** Why did Galileo's ideas represent a threat to the Catholic Church?
2. **Explaining** What did Galileo suggest that his opponents should do before dismissing his ideas?

TURNING POINT — THE SCIENTIFIC REVOLUTION

Rediscovered in the thirteenth century, the ideas of ancient philosophers, such as Aristotle and Plato, dominated European thought until the sixteenth century. Then scientists such as Copernicus, Kepler, Galileo, and Newton set the Western world on a new path known as the Scientific Revolution. In addition to observing the natural world, as the ancient philosophers did, they designed experiments to test possible explanations for what they observed.

In the eighteenth century, a group of intellectuals applied this scientific method to help understand other aspects of life. Hoping to improve society, these thinkers began what came to be called the Age of Enlightenment.

The Scientific Revolution and the Enlightenment created a new view of the universe and society in the 1600s and 1700s.

Galileo (1564–1642): confirmed the heliocentric universe; tied laws of planetary motion to motion on Earth

VIEWS OF ASTRONOMY

	ANCIENT PHILOSOPHERS	SCIENTISTS OF THE SCIENTIFIC REVOLUTION
Universe	Earth-centered	Sun-centered
Stars and planets	Pure orbs of light; move in perfect circles	Made of material substance; move in elliptical orbits
Motion	All motion caused by a prime mover (supreme being)	Gravity governs motion of objects on Earth and of planetary bodies
Method of Investigation	Observation of natural events; experiments alter natural conditions and thus would not reveal true nature of things	Observation of natural events; conduct experiments to test possible explanations

CRITICAL THINKING SKILLS

1. **Explaining** Why did the ancient philosophers object to experiments?
2. **Analyzing** In what ways did the Scientific Revolution serve as a turning point in history?

Breakthroughs in Medicine

The teachings of Galen, a Greek physician in the A.D. 100s, dominated medicine in the Late Middle Ages. Relying on animal, rather than human, dissection to picture human anatomy, Galen was wrong in many instances.

In the sixteenth century, a revolution in medicine began. Andreas Vesalius and William Harvey added to the understanding of human anatomy. By dissecting human bodies at the University of Padua, Vesalius accurately described the individual organs and general structure of the human body. William Harvey showed that the heart—not the liver, as Galen had thought—was the beginning point for the circulation of blood. He also proved that the same blood flows through the veins and arteries and makes a complete circuit through the body.

Breakthroughs in Chemistry

Robert Boyle was one of the first scientists to conduct controlled experiments in chemistry. His work on the properties of gases led to Boyle's Law—the volume of a gas varies with the pressure exerted on it. In the eighteenth century, Antoine Lavoisier invented a system for naming chemical elements still used today. Many people consider him the founder of modern chemistry.

✓ **Reading Check** **Explaining** How was Vesalius able to add to knowledge of anatomy?

Women's Contributions

MAIN IDEA Women scientists faced obstacles to practicing what they had learned.

HISTORY & YOU Do you recall how the Chinese and Japanese societies restricted the roles of women? Read to learn how two European women contributed to science.

Although scholarship was considered the exclusive domain of men, many women contributed to the Scientific Revolution. For example, Margaret Cavendish, a philosopher, and Maria Winkelmann, an astronomer, helped advance science through their writings and their work.

Margaret Cavendish

One of the most prominent female scientists of the seventeenth century, **Margaret Cavendish,** came from an English aristocratic family. Tutored at home, she studied subjects considered suitable for girls of proper upbringing—music, dancing, reading, and needlework. She was not formally educated in the sciences. However, Cavendish wrote a number of works on scientific matters, including *Observations Upon Experimental Philosophy.*

In her work, Cavendish was especially critical of the growing belief that humans, through science, were the masters of nature:

PRIMARY SOURCE

"We have no power at all over natural causes and effects . . . for man is but a small part, his powers are but particular actions of Nature, and he cannot have a supreme and absolute power."

—Margaret Cavendish, 1623–1673

Cavendish published under her own name at a time when most female writers had to publish anonymously. Her contribution to philosophy is widely recognized today; however, many intellectuals of the time did not take her work seriously.

Maria Winkelmann

In Germany, many of the women who were involved in science were astronomers.

These women had received the opportunity to become astronomers from working in family observatories where their fathers or husbands trained them. Between 1650 and 1710, women made up 14 percent of all German astronomers.

The most famous of the female astronomers in Germany was **Maria Winkelmann.** She received training in astronomy from a self-taught astronomer. When she married Gottfried Kirch, Prussia's foremost astronomer, she became his assistant and began to practice astronomy.

Winkelmann made some original contributions to astronomy, including the discovery of a comet. Her husband described the discovery:

PRIMARY SOURCE

"Early in the morning (about 2:00 A.M.) the sky was clear and starry. Some nights before, I had observed a variable star, and my wife (as I slept) wanted to find and see it for herself. In so doing, she found a comet in the sky. At which time she woke me, and I found that it was indeed a comet. . . . I was surprised that I had not seen it the night before."

—Gottfried Kirch, Winkelmann's astronomer husband

When her husband died, Winkelmann applied for a position as assistant astronomer at the Berlin Academy. She was highly qualified, but as a woman—with no university degree—she was denied the post. Members of the Berlin Academy feared that they would set a bad example by hiring a woman. "Mouths would gape," they said, by which they meant that members of the academy would be appalled.

Winkelmann's problems with the Berlin Academy reflect the obstacles women faced in being accepted as scientists. Such work was considered to be chiefly for males. In the view of most people in the seventeenth century, a life devoted to any kind of scholarship was at odds with the domestic duties women were expected to perform.

✓ **Reading Check** **Summarizing** What did Margaret Cavendish and Maria Winkelmann contribute to the Scientific Revolution?

Philosophy and Reason

MAIN IDEA Scientists came to believe that reason is the chief source of knowledge.

HISTORY & YOU Your computer stores much information, but can it use reason? Read to learn how human reason became central to the search for knowledge.

New conceptions of the universe brought about by the Scientific Revolution strongly influenced the Western view of humankind.

Descartes and Rationalism

Nowhere is this influence more evident than in the work of the seventeenth-century French philosopher **René Descartes** (day•KAHRT). Descartes began by thinking and writing about the doubt and uncertainty that seemed to be everywhere in the confusion of the seventeenth century. He ended with a philosophy that dominated Western thought until the twentieth century.

The starting point for Descartes's new system was doubt. In his most famous work, *Discourse on Method,* written in 1637, Descartes decided to set aside all that he had learned and to begin again. One fact seemed to him to be beyond doubt—his own existence:

PRIMARY SOURCE

"But I immediately became aware that while I was thus disposed to think that all was false, it was absolutely necessary that I who thus thought should be something; and noting that this truth I think, therefore I am, was so steadfast and so assured . . . I concluded that I might without scruple accept it as being the first principle of the philosophy I was seeking."

—René Descartes, *Discourse on Method*

Descartes emphasized the importance of his own mind. He asserted that he would accept only those things that his reason said were true.

From his first principle—"I think, therefore I am"—Descartes used his reason to

SCIENCE, TECHNOLOGY, & SOCIETY

The Scientific Method

Bacon's "guarded" method began a systematic approach to collecting and analyzing evidence that today is known as the scientific method.

"The present discoveries in science are such as lie immediately beneath the surface of common notions [beliefs]. It is necessary, however, to penetrate the more secret and remote parts of nature, in order to abstract both notions and axioms [principles] from things, by a more certain and guarded [careful] method."

—Francis Bacon, *Novum Organum,* 1620

Flowchart of the Scientific Method

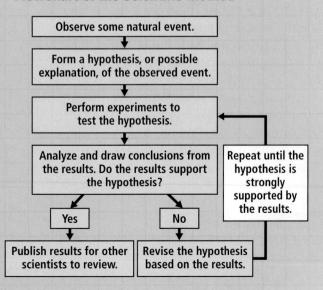

Observe some natural event.

Form a hypothesis, or possible explanation, of the observed event.

Perform experiments to test the hypothesis.

Analyze and draw conclusions from the results. Do the results support the hypothesis?

Repeat until the hypothesis is strongly supported by the results.

Yes — No

Publish results for other scientists to review.

Revise the hypothesis based on the results.

CRITICAL THINKING SKILLS

Scientists carefully review the work of other scientists and test the hypothesis themselves. The scientific community accepts the hypothesis only when the results of a large number of experiments by many scientists support it.

1. **Explaining** What do scientists do when the results of their experiments disagree with their proposed explanation?

2. **Analyzing** How does the scientific method help to arrive at a true explanation of a natural event?

arrive at a second principle. He argued that because "the mind cannot be doubted but the body and material world can, the two must be radically different."

From this idea came the principle of the separation of mind and matter (and of mind and body). Descartes's idea that mind and matter were completely separate allowed scientists to view matter as dead or inert. That is, matter was something that was totally detached from the mind and that could be investigated independently by reason.

Descartes has rightly been called the father of modern **rationalism.** This system of thought is based on the belief that reason is the chief source of knowledge.

Bacon and the Scientific Method

During the Scientific Revolution, people became concerned about how they could best understand the physical world. The result was the creation of the **scientific method**—a systematic procedure for collecting and analyzing evidence. The scientific method was crucial to the evolution of science in the modern world.

The person who developed the scientific method was actually not a scientist. **Francis Bacon** was an English philosopher with few scientific credentials. He believed that scientists should not rely on the ideas of ancient authorities. Instead, they should learn about nature by using **inductive reasoning**—proceeding from the particular to the general.

Before beginning this reasoning, scientists try to free their minds of opinions that might distort the truth. Then they start with detailed facts and proceed toward general principles. From observing natural events, scientists propose hypotheses (theories), or possible explanations, for the events. Then systematic observations and carefully organized experiments to test the hypotheses would lead to correct general principles.

Bacon was clear about what he believed his scientific method could accomplish. He stated that "the true and lawful goal of the sciences is none other than this: that human life be endowed with new discoveries and power." He was much more concerned with practical matters than pure science.

Bacon wanted science to benefit industry, agriculture, and trade. He said, "I am laboring to lay the foundation, not of any sect or doctrine, but of human utility and power."

How would this "human power" be used? Bacon believed it could be used to "conquer nature in action." The control and domination of nature became an important concern of science and the technology that accompanied it.

✓ Reading Check **Summarizing** What are the characteristics of the scientific method?

SECTION **1** **REVIEW**

Vocabulary

1. **Explain** the significance of: philosopher, geocentric, sphere, Nicolaus Copernicus, heliocentric, Johannes Kepler, Galileo Galilei, Isaac Newton, universal law of gravitation, Margaret Cavendish, Maria Winkelmann, René Descartes, rationalism, scientific method, Francis Bacon, inductive reasoning.

Main Ideas

2. **Summarize** the changes in the fifteenth and sixteenth centuries that helped the natural philosophers develop new views.

3. **Identify** examples of new ideas in the form of scientific discoveries or innovations that appeared during the 1500s and 1600s. Use a diagram like the one below to identify the ideas and the changes they produced.

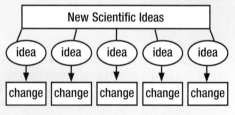

New Scientific Ideas

idea | idea | idea | idea | idea

change | change | change | change | change

4. **Describe** the obstacles that women in the 1600s and 1700s faced in being accepted as scientists.

Critical Thinking

5. **The BIG Idea** **Contrasting** Contrast the Ptolemaic and Copernican universes.

6. **Analyzing** Why did the Catholic Church condemn Galileo's work?

7. **Analyzing Visuals** Examine the painting of Galileo on page 306. Explain why you think the artist chose to pose Galileo as he did.

Writing About History

8. **Expository Writing** Research and write an essay about the contributions of Copernicus, Galileo, Newton, or Cavendish to the Scientific Revolution.

History ONLINE

For help with the concepts in this section of *Glencoe World History— Modern Times,* go to glencoe.com and click Study Central.

The Enlightenment

GUIDE TO READING

The BIG Idea
Ideas, Beliefs, and Values Enlightenment thinkers, or philosophes, believed all institutions should follow natural laws to produce the ideal society.

Content Vocabulary
- philosophe *(p. 312)*
- separation of powers *(p. 312)*
- deism *(p. 312)*
- laissez-faire *(p. 314)*
- social contract *(p. 315)*
- salon *(p. 316)*

Academic Vocabulary
- generation *(p. 312)*
- arbitrary *(p. 315)*

People and Places
- John Locke *(p. 310)*
- Montesquieu *(p. 312)*
- Voltaire *(p. 312)*
- Denis Diderot *(p. 313)*
- Adam Smith *(p. 314)*
- Cesare Beccaria *(p. 314)*
- Jean-Jacques Rousseau *(p. 315)*
- Paris *(p. 315)*
- Mary Wollstonecraft *(p. 315)*
- London *(p. 316)*
- John Wesley *(p. 317)*

Reading Strategy
Summarizing Information As you read, use a diagram like the one below to list some of the main ideas introduced during the Enlightenment.

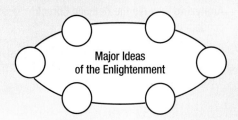

Major Ideas
of the Enlightenment

Applying the scientific method to their physical world, Enlightenment thinkers, or philosophes, reexamined all aspects of life—from government and justice to religion and women's rights. They created a movement that influenced the entire Western world.

Path to the Enlightenment

MAIN IDEA Eighteenth-century intellectuals used the ideas of the Scientific Revolution to reexamine all aspects of life.

HISTORY & YOU Do you think you were born with some knowledge, or did you learn everything you know? Read about John Locke's idea that when each of us is born, the mind is a tabula rasa, or blank slate.

The Enlightenment was an eighteenth-century philosophical movement of intellectuals who were greatly impressed with the achievements of the Scientific Revolution. One of the favorite words of these intellectuals was *reason*. By this, they meant the application of the scientific method to an understanding of all life. They hoped that by using the scientific method, they could make progress toward a better society than the one they had inherited. *Reason, natural law, hope, progress*—these were common words to the thinkers of the Enlightenment. The ideas of the Enlightenment would become a force for reform and eventually revolution.

John Locke

The intellectuals of the Enlightenment were especially influenced by the ideas of two seventeenth-century Englishmen, **John Locke** and Isaac Newton. In his *Essay Concerning Human Understanding*, Locke argued that every person was born with a tabula rasa, or blank mind:

PRIMARY SOURCE

"Let us then suppose the mind to be . . . white paper, void of all characters, without any ideas. How comes it to be furnished? Whence has it all the materials of reason and knowledge? To this I answer, in one word, from experience. . . . Our observation, employed either about external sensible objects or about the internal operations of our minds perceived and reflected on by ourselves, is that which supplies our understanding with all the materials of thinking."

—John Locke, *Essay Concerning Human Understanding*

Locke's ideas suggested that people were molded by the experiences that came through their senses from the surrounding world.

EUROPE AND THE AGE OF ENLIGHTENMENT

Uppsala
Stockholm
St. Petersburg
Glasgow
Edinburgh
Copenhagen
North Sea
Gdańsk
Cambridge
Amsterdam
Berlin
Oxford
Leiden
Warsaw
London
Greenwich
Göttingen
Halle
Leipzig
Paris
Frankfurt
Prague
Kraków
Strasbourg
Munich
Vienna
Geneva
Turin
Padua
Bologna
Pisa
Florence
Corsica
Lisbon
Madrid
Rome
Sardinia

ATLANTIC OCEAN

Sicily

50°N
40°N
10°W
0°
10°E
20°E
30°E

	Academy of Science
	Observatory
	Palace inspired by Versailles
	Publication of scientific or philosophical journals
	University

0   400 kilometers
0   400 miles
Lambert Azimuthal Equal-Area projection

Geography SKILLS

1. **Place** Based on the information given on this map, what did London and Berlin have in common during the Enlightenment?

2. **Regions** Pose and answer a question about the geographic distribution shown on this map.

Enlightenment thinkers began to believe that if environments were changed and people were exposed to the right influences, then people could be changed to create a new—and better—society.

Isaac Newton

The ideas of Isaac Newton also greatly influenced eighteenth-century intellectuals. As you read earlier, Newton believed that the physical world and everything in it was like a giant machine. His "world-machine" operated according to natural laws, which could be uncovered through systematic investigation.

The Enlightenment thinkers reasoned that if Newton was able to discover the natural laws that governed the physical world, then by applying his scientific methods, they would be able to discover the natural laws that governed human society. If all institutions would then follow these natural laws, the result would be an ideal society.

✓**Reading Check** **Explaining** What did Enlightenment thinkers hope to accomplish?

Ideas of the Philosophes

MAIN IDEA The philosophes wanted to create a better society.

HISTORY & YOU Do you remember what a monarchy is? Read to learn about two other forms of government.

The intellectuals of the Enlightenment were known by the French word **philosophe** (FEE•luh•ZAWF), meaning "philosopher." Not all philosophes were French, however, and few were philosophers in the strict sense of the term. They were writers, professors, journalists, economists, and above all, social reformers. They came chiefly from the nobility and the middle class.

Most leaders of the Enlightenment were French, although the English had provided the philosophical inspiration for the movement. It was the French philosophes who affected intellectuals elsewhere and created a movement that influenced the entire Western world.

The Role of Philosophy

To the philosophes, the role of philosophy was to change the world. One writer said that the philosophe is one who "applies himself to the study of society with the purpose of making his kind better and happier." One conducts this study by using reason, or an appeal to facts. A spirit of rational criticism was to be applied to everything, including religion and politics.

The philosophes often disagreed. Spanning almost a century, the Enlightenment evolved over time. Each succeeding **generation** became more radical as it built on the contributions of the previous one. A few people, however, dominated the landscape—Montesquieu (MAHN•tuhs•KYOO), Voltaire, and Diderot (dee•DROH).

Montesquieu

Charles-Louis de Secondat, the baron de **Montesquieu**, was a French noble. His famous work *The Spirit of the Laws* (1748) was a study of governments. In it, Montesquieu used the scientific method to try to find the natural laws that govern the social and political relationships of human beings.

Montesquieu identified three basic kinds of governments: (1) republics, suitable for small states; (2) despotism, appropriate for large states; and (3) monarchies, ideal for moderate-sized states. He used England as an example of a monarchy.

Montesquieu stated that England's government had three branches: the executive (the monarch), the legislative (Parliament), and the judicial (the courts of law). The government functioned through a **separation of powers.** In this separation, the executive, legislative, and judicial powers of the government limit and control each other in a system of checks and balances. By preventing any one person or group from gaining too much power, this system provides the greatest freedom and security for the state.

The system of checks and balances through separation of powers was Montesquieu's most lasting contribution to political thought. Translation of his work into English made it available to American philosophes, who worked his principles into the United States Constitution.

Voltaire

The greatest figure of the Enlightenment was François-Marie Arouet, known simply as **Voltaire.** A Parisian, Voltaire came from a prosperous middle-class family. His numerous writings brought him both fame and wealth.

Voltaire was especially well known for his criticism of Christianity and his strong belief in religious toleration. He fought against religious intolerance in France. In 1763 he penned his *Treatise on Toleration*, in which he reminded governments that "all men are brothers under God."

Throughout his life, Voltaire championed **deism,** an eighteenth-century religious philosophy based on reason and natural law. Deism built on the idea of the Newtonian world-machine. In the Deists' view, a mechanic (God) had created the universe. To Voltaire and most other philosophes, the universe was like a clock. God, the clockmaker, had created it, set it in motion, and allowed it to run without his interference and according to its own natural laws.

Diderot

Denis Diderot went to the University of Paris. His father hoped Denis would pursue a career in law or the Church. He did neither. Instead, he became a writer. He studied and read in many subjects and languages.

Diderot's most famous contribution to the Enlightenment was the *Encyclopedia, or Classified Dictionary of the Sciences, Arts, and Trades,* a 28-volume collection of knowledge that he edited. Published between 1751 and 1772, the *Encyclopedia,* according to Diderot, was to "change the general way of thinking."

The *Encyclopedia* became a weapon against the old French society. Many of its articles attacked religious superstition and supported religious toleration. Others called for social, legal, and political reforms. Sold to doctors, clergymen, teachers, and lawyers, the *Encyclopedia* spread Enlightenment ideas.

✓ **Reading Check** **Stating** What ideas did Montesquieu add to the Enlightenment?

New Social Sciences

MAIN IDEA The belief in logic and reason promoted the beginnings of social sciences.

HISTORY & YOU What do you think is the purpose of punishing criminals? Read to learn about arguments against extreme punishments.

The philosophes, as we have seen, believed that Newton's methods could be used to discover the natural laws underlying all areas of human life. This led to what we would call the social sciences—areas such as economics and political science.

Smith on Economics

The Physiocrats and Scottish philosopher Adam Smith have been viewed as the founders of the modern social science of economics. The Physiocrats, a French group, were interested in identifying the natural economic laws that governed human society. They maintained that if individuals were free to pursue their own economic self-interest, all society would benefit.

PEOPLE in HISTORY

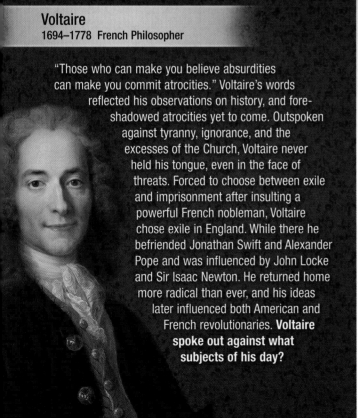

Voltaire
1694–1778 French Philosopher

"Those who can make you believe absurdities can make you commit atrocities." Voltaire's words reflected his observations on history, and foreshadowed atrocities yet to come. Outspoken against tyranny, ignorance, and the excesses of the Church, Voltaire never held his tongue, even in the face of threats. Forced to choose between exile and imprisonment after insulting a powerful French nobleman, Voltaire chose exile in England. While there he befriended Jonathan Swift and Alexander Pope and was influenced by John Locke and Sir Isaac Newton. He returned home more radical than ever, and his ideas later influenced both American and French revolutionaries. **Voltaire spoke out against what subjects of his day?**

Adam Smith
1723–1790 Scottish Economist and Philosopher

"No society can surely be happy, of which the far greater part of the members are poor and miserable." Someone reading this quote might think it originated with an American patriot or a French revolutionary. However, it actually came from Adam Smith, widely regarded as "the father of capitalism." Besides being the architect of the laissez-faire doctrine of government non-interference with commerce, and an opponent of heavy government taxation, Smith was also an outspoken advocate for ethical standards in society. His friends included Voltaire, Benjamin Franklin, and David Hume, three of the late eighteenth century's most revolutionary thinkers. **How did Adam Smith feel about the role of government?**

Laissez-Faire Economics

Mercantilism

A nation's wealth is measured by:
- the amount of gold and silver in its treasury

To increase wealth, government must:
- encourage exports to bring in gold and silver
- restrict imports to avoid draining away gold and silver
- grant monopolies and financial support to local businesses to give them an advantage over foreign competition

Laissez-Faire Economics

A nation's wealth is measured by:
- its annual output of goods and services

To increase wealth, government must:
- impose no restrictions on trade, allowing it to operate freely
- provide no support or monopoly advantages for local businesses, so that competition can occur freely

Adam Smith's *Wealth of Nations* (1776), inspired a major shift in economic theory and practice. In it, he argued that the desire for personal gain drives economic activity and that this leads to competition. He believed that allowing this competition to operate without government interference would benefit society in several ways:

- Prices are kept lower.
- Production is more efficient as businesses reduce costs to increase profit.
- Labor and capital are directed to the most profitable industries.

Unintentionally then, the pursuit of self-interest benefits all of society. In Smith's words:

"Every individual . . . neither intends to promote the public interest, nor knows how much his is promoting it. . . . [H]e intends only his own gain, and he is in this . . . led by an invisible hand to promote and end which was no part of his intention."

CRITICAL THINKING SKILLS

1. **Identifying** According to Adam Smith, why do people produce and sell products?
2. **Making Inferences** What do you think Smith means by "an invisible hand"?

The state, then, should not interrupt the free play of natural economic forces by imposing regulations on the economy. Instead, the state should leave the economy alone. This doctrine became known by its French name, **laissez-faire** (LEH•SAY FEHR), meaning "to let (people) do (what they want)."

The best statement of laissez-faire was made in 1776 by **Adam Smith** in his famous work, *The Wealth of Nations.* Like the Physiocrats, Smith believed that the state should not interfere in economic matters. Indeed, Smith gave to government only three basic roles. First, it should protect society from invasion (the function of the army). Second, the government should defend citizens from injustice (the function of the police). And finally, it should keep up certain public works that private individuals alone could not afford—roads and canals, for example—but which are necessary for social interaction and trade.

Beccaria on Justice

By the eighteenth century, most European states had developed a system of courts to deal with the punishment of crime. Punishments were often cruel. The primary reason for extreme punishments was the need to deter crime in an age when a state's police force was too weak to capture criminals.

One philosophe who proposed a new approach to justice was **Cesare Beccaria.** In his essay *On Crimes and Punishments* (1764), Beccaria argued that punishments should not be exercises in brutality. He also opposed capital punishment. He did not believe that it stopped others from committing crimes. Moreover, it set an example of barbarism: "Is it not absurd, that the laws, which punish murder, should, in order to prevent murder, publicly commit murder themselves?"

✓ Reading Check **Explaining** What is the concept of laissez-faire?

The Spread of Ideas

MAIN IDEA From the upper classes to the middle classes and from salons to pulpits, the ideas of the Enlightenment spread.

HISTORY & YOU How would your life change if you had no way to communicate—no e-mail, no phone? Learn how newspapers and magazines spread Enlightenment ideas.

By the late 1760s, a new generation of philosophes had come to maturity. Ideas about liberty, education, and the condition of women were spread through an increasingly literate society.

The Social Contract

The most famous philosophe of the later Enlightenment was **Jean-Jacques Rousseau** (ru•SOH). The young Rousseau wandered through France and Italy holding various jobs. Eventually he made his way to **Paris,** where he was introduced into the circle of the philosophes. He did not like city life, however, and often withdrew into long periods of solitude.

In his *Discourse on the Origins of the Inequality of Mankind,* Rousseau argued that people had adopted laws and government in order to preserve their private property. In the process, they had become enslaved by government. What, then, should people do to regain their freedom?

In his major work *The Social Contract,* published in 1762, Rousseau presented his concept of the **social contract.** Through a social contract, an entire society agrees to be governed by its general will. Individuals who wish instead to follow their own self-interests must be forced to abide by the general will. "This means nothing less than that [they] will be forced to be free," said Rousseau. Thus, liberty is achieved by being forced to follow what is best for "the general will" because the general will represents what is best for the entire community.

Another important work by Rousseau is *Émile.* Written in the form of a novel, the work is a general discussion "on the education of the natural man." Rousseau argues that education should foster, and not restrict, children's natural instincts.

Unlike many Enlightenment thinkers, Rousseau believed that emotions, as well as reason, were important to human development. He sought a balance between heart and mind, between emotions and reason.

Rousseau did not necessarily practice what he preached. His own children were sent to orphanages, where many children died at a young age. Rousseau also viewed women as being "naturally" different from men: "To fulfill her functions, . . . [a woman] needs a soft life. . . . How much care and tenderness does she need to hold her family together." To Rousseau, women should be educated for their roles as wives and mothers by learning obedience and the nurturing skills that would enable them to provide loving care for their husbands and children. Not everyone in the eighteenth century agreed with Rousseau's views about women, however.

Women's Rights

For centuries, male intellectuals had argued that the nature of women made them inferior to men and made male domination of women necessary. By the eighteenth century, however, female thinkers began to express their ideas about improving the condition of women. **Mary Wollstonecraft,** an English writer, advanced the strongest statement for the rights of women. Many see her as the founder of the modern European and American movements for women's rights.

In *A Vindication of the Rights of Women,* Wollstonecraft identified two problems with the views of many Enlightenment thinkers. She noted that the same people who argued that women must obey men also said that government based on the **arbitrary** power of monarchs over their subjects was wrong. Wollstonecraft pointed out that the power of men over women was equally wrong.

Wollstonecraft further argued that the Enlightenment was based on an ideal of reason in all human beings. Therefore, because women have reason, they are entitled to the same rights as men. Women, Wollstonecraft declared, should have equal rights in education, as well as in economic and political life.

The Growth of Reading

Of great importance to the Enlightenment was the spread of its ideas to the literate elite of European society. Especially noticeable in the eighteenth century was the growth of both publishing and the reading public. The number of titles issued each year by French publishers rose from 300 in 1750 to about 1,600 in the 1780s. Books had previously been aimed at small groups of the educated elite. Now, many books were directed at the new reading public of the middle classes, which included women and urban artisans.

An important aspect of the growth of publishing and reading in the eighteenth century was the development of magazines and newspapers for the general public. In Great Britain, an important center for the new magazines, 25 periodicals were published in 1700, 103 in 1760, and 158 in 1780.

The first daily newspaper was printed in **London** in 1702. Newspapers were relatively cheap and were even provided free in many coffeehouses.

The Salon

Enlightenment ideas were also spread through the salon. **Salons** were the elegant drawing rooms of the wealthy upper class's great urban houses. Invited guests gathered in these salons and took part in conversations that were often centered on the new ideas of the philosophes. The salons brought writers and artists together with aristocrats, government officials, and wealthy middle-class people.

The women who hosted the salons were in a position to sway political opinion and influence literary and artistic taste. For example, Marie-Thérèse de Geoffrin, wife of a wealthy merchant, hosted salons.

INFOGRAPHICS

John Wesley Brings a New Message of Salvation

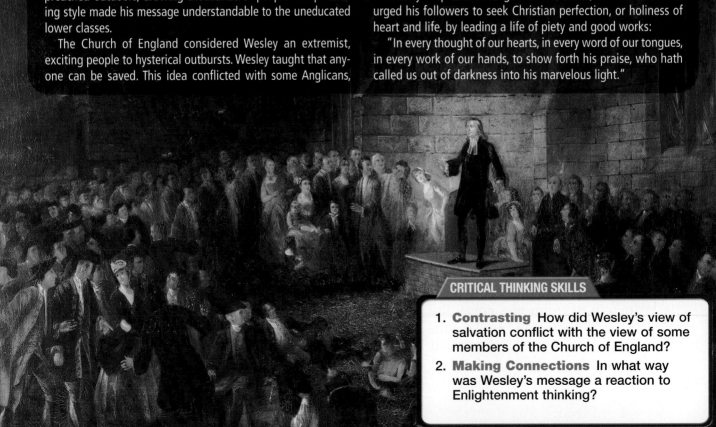

John Wesley (1703–1791), the founder of Methodism, brought religious revival to the people of England. Wesley often preached outdoors, drawing thousands of people. His preaching style made his message understandable to the uneducated lower classes.

The Church of England considered Wesley an extremist, exciting people to hysterical outbursts. Wesley taught that anyone can be saved. This idea conflicted with some Anglicans, who believed that God had already determined who would be saved and who would not.

Wesley emphasized religion of the heart, not the mind. He urged his followers to seek Christian perfection, or holiness of heart and life, by leading a life of piety and good works:

"In every thought of our hearts, in every word of our tongues, in every work of our hands, to show forth his praise, who hath called us out of darkness into his marvelous light."

CRITICAL THINKING SKILLS

1. **Contrasting** How did Wesley's view of salvation conflict with the view of some members of the Church of England?
2. **Making Connections** In what way was Wesley's message a reaction to Enlightenment thinking?

These gatherings at her fashionable home in Paris became the talk of France and of all Europe.

Distinguished foreigners competed to receive invitations to the salons. These gatherings helped spread the ideas of the Enlightenment.

Religion in the Enlightenment

Although many philosophes attacked the Christian churches, most Europeans in the eighteenth century were still Christians. Many people also sought a deeper personal devotion to God.

The Catholic parish church remained an important center of life. How many people went to church regularly is unknown, but 90 to 95 percent of Catholic populations went to mass on Easter Sunday.

After the initial religious fervor that created Protestantism in the sixteenth century, Protestant churches settled into well-established patterns often controlled or influenced by state authorities. Many Protestant churches were lacking in religious enthusiasm. The desire of ordinary Protestants for greater depths of religious experience led to new religious movements.

In England, the most famous new religious and evangelical movement—Methodism—was the work of **John Wesley,** an Anglican minister. Wesley had a mystical experience in which "the gift of God's grace" assured him of salvation. This experience led him to become a missionary to the English people to bring them the "glad tidings" of salvation.

Since many Anglican churches were closed to him, Wesley preached to the masses in open fields, in halls, or in cottages. He preached wherever an assembly could gather. Wesley traveled constantly, generally on horseback, and often preached two or three times a day. He appealed especially to the lower classes. He tried, he said, "to lower religion to the level of the lowest people's capacities."

His sermons often caused people to have conversion experiences. Many converts then joined Methodist societies to do good works. One notable reform they influenced was the abolition of the slave trade in the early 1800s. Christian reformers were also important in the American movement to abolish slavery.

Wesley's Methodism gave the lower and middle classes in English society a sense of purpose and community. Methodists stressed the importance of hard work and spiritual contentment rather than demands for political equality. After Wesley's death, Methodism became a separate Protestant group. Methodism proved that the need for spiritual experience had not been eliminated by the eighteenth-century search for reason.

✓ Reading Check **Evaluating** How did Mary Wollstonecraft use the Enlightenment ideal of reason to advocate rights for women?

Vocabulary

1. **Explain** the significance of: John Locke, philosophe, generation, Montesquieu, separation of powers, Voltaire, deism, Denis Diderot, laissez-faire, Adam Smith, Cesare Beccaria, Jean-Jacques Rousseau, Paris, social contract, Mary Wollstonecraft, arbitrary, London, salon, John Wesley.

Main Ideas

2. **Explain** the influence of John Locke and Isaac Newton on Enlightenment thinkers.

3. **Name** the social classes to which most philosophes belonged.

4. **Identify** factors that helped spread Enlightenment ideas through Europe by using a diagram like the one below.

> Factors that Spread Enlightenment

Critical Thinking

5. **The BIG Idea** **Evaluating** What did Rousseau mean when he stated that if individuals wanted to pursue their own self-interests at the expense of the common good, they "will be forced to be free"? Do you agree or disagree? Why?

6. **Comparing and Contrasting** How are the branches of the U.S. government similar to the branches Montesquieu identified? How are they different?

7. **Analyzing Visuals** Examine the painting of John Wesley on page 316. Explain why the painting shows Wesley preaching outdoors.

Writing About History

8. **Persuasive Writing** Mary Wollstonecraft argued that women are entitled to the same rights as men. Do you believe this to be true? Do you believe women are accorded equal rights today? Present your argument in an essay with evidence.

History ONLINE

For help with the concepts in this section of *Glencoe World History— Modern Times,* go to glencoe.com and click Study Central.

The Impact of the Enlightenment

GUIDE TO READING

The BIG Idea
Ideas, Beliefs, and Values Europe's individual nations were chiefly guided by the self-interest of their rulers.

Content Vocabulary
• enlightened absolutism *(p. 318)*
• rococo *(p. 326)*

Academic Vocabulary
• rigid *(p. 320)*   • unique *(p. 326)*

People and Places
• Frederick the Great *(p. 320)*
• Maria Theresa *(p. 320)*
• Catherine the Great *(p. 321)*
• Balthasar Neumann *(p. 326)*
• Antoine Watteau *(p. 326)*
• Giovanni Battista Tiepolo *(p. 326)*
• Johann Sebastian Bach *(p. 327)*
• George Handel *(p. 327)*
• Joseph Haydn *(p. 327)*
• Wolfgang Mozart *(p. 327)*
• Henry Fielding *(p. 327)*

Reading Strategy
Describing As you read, use a chart like the one below to list the conflicts of the Seven Years' War. Include the countries involved and where the conflicts were fought.

Conflicts of the Seven Years' War

Enlightenment ideas had an impact on the politics and arts of eighteenth-century Europe. While they liked to talk about enlightened reforms, most rulers were more interested in the power and stability of their nations. Their desire for balancing power, however, could also lead to war. The Seven Years' War became global as war broke out in Europe, India, and North America.

Enlightenment and Absolutism

MAIN IDEA Philosophes believed that, in order to reform society based on Enlightenment ideals, people should be governed by enlightened rulers.

HISTORY & YOU Have you ever ignored good advice? Why? Read to learn why European rulers considered but ultimately ignored the advice of the philosophes.

Enlightenment thought influenced European politics in the eighteenth century. The philosophes believed in natural rights for all people. These rights included equality before the law; freedom of religious worship; freedom of speech; freedom of the press; and the rights to assemble, hold property, and pursue happiness. As the American Declaration of Independence expressed, "We hold these truths to be self-evident, that all men are created equal; that they are endowed by their creator with certain unalienable rights; that among these are life, liberty and the pursuit of happiness."

To establish and preserve these natural rights, most philosophes believed that people needed to be governed by enlightened rulers. Enlightened rulers are monarchs who allow religious toleration, freedom of speech and of the press, and the rights of private property. They nurture the arts, sciences, and education. Above all, enlightened rulers obey the laws and enforce them fairly for all subjects. Only strong, enlightened monarchs could reform society.

Enlightened Absolutism

Many historians once assumed that a new type of monarchy, which they called **enlightened absolutism,** emerged in the later eighteenth century. In the system of enlightened absolutism, rulers tried to govern by Enlightenment principles while maintaining their royal powers. Did Europe's rulers, however, actually follow the advice of the philosophes and become enlightened? To answer this question, we examine three states—Prussia, Austria, and Russia.

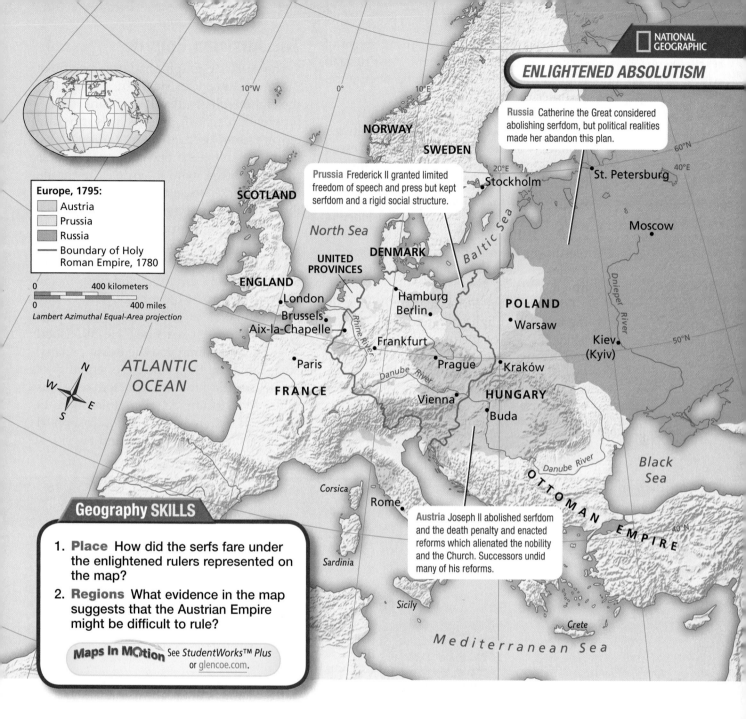

ENLIGHTENED ABSOLUTISM

Russia Catherine the Great considered abolishing serfdom, but political realities made her abandon this plan.

Prussia Frederick II granted limited freedom of speech and press but kept serfdom and a rigid social structure.

Austria Joseph II abolished serfdom and the death penalty and enacted reforms which alienated the nobility and the Church. Successors undid many of his reforms.

Europe, 1795:
- Austria
- Prussia
- Russia
- Boundary of Holy Roman Empire, 1780

0   400 kilometers
0   400 miles
Lambert Azimuthal Equal-Area projection

NORWAY
SWEDEN
SCOTLAND
North Sea
Baltic Sea
Stockholm
St. Petersburg
Moscow
DENMARK
UNITED PROVINCES
ENGLAND
Hamburg
Berlin
POLAND
Warsaw
London
Brussels
Aix-la-Chapelle
Frankfurt
Prague
Kraków
Kiev (Kyiv)
ATLANTIC OCEAN
Paris
FRANCE
Danube River
Vienna
Buda
HUNGARY
Rhine River
Dnieper River
Corsica
Rome
Black Sea
OTTOMAN EMPIRE
Sardinia
Sicily
Crete
Mediterranean Sea
Danube River

Geography SKILLS

1. **Place** How did the serfs fare under the enlightened rulers represented on the map?

2. **Regions** What evidence in the map suggests that the Austrian Empire might be difficult to rule?

Maps In Motion See *StudentWorks™ Plus* or glencoe.com.

Prussia: Army and Bureaucracy

Two able Prussian kings, Frederick William I and Frederick II, made Prussia a major European power in the eighteenth century. Frederick William I maintained a highly efficient bureaucracy of civil service workers. They observed the supreme values of obedience, honor, and, above all, service to the king. As Frederick William asserted: "One must serve the king with life and limb, . . . and surrender all except salvation. The latter is reserved for God. But everything else must be mine."

Frederick William's other major concern was the army. By the end of his reign in 1740, he had doubled the army's size. Although Prussia was tenth in physical size and thirteenth in population in Europe, it had the fourth-largest army after France, Russia, and Austria. The Prussian army, because of its size and its reputation as one of the best in Europe, was the most important institution in the state.

Members of the nobility, who owned large landed estates with many serfs, were the officers in the Prussian army.

These officers, too, had a strong sense of service to the king or state. As Prussian nobles, they believed in duty, obedience, and sacrifice.

Frederick II, or **Frederick the Great,** was one of the best educated and most cultured monarchs of the time. He was well versed in Enlightenment ideas and even invited the French philosophe Voltaire to live at his court for several years.

Frederick was a dedicated ruler. He, too, enlarged the Prussian army by actively recruiting the nobility into civil service. Frederick kept a strict watch over the bureaucracy.

For a time, Frederick seemed quite willing to make enlightened reforms. He abolished the use of torture except in treason and murder cases. He also granted limited freedom of speech and press, as well as greater religious toleration. However, Frederick kept Prussia's serfdom and **rigid** social structure intact and avoided any additional reforms.

The Austrian Empire

The Austrian Empire had become one of the great European states by the start of the eighteenth century. It was hard to rule, however, because it was a sprawling empire composed of many nationalities, languages, religions, and cultures. Empress **Maria Theresa,** who inherited the throne in 1740, worked to centralize and strengthen the state. She was not open to the philosophes' calls for reform, but she worked to improve the condition of the serfs.

Her son, Joseph II, believed in the need to sweep away anything standing in the path of reason: "I have made Philosophy the lawmaker of my empire." Joseph's reforms were far-reaching. He abolished serfdom and eliminated the death penalty. He established the principle of equality of all before the law and enacted religious reforms, including religious toleration. In his effort to change Austria, Joseph II issued thousands of decrees and laws.

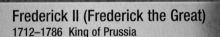

PEOPLE *in* HISTORY

Frederick II (Frederick the Great)
1712–1786 King of Prussia

When Napoleon visited the tomb of Frederick the Great in 1807, he remarked, "Gentlemen, if this man were still alive, I would not be here." This was high praise, especially considering that Prussia's Frederick II cared more about the arts, music, and philosophy than about warfare. Frederick was a flute player and composer who liked to surround himself with French intellectuals. Although cultural and intellectual pursuits remained his major interests, Frederick's leadership qualities began to emerge early in his reign. Under his 46-year rule, Prussia became a major military power with brilliantly executed victories that thwarted the expansion of the powerful Hapsburg Empire. **How did Prussia change under the leadership of Frederick II?**

Maria Theresa
1717–1780 Ruler of the Austrian Empire

Maria Theresa married at age 18. She remained devoted to her husband, Francis Stephen, throughout their 29-year marriage. She bore 16 children, many of whom would later become rulers of European nations or spouses of rulers. When her father, Charles VI of Austria, died in 1740, she became the only woman to rule during the 650-year Hapsburg dynasty. She enacted some reforms during her reign, but she never wavered from her belief in the legitimate right of monarchs to rule. Throughout her life, Maria Theresa showered her children with practical advice—especially her youngest daughter. This daughter would later fall victim to the anti-royalty hysteria of the French Revolution. Her name was Marie Antoinette. **What form of government did Maria Theresa support?**

Joseph's reform program largely failed. He alienated the nobles by freeing the serfs. He alienated the Catholic Church with his religious reforms. Even the serfs were unhappy because they could not understand the drastic changes. Joseph realized his failure when he wrote his own epitaph for his gravestone: "Here lies Joseph II who was unfortunate in everything that he undertook." His successors undid almost all of Joseph II's reforms.

Catherine the Great

In Russia, Peter the Great was followed by six weak successors who were often put in power and deposed by the palace guard. A group of nobles murdered the last of these six successors, Peter III. His German wife emerged as ruler of all the Russians.

Catherine II, or **Catherine the Great**, ruled Russia from 1762 to 1796. She was an intelligent woman who was familiar with the works of the philosophes and seemed to favor enlightened reforms. She invited the French philosophe Denis Diderot to Russia and urged him to speak frankly "as man to man." Diderot did so, outlining an ambitious program of reform. Catherine, however, was skeptical. Diderot's impractical theories, she said, "would have turned everything in my kingdom upside down." She did consider the idea of a new law code that would recognize the principle of the equality of all people in the eyes of the law.

In the end, however, Catherine did nothing because she knew that her success depended on the support of the Russian nobility. Catherine's policy of favoring the landed nobility led to worse conditions for the Russian peasants and eventually to rebellion. Led by an illiterate Cossack (a Russian warrior), Yemelyan Pugachov, the rebellion spread across southern Russia, but soon collapsed. Catherine took stronger measures against the peasants. All rural reform was halted; serfdom was expanded into newer parts of the empire.

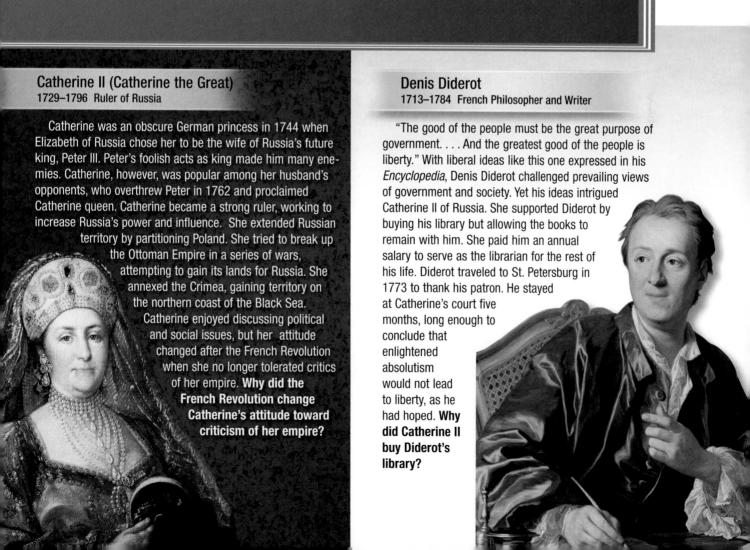

Catherine II (Catherine the Great)
1729–1796 Ruler of Russia

Catherine was an obscure German princess in 1744 when Elizabeth of Russia chose her to be the wife of Russia's future king, Peter III. Peter's foolish acts as king made him many enemies. Catherine, however, was popular among her husband's opponents, who overthrew Peter in 1762 and proclaimed Catherine queen. Catherine became a strong ruler, working to increase Russia's power and influence. She extended Russian territory by partitioning Poland. She tried to break up the Ottoman Empire in a series of wars, attempting to gain its lands for Russia. She annexed the Crimea, gaining territory on the northern coast of the Black Sea. Catherine enjoyed discussing political and social issues, but her attitude changed after the French Revolution when she no longer tolerated critics of her empire. **Why did the French Revolution change Catherine's attitude toward criticism of her empire?**

Denis Diderot
1713–1784 French Philosopher and Writer

"The good of the people must be the great purpose of government. . . . And the greatest good of the people is liberty." With liberal ideas like this one expressed in his *Encyclopedia*, Denis Diderot challenged prevailing views of government and society. Yet his ideas intrigued Catherine II of Russia. She supported Diderot by buying his library but allowing the books to remain with him. She paid him an annual salary to serve as the librarian for the rest of his life. Diderot traveled to St. Petersburg in 1773 to thank his patron. He stayed at Catherine's court five months, long enough to conclude that enlightened absolutism would not lead to liberty, as he had hoped. **Why did Catherine II buy Diderot's library?**

Catherine proved to be a worthy successor to Peter the Great in her policies of territorial expansion. Russia spread southward to the Black Sea by defeating the Turks under Catherine's rule. To the west, Russia gained about 50 percent of Poland's territory.

Enlightened Absolutism?

Of the rulers we have discussed, only Joseph II sought truly radical changes based on Enlightenment ideas. Both Frederick II and Catherine II liked to talk about enlightened reforms. They even attempted some, but their interest in strengthening the state and maintaining the existing system took priority.

In fact, all three of these enlightened absolutists—Frederick, Joseph, and Catherine—were guided primarily by their interest in the power and welfare of their state. When they did manage to strengthen their position as rulers, they did not use their enhanced position to undertake enlightened reforms to benefit their subjects. Rather, their power was used to collect more taxes and thus to create armies, to wage wars, and to gain even more power.

The philosophes condemned war as a foolish waste of life and resources. Despite their words, the rivalry among states that led to costly struggles remained unchanged in eighteenth-century Europe. Europe's self-governing, individual states were chiefly guided by the self-interest of their rulers.

The eighteenth-century monarchs were concerned with the balance of power. This concept proposed that states should have equal power in order to prevent any one from dominating the others. This desire for a balance of power, however, did not imply a desire for peace. Large armies created to defend a state's security were often used to conquer new lands as well. As Frederick II of Prussia remarked, "The fundamental rule of governments is the principle of extending their territories."

✓ **Reading Check** **Evaluating** What effect did enlightened reforms have in Prussia, Austria, and Russia?

The Seven Years' War

MAIN IDEA The Seven Years' War (1756–1763) became global as new alliances were formed and as war broke out in Europe, India, and North America.

HISTORY & YOU Do you and your classmates form friendship groups based on common interests? Read to learn about the changing alliances among European powers.

The stage was set for the Seven Years' War, when, in 1740, a major war broke out in connection with the succession to the Austrian throne.

Austrian Succession

When the Austrian emperor Charles VI died without a male heir, his daughter, Maria Theresa, succeeded him. King Frederick II of Prussia took advantage of the confusion surrounding the succession of a woman to the throne by invading Austrian **Silesia.** By this action, Frederick clearly stated that he did not recognize the legitimacy of the empress of Austria. France then entered the war against Austria, its traditional enemy. In turn, Maria Theresa allied with Great Britain.

The War of the Austrian Succession (1740 to 1748) was fought in three areas of the world. In Europe, Prussia seized Silesia while France occupied the Austrian Netherlands. In Asia, France took Madras (today called Chennai) in India from the British. In North America, the British captured the French fortress of Louisbourg at the entrance to the St. Lawrence River.

After seven years of warfare, all parties were exhausted and agreed to the Treaty of Aix-la-Chapelle in 1748. This treaty guaran-teed the return of all occupied territories except Silesia to their original owners. Prussia's refusal to return Silesia meant yet another war between Prussia and Austria.

Maria Theresa refused to accept the loss of Silesia. She rebuilt her army while working diplomatically to separate Prussia from its chief ally, France. In 1756 her hopes were realized when a diplomatic revolution reversed two longstanding alliances. How did this change come about?

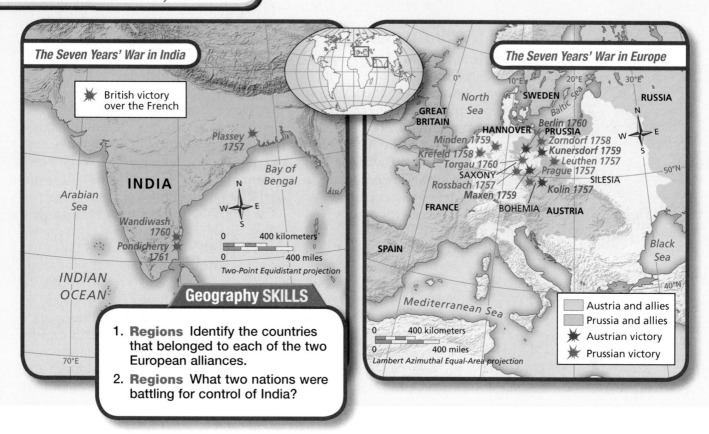

The Seven Years' War in India

✳ British victory over the French

Plassey 1757

Bay of Bengal

INDIA

Arabian Sea

Wandiwash 1760

Pondicherry 1761

INDIAN OCEAN

0   400 kilometers
0   400 miles
Two-Point Equidistant projection

70°E

The Seven Years' War in Europe

SWEDEN   RUSSIA

North Sea

GREAT BRITAIN

HANNOVER   PRUSSIA

Berlin 1760
Minden 1759   Zorndorf 1758
Krefeld 1758   Kunersdorf 1759
Torgau 1760   ✳ Leuthen 1757
SAXONY   Prague 1757   SILESIA
Rossbach 1757   Kolin 1757
Maxen 1759

FRANCE   BOHEMIA   AUSTRIA

SPAIN

Black Sea

Mediterranean Sea

0   400 kilometers
0   400 miles
Lambert Azimuthal Equal-Area projection

Austria and allies
Prussia and allies
✳ Austrian victory
✳ Prussian victory

Geography SKILLS

1. **Regions** Identify the countries that belonged to each of the two European alliances.
2. **Regions** What two nations were battling for control of India?

The War in Europe

French-Austrian rivalry had been a fact of European diplomacy since the late sixteenth century. However, two new rivalries now replaced the old one: the rivalry of Britain and France over colonial empires and the rivalry of Austria and Prussia over Silesia.

France abandoned Prussia and allied with Austria. Russia, which saw Prussia as a major threat to Russian goals in central Europe, joined the new alliance with France and Austria. In turn, Britain allied with Prussia. This diplomatic revolution of 1756 led to another worldwide war. The war had three major areas of conflict: Europe, India, and North America.

Europe witnessed the clash of the two major alliances: the British and Prussians against the Austrians, Russians, and French. Frederick the Great of Prussia was admired as a great tactical genius. His superb army and military skill enabled Frederick to defeat the Austrian, French, and Russian armies for a time. His forces were under attack from three different directions, however, and were gradually worn down.

Frederick faced disaster until Peter III, a new Russian czar who greatly admired Frederick, withdrew Russian troops from the conflict and from the Prussian lands that the Russians had occupied. This withdrawal created a stalemate and led to the desire for peace. The European war ended in 1763. All occupied territories were returned to their original owners, except Silesia. Austria officially recognized Prussia's permanent control of Silesia.

The War in India

The struggle between Britain and France that took place in the rest of the world had more decisive results. Known as the Great War for Empire, it was fought in India and North America. The French had returned Madras to Britain after the War of the Austrian Succession, but the struggle in India continued. The British ultimately won out, not because they had better forces but because they were more persistent.

With the Treaty of Paris in 1763, the French withdrew and left India to the British.

The War in North America

The greatest conflicts of the Seven Years' War took place in North America. On the North American continent, the French and British colonies were set up differently. The French government administered French North America (Canada and Louisiana) as a vast trading area. It was valuable for its fur, leather, fish, and timber. Because the French state was unable to get people to move to North America, its colonies were thinly populated.

British North America consisted of thirteen prosperous colonies on the eastern coast of what is now the United States. Unlike the French colonies, the British colonies were more populated, containing more than one million people by 1750.

The British and French fought over two main areas in North America. One consisted of the waterways of the Gulf of St. Lawrence, which were protected by the fortress of Louisbourg and by forts that guarded French Quebec. The other area they fought over was the unsettled Ohio River valley. The French began to move down from Canada and up from Louisiana to establish forts in the Ohio River valley. This French activity threatened to cut off the British settlers in the thirteen colonies from expanding into this vast area. The French were able to gain the support of the Native Americans who lived there. As traders and not settlers, the French were viewed by Native Americans with less hostility than the British.

The French scored a number of victories, at first. British fortunes were revived, however, by the efforts of William Pitt the Elder, Britain's prime minister. Pitt was convinced that the French colonial empire would have to be destroyed for Britain to create its own colonial empire. Pitt's policy focused on doing little in the European theater of war while putting resources into the colonial war, especially through the use of the British navy. The French had more troops in North America but not

POLITICAL CARTOONS   PRIMARY SOURCE

The Seven Years' War in North America

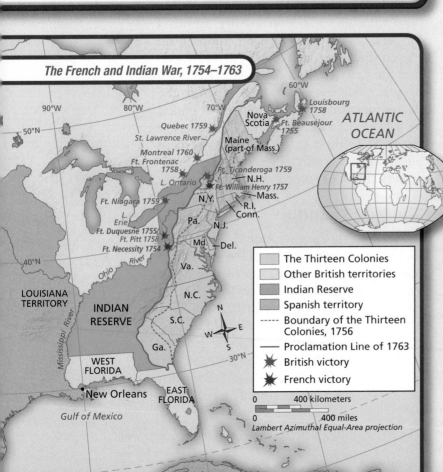

The rivalry between France and Britain for territories brought the Seven Years' War to North America. Known here as the French and Indian War, it began in the Ohio River valley. When the French built a fort in an area claimed by Virginia, the governor of Virginia sent 21-year-old George Washington to warn the French to leave.

> "They [the French] told me it was their absolute Design to take Possession of the Ohio.... They pretended to have an undoubted right to the river from a Discovery made by one La Sol [La Salle] 60 Years ago, & the use of this Expedition is to prevent our Settling on the River or Waters of it. . . ."
>
> —George Washington, *Diaries of George Washington*, 1753

In May 1754, George Washington, commanding a small force of Virginians, surprised French troops on the eastern side of the Ohio River and drove them out. Washington's men built a fort there, which they named Fort Necessity. The French soon regrouped, however. They captured Fort Necessity in July 1754. The French and Indian War was underway.

enough naval support. The defeat of French fleets in major naval battles gave the British an advantage. Without their fleets, the French could not easily reinforce their forts.

A series of British victories soon followed. In 1759 British forces under General Wolfe defeated the French under General Montcalm on the Plains of Abraham, outside Quebec. Both generals died in the battle. The British went on to seize Montreal, the Great Lakes area, and the Ohio River valley. The French were forced to make peace.

By the Treaty of Paris, the French transferred Canada and the lands east of the Mississippi to England. Spain, ally of the French, transferred Spanish Florida to British control. In return, the French gave their Louisiana territory to the Spanish. By 1763, Great Britain had become the world's greatest colonial power.

✓**Reading Check** **Explaining** How did Great Britain become the world's greatest colonial power?

Enlightenment and Arts

MAIN IDEA The eighteenth century was a great period in the history of European architecture, art, music, and literature.

HISTORY & YOU What style of music is most popular with your friends? Which musicians are the best examples of this style? Read to learn about popular music and musicians of the eighteenth century.

The ideas of the Enlightenment also had an impact on the world of culture. Eighteenth-century Europe witnessed both traditional practices and important changes in art, music, and literature.

Architecture and Art

The palace of Louis XIV at Versailles, in France, had made an enormous impact on Europe. The Austrian emperor, the Swedish king, and other European rulers also built grand residences. These palaces were modeled more on the Italian baroque style of the 1500s and 1600s than on the late seventeenth-century French classical style of Versailles.

To show the danger of disunity, Franklin drew an image of a snake cut into eight sections. The sections represented the eleven colonies that had joined the Albany Congress (the New England colonies were combined).

In 1754, as war with France loomed, Benjamin Franklin realized that the American colonies must band together for their mutual defense. Franklin published this cartoon—America's first political cartoon—to gain support for an association among the colonies called the Albany Congress.

Although the Albany Plan of Union drawn up by the congress was never formally adopted, it was the forerunner of the first constitution of the United States. Although the war ended their empire in North America, the French would later take their revenge by fighting on the American side in the American Revolution.

CRITICAL THINKING SKILLS

1. **Explaining** Why did the governor of Virginia send George Washington to talk to the French?
2. **Predicting** Based on their activities in the French and Indian War, what roles do you think Washington and Franklin would play in the American Revolution?

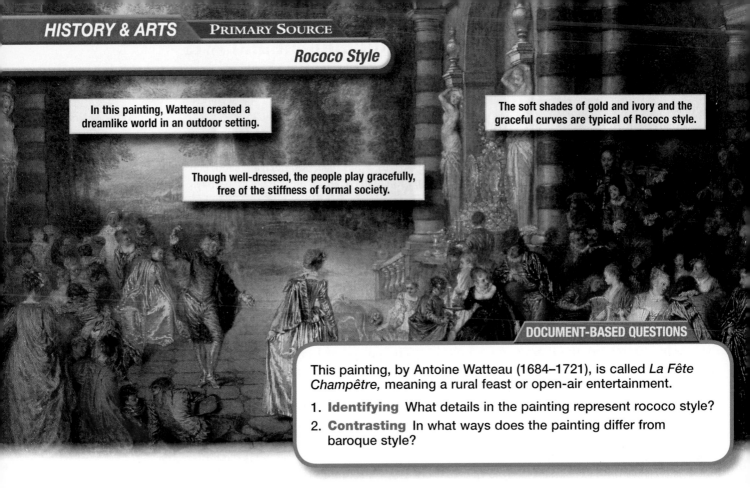

In this painting, Watteau created a dreamlike world in an outdoor setting.

The soft shades of gold and ivory and the graceful curves are typical of Rococo style.

Though well-dressed, the people play gracefully, free of the stiffness of formal society.

DOCUMENT-BASED QUESTIONS

This painting, by Antoine Watteau (1684–1721), is called *La Fête Champêtre*, meaning a rural feast or open-air entertainment.

1. **Identifying** What details in the painting represent rococo style?
2. **Contrasting** In what ways does the painting differ from baroque style?

Thus, a **unique** architectural style was created. Architects might choose traditional, classical, or any combination, but usually on a grand scale.

One of the greatest architects of the eighteenth century was **Balthasar Neumann.** Neumann's two masterpieces are the Church of the Fourteen Saints in southern Germany and the Residence, the palace of the prince-bishop of Würzburg. In these buildings, secular and spiritual become one, as lavish and fanciful ornament, light, bright colors, and elaborate detail greet the visitor. Inside the church, a pilgrim in search of holiness is struck by the incredible richness of detail.

The baroque and neoclassical styles that had dominated seventeenth-century art continued into the eighteenth century. By the 1730s, however, a new artistic style, known as **rococo,** had spread all over Europe.

Unlike the baroque style, which stressed grandeur and power, rococo emphasized grace, charm, and gentle action. Rococo made use of delicate designs colored in gold with graceful curves. The rococo style was highly secular. Its lightness and charm spoke of the pursuit of pleasure, happiness, and love.

Rococo's appeal is evident in the work of **Antoine Watteau.** In his paintings, gentlemen and ladies in elegant dress reveal a world of upper-class pleasure and joy. Underneath that exterior, however, is an element of sadness. The artist suggests such sadness in his paintings by depicting the fragility and passing nature of pleasure, love, and life. One of his masterpieces, the *Embarkation for Cythera,* shows French rococo at its peak.

Another aspect of rococo was a sense of enchantment and enthusiasm, especially evident in the work of **Giovanni Battista Tiepolo.** He brought fresco painting to new heights of dramatic effect with numerous active figures that are ranged in vivid pastels across vast, airy spaces. Many of Tiepolo's paintings came to adorn the walls and ceilings of churches and palaces. His masterpiece, *Allegory of the Planets and Continents,* adorns the ceiling of the bishop's residence at Würzburg. This painting is the largest ceiling fresco in the world at 7,287 square feet (677 sq. m).

History ONLINE
Student Web Activity—
Visit glencoe.com and complete the activity on rococo style.

Music

Eighteenth-century Europe produced some of the world's most enduring music. In the first half of the century, two composers—Johann Sebastian Bach and George Frideric Handel—stand out as musical geniuses.

Bach, a renowned organist as well as a composer, spent his entire life in Germany. While he was music director at the Church of Saint Thomas in Leipzig, he composed his *Mass in B Minor* and other works that gave him the reputation of being one of the greatest composers of all time.

Handel was a German who spent much of his career in England. He is probably best known for his religious music. Handel's *Messiah* has been called a rare work that appeals immediately to everyone and yet is a masterpiece of the highest order.

Bach and Handel perfected the baroque musical style. Two geniuses of the second half of the eighteenth century, Franz Joseph Haydn and Wolfgang Amadeus Mozart, were innovators who wrote music called classical rather than baroque.

Haydn spent most of his adult life as musical director for wealthy Hungarian princes. Visits to England introduced him to a world where musicians wrote for public concerts rather than princely patrons. This "liberty," as he called it, led him to write two great works, *The Creation* and *The Seasons.*

Mozart was truly a child prodigy. His failure to get a regular patron to support him financially made his life miserable. Nevertheless, he wrote music passionately. His works *The Marriage of Figaro, The Magic Flute,* and *Don Giovanni* are three of the world's greatest operas. Haydn remarked to Mozart's father, "Your son is the greatest composer known to me."

Literature

In the eighteenth century, European novelists began to choose realistic social themes over the past century's focus on heroic deeds and the supernatural. Novels were especially attractive to a growing number of middle-class readers.

The English writer **Henry Fielding** wrote novels about people without morals who survive by their wits. Fielding's best-known work is *The History of Tom Jones, a Foundling,* which describes the adventures of a young scoundrel. In a number of hilarious episodes, Fielding presents scenes of English life from the slums of London to the country houses of the English aristocracy. His characters reflect real types in eighteenth-century English society.

✓ Reading Check **Identifying** What are the characteristics of the rococo style of art?

Vocabulary

1. **Explain** the significance of: enlightened absolutism, Frederick the Great, Maria Theresa, Catherine the Great, Balthasar Neumann, rococo, Antoine Watteau, Giovanni Battista Tiepolo, Johann Sebastian Bach, George Handel, Joseph Haydn, Wolfgang Mozart, Henry Fielding.

Main Ideas

2. **Summarize** the reforms of Joseph II of Austria, Frederick II of Prussia, and Catherine II of Russia by using a chart like the one below.

Joseph II	Frederick II	Catherine II

3. **List** all the countries in the world that fought in the Seven Years' War. Which country gained the most territory?

4. **Identify** two composers who led the shift from baroque to classical music.

Critical Thinking

5. **The BIG Idea** **Analyzing** Why were Enlightenment ideals never fully practiced by eighteenth-century rulers?

6. **Drawing Conclusions** Describe the characteristics of an ideal enlightened ruler. Did any of the eighteenth-century rulers discussed in this section have these traits?

7. **Analyzing Visuals** Examine the painting by Watteau on page 326. What choices do you think the artist made to incorporate rococo style into the scene?

Writing About History

8. **Expository Writing** Listen to a selection of medieval religious music and of Mozart's *The Magic Flute.* Write an essay describing how the two pieces are similar and different. What kind of emotion does each piece convey?

History ONLINE

For help with the concepts in this section of *Glencoe World History—Modern Times,* go to glencoe.com and click Study Central.

The 18th-Century Salon

The French word *salon* refers to a parlor or living room, a main gathering space in a private home. In the 18th century, the salons became gathering places for intellectual conversation. Writers, scientists, and philosophers met weekly to discuss important discoveries and new works of poetry and theater.

The king's private space was separate from most courtiers.

The most trusted courtiers stood near the king.

Molière, a French playwright, meets with his patron, Louis XIV.

▲ *Molière received by Louis XIV,* by Jean Hégesippe Vetter

THE SHORTCOMINGS OF LIFE AT COURT

The king's court was a very formal place. There were strict rules about how courtiers had to dress, when and where they could sit, and when and where they could speak to certain people. Even courtiers who had the privilege of joining a conversation chose their words carefully. Some topics were objectionable to Church authorities or high-ranking nobility. Court gossip and intrigue often dominated discussion.

The salon of Madame de Geoffrin, an early, but not the original, gathering of thinkers. Most salon hosts were women, while guests were mostly men.

Participants came from the middle class as well as the aristocracy.

In the salon, a guest's good manners and original thought were highly prized displays of the guest's wealth and standing.

▲ *Reading of Voltaire's tragedy, "L'Orphelin de la Chine" at the salon of Madame de Geoffrin,* by Anicet Charles Gabriel Lemonnier

1. **Expressing** What ideas about government in France can you form by looking at this representation of the king?

2. **Speculating** In Madame de Geoffrin's salon, many specialties and interests were represented by the participants. Do you think such wide-ranging discussions helped or distracted each participant in his studies and writing?

A GOLDEN AGE OF CONVERSATION

Madame de Geoffrin (1699–1777) made two important salon innovations. She focused on an early afternoon meal, instead of a late dinner, allowing an entire afternoon of conversation. She also introduced a regular weekly schedule of themes, with days devoted to the visual arts and literature. She was remembered as a generous listener, and she had a talent for saying just enough, at the right time, to keep a conversation moving.

The American Revolution

GUIDE TO READING

The BIG Idea
Self-Determination The American Revolution and the formation of the United States of America seemed to confirm premises of the Enlightenment.

Content Vocabulary
• federal system *(p. 333)*

Academic Vocabulary
• amendment *(p. 333)* • guaranteed *(p. 333)*

People, Places, and Events
• Hanoverians *(p. 330)*
• Robert Walpole *(p. 330)*
• George Washington *(p. 332)*
• Declaration of Independence *(p. 332)*
• Thomas Jefferson *(p. 332)*
• Yorktown *(p. 332)*
• Bill of Rights *(p. 334)*

Reading Strategy
Summarizing Information As you read, use a chart like the one below to identify key aspects of the government created by the American colonists.

The ideas of the Enlightenment had clearly made an impact on the colonies in North America. In response to unfair taxation and other issues, the colonists revolted against British rule, formed their own army, and declared their independence. Many Europeans saw the American Revolution as the embodiment of the Enlightenment's political dreams.

Britain and the American Revolution

MAIN IDEA Drawing on the theory of natural rights, the Declaration of Independence declared the colonies to be independent of Britain.

HISTORY & YOU What comes to mind when you celebrate the Fourth of July? Learn why the colonists declared their independence.

The United Kingdom of Great Britain came into existence in 1707, when the governments of England and Scotland were united. The term *British* came to refer to both the English and the Scots.

In eighteenth-century Britain, the monarch and the Parliament shared power, with Parliament gradually gaining the upper hand. The monarch chose ministers, who were responsible to the Crown. These ministers set policy and guided Parliament. Having the power to make laws, levy taxes, and pass the budget, Parliament indirectly influenced the ministers of the monarch.

In 1714 a new dynasty—the **Hanoverians**—was established when the last Stuart ruler, Queen Anne, died without an heir. The crown was offered to her nearest relatives, Protestant rulers of the German state of Hanover. The first Hanoverian king, George I, did not speak English. Neither the first nor the second George knew the British system well, so their chief ministers were allowed to deal with Parliament.

Robert Walpole served as head of cabinet (later called prime minister) from 1721 to 1742. Walpole pursued a peaceful foreign policy. However, growing trade and industry led to an ever-increasing middle class. The middle class favored expansion of trade and of Britain's world empire. They found a spokesman in William Pitt the Elder, who became head of cabinet in 1757. He expanded the British Empire by acquiring Canada and India in the Seven Years' War.

In North America, then, Britain controlled Canada as well as the thirteen colonies on the eastern coast of what is now the United States. The British colonies were well populated, containing more than one million people by 1750. They were also prosperous. The British Board of Trade, the Royal Council, and Parliament

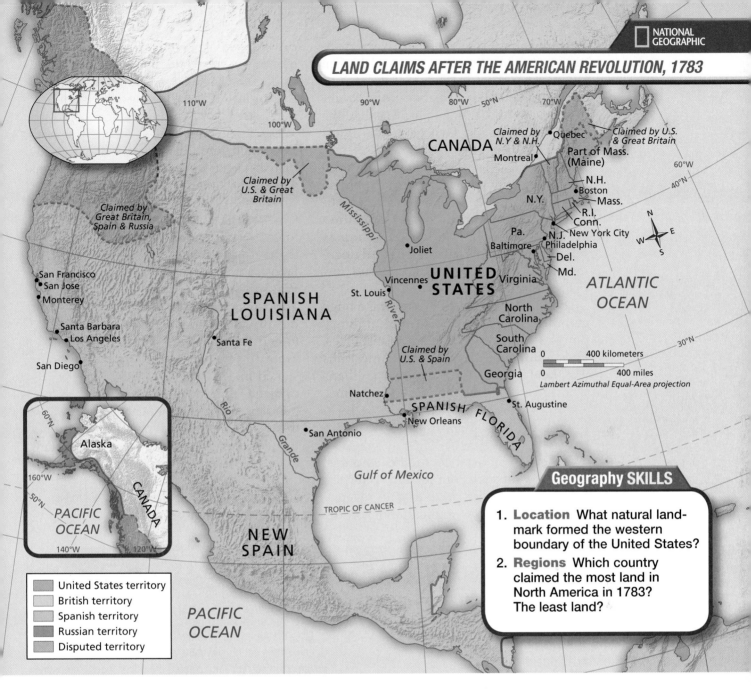

LAND CLAIMS AFTER THE AMERICAN REVOLUTION, 1783

Claimed by
U.S. & Great
Britain

Claimed by
Great Britain,
Spain & Russia

CANADA

Claimed by
N.Y & N.H.

Quebec

Claimed by U.S.
& Great Britain

Part of Mass.
(Maine)

Montreal

N.H.

Boston

N.Y.

Mass.

R.I.

Conn.

Pa.

N.J. New York City

Philadelphia

Baltimore

Del.

Md.

Joliet

SPANISH
LOUISIANA

UNITED
STATES

Virginia

ATLANTIC
OCEAN

Vincennes

St. Louis

North
Carolina

San Francisco
San Jose
Monterey

Santa Barbara
Los Angeles

Santa Fe

Claimed by
U.S. & Spain

South
Carolina

Georgia

San Diego

Natchez

SPANISH FLORIDA

St. Augustine

New Orleans

San Antonio

0   400 kilometers

0   400 miles

Lambert Azimuthal Equal-Area projection

Mississippi

River

Rio

Grande

Alaska

CANADA

PACIFIC
OCEAN

Gulf of Mexico

TROPIC OF CANCER

NEW
SPAIN

PACIFIC
OCEAN

Geography SKILLS

1. **Location** What natural land-mark formed the western boundary of the United States?

2. **Regions** Which country claimed the most land in North America in 1783? The least land?

United States territory
British territory
Spanish territory
Russian territory
Disputed territory

in theory controlled the colonies. In actuality, the colonies had legislatures that tended to act independently. Merchants in port cities such as Boston, New York City, and Charleston did not want the British government to run their affairs.

The American Revolution Begins

After the Seven Years' War, British leaders wanted to get new revenues from the colonies. These revenues would then be used to cover war costs. They would also pay for the expenses of maintaining an army to defend the colonies.

In 1765 Parliament imposed the Stamp Act on the colonies. The act required certain printed materials, such as legal documents and newspapers, to carry a stamp showing that a tax had been paid to Britain. Opposition was widespread and often violent. The act was repealed in 1766, ending the immediate crisis, but the cause of the dispute was not resolved.

Crisis followed crisis in the 1770s. To counteract British actions, the colonies organized the First Continental Congress, which met in Philadelphia in September 1774. Members urged colonists to "take up arms and organize militias."

Fighting finally erupted between colonists and the British army in April 1775 in Lexington and Concord, Massachusetts. Meeting soon afterward, the Second Continental Congress set up an army, called the Continental Army. **George Washington** served as its commander in chief.

More than a year passed before the colonies declared independence from the British Empire. On July 4, 1776, the Second Continental Congress approved the **Declaration of Independence** written by **Thomas Jefferson.** With this stirring political document, the American Revolution had formally begun.

The war against Great Britain was a huge gamble. Britain was a strong military power with enormous financial resources. The Continental Army of the Americans was made up of undisciplined civilians who agreed to serve for only a short time.

British Defeat

Of great importance to the colonies' cause was support from foreign countries. These nations were eager to gain revenge for earlier defeats at the hands of the British. The French supplied arms and money to the rebels. French officers and soldiers also served in Washington's army. In February 1778, following a British defeat, the French granted diplomatic recognition to the new United States. When Spain and the Dutch Republic entered the war, the British faced war with the Europeans as well as the Americans.

When General Cornwallis was forced to surrender to the American and French forces under Washington at **Yorktown** in 1781, the British decided to end the war. The Treaty of Paris, signed in 1783, recognized the independence of the American colonies. The treaty also granted the Americans control of the western territory from the Appalachians to the Mississippi River.

✓ **Reading Check** **Explaining** Why did foreign countries support the Americans?

CONNECTING TO THE UNITED STATES

➤GUARANTEED FREEDOMS

- **Freedom of Religion**
- **Freedom of Speech**
- **Freedom of Peaceable assembly**

After the American Revolution, the founders of the new United States set up a system whereby its citizens could govern themselves. They created the Bill of Rights to ensure individual liberties for future generations. Today, in the wake of terrorist attacks on U.S. soil, security has become a top priority for many Americans. Will new security measures encroach on the liberties that our revolutionary ancestors fought for and guaranteed in the Bill of Rights?

CONNECTING TO TODAY

1. **Analyzing** How has the search for terrorists impacted American liberty?

2. **Applying** In a 1929 case, U.S. Supreme Court Justice Holmes stated his understanding of free speech: ". . . the principle of free thought—not free thought for those who agree with us, but freedom for the thought that we hate." Give an example that applies this principle to today.

The Birth of a New Nation

MAIN IDEA The formation of the United States convinced many eighteenth-century philosophes that a new age and a better world could be created.

HISTORY & YOU Recall the philosopher Rousseau's concept of the social contract. Read to learn how the new United States set up government by the general will of the people.

After throwing off oppressive rule, the former colonies, now states, feared a strong central government. Thus, their first constitution, the Articles of Confederation (1781), created a government that lacked the power to deal with the nation's problems. In 1787, delegates met in Philadelphia at the Constitutional Convention to revise the Articles of Confederation. The delegates decided to write a plan for an entirely new government.

The Constitution

The proposed Constitution created a **federal system** in which the national government and the state governments shared power. Based on Montesquieu's ideas, the national, or federal, government was separated into three branches: executive, legislative, and judicial. Each branch had some power to check, or restrain, acts of the other branches.

A president served as the chief executive in the executive branch. The legislative branch consisted of elected representatives in two houses—the Senate and the House of Representatives. The Supreme Court and other courts formed the judicial branch. After ratification, or approval, by 9 of the 13 states, the Constitution took effect.

The Bill of Rights

As promised during negotiations over ratification, the new Congress proposed 12 **amendments** to the Constitution. The states approved 10 of the amendments. Together, these amendments became known as the **Bill of Rights.**

These 10 amendments **guaranteed** freedom of religion, speech, press, petition, and assembly. They gave Americans the right to bear arms and to be protected against unreasonable searches and arrests. They guaranteed trial by jury, due process of law, and the protection of property rights.

Many of the rights in the Bill of Rights were derived from the natural rights proposed by the eighteenth-century philosophes. Many European intellectuals saw the American Revolution as the embodiment of the Enlightenment's political dreams. The premises of the Enlightenment seemed confirmed. A new age and a better world could be achieved.

✓ Reading Check **Identifying** What was the main weakness of the Articles of Confederation?

SECTION 4 REVIEW

Vocabulary
1. **Explain** the significance of: Hanoverians, Robert Walpole, George Washington, Declaration of Independence, Thomas Jefferson, Yorktown, federal system, amendment, Bill of Rights, guaranteed.

Main Ideas
2. **Explain** why England wanted revenues from the American colonies.
3. **Explain** the purpose of the Stamp Act.
4. **Summarize** the rights and freedoms guaranteed by the American Bill of Rights by using a chart like the one below.

Guarantees of the Bill of Rights

Critical Thinking
5. **The BIG Idea** **Making Inferences** Why did many Europeans see the American Revolution as the embodiment of the Enlightenment's political dreams?
6. **Analyzing** If going to war with the British was such a huge gamble, why then did the colonists win?
7. **Analyzing Visuals** Study the photograph on page 332. What does the body language of the people in the photograph suggest to you?

Writing About History
8. **Expository Writing** Do further research on how the French supported the colonies during the American Revolution. Then write an essay analyzing the importance of the French assistance to the colonists.

History ONLINE

For help with the concepts in this section of *Glencoe World History—Modern Times*, go to glencoe.com and click Study Central.

STUDY TO GO

You can study anywhere, anytime by downloading quizzes and flash cards to your PDA from glencoe.com.

THE SCIENTIFIC REVOLUTION

- The Scientific Revolution changed the way Europeans viewed their world.
- Copernicus, Kepler, and Galileo provided new explanations of the universe.
- Breakthroughs in chemistry and medicine changed the understanding of human anatomy.
- Women scientists made important advances, but faced many obstacles.

COPERNICUS STUDIES THE NIGHT SKY

Niclaus Copernicus proposed a heliocentric explanation of the universe.

CATHERINE THE GREAT INVITES PHILOSOPHE DENIS DIDEROT TO RUSSIA

Like most rulers of her time, Catherine the Great outwardly supported Enlightenment ideas but did not always act upon them.

THE ENLIGHTENMENT

- Philosophes applied the scientific method to examine government, justice, and religion.
- The ideas of the Enlightenment became a force for social reform.
- Some rulers considered governing by Enlightenment principles but ultimately were more interested in maintaining power.
- Architecture, art, music, and literature were influenced by Enlightenment ideas.

THE AMERICAN REVOLUTION

- American colonists revolted against British rule.
- France, Spain, and the Dutch Republic helped the American colonies win independence.
- Many believed the American Revolution confirmed Enlightenment principles.

THE BRITISH SURRENDER AT YORKTOWN, VIRGINIA

British Lord Cornwallis surrenders to George Washington.

STANDARDIZED TEST PRACTICE

TEST-TAKING **TIP**

With a time line question, you may need to make an inference. Look for clues in the test question and time line. In this case, think about what the events on the time line have in common. These clues can help you make an inference that the time line supports.

Reviewing Vocabulary

Directions: Choose the word or words that best complete the sentence.

1. Monarchs who practiced _____ tried to govern by Enlightenment principles.

  A social contract law

  B deism

  C separation of powers

  D enlightened absolutism

2. A systematic procedure for collecting and analyzing evidence is known as the _____ method.

  A inductive

  B scientific

  C rational

  D gravitational

3. The _____ system is the sun-centered concept of the universe.

  A geocentric

  B Ptolemaic

  C heliocentric

  D Newtonian

4. The translation of _____ means "to let (people) do (what they want)."

  A laissez-faire

  B rousseau

  C salon

  D philosophe

Reviewing Main Ideas

Directions: Choose the best answers to the following questions.

Section 1 *(pp. 302–309)*

5. Galileo's observations disproved one aspect of Ptolemy's universe by showing for the first time which characteristic of heavenly bodies?

  A They revolve around the sun.

  B They are made of material substance.

  C They revolve in elliptical orbits.

  D They are pure orbs of light.

6. Who discovered that blood completes a circuit through the body?

  A Andreas Vesalius

  B Galen

  C William Harvey

  D Robert Boyle

7. Which philosopher is noted for the statement "I think, therefore I am"?

  A Francis Bacon

  B Aristotle

  C René Descartes

  D John Locke

Section 2 *(pp. 310–317)*

8. Who argued that every person was born with a tabula rasa, or blank mind?

  A Voltaire

  B John Locke

  C Adam Smith

  D Denis Diderot

Need Extra Help?								
If You Missed Questions . . .	1	2	3	4	5	6	7	8
Go to Page . . .	318	309	304	314	304	306	308	310

9. What was Montesquieu's most lasting contribution to political thought?

   A Deism

   B Laissez-faire doctrine

   C System of checks and balances through separation of powers

   D 28-volume *Encyclopedia*

Section 3 *(pp. 318–327)*

10. Which of the following leaders sought truly radical changes based on Enlightenment ideas?

    A Joseph II

    B Frederick the Great

    C Catherine the Great

    D Maria Theresa

11. The Seven Years' War took place in three main regions of the world: Europe, North America, and which of the following?

    A Latin America

    B Australia

    C India

    D Africa

Section 4 *(pp. 330–333)*

12. Who commanded the Continental Army?

    A Thomas Jefferson

    B General Cornwallis

    C George Washington

    D Robert Walpole

13. How many constitutional amendments are in the U.S. Bill of Rights?

    A 13

    B 5

    C 9

    D 10

Critical Thinking

Directions: Choose the best answers to the following questions.

14. Which of the following is an example of checks and balances at work in the United States government?

    A The national and state governments share power.

    B Congress is separated into two houses, the Senate and the House of Representatives.

    C The president can veto, or reject, an act of Congress.

    D Representatives to Congress are elected by a vote of the people.

Base your answer to question 15 on the time line below and on your knowledge of world history.

Selected Milestones in Political Thought

1762
The Social Contract describes Rousseau's belief that governments are created from the people's general will

1776
The Declaration of Independence asserts the right to overthrow an unjust king

1792
Mary Wollstonecraft argues for equal rights for women

---

15. Which of the following statements is supported by the information on the time line?

    A Most Europeans supported their monarchs.

    B Many people questioned the nature of their governments.

    C Enlightenment thinkers embraced the women's movement.

    D Only men thought and wrote about politics.

Need Extra Help?

If You Missed Questions . . .	9	10	11	12	13	14	15
Go to Page . . .	312	322	323	332	333	333	336

16. The philosophes compared the universe to a clock. Which of the following statements best explains this comparison?

   A The creator of the universe makes events occur on a predictable schedule.

   B The universe is a machine that requires power to operate properly.

   C Once set in motion, the universe operates without further help from its creator.

   D The universe runs in mysterious ways that only its creator can understand.

17. Which concept below conformed to the teaching of the Catholic Church in the eighteenth century?

   A A heliocentric universe

   B The universal law of gravitation

   C Rationalism

   D A geocentric universe

Base your answer to question 18 on the map below and on your knowledge of world history.

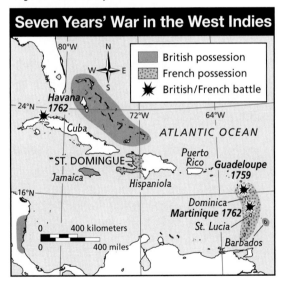

Seven Years' War in the West Indies

18. What battle was fought on the island of Cuba?

   A Hispaniola

   B Havana

   C Guadeloupe

   D Martinique

Document-Based Questions

Directions: Analyze the document and answer the short answer questions that follow the document.

John Locke greatly influenced eighteenth-century intellectuals. The quote below comes from Locke's famous work *Essay Concerning Human Understanding.*

> *"Let us then suppose the mind to be, as we say, white paper, void of all characters, without any ideas. How comes it to be furnished? Whence has it all the materials of reason and knowledge? To this I answer, in one word, from experience. . . . Our observation, employed either about external sensible objects or about the internal operations of our minds perceived and reflected on by ourselves, is that which supplies our understanding with all the materials of thinking."*

19. According to Locke, what one word describes how the blank mind becomes knowledgeable?

20. Paraphrase Locke's explanation of how the mind gains "all the materials of thinking."

Extended Response

21. The ideas of Montesquieu, Voltaire, and Rousseau influenced the development of the Constitution of the United States. Explain how the ideas of each person apply to the United States government.

History ONLINE
For additional test practice, use Self-Check Quizzes—Chapter 10 at glencoe.com.

Need Extra Help?						
If You Missed Questions . . .	16	17	18	19	20	21
Go to Page . . .	312	304	324	310	310	312

STOP

CHAPTER 11

The French Revolution and Napoleon 1789–1815

Section 1 The French Revolution Begins

Section 2 Radical Revolution

Section 3 The Age of Napoleon

MAKING CONNECTIONS

What makes a nation?

The Arc de Triomphe is one of the national symbols of France. It was commissioned by Napoleon in 1806 to commemorate his Grand Army. Can you name some other national symbols of France? In this chapter you will learn how France became a nation.

- What are some national symbols of the United States?
- What are the characteristics of a nation?
- What is nationalism?

FRANCE ▶

1789
French Revolution begins

1793
King Louis XVI executed; Reign of Terror begins

1799
Napoleon leads coup d'état that topples French government

1790 — 1800

THE WORLD ▶

1789
George Washington inaugurated as first U.S. president

1803
United States purchases Louisiana Territory from France

338

1812
Napoleon invades Russia

1815
Napoleon defeated at the Battle of Waterloo

1815

1810
Hidalgo leads Mexican independence movement

FOLDABLES™
Study Organizer

Identifying Create a Four-Door Book to record *who, what, when,* and *where* facts while you read about Napoleon Bonaparte.

Who	What
When	Where

History ONLINE

Chapter Overview—Visit glencoe.com to preview Chapter 11.

The French Revolution Begins

GUIDE TO READING

The BIG Idea
Struggle for Rights Social inequality and economic problems contributed to the French Revolution.

Content Vocabulary
- estate *(p. 340)*
- taille *(p. 340)*
- bourgeoisie *(p. 342)*
- sans-culottes *(p. 347)*

Academic Vocabulary
- consumer *(p. 341)*
- exclusion *(p. 345)*

People and Events
- Louis XVI *(p. 342)*
- Tennis Court Oath *(p. 343)*
- Declaration of the Rights of Man and the Citizen *(p. 345)*
- Olympe de Gouges *(p. 345)*

Reading Strategy
Explaining As you read, use a diagram like the one below to help you study.

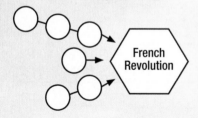

French Revolution

The year 1789 witnessed two far-reaching events: the beginning of a new United States of America and the beginning of the French Revolution. Compared with the American Revolution, the French Revolution was more complex and more radical. The French Revolution established both a new political order and a new social order. For that reason, it is considered a turning point in European history.

Background to the Revolution

MAIN IDEA The Third Estate, the vast majority of the French people, was heavily taxed and discontented.

HISTORY & YOU What if you had no say in family concerns despite doing all the household chores? Learn how the French people reacted to having no say in their government.

French society had changed little since medieval times. Feudalism established the privileges and obligations of the three main social classes. Although there were clergy and wealthy landowners in the American colonies, there were no laws giving them special status, unlike the class system in France. This social injustice caused unrest in eighteenth-century France.

France's Three Estates

Since the Middle Ages, France's population had been divided by law into one of three status groups, or **estates.** The First Estate consisted of the clergy, the Second Estate the nobles, and the Third Estate everyone else. Thus the Third Estate included anyone from the lowliest peasant to the wealthiest merchant.

The First Estate, or clergy, numbered about 130,000 out of a total population of 27 million and owned about 10 percent of the land. The clergy were radically divided. The higher clergy—cardinals, bishops, and heads of monasteries—were from noble families and shared their outlook and interests. The parish priests were often poor and from the class of commoners.

The Second Estate, or nobility, numbered about 350,000 and owned about 25 to 30 percent of the land. They played a crucial role in society in the 1700s. They held leading positions in the government, in the military, in the law courts, and in the Roman Catholic Church. Despite controlling most of the wealth of the kingdom, neither the clergy nor the nobles had to pay the **taille** (TAH•yuh), France's chief tax.

France's Three Estates

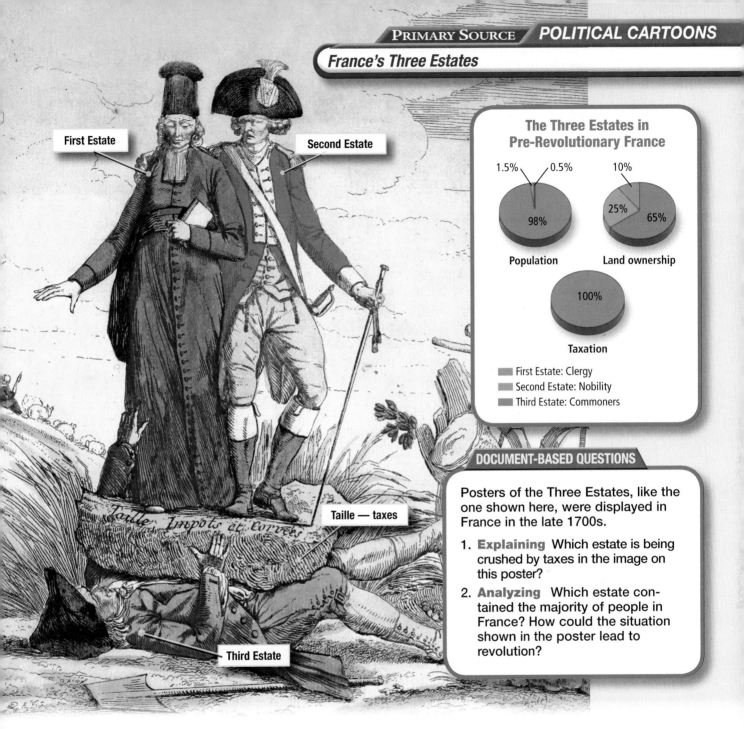

First Estate

Second Estate

The Three Estates in Pre-Revolutionary France

1.5% 0.5%

98%

Population

10%

25% 65%

Land ownership

100%

Taxation

First Estate: Clergy
Second Estate: Nobility
Third Estate: Commoners

Taille — taxes

Taille Impots et corvées

Third Estate

DOCUMENT-BASED QUESTIONS

Posters of the Three Estates, like the one shown here, were displayed in France in the late 1700s.

1. **Explaining** Which estate is being crushed by taxes in the image on this poster?

2. **Analyzing** Which estate contained the majority of people in France? How could the situation shown in the poster lead to revolution?

Unlike the First and Second Estates, the Third Estate was divided by vast differences in occupation, level of education, and wealth. Peasants made up 75 to 80 percent of the Third Estate and owned about 35 to 40 percent of the land; middle-class members of the Third Estate owned the rest. At least half of the peasants had little or no land to live on.

All peasants owed certain duties to the nobles, which were a holdover from medieval times when serfdom was widespread. For example, a peasant had to pay a fee to grind his flour or press his grapes because the local lord controlled the flour mill and wine press. When the harvest time came, the peasant had to work a certain number of days harvesting the noble's crop. Peasants fiercely resented these duties.

Another part of the Third Estate consisted of urban craftspeople, shopkeepers, and workers. These people, too, were struggling to survive. In the 1700s, the price of **consumer** goods increased much faster than wages, which left these urban groups with decreased buying power.

The struggle for survival led many of these people to play an important role in the revolution, especially in Paris.

The **bourgeoisie** (BURZH•WAH•ZEE), or middle class, was another part of the Third Estate. This group included about 8 percent of the population, or 2.3 million people. They owned about 20 to 25 percent of the land. The bourgeoisie included merchants, bankers, and industrialists, as well as professional people—lawyers, holders of public offices, doctors, and writers.

The middle class was unhappy with the privileges held by nobles. They did not want to abolish the nobility, however, but to better their own position. Some bourgeoisie had managed to become nobles by being appointed to public offices that conferred noble status. About 6,500 new nobles had been created by appointment during the 1700s.

The bourgeoisie also shared certain goals with the nobles. Both were drawn to the new political ideas of the Enlightenment. In addition, both groups were increasingly upset with a monarchical system resting on privileges and on an old and rigid social order. The opposition of these elites to the old order led them to take drastic action against the absolute monarchy of **Louis XVI**.

Financial Crisis

Social conditions, then, formed a long-standing background to the French Revolution. The immediate cause of the revolution was the near collapse of the French budget. Although the economy had been expanding for fifty years, there were periodic crises. Bad harvests in 1787 and 1788 and a slowdown in manufacturing led to food shortages, rising prices for food, and unemployment. One English traveler commented on the misery of French peasants:

<u>**PRIMARY SOURCE**</u>

"All the country girls and women are without shoes or stockings; and the plowmen at their work have neither shoes nor stockings to their feet. This is a poverty that strikes at the root of national prosperity."

—an English traveler in France

On the eve of the revolution, the French economy was in crisis. Despite these problems, the French king and his ministers continued to spend enormous sums of money on wars and court luxuries. The queen, Marie Antoinette, was especially known for her extravagance and this too caused popular resentment. When the government decided to spend huge sums to help the American colonists against Britain, the budget went into total crisis.

With France on the verge of financial collapse, Louis XVI was forced to call a meeting of the Estates-General, representatives of all three estates meeting together, to raise new taxes. The Estates-General had not met since 1614 because French kings were so powerful.

✓ **Reading Check** **Identifying** What groups were part of the Third Estate?

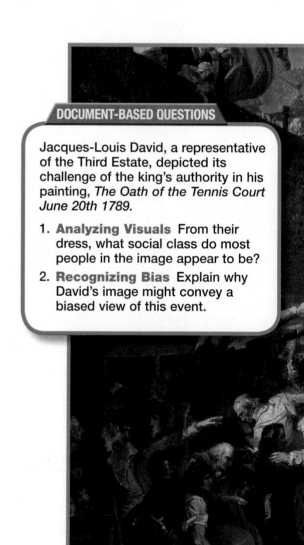

DOCUMENT-BASED QUESTIONS

Jacques-Louis David, a representative of the Third Estate, depicted its challenge of the king's authority in his painting, *The Oath of the Tennis Court June 20th 1789.*

1. **Analyzing Visuals** From their dress, what social class do most people in the image appear to be?

2. **Recognizing Bias** Explain why David's image might convey a biased view of this event.

From Estates-General to National Assembly

MAIN IDEA The Third Estate claimed the right to have its votes count as much as those of the First and Second Estates.

HISTORY & YOU Have you heard about a riot and wondered what made people take to the streets? Learn why Parisian workers rioted in the summer of 1789.

Louis XVI called a meeting of the Estates-General at Versailles on May 5, 1789. In the Estates-General, the First and Second Estates each had about 300 representatives. The Third Estate had almost 600 representatives. Most of the Third Estate wanted to set up a constitutional government that would make the clergy and nobility pay taxes, too.

From the start, there were arguments about voting. Traditionally, each estate had one vote—the First and Second Estates could outvote the Third Estate two to one. The Third Estate demanded instead that each deputy have one vote. Under this new system, with the help of a few nobles and clerics, the Third Estate would then have a majority vote. The king stated that he favored the current system.

On June 17, 1789, the Third Estate boldly declared that it was the National Assembly and would draft a constitution. Three days later, on June 20, its deputies arrived at their meeting place, only to find the doors had been locked. They then moved to a nearby indoor tennis court and swore that they would continue meeting until they had a new constitution. The oath they swore is known as the **Tennis Court Oath.**

PRIMARY SOURCE / **HISTORY & ARTS**

Tennis Court Oath

When the 600 delegates were locked out of Versailles, they walked to a nearby tennis court where they swore to meet until they had a constitution.

Bailly, the National Assembly's president, led the Tennis Court Oath.

Some clergy and nobles joined in the Oath.

Louis XVI prepared to use force against the Third Estate. On July 14, 1789, about 900 Parisians gathered in the courtyard of the Bastille (ba•STEEL)—an old fortress, used as a prison and armory. The price of bread had reached record highs so the crowd was hungry and agitated. According to rumor, the king's troops were coming, and there was ammunition in the Bastille. A group of attackers managed to lower the two drawbridges over the moat. Members of the French Guard joined the attack. After four hours of fighting, the prison warden surrendered. The rebels released the seven prisoners and cut off the prison warden's head. Angered that there were no munitions, the crowd demolished the Bastille brick by brick. Paris was abandoned to the rebels.

When King Louis XVI returned to his palace at Versailles after a day of hunting, the duc de la Rochefoucauld-Liancourt told him about the fall of the Bastille. Louis is said to have exclaimed, "Why, this is a revolt." "No, Sire," replied the duke. "It is a revolution."

Louis XVI was informed that he could no longer trust royal troops to shoot at the mob. The king's authority had collapsed in Paris. Meanwhile, all over France, revolts were breaking out. Popular hatred of the entire landholding system, with its fees and obligations, had finally spilled over into action.

Peasant rebellions became part of the vast panic known as the Great Fear. The peasants feared that the work of the National Assembly would be stopped by foreign armies. Rumors spread from village to village that foreign troops were on the way to put down the revolution. The peasants reacted by breaking into the houses of the lords to destroy the records of their obligations.

✓ **Reading Check** **Examining** Why did the Third Estate object to how votes were counted in the Estates-General?

HISTORY & ARTS **PRIMARY SOURCE**

The King Concedes

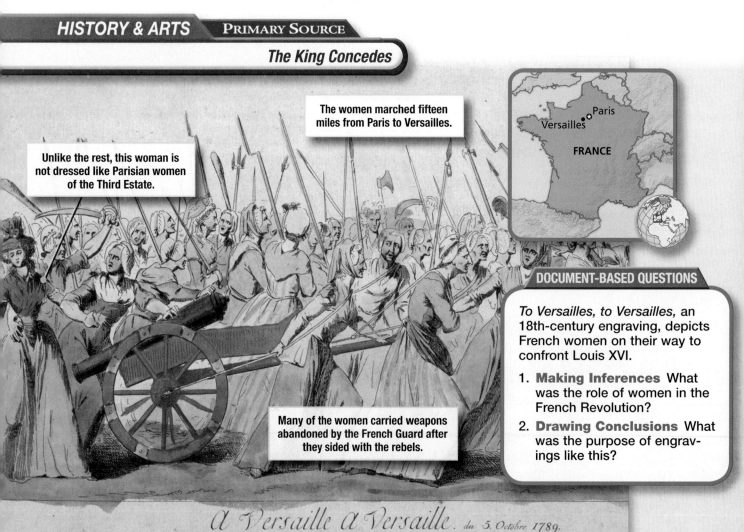

The women marched fifteen miles from Paris to Versailles.

Unlike the rest, this woman is not dressed like Parisian women of the Third Estate.

FRANCE
Paris
Versailles

Many of the women carried weapons abandoned by the French Guard after they sided with the rebels.

a Versaille a Versaille. du 5. Octobre 1789.

DOCUMENT-BASED QUESTIONS

To Versailles, to Versailles, an 18th-century engraving, depicts French women on their way to confront Louis XVI.

1. **Making Inferences** What was the role of women in the French Revolution?

2. **Drawing Conclusions** What was the purpose of engravings like this?

End of the Old Regime

MAIN IDEA The National Assembly affirmed the "rights of man" and set up a limited monarchy in the Constitution of 1791.

HISTORY & YOU How did George III react to the Declaration of Independence? Read how Louis XVI reacted to the events of 1789.

The National Assembly reacted to news of peasant rebellions and rumors of a possible foreign invasion. On August 4, 1789, the National Assembly decided to abolish all legal privileges of the nobles and clergy.

Declaration of the Rights of Man

On August 26, the National Assembly adopted the **Declaration of the Rights of Man and the Citizen.** Inspired by the English Bill of Rights of 1689 and by the American Declaration of Independence and Constitution, this charter of basic liberties began with "the natural and imprescriptible rights of man" to "liberty, property, security, and resistance to oppression."

Reflecting Enlightenment thought, the declaration proclaimed that all men were free and equal before the law, that appointment to public office should be based on talent, and that no group should be exempt from taxation. Freedom of speech and of the press were affirmed.

The declaration raised an important issue. Should equal rights include women? Many deputies agreed, provided that, as one man said, "women do not hope to exercise political rights and functions." One writer, **Olympe de Gouges,** refused to accept this **exclusion** of women. Echoing the words of the official declaration, she wrote:

PRIMARY SOURCE

"Believing that ignorance, omission, or scorn for the rights of woman are the only causes of public misfortunes and of the corruption of governments, the women have resolved to set forth in a solemn declaration the natural, inalienable, and sacred rights of woman in order that this declaration, constantly exposed before all the members of the society, will ceaselessly remind them of their rights and duties."

—from *Declaration of the Rights of Woman and the Female Citizen,* Olympe de Gouges, 1791

The King Concedes

In the meantime, Louis XVI remained at Versailles. Used to the absolutist system, he stubbornly refused to accept the National Assembly's decrees. On October 5, however, thousands of Parisian women—described by an eyewitness as "detachments of women coming up from every direction, armed with broomsticks, lances, pitchforks, swords, pistols and muskets"—marched to Versailles. Some of the women then met with the king. They told him that their children were starving because there was no bread. These women forced Louis to accept the new decrees.

Now the crowd insisted that the king and his family come to Paris to show support for the National Assembly. If the king was not under their close watch, they feared he would rouse the kings and princes from other countries to oppose reform.

On October 6, the king and his family returned to Paris. As a goodwill gesture, they brought wagonloads of flour from the palace storehouse. They were escorted by women who chanted: "We are bringing back the baker, the baker's wife, and the baker's boy." The king, the queen, and their son were now virtual prisoners in Paris.

Church Reforms

Under the old regime, the Catholic Church had been an important pillar of the social and political system. The revolutionaries felt they had to reform it too. The new revolutionary government had another serious motivation, however: the need for money. By seizing and selling off Church lands, the National Assembly was able to increase the state's revenues.

Finally, the Church was formally brought under the control of the state. A law was passed called the Civil Constitution of the Clergy. It said that bishops and priests were to be elected by the people, not appointed by the pope and the Church hierarchy. The state would also pay the salaries of the bishops and priests. Because of these changes, many Catholics became enemies of the revolution.

See page R43 to read excerpts from Olympe de Gouges's *Declaration of the Rights of Woman and the Female Citizen* in the **Primary Source and Literature Library.**

New Constitution and New Fears

The new Constitution of 1791 set up a limited monarchy. There was still a king, but a Legislative Assembly would make the laws. The new body was designed to be conservative. First, only the so-called "active" citizens—men over 25 who paid a certain amount of taxes—could vote. All others were considered "passive" citizens with equal rights but no vote. Second, the method of choosing its 745 deputies meant that only relatively wealthy people would serve. Not only the clergy, but also government officials and judges, would be elected. Local governments were put in charge of taxation. The influence of the new government began to spread throughout France.

By 1791, the "ancien régime," or old order, had been destroyed, but the new government did not have universal support. Political radicals and economically disadvantaged people wanted more reform. The king detested the new government's regulation of the Church and his loss of absolute power. While Louis resisted the new constitution, family members and advisers urged him to take more action.

In June 1791, the royal family attempted to flee France in disguise. They almost succeeded in reaching allies in the east, but they were recognized and were captured at Varennes and brought back to Paris. In this unsettled situation, the new Legislative Assembly met for the first time in October 1791 and amended the constitution to allow for trying the king if he turned against the nation. Although Louis XVI publicly swore to uphold the new constitution, the constitutional monarchy seemed already doomed.

CONNECTING TO THE UNITED STATES

REVOLUTIONARY IDEAS

Dr. Martin Luther King, Jr., was an important spokesman for the civil rights movement in the United States in the 1960s. The purpose of the civil rights movement was to gain equal rights for African Americans. These were the same rights that the French Third Estate had fought for nearly 200 years earlier. However, Dr. King advocated nonviolent protest to accomplish these goals.

- **All men are created equal**

- **All men have basic rights to liberty, property, and life**

Dr. King delivered his famous "I Have A Dream" speech at the Lincoln Memorial in Washington, D.C., in 1963 during the march for jobs and freedom. ▼

CONNECTING TO TODAY

1. **Comparing and Contrasting** What are some similarities and differences between the American civil rights movement and the French Revolution?

2. **Making Inferences** Why could a nonviolent approach to change succeed in the United States in the 1960s, but not in France in the late 1700s?

War with Austria

Over time, some European leaders began to fear that revolution would spread to their countries. The rulers of Austria and Prussia even threatened to use force to restore Louis XVI to full power. Insulted by this threat and fearing attack, the Legislative Assembly decided to strike first, declaring war on Austria in the spring of 1792. The French fared badly in the initial fighting. A frantic search for scapegoats began. One observer in France noted:

PRIMARY SOURCE

"Everywhere you hear the cry that the king is betraying us, the generals are betraying us, that nobody is to be trusted; . . . that Paris will be taken in six weeks by the Austrians. . . . We are on a volcano ready to spout flames."

—An observer, 1792

Rise of the Paris Commune

In the spring of 1792, angry citizens demonstrated to protest food shortages and defeats in the war. In August, Paris radicals again decided the fate of the revolution. They declared themselves a commune—a popularly run city council—and organized a mob attack on the royal palace and Legislative Assembly.

The French Revolution was entering a more radical and violent stage. Members of the new Paris Commune took the king captive. They forced the Legislative Assembly to suspend the monarchy and to call for a National Convention. This time they wanted a more radical change. All the representatives who would decide the nation's future would be elected through universal male suffrage, in which all adult males had the right to vote. This would broaden the group of voters to include men who did not meet the initial standards for citizenship established by the Assembly.

Many members of the Paris Commune proudly called themselves **sans-culottes,** meaning "without breeches." They wore long trousers, not the knee-length breeches of the nobles, which identified them as ordinary patriots without fine clothes. Often, sans-culottes are depicted as poor workers, but many were merchants or artisans—the elite of their neighborhoods. The revolution was entering a more radical phase because of the threat of foreign intervention to reestablish the monarchy and because economic conditions in France showed little improvement. This led to calls for new measures to be taken to secure the future of the revolution and improve the living conditions of the people in France.

✓ **Reading Check** **Evaluating** What was the significance of the Constitution of 1791?

Vocabulary

1. **Explain** the significance of: estate, taille, consume, bourgeoisie, Louis XVI, Tennis Court Oath, Declaration of the Rights of Man and the Citizen, Olympe de Gouges, exclusion, sans-culottes.

Main Ideas

2. **List** the reasons for the near collapse of government finances in France.

3. **Explain** why the Catholic Church was targeted for reform.

4. **Identify** five occasions when different groups expressed concern for equality during the revolution using a web diagram.

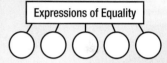

Expressions of Equality

Critical Thinking

5. **The BIG Idea** **Summarizing** What were the main affirmations of the Declaration of the Rights of Man and the Citizen?

6. **Explaining** How were the social and political concerns among the Three Estates different?

7. **Analyzing Visuals** Examine the painting of the Tennis Court Oath shown on page 343. How does David's painting reflect the ideals of the French Revolution?

Writing About History

8. **Persuasive Writing** Olympe de Gouges wrote that "ignorance, omission, or scorn for the rights of woman are the only causes of public misfortunes and of the corruption of governments." Do you agree or disagree? Write a paragraph supporting your point of view.

History ONLINE

For help with the concepts in this section of *Glencoe World History—Modern Times,* go to glencoe.com and click Study Central.

Social History

A Revolution In Clothing

Throughout history, clothing has communicated a person's social status, age, gender, marital status, and ethnicity. Before the French Revolution, some of the Third Estate tried to dress like the nobility. After the revolution, as the Third Estate gained power, their clothing became the style to copy.

SECOND ESTATE

Wigs or hair were layered into powdered curls. Sometimes a hat with feathers was pinned on top.

Hats were worn on top of elaborate wigs or carried as an accessory.

According to the sumptuary laws, only noblemen could carry swords.

Hoops, crumpled paper, or padding was used to enlarge and fluff the skirt.

Noblemen wore knee-length, tight-fitting breeches. Both men and women wore silk stockings.

Only nobility could wear satin, lace, and fur according to the sumptuary laws.

SUMPTUARY LAWS

Before the French Revolution outlawed social classes, sumptuary laws dictated which materials, styles, and accessories could be worn by each estate. Even poorer nobles, who did not have many clothes, dressed in expensive fabrics. The bourgeoisie, wealthier members of the Third Estate, tried to imitate the style of the Second Estate. Only the sumptuary laws prevented the bourgeoisie from "impersonating" a member of the nobility.

Blue, white, and red were symbolic colors of the revolution. It was patriotic to wear the *bonnet rouge*, or red cap, with a circular badge known as a tricolor cockade.

Women of the Third Estate wore a hat with a badge and their hair loose.

THIRD ESTATE

Revolutionary women wore man-styled jackets over their dresses.

Revolutionaries made a political statement by wearing longer trousers. These men became known as the sans-culottes—without breeches.

Practical fabrics and plain styles replaced expensive fabrics and fussy styles.

Both men and women shunned high heels and wore more practical leather or wooden shoes.

REVOLUTIONARY WEAR

During the Reign of Terror, a fashion statement became a political statement. Former nobles and wealthy bourgeoisie learned to avoid extravagant clothing. People wearing lavish clothes were often singled out for persecution, even execution. Revolutionary wear was simple, peasant garb in patriotic colors. Some revolutionary attire stayed in style, like the *pantelons,* or trousers.

ANALYZING VISUALS

1. **Comparing** Who sets fashion trends today, and who inspired fashion in the 1700s?

2. **Making Inferences** How do today's clothing styles make political or social statements?

Radical Revolution and Reaction

GUIDE TO READING

The BIG Idea
Struggle for Rights Radical groups controlled the revolution, which many people in France and abroad opposed.

Content Vocabulary
• faction *(p. 351)*
• elector *(p. 357)*
• coup d'état *(p. 357)*

Academic Vocabulary
• domestic *(p. 352)*   • external *(p. 352)*

People and Events
• Georges Danton *(p. 350)*
• Jean-Paul Marat *(p. 350)*
• Jacobins *(p. 351)*
• Committee of Public Safety *(p. 352)*
• Maximilien Robespierre *(p. 352)*
• Reign of Terror *(p. 353)*
• Directory *(p. 353)*

Reading Strategy
Classifying As you read, create a diagram like the one below to help you study.

Actions taken by the National Convention
1.
2.
3.
4.

Just as in the American Revolution, participants in the French Revolution had different ideas about how to carry out revolutionary ideas and achieve their goals. The revolution tore France's political, economic, and social structure apart, which made neighboring countries nervous. The French Revolution became more radical because of internal divisions and because of fear of foreign invasion.

The Move to Radicalism

MAIN IDEA When the new government was faced with many internal crises and external threats, it broke into factions.

HISTORY & YOU How does our Congress work to solve problems and pass laws? Read how various factions tried to take power in France.

After his flight to Varennes, Louis XVI remained on the throne for a year, but it was a chaotic year. Unrest was fueled by continuing food shortages, military setbacks, and rumors of royalist conspiracies. By August of 1792, the monarchy was over. Rallied by the newly appointed minister of justice, **Georges Danton**, the sans-culottes attacked the palace, and the royal family had to seek protection from the Legislative Assembly.

The powerful Paris Commune forced the Legislative Assembly to call a National Convention. Before the Convention could meet, panic and fear again gripped Paris. Rumors spread that imprisoned nobles and other traitors were conspiring to defeat the revolution. Violence erupted in the streets in September, leaving thousands dead. New leaders of the people emerged, including **Jean-Paul Marat,** who published a radical journal called *Friend of the People*. Marat defended the September massacres.

Soon the life of the king was at risk. The buildup to his execution began with the elections for a new National Convention.

The First Republic

In September 1792, the newly elected National Convention began meeting. The Convention had been called to draft a new constitution, but it also served as the ruling body of France. It was dominated by lawyers, professionals, and property owners. Two-thirds of its deputies were under the age of 45, but most had some political experience as a result of the revolution. Almost all distrusted the king. It was therefore no surprise that the National Convention's first major step on September 21 was to abolish the monarchy and establish a republic, the French Republic.

EYEWITNESS ACCOUNT

King Beheaded!

In a letter, Philipe Pinel, a physician, described the king's execution:

"... [Louis XVI] looked at the scaffold without flinching. The executioner at once proceeded to perform the customary rite by cutting off the King's hair, which he put in his pocket. Louis then walked up onto the scaffold. The air was filled with the roll of numerous drums . . . with such force that Louis's voice was drowned and it was only possible to catch a few stray words like 'I forgive my enemies'. . .

. . . Louis was fastened onto the deadly plank of the machine they call the guillotine and his head was cut off so quickly that he could hardly have suffered. This at least is a merit belonging to the murderous instrument . . . The executioner immediately lifted the head from the sack into which it fell automatically and displayed it [the head] to the people. . . .

As soon as the execution had taken place, the expression on the faces of many spectators changed . . . and [they] fell to crying, 'Vive la Nation!' . . . but a great number withdrew, their spirits racked with pain, to shed tears in the bosom of their families. As decapitations could not be performed without spilling blood on the scaffold many persons hurried to the spot to dip the end of their handkerchief or a piece of paper in it, to have a reminder of this memorable event."

DOCUMENT-BASED QUESTIONS

This popular print by Faucher-Gudin depicts Louis XVI's execution on January 21, 1793.

1. **Predicting** What does the mood after the execution reveal about the next phase of the revolution?

2. **Evaluating** Is it significant that Louis XVI's execution followed almost the same procedure as everyone else's? Why or why not?

The Fate of the King

After 1789, citizens had enthusiastically formed political clubs of varying social and political views. Many deputies belonged to these clubs. The Girondins (juh•RAHN•duhns) tended to represent areas outside Paris. They feared the radical mobs of Paris and leaned toward keeping the king alive. The Mountain represented the interests of radicals in Paris, and many belonged to the

Jacobins (JA•kuh•buhns) club. Increasingly they felt the king needed to be executed to ensure he was not a rallying point for opponents of the republic.

Both **factions,** or dissenting groups, tried to influence the "plain," the majority of deputies who did not belong to any political club. In early 1793, the Mountain convinced the Convention to pass a decree condemning Louis XVI to death.

On January 21, the king was beheaded on the guillotine. Revolutionaries had adopted this machine because it killed quickly and, they believed, humanely. The king's execution created new enemies for the revolution, both at home and abroad. A new crisis was at hand.

The execution of King Louis XVI pushed the revolution into a new radical phase. Henry de Firmont, a Catholic priest, was present at the king's execution. He describes the events he witnessed:

PRIMARY SOURCE

"The path leading to the scaffold was extremely rough and difficult to pass; the King was obliged to lean on my arm, and from the slowness with which he proceeded, I feared for a moment that his courage might fail; but what was my astonishment, when arrived at the last step, he suddenly let go of my arm, and I saw him cross with a firm foot the breadth of the whole scaffold; and in a loud voice, I heard him pronounce distinctly these words: 'I die innocent of all the crimes laid to my charge; I pardon those who had occasioned my death; and I pray to God that the blood you are going to shed may never be visited on France.'"

—Henry de Firmont

Crises and Responses

Disputes between the Girondins and the Mountain blocked the writing of a constitution. The Paris Commune pressured the National Convention to adopt more radical measures: price controls on food and universal male suffrage. Peasants in western France and inhabitants of major provincial cities refused to accept the authority of the Convention. Uprisings began in the west and spread to the south.

After Louis XVI was executed, a coalition of Austria, Prussia, Spain, Portugal, Britain, and the Dutch Republic took up arms against France. The French armies began to fall back. By late spring 1793, the coalition was poised to invade. It seemed possible that the revolution would be destroyed, and the old regime reestablished. Confronted with **domestic** uprisings and **external** threats, the National Convention gave the **Committee of Public Safety** broad powers. This was dominated by Georges Danton, then by the radical Jacobin **Maximilien Robespierre.**

✓ **Reading Check** **Examining** What were the differences between the Girondins and the Mountain?

PEOPLE *in* HISTORY

Jean-Paul Marat
1743–1793 French Revolutionary

Marat earned his nickname "drinker of blood" by urging the poor to take what they needed by force. As a radical Jacobin, Marat condemned the moderate Girondins. In *The Death of Marat*, Jacques-Louis David painted the murder scene and portrayed Marat as a martyr to the revolution. Marat often worked in his bathtub to soothe a skin condition. In Marat's hand is a letter from Charlotte Corday, a Girondin sympathizer, who asked for an appointment with him. Corday stabbed Marat in the bathtub and later stood trial for her crime. **Why did Marat condemn the approach of the Girondins?**

Maximilien Robespierre
1758–1794 French Revolutionary

Robespierre was one of the revolution's most important leaders and a radical Jacobin. He drew his power from the Paris Commune and the support of the sans-culottes. In the National Convention, he preached democracy and universal male suffrage. His nickname was "The Incorruptible" because of his reputation for integrity. His weaknesses were self-righteousness and not tolerating any difference of opinion. Robespierre said, "How can one reproach a man who has truth on his side?" His passion in pursuing the Reign of Terror frightened many and led to his arrest and execution. **How were Robespierre's views different from other revolutionaries?**

The Reign of Terror

MAIN IDEA While the Committee of Public Safety was in power, thousands were executed.

HISTORY & YOU Can you name a government that has executed its critics? Learn about the effects of the executions in France.

For roughly a year during 1793 and 1794, the Committee of Public Safety took control of the government. To defend France from domestic threats, the Committee adopted policies that became known as the **Reign of Terror.**

Crushing Rebellion

As a temporary measure, revolutionary courts were set up to prosecute counter-revolutionaries and traitors. Throughout France, almost 40,000 people were killed during the Reign of Terror. Of those, 16,000 people, including Marie Antoinette and Olympe de Gouges, died by the guillotine. Most executions occurred in towns that had openly rebelled against the Convention.

Revolutionary armies were set up to bring rebellious cities under the control of the National Convention. When the Committee of Public Safety decided to make an example of Lyon, 1,880 citizens of that city were executed. When guillotining proved too slow, grapeshot (a cluster of small iron balls) was used to shoot the condemned into open graves. A foreign witness wrote:

PRIMARY SOURCE

"Whole ranges of houses, always the most handsome, burnt. The churches, convents, and all the dwellings of the former patricians were in ruins. When I came to the guillotine, the blood of those who had been executed a few hours beforehand was still running in the street. . . . I said to a group of sans-culottes that it would be decent to clear away all this human blood. Why should it be cleared? one of them said to me. It's the blood of aristocrats and rebels. The dogs should lick it up."
—a German observer at Lyon, 1793

In western France, too, revolutionary armies were brutal in defeating rebels. The commander of the revolutionary army ordered that no mercy be given: "The road is strewn with corpses. Women, priests, monks, children, all have been put to death. I have spared nobody." Perhaps the most notorious violence occurred in Nantes, where victims were executed by being sunk in barges in the Loire River.

People from all classes were killed during the Terror. Clergy and nobles made up about 15 percent of the victims, while the rest were from the Third Estate. The Committee of Public Safety held that all this bloodletting was only temporary. Once the war and domestic crisis were over, the true "Republic of Virtue" would follow, and the Declaration of the Rights of Man and the Citizen would be realized. Robespierre wrote:

PRIMARY SOURCE

". . . [T]he springs of popular government in revolution are at once virtue and terror: virtue, without which terror is fatal; terror, without which virtue is powerless. Terror is nothing other than justice, prompt, severe, inflexible; it is therefore an emanation of virtue."
—Robespierre

The Republic of Virtue

In addition to the Terror, the Committee of Public Safety took other steps to control and shape a French society. Robespierre called this new order the Republic of Virtue—a democratic republic composed of good citizens. As outward signs of support for the republic, the titles "citizen" and "citizeness" were to replace "mister" and "madame." Women wore long dresses inspired by the clothing worn in the ancient Roman Republic.

Good citizens would be formed by good education. A law aimed at primary education for all was passed but not widely implemented. Another law abolished slavery in French colonies.

Because people were alarmed about high inflation, the Committee tried to control the prices of essential goods like food, fuel, and clothing. The controls did not work well, however, because the government had no way to enforce them.

From the beginning, women had been active participants in the revolution, although they had no official power.

During the radical stage of the revolution, women observed sessions of the National Convention and were not shy about making their demands.

In 1793, two women founded the Society for Revolutionary Republican Women in Paris. Most members were working-class women who asserted that they were ready to defend the republic. Most men, however, believed that women should not participate in either politics or the military.

The Convention also pursued a policy of de-Christianization. Its members believed that the religion encouraged superstition, rather than the use of reason. The word *saint* was removed from street names, churches were looted and closed by revolutionary armies, and priests were encouraged to marry. In Paris, the cathedral of Notre Dame, the center of the Catholic religion in France, was designated a "temple of reason." In November 1793, a public ceremony dedicated to the worship of reason was held in the former cathedral. Patriotic young girls dressed in white dresses paraded before a temple of reason where the high altar had once stood.

Another example of de-Christianization was the adoption of a new calendar. Years would no longer be numbered from the birth of Christ but from September 22, 1792—the first day of the French Republic and the autumnal equinox. The calendar contained 12 months. Each month consisted of three 10-day weeks, with the tenth day of each week a day of rest.

The months were given new names that referred to agriculture or the climate. *Vendémiaire,* which started in September, meant "vintage time." These changes in the calendar had a significant effect on religion in France, eliminating Sundays, Sunday worship services, and church holidays.

Robespierre came to realize, however, that most French people would not accept these efforts at de-Christianization. France was still overwhelmingly Catholic.

✓ **Reading Check** **Analyzing** How did the Committee of Public Safety identify enemies of the state?

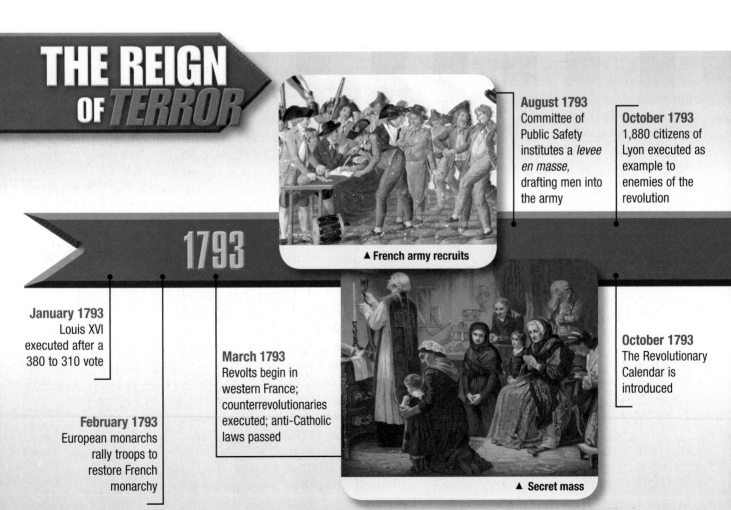

THE REIGN OF TERROR

1793

August 1793
Committee of Public Safety institutes a *levee en masse,* drafting men into the army

October 1793
1,880 citizens of Lyon executed as example to enemies of the revolution

▲ French army recruits

▲ Secret mass

January 1793
Louis XVI executed after a 380 to 310 vote

February 1793
European monarchs rally troops to restore French monarchy

March 1793
Revolts begin in western France; counterrevolutionaries executed; anti-Catholic laws passed

October 1793
The Revolutionary Calendar is introduced

A Nation in Arms

MAIN IDEA A huge revolutionary army defended France against invasion.

HISTORY & YOU How would you feel if every young person in your town was drafted? Read to learn the French reaction to a national draft in 1793.

As foreign troops gathered on its borders, the revolution seemed to be in danger. To save the republic, the Committee of Public Safety issued a decree to raise an army:

PRIMARY SOURCE

"Young men will fight, young men are called to conquer. Married men will forge arms, transport military baggage and guns and will prepare food supplies. Women, who at long last are to take their rightful place in the revolution and follow their true destiny, will forget their futile tasks: their delicate hands will work at making clothes for soldiers; they will make tents and they will extend their tender care to shelters where the defenders of the Patrie [homeland] will receive the help that their wounds require. Children will make lint of old cloth. It is for them that we are fighting: children, those beings destined to gather all the fruits of the revolution, will raise their pure hands toward the skies. And old men, performing their missions again, as of yore, will be guided to the public squares of the cities where they will kindle the courage of young warriors and preach the doctrines of hate for kings and the unity of the Republic."
—from the mobilization decree, August 23, 1793

Rise of the Revolutionary Army

In less than a year, the new French government had raised a huge army—by September 1794, it had over a million soldiers. It was the largest army ever seen in Europe, and it pushed the invaders back across the Rhine. It even conquered the Austrian Netherlands. In earlier times, wars were the business of rulers who fought rivals with professional soldiers. The new French army was created by a people's government. Its wars were people's wars.

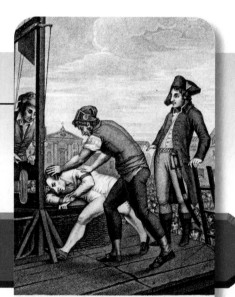
▲ Robespierre at the guillotine

1794

February 1794
Robespierre addresses "On Political Morality" to the Convention, stating that a combination of virtue and terror would save the Republic from its enemies

July 1794
Committee of Public Safety orders Robespierre's execution

June 1794
Law of 22 Prairial gives Robespierre more power; French army ends threat of foreign invasion

August 1794
Law of 22 Prairial repealed; release of prisoners begins

▲ French victory at Fleurus

Analyzing TIME LINES

1. **Determining Cause and Effect** What did the execution of Louis XVI set in motion in France and in the rest of Europe?

2. **Drawing Conclusions** Explain why the Reign of Terror came to an end.

End of the Terror

By the summer of 1794, the French had largely defeated their foreign foes. There was less need for the Reign of Terror, but it continued nonetheless. Robespierre was obsessed with ridding France of all the corrupt elements. Only then could the Republic of Virtue follow.

In June 1794, the Law of 22 Prairial was passed, which gave Robespierre more power to arrest and execute enemies of the revolution. Deputies in the National Convention who feared Robespierre decided to act, lest they be the next victims. They gathered enough votes to condemn him, and Robespierre was guillotined on July 28, 1794.

After the death of Robespierre, the Jacobins lost power and more moderate middle-class leaders took control. The Reign of Terror came to a halt. In August 1794, the Law of 22 Prairial was repealed and the release of prisoners began.

✓ **Reading Check** **Evaluating** How did the revolutionary army help to create nationalism?

POLITICAL CARTOONS   PRIMARY SOURCE

Evaluating the Terror

"—all perished, all—
Friends, enemies, of all parties, ages, ranks,
Head after head, and never heads enough
For those that bade them fall."

—William Wordsworth, *The Prelude, Book X, Residence in France*

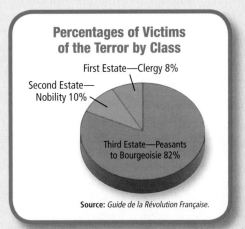

Percentages of Victims of the Terror by Class

First Estate—Clergy 8%

Second Estate—Nobility 10%

Third Estate—Peasants to Bourgeoisie 82%

Source: *Guide de la Révolution Française.*

DOCUMENT-BASED QUESTIONS

The *Radical's Arms* by George Cruikshank shows the British view of the Reign of Terror. The banner above the guillotine reads, "No God! No King! No Religion! No Constitution!"

1. **Identifying Points of View** What opinion of the Terror do Wordsworth and Cruikshank share?

2. **Making Inferences** Wordsworth's poem seems to indicate that "all parties, ages, ranks" suffered equally during the Terror. Does this chart and the one on page 577 support or challenge this view?

The Radical's Arms.

The Directory

MAIN IDEA The Constitution of 1795 set up a new government, but it was unable to inspire trust or solve economic problems.

HISTORY & YOU What kind of government did Americans have after 1781? Read to learn about France's government after Robespierre.

With the Terror over, the National Convention moved in a more conservative direction. First, it restricted the power of the Committee of Public Safety. Next, churches were allowed to reopen. Finally, a new constitution was created.

To keep any one political group from gaining control, the Constitution of 1795 set up two legislative houses. A lower house, the Council of 500, drafted laws. An upper house of 250, the Council of Elders, accepted or rejected proposed laws.

The method for election shows that the new government was much more conservative than the government of Robespierre. Members of both houses were chosen by **electors,** or qualified voters. Only those who owned or rented property worth a certain amount could be electors—only 30,000 people in the whole nation qualified. This was a significant change from the universal male suffrage the Paris Commune had demanded.

Under the new constitution, the executive was a committee of five called the **Directory.** The Council of Elders chose the Directors from a list presented by the Council of 500. The Directory, which lasted from 1795 to 1799, became known mainly for corruption. People reacted against the sufferings and sacrifices that had been demanded in the Reign of Terror. Some people made fortunes from government contracts or by loaning the government money at very high interest rates. They took advantage of the government's severe money problems during these difficult times.

At the same time, the government of the Directory faced political enemies from both conservatives and radicals. Some people wanted to bring back the monarchy, while others plotted to create a more radical regime like Robespierre's. Likewise, economic problems continued with no solution in sight. Finally, France was still conducting expensive wars against foreign enemies.

To stay in power, the Directory began to rely on the military, but one military leader turned on the government. In 1799 the successful and popular general Napoleon Bonaparte toppled the Directory in a **coup d'état** (KOO day•TAH), a sudden overthrow of the government. Napoleon then seized power.

✓ **Reading Check** **Describing** Describe the government that replaced the National Convention.

Vocabulary

1. **Explain** the significance of: Georges Danton, Jean-Paul Marat, Jacobins, faction, domestic, external, Committee of Public Safety, Maximilien Robespierre, Reign of Terror, elector, Directory, coup d'état.

Main Ideas

2. **How** were most members of the National Convention elected in 1792 alike in their political views?

3. **Explain** both the similarities and the differences between the Girondins and the Mountain.

4. **Use** a table like the one below to contrast government policy during and after the rule of Robespierre.

During	After

Critical Thinking

5. **The BIG Idea** **Examining** Did the French Republic live up to the revolution's ideals of Liberty, Equality, and Fraternity? Write a paragraph to support your opinion.

6. **Summarizing** What conditions led to the Reign of Terror? How did the Committee of Public Safety defend its brutal actions against the people?

7. **Analyzing Visuals** Examine the painting shown on page 352. Explain whether you think this is a realistic depiction of Marat's murder or whether the artist is promoting a particular version of events.

Writing About History

8. **Expository Writing** Propaganda is information spread to help or hurt a cause. How does the mobilization decree quoted on page 355 fit the definition of propaganda? Support your argument in an essay.

History ONLINE

For help with the concepts in this section of *Glencoe World History— Modern Times,* go to glencoe.com and click Study Central.

Who Should Be a Citizen?

What is a citizen? One definition is a free person who owes loyalty to a nation and who receives protection, rights, and privileges in return.

Who should be a citizen? At the time of the American Revolution only free, white adult males who owned property or paid taxes could vote. By 1870, all adult males "regardless of race, color, or previous condition of servitude" were granted the right to vote, but it was 1920 before American women could vote.

In France, the Declaration of the Rights of Man and the Citizen addressed social distinctions, but opinions differed on how to interpret the document. Read the excerpts from Robespierre and d'Aelders and study Fragonard's painting to see how they viewed citizenship and the continuing struggle for rights.

SOURCE 1

In this speech from October 1789, Maximilien Robespierre stated his view on property requirements for holding office and voting.

All citizens, whoever they are, have the right to aspire to all levels of office-holding. Nothing is more in line with your declaration of rights, according to which all privileges, all distinctions, all exceptions must disappear. The Constitution establishes that **sovereignty**[1] resides in the people, in all the individuals of the people. Each individual therefore has the right to participate in making the law which governs him and in the administration of the public good which is his own. If not, it is not true that all men are equal in rights, that every man is a citizen. If he who only pays a tax equivalent to a day of work has fewer rights than he who pays the equivalent to three days of work, and he who pays at the level of ten days has more rights than he whose tax only equals that value of three, then he who enjoys 100,000 livres [French pounds] of revenue has 100 times as many rights as he who only has 1,000 livres of revenue. It follows from all your **decrees**[2] that every citizen has the right to participate in making the law and consequently that of being an elector or eligible for office without the distinction of wealth.

SOURCE 2

Etta Palm d'Aelders was a woman active in a reform group called the Cercle Social (Social Circle). D'Aelders expressed her opinions in "The Injustices of the Laws and Favor of Men at the Expense of Women" (December, 1790).

Do not be just by halves, Gentlemen; . . . justice must be the first virtue of free men, and justice demands that the laws be the same for all beings, like the air and the sun. And yet everywhere, the laws favor men at the expense of women, because everywhere power is in your hands. What! Will free men, an enlightened people living in a century of enlightenment and philosophy, will they **consecrate**[3] what has been the abuse of power in a century of ignorance? . . .

The prejudices with which our sex has been surrounded—supported by unjust laws which only accord us a secondary existence in society and which often force us into the humiliating necessity of winning over the **cantankerous**[4] and ferocious character of a man, who, by the greed of those close to us has become our master—those prejudices have changed what was for us the sweetest and most saintly of duties, those of wife and mother, into a painful and terrible slavery. . . .

Oh! Gentlemen, if you wish us to be enthusiastic about the happy constitution that gives back men their rights, then begin by being just toward us. From now on we should be your voluntary companions and not your slaves. Let us merit your attachment!

[1] **sovereignty:** power; authority
[2] **decrees:** authoritative decisions; declarations

[3] **consecrate:** make sacred
[4] **cantankerous:** having a bad disposition; quarrelsome

▲ *Boissy d'Anglas salutes the head of the deputy Feraud, May 20, 1795,* by Alexandre Fragonard.

SOURCE 3

On May 20, 1795, an angry mob in the Convention hacked the head off deputy Feraud and presented it to the chairman, Boissy d'Anglas, who saluted the head. After this incident, d'Anglas presented measures to prevent the return of the Reign of Terror and to take precautions against **anarchy**[5].

Usually the crowds in the balcony were merely rowdy, insulting and threatening the deputies. At times like the one in the painting, they became a mob, invading the chamber and killing deputies with whom they disagreed. Some leaders thought the poor and the uneducated would take over the government, leading to violence and disorder. They feared "mob rule."

[5] **anarchy:** state of lawlessness based on lack of government authority

---

DOCUMENT-BASED QUESTIONS

1. **Analyzing** What does Robespierre think about basing citizenship on whether a person has property or pays taxes?

2. **Explaining** What does d'Aelders mean by women's "secondary existence in society"?

3. **Drawing Inferences** What do you think Fragonard's opinion might have been of universal suffrage—the right of all citizens to vote?

4. **Comparing** Although Robespierre was not a supporter of equal rights for women, list some similarities between his and d'Aelders's arguments.

5. **Contrasting** How does d'Aelders portrayal of women contrast with Fragonard's?

6. **Drawing Conclusions** Does universal suffrage mean anarchy or mob rule? How would you answer the question "Who should be a citizen?" Which source has a position most like your own?

The Age of Napoleon

Napoleon Bonaparte dominated French and European history from 1799 to 1815. During his reign Napoleon built and lost an empire and also spread ideas about nationalism in Europe.

GUIDE TO READING

The BIG Idea
Self-Determination As Napoleon built his empire across Europe, he also spread the revolutionary idea of nationalism.

Content Vocabulary
- consulate *(p. 362)*
- nationalism *(p. 366)*

Academic Vocabulary
- capable *(p. 363)*
- liberal *(p. 365)*

People and Events
- Napoleon Bonaparte *(p. 360)*
- Civil Code *(p. 363)*
- Anne-Louise-Germaine de Staël *(p. 363)*
- Duke of Wellington *(p. 367)*

Reading Strategy
Explaining As you read, use a diagram like the one below to help your study.

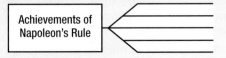

Achievements of Napoleon's Rule

The Rise of Napoleon

MAIN IDEA Napoleon, a popular general, overthrew the Directory, set up a new government, and eventually took complete power.

HISTORY & YOU What qualities do you look for in a political leader? Learn what made the French follow Napoleon.

Napoleon Bonaparte's role in the French Revolution is complex. In one sense, he brought it to an end when he came to power in 1799. Yet he was a child of the revolution as well. Without it, he would never have risen to power, and he himself never failed to remind the French that he had preserved the best parts of the revolution during his reign as emperor.

Early Life
Napoleon was born in 1769 in Corsica, an island in the Mediterranean, only a few months after France had annexed the island. His father came from minor nobility in Italy, but the family was not rich. Napoleon was talented, however, and won a scholarship to a famous military school.

When he completed his studies, Napoleon was commissioned as a lieutenant in the French army. Although he became one of the world's greatest generals and a man beloved by his soldiers, there were few signs of his future success at this stage. He spoke with an Italian accent and was not popular with his fellow officers.

Napoleon devoted himself to his goals. He read what French philosophers had to say about reason, and he studied famous military campaigns. When revolution and war with Europe came about, there were many opportunities for Napoleon to use his knowledge and skills.

Military Successes
Napoleon rose quickly through the ranks. In 1792 he became a captain. Two years later, at age 24, the Committee of Public Safety made him a brigadier general. In 1796 he became commander of the French armies in Italy. There Napoleon won a series of battles with qualities he became famous for—speed, surprise, and decisive action. Napoleon defeated the armies of the Papal States and

Napoleon's mother actually did not attend, but Napoleon told David to add her.

New crowns were made because the originals were lost during the revolution.

The Coronation of the Emperor Napoleon I

Pope Pius VII is shown giving his blessing.

David and his students painted 191 portraits, including Josephine's children, Napoleon's siblings, David's family, and important dignitaries.

DOCUMENT-BASED QUESTIONS

This detail of *The Coronation of the Emperor Napoleon I* by Jacques-Louis David shows Napoleon crowning the Empress Josephine on December 2, 1804. The complete painting, located at the Louvre, is 20 feet by 32 feet.

1. **Describing** How is Napoleon portrayed in this painting?
2. **Making Inferences** How does the painting glorify and legitimize the Empire?

their Austrian allies. These victories gave France control of northern Italy. Throughout the Italian campaigns, Napoleon's energy and initiative earned him the devotion of his troops. His keen intelligence, ease with words, and supreme self-confidence allowed him to win the support of those around him.

In 1797 he returned to France as a hero. He was given command of an army in training to invade Britain, but he knew the French could not carry out that invasion.

Instead, Napoleon suggested striking indirectly at Britain by taking Egypt.

Egypt lay on the route to India, a major source of British wealth and therefore one of Britain's most important colonies. Napoleon's goal of taking Egypt was never met, however. The British were a great sea power and controlled the Mediterranean. By 1799, the British had defeated the French naval forces supporting Napoleon's army in Egypt. Seeing certain defeat, Napoleon abandoned his army and returned to Paris.

Consul and Emperor

In Paris, Napoleon took part in the coup d'état of 1799 that overthrew the Directory and set up a new government, the **consulate**. In theory, it was a republic, but, in fact, Napoleon held absolute power. Napoleon was called first consul, a title borrowed from ancient Rome. He appointed officials, controlled the army, conducted foreign affairs, and influenced the legislature. In 1802 Napoleon was made consul for life. Two years later, he crowned himself Emperor Napoleon I.

✓**Reading Check** **Describing** What personal qualities gained Napoleon so much popular support?

Napoleon's Domestic Policies

MAIN IDEA Napoleon brought stability to France and established a single law code that recognized the equality of all citizens before the law.

HISTORY & YOU How would you feel if a government official checked all your mail before you read it? Read how many of Napoleon's policies reduced freedom.

Napoleon once claimed that he had preserved the gains of the revolution. Since he destroyed the republican form of government when he took power, how could Napoleon make this assertion? As we look

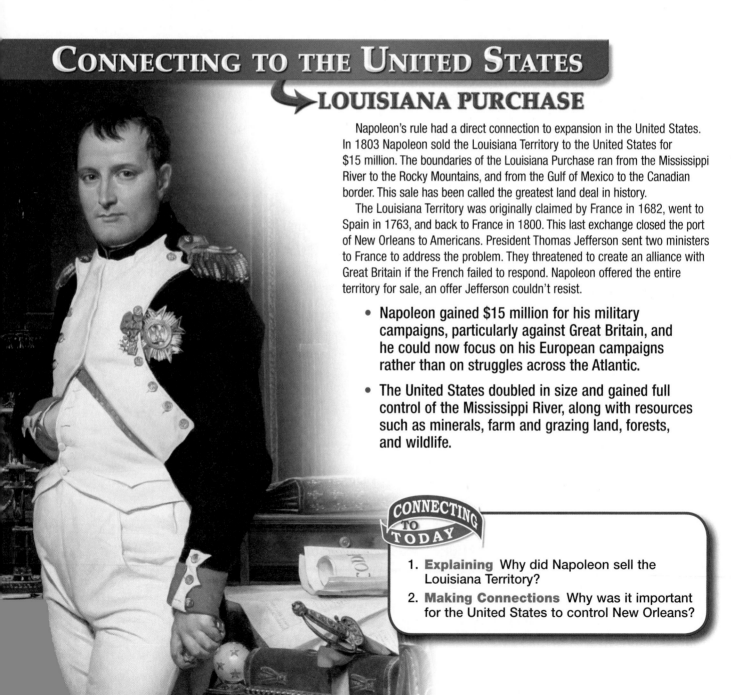

CONNECTING TO THE UNITED STATES

⤷LOUISIANA PURCHASE

Napoleon's rule had a direct connection to expansion in the United States. In 1803 Napoleon sold the Louisiana Territory to the United States for $15 million. The boundaries of the Louisiana Purchase ran from the Mississippi River to the Rocky Mountains, and from the Gulf of Mexico to the Canadian border. This sale has been called the greatest land deal in history.

The Louisiana Territory was originally claimed by France in 1682, went to Spain in 1763, and back to France in 1800. This last exchange closed the port of New Orleans to Americans. President Thomas Jefferson sent two ministers to France to address the problem. They threatened to create an alliance with Great Britain if the French failed to respond. Napoleon offered the entire territory for sale, an offer Jefferson couldn't resist.

- Napoleon gained $15 million for his military campaigns, particularly against Great Britain, and he could now focus on his European campaigns rather than on struggles across the Atlantic.

- The United States doubled in size and gained full control of the Mississippi River, along with resources such as minerals, farm and grazing land, forests, and wildlife.

CONNECTING TO TODAY

1. **Explaining** Why did Napoleon sell the Louisiana Territory?
2. **Making Connections** Why was it important for the United States to control New Orleans?

at Napoleon's domestic policies, it will be possible to judge whether the emperor's claims had any merit.

Peace with the Church

One of Napoleon's first moves at home was to establish peace with the Catholic Church, the oldest enemy of the revolution. In matters of religion, Napoleon himself was a man of the Enlightenment. He believed in reason and felt that religion was at most a social convenience. Since most of the French were Catholic, Napoleon felt it was good policy to mend relations with the Church.

In 1801 Napoleon came to an agreement with the pope, which recognized Catholicism as the religion of a majority of the French people. In return, the pope would not ask for the return of the church lands seized in the revolution.

With this agreement, the Catholic Church was no longer an enemy of the French government. It also meant that people who had acquired church lands in the revolution became avid supporters of Napoleon.

Codification of the Laws

Napoleon's most famous domestic achievement was to codify the laws. Before the revolution, France had almost 300 different legal systems. During the revolution, efforts were made to prepare a single law code for the entire nation. However, the work was not completed until Napoleon's reign.

Seven law codes were created, but the most important was the **Civil Code,** or Napoleonic Code, introduced in 1804. It preserved many of the principles that the revolutionaries had fought for: equality of all citizens before the law; the right of the individual to choose a profession; religious toleration; and the abolition of serfdom and all feudal obligations.

For women and children, the Civil Code was a step back. During the radical stage of the revolution, new laws had made divorce easier and allowed children, even daughters, to inherit property on an equal basis. The Civil Code undid these laws. Women were now "less equal than men."

When they married, they lost control over any property they had. They could not testify in court, and it became more difficult for them to begin divorce proceedings. In general, the code treated women like children, who needed protection and who did not have a public role.

A New Bureaucracy

Napoleon is also well known because he created a strong, centralized administration. He focused on developing a bureaucracy of **capable** officials. Early on, the regime showed that it did not care about rank or birth. Public officials and military officers alike were promoted based on their ability. Opening careers to men of talent was a reform that the middle class had clamored for before the revolution.

Napoleon also created a new aristocracy based on meritorious service to the nation. Between 1808 and 1814, Napoleon created about 3,200 nobles. Nearly 60 percent were military officers, while the rest were civil service or state and local officials. Socially, only 22 percent of this new aristocracy were from noble families of the old regime; about 60 percent were middle class in origin.

Preserver of the Revolution?

In his domestic policies, then, Napoleon did keep some major reforms of the French Revolution. Under the Civil Code, all citizens were equal before the law. The concept of opening government careers to more people was another gain of the revolution that he retained.

On the other hand, Napoleon destroyed some revolutionary ideals. Liberty was replaced by a despotism that grew increasingly arbitrary, in spite of protests by such citizens as the prominent writer **Anne-Louise-Germaine de Staël**. Napoleon shut down 60 of France's 73 newspapers and banned books, including de Staël's. He insisted that all manuscripts be subjected to government scrutiny before they were published. Even the mail was opened by government police.

✓ Reading Check **Evaluating** What was the overall effect of Napoleon's Civil Code?

History ONLINE

Student Web Activity— Visit the Glencoe World History Web site at glencoe.com and click on **Chapter 11 —Student Web Activity** to learn more about Napoleon Bonaparte.

TURNING POINT

SPREADING THE PRINCIPLES OF THE REVOLUTION

As a result of his conquests, Napoleon spread revolutionary ideals and nationalism throughout Europe. To ensure loyalty, Napoleon installed his relatives on the thrones of the lands he conquered. When Napoleon named his brother Jerome king of Westphalia, he explained the importance of spreading the principles of the French Revolution.

"What the peoples of Germany desire most impatiently is that talented commoners should have the same right to your esteem and to public employments as the nobles, that any trace of serfdom . . . should be completely abolished. . . . The peoples of Germany, the peoples of France, of Italy, of Spain all desire equality and liberal ideas. . . . The buzzing of the privileged classes is contrary to the general opinion. Be a constitutional king."

—Napoleon Bonaparte

NAPOLEON'S FAMILY & HIS EMPIRE (1799–1812)

RELATIVE	TITLE	DATE
A Caroline [sister] & Joachim Murat	Duke and Duchess of Berg	1806
B Jerome [brother] Bonaparte	King of Westphalia	1807
C Elisa [sister] Bacciochi	Princess of Lucca and Piombino	1806
	Duchess of Tuscany	1809
D Caroline [sister] & Joachim Murat	King and Queen of Naples	1808
E Pauline [sister] Borghese	Duchess of Guastalla	1806
F Prince Eugène de Beauharnais [Napoleon's stepson]	Viceroy of Italy	1805–
	Prince of Venice	1807
G Louis [brother] Bonaparte & Hortense de Beauharnais [Napoleon's stepdaugher]	King and Queen of Holland	1806– 1810
H Joseph [brother] Bonaparte	King of Spain	1806

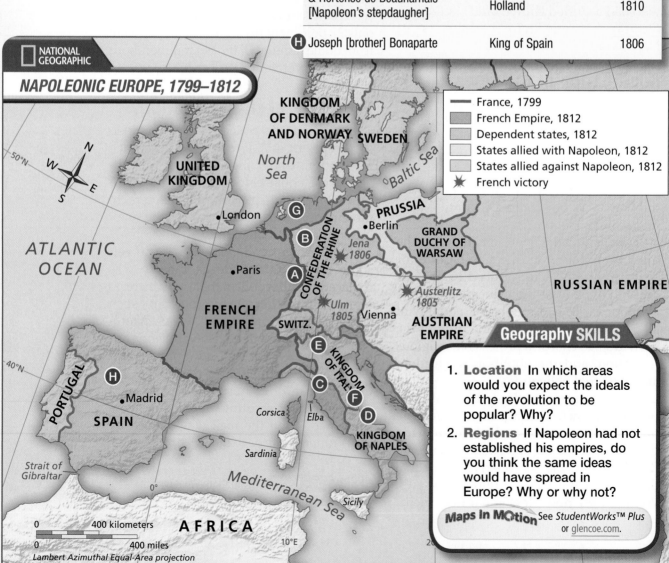

NATIONAL GEOGRAPHIC

NAPOLEONIC EUROPE, 1799–1812

— France, 1799
French Empire, 1812
Dependent states, 1812
States allied with Napoleon, 1812
States allied against Napoleon, 1812
✳ French victory

KINGDOM OF DENMARK AND NORWAY · SWEDEN · North Sea · Baltic Sea · UNITED KINGDOM · London · PRUSSIA · Berlin · GRAND DUCHY OF WARSAW · ATLANTIC OCEAN · CONFEDERATION OF THE RHINE · Jena 1806 · Paris · FRENCH EMPIRE · Austerlitz 1805 · RUSSIAN EMPIRE · Ulm 1805 · Vienna · SWITZ. · AUSTRIAN EMPIRE · KINGDOM OF ITALY · PORTUGAL · Madrid · SPAIN · Corsica · Elba · Sardinia · KINGDOM OF NAPLES · Strait of Gibraltar · Mediterranean Sea · Sicily · AFRICA

0   400 kilometers
0   400 miles
Lambert Azimuthal Equal-Area projection

Geography SKILLS

1. **Location** In which areas would you expect the ideals of the revolution to be popular? Why?

2. **Regions** If Napoleon had not established his empires, do you think the same ideas would have spread in Europe? Why or why not?

Maps In Motion See StudentWorks™ Plus or glencoe.com.

Napoleon's Empire

MAIN IDEA As Napoleon conquered Europe, he spread nationalist ideas. Inspired by those ideas, conquered peoples resisted Napoleon's armies and helped bring about the collapse of his empire.

HISTORY & YOU How would Americans react to a foreign country dictating trade policy to their government? Read how Napoleon tried to bar trade with Britain.

Napoleon is, of course, known less for his domestic policies than for his military leadership. His conquests began soon after he rose to power.

Building the Empire

When Napoleon became consul in 1799, France was at war with a European coalition of Russia, Great Britain, and Austria. Napoleon realized the need for a pause in the war. "The French Revolution is not finished," he said, "so long as the scourge of war lasts. . . . I want peace, as much to settle the present French government, as to save the world from chaos." In 1802 a peace treaty was signed, but it did not last long. War with Britain broke out again in 1803. Gradually, Britain was joined by Austria, Russia, Sweden, and Prussia. In a series of battles at Ulm, Austerlitz, Jena, and Eylau from 1805 to 1807, Napoleon's Grand Army defeated the Austrian, Prussian, and Russian armies.

From 1807 to 1812, Napoleon was the master of Europe. His Grand Empire was composed of three major parts: the French Empire, dependent states, and allied states. The French Empire was the inner core of the Grand Empire. It consisted of an enlarged France extending to the Rhine in the east and including the western half of Italy north of Rome.

Dependent states were kingdoms ruled by relatives of Napoleon. Eventually these included Spain, Holland, the kingdom of Italy, the Swiss Republic, the Grand Duchy of Warsaw, and the Confederation of the Rhine—a union of all German states except Austria and Prussia.

Allied states were countries defeated by Napoleon and then forced to join his struggle against Britain. These states included Prussia, Austria, Russia, and Sweden.

Spreading the Principles of the Revolution

Within his empire, Napoleon sought to spread some of the principles of the French Revolution, including legal equality, religious toleration, and economic freedom. In the inner core and dependent states of his Grand Empire, Napoleon tried to destroy the old order. The nobility and the clergy everywhere in these states lost their special privileges. Napoleon decreed equality of opportunity with offices open to those with ability, equality before the law, and religious toleration. The spread of French revolutionary principles was an important factor in the development of **liberal** traditions in these countries.

Like Hitler 130 years later, Napoleon hoped that his Grand Empire would last for centuries, but his empire collapsed almost as rapidly as it was formed. Two major reasons help explain this collapse: Britain's ability to resist Napoleon and the rise of nationalism.

British Resistance

Napoleon was never able to conquer Great Britain because of its sea power, which made it almost invulnerable. Napoleon hoped to invade Britain, but the British defeated the combined French-Spanish fleet at Trafalgar in 1805. This battle ended Napoleon's plans for invasion.

Napoleon then turned to his Continental System to defeat Britain. The aim of the Continental System was to stop British goods from reaching the European continent to be sold there. By weakening Britain economically, Napoleon would destroy its ability to wage war.

The Continental System also failed. Allied states resented being told by Napoleon that they could not trade with the British. Some began to cheat. Others resisted. Furthermore, new markets in the Middle East and in Latin America gave Britain new outlets for its goods. Indeed, by 1810, British overseas exports were at near-record highs.

Nationalism

A second important factor in the defeat of Napoleon was nationalism. **Nationalism** is the sense of unique identity of a people based on common language, religion, and national symbols. Nationalism was one of the most important forces of the nineteenth century. A new era was born when the French people decided that they were the nation.

Napoleon marched his armies through the Germanies, Spain, Italy, and Poland, arousing new ideas of nationalism in two ways. First, the conquered peoples became united in their hatred of the invaders. Second, the conquered peoples saw the power and strength of national feeling. It was a lesson not lost on them or their rulers.

✓**Reading Check** **Explaining** Why did being a sea power help Britain to survive an attack by the French?

The Fall of Napoleon

MAIN IDEA After major losses in Russia and Austria, Napoleon was defeated at Waterloo.

HISTORY & YOU Today there are some rulers who go into exile to avoid prosecution in their homelands. Read why in 1815 the French government exiled Napoleon.

Napoleon's downfall began in 1812 when he decided to invade Russia. Within only a few years, his fall was complete.

Disaster in Russia

The Russians had refused to remain in the Continental System, leaving Napoleon with little choice but to invade. He knew the risks in invading such a large country, but he also knew that if he did not punish

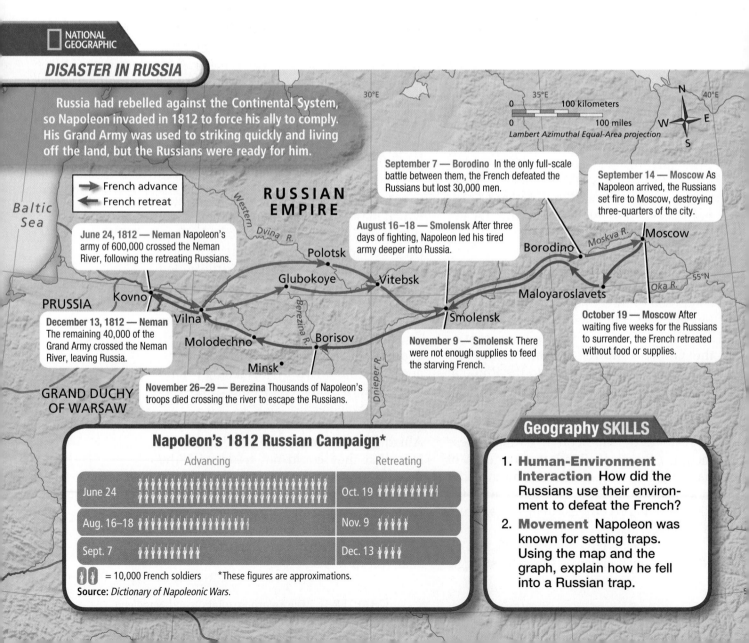

NATIONAL GEOGRAPHIC

DISASTER IN RUSSIA

Russia had rebelled against the Continental System, so Napoleon invaded in 1812 to force his ally to comply. His Grand Army was used to striking quickly and living off the land, but the Russians were ready for him.

→ French advance
← French retreat

RUSSIAN EMPIRE

September 7 — Borodino In the only full-scale battle between them, the French defeated the Russians but lost 30,000 men.

September 14 — Moscow As Napoleon arrived, the Russians set fire to Moscow, destroying three-quarters of the city.

June 24, 1812 — Neman Napoleon's army of 600,000 crossed the Neman River, following the retreating Russians.

August 16–18 — Smolensk After three days of fighting, Napoleon led his tired army deeper into Russia.

December 13, 1812 — Neman The remaining 40,000 of the Grand Army crossed the Neman River, leaving Russia.

October 19 — Moscow After waiting five weeks for the Russians to surrender, the French retreated without food or supplies.

November 9 — Smolensk There were not enough supplies to feed the starving French.

November 26–29 — Berezina Thousands of Napoleon's troops died crossing the river to escape the Russians.

Baltic Sea · PRUSSIA · Kovno · Vilna · Molodechno · Minsk · Polotsk · Glubokoye · Vitebsk · Borisov · Smolensk · Borodino · Maloyaroslavets · Moscow · GRAND DUCHY OF WARSAW · Western Dvina R. · Berezina R. · Dnieper R. · Moskva R. · Oka R.

30°E · 35°E · 40°E · 55°N

0   100 kilometers
0   100 miles
Lambert Azimuthal Equal-Area projection

Napoleon's 1812 Russian Campaign*

	Advancing		Retreating
June 24	𝄪𝄪𝄪𝄪𝄪𝄪𝄪𝄪𝄪𝄪𝄪𝄪𝄪𝄪𝄪𝄪𝄪𝄪𝄪𝄪𝄪𝄪𝄪𝄪𝄪𝄪𝄪𝄪𝄪𝄪	Oct. 19	𝄪𝄪𝄪𝄪𝄪
Aug. 16–18	𝄪𝄪𝄪𝄪𝄪𝄪𝄪𝄪𝄪𝄪𝄪𝄪	Nov. 9	𝄪𝄪
Sept. 7	𝄪𝄪𝄪𝄪𝄪	Dec. 13	𝄪𝄪

👤👤 = 10,000 French soldiers   *These figures are approximations.
Source: *Dictionary of Napoleonic Wars.*

Geography SKILLS

1. **Human-Environment Interaction** How did the Russians use their environment to defeat the French?

2. **Movement** Napoleon was known for setting traps. Using the map and the graph, explain how he fell into a Russian trap.

the Russians for ignoring the Continental System, other nations would follow suit.

In June 1812, a Grand Army of more than 600,000 men entered Russia. Napoleon's hopes depended on a quick victory over the Russians. The Russian forces, however, refused to do battle. Instead they retreated for hundreds of miles. As they retreated, they burned their own villages and countryside to keep Napoleon's army from finding food. When the Russians did fight at Borodino, Napoleon's forces won an indecisive victory, which cost many lives.

When the Grand Army finally reached Moscow, they found the city ablaze. Lacking food and supplies for his army, Napoleon abandoned the Russian capital in late October. As the winter snows began, Napoleon led the "Great Retreat" west across Russia. Thousands of soldiers starved and froze along the way. Fewer than 40,000 of the original 600,000 soldiers arrived back in Poland in January 1813.

This military disaster led other European states to rise up and attack the crippled French army. Paris was captured in March 1814. Napoleon was soon sent into exile on the island of Elba, off the northwest coast of Italy. The victorious powers restored monarchy to France in the person of Louis XVIII, brother of the executed king, Louis XVI.

The Final Defeat

The new king had little support, and the French people were not ready to surrender the glory of empire. Nor was Napoleon ready to give up. Restless in exile, he left the island of Elba and slipped back into France. The new king sent troops to capture Napoleon, who opened his coat and addressed them: "Soldiers of the 5th regiment, I am your Emperor. . . . If there is a man among you [who] would kill his Emperor, here I am!"

No one fired a shot. Shouting "Vive l'Empereur! Vive l'Empereur!"—"Long live the Emperor! Long live the Emperor!"—the troops went over to his side. On March 20, 1815, Napoleon entered Paris in triumph.

Russia, Great Britain, Austria, and Prussia responded to Napoleon's return. They again pledged to defeat the man they called the "Enemy and Disturber of the Tranquility of the World." Meanwhile, Napoleon raised another French army of devoted veterans who rallied from all over France. He then readied an attack on the allied troops stationed across the border in Belgium.

At Waterloo in Belgium on June 18, 1815, Napoleon met a combined British and Prussian army under the **Duke of Wellington** and suffered a bloody defeat. This time, the victorious allies exiled him to St. Helena, a small island in the south Atlantic. Napoleon remained in exile until his death in 1821, but his memory haunted French political life for many decades.

 **Reading Check** Examining Why did Napoleon invade Russia?

SECTION 3 REVIEW

Vocabulary

1. **Explain** the significance of: Napoleon Bonaparte, consulate, Civil Code, capable, Anne-Louise-Germaine de Staël, liberal, nationalism, Duke of Wellington.

Main Ideas

2. What were four major principles that were reflected in the Civil Code?

3. List the powers Napoleon exercised as first consul.

4. Using a diagram like this one, identify the reasons for the rise and fall of Napoleon.

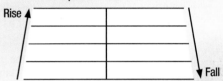
Napoleon's Rise and Fall

Critical Thinking

5. **The BIG Idea** Summarizing How did nationalism unify the people in countries that Napoleon invaded? Write a paragraph defining the importance of nationalism to the ultimate downfall of Napoleon.

6. **Connecting Events** How did the principles of the French Revolution spread throughout Europe?

7. **Analyzing Visuals** Examine the portrait on page 362. How does David portray Napoleon, and why do you think Napoleon wanted artists to produce paintings like this one?

Writing About History

8. **Persuasive Writing** Was Napoleon an enlightened ruler or a tyrant? Write a paper supporting your view. Be sure to include pertinent information about Napoleon's Civil Code.

History ONLINE

For help with the concepts in this section of *Glencoe World History—Modern Times*, go to glencoe.com and click Study Central.

You can study anywhere, anytime by downloading quizzes and flash cards to your PDA from glencoe.com.

CAUSES of the French Revolution

- France was ruled by absolute monarchy.
- A rigid social class system existed.
- The government was bankrupt.
- The Third Estate had no voice in government.
- Bad harvests, rising food prices, and unfair taxation caused civil unrest.
- The political goals of the nobility and middle class challenged the monarchy.

PLACE LOUIS XV, NEAR THE LOUVRE PALACE, PARIS, IN 1775

Statue of King Louis XV

PLACE LOUIS XV BECAME PLACE DE LA RÉVOLUTION IN 1792.

The guillotine replaced the statue of King Louis XV.

SHORT-TERM EFFECTS of the French Revolution

- The end of the monarchy caused initial chaos.
- France was attacked by foreign countries.
- The beheading of royals and the Reign of Terror led to internal disorder.
- Napoleon seized power and became emperor of France.

LONG-TERM EFFECTS of the French Revolution

- Napoleon's army conquered other countries and changed many traditional political and class systems.
- French armies spread nationalism and Enlightenment ideals to other countries.

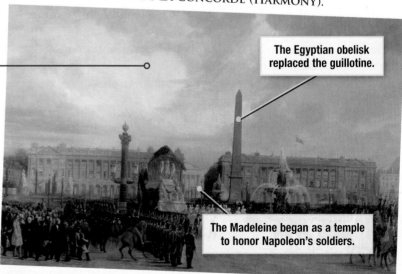

PLACE DE LA RÉVOLUTION BECAME PLACE DE LA CONCORDE (HARMONY).

The Egyptian obelisk replaced the guillotine.

The Madeleine began as a temple to honor Napoleon's soldiers.

STANDARDIZED TEST PRACTICE

TEST-TAKING TIP

As you read a primary source, pause when you reach an unfamiliar word and make sure you understand what the word refers to. Doing so will help you find the answer to a test question more easily.

Reviewing Vocabulary

Directions: Choose the word or words that best complete the sentence.

1. Paris Commune members, many of whom were called _____, considered themselves ordinary patriots.

  A priests

  B sans-culottes

  C aristocrats

  D bureaucrats

2. One of three classes into which French society was divided before the revolution is referred to as a/an _____.

  A taille

  B estate

  C faction

  D assembly

3. A/an _____ is a sudden overthrow of the government.

  A election

  B rebellion

  C coup d'état

  D crowning

4. In 1799 Napoleon headed a new government called the _____.

  A consulate

  B Reign of Terror

  C Glorious Revolution

  D Republic of Virtue

Reviewing Main Ideas

Directions: Choose the best answers to the following questions.

Section 1 *(pp. 340–347)*

5. Who called a meeting of the Estates-General in 1789?

  A Members of the First Estate

  B Members of the Third Estate

  C King Louis XVI

  D Olympe de Gouges

6. Which right did the Third Estate claim in the National Assembly?

  A To have freedom of religion

  B To have access to the Louvre

  C To have their votes count as much as the other Estates

  D To form their own militia

7. The Constitution of 1791 set up which form of government?

  A A limited monarchy

  B An absolute monarchy

  C A democracy

  D A republic

Section 2 *(pp. 350–357)*

8. What did the European nations that opposed the revolution threaten to do?

  A Execute Louis XVI

  B Form a Republic of Virtue

  C Take away France's territories

  D Invade France

Need Extra Help?								
If You Missed Questions . . .	1	2	3	4	5	6	7	8
Go to Page . . .	347	340	357	362	342	343	346	355

9. Thousands of people who opposed the government were executed when _____ was in power.

   A Louis XVI

   B the Estates-General

   C the Committee of Public Safety

   D Napoleon

10. What event happened at the end of the Reign of Terror?

    A The execution of King Louis XVI

    B The creation of the Committee of Public Safety

    C The execution of Maximilien Robespierre

    D Napoleon's overthrow of the Directory

Section 3 *(pp. 360–367)*

11. What is one of the changes Napoleon's law code brought to France?

    A It strengthened the power of the clergy.

    B It furthered women's rights.

    C It stated all citizens were equal before the law.

    D It preserved traditional French society.

12. What was the goal of the Continental System?

    A Codify laws throughout Europe

    B Cut off trade between Britain and France's allies

    C Conquer Russia

    D Create a strong, centralized bureaucracy in Europe

13. Where was Napoleon defeated for the final time?

    A Annecy in France

    B Waterloo in Belgium

    C Leipzig in Germany

    D Moscow in Russia

Critical Thinking

Directions: Choose the best answers to the following questions.

14. Why was the French invasion of Russia a failure?

    A England came to Russia's aid.

    B Napoleon was defeated before he could invade.

    C Barriers kept the French army from entering Russia.

    D Brutal weather and Russia's vast area made victory impossible.

Base your answers to questions 15 and 16 on the map below and your knowledge of world history.

Reign of Terror

• Center of execution

15. Which city was not a center of execution?

    A Marseille

    B Nantes

    C Versailles

    D Bordeaux

16. What do the locations of the centers of execution reveal about the influence of the Reign of Terror in France?

    A It affected all of France.

    B It only affected Paris.

    C It only affected people outside of France.

    D It only affected people in western France.

Need Extra Help?								
If You Missed Questions . . .	9	10	11	12	13	14	15	16
Go to Page . . .	353	356	363	365	367	366	370	370

17. Why did the National Convention decide to execute Robespierre?

   A He was a member of the royal family.

   B They feared that he sold secrets to Britain.

   C He led the attack on the Bastille.

   D They feared his power and his fanaticism.

Analyze the cartoon and answer the question that follows. Base your answer on the cartoon and on your knowledge of world history.

tôt tôt tôt
batter chaud
tôt tôt tôt
bon Courage
il faut avoir cœur à l'ouvrage.

▲ *The Estates-General forging a new constitution*

18. What opinion is the cartoonist expressing?

   A France is filled with hardworking citizens.

   B France is being destroyed by fighting between the Three Estates.

   C France's Three Estates worked together to create a document.

   D France's Third Estate works harder since his hammer is on the anvil.

Document-Based Questions

Directions: Analyze the document and answer the short answer questions that follow the document.

While emperor, Napoleon attempted to spread some ideals of the French Revolution to other nations. He shares these ideas with his brother Jerome, the new King of Westphalia:

> *"What the peoples of Germany desire most impatiently is that talented commoners should have the same right to your esteem and to public employments as the nobles, that any trace of serfdom and of an intermediate hierarchy between the sovereign and the lowest class of the people should be completely abolished. The benefits of the Code Napoleon, the publicity of judicial procedure, the creation of juries must be so many distinguishing marks of your monarchy."*

19. What does Napoleon say that the people of Germany want and do not want?

20. What were Napoleon's views about how civil and military workers should be hired and promoted? Where in this quote does Napoleon refer to these views?

21. In the quotation, Napoleon addresses "the peoples of Germany." How would the nobles of various German states be likely to respond to what he is telling German peoples and why?

Extended Response

22. Between 1789 and 1812 France went through dramatic shifts in systems of government. The goals of Napoleon varied from the goals of the National Assembly. Choose a period of government during the French Revolution or the Napoleonic Empire and explain why it was the most influential.

History ONLINE

For additional test practice, use Self-Check Quizzes—Chapter 11 at **glencoe.com**.

Need Extra Help?						
If You Missed Questions . . .	17	18	19	20	21	22
Go to Page . . .	351	343	371	371	371	368

TIME NOTEBOOK

House Beautiful

Incurable romantics just might rate the Taj Mahal the greatest wonder of the world. It was built by the Mogul emperor Shah Jahan as a tribute to his late wife, Queen Mumtaz Mahal, and contains her mausoleum. Work on this love letter of a marble building began in 1626 in Agra. It took 20,000 workers 22 years to complete it. For kings and queens looking to create an architectural splash, the Taj is a tough act to follow.

GETTY IMAGES

Stone Work

When Napoleon invaded Egypt in 1798, he wanted to rock their world. That hasn't happened. But now, a year later, his army has found a rock that could shake up our world. French soldiers unearthed the stone near the Egyptian town of Rosetta. One side of it is covered with inscriptions written in Greek, Egyptian as spoken in ancient times, and Egyptian hieroglyphics. No one has yet been able to translate hieroglyphics. If all three inscriptions are the same message, scholars could use the Greek words to decode the hieroglyphics. If that ever happens, this "Rosetta Stone" may be the key to understanding ancient Egypt.

VISUAL ARTS LIBRARY (LONDON)/ALAMY

VERBATIM

❝ So far as he is able, a prince should stick to the path of good but, if the necessity arises, he should know how to follow evil. **❞**

NICCOLÒ MACHIAVELLI,
from his book The Prince, *explaining how to succeed in politics*

❝ Here stand I. I can do no other. God help me. Amen. **❞**

MARTIN LUTHER,
who supposedly uttered these words to Charles II at the Diet of Worms, in refusing to back down from his criticisms of the Catholic Church

❝ The people of the various provinces are strictly forbidden to have in their possession any swords, short swords, bows, spears, firearms, or other types of arms. The possession of unnecessary implements makes difficult the collection of taxes and dues and tends to foment uprisings. **❞**

TOYOTOMI HIDEYOSHI,
whose military victories in Japan's provinces allowed him to rule a unified country until his death in 1598

❝ If I have seen further, it is by standing on the shoulders of giants. **❞**

SIR ISAAC NEWTON,
stating modestly that his discoveries owe a debt to the work of earlier scientists

❝ It will appear from everything which I have said, that it is not regulation [of the slave trade], it is not mere palliatives, that can cure this enormous evil. Total abolition is the only possible cure for it. **❞**

WILLIAM WILBERFORCE,
leader of the antislavery movement in England, in a stirring speech given in the House of Commons in 1789

SCHOOL DAZE

In Elizabethan England today, most school kids focus on learning to speak and read Latin. After all, courses in universities are taught in that language. But English royalty is expected to have a more wide-ranging education. At right is a typical day for a young royal taught by a private tutor at home.

Morning (7:30 to 1:00):
Dancing, Breakfast, French, Latin, Writing, Drawing, Prayers, Recreation, Dinner

Afternoon (1:00 to 5:30):
Cosmography (the study of Earth and the heavens), Latin, French, Writing, Prayers, Recreation, Supper

BRAND X PICTURES/ALAMY IMAGES

THE ULTIMATE RENAISSANCE MAN

Leonardo da Vinci is celebrated for his paintings and drawings. But less widely appreciated is the fabulous Florentine's talent as an inventor. In his many notebooks, Leonardo has sketched and described in detail an incredible array of devices. Here is just a small sample of his output. But beware: one of these inventions is an invention of ours. Which one?

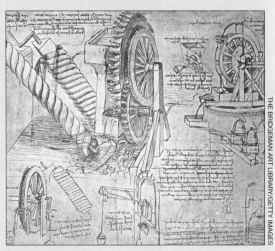

THE BRIDGEMAN ART LIBRARY/GETTY IMAGES

1. Parachute
2. Giant crossbow
3. Flying ship
4. Wristwatch
5. Self-propelled car
6. Drilling machine
7. Military tank
8. Paddleboat
9. Diving bell
10. Machine gun
11. Printing press
12. Helicopter

Answer: 4

BY THE NUMBERS

5 The number of moons first observed by Galileo through a telescope, in 1610, which proves that not all heavenly bodies orbit the Earth, as has previously been believed

3,500,000– 6,000,000 The number of people killed in the Napoleonic Wars, which took place between 1804 and 1815

224 The number of days it took Columbus to sail from Europe to the Americas and back

2,000 The number of pounds of sugar that Dutch merchants charged for one enslaved African in 1654

Milestones

DIED. AKBAR THE MAGNIFICENT, in 1605, Mogul ruler of most of northern India. This great Muslim leader set up an efficient system of government and severely punished corruption by those in power. He taxed Muslims and non-Muslims alike. A tolerant ruler, he allowed Hindus great control of their territories and so gained their loyalty.

THE BRIDGEMAN ART LIBRARY/GETTY IMAGES

FOUNDED. THE ROYAL AFRICAN COMPANY, in 1672. The British government has given the company exclusive permission to trade in slaves. The company expects to transport an average of 5,000 enslaved persons a year from Africa.

SIGNED. THE TREATY OF TORDESILLAS in 1494, by Spain and Portugal, which divides the world into two halves along an imaginary line curving north and south through the Atlantic Ocean. Every new land discovered west of the line will belong to Spain. Everything east of it will belong to Portugal, which

can now grab unclaimed areas of Africa and a small part of South America. Spain seems to have gotten the short end of the stick: It's unlikely that any valuable lands will be found beyond the Atlantic.

DISCOVERED. How blood moves through the human body, by William Harvey. In a book published in 1628, the English scientist nixes the idea that arteries pump blood. He says that the heart circulates blood and that vessels return it to the heart for recirculation. Many doctors have given Harvey's theories their heartfelt recommendation.

CRITICAL THINKING

1. **Analyzing Information** In what way might the Rosetta Stone be helpful to historians?

2. **Drawing Conclusions** Why did some people think that the Treaty of Tordesillas favored Portugal over Spain?

UNIT 3

An Era of European Imperialism

1800–1914

▶ Why It Matters

The period of world history from 1800 to 1914 was characterized by two major developments: the growth of industrialization and Western domination of the world. The Industrial Revolution became one of the major forces for change, leading Western civilization into the industrial era that has characterized the modern world. At the same time, the Industrial Revolution created the technological means, including new weapons, by which the West achieved domination over much of the rest of the world.

CHAPTER 12   INDUSTRIALIZATION AND NATIONALISM
1800–1870

CHAPTER 13   MASS SOCIETY AND DEMOCRACY
1870–1914

CHAPTER 14   THE HEIGHT OF IMPERIALISM
1800–1914

CHAPTER 15   EAST ASIA UNDER CHALLENGE
1800–1914

Railways, like this one at London Paddington Station, were integral to the success of the Industrial Revolution in Great Britain.

Industrialization and Nationalism 1800–1870

Section 1 The Industrial Revolution

Section 2 Reaction and Revolution

Section 3 National Unification and the Nationalism

Section 4 Romanticism and Realism

MAKING CONNECTIONS

How do events influence culture?

In 1834, fire destroyed the original Houses of Parliament in Britain. Reflecting the influence of the romantics, architects used neo-Gothic style—an imitation of the medieval Gothic style—to rebuild these landmarks and add Big Ben. In this chapter, you will learn how romanticism emerged from the turmoil of the Industrial Revolution.

- Review the description of Gothic style in Chapter 4. What elements of Gothic style do you see in the photo of the Houses of Parliament and clock tower?
- How has the development of the Internet affected today's culture?

EUROPE AND THE
UNITED STATES ▶

1804
Richard Trevithick's
steam locomotive
runs on an industrial
rail-line in Britain

1814
Congress of
Vienna meets

1848
Revolutions erupt in
Europe, beginning
with the overthrow
of Louis-Philippe

1800   1820   1840

THE WORLD ▶

1821
Mexico declares
independence from Spain

1839
Opium War
begins in China

1865
Confederate forces
surrender, ending the
American Civil War

1871
German
unification
achieved under
William I

1860   1880

1869
Suez Canal
completed

History **ONLINE**
Chapter Overview—Visit glencoe.com to preview Chapter 12.

FOLDABLES™
Study Organizer

Describing Create a
Layered-Look Book
to record notes about
the ideologies of
the 1800s.

Ideologies

Conservatism

Nationalism

Liberalism

The Industrial Revolution

GUIDE TO READING

The BIG Idea
New Technologies The Industrial Revolution changed the way people lived and worked.

Content Vocabulary
- enclosure movement *(p. 378)*
- capital *(p. 378)*
- entrepreneurs *(p. 378)*
- cottage industry *(p. 379)*
- puddling *(p. 380)*
- industrial capitalism *(p. 384)*
- socialism *(p. 385)*

Academic Vocabulary
- derived *(p. 380)*
- hypothetical *(p. 385)*

People and Places
- James Watt *(p. 380)*
- Manchester *(p. 381)*
- Liverpool *(p. 381)*
- Robert Fulton *(p. 383)*
- Robert Owen *(p. 385)*

Reading Strategy
Categorizing Information As you read, use a table like the one below to name important inventors mentioned in this section and their inventions.

Inventors	Inventions

Beginning in Great Britain during the late eighteenth century, the Industrial Revolution led to the industrialization that shaped the modern world. Europe saw a shift from an economy based on farming and handicrafts to an economy based on manufacturing by machines in factories.

The Industrial Revolution in Great Britain

MAIN IDEA With its plentiful natural resources, workers, wealth, and markets, Great Britain became the starting place of the Industrial Revolution.

HISTORY & YOU Think about how computers are rapidly changing today's world. Read to understand how the Industrial Revolution changed life in the nineteenth century.

The Industrial Revolution began in Great Britain in the 1780s and took several decades to spread to other Western nations. Several factors contributed to make Great Britain the starting place.

First, agricultural practices in the eighteenth century had changed. Expansion of farmland, good weather, improved transportation, and new crops such as the potato dramatically increased the food supply. More people could be fed at lower prices with less labor. Now even ordinary British families could use some of their income to buy manufactured goods.

Second, with the increased food supply, the population grew. Parliament passed **enclosure movement** laws in the 1700s. When landowners fenced off common lands, many peasants had to move to towns, giving Britain a plentiful supply of labor.

Third, Britain had a ready supply of money, or **capital**, to invest in the new industrial machines and factories. Many British people were wealthy. The **entrepreneurs** found new business opportunities and new ways to make profits.

Fourth, Britain had plentiful natural resources. The country's rivers provided water power for the new factories. These waterways provided a means for transporting raw materials and finished products. Britain also had abundant supplies of coal and iron ore, essential in manufacturing processes.

Finally, a supply of markets gave British manufacturers a ready outlet for their goods. Britain had a vast colonial empire, and British ships could transport goods anywhere in the world. Also, because of population growth and cheaper food at home, domestic markets increased. A growing demand for cotton cloth led British manufacturers to look for ways to increase production.

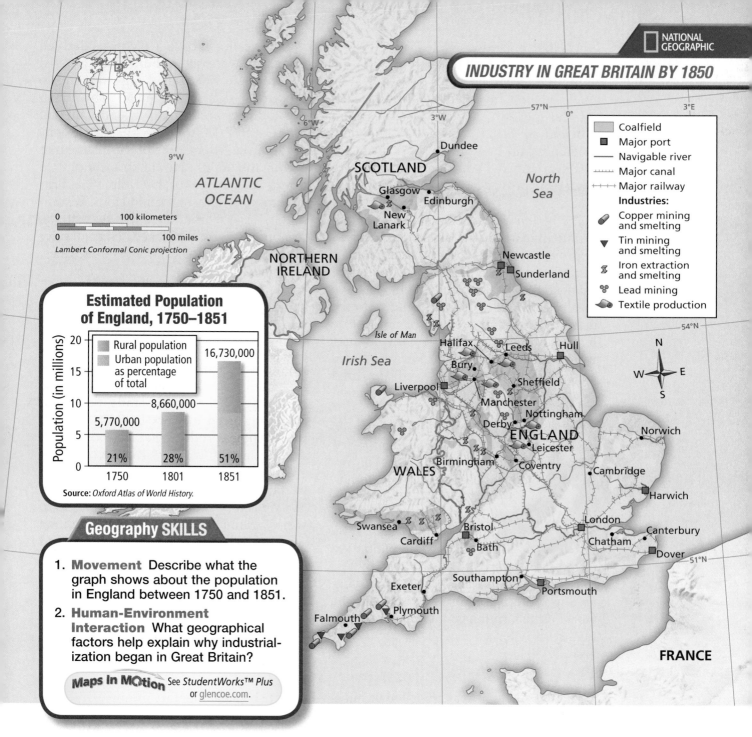

Legend

- Coalfield
- ■ Major port
- — Navigable river
- ⊢⊢⊢ Major canal
- +++ Major railway

Industries:
- Copper mining and smelting
- ▼ Tin mining and smelting
- Iron extraction and smelting
- Lead mining
- Textile production

Estimated Population of England, 1750–1851

Population (in millions)

- Rural population
- Urban population as percentage of total

1750	1801	1851
5,770,000	8,660,000	16,730,000
21%	28%	51%

Source: *Oxford Atlas of World History.*

Geography SKILLS

1. **Movement** Describe what the graph shows about the population in England between 1750 and 1851.

2. **Human-Environment Interaction** What geographical factors help explain why industrialization began in Great Britain?

Maps In Motion See *StudentWorks™ Plus* or glencoe.com.

Changes in Cotton Production

In the eighteenth century, Great Britain had surged way ahead in the production of inexpensive cotton goods. The manufacture of cotton cloth was a two-step process. First, spinners made cotton thread from raw cotton. Then, weavers wove the cotton thread into cloth on looms. In the eighteenth century, individuals spun the thread and then wove the cloth in their rural cottages. This production method was thus called a **cottage industry.**

A series of technological advances in the eighteenth century made cottage industry inefficient. First, the invention of the "flying shuttle" made weaving faster. Now, weavers needed more thread from spinners because they could produce cloth at a faster rate.

In 1764 James Hargreaves had invented a machine called the spinning jenny, which met this need. Other inventors made similar contributions. The spinning process became much faster. In fact, spinners produced thread faster than weavers could use it.

Another invention made it possible for the weaving of cloth to catch up with the spinning of thread. This was a water-powered loom invented by Edmund Cartwright in 1787. It now became more efficient to bring workers to the new machines and have them work in factories near streams and rivers, which were used to power many of the early machines.

The cotton industry became even more productive when the steam engine was improved in the 1760s by **James Watt**, a Scottish engineer. In 1782, Watt made changes that enabled the engine to drive machinery. Steam power could now be used to spin and weave cotton. Before long, cotton mills using steam engines were found all over Britain. Because steam engines were fired by coal, not powered by water, they did not need to be located near rivers.

British cotton cloth production increased dramatically. In 1760, Britain had imported 2.5 million pounds (1.14 million kg) of raw cotton, which was used to produce cloth in cottage industries. In 1787, the British imported 22 million pounds (10 million kg) of cotton, most of it spun on machines. By 1840, 366 million pounds (166 million kg) of cotton were imported each year. By this time, cotton cloth was Britain's most valuable product. Sold everywhere in the world, British cotton goods were produced mainly in factories.

The Coal and Iron Industries

The steam engine was crucial to Britain's Industrial Revolution. For fuel, the engine depended on coal, a substance that seemed then to be unlimited in quantity. The success of the steam engine increased the need for coal and led to an expansion in coal production. New processes using coal aided the transformation of another industry—the iron industry.

Britain's natural resources included large supplies of iron ore. At the beginning of the eighteenth century, the basic process of producing iron had changed little since the Middle Ages. A better quality of iron was produced in the 1780s when Henry Cort developed a process called **puddling**.

In this process, coke, which was **derived** from coal, was used to burn away impurities in crude iron, called pig iron, and to produce an iron of high quality. The British iron industry boomed. In 1740, Britain had produced 17,000 tons (15,419 metric tons or t) of iron. After Cort's process came into use in the 1780s, production jumped to nearly 70,000 tons (63,490 t). In 1852, Britain produced almost 3 million tons (2.7 million t)—more iron than the rest of the combined world produced. High-quality iron was used to build new machines, especially trains.

The New Factories

The factory was another important element in the Industrial Revolution. From its beginning, the factory created a new labor system. Factory owners wanted to use their new machines constantly. So, workers were forced to work in shifts to keep the machines producing at a steady rate.

Early factory workers came from rural areas where they were used to periods of hectic work, followed by periods of inactivity. Factory owners wanted workers to work without stopping. They disciplined workers to a system of regular hours and repetitive tasks. Anyone who came to work late was fined or quickly fired for misconduct, especially for drunkenness. One early industrialist said that his aim was "to make the men into machines that cannot err."

Discipline of factory workers, especially of children, was often harsh. A report from a British parliamentary inquiry into the condition of child factory workers stated:

PRIMARY SOURCE

" . . . provided a child should be drowsy, the overlooker walks round the room . . . and he touches the child on the shoulder, and says, 'Come here.' In a corner of the room there is an iron cistern; it is filled with water; he takes this boy, and takes him up by the legs, and dips him over head in the cistern, and sends him to work for the remainder of the day. . . ."

In some factories, children were often beaten with a rod or whipped to keep them at work.

Railroads

In the eighteenth century, more efficient means of moving resources and goods developed. Railroads were particularly important to the success of the Industrial Revolution.

Richard Trevithick, an English engineer, built the first steam locomotive. In 1804, Trevithick's locomotive ran on an industrial rail-line in Britain. It pulled 10 tons (9 t) of ore and 70 people at 5 miles (8.05 km) per hour. Better locomotives soon followed. In 1813, George Stephenson built the *Blucher,* the first successful flanged-wheel locomotive. With its flanged wheels, the *Blucher* ran on *top* of the rails instead of in sunken tracks.

The success of Stockton & Darlington, the first true railroad, encouraged investors to link by rail the rich cotton-manufacturing town of **Manchester** with the thriving port of **Liverpool,** a distance of 32 miles (51.5 km). In 1829, the investors sponsored a competition to find the most suitable locomotive to do the job. They selected the *Rocket*.

TURNING POINT

INDUSTRIALIZATION — TRANSFORMS SOCIETY

The Industrial Revolution in Europe began the shift from an agricultural to an industrial economy. Starting in Great Britain, it transformed not only where people worked but also the nature of work itself.

SOCIAL CHANGES OF INDUSTRIALIZATION

Before the Industrial Revolution
- Agricultural work on farms and in homes predominated; cottage industry took place in homes.
- Most people lived in rural areas.
- Single workers or families produced an entire product.

During and After the Industrial Revolution
- Manufacturing predominated, with workers placed in factories; cottage industry declined or disappeared.
- Workers migrated to work in city factories, causing explosive growth, overcrowding, and filthy conditions.
- Factories practiced division of labor. Each worker performed one task in the production process. These tasks were often repetitive and boring.
- Factory work required long hours under harsh working conditions.
- Child labor occurred on a large scale. Women and children were usually paid lower wages.

The new industrial workers included children as young as seven years old, as shown in this image of child workers carrying clay in a British brickyard.

DOCUMENT-BASED QUESTIONS

1. **Contrasting** How did factory tasks differ from traditional work?

2. **Making Inferences** How do you think industrialization affected people's attitudes about work? What specific changes would workers have disliked?

The *Rocket* sped along at 16 miles (25.7 km) per hour while pulling a 40-ton (36-t) train. Within 20 years, locomotives were able to reach 50 miles (80.5 km) per hour, an incredible speed. In 1840, Britain had almost 2,000 miles (3,218 km) of railroads. In 1850, more than 6,000 miles (9,654 km) of railroad track crisscrossed much of that country.

Railroad expansion caused a ripple effect in the economy. Building railroads created new jobs for farm laborers and peasants. Less expensive transportation led to lower-priced goods, thus creating larger markets. More sales meant more factories and more machinery. Business owners could reinvest their profits in new equipment, adding to the growth of the economy. This type of regular, ongoing economic growth became a basic feature of the new industrial economy.

✓ **Reading Check** **Describing** How were adult and child factory workers disciplined?

The Spread of Industrialization

MAIN IDEA The pace of industrialization in Europe and the United States depended on many factors, including government policy.

HISTORY & YOU Recall how the Enlightenment spread through Europe. Read about the factors that help explain why nations adapt to change at different speeds.

The world's first industrial nation, Great Britain, was also the richest nation by the mid-nineteenth century. It produced one-half of the world's coal and manufactured goods. Its cotton industry alone in 1850 was equal in size to the industries of all other European countries combined.

Europe

The Industrial Revolution spread to the rest of Europe at different times and speeds. First to be industrialized in continental

SCIENCE, TECHNOLOGY, & SOCIETY

The Power of Steam

Steam power helped drive the Industrial Revolution. Its impact was evident in factories and on the farm.

No innovation was more crucial to the Industrial Revolution than the steam engine. Steam power transformed both farm production and the transportation system. Steam-powered locomotives could deliver raw materials to factories and finished goods to market faster than ever before.

Farming had always been labor-intensive, but now farmers were able to haul the portable steam engine to the fields to power tools. Another step forward came in 1842 when a British company developed a self-propelled steam engine that could pull a plow. It paved the way for tractors and other machinery. Farm efficiency shot up dramatically.

George Stephenson's Rocket carried cotton goods from Manchester to the port of Liverpool.

CRITICAL THINKING SKILLS

1. **Explaining** Why was a rail connection to Liverpool important to manufacturers in Manchester?
2. **Determining Cause and Effect** In what way was the development of the steam engine a cause of the Industrial Revolution?

Europe were Belgium, France, and the German states. In these places, governments actively encouraged industrialization. For example, governments provided funds to build roads, canals, and railroads. By 1850, a network of iron rails spread across Europe.

North America

An Industrial Revolution also occurred in the United States. In 1800, 5 million people lived in the United States, and 6 out of every 7 American workers were farmers. No city had more than 100,000 people. By 1860, the population had grown to 30 million people. Cities had also grown. Nine cities had populations over 100,000. Only 50 percent of American workers were farmers.

A large country, the United States needed a good transportation system to move goods across the nation. Thousands of miles of roads and canals were built to link east and west. **Robert Fulton** built the first paddle-wheel steamboat, the *Clermont,* in 1807. Steamboats made transportation easier on the waterways of the United States.

Most important in the development of an American transportation system was the railroad. It began with fewer than 100 miles (160.9 km) of track in 1830. By 1860, about 30,000 miles (48,270 km) of railroad track covered the United States. The country became a single massive market for the manufactured goods of the Northeast.

Labor for the growing number of factories in the Northeast came chiefly from the farm population. Women and girls made up a large majority of the workers in large textile (cotton and wool) factories.

Factory owners sometimes sought entire families, including children, to work in their factories. One advertisement in a newspaper in the town of Utica, New York, read: "Wanted: A few sober and industrious families of at least five children each, over the age of eight years, are wanted at the cotton factory in Whitestown. Widows with large families would do well to attend this notice."

✓ Reading Check **Evaluating** Why was the railroad important to the industrialization of the United States?

Social Impact in Europe

MAIN IDEA Industrialization urbanized Europe and created new social classes, as well as the conditions for the rise of socialism.

HISTORY & YOU Do you know people who run their own businesses? Read to learn how early entrepreneurs contributed to the Industrial Revolution.

The Industrial Revolution drastically changed the social life of Europe and the world. In the first half of the nineteenth century, cities grew and two social classes—the industrial middle class and the industrial working class—emerged.

Growth of Population and Cities

European population stood at an estimated 140 million in 1750. By 1850, the population had almost doubled to 266 million. The key to this growth was a decline in death rates, wars, and diseases such as smallpox and plague. With increased food supplies, more people were better fed and more resistant to disease. Famine largely disappeared from Western Europe. The Irish potato famine proved an exception. The Irish depended on the potato for food. When a fungus infected crops in the 1840s, almost a million Irish people died. A million more emigrated, many to the United States.

European cities and towns dramatically grew. Industrialization spurred this growth. By 1850, British and Belgian cities were home to many industries. With the steam engine, factory owners could locate their plants in cities. People moved from the country to the cities to find work.

In 1800, Great Britain had one major city, London, with a population of about 1 million. Six cities had populations between 50,000 and 100,000. By 1850, London's population had swelled to about 2.5 million. Nine cities had populations over 100,000, and eighteen cities had populations between 50,000 and 100,000. Also, over 50 percent of the British population lived in towns and cities. In other European countries, urban populations grew less dramatically.

The rapid growth of cities in the first half of the nineteenth century led to pitiful living conditions for many. These conditions prompted urban reformers to call on local governments to clean up their cities. Reform would be undertaken in the second half of the nineteenth century.

The Industrial Middle Class

The Middle Ages saw the rise of commercial capitalism, an economic system based on trade. **Industrial capitalism**, an economic system based on industrial production, rose during the Industrial Revolution and produced a new middle-class group—the industrial middle class.

In the Middle Ages, the bourgeois, or middle-class person, was the burgher or town dweller. The bourgeois were merchants, officials, artisans, lawyers, or intellectuals. Later, the term *bourgeois* came to include people involved in industry and banking, as well as professionals such as lawyers, teachers, or doctors.

The new industrial middle class was made up of the people who built the factories, bought the machines, and developed the markets. They had initiative, vision, ambition, and, often, greed. One said, "Getting of money … is the main business of the life of men."

The Industrial Working Class

The Industrial Revolution also created a working class that faced wretched working conditions. Work hours ranged from 12 to 16 hours a day, 6 days a week. There was no security of employment and no minimum wage.

The worst conditions were in the cotton mills. One report noted that "in the cotton-spinning work, these creatures are kept, 14 hours in each day, locked up, summer and winter, in a heat of from 80 to 84 degrees." Mills were also dirty, dusty, dangerous, and unhealthy.

Conditions in the coal mines were also harsh. Steam-powered engines lifted the

---

POLITICAL CARTOONS · PRIMARY SOURCE

The Irish Potato Famine

The Irish depended on the potato as their main food source. When a fungus infected the potato in 1845 and again in 1846 and 1848, it spelled disaster. The potato famine of 1845 alone killed one million people. Millions more emigrated during the 1840s, most to the United States. Between 1841 and 1851, Ireland's population actually dropped—from 8.2 to 6.5 million.

The British government did little to relieve the suffering, in part because it believed free trade forbade government interference. Irish resentment at the British failure to help them has been passed on to later generations. For decades, right down to our own day, this resentment has fueled Irish nationalist movements like the IRA (Irish Republican Army).

Homeless Irish family on the streets.

A sign warning off the many homeless beggars.

The shovel was regarded as a symbol of labor.

HERE AND THERE;

DOCUMENT-BASED QUESTIONS

A cartoon in the July 15, 1848, Punch magazine compares an Irish and an American family. The full caption was "Here and There; or Emigration, a Remedy."

1. **Interpreting** Why might this cartoon have helped convince Irish people to immigrate to the United States?
2. **Explaining** How did the Irish potato famine contribute to Irish nationalism?

coal from the mines to the top, but the men inside the mines dug out the coal. Dangerous conditions, including cave-ins, explosions, and gas fumes (called "bad air"), were a way of life. The cramped conditions in mines and their constant dampness led to workers' deformed bodies and ruined lungs.

When the Factory Act of 1833 limited child labor, women made up the difference. Women were 50 percent of the British labor force in textile factories. Mostly unskilled, they were paid half or less than half of what men received.

The employment of children and women was a carry-over from the cottage industry where the family worked together. When the work hours of children and women were limited, a new pattern of work emerged. Men now earned most of the family income by working outside the home. Women took over daily care of the family and performed low-paying jobs that could be done in the home. This made it possible for women to continue to help with the family's financial survival.

Early Socialism

The transition to factory work was not easy. Although workers' lives eventually improved, they suffered terribly during the early period of industrialization. Their family life was disrupted, they were separated from the countryside, their hours were long, and their pay was low.

Some reformers opposed such a destructive capitalistic system and advocated **socialism.** In this economic system, society—usually in the form of the government—owns and controls some means of production such as factories and utilities. This public ownership of the means of production, it was believed, would allow wealth to be distributed more equitably to everyone.

Early socialists wrote books about the ideal society that might be created. In this **hypothetical** society, workers could use their abilities and everyone's needs would be met. Later socialists said these were impractical dreams. Karl Marx contemptuously labeled the earlier reformers utopian socialists. (He borrowed the term from *Utopia,* a work describing an ideal society by Sir Thomas More.) To this day we refer to the early socialists in this way.

Robert Owen, a British cotton manufacturer, was one utopian socialist. He believed that humans would show their natural goodness if they lived in a cooperative environment. Owen transformed the squalid factory town of New Lanark (Scotland) into a flourishing community. He created a similar community at New Harmony, Indiana, in the United States in the 1820s. New Harmony failed because not everyone was as committed to sharing as Owen was.

✓ **Reading Check** **Describing** How did socialists respond to new and harsh working conditions?

Vocabulary

1. **Explain** the significance of: enclosure movement, capital, entrepreneurs, cottage industry, James Watt, puddling, derived, Manchester, Liverpool, Robert Fulton, industrial capitalism, socialism, hypothetical, Robert Owen.

Main Ideas

2. **Describe** four factors that contributed to making Great Britain the starting place for the Industrial Revolution.

3. **Explain** how government policy influenced the spread of industrialization in Europe.

4. **Summarize** the population growth of Great Britain's cities by using a chart similar to the one below.

Population Growth of Great Britain's Cities, 1800–1850		
City	1800	1850
London's population		
No. of cities with population over 100,000		
No. of cities with population between 50,000 and 100,000		

Critical Thinking

5. **The BIG Idea** **Determining Cause and Effect** Analyze the causes and effects of the Industrial Revolution.

6. **Identifying Points of View** How might the industrial middle class and working class have differed in their views of early industrialization?

7. **Analyzing Visuals** What purpose do you think the engraver had in creating the image on page 381? What kind of images of child labor do you see in the news today?

Writing About History

8. **Informative Writing** You are a nineteenth-century journalist. Write a brief article depicting the working conditions in cotton mills and an explanation of how owners defend such conditions.

History ONLINE

For help with the concepts in this section of *Glencoe World History—Modern Times,* go to glencoe.com and click Study Central.

Describe the Lives of Workers in the Early 1800s

What hardships did industrialization create for workers? Though it transformed the British economy, industrialization had a drastic social impact on the working people of England.

How did industrialization affect living conditions? The Industrial Revolution not only brought waves of new factories, it caused masses of workers to move to the cities to find jobs at these factories. Both developments had a profound impact on the lives of England's workers.

The Industrial Revolution altered both the working and living conditions of Britain's working class. Read the excerpts and study the illustration to learn more about how industrialization impacted the people of England during the first half of the nineteenth century.

SOURCE 1

Miner Betty Harris, 37, gave testimony to an 1842 Royal Commission investigating conditions in British mines.

I was married at 23, and went into a **colliery**[1] when I was married. I . . . can neither read nor write. . . . I am a **drawer**[2], and work from 6 in the morning to 6 at night. Stop about an hour at noon to eat my dinner; have bread and butter for dinner; I get no drink. . . .

I have a belt round my waist, and a chain passing between my legs, and I go on my hands and feet. The road is very steep, and we have to hold by a rope; and when there is no rope, by anything we can catch hold of. There are six women and about six boys and girls in the pit I work in; it is very hard work for a woman. The pit is very wet where I work, and the water comes over our clog-tops always, and I have seen it up to my thighs; it rains in at the roof terribly. My clothes are wet through almost all day long. . . .

My cousin looks after my children in the day time. I am very tired when I get home at night; I fall asleep sometimes before I get washed. . . . the belt and chain is worse when we are **in the family way**[3]. My feller (husband) has beaten me many a times for not being ready.

SOURCE 2

German socialist Friedrich Engels, co-founder of Marxism, described industrial Manchester in his book, *The Condition of the Working-Class in England in 1844.*

The first court below Ducie Bridge . . . was in such a state at the time of the cholera that the sanitary police ordered it evacuated, swept, and disinfected with **chloride of lime**[4]. . . . At the bottom flows, or rather stagnates, the Irk, a narrow, coal-black, foul-smelling stream, full of debris and refuse, which it deposits on the shallower right bank. . . .

Above the bridge are **tanneries**[5], **bone mills**[6], and gasworks, from which all drains and refuse find their way into the Irk, which receives further the contents of all the neighboring sewers and **privies**[7]. . . . Below the bridge you look upon the piles of debris, the refuse, the filth, and offal from the courts on the steep left bank; here each house is packed close behind its neighbor and a piece of each is visible, all black, smoky, crumbling, ancient, with broken panes and window frames. . . .

Such is the Old Town of Manchester . . . [in] defiance of all considerations of cleanliness, ventilation, and health which characterize the construction of this single district, containing at least twenty to thirty thousand inhabitants.

[1] **colliery:** coal mine and its connected buildings
[2] **drawer:** worker who pulled coal tubs in a mine; tubs were attached to the drawer's belt with a chain

[3] **in the family way:** pregnant
[4] **chloride of lime:** bleaching powder
[5] **tanneries:** buildings where skins and hides are tanned

▲ Girls and women worked at "Carding, Drawing, and Roving" in a nineteenth-century English cotton mill.

SOURCE 3

A series of inventions in the late 1700s revolutionized the cotton industry in England. These new machines dramatically increased textile production and marked the end of the home-based system of textile production. By the early 1800s, textile workers had to work in factories where they operated large machines for long hours in hot temperatures.

The above print of a cotton mill appears in the book *History of the Cotton Manufacture in Great Britain* (London, 1835), by Edward Baines. The image shows the belts that connected the machines to a pulley system. A steam engine rotated the wheels on the shaft to power the machines. Note how close the female workers' hands, hair, and clothing are to the rotating gears.

---

[6] **bone mills:** mills that convert animal bones into fertilizer
[7] **privies:** outhouses

DOCUMENT-BASED QUESTIONS

1. **Calculating** How many hours did Betty Harris work each day?

2. **Recognizing Bias** How could Engels's background have affected his assessment of Manchester? How might a description of the city written by a factory owner contrast from that written by Engels?

3. **Assessing** How does Baines depict the working environment in the cotton mill? Is it safe or dangerous?

4. **Comparing and Contrasting** What do Harris's testimony and the above print suggest about how the work experience for women in mines and cotton mills was similar and different?

5. **Synthesizing** How could Engels have used Harris's testimony to support his main point about industrialization?

6. **Problem-Solving** Describe the lives of England's workers in the early 1800s. If you were an adviser to the British government in 1845, what changes would you have recommended?

Reaction and Revolution

GUIDE TO READING

The BIG Idea
Self-Determination In 1848, liberals and nationalists rebelled against many of the conservative governments of Europe.

Content Vocabulary
- conservatism *(p. 388)*
- principle of intervention *(p. 389)*
- liberalism *(p. 390)*
- universal male suffrage *(p. 392)*
- multinational state *(p. 393)*

Academic Vocabulary
- constitution *(p. 390)* • radical *(p. 392)*

People, Places, and Events
- Congress of Vienna *(p. 388)*
- Klemens von Metternich *(p. 388)*
- Vienna *(p. 388)*
- Bill of Rights *(p. 390)*
- Louis-Napoleon *(p. 392)*
- German Confederation *(p. 392)*
- Prague *(p. 393)*

Reading Strategy
Summarizing Information As you read, use a chart like the one below to summarize the causes of the revolutions in France in 1830 and 1848.

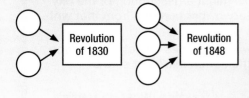

After the turmoil of the French revolutionary years, European rulers wanted to return to a conservative order and to keep a balance of power among nations. Liberals and nationalists, however, struggled to achieve more liberal governments and new nations. Their struggle led eventually to the revolutions that swept across much of Europe in 1848.

The Congress of Vienna

MAIN IDEA After Napoleon's defeat, the victors met and redrew the map of Europe to create a balance of power and to strengthen conservatism.

HISTORY & YOU Does the United Nations intervene in international disputes? Read about decisions that the great powers made at the Congress of Vienna and their effect on Europe.

After the defeat of Napoleon, European rulers moved to restore the old order. This was the goal of the victors—Great Britain, Austria, Prussia, and Russia—when they met at the **Congress of Vienna** in September 1814 to arrange a final peace settlement.

The haughty Austrian foreign minister, Prince **Klemens von Metternich** (MEH•tuhr•nihk), was the most influential leader at that meeting in **Vienna**. Metternich claimed that the principle of legitimacy guided him. He meant that lawful monarchs from the royal families who had ruled before Napoleon would be restored to their positions of power. This, they believed, would ensure peace and stability in Europe. The victorious powers had already restored the Bourbon king to the French throne in 1814.

Practical considerations of power were addressed at the Congress of Vienna. The great powers rearranged territories in Europe, believing that this would form a new balance of power. The powers at Vienna wanted to keep any one country from dominating Europe. This meant balancing political and military forces that guaranteed the independence of the great powers. To balance Russian territorial gains, for example, new territories were given to Prussia and Austria.

Conservatism and the Balance of Power

The arrangements worked out at the Congress of Vienna were a victory for rulers who wanted to contain the forces of change that the French Revolution had unleashed. These rulers, like Metternich, believed in the political philosophy known as **conservatism.**

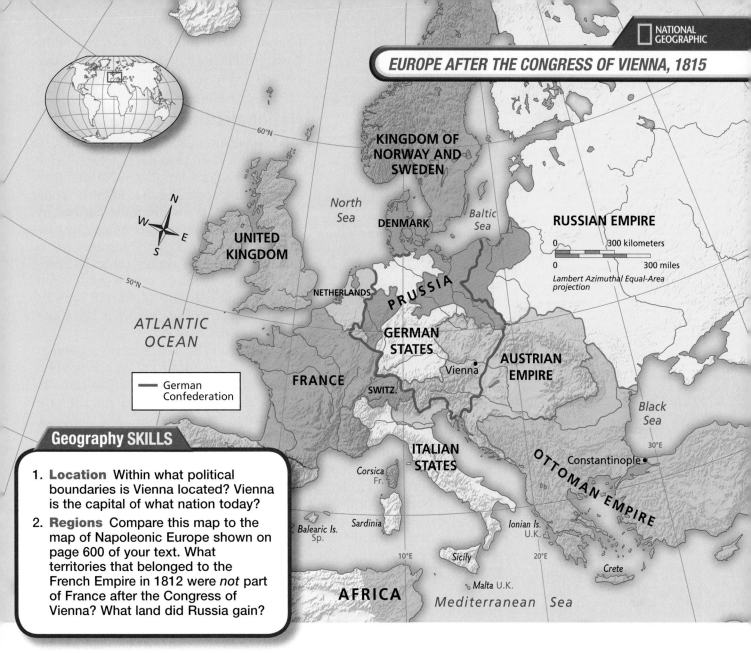

EUROPE AFTER THE CONGRESS OF VIENNA, 1815

KINGDOM OF
NORWAY AND
SWEDEN

North
Sea

Baltic
Sea

DENMARK

RUSSIAN EMPIRE

0   300 kilometers

0   300 miles

*Lambert Azimuthal Equal-Area
projection*

UNITED
KINGDOM

NETHERLANDS

PRUSSIA

ATLANTIC
OCEAN

GERMAN
STATES

Vienna

AUSTRIAN
EMPIRE

FRANCE

SWITZ.

Black
Sea

30°E

— German
Confederation

Geography SKILLS

1. **Location** Within what political boundaries is Vienna located? Vienna is the capital of what nation today?

2. **Regions** Compare this map to the map of Napoleonic Europe shown on page 600 of your text. What territories that belonged to the French Empire in 1812 were *not* part of France after the Congress of Vienna? What land did Russia gain?

ITALIAN
STATES

Corsica
Fr.

Constantinople

OTTOMAN EMPIRE

Balearic Is.
Sp.

Sardinia

Ionian Is.
U.K.

10°E

Sicily

20°E

Crete

Malta U.K.

AFRICA

Mediterranean Sea

60°N

50°N

Conservatism is based on tradition and a belief in the value of social stability. Most conservatives at that time favored obedience to political authority. They also believed that organized religion was crucial to keep order in society. Conservatives hated revolutions and were unwilling to accept demands from people who wanted either individual rights or representative governments.

To maintain the new balance of power, Great Britain, Russia, Prussia, and Austria (and later France) agreed to meet at times. The purpose of these conferences was to take steps needed to maintain peace in Europe. These meetings came to be called the Concert of Europe.

Principle of Intervention

Eventually, the great powers adopted a **principle of intervention.** According to this principle, the great powers had the right to send armies into countries where there were revolutions in order to restore legitimate monarchs to their thrones. Refusing to accept the principle, Britain argued that the great powers should not interfere in the internal affairs of other states. The other great powers, however, used military forces to crush revolutions in Spain and Italy, as well as to restore monarchs to their thrones.

✓ **Reading Check** **Analyzing** What were the goals of European leaders at the Congress of Vienna?

Forces of Change

MAIN IDEA Liberals and nationalists opposed the existing political system and threatened the conservative regimes.

HISTORY & YOU What do you have in common with other Americans? Learn how a common language, religion, and customs led people to form loyalty to a nation.

Between 1815 and 1830, conservative governments throughout Europe worked to maintain the old order. However, powerful forces for change—known as liberalism and nationalism—were also at work.

Liberalism

Liberalism is a political philosophy that grew out of the Enlightenment. **Liberalism** held that people should be as free as possible from government restraint.

Liberals had a common set of political beliefs. Chief among them was the protection of civil liberties, or the basic rights of all people. These civil liberties included equality before the law and freedom of assembly, speech, and the press. Liberals believed that all these freedoms should be guaranteed by a written document such as the American **Bill of Rights.**

Most liberals wanted religious toleration for all, as well as separation of church and state. Liberals also demanded the right of peaceful opposition to the government. They believed that a representative assembly (legislature) elected by qualified voters should make laws.

Many liberals, then, favored government ruled by a **constitution,** such as in a constitutional monarchy in which a constitution regulates a king. They believed that written constitutions would guarantee the rights they sought to preserve.

Liberals did not, however, believe in a democracy in which everyone had a right to vote. They thought that the right to vote and hold office should be open only to men of property. Liberalism, then, was tied to middle-class men, especially industrial middle-class men, who wanted voting rights for themselves so they could share power with the landowning classes. The liberals feared mob rule and had little desire to let the lower classes share that power.

Nationalism

Nationalism was an even more powerful force for change in the nineteenth century than was liberalism. Nationalism arose when people began to identify themselves as part of a community defined by a distinctive language, common institution, and customs. This community is called a nation. In earlier centuries, people's loyalty went to a king or to their town or region. In the nineteenth century, people began to feel that their chief loyalty was to the nation.

Nationalism did not become a popular force for change until the French Revolution. From then on, nationalists came to believe that each nationality should have its own government. Thus, the Germans, who were separated into many principalities, wanted national unity in a German nation-state with one central government. Subject peoples, such as the Hungarians, wanted the right to establish their own governments rather than be subject to the Austrian emperor.

Nationalism, then, was a threat to the existing political order. A united Germany, for example, would upset the balance of power set up at the Congress of Vienna in 1815. At the same time, an independent Hungarian state would mean the breakup of the Austrian Empire. Conservatives feared such change and thus tried hard to repress nationalism.

In the first half of the nineteenth century, nationalism found a strong ally in liberalism. Most liberals believed that freedom could only be possible in people who ruled themselves. Each group of people should have its own state. No state should attempt to dominate another state. The association with liberalism meant that nationalism had a wider scope.

Revolutionary Outbursts

Beginning in 1830, the forces of change— liberalism and nationalism—began to break through the conservative domination of

Europe. In France, liberals overthrew the Bourbon monarch Charles X in 1830 and established a constitutional monarchy. Political support for the new monarch, Louis Philippe, a cousin of Charles X, came from the upper-middle class.

In the same year, 1830, three more revolutions occurred. Nationalism was ·the chief force in all three of them. Belgium, which had been annexed to the former Dutch Republic in 1815, rebelled and created an independent state. In Poland and Italy, which were both ruled by foreign powers, efforts to break free were less successful. Russians crushed the Polish attempt to establish an independent Polish nation. Meanwhile Austrian troops marched south and put down revolts in a number of Italian states.

✓ Reading Check **Evaluating** How did liberalism and nationalism present a challenge to the conservative domination of Europe in the early 1800s?

The Revolutions of 1848

MAIN IDEA Beginning in France in 1848, the spirit of revolution spread quickly over Europe, but the uprisings were largely suppressed.

HISTORY & YOU Can you imagine living without the rights guaranteed in the Constitution? In 1848, popular uprisings in Europe hoped to win such rights.

The conservative order still dominated much of Europe as the midpoint of the nineteenth century approached. However, the forces of liberalism and nationalism continued to grow. These forces of change erupted once more in the revolutions of 1848.

Another French Revolution

Revolution in France once again sparked revolution in other countries. Severe economic problems beginning in 1846 brought untold hardship in France to the lower-middle class, workers, and peasants.

PRIMARY SOURCE / HISTORY & ARTS

The Overthrow of King Louis Philippe

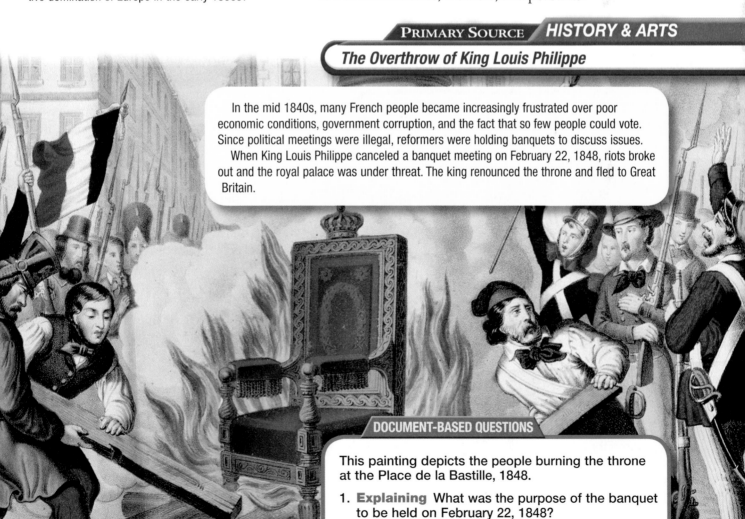

In the mid 1840s, many French people became increasingly frustrated over poor economic conditions, government corruption, and the fact that so few people could vote. Since political meetings were illegal, reformers were holding banquets to discuss issues.

When King Louis Philippe canceled a banquet meeting on February 22, 1848, riots broke out and the royal palace was under threat. The king renounced the throne and fled to Great Britain.

DOCUMENT-BASED QUESTIONS

This painting depicts the people burning the throne at the Place de la Bastille, 1848.

1. **Explaining** What was the purpose of the banquet to be held on February 22, 1848?

2. **Analyzing Visuals** How would you describe the symbolic meaning of this painting?

At the same time, members of the middle class clamored for the right to vote. The government of Louis Philippe refused to make changes, and opposition grew.

The monarchy was finally overthrown in 1848. A group of moderate and **radical** republicans set up a provisional, or temporary, government. The republicans were people who wished France to be a republic—a government in which leaders are elected.

The provisional government called for the election of representatives to a Constituent Assembly that would draw up a new constitution. Election was to be by **universal male suffrage,** meaning all adult men could vote.

The provisional government also set up national workshops to provide work for the unemployed. From March to June, the number of unemployed enrolled in the national workshops rose from about 66,000 to almost 120,000. This emptied the treasury and frightened the moderates, who reacted by closing the workshops on June 21.

The workers refused to accept this decision and poured into the streets. In four days of bitter and bloody fighting, government forces crushed the working-class revolt. Thousands were killed and thousands more were sent to the French prison colony of Algeria in northern Africa.

The new constitution, ratified on November 4, 1848, set up a republic called the Second Republic. The Second Republic had a single legislature elected by universal male suffrage. A president, also chosen by universal male suffrage, served for four years. In the elections for the presidency held in December 1848, Charles Louis Napoleon Bonaparte (called **Louis-Napoleon**), the nephew of the famous French ruler, won a resounding victory.

Trouble in the German States

News of the 1848 revolution in France led to upheaval in other parts of Europe. The Congress of Vienna in 1815 had recognized the existence of 38 independent German states (called the **German Confederation**). Of these, Austria and Prussia were the two great powers. The other states varied in size.

In 1848, cries for change led many German rulers to promise constitutions, a free press, jury trials, and other liberal reforms. In May 1848, an all-German parliament, called the Frankfurt Assembly, was held to fulfill a liberal and nationalist dream—the preparation of a constitution for a new united Germany. The Frankfurt Assembly's proposed constitution provided for a German state with a parliamentary government and a hereditary emperor ruling under a limited monarchy. The constitution also allowed for direct election of deputies to the parliament by universal male suffrage.

Ultimately, however, the Frankfurt Assembly failed to gain the support needed to achieve its goal. Frederick William IV of Prussia, to whom the throne was offered, refused to accept the crown from a popularly elected assembly. Thus, the assembly members had no real means of forcing the German rulers to accept their drafted constitution. German unification was not achieved.

NATIONAL GEOGRAPHIC

NATIONALITIES IN AUSTRIA-HUNGARY, MID-1800S

Boundary:
— of Austria-Hungary
— between Austria & Hungary

Ethnic background of majority of population:

Croat	Romanian
Czech	Romansch
German	Ruthenian
Italian	Serb
Magyar	Slovak
Pole	Slovene

Geography SKILLS

1. **Place** Name three nationalities in Hungary.
2. **Regions** Why might the ethnic makeup shown on this map lead to conflict within the empire?

Revolutions in Central Europe

The Austrian Empire also had its problems. The empire was a **multinational state**—a collection of different peoples including Germans, Czechs, Magyars (Hungarians), Slovaks, Romanians, Slovenes, Poles, Croats, Serbians, Ruthenians (Ukrainians), and Italians. Only the German-speaking Hapsburg dynasty held the empire together. The Germans, though only a quarter of the population, played a leading role in governing the Austrian Empire.

In March 1848, demonstrations erupted in the major cities. To calm the demonstrators, the Hapsburg court dismissed Metternich, the Austrian foreign minister, who fled to England. In Vienna, revolutionary forces took control of the capital and demanded a liberal constitution. To appease the revolutionaries, the government gave Hungary its own legislature. In Bohemia, the Czechs clamored for their own government.

Austrian officials had made concessions to appease the revolutionaries but were determined to reestablish their control over the empire. In June 1848, Austrian military forces crushed the Czech rebels in **Prague.** By the end of October, the rebels in Vienna had been defeated as well. With the help of a Russian army of 140,000 men, the Hungarian revolutionaries were finally subdued in 1849. The revolutions in the Austrian Empire had failed.

Revolts in the Italian States

The Congress of Vienna had set up nine states in Italy. These states included the Kingdom of Piedmont in the north; the Two Sicilies (Naples and Sicily); the Papal States; a handful of small states; and the northern provinces of Lombardy and Venetia, which were now part of the Austrian Empire.

In 1848, a revolt broke out against the Austrians in Lombardy and Venetia. Revolutionaries in other Italian states also took up arms and sought to create liberal constitutions and a unified Italy. By 1849, however, the Austrians had reestablished complete control over Lombardy and Venetia. The old order also prevailed in the rest of Italy.

Throughout Europe in 1848, popular revolts started upheavals that had led to liberal constitutions and liberal governments. However, moderate liberals and more radical revolutionaries were soon divided over their goals, and so conservative rule was reestablished. Even with the reestablishment of conservative governments, however, the forces of nationalism and liberalism continued to influence political events.

✓ Reading Check **Identifying** What countries experienced revolutions in 1848?

Vocabulary
1. **Explain** the significance of: Congress of Vienna, Klemens von Metternich, Vienna, conservatism, principle of intervention, liberalism, Bill of Rights, constitution, radical, universal male suffrage, Louis-Napoleon, German Confederation, multinational state, Prague.

Main Ideas
2. **Explain** how the Congress of Vienna achieved and maintained a balance of power.

3. **Summarize** the ideologies of conservatism, liberalism, and nationalism by using a chart like the one below.

Conservatism	Liberalism	Nationalism

4. **List** the different peoples living in the Austrian Empire.

Critical Thinking
5. **The BIG Idea** **Analyzing** How did the social and economic changes from the Industrial Revolution contribute to the spread of liberalism?

6. **Hypothesizing** Why did Great Britain not join the revolutions that spread through Europe in 1848?

7. **Analyzing Visuals** Examine the painting on page 391. If you did not already know, how could you tell the social class of the revolutionaries by their dress?

Writing About History
8. **Expository Writing** Select one of the following ideologies: conservatism, liberalism, or nationalism. Write an essay in which you identify contemporary ideas influenced by that ideology.

History ONLINE

For help with the concepts in this section of *Glencoe World History— Modern Times,* go to glencoe.com and click Study Central.

National Unification and Nationalism

GUIDE TO READING

The BIG Idea

Self-Determination In the mid-1800s, the Germans and Italians created their own nations. However, not all national groups were able to reach that goal.

Content Vocabulary

- militarism *(p. 396)*
- kaiser *(p. 397)*
- plebiscite *(p. 399)*
- emancipation *(p. 400)*
- abolitionism *(p. 401)*
- secede *(p. 401)*

Academic Vocabulary

- unification *(p. 395)*
- regime *(p. 399)*

People and Places

- Piedmont *(p. 395)*
- Giuseppe Garibaldi *(p. 396)*
- Otto von Bismarck *(p. 396)*
- Alsace *(p. 397)*
- Lorraine *(p. 397)*
- Queen Victoria *(p. 398)*
- Budapest *(p. 399)*
- Czar Alexander II *(p. 400)*

Reading Strategy

Summarizing Information
As you read, use a table like the one below to list the changes that took place in the indicated countries during the nineteenth century.

Great Britain	France	Austrian Empire	Russia

Although the revolutions of 1848 had failed, the forces of nationalism and liberalism remained powerful for the rest of the nineteenth century. Italy and Germany were unified, and Great Britain and France became more liberal, while Austria and Russia remained authoritarian by the end of the nineteenth century.

Toward National Unification

MAIN IDEA The rise of nationalism led to the unification of Italy and Germany.

HISTORY & YOU What have you achieved as a member of a group that you could not have achieved on your own? Learn how determined leadership and strong military effort resulted in the unification of the Italian and German states.

The revolutions of 1848 had failed. By 1871, however, both Germany and Italy would be unified. The changes that made this possible began with the Crimean War.

Breakdown of the Concert of Europe

The Crimean War was the result of a long-term struggle between Russia and the Ottoman Empire. The Ottoman Empire, centered in what is now Turkey, had long controlled most of the Balkans in southeastern Europe. By 1800, however, the Ottoman Empire was in decline. Its authority over Balkan territories began to weaken.

Russia was a nation with little access to warm-water ports. It had always coveted territory in the Balkans. Having this territory would allow Russian ships to sail through the Dardanelles, the straits between the Black Sea and the Mediterranean. If Russia could achieve this goal, it would become the major power in eastern Europe and would even be able to challenge British naval control of the eastern Mediterranean. Other European nations feared Russian ambitions but also hoped to gain some territory if the Ottoman Empire collapsed.

In 1853, the Russians invaded the Turkish Balkan provinces of Moldavia and Walachia. In response, the Ottoman Turks declared war on Russia. Great Britain and France, fearful of Russian gains, declared war on Russia the following year. This conflict came to be called the Crimean War.

The Crimean War was named for the Russian peninsula in the Black Sea where important battles took place. The war was poorly planned and poorly fought. Eventually, heavy losses caused the Russians to seek peace. By the Treaty of Paris, signed in March 1856, Russia agreed to allow Moldavia and Walachia to be placed under the protection of all the great powers.

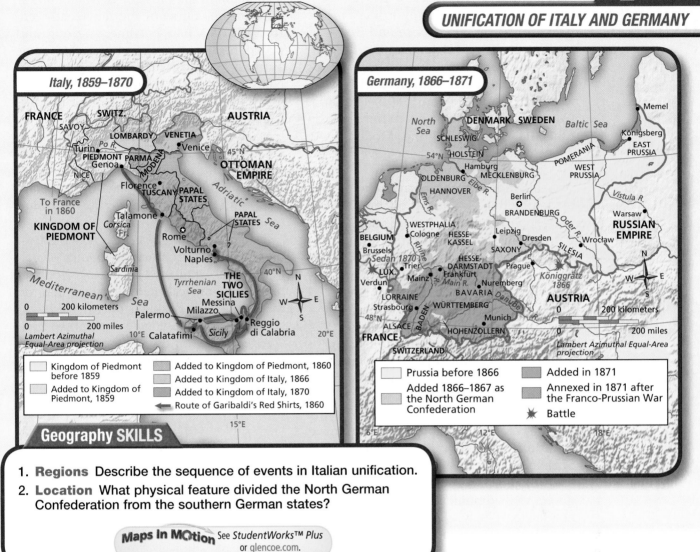

Italy, 1859–1870

FRANCE
SWITZ.
AUSTRIA
SAVOY
LOMBARDY
VENETIA
Turin
Po R.
Venice
45°N
PIEDMONT PARMA
Genoa
MODENA
OTTOMAN
EMPIRE
NICE
Florence
TUSCANY PAPAL
STATES
Adriatic
To France
in 1860
Talamone
PAPAL
STATES
Sea
KINGDOM OF
PIEDMONT
Corsica
(Fr.)
Rome
Volturno
Naples
Sardinia
40°N
THE
TWO
SICILIES
Tyrrhenian
Sea
N
Mediterranean
Sea
Messina
Milazzo
W E
S
0   200 kilometers
Palermo
Reggio
di Calabria
0   200 miles
10°E
Calatafimi
Sicily
20°E
*Lambert Azimuthal
Equal-Area projection*

15°E

	Kingdom of Piedmont before 1859		Added to Kingdom of Piedmont, 1860
	Added to Kingdom of Piedmont, 1859		Added to Kingdom of Italy, 1866
			Added to Kingdom of Italy, 1870
		←	Route of Garibaldi's Red Shirts, 1860

Germany, 1866–1871

Memel
North
Sea
DENMARK SWEDEN
Baltic Sea
SCHLESWIG
Königsberg
54°N
HOLSTEIN
POMERANIA
EAST
PRUSSIA
Hamburg
WEST
PRUSSIA
OLDENBURG
MECKLENBURG
Elbe R.
HANNOVER
Ems R.
Berlin
BRANDENBURG
Vistula R.
Warsaw
WESTPHALIA
Oder R.
RUSSIAN
EMPIRE
BELGIUM
Cologne
HESSE-
KASSEL
Leipzig
Dresden
Wrocław
SILESIA
Brussels
Rhine R.
SAXONY
Sedan 1870
HESSE-
DARMSTADT
Prague
Königgrätz
1866
LUX.
Trier
Frankfurt
Main R.
Nuremberg
Danube
N
Verdun
Mainz
BAVARIA
AUSTRIA
W E
LORRAINE
Strasbourg
WÜRTTEMBERG
S
48°N
BADEN
Munich
0   200 kilometers
ALSACE
HOHENZOLLERN
0   200 miles
FRANCE
*Lambert Azimuthal Equal-Area
projection*
SWITZERLAND
6°E
12°E
18°E

	Prussia before 1866		Added in 1871
	Added 1866–1867 as the North German Confederation		Annexed in 1871 after the Franco-Prussian War
		✹	Battle

Geography SKILLS

1. **Regions** Describe the sequence of events in Italian unification.
2. **Location** What physical feature divided the North German Confederation from the southern German states?

Maps In MOtion See *StudentWorks™ Plus* or glencoe.com.

The effect of the Crimean War was to destroy the Concert of Europe. Austria and Russia, the chief powers maintaining the status quo before the 1850s, were now enemies. Austria, with its own interests in the Balkans, had refused to support Russia in the Crimean War. A defeated and humiliated Russia withdrew from European affairs for the next 20 years. Austria now had no friends among the great powers. This situation opened the door to the **unification** of Italy and Germany.

Italian Unification

In 1850, Austria was still the dominant power on the Italian Peninsula. After the failure of the revolution of 1848, people began to look to the northern Italian state of **Piedmont** for leadership in achieving the unification of Italy. The royal house of Savoy ruled the Kingdom of Piedmont. Included in the kingdom were Piedmont, the island of Sardinia, Nice, and Savoy. The ruler of the kingdom, beginning in 1849, was King Victor Emmanuel II.

The king named Camillo di Cavour his prime minister in 1852. Cavour was a dedicated political leader. As prime minister, he pursued a policy of economic expansion to increase government revenues and enable the kingdom to equip a large army. Cavour, however, knew that Piedmont's army was not strong enough to defeat the Austrians. So, he made an alliance with the French emperor Louis-Napoleon. Cavour then provoked the Austrians into declaring war in 1859.

Following that conflict, a peace settlement gave Nice and Savoy to the French. Cavour had promised Nice and Savoy to the French in return for making the alliance. Lombardy, which had been under Austrian control, was given to Piedmont. Austria retained control of Venetia. Cavour's success caused nationalists in other Italian states (Parma, Modena, and Tuscany) to overthrow their governments and join their states to Piedmont.

Meanwhile, in southern Italy, a new leader of Italian unification had arisen. **Giuseppe Garibaldi,** a dedicated Italian patriot, raised an army of a thousand volunteers. They were called Red Shirts because of the color of their uniforms.

A branch of the Bourbon dynasty ruled the Two Sicilies (Sicily and Naples), and a revolt had broken out in Sicily against the king. Garibaldi's forces landed in Sicily and, by the end of July 1860, controlled most of the island. In August, Garibaldi and his forces crossed over to the mainland and began a victorious march up the Italian Peninsula. Naples and the entire Kingdom of the Two Sicilies fell in early September.

Garibaldi chose to turn over his conquests to Piedmont. On March 17, 1861, a new state of Italy was proclaimed under King Victor Emmanuel II. The task of unification was not yet complete, however. Austria still held Venetia in the north; and Rome was under the control of the pope, supported by French troops.

The Italians gained control of Venetia as a result of a war between Austria and Prussia. In the Austro-Prussian War of 1866, the new Italian state allied with Prussia. Prussia won the war, and the Italians were given Venetia.

In 1870, during the Franco-Prussian War, French troops withdrew from Rome. Their withdrawal enabled the Italian army to annex Rome on September 20, 1870. Rome became the capital of the united Italian state.

German Unification

After the Frankfurt Assembly failed to achieve German unification in 1848 and 1849, Germans looked to Prussia for leadership in the cause of German unification. In the course of the nineteenth century, Prussia had become a strong and prosperous state. Its government was authoritarian. The Prussian king had firm control over both the government and the army. Prussia was also known for its **militarism,** or reliance on military strength.

In the 1860s, King William I tried to enlarge the Prussian army. When the Prussian legislature refused to levy new taxes for the proposed military changes, William I appointed a new prime minister, Count **Otto von Bismarck.**

Bismarck has often been seen as the foremost nineteenth-century practitioner of realpolitik—the "politics of reality," or politics based on practical matters rather than on theory or ethics. Bismarck openly voiced his strong dislike of anyone who opposed him.

After his appointment, Bismarck ignored the legislative opposition to the military reforms. He argued instead that "Germany does not look to Prussia's liberalism but to her power." Bismarck proceeded to collect taxes and strengthen the army. From 1862 to 1866, Bismarck governed Prussia without approval of the parliament. In the meantime, he followed an active foreign policy, which soon led to war.

After defeating Denmark with Austrian help in 1864, Prussia gained control of the duchies of Schleswig and Holstein. Bismarck then created friction with the Austrians and forced them into a war on June 14, 1866. The Austrians, no match for the well-disciplined Prussian army, were defeated on July 3.

Prussia now organized the German states north of the Main River into the North German Confederation. The southern German states, which were largely Catholic, feared Protestant Prussia. However, they also feared France, their western neighbor. As a result, they agreed to sign military alliances with Prussia for protection against France.

Prussia now dominated all of northern Germany, and the growing power and military might of Prussia worried France. Bismarck was aware that France would never be content with a united German state to its east because of the potential threat to French security.

In 1870, Prussia and France became embroiled in a dispute over the candidacy of a relative of the Prussian king for the throne of Spain. Taking advantage of the situation, Bismarck goaded the French into declaring war on Prussia on July 19, 1870. This conflict was called the Franco-Prussian War.

The French proved to be no match for the better led and better organized Prussian forces. The southern German states honored their military alliances with Prussia and joined the war effort against the French. Prussian armies advanced into France. At Sedan, on September 2, 1870, an entire French army and the French ruler, Napoleon III, were captured.

Paris finally surrendered on January 28, 1871. An official peace treaty was signed in May. France had to pay 5 billion francs (about $1 billion) and give up the provinces of **Alsace** and **Lorraine** to the new German state. The loss of these territories left the French burning for revenge.

Even before the war had ended, the southern German states had agreed to enter the North German Confederation. On January 18, 1871, Bismarck and 600 German princes, nobles, and generals filled the Hall of Mirrors in the palace of Versailles, 12 miles outside Paris. William I of Prussia was proclaimed **kaiser,** or emperor, of the Second German Empire (the first was the medieval Holy Roman Empire).

The Prussian monarchy and the Prussian army had achieved German unity. The authoritarian and militaristic values of Prussia were triumphant in the new German state. With its industrial resources and military might, the new state had become the strongest power on the European continent.

✓ **Reading Check** **Explaining** How did the Crimean War destroy the Concert of Europe?

PEOPLE *in* HISTORY

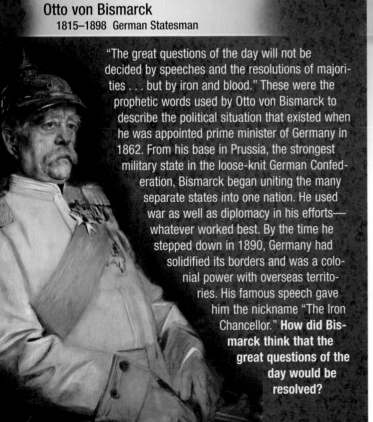

Otto von Bismarck
1815–1898 German Statesman

"The great questions of the day will not be decided by speeches and the resolutions of majorities . . . but by iron and blood." These were the prophetic words used by Otto von Bismarck to describe the political situation that existed when he was appointed prime minister of Germany in 1862. From his base in Prussia, the strongest military state in the loose-knit German Confederation, Bismarck began uniting the many separate states into one nation. He used war as well as diplomacy in his efforts— whatever worked best. By the time he stepped down in 1890, Germany had solidified its borders and was a colonial power with overseas territories. His famous speech gave him the nickname "The Iron Chancellor." **How did Bismarck think that the great questions of the day would be resolved?**

Giuseppe Garibaldi
1807–1882 Italian Patriot

"The slave shall show at last to his free brothers a sharpened sword forged from the links of his fetters." With these words, Giuseppe Garibaldi rallied his troops against the Bourbon French occupiers of his beloved Italy. Honored as "The Hero of Two Continents" after fighting for freedom in Brazil and Uruguay in the 1840s, Garibaldi conquered Sicily and southern Italy in 1860, triumphantly entering Naples as a liberator. Then, having no political ambitions, he turned his conquests over to King Victor Emmanuel II. Quietly retiring to his native island of Caprera, he was called back into military service soon afterward and continued fighting until Italy was completely free. **Why did Garibaldi turn over his conquests to Victor Emmanuel?**

Nationalism and Reform in Europe

MAIN IDEA While Italy and Germany were being unified, other states in Europe were also changing.

HISTORY & YOU Have you ever been to Paris or seen it depicted in the movies? Read about why the wide boulevards and public squares were originally built.

After 1848, Great Britain became more liberal, while the governments of France, Austria, and Russia grew more authoritarian.

Great Britain

Great Britain managed to avoid the revolutionary upheavals of the first half of the nineteenth century. In 1815, aristocratic landowning classes, which dominated both houses of Parliament, governed Great Britain. In 1832, Parliament passed a bill that increased the number of male voters.

The new voters were chiefly members of the industrial middle class. By giving the industrial middle class an interest in ruling, Britain avoided revolution in 1848. In the 1850s and 1860s, Parliament continued to make social and political reforms that helped the country to remain stable. However, despite reforms, Britain saw a rising Irish nationalist movement demanding increased Irish control over Irish internal affairs.

Another reason for Britain's stability was its continuing economic growth. By 1850, industrialization had brought prosperity to the British middle class. After 1850, real wages of workers rose significantly, enabling the working classes to share the prosperity.

Queen Victoria, whose reign from 1837 to 1901 was the longest in English history, well reflected the British feeling of national pride. Victoria's sense of duty and moral respectability reflected the attitudes of her age, later known as the Victorian Age.

POLITICAL CARTOONS   PRIMARY SOURCE

Political Reform in Great Britain

The Reform Act of 1832 gave voting rights to many men of the industrial middle class, yet it excluded six out of seven adult males. Pressure to extend voting rights down the social ladder led to the Reform Act of 1867. In his book *The English Constitution* (1867), Walter Bagehot described the possible effects of the Reform Act of 1867:

"... The Reform Act of 1867 has, I think, unmistakably completed the effect which the Act of 1832 began, but left unfinished. The middle class element has gained greatly by the second change, and the aristocratic element has lost greatly.... As a theoretical writer I can venture to say, what no elected member of Parliament, Conservative or Liberal, can venture to say, that I am exceedingly afraid of the ignorant multitude of the new constituencies...."

The figure on the horse represents Britain.

In the background are Lord Derby and other members of Parliament.

The horse and rider are jumping into the darkness labeled REFORM.

The face is Prime Minister Benjamin Disraeli, who sponsored the Reform Act of 1867, which added millions of working-class men to the voting lists.

A LEAP IN THE DARK.

DOCUMENT-BASED QUESTIONS

This cartoon focuses on a comment by Lord Derby that the Reform Act of 1867 was "a leap in the dark."

1. **Explaining** Why is Britain shielding her eyes in the cartoon?

2. **Analyzing Primary Sources** Why were many members of the ruling class uneasy about the new law?

France

In France, events after the revolution of 1848 moved toward the restoration of the monarchy. Four years after his election as president in 1848, Louis-Napoleon returned to the people to ask for the restoration of the empire. In this **plebiscite**, or popular vote, 97 percent responded with a yes vote. On December 2, 1852, Louis-Napoleon assumed the title of Napoleon III, Emperor of France. (The first Napoleon had named his son as his successor and had given him the title of Napoleon II. Napoleon II never ruled France, however.) The Second Empire had begun.

The government of Napoleon III was clearly authoritarian. As chief of state, Napoleon III controlled the armed forces, police, and civil service. Only he could introduce legislation and declare war. The Legislative Corps gave an appearance of representative government, because the members of the group were elected by universal male suffrage for six-year terms. However, they could neither initiate legislation nor affect the budget.

Napoleon III completely controlled the government and limited civil liberties. Nevertheless, the first five years of his reign were a spectacular success. To distract the public from their loss of political freedom, he focused on expanding the economy. Government subsidies helped foster the rapid construction of railroads, harbors, roads, and canals. Iron production tripled.

In the midst of this economic expansion, Napoleon III also carried out a vast rebuilding of the city of Paris. The old Paris of narrow streets and walls was replaced by a modern Paris of broad boulevards, spacious buildings, public squares, an underground sewage system, a new public water supply system, and gaslights. The new Paris served a military purpose as well. Broad streets made it more difficult for would-be rebels to throw up barricades and easier for troops to move rapidly through the city in the event of revolts.

In the 1860s, opposition to some of Napoleon's economic and governmental policies arose. In response, Napoleon III began to liberalize his **regime.** For example, he gave the legislature more power. In a plebiscite held in 1870, the French people gave Napoleon another victory. This triumph was short-lived, however. After the French were defeated in the Franco-Prussian War in 1870, the Second Empire fell.

The Austrian Empire

Nationalism, a major force in nineteenth-century Europe, presented special problems for the Austrian Empire. That was because the empire contained so many different ethnic groups, and many were campaigning for independence. Yet the Austrian Empire had managed to frustrate their desires.

After the Hapsburg rulers crushed the revolutions of 1848 and 1849, they restored centralized, autocratic government to the empire. Austria's defeat at the hands of the Prussians in 1866, however, forced the Austrians to make concessions to the fiercely nationalistic Hungarians.

The result of these concessions was the Compromise of 1867. This compromise created the dual monarchy of Austria-Hungary. Each of these two components of the empire now had its own constitution, its own legislature, its own government bureaucracy, and its own  capital (Vienna for Austria and **Budapest** for Hungary). Holding the two states together were a single monarch (Francis Joseph was both emperor of Austria and king of Hungary) and a common army, foreign policy, and system of finances.

In domestic affairs, then, the Hungarians had become an independent nation. The compromise, of course, did not satisfy the other nationalities that made up the multinational Austro-Hungarian Empire.

Russia

At the beginning of the nineteenth century, Russia was overwhelmingly rural, agricultural, and autocratic. The Russian czar was still regarded as a divine-right monarch with unlimited power. However, the Russian government faced challenges.

See page R46 to read excerpts from Czar Alexander II's *Imperial Decree to Free the Serfs* in the **Primary Source and Literature Library.**

It used soldiers, secret police, repression, and censorship to withstand the revolutionary fervor of the early 1800s.

In 1856, however, as described earlier, the Russians suffered a humiliating defeat in the Crimean War. Even staunch conservatives realized that Russia was falling hopelessly behind the western European powers. **Czar Alexander II** decided to make some reforms.

Serfdom, the largest problem in czarist Russia, was not just a humanitarian issue, but a complicated one that affected the economic, social, and political future of Russia. On March 3, 1861, Alexander issued an **emancipation** edict, which freed the serfs. Peasants could now own property and marry as they chose. The government provided land for the peasants by buying it from the landlords.

The new land system, however, was not that helpful to the peasants. The landowners often kept the best lands for themselves. The Russian peasants soon found that they did not have enough good land to support themselves. Emancipation, then, led not to a free, landowning peasantry but to an unhappy, land-starved peasantry that largely followed old ways of farming.

Alexander II attempted other reforms as well, but he soon found that he could please no one. Reformers wanted more changes and a faster pace for change. Conservatives thought that the czar was trying to destroy the basic institutions of Russian society. A group of radicals assassinated Alexander II in 1881. His son, Alexander III, became the successor to the throne. Alexander III turned against reform and returned to the old methods of repression.

✓ **Reading Check** **Examining** What concessions did the Hungarians gain from Austria in the Compromise of 1867?

CONNECTING TO THE UNITED STATES

NURSING AND PUBLIC HEALTH

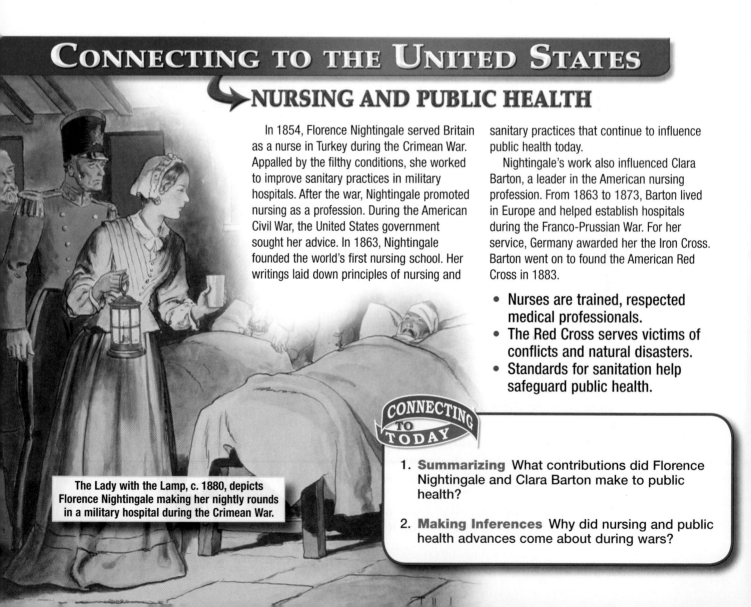

In 1854, Florence Nightingale served Britain as a nurse in Turkey during the Crimean War. Appalled by the filthy conditions, she worked to improve sanitary practices in military hospitals. After the war, Nightingale promoted nursing as a profession. During the American Civil War, the United States government sought her advice. In 1863, Nightingale founded the world's first nursing school. Her writings laid down principles of nursing and sanitary practices that continue to influence public health today.

Nightingale's work also influenced Clara Barton, a leader in the American nursing profession. From 1863 to 1873, Barton lived in Europe and helped establish hospitals during the Franco-Prussian War. For her service, Germany awarded her the Iron Cross. Barton went on to found the American Red Cross in 1883.

- **Nurses are trained, respected medical professionals.**
- **The Red Cross serves victims of conflicts and natural disasters.**
- **Standards for sanitation help safeguard public health.**

The Lady with the Lamp, c. 1880, depicts Florence Nightingale making her nightly rounds in a military hospital during the Crimean War.

CONNECTING TO TODAY

1. **Summarizing** What contributions did Florence Nightingale and Clara Barton make to public health?

2. **Making Inferences** Why did nursing and public health advances come about during wars?

Nationalism in the United States

MAIN IDEA Unified by the War of 1812, the United States later entered a bloody civil war that lasted from 1861 to 1865.

HISTORY & YOU Do you recall the upheaval of the American and French Revolutions? Read how the United States responded to national upheaval in the 1800s.

The United States Constitution committed the nation to liberalism and nationalism. Yet national unity did not come easily.

Two factions fought bitterly about the division of power in the new government. The Federalists favored a strong central government. The Republicans, fearing central power, wanted the federal government to be subordinate to the state governments. These divisions had ended with the War of 1812 against the British. This surge of national feeling served to cover up the nation's divisions.

By the mid-nineteenth century, slavery had become a threat to American unity. Four million enslaved African Americans were in the South by 1860, compared with one million in 1800.

The South's economy was based on growing cotton on plantations, chiefly by slave labor. The cotton economy and plantation-based slavery were closely related. The South was determined to maintain them. At the same time, **abolitionism,** a move-  ment to end slavery, arose in the North and challenged the Southern way of life.

As opinions over slavery grew more divided, compromise became less possible. Abraham Lincoln said in a speech in 1858 that "this government cannot endure permanently half slave and half free." When Lincoln was elected president in November 1860, war became certain.

On December 20, 1860, South Carolina voted to **secede,** or withdraw, from the United States. In February 1861, six more Southern states did the same. A rival nation—the Confederate States of America—was formed. In April, fighting erupted between North and South—the Union and the Confederacy.

The American Civil War (1861 to 1865) was an extraordinarily bloody struggle. Lincoln's Emancipation Proclamation declared most of the nation's enslaved people "forever free." The surrender of Confederate forces on April 9, 1865, meant that the United States would be "one nation, indivisible." National unity had prevailed.

✓ Reading Check **Explaining** Why did the election of Abraham Lincoln make civil war certain in the United States?

Vocabulary

1. **Explain** the significance of: unification, Piedmont, Giuseppe Garibaldi, militarism, Otto von Bismarck, Alsace, Lorraine, kaiser, Queen Victoria, plebiscite, regime, Budapest, Czar Alexander II, emancipation, abolitionism, secede.

Main Ideas

2. **Summarize** Bismarck's and Cavour's methods for achieving unification in Germany and Italy by using a Venn diagram like the one below.

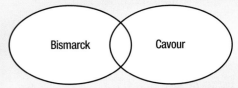

3. **Describe** the authoritarian aspects of Napoleon III's rule.

4. **Contrast** the views of the Federalists and Republicans in the United States.

Critical Thinking

5. **The BIG Idea** **Analyzing** Explain how liberalism affected events in Great Britain during the nineteenth century.

6. **Making Inferences** Why did Alexander III of Russia turn against the reforms of his father?

7. **Analyzing Visuals** Examine the political cartoon on page 398. How has the artist portrayed the relationship of the prime minister, Britain, and Parliament?

Writing About History

8. **Expository Writing** Write an essay comparing Bismarck and Napoleon III. Discuss events that occurred while they were in power and the impact of their leadership.

History ONLINE

For help with the concepts in this section of *Glencoe World History—Modern Times,* go to glencoe.com and click Study Central.

Romanticism and Realism

GUIDE TO READING

The BIG Idea
New Technologies Artistic movements are influenced by the society around them. Romanticism was in part a reaction to the Industrial Revolution, while advances in science contributed to a new movement called realism.

Content Vocabulary
- romanticism *(p. 402)*
- secularization *(p. 405)*
- organic evolution *(p. 406)*
- natural selection *(p. 406)*
- realism *(p. 407)*

Academic Vocabulary
- individuality *(p. 402)*   • approach *(p. 405)*

People and Places
- Ludwig van Beethoven *(p. 403)*
- Louis Pasteur *(p. 405)*
- Charles Darwin *(p. 405)*
- Charles Dickens *(p. 407)*

Reading Strategy
Summarizing Information
As you read, use a table like the one below to list popular literature from the romantic and realist movements.

Romanticism	Realism

Romanticism was a reaction to the Enlightenment and to the Industrial Revolution. Romantics believed that emotions, rather than reason, should guide them. By the mid-nineteenth century, romanticism had given way to a new movement called realism. Realists focused on the everyday world and ordinary people.

Romanticism

MAIN IDEA In the arts, romanticism stressed individualism and emotion instead of the Enlightenment's focus on universalism and reason.

HISTORY & YOU Do you and your friends dress differently from your parents? Perhaps you are expressing your individuality, as the romantics did in their time. Read to learn what romantics of the eighteenth century valued.

At the end of the eighteenth century, a new intellectual movement, known as **romanticism,** emerged as a reaction to the ideas of the Enlightenment. The Enlightenment had stressed reason as the chief means for discovering truth. The romantics emphasized feelings, emotion, and imagination as sources of knowing.

The romantics believed that emotion and sentiment were only understandable to the person experiencing them. In their novels, romantic writers created figures who were often misunderstood and rejected by society but who continued to believe in their own worth through their inner feelings.

Romantics also valued individualism, the belief in the uniqueness of each person. Many romantics rebelled against middle-class conventions. Male romantics grew long hair and beards and both men and women wore outrageous clothes to express their **individuality.**

Many romantics had a passionate interest in the past ages, especially the medieval era. They felt it had a mystery and interest in the soul that their own industrial age did not. Romantic architects revived medieval styles and built castles, cathedrals, city halls, parliamentary buildings, and even railway stations in a style called neo-Gothic. The British Houses of Parliament in London are a prime example of this architectural style.

Romanticism in Art and Music

Romantic artists shared at least two features. First, to them, all art was a reflection of the artist's inner feelings. A painting should mirror the artist's vision of the world and be the instrument of the artist's own imagination. Second, romantic artists abandoned classical reason for warmth and emotion.

Romanticism: The Prisoner of Chillon

In 1816, English poet Lord Byron (1788–1824) visited the Castle of Chillon in Switzerland. The story of Swiss patriot François Bonivard, a political prisoner in its dungeon for four years (1532–1536), inspired Byron to pen the moving poem "The Prisoner of Chillon" (1820). Here is an excerpt.

> "… They chain'd us each to a column stone,
> And we were three—yet, each alone,
> We could not move a single pace,
> We could not see each other's face,
> But with that pale and livid light
> That made us strangers in our sight:
> And thus together—yet apart,
> Fetter'd in hand, but join'd in heart."

DOCUMENT-BASED QUESTIONS

Eugène Delacroix painted the *Prisoner of Chillon* in 1834 in response to a poem by Byron.

1. **Interpreting** Describe the feelings you get from the poem and the painting.

2. **Making Connections** What might have inspired Byron and Delacroix to address the story of a long-ago prisoner?

Eugène Delacroix (DEH•luh•KWAH) was one of the most famous romantic painters from France. His paintings showed two chief characteristics: a fascination with the exotic and a passion for color. His works reflect his belief that "a painting should be a feast to the eye."

Many of Delacroix's paintings depicted scenes of uprisings against tyrants. His most influential work is perhaps *Liberty Leading the People*. In this painting, a woman holding a red banner is the symbol of liberty. She is leading revolutionaries forward during battle. After his travels to Spain and North Africa, Delacroix painted the animals he had seen there. *The Lion Hunt* is a good example of his later subjects.

In music, too, romantic trends dominated the first half of the nineteenth century. One of the most famous composers of this era was **Ludwig van Beethoven**. Some have called him a bridge between classical and romantic music. Others argue that he was such a rare genius he cannot be easily classified.

Beethoven's early work fell largely within the classical form of the eighteenth century. However, his *Third Symphony* embodied the elements of romanticism with powerful melodies that created dramatic intensity.

In one way, Beethoven was definitely a romantic. He thought of himself as an artist, not a craftsman. He had an intense and difficult personality but was committed to writing music that reflected his deepest feelings. "I must write, for what weighs on my heart, I must express."

Romanticism in Literature

Like the visual arts, the literary arts were deeply affected by romanticism and reflected a romantic interest in the past. Sir Walter Scott's *Ivanhoe,* for example, a best-seller in the early 1800s, told of clashes between knights in medieval England. Many romantic writers chose medieval subjects and created stories that expressed their strong nationalism.

An attraction to the exotic and unfamiliar gave rise to Gothic literature. Chilling examples are Mary Shelley's *Frankenstein*

HISTORY & ARTS　　PRIMARY SOURCE

A Romantic Response to Industrialization

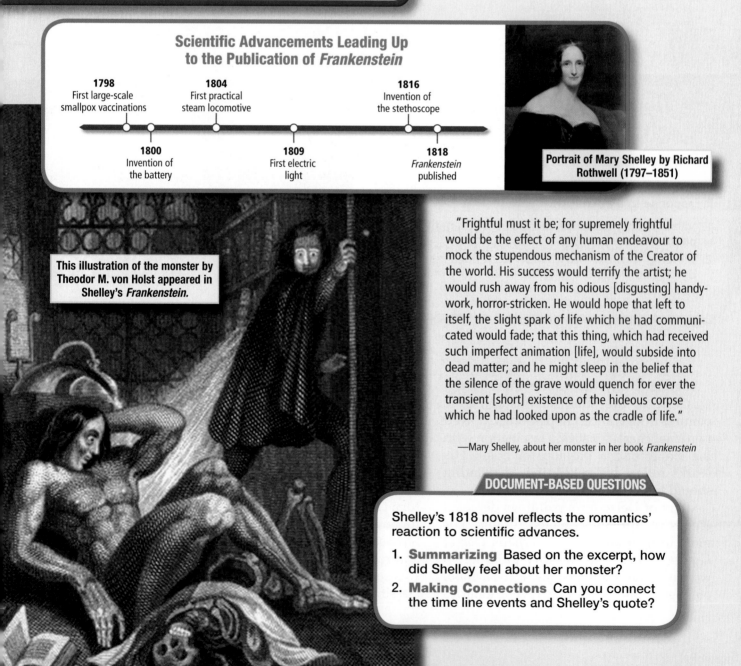

Scientific Advancements Leading Up to the Publication of *Frankenstein*

1798 First large-scale smallpox vaccinations

1804 First practical steam locomotive

1816 Invention of the stethoscope

1800 Invention of the battery

1809 First electric light

1818 *Frankenstein* published

Portrait of Mary Shelley by Richard Rothwell (1797–1851)

This illustration of the monster by Theodor M. von Holst appeared in Shelley's *Frankenstein.*

"Frightful must it be; for supremely frightful would be the effect of any human endeavour to mock the stupendous mechanism of the Creator of the world. His success would terrify the artist; he would rush away from his odious [disgusting] handy-work, horror-stricken. He would hope that left to itself, the slight spark of life which he had communicated would fade; that this thing, which had received such imperfect animation [life], would subside into dead matter; and he might sleep in the belief that the silence of the grave would quench for ever the transient [short] existence of the hideous corpse which he had looked upon as the cradle of life."

—Mary Shelley, about her monster in her book *Frankenstein*

DOCUMENT-BASED QUESTIONS

Shelley's 1818 novel reflects the romantics' reaction to scientific advances.

1. **Summarizing** Based on the excerpt, how did Shelley feel about her monster?
2. **Making Connections** Can you connect the time line events and Shelley's quote?

in Britain and Edgar Allen Poe's short stories of horror in the United States. Some romantics even sought the unusual in their own lives. They explored their dreams and nightmares and sought altered states of consciousness.

For the true romantic, poetry was the ideal art form. The romantics viewed poetry as the direct expression of the soul. Romantic poetry gave expression to one of the most important characteristics of romanticism—its love of nature. Romantics believed that nature served as a mirror into which humans could look to learn about themselves. This is especially evident in the poetry of William Wordsworth, the foremost English romantic poet of nature.

Wordsworth's experience of nature was almost mystical:

PRIMARY SOURCE

"One impulse from a vernal wood
May teach you more of man,
Of moral evil and of good,
Than all the sages can."
—William Wordsworth

The worship of nature also caused Wordsworth and other romantic poets to be critical of eighteenth-century science, which, they believed, had reduced nature to a cold object of study. To Wordsworth, the scientists' dry, mathematical **approach** left no room for the imagination or for the human soul.

The human soul was a source of expression for William Blake, a poet and artist connected with romanticism. Blake's *Songs of Innocence*, read in conjunction with his *Songs of Experience*, express what Blake called "the two contrary states of the human soul."

Many romantics were convinced that industrialization would cause people to become alienated from their inner selves and from the natural world. This idea shows up in Mary Shelley's novel *Frankenstein*: When science dares to try and conquer nature, a monster is created.

✓ **Reading Check** **Examining** How did the popularity of *Ivanhoe* reflect the interests of the nineteenth century?

New Age of Science

MAIN IDEA Rapid advances in science and technology fueled industrial growth, made medical care more effective, and challenged religious faith.

HISTORY & YOU When you get sick, do you take antibiotics to kill the germs? Learn how discoveries, such as the existence of germs, changed society in the 1800s.

The Scientific Revolution had created a modern, rational approach to the study of the natural world. For a long time, only the educated elite understood its importance. With the Industrial Revolution, however, came a heightened interest in scientific research. By the 1830s, new discoveries in science had led to many practical benefits that affected all Europeans. Science came to have a greater and greater impact on people.

New Discoveries

In biology, the Frenchman **Louis Pasteur** proposed the germ theory of disease, which was crucial to the development of modern scientific medical practices. In chemistry, the Russian Dmitry Mendeleyev in the 1860s classified all the material elements then known on the basis of their atomic weights. In Great Britain, Michael Faraday put together a primitive generator that laid the foundation for the use of electric current.

Dramatic material benefits such as these led Europeans to have a growing faith in science. This faith, in turn, undermined the religious faith of many people. It is no accident that the nineteenth century was an age of increasing **secularization,** indifference to or rejection of religion in the affairs of the world. For many people, truth was now to be found in science and the concrete material existence of humans.

Charles Darwin

More than anyone else, it was **Charles Darwin** who promoted the idea that humans are material beings who are part of the natural world. In 1859, Charles Darwin published his book *On the Origin of Species by Means of Natural Selection.*

Realist artists depicted the everyday life of ordinary people with photographic realism.

DOCUMENT-BASED QUESTIONS

French realist Gustave Courbet preferred to portray the common people, as here in *The Stonebreakers* (1849) where workers are repairing a road.

1. **Contrasting** In what ways does this painting illustrate Courbet's rejection of romanticism?
2. **Interpreting** What do you think was Courbet's goal in portraying a scene?

The basic idea of this book was that each species, or kind, of plant and animal had evolved over a long period of time from earlier, simpler forms of life. Darwin called this principle **organic evolution.**

How did this natural process work? According to Darwin, in every species, "many more individuals of each species are born than can possibly survive." This results in a "struggle for existence." Darwin believed that some organisms are born with variations, or differences, that make them more adaptable to their environment than other organisms, a process that Darwin called **natural selection.**

Those organisms that are naturally selected for survival ("survival of the fittest") reproduce and thrive. The unfit do not survive. The fit that survive pass on the variations that enabled them to survive until, according to Darwin, a new, separate species emerges. In *The Descent of Man*, published in 1871, Darwin argued that human beings had animal origins and

were not an exception to the rule governing other species.

Darwin's ideas raised a storm of controversy. Some people did not take his ideas seriously. Other people objected that Darwin's theory made human beings ordinary products of nature rather than unique creations of God. Others were bothered by his idea of life as a mere struggle for survival. "Is there a place in the Darwinian world for moral values?" they asked. Some believers felt Darwin had not acknowledged God's role in creation. Some detractors scorned Darwin and depicted him unfavorably in cartoons. Gradually, however, many scientists and other intellectuals came to accept Darwin's theory. His theory changed thinking in countless fields from biology to anthropology.

✓ Reading Check **Describing** How did the theory of natural selection influence the way people saw the world?

Realism

MAIN IDEA The rise of science encouraged writers and artists to create realistic works that portrayed even the poor and degraded in society.

HISTORY & YOU Do you enjoy lifelike video games? What details make these games so realistic? Learn about the details that created realism in nineteenth century art and literature.

The belief that the world should be viewed realistically, a view frequently expressed after 1850, was closely related to the scientific outlook. In politics, Bismarck had practiced the "politics of reality." In the literary and visual arts, **realism** became a movement as well.

Realism in Literature

The literary realists of the mid-nineteenth century rejected romanticism. They wanted to write about ordinary characters from life, not romantic heroes in exotic settings. They also tried to avoid emotional language by using precise description. They preferred novels to poems.

Many literary realists combined their interest in everyday life with an examination of social issues. These artists expressed their social views through their characters.

The French author Gustave Flaubert, who was a leading novelist of the 1850s and 1860s, perfected the realist novel. His work Madame Bovary presents a critical description of small-town life in France.

In Great Britain, **Charles Dickens** became a huge success with novels that showed the realities of life for the poor in the early Industrial Age. Novels such as *Oliver Twist* and *David Copperfield* created a vivid picture of the brutal life of London's poor, as well as of their humor and humanity. In fact, his characters were so sympathetic that they helped inspire social reform.

Realism in Art

In art, too, realism became dominant after 1850. Realist artists sought to show the everyday life of ordinary people and the world of nature with photographic realism.

The French painter Gustave Courbet was the most famous artist of the realist school. He loved to portray scenes from everyday life. His subjects were factory workers and peasants. "I have never seen either angels or goddesses, so I am not interested in painting them," Courbet once commented. There were those who objected to Courbet's "cult of ugliness" and who found such scenes of human misery scandalous. To Courbet, however, no subject was too ordinary, too harsh, or too ugly.

✓ Reading Check **Evaluating** What factors helped to produce the movement known as realism?

SECTION 4 REVIEW

Vocabulary
1. **Explain** the significance of: romanticism, individuality, Ludwig van Beethoven, approach, Louis Pasteur, secularization, Charles Darwin, organic evolution, natural selection, realism, Charles Dickens.

Main Ideas
2. **List** the values of the romantics.
3. **Summarize** the discoveries that scientists made in the mid-nineteenth century by using a chart like the one below.

Scientist	Discovery
Pasteur	
Mendeleyev	
Faraday	
Darwin	

4. **Explain** why Charles Dickens's novels helped inspire social reform.

Critical Thinking
5. **The BIG Idea** **Comparing and Contrasting** How did romanticism compare to the ideas of the Enlightenment?
6. **Assessing** How did scientific developments affect the cultural movements of the nineteenth century?
7. **Analyzing Visuals** Compare Delacroix's *Prisoner of Chillon* on page 403 with *The Stonebreakers* on page 406. From the paintings, how would you explain why we say that Delacroix is a romantic, and Courbet is a realist?

Writing About History
8. **Expository Writing** Read poetry by two different poets of romanticism. Write a paper describing the elements of romanticism found in the poems. Be sure to include quotations.

History ONLINE

For help with the concepts in this section of *Glencoe World History— Modern Times*, go to **glencoe.com** and click Study Central.

Social History

A Showcase for Industry and Progress

On May 1, 1851, the Great Exhibition opened in London's Hyde Park. The first international exhibition of its kind, the Great Exhibition displayed thousands of industrial innovations and manufactured goods from around the globe. This event displayed Great Britain's influential position as the "workshop of the world." Perhaps the crowning achievement of the Great Exhibition was the exhibition hall itself—the world's first prefabricated building, constructed of iron and glass and called "the Crystal Palace."

Over 6 million people of all classes, many from European cities, visited the Great Exhibition during the 141 days that it was open.

Thirty-two countries from Europe, America, Africa, and Asia took part in the exhibition. Fourteen thousand exhibitors displayed their products.

Stop the Presses

Much was written about the Great Exhibition and the Crystal Palace, including an opening-day ode by William Makepeace Thackeray that expressed the general public's sense of awe at the sight of the exhibition hall and the products on display "from Mississippi and from Nile—from Baltic, Ganges, Bosporus." Not everyone was impressed, however. Of the Crystal Palace, the artist Leigh Hunt wrote, "It was neither crystal nor a palace." The art critic John Ruskin said it looked like "a huge greenhouse."

Within its giant iron frame of 2,300 girders, the Crystal Palace contained nearly 300,000 panes of glass.

Two thousand laborers built the Crystal Palace in nine months—a record in 1851.

New products exhibited included false teeth, rubber goods, hydraulic presses, automated spinning machines, steam engines and pumps, and an early submarine.

MASS-PRODUCED GOODS

Because of Britain's access to raw materials from its colonies and because of the inventions and improvements in machinery during the Industrial Revolution, the thousands of products on display at the Great Exhibition had been mass-produced and were affordable to the average consumer. At the opening ceremony, Prince Albert of Great Britain stressed this point: "The products of all quarters of the globe are placed here at our disposal. And we have only to choose that which is best and cheapest for our purposes...."

ANALYZING VISUALS

1. **Comparing** If an international exhibition like this were held today, what kinds of innovative products might be on display? What types of industries would be represented?

2. **Inferring** Which country today might be called "the workshop of the world"? Explain why.

CHAPTER 12 Visual Summary

STUDY TO GO You can study anywhere, anytime by downloading quizzes and flash cards to your PDA from glencoe.com.

INDUSTRIALIZATION Transformed Society

- The Industrial Revolution began in Great Britain and spread throughout Europe and the United States.
- New technologies improved the production and transportation of goods.
- Workers migrated to cities as economies shifted from being farm-based to factory-based.
- As cities grew, an industrial middle class and an industrial working class emerged.

NEW TECHNOLOGIES DROVE INDUSTRIALIZATION

The new process of "puddling" helped factories make high-quality iron to build locomotives and machinery.

THE GERMAN STATES UNIFIED

A ceremony at the palace of Versailles installed William I as kaiser of the Second German Empire.

IDEOLOGIES Arising From the Industrial Revolution

- Harsh conditions in factories made socialism attractive.
- Liberalism and nationalism threatened conservative governments, leading to the revolutions of 1830 and 1848.
- Liberal reforms helped Great Britain to avoid revolution, while France, Austria, and Russia grew more authoritarian.
- The Crimean War broke down the Concert of Europe, enabling nationalists to unify Germany and Italy.

CULTURAL MOVEMENTS Arising From the Industrial Revolution

- Romanticism emphasized emotions and individuality in response to the Enlightenment's emphasis on reason.
- The Industrial Revolution heightened interest in scientific research.
- Growing confidence in science undermined religious faith, leading to increased secularization.
- Interest in science led to the realism movement, featuring ordinary people instead of romantic heroes.

REALISM IN LITERATURE: THE NOVEL MADAME BOVARY

In *Madame Bovary,* the tale ends in tragedy when Emma Bovary escapes what she views as her ordinary, unhappy life.

STANDARDIZED TEST PRACTICE

TEST-TAKING  TIP

When a question asks for an answer that is supported by information presented in a table, find the answer choice that is *proven true* by the information in the table.

Reviewing Vocabulary

Directions: Choose the word or words that best complete the sentence.

1. Another word for *popular vote* is _____.

A emancipation

B plebiscite

C secession

D kaiser

2. _____ evolution means that plant and animal species have evolved over a long period of time from earlier, simpler forms.

A Natural

B Sequential

C Environmental

D Organic

3. _____ is based on tradition and social stability.

A Liberalism

B Conservatism

C Socialism

D Abolitionism

4. Under _____, the public—generally the government—owns the means of production.

A romanticism

B liberalism

C socialism

D conservatism

Reviewing Main Ideas

Directions: Choose the best answers to the following questions.

Section 1 *(pp. 378–385)*

5. Which engineer improved the steam engine so it could drive machinery?

A James Watt

B Robert Fulton

C Henry Cort

D Robert Owen

6. From where did labor for the factories in the United States mostly come?

A Factories from the Northeast

B Native American population

C Southern cities

D Farm population

7. In what did industrialization trigger a dramatic increase?

A Diseases

B City populations

C Agricultural jobs

D Death rates

Section 2 *(pp. 388–393)*

8. Who was the most influential leader at the Congress of Vienna meeting in 1814?

A Charles X

B Louis-Napoleon

C Klemens von Metternich

D Ludwig van Beethoven

Need Extra Help?								
If You Missed Questions . . .	1	2	3	4	5	6	7	8
Go to Page . . .	399	406	408	385	380	383	383	388

 GO ON

9. What ideology or ideologies were behind the 1830 revolutions?

   A Radicalism

   B Liberalism and nationalism

   C Socialism

   D Romanticism

Section 3 *(pp. 394–401)*

10. Who was the politician who practiced realpolitik?

   A Camillo di Cavour

   B Giuseppe Garibaldi

   C Otto von Bismarck

   D Klemens von Metternich

11. What was the largest problem in czarist Russia?

   A Poor soil

   B Czar Alexander II

   C Romanticism

   D Serfdom

Section 4 *(pp. 402–407)*

12. What did romantics view as the direct expression of the soul?

   A Prose

   B Poetry

   C Liberalism

   D Nature

13. Who classified all the material elements known in the 1860s based on their atomic weights?

   A Louis Pasteur

   B Michael Faraday

   C Dimitry Mendeleyev

   D Robert Fulton

Critical Thinking

Directions: Choose the best answers to the following questions.

Use the following information to answer question 14.

American Civil War Casualties (1861–1865)

Type of Casualty	Union	Confederate	Total
Combat	110,070	74,524	184,594
Other*	249,458	124,000	373,458
TOTALS	359,528	198,524	558,052

*Includes deaths from disease, hardship, and accidents and includes losses among prisoners of war.

14. Which of the following statements is supported by the information in the table?

   A There were more than a million casualties in the Civil War.

   B Confederate forces had more casualties overall than did Union forces.

   C More Confederate soldiers died in combat than did Union soldiers.

   D Most soldiers died from causes other than actual combat.

15. Why were factory workers forced to work in shifts?

   A To keep the machines producing at a steady rate

   B Because women had to stay at home with their children

   C Because workers did not want to rise early

   D To give them diversity in the tasks performed

16. Why did the liberals favor a government ruled by a constitution?

   A To give everyone the right to vote

   B To guarantee the rights they sought to preserve

   C To do away with the need of a monarch

   D To let the lower classes share power

Need Extra Help?								
If You Missed Questions . . .	9	10	11	12	13	14	15	16
Go to Page . . .	391	396	399	405	405	406	380	390

17. Why did the literary realists of the mid-nineteenth century prefer novels to poems?

   A Gothic novels were far more popular than poetry.

   B No one knew how to write poetry.

   C They could express their social views through their characters.

   D They wanted to convey emotions with as few words as possible.

Use the map and answer question 18.

Revolutions in Europe, 1848–1849

Center of revolution

18. How far south did the revolutions of 1848–1849 extend?

   A Naples

   B Buda

   C Florence

   D Palermo

Document-Based Questions

Directions: Analyze the document and answer the short-answer questions that follow the document.

William Wordsworth, the foremost English romantic poet of nature, wrote the *Lyrical Ballads*. Among those ballads is "The Tables Turned." Read the following excerpt.

> "One impulse from a vernal wood
> May teach you more of man,
> Of moral evil and of good,
> Than all the sages can.
> Sweet is the lore which Nature brings;
> Our meddling intellect
> Mis-shapes the beauteous forms of things:—
> We murder to dissect.
> Enough of Science and of Art;
> Close up those barren leaves;
> Come forth, and bring with you a heart
> That watches and receives."

19. What characteristic of romantic poetry is evident in Wordsworth's poem?

20. What message is Wordsworth trying to convey?

Extended Response

21. Literature reflects the concerns that people have about their society. How did the political, economic, and social injustices that existed during the nineteenth century contribute to romanticism and realism?

History ONLINE

For additional test practice, use Self-Check Quizzes—Chapter 12 at glencoe.com.

Need Extra Help?					
If You Missed Questions . . .	17	18	19	20	21
Go to Page . . .	407	411	411	411	402

STOP

CHAPTER 13

Mass Society and Democracy 1870–1914

Section 1 The Growth of Industrial Prosperity

Section 2 The Emergence of Mass Society

Section 3 The National State and Democracy

Section 4 Toward the Modern Consciousness

What events can affect the entire world?

The 1900 World's Fair in Paris, shown in this photo, celebrated the achievements of the 1800s. The fair showcased inventions of the Second Industrial Revolution, especially those using the newly discovered power of electricity. In this chapter, you will learn about the causes and effects of the Second Industrial Revolution.

- Name another event that draws participants from around the world. What is the significance of the event?
- What are some technologies invented in your lifetime? How have they influenced your life?

EUROPE AND THE UNITED STATES ▶

1875
German Social Democratic Party emerges

1878
Thomas Edison forms the Edison Electric Light Company in New York

1890
Emperor William II fires Otto von Bismarck

1870   1885

THE WORLD ▶

1885
Indian National Congress forms

1894
China and Japan go to war over Korea

1905
"Bloody Sunday" in St. Petersburg, Russia

Souscrivez à
L'Emprunt de la "Victoire"

1914
World War I begins

1900 ○——————————————○ 1915

1914
Panama Canal opens

FOLDABLES™
Study Organizer

Second Industrial Revolution	Before Revolution	After Revolution
Job Opportunities for Women		
Marriage and family		
Women's Rights		

Comparing Opportunities
Create a Folded Table and use it to examine the lives of women before and after the Second Industrial Revolution. Include job opportunities for women, marriage and women's role in family life, and women's rights.

History ONLINE

Chapter Overview—Visit glencoe.com to preview Chapter 13.

The Growth of Industrial Prosperity

GUIDE TO READING

The BIG Idea
New Technologies Industrialization led to dramatic increases in productivity and to new political theories and social movements.

Content Vocabulary
- assembly line *(p. 419)*
- mass production *(p. 419)*
- bourgeoisie *(p. 420)*
- proletariat *(p. 420)*
- dictatorship *(p. 420)*
- revisionists *(p. 421)*

Academic Vocabulary
- financier *(p. 416)*
- transition *(p. 419)*

People and Places
- Thomas Edison *(p. 416)*
- Alexander Graham Bell *(p. 417)*
- Guglielmo Marconi *(p. 417)*
- Karl Marx *(p. 419)*

Reading Strategy
Determining Cause and Effect As you read, complete a diagram like the one below showing the cause and effect relationship between the resources and the products produced.

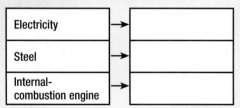

Electricity	→	
Steel	→	
Internal-combustion engine	→	

By the late nineteenth century, the Second Industrial Revolution made the economies of most European nations even more productive. Electricity and the internal-combustion engine transformed most of the European world into industrialized societies. However, the transition was not easy for workers. Many sought reform through trade unions or socialism to improve their lives.

The Second Industrial Revolution

MAIN IDEA In Western Europe, the introduction of electricity, chemicals, and petroleum triggered the Second Industrial Revolution, and a world economy began to develop.

HISTORY & YOU Does your life come to a halt when the power goes out? Read to learn when electricity first became a part of everyday life.

In the late nineteenth century, the belief in progress was so strong in the West that it was almost a religion. Europeans and Americans had been impressed by the stunning bounty of the Second Industrial Revolution. The first Industrial Revolution had given rise to textiles, railroads, iron, and coal. In the Second Industrial Revolution, steel, chemicals, electricity, and petroleum were the keys to making economies even more productive.

New Products

One major change in industry between 1870 and 1914 was the substitution of steel for iron. Steel was used in the building of lighter, smaller, and faster machines and engines. It was also used in railways, ships, and weapons. In 1860 Great Britain, France, Germany, and Belgium produced 125,000 tons (112,500 t) of steel. By 1913, the total was an astounding 32 million tons (29 million t).

Electricity was a major new form of energy that proved valuable. It was easily converted into other energy forms such as heat, light, and motion. Electricity also moved easily through space by means of wires. In the 1870s, the first practical generators of electrical current were developed. By 1910, hydroelectric power stations and coal-fired, steam-generating plants connected homes and factories to a single, common source of power.

Electricity gave birth to a series of inventions. Homes and cities began to have electric lights when **Thomas Edison** in the United States and Joseph Swan in Great Britain created the light bulb. Edison patented the first commercially practical incandescent light. In 1878, with the help of several **financiers**, including

ATLANTIC OCEAN

NORWAY
Stockholm
St. Petersburg
SWEDEN
DENMARK
Moscow
UNITED KINGDOM
London
NETH.
Berlin
BELG.
GERMAN EMPIRE
Warsaw
RUSSIAN EMPIRE
Breslau
Paris
Nuremberg
FRANCE
Vienna
Limoges
SWITZ.
St. Étienne
Toulouse
AUSTRO-HUNGARIAN EMPIRE
ROMANIA
Lisbon
Madrid
Marseille
ITALY
Belgrade
SERBIA
Black Sea
PORTUGAL
SPAIN
Barcelona
Corsica
MONTENEGRO
BULGARIA
Constantinople (İstanbul)
Sardinia
Rome
Naples
ALBANIA
Salerno
GREECE
OTTOMAN EMPIRE
Balearic Is.
Sicily
Malta U.K.
Crete
Cyprus U.K.
North Sea
Baltic Sea
Elbe R.
Seine R.
Danube R.
Po R.
Ebro R.
Dnieper R.
Mediterranean Sea

AFRICA

Geography SKILLS

1. **Human-Environment Interaction** Locate the areas that have the heaviest concentrations of industry. What geographic factors could have helped these areas become heavily industrialized?

2. **Place** Use the information provided in this map to create a chart that shows the type of industry in each European country.

Maps In Motion See StudentWorks™ Plus or glencoe.com.

Industrial concentration:
☐ Area
• City

Industry:
🧪 Chemicals
⚡ Electricity
🛢 Petroleum
⚙ Steel

0   400 kilometers
0   400 miles
Lambert Azimuthal Equal-Area projection

J. P. Morgan, Edison formed the Edison Electric Light Company in New York City. It was during this time that Edison remarked, "We will make electricity so cheap that only the rich will burn candles."

A revolution in communications also began. **Alexander Graham Bell** invented the telephone in 1876. **Guglielmo Marconi** sent the first radio waves across the Atlantic in 1901. Marconi made this report of his remarkable discovery:

PRIMARY SOURCE

"Shortly before mid-day I placed the single earphone to my ear and started listening. . . . I was at last on the point of putting . . . my beliefs to the test. . . . The electric waves sent out into space from Britain had traversed the Atlantic—the distance . . . of 1,700 miles [2,735 km]—It was an epoch in history. I now felt for the first time absolutely certain the day would come when mankind would be able to send messages without wires . . . between the farthermost ends of the earth."

By the 1880s, streetcars and subways powered by electricity had appeared in major European cities. Electricity transformed the factory as well. Conveyor belts, cranes, and machines could all be powered by electricity. With electric lights, factories could remain open 24 hours a day.

The development of the internal-combustion engine, fired by oil and gasoline, provided a new source of power in transportation. This engine gave rise to ocean liners with oil-fired engines, as well as to the airplane and the automobile. In 1903

Orville and Wilbur Wright made the first flight in a fixed-wing plane at Kitty Hawk, North Carolina. In 1919 the first regular passenger air service was established.

New Patterns

Industrial production grew at a rapid pace because of greatly increased sales of manufactured goods. Europeans could afford to buy more consumer products for several reasons. Wages for workers increased after 1870. In addition, prices for

SCIENCE, TECHNOLOGY, & SOCIETY

The Automobile: Technology That Changed the Global Landscape

Henry Ford and his son Edsel in a Model F Ford, 1905

Early cars were handmade and expensive. Only several hundred were sold between 1893 and 1901. In 1908, an American, Henry Ford, revolutionized the car industry by using an assembly line to mass-produce his Model T. The assembly line cut production costs, enabling Ford to lower prices. By 1916, Ford's factories were producing 735,000 cars a year.

The automobile transformed city life. No longer limited by a transportation system centered on rail lines and streetcars, people could live and work where they wanted. New, broader markets opened to business. Suburbs expanded, new roads were built, and traffic and air pollution increased. Today, nearly 58 million new vehicles hit the road each year worldwide.

CRITICAL THINKING SKILLS

1. **Identifying** How did the automobile accelerate change in the business world?
2. **Evaluating** What are the major benefits and costs of automotive technology?

manufactured goods were lower because of reduced transportation costs. One of the biggest reasons for more efficient production was the **assembly line,** a new manufacturing method pioneered by Henry Ford in 1913. The assembly line allowed a much more efficient **mass production** of goods.

In the cities, the first department stores began to sell a new range of consumer goods. These goods—clocks, bicycles, electric lights, and typewriters, for example—were made possible by the steel and electrical industries.

Not everyone benefited from the Second Industrial Revolution. By 1900, Europe was divided into two economic zones. Great Britain, Belgium, France, the Netherlands, Germany, the western part of the Austro-Hungarian Empire, and northern Italy made up an advanced industrialized core. These nations had a high standard of living and decent systems of transportation.

Another part of Europe was still largely agricultural. This was the little-industrialized area to the south and east. It consisted of southern Italy, most of Austria-Hungary, Spain, Portugal, the Balkan kingdoms, and Russia. These countries provided food and raw materials for the industrial countries and had a much lower standard of living than the rest of Europe.

Toward a World Economy

The Second Industrial Revolution, combined with the growth of transportation by steamship and railroad, fostered a true world economy. By 1900, Europeans were receiving beef and wool from Argentina and Australia, coffee from Brazil, iron ore from Algeria, and sugar from Java.

European capital was also invested abroad to develop railways, mines, electrical power plants, and banks. Of course, foreign countries also provided markets for Europe's manufactured goods. With its capital, industries, and military might, Europe dominated the world economy by the beginning of the twentieth century.

✓ **Reading Check** **Explaining** Why did Europe dominate the world economy by the beginning of the twentieth century?

The Working Class

MAIN IDEA Industrialization gave some a higher standard of living, but struggling workers turned to trade unions or socialism to improve their lives.

HISTORY & YOU Have you ever seen striking workers walking a picket line? Read to learn how trade unions first formed to help workers win better working conditions.

The **transition** to an industrialized society was very hard on workers. It made their lives difficult and forced them to live in crowded slums. They had to work long hours at mind-numbing tasks. This transition eventually gave workers a higher standard of living.

Goals for Reform

Reformers of this era believed that industrial capitalism was heartless and brutal. They wanted a new kind of society. Some reformers were moderates. They were willing to work within the system for gradual changes such as fewer hours, better benefits, and safe working conditions. Often they used trade unions to achieve these practical goals.

Other reformers were more radical. They wanted to abolish the capitalist system entirely and create a socialist system. To achieve this goal, they supported socialist parties. Socialist parties emerged after 1870, but the theory on which they were based came largely from Karl Marx. One form of Marxist socialism was eventually called communism (see Chapter 17).

Marx's Theory

In 1848 *The Communist Manifesto* was published. It was written by two Germans, **Karl Marx** and Friedrich Engels, who were appalled at the horrible conditions in the industrial factories. They blamed the system of industrial capitalism for these conditions.

Marx believed that all of world history was a "history of class struggles." According to Marx, oppressor and oppressed have always "stood in constant opposition to one another." One group—the oppressors—owned the means of production, such as land, raw materials, money, and so forth.

The German word
Freiheit means liberty.

In this passage from *The Communist Manifesto*, Karl Marx and Friedrich Engels express their belief that a classless society would be the end product of the struggle between the bourgeoisie and the proletariat.

"[T]he first step in the revolution by the working class is to raise the proletariat to the position of the ruling class. . . . The proletariat will use its political supremacy to wrest, by degrees, all capital from the bourgeoisie, to centralize all instruments of production in the hands of the State, i.e., of the proletariat organized as the ruling class; and to increase the total productive forces as rapidly as possible. . . . The proletarians have nothing to lose but their chains. They have a world to win."

The Communist Manifesto ends with a call to unity: "Workers of All Countries, Unite!"

DOCUMENT-BASED QUESTIONS

The German Social Democratic Party was the most important party to emerge based on Marx's ideas. This German poster from 1904 proclaims "Proletarians of the World, Unite!"

1. **Summarizing** What is the central message of the poster? Describe how the images create this message.

2. **Synthesizing** Describe the goals of the revolution that Marx and Engels discuss in the excerpt.

This gave them the power to control government and society. The other group, who owned nothing and who depended on the owners of the means of production, was the oppressed.

In the industrialized societies of Marx's day, the class struggle continued. Around him, Marx believed he saw a society that was "more and more splitting up into two great hostile camps, into two great classes directly facing each other: Bourgeoisie and Proletariat." The **bourgeoisie**—the middle class—were the oppressors. The **proletariat** (PROH•luh•TEHR•ee•uht)—the working class—were the oppressed.

Marx predicted that the struggle between the two groups would finally lead to an open revolution. The proletariat would violently overthrow the bourgeoisie. After their victory, the proletariat would form a **dictatorship** (a government in which a person or small group has absolute power) to organize the means of production. However, since the proletariat victory would essentially abolish the economic differences that create separate social classes, Marx believed that the final revolution would ultimately produce a classless society. The state itself, which had been a tool of the bourgeoisie, would wither away.

Socialist Parties

In time, working-class leaders formed socialist parties based on Marx's ideas. Most important was the German Social Democratic Party (SPD), which emerged in 1875. Under the direction of its Marxist leaders, the SPD advocated revolution while organizing itself into a mass political party that competed in elections for the German parliament. Once in parliament, SPD delegates worked to pass laws that would improve conditions for the working class.

In spite of government efforts to destroy it, the German Social Democratic Party grew. When it received four million votes in the 1912 elections, it became the largest single party in Germany. Because the German constitution gave greater power to the upper house and the German emperor, the SPD was not able to bring about the kind of changes it wanted.

Socialist parties also emerged in other European states. In 1889 leaders of the various socialist parties joined together and formed the Second International. This was an association of national socialist groups that would fight against capitalism worldwide. (The First International had failed in 1872.)

Marxist parties were divided over their goals. Pure Marxists thought that capitalism could only be defeated by a violent revolution. Other Marxists, called **revisionists,** rejected the revolutionary approach. They argued that workers must continue to organize in mass political parties and even work with other parties to gain reforms. As workers received the right to vote, revisionists believed, they could achieve their aims by working within democratic systems.

Trade Unions

Another force working for evolutionary, rather than revolutionary, socialism was the trade union, or labor union. To improve their conditions, workers organized in a union. Then the union had to get the employer to recognize its right to represent workers in collective bargaining. This is a process whereby union representatives negotiate with employers over wages and hours.

The right to strike was another important part of the trade union movement. In a strike, a union calls on its members to stop work in order to pressure employers to meet their demands for higher wages or improved factory safety. At first, laws were passed that made strikes illegal under any circumstances. In Great Britain, unions won the right to strike in the 1870s. By 1914, there were almost four million workers in British trade unions. In the rest of Europe, trade unions had varying degrees of success in helping workers achieve a better life.

✓ Reading Check **Summarizing** How would you summarize Marx's theory as expressed in *The Communist Manifesto?*

Vocabulary

1. **Explain** the significance of: Thomas Edison, financier, Alexander Graham Bell, Guglielmo Marconi, assembly line, mass production, transition, Karl Marx, bourgeoisie, proletariat, dictatorship, revisionists.

Main Ideas

2. **Explain** how the assembly line increased production.

3. **Summarize** how Europe dominated the world economy by the beginning of the twentieth century. Use a chart like the one below to make your summary.

Transportation	
Capital	
Foreign markets	

4. **Describe** how Marx's ideas came to directly impact society.

Critical Thinking

5. **The BIG Idea** **Making Inferences** Explain whether you think there is a relationship between the large number of technical innovations made during this period and the growing need for labor reforms and unions.

6. **Differentiating** How did the two Industrial Revolutions differ?

7. **Analyzing Visuals** Examine the Socialist poster on page 420. What feelings might this poster create in members of the bourgeoisie? Why?

Writing About History

8. **Expository Writing** After Marconi's first transmission across radio waves, he said, "I now felt for the first time absolutely certain the day would come when mankind would be able to send messages without wires. . . ." Write a paragraph about how this was a prophecy of technology to come.

History ONLINE

For help with the concepts in this section of *Glencoe World History—Modern Times*, go to glencoe.com and click Study Central.

The Emergence of Mass Society

GUIDE TO READING

The BIG Idea
Ideas, Beliefs, and Values The Second Industrial Revolution resulted in an increased urban population, a growing working class, and an increased awareness of women's rights.

Content Vocabulary
• feminism *(p. 426)*
• suffrage *(p. 427)*
• literacy *(p. 429)*

Academic Vocabulary
• advocate *(p. 426)*   • passive *(p. 429)*

People and Places
• Frankfurt *(p. 423)*
• Amalie Sieveking *(p. 427)*
• Florence Nightingale *(p. 427)*
• Clara Barton *(p. 427)*
• Emmeline Pankhurst *(p. 427)*

Reading Strategy
Summarizing Information As you read, complete a chart like the one below summarizing the divisions among the social classes.

Social Classes		
Working	Middle	Wealthy

During the nineteenth century, a vast number of people migrated to cities. The increasing urban population led governments to improve public health and sanitation services. Women began to advocate for their rights, leisure time increased, and many Western governments financed public education.

The New Urban Environment

MAIN IDEA As workers migrated to cities, local governments had to solve urgent public health problems; and their solutions allowed cities to grow even more.

HISTORY & YOU When you attend a crowded event, what kinds of problems arise from having so many people in one place? Read about the problems of overcrowded cities of the late 1800s.

By the end of the nineteenth century, the new industrial world had led to the emergence of a mass society in which the condition of the majority—the lower classes—was demanding some governmental attention. Governments now had to consider how to appeal to the masses, rather than just to the wealthier citizens. Housing was one area of great concern. Crowded quarters could easily spread disease. An even bigger threat to health was public sanitation.

Growth of Urban Populations

With few jobs available in the countryside, people from rural areas migrated to cities to find work in the factories or, later, in blue-collar industries. As a result of this vast migration, more and more people lived in cities. In the 1850s, urban dwellers made up about 40 percent of the English population, 15 percent in France, 10 percent in Prussia (Prussia was the largest German state), and 5 percent in Russia. By 1890, urban dwellers had increased to about 60 percent in England, 25 percent in France, 30 percent in Prussia, and 10 percent in Russia. In industrialized nations, cities grew tremendously. Between 1800 and 1900, the population in London grew from 960,000 to 6,500,000.

Improvements in Public Health and Sanitation

Cities also grew faster in the second half of the nineteenth century because of improvements in public health and sanitation. Thus, more people could survive living close together. Improvements came only after reformers in the 1840s urged local governments to do something about the filthy living conditions that caused disease. For example, cholera had ravaged Europe in the early 1830s and 1840s. Contaminated water in the overcrowded cities had spread the deadly disease.

EUROPEAN POPULATION GROWTH AND RELOCATION, 1820–1900

1820

ATLANTIC OCEAN

SWEDEN

North Sea • DENMARK

Baltic Sea

RUSSIAN EMPIRE

UNITED KINGDOM

London

NETH. • Amsterdam

Berlin

Brussels

Rhine R.

50°N

Paris

GERMAN CONFEDERATION

Seine R.

Loire R.

Danube R.

FRANCE

Geneva • SWITZ.

Vienna

AUSTRIAN EMPIRE

Po R.

PORTUGAL

Madrid

Ebro R.

Corsica

ITALY

Rome

Lisbon SPAIN

0°

Sardinia

Sicily

Mediterranean Sea

Crete

Inhabitants per square mile:
- Fewer than 20
- 20–50
- 50–100
- More than 100

0   400 kilometers
0   400 miles

Lambert Azimuthal Equal-Area projection

30°N   10°E   20°E

1900

ATLANTIC OCEAN

SWEDEN

North Sea • DENMARK

Baltic Sea

RUSSIAN EMPIRE

UNITED KINGDOM

London

NETH. • Amsterdam

Berlin

Brussels BELG.

GERMAN EMPIRE

Rhine R.

50°N

Paris

Loire R.

Danube R.

FRANCE

Geneva • SWITZ.

Vienna

AUSTRO-HUNGARIAN EMPIRE

Po R.

PORTUGAL

Madrid

Ebro R.

Corsica

ITALY

Rome

Lisbon SPAIN

0°

Sardinia

Mediterranean Sea

20°E

Inhabitants per square mile:
- Fewer than 20
- 20–50
- 50–100
- More than 100

0   400 kilometers
0   400 miles

Azimuthal Equal-Area projection

10°E   30°N

Geography SKILLS

1. **Movement** Describe how population density changed in Italy between 1820 and 1900.
2. **Human-Environment Interaction** Analyze the relationship between the population densities shown here and the areas of industrial concentration shown on the map on page 417.

Maps In MOtion See *StudentWorks™ Plus* or glencoe.com.

On the advice of reformers, city governments created boards of health to improve housing quality. Medical officers and building inspectors inspected dwellings for public health hazards. Building regulations required running water and internal drainage systems for new buildings.

Clean water and an effective sewage system were critical to public health. The need for freshwater was met by a system of dams and reservoirs that stored the water. Aqueducts and tunnels then carried water from the countryside to the city and into homes. Gas heaters, and later electric heaters, made regular hot baths possible.

The treatment of sewage was improved by building underground pipes that carried raw sewage far from the city for disposal. A public campaign in **Frankfurt**, Germany featured the slogan "from the toilet to the river in half an hour."

✓ **Reading Check** **Explaining** Why did cities grow so quickly in the 1800s?

Social Structure

MAIN IDEA European society comprised three broad social classes—upper, middle, and lower.

HISTORY & YOU Do you think of yourself as middle class? Learn how your great-great-grandparents might have viewed themselves.

After 1871, most people enjoyed a higher standard of living. Still, great poverty remained in Western society. Between the few who were rich and the many who were poor existed several middle-class groups.

The New Elite

At the top of European society stood a wealthy elite. This group made up only 5 percent of the population but controlled from 30 to 40 percent of the wealth. During the 1800s, the most successful industrialists, bankers, and merchants—the wealthy upper-middle class—had joined with the landed aristocracy to form this new elite. Whether aristocratic or upper-middle class in background, members of the elite became leaders in the government and military.

Marriage also served to unite the two groups. Daughters of business tycoons gained aristocratic titles, and aristocratic heirs gained new sources of cash. For example, when wealthy American Consuelo Vanderbilt married the British duke of Marlborough, the new duchess brought approximately $10 million to the marriage.

The Middle Classes

The middle classes consisted of a variety of groups. Below the upper-middle class, which formed part of the new elite, was a middle group that included lawyers, doctors, members of the civil service, business managers, engineers, architects, accountants, and chemists. Beneath this solid and comfortable middle group was a lower-middle class of small shopkeepers, traders, and prosperous farmers.

The Second Industrial Revolution produced a new group of white-collar workers between the lower-middle class and the lower classes. This group included traveling salespeople, bookkeepers, telephone operators, department store salespeople, and secretaries. Although not highly paid, these white-collar workers were often committed to middle-class ideals.

The middle classes shared a certain lifestyle with values that dominated much of nineteenth-century society. Members of the middle class liked to preach their worldview both to their children and to the upper and lower classes of their society. This was especially evident in Victorian Britain, often considered a model of middle-class society.

The European middle classes believed in hard work, which was open to everyone and guaranteed to have positive results. Outward appearances were also very important to the middle classes. The etiquette book *The Habits of Good Society* was a best-seller.

The Working Classes

Below the middle classes on the social scale were the working classes—also referred to as the lower classes—which made up almost 80 percent of the European population. These classes included landholding peasants, farm laborers, and sharecroppers, especially in eastern Europe.

The urban working class consisted of many different groups. They might be skilled artisans or semiskilled laborers, but many were unskilled day laborers or domestic servants. In Britain in 1900, one out of every seven employed persons was a domestic servant. Most servants were women.

After 1870, urban workers began to live more comfortably. Reforms created better living conditions in cities. In addition, a rise in wages, along with a decline in many consumer costs, made it possible for workers to buy more than just food and housing. Workers now had money to buy extra clothes or pay to entertain themselves in their few leisure hours. Because workers had organized and conducted strikes, they had won the 10-hour workday with a Saturday afternoon off.

✓ Reading Check **Identifying** Name the major groups in the social structure of the late nineteenth century.

Women's Experiences

MAIN IDEA Attitudes toward women changed as they moved into white-collar jobs, received more education, and began campaigning for the right to vote.

HISTORY & YOU Do you think of any jobs as "women's work"? Read to learn how women started to expand their options in the late 1800s.

In 1800 women were mainly defined by their family and household roles. The vast majority of women throughout Europe and the United States had no legal identity apart from their husbands. Married women could not be a party in a lawsuit, could not sit on a jury, could not hold property in their own names, and could not write a will.

Women in the early nineteenth century remained legally inferior and economically dependent on men. In the course of the nineteenth century and during the Second Industrial Revolution, women struggled to change their status.

New Job Opportunities

During much of the nineteenth century, working-class groups maintained the belief that women should remain at home to bear and nurture children and should not be allowed in the industrial workforce.

The Second Industrial Revolution, however, opened the door to new jobs for women. There were not enough men to fill the relatively low-paid, white-collar jobs being created, so employers began to hire women. Both industrial plants and retail shops needed clerks, typists, secretaries, file clerks, and salesclerks.

The expansion of government services created some job opportunities for women.

CONNECTING TO THE UNITED STATES

⤷ WOMEN'S RIGHTS

In the 1840s and 1850s, the call for equal political rights for women grew louder in Europe and in the United States. In 1848 the first convention for women's rights took place in Seneca Falls, New York. The suffrage movement grew, and in 1920 the Nineteenth Amendment to the U.S. Constitution granted women the right to vote.

The next major turning point for women came in the 1960s. The Equal Pay Act of 1963 protects against wage discrimination. Title VII of the Civil Rights Act of 1964 prohibits employment discrimination. And in 1972, Title IX Education Amendments assured equal treatment and opportunity for women in education and athletics.

- Right to vote
- Equal opportunity in employment
- Equal pay for equal work
- Equal opportunity in school academics and athletics

CONNECTING TO TODAY

1. **Specifying** How does Title IX legislation affect your school or you personally? Give one specific example.

2. **Contrasting** How do attitudes about a woman's role today in the United States differ from those of the 1800s?

Women could be secretaries and telephone operators, and also took jobs in education, health, and social services. While some middle-class women held these jobs, they were mainly filled by the working class who aspired to a better quality of life.

The Marriage Ideal

Many people in the nineteenth century believed in the ideal expressed in Lord Tennyson's *The Princess*, published in 1847:

PRIMARY SOURCE

"Man for the field and woman for the hearth:
Man for the sword and for the needle she:
Man with the head and woman with the heart:
Man to command and woman to obey."

This view of the sexes was strengthened during the Industrial Revolution. As the chief family wage earners, men worked outside the home. Women were left to care for the family.

Throughout the 1800s, marriage remained the only honorable and available career for most women. There was also one important change. The number of children born to the average woman began to decline—the most significant development in the modern family. This decline in the birthrate was tied to improved economic conditions, as well as to increased use of birth control. In 1882 Europe's first birth control clinic was founded in Amsterdam.

See page R47 to read excerpts from an article on working women in the **Primary Source and Literature Library.**

The Family Ideal

The family was the central institution of middle-class life. With fewer children in the family, mothers could devote more time to child care and domestic leisure. The middle-class family fostered an ideal of togetherness. The Victorians created the family Christmas with its Yule log, tree, songs, and exchange of gifts. By the 1850s, Fourth of July celebrations in the United States had changed from wild celebrations to family picnics.

The lives of working-class women were different from those of their middle-class counterparts. Most working-class women had to earn money to help support their families. While their earnings averaged only a small percentage of their husbands's earnings, the contributions of working-class women made a big difference in the economic survival of their families. Daughters in working-class families were expected to work until they married. After marriage, many women often did small jobs at home to support the family.

For working-class women who worked away from the home, child care was a concern. Older siblings, other relatives, or neighbors often provided child care while the mothers worked. Some mothers sent their children to dame schools in which other women provided in-home child care, as well as some basic literacy instruction.

For the children of the working classes, childhood was over by the age of 9 or 10. By this age, children often became apprentices or were employed in odd jobs.

Between 1890 and 1914, however, family patterns among the working class began to change. Higher-paying jobs in heavy industry and improvements in the standard of living made it possible for working-class families to depend on the income of husbands alone.

By the early twentieth century, some working-class mothers could afford to stay at home, following the pattern of middle-class women. At the same time, working-class families aspired to buy new consumer products, such as sewing machines and cast-iron stoves.

Women's Rights

Modern **feminism,** or the movement for women's rights, had its beginnings during the Enlightenment. At this time, some women **advocated** equality for women based on the doctrine of natural rights.

In the 1830s, a number of women in the United States and Europe argued for the right of women to own property and to divorce. By law, a husband had almost complete control over his wife's property. These early efforts were not very successful, however. Married women in Great Britain did not win the right to own some property until 1870.

The fight for property rights was only the beginning of the women's movement. Some middle- and upper-middle-class

Britain's Suffragists

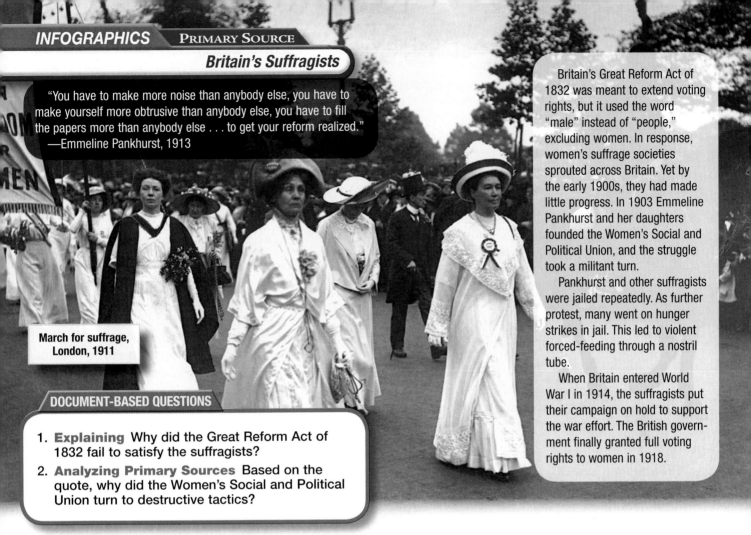

"You have to make more noise than anybody else, you have to make yourself more obtrusive than anybody else, you have to fill the papers more than anybody else . . . to get your reform realized."
—Emmeline Pankhurst, 1913

March for suffrage, London, 1911

Britain's Great Reform Act of 1832 was meant to extend voting rights, but it used the word "male" instead of "people," excluding women. In response, women's suffrage societies sprouted across Britain. Yet by the early 1900s, they had made little progress. In 1903 Emmeline Pankhurst and her daughters founded the Women's Social and Political Union, and the struggle took a militant turn.

Pankhurst and other suffragists were jailed repeatedly. As further protest, many went on hunger strikes in jail. This led to violent forced-feeding through a nostril tube.

When Britain entered World War I in 1914, the suffragists put their campaign on hold to support the war effort. The British government finally granted full voting rights to women in 1918.

DOCUMENT-BASED QUESTIONS

1. **Explaining** Why did the Great Reform Act of 1832 fail to satisfy the suffragists?
2. **Analyzing Primary Sources** Based on the quote, why did the Women's Social and Political Union turn to destructive tactics?

women fought for and gained access to universities. Others sought entry into occupations dominated by men.

Though training to become doctors was largely closed to women, some entered the medical field by becoming nurses. In Germany, **Amalie Sieveking** was a nursing pioneer who founded the Female Association for the Care of the Poor and Sick in Hamburg. More famous is the British nurse **Florence Nightingale.** Her efforts during the Crimean War (1853–1856), combined with those of **Clara Barton** in the U.S. Civil War (1861–1865), transformed nursing into a profession of trained, middle-class "women in white."

By the 1840s and 1850s, the movement for women's rights expanded as women called for equal political rights. They believed that **suffrage,** the right to vote, was the key to improving their overall position. Members of the women's movement, called suffragists, had one basic aim: the right of women to full citizenship in the nation-state.

The British women's movement was the most active in Europe. The Women's Social and Political Union, founded in 1903 by **Emmeline Pankhurst** and her daughters, used unusual publicity stunts to call attention to its demands. Its members pelted government officials with eggs, chained themselves to lampposts, burned railroad cars, and smashed the windows of fashionable department stores. British police answered with arrests and brutal treatment of leading activists.

Before World War I, demands for women's rights echoed throughout Europe and the United States. Before 1914, however, women had the right to vote in only a few nations, such as Norway and Finland, along with some American states. It took the upheaval of World War I to make male-dominated governments give in on this basic issue.

✓ **Reading Check** **Identifying** What was the basic aim of the suffragists?

Education and Leisure

MAIN IDEA As a result of industrialization, the levels of education rose. People's lives became more clearly divided into periods of work and leisure.

HISTORY & YOU How would our society change if a college education was required? Read about the era when an elementary education became required by law.

Universal education was a product of the mass society of the late nineteenth and early twentieth centuries. Before that time, education was reserved mostly for the elite and the wealthier middle class. Between 1870 and 1914, however, most Western governments began to finance a system of primary education. Boys and girls between the ages of 6 and 12 were required to attend these schools. States also took responsibility for training teachers by setting up teacher-training schools.

Public Education

Why did Western nations make this commitment to public education? One reason was industrialization. In the first Industrial Revolution, unskilled labor (workers without training or experience) was able to meet factory needs. The new firms of the Second Industrial Revolution, however, needed trained, skilled workers. Boys and girls with an elementary education now had new job possibilities beyond their villages or small towns. These included white-collar jobs in railways, post offices, schools, and hospitals.

The chief motive for public education, however, was political. Giving more people the right to vote created a need for better-educated voters. Even more important was the fact that primary schools instilled patriotism. As people lost their ties to local regions and even to religion, nationalism gave them a new faith.

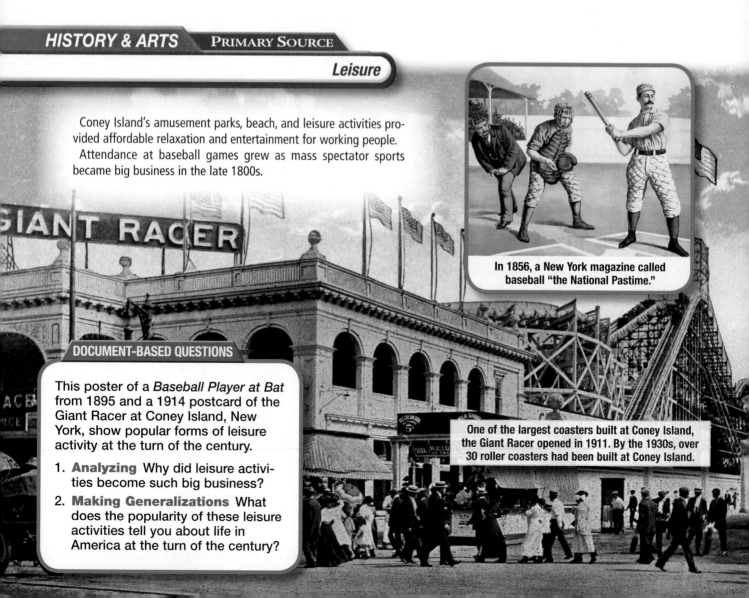

HISTORY & ARTS   PRIMARY SOURCE

Leisure

Coney Island's amusement parks, beach, and leisure activities provided affordable relaxation and entertainment for working people. Attendance at baseball games grew as mass spectator sports became big business in the late 1800s.

In 1856, a New York magazine called baseball "the National Pastime."

One of the largest coasters built at Coney Island, the Giant Racer opened in 1911. By the 1930s, over 30 roller coasters had been built at Coney Island.

DOCUMENT-BASED QUESTIONS

This poster of a *Baseball Player at Bat* from 1895 and a 1914 postcard of the Giant Racer at Coney Island, New York, show popular forms of leisure activity at the turn of the century.

1. **Analyzing** Why did leisure activities become such big business?

2. **Making Generalizations** What does the popularity of these leisure activities tell you about life in America at the turn of the century?

Compulsory elementary education created a demand for teachers, and most of them were women. Many men saw teaching as a part of women's "natural role" as nurturers of children. Women were also paid lower salaries than men, which in itself was a strong incentive for states to set up teacher-training schools for women. The first women's colleges were really teacher-training schools.

The most immediate result of public education was an increase in **literacy,** or the ability to read. In Western and central Europe most adults could read by 1900. In contrast, the story was very different where governments did not promote education. For example, only about 20 percent of adults in Serbia and Russia could read.

Once literacy expanded, a mass media developed. Newspapers sprang up to appeal to this new reading public. In London, papers such as the *Evening News* (1881) and the *Daily Mail* (1896) sold millions of copies each day. These newspapers were all written in an easily understood style. They were also sensationalistic—that is, they provided gossip and gruesome details of crimes.

New Forms of Leisure

People read this new kind of newspaper in their leisure time. There were other new forms of leisure, too. Amusement parks, dance halls, and organized team sports, for example, became enjoyable ways for people to spend their leisure hours.

These forms of leisure were new in several ways. First, leisure was now seen as what people did for fun after work. In an older era, work and leisure time were not so clearly defined. During the era of cottage industries, family members might chat or laugh while they worked on cloth in their homes. Now free time was more closely scheduled and more often confined to evening hours, weekends, and perhaps a week in the summer.

Second, the new forms of leisure tended to be **passive,** not participatory. Instead of doing a folk dance on the town square, a young woman sat in a Ferris wheel and was twirled around by a huge machine. Instead of playing a game of tug-of-war at the town fair, a young man sat on the sidelines at a cricket match and cheered his favorite team to victory.

A third change in leisure during this era was that people more often paid for many of their leisure activities. It cost money to ride a merry-go-round or Ferris wheel at Coney Island. This change was perhaps the most dramatic of all. Business entrepreneurs created amusement parks and professional sports teams in order to make a profit. Whatever would sell, they would promote.

✓ **Reading Check** **Describing** How did leisure activities change in the late nineteenth and early twentieth centuries?

Vocabulary

1. **Explain** the significance of: Frankfurt, feminism, advocate, Amalie Sieveking, Florence Nightingale, Clara Barton, suffrage, Emmeline Pankhurst, literacy, passive.

Main Ideas

2. **Summarize** the results of nineteenth-century urban reforms by using a diagram like the one below.

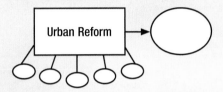

3. **Identify** the class to which each of these workers belonged in nineteenth-century European society: architect, shopkeeper, semiskilled laborer, successful industrialist.

4. **Explain** why the birthrate declined during the 1800s.

5. **Define** the term *universal education.* Why did industry help propel the movement for universal education?

Critical Thinking

6. **The BIG Idea** **Analyzing** Why have certain occupations such as elementary teaching and nursing historically been dominated by women?

7. **Speculating** Why do governments fund and promote literacy programs?

8. **Analyzing Visuals** Examine the two images on page 428. How do these activities differ from leisure activities of the past?

Writing About History

9. **Persuasive Writing** The feminist movement changed the role of women. In an essay, argue whether these changes were positive or negative.

History ONLINE

For help with the concepts in this section of *Glencoe World History— Modern Times,* go to glencoe.com and click Study Central.

Social History

At Home in London, 1890

By 1890, London was becoming a modern industrial city. Aggressive rebuilding programs had made workers' slums into working-class neighborhoods. Class differences, marked by how industrialists and laborers lived, remained clear. However, modern city services allowed everyone to live in a safer, cleaner environment.

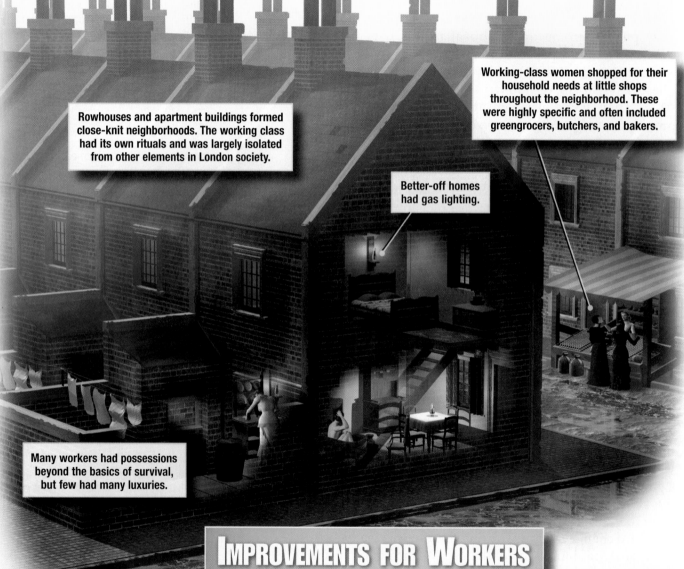

Rowhouses and apartment buildings formed close-knit neighborhoods. The working class had its own rituals and was largely isolated from other elements in London society.

Working-class women shopped for their household needs at little shops throughout the neighborhood. These were highly specific and often included greengrocers, butchers, and bakers.

Better-off homes had gas lighting.

Many workers had possessions beyond the basics of survival, but few had many luxuries.

IMPROVEMENTS FOR WORKERS

Working-class life remained dirty and difficult for many Londoners. Substance abuse, crime, and poverty remained serious problems. Rickety and filthy tenements were still home to people who failed to find decent wages or work at all. Other homes were well-built and offered water and sewer service. For workers with steady jobs and permanent homes, the Second Industrial Revolution offered a stable and improving life.

The homes of wealthy industrialists included furnishings from all over the British Empire.

The Victorian style in architecture and decorating tended to be very formal.

Wealthy Victorians enjoyed intricate patterns in wallpaper and furniture upholstery.

The telephone was one of many luxurious gadgets that later became common in English homes.

LUXURIES FOR INDUSTRIAL OWNERS

The owners of successful mills and industrial works enjoyed a luxurious lifestyle in the best neighborhoods of London. Their homes featured every modern convenience. The nobility's old stigma against the capitalist class had relaxed somewhat. Industrialists and nobles intermarried. The captains of industry sought social status. The aristocracy sought cash reserves and the opportunity to become leaders in the new economy.

ANALYZING VISUALS

1. **Describing** In what ways had London become a modern city by 1890?

2. **Contrasting** How were the homes of successful industrialists different from those of laborers?

The National State and Democracy

GUIDE TO READING

The BIG Idea

Competition Among Countries
While democracy triumphed in Western Europe, authoritarianism prevailed in central and eastern Europe, and industrialization swept the United States. International rivalries set the stage for war.

Content Vocabulary
• ministerial responsibility *(p. 432)*
• Duma *(p. 434)*

Academic Vocabulary
• insecure *(p. 435)*   • controversy *(p. 437)*

People and Places
• Otto von Bismarck *(p. 434)*
• William II *(p. 434)*
• Francis Joseph *(p. 434)*
• Nicholas II *(p. 434)*
• St. Petersburg *(p. 434)*
• Queen Liliuokalani *(p. 435)*
• Montenegro *(p. 437)*

Reading Strategy
Summarizing Information As you read, complete a diagram like the one below listing the countries in each alliance.

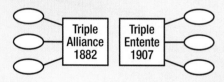

During the late nineteenth and early twentieth centuries, democracy expanded in Western Europe, while the old order preserved authoritarianism in central and eastern Europe. During this time, the United States recovered from the Civil War and became the world's richest nation. Meanwhile, international rivalries began to set the stage for World War I.

Western Europe and Political Democracy

MAIN IDEA Growing prosperity after 1850 contributed to the expansion of democracy in Western Europe.

HISTORY & YOU Which political party does your family support? Read about political parties in Western Europe in the late 1800s.

By the late nineteenth century, especially in Western Europe, there were many signs that political democracy was expanding. First, universal male suffrage laws were passed. Second, the prime minister was responsible to the popularly elected legislative body, not to the king or president. This principle is called **ministerial responsibility,** which is crucial for democracy. Third, mass political parties formed. As more men, and later women, could vote, parties created larger organizations and found ways to appeal to many who were now part of the political process.

Great Britain

Before 1871 Great Britain had a working two-party parliamentary system. These two parties—the Liberals and Conservatives—competed to pass laws that expanded the right to vote. Reform acts in 1867 and 1884 increased the number of adult male voters.

With political democracy established, social reforms for the working class soon followed. The working class in Great Britain supported the Liberal Party. Two developments made Liberals fear losing this support. First, the trade unions grew, and they favored a more radical change of the economic system. Second, in 1900, the Labour Party emerged and dedicated itself to the interests of workers. To retain the workers' support, the Liberals voted for social reforms, such as unemployment benefits and old age pensions.

France

In France, the collapse of Louis-Napoleon's Second Empire left the country in confusion. Finally, in 1875, the Third Republic gained a republican constitution. The new government had a

Austro-Hungarian Empire

French Empire

German Empire

Kingdom of Italy

Ottoman Empire

Russian Empire

Geography SKILLS

1. **Location** Which three empires extend beyond the area shown on this map?

2. **Human-Environment Interaction** Which empire do you think would be most likely to have to invade another empire to expand its own boundaries? Explain.

president and a legislature made up of two houses. The upper house, or Senate, was conservative and elected by high-ranking officials. All adult males voted for members of the lower house, the Chamber of Deputies. A premier (or prime minister), who led the government, was responsible to the Chamber of Deputies, not to the president.

France failed to develop a strong parliamentary system. The existence of a dozen political parties forced the premier to depend on a coalition of parties to stay in power. Nevertheless, by 1914, the Third Republic had the loyalty of most voters.

Italy

Italy had emerged by 1870 as a united national state. However, there was little national unity because of the great gulf between the poverty-stricken south and the industrialized north. Constant turmoil between labor and industry weakened the social fabric of the nation. Even universal male suffrage, granted in 1912, did little to halt the widespread government corruption and weakness.

✓**Reading Check** **Summarizing** What is the principle of ministerial responsibility?

Central and Eastern Europe: The Old Order

MAIN IDEA Although Germany, Austria-Hungary, and later Russia instituted elections and parliaments, real power remained in the hands of emperors and elites.

HISTORY & YOU Does your school have a student council? What is its role? Read to learn about the political structures in central and eastern Europe in the late 1800s.

Central and eastern Europe had more conservative governments than did Western Europe. Germany, the Austro-Hungarian Empire, and Russia were less industrialized, and education was not widely available. It was easier, then, for the old ruling groups to continue to dominate politics.

Germany

The constitution of the new imperial Germany that **Otto von Bismarck** began in 1871 set up a two-house legislature. The lower house, the Reichstag, was elected on the basis of universal male suffrage.

Ministers of government, however, were responsible not to the parliament, but to the emperor, who controlled the armed forces, foreign policy, and the bureaucracy. As chancellor (prime minister), Bismarck worked to keep Germany from becoming a democracy.

By the reign of **William II,** emperor from 1888 to 1918, Germany had become the strongest military and industrial power in Europe. With the expansion of industry and cities came demands for democracy.

Conservative forces—especially the land-owning nobility and big industrialists—tried to thwart the movement for democracy by supporting a strong foreign policy. They believed that expansion abroad would increase their profits and would also divert people from pursuing democratic reforms.

Austro-Hungarian Empire

After the creation of the dual monarchy of Austria-Hungary in 1867, Austria enacted a constitution that, in theory, set up a parliamentary system with ministerial responsibility. In reality, the emperor, **Francis Joseph,** largely ignored this system. He appointed and dismissed his own ministers and issued decrees, or laws, when the parliament was not in session.

The empire remained troubled by conflicts among its ethnic groups. A German minority governed Austria but felt increasingly threatened by Czechs, Poles, and other Slavic groups within the empire. Representatives of these groups in the parliament agitated for their freedom, which encouraged the emperor to ignore the parliament and govern by imperial decrees.

Unlike Austria, Hungary had a parliament that worked. It was controlled by landowners who dominated the peasants and ethnic groups.

Russia

In Russia, **Nicholas II** began his rule in 1894 believing that the absolute power of the czars should be preserved. "I shall maintain the principle of autocracy just as firmly and unflinchingly as did my unforgettable father." Conditions were changing, however.

By 1900, Russia had become the fourth-largest producer of steel. With industrialization came factories, an industrial working class, and pitiful working and living conditions. Socialist parties developed, including the Marxist Social Democratic Party, but government repression forced them underground.

Growing discontent and opposition to the czarist regime finally exploded. On January 22, 1905, a massive procession of workers went to the Winter Palace in **St. Petersburg** to present a petition of grievances to the czar. Troops opened fire on the peaceful demonstration, killing hundreds. This "Bloody Sunday" caused workers throughout Russia to call strikes.

Nicholas II was eventually forced to grant civil liberties and to create a legislative assembly, called the **Duma.** By 1907, however, the czar had already curtailed the power of the Duma and again used the army and bureaucracy to rule Russia.

✓ Reading Check **Identifying** What was the role of the Duma in the Russian government?

The United States

MAIN IDEA In the United States, the Second Industrial Revolution produced wealth that was more concentrated than it was in Europe.

HISTORY & YOU Can you name territories that are part of the United States today but are not states? Read how the Unitd States acquired territories in the late 1800s.

Civil war had not destroyed the national unity of the United States. Between 1870 and 1914, the country became an industrial power with an empire.

Aftermath of the Civil War

Four years of bloody civil war had preserved the American nation. However, the old South had been destroyed.

In 1865 the Thirteenth Amendment to the Constitution was passed, abolishing slavery. Later, the Fourteenth and Fifteenth Amendments gave citizenship to African Americans and the right to vote to African American males. New state laws in the South, however, soon stripped African Americans of the right to vote. By 1880, supporters of white supremacy were back in power everywhere in the South.

Economy

Between 1860 and 1914, the United States shifted from a farm-based economy to an industrial economy. American steel and iron production was the best in the world in 1900. Carnegie Steel Company alone produced more steel than all of Great Britain. As in Europe, industrialization in the United States led to urbanization. By 1900, the United States had three cities with populations over 1 million, with New York reaching 4 million.

In 1900 the United States was the world's richest nation, but the richest 9 percent of Americans owned 71 percent of the wealth. Many workers labored in unsafe factories, and devastating cycles of unemployment made them **insecure.** Many tried to organize unions, but the American Federation of Labor represented only 8.4 percent of the labor force.

Expansion Abroad

In the late 1800s, the United States began to expand abroad. The Samoan Islands in the Pacific were the first important U.S. colony. By 1887, Americans controlled the sugar industry on the Hawaiian Islands.

As more Americans settled in Hawaii, they wanted political power. When **Queen Liliuokalani** (lih•LEE•uh•woh•kuh•LAH•nee) tried to strengthen the monarchy to keep the islands under her people's control, the United States sent military forces to the islands. The queen was deposed and the United States annexed Hawaii in 1898.

In 1898 the United States defeated Spain in the Spanish-American War. As a result, the United States acquired the former Spanish possessions of Puerto Rico, Guam, and the Philippines. By the beginning of the twentieth century, the United States, the world's richest nation, had an empire.

✓ Reading Check **Identifying** Name the territories that the United States acquired in 1898.

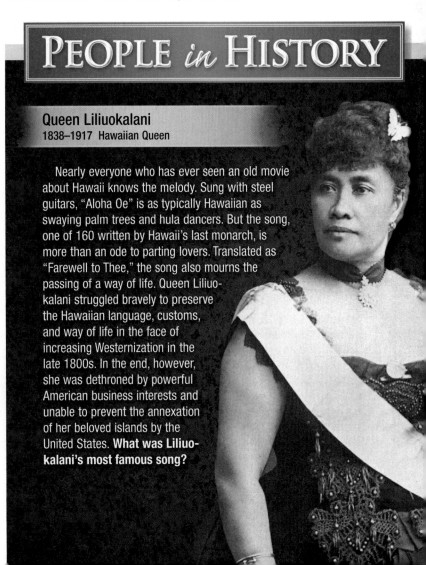

PEOPLE in HISTORY

Queen Liliuokalani
1838–1917 Hawaiian Queen

Nearly everyone who has ever seen an old movie about Hawaii knows the melody. Sung with steel guitars, "Aloha Oe" is as typically Hawaiian as swaying palm trees and hula dancers. But the song, one of 160 written by Hawaii's last monarch, is more than an ode to parting lovers. Translated as "Farewell to Thee," the song also mourns the passing of a way of life. Queen Liliuokalani struggled bravely to preserve the Hawaiian language, customs, and way of life in the face of increasing Westernization in the late 1800s. In the end, however, she was dethroned by powerful American business interests and unable to prevent the annexation of her beloved islands by the United States. **What was Liliuokalani's most famous song?**

International Rivalries

MAIN IDEA The German emperor pursued aggressive foreign policies that divided Europe into two hostile alliance systems.

HISTORY & YOU Remember how the Great Powers acted together in the early 1800s? Read to learn how the Great Powers divided into two hostile camps after the 1890s.

Otto von Bismarck realized that Germany's emergence in 1871 as the most powerful state in continental Europe had upset the balance of power established at Vienna in 1815. Fearing that France intended to create an anti-German alliance, Bismarck made a defensive alliance with Austria-Hungary in 1879. In 1882 Italy joined this alliance.

This Triple Alliance thus united the powers of Germany, Austria-Hungary, and Italy in a defensive alliance against France. At the same time, Bismarck maintained a separate treaty with Russia and tried to remain on good terms with Great Britain.

New Directions: William II

In 1890 Emperor William II fired Bismarck and took control of Germany's foreign policy. The emperor embarked on an activist policy dedicated to enhancing German power. He wanted, as he put it, to find Germany's rightful "place in the sun."

One of the changes William made in foreign policy was to drop the treaty with Russia. Almost immediately, in 1894, France formed an alliance with Russia. Germany thus had a hostile power on her western border and on her eastern border—exactly the situation Bismarck had feared!

Over the next decade, German policies abroad caused the British to draw closer to France. By 1907, an alliance of Great Britain, France, and Russia—the Triple Entente—stood opposed to the Triple Alliance of Germany, Austria-Hungary, and Italy.

Europe was now dangerously divided into two opposing camps that became more and more unwilling to compromise. A series of crises in the Balkans between 1908 and 1913 set the stage for World War I.

POLITICAL CARTOONS   PRIMARY SOURCE

William II Fires Bismarck

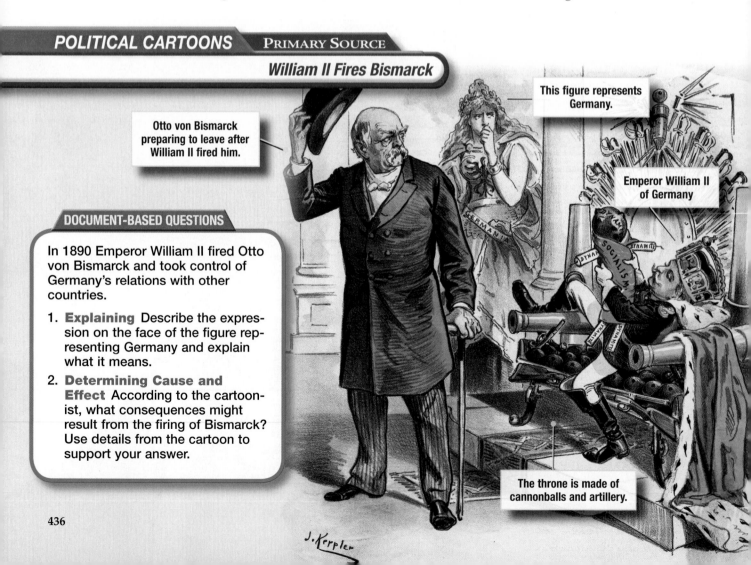

Otto von Bismarck preparing to leave after William II fired him.

This figure represents Germany.

Emperor William II of Germany

The throne is made of cannonballs and artillery.

DOCUMENT-BASED QUESTIONS

In 1890 Emperor William II fired Otto von Bismarck and took control of Germany's relations with other countries.

1. **Explaining** Describe the expression on the face of the figure representing Germany and explain what it means.

2. **Determining Cause and Effect** According to the cartoonist, what consequences might result from the firing of Bismarck? Use details from the cartoon to support your answer.

J. Keppler

Crises in the Balkans

During the nineteenth century, the Ottoman Empire that had once been strong enough to threaten Europe began to fall apart. Most of its Balkan provinces were able to gain their freedom.

As this was happening, however, two Great Powers saw their chance to gain influence in the Balkans: Austria and Russia. Their rivalry over the Balkans was one of the causes of World War I.

By 1878, Greece, Serbia, Romania, and **Montenegro** had become independent. Bulgaria did not become totally independent but was allowed to operate autonomously under Russian protection. The Balkan territories of Bosnia and Herzegovina were placed under the protection of Austria-Hungary.

In 1908 Austria-Hungary took the drastic step of annexing Bosnia and Herzegovina. This step led to a **controversy** with international complications that threatened to end in a general European war. This controversy was known as the Bosnian Crisis.

Serbia was outraged. The annexation of Bosnia and Herzegovina, two Slavic-speaking territories, dashed the Serbians' hopes of creating a large Serbian kingdom that would include most of the southern Slavs.

The Russians, self-appointed protectors of their fellow Slavs, supported the Serbs and opposed the annexation. Backed by the Russians, the Serbs prepared for war against Austria-Hungary. At this point, Emperor William II of Germany demanded that the Russians accept Austria-Hungary's annexation of Bosnia and Herzegovina or face war with Germany.

Weakened from their defeat in the Russo-Japanese War in 1905, the Russians backed down but vowed revenge. Two wars between Balkan states in 1912 and 1913 further embittered the inhabitants and created more tensions among the great powers.

The Serbs blamed their inability to create a large Serbian kingdom on Austria-Hungary. At the same time, Austria-Hungary was convinced that Serbia and Serbian nationalism were mortal threats to its empire and must be crushed at some point.

As Serbia's chief supporters, the Russians were angry and determined not to back down again in the event of another confrontation with Austria-Hungary or Germany in the Balkans. Finally, the allies of Austria-Hungary and Russia were determined to support their respective allies more strongly in another crisis. By the beginning of 1914, these countries viewed each other with suspicion. It would not take much to ignite the Balkan "powder keg."

✓ Reading Check **Explaining** Why were the Serbs outraged when Austria-Hungary annexed Bosnia and Herzegovina?

SECTION 3 REVIEW

Vocabulary
1. **Explain** the significance of: ministerial responsibility, Otto von Bismarck, William II, Francis Joseph, Nicholas II, St. Petersburg, Duma, insecure, Queen Liliuokalani, Montenegro, controversy.

Main Ideas
2. **Explain** why France did not develop a strong parliamentary system.

3. **List** the series of events leading to unrest in Russia at the start of the 1900s. What were the results of "Bloody Sunday"?

4. **Describe** how the United States became an industrial power. What problems did industrialization cause in the United States, and how did people attempt to solve some of these problems?

5. **Identify** the effects of William II's foreign policy by using a diagram like this one.

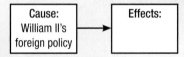

Cause: William II's foreign policy → Effects:

Critical Thinking
6. **The BIG Idea** **Evaluating** Which country do you think had a stronger democracy at the end of the nineteenth century, France or England? Why?

7. **Comparing and Contrasting** Use this chapter and Chapter 10 to compare and contrast the systems of government in France and the United States.

8. **Analyzing Visuals** Examine the political cartoon on page 436. Why do you think the cartoonist depicted William II as childlike?

Writing About History
9. **Expository Writing** Do some research about recent conflicts in the Balkans. Write one or two paragraphs comparing the causes of the recent conflicts with the causes of the conflicts between Balkan countries in the early 1900s.

History ONLINE

For help with the concepts in this section of *Glencoe World History— Modern Times,* go to glencoe.com and click Study Central.

Toward the Modern Consciousness

GUIDE TO READING

The BIG Idea
Ideas, Beliefs, and Values Radical changes in the economic and social structure of the West was matched by equally dramatic artistic and intellectual changes.

Content Vocabulary
- modernism *(p. 438)*
- psychoanalysis *(p. 441)*
- Social Darwinism *(p. 442)*
- pogroms *(p. 443)*
- Zionism *(p. 443)*

Academic Vocabulary
- abstract *(p. 440)*
- intensity *(p. 443)*

People and Places
- France *(p. 438)*
- Claude Monet *(p. 438)*
- Pablo Picasso *(p. 439)*
- Frank Lloyd Wright *(p. 440)*
- Marie Curie *(p. 440)*
- Albert Einstein *(p. 440)*
- Sigmund Freud *(p. 441)* • Vienna *(p. 441)*

Reading Strategy
Identifying Information As you read, complete a chart like the one below that lists an artist and a characteristic of the art movement indicated.

Impressionism		
Post-Impressionism		
Cubism		
Abstract painting		

During the late nineteenth and early twentieth centuries, people moved toward a modern consciousness. Their changing worldview was expressed in innovative art movements. Developments in the sciences also changed how people saw themselves and their world. Some people took nationalism to the extreme. They advocated Social Darwinism to justify the dominance of Western nations.

The Culture of Modernity

MAIN IDEA Dramatic innovation occurred in literature, the visual arts, and music in the late 1800s.

HISTORY & YOU How can you tell that student artwork is from your era? Read to learn how artists express the society they know.

Between 1870 and 1914, many writers and artists rebelled against the traditional literary and artistic styles that had dominated European cultural life since the Renaissance. The changes they produced have since been called **modernism.**

Literature

Western novelists and poets who followed the naturalist style felt that literature should be realistic and address social problems. Henrik Ibsen and Émile Zola, for example, explored the role of women in society, alcoholism, and the problems of urban slums in their work.

The symbolist writers had a different idea about what was real. Inspired by Sigmund Freud, they believed the external world, including art, was only a collection of symbols reflecting the true reality—the human mind. Art, the symbolists believed, should function for its own sake, not criticize or seek to understand society.

Painting

Since the Renaissance, Western artists had tried to represent reality as accurately as possible. By the late 1800s, artists were seeking new forms of expression to reflect their changing worldviews.

Impressionism was a movement that began in **France** in the 1870s, when a group of artists rejected traditional indoor studios and went to the countryside to paint nature directly. One important impressionist is **Claude Monet** (moh•NAY), who painted pictures that captured the interplay of light, water, and sky. Other impressionist painters include Pierre-Auguste Renoir (REHN•WAHR) and Berthe Morisot.

Impressionists and Postimpressionists

Van Gogh painted this view from his window at an asylum, a year before his suicide. His thick, agitated brush strokes and intense colors reflect his emotions.

The sketch-like quality of Monet's painting reflects the social upheaval of the late 1800s.

DOCUMENT-BASED QUESTIONS

Impressionists presented their impression of a scene at a given moment in time. This is captured in *Impression Sunrise* (1872) by Claude Monet (1840–1926). Postimpressionists painted their emotional or spiritual reaction to a scene. Vincent van Gogh (1853-1890) captures this in *The Starry Night* (1889).

1. **Expressing** Given the conditions under which he painted *The Starry Night*, how does van Gogh's painting convey his emotions?
2. **Comparing and Contrasting** In what ways are impressionism and post-impressionism similar? In what ways are they different?

In the 1880s, a new movement, known as postimpressionism, arose in France and soon spread. Painters Paul Cezanne and Vincent van Gogh used color and structure to express a mood. For van Gogh, art was a spiritual experience. He was especially interested in color and believed that it could act as its own form of language. Van Gogh maintained that artists should paint what they feel.

By the early 1900s, artists were no longer convinced that their main goal was to represent reality. This was especially true in the visual arts. One reason for the decline of realism in painting was photography. Invented in the 1830s, photography gained wide popularity after George Eastman created the first Kodak camera in 1888.

Artists tended to focus less on mirroring reality, which the camera could do, and more on creating reality. Painters and sculptors, like the symbolist writers of the time, looked for meaning in individual consciousness. Between 1905 and 1914, this search for individual expression created modern art. One of the most outstanding features of modern art is the attempt of the artist to avoid "visual reality."

By 1905, **Pablo Picasso**, an important figure in modern art was beginning his career. Picasso was a Spaniard who settled in Paris. He painted in a remarkable variety

History ONLINE
Student Web Activity—
Visit glencoe.com and complete the activity on impressionism.

of styles and even created a new style—cubism. Cubism used geometric designs to re-create reality in the viewer's mind. In his paintings, Picasso attempted to view human form from many sides. In this aspect, he seems to have been influenced by Albert Einstein's increasingly popular theory of relativity.

Abstract painting emerged around 1910. Wassily Kandinsky, a Russian who worked in Germany, was one of the first to use an abstract style. Kandinsky sought to avoid visual reality altogether. He believed that art should speak directly to the soul. To do so, it must use only line and color.

Architecture

Modernism in the arts revolutionized architecture and gave rise to a new principle known as functionalism. Functionalism was the idea that buildings, like the products of machines, should be functional, or useful. Buildings should fulfill the purposes for which they were built. All unnecessary ornamentation should be stripped away.

The United States was a leader in the new architecture. The country's rapid urban growth and lack of any architectural tradition allowed for new building methods. Architects, led by Louis H. Sullivan, used reinforced concrete, steel frames, and electric elevators to build skyscrapers virtually free of ornamentation. One of Sullivan's pupils was **Frank Lloyd Wright,** who pioneered the building of American homes with long geometric lines and overhanging roofs.

Music

At the beginning of the twentieth century, developments in music paralleled those in painting. The music of the Russian composer Igor Stravinsky exploited expressive sounds and bold rhythms.

Stravinsky's ballet *The Rite of Spring* revolutionized music. When it was performed in Paris in 1913, the sounds and rhythms of the music and dance caused a near riot by an outraged audience.

✓Reading Check **Explaining** How did the impressionists radically change the art of painting in the 1870s?

Uncertainty Grows

MAIN IDEA Scientific discoveries in this period had a profound impact on how people saw themselves and their world.

HISTORY & YOU Has someone you know had radiation treatment for cancer? Read about a discovery that led to this treatment.

Science was one of the chief pillars supporting the optimistic worldview that many Westerners shared in the 1800s. Science, supposedly based on hard facts and cold reason, offered a certainty of belief in nature's orderliness. Many believed that by applying already known scientific laws, humans could completely understand the physical world and reality.

Curie and the Atom

Throughout much of the 1800s, Westerners believed in a mechanical conception of the universe that was based on the ideas of Isaac Newton. In this perspective, the universe was viewed as a giant machine. Time, space, and matter were objective realities existing independently of those observing them. Matter was thought to be made of solid material bodies called atoms.

These views were seriously questioned at the end of the nineteenth century. The French scientist **Marie Curie** discovered that an element called radium gave off energy, or radiation, that apparently came from within the atom itself. Atoms were not simply hard material bodies but small, active worlds.

Einstein and Relativity

In the early twentieth century, **Albert Einstein,** a German-born scientist, provided a new view of the universe. In 1905 Einstein published his special theory of relativity, which stated that space and time are not absolute but are relative to the observer.

According to this theory, neither space nor time has an existence independent of human experience. As Einstein later explained to a journalist, "It was formerly believed that if all material things disappeared out of the universe, time and space would be left. According to the relativity theory, however, time and space disappear together with the things." Moreover, matter and energy reflect the relativity of time and space. Einstein concluded that matter is just another form of energy. The vast energies contained within the atom were explained, and the Atomic Age began. To some, however, a relative universe—unlike Newton's universe—was one without certainty.

Freud and Psychoanalysis

Sigmund Freud (FROYD), a doctor from **Vienna,** proposed theories regarding the nature of the human mind. Freud's ideas, like the new physics, added to the uncertainties of the age. His major theories were published in 1900 in *The Interpretation of Dreams.*

According to Freud, human behavior was strongly determined by past experiences and internal forces of which people were largely unaware. Repression of such experiences began in childhood, so he devised a method—known as **psychoanalysis**—by which a therapist and patient could probe deeply into the patient's memory. In this way, they could retrace the chain of repressed thoughts all the way back to their childhood origins. If the patient's conscious mind could be made aware of the unconscious and its repressed contents, the patient could be healed.

✓ **Reading Check** **Summarizing** What is Freud's theory of the human unconscious?

FREUD: IN SEARCH OF THE UNCONSCIOUS

Rapid advances in science, psychology, and the arts caused people to question previous knowledge and created a culture of modernity. While scientists such as Marie Curie and Albert Einstein were reshaping people's understanding of the external world, Sigmund Freud was shaping their perceptions of the internal world—the inner workings of the mind.

Freud believed that the mind has both conscious and unconscious parts, and that the unconscious controls many human behaviors. Painful memories from childhood become rooted, or repressed, in the unconscious, leading to mental illness. To help the person heal, these memories must be brought to conscious awareness. Freud believed that memories buried in the unconscious emerge in disguised form in dreams. One way to gain access to repressed memories, then, is to interpret dreams.

Freud's ideas prompted a new way of looking at human behavior as the result of unconscious drives and the experiences that shape them. His theories form the basis of modern psychoanalysis, but his influence extends into many fields.

Freud compared the parts of the mind to an iceberg.

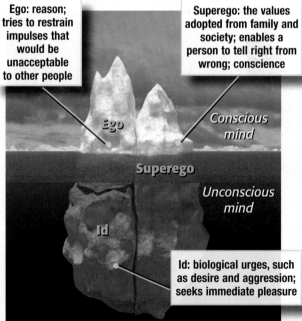

Ego: reason; tries to restrain impulses that would be unacceptable to other people

Superego: the values adopted from family and society; enables a person to tell right from wrong; conscience

Conscious mind

Unconscious mind

Id: biological urges, such as desire and aggression; seeks immediate pleasure

DOCUMENT-BASED QUESTIONS

1. **Identifying** According to the diagram, which part of the mind is completely unconscious?

2. **Analyzing** Suppose a person never learned society's values. How might that person behave?

Extreme Nationalism

MAIN IDEA In the late 1800s, extreme nationalism was reflected in the movements of Social Darwinism and anti-Semitism.

HISTORY & YOU What do you think qualifies someone to be an American? Read to learn how some thinkers in the late 1800s felt national identity should be determined.

Nationalism became more intense in many countries in the late 1800s. For some Europeans, loyalty to their nation became an anchor, almost a religious faith. Preserving their nation's status and their national traditions counted above everything else.

Social Darwinism and Racism

Social Darwinism was a theory used to justify the dominance of Western nations in the late nineteenth century. Certain thinkers claimed that it was valid science to apply Darwin's theory of natural selection to modern human societies. In fact, this was not good science, but what today might be called "junk science," or faulty science.

A British philosopher, Herbert Spencer, argued that social progress came from "the survival of the fittest"—that is, the strong advanced while the weak declined. This kind of thinking allowed some people to reject the idea that they should take care of the less fortunate.

Extreme nationalists also used Social Darwinism. They said that nations, too, were engaged in a "struggle for existence" in which only the fittest nations would survive. The German general Friedrich von Bernhardi argued in 1907: "War is a biological necessity of the first importance, . . . since without it an unhealthy development will follow, which excludes every advancement of the race, and therefore all real civilization. War is the father of all things."

Perhaps nowhere was the combination of extreme nationalism and racism more evident than in Germany. One of the chief exponents of German racism was Houston Stewart Chamberlain, a Briton who became a German citizen and an extreme nationalist. Chamberlain believed that the ancestors of modern-day Germanic peoples were the Aryans, a tribal people from Central

PEOPLE in HISTORY

Herbert Spencer
1820–1903 British Philosopher

When Charles Darwin unveiled his theory of evolution in 1859, Herbert Spencer was one of his strongest believers. Spencer was renowned in Victorian England for his writings and observations on the human condition. He adapted Darwin's theory to his own conclusions. Thus developed the school of thought known as Social Darwinism. In fact, one of Darwin's most famous quotes, "survival of the fittest," actually originated with Spencer. Spencer's theories had a great impact in the United States during the Industrial Revolution. Wealthy tycoons adapted his theories to justify their success and lofty status. In Europe, Social Darwinism was used to justify the imbalance of power among nations. **What famous quote did Spencer originate?**

Theodor Herzl
1860–1904 Founder of Zionism

Dramatic events often lead to decisive political actions. Such was the case in 1894, when a young Hungarian-born Jewish journalist named Theodor Herzl was in Paris during the trial of Captain Alfred Dreyfus. A Jewish officer in the French army, Dreyfus was unjustly accused of treason. Herzl heard mobs shouting, "Death to the Jews." This incident led Herzl to resolve that there could be only one solution to the Jewish plight in Europe: mass immigration to a land that they could call their own. Herzl became the founder of the Zionist movement. In 1948 Zionism achieved Herzl's dream— the establishment of the Jewish state of Israel. **What incident triggered Herzl's desire to establish a Jewish homeland?**

Asia who were thought to have migrated to northern India, Iran, and parts of Europe around 2000 B.C. Chamberlain thought the Aryans were the original creators of Western culture. He further believed that Jews were the enemy out to destroy the "superior" Aryans.

Anti-Semitism and Zionism

Anti-Semitism, or hostility toward and discrimination against Jews, was not new to Europe. Since the Middle Ages, the Jews had been falsely portrayed by Christians as the murderers of Jesus Christ and subjected to mob violence. Their rights had been restricted. They had been physically separated from Christians by being required to live in areas of cities known as ghettos.

By the 1830s, the lives of many Jews had improved. They had legal equality in many European countries. They became bankers, lawyers, scientists, and scholars and were absorbed into the national culture. Old prejudices were still very much alive, though, and anti-Semitism grew stronger in the late 1800s.

The **intensity** of anti-Semitism was evident from the Dreyfus affair in France. In 1894, a military court found Dreyfus, a captain in the French general staff, guilty of selling army secrets. During the trial, angry right-wing mobs yelled anti-Semitic sayings such as "Death to the Jews." After the trial, evidence emerged that proved Dreyfus innocent. A wave of public outcry finally forced the government to pardon Dreyfus in 1899.

In Germany and Austria-Hungary during the 1880s and 1890s, new parties arose that used anti-Semitism to win the votes of people affected by economic problems and blamed those problems on Jews. However, the worst treatment of Jews at the turn of the century occurred in Russia. Persecutions and **pogroms,** or organized massacres, were widespread.

Hundreds of thousands of Jews decided to emigrate to escape the persecution. Many went to the United States. Some Jews, probably about 25,000, immigrated to Palestine, which became home for a Jewish nationalist movement called **Zionism.**

For many Jews, Palestine, the land of ancient Israel, had long been the land of their dreams. A key figure in the growth of political Zionism was Theodor Herzl, who stated in his book *The Jewish State* (1896), "The Jews who wish it will have their state."

Settlement in Palestine was difficult, however, because it was then part of the Ottoman Empire, which was opposed to Jewish immigration. Although 3,000 Jews went annually to Palestine between 1904 and 1914, the Zionist desire for a homeland in Palestine remained only a dream on the eve of World War I.

✓ **Reading Check** Analyzing Why did some Jews move to Palestine?

Vocabulary

1. **Explain** the significance of: modernism, France, Claude Monet, Pablo Picasso, abstract, Frank Lloyd Wright, Marie Curie, Albert Einstein, Sigmund Freud, Vienna, psychoanalysis, Social Darwinism, intensity, pogroms, Zionism.

Main Ideas

2. **List** some modernist movements in the arts and an individual associated with each movement. Use a chart like the one below.

Field	Movement	Individual
Literature		
Art		
Architecture		
Music		

3. **Summarize** Albert Einstein's theory of relativity.

4. **Explain** how some people applied Darwin's theory of natural selection to modern human societies.

Critical Thinking

5. **The BIG Idea** Making Connections Why are times of political and economic change often associated with times of artistic change?

6. **Analyzing** What do you think General Friedrich von Bernhardi meant when he said, "War is a biological necessity of the first importance"?

7. **Analyzing Visuals** Examine the painting by Monet on page 439. What time of day do you think it depicts? How might the scene change if Monet painted it at a different time of day?

Writing About History

8. **Expository Writing** Research the symbolist writers. Who were they and what did they write about? Write a short biography about one symbolist. Include the titles of this symbolist's best-known works.

History ONLINE

For help with the concepts in this section of *Glencoe World History—Modern Times*, go to glencoe.com and click Study Central.

You can study anywhere, anytime by downloading quizzes and flash cards to your PDA from glencoe.com.

THE FIRST ELECTRIC STREETCAR

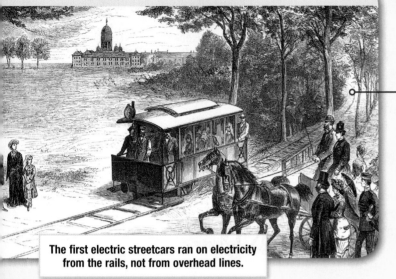

The first electric streetcars ran on electricity from the rails, not from overhead lines.

ECONOMIC CAUSES AND EFFECTS of the Second Industrial Revolution

- Steel, chemicals, electricity, and petroleum led a new wave of economic growth in the late 1800s.
- The introduction of assembly lines made mass production of goods more efficient.
- Industrialization raised the standard of living for many people in Europe.
- Harsh conditions caused many people to turn to socialism and trade unions.
- By the early 1900s, Europe dominated the world economy.

SOCIAL EFFECTS of the Second Industrial Revolution

- The rapid growth of cities forced local governments to improve public health and sanitation services.
- Europe's small elite class controlled much of the wealth; the working classes made up around 80 percent of the European population.
- Women began to push for the right to vote.
- The work of Curie, Einstein, and Freud led many people, including artists, to question the nature of reality.

THE PARIS TELEPHONE EXCHANGE, 1904

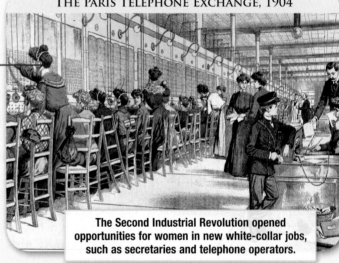

The Second Industrial Revolution opened opportunities for women in new white-collar jobs, such as secretaries and telephone operators.

FIRST WAR OF THE BALKANS, 1912

Two news reporters making a film recoil from an exploding grenade.

INTERNATIONAL RIVALRIES Set the Stage for War

- Democracy expanded in Western Europe, while Central and Eastern Europe remained authoritarian.
- Germany, Austria-Hungary, and Italy formed a defensive alliance called the Triple Alliance.
- France joined Britain and Russia in the Triple Entente.
- The rivalry between Austria and Russia for influence in the Balkans pushed a dangerously divided Europe toward war.

STANDARDIZED TEST PRACTICE

TEST-TAKING TIP

Look at each answer choice carefully. By eliminating answer choices that you know are incorrect, you can improve your chances of identifying the correct answer.

Reviewing Vocabulary

Directions: Choose the word or words that best complete the sentence.

1. The practice of _____ responsibility is crucial for democracy.

A administrative

B judicial

C ministerial

D dictatorial

2. Karl Marx used the term _____ to mean the working class.

A proletariat

B bourgeoisie

C suffrage

D Zionist

3. _____ is a Jewish nationalist movement.

A Liberalism

B Modernism

C Socialism

D Zionism

4. The movement for women's rights is known as modern _____.

A socialism

B feminism

C suffrage

D realism

Reviewing Main Ideas

Directions: Choose the best answers to the following questions.

Section 1 *(pp. 416–421)*

5. Who pioneered the assembly line?

A Thomas Edison

B Robert Fulton

C Henry Ford

D Clara Barton

6. What is the process used in negotiations between union representatives and employers?

A Collective bargaining

B Collective negotiating

C Bartering

D Selective hearing

Section 2 *(pp. 422–429)*

7. By 1890, urban dwellers in England had increased to about what percentage of the population?

A 80 percent

B 40 percent

C 60 percent

D 10 percent

8. Which social classes made up almost 80 percent of the European population in the late nineteenth century?

A Upper-middle

B Middle

C Elite

D Working

Need Extra Help?								
If You Missed Questions . . .	1	2	3	4	5	6	7	8
Go to Page . . .	432	420	443	426	419	421	422	424

9. By the 1850s, what right did many women believe they had to win in order to improve the overall position of women?

   A Right to own property

   B Right to vote

   C Right to divorce

   D Right to work

Section 3 *(pp. 432–437)*

10. While ruling Great Britain from 1906 to 1914, what party passed social reforms to retain the support of the workers?

    A Liberal

    B Socialist

    C Labour

    D Conservative

11. What two territories did Austria-Hungary annex in 1908?

    A Bosnia and Romania

    B Bulgaria and Montenegro

    C Bosnia and Herzegovina

    D Serbia and Montenegro

Section 4 *(pp. 438–443)*

12. What new style of art did Pablo Picasso create?

    A Abstraction

    B Idealism

    C Baroque

    D Cubism

13. What theory did some people use to justify the dominance of Western nations?

    A Laissez-faire

    B Social Darwinism

    C Marxism

    D Zionism

Critical Thinking

Directions: Choose the best answers to the following questions.

Use the following graph to answer question 14.

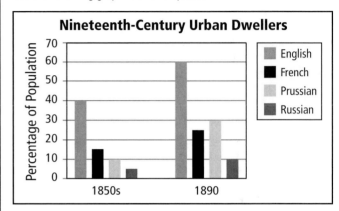

14. Which of the following statements is supported by the information in the graph?

    A There were fewer urban dwellers in 1890 than in the 1850s.

    B In 1890 more people lived in English cities than in Prussian cities.

    C The number of Prussian and English urban dwellers each rose 20 percent between the 1850s and 1890.

    D The number of urban dwellers increased by a larger percentage in Russia than in England.

15. Why did many conservatives in Germany support a policy of expansion in the late nineteenth century?

    A To divert people from seeking democracy

    B To force Otto von Bismarck from power

    C To promote socialism in Germany

    D To preserve absolute power of the emperor

16. Why did governments back public education?

    A To gain public support for political parties

    B To create more jobs for teachers

    C To appease the working classes

    D To increase the number of literate voters

Need Extra Help?								
If You Missed Questions . . .	9	10	11	12	13	14	15	16
Go to Page . . .	427	432	437	440	442	446	434	428

17. Why did the Balkans split into different factions during the late nineteenth century?

A Because the United States won the Spanish-American War

B Because the Ottoman Empire began to fall apart

C Because Serbia dominated the region

D Because Nicholas II of Russia was oppressive

Base your answer to question 18 on the cartoon below and on your knowledge of world history.

"ALL TOGETHER NOW! STOP HER!"

18. What opinion is the cartoonist expressing?

A The women's movement has no opposition to its petition for suffrage.

B Women have no right to force society to grant them suffrage.

C The suffrage movement has gained sufficient force to crush the opposition.

D Open-toe shoes show the immorality of the woman suffrage movement.

Document-Based Questions

Directions: Analyze the document and answer the short answer questions that follow the document. Base your answers on the document and on your knowledge of world history.

When workers gathered outside the Winter Palace in St. Petersburg on January 22, 1905, to present their grievances to Czar Nicholas II, troops fired into the crowd of peaceful demonstrators. One demonstrator described what happened.

> *"We were not more than thirty yards from the soldiers, being separated from them only by the bridge over the Tarakanovskii Canal, when suddenly, without any warning and without a moment's delay, was heard the dry crack of many rifle-shots. . . . A little boy of ten years, who was carrying a church lantern, fell pierced by a bullet. Both the [black]smiths who guarded me were killed, as well as all those who were carrying the icons and banners; and all these emblems now lay scattered on the snow. The soldiers were actually shooting into the courtyards of the adjoining houses, where the crowd tried to find refuge."*

19. To what historical event is the demonstrator an eye witness?

20. What does the imagery of the emblems being scattered in the snow seem to say?

Extended Response

21. Advances in science can sometimes change how people view their world and their universe. Compare and contrast Einstein's and Newton's understandings of the universe. Explain how they differ and how they are related.

History ONLINE

For additional test practice, use Self-Check Quizzes—Chapter 13 at glencoe.com.

Need Extra Help?					
If You Missed Questions . . .	17	18	19	20	21
Go to Page . . .	437	447	447	447	440

The Height of Imperialism 1800–1914

Section 1 Colonial Rule in Southeast Asia

Section 2 Empire Building in Africa

Section 3 British Rule in India

Section 4 Nation Building in Latin America

MAKING CONNECTIONS

What significance can a building convey?

The Victoria Memorial, shown in this photo, was built in honor of Queen Victoria, who was named the Empress of India after the Sepoy Mutiny. A symbol of British dominance in India, the memorial was built by several Indian states that were eager to gain political favor. In this chapter you will learn about European dominance not only in India, but also in Africa, Asia, and Latin America.

- What modern buildings do you know of that symbolize power or dominance?
- The Taj Mahal in India was built in memory of one of Shah Jahan's wives. What other buildings around the world honor individuals?

AFRICA, ASIA, AND
LATIN AMERICA ▶

1804
Haiti becomes first independent state in Latin America

1841
Explorer David Livingstone arrives in Africa

1800   1830   1860

THE WORLD ▶

1812
Napoleon invades Russia

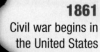

1861
Civil war begins in the United States

1874
Great Britain
annexes the
west coastal
states of Africa

1890

1900
Most of Southeast
Asia is under
Western rule

1914

1915
Gandhi revives
India's movement
for independence

1921
Chinese Communist
Party is formed

FOLDABLES
Study Organizer

Comparing and Contrasting Ask students to create a Venn diagram using a Three-Tab book to make a close comparison of the revolts in Mexico and South America. The over-lapping area of the ovals should include characteristics that both revolts had in common.

Revolts in Mexico

Both

Revolts in South America

History ONLINE

Chapter Overview—Visit glencoe.com to preview Chapter 14.

Colonial Rule in Southeast Asia

During the nineteenth century, many Western powers scrambled for new territories in Southeast Asia and Africa. Governing by either indirect or direct rule, the Western powers controlled the governments and economies of their colonies. Some territories resisted colonial rule, but most early resistance movements failed.

GUIDE TO READING

The BIG Idea
Competition Among Countries
Through the new imperialism, Westerners controlled vast territories, exploited native populations, and opened markets for European products.

Content Vocabulary
- imperialism *(p. 450)*
- racism *(p. 451)*
- protectorate *(p. 452)*
- indirect rule *(p. 454)*
- direct rule *(p. 454)*

Academic Vocabulary
- exploit *(p. 454)*
- export *(p. 454)*

People and Places
- Singapore *(p. 452)*
- Burma *(p. 452)*
- Thailand *(p. 452)*
- King Mongkut *(p. 452)*
- King Chulalongkorn *(p. 452)*
- Commodore George Dewey *(p. 452)*
- Philippines *(p. 453)*
- Emilio Aguinaldo *(p. 453)*

Reading Strategy
Identifying Information Make a chart showing which countries controlled what parts of Southeast Asia.

Spain (until 1898)	
Netherlands	
United States (after 1898)	
France	
Great Britain	

The New Imperialism

MAIN IDEA Under new imperialism, European countries began to seek additional territory.

HISTORY & YOU Do you remember how the Industrial Revolution created demand for raw materials and new markets? Read to learn how European countries used new imperialism to meet these needs.

In the nineteenth century, a new phase of Western expansion began. European nations began to view Asian and African societies as a source of industrial raw materials and a market for Western manufactured goods.

The Scramble for Territories

In the 1880s, European states began an intense scramble for overseas territory. **Imperialism,** the extension of a nation's power over other lands, was not new. Europeans had set up colonies and trading posts in North America, South America, and Africa by the sixteenth century.

However, the imperialism of the late nineteenth century, called the "new imperialism" by some, was different. Earlier, European states had been content, especially in Africa and Asia, to set up a few trading posts where they could carry on trade and perhaps some missionary activity. Now they sought nothing less than direct control over vast territories.

Motives for Imperialism

Why did Westerners begin to increase their search for colonies after 1880? There was a strong economic motive. Capitalist states in the West were looking for both markets and raw materials such as rubber, oil, and tin for their industries. The issue was not simply an economic one, however. European nation-states were involved in heated rivalries. They acquired colonies abroad in order to gain an advantage over their rivals. Colonies were also a source of national prestige. To some people, in fact, a nation could not be great without colonies.

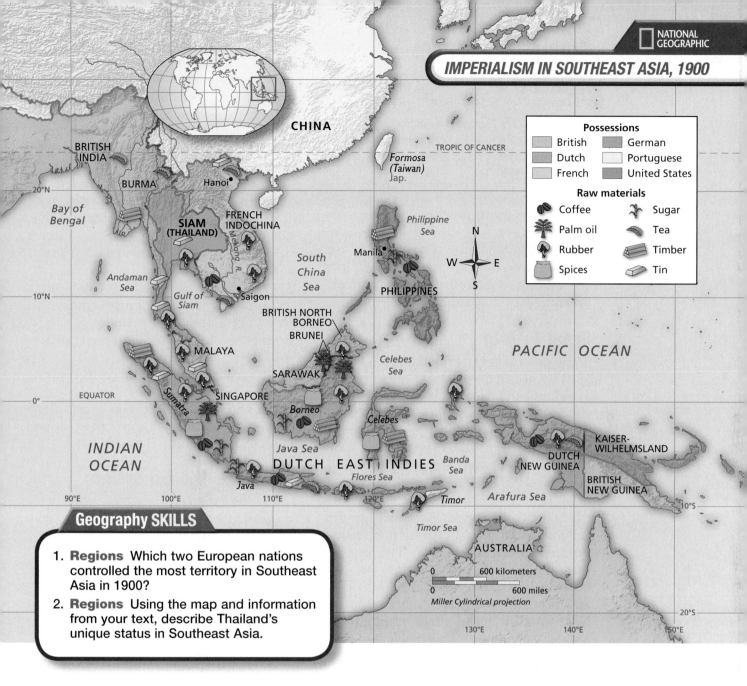

IMPERIALISM IN SOUTHEAST ASIA, 1900

CHINA

BRITISH INDIA

BURMA

Hanoi

SIAM (THAILAND)

FRENCH INDOCHINA

Saigon

Bay of Bengal

Andaman Sea

Gulf of Siam

Mekong R.

MALAYA

SINGAPORE

Sumatra

Java

INDIAN OCEAN

EQUATOR

DUTCH EAST INDIES

Java Sea

Borneo

SARAWAK

BRUNEI

BRITISH NORTH BORNEO

Celebes Sea

Celebes

Flores Sea

Banda Sea

Timor

Timor Sea

TROPIC OF CANCER

Formosa (Taiwan) Jap.

Manila

Philippine Sea

South China Sea

PHILIPPINES

PACIFIC OCEAN

DUTCH NEW GUINEA

KAISER-WILHELMSLAND

BRITISH NEW GUINEA

Arafura Sea

AUSTRALIA

Possessions

British	German
Dutch	Portuguese
French	United States

Raw materials

Coffee	Sugar
Palm oil	Tea
Rubber	Timber
Spices	Tin

N
W E
S

0   600 kilometers
0   600 miles
Miller Cylindrical projection

90°E   100°E   110°E   120°E   130°E   140°E   150°E
20°N
10°N
0°
10°S
20°S

Geography SKILLS

1. **Regions** Which two European nations controlled the most territory in Southeast Asia in 1900?
2. **Regions** Using the map and information from your text, describe Thailand's unique status in Southeast Asia.

In addition, imperialism was tied to Social Darwinism and racism. Social Darwinists believed that in the struggle between nations, the fit are victorious. **Racism** is the belief that race determines traits and capabilities. Racists erroneously believe that particular races are superior or inferior.

Racist beliefs have led to the use of military force against other nations. One British professor argued in 1900, "The path of progress is strewn with the wrecks of nations; traces are everywhere to be seen of the [slaughtered remains] of inferior races. Yet these dead people are, in very truth, the stepping stones on which

mankind has arisen to the higher intellectual and deeper emotional life of today."

Some Europeans took a more religious and humanitarian approach to imperialism. They believed Europeans had a moral responsibility to civilize primitive people. They called this responsibility the "white man's burden." To some, this meant bringing the Christian message to the "heathen masses." To others, it meant bringing the benefits of Western democracy and capitalism to these societies.

✓**Reading Check** **Describing** What were four primary motivations for the new imperialism?

Colonial Takeover

MAIN IDEA Rivalries for overseas territories led to Western dominance of Southeast Asia.

HISTORY & YOU Does your school have a sports rivalry with another school? Read to learn how the rivalry between Great Britain and France led to conquests in Southeast Asia.

The new imperialism of the late nineteenth century was evident in Southeast Asia. In 1800, the Europeans ruled only two societies in this area: the Spanish Philippines and the Dutch East Indies. By 1900, virtually the entire area was under Western rule.

Great Britain

The process began with Great Britain. In 1819 Great Britain sent Sir Thomas Stamford Raffles to found a new colony on a small island at the tip of the Malay Peninsula. Called **Singapore** ("city of the lion"), in the new age of steamships, it soon became a major stopping point for traffic going to or from China. Raffles was proud of his new city. He wrote about Singapore to a friend in England: "Here all is life and activity; and it would be difficult to name a place on the face of the globe with brighter prospects."

During the next few decades, the British advance into Southeast Asia continued. Next to fall was the kingdom of **Burma** (modern Myanmar). Britain wanted control of Burma in order to protect its possessions in India. It also sought a land route through Burma into south China. Although the difficult terrain along the frontier between Burma and China caused this effort to fail, British activities in Burma led to the collapse of the Burmese monarchy. Britain soon established control over the entire country.

France

France, which had some missionaries operating in Vietnam, nervously watched the British advance into Burma. The local Vietnamese authorities, who viewed Christianity as a threat to Confucian doctrine, persecuted the French missionaries. However, Vietnam failed to stop the Christian missionaries. Vietnamese internal rivalries divided the country into two separate governments—the north and the south.

France was especially alarmed by British attempts to monopolize trade. To stop any British move into Vietnam, the French government decided in 1857 to force the Vietnamese to accept French protection.

The French eventually succeeded in making the Vietnamese ruler give up territories in the Mekong River delta. The French occupied the city of Saigon and, during the next 30 years, extended their control over the rest of the country. In 1884 France seized the city of Hanoi and later made the Vietnamese empire a French **protectorate**—a political unit that depends on another government for its protection.

In the 1880s, France extended its control over neighboring Cambodia, Annam, Tonkin, and Laos. By 1887, France included all of its new possessions in a new Union of French Indochina.

Thailand—the Exception

After the French conquest of Indochina, **Thailand** (then called Siam) was the only remaining free state in Southeast Asia. During the last quarter of the nineteenth century, British and French rivalry threatened to place Thailand, too, under colonial rule.

Two remarkable rulers were able to prevent that from happening. One was **King Mongkut** (known to theatergoers as the king in *The King and I*), and the other was his son, **King Chulalongkorn.** Both promoted Western learning and maintained friendly relations with the major European powers. In 1896 Britain and France agreed to maintain Thailand as an independent buffer state between their possessions in Southeast Asia.

The United States

One final conquest in Southeast Asia occurred at the end of the nineteenth century. In 1898, during the Spanish-American War, United States naval forces under **Commodore George Dewey** defeated the Spanish fleet in Manila Bay.

Believing it was his moral obligation to "civilize" other parts of the world, President

William McKinley decided to turn the **Philippines,** which had been under Spanish control, into an American colony. This action would also prevent the area from falling into the hands of the Japanese. In fact, the islands gave the United States a convenient jumping-off point for trade with China.

This mixture of moral idealism and desire for profit was reflected in a speech given in the U.S. Senate in January 1900 by Senator Albert Beveridge of Indiana:

PRIMARY SOURCE

"Mr. President, the times call for candor. The Philippines are ours forever. And just beyond the Philippines are China's unlimited markets. We will not retreat from either. We will not abandon an opportunity in [Asia]. We will not renounce our part in the mission of our race, trustee, under God, of the civilization of the world."
—Senator Albert Beveridge, 1900

The Filipinos did not agree with the American senator. **Emilio Aguinaldo** (AH•gee•NAHL•doh) was the leader of a movement for independence in the Philippines. He began his revolt against the Spanish and went into exile in 1898. When the United States acquired the Philippines, Aguinaldo continued the revolt and set himself up as the president of the Republic of the Philippines. Led by Aguinaldo, the guerrilla forces fought bitterly against the United States troops to establish their independence.

The fight for Philippine independence resulted in three years of bloody warfare. However, the United States defeated the guerrilla forces, and President McKinley had his stepping-stone to the rich markets of China.

✓ **Reading Check** **Identifying** What spurred Britain to control Singapore and Burma?

POLITICAL CARTOONS   PRIMARY SOURCE

The New Imperialism

Uncle Sam, representing the United States

William II of Germany

John Bull, representing Great Britain

figure representing France

Major Regions of European Control

	Southeast Asia	Africa	India
Belgium		🏴	
Britain	🏴	🏴	🏴
France	🏴	🏴	
Germany		🏴	
Italy		🏴	
Netherlands	🏴		
Portugal	🏴	🏴	
Spain	🏴	🏴	

DOCUMENT-BASED QUESTIONS

This *Life* magazine cartoon from 1899, *White(!) Man's Burden,* appeared as Americans were fighting native peoples for control of the Philippines. As the chart shows, Europeans already had their colonial empires.

1. **Identifying** Who do the carriers in the cartoon represent?
2. **Identifying Points of View** What did "the white man's burden" mean to supporters of imperialism? What does it mean in the cartoon?

Colonial Regimes

MAIN IDEA European countries controlled the governments and economies of their colonies in Southeast Asia.

HISTORY & YOU Does your school's student council have the power to run the school? Read to learn about European rule in Southeast Asia.

Western powers governed their new colonial empires by either indirect or direct rule. Their chief goals were to **exploit** the natural resources of the lands and to open up markets for their own manufactured goods.

Indirect and Direct Rule

Sometimes a colonial power could realize its goals by cooperating with local political elites. For example, the Dutch East India Company used **indirect rule** in the Dutch East Indies. Under indirect rule, local rulers were allowed to keep their authority and status in a new colonial setting. This made access to the region's natural resources easier. Indirect rule was cheaper because fewer officials had to be trained and it affected local culture less.

However, indirect rule was not always possible. Some local elites resisted the foreign conquest. In these cases, the local elites were replaced with British officials. This system is called **direct rule.** For example, Great Britain administered Burma directly through its colonial government in India. In Indochina, France used both systems. It imposed direct rule in southern Vietnam, but ruled indirectly through the emperor in northern Vietnam.

To justify their conquests, Western powers spoke of bringing the blessings of Western civilization to their colonial subjects, including representative government. However, many Westerners came to fear the idea of native peoples (especially educated ones) being allowed political rights.

Colonial Economies

The colonial powers did not want their colonists to develop their own industries. Thus, colonial policy stressed the **export** of raw materials. This policy often led to some form of plantation agriculture. Peasants worked as wage laborers on the foreign-owned plantations. Plantation owners kept wages at poverty levels to increase profits. Conditions on plantations were often so unhealthy that thousands died. Also, peasants bore the burden of high taxes.

Nevertheless, colonial rule did bring some benefits to Southeast Asia. A modern economic system began there. Colonial governments built railroads, highways, and other structures that benefited native peoples as well as colonials. The development of an export market helped create an entrepreneurial class in rural areas. In the Dutch East Indies, for example, small growers of rubber, palm oil, coffee, tea, and spices began to share in the profits of the colonial enterprise. Most of the profits, however, were taken back to the colonial mother country.

✓ **Reading Check** **Explaining** How did colonial powers justify their rule?

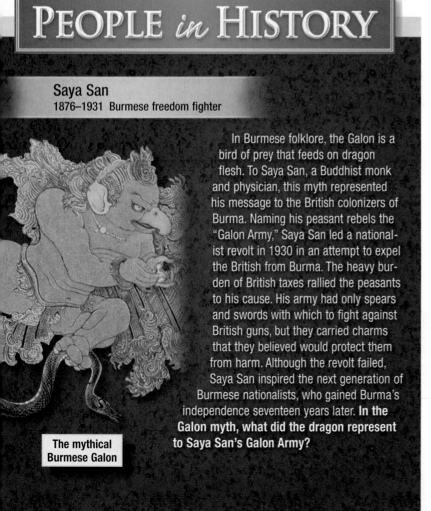

PEOPLE *in* HISTORY

Saya San
1876–1931 Burmese freedom fighter

In Burmese folklore, the Galon is a bird of prey that feeds on dragon flesh. To Saya San, a Buddhist monk and physician, this myth represented his message to the British colonizers of Burma. Naming his peasant rebels the "Galon Army," Saya San led a nationalist revolt in 1930 in an attempt to expel the British from Burma. The heavy burden of British taxes rallied the peasants to his cause. His army had only spears and swords with which to fight against British guns, but they carried charms that they believed would protect them from harm. Although the revolt failed, Saya San inspired the next generation of Burmese nationalists, who gained Burma's independence seventeen years later. **In the Galon myth, what did the dragon represent to Saya San's Galon Army?**

The mythical Burmese Galon

Resistance to Colonial Rule

MAIN IDEA Native peoples had varying levels of success resisting colonial rule in Southeast Asia.

HISTORY & YOU Do you know of any occupied countries today that object to foreign rule? Read to learn how countries in Southeast Asia resisted the rule of European powers.

Many subject peoples in Southeast Asia resented being governed by Western powers. At first, resistance came from the existing ruling class. In Burma, for example, the monarch himself fought Western domination. By contrast, in Vietnam, after the emperor had agreed to French control of his country, a number of government officials set up an organization called Can Vuoug ("Save the King"). They fought against the French without the emperor's help.

Sometimes, resistance to Western control took the form of peasant revolts. Under colonial rule, peasants were often driven off the land to make way for plantation agriculture. Angry peasants then vented their anger at the foreign invaders. For example, in Burma, in 1930 the Buddhist monk Saya San led a peasant uprising against the British colonial regime many years after the regime had completed its takeover.

Early resistance movements failed. They were overcome by Western powers. At the beginning of the twentieth century, a new kind of resistance began to emerge that was based on the force of nationalism. The leaders were often from a new class that the colonial rule had created: westernized intellectuals in the cities.

In many cases, this new urban middle class—composed of merchants, clerks, students, and professionals—had been educated in Western-style schools. They were the first generation of Asians to embrace the institutions and values of the West. Many spoke Western languages and worked in jobs connected with the colonial regimes.

At first, many of the leaders of these movements did not focus clearly on the idea of nationhood. Instead, they simply tried to defend the economic interests or religious beliefs of the native peoples. In Burma, for example, students at the University of Rangoon formed an organization to protest against official persecution of the Buddhist religion and British lack of respect for local religious traditions. They protested against British arrogance and failure to observe local customs in Buddhist temples. Not until the 1930s, however, did these resistance movements, such as those begun in Burma, begin to demand national independence.

✓ Reading Check **Summarizing** Explain three forms of resistance to Western domination.

Vocabulary

1. **Explain** the significance of: imperialism, racism, Singapore, Burma, protectorate, Thailand, King Mongkut, King Chulalongkorn, Commodore George Dewey, Philippines, Emilio Aguinaldo, exploit, indirect rule, direct rule, export.

Main Ideas

2. **Explain** how the new imperialism differed from old imperialism.

3. **Identify** how each area listed below was ruled—direct or indirect rule—and which European power ruled it.

Country	Direct	Indirect	Ruling Power
Dutch East Indies			
Burma			
Southern provinces in Mekong Delta			
Northern Vietnam			

4. **List** some benefits colonial rule brought to Southeast Asia. Do you think these benefits outweighed the disadvantages? Explain.

Critical Thinking

5. **The BIG Idea** **Making Inferences** Why were resistance movements often led by native leaders who had been educated in the West? How did their goals change over time?

6. **Determining Effect** Identify the effects of colonial rule on the colonies.

Analyzing Visuals

7. **Analyzing Visuals** Explain which features are used in the map on page 451 to present information visually, without the use of text.

Writing About History

8. **Expository Writing** Use varied media to determine how Filipino political groups today view the relationship between their country and the United States. Write an essay based on your findings.

History ONLINE

For help with the concepts in this section of *Glencoe World History—Modern Times*, go to glencoe.com and click Study Central.

Empire Building in Africa

GUIDE TO READING

The BIG Idea
Competition Among Countries
Virtually all of Africa was under European rule by 1900.

Content Vocabulary
- annexed *(p. 456)*
- indigenous *(p. 460)*

Academic Vocabulary
- uncharted *(p. 459)*
- traditions *(p. 462)*

People
- Muhammad Ali *(p. 457)*
- David Livingstone *(p. 459)*
- Henry Stanley *(p. 459)*
- Zulu *(p. 460)*

Reading Strategy
Categorizing Information As you read, make a chart like the one below showing which countries controlled what parts of Africa.

Western Power	Area of Africa
Belgium	
Britain	
France	
Germany	

During the late nineteenth century, the major European powers scrambled to colonize Africa. Virtually all of Africa was under European rule by 1900. Maintaining that rule was not easy, however. African nationalism emerged during the early part of the twentieth century.

West Africa and North Africa

MAIN IDEA European countries exercised increasing control over West Africa and North Africa, especially once the Suez Canal was completed.

HISTORY & YOU Do you take the long way to get to a destination, or do you look for shortcuts? Read about how Europeans constructed a shortcut for ships through Egypt.

Before 1880, Europeans controlled little of the African continent directly. They were content to let African rulers and merchants represent European interests. Between 1880 and 1900, however, Great Britain, France, Germany, Belgium, Italy, Spain, and Portugal, spurred by intense rivalries among themselves, placed virtually all of Africa under European rule.

West Africa

Europeans had a keen interest in Africa's raw materials, especially those of West Africa—peanuts, timber, hides, and palm oil. Earlier in the nineteenth century, Europeans had profited from the slave trade in this part of Africa. By the late 1800s, however, trade in enslaved people had virtually ended. As the slave trade declined, Europe's interest in other forms of trade increased. The growing European presence in West Africa led to increasing tensions with African governments in the area.

For a long time, most African states were able to maintain their independence. However, in 1874 Great Britain **annexed** (incorporated a country within a state) the west coastal states as the first British colony of Gold Coast. At about the same time, Britain established a protectorate in Nigeria. By 1900, France had added the huge area of French West Africa to its colonial empire. This left France in control of the largest part of West Africa. In addition, Germany controlled Togo, Cameroon, German Southwest Africa, and German East Africa.

North Africa

Egypt had been part of the Ottoman Empire, but as Ottoman rule declined, the Egyptians sought their independence. In 1805

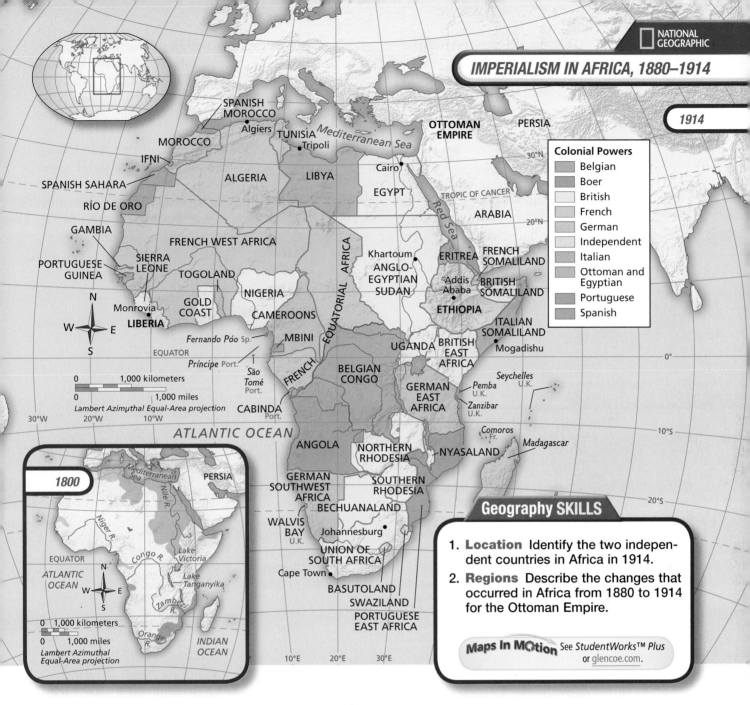

IMPERIALISM IN AFRICA, 1880–1914

1914

Colonial Powers
- Belgian
- Boer
- British
- French
- German
- Independent
- Italian
- Ottoman and Egyptian
- Portuguese
- Spanish

SPANISH MOROCCO
Algiers
MOROCCO
TUNISIA
Tripoli
Mediterranean Sea
OTTOMAN EMPIRE
PERSIA
IFNI
Cairo
30°N
SPANISH SAHARA
ALGERIA
LIBYA
EGYPT
TROPIC OF CANCER
RÍO DE ORO
ARABIA
20°N
Red Sea
GAMBIA
FRENCH WEST AFRICA
Khartoum
ERITREA
FRENCH SOMALILAND
PORTUGUESE GUINEA
SIERRA LEONE
TOGOLAND
ANGLO-EGYPTIAN SUDAN
Addis Ababa
BRITISH SOMALILAND
NIGERIA
EQUATORIAL AFRICA
ETHIOPIA
Monrovia
GOLD COAST
ITALIAN SOMALILAND
LIBERIA
CAMEROONS
UGANDA
BRITISH EAST AFRICA
Mogadishu
Fernando Póo Sp.
MBINI
EQUATOR
FRENCH
Príncipe Port.
São Tomé Port.
BELGIAN CONGO
GERMAN EAST AFRICA
Seychelles U.K.
Pemba U.K.
Zanzibar U.K.
CABINDA Port.
ATLANTIC OCEAN
Comoros Fr.
Madagascar
10°S
ANGOLA
NORTHERN RHODESIA
NYASALAND
GERMAN SOUTHWEST AFRICA
SOUTHERN RHODESIA
20°S
BECHUANALAND
WALVIS BAY U.K.
Johannesburg
UNION OF SOUTH AFRICA
Cape Town
BASUTOLAND
SWAZILAND
PORTUGUESE EAST AFRICA

0 1,000 kilometers
0 1,000 miles
Lambert Azimuthal Equal-Area projection

1800
Mediterranean Sea
PERSIA
Niger R.
Nile R.
Congo R.
Lake Victoria
EQUATOR
ATLANTIC OCEAN
Lake Tanganyika
Zambezi R.
Orange R.
INDIAN OCEAN
0 1,000 kilometers
0 1,000 miles
Lambert Azimuthal Equal-Area projection

Geography SKILLS

1. **Location** Identify the two independent countries in Africa in 1914.
2. **Regions** Describe the changes that occurred in Africa from 1880 to 1914 for the Ottoman Empire.

Maps In MOtion See StudentWorks™ Plus or glencoe.com.

an officer of the Ottoman army named **Muhammad Ali** seized power and established a separate Egyptian state.

During the next 30 years, Muhammad Ali introduced a series of reforms to bring Egypt into the modern world. He modernized the army, set up a public school system, and helped create small industries that refined sugar, produced textiles and munitions, and built ships.

The growing economic importance of the Nile Valley in Egypt, along with the development of steamships, gave Europeans the desire to build a canal east of Cairo to connect the Mediterranean and Red

Seas. In 1854 a French entrepreneur, Ferdinand de Lesseps, signed a contract to begin building the Suez Canal. The canal was completed in 1869.

The British took an active interest in Egypt after the Suez Canal was opened. Believing that the canal was its "lifeline to India," Great Britain tried to gain as much control as possible over the canal area.

In 1875 Britain bought Egypt's share in the Suez Canal. When an Egyptian army revolt against foreign influence broke out in 1881, Britain suppressed the revolt. Egypt became a British protectorate in 1914.

The British believed that they should also control the Sudan, south of Egypt, to protect their interests in Egypt and the Suez Canal. In 1881 Muslim cleric Muhammad Ahmad, known as the Mahdi (in Arabic, "the rightly guided one"), launched a revolt that brought much of the Sudan under his control.

Britain sent a military force under General Charles Gordon to restore Egyptian authority over the Sudan. However, Muhammad Ahmad's troops wiped out Gordon's army at Khartoum in 1885. General Gordon himself died in the battle. Not until 1898 were British troops able to seize the Sudan.

The French also had colonies in North Africa. In 1879, after about 150,000 French people had settled in the region of Algeria, the French government established control there. Two years later, France imposed a protectorate on neighboring Tunisia. In 1912 France established a protectorate over much of Morocco.

Italy joined the competition for colonies in North Africa by attempting to take over Ethiopia. In 1896, however, the Italian invading forces were defeated. Italy now was the only European state defeated by an African state. This humiliating loss led Italy to try again in 1911. Italy invaded and seized Turkish Tripoli, which it renamed Libya.

✓**Reading Check** **Explaining** Why did the British set up settlements in Africa?

INFOGRAPHICS

The Suez Canal Opens for Business

The Suez Canal, built by the French using Egyptian labor, was completed in 1869. This waterway linked the Mediterranean Sea and Red Sea. Instead of sailing around Africa, European ships could now pass through the canal to reach eastern Asia in much less time.

At this time, demand for Egyptian cotton made Egypt's economy strong. Egypt's ruler,

Khedive Ismā'īl, spent large sums on modernizing his country, building roads, railways, and factories. By the 1870s, however, economic conditions had worsened, forcing Egypt to borrow from foreigners to pay for these projects. To help pay the debt, Ismā'īl sold Egypt's share of the Suez Canal to Britain in 1875.

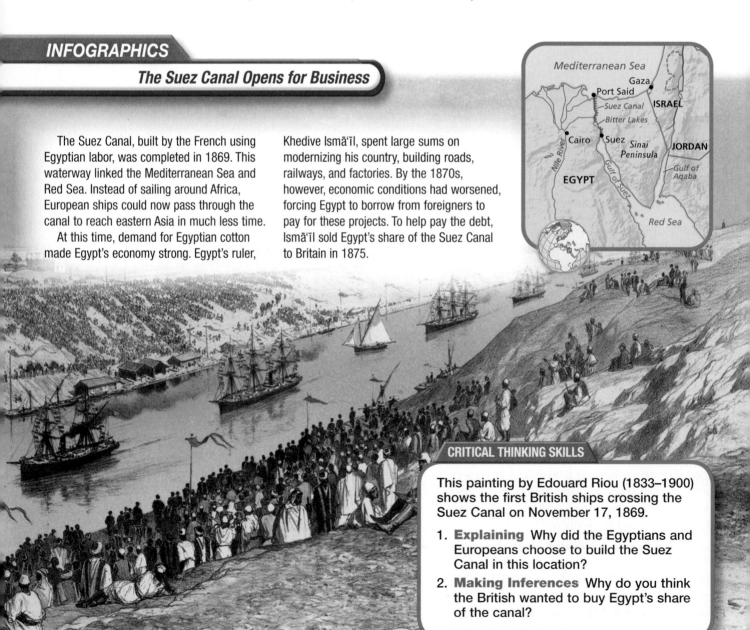

CRITICAL THINKING SKILLS

This painting by Edouard Riou (1833–1900) shows the first British ships crossing the Suez Canal on November 17, 1869.

1. **Explaining** Why did the Egyptians and Europeans choose to build the Suez Canal in this location?

2. **Making Inferences** Why do you think the British wanted to buy Egypt's share of the canal?

Central and East Africa

MAIN IDEA European powers competed for colonies in Central Africa and East Africa.

HISTORY & YOU Have you ever read a description of a far-off land that made you want to see it for yourself? Read to learn how reports of explorers stirred European interest in Africa.

Central Africa

Central African territories were soon added to the list of European colonies. Explorers aroused popular interest in the dense tropical jungles of Central Africa. **David Livingstone** was one such explorer. He arrived in Africa in 1841 as a 27-year-old medical missionary. During the 30 years he spent in Africa, Livingstone trekked through **uncharted** regions. He sometimes traveled by canoe, but mostly Livingstone walked and spent much of his time exploring the interior of the continent.

During his travels through Africa, Livingstone made detailed notes of his discoveries. He sent this information back to London whenever he could. The maps of Africa were often redrawn based on Livingstone's reports. A major goal of Livingstone's explorations was to find a navigable river that would open Central Africa to European commerce and to Christianity.

When Livingstone disappeared for awhile, an American newspaper, the *New York Herald,* hired a young journalist, **Henry Stanley,** to find the explorer. Stanley did find him, on the eastern shore of Lake Tanganyika. Overwhelmed by finding Livingstone alive if not well, Stanley greeted the explorer with these now-famous words, "Dr. Livingstone, I presume?"

After Livingstone's death in 1873, Stanley remained in Africa to carry on the great explorer's work. Unlike Livingstone, however, Henry Stanley had a strong dislike of Africa. He once said, "I detest the land most heartily."

In the 1870s, Stanley explored the Congo River in Central Africa and sailed down it to the Atlantic Ocean. Soon, he was encouraging the British to send settlers to the Congo River basin. When Britain refused, Stanley turned to King Leopold II of Belgium.

King Leopold II was the real driving force behind the colonization of Central Africa. He rushed enthusiastically into the pursuit of an empire in Africa. "To open to civilization," he said, "the only part of our globe where it has not yet penetrated, to pierce the darkness which envelops whole populations, is a crusade, if I may say so, a crusade worthy of this century of progress." Profit, however, was equally important to Leopold. In 1876 he hired Henry Stanley to set up Belgian settlements in the Congo.

Leopold's claim to the vast territories of the Congo aroused widespread concern among other European states. France, in particular, rushed to plant its flag in the heart of Africa. Leopold ended up with the territories around the Congo River. France occupied the areas farther north.

East Africa

By 1885, Britain and Germany had become the chief rivals in East Africa. Germany came late to the ranks of the imperialist powers. At first, the German chancellor Otto von Bismarck had downplayed the importance of colonies. As more and more Germans called for a German empire, however, Bismarck became a convert to colonialism. As he expressed it, "All this colonial business is a sham, but we need it for the elections."

In addition to its West African holdings, Germany tried to develop colonies in East Africa. Most of East Africa had not yet been claimed by any other power. However, the British were also interested in the area because control of East Africa would connect the British Empire in Africa from South Africa to Egypt. Portugal and Belgium also claimed parts of East Africa.

To settle conflicting claims, the Berlin Conference met in 1884 and 1885. The conference officially recognized both British and German claims for territory in East Africa. Portugal received a clear claim on Mozambique. No African delegates, however, were present at this conference.

✓ Reading Check **Examining** What effect did King Leopold II have on European colonization of the Congo River basin?

South Africa

MAIN IDEA European powers quickly came to dominate the region of South Africa.

HISTORY & YOU Have you and a good friend ever disagreed so hotly on an issue that you parted ways? Read to learn about how the Boers came to revolt against British rule in South Africa.

Nowhere in Africa did the European presence grow more rapidly than in the south. By 1865, the total white population of South Africa had risen to nearly 200,000 people.

The Boers, or Afrikaners—as the descendants of the original Dutch settlers were called—had occupied Cape Town and surrounding areas in South Africa since the seventeenth century. During the Napoleonic Wars, however, the British seized these lands from the Dutch. Afterward, the British encouraged settlers to come to what they called Cape Colony.

The Boer Republics

In the 1830s, disgusted with British rule, the Boers moved from the coastal lands and headed northward on the Great Trek. Altogether one out of every five Dutch-speaking South Africans joined the trek. Their parties eventually settled in the region between the Orange and Vaal (VAHL) Rivers and in the region north of the Vaal River. In these areas, the Boers formed two independent republics—the Orange Free State and the Transvaal (later called the South African Republic).

The Boers believed that white superiority was ordained by God. They denied non-Europeans any place in their society, other than as laborers or servants. As they settled the lands, the Boers put many of the **indigenous** peoples, those native to a region, in these areas on reservations.

The Boers had frequently battled the indigenous **Zulu** people. In the early nineteenth century, the Zulu, under a talented

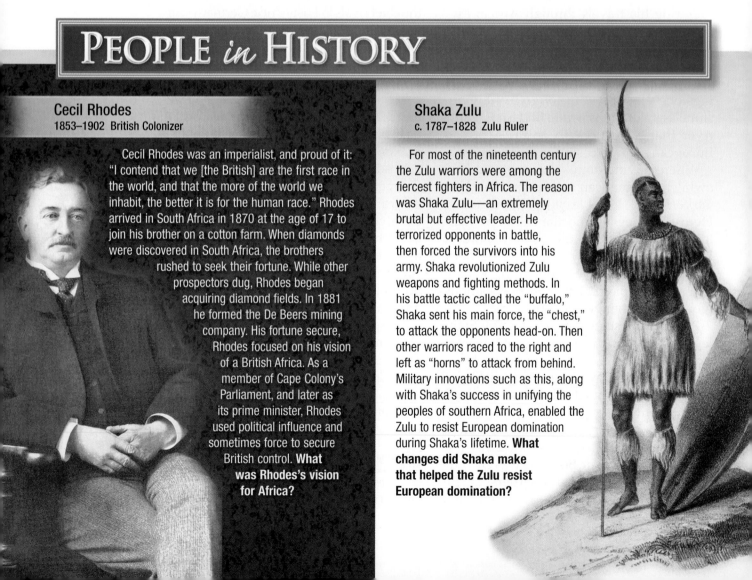

PEOPLE in HISTORY

Cecil Rhodes
1853–1902 British Colonizer

Cecil Rhodes was an imperialist, and proud of it: "I contend that we [the British] are the first race in the world, and that the more of the world we inhabit, the better it is for the human race." Rhodes arrived in South Africa in 1870 at the age of 17 to join his brother on a cotton farm. When diamonds were discovered in South Africa, the brothers rushed to seek their fortune. While other prospectors dug, Rhodes began acquiring diamond fields. In 1881 he formed the De Beers mining company. His fortune secure, Rhodes focused on his vision of a British Africa. As a member of Cape Colony's Parliament, and later as its prime minister, Rhodes used political influence and sometimes force to secure British control. **What was Rhodes's vision for Africa?**

Shaka Zulu
c. 1787–1828 Zulu Ruler

For most of the nineteenth century the Zulu warriors were among the fiercest fighters in Africa. The reason was Shaka Zulu—an extremely brutal but effective leader. He terrorized opponents in battle, then forced the survivors into his army. Shaka revolutionized Zulu weapons and fighting methods. In his battle tactic called the "buffalo," Shaka sent his main force, the "chest," to attack the opponents head-on. Then other warriors raced to the right and left as "horns" to attack from behind. Military innovations such as this, along with Shaka's success in unifying the peoples of southern Africa, enabled the Zulu to resist European domination during Shaka's lifetime. **What changes did Shaka make that helped the Zulu resist European domination?**

ruler named Shaka, had carved out their own empire. Even after Shaka's death, the Zulu remained powerful. Finally, in the late 1800s, the British military became involved in conflicts with the Zulu, and the Zulu were defeated.

Cecil Rhodes

In the 1880s, British policy in South Africa was influenced by Cecil Rhodes. Rhodes had founded diamond and gold companies that had made him a fortune. He gained control of a territory north of the Transvaal, which he named Rhodesia after himself.

Rhodes was a great champion of British expansion. He said once, "I think what [God] would like me to do is to paint as much of Africa British red as possible." One of Rhodes's goals was to create a series of British colonies "from the Cape to Cairo"—all linked by a railroad.

Rhodes's ambitions eventually led to his downfall in 1896. The British government forced him to resign as prime minister of Cape Colony after discovering that he planned to overthrow the Boer government of the South African Republic without his government's approval. The British action was too late to avoid a war between the British and the Boers, however.

The Boer War

This war, called the Boer War, dragged on from 1899 to 1902. Fierce guerrilla resistance by the Boers angered the British. They responded by burning crops and herding about 120,000 Boer women and children into detention camps, where lack of food caused some 20,000 deaths. Eventually, the vastly larger British army won. A peace treaty was signed in 1902.

In 1910 the British created an independent Union of South Africa, which combined the old Cape Colony and the Boer republics. The new state would be a self-governing nation within the British Empire. To appease the Boers, the British agreed that only whites, with a few propertied Africans, would vote.

✓Reading Check **Explaining** What were the causes of the Boer War?

Effects of Imperialism

MAIN IDEA Using direct or indirect rule, European nations exploited Africa, and their governance stimulated African nationalism.

HISTORY & YOU How do you feel when someone treats you with an air of superiority? Read to learn how European attitudes toward Africans stirred nationalist feelings.

By 1914, Great Britain, France, Germany, Belgium, Italy, Spain, and Portugal had divided up Africa. Only Liberia, which had been created as a homeland for the formerly enslaved persons of the United States, and Ethiopia remained free states. Native peoples who dared to resist were devastated by the Europeans' superior military force.

Colonial Rule in Africa

As was true in Southeast Asia, most European governments ruled their new territories in Africa with the least effort and expense possible. Indirect rule meant relying on existing political elites and institutions. The British especially followed this approach. At first, in some areas, the British simply asked a local ruler to accept British authority and to fly the British flag over official buildings.

The concept of indirect rule was introduced in the Islamic state of Sokoto, in northern Nigeria, beginning in 1903. This system of indirect rule in Sokoto had one good feature: it did not disrupt local customs and institutions. However, it did have some unfortunate consequences.

The system of indirect rule was basically a fraud because British administrators made all major decisions. The native authorities served chiefly to enforce those decisions.

Another problem was that the policy of indirect rule kept the old African elite in power. Such a policy provided few opportunities for ambitious and talented young Africans from outside the old elite. In this way British indirect rule sowed the seeds for class and tribal tensions, which erupted after independence came in the twentieth century.

Most other European nations governed their African possessions through a form of direct rule. This was true in the French colonies. At the top was a French official, usually known as a governor-general. He was appointed from Paris and governed with the aid of a bureaucracy in the capital city of the colony.

The French ideal was to assimilate African subjects into French culture rather than preserve native **traditions.** Africans were eligible to run for office and even serve in the French National Assembly in Paris. A few were also appointed to high-powered positions in the colonial administration.

Rise of African Nationalism

As in Southeast Asia, a new class of leaders emerged in Africa by the beginning of the twentieth century. Educated in colonial schools or in Western nations, they were the first generation of Africans to know a great deal about the West.

The members of this new class admired Western culture and sometimes disliked the ways of their own countries. They were eager to introduce Western ideas and institutions into their own societies. Still, many of these new leaders came to resent the foreigners and their arrogant contempt for African peoples. These intellectuals recognized the gap between theory and practice

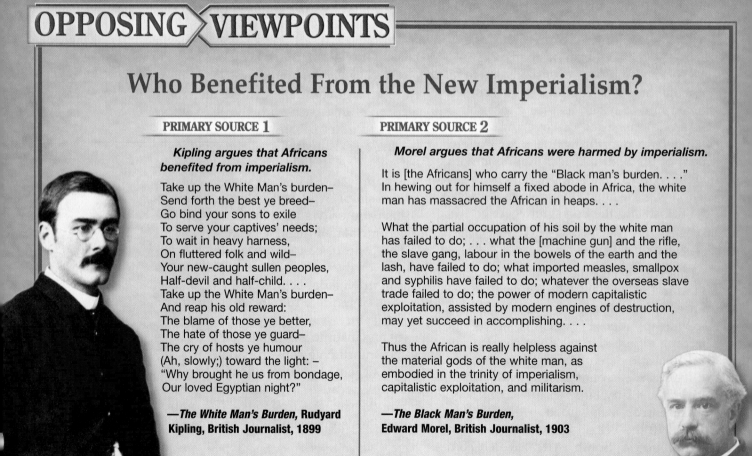

OPPOSING VIEWPOINTS

Who Benefited From the New Imperialism?

PRIMARY SOURCE 1

Kipling argues that Africans benefited from imperialism.

Take up the White Man's burden–
Send forth the best ye breed–
Go bind your sons to exile
To serve your captives' needs;
To wait in heavy harness,
On fluttered folk and wild–
Your new-caught sullen peoples,
Half-devil and half-child. . . .
Take up the White Man's burden–
And reap his old reward:
The blame of those ye better,
The hate of those ye guard–
The cry of hosts ye humour
(Ah, slowly;) toward the light: –
"Why brought he us from bondage,
Our loved Egyptian night?"

—*The White Man's Burden,* Rudyard Kipling, British Journalist, 1899

PRIMARY SOURCE 2

Morel argues that Africans were harmed by imperialism.

It is [the Africans] who carry the "Black man's burden. . . ." In hewing out for himself a fixed abode in Africa, the white man has massacred the African in heaps. . . .

What the partial occupation of his soil by the white man has failed to do; . . . what the [machine gun] and the rifle, the slave gang, labour in the bowels of the earth and the lash, have failed to do; what imported measles, smallpox and syphilis have failed to do; whatever the overseas slave trade failed to do; the power of modern capitalistic exploitation, assisted by modern engines of destruction, may yet succeed in accomplishing. . . .

Thus the African is really helpless against the material gods of the white man, as embodied in the trinity of imperialism, capitalistic exploitation, and militarism.

—*The Black Man's Burden,* Edward Morel, British Journalist, 1903

DOCUMENT-BASED QUESTIONS

1. **Interpreting** What was the impact of imperialism on the colonized territories in Africa, according to Morel?
2. **Analyzing** Quote lines in Rudyard Kipling's poem that reflect his view of the colonized peoples. What values did Kipling assume his readers shared with him?

in colonial policy. Westerners had exalted democracy, equality, and political freedom but did not apply these values in the colonies.

There were few democratic institutions. Native peoples could have only low-paying jobs in the colonial bureaucracy. To many Africans, colonialism had meant the loss of their farmlands or employment on plantations or in factories run by foreigners. Some lost even more, as Lobengula, a southern African king, told Britain's Queen Victoria in this letter:

PRIMARY SOURCE

"Some time ago a party of men came to my country, the principal one appearing to be a man called Rudd. They asked me for a place to dig for gold, and said they would give me certain things for the right to do so. I told them to bring what they could give and I would show them what I would give. A document was written and presented to me for signature. I asked what it contained, and was told that in it were my words and the words of those men. I put my hand to it. About three months afterwards I heard from other sources that I had given by the document the right to all the minerals of my country."

—*The Imperialism Reader*, Louis L. Snyder, ed.

Middle-class Africans did not suffer as much as poor African peasant plantation workers. However, members of the middle class also had complaints. They usually qualified only for menial jobs in the government or business. Even then, their salaries were lower than those of Europeans in similar jobs.

Europeans expressed their superiority over Africans in other ways. Segregated clubs, schools, and churches were set up as more European officials brought their wives and began to raise families. Europeans were also condescending in their relationships with Africans. For instance, Europeans had a habit of addressing Africans by their first names or calling an adult male "boy."

Such conditions led many members of the new urban educated class to feel great confusion toward their colonial rulers and the civilization the colonists represented. The educated Africans were willing to admit the superiority of many aspects of Western culture. However, these intellectuals fiercely hated colonial rule and were determined to assert their own nationality and cultural destiny. Out of this mixture of hopes and resentments emerged the first stirrings of modern nationalism in Africa.

During the first quarter of the twentieth century, resentment turned to action. Across Africa, native peoples began to organize political parties and movements seeking the end of foreign rule. They wanted to be independent and self-governed.

✓ Reading Check **Evaluating** Why were many African intellectuals frustrated by colonial policy?

SECTION 2 REVIEW

Vocabulary
1. **Explain** the significance of: annexed, Muhammad Ali, David Livingstone, uncharted, Henry Stanley, indigenous, Zulu, traditions.

Main Ideas
2. **Explain** why the British were so interested in controlling the Sudan.

3. **Name** a major goal that David Livingstone had for exploring Central Africa.

4. **List** the ways in which the French system of direct rule included Africans. Use a chart like the one below.

Roles of Africans in the French System of Direct Rule
1.
2.
3.
4.

Critical Thinking
5. **The BIG Idea** **Drawing Conclusions** What can you conclude from the fact that African delegates were not included in the Berlin Conference of 1884?

6. **Making Inferences** Why do you think the Boers resisted British rule?

7. **Analyzing Visuals** Examine the painting of the Suez Canal on page 458. How do you think the artist's portrayal of the scene provides a sense of setting and perspective? What elements suggest a time frame for the scene?

Writing About History
8. **Expository Writing** Research the importance of the Suez Canal today. Write a paper comparing the present-day significance of the canal to its historical significance.

History ONLINE

For help with the concepts in this section of *Glencoe World History—Modern Times*, go to glencoe.com and click Study Central.

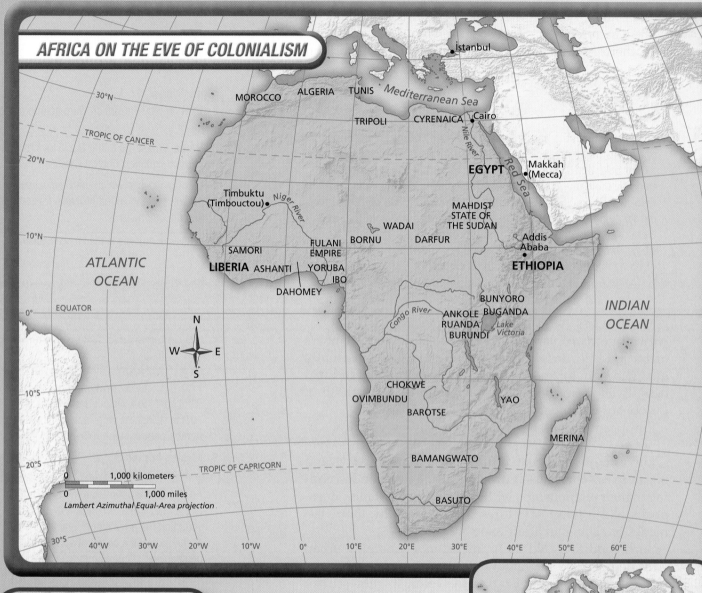

AFRICA ON THE EVE OF COLONIALISM

İstanbul

MOROCCO   ALGERIA   TUNIS   Mediterranean Sea

30°N

TROPIC OF CANCER   TRIPOLI   CYRENAICA   Cairo

20°N   EGYPT   Makkah (Mecca)

Timbuktu (Timbouctou)   Niger River

MAHDIST STATE OF THE SUDAN   Red Sea   Nile River

10°N   WADAI   BORNU   DARFUR   Addis Ababa

FULANI EMPIRE   ETHIOPIA

ATLANTIC OCEAN   SAMORI

LIBERIA   ASHANTI   YORUBA

IBO

DAHOMEY

EQUATOR   0°   ANKOLE   BUNYORO   BUGANDA   INDIAN OCEAN

RUANDA   Lake Victoria

Congo River   BURUNDI

10°S   CHOKWE

OVIMBUNDU   YAO

BAROTSE

MERINA

20°S   TROPIC OF CAPRICORN   BAMANGWATO

0   1,000 kilometers
0   1,000 miles
Lambert Azimuthal Equal-Area projection

BASUTO

30°S

40°W   30°W   20°W   10°W   0°   10°E   20°E   30°E   40°E   50°E   60°E

◀ In 1869, completion of the Suez Canal allowed ships to sail from Europe to Asia without going all the way around the southern tip of Africa.

By 1914, almost the entire continent was divided into European colonies. ▶

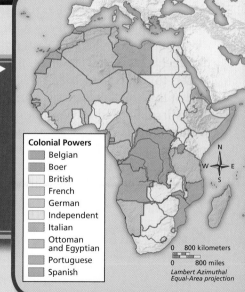

Colonial Powers

Belgian
Boer
British
French
German
Independent
Italian
Ottoman and Egyptian
Portuguese
Spanish

0   800 kilometers
0   800 miles
Lambert Azimuthal Equal-Area projection

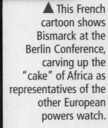

▲ This French cartoon shows Bismarck at the Berlin Conference, carving up the "cake" of Africa as representatives of the other European powers watch.

◄ Ethiopian Emperor Menelik defeated Italian forces in the Battle of Adwa in 1896, ending Italy's hopes of expanding its East African colonial empire.

THE SCRAMBLE FOR AFRICA

Interest in Africa Grows By the late 1800s, the Industrial Revolution had spread throughout Europe. Industrialized nations became economic rivals as they sought new markets in Africa for their manufactured goods and raw materials for production at home. Africa had rubber, ivory, minerals, and other natural resources as well as largely untapped markets for European products. Many Europeans also saw colonies as a way to assert their nation's status as a world power.

Advances in transportation and technology fueled interest in African colonization. As steamships replaced sailing ships, travel to Africa became faster. Construction of the Suez Canal made Africa part of a key trade route to India. New medicines increased protection against malaria and other tropical diseases, making colonization safer.

The Berlin Conference At talks in Berlin hosted by German chancellor Otto von Bismarck, delegates sought an orderly "carving up" of the African interior. Most shared the views of Belgian King Leopold II, who wrote, "I don't want to miss the chance of getting us a slice of this magnificent African cake." European powers haggled back and forth over geographic boundaries for their African colonies, but avoided direct conflict.

New National Boundaries By 1914, Europeans had redrawn the map of Africa. National boundaries largely ignored the location of ethnic, linguistic, and religious groups within each region. People in the Belgian Congo, for example, spoke over 200 different languages. New borders divided African kingdoms and tribes or put together ethnic groups with little knowledge of each other's languages and customs. These changes had an impact on the peoples of Africa long after colonial rule ended.

Geography SKILLS

1. **Place** What are key factors in the decision of European governments to colonize Africa after the Industrial Revolution?

2. **Human-Environmental Interaction** What effect might the redrawing of national boundaries by Europeans have on nation-building in African countries?

British Rule in India

The British brought order and stability to India, but India paid a high price for British rule. The mistrust and cultural differences between the British and Indians sparked an independence movement and renewed interest among Indians in their culture and history.

GUIDE TO READING

The BIG Idea
Struggle for Rights The British brought stability to India but destroyed native industries and degraded Indians.

Content Vocabulary
- sepoys *(p. 466)*
- viceroy *(p. 468)*

Academic Vocabulary
- civil *(p. 468)*
- estate *(p. 471)*

People, Places, and Events
- Kanpur *(p. 467)*
- Queen Victoria *(p. 467)*
- Bombay *(p. 469)*
- Indian National Congress *(p. 469)*
- Mohandas Gandhi *(p. 470)*
- Rabindranath Tagore *(p. 471)*

Reading Strategy
Determining Cause and Effect As you read, use a chart like the one below to identify some causes and effects of British influence on India.

Cause	Effect
1. British textiles	
2. cotton crops	
3. school system	
4. railroad, telegraph, telephone services	

The Sepoy Mutiny

MAIN IDEA Mistrust and cultural differences between the British and Indians led to violent conflict.

HISTORY & YOU Does your family follow certain traditions or religious practices? Read to learn how cultural differences helped ignite an Indian rebellion in 1857.

Over the course of the eighteenth century, British power in India had increased while the power of the Mogul rulers had declined (see Chapter 8). The British government gave a trading company, the British East India Company, power to become actively involved in India's political and military affairs. To rule India, the British East India Company had its own soldiers and forts. It also hired Indian soldiers, known as **sepoys,** to protect the company's interests in the region.

Events Leading to Revolt

In 1857 a growing Indian distrust of the British led to a revolt. The British call the revolt the Sepoy Mutiny. Indians call it the First War of Independence. Neutral observers label it the Great Rebellion.

The major immediate cause of the revolt was a rumor that the troops' new rifle cartridges were greased with cow and pig fat. The cow was sacred to Hindus. The pig was taboo to Muslims. To load a rifle at that time, soldiers had to bite off the end of the cartridge. To the sepoys, touching these greased cartridges to their lips would mean that they were polluted.

A group of sepoys at an army post in Meerut, near Delhi, refused to load their rifles with the cartridges. The British charged them with mutiny, publicly humiliated them, and put them in prison. This treatment of their comrades enraged the sepoy troops in Meerut. They went on a rampage, killing 50 European men, women, and children. Soon other Indians joined the revolt, including Indian princes whose land the British had taken.

Within a year, however, Indian troops loyal to the British and fresh British troops had crushed the rebellion. Although Indian troops fought bravely and outnumbered the British by about 230,000 to 45,000, they were not well organized. Rivalries between

Causes of the Sepoy Mutiny

- Increased British power in India; decreased power for Mogul rulers
- Growing distrust of British
- British disrespect for Indian religions and culture

Effects

- End of the Mogul Empire
- Beginning of direct British rule in India
- Indian nationalist movement

Troops Employed in British India, 1857

Royal troops
8.7% (24,263)

East India Company, European troops
7.7% (21,259)

East India Company, Sepoy troops
83.6% (232,224)

Source: *Statistical Abstract Relating to British India from 1840 to 1865.*

CRITICAL THINKING SKILLS

Charles Canning was the British governor-general in India. After the British crushed the sepoy uprising, Canning declared that any mutineer who had not committed murder could be spared execution. The *Times* of London called this decree the "clemency of Canning."

1. **Identifying** The sepoys made up what percentage of the troops of the British East India Company in 1857?

2. **Analyzing** What British attitude toward the sepoys does the cartoon show? Describe details from the cartoon that reveal this attitude.

The Great Rebellion in India

The caption of *The Clemency of Canning* (1857) reads, "Well, then, they shan't blow him from nasty guns; but he must promise to be a good little sepoy."

a sepoy

Governor General Charles Canning

THE CLEMENCY OF CANNING.

Hindus and Muslims kept the Indians from working together.

Atrocities were terrible on both sides. At **Kanpur** (Cawnpore), Indians massacred 200 defenseless women and children in a building known as the House of the Ladies. Recapturing Kanpur, the British took their revenge before executing the Indians.

Effects of the Revolt

As a result of the uprising, the British Parliament transferred the powers of the East India Company directly to the British government. In 1876 **Queen Victoria** took the title Empress of India. The people of India were now her colonial subjects, and India became her "Jewel in the Crown."

Although the rebellion failed, it helped to fuel Indian nationalism. The rebellion marked the first significant attempt by the people of South Asia to throw off British rule. Later, a new generation of Indian leaders would take up the cause.

✓ Reading Check **Describing** What were some effects of the Great Rebellion?

British Colonial Rule

MAIN IDEA The British brought order and stability to India, but they also hurt India's economy and degraded the Indian people.

HISTORY & YOU Do people in your life have both a positive and a negative influence on you? Read to learn how British rule in India had both positive and negative results for India.

See page R47 to read excerpts from Dadabhai Naroji's *The Impact of British Rule in India* in the **Primary Sources and Literature Library.**

After the Sepoy Mutiny, the British government began to rule India directly. They appointed a British official known as a **viceroy** (a governor who ruled as a representative of a monarch). A British **civil** service staff assisted the viceroy. This staff of about 3,500 officials ruled almost 300 million people, the largest colonial population in the world. British rule involved both benefits and costs for Indians.

Benefits of British Rule

British rule in India had several benefits for subjects. It brought order and stability to a society badly divided into many states with different political systems. It also led to a fairly honest, efficient government.

Through the efforts of the British administrator and historian Lord Thomas Macaulay, a new school system was set up. The new system used the English language, as Macaulay explained:

PRIMARY SOURCE

"What then shall the language of education be? [Some] maintain that it should be the English. The other half strongly recommend the Arabic and Sanskrit. The whole question seems to me to be, which language is the best worth knowing? . . . It is, I believe, no exaggeration to say that all the historical information which has been collected from all the books written in the Sanskrit language is less valuable than what may be found in short textbooks used at preparatory schools in England."
—*A New History of India*, Stanley Wolpert, 1977

The goal of the new school system was to train Indian children to serve in the government and army. The new system served only elite, upper-class Indians, however. Ninety percent of the population remained uneducated and illiterate.

Railroads, the telegraph, and a postal service were introduced to India shortly after they appeared in Great Britain. In 1853 the first trial run of a passenger train traveled the short distance from Bombay to Thane. By 1900, 25,000 miles (40,225 km) of railroads crisscrossed India.

Costs of British Rule

The Indian people, however, paid a high price for the peace and stability brought by British rule. Perhaps the greatest cost was economic. British entrepreneurs and a small number of Indians reaped financial benefits from British rule, but it brought hardship to millions of others in both the cities and the countryside. British manufactured goods destroyed local industries. British textiles put thousands of women out of work and severely damaged the Indian textile industry.

In rural areas, the British sent the zamindars to collect taxes. The British believed that using these local officials would make it easier to collect taxes from the peasants. However, the zamindars in India took advantage of their new authority. They increased taxes and forced the less fortunate peasants to become tenants or lose their land entirely. Peasant unrest grew.

The British also encouraged many farmers to switch from growing food to growing cotton. As a result, food supplies could not keep up with the growing population. Between 1800 and 1900, 30 million Indians died of starvation.

Finally, British rule was degrading, even for the newly educated upper classes who benefited the most from it. The best jobs and the best housing were reserved for Britons. Although many British colonial officials sincerely tried to improve the lot of the people in India, British arrogance cut deeply into the pride of many Indians.

The British also showed disrespect for India's cultural heritage. The Taj Mahal, for example, was built as a tomb for the beloved wife of an Indian ruler. The British used it as a favorite site for weddings and parties. Many partygoers even brought hammers to chip off pieces as souvenirs. British racial attitudes led to the rise of an Indian nationalist movement.

✓ Reading Check **Examining** How was British rule degrading to Indians?

Indian Nationalists

MAIN IDEA The British presence in India led to an Indian independence movement.

HISTORY & YOU What methods did Martin Luther King, Jr., use in the civil rights movement of the 1960s? Read to learn about Gandhi, the Indian leader who first practiced nonviolent protest.

The first Indian nationalists were upper-class and English-educated. Many of them were from urban areas, such as **Bombay** (Mumbai), Madras (Chennai), and Calcutta (Kolkata). Some were trained in British law and were members of the civil service.

At first, many Indian nationalists preferred reform to revolution. However, the slow pace of reform convinced many that relying on British goodwill was futile. In 1885 a small group of Indians met in Bombay to form the **Indian National Congress** (INC). The INC did not demand immediate independence. Instead, it called for a share in the governing process.

The INC had difficulties because of religious differences. The INC sought independence for all Indians, regardless of class or religious background. However, many of its leaders were Hindu and reflected Hindu concerns. Later, Muslims called for the creation of a separate Muslim League.

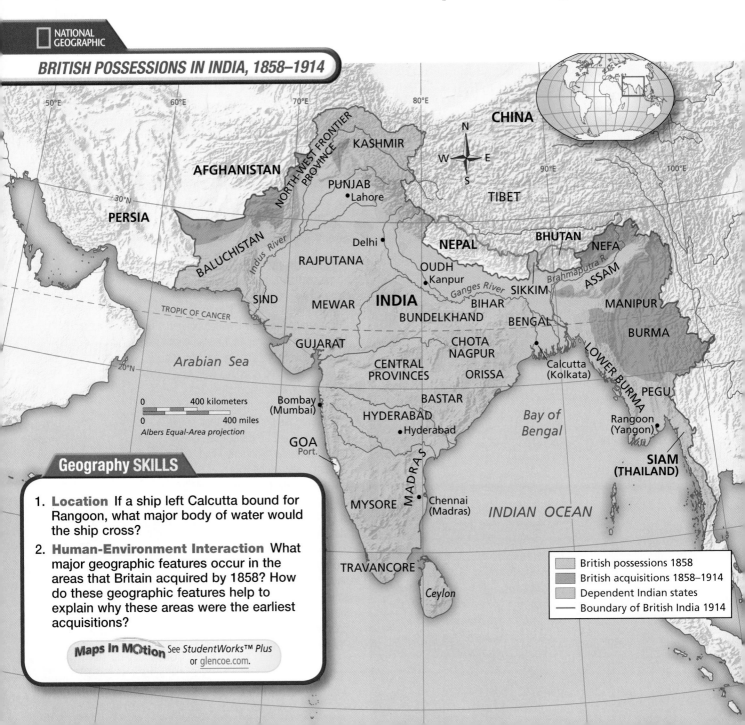

NATIONAL GEOGRAPHIC

BRITISH POSSESSIONS IN INDIA, 1858–1914

Map legend:
- British possessions 1858
- British acquisitions 1858–1914
- Dependent Indian states
- Boundary of British India 1914

0 400 kilometers
0 400 miles
Albers Equal-Area projection

Geography SKILLS

1. **Location** If a ship left Calcutta bound for Rangoon, what major body of water would the ship cross?

2. **Human-Environment Interaction** What major geographic features occur in the areas that Britain acquired by 1858? How do these geographic features help to explain why these areas were the earliest acquisitions?

Maps In Motion See *StudentWorks™ Plus* or glencoe.com.

Such a league would represent the interests of the millions of Muslims in Indian society.

In 1915 the return of a young Hindu from South Africa brought new life to India's struggle for independence. **Mohandas Gandhi** was born in 1869 in Gujarat, in western India. He studied in London and became a lawyer. In 1893 he went to South Africa to work in a law firm serving Indian workers there. He soon learned of the racial exploitation of Indians living in South Africa.

On his return to India, Gandhi became active in the independence movement. Using his experience in South Africa, he began a movement based on nonviolent resistance. Its aim was to force the British to improve the lot of the poor and to grant independence to India. Ultimately, Gandhi's movement led to Indian independence.

✓ Reading Check **Describing** Who were the first Indian nationalists?

Colonial Indian Culture

MAIN IDEA British rule sparked renewed interest among Indians in their own culture and history.

HISTORY & YOU Do you know where your ancestors came from? Are you curious about your cultural roots? Read to learn about an Indian author who helped awaken a new interest in Indian culture in the early 1900s.

The love-hate tension in India that arose from British domination led to a cultural awakening as well. The cultural revival began in the early nineteenth century with the creation of a British college in Calcutta. A local publishing house was opened. It issued textbooks on a variety of subjects, including the sciences, Sanskrit, and Western literature. The publisher also printed grammars and dictionaries in various Indian languages.

This revival soon spread to other regions of India. It led to a search for a new national

PEOPLE in HISTORY

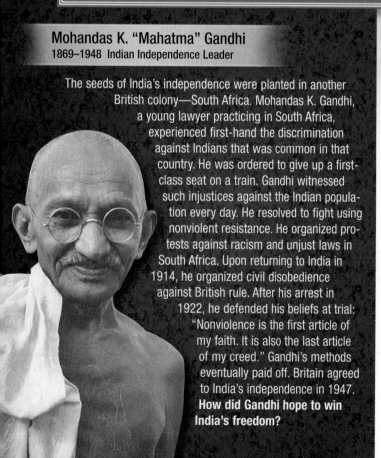

Mohandas K. "Mahatma" Gandhi
1869–1948 Indian Independence Leader

The seeds of India's independence were planted in another British colony—South Africa. Mohandas K. Gandhi, a young lawyer practicing in South Africa, experienced first-hand the discrimination against Indians that was common in that country. He was ordered to give up a first-class seat on a train. Gandhi witnessed such injustices against the Indian population every day. He resolved to fight using nonviolent resistance. He organized protests against racism and unjust laws in South Africa. Upon returning to India in 1914, he organized civil disobedience against British rule. After his arrest in 1922, he defended his beliefs at trial: "Nonviolence is the first article of my faith. It is also the last article of my creed." Gandhi's methods eventually paid off. Britain agreed to India's independence in 1947. **How did Gandhi hope to win India's freedom?**

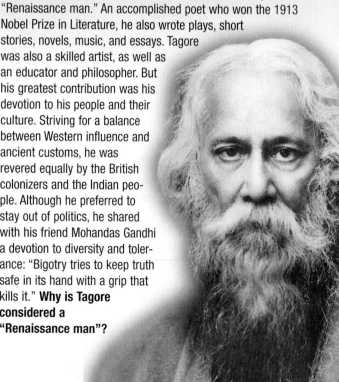

Rabindranath Tagore
1861–1941 Indian Writer and Social Reformer

Rabindranath Tagore was India's version of the European "Renaissance man." An accomplished poet who won the 1913 Nobel Prize in Literature, he also wrote plays, short stories, novels, music, and essays. Tagore was also a skilled artist, as well as an educator and philosopher. But his greatest contribution was his devotion to his people and their culture. Striving for a balance between Western influence and ancient customs, he was revered equally by the British colonizers and the Indian people. Although he preferred to stay out of politics, he shared with his friend Mohandas Gandhi a devotion to diversity and tolerance: "Bigotry tries to keep truth safe in its hand with a grip that kills it." **Why is Tagore considered a "Renaissance man"?**

identity and a modern literary expression. Indian novelists and poets began writing historical romances and epics. Some wrote in English, but most were uncomfortable with a borrowed colonial language. They preferred to use their own regional tongues.

Nationalist Newspapers

Printed in the various regional Indian languages, newspapers were a common medium used to arouse mass support for nationalist causes. These newspapers reached the lower-middle-class populations—tens of thousands of Indians who had never learned a word of English.

In his newspaper *Kesari* ("The Lion"), journalist Balwantrao Gangadhar Tilak used innuendo (suggestion) to convey the negative feelings about the British without ever writing anything disloyal. G. S. Aiyar, editor of the popular *Swadeshamitram* ("Friend of Our Own Nation"), organized the Triplicane Literary Society. At these meetings, the region's young intellectuals gathered to discuss poetry and politics.

Tagore

The most famous Indian author was **Rabindranath Tagore,** winner of the Nobel Prize in Literature in 1913. A great writer and poet, Tagore had many talents. He was also a social reformer, spiritual leader, educator, philosopher, singer, painter, and international spokesperson for the moral concerns of his age. He set to music the Bengali poem *Bande Mataram* ("Hail to Thee, Mother"), which became Indian nationalism's first anthem. Tagore liked to invite the great thinkers of the time to his expansive country home, or **estate.** There he set up a school that became an international university.

Tagore's life mission was to promote pride in a national Indian consciousness in the face of British domination. He wrote a widely read novel in which he portrayed the love-hate relationship of India toward its colonial mentor. The novel reflected an Indian people who admired and imitated the British but who agonized over how to establish their own identity.

Tagore, however, was more than an Indian nationalist. His life's work was one long prayer for human dignity, world peace, and the mutual understanding and union of East and West. As he once said,

PRIMARY SOURCE

"It is my conviction that my countrymen will truly gain their India by fighting against the education that teaches them that a country is greater than the ideals of humanity."

—Rabindranath Tagore

✓**Reading Check** **Comparing** How did the nationalist movement parallel cultural developments in India?

SECTION 3 REVIEW

Vocabulary

1. **Explain** the significance of: sepoys, Kanpur, Queen Victoria, viceroy, civil, Bombay, Indian National Congress, Mohandas Gandhi, Rabindranath Tagore, estate.

Main Ideas

2. **Identify** the event that ignited sepoy discontent into a full-scale mutiny.

3. **Illustrate** the percentage of India's population that died of starvation in the 1800s. Use a graph like the one below.

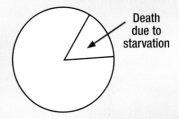

Death due to starvation

4. **State** the aim of Mohandas Gandhi's nonviolent resistance movement.

Critical Thinking

5. **The BIG Idea** **Predicting Consequences** Many British lived in India for decades. Do you think living in India would have changed British attitudes toward Indians? Explain.

6. **Drawing Conclusions** Do you think the benefits of British rule to India outweighed its costs? Support your answer.

7. **Analyzing Visuals** Study the photograph of Tagore on page 470. Describe some aspect of the photo that you believe provides a clue to Tagore's personality.

Writing About History

8. **Descriptive Writing** Imagine you are a member of India's upper class. You have just attended a reception at the home of a British official. Describe in writing your impressions of the home, making a comparison to your own residence.

History ONLINE

For help with the concepts in this section of *Glencoe World History— Modern Times,* go to glencoe.com and click Study Central.

Nation Building in Latin America

The success of the American Revolution and the ideals of the French Revolution spread throughout Latin America. One by one the Latin American countries gained their independence from colonial rule. However, with that independence came the realization that they had exchanged being political colonies of the Western powers to being their economic allies, dependent on their former rulers.

GUIDE TO READING

The BIG Idea
Self-Determination Latin American countries gained their independence but became economically dependent on Western powers.

Content Vocabulary
- *peninsulares (p. 472)*
- *creoles (p. 472)*
- *mestizos (p. 473)*
- *caudillos (p. 475)*
- *cash crops (p. 476)*

Academic Vocabulary
- *intervention (p. 475)*
- *redistribution (p. 476)*

People, Places, and Events
- José de San Martín (p. 474)
- Simón Bolívar *(p. 474)*
- Monroe Doctrine (p. 475)
- Antonio López de Santa Anna *(p. 475)*
- Benito Juárez *(p. 476)*
- Puerto Rico *(p. 477)*
- Panama Canal *(p. 477)*
- Haiti *(p. 477)*
- Nicaragua *(p. 478)*

Reading Strategy
Comparing and Contrasting As you read, create a Venn diagram comparing and contrasting colonial rule in Africa and in Latin America.

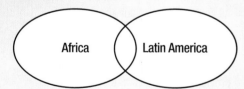

Africa — Latin America

Nationalist Revolts

MAIN IDEA Revolutionary ideas in Latin America were sparked by the successes of revolutions in North America.

HISTORY & YOU Who do you think of as heroes of the American struggle for independence? George Washington? Patrick Henry? Read to learn about the heroes of Latin American independence.

By the end of the eighteenth century, the political ideals stemming from the revolution in North America put European control of Latin America in peril. Latin America's social class structure played a big role in how the nineteenth-century revolutions occurred and what they achieved.

Social classes divided colonial Latin America. *Peninsulares* were Spanish and Portuguese officials who resided temporarily in Latin America for political and economic gain. At the top of the class structure, *peninsulares* dominated Latin America. They held all important positions. Creoles controlled land and business and resented the *peninsulares*. The *peninsulares* regarded the creoles as second-class citizens. Mestizos were the largest group. They worked as servants or laborers.

Prelude to Revolution

Creoles were the descendants of Europeans born in Latin America who lived there permanently. The creoles especially favored the revolutionary ideals of equality of all people in the eyes of the law, free trade, and a free press. The creoles disliked the domination of their trade by Spain and Portugal. When Napoleon overthrew the monarchies of Spain and Portugal, the authority of their colonial empires was severely weakened. Then, between 1807 and 1825, a series of revolts enabled most of Latin America to become independent.

Before the main independence movements began, an unusual revolution took place. In the French colony of Saint Domingue, on the island of Hispaniola, François-Dominique Toussaint-Louverture

EUROPEAN COLONIES IN LATIN AMERICA

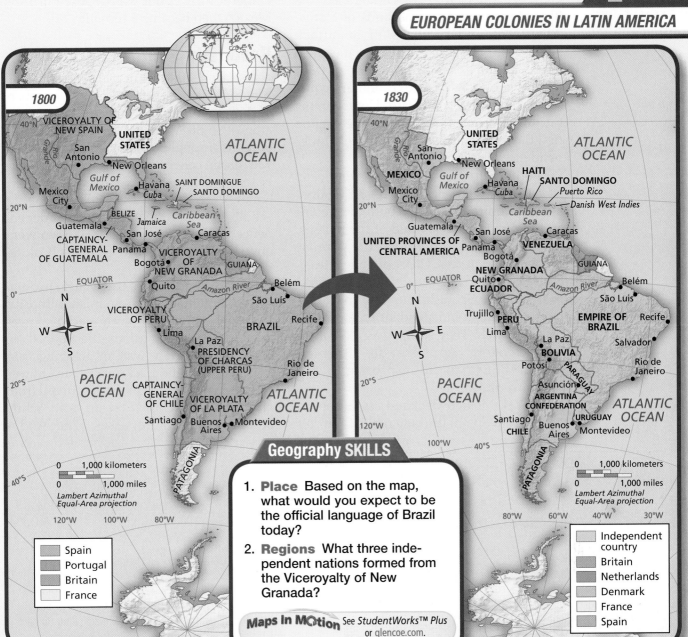

1800

1830

Geography SKILLS

1. **Place** Based on the map, what would you expect to be the official language of Brazil today?

2. **Regions** What three independent nations formed from the Viceroyalty of New Granada?

Maps In Motion See *StudentWorks™ Plus* or glencoe.com.

1800 legend:
- Spain
- Portugal
- Britain
- France

1830 legend:
- Independent country
- Britain
- Netherlands
- Denmark
- France
- Spain

(TOO•SAN LOO•vuhr•TYUR) led more than 100,000 slaves in revolt. They seized control of all of Hispaniola. On January 1, 1804, the western part of Hispaniola, now called Haiti, announced its freedom. Haiti became the first independent state in Latin America.

Revolt in Mexico

Beginning in 1810, Mexico, too, experienced a revolt. The first real hero of Mexican independence was Miguel Hidalgo. A parish priest, Hidalgo lived in a village about 100 miles (160 km) from Mexico City.

Hidalgo had studied the French Revolution. He roused the local Native Americans and **mestizos** (people of mixed European and Native American descent) to free themselves from the Spanish:

PRIMARY SOURCE

"My children, this day comes to us as a new dispensation. Are you ready to receive it? Will you be free? Will you make the effort to recover from the hated Spaniards the lands stolen from your forefathers 300 years ago?"

—Miguel Hidalgo, September 16, 1810

History ONLINE

Student Web Activity—
Visit glencoe.com and complete the activity on independence movements in Latin America.

CHAPTER 14 The Height of Imperialism **473**

On September 16, 1810, Hidalgo led this ill-equipped army of thousands of Native Americans and mestizos in an attack against the Spaniards. He was an inexperienced military leader, however, and his forces were soon crushed. A military court sentenced Hidalgo to death. However, his memory lives on. In fact, September 16, the first day of the uprising, is Mexico's Independence Day.

The participation of Native Americans and mestizos in Mexico's revolt against Spanish control frightened both the creoles and the *peninsulares.* Afraid of the masses, they cooperated in defeating the popular revolutionary forces. Conservative elites—both creoles and *peninsulares*—then decided to overthrow Spanish rule. The conservatives wanted an independent nation ruled by a monarch. They selected a creole military leader, Agustín de Iturbide (EE•tur•BEE•thay), to help bring in this new government.

In 1821 Mexico declared its independence from Spain. Iturbide named himself emperor in 1822 but was deposed in 1823. Mexico then became a republic.

Revolts in South America

José de San Martín of Argentina and **Simón Bolívar** of Venezuela, both members of the creole elite, were hailed as the "Liberators of South America." These men led revolutions throughout the continent. José de San Martín believed that the Spaniards must be removed from all of South America if any South American nation was to be free.

Bolívar began the struggle for independence in Venezuela in 1810. He then went on to lead revolts in New Granada (Colombia) and Ecuador.

By 1810, the forces of San Martín had liberated Argentina from Spanish authority. In January 1817, San Martín led his forces over the Andes to attack the Spanish in Chile. The journey was an amazing feat. Two-thirds of the pack mules and horses died during the trip. Soldiers suffered from lack of oxygen and severe cold while crossing mountain passes. The Andes

PEOPLE *in* HISTORY

José de San Martín
1778–1850 South American Liberator

José de San Martín was born in Argentina, but learned his military skills in the Spanish army. After Napoleon occupied Spain, he witnessed the uprising of Spanish patriots against French occupation. He began to sympathize with the independence movement in America. In Spain, he met with creole revolutionaries. Years later he wrote about this turning point in his life: ". . . [K]nowing of the first movements of Caracas, Buenos Aires and elsewhere we resolved to return each to our country of birth, in order to offer our services to the struggle. . . ." San Martín returned to Argentina and organized the resistance. After freeing Argentina, he led his troops across the Andes to free Chile. Later, he helped liberate Peru. **How did the French occupation of Spain influence San Martín?**

Simón Bolívar
1783–1830 South American Liberator

Son of a wealthy Venezuelan family, Simón Bolívar read books by European writers that described "the rights of man" and free republics. While visiting Rome, Bolívar gazed at the ruins of the great civilization and said to Rodriguez, "I swear . . . by my honor and my country, that I shall never allow my hands to be idle . . . until I have broken the shackles which bind us to Spain." Returning home, Bolívar raised an army. By the mid-1820s his forces had freed five nations. Bolívar dreamed of a "Gran Colombia," a vast union of South American states. But soon after Bolívar became president of Gran Colombia, civil wars tore the union apart. Although unification failed, Bolívar had set South America on the path of freedom. **What influences helped to motivate Bolívar?**

mountains were more than two miles (3.2 km) above sea level.

The arrival of San Martín's forces in Chile completely surprised the Spaniards. Spanish forces were badly defeated at the Battle of Chacabuco on February 12, 1817. In 1821 San Martín moved on to Lima, Peru, the center of Spanish authority.

San Martín was convinced that he could not complete the liberation of Peru alone. He welcomed the arrival of Simón Bolívar and his forces. Bolívar, the "Liberator of Venezuela," took on the task of crushing the last significant Spanish army at Ayacucho on December 9, 1824.

By the end of 1824, Peru, Uruguay, Paraguay, Colombia, Venezuela, Argentina, Bolivia, and Chile had all become free of Spain. Earlier, in 1822, the prince regent of Brazil had declared Brazil's independence from Portugal. The Central American states had become independent in 1823. In 1838 and 1839, they divided into five republics: Guatemala, El Salvador, Honduras, Costa Rica, and Nicaragua.

Threats to Independence

In the early 1820s, only one major threat remained to the newly won independence of the Latin American states. Members of the Concert of Europe favored the use of troops to restore Spanish control in Latin America. The British, who wished to trade with Latin America, disagreed. They proposed joint action with the United States against any European moves against Latin America.

Distrustful of British motives, James Monroe, the president of the United States, acted alone in 1823. In the **Monroe Doctrine,** he guaranteed the independence of the new Latin American nations. The Monroe Doctrine also strongly warned against any European **intervention** in the Americas.

More important to Latin American independence than American words, however, was the British navy. Other European powers feared the power of the British navy, which stood between Latin America and any planned European invasion force.

✓ **Reading Check** **Evaluating** How did the French Revolution help inspire the revolution in Mexico?

Nation Building

MAIN IDEA After they became independent, Latin American nations faced a staggering range of problems.

HISTORY & YOU Do you feel independent yet still depend on your parents in some ways, such as for money? Read how Latin America returned to economic dependence.

The new Latin American nations faced a number of serious problems between 1830 and 1870. The wars for independence had resulted in a staggering loss of people, property, and livestock. Unsure of their precise boundaries, the new nations went to war with one another to settle border disputes. Poor roads, a lack of railroads, thick jungles, and mountains made communication, transportation, and national unity difficult. During the course of the nineteenth century, the new Latin American nations would become economically dependent on Western nations once again.

Rule of the Caudillos

Most of the new nations of Latin America began with republican governments, but they had no experience in self-rule. Soon after independence, strong leaders known as **caudillos** gained power.

Caudillos ruled chiefly by military force and were usually supported by the landed elites. Many kept the new national states together. Some were also modernizers who built roads and canals, ports, and schools. Others were destructive.

Antonio López de Santa Anna, for example, ruled Mexico from 1833 to 1855. During this time, he served as president for 11 two-year terms. Calling himself the "Napoleon of the West," Santa Anna misused state funds, halted reforms, and created chaos. As one historian judged, "Any progress in Mexico achieved during the era of Santa Anna had nothing to do with him."

In 1835 American settlers in the Mexican state of Texas revolted against Santa Anna's rule. Texas gained its independence in 1836 and United States statehood followed in 1845. War between Mexico and the United States soon followed (1846–1848).

Mexico was defeated and lost almost one-half of its territory to the United States in the Mexican War.

Fortunately for Mexico, Santa Anna's disastrous rule was followed by a period of reform from 1855 to 1876. This era was dominated by **Benito Juárez,** a Mexican national hero. The son of Native American peasants, President Juárez brought liberal reforms to Mexico. Some of Juárez's Laws of Reform included separation of church and state, toleration of all faiths, curbing the power of the military, an educational system for all of Mexico, and the **redistribution** of land to the poor.

Other caudillos, such as Juan Manuel de Rosas in Argentina, were supported by the masses. These caudillos became extremely popular and brought about radical change. Unfortunately, the caudillo's authority depended on his personal power. When he died or lost power, civil wars for control of the country often erupted.

A New Imperialism

Political independence brought economic independence, but old patterns were quickly reestablished. Instead of Spain and Portugal, Great Britain and the United States now dominated the Latin American economy.

Great Britain dominated trade in Latin America for most of the nineteenth century. British merchants moved into Latin America in large numbers, and British investors poured in funds. By the late 1920s, the United States replaced Europe as the source of loans and investments. Direct U.S. investments in Latin America reached $3.5 billion, out of a world total of $7.5 billion.

American, British, and other foreign investors built transportation and communication systems and power plants. These investors also introduced new technologies such as refrigeration, steam engines, and mining equipment. These innovations led to increased production of export commodities such as wheat, tobacco, wool, sugar, coffee, and hides. At the same time, Latin American countries imported finished consumer goods, especially textiles, and had limited industry.

Economic Dependence

The emphasis on exporting raw materials and importing finished products ensured the ongoing domination of the Latin American economy by foreigners who reaped many benefits and profits. On the other hand, most Latin American countries experienced uneven economic development since they were almost wholly dependent on the sale or export of two or three **cash crops**—crops that are grown for sale rather than for personal use. A drop in world prices for the crops or failed harvests could be devastating to an economy based on cash crops.

Latin American countries remained economically dependent on Western nations, even though they were no longer colonies. In Central America and the Caribbean, export economies still dominated long into the 1900s. In some areas, such as in Cuba with sugar, in Brazil with coffee, and in Central America with bananas, an entire national economy continued to depend on a single cash crop.

Persistent Inequality

A fundamental problem for all of the new Latin American nations was the domination of society by the landed elites. Large estates remained a way of life in Latin America. By 1848, for example, the Sánchez Navarro family in Mexico possessed 17 estates made up of 16 million acres (6,480,000 ha). Latin American estates were often so large that they could not be farmed efficiently.

Land remained the basis of wealth, social prestige, and political power throughout the nineteenth century. Landed elites ran governments, controlled courts, and kept a system of inexpensive labor. These landowners made enormous profits by growing single cash crops, such as coffee for export. Most of the population had no land to grow basic food crops. As a result, the masses experienced dire poverty.

✓ Reading Check **Describing** What were some of the difficulties that the new Latin American republics faced?

Change in Latin America

MAIN IDEA Many Latin American governments patterned their new constitutions after the United States constitution.

HISTORY & YOU Can you think of a recent example when the United States demonstrated its power in the world? Read to learn how the United States extended its influence over countries in Latin America.

After 1870, Latin American governments, led by large landowners, wrote constitutions similar to those of the United States and European democracies. The ruling elites were careful to keep their power by limiting voting rights, however.

The U.S. in Latin America

By 1900, the United States had emerged as a world power. It began to intervene in the affairs of its southern neighbors. As a result of the Spanish-American War (1898), Cuba became a protectorate of the United States. That same year **Puerto Rico** was also annexed to the United States.

In 1903 President Theodore Roosevelt supported a rebellion that allowed Panama to separate from Colombia and establish a new nation. In return, the United States was granted control of a 10-mile strip of land running from coast to coast. There the United States built the **Panama Canal,** which opened in 1914 and was one of the greatest engineering feats in the world at that time.

American Investments

American investments in Latin America soon expanded, as did the resolve to protect those investments. Beginning in 1898, U.S. military forces were sent to Cuba, Mexico, Guatemala, Honduras, Nicaragua, Panama, Colombia, Haiti, and the Dominican Republic to protect American interests.

Some expeditions stayed for years. U.S. Marines were in **Haiti** from 1915 to 1934 and in **Nicaragua** from 1912 to 1933.

POLITICAL CARTOONS   PRIMARY SOURCE

The Monroe Doctrine and Roosevelt Corollary

President Theodore Roosevelt

MONROE DOCTRINE

U.S.

CLAIMS

REPUBLIC OF SANTO DOMINGO

EUROPE

In 1823 President James Monroe declared that Europeans may not interfere in the affairs of any nation in the Western Hemisphere. His intent was to protect U.S. interests in Latin America by discouraging further European colonization. In 1904 President Theodore Roosevelt took the policy a step further. At the time, European powers threatened to send warships to Santo Domingo to collect debts owed them. In a statement that became known as the Roosevelt Corollary to the Monroe Doctrine, Roosevelt claimed that the United States could intervene in any Latin American nation guilty of "chronic misconduct" (such as the inability to repay debts). The United States then took control of debt collection in the Dominican Republic.

DOCUMENT-BASED QUESTIONS

This cartoon, titled *Hands Off!*, illustrates one view of U.S. intervention in Latin America.

1. **Analyzing Visuals** How is the Latin American portrayed in this cartoon? What does this portrayal suggest about the reasons for U.S. imperialism in Latin America?

2. **Making Inferences** How do you think United States intervention might have affected Latin American nations?

Pancho Villa

Emiliano Zapata

Constitution of 1917

- established a federal government, with separation of powers and a bill of rights
- limited president's term in office
- granted universal male suffrage
- gave workers the right to form unions
- set a minimum wage and maximum hours
- prohibited pay discrimination based on race, ethnicity, or gender
- established a social security system
- stated that Mexico's natural resources belong to the Mexican people, not to foreign investors
- limited foreign land ownership
- restored lands to Native Americans

▲ Revolutionary leaders, such as "Pancho" Villa and Emiliano Zapata, raised armies from the discontented rural poor to fight for land reform. Zapata coined the revolutionary war slogan, "¡Tierra y Libertad!" which means "Land and Liberty!"—a cry still heard in Mexico to protest injustice.

Effects of the Mexican Revolution

The Constitution of 1917 set down many of the goals of the revolution. For revolutionary leaders, the goal was political reform. For peasants, it was about land reform. It would take decades for the reforms to take hold fully. Still, this constitution—the "fruit" of the Mexican Revolution—laid the groundwork for positive change. Eventually, the revolution helped to bring about a more democratic and politically stable Mexico.

CRITICAL THINKING SKILLS

1. **Identify** What are two signs of nationalism in the Mexican Constitution of 1917?
2. **Making Inferences** How well did the Mexican Revolution achieve its goals?

Increasing numbers of Latin Americans began to resent this interference from the "big bully" to the north.

Revolution in Mexico

In some countries, large landowners supported dictators who looked out for the interests of the ruling elite. Porfirio Díaz, who ruled Mexico between 1877 and 1911, created a conservative, centralized government. The army, foreign capitalists, large landowners, and the Catholic Church supported Díaz. All these groups benefited from their alliance with Díaz. However, growing forces for change in Mexico led to a revolution.

During Díaz's dictatorial reign, the wages of workers had declined. Ninety-five percent of the rural population owned no land, whereas about 1,000 families owned almost all of Mexico. A liberal landowner, Francisco Madero, forced Díaz from power in 1911. The door to a wider revolution then opened.

Madero made a valiant effort to handle the revolutionary forces at work. He put some of the best officials in his administration, and he sought a balance in dealing with foreign interests. However, his efforts proved ineffective.

The northern states were in near anarchy as Pancho Villa's armed masses of bandits swept the countryside. The federal army was full of hard-minded generals who itched to assert their power. Even the liberal politicians and idealists found fault with Madero for not solving all of the country's problems at once.

Madero's ineffectiveness created a demand for agrarian reform. This new call for reform was led by Emiliano Zapata. Zapata aroused the masses of landless peasants and began to seize and redistribute the estates of wealthy landholders. While Madero tried to reach an agreement with him for land reforms, Zapata refused to disarm his followers.

Between 1910 and 1920, the Mexican Revolution caused great damage to the Mexican economy. Finally, a new constitution was enacted in 1917. This constitution set up a government led by a president. It also created land-reform policies, established limits on foreign investors, and set an agenda to help the workers.

The revolution also led to an outpouring of patriotism throughout Mexico. National pride was evident, for example, as intellectuals and artists sought to capture what was unique about Mexico, with special emphasis on its past.

Prosperity and Social Change

After 1870, Latin America began an age of prosperity based to a large extent on the export of a few basic items. These included wheat and beef from Argentina, coffee from Brazil, coffee and bananas from Central America, and sugar and silver from Peru. These foodstuffs and raw materials were largely exchanged for finished goods—textiles, machines, and luxury items—from Europe and the United States. After 1900, Latin Americans also increased their own industrialization. They built factories to produce textiles, foods, and construction materials.

One result from the prosperity of increased exports was growth in the middle sectors (divisions) of Latin American society. Lawyers, merchants, shopkeepers, businesspeople, schoolteachers, professors, bureaucrats, and military officers increased in numbers. After 1900, these middle sectors of society continued to expand.

Middle-class Latin Americans shared some common characteristics. They lived in cities and sought education and decent incomes. They also saw the United States as a model, especially in regard to industrialization. The middle class sought liberal reform, not revolution. Once they had the right to vote, they generally sided with the landholding elites.

✓ **Reading Check** **Evaluating** What caused the growth of a middle class in Latin America?

Vocabulary
1. **Explain** the significance of: *peninsulares*, creoles, mestizos, José de San Martín, Simón Bolívar, Monroe Doctrine, intervention, caudillos, Antonio López de Santa Anna, Benito Juárez, redistribution, cash crops, Puerto Rico, Panama Canal, Haiti, Nicaragua.

Main Ideas
2. **Describe** the social classes of Latin America.

3. **Explain** how Latin American countries would often determine the next ruler after a caudillo died.

4. **Identify** the country that exported each product group listed in the chart below.

Product	Country
coffee	
bananas and coffee	
beef and wheat	
sugar and silver	

Critical Thinking
5. **The BIG Idea** **Determining Cause and Effect** How did persistent inequality contribute to the failure of democracy in the young Latin American nations?

6. **Making Inferences** Why do you think Theodore Roosevelt supported Panama's rebellion to win independence from Colombia?

7. **Analyzing Visuals** Examine the group photograph on page 478. What do you think you can determine about the subjects of the photo from the way they are dressed?

Writing About History
8. **Expository Writing** Why did Latin American countries remain economically dependent on Western nations when they were no longer political colonies? Write a brief essay explaining why this happened.

History ONLINE

For help with the concepts in this section of *Glencoe World History—Modern Times*, go to glencoe.com and click Study Central.

Indochina: French Colonialism in Vietnam

In the 1860s, France began to gain influence in Vietnam, and in 1887, Vietnam officially fell under French political domination and economic exploitation. French intervention divided Vietnamese society. Colonial policies benefited some Vietnamese, while others called for independence.

The wet-farming of rice was, and still is, an economic essential for Vietnam.

A Buddhist nun. The other traditional Vietnamese religion is Confucianism.

Vietnamese can be written in a traditional script or in Western letters. Nationalists adopted Western printing for journals promoting independence.

TRADITIONAL SOCIETY

Rice became an export crop to make money for French landowners. Large numbers of landless peasants worked big estates as they had for centuries, so traditional society remained mostly intact, though now the peasants sometimes faced rice shortages. The French did not preserve the traditional Confucian scholar officials, as they were the first to call for Vietnamese independence. Without these teachers, the country's historically high rate of literacy fell drastically.

Colonial architecture, seen in the Hanoi Cathedral, remains part of Vietnam's cultural heritage today.

Vietnamese Catholic converts were given land and administrative positions by the French.

The French used the traditional social order and modern military power to maintain control.

FRUSTRATIONS OF COLONIALISM

The French greatly increased the amount of rice land, but either sold it to the highest-bidding Vietnamese landlord or gave it to French speculators. The Vietnamese were shut out of trade and industry. They were denied civil liberties and participation in government. Most Vietnamese worked harder and received less in return. After 1900, new nationalist leaders began to look beyond the old monarchy for inspiration.

ANALYZING VISUALS

1. **Describing** What do the tools and equipment of traditional farming indicate about peasant life in colonial Vietnam?

2. **Assessing** What were some of the affects of colonial rule on the Vietnamese people?

CHAPTER **14** Visual Summary

You can study anywhere, anytime by downloading quizzes and flash cards to your PDA from glencoe.com.

SOUTHEAST ASIA AND AFRICA and New Imperialism

- Under new imperialism, European nations came to rule virtually all of Southeast Asia and Africa by 1900.
- European countries controlled the economies and governments of the Asian colonies.
- Some Southeast Asians resisted colonial rule more successfully than others.
- Europeans used direct and indirect rule to exploit Africa. Resentment led to African nationalism.

THE INAUGURATION OF THE SUEZ CANAL

The Suez Canal made control of Egypt even more desirable to European rivals.

THE SIEGE OF DELHI

British forces storm the Cashmere Gate to reclaim the city of Delhi after the Sepoy Mutiny.

INDIA and New Imperialism

- Indian mistrust of the British and cultural differences led to the Sepoy Mutiny.
- After the mutiny, Britain stabilized India but hurt the economy and degraded the Indians.
- Resistance to British rule led to an independence movement guided by Mohandas Gandhi, which was ultimately successful.

LATIN AMERICA and New Imperialism

- Inspired by the American and French Revolutions, Latin Americans started their own revolts for independence.
- Latin American nations wrote constitutions similar to the constitution of the United States.
- After gaining independence, Latin American nations experienced staggering economic and political problems.

HARVESTING COFFEE IN BRAZIL

In the spirit of new imperialism, Great Britain made economic colonies out of Latin America and took advantage of its raw materials such as coffee.

STANDARDIZED TEST PRACTICE

TEST-TAKING TIP

If you do not immediately know the right answer to a question, look at each answer choice carefully. Try to recall the context in which these events were discussed in class. Remembering this context may help you eliminate incorrect answer choices.

Reviewing Vocabulary

Directions: Choose the word or words that best complete the sentence.

1. _____ controlled land and business in Latin America but were regarded as second-class citizens by European officials there.

   A *Peninsulares*

   B Creoles

   C Mestizos

   D Caudillos

2. The British East India Company hired Indian soldiers called _____ to protect its interests in India.

   A caudillos

   B viceroys

   C mestizos

   D sepoys

3. A political unit that depends on another government for protection is known as _____.

   A a colony

   B an annex

   C a protectorate

   D a territory

4. The Boers fought with many _____ people, especially the Zulu of South Africa.

   A imperialist

   B indigenous

   C colonial

   D racist

Reviewing Main Ideas

Directions: Choose the best answers to the following questions.

Section 1 *(pp. 450–455)*

5. Unlike earlier imperialism, which desire became a motive for the new imperialism of the late nineteenth century?

   A To control large territories directly

   B To trade with faraway lands

   C To set up colonies in other lands

   D To convert primitive people to Christianity

6. What nation forced Vietnam to become its protectorate to prevent a rival power from expanding in the region?

   A Britain

   B France

   C United States

   D Netherlands

Section 2 *(pp. 456–463)*

7. Which of the following connects the Mediterranean and Red Sea?

   A Panama Canal

   B Dardanelles

   C Bosporus

   D Suez Canal

8. Who were the Afrikaners?

   A The caudillos

   B The Zulu

   C The Boers

   D The Tutsi

Need Extra Help?								
If You Missed Questions . . .	1	2	3	4	5	6	7	8
Go to Page . . .	472	466	452	460	450	453	457	460

 GO ON

9. Which country ruled its African possessions through direct rule?

A France

B United States

C Great Britain

D Poland

Section 3 (pp. 466–471)

10. What colony did Queen Victoria consider her "Jewel in the Crown"?

A South Africa

B India

C Burma

D New England

11. Which famous leader used nonviolent resistance to help win independence for India?

A Rabindranath Tagore

B G. S. Aiyar

C Mohandas Gandhi

D Balwantrao Gangadhar Tilak

Section 4 (pp. 472–479)

12. Who led his forces over the Andes, surprising Spanish troops and winning independence for Chile?

A Simón Bolívar

B Miguel Hidalgo

C Antonio López de Santa Anna

D José de San Martín

13. As a result of a slave revolt led by François-Dominique Toussaint-Louverture, which of the following became Latin America's first independent nation?

A Bolivia

B Brazil

C Mexico

D Haiti

Critical Thinking

Directions: Choose the best answers to the following questions.

Use the following map to answer question 14.

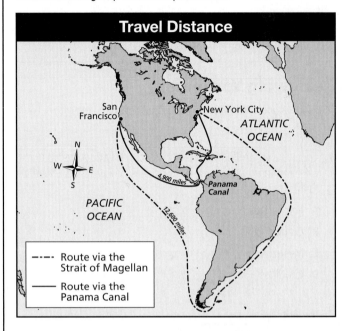

Travel Distance

14. Why is the Panama Canal important to the United States?

A It is the only way to get from New York City to San Francisco.

B It makes travel by sea from New York City to San Francisco possible.

C It connects the east and west coasts of the United States to Latin American ports.

D It shortens the sailing distance between the east and west coasts of the United States.

15. Which of the following was a result of the Sepoy Mutiny?

A The rise of an Indian nationalist movement

B The end of British direct rule in India

C The end of recruiting Indian troops for the British army

D The return of the Mogul ruler

Need Extra Help?							
If You Missed Questions . . .	9	10	11	12	13	14	15
Go to Page . . .	462	467	470	474	473	473	467

GO ON

16. Which of the following is a major reason why Latin American countries remained economically dependent after political independence?

A They imported raw materials and exported finished goods.

B They grew food instead of cash crops.

C They built factories instead of boosting farm production.

D They exported raw materials and imported finished goods.

17. "Europeans have a moral responsibility to civilize primitive people." This statement best expresses which of the following concepts?

A Social Darwinism

B nationalism

C the "white man's burden"

D the Monroe Doctrine

Analyze the chart and answer the question that follows. Base your answer on the chart and on your knowledge of world history.

Height of European Imperialism

European Power	Having Colonies in . . .		
	Southeast Asia	Africa	India
Britain	X	X	X
Belgium		X	
France	X	X	
Germany		X	
Italy		X	
Netherlands	X	X	
Portugal	X	X	
Spain	X	X	

18. A common phrase in the late nineteenth century was "the sun never sets on the _____ empire." To which country in the chart does this phrase refer?

A Spain

B France

C Germany

D Britain

Document-Based Questions

Directions: Analyze the document and answer the short answer questions that follow the document. Base your answers on the document and on your knowledge of world history.

Miguel Hidalgo, a parish priest living in a small village about 100 miles from Mexico City, had studied the French Revolution. Hidalgo roused the local Native Americans and mestizos to free themselves from Spanish rule. On September 16, 1810, Hidalgo's army attacked the Spaniards.

> *"My children, this day comes to us as a new dispensation. Are you ready to receive it? Will you be free? Will you make the effort to recover from the hated Spanish the lands stolen from your forefathers 300 years ago?"*

19. What emotions is Hidalgo trying to arouse?

20. Do you believe that Native Americans in North America are justified in feeling that their lands were stolen? Why or why not?

Extended Response

21. Colonialism affected people differently. Some thrived, while others suffered. Discuss the various concerns of people under colonial rule. Did social class affect how members of the native population viewed colonial rule? How were the concerns of different social classes similar? How were they different?

History ONLINE

For additional test practice, use Self-Check Quizzes—Chapter 14 at glencoe.com.

Need Extra Help?						
If You Missed Questions . . .	16	17	18	19	20	21
Go to Page . . .	476	451	485	485	485	454

STOP

CHAPTER 15

East Asia Under Challenge 1800–1914

Section 1 The Decline of the Qing Dynasty

Section 2 Revolution in China

Section 3 Rise of Modern Japan

MAKING CONNECTIONS

In what ways can one culture influence another?

During the Meiji Restoration, the imperial court was moved to the shogun's palace in Edo (now Tokyo). The palace was eventually replaced with the Japanese Imperial Palace, which houses the emperor and his family today. It has been rebuilt many times due to fires and war. It has been restored using traditional Japanese architecture. In this chapter you will learn how Japan emerged as an industrial society.

- What elements of traditional Japanese culture were affected by ideas of Western civilization?
- How has Japanese culture influenced life in the United States?

CHINA AND JAPAN ▶

THE WORLD ▶

| 1800 | 1830 | | | 1860 | |

1839
Opium War
begins in China

1853
U.S. asks
Japan to open
foreign relations

1867
Meiji
Restoration
begins in
Japan

1848
Nationalist revolutions
erupt in Europe

1879
Thomas Edison develops
the electric lightbulb

1899
Open Door Policy
with China
established

1911
Followers of
Sun Yat-sen launch
Chinese rebellion

1890   **1920**

1902
Africans defeated
in the Boer War

FOLDABLES™
Study Organizer

Japan
Before...   Japan
After...

Western Influence

**Identifying Cause
and Effect**
Create a Two-Tab Book to compare and
contrast Japan before and after Western
influence. Record differences in daily life,
women's roles, politics, and economics.

History ONLINE
Chapter Overview—Visit glencoe.com to preview Chapter 15.

The Decline of the Qing Dynasty

GUIDE TO READING

The BIG Idea
Competition Among Countries
As the Qing dynasty declined, Western nations increased their economic involvement with China.

Content Vocabulary
- extraterritoriality (p. 490)
- self-strengthening (p. 492)
- spheres of influence (p. 493)
- Open Door policy (p. 495)
- indemnity (p. 495)

Academic Vocabulary
- highlighted (p. 489)
- exclusive (p. 493)

People and Places
- Guangzhou (p. 489)
- Chang Jiang (p. 490)
- Hong Kong (p. 490)
- Hong Xiuquan (p. 490)
- Guang Xu (p. 493)
- Empress Dowager Ci Xi (p. 493)
- John Hay (p. 494)

Reading Strategy
Comparing and Contrasting As you read, create a chart like the one below to compare the Tai Ping and Boxer Rebellions.

	Tai Ping	Boxer
Reforms Demanded		
Method Used		
Outcomes		

China preferred to keep its culture free of Western influences. However, as the Qing government grew more unstable, the Western powers and Japan tightened their hold on the Chinese Empire. Foreign powers created spheres of influence and followed an Open Door policy to secure trading rights. The Chinese resisted but were eventually overcome, weakening the imperial government even more.

Causes of Decline

MAIN IDEA Pressure from the West and corruption and unrest from within led to the decline of the Qing dynasty.

HISTORY & YOU In grade school, did you ever see a bully use force to get something he wanted? Read to learn how Western powers used force to get what they wanted from China.

In 1800, after a long period of peace and prosperity, the Qing dynasty of the Manchus was at the height of its power. A little over a century later, however, humiliated and harassed by the Western powers, the Qing dynasty collapsed.

External and Internal Pressure

One important reason for the abrupt decline and fall of the Qing dynasty was the intense external pressure that the modern West applied to Chinese society. However, internal problems that the government was slow to address also played a role. For instance, Zhang Zhidong, a court official, argued against political reform:

PRIMARY SOURCE

"The doctrine of people's rights will bring us not a single benefit but a hundred evils. Are we going to establish a parliament? . . . there are still many today who are content to be vulgar and rustic. They are ignorant of the general situation in the world, they do not understand the basic system of the state. . . . Even supposing the confused and clamorous people are assembled in one house, for every one of them who is clear-sighted, there will be a hundred others whose vision is clouded; they will converse at random . . .—what use will it be?"

—*China's Response to the West: A Documentary Survey, 1839–1923,* Ssu-yu Teng and John K. Fairbank, eds., 1970

After an extended period of growth, the Qing dynasty began to suffer from corruption, peasant unrest, and incompetence. These weaknesses were made worse by rapid growth in the country's

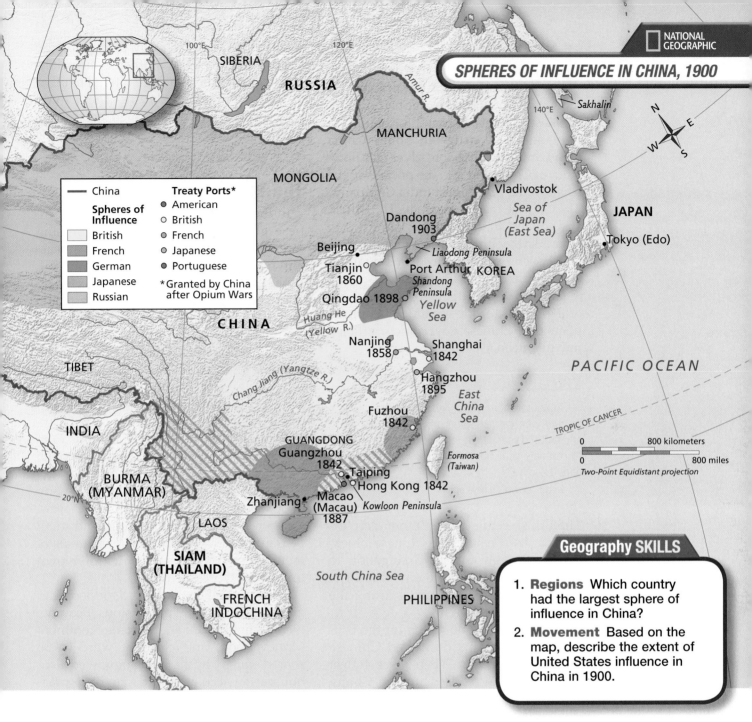

SPHERES OF INFLUENCE IN CHINA, 1900

100°E   120°E

SIBERIA

RUSSIA

MANCHURIA

Amur R.

140°E   Sakhalin

MONGOLIA

Vladivostok

China —   **Treaty Ports***
Spheres of Influence   ● American
    ○ British
☐ British   ● French
☐ French   ● Japanese
☐ German   ● Portuguese
☐ Japanese   *Granted by China after Opium Wars
☐ Russian

Dandong
1903

Sea of Japan (East Sea)

JAPAN

Tokyo (Edo)

Beijing

Liaodong Peninsula

Tianjin
1860

Port Arthur   KOREA

Shandong Peninsula

Qingdao 1898

Yellow Sea

CHINA

Huang He (Yellow R.)

Nanjing
1858

Shanghai
1842

PACIFIC OCEAN

TIBET

Chang Jiang (Yangtze R.)

Hangzhou
1895

East China Sea

Fuzhou
1842

INDIA

GUANGDONG
Guangzhou
1842

Formosa (Taiwan)

TROPIC OF CANCER

0   800 kilometers
0   800 miles

Two-Point Equidistant projection

20°N

BURMA
(MYANMAR)

Taiping
Hong Kong 1842

Zhanjiang

Macao
(Macau)
1887

Kowloon Peninsula

LAOS

SIAM
(THAILAND)

South China Sea

PHILIPPINES

FRENCH
INDOCHINA

Geography SKILLS

1. **Regions** Which country had the largest sphere of influence in China?

2. **Movement** Based on the map, describe the extent of United States influence in China in 1900.

---

population. By 1900, there were 400 million people in China. Population growth created a serious food shortage, and many people died of starvation. The ships, guns, and ideas of foreigners **highlighted** the growing weakness of the Qing dynasty and probably hastened its end.

By 1800, Europeans had been in contact with China for more than 200 years. Wanting to limit contact with outsiders, the Qing dynasty had restricted European merchants to a small trading outlet at **Guangzhou** (GWONG•JO), or Canton. The merchants could deal with only a few Chinese firms. The British did not like this arrangement.

Britain had an unfavorable trade balance with China. That is, they imported more goods from China than they exported to China. Britain had to pay China with silver for the difference between its imports—tea, silk, and porcelain—from China and its exports—Indian cotton—to China. At first, the British tried to negotiate with the Chinese to improve the trade imbalance. When negotiations failed, the British turned to trading opium.

History ONLINE

Student Web Activity—

Visit glencoe.com and complete the activity on Western influence in China.

The Opium War

Opium was grown in northern India under the sponsorship of the British East India Company and then shipped directly to Chinese markets. Demand for opium—a highly addictive drug—in South China jumped dramatically. Soon, silver was flowing out of China and into the pockets of the officials of the British East India Company.

The Chinese reacted strongly. The British were not the first to import opium into China. The Chinese government had already seen opium's dangerous qualities and had made its trade illegal. They appealed to the British government on moral grounds to stop the traffic in opium. Lin Zexu, a Chinese government official, wrote to Queen Victoria:

PRIMARY SOURCE

"Suppose there were people from another country who carried opium for sale to England and seduced your people into buying and smoking it; certainly your honorable ruler would deeply hate it and be bitterly aroused."
—Lin Zexu, a Chinese official

The British refused to halt their activity, however. As a result, the Chinese blockaded the foreign area in Guangzhou to force traders to surrender their opium. The British responded with force, starting the Opium War (1839–1842).

The Chinese were no match for the British. British warships destroyed Chinese coastal and river forts. When a British fleet sailed almost unopposed up the **Chang Jiang** (Yangtze River) to Nanjing, the Qing dynasty made peace.

In the Treaty of Nanjing in 1842, the Chinese agreed to open five coastal ports to British trade, limit taxes on imported British goods, and pay for the costs of the war. China also agreed to give the British the island of **Hong Kong.** Nothing was said in the treaty about the opium trade. Moreover, in the five ports, Europeans lived in their own sections and were subject not to Chinese laws but to their own laws—a practice known as **extraterritoriality.**

The Opium War marked the beginning of the establishment of Western influence in China. For the time being, the Chinese dealt with the problem by pitting foreign countries against one another. Concessions granted to the British were offered to other Western nations, including the United States. Soon, thriving foreign areas were operating in the five treaty ports along the southern Chinese coast.

The Tai Ping Rebellion

In the meantime, the failure of the Chinese government to deal with pressing internal economic problems led to a peasant revolt, known as the Tai Ping (TIE PING) Rebellion (1850–1864). It was led by **Hong Xiuquan,** a Christian convert who viewed himself as a younger brother of Jesus Christ.

Hong was convinced that God had given him the mission of destroying the Qing dynasty. Joined by great crowds of peasants, Hong captured the town of Yongan and proclaimed a new dynasty, the Heavenly Kingdom of Great Peace (*Tai Ping Tianguo* in Chinese—hence the name *Tai Ping Rebellion*).

The Tai Ping Rebellion appealed to many people because it called for social reforms. These reforms included giving land to all peasants and treating women as equals of men. Women even served in their own units in the Tai Ping army.

Hong's rebellion also called for people to give up their private possessions. Peasants were to hold lands and farms in common. Money, food, and clothing were to be shared equally by all. Hong outlawed alcohol and tobacco and eliminated the practice of binding women's feet. The Chinese Communist Revolution of the twentieth century (see Chapter 24) would have similar social goals.

In March 1853, the rebels seized Nanjing, the second largest city of the empire, and massacred 25,000 men, women, and children. The revolt continued for 10 more years but gradually began to fall apart. Europeans came to the aid of the Qing dynasty when they realized the destructive nature of the Tai Ping forces. As one British observer noted, there was no hope "of any good ever coming of the rebel movement. They do nothing but burn, murder, and destroy."

The Opium War

The Turks and Arabs were the first to trade opium in China. China's emperors tried to stop the spreading addiction but failed. Then in the 1830s, an official named Lin Zexu went after the traders. First he wrote to Queen Victoria, but she did not respond. Then he demanded that British merchants surrender a cargo of opium and dumped it into the sea. The outraged British sent warships and overwhelmed the Chinese, who were forced to sign the Treaty of Nanjing. This was the first of several unequal treaties the Chinese signed in the 1800s.

The Chinese war junks were no match for the superior firepower of the British ships.

The British steamship *Nemesis* was constructed of iron and armed with modern cannons.

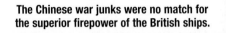

Opium Imported into China
(1 chest = approximately 135 pounds)

YEAR	NUMBER OF CHESTS PER YEAR
1729	200
1767	1,000
1830	10,000
1838	40,000

DOCUMENT-BASED QUESTIONS

This illustration, by E. Duncan, shows the British steamship *Nemesis* destroying Chinese war junks in Anson's Bay, 1841.

1. **Explaining** What is an unequal treaty? How does the illustration help to explain why China accepted an unequal treaty?
2. **Making Inferences** Do you think the British had mixed feelings about the Opium War? Explain.

In 1864, Chinese forces, with European aid, recaptured Nanjing and destroyed the remaining rebel force. The Tai Ping Rebellion was one of the most devastating civil wars in history. As many as 20 million people died during the 14-year struggle.

China's ongoing struggle with the West prevented the Qing dynasty from dealing effectively with the internal unrest. Beginning in 1856, the British and the French applied force to gain greater trade privileges. As a result of the Treaty of Tianjin in 1858, the Chinese agreed to legalize the opium trade and to open new ports to foreign trade. They also surrendered the Kowloon Peninsula to Great Britain. When the Chinese resisted parts of the treaty, the British seized Beijing in 1860.

Efforts at Reform

By the late 1870s, the Qing dynasty was in decline. Unable to restore order themselves, government troops had relied on forces recruited by regional warlords to help fight the Tai Ping Rebellion. To finance their armies, the warlords had collected taxes from local people. After the revolt, many of these warlords kept their armies.

With the support of the local gentry, the regional warlords continued to collect local taxes for their own use.

In its weakened state, the Qing court finally began to listen to the appeals of reform-minded officials. The reformers called for a new policy they called **"self-strengthening."** That is, China should adopt Western technology but keep its Confucian values and institutions.

Some reformers wanted to change China's traditional political institutions by introducing democracy. However, such ideas were too radical for most reformers. During the last quarter of the nineteenth century, the Chinese government tried to modernize China's military forces and build up industry without touching the basic elements of Chinese civilization. Railroads, weapons factories, and shipyards were built. However, the Chinese value system remained unchanged.

✓**Reading Check** **Summarizing** What did Britain do to fix their trade imbalance with China?

The Advance of Imperialism

MAIN IDEA Western nations and Japan set up spheres of influence in China to gain exclusive trading rights.

HISTORY & YOU Have you noticed that when a group considers options, a strong voice often sways its decision? Read how the emperor's aunt blocked reforms in China.

In the end, however, the changes did not help the Qing stay in power. The European advance into China continued during the last two decades of the nineteenth century. Internal conditions also continued to deteriorate.

Mounting Pressures

In the north and northeast, Russia took advantage of the Qing dynasty's weakness to force China to give up territories north of the Amur River in Siberia. Russia wanted both Manchuria and Mongolia and even had designs on Korea. Russia's designs on

PEOPLE in HISTORY

Guang Xu
1871–1908 Chinese Emperor

Attendants brought foreign mechanical toys to entertain the baby Emperor Guang Xu. As he grew, he became fascinated with Western inventions—telephones, phonographs, and bicycles. These influences convinced Guang Xu to set up a new educational system in China. Another factor played a key role as well—growing foreign intrusion: "Our scholars are now without solid and practical education; our artisans are without scientific instructors; when compared with other countries we soon see how weak we are. Does anyone think that our troops are as well drilled or as well led as those of the foreign armies? or that we can successfully stand against them? Changes must be made. . . ." **Why did Guang Xu set up a new educational system?**

Ci Xi
1835–1908 Chinese Empress

Though never the official ruler of China, Ci Xi was the power behind the throne for 47 years. When her young son became emperor, Ci Xi had herself appointed regent. After her son died, she appointed her four-year-old nephew, Guang Xu, to the throne, but continued as regent. When Guang Xu came of age, Ci Xi supposedly retired. But when he began making reforms, Ci Xi had him overthrown and resumed her regency. "I have often thought that I am the cleverest woman who ever lived . . . I have 400 million people all dependent on my judgment." She opposed modernization and supported the Boxers in their ill-fated rebellion against Western colonizers in 1900. Afterwards, she recognized the need to modernize, but too late to save the Qing dynasty. **How did Ci Xi react to the reforms of Guang Xu?**

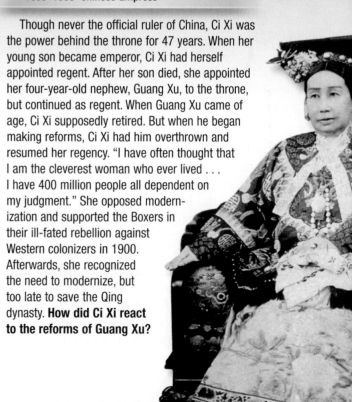

Korea threatened the Japanese. When Russia took military control of Manchuria, Britain signed an alliance with Japan. In Tibet, a struggle between Russia and Great Britain kept both powers from seizing the territory outright. This allowed Tibet to become free from Chinese influence.

Between the years of 1886 and 1895, the foreign powers tightened their hold on the Chinese Empire. Britain annexed Burma, made Sikkim a protectorate, and obtained the Tibetan town of Yadong, opening it to foreign trade. France occupied Laos in 1893. The Russian Trans-Siberian railway reached Lake Baikal by 1895.

Even more ominous changes were taking place in the Chinese heartland. European states began to create **spheres of influence,** areas where the imperial powers had **exclusive** trading rights. After the Tai Ping Rebellion, warlords in the provinces began to negotiate directly with foreign nations. In return for money, the warlords granted these nations exclusive trading rights or railroad-building and mining privileges. In this way, Britain, France, Germany, Russia, and Japan all established spheres of influence in China.

In 1894, another blow furthered the disintegration of the Qing dynasty. The Chinese went to war with Japan over Japanese inroads into Korea, a land that the Chinese had controlled for a long time. The Chinese were soundly defeated. As a reward, Japan demanded and received the island of Taiwan (known to Europeans at the time as Formosa) and the Liaodong (LYOW•DOONG) Peninsula. Fearing Japan's growing power, however, the European powers forced Japan to give the Liaodong Peninsula back to China.

New pressures for Chinese territory soon arose. In 1897, Chinese rioters murdered two German missionaries. Germany used this as a pretext to demand territories in the Shandong (SHON•DOONG) Peninsula. When the Chinese government approved the demand, other European nations made new claims on Chinese territory.

Internal Crisis

This latest scramble for territory took place at a time of internal crisis in China.

In June 1898, the young emperor **Guang Xu** (GWANG SHYOO) launched a massive reform program based on changes in Japan (see the discussion later in this chapter). During the following weeks, known as the One Hundred Days of Reform, the emperor issued edicts calling for major political, administrative, and educational reforms. With these reforms, Guang Xu intended to modernize government bureaucracy by following Western models. He also wanted to adopt a new educational system that would replace the traditional civil service examinations. His reforms included the adoption of Western-style schools and banks, and the institution of a free press. Guang Xu also intended to train the military to use modern weapons and Western fighting techniques.

Many conservatives at court, however, opposed these reforms. They saw little advantage in copying the West. As one said, "An examination of the causes of success and failure in government reveals that . . . the adoption of foreignism leads to disorder." According to this conservative, traditional Chinese rules needed to be reformed and not rejected in favor of Western changes.

Most important, **Empress Dowager Ci Xi** (TSUH•SEE), the emperor's aunt, opposed the new reform program. Ci Xi became a dominant force at court and opposed the emperor's reforms. With the aid of the imperial army, she eventually imprisoned the emperor. Other supporters of the reform were imprisoned, exiled, or prosecuted. These actions ended Guang Xu's reforms.

While Guang Xu's reform efforts aroused popular sympathy, they had limited support within Chinese society overall. His hasty measures damaged the careers of many scholars, losing much support for the reforms. Also, the reform efforts neglected agriculture, which was very important to China's future, and focused too heavily on the elite classes. Most notably, the reformers in power could not end foreign influence. Concluding that peaceful reform could never be achieved, some reformers began to consider revolution.

✓ **Reading Check** **Examining** What nations established spheres of influence in China?

Responses to Imperialism

MAIN IDEA The United States proposed an Open Door policy to guarantee it would have equal trading rights with European countries in China.

HISTORY & YOU What does an open door suggest to you? Read to learn how and why the United States proposed an Open Door policy in China.

As foreign pressure on the Qing dynasty grew stronger, both Great Britain and the United States feared that other nations would overrun the country should the Chinese government collapse. The annexation of Hawaii and the Philippines had encouraged the expansion of American interests in the Pacific. The United States now was fully engaged in expanding its stake in the global marketplace.

In 1899, U.S. secretary of state **John Hay** wrote a note to Britain, Russia, Germany, France, Italy, and Japan. Hay asked each country to respect equal trading opportunities in China. He also asked the powers with a sphere of influence not to set tariffs that would give an unfair advantage to the citizens of their own country. This note was not shown to the Chinese government. When none of the other imperialist governments expressed opposition to the idea, Hay proclaimed that all major states with economic interests in China had agreed that the country should have an Open Door policy.

POLITICAL CARTOONS   PRIMARY SOURCE

Open Door Policy

China is represented as a Chinese-style building, with dragons and an ornately carved door.

Guns, bayonets, and a German-style helmet appear in the open door.

Uncle Sam is shown as a traveling salesman.

Rogers: the Open Door.

In 1899 U.S. secretary of state John Hay sent notes to the major powers asking them to uphold "Chinese territorial and administrative" integrity and guarantee "equal and impartial trade with all parts of the Chinese Empire." Despite a general lack of response, Hay announced in 1900 that his Open Door policy had been approved.

After the Boxer Rebellion broke out, Hay promoted the following policy in a letter to various U.S. embassies:

"[T]he policy of the government of the United States is to seek a solution which may bring about permanent safety and peace to China, preserve Chinese territorial and administrative entity, protect all rights guaranteed to friendly powers by treaty and international law, and safeguard for the world the principle of equal and impartial trade with all parts of the Chinese Empire."

DOCUMENT-BASED QUESTIONS

To trade with China, the United States had to confront the European powers already established there.

1. **Analyzing** Why is Uncle Sam shown here with a briefcase and an umbrella?
2. **Predicting** What do you think would have happened if the United States had not stepped in with its Open Door policy?

Opening the Door to China

In part, the **Open Door policy** reflected American concern for the survival of China. However, it also reflected the interests of some U.S. trading companies. These companies wanted to operate in open markets and disliked the existing division of China into separate spheres of influence dominated by individual states.

The Open Door policy did not end the system of spheres of influence. However, it did reduce restrictions on foreign imports imposed by the dominating power within each sphere. The Open Door policy also helped to reduce imperialist hysteria over access to the China market. The policy lessened fears in Britain, France, Germany, and Russia that other powers would take advantage of China's weakness and attempt to dominate the China market for themselves.

The Boxer Rebellion

The Open Door policy came too late to stop the Boxer Rebellion. Boxer was the popular name given to members of a secret organization called the Society of Harmonious Fists. Members practiced a system of exercise—a form of shadowboxing, or boxing with an imaginary opponent— that they thought would protect them from bullets.

The Boxers were upset by the foreign takeover of Chinese lands. Their slogan was "destroy the foreigner." They especially disliked Christian missionaries and Chinese converts to Christianity who seemed to threaten Chinese traditions. At the beginning of 1900, Boxer bands roamed the countryside and slaughtered foreign missionaries and Chinese Christians. Their victims also included foreign businessmen and even the German envoy to Beijing.

Response to the killings of missionaries and Chinese Christians was immediate and overwhelming. When William II, emperor of Germany, learned of the envoy's fate, he sent German troops to China and declared:

PRIMARY SOURCE

"Show no mercy! Take no prisoners! . . . the Huns of King Attila made a name for themselves . . . impose the name of Germany in China . . . in such a way that no Chinese will ever dare look askance at a German again."

—Jean Chesneaux, Marianne Bastid, and Marie-Claire Bergère, *China: From the Opium Wars to the 1911 Revolution*

An allied army consisting of 20,000 British, French, German, Russian, American, and Japanese troops attacked Beijing in August 1900. The army restored order and demanded more concessions from the Chinese government. The Chinese government was forced to pay a heavy **indemnity**—a payment for damages—to the powers that had crushed the uprising. The imperial government was now weaker than ever.

✓ Reading Check **Explaining** How did the Boxers get their name?

SECTION 1 REVIEW

Vocabulary

1. **Explain** the significance of: highlighted, Guangzhou, Chang Jiang, Hong Kong, extraterritoriality, Hong Xiuquan, self-strengthening, spheres of influence, exclusive, Guang Xu, Empress Dowager Ci Xi, John Hay, Open Door policy, indemnity.

Main Ideas

2. **Summarize** the factors that led to the decline of the Qing dynasty by using a diagram like the one below.

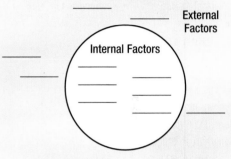

3. **Explain** how Western nations and Japan gained exclusive trading rights in China.

4. **List** the countries that supplied troops for the allied army, which was formed to fight the Boxers in 1900.

Critical Thinking

5. **The BIG Idea** **Making Inferences** Why did European nations agree to follow the Open Door policy proposed by the U.S.?

6. **Drawing Conclusions** Why did foreign powers help the Chinese government put down the Boxer Rebellion?

7. **Analyzing Visuals** In what ways does the cartoon on page 494 depict China as a difficult place in which to gain entry?

Writing About History

8. **Expository Writing** Using outside sources, research, write, and present a report on the effects of population growth on modern China. Include government laws to curtail population growth and explain the consequences of disobeying these laws.

History ONLINE

For help with the concepts in this section of *Glencoe World History— Modern Times*, go to glencoe.com and click Study Central.

Revolution in China

GUIDE TO READING

The BIG Idea
Self-Determination Reforms led to a revolution in China, and the arrival of Westerners brought changes to its culture and economy.

Content Vocabulary
• provincial *(p. 496)* • commodities *(p. 499)*

Academic Vocabulary
• phase *(p. 497)* • motive *(p. 499)*

People and Places
• Sun Yat-sen *(p. 496)*
• Henry Pu Yi *(p. 498)*
• General Yuan Shigai *(p. 498)*
• Shanghai *(p. 500)*
• Wuhan *(p. 500)*

Reading Strategy
Comparing and Contrasting As you read, create a chart like the one below listing the reforms requested by Sun Yat-sen and those implemented by Empress Dowager Ci Xi.

Sun Yat-sen's Proposals	Empress Dowager Ci Xi's Reform

After the Boxer Rebellion failed, China made desperate reform efforts. However, when Empress Dowager Ci Xi died in 1908, the Qing dynasty was near collapse. China slipped into revolution and civil war. Early twentieth-century Chinese culture reflected the country's struggle between the old and the new as Confucian social ideas declined and Western influences increased.

The Fall of the Qing

MAIN IDEA Sun Yat-sen led a successful revolution to end the Qing dynasty, but he was unable to establish a stable government.

HISTORY & YOU Do you find it hard to change, once you are used to doing things a certain way? Read to learn how resistance to change led to the downfall of the Qing dynasty.

After the Boxer Rebellion, the Qing dynasty in China tried desperately to reform itself. Empress Dowager Ci Xi, who had long resisted suggestions from her advisers for change, now embraced a number of reforms in education, administration, and the legal system.

A new educational system based on the Western model replaced the civil service examination system. In 1909, legislative assemblies were formed at the **provincial,** or local, level. Elections for a national assembly were even held in 1910.

The emerging new elite, composed of merchants, professionals, and reform-minded gentry, soon became impatient with the slow pace of political change. They were angry when they discovered that the new assemblies were not allowed to pass laws but could only give advice to the ruler. Moreover, the recent reforms had done nothing for the peasants, artisans, and miners, whose living conditions were getting worse as taxes increased. Unrest grew in the countryside as the dynasty continued to ignore deep-seated resentments.

The Rise of Sun Yat-sen

The first signs of revolution appeared during the last decade of the nineteenth century, when the young radical **Sun Yat-sen** formed the Revive China Society. Sun Yat-sen believed that the Qing dynasty was in a state of decay and could no longer govern the country. Unless the Chinese were united under a strong government, they would remain at the mercy of other countries. Although Sun believed that China should follow the pattern of Western countries, he also knew that the Chinese people were hardly ready for democracy.

Sun instead developed a three-stage reform process. The first stage would be a military takeover. In the second stage, a

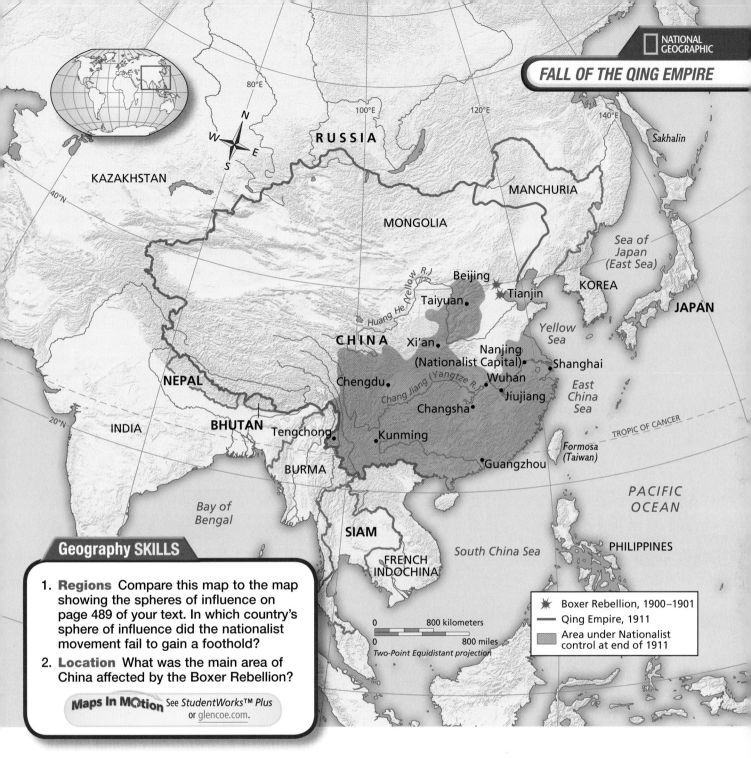

Sakhalin

80°E

100°E

120°E

140°E

RUSSIA

KAZAKHSTAN

40°N

MANCHURIA

MONGOLIA

Sea of
Japan
(East Sea)

Beijing

Tianjin

KOREA

Taiyuan

JAPAN

Huang He (Yellow R.)

CHINA

Xi'an

Yellow
Sea

Nanjing
(Nationalist Capital)

Shanghai

Chengdu

Wuhan

NEPAL

Chang Jiang (Yangtze R.)

Jiujiang

East
China
Sea

Changsha

20°N

BHUTAN

Tengchong

Kunming

TROPIC OF CANCER

INDIA

Formosa
(Taiwan)

BURMA

Guangzhou

Bay of
Bengal

PACIFIC
OCEAN

SIAM

South China Sea

PHILIPPINES

**FRENCH
INDOCHINA**

0   800 kilometers

0   800 miles

Two-Point Equidistant projection

✴ Boxer Rebellion, 1900–1901

— Qing Empire, 1911

▨ Area under Nationalist
control at end of 1911

Geography SKILLS

1. **Regions** Compare this map to the map showing the spheres of influence on page 489 of your text. In which country's sphere of influence did the nationalist movement fail to gain a foothold?

2. **Location** What was the main area of China affected by the Boxer Rebellion?

Maps In MOtion See *StudentWorks™ Plus* or glencoe.com.

transitional **phase,** Sun's own revolutionary party would prepare the people for democratic rule. The final stage called for establishment of a constitutional democracy.

At a convention in Tokyo in 1905, Sun united members of radical groups from across China and formed the Revolutionary Alliance, which eventually became the Nationalist Party. In presenting his program, Sun Yat-sen called for the following changes:

PRIMARY SOURCE

"Establish the Republic: Now our revolution is based on equality, in order to establish a republican government. All our people are equal and all enjoy political rights. . . . Equalize land ownership: The good fortune of civilization is to be shared equally by all the people of the nation. . . . Its [the land's] present price shall be received by the owner, but all increases in value . . . after the revolution shall belong to the state, to be shared by all the people."

—*Sources of Chinese Tradition,* W.T. de Bary et al., eds., 1960

Sun's new organization advocated his Three People's Principles, which promoted nationalism, democracy, and the right for people to pursue their own livelihoods. Although the new organization was small, it benefited from the rising discontent generated by the Qing dynasty's failure to improve conditions in China.

The Revolution of 1911

The Qing dynasty was near its end. In 1908, Empress Dowager Ci Xi died. Her nephew Guang Xu, a prisoner in the palace, died one day before his aunt. The throne was now occupied by China's "last emperor," the infant **Henry Pu Yi.**

In October 1911, followers of Sun Yat-sen launched an uprising in central China. At the time, Sun was traveling in the United States. Thus, the revolt had no leader, but the government was too weak to react. The Qing dynasty collapsed, opening the way for new political forces.

Sun's party had neither the military nor the political strength to form a new government. The party was forced to turn to a member of the old order, **General Yuan Shigai** (YOO•AHN SHUR•GIE), who controlled the army.

Yuan was a prominent figure in military circles, and he had been placed in charge of the imperial army sent to suppress the rebellion. Instead, he abandoned the government and negotiated with members of Sun Yat-sen's party. General Yuan agreed to serve as president of a new Chinese republic and to allow the election of a legislature. Sun himself arrived in China in January 1912, after reading about the revolution in a Denver, Colorado, newspaper.

In the eyes of Sun Yat-sen's party, the events of 1911 were a glorious revolution that ended 2,000 years of imperial rule. However, the 1911 uprising was hardly a revolution. It produced no new political or social order. Sun Yat-sen and his followers still had much to accomplish.

PEOPLE in HISTORY

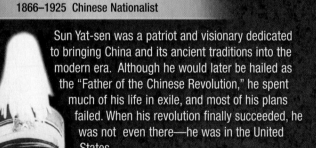

Sun Yat-sen
1866–1925 Chinese Nationalist

Sun Yat-sen was a patriot and visionary dedicated to bringing China and its ancient traditions into the modern era. Although he would later be hailed as the "Father of the Chinese Revolution," he spent much of his life in exile, and most of his plans failed. When his revolution finally succeeded, he was not even there—he was in the United States.

Sun hoped to create a modern republic in China, but he would never fully realize his dream. Two years before his death, he wrote: "Following China's war with France (1883-1884) I made up my mind to devote myself to the revolution. . . . Up to present the task of revolution, however, has not yet been completed. A span of thirty-seven years of my revolutionary work is to be chronicled by future historians. . . ." **What was Sun Yat-sen's dream for China?**

General Yuan Shigai
1859–1916 Chinese military ruler

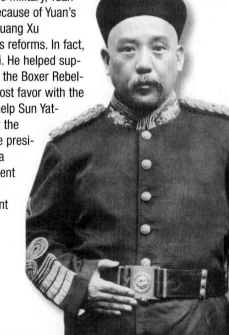

In the late 1800s, Japan and China competed for influence in Korea. There, a young Chinese diplomat, Yuan Shigai, learned how to manipulate political and military power to serve his own ends. After war with Japan destroyed the Chinese military, Yuan modernized a new force. Because of Yuan's military reforms, Emperor Guang Xu assumed Yuan supported his reforms. In fact, Yuan remained loyal to Ci Xi. He helped suppress the reforms and later, the Boxer Rebellion. When Ci Xi died, Yuan lost favor with the Qing rulers. He decided to help Sun Yat-sen's nationalists overthrow the emperor in exchange for the presidency. Yuan's opposition to a republican form of government soon became clear. He dissolved the elected parliament and tried to take the title of emperor, triggering a revolt. **What led to the revolt against Yuan's rule?**

The Revolutionary Alliance was supported mainly by an emerging urban middle class, and its program was based largely on Western liberal democratic principles. However, the urban middle class in China was too small to support a new political order. Most of the Chinese people still lived on the land, and few peasants supported Sun Yat-sen's party. In effect, then, the events of 1911 were less a revolution than a collapse of the old order.

An Era of Civil War

After the collapse of the Qing dynasty, the military took over. Sun Yat-sen and his colleagues had accepted General Yuan Shigai as president of the new Chinese republic in 1911 because they lacked the military force to compete with his control over the army. Many feared that if the revolt lapsed into chaos, the Western powers would intervene. If that happened, the last shreds of Chinese independence would be lost. However, even the general's new allies distrusted his **motives.**

Yuan understood little of the new ideas sweeping into China from the West. He ruled in a traditional manner and even tried to set up a new imperial dynasty. The reformers hated Yuan for using murder and terror to destroy the new democratic institutions. The traditionalists (those who supported the Qing) hated Yuan for being disloyal to the dynasty he had served.

Yuan's dictatorial efforts rapidly led to clashes with Sun's party, now renamed the *Guomindang,* or Nationalist Party. When Yuan dissolved the new parliament, the Nationalists launched a rebellion. The rebellion failed, and Sun Yat-sen fled to Japan.

Yuan was strong enough to brush off the challenge from the revolutionary forces, but he could not turn back history. He died in 1916 and was succeeded by one of his officers. Over the next several years, China slipped into civil war as the power of the central government disintegrated and military warlords seized power in the provinces. Their soldiers caused massive destruction throughout China.

✓ **Reading Check** **Explaining** Why did rebellions occur after General Yuan Shigai became president?

Cultural Changes

MAIN IDEA Western culture had a dramatic effect on many Chinese people, especially those living in cities.

HISTORY & YOU Can you identify foreign influences on your lifestyle? Read to learn how Westerners influenced Chinese culture.

Western influences forced the Chinese to adapt to new ways of thinking and living. Early twentieth-century Chinese culture reflected the struggle between Confucian social ideas and those of the West. These changes were most striking in the cities.

Society in Transition

When European traders began to move into China in greater numbers in the mid-1800s, Chinese society was already in a state of transition. The growth of industry and trade was especially noticeable in the cities, where a national market for such **commodities**—marketable products—as oil, copper, salt, tea, and porcelain had appeared.

The Chinese economy had never been more productive. Faster and more reliable transportation and a better system of money and banking had begun to create the foundation for a money economy. Foreign investments in China grew rapidly, and the money went into modernizing the Chinese economy. New crops brought in from abroad increased food production and encouraged population growth.

The coming of Westerners to China affected the Chinese economy in three ways. Westerners: (1) introduced modern means of transportation and communications; (2) created an export market; and (3) integrated the Chinese market into the nineteenth-century world economy.

To some, these changes were beneficial. Shaking China out of its old ways quickened a process of change that had already begun. Western influences forced the Chinese to adopt new ways of thinking and acting, and Western ideas stimulated the desire to modernize. Westerners also provided something else to the Chinese.

They gave them a model, funds, and the technical knowledge to modernize.

At the same time, however, China paid a heavy price for the new ways. Imperialism imposed a state of dependence on China, and many Chinese were exploited. In these ways, imperialism condemned the country to a condition of underdevelopment. Its local industry was largely destroyed. Also, many of the profits in the new economy went to foreign countries rather than back into the Chinese economy.

During the first quarter of the twentieth century, the pace of change in China quickened even more. After World War I, which temporarily drew foreign investment out of the country, Chinese businesspeople began to develop new ventures. **Shanghai** became the bastion of the new bourgeoisie. People lived in Shanghai at the same rhythm they lived in other modern cities. **Wuhan**, Tianjin, and Guangzhou also became major industrial and commercial

centers with a growing middle class and an industrial working class.

Culture in Transition

In 1800, daily life for most Chinese was the same as it had been for centuries. Most were farmers, living in millions of villages in rice fields and on hillsides throughout the countryside. A farmer's life was governed by the harvest cycle, village custom, and family ritual. A few men were educated in the Confucian classics. Women remained in the home or in the fields. All children were expected to obey their parents, and wives were expected to submit to the wishes of their husbands.

A visitor to China 125 years later would have seen a different society, although it would still have been recognizably Chinese. The changes were most striking in the cities. Here the educated and wealthy had been visibly affected by the growing

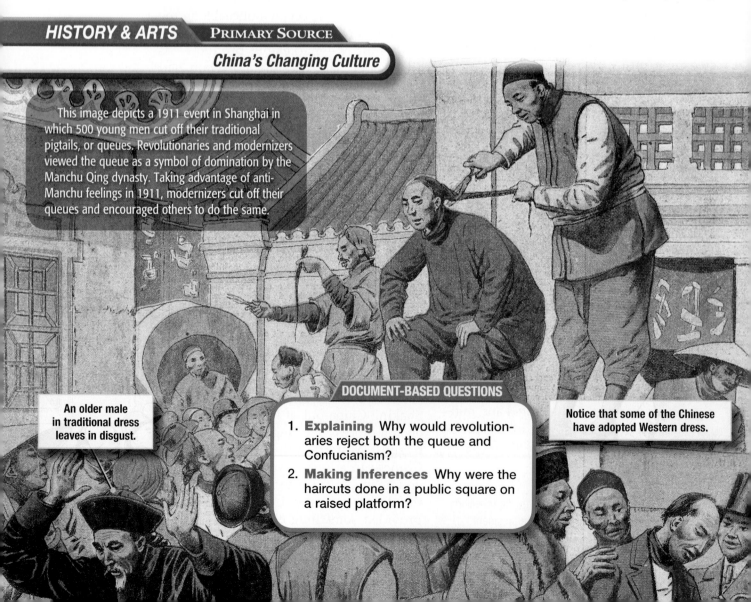

HISTORY & ARTS   PRIMARY SOURCE

China's Changing Culture

This image depicts a 1911 event in Shanghai in which 500 young men cut off their traditional pigtails, or queues. Revolutionaries and modernizers viewed the queue as a symbol of domination by the Manchu Qing dynasty. Taking advantage of anti-Manchu feelings in 1911, modernizers cut off their queues and encouraged others to do the same.

An older male in traditional dress leaves in disgust.

Notice that some of the Chinese have adopted Western dress.

DOCUMENT-BASED QUESTIONS

1. **Explaining** Why would revolutionaries reject both the queue and Confucianism?

2. **Making Inferences** Why were the haircuts done in a public square on a raised platform?

Western cultural presence. Confucian social ideas were declining rapidly in influence, and those of Europe and North America were on the rise.

Nowhere in China was the struggle between old and new more visible than in the culture. Radical reformers wanted to eliminate traditional culture, condemning it as an instrument of oppression. They were interested in creating a new China that would be respected by the modern world.

The first changes in traditional culture came in the late nineteenth century. Intellectuals began to introduce Western books, paintings, music, and ideas to China. By the first quarter of the twentieth century, China was flooded by Western culture as intellectuals called for a new culture based on that of the modern West.

Western literature and art became popular in China, especially among the urban middle class. Traditional culture, however, remained popular with the more conservative elements of the population, especially in rural areas. Most creative artists followed foreign trends, while traditionalists held on to Chinese culture.

Literature in particular was influenced by foreign ideas. Western novels and short stories began to attract a larger audience. Although most Chinese novels written after World War I dealt with Chinese subjects, they reflected the Western tendency toward a realistic portrayal of society. Often, they dealt with the new Westernized middle class. Most of China's modern authors showed a clear contempt for the past.

Mao Dun became known as one of China's best modern novelists. *Midnight,* Dun's most popular work, was also published in French and English. A naturalistic novel, *Midnight* described the changing customs of Shanghai's urban elites.

Ba Jin, the author of numerous novels and short stories, was one of China's foremost writers at the turn of the century. Born in 1904, Ba Jin was well attuned to the rigors and expected obedience of Chinese family life. In his trilogy, *Family, Spring,* and *Autumn,* he describes the disintegration of traditional Confucian ways as the younger members of a large family attempt to break away from their elders.

Ba Jin dedicated most of his energy to writing. He would sometimes retreat to his study to write for a whole year. Ba Jin once described his compulsion to express himself:

PRIMARY SOURCE

"Before my eyes are many miserable scenes, the suffering of others and myself forces my hands to move. I become a machine for writing."

—Ba Jin, *China Daily*

✓ **Reading Check** **Describing** What effects did Western culture have on China?

SECTION 2 REVIEW

Vocabulary
1. **Explain** the significance of: provincial, Sun Yat-sen, phase, Henry Pu Yi, General Yuan Shigai, motive, commodities, Shanghai, Wuhan.

Main Ideas
2. **List** the three stages in Sun Yat-sen's process for reform. What principles did he hope to promote in China?

3. **Describe** the attitudes toward Western culture held by Chinese in rural and urban areas. Which of these two groups do you think benefited more from Western involvement in China?

4. **Summarize** the changes resulting from European traders's contact with China in the mid-nineteenth century, using a diagram like the one below.

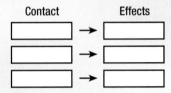

Contact → Effects

Critical Thinking
5. **The BIG Idea** **Sequencing** Why did the reforms introduced by Empress Dowager Ci Xi and General Yuan Shigai fail to improve the way China was governed?

6. **Defending** Foreign imperialism offered China more advantages than disadvantages. Defend this position.

7. **Analyzing Visuals** What elements in the image on page 500 reflect China's struggle between the old and the new?

Writing About History
8. **Expository Writing** Research and compare the reasons why both the United States and China experienced civil war. Write an essay offering alternatives to war that might have solved the internal problems of one of the two nations.

History ONLINE

For help with the concepts in this section of *Glencoe World History— Modern Times,* go to glencoe.com and click Study Central.

Rise of Modern Japan

GUIDE TO READING

The BIG Idea
Competition Among Countries
Western intervention opened Japan to trade, and the interaction between Japan and Western nations led to a modern industrial Japanese society.

Content Vocabulary
• concessions *(p. 502)*   • prefectures *(p. 504)*

Academic Vocabulary
• subsidy *(p. 505)*   • context *(p. 507)*

People and Places
• Matthew Perry *(p. 502)*
• Edo Bay *(p. 502)*
• Millard Fillmore *(p. 502)*
• Kyōto *(p. 503)*
• Mutsuhito *(p. 504)*
• Edo *(p. 504)*
• Ito Hirobumi *(p. 504)*
• Port Arthur *(p. 507)*

Reading Strategy
Categorizing Information As you read, create a table like the one below listing the promises contained in the Charter Oath of 1868 and the provisions of the Meiji constitution of 1890.

Charter Oath	Constitution

In the mid-nineteenth century, the United States forced Japan to open its doors to trade with Western nations. After the Sat-Cho alliance overthrew the shogun, the Meiji Restoration began. Japan emerged as a modern industrial society.

Japan Responds to Foreign Pressure

MAIN IDEA Under military pressure from the United States, Japan signed the Treaty of Kanagawa, which opened two ports to Western trade.

HISTORY & YOU What products would you have to give up if the United States stopped importing foreign goods? Read to find out why Japan decided to open its ports to trade with other countries.

By the end of the nineteenth century, Japan was emerging as a modern imperialist power. The Japanese followed the example of Western nations, while trying to preserve Japanese values.

An End to Isolation

By 1800, the Tokugawa shogunate had ruled Japan for 200 years. The Tokugawa had maintained an isolationist policy, keeping formal relations only with Korea and allowing only Dutch and Chinese merchants at Nagasaki. Western nations wanted to end Japan's isolation, believing that the expansion of trade on a global basis would benefit all nations.

The first foreign power to succeed with Japan was the United States. In the summer of 1853, Commodore **Matthew Perry** arrived in **Edo Bay** (now Tokyo Bay) with an American fleet of four warships. Perry sought "to bring a singular and isolated people into the family of civilized nations." Perry brought a letter from President **Millard Fillmore,** asking the Japanese for better treatment of sailors shipwrecked on the Japanese islands. (Foreign sailors shipwrecked in Japan were treated as criminals and exhibited in public cages.) He also asked to open foreign relations between the United States and Japan. Perry returned about six months later for an answer, this time with a larger fleet. Having discussed the issue, some shogunate officials recommended **concessions,** or political compromises. The guns of Perry's ships ultimately made Japan's decision.

Under military pressure, Japan agreed to the Treaty of Kanagawa with the United States. The treaty provided for the return of shipwrecked American sailors, opened two ports to Western traders, and established a U.S. consulate in Japan. In 1858, U.S. consul Townsend Harris signed a more detailed treaty. It called for the opening of several new ports to U.S. trade and residence, as well as an exchange

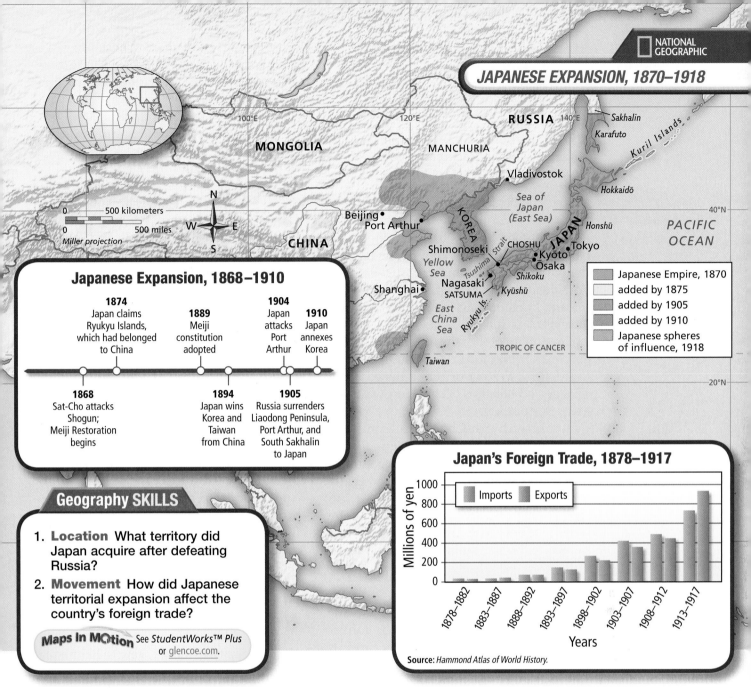

JAPANESE EXPANSION, 1870–1918

RUSSIA

Sakhalin
Karafuto
Kuril Islands

MONGOLIA

MANCHURIA

Vladivostok

Sea of
Japan
(East Sea)

Hokkaidō

PACIFIC
OCEAN

40°N

Beijing
Port Arthur

KOREA

Shimonoseki
Yellow
Sea

CHOSHU
JAPAN
Kyōto
Tokyo
Osaka

Honshū

CHINA

Nagasaki
SATSUMA

Shikoku
Kyūshū

Shanghai

East
China
Sea

Ryukyu Is.

Tsushima Strait
Tsushima

TROPIC OF CANCER

Taiwan

20°N

140°E

100°E   120°E

Japanese Expansion, 1868–1910

1874 Japan claims Ryukyu Islands, which had belonged to China	**1889** Meiji constitution adopted	**1904** Japan attacks Port Arthur **1910** Japan annexes Korea

1868 Sat-Cho attacks Shogun; Meiji Restoration begins

1894 Japan wins Korea and Taiwan from China

1905 Russia surrenders Liaodong Peninsula, Port Arthur, and South Sakhalin to Japan

Legend:
- Japanese Empire, 1870
- added by 1875
- added by 1905
- added by 1910
- Japanese spheres of influence, 1918

0   500 kilometers
0   500 miles
Miller projection

N
W   E
S

Geography SKILLS

1. **Location** What territory did Japan acquire after defeating Russia?
2. **Movement** How did Japanese territorial expansion affect the country's foreign trade?

Maps In MOtion See *StudentWorks™ Plus* or glencoe.com.

Japan's Foreign Trade, 1878–1917

Millions of yen: 1000, 800, 600, 400, 200, 0

■ Imports   ■ Exports

Years: 1878–1882, 1883–1887, 1888–1892, 1893–1897, 1898–1902, 1903–1907, 1908–1912, 1913–1917

Source: *Hammond Atlas of World History.*

of ministers. Japan soon signed similar treaties with several European nations.

Resistance to the New Order

Resistance to opening foreign relations was especially strong among the samurai warriors in two southern territories, Satsuma and Choshu. In 1863, the Sat-Cho alliance (from Satsuma-Choshu) forced the shogun to promise to end relations with the West. The rebellious groups soon showed their weakness, however. They had no experience with Western military pressure. When Choshu troops fired on Western ships in the Strait of Shimonoseki,

the Westerners fired back. The Choshu fortifications were destroyed.

The incident made the Sat-Cho alliance more determined not to give in to the West. When the shogun did not take a stronger position against the foreigners, the Sat-Cho leaders demanded that he resign and restore the emperor's power. In January 1868, the Sat-Cho attacked the shogun's palace in **Kyōto.** After a few weeks, the shogun's forces collapsed, ending the shogunate system and beginning the Meiji Restoration.

✓**Reading Check** **Identifying** What events led to the collapse of the shogunate system in Japan?

The Meiji Restoration

MAIN IDEA The Meiji government attempted to modernize Japan's political, economic, and social structures.

HISTORY & YOU What views did American political parties express in the last election? Read to learn about the issue that gave rise to Japan's first political parties.

The Sat-Cho leaders had genuinely mistrusted the West, but they soon realized that Japan must change to survive. The new leaders embarked on a policy of reform, transforming Japan into a modern industrial nation.

The symbol of the new era was the young emperor **Mutsuhito.** He called his reign the Meiji (MAY•jee), or "Enlightened Rule." This period has thus become known as the Meiji Restoration.

Of course, the Sat-Cho leaders controlled the Meiji ruler, just as the shogunate had controlled earlier emperors. In recognition of the real source of political power, the capital was moved from Kyōto to **Edo** (now named Tokyo), the location of the new leaders. The imperial court was moved to the shogun's palace in the center of the city.

Transformation of Politics

Once in power, the new leaders moved first to abolish the old order and to strengthen power in their hands. To undercut the power of the daimyo—the local nobles—the new leaders stripped these great lords of the titles to their lands in 1871. As compensation, the lords were given government bonds and were named governors of the territories formerly under their control. The territories were now called **prefectures.**

The Meiji reformers set out to create a modern political system based on the Western model. In 1868, the new leaders signed a Charter Oath, in which they promised to create a new legislative assembly within the framework of continued imperial rule. Although the daimyo were given senior positions in the new government, the modernizing leaders from the Sat-Cho

group held the key posts. The country was divided into 75 prefectures. (The number was reduced to 45 in 1889 and remains at that number today.)

During the next 20 years, the Meiji government undertook a careful study of Western political systems. A commission under **Ito Hirobumi** traveled to Great Britain, France, Germany, and the United States to study their governments.

As the process evolved, two main factions appeared, the Liberals and the Progressives. The Liberals wanted political reform based on the Western liberal democratic model, which vested supreme authority in the parliament as the representative of the people. The Progressives wanted power to be shared between the legislative and executive branches, with the executive branch having more control.

During the 1870s and 1880s, these factions fought for control. In the end, the Progressives won. The Meiji constitution, adopted in 1889, was modeled after that of Imperial Germany. Most authority was given to the executive branch.

In theory, the emperor exercised all executive authority, but in practice he was a figurehead. Real executive authority rested in the hands of a prime minister and his cabinet of ministers. These ministers were handpicked by the Meiji leaders.

Under the new constitution, the upper house included royal appointments and elected nobles, while the lower house was elected. The two houses were to have equal legislative powers.

The final result was a political system that was democratic in form but authoritarian in practice. Although modern in external appearance, it was still traditional because power remained in the hands of a ruling oligarchy (the Sat-Cho leaders). Although a new set of institutions and values had emerged, the system allowed the traditional ruling class to keep its influence and economic power.

Meiji Economics

The Meiji leaders also set up a land reform program, which made the traditional lands of the daimyo into the private property of the peasants. The Meiji leaders then levied a new land tax, which was set at an annual rate of three percent of the estimated value of the land. The new tax was an excellent source of revenue for the government. However, it was quite burdensome for the farmers.

Under the old system, farmers had paid a fixed percentage of their harvest to the landowners. In bad harvest years, they had owed little or nothing. Under the new system, the farmers had to pay the land tax every year, regardless of the quality of the harvest.

As a result, in bad years, many peasants were unable to pay their taxes. This forced them to sell their lands to wealthy neighbors and become tenant farmers who paid rent to the new owners. By the end of the nineteenth century, about 40 percent of all farmers were tenants.

With its budget needs met by the land tax, the government turned to the promotion of industry. The chief goal of the reformers was to create a "rich country and a strong state" to guarantee Japan's survival against the challenge of Western nations.

The Meiji government gave **subsidies** to needy industries, provided training and foreign advisers, improved transportation and communications, and started a new educational system that stressed applied science. By 1900, Japan's industrial sector was beginning to grow. Besides tea and silk, other key industries were weapons, shipbuilding, and sake (SAH•kee), or Japanese rice wine.

From the start, a unique feature of the Meiji model of industrial development was the close relationship between government and private business. The government encouraged the development of new industries by providing businesspeople with money and privileges. Once an individual enterprise or industry was on its feet, it was turned over entirely to private ownership. Even then, however, the government continued to play some role in the industry's activities.

CONNECTING TO THE UNITED STATES

MADE IN JAPAN

In the nineteenth century, the Meiji government opened Japan to trade with the outside world. Today, Japan is the fourth-largest trading partner of the United States. A strong work ethic and mastery of technology combined with a government-industry partnership have helped Japan become the world's third-largest economy. Some Japanese companies have grown into multinational corporations, with offices and factories all over the world. For example, Japan's Toyota Company is the fourth-largest carmaker in the United States. By 2006, Toyota had 12 plants in the United States and Canada.

This photo shows Japanese workers assembling cell phones.

Common Japanese products sold to Americans:

- Nintendo Game Boys
- Sega video games
- Sony televisions and cameras
- Honda and Toyota cars
- Panasonic phones and DVD players

CONNECTING TO TODAY

1. **Applying** Name a Japanese product that you own or use often.

2. **Making Inferences** Why do you think Toyota has located factories in the United States?

The Westernization of Japan

Japanese artist Hiroshige III created these woodblock prints just seven years after the Meiji Restoration opened the door to Western trade and ideas. The artist recorded a changing Japan. Western technology, such as railways and telegraph wires, connected the country. Western styles of architecture and clothing mixed with traditional Japanese styles. This style of Japanese print, called *ukiyo-e* ("pictures of the floating world"), also influenced Western art. These prints made a big impact on French impressionists like Claude Monet and Edgar Degas, who imitated their use of a flatter perspective and asymmetrical composition.

Tokyo-Yokohama railway

Western-style dress

Telegraph wires

Western-style houses

DOCUMENT-BASED QUESTIONS

This series of prints, called *"Famous Places on the Tokaido: a Record of the Process of Reform"* (1875), shows evidence of Western influence on Japanese life.

1. **Identifying** What style of Western art did Hiroshige's work influence?
2. **Identifying Points of View** Based on these prints, how did Western ideas affect Japan? Explain.

Military and Education

The Meiji reformers also transformed other institutions. A key focus of their attention was the military. The reformers were well aware that Japan would need a modern military force to compete with the West.

A new imperial army based on compulsory military service was formed in 1871. All Japanese men now served for three years. The new army was well equipped with modern weapons.

Education also changed. The Meiji leaders realized the need for universal education, including instruction in modern technology. A new ministry of education, established in 1871, adopted the American model of elementary schools, secondary schools, and universities. It brought foreign specialists to Japan to teach and it sent many students to study abroad.

Much of the content of the new educational system was Western in inspiration. However, a great deal of emphasis was still placed on the virtues of loyalty to the family and community. Loyalty to the emperor was especially valued.

Modern Social Structure

Before the Meiji reforms, the lives of all Japanese people were determined by their membership in a family, village, and social class. Japanese society was highly hierarchical. Belonging to a particular social class determined a person's occupation and social relationships with others.

Women were especially limited by the "three obediences": child to father, wife to husband, and widow to son. Husbands could easily obtain a divorce; wives could not. Marriages were arranged, and the average marital age of females was 16 years. Females did not share inheritance rights with males. Few received any education outside the family.

The Meiji Restoration had a marked effect on the traditional social system in Japan. Special privileges for the aristocracy were abolished. For the first time, women were allowed to seek an education. As the economy shifted from an agricultural to an industrial base, thousands of Japanese began to get new jobs and establish new social relationships.

Western fashions and culture became the rage. The ministers of the first Meiji government were known as the "dancing cabinet" because they loved Western-style ballroom dancing. A new generation of modern boys and girls began to imitate the clothing styles, eating habits, hairstyles, and social practices of European and American young people. The game of baseball was imported from the United States.

The social changes brought about by the Meiji Restoration also had a less attractive side. Many commoners were ruthlessly exploited in the coal mines and textile mills. Workers labored up to 20 hours a day, often under conditions of incredible hardship. Coal miners employed in Nagasaki worked in temperatures up to 130 degrees Fahrenheit (54 degrees C). When they tried to escape, they were shot.

Resistance to such conditions was not unknown. In many areas, villagers sought new political rights and demanded increased attention to human rights. A popular rights movement of the 1870s laid the groundwork for one of Japan's first political parties. It campaigned for a government that would reflect the will of the people.

The transformation of Japan into a "modern society" did not detach the country entirely from its old values, however. Traditional values based on loyalty to the family and community were still taught in the new schools.

Traditional Japanese values were also given a firm legal basis in the 1889 constitution, which limited the right to vote to men. The Civil Code of 1898 played down individual rights and placed women within the **context** of their family role.

✓ Reading Check **Explaining** How was Japan's government structured under the Meiji constitution?

Joining the Imperialists

MAIN IDEA By the early 1900s, Japan strengthened its military and started building an empire.

HISTORY & YOU What benefits did the British receive from their colonies in America? Read to find out why Japan wanted colonies.

The Japanese soon copied the imperialist Western approach to foreign affairs. A small, densely populated nation, Japan lacked resources and had no natural room to expand. The Japanese knew that Western nations had amassed some of their wealth and power because of their colonies. Those colonies had provided sources of raw materials, inexpensive labor, and markets for manufactured products. To compete, Japan also wanted to expand.

Beginnings of Expansion

The Japanese began their program of territorial expansion close to home. In 1874, Japan claimed control of the Ryukyu (ree•YOO•KYOO) Islands, which belonged to the Chinese Empire. Two years later, Japan's navy forced the Koreans to open their ports to Japanese trade. The Chinese grew concerned by Japan's growing influence there.

In the 1880s, Chinese-Japanese rivalry over Korea intensified. In 1894, the two nations went to war, and Japan won. In the treaty ending the war, China recognized Korea's independence. China also ceded (transferred) Taiwan and the Liaodong Peninsula, with its strategic naval base at **Port Arthur,** to Japan. In time, the Japanese gave the Liaodong Peninsula back to China.

Rivalry with Russia over influence in Korea had led to increasingly strained relations. The Russians thought little of the Japanese and even welcomed the possibility of war. One adviser to Nicholas II said, "We will only have to throw our caps at them and they will run away."

War with Russia

In 1904, Japan launched a surprise attack on the Russian naval base at Port Arthur, which Russia had taken from China in 1898. The Russian troops proved to be inferior.

The Russian commander in chief said, "It is impossible not to admire the bravery and activity of the Japanese. The attack of the Japanese is a continuous succession of waves, and they never relax their efforts by day or by night."

In the meantime, Russia had sent its Baltic fleet halfway around the world to East Asia, only to be defeated by the new Japanese navy off the coast of Japan. After their defeat, the Russians agreed to a humiliating peace in 1905. They gave the Liaodong Peninsula back to Japan, as well as the southern part of Sakhalin (SA•kuh•LEEN), an island north of Japan. The Japanese victory stunned the world. Japan had become one of the great powers.

U.S. Relations

When Japan established a sphere of influence in Korea, the United States recognized Japan's role there. In return, Japan recognized American authority in the Philippines. In 1910, Japan annexed Korea outright.

Some Americans began to fear the rise of Japanese power in East Asia. Japan resented U.S. efforts to restrict immigration. In 1907, President Theodore Roosevelt made a "gentlemen's agreement" with Japan that essentially stopped Japanese immigration to the United States.

✓ **Reading Check** **Explaining** Why did Japan turn itself into an imperialist power?

JAPAN BECOMES AN IMPERIAL POWER

When Matthew Perry's fleet steamed into Edo Bay in 1854, the Japanese saw "giant dragons puffing smoke." Never before had they seen ships powered by steam or carrying such large guns. The Japanese soon began to modernize their military.

After a decisive victory over China in 1894, Japan gained territory and influence in Korea. Russia, however, remained a formidable rival blocking Japan's ambitions in Korea and Manchuria.

In 1904, Japan unleashed its technologically advanced navy on the Russian naval base at Port Arthur, in Manchuria. This battle began the Russo-Japanese War. Japan's victory in the war stunned the world.

SIGNIFICANCE OF THE RUSSO-JAPANESE WAR OF 1904–1905
Marked the first victory of an Asian nation over a European power in modern times
Made Japan one of the world's great powers
Gave Japan a foothold in Manchuria
Reinforced Japan as the dominant power in Korea
Ended Russia's expansion in East Asia

DOCUMENT-BASED QUESTIONS

This woodcut shows Japanese warships engaging the Russian fleet at Port Arthur in 1904.

1. **Explaining** How did the Russo-Japanese War affect the balance of power in East Asia?

2. **Analyzing** Why do you think Japan's victory in the Russo-Japanese War stunned the world?

Culture in an Era of Transition

MAIN IDEA The culture of Western nations greatly influenced Japanese traditional culture.

HISTORY & YOU Do you own anything made in Japan? Read to learn about early cultural contact between the United States and Japan.

Contact with Western nations greatly influenced Japanese culture during the late-nineteenth and early-twentieth centuries. From literature to architecture, the Japanese copied Western techniques and styles. The exchange of cultures went both ways, however. Japanese art also influenced Westerners.

New Western Model

The wave of Western technology and ideas that entered Japan in the last half of the nineteenth century greatly altered the shape of traditional Japanese culture. Literature was especially affected. Dazzled by European literature, Japanese authors began translating and imitating the imported models.

The novel showed the greatest degree of change. People began to write novels that were patterned after the French tradition of realism. Naturalist Japanese authors tried to present existing social conditions and the realities of war as objectively as possible.

Other aspects of Japanese culture were also changed. The Japanese invited technicians, engineers, architects, and artists from Europe and the United States to teach their "modern" skills to eager Japanese students. The Japanese copied Western artistic techniques and styles. Huge buildings of steel and reinforced concrete, adorned with Greek columns, appeared in many Japanese cities.

A Return to Tradition

A national reaction had begun by the end of the nineteenth century, however. Many Japanese artists began to return to older techniques. In 1889, the Tokyo School of Fine Arts was established to promote traditional Japanese art. Japanese artists searched for a new but truly Japanese means of expression. Some artists tried to bring together native and foreign techniques. Others returned to past artistic traditions for inspiration.

Cultural exchange also went the other way. Japanese arts and crafts, porcelains, textiles, fans, folding screens, and woodblock prints became fashionable in Europe and North America. Japanese gardens, with their close attention to the positioning of rocks and falling water, became especially popular in the United States.

✓ Reading Check **Describing** What effect did Japanese culture have on other nations?

SECTION 3 REVIEW

Vocabulary
1. **Explain** the significance of: Matthew Perry, Edo Bay, Millard Fillmore, concessions, Kyōto, Mutsuhito, Edo, prefectures, Ito Hirobumi, subsidy, context, Port Arthur.

Main Ideas
2. **Identify** the benefits that the Treaty of Kanagawa granted to the United States.

3. **Explain** how Japan's Liberals and Progressives differed on the question of which government branch should hold the most power. Which group won?

4. **Illustrate** the results of Western influence on Japanese culture by using a diagram like the one below.

Western Influence on Japanese Culture

Critical Thinking
5. **The BIG Idea** **Evaluating** How did the Japanese land reform program create internal problems?

6. **Comparing** Compare the rights of Japanese women before and after the Meiji Restoration.

7. **Analyzing Visuals** Examine the images on page 506. How do these prints show a mixing of Western and Japanese cultures?

Writing About History
8. **Persuasive Writing** Pretend that you wish to study abroad in China or Japan. Write a letter of application stating which country you would like to visit and why. State what you hope to learn while abroad, and how you would overcome or minimize the drawbacks of being a foreign student.

History ONLINE

For help with the concepts in this section of *Glencoe World History—Modern Times*, go to glencoe.com and click Study Central.

Social History

Sumo Wrestling: The Sport of Giants

Wrestling in Asia began more than 2,400 years ago. In Japan, Shinto practices helped produce sumo by the third century A.D. By the eighth century, Japanese leaders were holding imperial sumo tournaments at court, while warriors embraced it as a martial art. Official rules made sumo a professional sport in the eighteenth century.

Major sumo tournaments in the 1800s were held in temporary open-air theaters built on Shinto temple grounds. These theaters could hold up to 3,000 spectators.

The roof over a sumo ring was designed to resemble a Shinto shrine. The four pillars represented the four seasons.

Sumo wrestlers were the earliest sports heroes in Japan and were especially popular with fans in their home province.

After 1780, four elders sat on the platform with their backs to the pillars. These sumo elders served as judges for the match.

THE NATIONAL SPORT OF JAPAN

Tanikaze Kajinosuke and Onogawa Kisaburo were the top sumo wrestlers of the late eighteenth century. Their intense rivalry greatly boosted the sport's popularity. In 1909, a new national stadium cemented sumo's status. Wrestlers eat a special diet to increase weight, while they train to build speed, power, and stamina. Underneath the exterior of a sumo wrestler is a muscular and agile body.

Referees wear heavy silk kimonos resembling those once worn by samurai and black imperial hats similar to those traditionally worn by Shinto priests.

In modern Japan, only sumo wrestlers are allowed to wear the topknot—the traditional symbol of samurai rank.

The loincloth worn by sumo wrestlers was first developed in the eighteenth century. When unfolded, the silk or cotton loincloth is 2.5 feet wide and more than 30 feet long.

A sumo wrestler wins a match by forcing his opponent out of the central circle or by forcing him to touch the ground with anything other than the soles of his feet.

Common sumo techniques include charging, pushing, sidestepping, slapping, and throwing. Matches are often over in a few seconds.

THE CEREMONY OF SUMO

Closely linked to Shinto roots, sumo includes centuries-old rituals. Before a match each contestant stamps on the floor and scatters salt around the ring to drive away demons and purify the competition area. Its link to the country's most ancient religion further strengthens the sport's place in Japanese culture. Sumo tournaments continue to draw capacity crowds and large television audiences.

ANALYZING VISUALS

1. **Interpreting** Why do you think modern sumo competitions continue to include Shinto rituals?

2. **Making Inferences** What does sumo wrestling reveal about the cultural significance of sports?

CHAPTER **15** Visual Summary

 You can study anywhere, anytime by downloading quizzes and flash cards to your PDA from glencoe.com.

SALE OF BRITISH GOODS TO CHINA

Britain established a sphere of influence in Guangzhou, China.

IMPERIALISM in China

- The Qing dynasty began to decline due to pressure from the West and internal corruption.
- Western nations and Japan created spheres of influence in China to gain exclusive trading rights.
- In order to secure its own trading rights, the United States proposed an Open Door trading policy.

REVOLUTION AND TRANSITION in China

- After China failed to reform, Sun Yat-sen led a rebellion that ended the Qing dynasty.
- Lacking military and political strength, Sun was unable to establish a stable government.
- European traders brought new ideas to China that changed the lives of many Chinese.

THE REVOLUTION OF 1911 BRINGS AN END TO THE QING DYNASTY

Imperial officials flee from the city of Tientsin during the Chinese revolution.

COMMODORE PERRY ARRIVES IN EDO BAY TO NEGOTIATE OPENING OF TRADE WITH JAPAN

Many credit Japan's rapid modernization to the Western technology that Perry introduced. Here he presents a model train to the Japanese.

TRADE AND IMPERIALISM of Japan

- After signing the Treaty of Kanagawa, Japan opened two ports for Western trade.
- The Meiji government tried to modernize its political, economic, and social structure.
- Japan built up its military and began expanding its territory.
- Western ideas and technology influenced Japanese culture.

STANDARDIZED TEST PRACTICE

TEST-TAKING TIP

When you read a map, pay careful attention to the title and to the map legend. The legend gives information crucial to understanding the map. The information in the legend may also help you eliminate answer choices that are incorrect.

Reviewing Vocabulary

Directions: Choose the word or words that best complete the sentence.

1. China formed legislative assemblies at the _____, or local, level.

   A provincial

   B global

   C regional

   D maritime

2. European states created _____ in China for their exclusive trading rights.

   A Open Door policies

   B self-strengthening policies

   C spheres of influence

   D extraterritoriality

3. Some shogunate officials recommended _____, or political compromises, to the U.S. trade proposals.

   A indemnities

   B prefectures

   C commodities

   D concessions

4. For damages that the Boxer Rebellion caused, China had to pay an _____.

   A invoice

   B indemnity

   C armistice

   D executive order

Reviewing Main Ideas

Directions: Choose the best answers to the following questions.

Section 1 *(pp. 488–495)*

5. The Qing dynasty restricted European merchants to a small trading outlet at what port?

   A Guangzhou

   B Chang Jiang

   C Hong Kong

   D Wuhan

6. Who led the Tai Ping Rebellion?

   A Henry Pu Yi

   B Hong Xiuquan

   C Guang Xu

   D Sun Yat-sen

7. Why did U.S. secretary of state John Hay propose the Open Door policy?

   A To gain a sphere of influence in China for the United States

   B To prevent a Chinese rebellion against Western imperialists

   C To prevent rival imperialists from expanding into other parts of Asia

   D To assure equal access to the Chinese market for all nations

Section 2 *(pp. 496–501)*

8. Who formed the Revolutionary Alliance in China in 1905?

   A Guang Xu

   B Henry Pu Yi

   C Sun Yat-sen

   D Hong Xiuquan

Need Extra Help?								
If You Missed Questions . . .	1	2	3	4	5	6	7	8
Go to Page . . .	496	493	502	495	489	490	494	497

9. Who was China's last emperor?

   A Sun Yat-sen

   B Henry Pu Yi

   C Ci Xi

   D Guang Xu

10. Early twentieth-century Chinese culture reflected a struggle between Western social ideas and what traditional Chinese beliefs?

    A Confucian

    B Shinto

    C Islamic

    D Hindu

Section 3 (pp. 502–509)

11. What United States president sent Matthew Perry to deliver a letter to Japan?

    A Theodore Roosevelt

    B James Monroe

    C Millard Fillmore

    D Woodrow Wilson

12. What does *Meiji* mean in English?

    A Enlightened reform

    B Majestic rule

    C Emancipated reform

    D Enlightened rule

13. The attack on Port Arthur began the war between what two nations?

    A Japan and Korea

    B China and Japan

    C Japan and Russia

    D China and Korea

Critical Thinking

Directions: Choose the best answers to the following questions.

Use the following map and your knowledge of world history to answer question 14.

Japanese Expansion 1873–1910

14. Which statement below is true?

    A Japan won a large amount of Manchuria territory from China.

    B Japan went to war with Russia after annexing Korea.

    C Japan won the Ryukyu Islands from Russia.

    D Japan won influence over Taiwan from China.

15. What is the main reason why Emperor Guang Xu's reform efforts failed?

    A Empress Dowager Ci Xi opposed them.

    B They favored agriculture, not the elite classes.

    C They ended the influence of foreigners.

    D The conservatives supported them.

Need Extra Help?							
If You Missed Questions . . .	9	10	11	12	13	14	15
Go to Page . . .	498	499	502	504	507	514	493

16. Why did Chinese reformers accept General Yuan Shigai as president of their new republic?

 A The majority of the peasants supported Yuan.

 B Yuan controlled the army.

 C The reformers trusted Yuan's clear support for democratic institutions.

 D Yuan promised to be an enlightened emperor.

17. Which statement below expresses a true comparison between the Boxer Rebellion and the Tai Ping Rebellion?

 A The Boxer Rebellion lasted longer than the Tai Ping Rebellion.

 B The Tai Ping Rebellion was aimed at the Qing dynasty, and the Boxer Rebellion was aimed at outsiders.

 C The leaders of both rebellions were anti-Christian.

 D The Tai Ping rebels were upset by the foreign takeover of Chinese lands, but the Boxer rebels sought social reforms.

The cartoon below, showing the Russian bear and a man representing Japan, was published just before the Russo-Japanese War. Base your answer to question 18 on this cartoon.

18. Which of the following statements best expresses the message in the cartoon?

 A Russia wants to provoke war, while Japan wants to avoid it.

 B If the confrontation leads to war, Japan will surely win.

 C Confronting Russia is a risky move for Japan.

 D The Russians fear Japanese military strength.

Document-Based Questions

Directions: Analyze the document and answer the short-answer questions that follow the document. Base your answers on the document and on your knowledge of world history.

Zhang Zhidong, a leading Chinese court official, argued:

> "The doctrine of people's rights will bring us not a single benefit but a hundred evils. Are we going to establish a parliament? Among the Chinese scholars and people there are still many today who are content to be vulgar and rustic. They are ignorant of the general situation in the world, they do not understand the basic system of the state."

19. What does Zhang Zhidong think about the Chinese people?

20. Based on what you have learned of the Qing dynasty, why would a court official be against forming a parliament? What did a parliament represent to Chinese traditionalists?

Extended Response

21. To build a "rich country and a strong state," the Japanese government subsidized (provided funds for) its industries. Evaluate the reasons for Japan's decision. The potential need for subsidy is not unique to Japan. Imagine that you are the president of a newly colonized island. Explain how you would promote the growth of industry on your island.

History ONLINE

For additional test practice, use Self-Check Quizzes—Chapter 15 at **glencoe.com**.

Need Extra Help?						
If You Missed Questions . . .	16	17	18	19	20	21
Go to Page . . .	498–499	490, 495	515	515	515	504

Step Lively!

Those looking to trip the light fantastic should head south of the border. In cities from Havana, Cuba, to Buenos Aires, Argentina, the exuberance and passion of Latin American countries is on display in their popular dances. A melting pot of African, native, and European cultures has produced many new styles of dance. Here are a few types of this fantastic footwork.

Tango: Workers created this dramatic dance in Buenos Aires, in the last quarter of the 19th century. It borrows from African rhythms and from such traditional dances as waltzes. As a couple moves around the dance floor, one partner may stop while the other dances around him or her.

Samba: This was once part of Carnival parades in Brazil. Dancers move their feet only a few inches and bend one knee at a time. They raise and lower their hips in time to the music.

Rumba: The rumba began in Havana in the 1890s as an Afro-Cuban dance. The dancers' movements are very slow and rhythmic, with much hip movement and boxlike steps.

Merengue: Originating in the Dominican Republic in the 18th century, the merengue is a series of fast steps. Partners stand side to side and circle each other in short steps, always holding each other's hands. Although the music is fast, the dancers keep their upper bodies still.

CHRISTEL GERSTENBERG/CORBIS

The tango

VERBATIM

" In a week, I suppose, I shall think it very natural, but the subservience of the natives to a handful of white men, who have got into this country, shocks me at the moment. "

FANNY EDEN,
*sister of a British official,
on arriving in India in 1836*

" Men of the South! It is better to die on your feet than to live on your knees. "

EMILIANO ZAPATA,
*guerrilla leader who fought in the
Mexican Revolution of 1911*

" An individual should not have too much freedom. A nation should have absolute freedom. "

SUN YAT-SEN,
*the leader of the Nationalist revolution
in China that toppled the imperial government and replaced it with a republic*

" It was the secrets of heaven and earth that I desired to learn. "

VICTOR FRANKENSTEIN,
*on his goal of bringing
the Monster to life, in the 1818 novel
Frankenstein, by Mary Shelley*

Q & A: AN ENGLISH FACTORY WORKER TELLS ALL

Not everyone's life has been improved by the Industrial Revolution. Take factory workers, for example. They must toil long hours in mind-numbing, often dangerous jobs. This eye-opening interview took place in 1832 between 53-year-old Charles Aberdeen, who started working in a cotton factory at the age of 12, and members of the British House of Commons.

Q [Parliament members]: Is [your job] dangerous employment?

A [Aberdeen]: Very dangerous [for new workers], but they get used to it.

Q: Are the hours shorter or longer at present, than when you were apprentice to a cotton mill?

A: Much the same. . . . I have done twice the quantity of work that I used to do, for less wages. Machines have been speeded.

Q: Has this increased labour any visible effect upon the appearance of the children?

A: It causes a paleness. A factory child may be known easily from another child that does not work in a factory.

Q: What is the age to which those that have been accustomed from early youth to work in factories survive?

A: I think that most of them die under forty.

CLASSIC IMAGE/ALAMY

STAPLETON COLLECTION/CORBIS

Spreading the Word

Great Britain has received more than trade benefits from India, its prize territory. The British Empire's "jewel in the crown" has given Britain the gift of words. Many Indian words have been incorporated into the English language, from curry to jungle. Here are just a few of these linguistic emigrants. However, one of the words is not Indian. Can you guess which?

1. bandanna
2. juggernaut
3. thug
4. pajamas
5. loot
6. khaki
7. shampoo
8. safari
9. candy
10. bungalow
11. guru
12. cot

Answer: 8

BY THE NUMBERS

8 Hours it took to take the first photograph, called a "heliograph," by Frenchman Joseph Niépce in 1826

90.4 Percentage of Africa controlled by colonial powers in 1900

3 The number of countries out of 13 on the South American mainland that have not gained independence at the end of the 19th century

285 Number of athletes that competed in the first modern Olympic Games, held in Athens, Greece, in 1896

POPPERFOTO/ALAMY

32 The millions of people who died from lack of food during famines in India between 1800 and 1900

Milestones

DIED. GEORGE GORDON, Lord Byron, in 1824, at age 36, after a brief illness. The English Romantic poet is one of today's most famous and controversial writers. Among his works are *Childe Harold's Pilgrimage* and *Don Juan.* Like the subjects of his writings, Byron was a rebellious antihero. At the time of Byron's death, he was fighting for Greece's independence from Turkey. To Greeks, he is not an anti-hero—he is a hero.

ABOLISHED. SLAVERY in the British Empire, by the Slavery Abolition Act of 1833. Slave holders have been paid for freeing the people they had enslaved. In one instance, the British government gave plantation owners in the Caribbean a total of 20 million pounds.

AWARDED. THE NOBEL PRIZE for Chemistry in 1911, to Marie Curie, for the discovery of the elements polonium and radium. Madame Curie is so intensely focused on her experiments with radium, she carries around test tubes of it and stores the radioactive material in her desk. This top scientist is sure to have an even more glowing future!

INFECTED. CATTLE IN AFRICA by a disease called rinderpest. By 1897, the contagious virus had killed between 90 and 95 percent of all cattle. It also took large numbers of buffalo, giraffes, antelopes, and warthogs. The epidemic has caused starvation among Africans and has also affected the social life of many ethnic groups: for cattle owners, their animals are an important source of wealth and power.

CRITICAL THINKING

1. **Identifying Central Issues** What conclusion do you think the members of the House of Commons who interviewed Charles Aberdeen came to about factory conditions?

2. **Hypothesizing** What social effects might the death of cattle have had on Africans?

UNIT 4

The Twentieth-Century Crisis
1914–1945

▶ Why It Matters

The period between 1914 and 1945 was one of the most destructive in the history of humankind. As many as 60 million people died as a result of World Wars I and II, the global conflicts that began and ended this era. As World War I was followed by revolutions, the Great Depression, totalitarian regimes, and the horrors of World War II, it appeared to many that European civilization had become a nightmare. By 1945, the era of European domination over world affairs had been severely shaken. With the decline of Western power, a new era of world history was about to begin.

CHAPTER 16   WAR AND REVOLUTION
              1914–1919

CHAPTER 17   THE WEST BETWEEN THE WARS
              1919–1939

CHAPTER 18   NATIONALISM AROUND THE WORLD
              1919–1939

CHAPTER 19   WORLD WAR II
              1939–1945

German troops march into Prague in 1939 during the Nazi invasion of Czechoslovakia, illustrating the upheaval of World War II.

CHAPTER 16

War and Revolution 1914–1919

Section 1 The Road to World War I

Section 2 World War I

Section 3 The Russian Revolution

Section 4 End of World War I

MAKING CONNECTIONS

How can new technology affect warfare?

In World War I, new war technology such as the tank and machine gun contributed to a loss of life never before experienced in war. Soldiers living in muddy trenches were exposed to rats, lice, and disease while constantly under threat of attack. In this chapter you will learn about many aspects of World War I and the Russian Revolution.

- What other inventions made World War I more devastating than previous wars?
- What new technologies have been used in more recent wars?

EUROPE AND THE UNITED STATES ▶

1914
Assassination of Archduke Ferdinand sparks WWI

1917
United States enters the war

The Russian Revolution begins

1914   1916

THE WORLD ▶

1912
Italians attempt to seize Libya during the Italian-Turkish War

1915
Armenians are victims of genocide by Turkey

1918
Germany
agrees
to truce

1919
U.S. President
Wilson helps
form the League
of Nations

1918

1918
Worldwide influenza
epidemic begins

1919
Gandhi begins his
nonviolent campaign in India

FOLDABLES™
Study Organizer

Pre-Revolution
and
Anti-Communist
Forces

Revolution
and
Communist
Forces

Russia

Analyzing Make a
Two-Tab Book to orga-
nize information you read about the
Russian Revolution. Under the first tab,
record political, social, and economic
events that led to the revolution. Under
the second tab, record political and military events that brought the Communists
to power.

History ONLINE

Chapter Overview—Visit glencoe.com to preview Chapter 16.

The Road to World War I

GUIDE TO READING

The BIG Idea
Competition Among Countries
Militarism, nationalism, and a crisis in the Balkans led to World War I.

Content Vocabulary
• conscription *(p. 523)*   • mobilization *(p. 525)*

Academic Vocabulary
• military *(p. 523)*   • complex *(p. 523)*

People, Places, and Events
• Triple Alliance *(p. 522)*
• Triple Entente *(p. 522)*
• Serbia *(p. 524)*
• Archduke Francis Ferdinand *(p. 524)*
• Bosnia *(p. 524)*
• Gavrilo Princip *(p. 524)*
• Emperor William II *(p. 524)*
• Czar Nicholas II *(p. 525)*
• General Alfred von Schlieffen *(p. 525)*

Reading Strategy
Determining Cause and Effect
As you read, create a diagram like the one below to identify the factors that led to World War I.

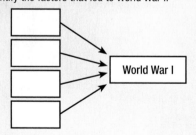

As European countries formed alliances and increased the sizes of their armed forces, they set the stage for a global war. All they needed was a good reason to mobilize troops. Another crisis in the Balkans in the summer of 1914 led directly to the conflict. When a Serbian terrorist assassinated Archduke Francis Ferdinand and his wife, the powder keg exploded.

Causes of the War

MAIN IDEA Nationalism, militarism, and a system of alliances contributed to the start of World War I.

HISTORY & YOU Have you ever defended a friend who was being criticized? Read to find out how a system of alliances led to the start of World War I.

Nineteenth-century liberals believed that if European states were organized along national lines, these states would work together and create a peaceful Europe. They were wrong. The system of nation-states that emerged in Europe in the last half of the nineteenth century led not to cooperation but to competition.

Nationalism and Alliances

Rivalries over colonies and trade grew during an age of frenzied nationalism and imperialist expansion. At the same time, Europe's great powers had been divided into two loose alliances. Germany, Austria-Hungary, and Italy formed the **Triple Alliance** in 1882. France, Great Britain, and Russia created the **Triple Entente** in 1907.

In the early years of the twentieth century, a series of crises tested these alliances. Especially troublesome were the crises in the Balkans between 1908 and 1913. These events left European states angry at each other and eager for revenge. Self-interest and success guided each state. They were willing to use war to preserve their power.

Nationalism in the nineteenth century had yet another serious result. Not all ethnic groups had become nations. Slavic minorities in the Balkans and the Hapsburg Empire, for example, still dreamed of their own national states. The Irish in the British Empire and the Poles in the Russian Empire had similar dreams.

Internal Dissent

National desires were not the only source of internal strife at the beginning of the 1900s. Socialist labor movements also had grown more powerful. The Socialists were increasingly inclined to use strikes, even violent ones, to achieve their goals.

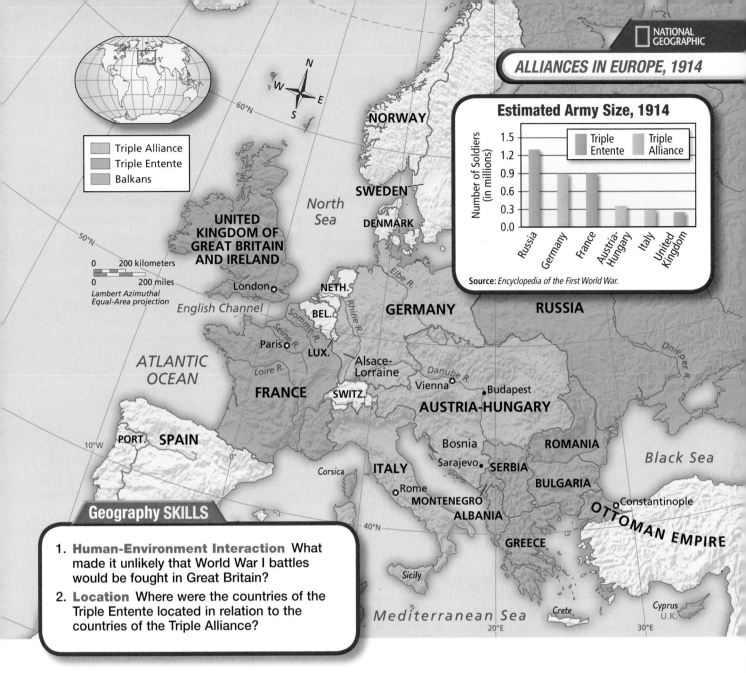

ALLIANCES IN EUROPE, 1914

Triple Alliance
Triple Entente
Balkans

Estimated Army Size, 1914

Number of Soldiers (in millions)

Triple Entente | Triple Alliance

Source: *Encyclopedia of the First World War.*

Geography SKILLS

1. **Human-Environment Interaction** What made it unlikely that World War I battles would be fought in Great Britain?

2. **Location** Where were the countries of the Triple Entente located in relation to the countries of the Triple Alliance?

Some conservative leaders, alarmed at the increase in labor strife and class division, feared that European nations were on the verge of revolution. This desire to suppress internal disorder may have encouraged various leaders to take the plunge into war in 1914.

Militarism

The growth of mass armies after 1900 heightened the existing tensions in Europe. These large armies made it obvious that if war did come, it would be highly destructive.

Most Western countries had established **conscription,** a **military** draft, as a regular practice before 1914. (The United States and

Britain were exceptions.) European armies doubled in size between 1890 and 1914.

Militarism—the aggressive preparation for war—was growing. As armies grew, so too did the influence of military leaders. They drew up vast and **complex** plans for quickly mobilizing millions of soldiers and enormous quantities of supplies in the event of war.

Fearing that any changes would cause chaos in the armed forces, military leaders insisted that their plans could not be altered. This left European political leaders with little leeway. In 1914 they had to make decisions for military instead of political reasons.

✓ **Reading Check** **Determining Cause and Effect** What were some major causes of World War I?

The Outbreak of War

MAIN IDEA Serbia's determination to become a large, independent state angered Austria-Hungary and started hostilities.

HISTORY & YOU What circumstances today might influence the United States to enter a war on behalf of an ally? Read to learn how an assassination led to a world war.

Militarism, nationalism, and the desire to stifle internal dissent may all have played a role in the starting of World War I. However, it was the decisions that European leaders made in response to a crisis in the Balkans that led directly to the conflict.

Assassination in Sarajevo

By 1914, Serbia, supported by Russia, was determined to create a large, independent Slavic state in the Balkans. Austria-Hungary, which had its own Slavic minorities to contend with, was equally determined to prevent that from happening.

On June 28, 1914, **Archduke Francis Ferdinand,** the heir to the throne of Austria-Hungary, and his wife Sophia visited the city of Sarajevo (SAR•uh•YAY•voh) in Bosnia. A group of conspirators waited there in the streets.

In that group was **Gavrilo Princip,** a 19-year-old Bosnian Serb. Princip was a member of the Black Hand, a Serbian terrorist organization that wanted Bosnia to be free of Austria-Hungary and to become part of a large Serbian kingdom. An assassination attempt earlier that morning by one of the conspirators had failed. Later that day, however, Princip succeeded in fatally shooting both the archduke and his wife.

Austria-Hungary Responds

The Austro-Hungarian government did not know whether or not the Serbian government had been directly involved in the archduke's assassination, but it did not care. Austrian leaders wanted to attack Serbia but feared that Russia would intervene on Serbia's behalf. So, they asked for—and received—the backing of their German allies. **Emperor William II** of Germany gave Austria-Hungary a "blank check," promising Germany's full support if war broke out between Russia and Austria-Hungary. On July 28, Austria-Hungary declared war on Serbia.

HISTORY & ARTS   PRIMARY SOURCE

Assassination of Francis Ferdinand

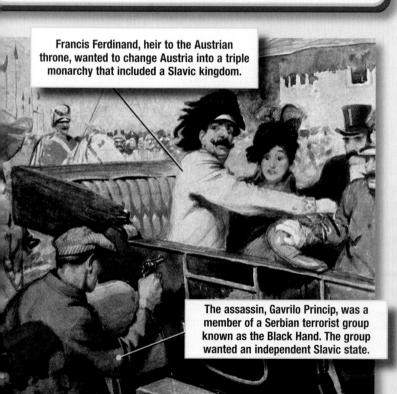

Francis Ferdinand, heir to the Austrian throne, wanted to change Austria into a triple monarchy that included a Slavic kingdom.

The assassin, Gavrilo Princip, was a member of a Serbian terrorist group known as the Black Hand. The group wanted an independent Slavic state.

The German ambassador at Vienna described Austria's reaction to the assassination:

"Here I hear even serious people express the desire of settling accounts with the Serbs once for all. A series of conditions should be sent to the Serbs, and if they do not accept these, energetic steps should be taken."
—Dispatch from the German ambassador at Vienna, July 10, 1914

DOCUMENT-BASED QUESTIONS

This 1914 illustration is by the American artist I. B. Hazelton.

1. **Making Inferences** Why did the Black Hand want to assassinate Archduke Francis Ferdinand?

2. **Determining Cause and Effect** What effect did the assassination have in Austria and the rest of Europe?

Russia Mobilizes

Russia was determined to support Serbia's cause. On July 28, **Czar Nicholas II** ordered partial mobilization of the Russian army against Austria-Hungary. **Mobilization** is the process of assembling troops and supplies for war. In 1914, mobilization was considered an act of war.

Leaders of the Russian army informed the czar that they could not partially mobilize. Their mobilization plans were based on a war against both Germany and Austria-Hungary. Mobilizing against only Austria-Hungary, they claimed, would create chaos in the army. Based on this claim, the czar ordered full mobilization of the Russian army on July 29, knowing that Germany would consider this order an act of war.

The Conflict Broadens

Indeed, Germany reacted quickly. The German government warned Russia that it must halt its mobilization within 12 hours. When Russia ignored this warning, Germany declared war on Russia on August 1.

Like the Russians, the Germans had a military plan. **General Alfred von Schlieffen** (SHLEE•fuhn) had helped draw up the plan, which was known as the Schlieffen Plan. It called for a two-front war with France and Russia since the two had formed a military alliance in 1894.

According to the Schlieffen Plan, Germany would conduct a small holding action against Russia while most of the German army would carry out a rapid invasion of France. This meant invading France by moving quickly along the level coastal area through Belgium. After France was defeated, the German invaders would move to the east against Russia.

Under the Schlieffen Plan, Germany could not mobilize its troops solely against Russia. Therefore, it declared war on France on August 3. About the same time, it issued an ultimatum to Belgium demanding that German troops be allowed to pass through Belgian territory.

On August 4, Great Britain declared war on Germany for violating Belgian neutrality. In fact, Britain, which was allied with France and Russia, was concerned about maintaining its own world power. As one British diplomat put it, if Germany and Austria-Hungary won the war, "what would be the position of a friendless England?" By August 4, all the Great Powers of Europe were at war.

✓ **Reading Check** **Evaluating** How did the Schlieffen Plan contribute to the outbreak of World War I?

Vocabulary

1. **Explain** the significance of: Triple Alliance, Triple Entente, conscription, military, complex, Serbia, Archduke Francis Ferdinand, Bosnia, Gavrilo Princip, Emperor William II, Czar Nicholas II, mobilization, General Alfred von Schlieffen.

Main Ideas

2. **List** the powers that formed the Triple Alliance and the Triple Entente.

3. **Explain** why Gavrilo Princip killed Archduke Francis Ferdinand.

4. **Identify** the series of decisions that European leaders made in 1914 that led directly to the outbreak of war. Use a diagram like the one below.

☐→☐→☐→☐→☐

Critical Thinking

5. **The BIG IDEA** **Analyzing** How did the creation of military plans help draw the nations of Europe into World War I? In your opinion, what should today's national and military leaders have learned from the military plans that helped initiate World War I? Explain your answer.

6. **Making Inferences** Why was the Austro-Hungarian government not really concerned whether Serbia itself was involved in Archduke Ferdinand's assassination?

7. **Analyzing Visuals** Examine the painting on page 524. How is Archduke Francis Ferdinand reacting to the assassin?

Writing About History

8. **Expository Writing** Some historians believe that the desire to suppress internal disorder may have encouraged leaders to enter the war. As an adviser, write a memo to your country's leader explaining how a war might help the domestic situation.

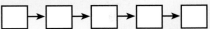

History ONLINE

For help with the concepts in this section of *Glencoe World History— Modern Times*, go to glencoe.com and click Study Central.

World War I

The war that many thought would be over in a few weeks lasted far longer, resulting in many casualties for both sides. The war widened, and the United States entered the fray in 1917. As World War I escalated, governments took control of their economies, rationing food and supplies and calling on civilians to work and make sacrifices for the war effort.

GUIDE TO READING

The BIG Idea

Devastation of War The stalemate at the Western Front led to a widening of World War I, and governments expanded their powers to accommodate the war.

Content Vocabulary

- propaganda *(p. 526)*
- trench warfare *(p. 527)*
- war of attrition *(p. 529)*
- total war *(p. 531)*
- planned economies *(p. 531)*

Academic Vocabulary

- target *(p. 529)*
- unrestricted *(p. 531)*

People, Places, and Events

- Marne *(p. 526)*
- Gallipoli *(p. 530)*
- Lawrence of Arabia *(p. 530)*
- Admiral Holtzendorf *(p. 531)*
- Woodrow Wilson *(p. 532)*

Reading Strategy

Organizing Information As you read, identify which countries belong to the Allies and the Central Powers. What country changed allegiance? What country withdrew from the war?

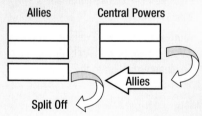

Allies   Central Powers

Allies

Split Off

1914 to 1915: Illusions and Stalemate

MAIN IDEA Trench warfare brought the war on the Western Front to a stalemate while Germany and Austria-Hungary defeated Russia on the Eastern Front.

HISTORY & YOU How do political campaigns influence voters? Read to learn how governments tried to influence public opinion before World War I.

Before 1914, many political leaders believed war to be impractical because it involved so many political and economic risks. Others believed that diplomats could easily prevent war. At the beginning of August 1914, both ideas were shattered. However, the new illusions that replaced them soon proved to be equally foolish.

Government **propaganda**—ideas spread to influence public opinion for or against a cause—had stirred national hatreds before the war. Now, in August 1914, the urgent pleas of European governments for defense against aggressors fell on receptive ears in every nation at war. Most people seemed genuinely convinced that their nation's cause was just.

A new set of illusions also fed the enthusiasm for war. In August 1914, almost everyone believed that the war would be over in a few weeks. After all, almost all European wars since 1815 had, in fact, ended in a matter of weeks. Both the soldiers who boarded the trains for the war front in August 1914 and the jubilant citizens who saw them off believed that the warriors would be home by Christmas.

The Western Front

German hopes for a quick end to the war rested on a military gamble. The Schlieffen Plan had called for the German army to make a vast encircling movement through Belgium into northern France. According to the plan, the German forces would sweep around Paris. This would enable them to surround most of the French army.

The German advance was halted a short distance from Paris at the First Battle of the **Marne** (September 6–10). To stop the Germans, French military leaders loaded 2,000 Parisian taxicabs with fresh troops and sent them to the front line.

WORLD WAR I IN EUROPE, 1914–1918

ATLANTIC
OCEAN

Sinking of
the *Lusitania*
May 7, 1915

UNITED
KINGDOM

North
Sea

NORWAY

SWEDEN

DENMARK

NETH.

London

Somme 1916

Nov. 1914

BEL.

Paris

Marne 1914, 1918

LUX.

Verdun 1916

FRANCE

SWITZ.

ITALY

Corsica

Sardinia

PORT.

SPAIN

SPANISH
MOROCCO

Morocco
Fr.

Algeria
Fr.

Tunisia
Fr.

Sicily

Baltic Sea

Masurian Lakes
1914

Aug. 1914

Tannenberg
1914

Berlin

GERMANY

Budapest

AUSTRIA-
HUNGARY

GALICIA

Jan. 1915

Jan. 1917

Sept. 1916

Caporetto
1917

Sarajevo

Oct. 1915

SERBIA

Jan. 1917

ROMANIA

BULGARIA

MONTENEGRO

Dec. 1915

GREECE

ALBANIA

OTTOMAN EMPIRE

Gallipoli
1915

Crete

Cyprus
U.K.

March 1918

Nov. 1915

RUSSIAN
EMPIRE

Black Sea

Nov. 1917

Oct. 1918

March 1918

Oct. 1918

March 1918

Caspian
Sea

Mediterranean Sea

Libya
Italy

0   200 kilometers

0   200 miles

Lambert Azimuthal
Equal-Area projection

Legend:
- Allies
- Central Powers
- Neutral nations
- Farthest advance of the Allies
- Farthest advance of the Central Powers
- British naval blockade
- German submarine war zone
- Treaty line of Brest-Litovsk
- Allied victory
- Central Powers victory
- Indecisive battle

Geography SKILLS

1. **Movement** Under the Schlieffen Plan, through which country did the Germans pass on the way to France?
2. **Place** How did the geographic characteristics of the United Kingdom affect its role in World War I?

Maps In Motion See *StudentWorks™ Plus* or glencoe.com.

The war quickly turned into a stalemate as neither the Germans nor the French could dislodge each other from the trenches they had dug for shelter. These trenches were ditches protected by barbed wire.

Two lines of trenches soon reached from the English Channel to the frontiers of Switzerland. The Western Front had become bogged down in **trench warfare.** Both sides were kept in virtually the same positions for four years.

The Eastern Front

Unlike the Western Front, the war on the Eastern Front was marked by mobility. The cost in lives, however, was equally enormous. At the beginning of the war, the Russian army moved into eastern Germany but was decisively defeated at the Battle of Tannenberg on August 30 and the Battle of Masurian Lakes on September 15. After these defeats, the Russians were no longer a threat to Germany.

Austria-Hungary, Germany's ally, fared less well at first. The Austrians had been defeated by the Russians in Galicia and thrown out of Serbia as well. To make matters worse, the Italians betrayed their German and Austrian allies in the Triple Alliance by attacking Austria in May 1915.

Italy thus joined France, Great Britain, and Russia, who had previously been known as the Triple Entente, but now were called the Allied Powers, or Allies.

By this time, the Germans had come to the aid of the Austrians. A German-Austrian army defeated the Russian army in Galicia and pushed the Russians far back into their own territory. Russian casualties stood at 2.5 million killed, captured, or wounded. The Russians had almost been knocked out of the war.

Encouraged by their success against Russia, Germany and Austria-Hungary, joined by Bulgaria in September 1915, attacked and eliminated Serbia from the war. Their successes in the east would enable the German troops to move back to the offensive in the west.

✓**Reading Check** **Contrasting** How did the war on the Eastern Front differ from the war on the Western Front?

The Great Slaughter

MAIN IDEA New weapons and trench warfare made World War I far more devastating than any previous wars.

HISTORY & YOU How do new inventions and strategies affect warfare today? Read on to learn about the new inventions and trench warfare that characterized the fighting in World War I.

On the Western Front, the trenches dug in 1914 had by 1916 become elaborate systems of defense. The Germans and the French each had hundreds of miles of trenches, which were protected by barbed-wire entanglements up to 5 feet (about 1.5 m) high and 30 yards (about 27 m) wide. Concrete machine-gun nests and other gun batteries, supported further back by heavy artillery, protected the trenches. Troops lived in holes in the ground, separated from each other by a strip of territory known as no-man's-land.

SCIENCE, TECHNOLOGY, & SOCIETY

The New Technology of World War I

Warfare in the trenches produced unimaginable horrors. Battlefields were hellish landscapes of barbed wire, shell holes, mud, and injured and dying men.

Trench warfare left World War I in stalemate, with neither side able to gain more than a few miles of ground. Both the Allied Powers and the Central Powers attempted to gain an advantage with new weapons and war machines. Machine guns, poison gas, fighter airplanes, and tanks were all introduced or vastly improved during World War I.

In the end, new technology did not break the stalemate. It did, however, cause the deadliest war the world had yet seen. Nearly 10 million people perished during World War I, which became known as "the war to end all wars."

Writer H. G. Wells described the impact of the new war technology:

"Now, there does not appear the slightest hope of any invention that will make war more conclusive or less destructive; there is, however, the clearest prospect in many directions that it may be more destructive and less conclusive. It will be dreadfuller and bitterer: its horrors will be less and less forgivable."

—H. G. Wells, "Civilization at the Breaking Point," *New York Times,* May 27, 1915

Machine guns could fire faster than other types of guns. Here, machine gunners wear masks to protect themselves from poison gas.

Tactics of Trench Warfare

Trench warfare baffled military leaders who had been trained to fight wars of movement and maneuver. At times, the high command on either side would order an offensive that would begin with an artillery barrage to flatten the enemy's barbed wire and leave the enemy in a state of shock. After "softening up" the enemy in this fashion, a mass of soldiers would climb out of their trenches with fixed bayonets and hope to work their way toward the enemy trenches.

The attacks rarely worked because men advancing unprotected across open fields could be fired at by the enemy's machine guns. In 1916 and 1917, millions of young men died in the search for the elusive breakthrough.

In just ten months at Verdun, France, 700,000 men lost their lives over a few miles of land in 1916. World War I had turned into a **war of attrition,** a war based on wearing the other side down by constant attacks and heavy losses.

War in the Air

By the end of 1915, airplanes had appeared on the battlefront for the first time in history. Planes were first used to spot the enemy's position. Soon, planes also began to attack ground **targets,** especially enemy communications.

Fights for control of the air occurred and increased over time. At first, pilots fired at each other with handheld pistols. Later, machine guns were mounted on the noses of planes, which made the skies considerably more dangerous.

The Germans also used their giant airships—the zeppelins—to bomb London and eastern England. This caused little damage but frightened many people. Germany's enemies, however, soon found that zeppelins, which were filled with hydrogen gas, quickly became raging infernos when hit by antiaircraft guns.

See page R50 to read an excerpt from Arthur Guy Empey's *Over the Top* in the **Primary Sources and Literature Library.**

✓**Reading Check** **Explaining** Why were military leaders baffled by trench warfare?

German fighter pilot Manfred von Richthofen, better known as the Red Baron, stands in front of a Fokker DV-II biplane. Planes such as this one gave the Germans an edge because they could fire a machine gun through the propeller.

In 1916 the British became the first to use armored tanks in war. Armor protected the tanks from machine gun fire. Caterpillar tracks allowed tanks to cross barbed-wire entanglements.

DOCUMENT-BASED QUESTIONS

1. **Explaining** How did each of the inventions shown here provide an advantage on the battlefield?

2. **Analyzing** What did H. G. Wells believe was the overall impact of the new war technology? Do you agree? Explain.

A World War

MAIN IDEA With the war at a stalemate, both the Allied Powers and the Central Powers looked for new allies to gain an advantage.

HISTORY & YOU In the American Revolution, what country provided aid to the colonists? Read to learn how nations looked for allies in World War I.

Because of the stalemate on the Western Front, both sides sought to gain new allies. Each side hoped new allies would provide a winning advantage, as well as a new source of money and war goods.

Widening of the War

Bulgaria entered the war on the side of the Central Powers, as Germany, Austria-Hungary, and the Ottoman Empire were called. Russia, Great Britain, and France—the Allied Powers—declared war on the Ottoman Empire.

The Allies tried to open a Balkan front by landing forces at **Gallipoli** (guh•LIH•puh•lee), southwest of Constantinople, in April 1915. However, the campaign proved disastrous, forcing the Allies to withdraw.

In return for Italy entering the war on the Allied side, France and Great Britain promised to let Italy have some Austrian territory. Italy on the side of the Allies opened up a front against Austria-Hungary.

By 1917, the war had truly become a world conflict. That year, while stationed in the Middle East, a British officer known as **Lawrence of Arabia** urged Arab princes to revolt against their Ottoman overlords. In 1918 British forces from Egypt mobilized troops from India, Australia, and New Zealand and destroyed the Ottoman Empire in the Middle East.

The Allies also took advantage of Germany's preoccupations in Europe and lack of naval strength to seize German colonies in the rest of the world. Japan, a British ally beginning in 1902, seized a number of

---

INFOGRAPHICS   PRIMARY SOURCE

The Sinking of the Lusitania

The sinking of the *Lusitania*, a British passenger ship, by a German submarine outraged people on both sides of the Atlantic. Anti-German riots broke out, and both Americans and Europeans called on President Woodrow Wilson to declare war against Germany. Germany, however, claimed that the *Lusitania* was a fair target because it was carrying a cargo of 173 tons of ammunition along with the civilian passengers.

On May 13, 1915, Wilson sent the first of four notes to Germany to protest the German violation of American neutrality. Two years later Wilson would list German submarine warfare as a reason for the U.S. entry into World War I.

The German embassy ran this notice in the *New York Times* on April 22, 1915. ▶

ADVERTISEMENT.

NOTICE!

TRAVELLERS intending to embark on the Atlantic voyage are reminded that a state of war exists between Germany and her allies and Great Britain and her allies; that the zone of war includes the waters adjacent to the British Isles; that, in accordance with formal notice given by the Imperial German Government, vessels flying the flag of Great Britain, or of any of her allies, are liable to destruction in those waters and that travellers sailing in the war zone on ships of Great Britain or her allies do so at their own risk.

IMPERIAL GERMAN EMBASSY
WASHINGTON, D. C., APRIL 22, 1915.

This early book by French historian and novelist Georges Toudouze calls the sinking of the *Lusitania* a "crime."

DOCUMENT-BASED QUESTIONS

1. **Identifying Points of View** What was Toudouze's point of view on the sinking of the *Lusitania*? Would the German embassy have agreed with that point of view? Explain.

2. **Determining Cause and Effect** What was an important political effect of the sinking of the *Lusitania*?

German-held islands in the Pacific. Australia seized German New Guinea.

Entry of the United States

At first, the United States tried to remain neutral. As World War I dragged on, however, it became more difficult to do so. The immediate cause of the United States's involvement grew out of the naval war between Germany and Great Britain.

Britain had used its superior naval power to set up a blockade of Germany. The blockade kept war materials and other goods from reaching Germany by sea. Germany had retaliated by setting up a blockade of Britain. Germany enforced its blockade with the use of **unrestricted** submarine warfare, which included the sinking of passenger liners.

On May 7, 1915, German forces sank the British ship *Lusitania*. About 1,100 civilians, including over 100 Americans, died. After strong protests from the United States, the German government suspended unrestricted submarine warfare in September 1915 to avoid antagonizing the United States further. Only once did the Germans and British engage in direct naval battle—at the Battle of Jutland on May 31, 1916, when neither side won a conclusive victory.

By January 1917, however, the Germans were eager to break the deadlock in the war. German naval officers convinced Emperor William II that resuming the use of unrestricted submarine warfare could starve the British into submission within six months. When the emperor expressed concern about the United States, **Admiral Holtzendorf** assured him, "I give your Majesty my word as an officer that not one American will land on the continent."

The German naval officers were quite wrong. The British were not forced to surrender, and the return to unrestricted submarine warfare brought the United States into the war in April 1917. U.S. troops did not arrive in large numbers in Europe until 1918. However, the entry of the United States into the war gave the Allied Powers a psychological boost and a major new source of money and war goods.

✓ **Reading Check** **Evaluating** Why did the Germans resort to unrestricted submarine warfare?

The Impact of Total War

MAIN IDEA World War I became a total war, with governments taking control of their economies and rationing civilian goods.

HISTORY & YOU Do you think the government should ever be allowed to censor what newspapers publish? Read to learn why many governments resorted to censorship and similar practices during World War I.

As World War I dragged on, it became a **total war** involving a complete mobilization of resources and people. It affected the lives of all citizens in the warring countries, however remote they might be from the battlefields.

Masses of men had to be organized, and supplies were manufactured and purchased for years of combat. (Germany alone had 5.5 million men in uniform in 1916.) This led to an increase in government powers and the manipulation of public opinion to keep the war effort going. The home front was rapidly becoming a cause for as much effort as the war front.

Increased Government Powers

Most people had expected the war to be short. Little thought had been given to long-term wartime needs. Governments had to respond quickly, however, when the new war machines failed to achieve their goals. Many more men and supplies were needed to continue the war effort. To meet these needs, governments expanded their powers. Countries drafted tens of millions of young men, hoping for that elusive breakthrough to victory.

Wartime governments throughout Europe also expanded their power over their economies. Free-market capitalistic systems were temporarily put aside. Governments set up price, wage, and rent controls. They also rationed food supplies and materials; regulated imports and exports; and took over transportation systems and industries. In effect, in order to mobilize all the resources of their nations for the war effort, European nations set up **planned economies**—systems directed by government agencies.

Under conditions of total war mobilization, the differences between soldiers at war and civilians at home were narrowed. In the view of political leaders, all citizens were part of a national army dedicated to victory. **Woodrow Wilson,** president of the United States, said that the men and women "who remain to till the soil and man the factories are no less a part of the army than the men beneath the battle flags."

Manipulation of Public Opinion

As the war continued and casualties grew worse, the patriotic enthusiasm that had marked the early stages of World War I waned. By 1916, there were signs that civilian morale was beginning to crack. War governments, however, fought back against growing opposition to the war.

Authoritarian regimes, such as those of Germany, Russia, and Austria-Hungary, relied on force to subdue their populations. Under the pressures of the war, however, even democratic states expanded their police powers to stop internal dissent. The British Parliament, for example, passed the Defence of the Realm Act (DORA). It allowed the government to arrest protesters as traitors. Newspapers were censored, and sometimes publication was suspended.

Wartime governments made active use of propaganda to increase enthusiasm for the war. At the beginning, public officials needed to do little to achieve this goal. The British and French, for example, exaggerated German atrocities in Belgium and found that their citizens were only too willing to believe these accounts.

As the war progressed and morale sagged, governments were forced to devise new techniques for motivating the people. In one British recruiting poster, for example, a small daughter asked her father, "Daddy, what did YOU do in the Great War?" while her younger brother played with toy soldiers.

CONNECTING TO THE UNITED STATES

THE INFLUENZA EPIDEMIC OF 1918

In the fall of 1918, just as World War I was winding down in Europe, a deadly influenza epidemic struck. Probably spread by soldiers returning from the front, it became the deadliest epidemic in history:

- **An estimated 675,000 Americans died, ten times as many as had died in the war.**
- **An estimated 50 million people died worldwide.**

Things could have been even worse. Because of the war, people were used to government restrictions. Public health departments were able to step in with measures to restrict contact. The war had also brought new technologies such as germ theory and antiseptics. These had saved lives in the battlefield and eventually would help save the world from this deadly epidemic.

Given the deadly spread of the 1918 influenza, scientists are keeping a close watch on today's flu viruses. With today's ease of air travel, a new virus could take only days to spread around the world.

◀ *Baseball players and spectators wear gauze masks to protect themselves from infection during the 1918 influenza epidemic.*

CONNECTING TO TODAY

1. **Hypothesizing** In the face of a deadly pandemic, do you think that people today would continue with normal activities such as spectator sports? Why or why not?

2. **Making Generalizations** How would a pandemic similar to the one in 1918 affect your life?

Total War and Women

World War I created new roles for women. Because so many men left to fight at the front, women were asked to take over jobs that had not been available to them before. Women were employed in jobs that had once been considered beyond their capacity.

These jobs included civilian occupations such as chimney sweeps, truck drivers, farm laborers, and factory workers in heavy industry. For example, 38 percent of the workers in the Krupp Armaments works in Germany in 1918 were women. Also, between 1914 and 1918 in Britain, the number of women working in public transport rose 14 times, doubled in commerce, and rose by nearly a third in industry.

The place of women in the workforce was far from secure, however. Both men and women seemed to expect that many of the new jobs for women were only temporary. This was evident in the British poem "War Girls," written in 1916:

PRIMARY SOURCE

"There's the girl who clips your ticket for the train,
And the girl who speeds the lift from floor to floor,
There's the girl who does a milk-round in the rain,
And the girl who calls for orders at your door.
Strong, sensible, and fit,
They're out to show their grit,
And tackle jobs with energy and knack.
No longer caged and penned up,
They're going to keep their end up
Till the khaki soldier boys come marching back."

At the end of the war, governments would quickly remove women from the jobs they had encouraged them to take earlier. The work benefits for women from World War I were short-lived as men returned to the job market. By 1919, there would be 650,000 unemployed women in Great Britain. Wages for the women who were still employed would be lowered.

Nevertheless, in some countries the role women played in wartime economies had a positive impact on the women's movement for social and political emancipation. The most obvious gain was the right to vote, which was given to women in Germany, Austria, and the United States immediately after the war. British women over 30 gained the vote, together with the right to stand for Parliament, in 1918.

Many upper- and middle-class women had also gained new freedoms. In ever-increasing numbers, young women from these groups took jobs, had their own apartments, and showed their new independence.

✓ **Reading Check** **Summarizing** What was the effect of total war on ordinary citizens?

Vocabulary

1. **Explain** the significance of: propaganda, Marne, trench warfare, war of attrition, target, Gallipoli, Lawrence of Arabia, unrestricted, Admiral Holtzendorf, total war, planned economies, Woodrow Wilson.

Main Ideas

2. **Explain** why governments often use propaganda during wartime.

3. **Describe** the trenches that both the Western Front and Eastern Front used in World War I.

4. **Illustrate,** by using a diagram similar to the one below, the ways in which government powers increased during the war.

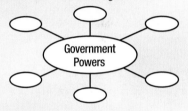

Government Powers

Critical Thinking

5. **The BIG Idea** **Assessing** What methods did governments use to counter the loss of enthusiasm and opposition to the war at home?

6. **Analyzing Primary Sources** How did Admiral Holtzendorf's assurance to the German emperor, "I give your Majesty my word as an officer that not one American will land on the continent" prove to be wrong?

7. **Analyzing Visuals** Explain why the war technology shown in the photograph on page 528 did not help break the World War I stalemate.

Writing About History

8. **Expository Writing** What lasting results occurred in women's rights due to World War I? What were the temporary results? Write an essay discussing the effect of the war on women's rights.

History ONLINE

For help with the concepts in this section of *Glencoe World History—Modern Times,* go to glencoe.com and click Study Central.

Technology and Trench Life Define Total War

The politicians and generals who led their nations into World War I anticipated an old fashioned conflict. But once the Allies and Germans reached a stalemate, the armies, for the first time, dug miles of trenches opposite one another as protection against exploding shells and machine-gun fire. Infantry soldiers rotated into and out of the trenches five days at a time. It was a world of mud and blood, poison gas and high-explosive shells overhead. The tedium of trench life was broken most often by one army or the other charging out of its trenches and into the enemy's barbed wire and machine guns.

Steel helmets protected infantrymen against shrapnel, high-speed splinters of metal from exploding shells.

Earthtones replaced vibrant blues and reds in infantry uniforms.

Machine guns shot down soldiers charging across the no-man's-land between opposing trenches in great numbers.

COLD COMFORT IN THE TRENCHES

Trenches provided infantry soldiers with their only protection against enemy fire. They were a necessary innovation for armies fighting in close contact with powerful and accurate weapons. Hot food was brought forward in containers to discourage cooking fires. In some places, soldiers fired at the enemy trenches at every opportunity. In others, enemies took a "live and let live" approach. These attitudes often depended upon the level of exhaustion the soldiers were feeling.

The area between opposing trenches was called no-man's-land.

Soldiers fixed bayonets, long knives, on front of their rifles to charge the enemy.

When possible, mud floors were covered with wooden planks.

Barbed wire in front of a trench slowed or stopped an enemy attack.

Gas masks provided the only hope of protection from the chlorine gas clouds that came before enemy charges.

TECHNOLOGY AND THE HORROR OF WAR

Tanks made their first appearance in battle during World War I. Though slow and cumbersome, they foreshadowed the destruction mechanized warfare would bring. Airplanes fought one another for the first time as well, and both sides experimented with bombs and machine guns in aerial attacks on ground positions. These applications of technology left a deep, terrifying impression on soldiers showing the dark side of industrialization.

ANALYZING VISUALS

1. **Comparing** How well do you think infantry soldiers' uniforms protected them from modern weapons? How has this changed since World War I, and why?

2. **Theorizing** Think about the images of early tanks and airplanes shown here. Why do these devices seem primitive to us today?

The Russian Revolution

GUIDE TO READING

The BIG Idea
Struggle for Rights The fall of the czarist regime and the Russian Revolution put the Communists in power in Russia.

Content Vocabulary
• soviets (p. 538)
• war communism (p. 541)

Academic Vocabulary
• revolution (p. 538)
• aid (p. 540)

People and Places
• Grigory Rasputin (p. 536)
• Alexandra (p. 536)
• Petrograd (p. 537)
• Aleksandr Kerensky (p. 538)
• Bolsheviks (p. 538)
• V. I. Lenin (p. 538)
• Ukraine (p. 540)
• Siberia (p. 540)
• Urals (p. 541)
• Leon Trotsky (p. 541)

Reading Strategy
Categorizing Information As you read, use a chart like the one below to identify the factors and events that led to Lenin coming to power in 1917.

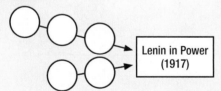

Lenin in Power (1917)

As the world anxiously waited to learn of developments along the fronts of World War I, Russia stirred internally with unrest. The Romanov dynasty of Russia ended when Czar Nicholas II stepped down and a provisional government was put in power. Seizing the opportunity that the instability offered, the Bolsheviks under V. I. Lenin overthrew the provisional government. By 1921, the Communists were in total command of Russia.

Background to Revolution

MAIN IDEA Worker unrest and the Russian czar's failures in the war led to revolution in March 1917.

HISTORY & YOU Recall the causes of the French Revolution. Then, read to learn what caused the Russian Revolution.

After its defeat by Japan in 1905, and the Revolution of 1905, Russia was unprepared both militarily and technologically for the total war of World War I. Russia had no competent military leaders. Even worse, Czar Nicholas II insisted on taking personal charge of the armed forces in spite of his obvious lack of ability and training.

In addition, Russian industry was unable to produce the weapons needed for the army. Supplies and munitions were rarely at the places where they needed to be. Many soldiers trained using broomsticks. Others were sent to the front without rifles and told to pick one up from a dead comrade.

Given these conditions, it is not surprising that the Russian army suffered incredible losses. Between 1914 and 1916, 2 million soldiers were killed, and another 4 to 6 million were wounded or captured. By 1917, the Russian will to fight had vanished.

Beginnings of Upheaval

An autocratic ruler, Czar Nicholas II relied on the army and bureaucracy to hold up his regime. He was further cut off from events when a man named **Grigory Rasputin** (ra•SPYOO•tuhn) began to influence the czar's wife, **Alexandra.**

Rasputin gained Alexandra's confidence through her son, Alexis, who had hemophilia (a deficiency in the ability of the blood to clot). Alexandra believed that Rasputin had extraordinary powers, for he alone seemed to be able to stop her son's bleeding. With the czar at the battlefront, Alexandra made all of the important decisions after consulting Rasputin. His influence made him an important power behind the throne. Rasputin often interfered in government affairs.

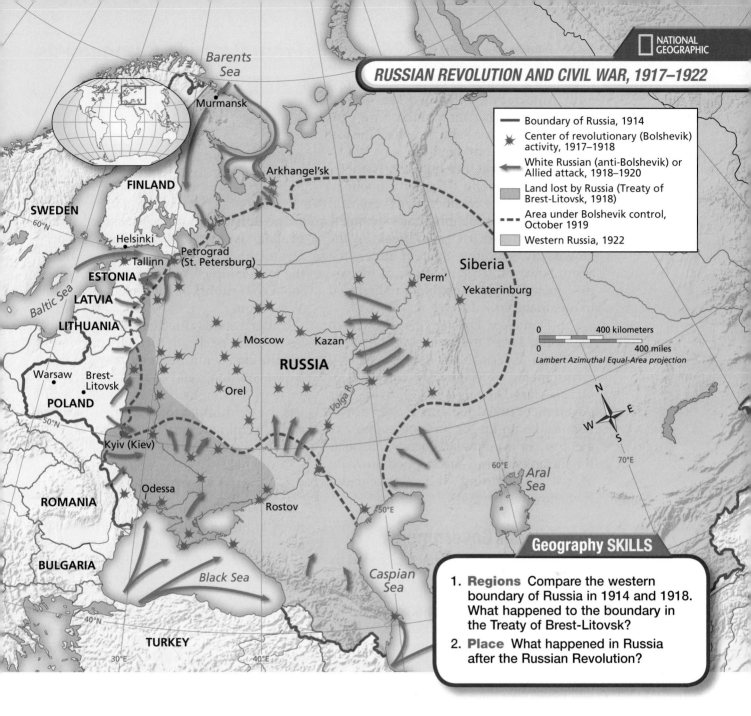

RUSSIAN REVOLUTION AND CIVIL WAR, 1917–1922

——	Boundary of Russia, 1914
✳	Center of revolutionary (Bolshevik) activity, 1917–1918
←	White Russian (anti-Bolshevik) or Allied attack, 1918–1920
▨	Land lost by Russia (Treaty of Brest-Litovsk, 1918)
- - -	Area under Bolshevik control, October 1919
▢	Western Russia, 1922

Barents Sea

Murmansk

FINLAND

SWEDEN
60°N

Helsinki

Arkhangel'sk

Tallinn

Petrograd (St. Petersburg)

Siberia

Perm'

Yekaterinburg

ESTONIA

Baltic Sea

LATVIA

LITHUANIA

Moscow   Kazan

RUSSIA

0   400 kilometers
0   400 miles
Lambert Azimuthal Equal-Area projection

Warsaw   Brest-Litovsk

Orel

Volga R.

POLAND
50°N

Kyiv (Kiev)

N
W   E
S

Odessa

60°E   Aral Sea   70°E

ROMANIA

Rostov

50°E

BULGARIA

Black Sea

Caspian Sea

40°N

TURKEY

30°E   40°E

Geography SKILLS

1. **Regions** Compare the western boundary of Russia in 1914 and 1918. What happened to the boundary in the Treaty of Brest-Litovsk?

2. **Place** What happened in Russia after the Russian Revolution?

As the leadership at the top stumbled its way through a series of military and economic disasters, the Russian people grew more and more upset with the czarist regime. Even conservative aristocrats who supported the monarchy felt the need to do something to save the situation. First, they assassinated Rasputin in December 1916. It was not easy to kill Rasputin. They shot him three times and then tied him up and threw him into the Neva River. Rasputin drowned but not before he had managed to untie the knots underwater. The killing of Rasputin occurred too late, however, to save the monarchy.

The March Revolution

At the beginning of March 1917, working-class women led a series of strikes in the capital city of **Petrograd** (formerly St. Petersburg). A few weeks earlier, the government had started bread rationing in Petrograd after the price of bread had skyrocketed.

Many of the women who stood in the lines waiting for bread were also factory workers who worked 12-hour days. Exhausted and distraught over their half-starving and sick children, the women finally revolted.

History ONLINE

Student Web Activity—
Visit glencoe.com and complete the activity on the Russian royal family.

On March 8, about 10,000 women marched through the city of Petrograd demanding "Peace and Bread" and "Down with Autocracy." Other workers joined them, and together they called for a general strike. The strike shut down all the factories in the city on March 10.

Alexandra wrote her husband Nicholas II at the battlefront: "This is a hooligan movement. If the weather were very cold they would all probably stay at home." Nicholas ordered troops to break up the crowds by shooting them if necessary. Soon, however, large numbers of the soldiers joined the demonstrators and refused to fire on the crowds.

The Duma, or legislative body, which the czar had tried to dissolve, met anyway. On March 12, it established the provisional government, which mainly consisted of middle-class Duma representatives. This government urged the czar to step down. Because he no longer had the support of the army or even the aristocrats, Nicholas II reluctantly agreed and stepped down on March 15, ending the 300-year-old Romanov dynasty.

Provisional Government

The provisional government, headed by **Aleksandr Kerensky** (keh•REHN•skee), now decided to carry on the war to preserve Russia's honor. This decision to remain in World War I was a major blunder. It satisfied neither the workers nor the peasants, who were tired and angry from years of suffering and wanted above all an end to the war.

The government was also faced with a challenge to its authority—the **soviets**. The soviets were councils composed of representatives from the workers and soldiers. The soviet of Petrograd had been formed in March 1917. At the same time, soviets sprang up in army units, factory towns, and rural areas. The soviets, largely made up of socialists, represented the more radical interests of the lower classes. One group—the Bolsheviks—came to play a crucial role.

✓ **Reading Check** **Identifying** Develop a sequence of events leading to the March Revolution.

From Czars to Communists

MAIN IDEA Lenin and the Bolsheviks gained control and quickly overthrew the provisional government.

HISTORY & YOU How has political change happened in the United States? Read to learn how Lenin proposed to make changes in Russia.

The **Bolsheviks** began as a small faction of a Marxist party called the Russian Social Democrats. The Bolsheviks came under the leadership of Vladimir Ilyich Ulyanov (ool•YAH•nuhf), known to the world as **V. I. Lenin**.

Under Lenin's direction, the Bolsheviks became a party dedicated to violent **revolution**. Lenin believed that only violent revolution could destroy the capitalist system. A "vanguard" (forefront) of activists, he said, must form a small party of well-disciplined, professional revolutionaries to accomplish the task.

Lenin and the Bolsheviks

Between 1900 and 1917, Lenin spent most of his time abroad. When the provisional government was formed in March 1917, he saw an opportunity for the Bolsheviks to seize power. In April 1917, German military leaders, hoping to create disorder in Russia, shipped Lenin to Russia. Lenin and his associates were in a sealed train to prevent their ideas from infecting Germany.

Lenin's arrival in Russia opened a new stage of the Russian Revolution. Lenin maintained that the soviets of soldiers, workers, and peasants were ready-made instruments of power. He believed that the Bolsheviks should work toward gaining control of these groups and then use them to overthrow the provisional government.

At the same time, the Bolsheviks reflected the discontent of the people. They promised an end to the war. They also promised to redistribute all land to the peasants, to transfer factories and industries from capitalists to committees of workers, and to transfer government power from the provisional government to the soviets. Three simple slogans summed up the Bolshevik program: "Peace, Land, Bread," "Worker Control of Production," and "All Power to the Soviets."

The Bolsheviks Seize Power

By the end of October, Bolsheviks made up a slight majority in the Petrograd and Moscow soviets. The number of party members had grown from 50,000 to 240,000. With Leon Trotsky, a dedicated revolutionary, as head of the Petrograd soviet, the Bolsheviks were in a position to claim power in the name of the soviets. During the night of November 6, Bolshevik forces seized the Winter Palace, the seat of the provisional government. The government quickly collapsed with little bloodshed.

This overthrow coincided with a meeting of the all-Russian Congress of Soviets, which represented local soviets countrywide. Outwardly, Lenin turned over the power of the provisional government to the Congress of Soviets. The real power, however, passed to a council headed by Lenin.

The Bolsheviks, who renamed themselves the Communists, still had a long way to go. Lenin had promised peace; and that, he realized, would not be an easy task.

TURNING POINT

THE RUSSIAN REVOLUTION

The Russian Revolution was the most violent and radical revolution since the French Revolution. In March 1917, the czar abdicated and a provisional government took control. Then, led by V. I. Lenin, the Bolsheviks seized power in November 1917. This marked a new era of Soviet rule. Russia had become the world's first socialist state, and Lenin intended for the revolution to spread.

The day after the Bolsheviks seized the Winter Palace, Lenin addressed the Russian people. In his speech he outlined the goals of the Bolsheviks. These goals threatened the governments of Western Europe:

"The first thing is the adoption of practical measures to realize peace. . . . We shall offer peace to the peoples of all the warring countries upon the basis of the Soviet terms— no annexations, no indemnities, and the right of self-determination of peoples. . . . This proposal of peace will meet with resistance on the part of the imperialist governments. . . . But we hope that revolution will soon break out in all the warring countries. This is why we address ourselves especially to the workers of France, England, and Germany."

—V. I. Lenin, quoted in *Ten Days that Shook the World,* by John Reed

The Winter Palace housed the provisional government after Nicholas stepped down. It had been the home of every Russian czar from Catherine the Great to Nicholas II.

DOCUMENT-BASED QUESTIONS

Georgiy Savitsky's painting *Assault on the Winter Palace* depicts the events of November 6, 1917.

1. **Analyzing** Why did the Bolsheviks choose the Winter Palace as the place to attack?

2. **Explaining** Why is the Russian Revolution considered a turning point?

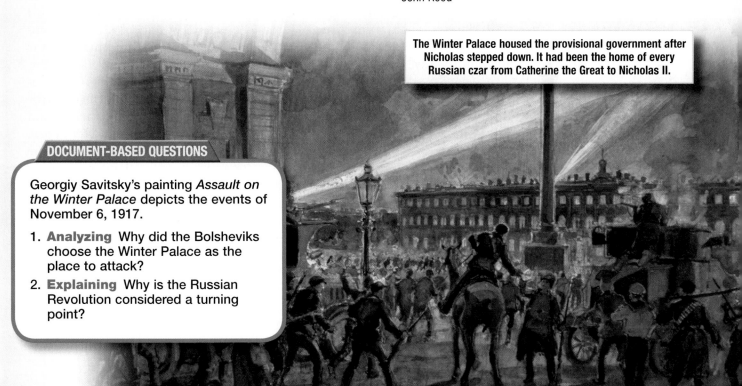

Factory smokestacks symbolize industrialization.

A blacksmith stands on the crown of the czar.

A peasant holds a sickle, a symbol of communism.

"Communism is Soviet power plus the electrification of the whole country. Otherwise the country remains small-peasant. . . . We are weaker than capitalism, not only on a world scale but also within the country. All this is well known. We recognize this and we are taking action to transform the small-peasant base into a heavy-industry base. Only when the country is electrified, when industry, agriculture, and transport are placed on the technical basis of modern heavy industry, will we have won decisively."
—V. I. Lenin, remarks to the Congress of Soviets, 1920

DOCUMENT-BASED QUESTIONS

Year of the Proletarian Dictatorship is a propaganda poster created in 1918 by the Russian artist Aleksandr Apsit. It illustrates some of the goals of the Communists after the Russian Revolution.

1. **Making Inferences** What were two major goals of the Communists after the Russian Revolution? Explain.

2. **Analyzing** Why do you think a communist revolution occurred in Russia rather than an industrialized nation?

It would mean the humiliating loss of much Russian territory. There was no real choice, however.

On March 3, 1918, Lenin signed the Treaty of Brest-Litovsk with Germany and gave up eastern Poland, **Ukraine**, Finland, and the Baltic provinces. To his critics, Lenin argued that it made no difference. The spread of the socialist revolution throughout Europe would make the treaty largely irrelevant. In any case, he had promised peace to the Russian people. Real peace did not come, however, because the country soon sank into civil war.

Civil War in Russia

Many people were opposed to the new Bolshevik, or Communist, government. These people included not only groups loyal to the czar but also liberal and anti-Leninist socialists. Liberals often supported a constitutional monarchy, while a number of socialists supported gradual reform. These socialists expected to work for a socialist state under more democratic leaders than Lenin. They were joined by the Allies, who were extremely concerned about the Communist takeover.

The Allies sent thousands of troops to various parts of Russia in the hope of bringing Russia back into the war. The Allied forces rarely fought on Russian soil, but they gave material aid to anti-Communist forces. Between 1918 and 1921, the Communist or Red Army fought on many fronts against these opponents.

The first serious threat to the Communists came from **Siberia**. An anti-Communist, or White, force attacked and advanced almost to the Volga River before being stopped. Attacks also came from the Ukrainians and from the Baltic regions. In mid-1919, White forces swept through Ukraine and advanced almost to Moscow before being pushed back.

By 1920, however, the major White forces had been defeated and Ukraine retaken. The next year, the Communist regime regained control over the independent nationalist governments in Georgia, Russian Armenia, and Azerbaijan (A•zuhr•by•JAHN).

The royal family was another victim of the civil war. After the czar abdicated, he, his wife, and their five children had been held as prisoners. In April 1918, they were moved to Yekaterinburg, a mining town in the **Urals**. On the night of July 16, members of the local soviet murdered the czar and his family and burned their bodies in a nearby mine shaft.

Triumph of the Communists

How had Lenin and the Communists triumphed in the civil war over such overwhelming forces? One reason was that the Red Army was a well-disciplined fighting force. This was largely due to the organizational genius of **Leon Trotsky**. As commissar of war, Trotsky reinstated the draft and insisted on rigid discipline. Soldiers who deserted or refused to obey orders were executed on the spot.

Furthermore, the disunity of the anti-Communist forces weakened their efforts. Political differences created distrust among the Whites. Some Whites insisted on restoring the czarist regime. Others wanted a more liberal and democratic program. The Whites, then, had no common goal.

The Communists, in contrast, had a single-minded sense of purpose. Inspired by their vision of a new socialist order, the Communists had both revolutionary zeal and strong convictions. They were also able to translate their revolutionary faith into practical instruments of power. A policy of **war communism**, for example, was used to ensure regular supplies for the Red Army. The government controlled the banks and most industries, seized grain from peasants, and centralized state administration under Communist control.

Another instrument was Communist revolutionary terror. A new Red secret police—known as the Cheka—began a Red Terror. Aimed at destroying all those who opposed the new regime (much like the Reign of Terror in the French Revolution), the Red Terror added an element of fear to the Communist regime.

Finally, foreign armies on Russian soil enabled the Communists to appeal to the powerful force of Russian patriotism. At one point, over 100,000 foreign troops—mostly Japanese, British, American, and French—were stationed in Russia in support of anti-Communist forces. Their presence made it easy for the Communist government to call on patriotic Russians to fight foreign attempts to control the country.

By 1921, the Communists were in total command of Russia. The Communist regime had transformed Russia into a centralized state dominated by a single party. The state was also largely hostile to the Allied Powers, because the Allies had tried to help the Communists' enemies in the civil war.

✓ Reading Check **Contrasting** Why did the Red Army prevail over the White forces?

Vocabulary

1. **Explain** the significance of: Grigory Rasputin, Alexandra, Petrograd, Aleksandr Kerensky, soviets, Bolsheviks, V. I. Lenin, revolution, Ukraine, Siberia, Urals, Leon Trotsky, war communism.

Main Ideas

2. **Explain** what the Petrograd women meant when they chanted "Peace and Bread" during their march.

3. **List** the steps that the Communists took to turn Russia into a centralized state dominated by one party. Use a chart like the one below.

Steps to Communist Control
1.
2.

4. **Specify** why Lenin accepted the loss of so much Russian territory in the Treaty of Brest-Litovsk.

Critical Thinking

5. **The BIG Idea** **Analyzing** How did the presence of Allied troops in Russia ultimately help the Communists?

6. **Identifying Central Issues** What led to Czar Nicholas II's downfall?

7. **Analyzing Visuals** Examine the painting on page 540. What does the red flag symbolize?

Writing About History

8. **Multimedia Presentation** Prepare a multimedia presentation comparing the economic, political, and social causes of the American, French, and Russian Revolutions.

History ONLINE

For help with the concepts in this section of *Glencoe World History—Modern Times*, go to glencoe.com and click Study Central.

End of World War I

GUIDE TO READING

The BIG Idea
Order and Security After the defeat of the Germans, peace settlements brought political and territorial changes to Europe and created bitterness and resentment in some nations.

Content Vocabulary
- armistice *(p. 544)*
- mandates *(p. 547)*
- reparations *(p. 545)*

Academic Vocabulary
- psychological *(p. 542)*
- cooperation *(p. 544)*

People and Places
- Erich Ludendorff *(p. 542)*
- Georges Clemenceau *(p. 545)*
- Kiel *(p. 544)*
- Alsace *(p. 546)*
- Friedrich Ebert *(p. 544)*
- Lorraine *(p. 546)*
- Poland *(p. 546)*
- David Lloyd George *(p. 545)*

Reading Strategy
Organizing Information At the Paris Peace Conference, the leaders of France, Britain, and the United States were motivated by different concerns. As you read, use a chart like the one below to identify the national interests of each country as it approached the peace deliberations.

France	Britain	United States

Governments, troops, and civilians were weary as World War I continued through 1917. Shortly after the United States entered the war, Germany made its final military gamble on the Western Front and lost. The war finally ended on November 11, 1918. The peace treaties were particularly harsh on Germany. New nations were formed, and a League of Nations was created to resolve future international disputes.

The Last Year of the War

MAIN IDEA The new German republic and the Allies signed an armistice, ending the war on November 11, 1918.

HISTORY & YOU Have you heard debates about how large the U.S. military budget should be? Read to understand the role of U.S. army support in the Allied victory of World War I.

The year 1917 had not been a good one for the Allies. Allied offensives on the Western Front had been badly defeated. The Russian Revolution, which began in November 1917, led to Russia's withdrawal from the war a few months later. The cause of the Central Powers looked favorable, although war weariness was beginning to take its toll.

On the positive side, the entry of the United States into the war in 1917 gave the Allies a much-needed **psychological** boost. The United States also provided fresh troops and material. In 1918, American troops would prove crucial.

A New German Offensive

For Germany, the withdrawal of the Russians offered new hope for a successful end to the war. Germany was now free to concentrate entirely on the Western Front. **Erich Ludendorff,** who guided German military operations, decided to make one final military gamble—a grand offensive in the west to break the military stalemate. In fact, the last of Germany's strength went into making this one great blow. The divisions were running low on provisions, reserves of soldiers were nearly depleted, and the German home front was tired of the war.

The German attack was launched in March 1918. By April, German troops were within about 50 miles (80 km) of Paris. However, the German advance was stopped at the Second Battle of the Marne on July 18. French, Moroccan, and American troops (140,000 fresh American troops had just arrived), supported by hundreds of tanks, threw the Germans back over the Marne. On August 8, the

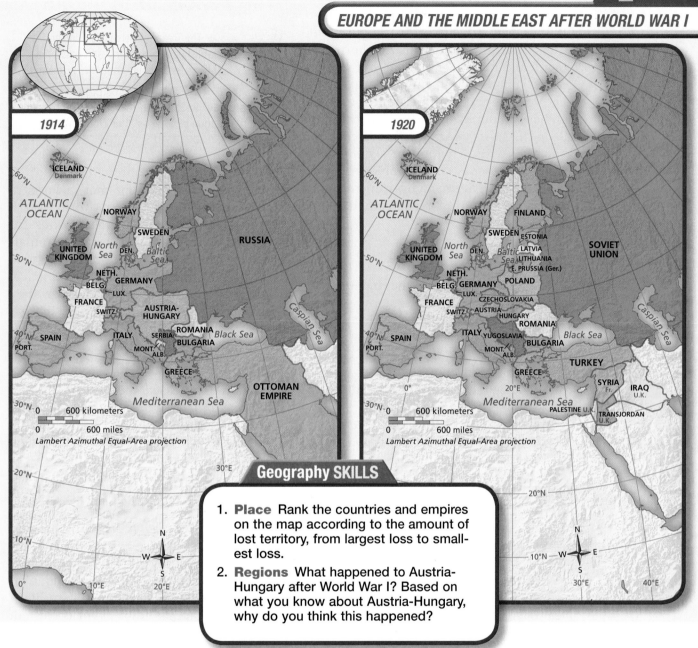

EUROPE AND THE MIDDLE EAST AFTER WORLD WAR I

1914

ICELAND
Denmark

ATLANTIC
OCEAN

NORWAY

SWEDEN

RUSSIA

UNITED
KINGDOM

North
Sea

DEN.

Baltic
Sea

NETH.

BELG.

GERMANY

LUX.

FRANCE

SWITZ.

AUSTRIA-
HUNGARY

Caspian Sea

SPAIN

ITALY

SERBIA

ROMANIA

Black Sea

MONT.

BULGARIA

PORT.

ALB.

GREECE

OTTOMAN
EMPIRE

Mediterranean Sea

0   600 kilometers

0   600 miles

Lambert Azimuthal Equal-Area projection

1920

ICELAND
Denmark

ATLANTIC
OCEAN

NORWAY

FINLAND

SWEDEN

ESTONIA

SOVIET
UNION

UNITED
KINGDOM

North
Sea

DEN.

Baltic
Sea

LATVIA

LITHUANIA

E. PRUSSIA (Ger.)

NETH.

BELG.

GERMANY

LUX.

POLAND

FRANCE

SWITZ.

CZECHOSLOVAKIA

AUSTRIA

HUNGARY

ROMANIA

Caspian Sea

SPAIN

ITALY

YUGOSLAVIA

Black Sea

MONT.

BULGARIA

PORT.

ALB.

TURKEY

GREECE

SYRIA
Fr.

IRAQ
U.K.

Mediterranean Sea

PALESTINE U.K.

TRANSJORDAN
U.K.

0   600 kilometers

0   600 miles

Lambert Azimuthal Equal-Area projection

Geography SKILLS

1. **Place** Rank the countries and empires on the map according to the amount of lost territory, from largest loss to smallest loss.

2. **Regions** What happened to Austria-Hungary after World War I? Based on what you know about Austria-Hungary, why do you think this happened?

forces met at the Second Battle of the Somme. Ludendorff wrote of this battle: "August 8 was the black day of the German army in the history of this war." Ludendorff admitted that his gamble had failed:

<u>**PRIMARY SOURCE**</u>

"The 8th of August put the decline of [our] fighting power beyond all doubt, and in such a situation as regards reserves, I had no hope of finding a strategic expedient whereby to turn the situation to our advantage."

—Erich Ludendorff, in *The Great War*, Correlli Barnett, 1980

A million American troops poured into France, and the Allies began an advance toward Germany. On September 29, 1918, General Ludendorff told German leaders that the war was lost. He demanded the government ask for peace at once.

Collapse and Armistice

German officials soon found that the Allies were unwilling to make peace with the autocratic imperial government of Germany. Reforms for a liberal government came too late for the tired, angry German people.

On November 3, 1918, sailors in the northern German town of **Kiel** mutinied. Within days, councils of workers and soldiers formed throughout northern Germany and took over civilian and military offices. Emperor William II gave in to public pressure and left the country on November 9. After William II's departure, the Social Democrats under **Friedrich Ebert** announced the creation of a democratic republic. Two days later, on November 11, 1918, the new German government signed an **armistice** (a truce, an agreement to end the fighting).

Revolutionary Forces

The war was over, but the revolutionary forces set in motion in Germany were not yet exhausted. A group of radical socialists, unhappy with the Social Democrats' moderate policies, formed the German Communist Party in December 1918. A month later, the Communists tried to seize power in Berlin.

The new Social Democratic government, backed by regular army troops, crushed the rebels and murdered Rosa Luxemburg and Karl Liebknecht (LEEP•KNEHKT), leaders of the German Communists. A similar attempt at Communist revolution in the city of Munich, in southern Germany, was also crushed.

The new German republic had been saved. The attempt at revolution, however, left the German middle class with a deep fear of communism.

Austria-Hungary, too, experienced disintegration and revolution. As war weariness took hold of the empire, ethnic groups increasingly sought to achieve their independence. By the time World War I ended, the Austro-Hungarian Empire had ceased to exist.

The empire had been replaced by the independent republics of Austria, Hungary, and Czechoslovakia, along with the large monarchical state called Yugoslavia. Rivalries among the nations that succeeded Austria-Hungary would weaken eastern Europe for the next 80 years.

✓ Reading Check **Describing** What happened within Germany after the armistice?

The Peace Settlements

MAIN IDEA The Treaty of Versailles punished Germany, established new nations, and created a League of Nations to solve international problems.

HISTORY & YOU What is the purpose of the United Nations today? Read to learn why the U.S. president wanted a League of Nations after World War I.

In January 1919, representatives of 27 victorious Allied nations met in Paris to make a final settlement of World War I. Over a period of years, the reasons for fighting World War I had changed dramatically. When European nations had gone to war in 1914, they sought territorial gains. By the beginning of 1918, however, they were also expressing more idealistic reasons for the war.

Wilson's Proposals

No one expressed these idealistic reasons better than the president of the United States, Woodrow Wilson. Even before the end of the war, Wilson outlined "Fourteen Points" to the United States Congress—his basis for a peace settlement that he believed justified the enormous military struggle being waged.

Wilson's proposals for a truly just and lasting peace included reaching the peace agreements openly rather than through secret diplomacy. His proposals also included reducing armaments (military forces or weapons) to a "point consistent with domestic safety" and ensuring self-determination (the right of each people to have their own nation).

Wilson portrayed World War I as a people's war against "absolutism and militarism." These two enemies of liberty, he argued, could be eliminated only by creating democratic governments and a "general association of nations." This association would guarantee "political independence and territorial integrity to great and small states alike."

Wilson became the spokesperson for a new world order based on democracy and international **cooperation.** When he arrived in Europe for the peace conference, Wilson was enthusiastically cheered by many

Europeans. President Wilson soon found, however, that more practical motives guided other states.

The Paris Peace Conference

Delegates met in Paris in early 1919 to determine the peace settlement. At the Paris Peace Conference, complications became obvious. For one thing, secret treaties and agreements that had been made before the war had raised the hopes of European nations for territorial gains. These hopes could not be ignored, even if they did conflict with the principle of self-determination put forth by Wilson.

National interests also complicated the deliberations of the Paris Peace Conference. **David Lloyd George,** prime minister of Great Britain, had won a decisive victory in elections in December 1918. His platform was simple: make the Germans pay for this dreadful war.

France's approach to peace was chiefly guided by its desire for national security. To **Georges Clemenceau** (KLEH•muhn•SOH), the premier of France, the French people had suffered the most from German aggression. The French desired revenge and security against future German attacks. Clemenceau wanted Germany stripped of all weapons, vast German payments—**reparations**—to cover the costs of the war, and a separate Rhineland as a buffer state between France and Germany.

The most important decisions at the Paris Peace Conference were made by Wilson, Clemenceau, and Lloyd George. Italy, as one of the Allies, was considered one of the Big Four powers. However, it played a smaller role than the other key powers— the United States, France, and Great Britain, who were called the Big Three. Germany was not invited to attend, and Russia could not be present because of its civil war.

In view of the many conflicting demands at the peace conference, it was no surprise that the Big Three quarreled. Wilson wanted to create a world organization, the League of Nations, to prevent future wars. Clemenceau and Lloyd George wanted to punish Germany. In the end, only compromise made it possible to achieve a peace settlement.

Wilson's wish that the creation of an international peacekeeping organization be the first order of business was granted. On January 25, 1919, the conference accepted the idea of a League of Nations. In return, Wilson agreed to make compromises on territorial arrangements. He did so because he believed that the League could later fix any unfair settlements.

Clemenceau also compromised to obtain some guarantees for French security. He gave up France's wish for a separate Rhineland and instead accepted a defensive alliance with Great Britain and the United States. However, the U.S. Senate refused to ratify this agreement, which weakened the Versailles peace settlement.

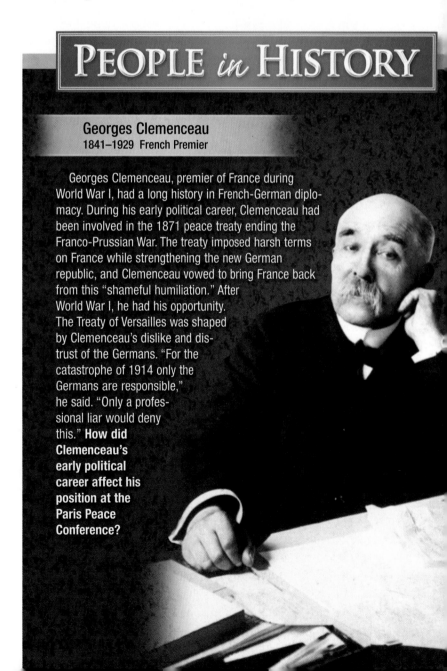

PEOPLE in HISTORY

Georges Clemenceau
1841–1929 French Premier

Georges Clemenceau, premier of France during World War I, had a long history in French-German diplomacy. During his early political career, Clemenceau had been involved in the 1871 peace treaty ending the Franco-Prussian War. The treaty imposed harsh terms on France while strengthening the new German republic, and Clemenceau vowed to bring France back from this "shameful humiliation." After World War I, he had his opportunity. The Treaty of Versailles was shaped by Clemenceau's dislike and distrust of the Germans. "For the catastrophe of 1914 only the Germans are responsible," he said. "Only a professional liar would deny this." **How did Clemenceau's early political career affect his position at the Paris Peace Conference?**

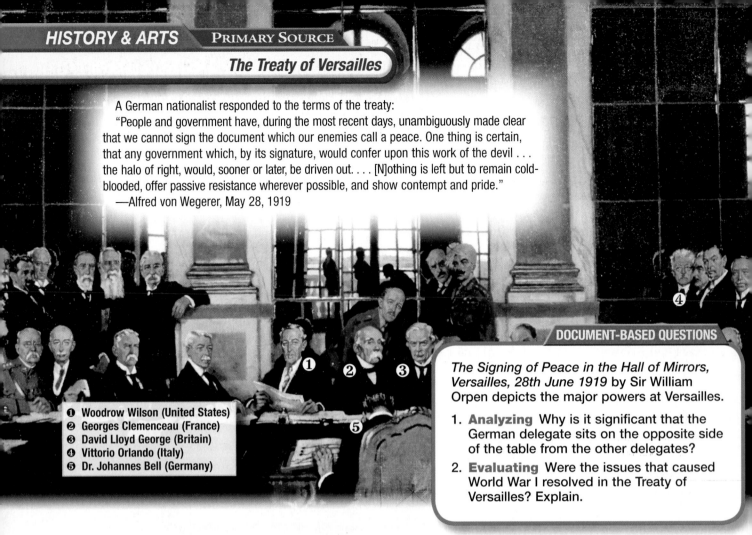

A German nationalist responded to the terms of the treaty:

"People and government have, during the most recent days, unambiguously made clear that we cannot sign the document which our enemies call a peace. One thing is certain, that any government which, by its signature, would confer upon this work of the devil . . . the halo of right, would, sooner or later, be driven out. . . . [N]othing is left but to remain cold-blooded, offer passive resistance wherever possible, and show contempt and pride."

—Alfred von Wegerer, May 28, 1919

❶ Woodrow Wilson (United States)
❷ Georges Clemenceau (France)
❸ David Lloyd George (Britain)
❹ Vittorio Orlando (Italy)
❺ Dr. Johannes Bell (Germany)

DOCUMENT-BASED QUESTIONS

The Signing of Peace in the Hall of Mirrors, Versailles, 28th June 1919 by Sir William Orpen depicts the major powers at Versailles.

1. **Analyzing** Why is it significant that the German delegate sits on the opposite side of the table from the other delegates?

2. **Evaluating** Were the issues that caused World War I resolved in the Treaty of Versailles? Explain.

The Treaty of Versailles

The final peace settlement of Paris consisted of five separate treaties with the defeated nations of Germany, Austria, Hungary, Bulgaria, and Turkey. The Treaty of Versailles with Germany was by far the most important.

The Germans considered it a harsh peace. They were especially unhappy with Article 231, the so-called War Guilt Clause, which declared that Germany (and Austria) were responsible for starting the war. The treaty ordered Germany to pay reparations for all damages that the Allied governments and their people had sustained as a result of the war.

The military and territorial provisions of the Treaty of Versailles also angered the Germans. Germany had to reduce its army to 100,000 men, cut back its navy, and eliminate its air force. **Alsace** and **Lorraine,** taken by the Germans from France in 1871, were now returned. Sections of eastern Germany were awarded to a new Polish state.

German land along the Rhine River became a demilitarized zone, stripped of all weapons and fortifications. This, it was hoped, would serve as a barrier to any future German moves against France. Although outraged by the "dictated peace," Germany accepted the treaty.

The Legacies of the War

The war, the Treaty of Versailles, and the separate peace treaties made with the other Central Powers redrew the map of eastern Europe. The German and Russian empires lost much territory. The Austro-Hungarian Empire disappeared.

New nation-states emerged from the lands of these three empires: Finland, Latvia, Estonia, Lithuania, **Poland,** Czechoslovakia, Austria, and Hungary. New territorial arrangements were also made in the Balkans. Romania acquired additional lands. Serbia formed the nucleus of a new state, called Yugoslavia, which combined Serbs, Croats, and Slovenes.

The principle of self-determination supposedly guided the Paris Peace Conference. However, the mixtures of peoples in eastern Europe made it impossible to draw boundaries along strict ethnic lines. Compromises had to be made, sometimes to satisfy the national interests of the victors. France, for example, had lost Russia as its major ally on Germany's eastern border. Thus, France wanted to strengthen and expand Poland, Czechoslovakia, Yugoslavia, and Romania as much as possible. Those states could then serve as barriers against Germany and Communist Russia.

As a result of compromises, almost every eastern European state was left with ethnic minorities: Germans in Poland; Hungarians, Poles, and Germans in Czechoslovakia; Hungarians in Romania, and Serbs, Croats, Slovenes, Macedonians, and Albanians in Yugoslavia. The problem of ethnic minorities within nations would lead to many later conflicts.

Yet another centuries-old empire—the Ottoman Empire—was broken up by the peace settlement. To gain Arab support against the Ottoman Turks during the war, the Western Allies had promised to recognize the independence of Arab states in the Ottoman Empire. Once the war was over, however, the Western nations changed their minds. France took control of Lebanon and Syria, and Britain received Iraq and Palestine.

These acquisitions were officially called **mandates.** Woodrow Wilson had opposed the outright annexation of colonial territories by the Allies. As a result, the peace settlement created the mandate system. According to this system, a nation officially governed another nation as a mandate on behalf of the League of Nations but did not own the territory.

World War I shattered the liberal, rational society that had existed in late nineteenth- and early twentieth-century Europe. The deaths of nearly 10 million people, as well as the incredible destruction caused by the war, undermined the whole idea of progress. Entire populations had participated in a devastating slaughter.

World War I was a total war—one that involved a complete mobilization of resources and people. As a result, the power of governments over the lives of their citizens increased. Freedom of the press and speech were limited in the name of national security. World War I made the practice of strong central authority a way of life.

The turmoil created by the war also seemed to open the door to even greater insecurity. Revolutions broke up old empires and created new states, which led to new problems. The hope that Europe and the rest of the world would return to normalcy was, however, soon dashed.

 **Reading Check** **Identifying** What clause in the Treaty of Versailles particularly angered the Germans?

SECTION 4 REVIEW

Vocabulary

1. **Explain** the significance of: psychological, Erich Ludendorff, Kiel, Friedrich Ebert, armistice, cooperation, David Lloyd George, Georges Clemenceau, reparations, Alsace, Lorraine, Poland, mandates.

Main Ideas

2. **Specify** why Erich Ludendorff's final military gamble failed for Germany.

3. **List** some of President Wilson's proposals for creating peace. Use a chart like the one below to make your list.

President Wilson's Proposals
1.
2.

4. **Explain** why the mandate system was created. Which countries became mandates? Which countries governed them?

Critical Thinking

5. **The BIG Idea** **Making Generalizations** Although Woodrow Wilson came to the Paris Peace Conference with high ideals, the other leaders had more practical concerns. Why do you think that was so?

6. **Comparing and Contrasting** Compare and contrast Wilson's Fourteen Points to the Treaty of Versailles.

7. **Analyzing Visuals** Examine the painting on page 546. What is the significance of the setting?

Writing About History

8. **Informative Writing** Suppose that you are a reporter for a large newspaper. You are sent to the Paris Peace Conference to interview one of the leaders of the Big Three. Prepare a written set of questions you would like to ask the leader you have selected.

History ONLINE

For help with the concepts in this section of *Glencoe World History—Modern Times*, go to glencoe.com and click Study Central.

STUDY TO GO You can study anywhere, anytime by downloading quizzes and flash cards to your PDA from glencoe.com.

THE CAUSES OF WORLD WAR I

- Nationalism contributed to the start of World War I, as rivals vied for colonies and trade.
- European nations increased the size of their militaries, heightening existing tensions.
- Serbia's desire for an independent state angered Austria-Hungary.

THE ASSASSINATION OF ARCHDUKE FERDINAND

Austria-Hungary declared war on Serbia after a Serbian terrorist killed the archduke.

GERMANS RETREAT DURING AN ALLIED AIR ATTACK, 1918

Soldiers struggled to adapt to new war technology such as the airplane.

The Reality of MODERN WARFARE

- Trench warfare brought the Western Front to a stalemate until new allies entered the war.
- Trench warfare and new technology caused a devastating loss of life.
- Governments took control of economies and rationed civilian goods, affecting all citizens.

THE RUSSIAN REVOLUTION and THE END OF WORLD WAR I

- Russia's failure in the war and worker unrest led to the Russian Revolution in 1917.
- Bolshevik overthrow of the provisional government led to civil war and eventual Communist control.
- A defeated Germany signed an armistice with the Allies, ending the war on November 11, 1918.
- The Treaty of Versailles punished Germany, formed new nations, and created the League of Nations to solve international problems.

RESULTS OF PEACE TREATIES AFTER WORLD WAR I

Germany was forced to destroy tanks and other military equipment to conform to the Treaty of Versailles.

STANDARDIZED TEST PRACTICE

TEST-TAKING

A date can be an important clue. When a question or answer contains a date, think about major events that occurred during or around that time. Then eliminate answer choices that do not reflect that history.

Reviewing Vocabulary

Directions: Choose the word or words that best complete the sentence.

1. Ideas that are spread to influence public opinion for or against a cause are known as _____.

   A ad campaigns

   B brochures

   C propaganda

   D newsletters

2. Germany had to make _____ to cover the costs of World War I.

   A reparations

   B credit card purchases

   C debts

   D border changes

3. _____ is the process of assembling troops and supplies to get ready for war.

   A Conscription

   B War communism

   C Armistice

   D Mobilization

4. The _____ were councils composed of representatives from Russian workers and soldiers.

   A czars

   B Duma

   C soviets

   D Bolsheviks

Reviewing Main Ideas

Directions: Choose the best answers to the following questions.

Section 1 *(pp. 522–525)*

5. To increase the size of their armies, many Western countries established which of the following?

   A A voluntary enlistment program

   B Their imperialistic goals

   C A conscription program

   D The Schlieffen Plan

6. When was Archduke Francis Ferdinand assassinated?

   A August 4, 1914

   B September 20, 1915

   C November 11, 1918

   D June 28, 1914

Section 2 *(pp. 526–533)*

7. During World War I, the Allies tried to open a Balkan front by landing forces at which city?

   A Gallipoli

   B Beirut

   C Sarajevo

   D Odessa

8. Who urged Arab princes to revolt against their Ottoman overlords in 1917?

   A Mohandas Gandhi

   B Lawrence of Arabia

   C Lord Chamberlain

   D Gavrilo Princip

Need Extra Help?								
If You Missed Questions . . .	1	2	3	4	5	6	7	8
Go to Page . . .	526	545	525	538	523	524	530	530

9. When did most British women gain the right to vote?

   A 1920

   B 1904

   C 1918

   D 1935

Section 3 (pp. 536–541)

10. In which city did Russian working-class women lead a series of strikes in March 1917?

    A Moscow

    B Berlin

    C Budapest

    D Petrograd

11. Which faction of a Marxist party came under the leadership of V. I. Lenin?

    A Bolsheviks

    B Stalinists

    C Zionists

    D Slavsheviks

Section 4 (pp. 542–547)

12. Under whose command did the German forces make one final military gamble to win the Western Front in 1918?

    A Adolf Hitler

    B Erich Ludendorff

    C Karl Liebknecht

    D Friedrich Ebert

13. What were Woodrow Wilson's proposals for a peace settlement called?

    A Germany's Nightmare

    B Twelve Points

    C Fourteen Points

    D The Peace Settlement

Critical Thinking

Directions: Choose the best answers to the following questions.

Use the following map to answer question 14.

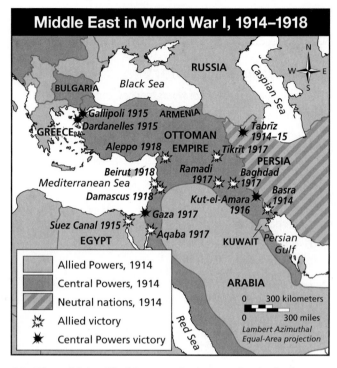

Middle East in World War I, 1914–1918

14. When did the Allied Powers win the most battles in the Middle East?

    A 1917

    B 1918

    C 1920

    D The Allied Powers and Central Powers won the same number of battles.

15. What major event resulted from the Balkan crises between 1908 and 1913?

    A The creation of a new Serbian kingdom

    B The assassination of Archduke Francis Ferdinand and his wife

    C The Berlin Conference of 1884

    D The end of the Romanov dynasty

Need Extra Help?							
If You Missed Questions . . .	9	10	11	12	13	14	15
Go to Page . . .	533	537	538	542	544	550	524

GO ON

16. Why did Russian conservative aristocrats kill Rasputin?

 A He was a holy person.

 B He had hemophilia.

 C He was Alexis's tutor.

 D He interfered too often in government affairs.

17. What slogan would best express Georges Clemenceau's motives at the Paris Peace Conference in 1919?

 A "Give Them Bread"

 B "Peace at Last"

 C "Revenge! Sweet Revenge!"

 D "Down with Autocracy"

Analyze the graph and answer the question that follows.

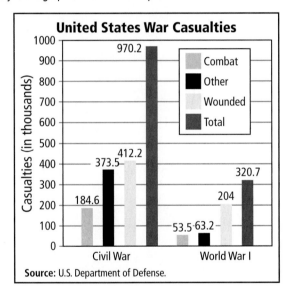

United States War Casualties

Source: U.S. Department of Defense.

18. Which of the following statements is based on the information in the graph?

 A There were approximately 1 million U.S. casualties in World War I.

 B Approximately 400,000 U.S. troops were wounded in World War I.

 C Compared to the total number of U.S. casualties in World War I, there were approximately 3 times the total number of casualties in the Civil War.

 D Total American casualties in World War I did not exceed 200,000.

Document-Based Questions

Directions: Analyze the document and answer the short answer questions that follow the document. Base your answers on the document and on your knowledge of world history.

Many Europeans saw the potential danger in the explosive situation between Serbia and Austria-Hungary. The British ambassador to Vienna, Austria, anticipated war in 1913.

> *"Serbia will some day set Europe by the ears, and bring about a universal war on the Continent. . . . I cannot tell you how exasperated people are getting here at the continual worry which that little country causes to Austria under encouragement from Russia. . . . It will be lucky if Europe succeeds in avoiding war as a result of the present crisis."*

19. Is the ambassador neutral in his comments, or does he favor one country over another?

20. Compare the ways in which the actual events that started World War I mirror the ambassador's concerns.

Extended Response

21. Both Britain and the United States passed laws during the war to silence opposition and censor the press. Are the ideals of a democratic government consistent with such laws? Provide arguments for and against.

History ONLINE

For additional test practice, use Self-Check Quizzes—Chapter 16 at glencoe.com.

Need Extra Help?						
If You Missed Questions . . .	16	17	18	19	20	21
Go to Page . . .	536	545	551	551	551	532

STOP

CHAPTER **17**

The West Between the Wars 1919–1939

Section 1 The Futile Search for Stability

Section 2 The Rise of Dictatorial Regimes

Section 3 Hitler and Nazi Germany

Section 4 Cultural and Intellectual Trends

MAKING CONNECTIONS

How can politics be reflected in sports?

Nazi leader Adolf Hitler wanted to use the 1936 Olympic Games in Berlin to show the superiority of the Aryan (German) race. However, African-American athlete Jesse Owens of the United States shattered that plan by winning four gold medals. In this chapter you will learn how Hitler and other leaders created totalitarian states.

- In the photograph, why is Jesse Owens (at center) saluting and why is Lutz Long (at right) extending his arm?
- Do you think national pride and politics or individual accomplishments are more important to Olympic athletes today?

EUROPE AND THE
UNITED STATES ▶

1922
Lenin and the
Communists
create the USSR

1926
Mussolini estab-
lishes a Fascist
dictatorship
in Italy

1929
U.S. stock market
crashes; Great
Depression begins

1919   1925   1930

THE WORLD ▶

1923
Nationalists and Communists
in China form an alliance

552

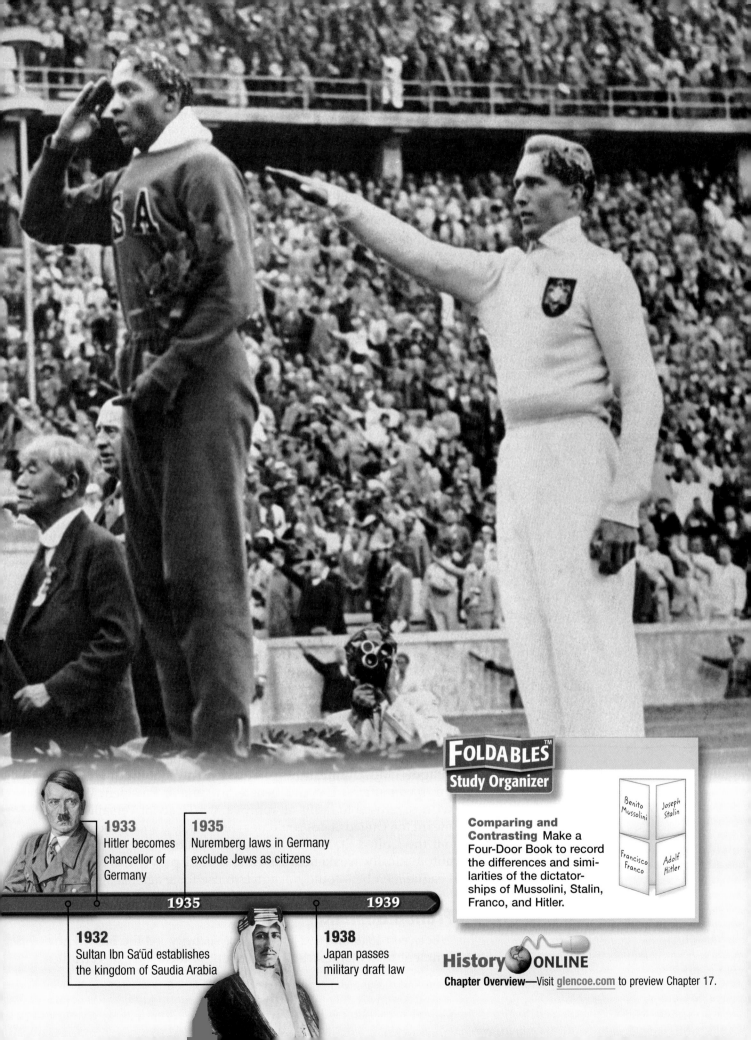

1933
Hitler becomes
chancellor of
Germany

1935
Nuremberg laws in Germany
exclude Jews as citizens

1935

1939

1932
Sultan Ibn Sa'ūd establishes
the kingdom of Saudia Arabia

1938
Japan passes
military draft law

FOLDABLES™
Study Organizer

Benito
Mussolini

Joseph
Stalin

Francisco
Franco

Adolf
Hitler

**Comparing and
Contrasting** Make a
Four-Door Book to record
the differences and simi-
larities of the dictator-
ships of Mussolini, Stalin,
Franco, and Hitler.

History ONLINE

Chapter Overview—Visit glencoe.com to preview Chapter 17.

The Futile Search for Stability

GUIDE TO READING

The BIG Idea
Competition Among Countries
Peace and prosperity were short-lived after World War I as a global depression weakened Western democracies.

Content Vocabulary
- depression *(p. 556)*
- collective bargaining *(p. 558)*
- deficit spending *(p. 559)*

Academic Vocabulary
- annual *(p. 555)*
- ratio *(p. 556)*

People, Places, and Events
- Ruhr Valley *(p. 555)*
- Dawes Plan *(p. 556)*
- Treaty of Locarno *(p. 556)*
- Switzerland *(p. 558)*
- Weimar Republic *(p. 558)*
- John Maynard Keynes *(p. 559)*
- Franklin Delano Roosevelt *(p. 559)*
- New Deal *(p. 559)*

Reading Strategy
Comparing and Contrasting As you read, use a table like the one below to compare France's Popular Front with the New Deal in the United States.

Popular Front	New Deal

The peace settlement of World War I left many nations unhappy, and the League of Nations proved unable to deal with the crises following the war. The brief period of prosperity that began in Europe during the early 1920s ended in 1929 with the beginning of the Great Depression. This economic collapse shook people's confidence in political democracy and paved the way for fear and the rise of extremist parties that offered solutions to the hardships that many were enduring.

Uneasy Peace, Uncertain Security

MAIN IDEA Discontent with the Treaty of Versailles and a weak League of Nations opened the door to new problems in the interwar years.

HISTORY & YOU Imagine how your life would change if the price of everything doubled each day. Read to learn how runaway inflation affected Germany after World War I.

The peace settlement at the end of World War I tried to fulfill nineteenth-century dreams of nationalism. It created new boundaries and new states. From the beginning, however, the settlement left nations unhappy. Border disputes poisoned relations in eastern Europe for years. Many Germans vowed to revise the terms of the Treaty of Versailles.

A Weak League of Nations

President Woodrow Wilson had realized that the peace settlement included unwise provisions that could serve as new causes for conflict. He had placed many of his hopes for the future in the League of Nations. This organization, however, was not very effective in maintaining the peace.

One problem was the failure of the United States to join the League. Most Americans wanted to avoid involvement in European affairs. The U.S. Senate, in spite of President Wilson's wishes, refused to ratify, or approve, the Treaty of Versailles. That meant the United States could not join the League of Nations. Without the United States, the League of Nations' effectiveness was automatically weakened. As time would prove, the remaining League members could not agree to use force against aggression.

French Demands

Between 1919 and 1924, desire for security led the French government to demand strict enforcement of the Treaty of Versailles.

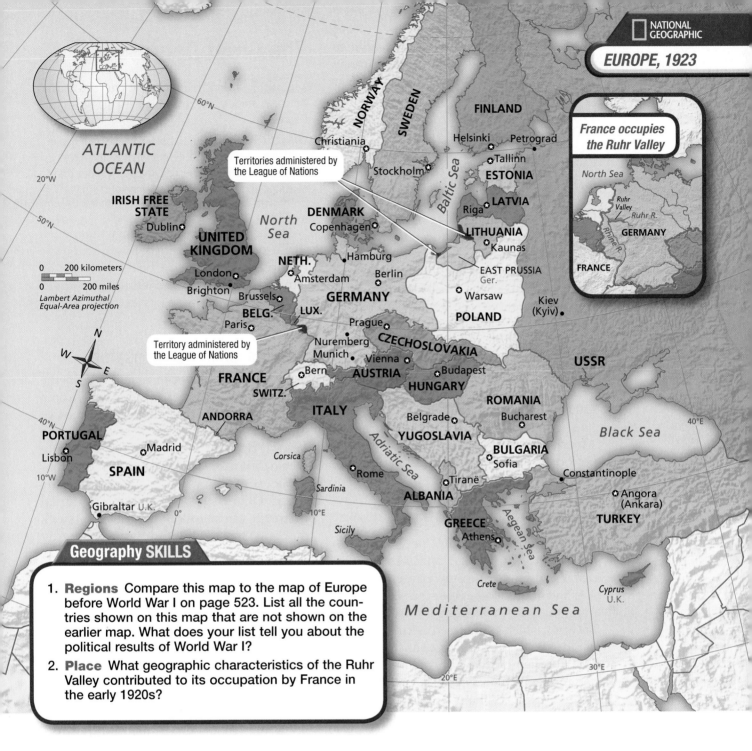

France occupies the Ruhr Valley

North Sea

Ruhr Valley

Ruhr R.

GERMANY

Rhine R.

FRANCE

ATLANTIC OCEAN

20°W

60°N

50°N

40°N

10°W

0°

NORWAY

Christiania

SWEDEN

Stockholm

FINLAND

Helsinki

Petrograd

Tallinn

ESTONIA

Riga

LATVIA

LITHUANIA

Kaunas

Baltic Sea

EAST PRUSSIA
Ger.

Warsaw

Kiev
(Kyiv)

IRISH FREE STATE

Dublin

UNITED KINGDOM

London

Brighton

North Sea

DENMARK

Copenhagen

NETH.

Amsterdam

Hamburg

Berlin

GERMANY

Territories administered by
the League of Nations

BELG.

Brussels

LUX.

Paris

Prague

Nuremberg

Munich

CZECHOSLOVAKIA

Vienna

POLAND

USSR

Territory administered by
the League of Nations

FRANCE

SWITZ.

Bern

AUSTRIA

Budapest

HUNGARY

ROMANIA

Bucharest

Black Sea

40°E

ANDORRA

ITALY

Belgrade

YUGOSLAVIA

BULGARIA

Sofia

Constantinople

PORTUGAL

Madrid

Lisbon

SPAIN

Corsica

Sardinia

Rome

Adriatic Sea

Tiranë

ALBANIA

GREECE

Athens

Aegean Sea

Angora
(Ankara)

TURKEY

Gibraltar U.K.

10°E

20°E

Sicily

Crete

Mediterranean Sea

Cyprus
U.K.

30°E

Geography SKILLS

1. **Regions** Compare this map to the map of Europe before World War I on page 523. List all the countries shown on this map that are not shown on the earlier map. What does your list tell you about the political results of World War I?

2. **Place** What geographic characteristics of the Ruhr Valley contributed to its occupation by France in the early 1920s?

This tough policy began with the issue of reparations (payments) that the Germans were supposed to make for the damage they had done in the war. In April 1921, the Allied Reparations Commission determined that Germany owed 132 billion German marks (33 billion U.S. dollars) for reparations, payable in **annual** installments of 2.5 billion marks.

The new German republic made its first payment in 1921. By the following year, however, the German government faced a financial crisis and announced that it could not pay any more reparations. Outraged, France sent troops to occupy the **Ruhr Valley**, Germany's chief industrial and mining center. France planned to collect reparations by using the Ruhr mines and factories.

Inflation in Germany

The German government adopted a policy of passive resistance to this French occupation. German workers went on strike.

The German government mainly paid their salaries by printing more paper money. This only added to the inflation (rise in prices) that had already begun in Germany by the end of the war.

The German mark soon became worthless. In 1914, 4.2 marks equaled 1 U.S. dollar. By November 1, 1923, it took 130 billion marks to equal 1 dollar. By the end of November, the **ratio** had increased to an incredible 4.2 trillion marks to 1 dollar.

Economic adversity led to political upheavals. Both France and Germany began to seek a way out of the disaster. In August 1924, an international commission produced a new plan for reparations. The **Dawes Plan,** named after the American banker who chaired the commission, first reduced reparations. It then coordinated Germany's annual payments with its ability to pay.

The Dawes Plan also granted an initial $200 million loan for German recovery. This loan soon opened the door to heavy American investment in Europe. A brief period of European prosperity followed, but it only lasted from 1924 to 1929.

The Treaty of Locarno

With prosperity came a new European diplomacy. The foreign ministers of Germany and France, Gustav Stresemann and Aristide Briand, fostered a spirit of cooperation. In 1925 they signed the **Treaty of Locarno,** which guaranteed Germany's new western borders with France and Belgium.

Many viewed the Locarno pact as the beginning of a new era of European peace. On the day after the pact was concluded, headlines in the *New York Times* read "France and Germany Ban War Forever." The London *Times* declared "Peace at Last." The new spirit of cooperation grew even stronger when Germany joined the League of Nations in March 1926.

Two years later, the Kellogg-Briand Pact brought even more hope. Sixty-three nations signed this accord and pledged "to renounce war as an instrument of national policy." Nothing was said, however, about what would be done if anyone violated the pact.

✓ **Reading Check** **Explaining** Why was the League of Nations unable to maintain peace?

The Great Depression

MAIN IDEA Underlying economic problems and an American stock market crisis triggered the Great Depression.

HISTORY & YOU The U.S. stock market plunged in 2001 after terrorist attacks, but what would have happened if it had collapsed? Read to find out the consequences of the 1929 stock market crash.

The brief period of prosperity that began in Europe in 1924 ended in an economic collapse that came to be known as the Great Depression. A **depression** is a period of low economic activity and rising unemployment.

Causes of the Depression

Two factors played a major role in the start of the Great Depression. First was a series of downturns in the economies of individual nations in the second half of the 1920s. Prices for farm products, especially wheat, fell rapidly due to overproduction.

The second factor that triggered the Great Depression was an international financial crisis involving the U.S. stock market. Much of the European prosperity between 1924 and 1929 was built on U.S. bank loans to Germany. Germany needed the U.S. loans to pay reparations to France and Great Britain. During the 1920s, the U.S. stock market boomed. By 1928, American investors pulled money out of Germany to invest it in the stock market. Then, in October 1929, the U.S. stock market crashed. Stock prices plunged.

In a panic, U.S. investors withdrew even more funds from Germany and other European markets. This withdrawal made the banks of Germany and other European states weak. The well-known Creditanstalt Bank in Vienna collapsed in May 1931. By then, trade was slowing, industrial production was declining, and unemployment was rising.

Responses to the Depression

Economic depression was not new to Europe. However, the extent of the economic downturn after 1929 truly made this the Great Depression. During 1932, the worst year of the Depression, nearly 1 in every 4 British workers was unemployed. About 5.5 million Germans, or roughly 30 percent of the German labor force, had no jobs. The unemployed and homeless filled the streets.

Governments did not know how to deal with the crisis. They lowered wages and raised tariffs to exclude foreign goods from home markets. These measures made the crisis worse and had serious political effects.

One effect of the economic crisis was increased government activity in the economy. Another effect was a renewed interest in Marxist ideas. Marx's prediction that capitalism would destroy itself through overproduction seemed to be coming true. Communism thus became more popular, especially among workers and intellectuals.

Finally, the Great Depression led masses of people to follow political leaders who offered simple solutions in return for dictatorial power. Everywhere, democracy seemed on the defensive in the 1930s.

✓ Reading Check Summarizing What were the results of the Great Depression?

TURNING POINT

POLITICAL EFFECTS OF THE GREAT DEPRESSION

The Great Depression left millions of people unemployed— and national economies in crisis. As government attempts to solve the economic problems failed, popular morale waned. Many people turned to Marxism for answers. Extremist political parties gained support by promising better times ahead. These results of the Great Depression were major factors leading to World War II.

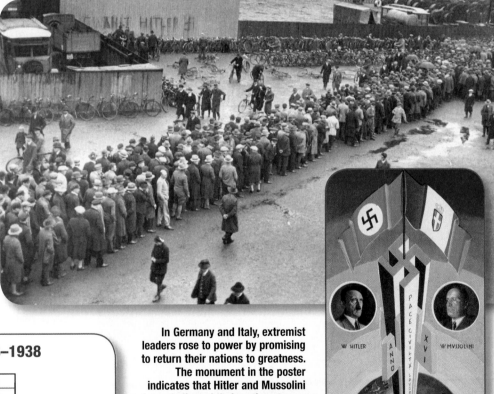

Long lines of unemployed German workers seeking food or jobs bore witness to the misery of the Great Depression. ▶

In Germany and Italy, extremist leaders rose to power by promising to return their nations to greatness. The monument in the poster indicates that Hitler and Mussolini have dedicated their nations to peace, civilization, and work. ▶

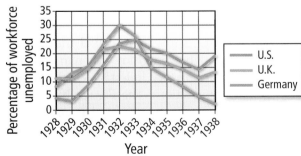

Unemployment, 1928–1938

Percentage of workforce unemployed (vertical axis: 0, 5, 10, 15, 20, 25, 30, 35)

Year (horizontal axis: 1928, 1929, 1930, 1931, 1932, 1933, 1934, 1935, 1936, 1937, 1938)

— U.S.
— U.K.
— Germany

Sources: *European Historical Statistics, 1750–1970; Historical Statistics of the United States.*

CRITICAL THINKING SKILLS

1. **Identifying** Name three political effects of the Great Depression.
2. **Predicting** How might post-Depression political developments have led nations to war?

Democratic States

MAIN IDEA Although new democracies were established in Europe after World War I, the Depression shook people's confidence in political democracy.

HISTORY & YOU When you get stuck on a homework problem, do you look for help? Read about economic problems that sent desperate Europeans searching for answers.

President Woodrow Wilson claimed that World War I had been fought to make the world safe for democracy. In 1919 his claim seemed justified. Most European states, both major and minor, had democratic governments.

In a number of states, women could now vote. Male political leaders had rewarded women for their contributions to the war effort by granting them voting rights. (However, women could not vote until 1944 in France, 1945 in Italy, and 1971 in **Switzerland**.)

In the 1920s, Europe seemed to be returning to the political trends of the prewar era—parliamentary regimes and the growth of individual liberties. This was not, however, an easy process. Four years of total war and four years of postwar turmoil made a "return to normalcy" difficult.

Germany

Imperial Germany ended in 1918 with Germany's defeat in the war. A German democratic state known as the **Weimar** (VY•MAHR) **Republic** was then created. The Weimar Republic was plagued by serious economic problems.

Germany experienced runaway inflation in 1922 and 1923. With it came serious social problems. Families on fixed incomes watched their life savings disappear.

To make matters worse, after a period of relative prosperity from 1924 to 1929, Germany was struck by the Great Depression. In 1930, unemployment had grown to 3 million people by March and to 4.38 million by December. The Depression paved the way for fear and the rise of extremist parties.

France

After the defeat of Germany, France became the strongest power on the European continent. However, France, too, suffered financial problems after the war. It needed to rebuild the areas that had been devastated in the war.

Because it had a more balanced economy than other nations, France did not begin to feel the full effects of the Great Depression until 1932. The economic instability it then suffered soon had political effects. During a 19-month period in 1932 and 1933, six different cabinets were formed as France faced political chaos. Finally, in June 1936, a coalition of leftist parties—Communists, Socialists, and Radicals—formed the Popular Front government.

The Popular Front started a program for workers that some have called the French New Deal. This program was named after the New Deal in the United States (discussed later in this section). The French New Deal gave workers the right to **collective bargaining** (the right of unions to negotiate with employers over wages and hours), a 40-hour workweek in industry, a two-week paid vacation, and a minimum wage.

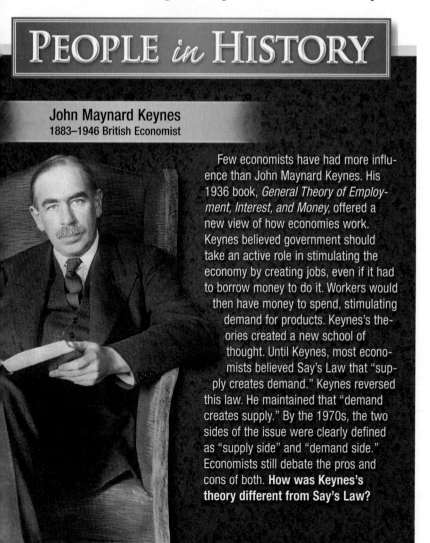

PEOPLE *in* HISTORY

John Maynard Keynes
1883–1946 British Economist

Few economists have had more influence than John Maynard Keynes. His 1936 book, *General Theory of Employment, Interest, and Money*, offered a new view of how economies work. Keynes believed government should take an active role in stimulating the economy by creating jobs, even if it had to borrow money to do it. Workers would then have money to spend, stimulating demand for products. Keynes's theories created a new school of thought. Until Keynes, most economists believed Say's Law that "supply creates demand." Keynes reversed this law. He maintained that "demand creates supply." By the 1970s, the two sides of the issue were clearly defined as "supply side" and "demand side." Economists still debate the pros and cons of both. **How was Keynes's theory different from Say's Law?**

Great Britain

Industries such as coal, steel, and textiles declined after the war, leading to a rise in unemployment. Two million Britons were out of work in 1921.

Britain experienced limited prosperity from 1925 to 1929. However, by 1929, Britain faced the growing effects of the Great Depression. The Labour Party failed to solve the nation's economic problems and fell from power in 1931. A new government, led by the Conservatives, claimed credit for bringing Britain out of the worst stages of the Depression by using the traditional policies of balanced budgets and protective tariffs.

Political leaders in Britain largely ignored the new ideas of a British economist, **John Maynard Keynes,** who published his *General Theory of Employment, Interest, and Money* in 1936. He condemned the old theory that, in a free economy, depressions should be left to resolve themselves without governmental interference. Keynes argued that unemployment came from a decline in demand, not from overproduction. Demand, in turn, could be increased by putting people back to work building highways and public buildings. If necessary, governments should finance such projects with **deficit spending,** or going into debt.

The United States

After Germany, no Western nation was more affected by the Great Depression than the United States. By 1932, U.S. industrial production had fallen almost 50 percent from its 1929 level. By 1933, there were more than 12 million unemployed.

Under these circumstances, the Democrat **Franklin Delano Roosevelt** won a landslide victory in the 1932 presidential election. Believing in free enterprise, Roosevelt believed that capitalism had to be reformed to save it. He pursued a policy of active government intervention in the economy, known as the **New Deal.**

The New Deal included an increased program of public works. The Works Progress Administration (WPA), established in 1935, was a government organization employing about three million people at its peak. Workers built bridges, roads, post offices, and airports.

The Roosevelt administration was also responsible for new social legislation that began the U.S. welfare system. In 1935 the Social Security Act created a system of old-age pensions and unemployment insurance.

The New Deal's reforms may have prevented a social revolution in the United States. However, it did not solve the unemployment problems. In 1938 American unemployment still stood at more than 10 million. Only World War II and the growth of weapons industries brought U.S. workers back to full employment.

✓ Reading Check **Summarizing** How did the German people respond to the Great Depression?

Vocabulary

1. **Explain** the significance of: annual, Ruhr Valley, ratio, Dawes Plan, Treaty of Locarno, depression, Switzerland, Weimar Republic, collective bargaining, John Maynard Keynes, deficit spending, Franklin Delano Roosevelt, New Deal.

Main Ideas

2. **List** the provisions of the Dawes Plan.

3. **Summarize** the causes of the Great Depression by using a diagram like the one below.

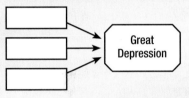

4. **Explain** the intent of the Roosevelt administration's New Deal.

Critical Thinking

5. **The BIG Idea** **Determining Cause and Effect** Explain how the Great Depression weakened Western democracies.

6. **Making Inferences** Why did the American public mostly oppose joining the League of Nations after World War I?

7. **Analyzing Visuals** Examine the photograph on page 557. What does it tell you about conditions in Germany during the Great Depression?

Writing About History

8. **Informative Writing** Research and write an essay that explains how the Great Depression caused extremist political parties to emerge throughout the world.

History ONLINE

For help with the concepts in this section of *Glencoe World History— Modern Times*, go to glencoe.com and click Study Central.

The Rise of Dictatorial Regimes

GUIDE TO READING

The BIG Idea
Human Rights By 1939, many European countries had adopted dictatorial regimes that aimed to control every aspect of their citizens' lives for state goals.

Content Vocabulary
- totalitarian state (p. 560)
- fascism (p. 561)
- collectivization (p. 564)

Academic Vocabulary
- unprecedented (p. 560)
- media (p. 563)

People, Places, and Events
- Russia (p. 560)
- Benito Mussolini (p. 561)
- New Economic Policy (p. 563)
- Politburo (p. 564)
- Joseph Stalin (p. 564)
- Five-Year Plans (p. 564)
- Francisco Franco (p. 567)
- Madrid (p. 567)

Reading Strategy
Categorizing Information As you read, use a web diagram like the one below to list methods Mussolini used to create a Fascist dictatorship.

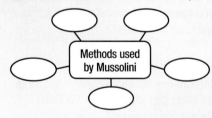
Methods used by Mussolini

After World War I, European democracy was under threat. France and Britain remained democratic, but in Italy and Russia, a new kind of dictatorship emerged with Mussolini's fascist state in Italy and Stalin's totalitarian rule in Russia. Other Western states like Spain tried to keep old elites in power with authoritarian regimes.

The Rise of Dictators

MAIN IDEA The totalitarian states did away with individual freedoms.

HISTORY & YOU What if you could listen only to government-sponsored programs? Read to learn about a form of government that controls all aspects of people's lives.

The apparent triumph of democracy in Europe in 1919 was very short-lived. By 1939, only two major European states—France and Great Britain—remained democratic. Italy, the Soviet Union, Germany, and many other European states adopted dictatorial regimes. These regimes took both old and new forms.

A new form of dictatorship was the modern totalitarian state. In a **totalitarian state,** the government aims to control the political, economic, social, intellectual, and cultural lives of its citizens. New totalitarian regimes pushed the central state's power far beyond what it had been in the past. These regimes wanted more than passive obedience. They wanted to conquer the minds and hearts of their subjects. They achieved this goal through mass propaganda techniques and high-speed modern communication. Modern technology also gave totalitarian states an **unprecedented** ability to impose their wishes on their subjects.

The totalitarian states were led by a single leader and a single party. They rejected the ideal of limited government power and the guarantee of individual freedoms. Instead, individual freedom was subordinated to the collective will of the masses. The leader determined that collective will, however. The masses were expected to be actively involved in achieving the state's goals. Those goals might include war, a socialist state, or a thousand-year empire like the one Adolf Hitler wanted to establish.

Fascism in Italy

Like other European countries, Italy experienced severe economic problems after World War I. Inflation grew, and both industrial and agricultural workers staged strikes. Socialists spoke of

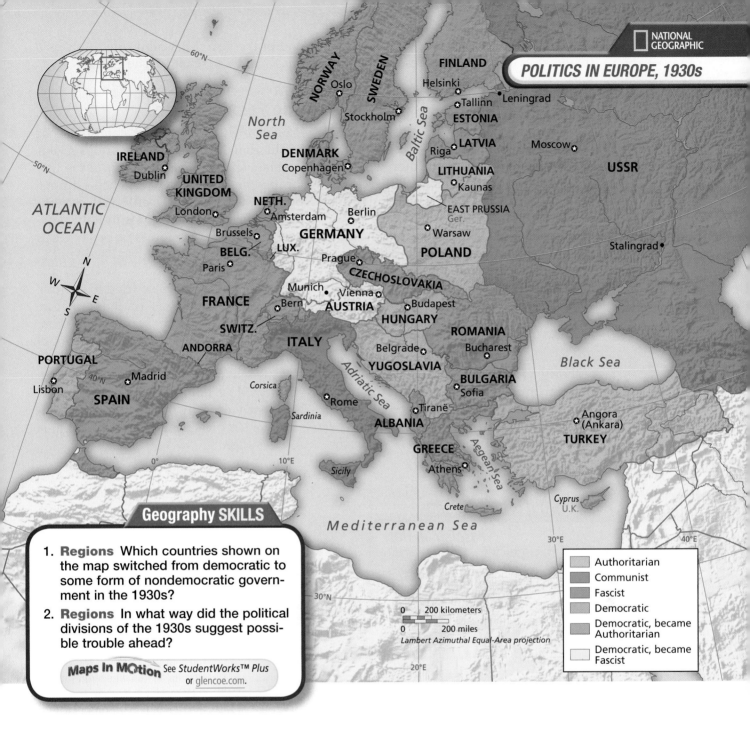

NORWAY
Oslo
SWEDEN
Stockholm
FINLAND
Helsinki
Leningrad
Tallinn
ESTONIA
North
Sea
Baltic Sea
Riga
LATVIA
Moscow
USSR
DENMARK
Copenhagen
LITHUANIA
Kaunas
IRELAND
Dublin
UNITED
KINGDOM
London
NETH.
Amsterdam
Berlin
EAST PRUSSIA
Ger.
Warsaw
Stalingrad
ATLANTIC
OCEAN
BELG.
Brussels
Paris
LUX.
GERMANY
Prague
POLAND
FRANCE
Bern
Munich
Vienna
CZECHOSLOVAKIA
AUSTRIA
Budapest
HUNGARY
ROMANIA
Bucharest
SWITZ.
ANDORRA
ITALY
Belgrade
YUGOSLAVIA
Black Sea
PORTUGAL
Lisbon
Madrid
SPAIN
Corsica
Sardinia
Rome
Adriatic Sea
Tiranë
ALBANIA
BULGARIA
Sofia
Angora
(Ankara)
TURKEY
GREECE
Athens
Aegean Sea
Sicily
Crete
Cyprus
U.K.
Mediterranean Sea

Geography SKILLS

1. **Regions** Which countries shown on the map switched from democratic to some form of nondemocratic government in the 1930s?

2. **Regions** In what way did the political divisions of the 1930s suggest possible trouble ahead?

Maps In MOtion See *StudentWorks™ Plus* or glencoe.com.

0   200 kilometers
0   200 miles
Lambert Azimuthal Equal-Area projection

- Authoritarian
- Communist
- Fascist
- Democratic
- Democratic, became Authoritarian
- Democratic, became Fascist

revolution. The middle class began to fear a Communist takeover like the one that had recently occurred in **Russia.** Industrial and agricultural strikes created more division. From this background of widespread unrest emerged Mussolini.

In the early 1920s, **Benito Mussolini** (MOO•suh•LEE•nee) set up the first European fascist movement in Italy. Mussolini began his political career as a Socialist. In 1919 he created a new political group, the *Fascio di Combattimento,* or League of Combat. *Fascism* comes from that name.

As a political philosophy, **fascism** (FA•SHIH•zuhm) glorifies the state above the individual by emphasizing the need for a strong central government led by a dictatorial ruler. In a fascist state, the government controls the people and stifles any opposition.

By 1922, Mussolini's movement was growing quickly. The middle-class fear of socialism, communism, and disorder made the Fascists increasingly attractive to many people. Mussolini knew that many Italians were still angry over the peace settlement.

The failure to receive more land under the treaty was a deep source of resentment. He knew nationalism was a powerful force and demanded more land for Italy. Mussolini converted thousands to the Fascist Party with his nationalistic appeals.

In 1922 Mussolini and the Fascists threatened to march on Rome if they were not given power. Victor Emmanuel III, the king of Italy, gave in and made Mussolini prime minister.

Mussolini used his position as prime minister to create a Fascist dictatorship. New laws gave the government the right to stop any publications that criticized the Catholic Church, the monarchy, or the state. The prime minister was made head of the government with the power to make laws by decree. The police were given unrestricted authority to arrest and jail anyone for either political or nonpolitical crimes.

In 1926 the Fascists outlawed all other political parties in Italy and established a secret police, known as the OVRA. By the end of the year, Mussolini ruled Italy as *Il Duce* (eel DOO•chay), "The Leader."

The Fascist State

Believing that the Fascist state should be totalitarian, Mussolini used various means to establish complete control over the Italian people. The OVRA watched citizens' political activities and enforced government policies. Police actions in Italy, however, were never as repressive or savage as those in Nazi Germany (discussed later in this chapter).

The Italian Fascists also tried to exercise control over all forms of mass **media**, including newspapers, radio, and film. The media was used to spread propaganda. Propaganda was intended to mold Italians into a single-minded Fascist community. Most Italian Fascist propaganda, however, was fairly basic and mainly consisted of simple slogans like "Mussolini Is Always Right."

INFOGRAPHICS · PRIMARY SOURCE

Fascism in Italy

In this poster, the background engraving is of Romulus and Remus, the mythological founders of Rome. Mussolini holds the fasces, a bundle of rods tied together with an ax. A symbol of ancient Rome's authority, the fasces was adopted by the Fascists as their symbol.

"Anti-individualistic, the Fascist conception of life stresses the importance of the State and accepts the individual only in so far as his interests coincide with those of the State. . . . War alone keys up all human energies to their maximum tension and sets the seal of nobility on those people who have the courage to face it."

—Benito Mussolini, "The Doctrine of Fascism," in *Italian Fascisms,* Adrian Lyttleton, ed., 1973

DOCUMENT-BASED QUESTIONS

1. **Explaining** How does Mussolini describe the role of the individual in the Fascist state?

2. **Making Connections** What is the significance of the background engraving in the poster?

The Fascists also used organizations to promote the ideals of fascism and to control the population. For example, by 1939, Fascist youth groups included about 66 percent of the population between the ages of 8 and 18. These youth groups particularly focused on military activities and values.

With these organizations, the Fascists hoped to create a nation of new Italians who were fit, disciplined, and war-loving. In practice, however, the Fascists largely maintained traditional social attitudes. This is especially evident in their policies regarding women. The Fascists portrayed the family as the pillar of the state. Seen as the foundation of the family, women were to be homemakers and mothers. According to Mussolini, these roles were "their natural and fundamental mission in life."

In spite of his attempts, Mussolini never achieved the degree of totalitarian control seen in Hitler's Germany or Stalin's Soviet Union (discussed later in this chapter). The Italian Fascist Party did not completely destroy the country's old power structure. Some institutions, including the armed forces, managed to keep most of their independence. Victor Emmanuel III was also retained as king.

Mussolini's compromise with the traditional institutions of Italy was especially evident in his dealings with the Catholic Church. Mussolini's regime recognized the sovereign independence of a small area within Rome known as Vatican City. The Church had claimed this area since 1870. In return, the pope recognized the Italian state. Mussolini's regime also gave the Church a large grant of money and recognized Catholicism as the "sole religion of the state." In return, the Catholic Church urged Italians to support the Fascist regime.

In all areas of Italian life under Mussolini and the Fascists, a large gap existed between Fascist ideals and practices. The Italian Fascists promised much but delivered considerably less. They would soon be overshadowed by a much more powerful fascist movement to the north—that of Adolf Hitler, a student and admirer of Mussolini.

✓ Reading Check **Examining** How did Mussolini gain power in Italy?

A New Era in the USSR

MAIN IDEA In the Soviet Union, Stalin maintained total power by murdering his political opponents.

HISTORY & YOU If a U.S. president dies in office, how is he or she replaced? Read to find out the difficulties for succession when Lenin died.

As discussed earlier, Lenin followed a policy of war communism during the civil war in Russia. The government controlled most industries and seized grain from peasants to ensure supplies for the army.

Once the war was over, peasants began to sabotage the Communist program by hoarding food. The situation became even worse when drought caused a terrible famine between 1920 and 1922. As many as 5 million lives were lost. With agricultural disaster came industrial collapse. By 1921, industrial output was only 20 percent of its 1913 level.

Russia was exhausted. A peasant banner proclaimed, "Down with Lenin and horse-flesh. Bring back the czar and pork." As Leon Trotsky said, "The country, and the government with it, were at the very edge of the abyss."

Lenin's New Economic Policy

In March 1921, Lenin pulled Russia back from the abyss. He abandoned war communism in favor of his **New Economic Policy** (NEP). The NEP was a modified version of the old capitalist system. Peasants were allowed to sell their produce openly. Retail stores, as well as small industries that employed fewer than 20 workers, could be privately owned and operated. Heavy industry, banking, and mines, however, remained in the hands of the government.

The Soviet Union

In 1922 Lenin and the Communists formally created a new state called the Union of Soviet Socialist Republics. The state is also known as the USSR (by its initials) or as the Soviet Union (by its shortened form). By that time, a revived market and a good harvest had brought an end to famine. Soviet agricultural production climbed to 75 percent of its prewar level.

Overall, the NEP saved the Soviet Union from complete economic disaster. Lenin and other leading Communists, however, intended the NEP to be only a temporary retreat from the goals of communism.

Industrialization

Lenin died in 1924. A struggle for power began at once among the seven members of the **Politburo** (PAH•luht•BYUR•oh)—the Communist Party's main policy-making body. The Politburo was severely divided over the future direction of the Soviet Union.

One group, led by Leon Trotsky, wanted to end the NEP and launch Russia on a path of rapid industrialization, chiefly at the expense of the peasants. This group also wanted to spread communism abroad. It believed that the revolution in Russia would not survive without other communist states.

Another group in the Politburo rejected the idea of worldwide communist revolution. Instead, it wanted to focus on building a socialist state in Russia and to continue Lenin's NEP. This group believed that rapid industrialization would harm the living standards of the Soviet peasants.

The Rise of Stalin

These divisions were further strained by an intense personal rivalry between Leon Trotsky and another Politburo member, **Joseph Stalin.** In 1924 Trotsky held the post of commissar of war. Stalin held the bureaucratic job of party general secretary. The general secretary appointed regional, district, city, and town party officials. Thus this bureaucratic job actually became the most important position in the party.

Stalin used his post as general secretary to gain complete control of the Communist Party. The thousands of officials Stalin appointed provided him with support in his bid for power. By 1929, Stalin had removed the Bolsheviks of the revolutionary era from the Politburo and had established a powerful dictatorship. Trotsky, pushed out of the party in 1927, eventually made his way to Mexico. There he was murdered in 1940, probably on Stalin's orders.

Five-Year Plans

The Stalin Era marked the beginning of an economic, social, and political revolution that was more sweeping in its results than were the revolutions of 1917. Stalin made a significant shift in economic policy in 1928 when he ended the NEP. That year he launched his First Five-Year Plan. The **Five-Year Plans** set economic goals for five-year periods. Their purpose was to transform Russia virtually overnight from an agricultural into an industrial country.

The First Five-Year Plan emphasized maximum production of military equipment and capital goods (goods devoted to the production of other goods, such as heavy machines). The plan quadrupled the production of heavy machinery and doubled oil production. Between 1928 and 1937, during the first two Five-Year Plans, steel production in Russia increased from 4 million to 18 million tons (3.6 to 16.3 million t) per year.

Costs of Industrialization

The social and political costs of industrialization were enormous. Little thought was given to caring for the expanded labor force in the cities. The number of workers increased by millions between 1932 and 1940. However, total investment in housing actually declined after 1929. The result was that millions of workers and their families lived in miserable conditions. Real wages in industry also declined by 43 percent between 1928 and 1940. Strict laws even limited where workers could move. To keep workers content, government propaganda stressed the need for sacrifice to create the new socialist state.

With rapid industrialization came an equally rapid collectivization of agriculture. **Collectivization** was a system in which private farms were eliminated. Instead, the government owned all of the land, and the peasants worked it.

The peasants resisted by hoarding crops and killing livestock. In response, Stalin stepped up the program. By 1930, 10 million peasant households had been collectivized. By 1934, 26 million family farms had been collectivized into 250,000 units.

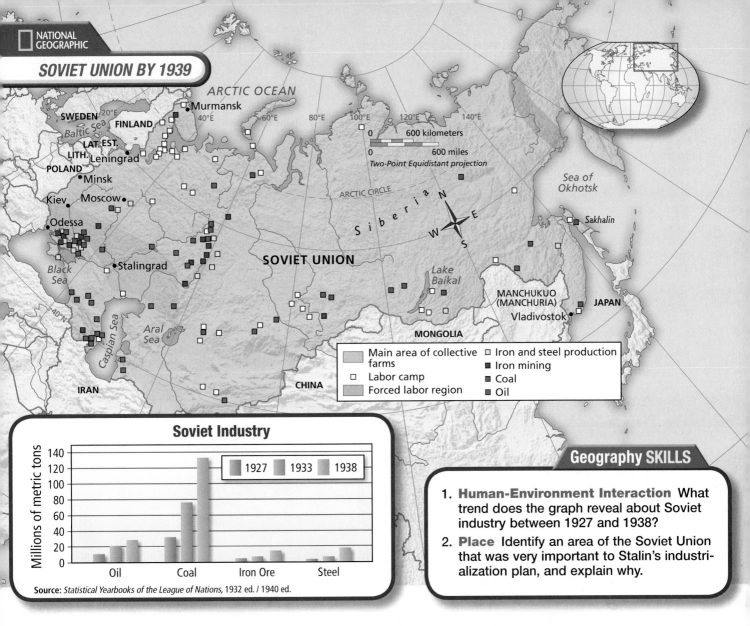

SOVIET UNION BY 1939

ARCTIC OCEAN

SWEDEN
FINLAND
Baltic Sea
LAT. EST.
LITH. Leningrad
POLAND
Minsk
Kiev
Moscow
Odessa
Black Sea
Stalingrad
Caspian Sea
Aral Sea
IRAN

Murmansk

ARCTIC CIRCLE

S i b e r i a

SOVIET UNION

Lake Baikal

MONGOLIA

CHINA

Sea of Okhotsk

Sakhalin

MANCHUKUO (MANCHURIA)

Vladivostok

JAPAN

0   600 kilometers
0   600 miles
Two-Point Equidistant projection

Legend:
- Main area of collective farms
- Labor camp
- Forced labor region
- Iron and steel production
- Iron mining
- Coal
- Oil

Soviet Industry

Millions of metric tons (y-axis: 0, 20, 40, 60, 80, 100, 120, 140)

Categories: Oil, Coal, Iron Ore, Steel

Legend: 1927, 1933, 1938

Source: *Statistical Yearbooks of the League of Nations,* 1932 ed. / 1940 ed.

Geography SKILLS

1. **Human-Environment Interaction** What trend does the graph reveal about Soviet industry between 1927 and 1938?
2. **Place** Identify an area of the Soviet Union that was very important to Stalin's industrialization plan, and explain why.

Costs of Stalin's Programs

Collectivization was done at tremendous cost. The hoarding of food and the slaughter of livestock led to widespread famine. Stalin himself is supposed to have said that 10 million peasants died in the famines of 1932 and 1933. Stalin gave the peasants only one concession. Each collective farm worker could have one tiny, privately owned garden plot.

Stalin's programs had other costs as well. To achieve his goals, Stalin strengthened his control over the party. Those who resisted were sent into forced labor camps in Siberia.

Stalin's desire to make all decisions led to purges, or removal, of the Old Bolsheviks. These people had been involved in the early days of the movement. Between 1936 and 1938, the most prominent Old Bolsheviks were put on trial and condemned to death.

During this time, Stalin purged army officers, diplomats, union officials, intellectuals, and ordinary citizens. An estimated 8 million Russians were arrested. Millions were sent to labor camps in Siberia; they never returned. Others were executed.

The Stalin era also overturned permissive social legislation enacted in the early 1920s. To promote equal rights for women, the Communists had made the divorce process easier. They had also encouraged women to work outside the home. After Stalin came to power, the family was praised as a small collective. Parents were responsible for teaching the values of hard work, duty, and discipline to their children.

✓ **Reading Check**   **Summarizing** What was Lenin's New Economic Policy?

Authoritarian States in the West

MAIN IDEA Authoritarian governments in the West worked to preserve the existing social order.

HISTORY & YOU If you were living in a new nation, what kind of government would you want? Read to learn about the types of governments adopted by new states in eastern Europe after World War I.

A number of governments in the Western world were not totalitarian but were authoritarian. These states adopted some of the features of totalitarian states, in particular, their use of police powers. However, these authoritarian governments did not want to create a new kind of mass society. Instead, they wanted to preserve the existing social order.

Eastern Europe

At first, it seemed that political democracy would become well established in eastern Europe after World War I. Austria, Poland, Czechoslovakia, Yugoslavia (known as the kingdom of the Serbs, Croats, and Slovenes until 1929), Romania, Bulgaria, and Hungary all adopted parliamentary systems. However, authoritarian regimes soon replaced most of these systems.

Parliamentary systems failed in most eastern European states for several reasons. These states had little tradition of political democracy. In addition, they were mostly rural and agrarian. Many of the peasants were illiterate (could not read or write). Large landowners still dominated most of the land, and they feared the peasants. Ethnic conflicts also threatened these countries.

HISTORY & ARTS   PRIMARY SOURCE

The Destruction of Guernica

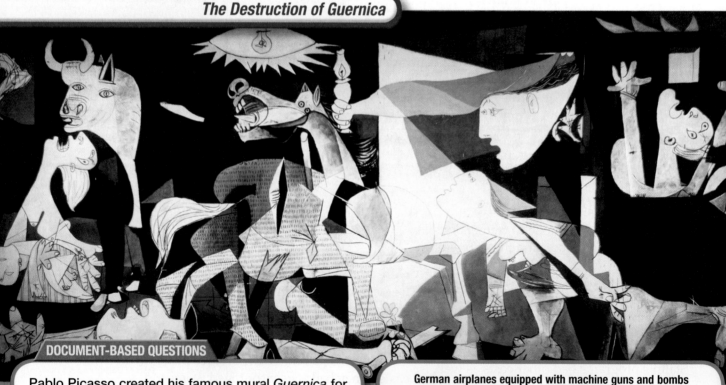

DOCUMENT-BASED QUESTIONS

Pablo Picasso created his famous mural *Guernica* for the 1937 World's Fair in Paris. "[In *Guernica*,] I clearly express my loathing for the military caste that has plunged Spain into a sea of suffering and death."

1. **Explaining** What effect did new war technology have in the battle at Guernica?

2. **Analyzing** What one word best describes your response to *Guernica?* Use details from the painting to explain how the artist creates this feeling.

German airplanes equipped with machine guns and bombs completely destroyed the small village of Guernica in April 1937 during the Spanish Civil War.

Powerful landowners, the churches, and even some members of the small middle class feared land reform. They also feared communist upheaval and ethnic conflict. These groups looked to authoritarian governments to maintain the old system. Only Czechoslovakia, which had a large middle class, a liberal tradition, and a strong industrial base, maintained its political democracy.

Spain

In Spain, too, political democracy failed to survive. Although the middle class and intellectuals supported the Second Republic, the new government began falling apart shortly after it was created in 1931. Rivalries between political parties and personal rivalries between their leaders tore Spain apart. Spain's Second Republic lasted only five years, three months, and three days.

Francisco Franco rose rapidly within the military ranks. He became Europe's youngest general. When chaos swept Spain, the Spanish military forces under Franco's leadership revolted against the democratic government in 1936. A brutal and bloody civil war began.

Foreign intervention complicated the Spanish Civil War. The fascist regimes of Italy and Germany aided Franco's forces. They sent him arms, money, and soldiers. Hitler used the Spanish Civil War as an opportunity to test the new weapons of his revived air force. German bombers destroyed the city of Guernica in April 1937. Spanish artist Pablo Picasso immortalized the horrible destruction in his mural *Guernica.*

The Spanish republican government was aided by 40,000 foreign volunteers. The Soviet Union sent in trucks, planes, tanks, and military advisers.

The Spanish Civil War came to an end when Franco's forces captured **Madrid** in 1939. In April of that year, Franco issued a statement:

PRIMARY SOURCE

"Today, the Red Army having been disarmed and captured, the National troops have reached their final military objectives. The war is over.—Burgos, April 1, 1939, the Year of Victory—Generalissimo Franco."

—*Portrait of Spain,* Francisco Franco, as quoted in Tad Szulc, 1972

Franco established a dictatorship that favored large landowners, businesspeople, and the Catholic clergy. Because Franco's dictatorship favored traditional groups and did not try to control every aspect of people's lives, it is an example of an authoritarian rather than a totalitarian regime.

✓ Reading Check   **Explaining** How did Czechoslovakia maintain its political democracy?

SECTION 2 REVIEW

Vocabulary

1. **Explain** the significance of: totalitarian state, unprecedented, Russia, Benito Mussolini, fascism, media, New Economic Policy, Politburo, Joseph Stalin, Five-Year Plans, collectivization, Francisco Franco, Madrid.

Main Ideas

2. **Describe** the methods used by a totalitarian state to control its people.

3. **Summarize,** by using a diagram like the one below, how Stalin changed the Soviet Union. Include the economic, social, and political results of his programs.

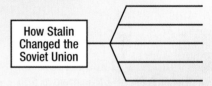

How Stalin Changed the Soviet Union

4. **List** the countries that participated in the Spanish Civil War.

Critical Thinking

5. **The BIG Idea** **Analyzing** Why do you think people supported dictatorial regimes?

6. **Evaluating** What was the goal of the Five-Year Plans during the 1920s and 1930s in the Soviet Union?

7. **Analyzing Visuals** Examine the painting *Guernica,* shown on page 566. How does the painting's abstract form help convey its message?

Writing About History

8. **Persuasive Writing** Imagine you are a middle-class Italian in the 1920s who is concerned about society. Write a letter to the editor of the local paper supporting Mussolini's new government.

History ONLINE

For help with the concepts in this section of *Glencoe World History—Modern Times,* go to glencoe.com and click Study Central.

Hitler and Nazi Germany

Recovering from the humiliating loss of World War I and from the Great Depression, Germans found extremist parties more attractive. Adolf Hitler's Nazi Party promised to build a new Germany, and his party's propaganda appealed to the German sense of national honor. The new Germany that Hitler envisioned did not include any group the Nazis considered inferior, especially the Jewish people.

GUIDE TO READING

The BIG Idea

Human Rights Hitler's totalitarian state was widely accepted, but German Jews and minorities were persecuted.

Content Vocabulary
- Nazi *(p. 568)*
- concentration camps *(p. 570)*
- Aryan *(p. 570)*

Academic Vocabulary
- require *(p. 573)*
- prohibit *(p. 573)*

People, Places, and Events
- Adolf Hitler *(p. 568)*
- Munich *(p. 568)*
- Reichstag *(p. 569)*
- Enabling Act *(p. 570)*
- Heinrich Himmler *(p. 570)*
- Nuremberg *(p. 573)*
- Nuremberg laws *(p. 573)*
- *Kristallnacht (p. 573)*

Reading Strategy

Categorizing Information As you read, use a chart like the one below to list anti-Semitic policies enforced by the Nazi Party.

Anti-Semitic Policies

Hitler and His Views

MAIN IDEA Adolf Hitler's ideas were based on racism and German nationalism.

HISTORY & YOU What would you say if you were asked whether you valued all types of people? Read on to learn about Hitler's ideology.

Adolf Hitler was born in Austria on April 20, 1889. Unsuccessful in school, he traveled to Vienna to become an artist but was rejected by the academy. Here he developed his basic social and political ideas. At the core of Hitler's ideas was racism, especially anti-Semitism (hostility toward Jews). Hitler was also an extreme nationalist who understood how political parties could effectively use propaganda and terror.

Hitler served four years on the Western Front during World War I. At the end of the war, Hitler remained in Germany and decided to enter politics. In 1919 he joined the little-known German Workers' Party, one of several right-wing extreme nationalist parties in **Munich.**

By the summer of 1921, Hitler had taken total control of the party. By then the party had been renamed the National Socialist German Workers' Party (NSDAP, an abbreviation of the German name), or **Nazi,** for short. Within two years, party membership had grown to 55,000 people, with 15,000 in the party militia. The militia was variously known as the SA, the Storm Troops, or the Brownshirts, after the color of their uniforms.

An overconfident Hitler staged an armed uprising against the government in Munich in November 1923. This uprising, called the Beer Hall Putsch, was quickly crushed, and Hitler was sentenced to prison. During his brief stay in jail, Hitler wrote *Mein Kampf,* or *My Struggle,* an account of his movement and its basic ideas.

In *Mein Kampf,* Hitler links extreme German nationalism, strong anti-Semitism, and anticommunism together by a Social Darwinian theory of struggle. This theory emphasizes the right of superior nations to lebensraum (LAY•buhnz•ROWM)—"living space"—through expansion. It also upholds the right of superior individuals to gain authoritarian leadership over the masses.

The Message of Nazism

Nazi banners adorn Nuremberg's medieval imperial castle. Below it is a map of Germany, with East Prussia separated from the rest of the country by Poland.

The Nazi eagle perched on a swastika was the formal symbol of the Third Reich. Behind it is the Third Reich battle flag.

This poster commemorates the 1934 Nuremberg Rally. Hitler considered Nuremberg to be "the most German of all cities." Starting in 1933, the year Hitler was appointed chancellor of Germany, annual Nazi Party rallies were held at Nuremberg.

The following excerpt is from the introductory chapter of a handbook given to Hitler Youth boys between the ages of 10 and 14. Nearly every German boy would have received a copy.

"Our beloved swastika flag appears at this time too. The Führer himself designed it. For us, it is more than an outward symbol. We National Socialists [Nazis] see our program in our flag. We see the social in the red, the movement's national thinking in the white, and in the swastika we see the symbol of the victory of Aryan humanity and the victory of productive humanity, which was always anti-Semitic and will always be anti-Semitic. When this flag flies, it is a parable of our desires: We think of national freedom and social justice, of racial purity and the victory of Nordic humanity. The swastika reminds us of the time when Nordic farmers and warriors marched to Italy and Greece. It was borne at the front of the soldiers as a holy symbol of the Germanic-German spirit."

—*The Life of the Führer*

DOCUMENT-BASED QUESTIONS

1. **Explaining** Based on the excerpt, what is the meaning of the swastika?
2. **Making Connections** Why does the excerpt refer to "Nordic farmers and warriors"?

Rise of Nazism

While in prison, Hitler realized that the Nazis would have to attain power by legal means, not by a violent overthrow of the Weimar Republic. Hitler knew that the Nazi Party would have to be a mass political party that could compete for votes with the other political parties.

Once out of prison, Hitler expanded the Nazi Party in Germany. By 1929, it had a national party organization. Three years later, it had 800,000 members and had become the largest party in the **Reichstag**—the German parliament.

No doubt, Germany's economic difficulties were a crucial factor in the Nazi rise to power. Unemployment had risen dramatically, growing from 4.35 million in 1931 to about 5.5 million by the winter of 1932. The Great Depression made extremist parties more attractive.

Hitler promised a new Germany that appealed to nationalism and militarism.

These appeals struck an emotional chord in his listeners. After attending one of Hitler's rallies, a schoolteacher in Hamburg said, "When the speech was over, there was roaring enthusiasm and applause.... How many look up to him with touching faith as their helper, their saviour, their deliverer from unbearable distress."

The Nazis Take Control

After 1930, the German government ruled by decree with the support of President Hindenburg. The Reichstag had little power. More and more, the right-wing elites of Germany—the industrial leaders, landed aristocrats, military officers, and higher bureaucrats—looked to Hitler for leadership. Under pressure, Hindenburg agreed to allow Hitler to become chancellor in 1933 and create a new government.

Within two months, Hitler had laid the foundation for the Nazi Party's complete control over Germany. The crowning step of Hitler's "legal seizure" of power came on March 23, 1933, when a two-thirds vote of the Reichstag passed the **Enabling Act**. This law gave the government the power to ignore the constitution for four years while it issued laws to deal with the country's problems. The Enabling Act also gave Hitler's later actions a legal basis. He no longer needed the Reichstag or President Hindenburg. In effect, Hitler became a dictator appointed by the parliamentary body itself.

With their new power, the Nazis quickly brought all institutions under their control. They purged the civil service of Jews and democratic elements. They set up prison camps called **concentration camps** for people who opposed them. Trade unions were dissolved. All political parties except the Nazis were abolished.

By the end of the summer of 1933, only seven months after being appointed chancellor, Hitler had established the basis for a totalitarian state. When Hindenburg died in 1934, the office of president was abolished. Hitler became sole ruler of Germany. People took oaths of loyalty to their *Führer* (FYUR•uhr), or "Leader."

✓ Reading Check **Examining** Why was the Enabling Act important to Hitler's success?

The Nazi State, 1933–1939

MAIN IDEA Hitler used anti-Semitism, economic policy, and propaganda to build a Nazi state.

HISTORY & YOU What if the U.S. president declared, "The time of personal happiness is over"? Read to learn how the German people reacted to a similar statement by Hitler.

Hitler wanted to develop a totalitarian state. He had not simply sought power for power's sake. He had a larger goal—the development of an **Aryan** racial state that would dominate Europe and possibly the world for generations to come. (*Aryan* is a term used to identify people speaking Indo-European languages. The Nazis misused the term by treating it as a racial designation and identifying the Aryans with the ancient Greeks and Romans and twentieth-century Germans and Scandinavians.)

Nazis thought the Germans were the true descendants and leaders of the Aryans and would create another empire like the one ruled by the ancient Romans. The Nazis believed that the world had already seen two German empires, or Reichs: the Holy Roman Empire and the German Empire of 1871 to 1918. It was Hitler's goal to create a Third Reich, the empire of Nazi Germany.

To achieve his goal, Hitler needed the active involvement of the German people. Hitler stated:

PRIMARY SOURCE

"We must develop organizations in which an individual's entire life can take place. Then every activity and every need of every individual will be regulated by the collectivity represented by the party. There is no longer any arbitrary will, there are no longer any free realms in which the individual belongs to himself. . . . The time of personal happiness is over."
—Adolf Hitler

The Nazis pursued the creation of the totalitarian state in a variety of ways. They employed economic policies, mass spectacles, and organizations—both old and new—to further Nazi goals. They also freely used terror. Policies toward women and, in particular, toward Jews reflected Nazi aims.

The State and Terror

Nazi Germany was the scene of almost constant personal and institutional conflict. Struggle was a basic feature of relationships within the party, within the state, and between party and state. Hitler, of course, was the ultimate decision maker and absolute ruler.

The *Schutzstaffeln* ("Guard Squadrons"), known simply as the SS, were an important force for maintaining order. The SS was originally created as Hitler's personal bodyguard. Under the direction of **Heinrich Himmler,** the SS came to control not only the secret police forces that Himmler had set up, but also the regular police forces.

The SS was based on two principles: terror and ideology. Terror included the instruments of repression and murder—secret police, criminal police, concentration camps, and later, execution squads and death camps (concentration camps where prisoners are killed). For Himmler, the chief goal of the SS was to further the Aryan master race.

INFOGRAPHICS   PRIMARY SOURCE

Himmler and the SS

"We have to know that the enemy during war is not only the enemy in the military sense, but also the ideological enemy. When I speak of enemies, I of course mean our natural enemy—Bolshevism led by international Jewry and Free Masons. . . . [Bolshevism] is the exact opposite of all which the Aryan people loves, cherishes and values. . . . We [Aryans] are more valuable because our blood enables us to be more inventive than the others, to lead our people better than the others, because we have better soldiers, better statesmen, a higher culture, a better character. We have better quality, if I now turn to your area, because the German soldier is more devoted to his duty, more decent and intelligent than the soldier of the other people."
—Heinrich Himmler, "Lecture on the Nature and Tasks of the SS," January 1937

DOCUMENT-BASED QUESTIONS

With the feared SS under his control, Heinrich Himmler pursued the Nazi goal of an Aryan master race.

1. **Specifying** According to Himmler, what political ideology was linked to Jews?
2. **Analyzing Primary Sources** How did Himmler use Nazi ideology to motivate the SS in this speech?

▲ *Heinrich Himmler at Nuremberg, mid-1930s*

Although anti-Semitic policies had been in effect in Germany since the Nazi takeover in 1933, the events of *Kristallnacht* signaled the start of a more violent era of anti-Semitism. Businesses could not reopen unless managed by non-Jews. Jews were banned from schools and most public places.

"Regards: Measures against Jews tonight. . . .

"a) Only such measures may be taken which do not jeopardize German life or property (for instance, burning of synagogues only if there is no danger of fires for the neighborhoods).

"b) Business establishments and homes of Jews may be destroyed but not looted. . . .

"c) In business streets special care is to be taken that non-Jewish establishments will be safeguarded at all cost against damage. . . .

"As soon as the events of this night permit the use of the designated officers, as many Jews, particularly wealthy ones, as the local jails will hold, are to be arrested in all districts."
—Directive from SS officer Reinhard Heydrich, November 10, 1938

Still visible in this burned synagogue is a *bimah*, a raised platform from which the Torah is read.

Kristallnacht was named for the shattered windows resulting from violence against Jews.

DOCUMENT-BASED QUESTIONS

1. **Hypothesizing** Why do you think Heydrich said that Jewish-owned stores and homes could be destroyed but not looted?

2. **Organizing** Research and create a time line of anti-Semitic Nazi policies in the years before *Kristallnacht*.

Economics and Spectacles

In the economic sphere, Hitler used public works projects and grants to private construction firms to put people back to work and end the Depression. A massive rearmament program, however, was the key to solving the unemployment problem.

Unemployment, which had reached more than 5 million people in 1932, dropped to 2.5 million in 1934 and less than 500,000 in 1937. The regime claimed full credit for solving Germany's economic woes. The new regime's part in bringing an end to the Depression was an important factor in leading many Germans to accept Hitler and the Nazis.

In addition, the Nazis used mass demonstrations and spectacles to make the German people an instrument of Hitler's policies. These meetings, especially the **Nuremberg** party rallies that were held every September, usually evoked mass enthusiasm and excitement.

The Nazi totalitarian state also controlled institutions, which included churches, schools, and universities. In addition, Nazi professional organizations and youth organizations taught Nazi ideals.

Women and Nazism

Women played a crucial role in the Aryan state as bearers of the children who, the Nazis believed, would bring about the triumph of the Aryan race. The Nazis believed men were destined to be warriors and political leaders, while women were meant to be wives and mothers. By preserving this clear distinction, each could best serve to "maintain the whole community."

Nazi ideas determined employment opportunities for women. Jobs in heavy industry, the Nazis thought, might hinder women from bearing healthy children. Certain professions, including university teaching, medicine, and law, were also considered unsuitable for women, especially married women. The Nazis instead encouraged women to pursue other occupations, such as social work and nursing. The Nazi regime pushed its campaign against working women with poster slogans such as "Get ahold of pots and pans and broom and you'll sooner find a groom!"

Anti-Semitic Policies

From its beginning, the Nazi Party reflected the strong anti-Semitic beliefs of Adolf Hitler. Once in power, the Nazis translated anti-Semitic ideas into anti-Semitic policies, including anti-Jewish boycotts and other measures.

In September 1935, the Nazis announced new racial laws at the annual party rally in Nuremberg. These **Nuremberg laws** defined who was considered a Jew—anyone with even one Jewish grandparent. They also excluded Jews from German citizenship, stripped Jews of their civil rights, and forbade marriages between Jews and German citizens. Jews could neither teach nor take part in the arts. Eventually, German Jews were also **required** to wear yellow Stars of David and to carry identification cards saying they were Jewish.

A more violent phase of anti-Jewish activity began on the night of November 9, 1938—*Kristallnacht*, or the "night of shattered glass." In a destructive rampage, Nazis burned synagogues and destroyed some 7,000 Jewish businesses. At least 100 Jews were killed. Thirty thousand Jewish males were rounded up and sent to concentration camps.

Kristallnacht led to further drastic steps. Jews were barred from all public transportation and all public buildings, including schools and hospitals. They were **prohibited** from owning, managing, or working in any retail store. The Jews were forced to clean up all the debris and damage due to *Kristallnacht*. Finally, under the direction of the SS, Jews were encouraged to "emigrate from Germany." The fortunate Jews were the ones who managed to escape from the country.

✔ **Reading Check** **Summarizing** What steps did Hitler take to establish a Nazi totalitarian state in Germany?

SECTION **3** REVIEW

Vocabulary
1. **Explain** the significance of: Adolf Hitler, Munich, Nazi, Reichstag, Enabling Act, concentration camps, Aryan, Heinrich Himmler, Nuremberg, Nuremberg laws, require, *Kristallnacht*, prohibit.

Main Ideas
2. **Summarize** the steps that Hitler took to become the sole ruler of Germany.

3. **Describe** the policies and programs that the Nazis used to create a Third Reich. Using a table like the one below, identify the goals for each policy or program.

Policy/Program	Goals

4. **List** the rights that the Nazi government took from the Jews.

Critical Thinking
5. **The BIG Idea** **Determining Cause and Effect** How did mass demonstrations and meetings contribute to the success of the Nazi Party?

6. **Drawing Conclusions** Why were the methods used by Himmler's SS effective in furthering Nazi goals?

7. **Analyzing Visuals** Examine the poster on page 569. Why is East Prussia shown as being separated from the rest of Germany?

Writing About History
8. **Expository Writing** Find a library book by a German who lived under Nazism. Read about the author's life. Write a report about whether that person could have resisted the government and why or why not.

History ONLINE

For help with the concepts in this section of *Glencoe World History— Modern Times*, go to glencoe.com and click Study Central.

Social History

The Hitler Youth

In a totalitarian state, every individual serves the state—there is no society apart from it. Just as there were Nazi organizations for teachers, farmers, and other groups, Hitler established an organization for young people between the ages of 10 and 18—the Hitler Youth. It was formed even before the Nazis gained power because Hitler recognized the importance of winning young people over to his ideas. Upon joining, a young person took an oath: "In the presence of the blood banner [Nazi flag] which represents our Führer, I swear to devote all my energies and my strength to the saviour of our country, Adolf Hitler. I am willing and ready to give up my life for him, so help me God."

The swastika was a symbol of the Nazi party.

The raised arm salute symbolized devotion to Adolf Hitler.

The Hitler Youth copied military discipline and stressed absolute obedience to the party.

MEMBERSHIP INCREASES

The Hitler Youth had 100,000 members when Hitler took power in January 1933. Membership jumped to 2 million by the end of the year and to 5.4 million by December 1936. The Nazis later banned competing youth organizations and, in March 1939, issued a decree requiring all German youths aged 10 to 18 to join the Hitler Youth. By the early years of World War II, about 90 percent of the country's young people belonged to the Hitler Youth.

Older boys learned to shoot small caliber rifles, while boys 14 and younger practiced with air guns.

Along with general military training, special divisions of the Hitler Youth included Flying, Naval, Motorized, Signal, Medical, and Musical Units.

The female division of the Hitler Youth was the League of German Girls. They learned obedience, duty, and how to be good mothers.

Sports and calisthenics were valued above other activities. The Third Reich needed men and women who were physically strong.

SERVING THE REICH

The goal of the Hitler Youth was to indoctrinate young Germans with Nazi ideology—hatred of Jews, glorification of the German nation, and worship of Hitler. Hitler Youth members participated in party rallies and parades, distributed party literature, and kept an eye on teachers and their curriculum for the Nazi party. The success of the organization was proven in World War II as young men eagerly signed up for the military, while youth on the home front collected scrap metal, served as air raid wardens, and helped wounded soldiers.

ANALYZING VISUALS

1. **Speculating** What elements in German society might have inspired young Germans to join the Hitler Youth before it became mandatory?

2. **Interpreting** How does the Hitler Youth organization reflect totalitarian ideas?

Cultural and Intellectual Trends

GUIDE TO READING

The BIG Idea
Ideas, Beliefs, and Values The destruction of World War I and the turmoil of the Great Depression profoundly affected the work of artists and intellectuals.

Content Vocabulary
- photomontage *(p. 578)*
- surrealism *(p. 579)*
- uncertainty principle *(p. 579)*

Academic Vocabulary
- assembly *(p. 577)*
- trend *(p. 578)*

People and Places
- Salvador Dalí *(p. 579)*
- James Joyce *(p. 579)*
- Dublin *(p. 579)*
- Hermann Hesse *(p. 579)*

Reading Strategy
Categorizing Information As you read, use a table like the one below to list literary works by Hesse and Joyce. Describe the techniques used in each work.

Literary Works	Techniques

Mass communications as a propaganda tool was born during World War I as governments worked to win citizen support for the war. In the 1920s and 1930s, people worldwide felt the effects of the Great Depression and political instability. The arts and sciences reflected the changes occurring in people's ideas about the world.

Mass Culture and Leisure

MAIN IDEA Hitler used radio and movies as propaganda tools to promote Nazism.

HISTORY & YOU How would you compare advertising in a democracy to propaganda in a totalitarian state? Read to find out how Hitler used movies to promote his beliefs.

A series of inventions in the late 1800s had led the way for a revolution in mass communications. Especially important was Marconi's discovery of wireless radio waves. A musical concert transmitted in June 1920 had a major impact on radio broadcasting. Broadcasting facilities were built in the United States, Europe, and Japan during 1921 and 1922. At the same time, the mass production of radios began. In 1926 there were 2.2 million radios in Great Britain. By the end of the 1930s, there were 9 million.

Although motion pictures had first emerged in the 1890s, full-length features did not appear until shortly before World War I. The Italian film *Quo Vadis* and the American film *Birth of a Nation* made it apparent that cinema was an important new form of mass entertainment.

By 1939, about 40 percent of adults in the more developed countries were attending a movie once a week. That figure had increased to 60 percent by the end of World War II.

Use of Radio and Movies for Propaganda

Of course, radio and the movies could be used for political purposes. Radio offered great opportunities for reaching the masses. This became obvious when it was discovered that Adolf Hitler's fiery speeches made just as great an impact on people when heard over the radio as they did in person. The Nazi regime encouraged radio listening by urging manufacturers to produce inexpensive radios that could be bought on an installment plan.

Film, too, had propaganda potential, a fact not lost on Joseph Goebbels (GUHR•buhlz), the propaganda minister of Nazi Germany. Believing that film was one of the "most modern and scientific

In 1934 Adolf Hitler commissioned Leni Riefenstahl to film the 1934 Nazi party rally in Nuremberg. The resulting film, *Triumph of the Will,* is considered one of the greatest documentary films of all time—and a chilling piece of Nazi propaganda.

Riefenstahl later said of the film, "It reflects the truth that was then, in 1934, history. It is therefore a documentary, not a propaganda film." It is true that the film is the record of an actual event that happened at a specific time. In that respect, it is a documentary. However, Riefenstahl's powerful and positive images of Hitler as a kind of savior make it propaganda. For example, at the beginning of the film, Hitler's plane descends from the sky almost like the chariot of a god coming to visit Earth. The film was edited and set to the music of Richard Wagner, building to a climax when Hitler takes the stand. In this way, it attempts to influence the audience's attitude toward the Nazis—which is the goal of propaganda.

Today many of Riefenstahl's films are considered masterpieces, in spite of the fact that they glorify the Nazis.

DOCUMENT-BASED QUESTIONS

1. **Identifying** How can you tell from the photo that this is a huge Nazi rally?
2. **Making Connections** How can a film be both a documentary and propaganda?

Director Leni Riefenstahl filming *Triumph of the Will* at the Luitpoldhain Arena in Nuremberg, 1934

means of influencing the masses," Goebbels created a special film division in his Propaganda Ministry. The film division supported the making of both documentaries—nonfiction films—and popular feature films that carried the Nazi message.

The Uses of Leisure

After World War I, the **assembly** line and mass production took hold in industry. More consumer goods were available, and more people could buy them because they had more income or credit. By 1920, the eight-hour day had been established for many workers. Gradually, it became the norm.

This new work pattern meant more free time for the leisure activities that had emerged by 1900. Professional sporting events were an important part of mass leisure. Travel was another favorite activity. Trains, buses, and cars made trips to beaches or holiday resorts popular and affordable.

Mass leisure offered new ways for totalitarian states to control the people. The Nazi regime, for example, adopted a program called *Kraft durch Freude* ("Strength through Joy"). The program offered a variety of leisure activities to fill the free time of the working class. These activities included concerts, operas, films, guided tours, and sporting events.

✓ **Reading Check** **Examining** How did the "Strength through Joy" program help support the Nazi regime?

Arts and Science

MAIN IDEA The art, literature, and scientific break-throughs produced after World War I both embraced the past and reflected uncertainty for the future.

HISTORY & YOU Can you think of a song, book, or movie that reflects the attitudes of your friends? Read to learn what art, literature, and science revealed about society in the years after World War I.

Four years of devastating war had left many Europeans with a profound sense of despair. The Great Depression and the growth of violent fascist movements only added to the despair created by the war. Many people began looking at themselves differently; their future seemed uncertain.

With political, economic, and social uncertainties came intellectual uncertainties. These were evident in the artistic, intellectual, and scientific achievements of the years following World War I.

Art: Nightmares and New Visions

After 1918, artistic **trends** mainly reflected developments made before the war. Abstract art, for example, became ever more popular. In addition, a prewar fascination with the absurd and the unconscious content of the mind seemed even more appropriate in light of the nightmare landscapes of the World War I battlefronts. "The world does not make sense, so why should art?" was a common remark. This sentiment gave rise to both the Dada movement and surrealism.

The dadaists were artists who were obsessed with the idea that life has no purpose. They were revolted by what they saw as the insanity of life and tried to express that feeling in their art. Dada artist Hannah Höch, for example, used **photomontage** (a picture made of a combination of photographs) to comment on women's roles in the new mass culture.

A more important artistic movement than dadaism was **surrealism.** By portraying the

CONNECTING TO THE UNITED STATES

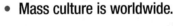

MASS CULTURE THEN AND NOW

By 1920, shorter workdays gave rise to mass culture. Huge movie palaces were built, and radio brought the world into people's homes. Magazines helped spread trends.

Today's mass culture often focuses more on private entertainment. People watch movies and television on tiny portable screens and listen to music through earbuds. Cultural trends spread over the Internet. American mass culture is exported around the world, where it is often embraced, but it has also provoked negative responses.

- Mass culture is a by-product of industrialization.
- Mass culture may have a public or private focus.
- Mass culture is worldwide.

1. **Contrasting** What is the biggest difference between early mass culture and mass culture today?

2. **Making Inferences** Why would some cultures react negatively to the Americanization that comes with the spread of American mass culture?

unconscious—fantasies, dreams, and even nightmares—the surrealists sought to show the greater reality that exists beyond the world of physical appearances. One of the world's foremost surrealist painters, the Spaniard **Salvador Dalí,** placed recognizable objects in unrecognizable relationships. Dalí created a strange world in which the irrational became visible.

Not everybody accepted modern art forms. Many people denounced what they saw as decay in the arts. In Germany, Hitler and the Nazis believed that they were creating a new and genuine German art to glorify heroic Germans. What the Nazis developed, however, was actually derived from nineteenth-century folk art and emphasized realistic scenes of everyday life.

Literature: The Search for the Unconscious

The interest in the unconscious also appeared in new literary techniques. "Stream of consciousness" was a technique used by writers to show the innermost thoughts of each character. The most famous example is the novel *Ulysses,* published by the Irish writer **James Joyce** in 1922. *Ulysses* tells the story of one day in the life of ordinary people in **Dublin.**

The novels of German writer **Hermann Hesse** reflect the influence of both Freud's psychology and Asian religions. His works often focus on the spiritual loneliness of modern human beings in a mechanized urban society. In *Siddhartha* and *Steppenwolf,* Hesse uses Buddhist ideas to show the psychological confusion of modern existence. Hesse's novels had a great impact on German youth in the 1920s. He won the Nobel Prize for literature in 1946.

The Heroic Age of Physics

The prewar physics revolution begun by Albert Einstein continued in the 1920s and 1930s. In fact, Ernest Rutherford, one of the physicists who showed that the atom could be split, called the 1920s the "heroic age of physics."

The unfolding new physics undermined the classical physics of Newton. Newtonian physics had made people believe that all phenomena could be completely defined and predicted. In 1927 German physicist Werner Heisenberg's **uncertainty principle** shook this belief. Physicists knew that atoms were made up of smaller parts (subatomic particles). The unpredictable behavior of these subatomic particles is the basis for the uncertainty principle. Heisenberg's theory essentially suggests that all physical laws are based on uncertainty. The theory's emphasis on randomness challenged Newtonian physics and, in a way, represented a new worldview. Thus, the principle of uncertainty fit in well with the other uncertainties of the interwar years.

✓ **Reading Check** **Explaining** How did Heisenberg's uncertainty principle challenge the Newtonian worldview?

Vocabulary

1. **Explain** the significance of: assembly, trend, photomontage, surrealism, Salvador Dalí, James Joyce, Dublin, Hermann Hesse, uncertainty principle.

Main Ideas

2. **Describe** the method the Nazi regime used to encourage radio listening.

3. **Identify** the artistic movements of this period, using a chart like the one below.

Artistic Movement	Description
	life has no purpose; expresses the insanity of life
	seeks a reality beyond the material world

4. **List** the qualities that the Nazis wanted German art to glorify.

Critical Thinking

5. **The BIG Idea** **Evaluating** What impact did technological advances in transportation and communication have on Western culture between the wars?

6. **Making Generalizations** Why do you think Hitler was so concerned with issues such as the content and style of art?

7. **Analyzing Visuals** Examine the Nazi rally photograph on page 577. Is this photograph a credible historical source? Why or why not?

Writing About History

8. **Informative Writing** Prepare a poster that shows the development of mass communication from the radio to modern technological advances in computers. Include photos and illustrations in your poster. Write a brief paragraph that summarizes twentieth-century innovations.

History ONLINE

For help with the concepts in this section of *Glencoe World History— Modern Times,* go to glencoe.com and click Study Central.

You can study anywhere, anytime by downloading quizzes and flash cards to your PDA from glencoe.com.

The AFTERMATH OF WAR and Impact of GLOBAL DEPRESSION

- Many nations were unhappy with the peace settlement after World War I.
- The crash of the U.S. stock market triggered a world-wide financial crisis and a global depression.
- The Great Depression made people doubt democracy and look to authoritarian leaders for simple solutions to problems.

THE GREAT DEPRESSION

The Great Depression caused many to live in squalor, as shown in this picture of "Hoover Village" in Central Park, New York City, 1931.

MUSSOLINI'S BLACKSHIRTS MARCH THE STREETS OF ROME ON OCTOBER 28, 1922

Mussolini used the Blackshirts to enforce the policies of his totalitarian regime.

TOTALITARIAN AND AUTHORITARIAN Governments in Europe Take Power

- Some nations in Europe replaced democracy with totalitarian governments.
- Mussolini's Fascist regime in Italy controlled citizens with mass propaganda.
- In the Soviet Union, Stalin gained control of the Communist Party, arresting or killing those who opposed him.

The Rise of NAZI GERMANY

- Losses in World War I and economic devastation led to political struggles in Germany.
- Hitler's Nazi Party created a totalitarian state based on racism and German nationalism.
- The Nazis enforced their will through secret police and concentration camps.

NAZI PARTY USES ANTI-SEMITIC POLICIES

This anti-Semitic banner hung outside Nazi headquarters in Nuremberg in 1935. It reads: "By resisting the Jews, I fight for the Lord."

STANDARDIZED TEST PRACTICE

TEST-TAKING TIP

If you do not know the right answer to a question, use common sense to eliminate answer choices that do not make sense. Recall the context in which the topic was discussed in class or in the textbook. This may help you eliminate incorrect answer choices.

Reviewing Vocabulary

Directions: Choose the word or words that best complete the sentence.

1. The Nazis imprisoned Jewish people in _____.

   A Reichstags

   B concentration camps

   C totalitarian states

   D Politburos

2. _____ is the term for a period of low economic activity and rising unemployment.

   A Collectivization

   B Inflation

   C Deficit spending

   D Depression

3. A picture made of a combination of photographs is known as a _____.

   A photomontage

   B propaganda film

   C mural

   D collage

4. _____ glorifies the state above the individual.

   A Racism

   B Fascism

   C Dadaism

   D Surrealism

Reviewing Main Ideas

Directions: Choose the best answers to the following questions.

Section 1 *(pp. 554–559)*

5. Why was the League of Nations weak?

   A It had too many members.

   B It had too few members.

   C The United States did not join it.

   D The Nazis took control of it.

6. Which of the following was a factor in triggering the Great Depression?

   A Economic downturns in individual nations

   B Renewed interest in Marxism among Germans

   C The policies of the New Deal

   D The rise of the Nazis and Fascists

Section 2 *(pp. 560–567)*

7. Who led the Fascist movement in Italy?

   A Adolf Hitler

   B Leon Trotsky

   C Francisco Franco

   D Benito Mussolini

8. What Soviet economic plan allowed some capitalism, with the state controlling large industries?

   A Fourteen Points

   B Five-Year Plans

   C New Economic Policy

   D New Deal

Need Extra Help?								
If You Missed Questions . . .	1	2	3	4	5	6	7	8
Go to Page . . .	570	556	578	561	554	556	561	563

9. In what country did Hitler test the new weaponry of Germany's air force?

  A France

  B Spain

  C Italy

  D Russia

Section 3 (pp. 568–573)

10. What group did Hitler claim would dominate Europe and the world?

  A Aryans

  B Socialists

  C Semites

  D Communists

11. What was the name of the Nazi attacks that destroyed some 7,000 Jewish businesses and burned synagogues?

  A *Nazionalnacht*

  B *Kristallnacht*

  C *Weimar*

  D *Mein Kampf*

Section 4 (pp. 576–579)

12. What was the Nazi "Strength through Joy" program?

  A A self-paced physical fitness program

  B A benefit for joining the SS

  C A use of religious experience to promote Nazi ideology

  D A variety of leisure activities for the working class

13. Who was the author of *Ulysses*?

  A Hermann Hesse

  B Salvador Dalí

  C James Joyce

  D Joseph Goebbels

Critical Thinking

Directions: Choose the best answers to the following questions.

Use the following map to answer question 14.

Spanish Civil War, 1936–1939

14. Based on the map, what territory did the Republicans control?

  A Several Mediterranean Sea ports

  B Several Pacific Ocean ports

  C A land route to Europe

  D Territory on the Atlantic coast

15. Which of the following is a true statement about industrialization in Stalinist Russia?

  A It emphasized consumer products over capital goods.

  B It was directed by the government.

  C It emphasized agricultural production over heavy industry.

  D It depended on technological innovations of the time.

Need Extra Help?							
If You Missed Questions . . .	9	10	11	12	13	14	15
Go to Page . . .	567	570	573	577	579	567	564

16. What is one reason why the German people supported the Nazis?

  A The Nazis promised peace in a time of turmoil.

  B The Nazis emphasized personal happiness.

  C The Nazis brought an end to the Depression.

  D The Nazis preached acceptance and toleration.

17. Whose work influenced the literary technique known as "stream of consciousness"?

  A Werner Heisenberg

  B Albert Einstein

  C Adolf Hitler

  D Sigmund Freud

In the cartoon below, the character on the left is British prime minister Neville Chamberlain. The character on the right is Benito Mussolini. The caption says, "Would you oblige me with a match, please?" Base your answer to question 18 on the cartoon.

WOULD YOU OBLIGE ME WITH A MATCH PLEASE ?

—David Low, *London Evening Standard* (February 25, 1938)

18. What is the message of the cartoon?

  A Chamberlain realizes that Mussolini is about to trick him.

  B Chamberlain is a more generous person than Mussolini.

  C Chamberlain is afraid to deny any request Mussolini makes.

  D Chamberlain is unaware of the danger Mussolini poses.

Document-Based Questions

Directions: Analyze the document and answer the short answer questions that follow the document. Base your answers on the document and on your knowledge of world history.

The following passage comes from the writing of Adolf Hitler before he rose to power.

> "The power which has always started the greatest religious and political avalanches in history rolling has from time immemorial been the magic power of the spoken word and that alone. The broad masses of the people can be moved only by the power of speech. All great movements are popular movements, volcanic eruptions of human passions and emotional sentiments, stirred either by the cruel goddess of distress or by the firebrand of the word hurled among the masses."
>
> —Adolf Hitler, as quoted in *The Rise of the Nazis*, Charles Freeman, 1988

19. Consider Germany's economic condition following World War I. To what does Hitler refer when he says "the cruel goddess of distress"?

20. How did Hitler plan to create a movement?

Extended Response

21. The Great Depression threw the world into a downturn as inflation and unemployment rose. Imagine that you are living in 1928. Assume that you know everything that is going to occur because of the Great Depression and that you have the ability to move to any major country in the world. Where would you go and why? Would being part of a particular social class influence your decision?

History ONLINE

For additional test practice, use Self-Check Quizzes—Chapter 17 at **glencoe.com**.

Need Extra Help?						
If You Missed Questions . . .	16	17	18	19	20	21
Go to Page . . .	572	579	583	569	569	556

STOP

CHAPTER 18

Nationalism Around the World 1919–1939

Section 1 Nationalism in the Middle East

Section 2 Nationalism in Africa and Asia

Section 3 Revolutionary Chaos in China

Section 4 Nationalism in Latin America

MAKING CONNECTIONS

How can nationalism affect a country?

Mexican president Lázaro Cárdenas sparked an era of change with policies promoting land reforms and workers' rights and limiting foreign investment—all goals of the Mexican Revolution. Known as the president who stood up to the United States, Cárdenas seized the property of foreign oil companies in Mexico. In this chapter you will learn how nationalist movements affected individual nations.

- How did nationalism influence the historical path of the world's nations?
- How does patriotism influence the behavior of Americans today?

THE WORLD ▶

1919
Comintern formed by Lenin

1921
Young Kikuyu Association protests British taxes in Africa

1927
Chiang Kai-shek organizes the Shanghai Massacre

1920   1925   1930

1919
League of Nations formed

1929
Great Depression begins

1933
Franklin D. Roosevelt announces the Good Neighbor policy

1939
British limit number of Jewish immigrants to Palestine

1935   1940

1939
World War II begins

FOLDABLES™
Study Organizer

Drawing Conclusions As you read, use a Four-Door Book to take notes about the leaders of the nationalist movements. Draw conclusions about what each leader sought to accomplish and what each ultimately achieved.

Mustafa Kemal (Atatürk)   Mohandas Ghandi

Lázaro Cárdenas   Harry Thuku

History ONLINE
Chapter Overview—Visit glencoe.com to preview Chapter 18.

Nationalism in the Middle East

GUIDE TO READING

The BIG Idea
Self-Determination After World War I, the quest for national self-determination led to the creation of Turkey, Iran, and Saudi Arabia. In the same period, the Balfour Declaration supported the creation of a national Jewish homeland in Palestine.

Content Vocabulary
- genocide *(p. 588)*
- ethnic cleansing *(p. 588)*

Academic Vocabulary
- legislature *(p. 586)*   • element *(p. 588)*

People and Places
- Abdülhamīd II *(p. 586)*   • Iran *(p. 589)*
- T. E. Lawrence *(p. 586)*   • Ibn Saʿūd *(p. 591)*
- Atatürk *(p. 589)*   • Saudi Arabia *(p. 591)*
- Tehran *(p. 589)*   • Palestine *(p. 591)*
- Reza Shah Pahlavi *(p. 589)*

Reading Strategy
Comparing and Contrasting As you read, make a Venn diagram like the one below comparing and contrasting the national policies of Atatürk and Reza Shah Pahlavi.

Atatürk | Reza Shah Pahlavi

The Ottoman Empire ended shortly after World War I. While the new Turkish Republic modernized, Persia evolved into the modern state of Iran and the kingdom of Saudi Arabia was established. In Palestine, tensions mounted as both Arabs and Jews viewed the area as their homeland.

Decline and Fall of the Ottoman Empire

MAIN IDEA The Ottoman Empire, which had been steadily declining since the late 1700s, finally ended after World War I.

HISTORY & YOU Do you think it is possible for an empire to exist in the world today? Read to learn about the fall of the Ottoman Empire.

The Ottoman Empire—which once had included parts of eastern Europe, the Middle East, and North Africa—had been growing steadily weaker. The empire's size had decreased dramatically during the nineteenth century. Greece achieved its independence during the course of the 1820s and 1830s, and the empire subsequently lost much more European territory. Ottoman rule also ended in North Africa.

In 1876 Ottoman reformers seized control of the empire's government and adopted a constitution that set up a **legislature.** However, the sultan they placed on the throne, **Abdülhamīd II,** suspended the new constitution. Abdülhamīd paid a high price for his authoritarian actions—he lived in constant fear of assassination. He kept a thousand loaded revolvers hidden throughout his guarded estate and insisted that his pets taste his food before he ate it.

The suspended constitution became a symbol of change to a group of reformers named the Young Turks. This group forced the restoration of the constitution in 1908 and deposed the sultan the following year. However, the Young Turks lacked strong support for their government. The stability of the empire was also challenged by many ethnic Turks who had begun to envision a Turkish state that would encompass all people of Turkish nationality.

Impact of World War I

The final blow to the old empire came from World War I. After the Ottoman government allied with Germany, the British sought to undermine Ottoman rule in the Arabian Peninsula by supporting Arab nationalist activities there. The nationalists were aided by the dashing British adventurer **T. E. Lawrence,** popularly known as "Lawrence of Arabia."

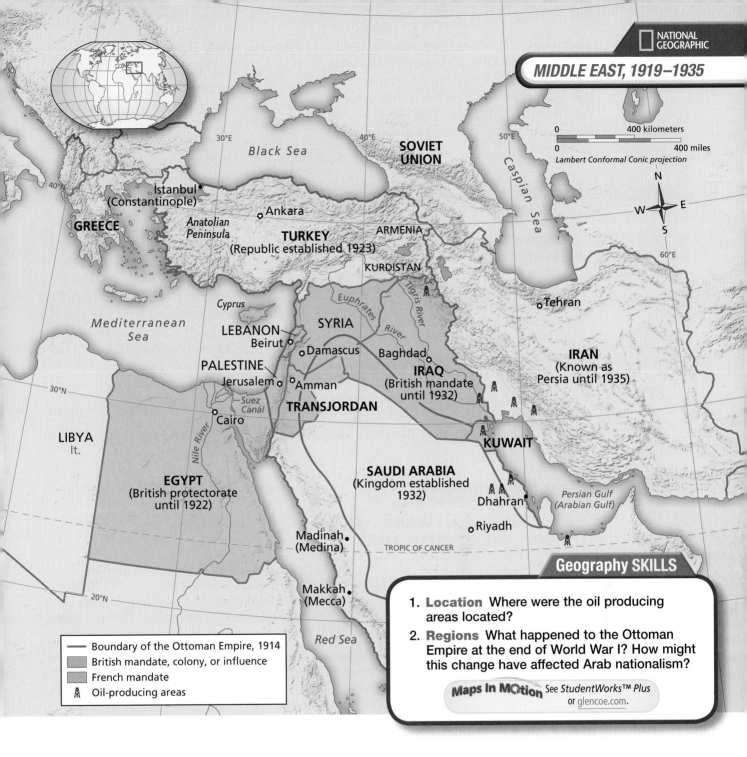

NATIONAL GEOGRAPHIC

MIDDLE EAST, 1919–1935

400 kilometers

400 miles

Lambert Conformal Conic projection

Black Sea

30°E

40°E

50°E

SOVIET UNION

İstanbul
(Constantinople)

Ankara

GREECE

Anatolian Peninsula

40°N

60°E

TURKEY
(Republic established 1923)

ARMENIA

Caspian Sea

KURDISTAN

Euphrates River

Tigris River

Cyprus

Mediterranean Sea

LEBANON
Beirut

SYRIA

Damascus

Baghdad

Tehran

IRAN
(Known as Persia until 1935)

PALESTINE
Jerusalem

Amman

IRAQ
(British mandate until 1932)

30°N

— Suez Canal

TRANSJORDAN

Cairo

Nile River

LIBYA
It.

KUWAIT

EGYPT
(British protectorate until 1922)

SAUDI ARABIA
(Kingdom established 1932)

Dhahran

Persian Gulf (Arabian Gulf)

Riyadh

Madinah
(Medina)

TROPIC OF CANCER

Makkah
(Mecca)

Red Sea

20°N

Boundary of the Ottoman Empire, 1914

British mandate, colony, or influence

French mandate

Oil-producing areas

Geography SKILLS

1. **Location** Where were the oil producing areas located?

2. **Regions** What happened to the Ottoman Empire at the end of World War I? How might this change have affected Arab nationalism?

Maps In MOtion See *StudentWorks™ Plus* or glencoe.com.

In 1916 Arabia declared its independence from Ottoman rule. British troops advanced from Egypt and seized Palestine. After suffering more than 300,000 deaths during the war, the Ottoman Empire made peace with the Allies in October 1918.

The Armenian Genocide

During the war the Ottoman Turks had alienated the Allies with their policies toward minority subjects, especially the Armenians. The Christian Armenian

minority had been pressing the Ottoman government for its independence for years. In 1915 the government began killing Armenian men and expelling women and children from the empire.

Within 7 months, 600,000 Armenians had been killed, and 500,000 had been deported (sent out of the country). Of those deported, 400,000 died while marching through the deserts and swamps of Syria and Mesopotamia. By September 1915, an estimated 1 million Armenians were dead.

They were victims of **genocide,** the deliberate mass murder of a particular racial, political, or cultural group. (A similar practice would be called **ethnic cleansing** in the Bosnian War of 1993–1996.) One eyewitness to the 1915 Armenian deportation said:

PRIMARY SOURCE

"[She] saw vultures hovering over children who had fallen dead by the roadside. She saw beings crawling along, maimed, starving and begging for bread. . . . [S]he passed soldiers driving before them . . . whole families, men, women and children, shrieking, pleading, wailing . . . setting out for exile into the desert from which there was no return."

—as quoted in *The First World War,* by Martin Gilbert

By 1918, another 400,000 Armenians had been massacred. Russia, France, and Britain denounced the Turkish actions as being "crimes against humanity and civilization." Because of the war, however, the killings continued.

The Turkish Republic

At the end of World War I, the tottering Ottoman Empire collapsed. Great Britain and France made plans to divide Ottoman territories in the Middle East. Only the area of present-day Turkey remained under Ottoman control. Then, Greece invaded Turkey and seized the western parts of the Anatolian Peninsula.

The invasion alarmed key **elements** in Turkey, who were organized under the leadership of the war hero Colonel Mustafa Kemal. Kemal summoned a national congress calling for the creation of an elected government and a new Republic of Turkey. His forces drove the Greeks from the Anatolian Peninsula. In 1923 the last of the Ottoman sultans fled the country, which was now declared to be the Turkish Republic. The Ottoman Empire had finally come to an end.

✓ **Reading Check** **Evaluating** How did the Ottoman Empire finally end?

HISTORY & ARTS   PRIMARY SOURCE

The Armenian Genocide

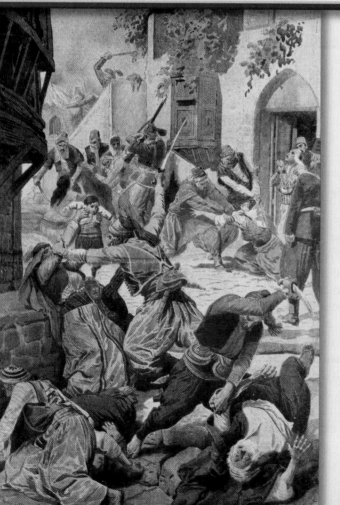

As the Ottoman Empire eroded, ethnic tensions increased. When the Committee of Union and Progress (CUP) seized power in 1913, leaders responded to Armenian calls for reform with force. Seeking a purely Turkish state, they began a campaign of genocide. Beginning in 1915, Armenian Christians were murdered, deported, and sent to concentration camps.

"The Ottoman Empire should be cleaned up of the Armenians and the Lebanese. We have destroyed the former by the sword, we shall destroy the latter through starvation."
—Enver Pasha, leader of the Young Turks, May 19, 1916

Allied with the Central Powers in World War I, CUP leaders massacred Armenians under the cover of war. Despite Allied warnings to end the genocide, the killing continued until 1919. To this day, Turkey refuses to acknowledge the Armenian genocide.

DOCUMENT-BASED QUESTIONS

The Massacre of the Armenians appeared in *Le Petit Journal* in France December 12, 1915. The lithograph shows the April 24, 1915, murder of 300 Armenian leaders, writers, and professionals as well as thousands of impoverished Armenians.

1. **Identifying** What elements of the lithograph create sympathy for the Armenians?
2. **Making Inferences** Why do you think Allied forces failed to intervene directly in the genocide?

Middle East Changes

MAIN IDEA Turkey's president Kemal changed the political system and the Turkish culture to create a modern state, while government and economic reforms changed Persia into the modern country of Iran.

HISTORY & YOU If you had the power to make your community more modern, what changes would you make? Read to learn about the modernization of Turkey and Persia.

While Turkey, Iran, and Saudi Arabia emerged as modern states, tensions mounted between the Jewish and Muslim inhabitants in Palestine.

The Modernization of Turkey

President Kemal was now popularly known as **Atatürk** (AT•uh•TUHRK), or "father Turk." Over the next several years, he tried to transform Turkey into a modern state. A democratic system was put in place, but Atatürk did not tolerate opposition and harshly suppressed his critics.

Atatürk's changes went beyond politics. Many Arabic elements were eliminated from the Turkish language, which was now written in the Roman alphabet. Popular education was introduced. All Turkish citizens were forced to adopt family (last) names, in the European style.

Atatürk also took steps to modernize Turkey's economy. Factories were established, and a five-year plan provided for state direction over the economy. Atatürk also tried to modernize farming, although he had little effect on the nation's peasants.

Perhaps the most significant aspect of Atatürk's reform program was his attempt to break the power of the Islamic religion. He wanted to transform Turkey into a secular state—a state that rejects religious influence on its policies. Atatürk said, "Religion is like a heavy blanket that keeps the people of Turkey asleep."

The caliphate was formally abolished in 1924. Men were forbidden to wear the fez, the brimless cap worn by Turkish Muslims. When Atatürk began wearing a Western panama hat, one of his critics remarked, "You cannot make a Turk into a Westerner by giving him a hat."

Women were forbidden to wear the veil, a traditional Islamic custom. New laws gave women marriage and inheritance rights equal to men's. In 1934 women received the right to vote. All citizens were also given the right to convert to other religions.

The legacy of Kemal Atatürk was enormous. In practice, not all of his reforms were widely accepted, especially by devout Muslims. However, most of the changes that he introduced were kept after his death in 1938. By and large, the Turkish Republic was the product of Atatürk's determined efforts.

The Beginnings of Modern Iran

A similar process of modernization was underway in Persia. Under the Qājār dynasty (1794–1925), the country had not been very successful in resolving its domestic problems. Increasingly, the dynasty had turned to Russia and Great Britain to protect itself from its own people, which led to a growing foreign presence in Persia. The discovery of oil in the southern part of the country in 1908 attracted more foreign interest. Oil exports increased rapidly, and most of the profits went to British investors.

The growing foreign presence led to the rise of a native Persian nationalist movement. In 1921 Reza Khan, an officer in the Persian army, led a military mutiny that seized control of **Tehran,** the capital city. In 1925 Reza Khan established himself as shah, or king, and was called **Reza Shah Pahlavi.** The name of the new dynasty he created, Pahlavi, was the name of the ancient Persian language.

During the next few years, Reza Shah Pahlavi tried to follow the example of Kemal Atatürk in Turkey. He introduced a number of reforms to strengthen and modernize the government, the military, and the economic system. Persia became the modern state of **Iran** in 1935.

Unlike Atatürk, Reza Shah Pahlavi did not try to destroy the power of Islamic beliefs. However, he did encourage the creation of a Western-style educational system and forbade women to wear the veil in public.

November 2nd, 1917

Dear Lord Rothschild,

I have much pleasure in conveying to you, on behalf of His Majesty's Government, the following declaration of sympathy with Jewish Zionist aspirations which has been submitted to, and approved by, the Cabinet.

" His Majesty's Government view with favour the establishment in Palestine of a national home for the Jewish people, and will use their best endeavours to facilitate the achievement of this object, it being clearly understood that nothing shall be done which may prejudice the civil and religious rights of existing non-Jewish communities in Palestine, or the rights and political status enjoyed by Jews in any other country."

I should be grateful if you would bring this declaration to the knowledge of the Zionist Federation.

Yours sincerely,

Arthur James Balfour

It was just a simple letter written by Arthur James Balfour, Britain's foreign secretary, to Lord Rothschild, a leader of the Jewish community in Britain. Yet relations in the Middle East today still reflect its impact.

By supporting the Zionist desire for a homeland in Palestine, Britain hoped to gain Jewish support for the Allies in World War I. The British also hoped that the settlement of Palestine by a Jewish population friendly to Britain would help protect British interests around the important Suez Canal.

A week after the letter was written, it was published in the *Times* of London. It became known as the Balfour Declaration. This letter became the basis of international support for the modern state of Israel.

CRITICAL THINKING SKILLS

1. **Explaining** In what way did the Balfour Declaration fall short of Zionist desires?
2. **Determining Cause and Effect** How did the Balfour Declaration affect events in the Middle East?

Foreign powers continued to harass Iran. To free himself from Great Britain and the Soviet Union, Reza Shah Pahlavi drew closer to Nazi Germany. During World War II, the shah rejected the demands of Great Britain and the Soviet Union to expel a large number of Germans from Iran. In response, Great Britain and the Soviet Union sent troops into the country. Reza Shah Pahlavi resigned in protest and was replaced by his son, Mohammad Reza Pahlavi.

Arab Nationalism

World War I offered the Arabs an excellent opportunity to escape from Ottoman rule. However, there was a question as to what would replace that rule. The Arabs were not a nation, though they were united by their language and their Islamic cultural and religious heritage. However, efforts by generations of political leaders to create a single Arab nation have been unsuccessful.

Because Britain had supported the efforts of Arab nationalists in 1916, the nationalists hoped this support would continue after the war ended. Instead, Britain made an agreement with France to create a number of mandates in the area. These mandates were former Ottoman territories that the new League of Nations now supervised. The League, in turn, granted its members the right to govern particular mandates. Iraq, Palestine, and Jordan were assigned to Great Britain; Syria and Lebanon, to France.

For the most part, Europeans created these Middle Eastern states. The Europeans determined the nations' borders and divided the peoples. In general, the people in these states had no strong identification with their designated country. However, a sense of Arab nationalism remained.

In the early 1920s, a reform leader, **Ibn Sa'ūd**, united Arabs in the northern part of the Arabian Peninsula. Devout and gifted, Ibn Sa'ūd (from whom came the name **Saudi Arabia**) won broad support. He established the kingdom of Saudi Arabia in 1932.

At first, the new kingdom, which consisted mostly of the vast central desert of the Arabian Peninsula, was desperately poor. Its main source of income came from the Muslim pilgrims who visited Makkah (Mecca) and Madinah (Medina). During the 1930s, however, U.S. prospectors began to explore for oil. Standard Oil made a successful strike at Dhahran, on the Persian Gulf, in 1938. Soon, the Arabian-American oil company Aramco was created. The isolated kingdom was suddenly flooded with Western oil industries that brought the promise of wealth.

The Problem of Palestine

The situation in **Palestine** complicated matters in the Middle East even more. While Palestine had been the home of the Jews in antiquity, Jews had been forced into exile in the first century A.D. A Jewish presence always remained, but Muslim Arabs made up about 80 percent of the region's population. In Palestine, the nationalism of Jews and Arabs came into conflict because both groups viewed the area as a potential national state.

Since the 1890s, the Zionist movement had advocated that Palestine should be established as a Jewish state. Jews recalled that the ancient state of Israel was located there. Arabs pointed out that their ancestors had also lived in Palestine for centuries.

The Balfour Declaration

As a result of the Zionist movement and growing anti-Semitism in Europe, more Jews began to migrate to Palestine. Then during World War I, the British government, hoping to win Jewish support for the Allies, issued the Balfour Declaration. It expressed support for a national home for the Jews in Palestine, but it also added that this goal should not undermine the rights of the non-Jewish peoples living there.

The Balfour Declaration drew even more Jews to Palestine. In 1933 the Nazi regime in Germany began policies that later led to the Holocaust and the murder of six million Jews. During the 1930s, many Jews fled to Palestine. Violence flared between Jewish and Muslim inhabitants.

Trying to end the violence, the British declared in 1939 that only 75,000 Jewish people would be allowed to immigrate to Palestine over the next five years; after that, no more Jews could do so. This decision, however, only intensified the tension and increased the bloodshed.

✓ **Reading Check** **Explaining** Why did the Balfour Declaration produce problems in Palestine?

SECTION 1 REVIEW

Vocabulary
1. **Explain** the significance of: legislature, Abdülhamīd II, T. E. Lawrence, genocide, ethnic cleansing, element, Atatürk, Tehran, Reza Shah Pahlavi, Iran, Ibn Sa'ūd, Saudi Arabia, Palestine.

Main Ideas
2. **Explain** how the Ottoman alliance with Germany in World War I contributed to the fall of the Ottoman Empire.

3. **Summarize** the steps Atatürk took to modernize Turkey, using a diagram like the one below.

Modernization of Turkey

4. **Explain** why more Jewish people began to migrate to Palestine.

Critical Thinking
5. **The BIG Idea** **Evaluating** Why was it difficult for the Arab peoples to form one nation?

6. **Making Connections** Why did foreign interest in Persia and Saudi Arabia increase in the first half of the twentieth century?

7. **Analyzing Visuals** Examine the illustration on page 588. Would a Turkish magazine have depicted this scene in the same way? Explain your answer.

Writing About History
8. **Expository Writing** Review information in your textbook about the fall of these two empires: the Han Dynasty (Chapter 1) and the Roman Empire (Chapter 2). Then create a multimedia presentation that compares the collapse of these empires to the fall of the Ottoman Empire.

For help with the concepts in this section of *Glencoe World History—Modern Times*, go to glencoe.com and click Study Central.

Nationalism in Africa and Asia

GUIDE TO READING

The BIG Idea
Self-Determination Nationalism led the people of Africa and Asia to seek independence.

Content Vocabulary
- Pan-Africanism *(p. 594)*   • *zaibatsu (p. 598)*
- civil disobedience *(p. 596)*

Academic Vocabulary
- volunteer *(p. 592)*   • compensation *(p. 593)*

People and Places
- Kenya *(p. 593)*
- W.E.B. Du Bois *(p. 594)*
- Marcus Garvey *(p. 594)*
- Ho Chi Minh *(p. 595)*
- Mohandas Gandhi *(p. 596)*
- Mahatma *(p. 596)*
- Jawaharlal Nehru *(p. 596)*
- Manchuria *(p. 599)*

Reading Strategy
Contrasting As you read, use a table like the one below to contrast the backgrounds and values of Gandhi and Nehru.

Mohandas Gandhi	Jawaharlal Nehru

Nationalism spread throughout Africa and Asia in the early twentieth century. Calls for independence came from a new generation of Western-educated African leaders. As communism spread in Asia, Mohandas Gandhi and Jawaharlal Nehru worked for the independence of India. Meanwhile, militarists gained control of the Japanese government.

African Independence Movements

MAIN IDEA After World War I, many Africans organized to end colonial rule in their countries.

HISTORY & YOU Have you ever worked with a group to promote a cause you believe in? Read to learn about ideas that inspired Africans to work toward independence after World War I.

Black Africans had fought in World War I in British and French armies. Many Africans hoped that independence after the war would be their reward. As one newspaper in the Gold Coast argued, if African **volunteers** who fought on European battlefields were "good enough to fight and die in the Empire's cause, they were good enough to have a share in the government of their countries." Most European leaders, however, were not ready to give up their colonies.

The peace settlement after World War I was a huge disappointment. Germany was stripped of its African colonies, but these colonies were awarded to Great Britain and France to be administered as mandates for the League of Nations. Britain and France now governed a vast portion of Africa.

African Protests

After World War I, Africans became more active politically. The foreign powers that had conquered and exploited Africa also introduced Western education. In educating Africans, the colonial system introduced them to the modern world and gave them visions of a world based on the ideals of liberty and equality. In Africa itself, the missionary schools taught these ideals to their pupils. The African students who studied abroad, especially in Britain and the United States, and the African soldiers who served in World War I learned new ideas about freedom and nationalism in the West. As more Africans became aware of the enormous gulf between Western ideals and practices, they decided to seek reform.

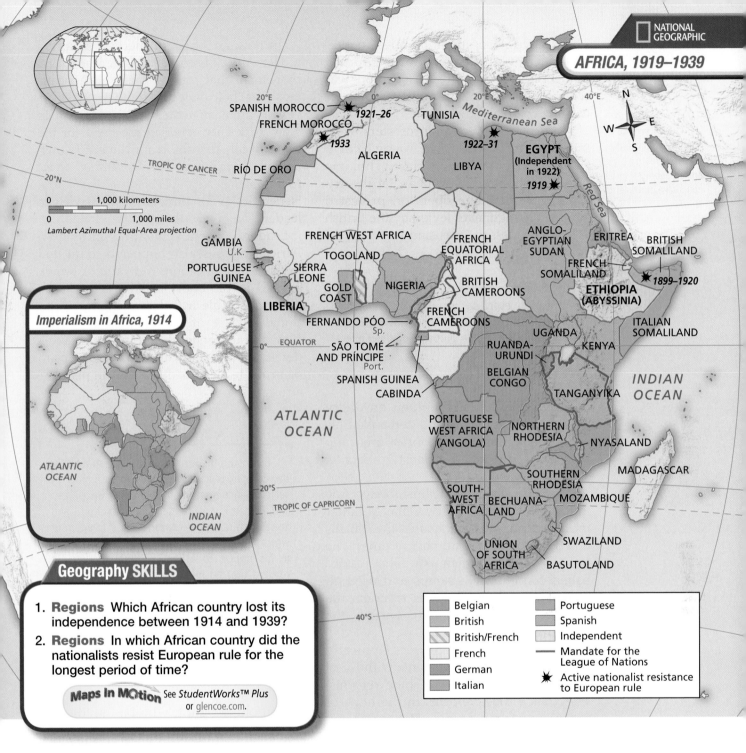

NATIONAL GEOGRAPHIC

AFRICA, 1919–1939

SPANISH MOROCCO — *1921–26*
FRENCH MOROCCO — *1933*
RÍO DE ORO
TUNISIA
ALGERIA
LIBYA — *1922–31*
EGYPT (Independent in 1922) — *1919*

Mediterranean Sea
Red Sea

TROPIC OF CANCER
20°N

0   1,000 kilometers
0   1,000 miles
Lambert Azimuthal Equal-Area projection

GAMBIA U.K.
PORTUGUESE GUINEA
SIERRA LEONE
GOLD COAST
LIBERIA
FERNANDO PÓO Sp.
SÃO TOMÉ AND PRÍNCIPE Port.
SPANISH GUINEA
CABINDA

FRENCH WEST AFRICA
TOGOLAND
NIGERIA
BRITISH CAMEROONS
FRENCH CAMEROONS
FRENCH EQUATORIAL AFRICA

ANGLO-EGYPTIAN SUDAN
ERITREA
FRENCH SOMALILAND
BRITISH SOMALILAND
ETHIOPIA (ABYSSINIA)
ITALIAN SOMALILAND — *1899–1920*

EQUATOR
0°

RUANDA-URUNDI
UGANDA
KENYA
BELGIAN CONGO
TANGANYIKA

INDIAN OCEAN

ATLANTIC OCEAN

PORTUGUESE WEST AFRICA (ANGOLA)
NORTHERN RHODESIA
NYASALAND
SOUTHERN RHODESIA
MOZAMBIQUE
MADAGASCAR
SOUTH-WEST AFRICA
BECHUANA-LAND
20°S
TROPIC OF CAPRICORN
UNION OF SOUTH AFRICA
SWAZILAND
BASUTOLAND

40°S

Imperialism in Africa, 1914

ATLANTIC OCEAN
INDIAN OCEAN

Geography SKILLS

1. **Regions** Which African country lost its independence between 1914 and 1939?

2. **Regions** In which African country did the nationalists resist European rule for the longest period of time?

Maps In Motion See *StudentWorks™ Plus* or glencoe.com.

Legend	
Belgian	Portuguese
British	Spanish
British/French	Independent
French	Mandate for the League of Nations
German	Active nationalist resistance to European rule
Italian	

Opposition to the British colonial administration escalated in Nigeria during and after World War I. Resistance was a combined effort of the traditional authority, the king of Lagos, and of educated Africans who wanted a democratic government. Leading the nationalists was Herbert Macaulay, a civil engineer who held a position in the colonial government. Macaulay and the editor of the *Lagos Weekly Record* carried on a years-long editorial campaign against the colonial government.

Political unrest also took place in **Kenya**. One of the most important issues concerned the redistribution of land. Large tracts of land on the highlands had been taken from black Africans and given to white settlers. The Africans had received little if any **compensation** for this land. Instead, they were forced to become squatters on the land they believed was their own.

During the 1920s, protest organizations, mostly founded by the Kikuyu, emerged in Kenya. These first groups were moderate.

History ONLINE

Student Web Activity—
Visit glencoe.com to learn how to create a multimedia presentation and create a presentation on nationalist movements.

The Kikuyu Association, founded in 1920 by farmers, was intent on blocking further land confiscation. This association was willing to work toward reform within the existing colonial structure.

Some of the Kenyan protesters were more radical, however. The Young Kikuyu Association, organized by Harry Thuku in 1921, challenged European authority. Thuku, a telephone operator, protested against the high taxes levied by the British rulers. His message was simple:

PRIMARY SOURCE

"Hearken, every day you pay . . . tax to the Europeans of Government. Where is it sent? It is their task to steal the property of the Kikuyu people."
—Harry Thuku

Thuku was arrested. When an angry crowd stormed the jail and demanded his release, government authorities fired into the crowd and killed at least 20 people. Thuku was sent into exile.

Libya also struggled against foreign rule in the 1920s. Forces led by Omar Mukhtar used guerrilla warfare against the Italians and defeated them a number of times. The Italians reacted ferociously. They established concentration camps and used all available modern weapons to crush the revolt. Mukhtar's death ended the movement.

Although colonial powers typically responded to such movements with force, they also began to make some reforms. They made these reforms in the hope of satisfying African peoples. Reforms, however, were too few and too late. By the 1930s, an increasing number of African leaders were calling for independence, not reform.

New Leaders

Calls for independence came from a new generation of young African leaders. Many had been educated abroad, in Europe and the United States. Those who had studied in the United States were especially influenced by the ideas of **W.E.B. Du Bois** and **Marcus Garvey.**

Du Bois, an African American educated at Harvard University, was the leader of a movement that tried to make all Africans aware of their own cultural heritage. Garvey, a Jamaican who lived in Harlem in New York City, stressed the need for the unity of all Africans, a movement known as **Pan-Africanism.** His *Declaration of the Rights of the Negro Peoples of the World,* issued in 1920, impacted later African leaders.

Leaders and movements in individual African nations also appeared. Educated in Great Britain, Jomo Kenyatta of Kenya argued in his book *Facing Mount Kenya* that British rule was destroying the traditional culture of the peoples of Africa. Kenyatta understood that it would take a determined effort to shake off European control. He described the African peoples' struggle:

PRIMARY SOURCE

"By driving the African off his ancestral lands, the Europeans have reduced him to a state of serfdom incompatible with human happiness. The African is conditioned, by the cultural and social institutions of centuries, to a freedom of which Europe has little conception, and it is not in his nature to accept serfdom forever. He realizes that he must fight unceasingly for his own complete emancipation [freedom]; for without this he is doomed to remain the prey of rival imperialisms, which in every successive year will drive their fangs more deeply into his vitality and strength."
—Jomo Kenyatta

Léopold Senghor, who had studied in France and written poetry about African culture, organized an independence movement in Senegal. Nnamdi Azikiwe, of Nigeria, began a newspaper, *The West African Pilot,* in 1937 and urged nonviolence as a method to gain independence. These are just a few of the leaders who worked to end colonial rule in Africa. Success, however, would not come until after World War II.

✓ **Reading Check** **Analyzing** Why did many Africans become more politically active after World War I?

Revolution in Asia

MAIN IDEA In the 1920s, the Comintern helped to spread communism throughout Asia.

HISTORY & YOU Do you remember the Marxist theory that industrial workers would defeat capitalism? Read to learn how Lenin's revised idea of Marxism was spread in Asia.

Before World War I, the Marxist doctrine of social revolution had no appeal for Asian intellectuals. After all, most Asian societies were still agricultural and hardly ready for revolution. That situation changed after the revolution in Russia in 1917. Lenin and the Bolsheviks showed that a revolutionary Marxist party could overturn an outdated system—even one that was not fully industrialized—and begin a new one.

In 1920 Lenin adopted a new revolutionary strategy aimed at societies outside the Western world. He spread the word of Karl Marx through the Communist International, or Comintern, a worldwide organization of Communist parties formed in 1919 to advance world revolution. Agents were trained in Moscow and then returned to their own countries to form Marxist parties. By the end of the 1920s, practically every colonial society in Asia had a Communist party.

How successful were these new parties? In some countries, the local Communists established a cooperative relationship with nationalist parties to struggle against Western imperialism. This was true in French Indochina. Moscow-trained **Ho Chi Minh** organized the Vietnamese Communists in the 1920s. The strongest Communist-nationalist alliance was formed in China (see Section 3). In most colonial societies, though, Communist parties of the 1930s failed to gain support among the majority of the population.

✓Reading Check **Evaluating** What was the relationship between communism and imperialism?

Ho Chi Minh: Vietnam's Communist Leader

A statue of Ho Chi Minh

Ho Chi Minh as a young man

At the Paris Peace Conference after World War I, Ho Chi Minh (1890–1969) tried to give U.S. president Woodrow Wilson a list of Vietnam's grievances against the French. Yet Wilson and the Allies chose not to address his concerns.

In the years following World War I, Ho continued to protest French colonialism in Vietnam. He also became increasingly drawn to the ideas of Lenin. Describing his reasons for becoming a Communist, he wrote:

"I loved and admired Lenin because he was a great patriot who liberated his compatriots. . . .
The reason for my joining the French Socialist Party was that these 'ladies and gentlemen' . . . had shown sympathy toward me—toward the struggle of the oppressed peoples."
—Ho Chi Minh, *The Path Which Led Me to Leninism*

In 1929 Ho formed the Indochinese Communist Party. He eventually rose to become president of Vietnam, as well as one of the most influential Communist leaders of the twentieth century. During his lifetime, Vietnam won independence from the French and fought a war over communism in Vietnam. Vietnam remains Communist today.

DOCUMENT-BASED QUESTIONS

1. **Interpreting** Why did Ho Chi Minh become a Communist leader?
2. **Evaluating** How might history have been different if Woodrow Wilson had not ignored Ho Chi Minh?

Indian Independence

MAIN IDEA Mohandas Gandhi and Jawaharlal Nehru led India's independence movement.

HISTORY & YOU Do your methods for solving a problem differ from those of your friends? Read to learn about Mohandas Gandhi's unusual methods.

Mohandas Gandhi had been active in the Indian National Congress and the movement for Indian self-rule before World War I. The Indian people had already begun to refer to him as India's "Great Soul," or **Mahatma**. After the war, Gandhi remained an important figure, and new leaders also arose.

Protest and Reform

Gandhi left South Africa in 1914. When he returned to India, he organized mass protests against British laws. A believer in nonviolence, Gandhi used the methods of **civil disobedience**—refusal to obey laws considered to be unjust.

In 1919 British troops killed hundreds of unarmed protesters in Amritsar, in northwestern India. Horrified at the violence, Gandhi briefly retreated from active politics, but was later arrested and imprisoned for his role in protests.

In 1935 Britain passed the Government of India Act. This act expanded the role of Indians in governing. Before, the Legislative Council could only give advice to the British governor. Now, it became a two-house parliament, and two-thirds of its Indian members were to be elected. Similar bodies were created at the provincial level. Five million Indians (still a small percentage of the population) were given the right to vote.

A Push for Independence

The Indian National Congress (INC), founded in 1885, sought reforms in Britain's government of India (see Chapter 14). Reforms, however, were no longer enough. Under its new leader, Motilal Nehru, the INC wanted to push for full independence.

Gandhi, now released from prison, returned to his earlier policy of civil disobedience. He worked hard to inform ordinary Indians of his beliefs and methods. It was wrong, he said, to harm any living being. Hate could only be overcome by love, and love, rather than force, could win people over to one's position.

Nonviolence was central to Gandhi's campaign of noncooperation and civil disobedience. To protest unjust British laws, Gandhi told his people: "Don't pay your taxes or send your children to an English-supported school. . . . Make your own cotton cloth by spinning the thread at home, and don't buy English-made goods. Provide yourselves with home-made salt, and do not buy government-made salt."

Britain had increased the salt tax and prohibited the Indians from manufacturing or harvesting their own salt. In 1930 Gandhi protested these measures. Accompanied by supporters, he walked to the sea on what became known as the Salt March. On reaching the coast, Gandhi picked up a pinch of salt. Thousands of Indians followed his act of civil disobedience. Gandhi and many other members of the INC were arrested.

New Leaders and Problems

In the 1930s, **Jawaharlal Nehru** entered the movement. The son of Motilal Nehru, Jawaharlal studied law in Great Britain. He was a new kind of Indian politician—upper class and intellectual.

The independence movement split into two paths. The one identified with Gandhi was religious, Indian, and traditional. The other, identified with Nehru, was secular, Western, and modern. The two approaches created uncertainty about India's future path.

In the meantime, another problem had arisen in the independence movement. Hostility between Hindus and Muslims had existed for centuries. Muslims were dissatisfied with the Hindu dominance of the INC and raised the cry "Islam is in danger."

By the 1930s, the Muslim League was under the leadership of Mohammed Ali Jinnah. The league believed in the creation of a separate Muslim state of Pakistan ("the land of the pure") in the northwest.

✓ **Reading Check** **Comparing** How did Nehru's approach differ from Gandhi's?

GANDHI AND NONVIOLENCE

We generally think of revolutions and independence movements as being violent. Yet Mohandas Gandhi, leader of India's independence movement, used a nonviolent approach—civil disobedience—to protest British control in India.

Gandhi's methods included boycotts of British goods and institutions as well as prolonged fasting (giving up food) to draw attention to issues. These protests eventually led to independence for India—and inspired civil rights leaders throughout the world.

In 1930 Gandhi launched a protest to oppose the British Salt Acts. These laws made it illegal to prepare salt from seawater, which would deprive the British government of tax revenue from its monopoly on the sale of salt. Gandhi set out with 78 followers for the coast to collect seawater to make salt. The British jailed Gandhi and more than 60,000 of his followers. Yet the protesters had sent a powerful message to the British. A year later, the government agreed to negotiate with Gandhi as the representative of the Indian National Congress.

Gandhi and his followers on the 200-mile (322-km) Salt March in 1930

This famous photo of Gandhi shows him with a spinning wheel, symbolizing the Indian boycott of British taxes on cloth.

Gandhi described the difference between nonviolence and other forms of protest:

"Passive resistance is a method of securing rights by personal suffering; it is the reverse of resistance by arms. . . . For instance, the Government of the day has passed a law which is applicable to me. I do not like it. If by using violence I force the Government to repeal the law, I am employing what may be termed body-force. If I do not obey the law and accept the penalty for its breach, I use soul-force. It involves sacrifice of self."

—Mohandas K. Gandhi, *Non-Violence (Satyagraha)*

DOCUMENT-BASED QUESTIONS

1. **Explaining** Explain how each photograph shows an example of nonviolence.
2. **Analyzing** In what ways was Gandhi's Indian independence movement a turning point in history?

A Militarist Japan

MAIN IDEA By the late 1920s, militant forces in Japan were campaigning for an end to peaceful policies.

HISTORY & YOU Do you own anything made by Sony, Mitsubishi, or Toshiba? Read to learn how Japan developed its modern industrial economy.

Japanese society developed along a Western model. The economic and social reforms launched during the Meiji Era led to increasing prosperity and a modern industrial and commercial sector.

A *Zaibatsu* Economy

In the Japanese economy, various manufacturing processes were concentrated within a single enterprise called the *zaibatsu,* a large financial and industrial corporation. These vast companies controlled major segments of the Japanese industrial sector. By 1937, the four largest *zaibatsu* (Mitsui, Mitsubishi, Sumitomo, and Yasuda) controlled 21 percent of the banking industry, 26 percent of mining, 35 percent of shipbuilding, and over 60 percent of paper manufacturing and insurance.

The concentration of wealth led to growing economic inequalities. City workers were poorly paid and housed. Economic crises added to this problem. After World War I, inflation in food prices led to food riots. A rapid increase in population led to food shortages. (The population of the Japanese islands increased from 43 million in 1900 to 73 million in 1940.) Later, when the Great Depression struck, workers and farmers suffered the most.

With hardships came calls for a return to traditional Japanese values. Traditionalists especially objected to the growing influence of Western ideas and values on Japanese educational and political systems. At the same time, many citizens denounced Japan's attempt to find security through cooperation with the Western powers. Instead, they demanded that Japan use its own strength to dominate Asia and meet its needs.

CONNECTING TO THE UNITED STATES

THE *ZAIBATSU* ECONOMY

▼ *American teenagers shopping for electronics at a mall in California*

During Japan's Meiji Era, family-controlled conglomerates known as *zaibatsu* began to form. By the time World War II began, four *zaibatsu* controlled much of Japan's banking, trade, and heavy industry. The Japanese government aided the growth of the *zaibatsu* by granting monopolies and special privileges in return for their help with government projects.

After World War II, the Allies broke up the *zaibatsu.* In the 1950s, however, new groups called *keiretsu* formed, based on the old *zaibatsu* and often retaining their old names. By pooling their resources, the *keiretsu* helped make Japan a global economic power. Today, Japanese *keiretsu* such as Mitsubishi, Mitsui, and Fuyo produce brands popular around the world.

- **Mitsubishi: Mitsubishi Electric, Mitsubishi Motors**
- **Mitsui: Fuji, Toshiba, Toyota**
- **Fuyo: Canon, Hitachi, Yamaha, Nissan, Ricoh**

CONNECTING TO TODAY

1. **Analyzing** What advantages aided the growth of the *zaibatsu* and *keiretsu* into powerful corporations?
2. **Identifying** Name three products made by Japanese *keiretsu* that are commonly sold in the United States.

Japan and the West

In the early twentieth century, Japan had difficulty finding sources of raw materials and foreign markets for its manufactured goods. Until World War I, Japan fulfilled these needs by seizing territories, such as Taiwan (Formosa), Korea, and southern Manchuria. This policy succeeded but aroused the concern of the Western nations.

The United States was especially concerned. It wanted to keep Japan open to U.S. trade. In 1922 the United States held a major conference of nations with interests in the Pacific. This conference achieved a nine-power treaty that recognized the territorial integrity of China and the maintenance of the Open Door policy. Japan agreed, in return for recognition of its control of southern Manchuria.

However, this agreement did not prove popular. Expansion into heavy industry, mining, and manufacture of appliances and automobiles needed resources not found in abundance in Japan. The Japanese government came under pressure to find new sources for raw materials abroad.

The Rise of Militarism

During the early 1900s, Japan had moved toward a more democratic government. The parliament and political parties grew stronger. The influence of the old ruling oligarchy, however, remained strong.

At the end of the 1920s, a militant group within the ruling party gained control of the political system. Some militants were civilians convinced that Western ideas had corrupted the parliamentary system. Others were military members angered by the cuts in military spending and the government's pacifist policies of the early 1920s.

During the early 1930s, civilians formed extremist patriotic organizations, such as the Black Dragon Society. Members of the army and navy created similar societies. One group of middle-level army officers invaded **Manchuria** without government approval in the autumn of 1931. Within a short time, all of Manchuria had been conquered. The Japanese government opposed the conquest, but the Japanese people supported it. Unable to act, the government was soon dominated by the military and other supporters of Japanese expansionism.

Japanese society was put on wartime status. A military draft law was passed in 1938. Economic resources were placed under strict government control. All political parties were merged into the Imperial Rule Assistance Association, which called for Japanese expansion abroad. Labor unions were disbanded. Education and culture were purged of most Western ideas. Militant leaders stressed traditional Japanese values.

✓ Reading Check **Examining** Why did the Japanese government shift to wartime status?

SECTION 2 REVIEW

Vocabulary
1. **Explain** the significance of: volunteer, Kenya, compensation, W.E.B. Du Bois, Marcus Garvey, Pan-Africanism, Ho Chi Minh, Mohandas Gandhi, Mahatma, civil disobedience, Jawaharlal Nehru, *zaibatsu*, Manchuria.

Main Ideas
2. **Identify** at least three leaders who worked to end colonial rule in Africa.

3. **Explain** how Lenin spread the ideas of Karl Marx.

4. **List** five events that contributed to Japan's becoming a military state in the 1930s. Use a diagram like the one below to make your list.

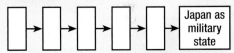

Critical Thinking
5. **The BIG Idea** **Comparing** What did young African leaders who wanted independence for their countries have in common?

6. **Contrasting** How did Gandhi's methods for achieving his nationalist goals differ from those of many other revolutionaries?

7. **Analyzing Visuals** Study the photograph and caption about Gandhi and the spinning wheel on page 597. Why do you think it has become famous?

Writing About History
8. **Expository Writing** Japanese conglomerates today are called *keiretsu*. Research one of them, such as Mitsui or Mitsubishi, and write two paragraphs comparing their operations to American industry.

History ONLINE

For help with the concepts in this section of *Glencoe World History— Modern Times,* go to glencoe.com and click Study Central.

Revolutionary Chaos in China

GUIDE TO READING

The BIG Idea
Order and Security During the 1920s, two men, Chiang Kai-shek and Mao Zedong, struggled to lead a new Chinese state.

Content Vocabulary
• guerrilla tactics *(p. 602)*
• redistribution of wealth *(p. 605)*

Academic Vocabulary
• cease *(p. 600)*   • eventually *(p. 601)*

People, Places, and Events
• Shanghai *(p. 600)*   • Nanjing *(p. 601)*
• Sun Yat-sen *(p. 600)*   • Mao Zedong *(p. 602)*
• Chang Jiang *(p. 600)*   • People's Liberation
• Chiang Kai-shek   Army (PLA) *(p. 603)*
  (p. 601)
• Shanghai Massacre *(p. 601)*

Reading Strategy
Summarizing Information As you read, make a cluster diagram like the one below showing the Confucian values that Chiang Kai-shek used to bring modern Western ideas into a culturally conservative population.

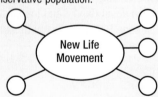

New Life Movement

In 1923 the Nationalist and Communist Parties formed an alliance to drive the imperialists out of China. Tensions between the two parties grew, however. Sun Yat-sen's successor, Chiang Kai-shek, struck against the Communists. Many Communists went into hiding or fled to the mountainous north, where Mao Zedong set up a Communist base.

Nationalists and Communists

MAIN IDEA Cooperating to drive the imperialists from China, the Nationalists and Communists then fought one another fiercely for the right to rule China.

HISTORY & YOU Can you work with people you do not trust? Learn how the alliance between the Nationalists and the Communists in China worked out.

Revolutionary Marxism had its greatest impact in China. By 1920, central authority had almost **ceased** to exist in China. Two political forces began to emerge as competitors for the right to rule China: Sun Yat-sen's Nationalist Party, which had been driven from the political arena several years earlier, and the Chinese Communist Party.

The Nationalist-Communist Alliance

In 1921 a group of young radicals, including several faculty and staff members from Beijing University, founded the Chinese Communist Party (CCP) in the commercial and industrial city of **Shanghai.** Comintern agents soon advised the new party to join with the more experienced Nationalist Party.

Sun Yat-sen, leader of the Nationalists (see Chapter 15), welcomed the cooperation. He needed the expertise that the Soviet Union could provide. His anti-imperialist words had alienated many Western powers. One English-language newspaper in Shanghai wrote: "All his life, all his influence, are devoted to ideas that keep China in turmoil, and it is utterly undesirable that he should be allowed to prosecute those aims here." In 1923 the two parties—Nationalists and Communists—formed an alliance to oppose the warlords and drive the imperialist powers out of China.

For over three years, the two parties overlooked their mutual suspicions and worked together. They formed a revolutionary army to march north and seize control over China. This Northern Expedition began in the summer of 1926. By the following spring, revolutionary forces had taken control of all of China south of the **Chang Jiang** (Yangtze River), including the major river ports of Wuhan and Shanghai.

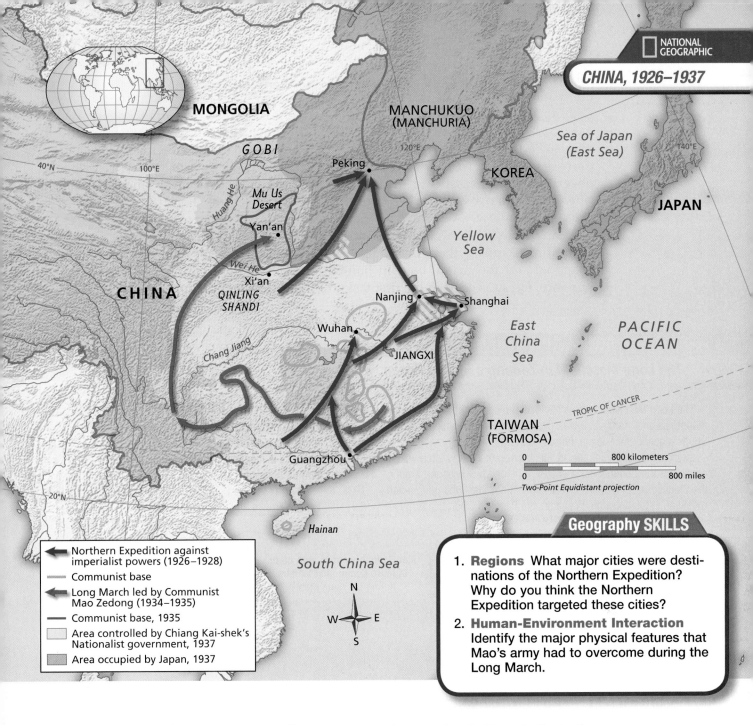

MONGOLIA

MANCHUKUO
(MANCHURIA)

GOBI

Sea of Japan
(East Sea)

KOREA

JAPAN

Huang He

*Mu Us
Desert*

Yan'an

Wei He

Xi'an

QINLING
SHANDI

CHINA

Peking

120°E

140°E

40°N

100°E

Yellow
Sea

Nanjing

Shanghai

Wuhan

JIANGXI

Chang Jiang

East
China
Sea

PACIFIC
OCEAN

TROPIC OF CANCER

TAIWAN
(FORMOSA)

Guangzhou

0   800 kilometers

0   800 miles

Two-Point Equidistant projection

Hainan

South China Sea

N
W   E
S

Legend:

→ Northern Expedition against
imperialist powers (1926–1928)

⁓ Communist base

→ Long March led by Communist
Mao Zedong (1934–1935)

— Communist base, 1935

☐ Area controlled by Chiang Kai-shek's
Nationalist government, 1937

☐ Area occupied by Japan, 1937

Geography SKILLS

1. **Regions** What major cities were desti-
nations of the Northern Expedition?
Why do you think the Northern
Expedition targeted these cities?

2. **Human-Environment Interaction**
Identify the major physical features that
Mao's army had to overcome during the
Long March.

Tensions between the parties **eventually** rose to the surface. Sun Yat-sen died in 1925, and General **Chiang Kai-shek** (JYAHNG KY•SHEHK) succeeded him as head of the Nationalist Party. Chiang pretended to support the alliance with the Communists until April 1927, when he struck against them in Shanghai, killing thousands. After the **Shanghai Massacre,** the Nationalist-Communist alliance ceased to exist.

In 1928 Chiang Kai-shek founded a new Chinese republic at **Nanjing.** During the next three years, he worked to reunify China. Although Chiang saw Japan as a

serious threat, he believed that the Communists were more dangerous. He once remarked that "the Communists are a disease of the heart."

The Communists in Hiding

After the Shanghai Massacre, most of the Communist leaders went into hiding in the city. There, they tried to revive the Communist movement among the working class. Shanghai was a rich recruiting ground for the party. People were discontented and looking for leadership.

Some party members fled to the mountainous Jiangxi (JYAHNG•SHEE) Province south of the Chang Jiang. They were led by the young Communist organizer **Mao Zedong** (MOW DZUH•DUNG). Unlike most other leading members of the Communist Party, Mao was convinced that a Chinese revolution would be driven by the poverty-stricken peasants in the countryside rather than by the urban working class.

Chiang Kai-shek now tried to root the Communists out of their urban base in Shanghai and their rural base in Jiangxi Province. He succeeded in the first task in 1931. Most party leaders in Shanghai were forced to flee to Mao's base in southern China.

Chiang Kai-shek then turned his forces against Mao's stronghold in Jiangxi Province. Chiang's forces far outnumbered Mao's, but Mao made effective use of **guerrilla tactics,** using unexpected methods like sabotage and deception to fight the enemy. Four slogans describe his methods: "When the enemy advances, we retreat! When the enemy halts and camps, we trouble them! When the enemy tries to avoid battle, we attack! When the enemy retreats, we pursue!"

INFOGRAPHICS   PRIMARY SOURCE

The Long March: Mao Zedong's Rise to Power

The Long March was physically demanding, zigzagging through mountains and marshes. It took over a year. Only one-tenth of the troops reached their destination in northern China.

Despite the great difficulty of the journey, the Long March was crucial for the Communists, because it helped build support among the Chinese people. Unlike the Nationalist soldiers, who often acted rudely and stole from the peasants, the People's Liberation Army (PLA) soldiers followed Mao's instructions to treat the peasants with respect. Their behavior helped the PLA gain the support of the masses, which would prove to be key to eventual victory.

Mao Zedong's leadership during the Long March also helped establish him as the clear leader of the Communists. In January 1935, the Red Army arrived in Zunyi. Soon, the Chinese Communist Party held a conference and elected Mao as party leader.

Mao Zedong (center) with other Chinese Communist leaders during the Long March

"The Long March is . . . a propaganda force. It has announced to some 200 million people . . . that the road of the Red Army is their only road to liberation. Without the Long March, how could the broad masses have learned so quickly about the existence of the great truth which the Red Army embodies?"

—Mao Zedong, report to a Communist Party conference, December 27, 1935

DOCUMENT-BASED QUESTIONS

1. **Determining Cause and Effect** What role did the Long March play in Mao's rise to power? How did it build support for the Communist cause?

2. **Analyzing** According to Mao in the quote to the left, what "great truth" did the Red Army embody?

The Long March

In 1934 Chiang's troops, with their superior military strength, surrounded the Communist base in Jiangxi and set up a blockade of the stronghold. With the villages behind Chiang's troops, no food or supplies could pass to the Communist base. Chiang even built small forts to prevent Communist raids. However, Mao's army, the **People's Liberation Army (PLA)**, broke through the Nationalist lines and began its famous Long March.

Both Mao and Chiang knew that unless Mao's army could cross the Chang Jiang, it would be wiped out. Mao's army began a desperate race. Moving on foot through mountains, marshes, rivers, and deserts, the army traveled almost 6,000 miles (9,600 km), averaging 24 miles (38 km) each day, to reach the last surviving Communist base in northwest China. All along those miles, Mao's troops had to fight Chiang's army.

Many of Mao's troops froze or starved. One survivor of the Long March told of soldiers eating their horses and wild vegetables once their grain was gone. Another survivor remembered:

PRIMARY SOURCE

"We were disheartened. Broken units. No food. The commanders dead. Only spirits got us through."

—Li Xiannian, as quoted in *The Long March: The Untold Story*, Harrison E. Salisbury

One year later, Mao's troops reached safety in the dusty hills of northern China. Of the 90,000 troops who had embarked on the journey, only 9,000 remained. In the course of the Long March, Mao Zedong had become the sole leader of the Chinese Communist Party. To people who lived at the time, it must have seemed that the Communist threat to the Nanjing regime was over. To the Communists, however, there remained hope for the future.

✓Reading Check **Explaining** Why did communism no longer seem a threat to China after the Long March?

The New China

MAIN IDEA Chiang Kai-shek was committed to building a new China with a republican government.

HISTORY & YOU How does a republic differ from a monarchy? Read what Chiang Kai-shek believed must happen before China could be a republic.

Even while trying to root out Mao's Communist forces, Chiang had been trying to build a new Chinese nation. He had publicly declared his commitment to Sun Yat-sen's plans for a republican government. But first, there would be a transitional period. In Sun's words:

PRIMARY SOURCE

"China . . . needs a republican government just as a boy needs school. As a schoolboy must have good teachers and helpful friends, so the Chinese people, being for the first time under republican rule, must have a farsighted revolutionary government for their training. This calls for the period of political tutelage, which is a necessary transitional stage from monarchy to republicanism. Without this, disorder will be unavoidable."

—Sun Yat-sen, as quoted in *Sources of Chinese Tradition*, William Theodore de Bary et al. (eds.)

In keeping with Sun's program, Chiang announced a period of political tutelage (training) to prepare the Chinese people for a final stage of constitutional government. Even the humblest peasant would be given time to understand the country's problems and the new government. In the meantime, the Nationalists would use their dictatorial power to carry out a land-reform program and to modernize industry.

A Class Divide

It would take more than plans on paper to create a new China, however. Years of neglect and civil war had severely weakened the political, economic, and social fabric of the nation. Most of the people who lived in the countryside were drained by warfare and civil strife. Rural peasants—up to 80 percent of China's population—were still very poor and overwhelmingly illiterate.

China's New Life Movement

FIFTEEN CENTS   January 3, 1938

TIME

The Weekly Newsmagazine

Painted for TIME by S. J. Woolf

Volume XXXI

MAN & WIFE OF THE YEAR
"Any sacrifice should not be regarded as too costly."
(See FOREIGN NEWS)

Number 1

Generalissimo and Madame Chiang Kai-shek were named *TIME*'s Man and Wife of the Year in 1938 for their leadership in China.

China in the early 1930s faced many social and economic problems, as Communists and Nationalists fought for control of the troubled nation. In 1934 Chiang Kai-shek and his wife Mei-ling formed a plan to rally the people against the Communists and increase Chinese national pride. Their New Life Movement called for a renewal of values such as social discipline, courtesy, and service. Four ancient Confucian virtues would serve as guides for living: Li (courtesy), I (duty), Lien (honesty), and Chih (honor).

The movement began with rules regulating clothing and prohibiting behavior such as spitting or smoking in public. The Chiangs hoped that adherence to these rules would unify the Chinese and prepare them to confront China's larger social and economic issues. Despite this grand vision, however, the New Life Movement became overly preoccupied with its rules for daily life. In the end it failed to grow into the larger social movement the Chiangs had envisioned.

". . . [T]he new life movement is based upon preservation of these four [Confucian] virtues, and it aims to apply them to actual, existing conditions, in order that the moral character of the nation shall attain the highest possible standard. The Generalissimo observed that communism crushed the spirit of the people."
—Madame Chiang Kai-shek, 1935

CRITICAL THINKING SKILLS

1. **Summarizing** What did the Chiangs hope to achieve with the New Life Movement?
2. **Making Inferences** Why do you think the Chiangs believed a return to ancient Confucian values would help reunify China?

Meanwhile, a Westernized middle class had begun to form in the cities. Here, observers would have believed that Chiang Kai-shek had lifted China into the modern world. Young people in the cities wore European clothes; they went to the movies and listened to the radio. It was here in the cities that the new government of Chiang Kai-shek found most of its support.

The Westernized middle class had little in common with the peasants in the countryside. They pursued the middle-class values of individual achievement and the accumulation of wealth.

Innovations and Traditions

Chiang Kai-shek was aware of the problem of introducing foreign ideas into a population that was still culturally conservative. Thus, while attempting to build a modern industrial state, he tried to bring together modern Western innovations with traditional Confucian values of hard work, obedience, and integrity. With his U.S.-educated wife Mei-ling Soong, Chiang set up a "New Life Movement." Its goal was to promote traditional Confucian social ethics, such as integrity, propriety, and righteousness. At the same time, it rejected what was viewed as the excessive individualism and material greed of Western capitalist values.

Chiang Kai-shek faced a host of other problems as well. The Nanjing government had total control over only a handful of provinces in the Chang Jiang valley. As we shall see in the next chapter, the Japanese threatened to gain control of northern China. The Great Depression was also having an ill effect on China's economy.

Limited Progress

In spite of all these problems, Chiang did have some success. He undertook a massive road-building project and repaired and extended much of the country's railroad system as well. More than 50,000 miles (80,467 km) of highways were built around and through the coastal areas. New factories, most of which the Chinese owned, were opened. Through a series of agreements, the foreign powers ended many of their leases, gave up extraterritorial rights, and returned the customs service to Chinese control. Chiang also established a national bank and improved the education system.

In other areas, Chiang was less successful and progress was limited. For example, a land-reform program was enacted in 1930, but it had little effect. Because Chiang's support came from the rural landed gentry, as well as the urban middle class, he did not press for programs that would lead to a **redistribution of wealth,** the shifting of wealth from a rich minority to a poor majority. For the peasants and poor townspeople, there was no real improvement under the Nanjing government.

The government was also repressive. Fearing Communist influence, Chiang suppressed all opposition and censored free expression. In doing so, he alienated many intellectuals and political moderates.

Sun Fo, Sun Yat-sen's son, expressed disapproval of the Nanjing government:

PRIMARY SOURCE

"We must frankly admit the fact that in these twenty years the machinery and practice of the Kuomintang [Chinese Nationalist Party] have turned in a wrong direction, inconsistent with the party constitution drafted by Dr. Sun Yat-sen in 1923 and contrary to the spirit of democracy."

—Sun Fo, as quoted in *China in Revolution*, John Robottom, 1969

✓ **Reading Check** **Identifying** What was the intended final stage of Chiang Kai-shek's reform program?

SECTION 3 REVIEW

Vocabulary

1. **Explain** the significance of: cease, Shanghai, Sun Yat-sen, Chang Jiang, eventually, Chiang Kai-shek, Shanghai Massacre, Nanjing, Mao Zedong, guerrilla tactics, People's Liberation Army (PLA), redistribution of wealth.

Main Ideas

2. **Explain** why the Communist Party allied with the Nationalist Party.

3. **Identify** the group of people that Mao Zedong believed would be the driving force behind the Chinese revolution.

4. **List** Chiang Kai-shek's successes during the 1930s. Use a diagram like the one below to make your list.

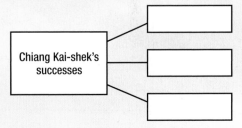

Critical Thinking

5. **The BIG Idea** **Analyzing** What did Mao's Long March accomplish?

6. **Making Inferences** Why did Chiang Kai-shek believe a period of political tutelage was necessary?

7. **Analyzing Visuals** Examine the magazine cover on page 604. How does this image illustrate the Chiangs' connection to the West?

Writing About History

8. **Persuasive Writing** Research how the United States supported Chiang Kai-shek and why. Write an editorial for or against the intervention of the United States in China.

History ONLINE

For help with the concepts in this section of *Glencoe World History— Modern Times*, go to glencoe.com and click Study Central.

Social History

The Two Chinas of the 1930s

In the 1930s, four-fifths of the Chinese population lived in rural areas. To build a strong modern nation, Chiang Kai-shek and the Nationalist government sharply increased the peasants' taxes. Because the projects primarily benefited the urban areas of the country, society was divided into two distinct sectors.

As China modernized in the 1930s, many young rural Chinese people moved to the cities to find jobs.

China's cities grew dramatically in the early twentieth century. The population of Shanghai, for example, had grown from 500,000 in 1895 to three million in the 1920s.

By the 1930s, automobiles were an increasingly common sight in Chinese cities.

Westernized fashions became popular with China's urban middle class.

URBAN CHINA

Western investments and technology helped stimulate industrial growth, modern banking, and commerce in China's urban areas. As the economy changed, wealth-building capitalist values spread among the growing urban middle class. Increasingly Westernized, the residents of China's cities grew further apart from the country's rural population.

Road-building projects extended into some rural areas in the 1930s. Many Chinese peasants, however, received no benefit from the government's modernization programs.

In the 1930s, extended peasant families lived in simple houses lacking electricity, plumbing, and glass windows.

Life in rural China was slow to change. Farmers in the 1930s still relied on pack animals and carts to transport goods to market.

Peasants wore broad-rimmed hats made of straw to shield themselves from the sun while working outside.

Chinese peasants relied on draft animals to work their fields.

RURAL CHINA

Though about half of China's farmers owned their own land, many peasants fell into debt. Bandits, natural disasters, and warfare added to the hardships facing them. Being forced to pay for projects that primarily benefited city dwellers created resentment among people in rural China. This discontent allowed the Chinese Communist Party to develop rural programs to win the support of the peasant masses.

ANALYZING VISUALS

1. **Contrasting** How was life in urban China in the 1930s different from life in rural China at that time?

2. **Speculating** How could modernization programs focusing on rural areas have more effectively benefited Chinese peasants in the 1930s?

Nationalism in Latin America

During the 1920s, U.S. investors poured funds directly into Latin American businesses. The Great Depression devastated Latin America's economy and created instability. This turmoil led to the creation of military dictatorships and authoritarian states in Latin America in the 1930s.

GUIDE TO READING

The BIG Idea
Order and Security In Latin America, the Great Depression made politics unstable, and in many cases, military dictatorships were the result.

Content Vocabulary
• oligarchy *(p. 611)*

Academic Vocabulary
• investor *(p. 608)*   • establish *(p. 611)*

People, Places, and Events
• Argentina *(p. 608)*
• Chile *(p. 608)*
• Brazil *(p. 608)*
• Peru *(p. 608)*
• Mexico *(p. 608)*
• Juan Vicente Gómez *(p. 609)*
• Good Neighbor policy *(p. 609)*
• Hipólito Irigoyen *(p. 611)*
• Getúlio Vargas *(p. 611)*
• Institutional Revolutionary Party (PRI) *(p. 611)*
• Lázaro Cárdenas *(p. 611)*
• PEMEX *(p. 612)*
• Diego Rivera *(p. 613)*

Reading Strategy
Summarizing Information As you read, make a chart like the one below listing the main exports of Latin America.

Country	Exports

The Latin American Economy

MAIN IDEA During the 1920s and 1930s, foreign investments and the Great Depression led some Latin American nations to emphasize domestic industry to balance the economy.

HISTORY & YOU Have you ever enjoyed a banana split? Most likely, the banana came from Latin America. Read to learn about Latin America's changing economic relationship with the United States.

At the beginning of the twentieth century, the Latin American economy was based largely on the export of foodstuffs and raw materials. Some countries relied on only one or two products for sale abroad. **Argentina,** for example, exported beef and wheat; **Chile,** nitrates and copper; **Brazil** and Caribbean nations, sugar; and Central America, bananas. A few reaped large profits from these exports. For most of the people, however, the returns were small.

Role of the United States
Beginning in the 1920s, the United States began to replace Great Britain as the major **investor** in Latin America. British investors had put money into stocks and other forms of investment that did not give them direct control of the companies. U.S. investors, however, put their funds directly into production facilities and actually ran the companies. In this way, large segments of Latin America's export industries fell into U.S. hands. A number of smaller Central American countries became independent republics. However, their economies often depended on wealthy nations. The U.S.-owned United Fruit Company, for example, owned land, packing plants, and railroads in Central America. American firms also gained control of the copper-mining industry in Chile and **Peru,** as well as of the oil industry in **Mexico,** Peru, and Bolivia.

Many Latin Americans resented U.S. control of Latin American industries. A growing nationalist awareness led many of them to view the United States as an imperialist power. It was not difficult for Latin American nationalists to show that profits from U.S. businesses were sometimes used to keep ruthless dictators in

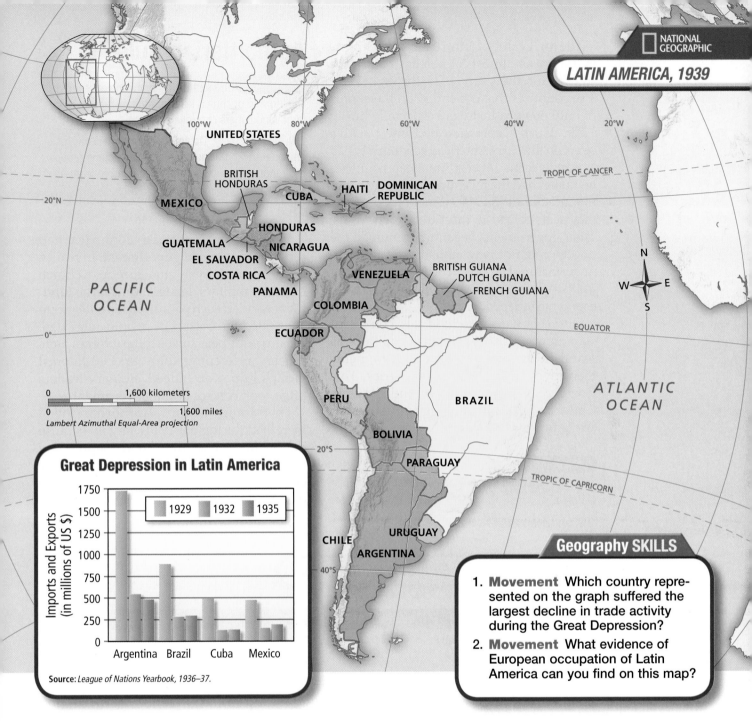

Great Depression in Latin America

Imports and Exports (in millions of US $)

Legend: 1929 1932 1935

Argentina   Brazil   Cuba   Mexico

Source: *League of Nations Yearbook, 1936–37.*

Geography SKILLS

1. **Movement** Which country represented on the graph suffered the largest decline in trade activity during the Great Depression?

2. **Movement** What evidence of European occupation of Latin America can you find on this map?

power. In Venezuela, for example, U.S. oil companies had close ties to the dictator **Juan Vicente Gómez.**

The United States had always cast a large shadow over Latin America. It had intervened militarily in Latin American affairs for years. This was especially true in Central America and the Caribbean. Many Americans considered both regions vital to U.S. security.

The United States made some attempts to change its relationship with Latin America in the 1930s. In 1933 President Franklin D. Roosevelt announced the **Good Neighbor policy,** rejecting the use of U.S. military force in Latin America on principle. Adhering to his word, the president withdrew the last United States Marines from Haiti in 1934. For the first time in 30 years, there were no U.S. troops in Latin American countries.

Impact of the Great Depression

The Great Depression was a disaster for Latin America's economy. Weak U.S. and European economies meant there was less demand for Latin American exports, especially coffee, sugar, metals, and meat.

The total value of Latin American exports in 1930 was almost 50 percent below the figures for the years 1925 through 1929. The countries that depended on the export of only one product were especially hurt.

The Great Depression had one positive effect on the Latin American economy. When exports declined, Latin American countries no longer had the revenues necessary to buy manufactured goods from abroad. Thus they were forced to meet their own needs. Their governments began to encourage the development of new industries to produce manufactured goods. The hope was that industrial development would bring greater economic independence.

Often, however, individuals could not start new industries because capital was scarce in the private sector. Governments then invested in the new industries. This led to government-run steel industries in Chile and Brazil and oil industries in Argentina and Mexico.

✓ **Reading Check** **Comparing** How did the U.S. method of investing in Latin America differ from that of Britain?

Authoritarian Rule

MAIN IDEA In most Latin American countries, a small group of church leaders, military leaders, and large landowners controlled politics.

HISTORY & YOU Do you think all Americans have an equal say in our government, or do some groups have more influence than others? Read to learn about Latin American politics in the 1930s.

Most Latin American countries had republican forms of government. In reality, however, a relatively small group of church officials, military leaders, and large land-owners ruled each country. This elite group controlled the masses of people, who were mostly poor peasants. Military forces were crucial in keeping these special-interest groups in power. Indeed, military leaders often took control of the government.

This trend toward authoritarianism increased during the 1930s, largely because of the impact of the Great Depression. Domestic instability caused by economic crises led to the creation of many military dictatorships in the early 1930s. This trend

INFOGRAPHICS

Selected Nationalist Movements in the Early Twentieth Century

	LATIN AMERICA			AFRICA AND ASIA			MIDDLE EAST		
Country	Argentina	Brazil	Mexico	Kenya	Libya	India	Turkey	Persia	Northern Arabian Peninsula
Leader	Argentine army; Group of United Officers	Getúlio Vargas	Lázaro Cárdenas	Harry Thuku (Young Kikuyu Association); Jomo Kenyatta	Omar Mukhtar	Mohandas Gandhi	Mustafa Kemal (Atatürk)	Reza Khan (Reza Shah Pahlavi)	Ibn Sa'ūd
Driving Force	Fear of workers; dissatisfaction with government	Bad economy	Foreign control of oil industry	High taxes; British rule	Italian rule	British rule	Greek seizure of Anatolian Peninsula	British and Soviet presence	European creation of states
Outcome	New governments (1930, 1943)	Vargas's New State (1938)	Seizure of oil and property (1938); PEMEX	Exile of Thuku (1922)	Revolt crushed (1920s)	Govern-ment of India Act (1935)	Turkish Republic (1923)	Iran (1935)	Saudi Arabia (1932)

Chart SKILLS

1. **Analyzing** What was the most frequent motivation for revolt in the countries identified above?
2. **Summarizing** How successful were those who sought to create a new nation or a new form of government?

was especially evident in Argentina, Brazil, and Mexico. Together, these nations possessed over half of the land and wealth of Latin America.

Argentina

Argentina was controlled by an **oligarchy,** a government where a select group of people exercises control. This oligarchy of large landowners who had grown wealthy from the export of beef and wheat failed to realize the growing importance of industry and cities in their country. It also ignored the growing middle class, which reacted by forming the Radical Party in 1890.

In 1916 **Hipólito Irigoyen** (ee•PAW•lee•TOH IHR•ih•GOH•YEHN), leader of the Radical Party, was elected president of Argentina. The Radical Party, however, feared the industrial workers, who were using strikes to improve their conditions. The party thus drew closer to the large landowners and became more corrupt.

The military was also concerned with the rising power of the industrial workers. In 1930 the Argentine army overthrew President Irigoyen and reestablished the power of the large landowners. Through this action, the military hoped to continue the old export economy and thus stop the growth of working-class power that would come with more industrialization.

During World War II, restless military officers formed a new organization, the Group of United Officers (GOU). They were unhappy with the government and overthrew it in June 1943. Three years later, one GOU member, Juan Perón, was elected president of Argentina (see Chapter 22).

Brazil

In 1889 the army had overthrown the Brazilian monarchy and **established** a republic. It was controlled chiefly by the landed elites, who had become wealthy from large coffee plantations.

By 1900, three-fourths of the world's coffee was grown in Brazil. As long as coffee prices remained high, the ruling oligarchy was able to maintain its power. The oligarchy largely ignored the growth of urban industry and the working class that came with it.

The Great Depression devastated the coffee industry. By the end of 1929, coffee prices had hit a record low. In 1930 a military coup made **Getúlio Vargas,** a wealthy rancher, president of Brazil. Vargas ruled Brazil from 1930 to 1945. Early in his rule, he appealed to workers by establishing an eight-hour day and a minimum wage.

Faced with strong opposition in 1937, Vargas made himself dictator. Beginning in 1938, he established his New State. It was basically an authoritarian state with some fascist-like features. Political parties were outlawed and civil rights restricted. Secret police silenced Vargas's opponents.

Vargas also pursued a policy of stimulating new industries. The government established the Brazilian steel industry and set up a company to explore for oil. By the end of World War II, Brazil had become Latin America's chief industrial power. In 1945 the army, fearing that Vargas might prolong his power illegally after calling for new elections, forced him to resign.

Mexico

Mexico was not an authoritarian state, but neither was it truly democratic. The Mexican Revolution of the early twentieth century had been the first significant effort in Latin America to overturn the system of large landed estates and raise the living standards of the masses (see Chapter 14). Out of the revolution had emerged a relatively stable political order.

The government was democratic in form. However, the official political party of the Mexican Revolution, known as the **Institutional Revolutionary Party,** or **PRI**, controlled the major groups within Mexican society. Every six years, party bosses of the PRI chose the party's presidential candidate. That candidate was then dutifully elected by the people.

A new wave of change began with **Lázaro Cárdenas** (KAHR•duhn•AHS), president of Mexico from 1934 to 1940. He moved to fulfill some of the original goals of the revolution. His major step was to distribute 44 million acres (17.8 million ha) of land to landless Mexican peasants. This action made him enormously popular with the peasants.

President Cárdenas also took a strong stand with the United States over oil. By 1900, Mexico was known to have enormous oil reserves, especially in the Gulf of Mexico. Over the next 30 years, oil companies from Britain and, in particular, the United States, made large investments in Mexico and the oil industry there. After a dispute with the foreign-owned oil companies over workers' wages, the Cárdenas government seized control of the oil fields and the property of the foreign-owned oil companies.

The U.S. oil companies were furious and asked President Franklin D. Roosevelt to intervene. He refused, reminding them of his promise in the Good Neighbor policy not to send U.S. troops into Latin America. Mexicans cheered Cárdenas as the president who had stood up to the United States.

Eventually, the Mexican government did pay the oil companies for their property. It then set up **PEMEX,** a national oil company, to run the oil industry. PEMEX did not do well at first, however, because exports fell. Still for many, PEMEX was a symbol of Mexican independence.

✓ **Reading Check** **Examining** How was the Mexican government democratic in form but not in practice?

HISTORY & ARTS   PRIMARY SOURCE

The Political Art of Diego Rivera

A2 Karl Marx holds a page from *The Communist Manifesto* calling for the formation of a new society

B1–B2 Workers in various fields, in typical poses and actions

A2–B2–B3 In compartments under Marx: (a) capitalists around a ticker-tape machine; (b) Mexican president Calles with his evil advisers, a general and a priest; (c) members of the upper class and the clergy behaving decadently

C2–C3 Reading and teaching revolutionary texts

A3 Communist flag

A3–A4 Mexico City burns in class warfare

B3–B4 A worker agitates a crowd

B3 Government troops put down a strike (*huelga*)

C3 Government troops attack peasants

DOCUMENT-BASED QUESTIONS

In 1929 Diego Rivera began to paint murals in the National Palace in Mexico City. The murals portray the history of Mexico from pre-Columbian times to the future. The mural above is called *Mexico Today and Tomorrow.*

1. **Identifying** Who does Rivera portray favorably in the mural?
2. **Recognizing Bias** How does Rivera reveal his political biases in the mural?

Culture in Latin America

MAIN IDEA Latin American artists adapted European modern art techniques to their own native roots.

HISTORY & YOU Think about the meaning of the word *abstract*. What would you expect "abstract art" to look like? Read to learn about abstract modern art in Latin America.

During the early twentieth century, European artistic and literary movements began to penetrate Latin America. In major cities, such as Buenos Aires in Argentina and São Paulo in Brazil, wealthy elites expressed interest in the work of modern artists.

Latin American artists went abroad and brought back modern techniques, which they often adapted to their own native roots. Modern artists, such as Roberto Matta from Chile and Carlos Merida from Guatemala, created abstract art, which did not closely resemble the way objects really appear. Gunther Gerzso, considered Mexico's most significant twentieth-century abstractionist, once said:

PRIMARY SOURCE

"Many people say I am an abstract painter. Actually, I think my paintings are very realistic. They are real because they express very accurately what I am all about, and in doing so they are to some degree about everybody else."

—Gunther Gerzso

Many artists and writers used their work to promote the emergence of a new national spirit. An example was the Mexican artist **Diego Rivera.** Rivera had studied in Europe, where he was especially influenced by fresco painting in Italy. After his return to Mexico, he developed a monumental style that filled wall after wall with murals. Rivera's wall paintings can be found in such diverse places as the Ministry of Education, the Chapel of the Agriculture School at Chapingo, and the Social Security Hospital. His works were aimed at the masses of people, many of whom could not read.

Rivera sought to create a national art that would portray Mexico's past, especially its Aztec legends, as well as Mexican festivals and folk customs. Rivera's work also carried a political and social message. Rivera did not want people to forget the Mexican Revolution, which had overthrown the large landowners and the foreign interests that supported them.

Rivera's work was often controversial. U.S. business tycoon Nelson Rockefeller hired Rivera to paint a mural on the wall of the RCA building at Rockefeller Center in New York City. Before Rivera finished, Rockefeller had the mural destroyed because it included a portrait of Soviet leader V. I. Lenin.

✓ Reading Check **Examining** How did Diego Rivera use his artistic talent as a political tool?

SECTION 4 REVIEW

Vocabulary

1. **Explain** the significance of: Argentina, Chile, Brazil, investor, Peru, Mexico, Juan Vicente Gómez, Good Neighbor policy, oligarchy, Hipólito Irigoyen, establish, Getúlio Vargas, Institutional Revolutionary Party (PRI), Lázaro Cárdenas, PEMEX, Diego Rivera.

Main Ideas

2. **Explain** why most individuals could not start new businesses in Latin America.

3. **List** the political struggles in Argentina and Brazil during the first half of the twentieth century. Use a table like the one below to make your list.

Argentina	Brazil

4. **Describe** how Diego Rivera portrayed Mexico's native roots.

Critical Thinking

5. **The BIG Idea Determining Cause and Effect** Why did the Great Depression cause many Latin American countries to try to gain more independence from foreign economic dominance?

6. **Making Predictions** How might the Cárdenas government's dispute with foreign-owned oil companies affect future foreign investment in Mexico?

7. **Analyzing Visuals** Choose one of the details from the painting on page 612 and explain why Diego Rivera chose to include it in this mural.

Writing About History

8. **Descriptive Writing** Using outside sources, find examples of Diego Rivera's murals. In an essay, compare his paintings to the frescoes of medieval Italian painters like Giotto. How do Rivera's murals reflect Italian influence? How are they different?

History ONLINE

For help with the concepts in this section of *Glencoe World History—Modern Times*, go to glencoe.com and click Study Central.

CHAPTER 18 Visual Summary

STUDY TO GO You can study anywhere, anytime by downloading quizzes and flash cards to your PDA from glencoe.com.

MAO ZEDONG ON THE LONG MARCH

Mao Zedong became the sole leader of the Chinese Communist Party.

THE MIDDLE EAST AND CHINA Influenced by Nationalism and Revolution

- The Ottoman Empire ended after World War I.
- Modernization and nationalist movements helped Turkey, Iran, and Saudi Arabia become modern states.
- In China, the Nationalist and Communist Parties formed a brief alliance to drive out imperialists.
- After the alliance split in China, the Communists went into hiding, and Chiang Kai-shek tried to build a republic.

AFRICA AND ASIA Influenced by Nationalism

- Nationalism led Africa and Asia to seek independence from colonial rule.
- Comintern spread Marxist ideas to Asia, resulting in Communist parties in all colonies.
- India's independence movement split into two paths, led by Gandhi and Nehru.
- Japan moved from a democratic government to a militaristic state.

CELEBRATIONS IN MOSCOW MARK THE SECOND MEETING OF THE COMMUNIST INTERNATIONAL

Agents were trained in Moscow and then sent back to Asia to form Communist parties.

OIL GUSHER IN MEXICO

The Mexican government nationalized the oil industry after Britain and the United States tried to control it.

LATIN AMERICA Influenced by Nationalism

- Latin American nationalists resented foreign investors and viewed them as imperialist powers.
- The Great Depression devastated Latin America's economy and created instability.
- Turmoil led to military dictatorships and authoritarian rule by small groups.
- Artists combined European modern art with their native culture, often promoting a national spirit.

STANDARDIZED TEST PRACTICE

TEST-TAKING

Read each answer choice carefully and eliminate any statements that you know are false. Getting rid of these wrong answer choices will help you find the correct answer.

Reviewing Vocabulary

Directions: Choose the word or words that best complete the sentence.

1. Mao Zedong used _____, or unexpected methods like sabotage and deception, to fight Chiang Kai-shek's forces.

   A trench warfare

   B guerrilla tactics

   C war of attrition

   D total war

2. What is the term for the deliberate mass murder of a particular racial, political, or cultural group?

   A Patricide

   B Suicide

   C Homicide

   D Genocide

3. In Argentina in the early 1930s, the _____ that controlled the government was made up of large landowners.

   A oligarchy

   B *zaibatsu*

   C hierarchy

   D bureaucracy

4. As a form of protest, Mohandas Gandhi advocated _____, or the refusal to obey laws considered to be unjust.

   A collective bargaining

   B extraterritoriality

   C civil disobedience

   D guerrilla tactics

Reviewing Main Ideas

Directions: Choose the best answers to the following questions.

Section 1 *(pp. 586–591)*

5. Between 1915 and 1918, what Christian minority group was targeted by the Ottoman Turks?

   A Armenians

   B Zionists

   C Slavs

   D Communists

6. Who began transforming Turkey into a modern state in the early 1920s?

   A Reza Shah Pahlavi

   B Ibn Sa'ūd

   C Mustafa Kemal

   D Abdülhamīd II

7. What British document supported the creation of a Jewish homeland in Palestine?

   A The Zionist Act

   B The Dawes Plan

   C The Palestine Act

   D The Balfour Declaration

Section 2 *(pp. 592–599)*

8. Who founded the Pan-Africanism movement?

   A Nnamdi Azikiwe

   B Marcus Garvey

   C Jomo Kenyatta

   D Léopold Senghor

Need Extra Help?								
If You Missed Questions . . .	1	2	3	4	5	6	7	8
Go to Page . . .	602	588	611	596	587	589	590	594

9. Where did some Indian Muslims want to form a separate state in the 1930s?

   A Pakistan

   B Taiwan (Formosa)

   C Palestine

   D Liberia

Section 3 (pp. 600–605)

10. In what city did Chiang Kai-shek form a new Chinese republic?

    A Beijing

    B Shanghai

    C Tianjin

    D Nanjing

11. Which of the following was a result of the Long March?

    A The Communists surprised the Nationalists in Jiangxi and drove them out.

    B The Communists formed an alliance with the Chinese Nationalists.

    C The Communists chose Mao Zedong as their leader.

    D The Communists lost the support of the rural peasants.

Section 4 (pp. 608–613)

12. Which of the following was part of the Good Neighbor policy in 1934?

    A The last U.S. investors left Latin America.

    B The last U.S. troops were removed from Latin America.

    C U.S. troops removed several ruthless Latin American dictators.

    D U.S. troops protected Latin America against European aggression.

13. Which Latin American countries were most harmed by the Great Depression?

    A Countries that exported a wide variety of foodstuffs and raw materials

    B Countries that had a large manufacturing base

    C Countries that depended on the export of only one product

    D Countries that had large government-run industries

Critical Thinking

Directions: Choose the best answers to the following questions.

Use the following map to answer question 14.

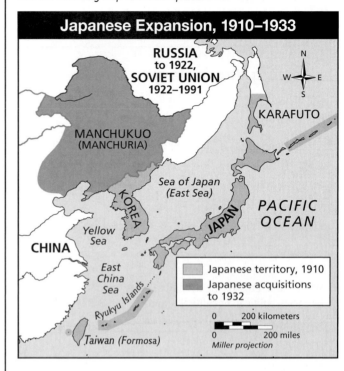

Japanese Expansion, 1910–1933

14. How did Japan's territory change between 1910 and 1933?

    A Japan acquired Manchuria in 1910, doubling its size.

    B Japan acquired Korea and Manchuria.

    C Japan gave up Manchuria, losing half its territory.

    D Japan acquired Manchuria by 1933, doubling its size.

15. Why did Chiang's land-reform program have little effect?

    A There was little unowned land to divide.

    B His council favored more land taxes.

    C His support came from the landed gentry.

    D He spent too much on building railways.

16. Why was Mexico not "truly democratic" in the 1930s?

    A There was a military dictatorship.

    B The authoritarian New State refused to hold elections.

    C There was a ruling oligarchy.

    D There was one dominant political party.

Need Extra Help?								
If You Missed Questions . . .	9	10	11	12	13	14	15	16
Go to Page . . .	596	601	603	609	610	616	605	611

GO ON

17. Which of the following statements represents an effect of the *zaibatsu* economy on Japan?

A Internal tension decreased, as economic success brought wealth to all social classes.

B Militarism increased, as Japan needed to expand to find resources to fuel its industries.

C Relations with other Asian nations improved, as trade among them increased.

D Population decreased, as fewer children were needed to work on family farms.

Base your answer to question 18 on the cartoon below and your knowledge of world history.

England's commercial interests in the Orient

John Bull (England)

ENGLAND'S COMMERCIAL INTERESTS IN THE ORIENT

Ottoman Turk

Armenia

John Bull hated to drop his bundle.

18. Which statement best expresses the cartoon's message?

A England will use its economic power to save the Armenians.

B England will not help the Armenians because it fears war with the Ottoman Turks.

C England's vast economic power will not be enough to save the Armenians.

D England will not give up its economic interests in the region to help the Armenians.

Document-Based Questions

Directions: Analyze the document and answer the short-answer questions that follow the document. Base your answers on the document and on your knowledge of world history.

In the fall of 1926, the young Communist Mao Zedong submitted a report to the Chinese Communist Party. In that report, Mao wrote:

> "In a very short time, in China's Central, Southern, and Northern provinces, several hundred million peasants will rise like a mighty storm, like a hurricane, a force so swift and violent that no power, however great, will be able to hold it back. They will smash all the restraints that bind them and rush forward along the road to liberation. They will sweep all the imperialists, warlords, corrupt officials, local tyrants, and evil gentry into their graves. . . . In force and momentum the attack is tempestuous; those who bow before it survive and those who resist perish."
> —Selected Works of Mao Tse-Tung, 1954

19. According to Mao Zedong, who would be the driving force in the Chinese revolution?

20. Why would this driving force in the revolution be so powerful?

Extended Response

21. Europeans created the Middle Eastern states of Iraq, Palestine, Jordan, Syria, and Lebanon from former Ottoman territories after World War I. The Europeans determined the borders and divided the peoples. Why might this national origin lead to future conflicts in the Middle East?

History ONLINE

For additional test practice, use Self-Check Quizzes— Chapter 18 at **glencoe.com**.

Need Extra Help?					
If You Missed Questions . . .	17	18	19	20	21
Go to Page . . .	598	617	617	617	587

CHAPTER 19

World War II 1939–1945

Section 1 Paths to War

Section 2 The Course of World War II

Section 3 The New Order and the Holocaust

Section 4 Home Front and Aftermath of War

MAKING CONNECTIONS

How can war affect civilians?

The German blitzkrieg quickly overwhelmed Poland, setting off the war in Europe. German troops paraded in Warsaw to celebrate their victory. The people of Poland soon experienced the terrors of Hitler's regime, suffering torture, forced deportation, slave labor, and execution. In this chapter you will learn about the course of World War II and its effects.

- What was the Holocaust and how did it affect the people of Nazi-occupied lands?
- How are conflicts today affecting civilian populations?

THE WORLD ▶

1939
Britain and France declare war on Germany

1941
Japanese attack Pearl Harbor

1939   1941

1939
Spanish Civil War ends

1940
France falls to Germany

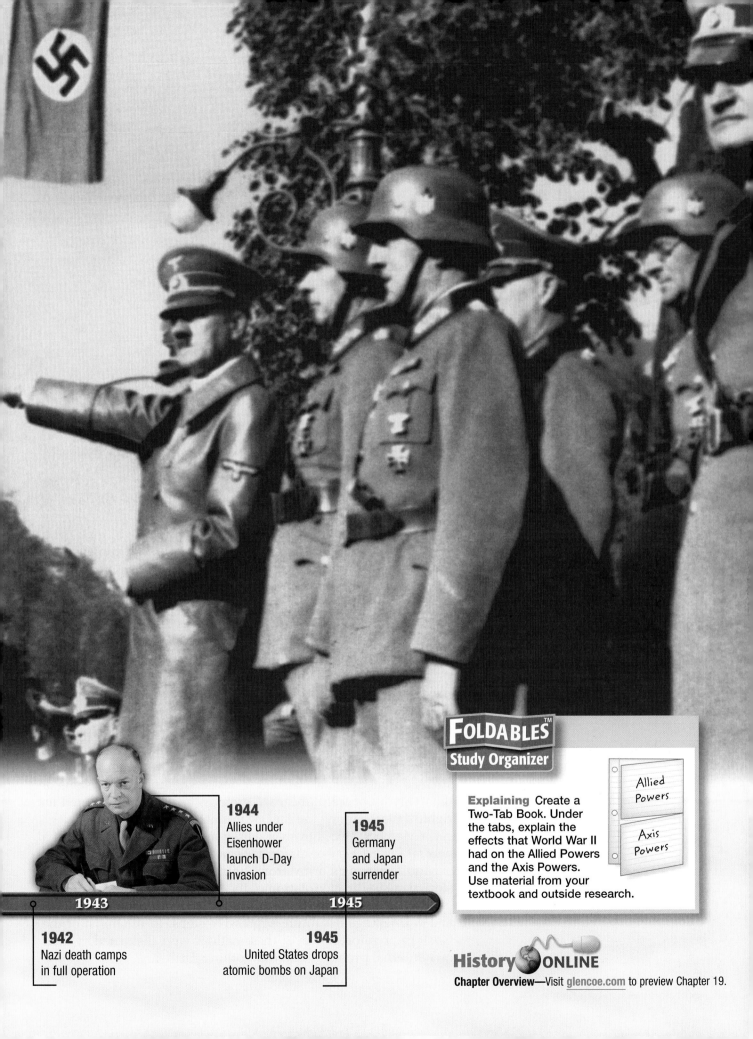

1944
Allies under
Eisenhower
launch D-Day
invasion

1945
Germany
and Japan
surrender

1943 — 1945

1942
Nazi death camps
in full operation

1945
United States drops
atomic bombs on Japan

FOLDABLES™
Study Organizer

Explaining Create a
Two-Tab Book. Under
the tabs, explain the
effects that World War II
had on the Allied Powers
and the Axis Powers.
Use material from your
textbook and outside research.

Allied
Powers

Axis
Powers

History ONLINE

Chapter Overview—Visit glencoe.com to preview Chapter 19.

Paths to War

GUIDE TO READING

The BIG Idea
Competition Among Countries
The ambitions of Japan and Germany paved the way for the outbreak of World War II.

Content Vocabulary
- demilitarized *(p. 621)*   • sanctions *(p. 625)*
- appeasement *(p. 621)*

Academic Vocabulary
- dominate *(p. 620)*
- violation *(p. 620)*

People and Places
- Adolf Hitler *(p. 620)*
- Rhineland *(p. 621)*
- Benito Mussolini *(p. 621)*
- Sudetenland *(p. 622)*
- Joseph Stalin *(p. 622)*
- Manchukuo *(p. 624)*
- Chiang Kai-shek *(p. 624)*
- New Order *(p. 625)*

Reading Strategy
Categorizing Information As you read, create a chart like the one below listing examples of Japanese aggression and German aggression prior to the outbreak of World War II.

Japanese Aggression	German Aggression

In the 1930s, both Germany and Japan invaded neighboring countries in an attempt to gain resources and land for their empires. Hitler allied with Italy, annexed Austria, and invaded Czechoslovakia. Japan made a quick conquest of Manchuria. At first, other world powers tried to ignore these acts of aggression. They wanted to avoid war—yet the path to war was already paved.

The German Path to War

MAIN IDEA Adolf Hitler's theory of racial domination laid the foundation for aggressive expansion outside of Germany.

HISTORY & YOU Have you ever lost a friend? Read to find out how Czechoslovakia was abandoned by its Western allies.

World War II in Europe had its beginnings in the ideas of **Adolf Hitler.** He believed that Germans belonged to a so-called Aryan race that was superior to all other races and nationalities. Consequently, Hitler believed that Germany was capable of building a great civilization. To be a great power, however, Germany needed more land to support a larger population.

Already in the 1920s, Hitler had indicated that a Nazi regime would find this land to the east—in the Soviet Union. Germany therefore must prepare for war with the Soviet Union. Once the Soviet Union had been conquered, according to Hitler, its land would be resettled by German peasants. The Slavic peoples could be used as slave labor to build the Third Reich, an Aryan racial state that Hitler thought would **dominate** Europe for a thousand years.

Hitler Violates Treaty

After World War I, the Treaty of Versailles had limited Germany's military power. As chancellor, Hitler, posing as a man of peace, stressed that Germany wished to revise the unfair provisions of the treaty by peaceful means. Germany, he said, only wanted its rightful place among the European states.

On March 9, 1935, however, Hitler announced the creation of a new air force. One week later, he began a military draft that would expand Germany's army from 100,000 to 550,000 troops. These steps were in direct **violation** of the Treaty of Versailles.

France, Great Britain, and Italy condemned Germany's actions and warned against future aggressive steps. In the midst of the Great Depression, however, these nations were distracted by their own internal problems and did nothing further.

Geography SKILLS

1. **Location** Approximately how much territory did Germany annex between 1936 and 1939? How did its size in 1939 compare to its size in 1935?

2. **Place** Use the maps to create a chart comparing German and Italian expansion. What reasons can you see for Germany being the more aggressive country in its expansion?

Maps In Motion See *StudentWorks™ Plus* or glencoe.com.

Legend:
- Germany, 1935
- German occupation, 1936
- German acquisitions, 1938–1939
- Italy and possessions, 1935
- Italian acquisitions, 1935–1939

Hitler was convinced that the Western states had no intention of using force to maintain the Treaty of Versailles. Hence, on March 7, 1936, he sent German troops into the **Rhineland.** The Rhineland was part of Germany; but, according to the Treaty of Versailles, it was a **demilitarized** area. That is, Germany was not permitted to have weapons or fortifications there. France had the right to use force against any violation of this provision but would not act without British support.

Great Britain did not support the use of force against Germany, however. The British government viewed the occupation of German territory by German troops as a reasonable action by a dissatisfied power. The London *Times* noted that the Germans were only "going into their own back garden." Great Britain thus began to practice a policy of **appeasement.** This policy was based on the belief that if European states satisfied the reasonable demands of dissatisfied powers, the dissatisfied powers would be content, and stability and peace would be achieved in Europe.

New Alliances

Meanwhile, Hitler gained new allies. **Benito Mussolini** of Italy had long dreamed of creating a new Roman Empire.

In October 1935, Mussolini's forces invaded Ethiopia. Angered by French and British opposition to his invasion, Mussolini welcomed Hitler's support. He began to draw closer to the German dictator.

In 1936 both Germany and Italy sent troops to Spain to help General Francisco Franco in the Spanish Civil War. In October 1936, Mussolini and Hitler made an agreement recognizing their common political and economic interests. One month later, Mussolini spoke of the new alliance between Italy and Germany, called the Rome-Berlin Axis. Also in November, Germany and Japan signed the Anti-Comintern Pact, promising a common front against communism.

Union with Austria

By 1937, Germany was once more a "world power," as Hitler proclaimed. He was convinced that neither France nor Great Britain would provide much opposition to his plans. In 1938 he decided to pursue one of his goals: *Anschluss* (AHN•shloos), or union, with Austria, his native land.

By threatening Austria with invasion, Hitler forced the Austrian chancellor to put Austrian Nazis in charge of the government. The new government promptly invited German troops to enter Austria and "help" in maintaining law and order. One day later, on March 13, 1938, after his triumphal return to his native land, Hitler annexed Austria to Germany.

Demands and Appeasement

Hitler's next objective was the destruction of Czechoslovakia. On September 15, 1938, he demanded that Germany be given the **Sudetenland,** an area in northwestern Czechoslovakia that was inhabited largely by Germans. He expressed his willingness to risk "world war" to achieve his objective.

At a hastily arranged conference in Munich, British, French, German, and Italian representatives did not object to Hitler's plans but instead reached an agreement that met virtually all of Hitler's demands. German troops were allowed to occupy the Sudetenland. The Czechs, abandoned by their Western allies, stood by helplessly.

The Munich Conference was the high point of Western appeasement of Hitler. When Neville Chamberlain, the British prime minister, returned to England from Munich, he boasted that the agreement meant "peace for our time." Hitler had promised Chamberlain that he would make no more demands. Like many others, Chamberlain believed Hitler's promises.

Great Britain and France React

In fact, Hitler was more convinced than ever that the Western democracies would not fight. Increasingly, he was sure that he could not make a mistake, and he had by no means been satisfied at Munich.

In March 1939, Hitler invaded and took control of Bohemia and Moravia in western Czechoslovakia. In the eastern part of the country, Slovakia became a puppet state controlled by Nazi Germany. On the evening of March 15, 1939, Hitler triumphantly declared in Prague that he would be known as the greatest German of them all.

At last, the Western states reacted to the Nazi threat. Hitler's aggression had made clear that his promises were worthless. When Hitler began to demand the Polish port of Danzig, Great Britain saw the danger and offered to protect Poland in the event of war. At the same time, both France and Britain realized that only the Soviet Union was powerful enough to help contain Nazi aggression. They began political and military negotiations with **Joseph Stalin,** the Soviet dictator.

Hitler and the Soviets

Meanwhile, Hitler continued to believe that the West would not fight over Poland. He now feared, however, that the West and the Soviet Union might make an alliance. Such an alliance could mean a two-front war for Germany. To prevent this possibility, Hitler made his own agreement with Stalin.

On August 23, 1939, Germany and the Soviet Union signed the Nazi-Soviet Non-aggression Pact. In it, the two nations promised not to attack each other. To get the nonaggression pact, Hitler offered

Stalin control of eastern Poland and the Baltic states. Because he expected to fight the Soviet Union anyway, it did not matter to Hitler what he promised—he was accustomed to breaking promises.

Germany Invades Poland

Hitler shocked the world when he announced the nonaggression pact. The treaty gave Hitler the freedom to attack Poland. He told his generals, "Now Poland is in the position in which I wanted her. . . . I am only afraid that at the last moment some swine will submit to me a plan for mediation."

Hitler need not have worried. On September 1, German forces invaded Poland. Two days later, Britain and France declared war on Germany.

✓**Reading Check** **Identifying** Where did Hitler believe he could find more "living space" to expand Germany?

The Japanese Path to War

MAIN IDEA The need for natural resources fueled the Japanese plan to seize other countries.

HISTORY & YOU Do you think countries should go to war over natural resources? Read to learn what happened between Japan and China when Japan needed certain natural resources in the 1930s.

On the night of September 18, 1931, Japanese soldiers, disguised as Chinese, blew up a small section of the Manchurian Railway near the city of Mukden. Japan owned this area, and the Japanese soldiers wanted to blame the "Mukden incident" on the Chinese. The Japanese army used this incident to justify its taking all of Manchuria in a series of rapid military advances.

Most Japanese were delighted about the apparently easy conquest of Manchuria. This was not surprising since Manchuria was far larger than Japan itself and had a population of 30 million Chinese.

PRIMARY SOURCE **POLITICAL CARTOONS**

The Nazi-Soviet Nonaggression Pact

For years, Great Britain and France had been attempting to make an alliance with the Soviet Union against Nazi Germany. Yet in August 1939, Hitler shocked the Western powers by making his own agreement with Stalin.

The Nazi-Soviet Nonaggression Pact was one of the last steps leading to World War II. By secretly agreeing to split eastern Europe with the Soviets, Hitler knew that he would not have to fight the Soviets when war began. He invaded Poland about a week after signing the Nonaggression Pact.

Despite the pact, Hitler did not intend to keep his promises to Stalin. The Nazi-Soviet alliance would last only until 1941, when Hitler invaded the Soviet Union.

CRITICAL THINKING SKILLS

This American cartoon satirizing the Nazi-Soviet Nonaggression Pact was published the day before Hitler invaded the Soviet Union—June 22, 1941.

1. **Determining Cause and Effect** How did the Nazi-Soviet Nonaggression Pact help lead to World War II?

2. **Interpreting** How did world reaction to the pact change between 1939 and 1941?

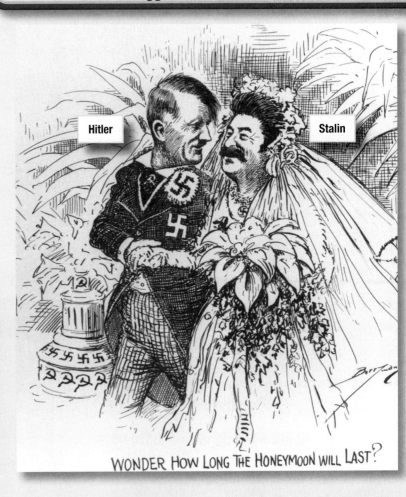

WONDER HOW LONG THE HONEYMOON WILL LAST?

The country also offered many resources the Japanese needed. After this conquest, the Japanese army became committed to an expansionist policy.

By September 1932, the Japanese army had formed Manchuria into a separate state and renamed it **Manchukuo.** They placed a puppet ruler, Henry Pu Yi, on the throne. As an infant, Henry Pu Yi had been China's "last emperor." He had abdicated that throne, however, following the revolution of 1911 in China.

Worldwide protests against the Japanese seizure of Manchuria led the League of Nations to send in investigators. When the investigators issued a report condemning the seizure, Japan withdrew from the League. The United States refused to recognize the Japanese takeover of Manchuria but was unwilling to threaten force.

Over the next several years, Japan continued its expansion and established control over the eastern part of Inner Mongolia and areas in north China around Beijing.

Neither the emperor nor government leaders could control the army. In fact, it was the army that established Japanese foreign policy. The military held the upper hand. By the mid-1930s, militants connected to the government and the armed forces had gained control of Japanese politics.

War with China

Chiang Kai-shek tried to avoid a conflict with Japan so that he could deal with what he considered the greater threat from the Communists. When clashes between Chinese and Japanese troops broke out, he sought to appease Japan by allowing it to govern areas in north China.

As Japan moved steadily southward, protests against Japanese aggression grew stronger in Chinese cities. In December 1936, Chiang ended his military efforts against the Communists and formed a new united front against the Japanese. In July 1937, Chinese and Japanese forces clashed south of Beijing and hostilities spread.

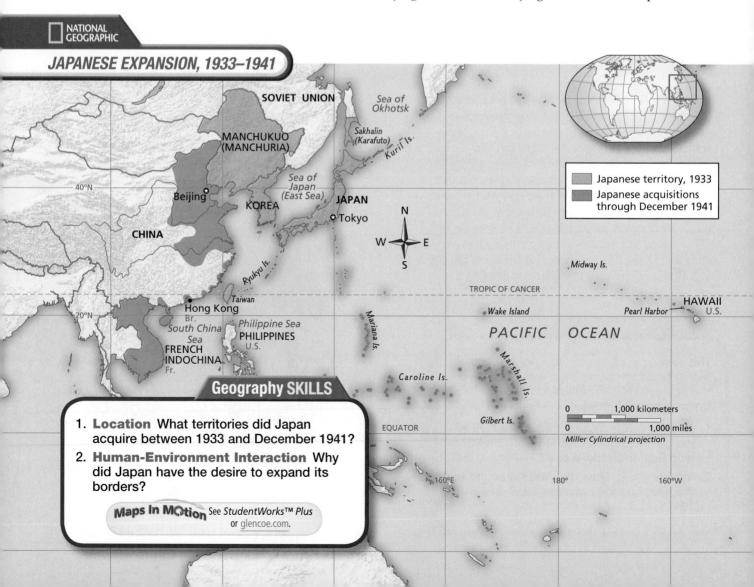

NATIONAL GEOGRAPHIC

JAPANESE EXPANSION, 1933–1941

Japanese territory, 1933

Japanese acquisitions through December 1941

Geography SKILLS

1. **Location** What territories did Japan acquire between 1933 and December 1941?

2. **Human-Environment Interaction** Why did Japan have the desire to expand its borders?

Maps In Motion See *StudentWorks™ Plus* or glencoe.com.

Japan had not planned to declare war on China. However, the 1937 incident eventually turned into a major conflict. The Japanese seized the Chinese capital of Nanjing in December. Chiang Kai-shek refused to surrender and moved his government upriver, first to Hankou, then to Chongqing. As the Japanese pushed onward, Chinese civilians experienced extreme brutality and aerial bombing. Although they were defeated, the Chinese continued to resist the Japanese for the entire course of the war.

The New Asian Order

Japanese military leaders had hoped to force Chiang to agree to join a **New Order** in East Asia, comprising Japan, Manchuria, and China. Japan would attempt to establish a new system of control in Asia with Japan guiding its Asian neighbors to prosperity. After all, who could better teach Asian societies how to modernize than the one Asian country that had already done it?

Part of Japan's plan was to seize Soviet Siberia, with its rich resources. During the late 1930s, Japan began to cooperate with Nazi Germany. Japan assumed that the two countries would ultimately launch a joint attack on the Soviet Union and divide Soviet resources between them.

When Germany signed the nonaggression pact with the Soviets in August 1939, Japanese leaders had to rethink their goals. Japan did not have the resources to defeat the Soviet Union without help. Thus, the Japanese became interested in the raw materials that could be found in Southeast Asia to fuel its military machine.

Japan Launches Attack

A move southward, however, would risk war with the European colonial powers and the United States. Japan's attack on China in the summer of 1937 had already aroused strong criticism, especially in the United States. Nevertheless, in the summer of 1940, Japan demanded the right to exploit economic resources in French Indochina.

The United States objected. It warned Japan that it would apply economic **sanctions**—restrictions intended to enforce international law—unless Japan withdrew from the area and returned to its borders of 1931. Japan badly needed the oil and scrap iron it was getting from the United States. Should these resources be cut off, Japan would have to find them elsewhere. Japan viewed the possibility of sanctions as a threat to its long-term objectives.

Japan was now caught in a dilemma. To guarantee access to raw materials in Southeast Asia, Japan had to risk losing raw materials from the United States. After much debate, Japan decided to launch a surprise attack on U.S. and European colonies in Southeast Asia.

✓ Reading Check **Explaining** Why did Japan want to establish a New Order in East Asia?

SECTION 1 REVIEW

Vocabulary
1. **Explain** the significance of: Adolf Hitler, dominate, violation, Rhineland, demilitarized, appeasement, Benito Mussolini, Sudetenland, Joseph Stalin, Manchukuo, Chiang Kai-shek, New Order, sanctions.

Main Ideas
2. **List** the reasons why Hitler's pact with Stalin caused Britain and France to declare war on Germany.

3. **Summarize,** by using a chart like the one below, the agreements in chronological order that encouraged Hitler's aggressive policies.

Agreements Encouraging Hitler's Aggressive Policies

4. **Explain** why Japan felt the need to control other nations.

Critical Thinking
5. **The BIG Idea** **Determining Cause and Effect** How did the ambitions of Germany and Japan lead to war?

6. **Comparing** Compare Hitler's annexation of Austria and occupation of the Sudetenland to Japan's plans for a New Order in East Asia.

7. **Analyzing Visuals** Examine the political cartoon on page 623. Why did the cartoonist depict Hitler and Stalin as husband and wife?

Writing About History
8. **Persuasive Writing** Imagine you are the editor of a British newspaper in 1938. Write an editorial that expresses your viewpoint on how war can be avoided.

History ONLINE

For help with the concepts in this section of *Glencoe World History—Modern Times*, go to glencoe.com and click Study Central.

What Were the Causes of World War II?

How did the international community try to prevent war? The League of Nations, disarmament conferences, and mutual defense treaties were efforts used in the 1920s and 1930s by the international community to maintain world peace.

Why did these efforts fail to prevent World War II? Japan, Italy, and Germany each used its military to occupy foreign territories in the 1930s. Their aggressive moves led to the outbreak of a global conflict by the end of the decade.

After World War I ended in 1918, global leaders resolved to prevent future wars. Nonetheless, only two decades later, the most destructive conflict in human history broke out. Read the excerpts and study the cartoon to learn more about the causes of World War II.

SOURCE 1

British historian Dr. G.P. Gooch addressed the threat of war in his 1938 article, "The Breakdown of the System of Collective Security."

Since the Allies declined to scale down their armaments to the German level, Germany was certain to climb towards theirs as soon as she felt strong enough to do so with **impunity**[1].

The Disarmament Conference which opened at Geneva in February 1932 had taken years to prepare, and it met too late. Even the chance of a limited agreement was lost owing to the lack of a strong lead at the outset by a Great Power . . . Each country was **virtuously**[2] ready for reductions in categories which were not of vital importance to itself, but stood out for those which it needed most. Thus Great Britain longed for the abolition of the submarine, which nearly starved us in 1917, while she clung to the **capital ship**[3]. . . .When the Conference adjourned for the summer holidays in 1932, it was clear that it had failed. In the autumn Germany retired, but was brought back by a promise of equality of status. . . . Such a system proved unattainable, and a year later Hitler's Germany withdrew not only from the Conference but from the League [of Nations] itself. . . . Since that moment Germany has been re-arming at feverish speed, and Europe is back again in its pre-War mood when everyone was afraid of Berlin. Our own colossal re-armament programme is the measure of our alarm.

SOURCE 2

The following passages are from 1938 diary entries of Victor Klemperer, a Jewish professor who lived in Nazi Germany.

The immense act of violence on the [German] **annexation**[4] of Austria, the immense increase in [Germany's] power both internally and externally, the defenseless trembling fear of England, France, etc. We shall not live to see the end of the Third Reich. . . .

The Third Reich will win again—whether by bluff or by force. . . . Chamberlain flies to Hitler for the second time tomorrow. England and France remain calm, in Dresden the **Sudeten German "Freikorps"**[5] is almost ready to invade [Czechoslovakia]. And the populace here is convinced that the Czechs alone are to blame and that Hitler loves peace. . . .

Four-power meeting[6] today [September 29] at three in Munich. Czechoslovakia continues to exist, Germany gets the Sudetenland, probably a colony as well. . . . For the populace on the front pages of the German press it is of course the absolute success of Hitler, the prince of peace and brilliant diplomat. . . . No shot is fired, and the [German] troops have been marching in since yesterday. Wishes for peace and friendship have been exchanged with England and France, Russia is cowering and silent, a zero. Hitler is being acclaimed even more extravagantly than in the Austria business.

---

[1] **impunity:** freedom from punishment
[2] **virtuously:** morally
[3] **capital ship:** large class warship, such as a battleship

[4] **annexation:** the act of incorporating new territory
[5] **Sudeten German "Freikorps":** German guerrilla force that sought to add the Sudetenland region to Germany

▲ The weakness of the League of Nations is illustrated in this 1931 cartoon, "Let Sam Do It," by Winsor McCay.

SOURCE 3

At the end of World War I, United States president Woodrow Wilson lobbied for the creation of an international organization to help prevent future conflicts. The League of Nations formed in 1919. Many Americans, however, feared that joining the League would drag the country into foreign wars. As a result, the U.S. Senate refused to allow the nation to become a member of the League.

In 1931, the League of Nations faced a major challenge to its ability to maintain world peace when Japan invaded China. Artist Winsor McCay published the above cartoon after Japanese soldiers captured Manchuria from the Chinese. The man standing on the right side of the cartoon, Uncle Sam, represents the United States.

---

6 **Four-power meeting:** meeting of Germany, Italy, France, and Britain to discuss Germany's claims to the Sudetenland

DOCUMENT-BASED QUESTIONS

1. **Explaining** According to Gooch, why did the Disarmament Conference in Geneva fail?

2. **Recognizing Bias** What does Klemperer suggest about how most Germans felt about Hitler in 1938? Why do you think the German populace felt that way about Hitler?

3. **Interpreting** What does McCay believe about the likelihood of stopping the conflict between Japan and China?

4. **Analyzing** Do Gooch and Klemperer primarily agree or disagree in their assessments of the threat to world peace in 1938?

5. **Comparing** What common point does each of the three sources make about the international efforts to prevent war in the 1930s?

6. **Drawing Conclusions** What were the causes of World War II? Do you think the Western powers could have prevented the war? Why or why not?

The Course of World War II

GUIDE TO READING

The BIG Idea
Devastation of War Allied perseverance, effective military operations, and Axis miscalculations brought the devastation of World War II to an end.

Content Vocabulary
- blitzkrieg *(p. 628)*
- neutrality *(p. 630)*
- isolationism *(p. 630)*
- partisans *(p. 635)*

Academic Vocabulary
- resolve *(p. 630)*
- involvement *(p. 630)*

People and Places
- Franklin D. Roosevelt *(p. 630)*
- Stalingrad *(p. 633)*
- Midway Island *(p. 633)*
- Douglas MacArthur *(p. 633)*
- Winston Churchill *(p. 634)*
- Normandy *(p. 634)*
- Harry S. Truman *(p. 635)*
- Hiroshima *(p. 635)*

Reading Strategy
Determining Cause and Effect
As you read, create a chart like the one below listing key events during World War II and their effect on the outcome of the war.

Event	Effect

The first years of World War II seemed to go in Hitler's favor. With his blitzkrieg, he had gained control of much of western and central Europe. Victories over Britain and Russia remained elusive, however. When the United States entered the war, the Allies agreed to fight until the Axis Powers surrendered unconditionally. Together, the Allies strengthened their strategies and stopped the advances of both the Germans and the Japanese. Germany surrendered on May 7, 1945, and Japan surrendered on August 14.

Europe at War

MAIN IDEA Germany used a "lightning war" to gain control of much of western and central Europe, but Britain was undefeated and German troops were stopped in Russia.

HISTORY & YOU Have you ever known two people who were fighting, but you refused to take sides? Read how the United States remained neutral even though the British asked for help.

Hitler stunned Europe with the speed and efficiency of the German attack on Poland. His **blitzkrieg**, or "lightning war," used armored columns, called panzer divisions, supported by airplanes. Each panzer division was a strike force of about 300 tanks with accompanying forces and supplies.

The forces of the blitzkrieg broke quickly through Polish lines and encircled the bewildered Polish troops. Regular infantry units then moved in to hold the newly conquered territory. Within four weeks, Poland had surrendered. On September 28, 1939, Germany and the Soviet Union divided Poland.

Hitler's Early Victories

After a winter of waiting (called the "phony war"), Hitler resumed the attack on April 9, 1940, with another blitzkrieg against Denmark and Norway. One month later, on May 10, Germany launched an attack on the Netherlands, Belgium, and France. The main assault was through Luxembourg and the Ardennes (ahr•DEHN) Forest. German panzer divisions broke through weak French defensive positions there and raced across northern France.

French and British forces were taken by surprise. Anticipating a German attack, France had built a defense system, called the Maginot Line, along its border with Germany. The line was a series of concrete and steel fortifications armed with heavy artillery.

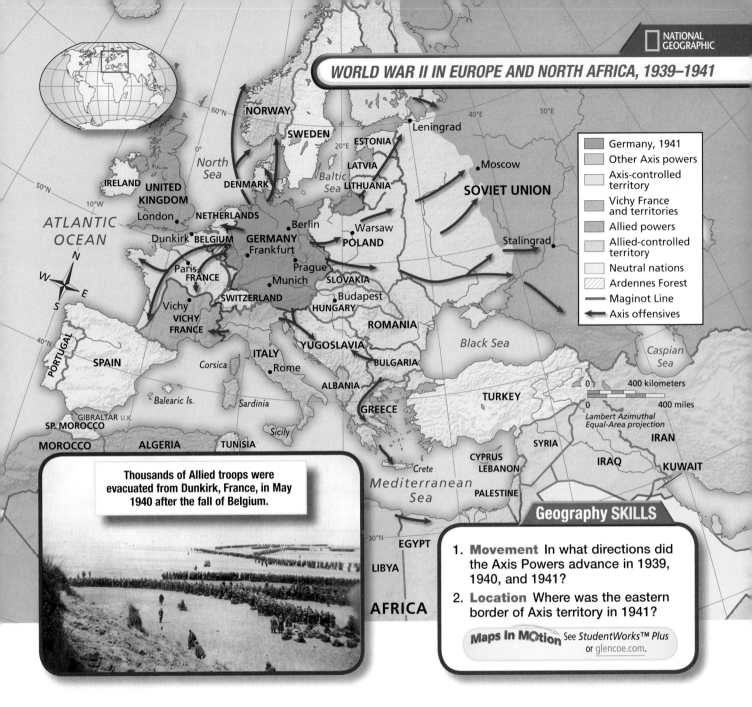

WORLD WAR II IN EUROPE AND NORTH AFRICA, 1939–1941

Legend:
- Germany, 1941
- Other Axis powers
- Axis-controlled territory
- Vichy France and territories
- Allied powers
- Allied-controlled territory
- Neutral nations
- Ardennes Forest
- Maginot Line
- Axis offensives

0 400 kilometers
0 400 miles
Lambert Azimuthal Equal-Area projection

Thousands of Allied troops were evacuated from Dunkirk, France, in May 1940 after the fall of Belgium.

Geography SKILLS

1. **Movement** In what directions did the Axis Powers advance in 1939, 1940, and 1941?
2. **Location** Where was the eastern border of Axis territory in 1941?

Maps In Motion See StudentWorks™ Plus or glencoe.com.

The Germans, however, decided not to cross the Maginot Line. Instead, they went around it and attacked France from its border with Belgium.

By going around the Maginot Line, the Germans split the Allied armies. French troops and the entire British army were trapped on the beaches of Dunkirk. Only through the heroic efforts of the Royal Navy and civilians in private boats did the British manage to evacuate 338,000 Allied (mostly British) troops.

One English skipper of a small boat who helped in that rescue described the scene:

PRIMARY SOURCE

"The soldiers were coming off the beach clinging to bits of wood and wreckage and anything that would float. As we got close enough we began … picking up as many as we could … [and taking] them off to one of the ships lying off in the deep water."

—Len Deighton, *Blood, Tears and Folly*, 1993

The French signed an armistice on June 22, 1940. German armies now occupied about three-fifths of France. An authoritarian regime under German control was set up over the remainder of the country.

It was known as Vichy France and was led by an aged French hero of World War I, Marshal Henri Pétain. Germany was now in control of western and central Europe, but Britain had still not been defeated. In fact, after Dunkirk, the British **resolve** heightened, and Britain appealed to the United States for help.

President **Franklin D. Roosevelt** denounced the aggressors, but the United States followed a strict policy of **isolationism**. A series of **neutrality** acts, passed in the 1930s, prevented the United States from taking sides or becoming involved in any European wars. Many Americans felt that the United States had been drawn into World War I due to economic **involvement** in Europe, and they wanted to prevent a recurrence. Roosevelt was convinced that the neutrality acts actually encouraged Axis aggression and wanted the acts repealed. They were gradually relaxed as the United States supplied food, ships, planes, and weapons to Britain.

The Battle of Britain

Hitler realized that an amphibious (land-sea) invasion of Britain could succeed only if Germany gained control of the air. At the beginning of August 1940, the Luftwaffe (LOOFT•vah•fuh)—the German air force—launched a major offensive. German planes bombed British air and naval bases, harbors, communication centers, and war industries.

The British fought back with determination. They were supported by an effective radar system that gave them early warning of German attacks. Nevertheless, by the end of August, the British air force had suffered critical losses.

In September, in retaliation for a British attack on Berlin, Hitler ordered a shift in strategy. Instead of bombing military targets, the Luftwaffe began massive bombing of British cities. Hitler hoped in this way to break British morale. Instead, because military targets were not being hit, the British were able to rebuild their air strength

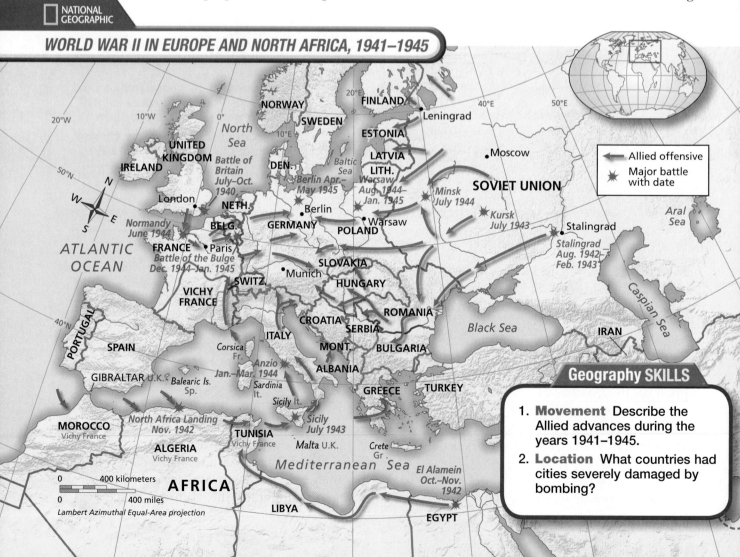

NATIONAL GEOGRAPHIC

WORLD WAR II IN EUROPE AND NORTH AFRICA, 1941–1945

Allied offensive

★ Major battle with date

Geography SKILLS

1. **Movement** Describe the Allied advances during the years 1941–1945.

2. **Location** What countries had cities severely damaged by bombing?

quickly. Soon, the British air force was inflicting major losses on Luftwaffe bombers. At the end of September, Hitler postponed the invasion of Britain indefinitely.

Attack on the Soviet Union

Although he had no desire for a two-front war, Hitler became convinced that Britain was remaining in the war only because it expected Soviet support. If the Soviet Union was smashed, Britain's last hope would be eliminated. Moreover, Hitler had convinced himself that the Soviet Union had a pitiful army and could be defeated quickly.

Hitler's invasion of the Soviet Union was scheduled for the spring of 1941, but the attack was delayed because of problems in the Balkans. Hitler had already gained the political cooperation of Hungary, Bulgaria, and Romania. However, the failure of Mussolini's invasion of Greece in 1940 had exposed Hitler's southern flank to British air bases in Greece. To secure his Balkan flank, Hitler therefore seized both Greece and Yugoslavia in April.

Reassured, Hitler invaded the Soviet Union on June 22, 1941. He believed that the Russians could still be decisively defeated before the brutal winter weather set in.

The massive attack stretched out along a front some 1,800 miles (about 2,900 km) long. German troops advanced rapidly, capturing two million Russian soldiers. By November, one German army group had swept through Ukraine. A second army was besieging the city of Leningrad, while a third approached within 25 miles (about 40 km) of Moscow, the Soviet capital.

An early winter and fierce Soviet resistance, however, halted the German advance. Because of the planned spring date for the invasion, the Germans had no winter uniforms. For the first time in the war, German armies had been stopped. A counterattack in December 1941 by a Soviet army came as an ominous ending to the year for the Germans.

✓ **Reading Check** **Evaluating** In the spring of 1941, what caused Hitler to delay his invasion of the Soviet Union? What halted the German advance once it had begun?

Japan at War

MAIN IDEA The Japanese attack on Pearl Harbor outraged Americans and led to the entry of the United States into the war.

HISTORY & YOU Do you think the terrorist attacks of 2001 unified Americans? Read to find out how the Japanese attack on Pearl Harbor affected American opinion about World War II.

On December 7, 1941, Japanese aircraft attacked the U.S. naval base at Pearl Harbor in the Hawaiian Islands. The same day, other Japanese units launched additional assaults on the Philippines and began advancing toward the British colony of Malaya. Soon after, Japanese forces invaded the Dutch East Indies and occupied a number of islands in the Pacific Ocean. In some cases, as on the Bataan Peninsula and the island of Corregidor in the Philippines, resistance was fierce. By the spring of 1942, however, almost all of Southeast Asia and much of the western Pacific had fallen into Japanese hands.

Japan's New "Community"

A triumphant Japan now declared the creation of a community of nations. The name given to this new "community" was the Greater East Asia Co-Prosperity Sphere. The entire region would now be under Japanese direction. Japan also announced its intention to liberate the colonial areas of Southeast Asia from Western colonial rule. These idealistic-sounding goals were immediately set aside. What Japan wanted from the region for the moment was to extract its resources for the Japanese war machine. Japan treated the countries under its rule as conquered lands.

Global War

Japanese leaders had hoped that their lightning strike at American bases would destroy the U.S. fleet in the Pacific. The Roosevelt administration, they thought, would now accept Japanese domination of the Pacific. The American people, in the eyes of Japanese leaders, were soft. Their easy, rich life had made them unable to fight.

The Japanese miscalculated, however. The attack on Pearl Harbor unified American opinion about becoming involved in the war. Once bitterly divided over participating in the war, the American people now took up arms. The United States joined with European nations and Nationalist China in a combined effort to defeat Japan.

Believing the American involvement in the Pacific would make the United States ineffective in the European theater of war, Hitler declared war on the United States four days after Pearl Harbor. Another European conflict had turned into a global war.

✓ **Reading Check** **Describing** By the spring of 1942, which territories did Japan control?

The Allies Advance

MAIN IDEA The Allied forces stopped the advance of the Germans and the Japanese.

HISTORY & YOU Have you ever had to overcome obstacles in order to achieve a goal? Read to find out how the Allied forces fought for the unconditional surrender of Germany and Japan at the end of World War II.

The entry of the United States into the war created a new coalition, the Grand Alliance. To overcome mutual suspicions, the three major Allies—Great Britain, the United States, and the Soviet Union— agreed to stress military operations and

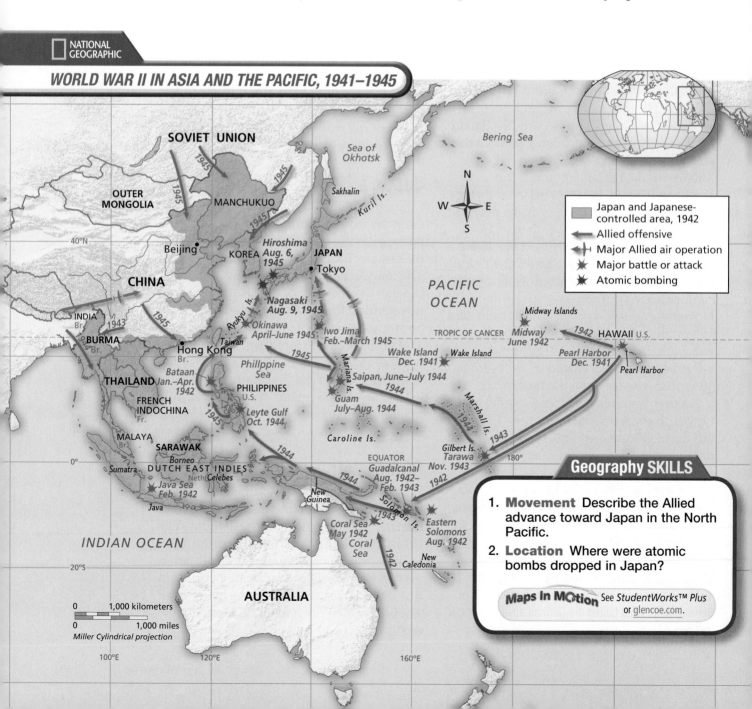

NATIONAL GEOGRAPHIC

WORLD WAR II IN ASIA AND THE PACIFIC, 1941–1945

Japan and Japanese-controlled area, 1942
Allied offensive
Major Allied air operation
Major battle or attack
Atomic bombing

SOVIET UNION

Sea of Okhotsk

Bering Sea

OUTER MONGOLIA

MANCHUKUO

Sakhalin

Kuril Is.

40°N

Beijing

Hiroshima Aug. 6, 1945

KOREA

JAPAN

Tokyo

CHINA

PACIFIC OCEAN

Nagasaki Aug. 9, 1945

Ryukyu Is.

Midway Islands

INDIA Br. 1943

Okinawa April–June 1945

Iwo Jima Feb.–March 1945

TROPIC OF CANCER Midway June 1942 HAWAII U.S.

BURMA Br.

Taiwan

Hong Kong Br.

1945

Phillppine Sea

Wake Island Dec. 1941 Wake Island

1942

Pearl Harbor Dec. 1941

Pearl Harbor

THAILAND

Bataan Jan.–Apr. 1942

PHILIPPINES U.S.

Mariana Is.

Saipan, June–July 1944

1944

FRENCH INDOCHINA Fr.

Leyte Gulf Oct. 1944

Guam July–Aug. 1944

Marshall Is.

1944

MALAYA Br.

Caroline Is.

1943

SARAWAK

Borneo

EQUATOR

Gilbert Is. Tarawa Nov. 1943

180°

0°

Sumatra

DUTCH EAST INDIES Neth.

Celebes

Guadalcanal Aug. 1942– Feb. 1943

Geography SKILLS

Java Sea Feb. 1942

1944

1942

Java

New Guinea

Solomon Is.

1943

Eastern Solomons Aug. 1942

1. **Movement** Describe the Allied advance toward Japan in the North Pacific.

INDIAN OCEAN

Coral Sea May 1942 Coral Sea

New Caledonia

1942

2. **Location** Where were atomic bombs dropped in Japan?

20°S

AUSTRALIA

Maps In MOtion See StudentWorks™ Plus or glencoe.com.

0   1,000 kilometers
0   1,000 miles
Miller Cylindrical projection

100°E   120°E   160°E

ignore political differences. At the beginning of 1943, the Allies agreed to fight until the Axis Powers—Germany, Italy, and Japan—surrendered unconditionally. The unconditional surrender principle, which required the Axis nations to surrender without any favorable condition, cemented the Grand Alliance by making it nearly impossible for Hitler to divide his foes.

The European Theater

Defeat was far from Hitler's mind at the beginning of 1942. As Japanese forces advanced into Southeast Asia and the Pacific, Hitler and his European allies continued fighting the war in Europe against the armies of Britain and the Soviet Union.

Until late 1942, it appeared that the Germans might still prevail on the battlefield. In North Africa, the Afrika Korps, German forces led by General Erwin Rommel, broke through the British defenses in Egypt and advanced toward Alexandria.

A renewed German offensive in the Soviet Union led to the capture of the entire Crimea in the spring of 1942. In August, Hitler boasted:

PRIMARY SOURCE

"As the next step, we are going to advance south of the Caucasus and then help the rebels in Iran and Iraq against the English. Another thrust will be directed along the Caspian Sea toward Afghanistan and India. Then the English will run out of oil. In two years we'll be on the borders of India. Twenty to thirty elite German divisions will do. Then the British Empire will collapse."

—*Spandau*, Albert Speer, trans. Richard Winston and Clara Winston, 1976

This would be Hitler's last optimistic outburst. By the fall of 1942, the war had turned against the Germans.

The Tide Turns

In North Africa, British forces had stopped Rommel's troops at El Alamein (EHL A•luh•MAYN) in the summer of 1942. The Germans then retreated back across the desert. In November 1942, British and American forces invaded French North Africa. They forced the German and Italian troops there to surrender in May 1943.

On the Eastern Front, after the capture of the Crimea, Hitler's generals wanted him to concentrate on the Caucasus and its oil fields. Hitler, however, decided that **Stalingrad,** a major industrial center on the Volga River, should be taken first.

In perhaps the most terrible battle of the war, between November 1942 and February 2, 1943, the Soviets launched a counterattack. German troops were stopped, then encircled, and supply lines were cut off, all in frigid winter conditions. The Germans were forced to surrender at Stalingrad. The entire German Sixth Army, considered the best of the German troops, was lost.

By February 1943, German forces in Russia were back to their positions of June 1942. By the spring of 1943, even Hitler knew that the Germans would not defeat the Soviet Union.

The Asian Theater

In 1942 the tide of battle in the East also changed dramatically. In the Battle of the Coral Sea on May 7 and 8, 1942, American naval forces stopped the Japanese advance and saved Australia from being invaded.

The turning point of the war in Asia came on June 4, at the Battle of **Midway Island.** U.S. planes destroyed four attacking Japanese aircraft carriers. The United States defeated the Japanese navy and established naval superiority in the Pacific.

By the fall of 1942, Allied forces in Asia were gathering for two operations. One, commanded by U.S. general **Douglas MacArthur,** would move into the Philippines through New Guinea and the South Pacific Islands. The other would move across the Pacific with a combination of U.S. Army, Marine, and Navy attacks on Japanese-held islands. The policy was to capture some Japanese-held islands and bypass others, "island hopping" up to Japan. After a series of bitter engagements in the waters off the Solomon Islands from August to November 1942, Japanese fortunes were fading.

✓ Reading Check) **Summarizing** Why was the German assault on Stalingrad a crushing defeat for the Germans?

Last Years of the War

MAIN IDEA Allied victories forced Germany and Japan to surrender unconditionally.

HISTORY & YOU Do the ends justify the means? Read about the decision to use the atomic bomb.

By the beginning of 1943, the tide of battle had turned against Germany, Italy, and Japan. Axis forces in Tunisia surrendered on May 13, 1943. The Allies then crossed the Mediterranean and carried the war to Italy, an area that **Winston Churchill** had called the "soft underbelly" of Europe. After taking Sicily, Allied troops began an invasion of mainland Italy in September.

The European Theater

After Sicily fell, King Victor Emmanuel II of Italy arrested Mussolini, but in a daring raid, the Germans liberated him. He was then made the head of a German puppet state in northern Italy as German troops moved in and occupied much of Italy.

The Germans set up defense lines in the hills south of Rome. The Allies advanced up the peninsula with heavy casualties, but they took Rome on June 4, 1944. By then, the Italian war was secondary as the Allied forces opened their long-awaited "second front" in western Europe.

Since the autumn of 1943, the Allies had planned an invasion of France from Great Britain, across the English Channel. Finally, on June 6, 1944 (D-Day), Allied forces under U.S. general Dwight D. Eisenhower landed on the **Normandy** beaches in history's greatest naval invasion. The Allies fought their way past hidden underwater mines, treacherous barbed wire, and horrible machine gun fire. Believing the battle was a diversion and the real invasion would occur elsewhere, the Germans responded slowly. This gave the Allied forces time to set up a beachhead. Within three months, the Allies had landed two million men and 500,000 vehicles. Allied forces then began pushing inland and broke through German defensive lines.

INFOGRAPHICS — PRIMARY SOURCE

D-Day: June 6, 1944

The D-Day invasion took place on five beaches along fifty miles of Normandy coast. More than 1,000 transports dropped paratroopers, while amphibious craft landed some 130,000 American, British, and Canadian troops on the code-named beaches (see map below). The combined D-Day invasion succeeded not only because of its sheer size, but because of great timing—the Allies attacked while many German forces were fighting the Soviets on the Eastern Front.

Amphibious ships

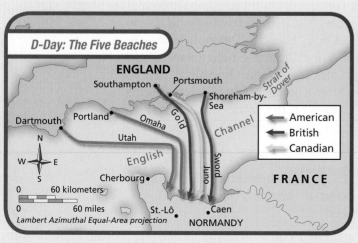

D-Day: The Five Beaches

ENGLAND
Southampton
Portsmouth
Shoreham-by-Sea
Strait of Dover
Dartmouth
Portland
Omaha
Gold
Utah
Channel
English
Sword
Juno
American
British
Canadian
N W E S
0   60 kilometers
0   60 miles
Lambert Azimuthal Equal-Area projection
Cherbourg
St.-Lô
Caen
NORMANDY
FRANCE

DOCUMENT-BASED QUESTIONS

1. **Identifying** What nations took part in the D-Day invasion?
2. **Making Inferences** How did the fact that the Germans were also fighting the Soviets affect the outcome of D-Day?

Allied troops liberated Paris by the end of August. In March 1945, they crossed the Rhine River and advanced into Germany. At the end of April 1945, Allied armies in northern Germany moved toward the Elbe River, where they linked up with the Soviets.

The Soviets had come a long way since the Battle of Stalingrad in 1943. The Soviets had soundly defeated the German forces at the Battle of Kursk (July 5 to 12), the greatest tank battle of World War II. Soviet forces now began a steady advance westward. Reoccupying the Ukraine by the end of 1943, they moved into the Baltic states by early 1944. Advancing along a northern front, Soviet troops occupied Warsaw in January 1945 and entered Berlin in April. Meanwhile, Soviet troops along a southern front swept through Hungary, Romania, and Bulgaria.

By January 1945, Adolf Hitler had moved into a bunker 55 feet (almost 17 m) under the city of Berlin. In his final political testament, Hitler, consistent to the end in his anti-Semitism, blamed the Jews for the war. He wrote, "Above all I charge the leaders of the nation and those under them to scrupulous observance of the laws of race and to merciless opposition to the universal poisoner of all peoples, international Jewry."

Hitler committed suicide on April 30, two days after Italian **partisans,** or resistance fighters, shot Mussolini. On May 7, 1945, Germany surrendered. The war in Europe was finally over.

The Asian Theater

The war in Asia continued. Beginning in 1943, U.S. forces went on the offensive and advanced across the Pacific. As the Allied military power drew closer to the main Japanese islands in the first months of 1945, **Harry S. Truman,** who had become president after Roosevelt died in April, had a difficult decision to make. Should he use newly developed atomic weapons to bring the war to an end? If the United States invaded Japan, Truman and his advisers had become convinced that American troops would suffer heavy casualties. At the time, however, only two bombs were available; no one knew how effective they would be.

Truman decided to use the bombs. The first bomb was dropped on the Japanese city of **Hiroshima** on August 6. Three days later, a second bomb was dropped on Nagasaki. Both cities were leveled. Thousands of people died immediately after the bombs were dropped. Thousands more died in later months from radiation. Japan surrendered on August 14.

World War II was finally over. Seventeen million had died in battle. Perhaps 20 million civilians had perished as well. Some estimates place total losses at 60 million.

✓ Reading Check **Identifying** What was the "second front" that the Allies opened in western Europe?

SECTION 2 REVIEW

Vocabulary
1. **Explain** the significance of: blitzkrieg, resolve, Franklin D. Roosevelt, isolationism, neutrality, involvement, Stalingrad, Midway Island, Douglas MacArthur, Winston Churchill, Normandy, partisans, Harry S. Truman, Hiroshima.

Main Ideas
2. **Explain** why Hitler ordered a shift in strategy after the Luftwaffe began bombing British cities. What was the outcome of this strategy?

3. **List** the series of events that began to turn the war against Germany in 1942. Use a chart like the one below to make your list.

Events That Turned the War Against Germany, 1942–1943
1.
2.

4. **Describe** how the war ended on the Asian front.

Critical Thinking
5. **The Big Idea** **Evaluating** How did the entry of the United States into World War II affect the war's progression and outcome?

6. **Sequencing** Put the events of World War II in chronological order.

7. **Analyzing Visuals** Examine the photograph on page 634. What was the purpose of the amphibious ships?

Writing About History
8. **Persuasive Writing** Imagine you are Harry S. Truman. You must end the war quickly on the Asian front, and you have decided to use the atomic bomb against Japan. You must convince your cabinet that your choice of action is the best alternative. Write a short essay defending your position.

History ONLINE

For help with the concepts in this section of *Glencoe World History—Modern Times*, go to glencoe.com and click Study Central.

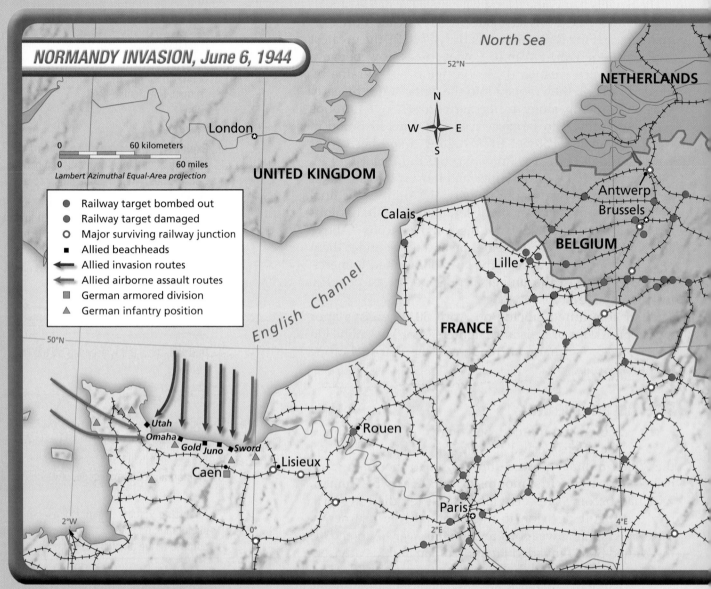

NORMANDY INVASION, June 6, 1944

North Sea

52°N

NETHERLANDS

London

UNITED KINGDOM

0 — 60 kilometers
0 — 60 miles
Lambert Azimuthal Equal-Area projection

Antwerp

Brussels

Calais

BELGIUM

Lille

● Railway target bombed out
● Railway target damaged
○ Major surviving railway junction
■ Allied beachheads
← Allied invasion routes
← Allied airborne assault routes
■ German armored division
▲ German infantry position

FRANCE

50°N

Utah
Omaha
Gold Juno Sword
Caen

Rouen

Lisieux

Paris

2°W

0°

2°E

4°E

English Channel

By 6 A.M. on D-day, tightly-packed landing craft were moving swiftly across the English Channel to the Normandy shore. During the invasion, about 7000 ships and landing craft carried more than 130,000 troops across the channel.

June 10: U.S. troops at Omaha Beach begin moving inland with their jeeps, tanks, and other heavy equipment offloaded from large supply ships anchored in the channel. ▶

Floating piers rose and fell with the tides.

▲ The Mulberry artificial harbor allowed ships to unload vast amounts of cargo.

◄ August 29: Normandy invasion troops and their reinforcements have fought their way across France and freed Paris from Nazi rule. These U.S. soldiers are marching in a parade celebrating the liberation of Paris.

THE NORMANDY INVASION

The Plan On D-Day, June 6, 1944, Allied troops took part in the largest sea assault in history. Code-named Operation Overlord, its goal was to gain a foothold on the Normandy coast in France. For the invasion, Allied leaders divided the coastline into five beaches code-named Utah, Omaha, Gold, Juno, and Sword. U.S. and British forces each took responsibility for two beaches. Canadian troops had one. The Allies worked hard to make the Germans think the invasion would take place near Calais. They sent out false radio reports and radar signals, and put fake tanks and trucks where German planes would easily spot them. Close to D-Day, the Allies increased bombing raids near Calais.

The Landing Although the invasion was set for June 5, bad weather led officials to delay it by a day. Once it began, thousands came ashore in wooden boats called landing craft. These boats picked up troops and supplies from larger ships in deeper water and dropped them off close to the shore. British and U.S. planes provided protective counterfire as soldiers ran from landing crafts to the beaches. Gliders or parachutes also landed on the beaches bringing men to fight alongside ground forces. In time the Allies built an artificial harbor out of concrete blocks and steel pontoons where many ships could unload supplies at the same time.

A Turning Point in the War Surprised that Allied troops had landed so far from Calais, the Germans reacted slowly. Before they had time to respond more forcefully, Allied troops had gained control of all five landing zones. With innovation and careful planning, a risky strategy became a winning one. The Normandy invasion marked the beginning of the end of the war.

Geography SKILLS

1. **Location** Why did Calais' location make it a likely place for the invasion?
2. **Human-Environmental Interaction** How did Allied leaders adapt their invasion strategy to the coastal area chosen for the Normandy invasion?

The New Order and the Holocaust

GUIDE TO READING

The BIG Idea
Human Rights Millions of people were forced to labor for the German and Japanese war machines. The Holocaust claimed the lives of six million Jews.

Content Vocabulary
- genocide *(p. 640)*
- collaborators *(p. 641)*

Academic Vocabulary
- ethnic *(p. 638)*
- occupation *(p. 639)*

People, Places, and Events
- Poland *(p. 638)*
- Heinrich Himmler *(p. 638)*
- Reinhard Heydrich *(p. 636)*
- Auschwitz *(p. 640)*
- Holocaust *(p. 641)*

Reading Strategy
Comparing and Contrasting As you read, use a Venn diagram like the one below to compare and contrast the New Order of Germany and the New Order of Japan.

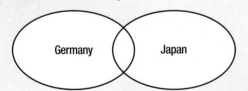

Germany | Japan

As World War II continued, Japan and Germany changed their domestic policies. Japan used the resources of conquered nations and forced millions to labor for its war machine. In Germany, the Nazis began a terrifying genocide, carried out by death squads and death camps. Nearly two out of every three European Jews died in the Holocaust.

The New Order in Europe

MAIN IDEA The German conquest of continental Europe forced millions of native peoples to work for the Nazi war machine.

HISTORY & YOU Recall how the ancient Romans conquered lands and then enslaved many of the people. Read to learn about the Nazi plan to use slave labor.

In 1942 the Nazi regime stretched across continental Europe from the English Channel in the west to the outskirts of Moscow in the east. Nazi-occupied Europe was largely organized in one of two ways. Nazi Germany directly annexed some areas, such as western Poland, and made them into German provinces. Most of occupied Europe, however, was run by German military or civilian officials with help from local people who collaborated with the Nazis.

Resettlement in the East

Nazi administration in the conquered lands to the east was especially ruthless. Seen as the "living space" for German expansion, these lands were populated, Nazis thought, by racially inferior Slavic peoples. Hitler's plans for an Aryan racial empire were so important to him that he and the Nazis began to put their racial program into effect soon after the conquest of **Poland.**

Heinrich Himmler, the leader of the SS, was in charge of German resettlement plans in the east. Himmler's task was to move the Slavic peoples out and replace them with Germans. Slavic peoples included Czech, Polish, Serbo-Croatian, Slovene, and Ukrainian. The resettlement policy was first applied to the lands of western Poland. One million Poles were uprooted and moved to southern Poland. Hundreds of thousands of **ethnic** Germans (German descendants who had migrated years ago from Germany to different parts of southern and eastern Europe) were brought in to colonize the German provinces in Poland. By 1942, two million ethnic Germans had been settled in Poland.

The invasion of the Soviet Union made the Nazis even more excited about German colonization. Hitler envisioned a colossal project of social engineering after the war. Poles, Ukrainians, and

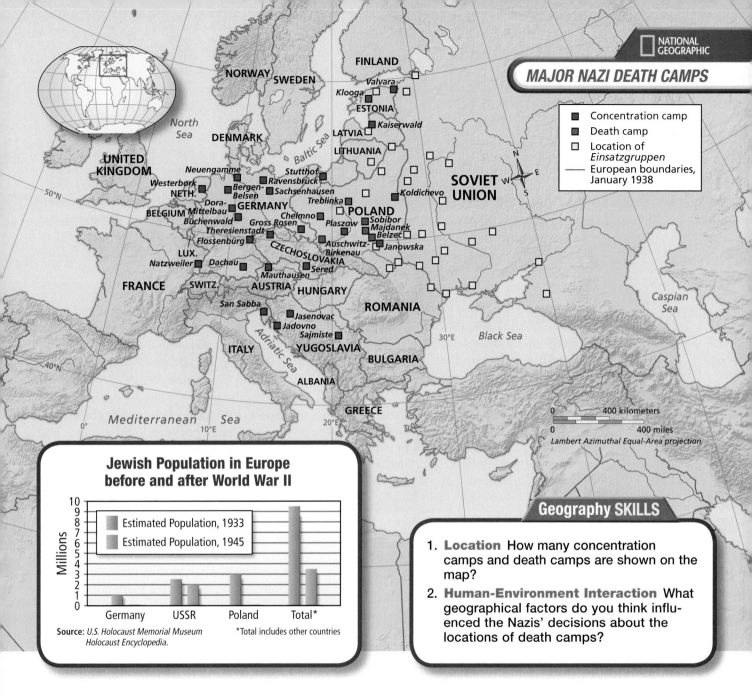

MAJOR NAZI DEATH CAMPS

FINLAND
NORWAY
SWEDEN
Valvara
Klooga
ESTONIA
Kaiserwald
DENMARK
LATVIA
LITHUANIA
UNITED KINGDOM
Neuengamme
Stutthof
Westerbork
Ravensbrück
NETH.
Bergen-Belsen
Sachsenhausen
Koldichevo
SOVIET UNION
Dora-Mittelbau
GERMANY
Treblinka
BELGIUM
Buchenwald
Chelmno
POLAND
Gross Rosen
Plaszow
Sobibor
Theresienstadt
Majdanek
Flossenbürg
Belzec
Auschwitz-Birkenau
Janowska
LUX.
CZECHOSLOVAKIA
Natzweiler
Dachau
Sered
FRANCE
SWITZ.
Mauthausen
AUSTRIA
HUNGARY
San Sabba
ROMANIA
Jasenovac
Jadovno
Sajmiste
Caspian Sea
ITALY
YUGOSLAVIA
Black Sea
BULGARIA
ALBANIA
GREECE
Mediterranean Sea

North Sea
Baltic Sea
Adriatic Sea

■ Concentration camp
■ Death camp
□ Location of *Einsatzgruppen*
— European boundaries, January 1938

50°N
40°N
0°
10°E
20°E
30°E

0   400 kilometers
0   400 miles
Lambert Azimuthal Equal-Area projection

Jewish Population in Europe before and after World War II

Millions (y-axis: 0–10)

Legend:
- Estimated Population, 1933
- Estimated Population, 1945

Categories: Germany, USSR, Poland, Total*

Source: *U.S. Holocaust Memorial Museum Holocaust Encyclopedia.*

*Total includes other countries

Geography SKILLS

1. **Location** How many concentration camps and death camps are shown on the map?
2. **Human-Environment Interaction** What geographical factors do you think influenced the Nazis' decisions about the locations of death camps?

Russians would be removed and become slave labor, according to Hitler's plan. German peasants would settle on the abandoned lands and "Germanize" them.

Himmler told a gathering of SS officers that 30 million Slavs might die to achieve this plan. He continued, "Whether nations live in prosperity or starve to death interests me only insofar as we need them as slaves for our culture. Otherwise it is of no interest."

Slave Labor in Germany

By the summer of 1944, seven million European workers labored in Germany. They made up 20 percent of Germany's labor force. Another seven million workers were forced to labor for the Nazis on farms, industries, and in military camps.

The use of forced labor caused many problems for Germany, however. Sending so many workers to Germany disrupted industrial production in the occupied countries that could have helped Germany. Then, too, the brutal way in which Germany recruited foreign workers led more and more people to resist the Nazi **occupation** forces.

✓ **Reading Check** **Describing** What was Hitler's vision for the residents of eastern Europe?

The Holocaust

MAIN IDEA Adolf Hitler's philosophy of Aryan superiority led to the Holocaust.

HISTORY & YOU Have you seen films about the Holocaust? Read to find out how the Nazis planned to exterminate the Jews.

No aspect of the Nazi New Order was more terrifying than the deliberate attempt to exterminate the Jews. Racial struggle was a key element in Hitler's world of ideas. To him, racial struggle was a clearly defined conflict of opposites. On one side were the Aryans, who were the creators of human cultural development, according to Hitler. On the other side were the Jews, and Hitler believed they were trying to destroy the Aryans.

Himmler and the SS closely shared Hitler's racial ideas. The SS was given responsibility for what the Nazis called their Final Solution to the Jewish problem. The Final Solution was **genocide** (physical extermination) of the Jewish people.

The *Einsatzgruppen*

Reinhard Heydrich, head of the SS's Security Service, had the task of administering the Final Solution. Heydrich created special strike forces, called *Einsatzgruppen,* to carry out Nazi plans. After the defeat of Poland, these forces rounded up all Polish Jews and put them in ghettos set up in a number of Polish cities. Conditions in the ghettos were horrible. Families were crowded together in unsanitary housing. The Nazis tried to starve residents by allowing only minimal amounts of food. In spite of their suffering, residents carried on, and some organized resistance against the Nazis.

In June 1941, the *Einsatzgruppen* were given the new job of acting as mobile killing units. These SS death squads followed the regular army's advance into the Soviet Union. Their job was to round up Jews in their villages, execute them, and bury them in mass graves. The graves were often giant pits dug by the victims themselves before they were shot.

The leader of one of these death squads described the mode of operation:

History ONLINE

Student Web Activity—
Visit glencoe.com and complete the activity on concentration camps.

PRIMARY SOURCE

"The unit selected for this task would enter a village or city and order the prominent Jewish citizens to call together all Jews for the purpose of resettlement. They were requested to hand over their valuables to the leaders of the unit, and shortly before the execution to surrender their outer clothing. The men, women, and children were led to a place of execution which in most cases was located next to a more deeply excavated anti-tank ditch. Then they were shot, kneeling or standing, and the corpses thrown into the ditch."
—*Nazi Conspiracy and Aggression,* vol. 5, 1946

The Death Camps

The *Einsatzgruppen* probably killed more than one million Jews. As appalling as that sounds, it was too slow by Nazi standards. They decided to kill the European Jewish population in specially built death camps.

Beginning in 1942, Jews from countries occupied by Germany (or sympathetic to Germany) were rounded up, packed like cattle into freight trains, and shipped to Poland. Six extermination centers were built in Poland for this purpose. The largest was **Auschwitz** (OWSH•vihts).

About 30 percent of the new arrivals at Auschwitz were sent to a labor camp, where many were starved or worked to death. The remainder of the people went to the gas chambers. Some inmates were subjected to cruel and painful "medical" experiments.

By the spring of 1942, the death camps were in full operation. First priority was given to the elimination of the Polish ghettos. By the summer of 1942, however, Jews were also being shipped from France, Belgium, and Holland. Even as the Allies were winning the war in 1944, Jews were being shipped from Greece and Hungary. In spite of Germany's desperate military needs, even late in the war when Germany was facing utter defeat, the Final Solution still had priority in using railroad cars to ship Jews to the death camps.

The Death Toll

The Germans killed approximately six million Jews, over three million of them in the death camps. Even in concentration camps that were not designed specifically for mass murder, large numbers of inmates were worked to death or subjected to deadly medical experiments. Virtually 90 percent of the Jewish populations of Poland, the Baltic countries, and Germany were killed. Overall, the Holocaust was responsible for the death of nearly two out of every three European Jews.

The Nazis were also responsible for the deliberate death by shooting, starvation, or overwork of at least another nine to ten million non-Jewish people. The Nazis considered the Roma (sometimes known as Gypsies), like the Jews, to be an alien race. About 40 percent of Europe's one million Roma were killed in the death camps.

The leading citizens of the Slavic peoples—the clergy, intellectuals, civil leaders, judges, and lawyers—were arrested and killed. Probably an additional four million Poles, Ukrainians, and Belorussians lost their lives as slave laborers. Finally, at least three to four million Soviet prisoners of war were killed.

This mass slaughter of European Jews is known as the **Holocaust.** Jews in and out of the camps attempted to resist the Nazis. Friends and even strangers aided some Jews, hiding them in villages or smuggling them into safe areas. Foreign diplomats would try to save Jews by issuing exit visas. The nation of Denmark saved almost its entire Jewish population.

Some people did not believe the accounts of death camps because, during World War I, allies had greatly exaggerated German atrocities to arouse enthusiasm for the war. Most often, people pretended not to notice what was happening. Even worse, **collaborators** (people who assisted the enemy) helped the Nazis hunt down Jews. Although the Allies were aware of the concentration camps and death camps, they chose to concentrate on ending the war. Not until after the war did the full extent of the horror and inhumanity of the Holocaust impress itself upon people's consciousness.

See page R51 to read excerpts from *The Holocaust—The Camp Victims* in the **Primary Source and Literature Library.**

Children in the War

Young people of all ages were also victims of the atrocities of World War II.

HISTORY & ARTS   PRIMARY SOURCE

The Final Solution at Auschwitz

Auschwitz was the largest and most notorious Nazi death camp. About 1.5 million people lost their lives there, most of them Jewish. The camp was located in Poland at the junction of 44 separate railroad tracks. These railroads transported Jews from all over Europe to Auschwitz.

Hungarian prisoners arrive at Auschwitz concentration camp.

Eyewitness account of an Auschwitz prisoner:

"Every day we saw thousands and thousands of innocent people disappear up the chimney. With our own eyes, we could truly fathom what it means to be a human being. There they came, men, women, children, all innocent. They suddenly vanished, and the world said nothing . . ."

—Filip Müller, Auschwitz prisoner

DOCUMENT-BASED QUESTIONS

1. **Describing** Use the photograph and quotations to write a brief description of the Nazi Final Solution at Auschwitz.

2. **Analyzing** How does Müller describe the victims at Auschwitz?

CONNECTING TO THE UNITED STATES

THE U.S. HOLOCAUST MEMORIAL MUSEUM

Since World War II, people have tried to understand the moral failure that allowed the Holocaust to happen. The word *genocide* was first used in 1944 to describe the Holocaust. The United Nations defined genocide as an attempt to destroy, in whole or in part, a national, ethnic, racial, or religious group. In recent years, genocide has taken place in the former Yugoslavia, Rwanda, and Darfur.

By learning about the past, we may be able to prevent future genocide. The U.S. Holocaust Memorial Museum in Washington, D.C., helps people remember and reflect upon the Holocaust.

- Educates people about the Holocaust
- Preserves the memory of those who suffered
- Encourages reflection and civic responsibility

A visitor tours the inside of the U.S. Holocaust Museum in Washington, D.C. ▶

CONNECTING TO TODAY

1. **Assessing** Why is it important to remember the Holocaust?
2. **Making Connections** Where has genocide taken place in recent years?

Because they were unable to work, Jewish children, along with their mothers, were the first ones selected for the gas chambers. Young Jewish males learned to look as adult as possible to survive. About 1.2 million Jewish children died in the Holocaust.

Many children were evacuated from cities during the war to avoid the bombing. The Germans created about 9,000 camps for children in the countryside. In Japan, 15,000 children were evacuated from Hiroshima before its destruction. The British moved about six million children and their mothers in 1939. Some British parents even sent their children to Canada and the United States. This, too, could be dangerous. When the ocean liner *Arandora Star* was hit by a German torpedo, it had 77 British children on board. They never made it to Canada.

Children evacuated to the countryside did not always see their parents again. In 1945 there were perhaps 13 million orphaned children in Europe.

In eastern Europe, it was children who especially suffered under German occupation. All secondary schools in German-occupied eastern Europe were closed. Their facilities and equipment were destroyed. Heinrich Himmler said that their education should consist only "in teaching simple arithmetic up to 500, the writing of one's name, and that God has ordered obedience to the Germans, honesty, diligence, and politeness. I do not consider an ability to read as necessary."

At times, young people were expected to fight in the war. In the last years of the war, Hitler Youth members, often only 14 or 15 years old, served in the front lines. Soviet Union children as young as 13 or 14 spied on German positions and worked with the resistance movement. Some were even given decorations for killing the enemy.

✓ **Reading Check** **Summarizing** What was the job of the *Einsatzgruppen*?

The New Order in Asia

MAIN IDEA The Japanese conquest of Southeast Asia forced millions of native peoples to work for the Japanese war machine.

HISTORY & YOU What if you were separated from your family and forced to work for a foreign country? Read to learn about Japanese policies in the occupied areas of Southeast Asia.

Japanese war policy in Asian areas occupied by Japan was basically defensive. Japan needed its new possessions to meet its growing need for raw materials, such as tin, oil, and rubber, and as markets for its manufactured goods. To organize these possessions, Japanese leaders included them in the Greater East Asia Co-Prosperity Sphere. This economic community supposedly would provide mutual benefits to the occupied areas and to Japan.

Japanese Colonial Policies

The Japanese had conquered Southeast Asia under the slogan "Asia for the Asiatics." Japanese officials in occupied territories promised that local governments would be established under Japanese control. In fact, real power rested with Japanese military authorities in each territory. In turn, the Army General Staff in Tokyo controlled the local Japanese military command. Japan used the economic resources of its colonies for its war machine and recruited the native peoples to serve in local military units or in public works projects. In some cases, these policies brought severe hardships to the native peoples. In Vietnam, for example, over a million people starved in 1944 and 1945 when Japanese officials forcibly took their rice and sold it abroad.

At first, many Southeast Asian nationalists took Japanese promises at face value and agreed to cooperate. Eventually, the nature of Japanese occupation policies became clear, and sentiment turned against Japan. Japanese officials provoked such attitudes by their contempt for local customs. Like the Germans, Japanese military forces often had little respect for the lives of their subject peoples. To help their war effort, the Japanese used labor forces composed of both prisoners of war and local peoples.

Such Japanese behavior created a dilemma for many nationalists. They had no desire to see the return of the colonial powers, but they did not like what the Japanese were doing. Some turned against the Japanese. Others simply did nothing. On the other hand, some nationalists tried to have it both ways. Indonesian patriots pretended to support Japan while actually sabotaging the Japanese administration.

✓ Reading Check **Examining** How did the Japanese treat the native peoples in occupied lands?

SECTION 3 REVIEW

Vocabulary
1. **Explain** the significance of: Poland, Heinrich Himmler, ethnic, occupation, genocide, Reinhard Heydrich, Auschwitz, Holocaust, collaborators.

Main Ideas
2. **Explain** how Hitler began putting his racial program into effect soon after he conquered Poland.

3. **Calculate** the death toll of Jewish and non-Jewish people while Hitler established his New Order. Use a table like the one below to make your calculation.

People	Number Killed
Total:	

4. **List** the reasons why the sentiment of people in Japanese-occupied areas turned against the Japanese.

Critical Thinking
5. **The BIG Idea** **Evaluating** How did the Holocaust impact Europe and the rest of the world? What lessons does the Holocaust have for us today?

6. **Recognizing Bias** Heinrich Himmler said this about the education of Slavic children: "I do not consider an ability to read as necessary." Why would Himmler say this?

7. **Analyzing Visuals** Examine the photograph on page 641. How were prisoners transported to Auschwitz?

Writing About History
8. **Descriptive Writing** Imagine you are a teen living in a Polish ghetto in 1940–1941. In a paragraph or two, describe your daily life—your meals, your quarters, your schooling, your family, and friends.

History ONLINE

For help with the concepts in this section of *Glencoe World History— Modern Times*, go to glencoe.com and click Study Central.

Home Front and Aftermath of War

GUIDE TO READING

The BIG Idea
Competition Among Countries After World War II, a new set of Cold War problems faced the international community.

Content Vocabulary
- mobilization (p. 644)
- kamikaze (p. 647)
- blitz (p. 648)
- Cold War (p. 650)

Academic Vocabulary
- widespread (p. 644)
- ideological (p. 650)

People and Places
- Albert Speer (p. 647)
- General Hideki Tōjō (p. 647)
- London (p. 648)
- Dresden (p. 648)

Reading Strategy
Comparing and Contrasting As you read, create a chart like the one below comparing and contrasting the impact of World War II on the lives of civilians.

Country	Impact on Lives of Civilians
Soviet Union	
United States	
Japan	
Germany	

During World War II, nations mobilized their people and geared their economies to war. While the troops fought, the citizens on the home front made personal sacrifices to produce the materials and supplies needed to fuel the war. Thousands lost their lives in bombing raids. Once the war ended, political tensions, suspicions, and conflicts of ideas led to a new struggle—the Cold War. The world seemed to be bitterly divided once again.

The Mobilization of Four Nations

MAIN IDEA The Soviet Union, the United States, Germany, and Japan all mobilized for the war with an emphasis on personal sacrifice.

HISTORY & YOU Do you believe that all citizens should cooperate during a national crisis? Read on to understand the feelings of sacrifice during the crisis of World War II.

Even more than World War I, World War II was a total war. Fighting was much more **widespread** and covered most of the world. Economic **mobilization** (the act of assembling and preparing for war) was more extensive; so, too, was the mobilization of women. The number of civilians killed—almost 20 million—was far higher. Many of these victims were children.

World War II had an enormous impact on civilian life in the Soviet Union, the United States, Germany, and Japan. We consider the home fronts of those four nations next.

The Soviet Union

Known to the Soviets as the Great Patriotic War, the German-Soviet war witnessed the greatest land battles in history, as well as incredible ruthlessness. The initial military defeats suffered by the Soviet Union led to drastic emergency measures that affected the lives of the civilian population. The city of Leningrad, for example, experienced 900 days of siege. Its inhabitants became so desperate for food that they even ate dogs, cats, and mice. Probably 1.5 million people died in the city.

As the German army made its rapid advance into Soviet territory, Soviet workers dismantled and shipped the factories in the western part of the Soviet Union to the interior—to the Urals, western Siberia, and the Volga regions. Machines were placed on the bare ground. As laborers began their work, walls went up around them.

Stalin called the widespread military and industrial mobilization of the nation a "battle of machines." The Soviets won, producing

In both the United States and the Soviet Union, civilians made vital contributions to the war effort. New groups of workers, including women, filled industrial jobs while young men served as soldiers on the front lines. Industrial jobs were of critical importance because they manufactured essential supplies for war, including airplanes, ships, and ammunition.

Women, old men, and teenagers filled most of the jobs in Soviet factories. Working hours were long, and there were no days off. Production did not stop during the frequent bombing raids. Output increased to four times its prewar levels.

This American poster features Rosie the Riveter, a symbol of the female industrial worker contributing to the war effort.

This 1944 Soviet World War II poster has a similar message as the American poster. The complete Russian slogan reads, "We will defend Leningrad! We will restore it!"

Mobilization for War

Source: *Economic History Review.*

DOCUMENT-BASED QUESTIONS

1. **Analyzing** What happened to the percentage of industrial workers between 1940 and 1943 in the United States and in the Soviet Union? Why?

2. **Comparing** Why do you think American and Soviet posters encouraged women to work in war-related jobs?

78,000 tanks and 98,000 artillery pieces. In 1943, 55 percent of the Soviet national income went for war materials, compared with 15 percent in 1940. As a result of the emphasis on military goods, Soviet citizens experienced severe shortages of both food and housing.

Soviet women played a major role in the war effort. Women and girls worked in industries, mines, and railroads. Overall, the number of women working in industry increased almost 60 percent. Soviet women were also expected to dig antitank ditches and work as air-raid wardens. In addition,

the Soviet Union was the only country in World War II to use women in battle. Soviet women served as snipers and also in aircrews of bomber squadrons.

The United States

The home front in the United States was quite different from that of the other major powers. The United States was not fighting on its own territory. Eventually, the United States became the arsenal of the Allied Powers; it produced much of the military equipment the Allies needed. The height of war production came in November 1943.

At that point, the country was building six ships a day and 96,000 planes per year.

The mobilization of the American economy and workforce resulted in some social turmoil, however. The construction of new factories created boomtowns. Thousands came there to work but then faced a shortage of houses and schools. Sixteen million men and women were enrolled in the military and moved frequently. Another 16 million, mostly wives and girlfriends of servicemen or workers looking for jobs, also moved around the country.

Over a million African Americans moved from the rural South to the cities of the North and West, looking for jobs in industry. The presence of African Americans in areas where they had not lived before led to racial tensions and sometimes even racial riots. In Detroit in June 1943, for example, white mobs roamed the streets attacking African Americans.

One million African Americans joined the military, where they served in segregated units. For some, this treatment led later to a fight for their civil rights.

Japanese Americans faced even more serious issues. On the West Coast, 110,000 Japanese Americans, 65 percent of whom had been born in the United States, were removed to camps surrounded by barbed wire and required to take loyalty oaths. Public officials claimed this policy was necessary for security reasons.

California governor Culbert Olson expressed the racism in this policy:

PRIMARY SOURCE

"[W]hen I look out at a group of Americans of German or Italian descent, I can tell whether they're loyal or not. I can tell how they think and even perhaps what they are thinking. But it is impossible for me to do this with inscrutable Orientals, and particularly the Japanese."

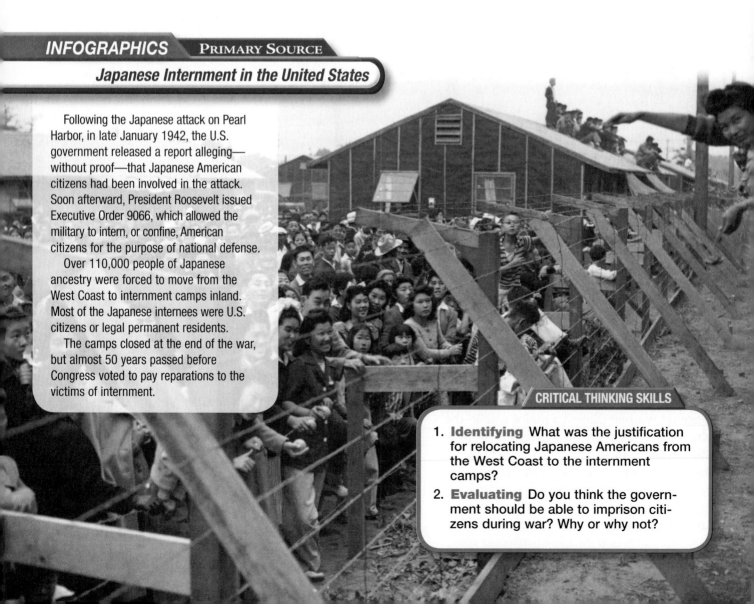

INFOGRAPHICS   PRIMARY SOURCE
Japanese Internment in the United States

Following the Japanese attack on Pearl Harbor, in late January 1942, the U.S. government released a report alleging—without proof—that Japanese American citizens had been involved in the attack. Soon afterward, President Roosevelt issued Executive Order 9066, which allowed the military to intern, or confine, American citizens for the purpose of national defense.

Over 110,000 people of Japanese ancestry were forced to move from the West Coast to internment camps inland. Most of the Japanese internees were U.S. citizens or legal permanent residents.

The camps closed at the end of the war, but almost 50 years passed before Congress voted to pay reparations to the victims of internment.

CRITICAL THINKING SKILLS

1. **Identifying** What was the justification for relocating Japanese Americans from the West Coast to the internment camps?

2. **Evaluating** Do you think the government should be able to imprison citizens during war? Why or why not?

Germany

In August 1914, Germans had enthusiastically cheered their soldiers marching off to war. In September 1939, the streets were quiet. Many Germans did not care. Even worse for the Nazi regime, many feared disaster.

Hitler was well aware of the importance of the home front. He believed that the collapse of the home front in World War I had caused Germany's defeat. In his determination to avoid a repetition of that experience, he adopted economic policies that may have cost Germany the war.

To maintain the morale of the home front during the first two years of the war, Hitler refused to cut consumer goods production or to increase the production of armaments. Blitzkrieg gave the Germans quick victories and enabled them to plunder the food and raw materials of conquered countries. In this way, they could avoid taking resources away from the civilian economy. After German defeats on the Russian front and the American entry into the war, however, the economic situation in Germany changed.

Early in 1942, Hitler finally ordered a massive increase in armaments production and in the size of the army. Hitler's architect, **Albert Speer,** was made minister for armaments and munitions in 1942. Speer was able to triple the production of armaments between 1942 and 1943, in spite of Allied air raids.

A total mobilization of the economy was put into effect in July 1944. Schools, theaters, and cafés were closed. By that time, though, total war mobilization was too late to save Germany from defeat.

Nazi attitudes toward women changed over the course of the war. Before the war, the Nazis had worked to keep women out of the job market. As the war progressed and more and more men were called up for military service, this position no longer made sense. Nazi magazines now proclaimed, "We see the woman as the eternal mother of our people, but also as the working and fighting comrade of the man."

In spite of this change, the number of women working in industry, agriculture, commerce, and domestic service increased only slightly. The total number of employed women in September 1944 was 14.9 million, compared with 14.6 million in May 1939. Many women, especially those of the middle class, did not want jobs, particularly not in factories.

Japan

When it entered the war with the United States, Japan already had an economy in high gear after four years of war with China. Wartime Japan was a highly mobilized society. To guarantee its control over all national resources, the government created a planning board to control prices, wages, labor, and resources. Traditional habits of obedience and hierarchy were used to encourage citizens to sacrifice their resources, and sometimes their lives, for the national cause.

The calls for sacrifice reached a high point in the final years of the war. Young Japanese were encouraged to volunteer to serve as pilots in suicide missions against U.S. fighting ships at sea. These pilots were known as **kamikaze,** or "divine wind." The name went back to the late thirteenth century when kamikazes (though not airborne) had saved Japan from Kublai Khan and the Mongols.

Japan was extremely reluctant to mobilize women on behalf of Japan's war effort. **General Hideki Tōjō,** prime minister from 1941 to 1944, opposed female employment. He argued that "the weakening of the family system would be the weakening of the nation. . . . [W]e are able to do our duties only because we have wives and mothers at home."

Female employment increased during the war, but only in such areas as the textile industry and farming, where women had traditionally worked. Instead of using women to meet labor shortages, the Japanese government brought in Korean and Chinese laborers.

When the Japanese Diet passed its new constitution in 1947, women were assured the right to vote. They were given full legal equality with men in every way.

✓ **Reading Check** **Evaluating** How did World War II contribute to racial tensions in the United States?

The Bombing of Cities

MAIN IDEA The bombing of cities in Britain, Germany, and Japan destroyed buildings and killed thousands of civilians.

HISTORY & YOU Has a relative told you about living someplace where military attacks were a threat? Read to learn about the bombing of cities during World War II.

Bombing was used in World War II against military targets, enemy troops, and civilian populations. Bombing made the home front a dangerous place.

A few bombing raids had been conducted in the last year of World War I, and the bombing of civilians had led to a public outcry. Bombing raids and the reaction to them gave rise to the argument that bombing civilian populations would be an effective way to force governments to make peace. As a result, European air forces began to develop long-range bombers in the 1930s.

Britain

The first sustained use of civilian bombing began in early September 1940. Londoners took the first heavy blows. For months, the German air force bombed **London** nightly. Thousands of civilians were killed or injured, and enormous damage was done. In spite of the extensive damage done to lives and property, Londoners' morale remained high.

The **blitz,** as the British called the German air raids, soon became a national experience. The blitz was carried to many other British cities and towns. The ability of Londoners to maintain their morale set the standard for the rest of the British population. The theory that the bombing of civilian targets would force peace was proved wrong.

Germany

The British failed to learn from their own experience, however. Churchill and his advisers believed that destroying German communities would break civilian morale and bring victory. Major bombing raids on German cities began in 1942. On May 31, 1942, Cologne became the first German city to be attacked by 1,000 bombers.

Bombing raids added an element of terror to the dire circumstances caused by growing shortages of food, clothing, and fuel. Germans especially feared the incendiary bombs, which created firestorms that swept through cities. The ferocious bombing of **Dresden** from February 13 to 15, 1945, created a firestorm that may have killed as many as 100,000 inhabitants and refugees.

Germany suffered enormously from the Allied bombing raids. Millions of buildings were destroyed; half a million civilians died. Nevertheless, it is highly unlikely that Allied bombing sapped the German morale. Instead, Germans, whether pro-Nazi or anti-Nazi, fought on stubbornly, often driven simply by a desire to live.

Nor did the bombing destroy Germany's industrial capacity. Production of war materials actually increased between 1942 and 1944, in spite of the bombing. However, the widespread destruction of transportation systems and fuel supplies made it extremely difficult for the new materials to reach the German military.

Japan

Japan was open to air raids toward the end of the war because its air force had almost been destroyed. Moreover, its crowded cities were built of flimsy materials that were especially vulnerable to fire.

Attacks on Japanese cities by the new U.S. B-29 Superfortresses, the biggest bombers of the war, had begun on November 24, 1944. By the summer of 1945, many of Japan's industries had been destroyed, along with one-fourth of its dwellings. To add to the strength of its regular army, the Japanese government decreed the mobilization of all people between the ages of 13 and 60 into a People's Volunteer Corps.

In Japan, the bombing of civilians reached a new level with the use of the first atomic bomb. Fearing high U.S. casualties in a land invasion of Japan, President Truman and his advisers decided to drop atomic bombs on Hiroshima and Nagasaki in August 1945.

✓ Reading Check **Explaining** Why were civilian populations bombed?

TURNING POINT

HIROSHIMA, NAGASAKI, AND THE NUCLEAR AGE

On August 6, 1945, the United States dropped an atomic bomb on Hiroshima, Japan. Of the city's 350,000 inhabitants, 190,000 died—some immediately and others after suffering the effects of radiation. Three days later, a second bomb was dropped on the city of Nagasaki. Japan's emperor soon surrendered, ending World War II in the Pacific.

The dropping of the atomic bombs in Japan marked the beginning of the Nuclear Age. Once the world had witnessed the deadly potential of nuclear energy, other countries raced to build their own nuclear weapons. In August 1949, the Soviet Union set off its first atomic bomb, starting an arms race with the United States that lasted for 40 years.

The standoff between the Soviet Union and the United States ended in the 1980s, but the nuclear weapons issue remains. Today many countries are working together to prevent the spread of nuclear weapons. After the destruction at Hiroshima, few nations want to risk another nuclear explosion. Yet because nuclear technology also has peaceful uses, such as generating electricity, controlling its use can be difficult.

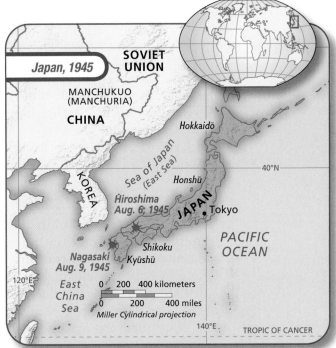

Destruction in Hiroshima, 1945

70,000 of Hiroshima's 76,000 buildings were flattened.

Five square miles of Hiroshima turned to ashes.

Nuclear bombs create large mushroom-shaped clouds, dropping deadly radioactive fallout.

CRITICAL THINKING SKILLS

1. **Determining Cause and Effect** What impact did the atomic bomb have upon the course of World War II?

2. **Identifying Central Issues** How did nuclear technology redefine the second half of the twentieth century?

Peace and a New War

MAIN IDEA Political tensions, suspicions, and a conflict of ideas led the United States and the Soviet Union into the Cold War.

HISTORY & YOU How do you treat people you do not trust? Read to learn how the United States and the Soviet Union reacted to one another in this era.

No real peace but a period of political tensions, known as the **Cold War,** followed the total victory of the Allies in World War II. An **ideological** conflict between the United States and the Soviet Union, the Cold War dominated world affairs until the end of the 1980s.

The Tehran Conference

Stalin, Roosevelt, and Churchill were the leaders of the Big Three (the Soviet Union, the United States, and Great Britain) of the Grand Alliance. They met at Tehran in November 1943 to decide the future course of the war. Their major tactical decision had concerned the final assault on Germany, an American-British invasion through France scheduled for the spring of 1944.

The acceptance of this plan had important consequences. It meant that Soviet and British-American forces would meet in defeated Germany along a north-south dividing line. Most likely, Soviet forces would liberate Eastern Europe. The Allies also agreed to a partition of postwar Germany.

The Yalta Conference

The Big Three powers met again at Yalta in southern Russia in February 1945. By then, the defeat of Germany was assured. The Western powers, having once believed that the Soviets were in a weak position, now faced the reality of 11 million Soviet soldiers taking possession of Eastern Europe and much of central Europe.

Stalin was deeply suspicious of the Western powers. He wanted a buffer to protect the Soviet Union from possible future Western aggression. This meant establishing pro-Soviet governments along the Soviet Union's borders.

Roosevelt, however, favored the idea of self-determination for Europe. This involved a pledge to help liberated Europe create "democratic institutions of their own choice" through free elections.

NATIONAL GEOGRAPHIC

EUROPE AFTER WORLD WAR II

0   400 kilometers
0   400 miles
Lambert Azimuthal Equal-Area projection

Area of Soviet influence
Area of Western influence

NORWAY
FINLAND
SWEDEN
North Sea
Baltic Sea
IRELAND UNITED KINGDOM   DENMARK
NETHERLANDS
SOVIET UNION
EAST GERMANY
Berlin POLAND
ATLANTIC OCEAN
BELGIUM
LUX. WEST GERMANY CZECHOSLOVAKIA
FRANCE SWITZ. AUSTRIA HUNGARY
ROMANIA
YUGOSLAVIA
PORTUGAL
SPAIN ITALY BULGARIA Black Sea
ALBANIA
Mediterranean Sea GREECE

Geography SKILLS

1. **Regions** Compare this map to the map on page 527 and identify the political changes in Europe from 1918 to 1945.

2. **Place** What happened to Germany's borders after World War II?

Roosevelt also agreed to Stalin's price for military aid against Japan: Sakhalin and the Kuril Islands, ruled by Japan, as well as two warm-water ports and railroad rights in Manchuria.

The creation of the United Nations was a major American concern at Yalta. Both Churchill and Stalin accepted Roosevelt's plans for the establishment of a United Nations organization and set the first meeting for San Francisco in April 1945.

The issues of Germany and Eastern Europe were treated less decisively. Once Germany surrendered unconditionally, the Big Three agreed to divide Germany into four zones, one each for the United States, Great Britain, France, and the Soviet Union to occupy and govern. Stalin compromised and agreed to free elections in Poland. However, it was clear that Stalin might not honor this provision for other Eastern European countries. The issue of free elections in Eastern Europe caused a serious split between the Soviets and Americans. This split became more evident when the Big Three next met at Potsdam, Germany.

The Potsdam Conference

The Potsdam Conference of July 1945 began in mistrust. Harry Truman, having succeeded Roosevelt, demanded free elections in Eastern Europe. Stalin responded, "A freely elected government in any of these East European countries would be anti-Soviet, and that we cannot allow." Stalin sought absolute security for the Soviets. Free elections would threaten his goal of controlling Eastern Europe. Short of an invasion by Western forces, nothing would undo developments in Eastern Europe. Very few supported such a policy of invasion.

The Allies did agree that trials should be held of leaders who had committed crimes against humanity during the war. In 1945 and 1946, Nazi leaders were tried and condemned at trials in Nuremberg, Germany. Trials were also held in Japan and Italy.

A New Struggle

A new struggle began. Many in the West thought Soviet policy was part of a worldwide Communist conspiracy. The Soviets viewed Western, and especially American, policy as nothing less than global capitalist expansionism.

The former British prime minister Winston Churchill declared that "an iron curtain" had "descended across the continent," dividing Europe into two hostile camps. Stalin branded Churchill's speech a "call to war with the Soviet Union." Only months after the world's most devastating conflict had ended, the world seemed to be bitterly divided once again.

✓ Reading Check **Identifying** What caused the major split between the United States and the Soviet Union following World War II?

SECTION 4 REVIEW

Vocabulary
1. **Explain** the significance of: widespread, mobilization, Albert Speer, kamikaze, General Hideki Tōjō, London, blitz, Dresden, Cold War, ideological.

Main Ideas
2. **Explain** how the Nazi attitude toward women changed over the course of World War II.
3. **List** the countries where bombing of heavily populated cities took place. Use a chart like the one below to make your list.

Country	City

4. **Summarize** the outcomes of the three conferences in which the Big Three (United States, Great Britain, and the Soviet Union) participated during and after World War II.

Critical Thinking
5. **The BIG Idea** **Drawing Conclusions** How did World War II affect the world balance of power? Which nations emerged from the conflict as world powers?
6. **Defending** General Hideki Tōjō argued that "the weakening of the family system would be the weakening of the nation." Is he right? Explain.
7. **Analyzing Visuals** Examine the photographs on page 649. In what ways did the nuclear blast in Hiroshima cause both immediate and long-term damage?

Writing About History
8. **Persuasive Writing** Could President Truman have dropped the atomic bombs on Japan not to end the war but to impress the Soviet Union with U.S. military power? Write an essay evaluating this hypothesis.

History ONLINE

For help with the concepts in this section of *Glencoe World History— Modern Times*, go to glencoe.com and click Study Central.

The Blitz: London's Finest Hour

In August 1940, the German air force launched a major bombing offensive against airfields and industrial targets in Great Britain. A month later, the Germans shifted their focus to civilian targets. On September 7, 1940, a thousand German warplanes rained bombs down upon London. This devastating attack marked the beginning of the London Blitz.

During air raids, underground tube stations (subway stops), like the one pictured below, were converted into bomb shelters.

Many underground shelters in London were equipped with air conditioning and first-aid stations.

Many Londoners who owned gardens sought refuge in Anderson shelters. These small structures, consisting of corrugated iron sheets, were buried four feet in the ground and then covered with soil. A single Anderson shelter could hold up to six people.

Shelters needed to accommodate large numbers of people. During an air raid, up to 1,000 Londoners crowded into the platforms, connection tunnels, and emergency stairs that comprised a tube station shelter.

SURVIVING THE BLITZ

The Germans bombed London on nearly a nightly basis between September and November 1940. Thousands of Londoners sought refuge in shelters. The Blitz caused other hardships. The destruction of factories and shops, plus hours spent in shelters, disrupted work schedules. Black-out ordinances kept all lights off after dark, causing traffic accidents. The horrific noise cost everyone much-needed sleep.

German bombs caused great destruction to the buildings of London. By the end of the Blitz, over one million homes in the city had been destroyed or damaged, creating a serious homelessness problem.

Prime Minister Winston Churchill was a symbol of British strength and determination during the Blitz.

Despite the hardships they faced, London men and women served as air-raid wardens, fire watchers, firemen, ambulance drivers, first-aid providers, and rescue workers to help their fellow citizens cope with the crisis.

Soon after the war began in September 1939, over a million Londoners, mostly mothers and children, moved to the countryside or Canada. A year later, the Blitz sparked another major evacuation of children and adults from London and other British cities.

Separated from their parents, many London children spent much of the war living with strangers in the countryside.

TURNING THE TIDE

German bombers claimed the lives of 14,000 Londoners during the Blitz, and many more were injured or left homeless. The city's morale remained strong, however. The Royal Air Force showed resolve, too, and shot down many of the attacking German bombers. In June 1941, Hitler launched his eventually disastrous campaign against the Soviet Union. Great Britain had survived its most serious threat of the war.

ANALYZING VISUALS

1. **Explaining** How did Londoners adjust to the threats created by the German bombing attacks?

2. **Analyzing** What does the London Blitz suggest about the effectiveness of bombing attacks upon a civilian population?

653

CHAPTER 19 Visual Summary

 You can study anywhere, anytime by downloading quizzes and flash cards to your PDA from glencoe.com.

THE BEGINNING of World War II

- Nazi Germany began an aggressive policy of expansion.
- After Germany invaded Poland, Britain and France declared war on Germany.
- Seeking access to natural resources, Japan seized Manchuria and North China.
- Japan launched a surprise attack on U.S. and European colonies in Southeast Asia in 1940.

GERMAN TANKS STREAM INTO POLAND, 1939

The invasion of Poland ignited the war in Europe.

ALLIED TROOPS LAND AT NORMANDY, 1944

Allies attacked Normandy from air and sea, beginning a sweep that would eventually defeat Nazi Germany.

THE COURSE of the War

- The German blitzkrieg subdued much of western and central Europe, but Germany could not defeat Britain or Russia.
- The Japanese attack at Pearl Harbor in 1941 brought the United States into the war.
- The Grand Alliance forced the unconditional surrender of the Axis Powers in 1945.
- After the war, political tensions between the United States and the Soviet Union led to the Cold War.

LIVES AFFECTED by War

- Germany and Japan forced people of conquered nations to labor for their war effort.
- Hitler's extremist racial views led to the Holocaust and death of millions.
- Civilians worked in war factories and endured shortages.
- Bombings targeted civilians as well as the military.
- Almost 20 million civilians died in the war.

NAZIS ROUND UP JEWS IN WARSAW, POLAND, 1943

Jewish children and their mothers were the first to be sent to the gas chambers.

STANDARDIZED TEST PRACTICE

TEST-TAKING TIP

When answering a test item involving a map, look at the map carefully. Pay attention to the title of the map and to the legends used to identify geographic areas. Use these clues to eliminate incorrect answer choices.

Reviewing Vocabulary

Directions: Choose the word or words that best complete the sentence.

1. Germany used a "lightning war," or _____, to gain control of Poland.

   A Luftwaffe

   B blitz

   C blitzkrieg

   D *Einsatzgruppen*

2. The period of political tensions between the United States and the Soviet Union following World War II was known as the _____.

   A Great Depression

   B Doctrine of Aggression

   C Potsdam Agreement

   D Cold War

3. _____ are restrictions intended to enforce international law.

   A Embargoes

   B Tariffs

   C Sanctions

   D Edicts

4. Hitler's Final Solution was _____ of the Jewish people.

   A genocide

   B patricide

   C suicide

   D isolationism

Reviewing Main Ideas

Directions: Choose the best answers to the following questions.

Section 1 *(pp. 620–625)*

5. What policy attempted to satisfy the reasonable demands of dissatisfied powers?

   A Easement

   B Appeasement

   C Isolationism

   D Colonization

6. What name did Japan give Manchuria?

   A Nagasaki

   B Hiroshima

   C Kimono

   D Manchukuo

Section 2 *(pp. 628–635)*

7. What event triggered the entry of the United States into World War II?

   A The blitz over London

   B The assassination of Franklin D. Roosevelt

   C The bombing of Pearl Harbor

   D The German invasion of Poland

8. In what city did Hitler lose his entire German Sixth Army?

   A Stalingrad

   B Dunkirk

   C Midway Island

   D Dresden

Need Extra Help?								
If You Missed Questions . . .	1	2	3	4	5	6	7	8
Go to Page . . .	628	650	625	640	621	624	631	633

GO ON

9. What battle in World War II is considered history's greatest naval invasion?

   A Battle of Dunkirk

   B D-Day

   C Battle of Midway

   D Battle of Kursk

Section 3 (pp. 638–643)

10. What was the name for the special strike forces who carried out the Final Solution?

    A *Kristallnacht*

    B Kamikaze

    C *Einsatzgruppen*

    D Luftwaffe

11. What economic community supposedly provided mutual benefits to Japan's occupied areas and to Japan?

    A The Greater East Asia Co-Prosperity Sphere

    B The East Asian Emporium

    C The Greater Eurasian Market

    D The Kamikaze Commerce

Section 4 (pp. 644–651)

12. What was the only country in World War II that used women in battle?

    A United States

    B Japan

    C Germany

    D Soviet Union

13. At which postwar conference did the Allies agree that war crime trials should be held?

    A Warsaw

    B Potsdam

    C Berlin

    D Versailles

Critical Thinking

Directions: Choose the best answers to the following questions.

Use the following map and your knowledge of world history to answer question 14.

German-Controlled Territory, 1943

14. How did geographic factors influence German military advances?

    A German troops had to cover long distances.

    B German supply lines were vulnerable and easily breached.

    C Colder climates created problems that the German military could not overcome.

    D The blitzkrieg relied on tanks that were most effective on flatter terrain.

15. What was the main reason for Hitler's advance into other lands?

    A He hated the French and Russians.

    B He wanted more seaports.

    C He wanted "living space" for German expansion.

    D He wanted to spread communism to all lands.

Need Extra Help?							
If You Missed Questions . . .	9	10	11	12	13	14	15
Go to Page . . .	634	640	643	645	651	628	638

GO ON

16. What was the main significance of the Nazi-Soviet Nonaggression Pact?

   A It gave Hitler the freedom to attack Poland.

   B It appeased the Western allies' fears of German aggression.

   C It postponed Japan's war with China.

   D It ended the United States's isolationist policy.

17. In reviewing the events of World War II, which item below has the events in the correct chronological order?

   A D-Day, bombing of Pearl Harbor, rescue at Dunkirk, bombing of Hiroshima

   B Rescue at Dunkirk, bombing of Pearl Harbor, D-Day, bombing of Hiroshima

   C Bombing of Pearl Harbor, D-Day, rescue at Dunkirk, bombing of Hiroshima

   D Bombing of Hiroshima, bombing of Pearl Harbor, rescue at Dunkirk, D-Day

Analyze the graph below and answer the question that follows. Base your answer on the chart and your knowledge of world history.

U.S. Unemployment Rates

Source: *Monthly Labor Review.*

18. Why did the unemployment rate rise steeply in 1932 and then plunge to below 1929 levels in 1945?

   A More people were without jobs in 1929 because of the Great Depression.

   B The unemployment rate rebounded to 10 percent in 1950.

   C The Great Depression began in 1929 and affected the economy for several years; the 1945 rate reflected that of a war economy.

   D The Cold War affected the unemployment rate of 1950.

Document-Based Questions

Directions: Analyze the document and answer the short answer questions that follow the document. Base your answers on the document and on your knowledge of world history.

Rudolf Höss, commanding officer at the Auschwitz death camp, described the experience awaiting the Jews when they arrived there:

> *"We had two SS doctors on duty at Auschwitz to examine the incoming transports of prisoners. The prisoners would be marched by one of the doctors who would make spot decisions as they walked by. Those who were fit for work were sent into the camp. Others were sent immediately to the extermination plants. Children of tender years were invariably exterminated since by reason of their youth they were unable to work. . . . At Auschwitz we fooled the victims into thinking that they were to go through a delousing process. Frequently they realized our true intentions and we sometimes had riots and difficulties due to that fact."*
>
> —Nazi Conspiracy and Aggression, vol. 6, 1946

19. What is the tone of Höss's description? What were his feelings toward the Jewish people?

20. According to Höss's description, who among the Jewish people were first sent to the extermination plants?

Extended Response

21. The Treaty of Versailles imposed harsh reparations on Germany after World War I. Hitler wanted changes. Analyze whether events leading to World War II, or even the war itself, would have occurred if England, France, and Italy had enforced the provisions of the Treaty of Versailles when Germany initially broke them.

History ONLINE

For additional test practice, use Self-Check Quizzes—Chapter 19 at **glencoe.com**.

Need Extra Help?						
If You Missed Questions . . .	16	17	18	19	20	21
Go to Page . . .	623	628	645	657	657	620

STOP

Whose House? Bauhaus!

The U.S. erects the tallest buildings. But the heights of modern architecture are being reached in Europe, by Bauhaus. Bauhaus is a design school founded in Germany in 1919. It is also the name of a revolutionary style of streamlined architecture produced by the school's teachers and students. "Bauhauses" have no ornamentation and reject the architecture of the past. This building style (examples below) may be the wave of the future. In the U.S., a few architects, such as Richard Neutra and Irving Gill, are also creating modernistic buildings, in what they call the International Style.

HEIDI JAMES/ALAMY

Tugendhat House, Brno, Czechoslovakia (1930)

Mies van der Rohe not only designed the house, he designed everything in it. He even indicated where to place the furniture. A home where you practically have to ask the architect's permission to move a chair may not be everyone's dream house.

FORESTIER YVES/CORBIS SYGMA

Bauhaus School, Dessau, Germany (1925)

Walter Gropius, the founder of Bauhaus, designed the school itself. Its flat roof reduces wind and rain damage. And it can also serve as a classroom or a garden. Many of the school's walls are glass so the classes are flooded with light. Who knew school could look this cool!

VERBATIM

❝ If you are lucky enough to have lived in Paris as a young man, then wherever you go for the rest of your life it stays with you, for Paris is a moveable feast. ❞

ERNEST HEMINGWAY,
one of many American writers who moved to Paris after World War I

❝ Beyond this day, no thinking person could fail to see what would happen. ❞

OSKAR SCHINDLER,
the German industrialist, who saved nearly 1,200 Jews who worked in his factory from being killed by the Nazis

❝ Every Communist must grasp the truth, 'Political power grows out of the barrel of a gun.' ❞

MAO ZEDONG,
leader of the Communist Party in China

❝ It is the policy of Africans to take the place of Europeans, but the real point of disagreement is as to the rate this process should proceed. The government feels this process is too fast. The people, that it is too slow. ❞

SIERRA LEONE *DAILY MAIL*,
in an article, 1936

LONDON CALLING

In 1940, Edward R. Murrow began giving Americans live, firsthand reports of what it's like to be in London during German bombing raids, called the blitz. The broadcasts have been building sympathy in the U.S. for England in its fight against the Nazis—exactly as Winston Churchill had predicted when he okayed Murrow's transmissions. Here is part of a broadcast Murrow made from London.

This is Trafalgar Square. The noise that you hear at the moment is the sound of the air raid sirens. A searchlight just burst into action off in the distance. One single beam sweeping the sky above me now. People are walking along quite quietly. We're just at the entrance of an air-raid shelter here and I must move this cable over just a bit so people can walk in. I'll let you hear the traffic and the sounds of the sirens for a moment. More searchlights coming into action. You see them reach straight up into the sky and occasionally they catch a cloud and seem to splash on the bottom of it. . . . One of the strangest sounds one can hear in London these days—or rather these dark nights—just the sound of footsteps walking along the street, like ghosts shod with steel shoes.

POPPERFOTO/ALAMY

MARY EVANS PICTURE LIBRARY/ALAMY

Tut, Tut

Curse of the pharaohs? Tosh! scoffs Howard Carter, who is alive and well. In 1922, the English archaeologist dug his way into King Tut's 3,000-year-old tomb located in Egypt's Valley of the Kings. The tomb contained treasures buried with the pharaoh. This excerpt from Carter's recent account of his discovery describes first entering the tomb.

With trembling hands I made a tiny breach in the upper left-hand corner [of the door]. Darkness and blank space, as far as an iron testing-rod could reach, showed that whatever lay beyond was empty … and then, widening the hole a little, I inserted [a] candle and peered in, Lord Carnarvon. . . . standing anxiously beside me to hear the verdict. At first I could see nothing, the hot air escaping from the chamber causing the candle flame to flicker, but presently, as my eyes grew accustomed to the light, details of the room within emerged slowly from the mist, strange animals, statues, and gold—everywhere the glint of gold. For the moment—an eternity it must have seemed to the others standing by—I was struck dumb with amazement, and when Lord Carnarvon, unable to stand the suspense any longer, inquired anxiously, "Can you see anything?" it was all I could do to get out the words, "Yes, wonderful things."

BY THE NUMBERS

250 The average length in yards of "no-man's land"—the space between the trenches of Allied and Central Powers—during World War I

70 million The number of soldiers and civilians killed in battle in World War I and World War II combined

500,000 The number of Africans who fought for France and Britain in World War II

HULTON-DEUTSCH COLLECTION/CORBIS

248 The number of miles that Gandhi, along with 78 supporters, walked in protest of Britain's salt tax and ban on Indians producing their own salt (which affects nearly everyone in India) in 1930. The 24-day march focused attention on the nation's independence movement.

6 The number of governments that ruled Chile between 1931 and 1932—a time of instability because of the Great Depression

Milestones

EMBALMED. V. I. LENIN, upon his death in 1924. The body of Lenin, the Communist leader of the Russian Revolution and first premier of the Soviet Union, has been preserved and placed on display in a mausoleum in Moscow's Red Square.

PROVED. ALBERT EINSTEIN'S THEORY OF RELATIVITY, by measurements taken during a solar eclipse in 1919. As Einstein's theory had predicted, light from distant stars bent around the sun due to gravity caused by the curving of space-time. Though scientists no longer doubt his theory, the general public remains relatively baffled.

WON. THE FIRST WORLD SOCCER TOURNAMENT, by host team Uruguay, which defeated Argentina 4 to 2, in 1930. Thirteen teams competed, but many European teams did not. They refused to make the three-week trip by boat to South America.

DESTROYED. Much of TOKYO AND YOKOHAMA by a powerful earthquake that struck the cities on September 1, 1923. The 8.3-magnitude trembler resulted in the deaths of nearly 100,000 people, with thousands more missing. Fires left hundreds of thousands of people homeless, as traditional paper and wood houses quickly burned.

CRITICAL THINKING

1. **Distinguishing Fact From Fiction** In "Whose House? Bauhaus!," can you give examples of facts and opinions?

2. **Determining Cause and Effect** How would Murrow's broadcast help Churchill's plans for drawing the United States into the war against Germany?

UNIT 5

Toward a Global Civilization
1945–Present

▶ Why It Matters

World War II can be seen as the end of European domination of the world. After the war, the Cold War rivalry between the United States and the Soviet Union forced nations to take sides. In the late 1980s, the Soviet Empire began to come apart, and the Cold War ended. World War II also undermined the colonial order in Asia and Africa. Most colonies in Asia and Africa would become independent nations.

CHAPTER 20 COLD WAR AND POSTWAR CHANGES
1945–1970

CHAPTER 21 THE CONTEMPORARY WESTERN WORLD
1970–PRESENT

CHAPTER 22 LATIN AMERICA
1945–PRESENT

CHAPTER 23 AFRICA AND THE MIDDLE EAST
1945–PRESENT

CHAPTER 24 ASIA AND THE PACIFIC
1945–PRESENT

CHAPTER 25 CHANGING GLOBAL PATTERNS

Afghan troops deploying to deal with the state of emergency in Kabul, Afghanistan, caused by the pullout of Soviet troops in 1989.

CHAPTER 20

Cold War and Postwar Changes 1945–1970

Section 1 Development of the Cold War

Section 2 The Soviet Union and Eastern Europe

Section 3 Western Europe and North America

MAKING CONNECTIONS

How can a nation defend itself in the nuclear age?

Cold War tensions due to the arms race and the Cuban missile crisis made Americans feel vulnerable to nuclear attack. Families built bomb shelters and children practiced "duck-and-cover" at school, as shown in the photo. In this chapter you will learn how political tensions between countries can pose a real threat of disaster.

- Why was the Cuban missile crisis such a threat to the United States?
- How does terrorism pose a threat today?

EUROPE,
THE SOVIET UNION,
AND THE UNITED STATES ▶

1945
Cold War begins

1947
President Truman establishes Truman Doctrine

1957
Soviets launch *Sputnik I*

1945	1950	1955

THE WORLD ▶

1947
India and Pakistan become independent nations

1956
Suez War begins in Egypt

1961
Berlin Wall is
constructed

1963
Martin Luther King,
Jr. leads march
on Washington

1960 — 1965 — 1970

1962
Arrest of African leader
Nelson Mandela

FOLDABLES™
Study Organizer

Causes | Effects
Cold War

**Identifying Cause
and Effect** Create
and use this Two-Tab Book to list the
causes and effects of the Cold War. For
each cause that you list, identify two or
more effects. List these in the Foldable in
a way so that you can easily identify the
effects that resulted from each cause.

History ✺ **ONLINE**

Chapter Overview—Visit glencoe.com to preview Chapter 20.

Development of the Cold War

GUIDE TO READING

The BIG Idea
Competition Among Countries
A period of conflict known as the Cold War developed between the United States and the Soviet Union after 1945, dividing Europe.

Content Vocabulary
- satellite states (p. 666)
- policy of containment (p. 666)
- arms race (p. 667)
- deterrence (p. 669)
- domino theory (p. 671)

Academic Vocabulary
- liberated (p. 664)
- nuclear (p. 667)

People, Places, and Events
- Truman Doctrine (p. 665)
- Dean Acheson (p. 666)
- Marshall Plan (p. 666)
- Berlin (p. 666)
- Federal Republic of Germany (p. 666)
- German Democratic Republic (p. 666)
- NATO (p. 668)
- Warsaw Pact (p. 668)
- SEATO (p. 669)
- CENTO (p. 669)
- Nikita Khrushchev (p. 669)

Reading Strategy
Summarizing As you read, use a table like the one below to list the American presidents who held office during this period and the major Cold War events that took place during their administrations.

President	Major Event

After World War II, the United States and the Soviet Union became fierce political rivals. Fearing the spread of communism in Europe, the United States began to send aid to countries that might otherwise have turned to communism. And in Cuba, the United States and the Soviet Union had a standoff that brought the world very close to nuclear war.

Confrontation of the Superpowers

MAIN IDEA After World War II, the United States and Soviet Union became fierce rivals.

HISTORY & YOU Have you ever had a rival? Read to learn how the rivalry between the United States and Soviet Union began.

Once the Axis Powers were defeated, the differences between the United States and the Soviet Union became clear. Stalin still feared the capitalist West, and U.S. as well as other Western leaders continued to fear communism. It should not surprise us that two such different systems would come into conflict.

For security reasons, the Soviet government refused to give up control of Eastern Europe after World War II. Nor were American leaders willing to give up the power and prestige the United States had gained throughout the world. Between 1945 and 1949, a number of events led these two superpowers (countries whose military power is combined with political influence) into conflict. As tensions increased, each side formed alliances. In 1949 the United States and its European allies formed the North Atlantic Treaty Organization (NATO). In 1955 the Soviet Union and its European allies began the Warsaw Pact.

Rivalry in Europe

Eastern Europe was the first area of disagreement. The United States and Great Britain believed that the **liberated** nations of Eastern Europe should freely determine their own governments. Stalin, fearful that these nations would be anti-Soviet if they were permitted free elections, opposed the West's plans. Having freed Eastern Europe from the Nazis, the Soviet army stayed in the conquered areas.

A civil war in Greece created another area of conflict between the superpowers. The Communist People's Liberation Army and anti-Communist forces supported by Great Britain fought for control of Greece in 1946. However, Britain had its own economic problems, which caused it to withdraw its aid from Greece.

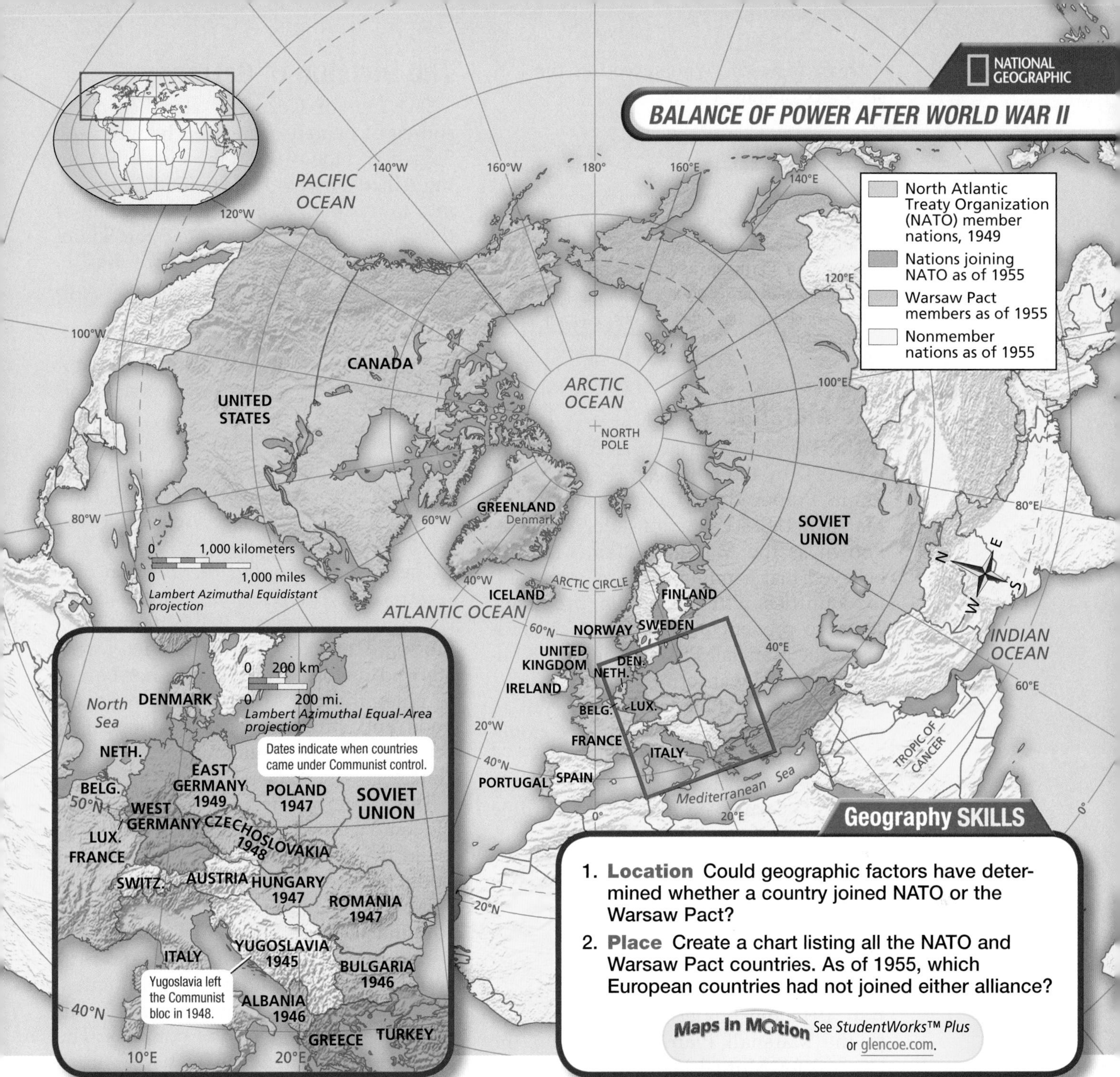
NATIONAL GEOGRAPHIC
BALANCE OF POWER AFTER WORLD WAR II
North Atlantic Treaty Organization (NATO) member nations, 1949
Nations joining NATO as of 1955
Warsaw Pact members as of 1955
Nonmember nations as of 1955
PACIFIC OCEAN
ARCTIC OCEAN
NORTH POLE
ATLANTIC OCEAN
INDIAN OCEAN
CANADA
UNITED STATES
GREENLAND Denmark
ICELAND
SOVIET UNION
FINLAND
NORWAY
SWEDEN
UNITED KINGDOM
IRELAND
DEN.
NETH.
BELG.
LUX.
FRANCE
PORTUGAL
SPAIN
ITALY
Mediterranean Sea
ARCTIC CIRCLE
TROPIC OF CANCER
0 1,000 kilometers
0 1,000 miles
Lambert Azimuthal Equidistant projection
140°W
160°W
180°
160°E
140°E
120°W
120°E
100°W
100°E
80°W
80°E
60°W
40°W
60°N
40°E
60°E
20°W
40°N
20°E
0°
20°N
North Sea
DENMARK
0 200 km
0 200 mi.
Lambert Azimuthal Equal-Area projection
Dates indicate when countries came under Communist control.
NETH.
BELG.
EAST GERMANY 1949
POLAND 1947
SOVIET UNION
50°N
WEST GERMANY
CZECHOSLOVAKIA 1948
LUX.
FRANCE
SWITZ.
AUSTRIA
HUNGARY 1947
ROMANIA 1947
ITALY
YUGOSLAVIA 1945
BULGARIA 1946
Yugoslavia left the Communist bloc in 1948.
ALBANIA 1946
40°N
GREECE
TURKEY
10°E
20°E

Geography SKILLS

1. **Location** Could geographic factors have determined whether a country joined NATO or the Warsaw Pact?
2. **Place** Create a chart listing all the NATO and Warsaw Pact countries. As of 1955, which European countries had not joined either alliance?

Maps In MOtion See *StudentWorks™ Plus* or glencoe.com.

The Truman Doctrine

President Harry S. Truman of the United States was alarmed by the British withdrawal and the possibility of Soviet expansion into the eastern Mediterranean. Addressing a joint session of Congress on March 12, 1947, Truman asked for $400 million in aid for Greece and Turkey. In requesting this aid, Truman established a policy known as the **Truman Doctrine.** He declared, "It must be the policy of the United States to support free peoples who are resisting attempted subjugation by armed minorities or by outside pressures."

Although Truman's request was for Greece and Turkey, the Truman Doctrine stated that the United States would also provide such aid to other countries threatened by Communist expansion. If the Soviet expansion was not stopped in Greece and Turkey, the Truman argument ran, then the United States would have to face the spread of communism.

Dean Acheson, who served as the U.S. secretary of state, explained:

PRIMARY SOURCE

"Like apples in a barrel infected by disease, the corruption of Greece would infect Iran and all the East . . . likewise Africa, Italy, France. . . . Not since Rome and Carthage had there been such a polarization of power on this earth."

—Quoted in *The Fifteen Weeks (February 21– June 5, 1947),* 2nd ed., Joseph M. Jones, 1964

The Marshall Plan

The Truman Doctrine was followed in June 1947 by the European Recovery Program. Proposed by General George C. Marshall, U.S. secretary of state, it is better known as the **Marshall Plan.** Marshall believed that communism was successful in countries with economic problems. Thus, to prevent the spread of communism, the Marshall Plan provided $13 billion to rebuild war-torn Europe.

The Marshall Plan was not meant to exclude the Soviet Union or its economically and politically dependent Eastern European **satellite states.** Those states refused to participate, however. According to the Soviet view, the Marshall Plan guaranteed "American loans in return for the relinquishing by the European states of their economic and later also their political independence." The Soviets saw the Marshall Plan as an attempt to buy the support of countries.

In 1949 the Soviet Union responded to the Marshall Plan by founding the Council for Mutual Economic Assistance (COMECON) for the economic cooperation of the Eastern European states. COMECON largely failed, however, because the Soviet Union was unable to provide much financial aid.

By 1947, the split in Europe between the United States and the Soviet Union had become a fact of life. In July 1947, George Kennan, a well-known U.S. diplomat with much knowledge of Soviet affairs, argued for a **policy of containment** to keep communism within its existing boundaries and prevent further Soviet aggressive moves. Containment became U.S. policy.

The Division of Germany

The fate of Germany also became a source of heated contention between the Soviets and the West. At the end of the war, the Allied Powers had divided Germany into four zones, each occupied by one of the Allies—the United States, the Soviet Union, Great Britain, and France. **Berlin,** located deep inside the Soviet zone, was also divided into four zones.

The foreign ministers of the four occupying powers met repeatedly in an attempt to arrive at a final peace treaty with Germany but had little success. By February 1948, Great Britain, France, and the United States were making plans to unify the three Western sections of Germany (and Berlin) and create a West German government.

The Soviets opposed the creation of a separate West German state. They attempted to prevent it by mounting a blockade of West Berlin. Soviet forces allowed neither trucks, trains, nor barges to enter the city's three Western zones. Food and supplies could no longer get through to the 2.5 million people in these zones.

The Western powers faced a dilemma. No one wanted another war, but how could the people in the Western zones of Berlin be kept alive when the whole city was blockaded inside the Soviet zone? The solution was the Berlin Airlift—supplies would be flown in by American and British airplanes. For more than 10 months, more than 200,000 flights carried 2.3 million tons (1.4 million t) of supplies. The Soviets, who wanted to avoid war as much as the Western powers, finally gave in and lifted the blockade in May 1949.

In September 1949, the **Federal Republic of Germany,** or West Germany, was formally created. Its capital was Bonn. Less than a month later, a separate East German state, the **German Democratic Republic,** was set up by the Soviets. East Berlin became its capital. Berlin was now divided into two parts, a reminder of the division of West and East.

✓ **Reading Check** **Describing** What was the intention of the Marshall Plan?

The Cold War Spreads

MAIN IDEA As Cold War tensions increased, nations were forced to choose to support the Soviet Union or the United States.

HISTORY & YOU Have you ever tried to gain supporters to help you win an argument? Read to learn how Communist and anti-Communist alliances formed as the Cold War spread.

In 1949 Chiang Kai-shek finally lost control of China, and the Communist Mao Zedong announced the formation of the People's Republic of China. Zedong's victory strengthened U.S. fears about the spread of communism. The Soviet Union also exploded its first atomic bomb in 1949.

The Arms Race

All too soon, the United States and the Soviet Union were becoming involved in a growing **arms race**, in which both countries built up their armies and weapons. **Nuclear** weapons became increasingly destructive as each superpower raced to build deadlier bombs.

Both sides came to believe that an arsenal of nuclear weapons would actually prevent war. They believed that if one nation attacked with nuclear weapons, the other nation would still be able to respond.

INFOGRAPHICS   PRIMARY SOURCE

The Berlin Airlift

On the morning of June 24, 1948, the Soviet Union cut off all rail, road, and water routes into West Berlin in an attempt to force the Allies to abandon the city. It was the first major crisis of the Cold War.

Lucius Clay, the military governor of the U.S. sector of West Germany, warned, "When Berlin falls, West Germany will be next." Military retaliation was unthinkable, however. The Soviet Union's armed forces were stronger than the combined forces of the West.

On July 1, the United States and Great Britain began sending cargo planes filled with food and supplies to the people of West Berlin. By winter, a plane was arriving every three minutes, 24 hours a day, delivering not just food but coal, newsprint—and even feed for the animals of the Berlin zoo. The Berlin Airlift was a success. The Soviets admitted defeat and lifted the blockade on May 12, 1949.

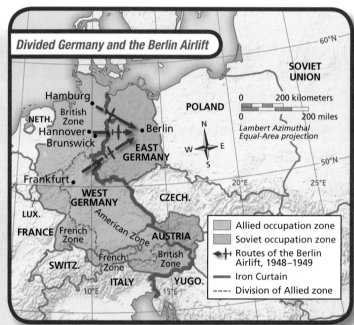

Divided Germany and the Berlin Airlift

- Allied occupation zone
- Soviet occupation zone
- ◄━┼ Routes of the Berlin Airlift, 1948–1949
- —— Iron Curtain
- - - - Division of Allied zone

Lambert Azimuthal Equal-Area projection

German children cheer an American cargo plane airlifting food and supplies to Berlin in 1948.

DOCUMENT-BASED QUESTIONS

1. **Analyzing Visuals** Why could the Allies not deliver food to West Berlin by land?
2. **Making Inferences** Why was the fate of Berlin important to the Allies and the Soviets?

TURNING POINT — THE SPREAD OF THE COLD WAR

In the decades after World War II, the Cold War between the United States and the Soviet Union spread, creating military alliances and defining the postwar era. Each superpower used military and economic aid to win the support of European nations. The United States also built alliances in Asia to contain the combined Communist threat of the Soviet Union and China.

In addition to these alliances, "hot" wars broke out in Asia. Korea and Vietnam were both divided between a Communist north and a free south. As conflicts arose there, the Soviet Union and the United States sent troops to prevent the other side from expanding.

In this Korean War photo, generals from North Korea and China are leaving a UN meeting protected by soldiers.

MAJOR DEVELOPMENTS IN THE COLD WAR, 1947–1973

1947	Truman Doctrine provides aid to Greece and Turkey.
	Marshall Plan provides aid to rebuild Europe after the war.
1948	Berlin Airlift begins.
1949	United States and its European allies form NATO.
	Communist leader Mao Zedong rises to power in China.
	Soviet Union explodes its first nuclear bomb.
1950–1953	United States, Soviet Union, and China intervene in Korean War.
1954	SEATO forms to prevent communism from spreading in Asia.
1955	Soviet Union and its European allies form the Warsaw Pact.
1959	CENTO forms to prevent Soviet Union from expanding to the south.
1961	Soviet Union builds the Berlin Wall.
1962	Cuban Missile Crisis brings the Soviet Union and the United States to the brink of nuclear war.
1964–1973	United States and Soviet Union intervene in Vietnam War; Vietnam falls to communism.

CRITICAL THINKING SKILLS

1. **Summarizing** What impact did the conflict between the superpowers have on the rest of the world?
2. **Analyzing** Why are the post–World War II years considered a turning point?

According to this policy, neither side could risk using their massive supplies of weapons for fear that the other side would retaliate and devastate the attacker.

New Military Alliances

The search for security during the Cold War led to the formation of new military alliances. The North Atlantic Treaty Organization (**NATO**) was formed in April 1949 when Belgium, Luxembourg, France, the Netherlands, Great Britain, Italy, Denmark, Norway, Portugal, and Iceland signed a treaty with the United States and Canada. All the powers agreed to provide mutual help if any one of them was attacked. A few years later, West Germany, Turkey, and Greece also joined.

In 1955 the Soviet Union joined with Albania, Bulgaria, Czechoslovakia, East Germany, Hungary, Poland, and Romania in a formal military alliance known as the **Warsaw Pact.** Now, Europe was once again divided into hostile alliance systems, just as it had been before World War I.

New military alliances spread to the rest of the world after the United States became involved in the Korean War (discussed in Chapter 24). The war began in 1950 as an attempt by the Communist government of North Korea, which was allied with the Soviet Union, to take over South Korea. The Korean War confirmed American fears of Communist expansion. More determined than ever to contain Soviet power, the United States extended its military alliances around the world.

To stem Soviet aggression in the East, the United States, Great Britain, France, Pakistan, Thailand, the Philippines, Australia, and New Zealand formed the Southeast Asia Treaty Organization **(SEATO).** The Central Treaty Organization **(CENTO),** which included Turkey, Iraq, Iran, Pakistan, Great Britain, and the United States, was meant to prevent the Soviet Union from expanding to the south. By the mid-1950s, the United States found itself in military alliances with 42 states around the world.

However strongly allied with other nations, the United States feared that the Soviet Union was gaining ground in the arms race. The Soviet Union had set off its first atomic bomb in 1949. In the early 1950s, both the Soviet Union and the United States developed the even more deadly hydrogen bomb. By the mid-1950s, both had intercontinental ballistic missiles (ICBMs) capable of sending bombs anywhere.

Both the United States and the Soviet Union now worked to build up huge arsenals of nuclear weapons. The search for security soon took the form of **deterrence.** This policy held that huge arsenals of nuclear weapons on both sides prevented war. The belief was that neither side would launch a nuclear attack, because both knew that the other side would be able to strike back with devastating power.

In 1957 the Soviets sent *Sputnik I,* the first human-made space satellite, to orbit Earth. New fears seized the American public. Did the Soviet Union have a massive lead in building missiles? Was there a "missile gap" between the United States and the Soviet Union?

A Wall in Berlin

Nikita Khrushchev (kroosh•CHAWF), who emerged as the new leader of the Soviet Union in 1955, tried to take advantage of the American concern over missiles to solve the problem of West Berlin. West Berlin remained a "Western island" of prosperity in the midst of the relatively poverty-stricken East Germany. Many East Germans, tired of Communist repression, managed to escape East Germany by fleeing through West Berlin.

Khrushchev realized the need to stop the flow of refugees from East Germany through West Berlin. In August 1961, the East German government began to build a wall separating West Berlin from East Berlin. Eventually it became a massive barrier guarded by barbed wire, floodlights, machine-gun towers, minefields, and vicious dog patrols. The Berlin Wall became a striking symbol of the division between the two superpowers.

The Cuban Missile Crisis

During the administration of John F. Kennedy, the Cold War confrontation between the United States and the Soviet Union reached frightening levels. In 1959 a left-wing revolutionary named Fidel Castro overthrew the Cuban dictator Fulgencio Batista and set up a Soviet-supported totalitarian regime in Cuba (see Chapter 29). Having a socialist regime with Communist contacts so close to the mainland was considered a threat to the security of the United States.

President Kennedy feared that if he moved openly against Castro, then the Soviets might retaliate by moving against Berlin. As a result, the stage might be set for the two superpowers to engage in a nuclear war.

For months, Kennedy considered alternatives. He finally approved a plan that the CIA had proposed. Exiled Cuban fighters would invade Cuba at the Bay of Pigs, on the Playa Girón and Playa Larga beaches. The purpose of the invasion was to cause a revolt against Castro.

The invasion was a disaster. One adviser informed Kennedy:

The Cuban Missile Crisis

Letter from Nikita Khrushchev to President John F. Kennedy, October 28, 1962:

"I appreciate your assurance that the United States will not invade Cuba. Hence, we have ordered our officers to stop building bases, dismantle the equipment, and send it back home.

We must not allow the situation to deteriorate, (but) eliminate hotbeds of tension, and we must see to it that no other conflicts occur which might lead to a world nuclear war."

DOCUMENT-BASED QUESTIONS

This American political cartoon was published on October 30, 1962. Two days earlier Nikita Khrushchev had agreed to the removal of Soviet missiles from Cuba.

1. **Explaining** What is Khrushchev preparing to do, and what does his action symbolize?
2. **Identifying Points of View** Look at the caption of the cartoon. What point is the cartoonist making about the Cuban missile crisis?

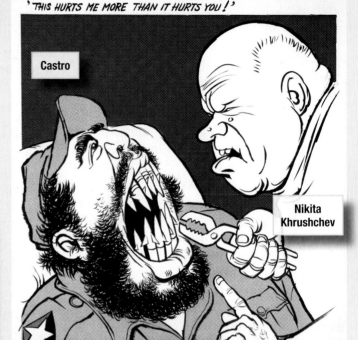

'THIS HURTS ME MORE THAN IT HURTS YOU!'

Castro

Nikita Khrushchev

Ed Valtman '62

Fidel Castro's teeth look like missiles.

PRIMARY SOURCE

"[T]he situation in Cuba is not a bit good. The Cuban armed forces are stronger, the popular response is weaker, and our tactical position is feebler than we had hoped. Tanks have done in one beachhead, and the position is precarious at the others."

—quote from an adviser to Kennedy

The invasion began on Sunday, April 16, 1961. By Wednesday, the exiled fighters began surrendering. One hundred and fourteen died; the rest were captured by Castro's troops.

After the Bay of Pigs, the Soviet Union sent advisers to Cuba. Then, in 1962, Khrushchev began to place nuclear missiles in Cuba. The missiles were meant to counteract U.S. nuclear weapons placed in Turkey, a country within easy range of the Soviet Union. Khrushchev said:

PRIMARY SOURCE

"Your rockets are in Turkey. You are worried by Cuba . . . because it is 90 miles from the American coast. But Turkey is next to us."

—Quoted in *Europe since 1945: An Introduction*, Peter Lane, 1985

The United States was not willing to allow nuclear weapons within such close striking distance of its mainland. In October 1962, Kennedy found out that Soviet ships carrying missiles were heading to Cuba. He decided to blockade Cuba to prevent the fleet from reaching its destination. This approach gave each side time to find a peaceful solution. Khrushchev agreed to turn back the fleet and remove Soviet missiles from Cuba if Kennedy pledged not to invade Cuba. Kennedy quickly agreed.

The Cuban missile crisis seemed to bring the world frighteningly close to nuclear war. Indeed, in 1992 a high-ranking Soviet officer revealed that short-range rockets armed with nuclear devices would have been used against U.S. troops if the United States had invaded Cuba, an option that Kennedy fortunately had rejected. The realization that the world might have been destroyed in a few days had a profound influence on both sides. A hotline communications system between Moscow and Washington, D.C., was installed in 1963. The two superpowers could now communicate quickly in times of crisis.

Vietnam and the Domino Theory

By that time, the United States had been drawn into a new struggle that had an important impact on the Cold War—the Vietnam War (see Chapter 24). In 1964, under President Lyndon B. Johnson, increasing numbers of U.S. troops were sent to Vietnam. Their purpose was to keep the Communist regime of North Vietnam from invading and gaining control of South Vietnam.

U.S. policy makers saw the conflict in terms of a **domino theory.** If the Communists succeeded in South Vietnam, the argument went, other countries in Asia would also fall (like dominoes) to communism.

Despite the massive superiority in equipment and firepower of the American forces, the United States failed to defeat the North Vietnamese. The growing number of American troops in Vietnam soon produced an antiwar movement in the United States, especially among college students of draft age. The mounting destruction of the conflict, seen on television, also turned American public opinion against the war.

President Johnson, condemned for his handling of the costly and indecisive war, decided not to run for reelection. Former vice president Richard M. Nixon won the election with his pledge to stop the war and bring the American people together. Ending the war was difficult, and Nixon's administration was besieged by antiwar forces.

Finally, in 1973 President Nixon reached an agreement with North Vietnam that allowed the United States to withdraw its forces. Within two years after the American withdrawal, Vietnam had been forcibly reunited by Communist armies from the North.

Despite the success of the North Vietnamese Communists, the domino theory proved unfounded. A split between Communist China and the Soviet Union put an end to the Western idea that there was a single form of communism directed by Moscow. Under President Nixon, American relations with China were resumed. New nations in Southeast Asia managed to avoid Communist governments.

Above all, Vietnam helped show the limitations of American power. By the end of the Vietnam War, a new era in American-Soviet relations had begun to emerge.

✓ Reading Check **Identifying** Name the military alliances formed during the Cold War.

Vocabulary

1. **Explain** the significance of: liberated, Truman Doctrine, Dean Acheson, Marshall Plan, satellite states, policy of containment, Berlin, Federal Republic of Germany, German Democratic Republic, arms race, nuclear, NATO, Warsaw Pact, SEATO, CENTO, deterrence, Nikita Khrushchev, domino theory.

Main Ideas

2. **Identify** the purpose of the Truman Doctrine.

3. **List** the countries in the military alliances formed during the Cold War. Use a table like the one below to make your list.

Alliance	Countries

4. **Explain** how television coverage affected the Vietnam War.

Critical Thinking

5. **The BIG Idea** **Evaluating** In your opinion, why did the United States assume global responsibility for containing communism?

6. **Making Connections** How did the Cold War confrontations affect the decision of the United States to move against Fidel Castro in Cuba? What was the outcome of that decision?

7. **Analyzing Visuals** Examine the photograph on page 667. What side of the conflict do you think the photographer supported? Explain your answer.

Writing About History

8. **Informative Writing** Imagine that you are a resident of Berlin in 1948. Write a letter to a friend living in another part of Germany explaining what is happening in Berlin and your reaction to the actions of the foreign governments involved.

History ONLINE

For help with the concepts in this section of *Glencoe World History—Modern Times*, go to glencoe.com and click Study Central.

GERMANY, 1950–1961

SWEDEN

DENMARK

North Sea

Baltic Sea

55°N

NETHERLANDS

WEST GERMANY

Berlin

EAST GERMANY

Elbe River

Oder River

POLAND

BELGIUM

Rhine River

Bonn

50°N

CZECHOLOVAKIA

LUXEMBOURG

FRANCE

Danube River

200 kilometers

200 miles

Lambert Conformal Conic projection

5°E   10°E   15°E

SWITZERLAND

AUSTRIA

HUNGARY

◄ August 13, 1961: East German soldiers set up barbed wire barriers to separate the Soviet sector from the rest of Berlin. West Berliners watch.

Berlin   EAST GERMANY

French Sector

British Sector

American Sector

Soviet Sector

Checkpoint Charlie (Foreigners and diplomats only)

Checkpoint Heinrich Heine Strasse (West German citizens only)

Metal supports hold barbed wire.

Steel tank traps stop tanks and other vehicles from crossing field.

▲ In December 1961, East German police narrowed or closed checkpoints at many border crossings between East and West Berlin.

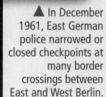

◄ October 1961: The Soviets and East Germans deny the right of a U.S. military officer to travel freely between East and West Berlin. For several hours U.S. and Soviet tanks face off against each other at Checkpoint Charlie.

THE BERLIN WALL

East German Flight After World War II from 1949 to 1961, about 2.5 million people fled East Germany. Most left to escape Communist rule, fearing growing economic hardships and political repression. Many emigrants were doctors, engineers, teachers, and other professionals. By August 1961 over 10,000 East Germans had fled in a single week. West Berlin was the main escape route, especially for the 60,000 East Berliners who worked in West Berlin. As the population loss began to cause economic problems, the East German government took action.

The Wall Goes Up On August 13, 1961, East German leaders ordered streets torn up and temporary roadblocks built. They halted all road traffic and train service between East and West Berlin and cut most telephone lines linking the divided city. The thousands of East Berliners who worked in West Berlin had to give up their jobs.

Work began at once on a permanent concrete block wall 15-feet high topped with barbed wire. Hundreds of watchtowers lined the wall, which stretched 28 miles through the city. Another 75-mile-long section of wall separated West Berlin from the surrounding East German countryside. To reach the wall, East Berliners had to cross a wide open area, often called the "death strip." Guards had orders to shoot anyone seen there. Close to 200 people died trying to escape.

A Changed City The Berlin Wall cut through almost two hundred streets as well as dozens of rail lines. Workers bricked over windows and doors of houses and churches and bulldozed parks near the wall. Until its fall 28 years later, the wall greatly affected both the land and people of Berlin.

Geography SKILLS

1. **Movement** Why did the East Germans extend the wall all the way around West Berlin as well as through the middle of the city?

2. **Movement** How did the separation of East and West Berlin by the wall affect the economic life of the city?

The Soviet Union and Eastern Europe

GUIDE TO READING

The BIG Idea
Self-Determination The Soviet Union faced revolts and protests in its attempt to gain and maintain control over Eastern Europe.

Content Vocabulary
- heavy industry *(p. 674)*
- de-Stalinization *(p. 675)*

Academic Vocabulary
- enhanced *(p. 674)*   • sole *(p. 674)*

People and Places
- Soviet Union *(p. 674)*   • Hungary *(p. 677)*
- Alexander
  Solzhenitsyn *(p. 675)*   • Czechoslovakia *(p. 677)*
- Albania *(p. 676)*   • Imre Nagy *(p. 677)*
- Yugoslavia *(p. 676)*   • Aleksandr Dubček *(p. 677)*
- Tito *(p. 676)*
- Poland *(p. 677)*

Reading Strategy
Categorizing Information As you read, use a diagram like the one below to identify how the Soviet Union carried out Communist policies.

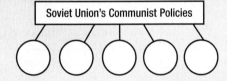

Soviet Union's Communist Policies

Stalin was a repressive leader who wanted to bring all of Eastern Europe under Soviet control. Many Communist countries came under Soviet control during this era, including Poland, Hungary, and Czechoslovakia. Albania and Yugoslavia remained independent. After Stalin's death, Nikita Khrushchev denounced the most brutal policies of the Stalin regime.

Postwar Soviet Leaders

MAIN IDEA The Soviet Union recovered rapidly after World War II, but it could not maintain high levels of industrial production.

HISTORY & YOU In a democracy, does new leadership mean a change in daily life? Read to learn how Stalin's death dramatically altered the Soviet Union.

World War II devastated the **Soviet Union.** To create a new industrial base, Stalin returned to the method that he had used in the 1930s. Soviet workers were expected to produce goods for export with little in return for themselves. The incoming capital from abroad could then be used to buy machinery and Western technology.

Economic recovery in the Soviet Union was spectacular in some respects. By 1950, Russian industrial production surpassed prewar levels by 40 percent. New power plants, canals, and giant factories were built. **Heavy industry** (the manufacture of machines and equipment for factories and mines) increased, chiefly for military benefit. The hydrogen bomb in 1953 and the first space satellite, *Sputnik I,* in 1957 **enhanced** the Soviet Union's reputation as a world power.

Yet the Soviet people were shortchanged. The production of consumer goods did not increase as much as heavy industry, and there was a housing shortage. As a British official in Moscow reported, "Every room is both a living room by day and a bedroom by night."

The Reign of Stalin

Stalin was the undisputed master of the Soviet Union. He distrusted competitors, exercised **sole** power, and had little respect for other Communist Party leaders. He is reported to have said to members of his inner circle in 1952, "You are as blind as kittens. What would you do without me?"

Stalin's suspicions added to the regime's increasing repression. In 1946 the government ordered all literary and scientific work to conform to the state's political needs. Along with this anti-

A Comparison of Market and Command Economics

Stalin's Soviet Union had a completely different economic system than that of Western Europe and the United States. Communist economies operate on the command system. This means the government makes all decisions about production—what will be produced, how much, how, and for whom. Command economies often focus either on heavy industry—as was the case in Stalin's Soviet Union—or on producing goods for export.

Capitalist economies, on the other hand, operate on the free market system, in which the means of production (such as factories) are owned by private citizens. Under capitalism, private owners and businesses invest their money in the hope of making a profit.

COMPARISON OF MARKET AND COMMAND ECONOMIES

	Market Economy (Capitalism)	Command Economy (Communism)
Ownership	Private ownership of property, means of production	Government control of property, means of production
Control	Private individuals and businesses make economic decisions, with little government intervention	Government makes all economic decisions
Market Forces	Supply and demand of goods	Government planning

DOCUMENT-BASED QUESTIONS

This 1951 Soviet propaganda poster is titled "Glory to Stalin, the great designer of Communism."

1. **Contrasting** What is the main difference between a command economy and a market economy?

2. **Analyzing** How does the poster and its title illustrate a command economy?

---

intellectual campaign came political terror. The threat of more purges in 1953 disappeared when Stalin died on March 5, 1955.

The Khrushchev Era

A group of leaders succeeded Stalin. However, the new general secretary of the Communist Party, Nikita Khrushchev, soon emerged as the chief Soviet policy maker. Once in power, Khrushchev took steps to undo some of the worst features of Stalin's regime.

At the Twentieth Congress of the Communist Party in 1956, Khrushchev condemned Stalin for his "administrative violence, mass repression, and terror." The process of eliminating the more ruthless policies of Stalin became known as **de-Stalinization.**

Khrushchev loosened government controls on literary and artistic works. In 1962, for example, he allowed the publication of *One Day in the Life of Ivan Denisovich*. This novel, written by **Aleksandr Solzhenitsyn** (SOHL•zhuh• NEET•suhn), is a grim portrayal of life in a Siberian labor camp.

History ONLINE

Student Web Activity—
Visit glencoe.com and complete the activity on the Cold War.

Many Soviets identified with Ivan as a symbol of the suffering endured under Stalin.

Khrushchev also tried to place more emphasis on producing consumer goods. He attempted to increase agricultural output by growing corn and cultivating vast lands east of the Ural Mountains. The attempt was not successful and damaged Khrushchev's reputation within the party. This failure, combined with increased military spending, hurt the Soviet economy. The industrial growth rate, which had soared in the early 1950s, now declined sharply from 13 percent in 1953 to 7.5 percent in 1964.

Foreign policy failures also damaged Khrushchev's reputation among his colleagues. His rash plan to place missiles in Cuba was the final straw. While he was away on vacation in 1964, a special meeting of the Soviet leaders voted him out of office (because of "deteriorating health") and forced him into retirement.

✓ **Reading Check** **Explaining** Why did the Soviet leaders vote Khrushchev out of power?

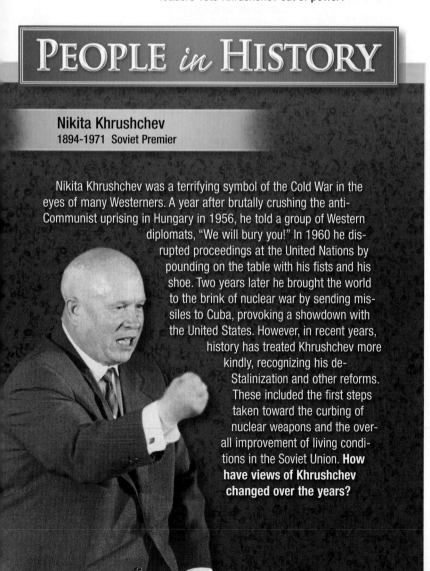

PEOPLE in HISTORY

Nikita Khrushchev
1894-1971 Soviet Premier

Nikita Khrushchev was a terrifying symbol of the Cold War in the eyes of many Westerners. A year after brutally crushing the anti-Communist uprising in Hungary in 1956, he told a group of Western diplomats, "We will bury you!" In 1960 he disrupted proceedings at the United Nations by pounding on the table with his fists and his shoe. Two years later he brought the world to the brink of nuclear war by sending missiles to Cuba, provoking a showdown with the United States. However, in recent years, history has treated Khrushchev more kindly, recognizing his de-Stalinization and other reforms. These included the first steps taken toward the curbing of nuclear weapons and the overall improvement of living conditions in the Soviet Union. **How have views of Khrushchev changed over the years?**

Eastern Europe

MAIN IDEA After World War II, Soviet control of Eastern Europe became firmly entrenched.

HISTORY & YOU During the age of imperialism, European powers controlled their colonial peoples in a number of ways. Read to learn how the Soviet Union maintained tight control over Eastern Europe.

At the end of World War II, Soviet military forces occupied all of Eastern Europe and the Balkans (except for Greece, Albania, and Yugoslavia). All of the occupied states came under Soviet control.

Communist Patterns of Control

The timetable of the Soviet takeover varied from country to country. Between 1945 and 1947, Soviet-controlled Communist governments became firmly entrenched in East Germany, Bulgaria, Romania, Poland, and Hungary. In Czechoslovakia, where there was a tradition of democracy and a multi-party system, the Soviets did not seize control of the government until 1948. At that time they dissolved all but the Communist Party.

Albania and Yugoslavia were exceptions to this pattern of Soviet dominance. During the war, both countries had strong Communist movements that resisted the Nazis. After the war, local Communist parties took control. The Stalinist-type regime in **Albania** grew more and more independent of the Soviet Union.

In **Yugoslavia,** Josip Broz, known as **Tito,** had led the Communist resistance movement. After the war, he created an independent Communist state in Yugoslavia. Stalin had hoped to control Yugoslavia, just as he controlled other Eastern European countries. Tito, however, refused to give in to Stalin's demands.

Tito gained the people's support by portraying the struggle as one of Yugoslav national freedom. Tito ruled Yugoslavia until his death in 1980. Although Yugoslavia had a Communist government, it was not a Soviet satellite state.

Between 1948 and Stalin's death in 1953, the Eastern European satellite states, directed by the Soviet Union, followed

Stalin's example. They instituted Soviet-type five-year plans with emphasis on heavy industry rather than consumer goods. They collectivized agriculture, eliminated all noncommunist parties, and set up the institutions of repression—secret police and military forces.

Revolts Against Communism

Communism did not develop deep roots among the peoples of Eastern Europe. Moreover, the Soviets exploited Eastern Europe economically for their own benefit and made living conditions harsh for most people.

After Stalin's death, many Eastern European states began to pursue a new course. In the late 1950s and 1960s, however, the Soviet Union made it clear—especially in **Poland, Hungary,** and **Czechoslovakia**—that it would not allow its Eastern European satellites to become independent of Soviet control.

In 1956, when protests erupted in Poland, the Polish Communist Party adopted a series of reforms and elected Władysław Gomułka as first secretary. Gomułka declared that Poland had the right to follow its own socialist path. However, the Poles pledged to remain loyal to the Warsaw Pact.

Unrest in Hungary, combined with economic difficulties, led to calls for revolt. **Imre Nagy,** the Hungarian leader, declared Hungary a free nation on November 1, 1956. He promised free elections, which could have meant the end of Communist rule in Hungary. Yet Khrushchev did not allow Hungary to be free. Three days after Nagy's declaration, the Soviet Army attacked Budapest, and the Soviets reestablished control. Nagy was seized by the Soviet military and executed two years later.

The situation in Czechoslovakia in the 1950s was different. Stalin had placed Antonín Novotný in power in 1953. By the late 1960s, however, Novotný had alienated many members of his own party and Czechoslovakia's writers. A writers' rebellion, which encouraged the people to take control of their own lives, led to Novotný's resignation in 1968.

Alexander Dubček (DOOB•chehk), first secretary of the Communist Party, introduced a number of reforms in 1968, including freedom of speech and press and freedom to travel abroad. He relaxed censorship and began to pursue an independent foreign policy. He also promised a gradual democratization of the Czechoslovakian political system. Dubček hoped to create "socialism with a human face."

A period of euphoria, known as the "Prague Spring," followed but it proved to be short-lived. To forestall the spreading of this "spring fever," the Soviet Army invaded Czechoslovakia in August 1968. It crushed the reform movement. Gustav Husák replaced Dubček, did away with his reforms, and reestablished the old order.

✓ **Reading Check** **Evaluating** What caused the battles between the Eastern European states and the Soviet Union?

Vocabulary

1. **Explain** the significance of: Soviet Union, heavy industry, enhanced, sole, de-Stalinization, Aleksandr Solzhenitsyn, Albania, Yugoslavia, Tito, Poland, Hungary, Czechoslovakia, Imre Nagy, Alexander Dubček.

Main Ideas

2. **Summarize** the steps that Khrushchev took to de-Stalinize the Soviet Union. Use a chart like the one below to make your summary.

Khrushchev's Steps to De-Stalinize the Soviet Union
1.
2.

3. **Name** two countries in Eastern Europe that resisted Soviet dominance.

4. **Explain** how Alexander Dubček created "socialism with a human face" in Czechoslovakia.

Critical Thinking

5. **The BIG Idea** **Analyzing** Why did Yugoslavia and Albania not come under the control of the Soviet Union?

6. **Making Connections** How did Aleksandr Solzhenitsyn aid in Khrushchev's de-Stalinization of the Soviet Union?

7. **Analyzing Visuals** Examine the 1951 Soviet poster on page 675. How do the workers appear to view Stalin?

Writing About History

8. **Informative Writing** You are a Western journalist in Hungary in 1956. Write an article for an American newspaper that describes the events leading to the Soviet attack on Budapest and predicting the effect it will have on the Cold War.

History ONLINE

For help with the concepts in this section of *Glencoe World History—Modern Times*, go to glencoe.com and click Study Central.

Western Europe and North America

Most Western European countries recovered rapidly from World War II. Some European nations found economic unity with the European Economic Community (EEC). The United States experienced an economic boom after World War II but reeled under social and political issues. Meanwhile, a consumer society and the women's liberation movement led to more changes.

GUIDE TO READING

The BIG Idea

Ideas, Beliefs, and Values Post-World War II societies rebuilt their economies and communities, but not without upheaval and change.

Content Vocabulary

- welfare state *(p. 680)*
- bloc *(p. 681)*
- real wages *(p. 681)*
- civil rights movement *(p. 682)*
- consumer society *(p. 684)*
- women's liberation movement *(p. 685)*

Academic Vocabulary

- recovery *(p. 678)*
- minimal *(p. 680)*

People and Places

- France *(p. 678)*
- Charles de Gaulle *(p. 678)*
- Christian Democratic Union (CDU) *(p. 679)*
- West Germany *(p. 679)*
- European Economic Community (EEC) *(p. 681)*
- John F. Kennedy *(p. 682)*
- Martin Luther King, Jr. *(p. 682)*
- Simone de Beauvoir *(p. 685)*

Reading Strategy

Categorizing Information As you read, use a table like the one below to list programs instituted by Great Britain, the United States, and Canada to promote social welfare.

Great Britain	United States	Canada

Western Europe: New Unity

MAIN IDEA After the end of World War II, most of Western Europe recovered economically and the region became more unified.

HISTORY & YOU How did Germany rebuild after World War I? Read to learn how Germany became divided after World War II.

With the economic aid of the Marshall Plan, the countries of Western Europe recovered relatively rapidly from the devastation of World War II. Between 1947 and 1950, European countries received $9.4 billion for new equipment and raw materials. By 1950, industrial output in Europe was 30 percent above prewar levels. This economic **recovery** continued well into the 1950s and 1960s. It was a time of dramatic economic growth and prosperity in Western Europe.

France and de Gaulle

The history of **France** for nearly a quarter of a century after the war was dominated by one man—the war hero **Charles de Gaulle**. In 1946 de Gaulle helped establish a new government, the Fourth Republic. That government, however, was largely ineffective.

In 1958 leaders of the Fourth Republic, frightened by bitter divisions caused by a crisis in the French colony of Algeria (see Chapter 23), asked de Gaulle to form a new government. That year, de Gaulle drafted a new constitution for the Fifth Republic that greatly enhanced the power of the president.

The French president would now have the right to choose the prime minister, dissolve parliament, and supervise both defense and foreign policy. French voters overwhelmingly approved the constitution, and de Gaulle became the first president of the Fifth Republic.

As the new president, de Gaulle wanted France to be great power once again. To achieve the status of a world power, de Gaulle invested heavily in nuclear arms. France exploded its first nuclear bomb in 1960.

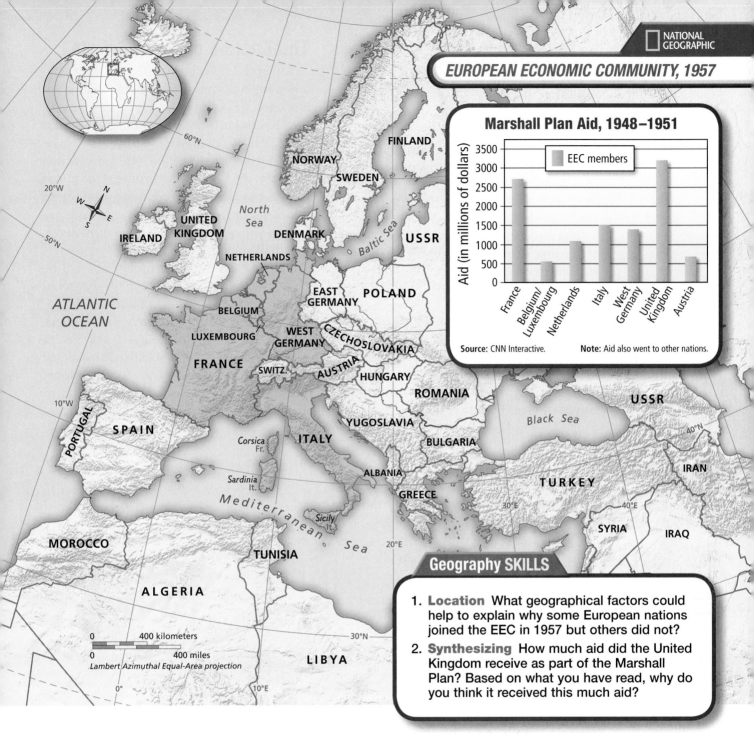

EUROPEAN ECONOMIC COMMUNITY, 1957

Marshall Plan Aid, 1948–1951

EEC members

(Bar chart: Aid in millions of dollars, values for France ~2700, Belgium/Luxembourg ~550, Netherlands ~1100, Italy ~1500, West Germany ~1400, United Kingdom ~3200, Austria ~650)

Source: CNN Interactive. **Note:** Aid also went to other nations.

Geography SKILLS

1. **Location** What geographical factors could help to explain why some European nations joined the EEC in 1957 but others did not?
2. **Synthesizing** How much aid did the United Kingdom receive as part of the Marshall Plan? Based on what you have read, why do you think it received this much aid?

During de Gaulle's presidency, the French economy grew at an annual rate of 5.5 percent, faster than that of the United States. France became a major industrial producer and exporter, especially of automobiles and weapons.

Nevertheless, problems remained. Large government deficits and a rise in the cost of living led to unrest. In May 1968, a series of student protests was followed by a general labor strike. Tired and discouraged, de Gaulle resigned from office in April 1969 and died within a year.

The Economic Miracle

The three Western zones of Germany were unified as the Federal Republic of Germany in 1949. From 1949 to 1963, Konrad Adenauer (A•duhn•owR), the leader of the **Christian Democratic Union** (CDU), served as chancellor (head of state). Adenauer sought respect for **West Germany.** He cooperated with the United States and other Western European nations and especially wanted to work with France—Germany's longtime enemy.

Under Adenauer, West Germany experienced an "economic miracle." This revival of the West German economy was largely guided by the minister of finance, Ludwig Erhard. Unemployment fell from 8 percent in 1950 to 0.4 percent in 1965. To maintain its economic expansion, West Germany even brought in hundreds of thousands of "guest" workers on visas from other countries such as Italy, Spain, Greece, Turkey, and Yugoslavia.

Adenauer resigned in 1963, after 14 years of guiding West Germany through its postwar recovery. Succeeding Adenauer as chancellor, Ludwig Erhard largely continued Adenauer's policies.

An economic downturn in the mid-1960s opened the door to the Social Democratic Party, which became the leading party in 1969. The Social Democrats, a moderate socialist party, were led by Willy Brandt, mayor of West Berlin.

The Decline of Great Britain

The end of World War II left Great Britain with massive economic problems. In elections held immediately after the war, the Labour Party overwhelmingly defeated Churchill's Conservative Party.

Under Clement Attlee, the new prime minister, the Labour government set out to create a modern **welfare state**—a state in which the government takes responsibility for providing citizens with services and a **minimal** standard of living.

In 1946 the new government passed the National Insurance Act and the National Health Service Act. The insurance act provided government funds to help the unemployed, the sick, and the aged. The health act created a system of socialized medicine that ensured medical care for everyone. The British welfare state became the norm for most European states after the war.

INFOGRAPHICS PRIMARY SOURCE

Political Change in Postwar Germany

The 1949 constitution of the German Federal Republic begins: "Human dignity shall be inviolable. To respect and protect it shall be the duty of all state authority." It goes on to list basic rights of all citizens, as well as the right to asylum, or protection, for anyone who has been persecuted for political reasons.

The words of the 1949 constitution are a reminder. During World War II, Hitler attempted to carry out the systematic murder of Europe's Jews. After the war, Germany and the world wanted to ensure that nothing like this could ever happen again.

In 1952 West German chancellor Konrad Adenauer signed an agreement to make reparations to Israel as compensation for taking in Holocaust survivors. West Germany and Israel did not establish diplomatic relations until 1964. Forty years later, German chancellor Gerhard Schröder acknowledged the nature of the two countries' relationship: "The relations between our two countries will always have a special character, shaped by the unspeakable crimes and suffering of the Shoa [Holocaust]."

Israeli president Moshe Katsav unveils the sign for a street in Berlin, Germany, named after the assassinated Israeli prime minister Yitzhak Rabin.

CRITICAL THINKING SKILLS

1. **Describing** What was the nature of diplomatic relations between Germany and Israel in 1952? 1964? Today?
2. **Making Connections** Based on the 1949 constitution, what do you think Germany learned from the Holocaust?

The cost of building a welfare state at home forced Britain to reduce expenses abroad. This meant dismantling the British Empire. Britain was forced to give in to the demands of many colonies for independence. Britain was no longer able to play the role of a world power.

Continuing economic problems brought the Conservatives back into power from 1951 to 1964. Although they favored private enterprise, the Conservatives accepted the welfare state and even extended it by financing an ambitious building program to improve British housing.

The Move Toward Unity

As we have seen, the divisions created by the Cold War led the nations of Western Europe to form the North Atlantic Treaty Organization in 1949. The destructiveness of two world wars caused many thoughtful Europeans to consider the need for some additional form of European unity. National feeling was still too powerful, however, for European nations to give up their political sovereignty. As a result, the desire for unity focused chiefly on the economic arena, not the political one.

In 1957 France, West Germany, the Benelux countries (Belgium, the Netherlands, and Luxembourg), and Italy signed the Rome Treaty. This treaty created the **European Economic Community** (EEC), also known as the Common Market.

The EEC was a free-trade area made up of the six member nations. These six nations would impose no tariffs, or import charges, on each other's goods. However, as a group, they would be protected by a tariff imposed on goods from non-EEC nations. In this way, the EEC encouraged cooperation among the member nations' economies. All the member nations benefited economically.

By the 1960s, the EEC had become an important trading **bloc** (a group of nations with a common purpose). In 1973 Britain, Denmark, and Ireland joined the EEC. With a total population of 165 million, the EEC was the world's largest exporter and purchaser of raw materials.

✓ **Reading Check** **Evaluating** Why did European unity come in the form of an economic alliance?

The U.S. after the War

MAIN IDEA In the years following World War II, the United States faced a range of difficult social and political issues.

HISTORY & YOU What social and political issues are under debate today? Read to learn about the controversies in American history from 1945 to 1970.

Between 1945 and 1970, the ideals of Franklin Delano Roosevelt's New Deal largely determined the patterns of American domestic politics. The New Deal had brought basic changes to American society. They included a dramatic increase in the role and power of the federal government, the rise of organized labor as a significant force in the economy and politics, the beginning of a welfare state, and a realization of the need to deal fairly with the concerns of minorities, especially African Americans.

The New Deal tradition in American politics was reinforced by the election of Democratic presidents—Harry S. Truman in 1948, John F. Kennedy in 1960, and Lyndon B. Johnson in 1964. Even the election of a Republican president, Dwight D. Eisenhower, in 1952 and 1956 did not change the basic direction of the New Deal. Eisenhower said:

PRIMARY SOURCE

"Should any political party attempt to abolish Social Security and eliminate labor laws, you would not hear of that party again in our political history."
—Dwight D. Eisenhower, 1954

An economic boom followed World War II. A shortage of consumer goods during the war had left Americans with both extra income and the desire to buy goods after the war. In addition, the growth of labor unions brought higher wages and gave more workers the ability to buy consumer goods. Between 1945 and 1973, **real wages** (the actual purchasing power of income) grew an average of 3 percent a year, the most prolonged advance ever in American history.

Prosperity was not the only characteristic of the early 1950s. Cold War struggles abroad led to the widespread fear that Communists had infiltrated the United States.

President Truman's attorney general warned that Communists were "everywhere—in factories, offices, butcher stores, on street corners, in private businesses." For many Americans, proof of this threat became more evident when thousands of American soldiers were sent to Korea to fight and die in a war against Communist aggression.

This climate of fear produced a dangerous political agitator, Senator Joseph R. McCarthy of Wisconsin. His charges that hundreds of supposed Communists were in high government positions helped create a massive "Red Scare"—fear of Communist subversion. Under McCarthy, several individuals, including intellectuals and movie stars, were questioned about alleged Communist activities. When McCarthy attacked "Communist conspirators" in the U.S. Army, he was condemned by the Senate in 1954. Very quickly, his anti-Communist crusade came to an end.

The 1960s and Civil Rights

The 1960s began on a youthful and optimistic note. At age 43, **John F. Kennedy** became the youngest elected president in the history of the United States. His administration was cut short when the president was killed by an assassin on November 22, 1963. Vice President Lyndon B. Johnson then became president. Johnson won a new term as president in a landslide victory in 1964.

President Johnson used his stunning victory to pursue the growth of the welfare state, begun in the New Deal. Johnson's programs included health care for the elderly, various measures to combat poverty, and federal assistance for education.

Johnson's other domestic passion was the **civil rights movement,** or equal rights for African Americans. The civil rights movement had its beginnings in 1954, when the United States Supreme Court ruled that the practice of racial segregation (separation) in public schools was illegal. According to Chief Justice Earl Warren, "separate educational facilities are inherently unequal." African Americans also boycotted segregated buses and other public places.

In August 1963, the Reverend **Martin Luther King, Jr.,** leader of a growing movement for racial equality, led a march on Washington, D.C., to dramatize the African American desire for equality. King advocated the principle of passive disobedience practiced by Mohandas Gandhi. King's march and his impassioned plea for racial equality had an electrifying effect on the American people. By the end of 1963, a majority of the American people called civil rights the most significant national issue.

President Johnson took up the cause of civil rights. The Civil Rights Act of 1964 created the machinery to end segregation and discrimination in the workplace and all public places. Then, the Voting Rights Act made it easier for African Americans to vote in Southern states.

Laws alone, however, could not guarantee the Great Society that Johnson talked about creating. He soon faced bitter social unrest.

Social Upheaval

In the North and West, local patterns of segregation led to higher unemployment rates for African Americans than for whites. In the summer of 1965, race riots broke out in the Watts district of Los Angeles. Thirty-four people died and over 1,000 buildings were destroyed.

In 1968 Martin Luther King, Jr., was assassinated. Riots hit over 100 cities, including Washington, D.C. The riots led to a "white backlash" (whites became less sympathetic to the cause of racial equality) and continued the racial division of the United States.

Antiwar protests also divided the American people. As the Vietnam War (see Chapter 24) progressed through the second half of the 1960s, the protests grew. Then, in 1970 four students at Kent State University were killed and nine others were wounded by the Ohio National Guard during a student demonstration. The tragedy startled the nation. Americans were less willing to continue the war.

The combination of antiwar demonstrations and riots in the cities caused many people to call for "law and order." This was the appeal used by Richard Nixon, the Republican presidential candidate in 1968. With Nixon's election in 1968, a shift to the political right in American politics began.

The Civil Rights Act of 1964 and the Voting Rights Acts

In August 1963, Martin Luther King, Jr., told the 250,000 people who had marched on Washington, D.C, for civil rights: "I am happy to join with you today in what will go down in history as the greatest demonstration for freedom in the history of our nation." He went on to deliver one of the most famous speeches of modern times—his "I Have a Dream" speech.

Within a year, Congress had passed the Civil Rights Act of 1964, which outlawed segregation and prohibited discrimination on the basis of "race, color, religion, or national origin." A year later, Congress passed the Voting Rights Act of 1965, which prohibited laws and practices that kept African Americans from voting.

The Reverend Martin Luther King, Jr. at the March on Washington, August 28, 1963

CRITICAL THINKING SKILLS

1. **Explaining** What was the connection between the 1964 Civil Rights Act and the 1965 Voting Rights Act?

2. **Determining Cause and Effect** What do you think was the effect of the March on Washington?

American-Canadian Relations

After the war, Canada began developing electronic, aircraft, nuclear, and chemical engineering industries on a large scale. Investment of capital from the United States led to U.S. ownership of Canadian businesses. Some Canadians feared American economic domination of Canada.

Canadians also worried about playing a secondary role politically and militarily to the United States. Canada established its own identity in world politics and government. For example, Canada was a founding member of the United Nations in 1945 and joined the North Atlantic Treaty Organization in 1949. Under Lester Pearson, the Liberal government laid the groundwork for Canada's welfare state. A national social security system (the Canada Pension Plan) and a national health insurance program were enacted.

✓ **Reading Check** **Identifying** Name President Johnson's two most important domestic policy goals.

Changing Values

MAIN IDEA After World War II, advances in technology and the struggle for rights led to rapid change in Western society.

HISTORY & YOU Have you or your family members ever used credit cards? Read to learn how buying on credit became widespread during the 1950s.

After World War II, Western society witnessed rapid change. Such new inventions as computers, televisions, and jet planes altered the pace and nature of human life. The rapid changes in postwar society led many to view it as a new society.

A New Social Structure

Postwar Western society was marked by a changing social structure. Especially noticeable were changes in the middle class. Traditional middle-class groups were made up of businesspeople, lawyers, doctors, and teachers. A new group of managers and technicians, hired by large companies and government agencies, now joined the ranks of the middle class.

Changes also occurred among the lower classes. The shift of people from rural to urban areas continued. The number of people in farming declined drastically. By the 1950s, the number of farmers in most parts of Europe had dropped by 50 percent. The number of industrial workers also began to decline as the amount of white-collar workers increased.

At the same time, a noticeable increase in the real wages of workers made it possible for them to imitate the buying patterns of the middle class. This led to what some observers have called the **consumer society**—a society preoccupied with buying goods.

Buying on credit became widespread in the 1950s. Workers could now buy such products as televisions, washing machines, refrigerators, vacuum cleaners, and stereos. The automobile was the most visible symbol of the new consumerism. In 1948 there were 5 million cars in all of Europe. By the 1960s, there were almost 45 million.

Women in the Postwar World

Women's participation in the world wars had resulted in several gains. They had achieved one of the major aims of the nineteenth-century feminist movement—the right to vote. After making important contributions in World War I, women had gained voting rights in many countries. Sweden, Great Britain, Germany, Poland, Hungary, Austria, and Czechoslovakia extended voting rights to women in 1918, followed by the United States in 1920. French women only gained the vote in 1944, while Italian women did so in 1945.

During World War II, women had entered the workforce in huge numbers. At the war's end, however, they were removed to provide jobs for soldiers returning home. For a time, women fell back into traditional roles. Birthrates rose, creating a "baby boom" in the late 1940s and the 1950s.

CONNECTING TO THE UNITED STATES

THE AMERICAN WOMEN'S MOVEMENT

In 1949 the French writer Simone de Beauvoir published her best-known work, *The Second Sex*, a philosophical look at women's role in society.

De Beauvoir helped reawaken the American women's movement, which had languished after they gained the right to vote in 1920.

In the 1960s and 1970s, the American women's movement focused on job discrimination. New laws made it illegal to pay a woman less than a man for the same job or to otherwise discriminate on the basis of sex.

- Women should demand equality with men
- Every person, regardless of sex, class, or age, should be able to define herself or himself

Male and female astronauts work side by side aboard the space shuttle Endeavor.

CONNECTING TO TODAY

1. **Explaining** Why did the women's movement slow down in the United States?
2. **Making Connections** What influence did Simone de Beauvoir's ideas have on the women's movement in the United States?

By the end of the 1950s, however, the birthrate had begun to fall and, with it, the size of families. The structure of the workplace changed once again as the number of married women in the workforce increased in both Europe and the United States. These women, especially working-class women, faced an old problem. They still earned less than men for equal work. For example, in the 1960s, women earned 60 percent of men's wages in Britain, 50 percent in France, and 63 percent in West Germany.

In addition, women still tended to enter traditionally female jobs. Many faced the double burden of earning income and raising a family. Such inequalities led increasing numbers of women to rebel. In the late 1960s came renewed interest in feminism, or the **women's liberation movement.**

Of great importance to the emergence of the postwar women's liberation movement was the work of **Simone de Beauvoir** (duh•boh•VWAHR). In 1949 she published *The Second Sex*. As a result of male-dominated societies, she argued, women were defined by their differences from men and consequently received second-class status. De Beauvoir influenced both the American and European women's movements.

Student Revolts

Before World War II, it was mostly members of Europe's wealthier classes who went to universities. After the war, European states encouraged more people to gain higher education by eliminating fees. As a result, enrollments from middle and lower classes grew dramatically. In France, 4.5 percent of young people went to universities in 1950. By 1965, the figure had increased to 14.5 percent.

There were problems, however. Many European university classrooms were overcrowded, and many professors paid little attention to their students. Growing discontent led to an outburst of student revolts in the late 1960s.

This student radicalism had several causes. Many protests were an extension of the revolts in American universities, often sparked by student opposition to the Vietnam War. Some students, particularly in Europe, believed that universities failed to respond to their needs or to the realities of the modern world. Others believed they were becoming small cogs in the large and impersonal bureaucratic wheels of the modern world.

Student protests of the 1960s and early 1970s caused many people to rethink basic assumptions. Student upheavals, however, were not a turning point in the history of postwar Europe, as some people thought at the time. As student rebels became middle-class professionals, revolutionary politics became mostly a memory.

✓ Reading Check **Identifying** What was the women's liberation movement trying to accomplish?

Vocabulary
1. **Explain** the significance of: recovery, France, Charles de Gaulle, Christian Democratic Union, West Germany, welfare state, minimal, European Economic Community, bloc, real wages, John F. Kennedy, civil rights movement, Martin Luther King, Jr., consumer society, women's liberation movement, Simone de Beauvoir.

Main Ideas
2. **Explain** why many British colonies gained their independence after World War II.

3. **List** some of the factors that caused social upheaval in the United States during the 1960s and early 1970s.

4. **Identify** factors leading to the postwar women's liberation movement. Use a diagram like the one below.

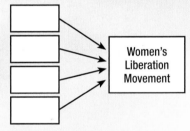

Critical Thinking
5. **The BIG Idea** **Assessing** Did the student revolts of this period contribute positively or negatively to society? Explain.

6. **Defending** Should the United States become a welfare state? Why or why not?

7. **Analyzing Visuals** What information does the photograph on page 683 provide about the March on Washington?

Writing About History
8. **Persuasive Writing** Write an essay that argues for or against the use of demonstrations, marches, and riots for changing public opinion and policy.

History ONLINE

For help with the concepts in this section of *Glencoe World History—Modern Times*, go to glencoe.com and click Study Central.

685

Popular Culture of the 1950s and 1960s

In the United States, an economic upturn after World War II sparked a baby boom and the growth of American suburbs. The new prosperity also freed many American teenagers from having to work full-time, resulting in a greater importance placed on secondary education. As a result, adolescents in white, suburban America became a clearly defined social group. This teenage culture was reflected in music, fashions, television shows, and leisure activities. Though the youth culture remained a distinct entity in American society, its values would change sharply over time.

Soda fountains, malt shops, and drugstore counters were popular locations for 1950s teenagers to gather for food and socializing.

Rock 'n' roll, record players, and jukeboxes made dancing a mainstay of teenage social life.

Clean-cut boys wore button-down shirts, khakis or gray flannel trousers, white socks and penny loafers.

Collar-length hairstyles, such as the flip, were popular among girls. Boys typically preferred to wear their hair short with a part on the side or as a flattop.

Girls commonly wore a blouse or a sweater paired with a dress or skirt that fell well below the knee. White bobby socks and penny loafers or saddle shoes completed the female teen's ensemble.

YOUTH CULTURE OF THE 1950S

For the first time, teenagers had the leisure time, money, and freedom to claim their own part of America's prosperous society. As the nation's youth culture became more defined, the goal of most teens was to fit in with their peers. Young people wanted to dress like their classmates, attend the same pep rallies, gather at the same soda shops, and listen to the same rock music. Some teenagers, however, cultivated a rebellious image. Known as "greasers," they wore jeans and T-shirts, combed their hair into ducktails, and some engaged in delinquent activities. Nonetheless, conformity and consumerism were defining elements of teenage culture of the 1950s.

By the middle 1960s, rock and folk festivals were common places to gather, establish a feeling of community, and take part in social protest activities.

Boys and girls in the 1960s increasingly wore their hair long.

Fashion fads among boys included jeans, tie-dyed shirts, paisley shirts, velvet trousers, bell-bottoms, Nehru jackets, and turtlenecks.

Free-flowing dance movements were a favorite form of personal expression in the 1960s.

Girls' fashions included beads and brightly colored miniskirts or short dresses. Sandals, or even going barefoot, also became popular.

YOUTH CULTURE OF THE 1960S

Inspired in part by the civil rights movement and the Vietnam War, teenagers in the 1960s increasingly rejected the traditional values of their parents. As the youth rebellion grew, a "generation gap" formed between young people and their parents. Teenagers held attitudes and opinions that older Americans did not understand or accept. The youth of the 1960s generally embraced individualism and free expression. This desire was reflected in the fashions and music popular among teens in the decade. Not all teenagers rebelled. Many young people in the 1960s retained traditional values, and sought a career in the nation's economy.

ANALYZING VISUALS

1. **Comparing** Despite the differences between the youth culture of the 1950s and 1960s, how were American teenagers in those two decades similar?

2. **Analyzing** How were the values held by teenagers in the 1950s and 1960s reflected in their clothing, personal appearance, and social activities?

687

You can study anywhere, anytime by downloading quizzes and flash cards to your PDA from glencoe.com.

THE BERLIN WALL

The Berlin Wall symbolized the division between the two superpowers.

POLITICAL DIVISION AND CONFLICT During the Cold War

- The United States and Soviet Union became fierce political rivals.
- The United States provided aid to countries threatened by Communist expansion.
- Each side formed alliances: NATO (the U.S. and its allies) and the Warsaw Pact (the Soviet Union and its allies).
- Political division led to a growing arms race, the Berlin Wall, and the Cuban missile crisis.

THE SOVIET UNION AND EASTERN EUROPE During the Cold War

- In its economy, the Soviet Union emphasized heavy industry, benefiting the military over average citizens.
- Stalin ruled by repression and political terror.
- Khrushchev tried to increase farm and consumer products, but his policies failed.
- The Soviet Union gained control over much of Eastern Europe.

HUNGARIAN UPRISING OF 1956

Hungarians declared their freedom, but the Soviet Army forcibly reestablished Communist control.

SEGREGATION BECOMES ILLEGAL IN PUBLIC SCHOOLS IN THE UNITED STATES

In this photo from 1954 soldiers escort African Americans to school.

WESTERN EUROPE AND NORTH AMERICA During the Cold War

- Economic aid from the Marshall Plan helped Western Europe recover from the devastation of war.
- Six nations formed the European Economic Community (EEC).
- In the United States, Cold War tensions led to war in Korea and the "Red Scare."
- New technology and civil rights struggles changed society.

STANDARDIZED TEST PRACTICE

TEST-TAKING TIP

A date can be an important clue. When a question contains a date, think about major events that occurred during or around that time. Then eliminate answer choices that do not reflect that history.

Reviewing Vocabulary

Directions: Choose the word or words that best complete the sentence.

1. _____ is the manufacture of machines and equipment for factories and mines.

   A Assembly line

   B Heavy industry

   C Light industry

   D Deterrence

2. In a _____ state, the government provides citizens with services and a minimal standard of living.

   A welfare

   B natural

   C socialist

   D communist

3. To keep communism within its existing boundaries, the United States followed a policy of _____.

   A encroachment

   B socialism

   C colonization

   D containment

4. A _____ is a group of nations with a common purpose.

   A consortium

   B bloc

   C satellite

   D region

Reviewing Main Ideas

Directions: Choose the best answers to the following questions.

Section 1 *(pp. 664–671)*

5. What is another name for the European Recovery Program of 1947?

   A Common Market

   B Truman Doctrine

   C Five-Year Plan

   D Marshall Plan

6. What is the name of the military alliance the Soviet Union made with seven nations in 1955?

   A Allied Pact

   B Nonaggression Pact

   C Warsaw Pact

   D Truman Pact

7. What did Nikita Khrushchev place in Cuba in 1962?

   A Soviet troops

   B Sugar reserves

   C Nuclear missiles

   D Exiled freedom fighters

Section 2 *(pp. 674–677)*

8. Who wrote *One Day in the Life of Ivan Denisovich*?

   A Aleksandr Solzhenitsyn

   B Adolf Hitler

   C Simone de Beauvoir

   D Ivan Denisovich

Need Extra Help?								
If You Missed Questions . . .	1	2	3	4	5	6	7	8
Go to Page . . .	674	680	666	681	666	668	670	675

GO ON

9. Which leader hoped to create "socialism with a human face" in Czechoslovakia?

  A Alexander Dubček

  B Nikita Khrushchev

  C Imre Nagy

  D Josip Broz

Section 3 *(pp. 678–685)*

10. Which postwar country experienced an "economic miracle"?

  A East Germany

  B West Germany

  C Hungary

  D Great Britain

11. Which American politician created a massive "Red Scare"—fear of Communist subversion—in the early 1950s?

  A Richard Nixon

  B Lyndon B. Johnson

  C Joseph R. McCarthy

  D Harry S. Truman

12. In which year was Martin Luther King, Jr., assassinated?

  A 1970

  B 1963

  C 1968

  D 1972

13. Who wrote *The Second Sex*?

  A Jacqueline Kennedy

  B Madame Gustav

  C Paulette de Vous

  D Simone de Beauvoir

Critical Thinking

Directions: Choose the best answers to the following questions.

Use the following map to answer question 14.

Cuban Missile Crisis, 1962

Legend:
- Soviet missile site
- U.S. blockade zone
- U.S. naval base

14. Where were the Soviet missile sites located?

  A In the Bahamas

  B Near Guantánamo Bay

  C In eastern Cuba

  D Near the Bay of Pigs

15. Why did the Soviet Union invade Hungary in 1956?

  A To stop a rebellion led by Alexander Dubček

  B To set up nuclear missiles aimed at Berlin

  C To maintain Communist rule

  D To stop a rebellion led by a group of writers

16. Which event caused a shift in U.S. politics to the political right?

  A The Cuban missile crisis

  B The election of Richard Nixon

  C Passage of the Civil Rights Act

  D The assassination of Martin Luther King, Jr.

Need Extra Help?								
If You Missed Questions . . .	9	10	11	12	13	14	15	16
Go to Page . . .	677	679	682	682	685	690	677	682

GO ON

17. What was the significance of intercontinental ballistic missiles (ICBMs) in the 1950s?

    A They sent missiles into space.

    B They were hydrogen bombs.

    C They could send bombs anywhere.

    D They were the first space satellites.

Analyze the chart below and answer the question that follows. Base your answer on the chart.

The British welfare state became the norm for most European states after World War II. The United States did not follow suit. As health-care costs continue to rise in the United States, so does the number of people who are without health insurance.

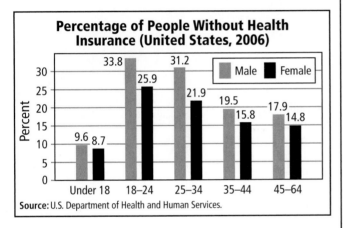

Percentage of People Without Health Insurance (United States, 2006)

Under 18: Male 9.6, Female 8.7
18–24: Male 33.8, Female 25.9
25–34: Male 31.2, Female 21.9
35–44: Male 19.5, Female 15.8
45–64: Male 17.9, Female 14.8

Source: U.S. Department of Health and Human Services.

18. According to the graph, which age group and gender has the highest percentage of people without health insurance?

    A 25-to-34-year-old males

    B 25-to-34-year-old females

    C 18-to-24-year-old females

    D 18-to-24-year-old males

Document-Based Questions

Directions: Analyze the document and answer the short answer questions that follow the document. Base your answers on the document and on your knowledge of world history.

Bob Dylan, recording artist, expressed the feeling of the younger generation with his song "The Times They Are a-Changin'," released in 1964.

The Times They Are a-Changin

Come gather round people
Wherever you roam
And admit that the waters
Around you have grown
And accept it that soon
You'll be drenched to the bone
If your time to you
Is worth savin'
Then you better start swimmin'
Or you'll sink like a stone
For the times they are a-changin' . . .

19. What is the tone of Dylan's lyrics? To whom does Dylan direct "come gather round"?

20. What does Dylan mean when he says "admit that the waters around you have grown"?

Extended Response

21. The Cuban missile crisis brought the world dangerously close to nuclear war. Explain how the politics of the Cold War affected both Kennedy's and Khrushchev's decisions leading to the crisis. What else could they have done to prevent the crisis?

History ONLINE

For additional test practice, use Self-Check Quizzes—Chapter 20 at **glencoe.com**.

Need Extra Help?					
If You Missed Questions . . .	17	18	19	20	21
Go to Page . . .	669	691	691	691	670

STOP

CHAPTER 21

The Contemporary Western World 1970–Present

Section 1 Decline of the Soviet Union

Section 2 Eastern Europe

Section 3 Europe and North America

Section 4 Western Society and Culture

MAKING CONNECTIONS
What did the Berlin Wall symbolize?

Shortly after the East German government opened the Berlin Wall's checkpoints in 1989, thousands of citizens mobbed the wall and began to tear it down. This photo shows East German border guards protecting the wall the morning before the first section fell. The fall of the Berlin Wall marked the end of the Cold War and served as the first step toward the reunification of Germany. In this chapter you will learn about political, economic, and social changes that have taken place in the contemporary Western world.

- What were the immediate effects of the fall of the Berlin Wall?
- How does the East-West split during the Cold War affect Germany today?

EUROPE,
THE SOVIET UNION,
AND THE UNITED STATES ▶

1974
Gerald Ford becomes U.S. president after Nixon resigns

1984
USSR boycotts Los Angeles Olympics

1990
Germany reunified

1970   1980   1990

THE WORLD ▶

1979
Mother Teresa wins Nobel Peace Prize

2002
Euro established
as common currency
in many Western
European nations

2004
Chechen rebels seize
Russian school;
many children die

2000

1995
Terrorists release deadly
chemicals in Tokyo subway

2002
China joins World
Trade Organization

FOLDABLES™
Study Organizer

Identifying Research
the historical role played
by Mikhail Gorbachev in
reshaping the Soviet
Union during the 1980s.
Organize the information
in a Four-Door Book using *Who*, *What*,
When, and *Where* categories.

Who | What
When | Where

History ONLINE

Chapter Overview—Visit glencoe.com to preview Chapter 21.

Decline of the Soviet Union

GUIDE TO READING

The BIG Idea
Self-Determination One of the largest empires in the world ended when the Soviet Union broke up in 1991.

Content Vocabulary
• détente *(p. 694)*
• dissidents *(p. 694)*
• perestroika *(p. 696)*

Academic Vocabulary
• participation *(p. 695)*   • responsive *(p. 696)*

People, Places, and Events
• Leonid Brezhnev   • Mikhail Gorbachev
  (p. 694)   *(p. 696)*
• Brezhnev Doctrine   • Boris Yeltsin *(p. 696)*
  (p. 694)   • Ukraine *(p. 696)*
• Afghanistan *(p. 695)*   • Belarus *(p. 696)*
• Ronald Reagan   • Vladimir Putin
  (p. 695)   *(p. 698)*

Reading Strategy
Comparing and Contrasting As you read, create a chart like the one below comparing the policies of Brezhnev and Gorbachev.

	Leonid Brezhnev	Mikhail Gorbachev
Foreign Policy		
Economic Policy		
Military Policy		
Personal Policy		

After Nikita Khrushchev was forced out of office, the Soviet Union experienced domestic and foreign problems. By the 1980s, the country was seriously ailing, and many believed that reform was necessary. That reform began under Mikhail Gorbachev's perestroika and continued with the breakup of the Soviet Union in 1991. Today, Russia has emerged as an economic power with its vast energy wealth.

The Soviet Union Under Stress

MAIN IDEA The Soviet Union could not survive a combination of domestic and foreign problems.

HISTORY & YOU What challenges does the U.S. president face today? Read to learn about the challenges faced by the Soviet leaders in the 1980s.

Between 1964 and 1982, drastic change in the Soviet Union had seemed highly unlikely. What happened to create such a dramatic turnaround by the late 1980s?

The Brezhnev Era

Alexei Kosygin and **Leonid Brezhnev** (BREHZH•NEHF) replaced Nikita Khrushchev when he was removed from office in 1964. Brezhnev emerged as the dominant leader in the 1970s. Determined to keep Eastern Europe in Communist hands, he was not interested in reform. He also insisted on the Soviet Union's right to intervene if communism was threatened in another Communist state (known as the **Brezhnev Doctrine**).

At the same time, Brezhnev benefited from **détente,** a relaxation of tensions and improved relations between the two superpowers. Roughly equal to the United States in nuclear arms, the Soviet Union felt more secure. As a result, its leaders relaxed their authoritarian rule. Brezhnev allowed more access to Western styles of music, dress, and art. However, he still punished **dissidents,** those who spoke out against the regime.

In his economic policies, Brezhnev continued to emphasize heavy industry. Two problems, however, weakened the Soviet economy. First, the central government was a huge, complex, but inefficient bureaucracy that led to indifference. Second, many collective farmers preferred working their own small private plots to laboring in the collective work brigades.

By the 1970s, the Communist ruling class in the Soviet Union had become complacent and corrupt. Party and state leaders, as well as army leaders and secret police (KGB), enjoyed a high

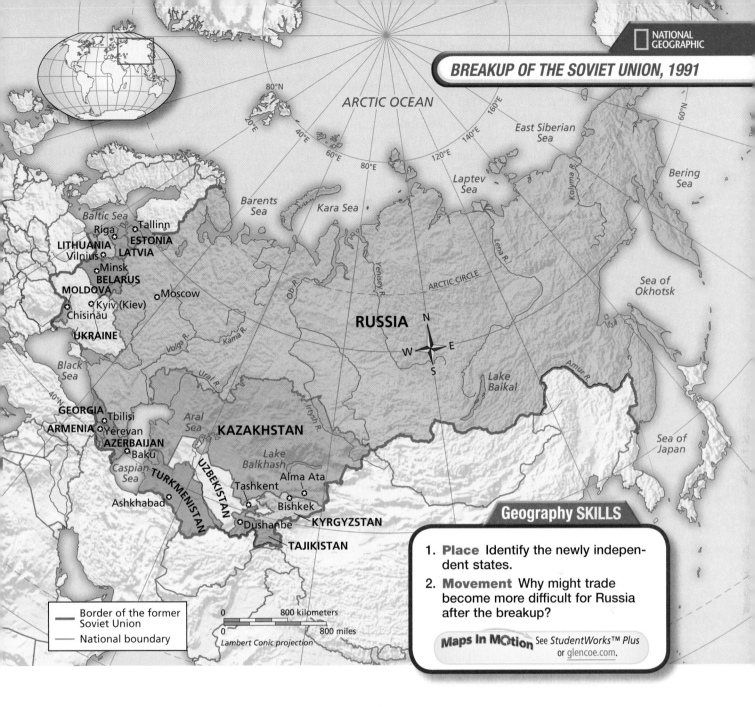

ARCTIC OCEAN

East Siberian Sea

Bering Sea

Laptev Sea

Barents Sea

Kara Sea

Sea of Okhotsk

Baltic Sea

Tallinn

Riga

ESTONIA

LITHUANIA   LATVIA

Vilnius

Minsk

BELARUS

MOLDOVA   Moscow

Kyiv (Kiev)

Chisinău

UKRAINE

RUSSIA

N
W   E
S

Black Sea

ARCTIC CIRCLE

Lake Baikal

Amur R.

Sea of Japan

GEORGIA   Tbilisi

Aral Sea

ARMENIA   Yerevan

AZERBAIJAN

Baku

Caspian Sea

TURKMENISTAN

UZBEKISTAN

KAZAKHSTAN

Lake Balkhash

Alma Ata

Tashkent

Ashkhabad

Bishkek

Dushanbe   KYRGYZSTAN

TAJIKISTAN

Ob. R.

Kama R.

Volga R.

Ural R.

Irtysh R.

Yenisey R.

Lena R.

Kolyma R.

Geography SKILLS

1. **Place** Identify the newly independent states.

2. **Movement** Why might trade become more difficult for Russia after the breakup?

Maps In Motion See *StudentWorks™ Plus* or glencoe.com.

— Border of the former Soviet Union

— National boundary

0   800 kilometers
0   800 miles
Lambert Conic projection

The Cold War Intensifies

standard of living. Regardless of the government's inefficiency and corruption, Brezhnev did not want to tamper with the party leadership and state bureaucracy.

By the 1970s, détente allowed U.S. grain and consumer goods to be sold to the Soviet Union. However, détente collapsed in 1979 when the Soviet Union invaded **Afghanistan.** A new period of East-West confrontation began.

The Soviet Union wanted to restore a pro-Soviet regime in Afghanistan. The United States viewed this as an act of expansion. To show his disapproval, President Jimmy Carter canceled U.S. **participation** in the 1980 Olympic Games to be held in Moscow. He also placed an embargo on the shipment of U.S. grain to the Soviets. Relations became even chillier when **Ronald Reagan** became president. He called the Soviet Union an "evil empire" and began a military buildup and a new arms race. Reagan also gave military aid to the Afghan rebels.

✓ **Reading Check** **Explaining** Why did détente between the Soviets and Americans end?

Gorbachev and Reform

MAIN IDEA Gorbachev's reforms contributed to the end of the Cold War and of the Soviet Union.

HISTORY & YOU Has a U.S. president ever changed the course of our nation? Read to learn how Mikhail Gorbachev changed the course of the USSR.

By 1980, the Soviet Union was ailing. It had a declining economy, a rise in infant mortality rates, a dramatic surge in alcoholism, and poor working conditions. Within the Communist Party, a small group of reformers emerged. One was **Mikhail Gorbachev** (GAWR•buh•CHAWF). When the party chose him as leader in March 1985, a new era began.

Gorbachev and Perestroika

From the start, Gorbachev preached the need for radical reforms based on **perestroika** (PEHR•uh•STROY•kuh), or restructuring. At first, this meant restructuring economic policy. Gorbachev wanted to start a market economy more **responsive** to consumers. It was to have limited free enterprise so that some businesses would be privately owned and operated.

Gorbachev soon realized, however, that an attempt to reform the economy would not work without political reform. Therefore, at the 1988 Communist Party conference, he set up a new Soviet parliament with elected members, the Congress of People's Deputies. It met in 1989, the first such meeting in the country since 1918.

Gorbachev then created a new state presidency as the leading executive office. Under the old system, the first secretary of the Communist Party (Gorbachev's position) had been the most important. In March 1990, Gorbachev became the Soviet Union's first—and last—president.

End of the Cold War

When Mikhail Gorbachev came to power in the Soviet Union, the Cold War suddenly ended. His "New Thinking"—his willingness to rethink Soviet foreign policy—led to stunning changes.

First, Gorbachev made an agreement with the United States in 1987, the Intermediate-Range INF Treaty, to eliminate intermediate-range nuclear weapons. Both superpowers wanted to slow down the arms race. They wanted to reduce their military budgets to solve domestic problems. Gorbachev hoped to focus resources on social and economic change. The United States wanted to balance its national debt, which had tripled during the Reagan presidency.

Gorbachev also stopped giving Soviet military support to Communist governments in Eastern Europe. This opened the door to the overthrow of Communist regimes. A mostly peaceful revolutionary movement swept through Eastern Europe in 1989. The reunification of Germany on October 3, 1990, was a powerful symbol of the end of the Cold War. In 1991 the Soviet Union was dissolved. The long rivalry between the two superpowers was over.

End of the Soviet Union

The Soviet Union included 92 ethnic groups and 112 different languages. As Gorbachev released the iron grip of the Communist Party, centered in Moscow, old ethnic tensions came to the fore. Nationalist movements began. In 1989 and 1990, calls for independence came first in Soviet Georgia and then in Latvia, Estonia, Moldavia, Uzbekistan, Azerbaijan, and Lithuania.

The conservative leaders of the traditional Soviet institutions—the army, government, KGB, and military industries—were worried. The breakup of the Soviet Union would end their privileges. On August 19, 1991, a group of these conservative leaders arrested Gorbachev and tried to seize power. The attempt failed, however, when **Boris Yeltsin,** president of the Russian Republic, and thousands of Russians bravely resisted the rebel forces in Moscow.

The Soviet republics now moved for complete independence. **Ukraine** voted for independence on December 1, 1991. A week later, the leaders of Russia, Ukraine, and **Belarus** announced that the Soviet Union had "ceased to exist."

✓ Reading Check **Explaining** How did Gorbachev contribute to the Soviet Union's breakup?

THE COLLAPSE OF THE SOVIET UNION

Soldiers and tanks move to Red Square to surround the Kremlin at the beginning of the August 1991 coup.

Mikhail Gorbachev's efforts at political reform began in 1988 with the creation of a new parliament through competitive elections. This Congress of People's Deputies included strong critics of the Communist Party leadership.

In 1989 reforms in the Soviet Union encouraged the satellite states of Eastern Europe to reject communism and elect their own democratic governments. Nationalist groups within the Soviet Union also began to call for independence.

The Soviet Union was made up of 15 separate republics, each with its own dominant ethnic group, a powerful force toward nationalism. To try to hold the Soviet Union together, Gorbachev negotiated the Union Treaty in 1991, which granted greater powers to the republics. Communist leaders were threatened by this agreement. They attempted a coup against Gorbachev in August 1991.

Though unsuccessful, the coup greatly weakened Gorbachev's political power since it was brought about by his supporters. It revealed the political weakness of the Soviet state. One by one, the Soviet republics began to declare their independence.

On December 25, 1991, Gorbachev resigned as president, and the flag of the Soviet Union was lowered for the last time over the Kremlin.

CRITICAL THINKING SKILLS

1. **Explaining** Why did independence movements arise in the Soviet republics?
2. **Making Inferences** Why do you think the failed 1991 coup hastened the breakup of the Soviet Union?

THE FORMER SOVIET REPUBLICS	
REPUBLIC	MAJOR ETHNIC GROUP
Russia	Russian (79.8%)
Ukraine	Ukrainian (77.8%)
Uzbekistan	Uzbek (80%)
Belarus	Belarusian (81.2%)
Kazakhstan	Kazakh (53.4%)
Azerbaijan	Azerbaijani (90.6%)
Georgia	Georgian (83.8%)
Tajikistan	Tajik (79.9%)
Armenia	Armenian (97.9%)
Lithuania	Lithuanian (83.4%)
Moldova	Moldavian (78.2%)
Turkmenistan	Turkmen (85%)
Kyrgyzstan	Kyrgyz (64.9%)
Latvia	Latvian (57.7%)
Estonia	Estonian (67.9%)

The New Russia

MAIN IDEA Although the country still faces some challenges, Russia has greatly improved economically.

HISTORY & YOU Has the cost of gasoline been in the news recently? Read to learn how Russia has become one of the largest exporters of oil.

Gorbachev resigned on December 25, 1991. He turned over his responsibilities as commander in chief to Boris Yeltsin, the new president of Russia. By the end of 1991, one of the largest empires in world history had ended.

Russia Under Yeltsin

Boris Yeltsin was committed to introducing a free market economy as quickly as possible, but the transition was not easy.

Economic hardships and social disarray were made worse by a dramatic rise in organized crime.

Another problem Yeltsin faced was in Chechnya, a province in the south that wanted to secede from Russia and become independent. Yeltsin used brutal force against the Chechens (CHEH•chuhnz) to keep the province as part of Russia. Yeltsin also dealt with former Soviet states like Poland, Hungary, and the Czech Republic who wanted to join NATO. Yeltsin opposed their wishes. However, in the 1990s, these countries eventually succeeded in joining NATO.

Russia Under Putin

At the end of 1999, Yeltsin resigned and was replaced by **Vladimir Putin,** who was elected president in 2000. Putin, a former

INFOGRAPHICS

Challenges for the New Russia

After playing a central role in the breakup of the Soviet Union, Boris Yeltsin became Russia's first elected leader in 1990. As president, he faced the difficult task of transforming the former communist state into a democratic, free-market state.

Unfortunately, the transition to capitalism did not go smoothly. Economic reforms caused inflation and unemployment, and Russians' quality of life plummeted. Yeltsin also struggled with political enemies and a violent rebellion in Chechnya.

In 1998 when Russia defaulted on billions of dollars in debts, the economy collapsed completely. At the end of 1999, Yeltsin resigned, handing over power to Prime Minister Vladimir Putin.

In his resignation speech, Yeltsin addressed the many challenges of his presidency:

"I want to ask for your forgiveness for the fact that many of the dreams we shared did not come true. And for the fact that what seemed simple to us turned out to be tormentingly difficult. I ask forgiveness for not justifying some hopes of those people who believed that at one stroke, in one spurt, we could leap from the gray, stagnant, totalitarian past into the light, rich, civilized future."
—Boris Yeltsin, December 31, 1999

Chechen fighters attack a Russian tank in Chechnya in 1995

Russians protest at the Winter Palace in St. Petersburg in January 1992. The sign demands that the country's leaders be punished for bringing poverty and hardship to the Russian people.

DOCUMENT-BASED QUESTIONS

1. **Identifying** What challenges did Russia face as it made the transition from communism to capitalism?

2. **Analyzing** Did Yeltsin believe he succeeded in transforming post-Soviet Russia? Explain.

KGB officer, was widely seen as someone who wanted to keep a tight rein on government power. In July 2001, Putin launched reforms to boost growth and budget revenues. The reforms included the free sale and purchase of land and tax cuts. Putin has also applied for Russia's admission to the World Trade Organization and has worked out a special partnership with the European Union. In spite of these changes, the business climate remains somewhat uncertain, and this has stifled foreign investment.

Since Putin's reforms, Russia has experienced a budget surplus and a growing economy. Russia can attribute a large part of its economic growth to its oil and gas exports. The country has an estimated 6 percent of the world's oil deposits and about 30 percent of the world's natural gas deposits.

In fact, Russia's energy wealth and control over export pipelines have made the country quite powerful. Increasingly, Russia has used its supplies of oil and gas as a political lever to wield power over former Soviet states and to influence world energy prices. For example, in 2006, Russia raised gas prices by about 100 percent for Ukraine, whose democratic government it opposed. A trans-Siberian oil pipeline, planned for 2008, will make Asia more dependent on Russian oil.

Even though it has made economic gains, Russia still faces some challenges. Rising alcoholism, criminal activities, and the decline of the traditional family system give Russians concern. Putin has tried to deal with these problems by centralizing his control over the government. Some observers have raised concerns that Putin grants even more influence to government forces that desire to reassert state control over the economy.

Other challenges for Russia are the ongoing turmoil in Chechnya and terrorism. In 2002 Chechen terrorists took about 600 Russians hostage in a Moscow theater. Between 2002 and 2004, terrorist attacks in Russia killed an estimated 500 people. Chechen rebels seized a school in the town of Beslan in 2004. When Russian troops moved in to end the siege, more than 300 died. Many were young schoolchildren. Although Russian troops killed the Chechen leader in 2006, the remaining insurgents have continued terrorist attacks in the North Caucasus region. Putin has refused to negotiate with the Chechen rebels.

Critics have questioned Putin's Chechnya policy, as well as how fully this event has been reported in state-owned media. In response, Putin cracked down on the media outlets. Observers in the West have been alarmed by his attack on democratic practices in Russia. However, many Russians support Putin's attempt to restore a sense of pride and discipline in Russian society.

✓ Reading Check **Identifying** What are some of the challenges that Russia still faces?

SECTION 1 REVIEW

Vocabulary

1. **Explain** the significance of: Leonid Brezhnev, Brezhnev Doctrine, détente, dissidents, Afghanistan, participation, Ronald Reagan, Mikhail Gorbachev, perestroika, responsive, Boris Yeltsin, Ukraine, Belarus, Vladimir Putin.

Main Ideas

2. **List** the problems that weakened the Soviet economy during the 1960s and 1970s. Use a chart like the one below to make your list.

Problems That Weakened the Soviet Economy, 1960s–1970s
1.
2.

3. **Explain** the role that nationalism played in the breakup of the Soviet Union.

4. **Summarize** the reforms that Vladimir Putin has made to keep Russia on a strong economic track.

Critical Thinking

5. **The BIG Idea** **Comparing** In what ways can the breakup of the Soviet Union be compared to that of the Roman Empire and the Han dynasty?

6. **Making Connections** Why did the former Soviet Union have problems adapting to a free-market economy?

7. **Analyzing Visuals** Examine the smaller photograph on page 698. Do the Chechen fighters and the Russian army appear to be equally well-armed?

Writing About History

8. **Expository Writing** Locate biographical information on Leonid Brezhnev, Mikhail Gorbachev, Boris Yeltsin, and Vladimir Putin. In an essay, analyze each leader's strengths and weaknesses.

History ONLINE

For help with the concepts in this section of *Glencoe World History— Modern Times*, go to glencoe.com and click Study Central.

Eastern Europe

GUIDE TO READING

The BIG Idea
Self-Determination Popular revolutions helped end Communist regimes in Eastern Europe.

Content Vocabulary
• ethnic cleansing *(p. 703)*
• autonomous *(p. 703)*

Academic Vocabulary
• demonstrations *(p. 700)*
• symbol *(p. 702)*

People and Places
• Lech Walesa *(p. 700)*
• Václav Havel *(p. 701)*
• Slobodan Milošević *(p. 703)*
• Bosnia-Herzegovina *(p. 703)*
• Kosovo *(p. 703)*

Reading Strategy
Categorizing Information As you read, use a chart like the one below to list reasons for and the results of revolution.

Country	Reasons for Revolution	Results of Revolution
Poland		
Czechoslovakia		
Romania		
East Germany		
Yugoslavia		

Soon after the Soviet Union withdrew troop support to its satellite countries, revolutions or demonstrations for independence broke out throughout Eastern Europe. In the shakedown, Germany united into one country, while all six republics that had formed Yugoslavia in 1918 became independent republics. The Iron Curtain finally broke down.

Revolutions in Eastern Europe

MAIN IDEA Without the backing of the Soviet Union, Communist regimes in Eastern Europe fell to popular revolutions.

HISTORY & YOU What is the meaning of the term "Iron Curtain"? Read to learn how the Iron Curtain was finally brought down.

When Gorbachev decided the Soviets would no longer send troops to support the governments of the satellite countries, revolutions broke out throughout Eastern Europe. A look at four Eastern European states shows how the process worked.

Poland

Workers' protests led to demands for change in Poland. In 1980, a worker named **Lech Walesa** (LEHK vah•LEHN•suh) organized a national trade union known as Solidarity. Solidarity gained the support of the workers and of the Roman Catholic Church, which was under the leadership of Pope John Paul II, the first Polish pope. Even when Walesa was arrested, the movement continued. Finally, in 1988, the Polish regime agreed to free parliamentary elections—the first free elections in Eastern Europe in 40 years. A new government was elected, ending 45 years of Communist rule.

In December 1990, Walesa was chosen as president. Poland's new path, however, was not easy. Rapid free-market reforms led to severe unemployment and popular discontent. Aleksander Kwasniewski, who succeeded Walesa, continued Poland's move toward an increasingly prosperous free-market economy. Current president Lech Kaczynski is emphasizing the need to combine modernization with tradition.

Czechoslovakia

The Soviets crushed and then repressed the Czechoslovakian reform movement of 1968. Writers and other intellectuals continued to oppose the government, but they at first had little success. Then in 1988 and 1989, mass **demonstrations** took place throughout

EASTERN EUROPE: THE TRANSITION FROM COMMUNISM

200 kilometers

200 miles

Lambert Azimuthal Equal-Area projection

POLAND
1980: Lech Walesa forms Solidarity, which becomes primary opposition to Communists.
1989: Communists defeated in general election; Solidarity forms government under Walesa.
1990: Solidarity wins first free elections.

SOVIET UNION

GERMANY
1989: Honecker resigns and the Berlin Wall falls.
1990: East and West Germany reunify in October.

ROMANIA
1989: A popular uprising leads to the execution of Ceausescu.
1990: Former Communists win disputed elections.
1992: First multi-party general election.
1996: Opposition wins elections and forms the first non-Communist government.

CZECHOSLOVAKIA
1989: Mass demonstrations in Prague. Non-Communist government formed; Vaclav Havel elected.
1990: First free elections.
1993: Slovakia and the Czech Republic separate.

HUNGARY
1989: Hungary lifts travel restrictions on East Germans.
1990: Democratic forum wins free elections.

YUGOSLAVIA
1989: Milošević elected president of Serbia.
1992: Fighting begins in Bosnia-Herzegovina.
1995: Bosnia-Herzegovina divided in half by Dayton Peace Accords.

(1990) Year of first multi-party elections

WEST GERMANY
EAST GERMANY (1990)
POLAND (1990)
CZECH REPUBLIC
CZECHOSLOVAKIA (1990)
SLOVAKIA
HUNGARY (1990)
SLOVENIA
CROATIA
VOJVODINA
YUGOSLAVIA (1990)
BOSNIA-HERZEGOVINA
SERBIA
ROMANIA (1992)
MONTENEGRO
KOSOVO
BULGARIA (1990)
ALBANIA (1991)
MACEDONIA

ALBANIA
1990: Democratic Party formed after pro-democracy demonstrations.
1991: Free elections won by the Communist Party.

BULGARIA
1989: United Democratic Front formed after the resignation of Zhivkov.
1990: Former Communists win free elections.
1991: United Democratic Front defeats Communists in legislative elections.

Geography SKILLS

1. **Place** What happened to Czechoslovakia and Yugoslavia after they held their first free elections?

2. **Evaluating** In some countries, Communists won the first free elections. Do you think this was a setback for democracy? Why or why not?

Czechoslovakia. By November 1989, crowds as large as 500,000 were forming in Prague.

In December 1989 the Communist government collapsed. At the end of that month, **Václav Havel** (VAHT•SLAHF HAH•vehl), a writer who had played an important role in bringing down the Communist government, became the new president. Havel was an eloquent spokesperson for Czech democracy and a new order in Europe.

The new government soon faced old ethnic conflicts. The two national groups, Czechs and Slovaks, agreed to a peaceful division of the country. Czechoslovakia split into the Czech Republic and Slovakia. Havel became the first president of the Czech Republic, and Michal Kovác became the first president of Slovakia.

Under the new president, Václav Klaus, the Czech Republic remains one of the most stable and prosperous economies of the post-Communist Eastern European states. Slovakia has mastered much of the difficult transition from a centrally planned economy to a modern market economy. However, President Ivan Gasparovic faces the challenge of Slovakia's high unemployment rate.

Romania

Communist leader Nicolae Ceauşescu (nee•kaw•LY chow•SHEHS•koo) ruled Romania with an iron grip, using secret police to crush all dissent. Nonetheless, opposition grew. His economic policies led to a sharp drop in living standards. Food shortages caused rationing. His bulldozing of entire villages to further urbanization plans angered the Romanian people.

One incident ignited the flames of revolution. In December 1989, the secret police murdered thousands of people who were peacefully demonstrating. Finally, the army refused to support any more repression. Ceauşescu and his wife were captured and executed. A new government was quickly formed.

Former Communists dominated the government until 1996. The current president, Traian Basescu, leads a country that is just beginning to show economic growth and the rise of a middle class.

German Reunification

Erich Honecker, head of the Communist Party in East Germany, ruled harshly. While many East Germans fled their country, others led mass demonstrations against the regime in 1989.

Once the Communist government opened its entire border with the West, thousands of East Germans swarmed across the border to reunite with their families and friends. People on both sides of the wall began tearing it down. Helpless, the government ordered the rest of the wall torn down. The Berlin Wall, long a **symbol** of the Cold War, was no more.

The reunification of Germany took place on October 3, 1990. What had seemed almost impossible became a reality—the countries of West and East Germany had reunited to form one Germany.

✓ **Reading Check** **Explaining** What did the fall of the Berlin Wall represent?

INFOGRAPHICS

The Fall of the Berlin Wall

Before the Berlin Wall was built, thousands of East Berliners fled to the West for the opportunities it had to offer. The East German government built the Berlin Wall in 1961 to stem this economic loss. The wall separated family members and friends for decades, and it became a symbol of Communist tyranny. On November 9, 1989, in response to mass protests, East Germany's Communist rulers opened the wall's gates. Soon after crowds began to climb the wall and to tear it down.

When Germany was reunified in 1990, Chancellor Helmut Kohl promised a transformation of the East that would take place within four years. However, it became apparent that rebuilding the East German economy could take many decades and have a high cost. Despite these challenges, all Germans now enjoy the same political freedoms as one nation.

Germans climbing over the Berlin Wall in November 1989

CRITICAL THINKING SKILLS

1. **Explaining** Why did East Germany build the Berlin Wall?
2. **Interpreting** Has German reunification been a success? Explain.

The Disintegration of Yugoslavia

MAIN IDEA Ethnic tensions led to armed conflict in Yugoslavia.

HISTORY & YOU Can you recall examples in your textbook of ethnic conflict? Read about ethnic cleansing in the Bosnian war.

Yugoslavia had a Communist government but was never a Soviet satellite state. By 1990, however, the Communist Party collapsed. The Yugoslav political scene was complex. **Slobodan Milošević** (slaw•BAW•dahn muh•LOH•suh•VIHCH), leader of Serbia, rejected efforts toward independence. In Milošević's view, the republics' borders first needed to be redrawn to form a new Greater Serbian state. When negotiations failed, Slovenia and Croatia declared their independence in June 1991. In September 1991, the Yugoslav army assaulted Croatia. Increasingly, Serbia, aided by Croatian Serbs, dominated the Yugoslav army. Serbian forces captured one-third of Croatia's territory before a cease-fire ended the conflict.

Wars in Bosnia and Kosovo

The Serbs next attacked **Bosnia-Herzegovina** and acquired 70 percent of Bosnian territory. Many Bosnians were Muslims. The Serbs followed a policy called **ethnic cleansing** toward Bosnians—killing or forcibly removing them from their lands. Ethnic cleansing revived memories of Nazi atrocities in World War II.

With support from NATO air attacks, Bosnian and Croatian forces regained considerable territory lost to Serbian forces. This forced the Serbs to sign a formal peace treaty that split Bosnia into a Serb republic and a Muslim-Croat federation. In 2006, about 30,000 NATO troops were still in Bosnia trying to keep the peace.

A new war erupted in 1998 over **Kosovo,** an **autonomous** or self-governing province within Yugoslavia. After Slobodan Milošević stripped Kosovo of its autonomy in 1989, groups of ethnic Albanians founded the Kosovo Liberation Army (KLA) and began a campaign against Serbian rule. To crush the KLA, Serb forces massacred ethnic Albanians. The United States and NATO allies worked on a settlement that would end the killing. The Albanians in Kosovo regained their autonomy in 1999. Milošević's rule ended in 2000. While on trial for his role in the massacre of Kosovo civilians, Milošević died in 2006.

Yugoslavia ceased to exist in 2004 when the government officially renamed the country Serbia and Montenegro. The people of Montenegro voted for independence in 2006. Thus, all six republics that formed Yugoslavia in 1918 were once again independent nations.

✓ Reading Check **Identifying** What events resulted from the disintegration of Yugoslavia?

SECTION 2 REVIEW

Vocabulary

1. **Explain** the significance of: Lech Walesa, demonstrations, Václav Havel, symbol, Slobodan Milošević, Bosnia-Herzegovina, ethnic cleansing, Kosovo, autonomous.

Main Ideas

2. **List** four Eastern European states discussed in this section that were Soviet satellite states. What events occurred in each state after the withdrawal of Soviet influence?

3. **Explain** why the Communist government ordered the Berlin Wall to be torn down.

4. **Summarize** the Yugoslav republics that wanted independence after 1990, the inhabitants of these republics (if listed), and the reasons the republics fought each other. Use a chart like the one below.

Republics	Inhabitants	Causes of Fighting

Critical Thinking

5. **The BIG Idea** **Analyzing** Why was the collapse of communism in the Soviet Union a turning point in history?

6. **Comparing** How is the ethnic cleansing of Bosnians similar to the Holocaust?

7. **Analyzing Visuals** Examine the photograph on page 702. Why is it significant that people are climbing over the wall?

Writing About History

8. **Informative Writing** Research and write an essay about the Polish Solidarity movement. Why was it successful? Be sure to discuss Lech Walesa's supporters, adversaries, and the status of the movement today.

History ONLINE

For help with the concepts in this section of *Glencoe World History—Modern Times*, go to glencoe.com and click Study Central.

Europe and North America

GUIDE TO READING

The BIG Idea
Ideas, Beliefs, and Values Postwar Western societies rebuilt their communities, but shifting social structures led to upheaval and change.

Content Vocabulary
• Thatcherism *(p. 707)*   • budget deficits *(p. 708)*

Academic Vocabulary
• currency *(p. 704)*   • shift *(p. 704)*

People, Places, and Events
• France *(p. 704)*
• West Germany *(p. 705)*
• Northern Ireland *(p. 707)*
• Margaret Thatcher *(p. 707)*
• Richard Nixon *(p. 707)*
• Watergate *(p. 707)*
• Gerald Ford *(p. 707)*
• Jimmy Carter *(p. 707)*
• Ronald Reagan *(p. 708)*
• Reagan Revolution *(p. 708)*
• George Bush *(p. 708)*
• Bill Clinton *(p. 708)*
• George W. Bush *(p. 709)*
• Pierre Trudeau *(p. 709)*

Reading Strategy
Comparing and Contrasting As you read, use a Venn diagram like the one below to compare and contrast economic policies of Thatcherism and those of the Reagan Revolution.

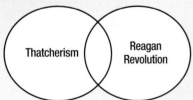

During the later decades of the twentieth century, the leaders of Western European countries faced many economic challenges. Germany, in particular, wrestled with social and economic problems caused by its unification. Meanwhile, in the United States, politics took a shift to the right; and Canada was divided on the Quebec secession debate.

Winds of Change in Western Europe

MAIN IDEA France, Great Britain, and Germany have all experienced economic upheavals and changes.

HISTORY & YOU Do you believe there should be a global currency? Read to learn how Europe adopted a single currency.

Between the early 1950s and late 1970s, Western Europe experienced virtually full employment. An economic downturn, however, occurred in the mid-1970s and early 1980s. Both inflation and unemployment rose dramatically, partly because of increases in oil prices after the Arab-Israeli conflict in 1973 (see Chapter 23). Western European economies recovered in the course of the 1980s, but problems remained.

The Western European nations moved toward a greater union of their economies after 1970. The European Economic Community (EEC) expanded in 1973 to include Great Britain, Ireland, and Denmark. By 1986, Spain, Portugal, and Greece had become members. Austria, Finland, and Sweden joined in 1995.

The EEC or European Community (EC) was chiefly an economic union. By 1992, it comprised 344 million people and was the world's largest single trading bloc. The Treaty on European Union, which went into effect on January 1, 1994, turned the EC into the European Union (EU). One of the EU's first goals was to establish a common **currency,** the euro. Twelve of the 15 EU nations abandoned their currency in favor of the euro on January 1, 2002.

The new goal of the EU was to add the states of Eastern and southeastern Europe to the union. In May 2004, the EU added ten new members, mostly from Eastern Europe.

Uncertainties in France

In **France,** a deteriorating economic situation in the 1970s caused a political **shift** to the left. By 1981, the Socialists gained power in the National Assembly. Socialist François Mitterrand was elected president. He initiated a number of measures to aid workers: an increased minimum wage, a 39-hour workweek, and higher taxes

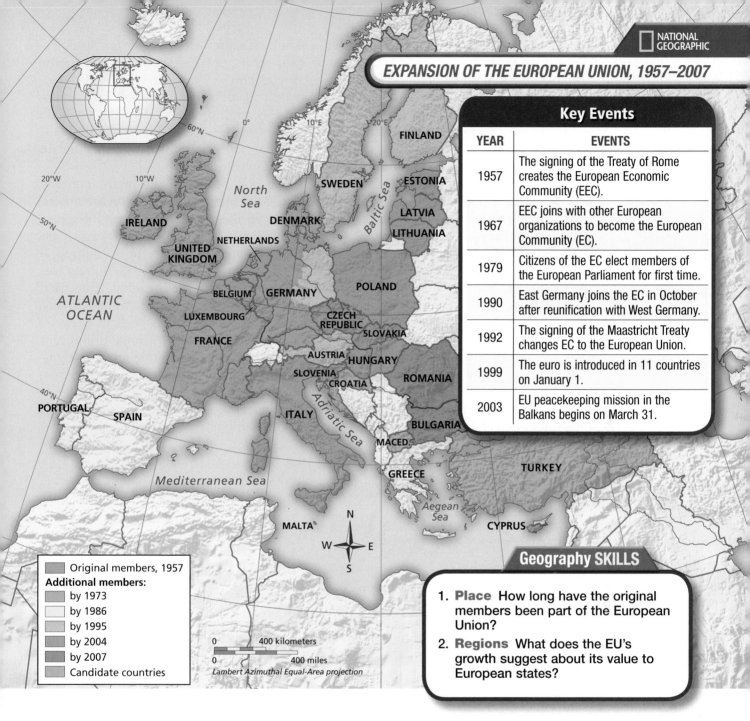

EXPANSION OF THE EUROPEAN UNION, 1957–2007

NATIONAL GEOGRAPHIC

Key Events

YEAR	EVENTS
1957	The signing of the Treaty of Rome creates the European Economic Community (EEC).
1967	EEC joins with other European organizations to become the European Community (EC).
1979	Citizens of the EC elect members of the European Parliament for first time.
1990	East Germany joins the EC in October after reunification with West Germany.
1992	The signing of the Maastricht Treaty changes EC to the European Union.
1999	The euro is introduced in 11 countries on January 1.
2003	EU peacekeeping mission in the Balkans begins on March 31.

Original members, 1957
Additional members:
by 1973
by 1986
by 1995
by 2004
by 2007
Candidate countries

0   400 kilometers
0   400 miles
Lambert Azimuthal Equal-Area projection

Geography SKILLS

1. **Place** How long have the original members been part of the European Union?
2. **Regions** What does the EU's growth suggest about its value to European states?

for the rich. The Socialist government also nationalized, or took over, major banks, the steel industry, the space and electronics industries, and insurance firms.

Socialist policies, however, largely failed to work, and France's economic decline continued. In 1993 French unemployment stood at 10.6 percent. In the elections in March of that year, the Socialists won only 28 percent of the vote. A coalition of conservative parties gained 80 percent of the seats in the National Assembly. The move to the right in France was strengthened when the conservative mayor of Paris,

Jacques Chirac, was elected president in May 1995 and reelected in 2002.

Reunification Woes

In 1969 the Social Democrats, a moderate Socialist party, replaced the Christian Democrats as the leading political party in **West Germany.** The first Social Democratic chancellor elected in West Germany was Willy Brandt. In December 1972 Brandt signed a treaty that led to greater contact between East Germany and West Germany. Economic, cultural, and personal ties between the countries were stronger as a result.

For his efforts, Brandt received the Nobel Peace Prize for 1971.

In 1982 the Christian Democratic Union of Helmut Kohl formed a new, more conservative government. Kohl was a smart politician who benefited greatly from an economic boom in the mid-1980s. Then events in East Germany led to the unexpected reunification of the two Germanies in 1990. With a population of 79 million people, the new Germany became the leading power in Europe.

The joy over reunification soon faded as new problems arose. It became clear that the rebuilding of eastern Germany would take far more money than had originally been thought.

Kohl's government was soon forced to face the politically undesirable task of raising taxes. In addition, the virtual collapse of the economy in eastern Germany had led to extremely high levels of unemployment and severe discontent. One result was a return to power for the Social Democrats, who were victorious in the 1998 elections. However, the Social Democrats had little success in solving Germany's economic woes. In 2005 Angela Merkel, leader of the Christian Democrats, became the first female chancellor in German history.

The collapse of the German economy also led to increasing attacks on foreigners. For years, illegal immigrants and foreigners seeking refuge had found haven in Germany because of its very liberal immigration laws. In 1992 over 440,000 immigrants came to Germany seeking refuge. Increased unemployment and economic problems, however, caused tensions to grow between some Germans and various immigrant groups. Attacks against foreigners by right-wing extremists—especially young neo-Nazis who believed in Hitler's idea of creating a pure Aryan race—became a part of German life.

INFOGRAPHICS

North African Immigration to France

Major migration to Europe took place after World War II. In the 1950s and 1960s, immigrant workers came to Western European nations to help fill the labor shortage. Most of these workers came from Africa and Asia—usually from former European colonies.

For example, many of the immigrant workers that came to France were from former French colonies that were Muslim, such as Algeria. It was assumed that most migrants would return home after a time; however, many stayed.

Immigration in France became a political issue in the 1970s when, due to recession, France tightened its immigration policy. By this time, Muslims had become more visible in French society. Some saw their lack of willingness to assimilate as a threat to the French national identity.

In an effort to separate church and state, a 2004 French law banned the wearing of headscarves by Muslims in French state schools. Muslim protesters said this denied them their freedom of religion. Similar cultural clashes have taken place across Europe in recent years.

Muslim women protest outside the French Embassy in London against the 2004 ban on wearing the *hijab*, or head scarf, in French state schools.

CRITICAL THINKING SKILLS

1. **Explaining** How did immigrant workers help Western Europe?
2. **Determining Cause and Effect** What kinds of tensions have arisen as a result of the migration of Muslims to Western Europe?

Great Britain and Thatcherism

Between 1964 and 1979, Great Britain's Conservative Party and Labour Party alternated being in power. One problem both parties had to face was the intense fighting between Catholics and Protestants in **Northern Ireland.** An ailing economy and frequent labor strikes were two other issues that the government struggled to solve.

In 1979 the Conservatives came to power under **Margaret Thatcher,** Britain's first female prime minister. Thatcher pledged to limit social welfare, to restrict union power, and to end inflation. Her main focus was privatization. As Thatcher said, "The State's job is to provide a proper framework of laws within which private enterprise can flourish, not to extend its powers by owning business." Although she did not eliminate the basic parts of the social welfare system, Thatcher did break the power of the labor unions and control inflation.

Thatcherism, as her economic policy was termed, improved the British economic situation, but at a price. Business investment and the number of small businesses increased substantially. The south of England, for example, prospered. Old industrial areas elsewhere, however, were beset by high unemployment, poverty, and even violence.

Thatcher dominated British politics in the 1980s. Only in 1990 did the Labour Party's fortunes seem to revive. At that time, Thatcher's government tried to replace local property taxes with a flat-rate tax payable by every adult. In 1990 antitax riots broke out. Thatcher's popularity fell, and she resigned as prime minister.

The Conservative Party, now led by John Major, failed to capture the imagination of most Britons. In new elections in 1997, the Labour Party won a landslide victory. Tony Blair, a moderate, became prime minister and instilled a new vigor on the political scene. By 2006, however, his ongoing support of the U.S. war in Iraq, when most Britons opposed it, caused his popularity to plummet.

✓ Reading Check **Identifying** What were the policies of Thatcherism?

The U.S. and Canada

MAIN IDEA The United States has moved toward the political right, and Quebec's status divides Canada.

HISTORY & YOU What if your state wanted to become an independent nation? Read to learn about Quebec's desire to secede from Canada.

U.S. politics shifted to the right in the mid-1970s as economic issues became the focus. Canadians were concerned about economic issues and the status of Quebec.

Nixon, Ford, and Carter

In his campaign for the presidency, **Richard Nixon** believed that "law and order" issues and a slowdown in racial desegregation would appeal to Southern whites. The South, once a stronghold for the Democrats, began to form a new allegiance to the Republican Party.

As president, Nixon used illegal methods to gain political information about his opponents. This led to the **Watergate** scandal. A group of men working for Nixon's reelection campaign broke into the Democratic National Headquarters, located in the Watergate Hotel in Washington, D.C. They were caught there trying to install electronic listening devices.

Nixon lied to the American public about his involvement in the affair. Secret tapes of his conversations in the White House, however, revealed the truth. On August 9, 1974, Nixon resigned rather than face possible impeachment.

Vice President **Gerald Ford** became president when Nixon resigned, only to lose in the 1976 election to the former governor of Georgia, **Jimmy Carter.** By 1980, the Carter administration was faced with two devastating problems. First, high inflation rates and a decline in average earnings were causing a drop in American living standards.

A crisis abroad erupted when the Iranian government of the Ayatollah Ruhollah Khomeini (koh•MAY•nee) (see Chapter 23) held 52 Americans hostage. Carter's inability to gain the release of the American hostages contributed to his loss to **Ronald Reagan** in the 1980 election.

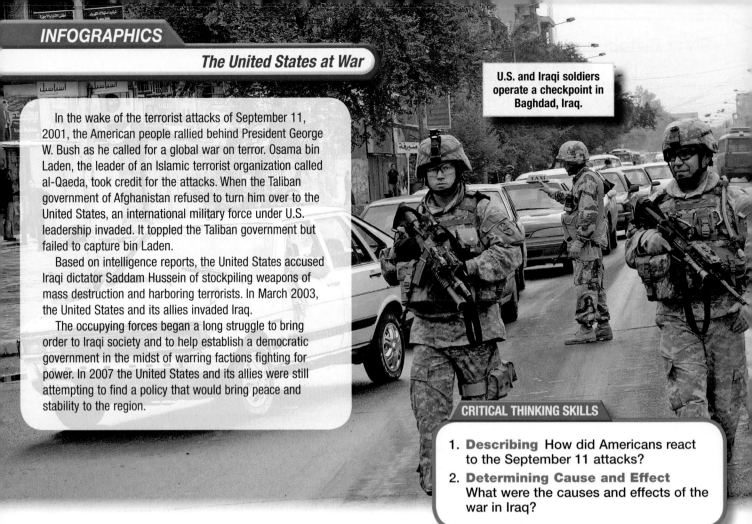

U.S. and Iraqi soldiers operate a checkpoint in Baghdad, Iraq.

In the wake of the terrorist attacks of September 11, 2001, the American people rallied behind President George W. Bush as he called for a global war on terror. Osama bin Laden, the leader of an Islamic terrorist organization called al-Qaeda, took credit for the attacks. When the Taliban government of Afghanistan refused to turn him over to the United States, an international military force under U.S. leadership invaded. It toppled the Taliban government but failed to capture bin Laden.

Based on intelligence reports, the United States accused Iraqi dictator Saddam Hussein of stockpiling weapons of mass destruction and harboring terrorists. In March 2003, the United States and its allies invaded Iraq.

The occupying forces began a long struggle to bring order to Iraqi society and to help establish a democratic government in the midst of warring factions fighting for power. In 2007 the United States and its allies were still attempting to find a policy that would bring peace and stability to the region.

CRITICAL THINKING SKILLS

1. **Describing** How did Americans react to the September 11 attacks?
2. **Determining Cause and Effect** What were the causes and effects of the war in Iraq?

Reagan, Bush, and Clinton

The **Reagan Revolution,** as it has been called, sent U.S. policy in new directions. Reversing decades of policy, Reagan cut back on the welfare state, decreasing spending on food stamps, school lunch programs, and job programs. At the same time, Reagan oversaw the largest peacetime military buildup in U.S. history.

Total federal spending rose from $631 billion in 1981 to over a trillion dollars by 1987. The spending policies of the Reagan administration produced record government **budget deficits.** A budget deficit exists when the government spends more than it collects in revenues. In the 1970s, the total deficit was $420 billion. Between 1981 and 1987, budget deficits were three times that amount.

George Bush, Reagan's vice president, succeeded him as president. Bush's inability to deal with the federal deficit and an economic downturn, however, allowed Democrat **Bill Clinton** to be elected president in 1992. Clinton claimed to be a new kind of Democrat, one who favored several Republican policies of the 1980s. This clearly said that the shift to the right in U.S. politics did not end with the election of a Democrat.

A lengthy economic revival won Clinton popular support, but his second term was overshadowed by charges of presidential misconduct. The House of Representatives voted two articles of impeachment—formal charges of misconduct—against him. After a bitter partisan struggle, he was acquitted in the Senate. Clinton's problems helped Republican **George W. Bush,** son of the first President Bush, to win the presidency in 2000.

Bush and 9/11

The new president soon found most of his attention directed to the problem of terrorism. Terrorists directed by Osama bin Laden hijacked four commercial jets in Boston, Newark, and Washington, D.C. The hijackers flew two of the airplanes directly into the World Trade Center towers in New York City. A third hijacked plane slammed into the Pentagon in Arlington, Virginia. The fourth plane crashed into an isolated field in Pennsylvania. In all, almost 3,000 people were killed that day.

After the attacks of September 11, President George W. Bush vowed to fight terrorism. In October 2001, he led a coalition of countries in a war against the Taliban in Afghanistan. The Taliban was a militant Islamic group that controlled Afghanistan and allowed Osama bin Laden to train his al-Qaeda terrorists there. After the defeat of the Taliban, the United States and its allies worked with Afghan leaders to create a new government.

In November 2004, Bush was narrowly elected to a second term. Two years later, however, his popularity plummeted as discontent grew over the Iraq War (see Chapter 23), financial corruption in the Republican Party, and the administration's poor handling of relief efforts after Hurricane Katrina.

Canada

During a major economic recession in Canada in the early 1960s, the Liberals came into power. **Pierre Trudeau** (TROO•DOH) became prime minister in 1968. Although from a French-Canadian background, Trudeau was dedicated to preserving a united Canada. At the same time, he acknowledged the rights of French-speaking Canadians. His government passed the Official Languages Act, which allowed both English and French to be used in the federal civil service. Trudeau's government also supported a vigorous program of industrialization.

In 1993 Canada approved the North American Free Trade Agreement (NAFTA), along with the United States and Mexico, to make trade easier and more profitable. Since many Canadians thought the agreement too favorable to the United States, Brian Mulroney lost popularity and the position of prime minister to Jean Chrétien, who was reelected in both 1997 and 2000. However, with a Conservative victory in 2006, Stephen Harper became the new prime minister.

The status of the French-speaking Quebec province has been an issue for decades. In 1995 Quebec voters only narrowly rejected secession. In 1998 Canada's Supreme Court ruled the government would have to agree to secession if Quebec voters supported it. However, that vote would have to be on a clear issue and with a clear majority. The debate still divides Canadians.

✓ Reading Check What was the purpose of Canada's Official Languages Act?

Vocabulary

1. **Explain** the significance of: currency, France, shift, West Germany, Northern Ireland, Margaret Thatcher, Thatcherism, Richard Nixon, Watergate, Gerald Ford, Jimmy Carter, Ronald Reagan, Reagan Revolution, budget deficits, George Bush, Bill Clinton, George W. Bush, Pierre Trudeau.

Main Ideas

2. **Summarize** the problems that Germany faced when it was unified in 1990. Use a chart like the one below to make your summary.

Problems Created by German Unification

3. **Identify** Margaret Thatcher. What role did she play in Britain's economic recovery?

4. **List** in chronological order by term the U.S. presidents beginning with Richard Nixon.

Critical Thinking

5. **The BIG Idea** **Determining Cause and Effect** What factors led to the economic downturn of the 1970s? How did European nations respond?

6. **Making Inferences** Why does Quebec wish to secede from Canada?

7. **Analyzing Visuals** Examine the photograph on page 706. What is the protesters' point of view? How do you know?

Writing About History

8. **Expository Writing** When a country faces economic problems, its inhabitants often blame a person or a group. Look up the word *scapegoating*. Do you think that the way some Germans treated foreigners in the 1990s is an example of scapegoating? Write an essay about this topic.

History ONLINE
For help with the concepts in this section of *Glencoe World History—Modern Times*, go to glencoe.com and click Study Central.

Western Society and Culture

GUIDE TO READING

The BIG Idea
New Technologies Trends in contemporary Western society include rapid changes in science and technology, changes in family structures and population trends, increased religious diversity, and a shared popular culture among nations.

Content Vocabulary
• gender stereotyping (p. 712)
• gender parity (p. 712)
• postmodernism (p. 713)
• popular culture (p. 713)
• cultural imperialism (p. 713))

Academic Vocabulary
• chemical (p. 710)   • globalization (p. 713)

People, Places, and Events
• Sputnik I (p. 710)   • Basque region (p. 715)
• Equal Pay Act (p. 712)   • Bloody Sunday
• Roe v. Wade (p. 712)   (p. 715)
• Munich (p. 713)

Reading Strategy
Categorizing Information As you read, complete a chart like the one below to list the issues and outcomes for the women's movement since 1970.

Issues	Outcomes

Among the effects of globalization is the spread of culture, and Western culture has expanded to and influenced most parts of the world. Western culture itself has undergone many changes these past few decades, most notably with changes in the family, in women's lives, and in religious trends. Not all people welcome Western culture; some see it as a challenge to their own culture and national identity.

The Quickening Pace of Change

MAIN IDEA The Western world has seen many technological and social changes, as well as changes in the family and in women's lives.

HISTORY & YOU How often do you use your cell phone? Read to learn how new technologies are transforming Western society.

Western societies have tended to pride themselves on expanding democracy and material progress. Since 1970, the pace of material change has quickened and promoted a global economy. An important question today is how this global economy will affect each country.

Science and Technology

Science and technology are important forces for change in today's world. During World War II, governments recruited scientists to develop new weapons, the most famous being the atomic bomb. By funding projects, governments created a new model for scientific research. Complex projects required not just teams of scientists. They also needed huge laboratories and sophisticated equipment that only governments or large corporations could fund.

A stunning example of such projects is the space race. In 1961 four years after the Soviet Union launched *Sputnik I,* President Kennedy predicted that Americans would land on the moon within a decade. The American moon landing happened in 1969.

Postwar science and technology led to rapid change. Many believed that scientific knowledge gave society the ability and the right to manipulate the environment for everyone's benefit. Critics in the 1960s and 1970s, however, argued that some technology had far-reaching effects that damaged the environment. The use of **chemical** fertilizers, for example, produced higher-yield crops but also destroyed the ecological balance of streams, rivers, and woodlands. In the early 2000s, debates over organic farming and genetically enhanced foods intensified. People continue to disagree over the role of science in food production.

Technology And The Environment

Power plants designed to generate electricity are a major source of greenhouse gases.

Electricity produced from the wind produces no greenhouse gas emissions.

Science and technology have changed the way we live. Yet one of the unfortunate side-effects of modern technology has been damage to the environment.

Global warming, for example, has been linked to emissions of carbon dioxide and other greenhouse gases from burning fossil fuels—coal, gas, and oil. These emissions have been blamed for rapid melting of the polar ice caps. This could cause sea levels to rise, which could have a devastating effect on populated coastal areas throughout the world.

In an attempt to slow global warming, some 141 countries have ratified the Kyoto Protocol, which calls on countries to cut air pollution. The United States has refused to sign, however, saying that the required changes would be too costly.

Iceland, on the other hand, had already begun to reduce its dependence on fossil fuels by introducing geothermal and hydroelectric power plants. Iceland has also announced that it will switch to hydrogen-powered vehicles.

Another clean source of energy is wind. Scientists estimate that one-third of the world's electricity could be supplied by wind generators by 2050. That would be enough to prevent 113 billion metric tons of carbon dioxide from entering the atmosphere each year. Wind farms like the one shown above have sprouted around the world—including in the United States.

CRITICAL THINKING SKILLS

1. **Identifying** What was the purpose of the Kyoto Protocol?
2. **Analyzing** Do you think that the Kyoto Protocol will accomplish its goal without the participation of the United States?

Changes in the Family

The Western world is also experiencing changing trends in marriage and divorce. Over the past 40 years, the number of people in Europe getting married has decreased. People also tend to get married at a slightly older age.

Between 1980 and 1995, for example, the average age of French women marrying for the first time went up from 23 to 27 years. The divorce rate, too, has gone up. Between 1970 and 1995, Belgium, France, the Netherlands, and the United Kingdom all saw enormous increases in divorce rates. These social trends have meant a lower birthrate and thus an older population overall.

Changes in Women's Lives

Women's changing roles in the workforce have also affected family size and thus population growth. More women work not only because they choose to, but to help support their families.

Since the 1970s, the number of women active in the workforce has continued to rise.

At the same time, more women went to college, and more of them pursued careers in law, medicine, and government.

The Women's Movement

In the 1960s and 1970s, the women's movement emerged in the United States. It quickly spread to Western Europe and in recent decades to other parts of the world. Supporters of the movement wanted to change the basic conditions of women's lives. They forced politicians to address "**gender stereotyping,**" restricting what a person could do just because of the person's gender. The United States passed the **Equal Pay Act** in 1963. It required women to be paid the same as men for performing the same work.

A controversial issue was abortion. In 1973 the U.S. Supreme Court legalized abortion in *Roe v. Wade*. While national health insurance covers abortion in most of Europe, the procedure is still hotly debated in the United States.

In the 1990s, there was a backlash against the women's movement. Some women urged a return to traditional roles. Others found ways to balance career and family. However, women in Western societies still earn much less on average than men. Many women face the burden of working outside the home while continuing to do most of the child rearing and domestic work.

To encourage women's roles in government, Norway and Denmark adopted **gender parity** policies in the 1970s. Women must make up either a certain number of the candidates in an election or a certain number of those elected. Other European nations followed suit.

✓ **Reading Check** **Identifying** How does gender stereotyping affect women's and men's roles?

INFOGRAPHICS

Women in the Workforce

Since the 1970s, Western countries have experienced an increased percentage of women in the workforce, due to the efforts of the international women's movement. Laws passed in the United States and Europe made it illegal to discriminate on the basis of gender. New laws also made it illegal to pay a woman less than a man for the same work.

Although women still make less money than men in Western countries, that pay gap is narrowing. In the United States, women earned 62 percent of what men earned in 1979, but that rose to 80 percent by 2004. In the United Kingdom, women earned 87.4 percent of what men earned in 2006. This represented the smallest pay gap ever recorded in the U.K.

Women demonstrating in London, 1971

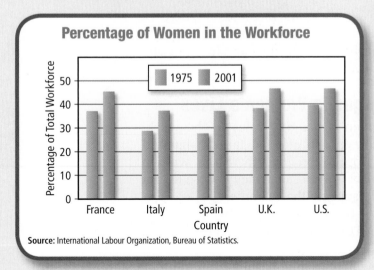

Percentage of Women in the Workforce

Percentage of Total Workforce — 1975 / 2001

France, Italy, Spain, U.K., U.S.

Country

Source: International Labour Organization, Bureau of Statistics.

CRITICAL THINKING SKILLS

1. **Identifying** What has been the general trend in employment of women in Western countries since the 1970s?

2. **Evaluating** How do you think the increase of women in the workforce has advanced the status of women in general?

Culture and Identity

MAIN IDEA Popular culture brings the world closer, but some nations want to maintain their own identities.

HISTORY & YOU Did you know that American movies can be seen all over the world? Read to learn how Western culture affects the world.

The effects of globalization are not limited to politics and economics. Western culture can now be mass-produced and marketed globally. However, the dominance of Western culture also raises some questions.

Trends in Art

The United States dominated the art world after World War II, and New York City became the artistic center of the Western world. Artists, from abstract expressionists like Jackson Pollock to postmodernists, expressed vibrantly and energetically the postwar culture.

Abstractionism dominated modern art after 1945. Abstract expressionists conveyed emotion and feeling. By the 1980s, postmodern styles emerged. **Postmodernism,** a revival of traditional elements and techniques, includes traditional painting styles and traditional crafts. Postmodern artists often create works that include elements of film, performance, popular culture, and sculpture. Today's artists use digital cameras and computer programs to produce interactive art forms. Viewers can influence the production of the art itself.

Popular Culture

Today people often talk about the movies they saw over the weekend or who won last night's football or basketball game before they talk about anything else. Music, movies, television, sports—all are part of our popular culture. Entertainment created for a profit and for a mass audience is known as **popular culture.**

Known throughout the world, American performers and filmmakers help spread American popular culture. From early rock 'n' roll to multimillion dollar musical acts of today, the world participates in America's musical pop culture.

Films also play a big role in spreading Western culture. In 2003 moviegoers around the world eagerly waited for the opening of the third and final installment of the *Lord of the Rings* trilogy, *The Return of the King*. The film's success is an example of the **globalization** of modern popular culture.

Television and sports have created a sense that Americans and Europeans share a culture. Europeans watch popular American shows like *ER* and become familiar with American brand names—and American attitudes about family, work, and money. As a cultural export, sports have become big business. Sports organizations receive most of their revenues from advertisers who pay millions to sponsor TV football, soccer, or baseball.

Sports have become big politics as well. The most telling example of how politics and sports mix came with the 1972 Olympic Games in **Munich.** There a Palestinian terrorist group seized 11 Israeli athletes as hostages. All of the hostages were killed. During the height of the Cold War, the USSR refused to participate in the 1984 Los Angeles Olympics after the United States boycotted the 1980 Moscow Olympics.

Some nations' peoples worry that American entertainment weakens their own language and culture. Critics refer to **cultural imperialism,** meaning that a Western nation controls other world cultures much as Western nations had controlled colonial governments. To protect their own musical heritage, the French even passed a law saying that at least 40 percent of radio time had to be reserved for French-language music.

Although Western music and movies may still dominate, trends in the opposite direction are developing. One trend is that non-Western music is being played in Western rock and pop. Paul Simon's *Graceland* was an early example. Simon spiced many of his songs with *mbaqanga*—the dance music of the black townships of South Africa. The reggae music native to Jamaica has an enormous following, especially with resistance movements. Finally, Latin pop has become so popular that there have been Latin Grammy awards since 1999.

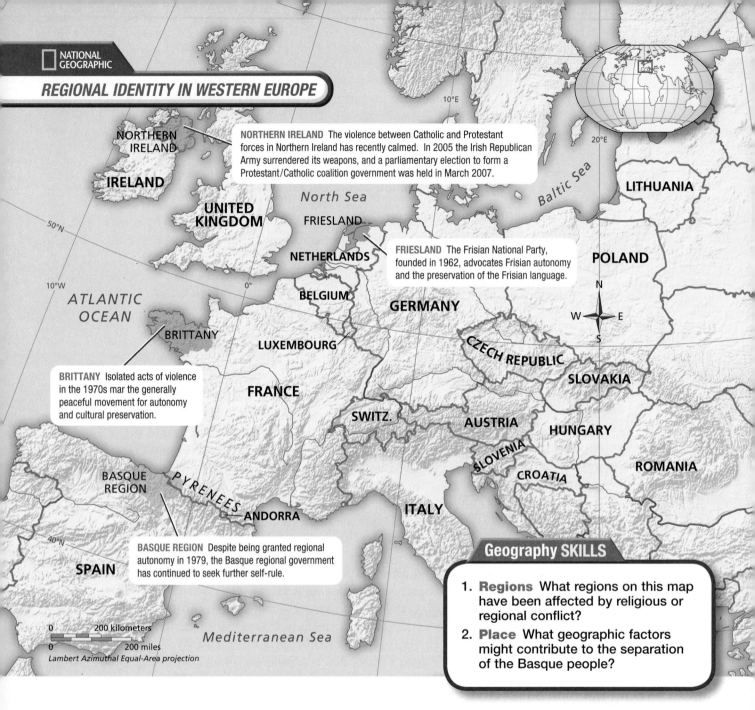

REGIONAL IDENTITY IN WESTERN EUROPE

NATIONAL GEOGRAPHIC

NORTHERN IRELAND The violence between Catholic and Protestant forces in Northern Ireland has recently calmed. In 2005 the Irish Republican Army surrendered its weapons, and a parliamentary election to form a Protestant/Catholic coalition government was held in March 2007.

FRIESLAND The Frisian National Party, founded in 1962, advocates Frisian autonomy and the preservation of the Frisian language.

BRITTANY Isolated acts of violence in the 1970s mar the generally peaceful movement for autonomy and cultural preservation.

BASQUE REGION Despite being granted regional autonomy in 1979, the Basque regional government has continued to seek further self-rule.

NORTHERN IRELAND
IRELAND
UNITED KINGDOM
North Sea
FRIESLAND
NETHERLANDS
BELGIUM
GERMANY
LUXEMBOURG
FRANCE
BRITTANY
SWITZ.
AUSTRIA
HUNGARY
SLOVENIA
CROATIA
ROMANIA
ITALY
BASQUE REGION
PYRENEES
ANDORRA
SPAIN
ATLANTIC OCEAN
Mediterranean Sea
Baltic Sea
LITHUANIA
POLAND
CZECH REPUBLIC
SLOVAKIA

10°E
20°E
50°N
10°W
0°
40°N

0   200 kilometers
0   200 miles
Lambert Azimuthal Equal-Area projection

Geography SKILLS

1. **Regions** What regions on this map have been affected by religious or regional conflict?
2. **Place** What geographic factors might contribute to the separation of the Basque people?

Religious Trends

From the Middle Ages through the early part of the twentieth century, Christianity dominated the spiritual life of Western society. After World War II, however, many immigrants from former colonies moved to Europe to find jobs. The result has been much greater religious diversity in Europe. Immigrants from Africa, for example, have established large Muslim communities in France, Germany, and Great Britain.

Many people define themselves through their religion, and it influences national customs and social attitudes. This is why some Europeans feel that non-Christian immigrants are threatening their culture.

There is a different trend in the United States. Since the 1980s, a Protestant revival has gathered strength translating into a political force in which conservative Christian groups play a larger role in American politics.

Religious trends in the United States and Europe have raised an important issue: what role should religion play in a democracy? In the United States, controversies have erupted over the precise extent to which religion and government should be separated. Conflicts have arisen, for example, about the place of prayer in public schools and the use of federal money to fund programs that certain Christians oppose.

In Europe, non-Christians struggle to find a balance between their identities as citizens of the West and as believers in a non-Christian religion. In France, for example, there is an ongoing struggle over whether Muslim girls should be allowed to wear headscarves to public schools.

Nationalism and Regional Identity

A global American-style culture is not the only challenge to national identity. Minorities in Europe want to preserve their culture or even have their own nation. Sometimes these are ethnic groups, and sometimes they are religious groups. These minorities use different tactics, from peaceful demonstrations to terrorism, to reach their goals.

Most minority movements are peaceful. In **Brittany**, a western region of France that is Celtic in its language and culture, local communities organize festivals called **Fest Noz** to celebrate their culture. These festivals feature traditional Breton costumes, music, and the Breton language, which closely resembles the Gaelic spoken in Ireland.

Some minorities use violence as a tool to win concessions or gain independence. The **Basque region** is in the western Pyrenees, and part of the territory belongs to Spain and part to France. Although most Basques accept the status quo and work peacefully to protect their language and culture, Basque extremists do not. The group Basque Fatherland and Liberty (ETA) employs violence.

Northern Ireland has also faced ongoing problems with violent extremists. In 1921 Ireland was partitioned between the independent Irish Republic, which is mostly Catholic, and Northern Ireland, which remained under British control. Northern Ireland has a powerful Protestant majority but also contains many Catholics.

Clashes between Catholics and Protestants in Northern Ireland escalated on January 30, 1972. On this date, which is known as "**Bloody Sunday,**" British troops fired on a crowd of civil rights protesters and killed 13 people.

For the next three decades, the Catholic Irish Republican Army (IRA) employed violence and terror in an effort to unite Northern Ireland with the Republic of Ireland. Often aimed against British officials or local Protestant leaders, this violence continued despite many peace talks. By 2000, about 3,600 people had been killed and 36,000 injured. Exhausted by years of violence, the two sides began talks in the 1990s, and signed the Good Friday Agreement in April 1998. The reluctance of the IRA and other militants to disarm, however, threatens the peace process.

✓ Reading Check **Explaining** Why did conflict between Catholics and Protestants in Northern Ireland begin?

Vocabulary
1. **Explain** the significance of: *Sputnik I*, chemical, gender stereotyping, Equal Pay Act, *Roe* v. *Wade*, gender parity, postmodernism, globalization, popular culture, Munich, cultural imperialism, Basque region, Bloody Sunday.

Main Ideas
2. **Explain** why some critics began to question the value of technological progress in postwar society. Give examples.

3. **List** the achievements of the women's movement during the 1960s and 1970s. Use a chart like the one below to make your list.

Achievements of the Women's Movement
1.
2.

4. **Define** cultural imperialism. How have some countries reacted to it?

Critical Thinking
5. **The BIG Idea** **Evaluating** Which medium—TV, films, sports, music—do you believe has the greatest effect on the cultures of other countries? In what ways?

6. **Making Generalizations** Why do some minorities use violence as a tool to gain independence?

7. **Analyzing Visuals** Do you think the women in the photograph on page 712 would be pleased with the status of women today? Why or why not?

Writing About History
8. **Descriptive Writing** Abstractionism, abstract expressionism, and pop art became popular art forms after World War II. Research these art forms and describe in an essay how they represent innovations.

History ONLINE

For help with the concepts in this section of *Glencoe World History— Modern Times*, go to  glencoe.com and click Study Central.

Rock 'n' Roll Around the World

The electric amplification of voices and strings allowed guitar-driven groups to produce a big sound with a few people. Worldwide, rock music combined with local traditions to create new musical forms. Rock 'n' roll let musicians experiment. These experiments allowed people from many cultures to feel like part of a worldwide movement.

◀ *The Platters*

In 1964, the British Invasion first defined rock 'n' roll as an international phenomenon.

Rock 'n' roll first appeared in the U.S. in the mid-1950s.

The Kinks ▶

ROCK 'N' ROLL'S SOCIAL IMPACT

Rock 'n' roll appealed to young people with a loud and heavy beat for dancing and lyrics about topics important to teens. Early rock 'n' rollers shocked white American parents in the 1950s and helped create a generation gap, a cultural separation between children and their parents. The music also brought African American influences to white audiences in the United States. Rhythm and blues music provided the roots of the 1950s rock 'n' roll sound. Over time, it would influence music throughout the world.

▼ *Bob Marley and the Wailers*

Ska, rocksteady, and reggae took rock influences and in turn influenced musicians in the U.S. and Britain.

In the 1970s, Afrobeat fused rock and jazz influences to Nigerian forms. Lyrics demanded personal freedoms and a just society.

Fela Kuti ▶

A GLOBAL EXCHANGE OF POPULAR MUSIC

Across Africa, the electric guitar and jazz and blues musical structures combined with local traditions to create a great many new forms, referred to collectively as Afropop. One example of Afropop is the Afrobeat style created by Fela Kuti. Likewise, the Jamaican innovators of ska and reggae helped a new generation of British and American youth form the styles of punk rock and hip-hop. The shrinking world of the past century has made popular music into a vehicle for cultural exchange and innovation.

ANALYZING VISUALS

1. **Making Connections** How does today's music affect society? How does it compare to the impact of rock 'n' roll in the 1950s?

2. **Assessing** In different decades and many countries, the electric guitar has become an essential element of popular music. What does this mean for the global exchange of culture?

CHAPTER 21 Visual Summary

 You can study anywhere, anytime by downloading quizzes and flash cards to your PDA from glencoe.com.

Economic and Political Change in the SOVIET UNION AND EASTERN EUROPE

- Gorbachev's reforms helped to end the Cold War and break up the Soviet Union.
- Communist regimes in Eastern Europe ended as the loss of Soviet support led to revolutions.
- Ethnic tensions in Yugoslavia led to conflicts in Bosnia and Kosovo.
- Energy resources support Russia's economy, but it still faces many economic and social problems.

DESTRUCTION OF THE BERLIN WALL

The fall of the Berlin Wall symbolized the end of the Cold War.

PROTESTANTS AND CATHOLICS CLASH IN NORTHERN IRELAND

Northern Ireland's Catholics wanted to unite with the Republic of Ireland, while Protestants preferred to remain part of Great Britain.

Economic and Social Issues in WESTERN EUROPE AND NORTH AMERICA

- U.S. president Richard Nixon resigned after the Watergate scandal.
- After reunification, Germany faced the cost of rebuilding the economy of eastern Germany.
- The EC became the European Union, and most members adopted the Euro.
- Canadians became divided over the possible secession of French-speaking Quebec.

The Spread and Transformation of WESTERN TECHNOLOGY AND CULTURE

- Significant changes in technology have revolutionized life in the Western world.
- The women's movement addressed issues of stereotyping, pay equality, abortion, and political parity.
- As popular culture brings the world closer, some nations and minority groups worry about loss of their cultural identity.

U.S. ASTRONAUTS FIRST TO WALK ON THE MOON

Revolutionary advances in science made space travel possible.

STANDARDIZED TEST PRACTICE

TEST-TAKING

If you do not know the correct answer to a question, read the answer choices carefully. Eliminate any statement that is historically incorrect. This will help you focus on the remaining answer choices and increase your chances of choosing the correct answer.

Reviewing Vocabulary

Directions: Choose the word (or words) that best completes the sentence.

1. A _____ exists when the government spends more than it collects in revenues.
   A red-line budget
   B budget deficit
   C surplus budget
   D balanced budget

2. Mikhail Gorbachev based his radical reforms on _____, or restructuring.
   A intifada
   B genestroika
   C restifada
   D perestroika

3. Kosovo was a self-governing province; that is, it was _____.
   A an autonomous province
   B a dependent province
   C a protectorate
   D a colonial territory

4. _____ policies require that women must make up either a certain number of the candidates in an election or a certain number of those elected.
   A Gender parity
   B Equality
   C Gender stereotyping
   D Discrimination

Reviewing Main Ideas

Directions: Choose the best answers to the following questions.

Section 1 *(pp. 694–699)*

5. What caused the Cold War to intensify in 1979?
   A Gorbachev's perestroika
   B U.S. invasion of Iraq
   C Boris Yeltsin's presidency of Russia
   D Soviet invasion of Afghanistan

6. Why did the Soviet Union and the United States sign the INF Treaty of 1987?
   A To extend aid to Afghanistan
   B To slow down the arms race
   C To build up their arsenals
   D To deter invasion from China

7. To what was Boris Yeltsin committed for improving Russia's economy?
   A Introducing a free-market economy
   B Allowing the Chechens their independence
   C Alowing the free sale and purchase of land
   D Using Russia's national resources as geopolitical leverage

Section 2 *(pp. 700–703)*

8. Who organized Solidarity in Poland?
   A Mikhail Gorbachev
   B Václav Havel
   C Lech Walesa
   D Václav Klaus

Need Extra Help?								
If You Missed Questions . . .	1	2	3	4	5	6	7	8
Go to Page . . .	708	696	703	712	695	696	698	700

9. Which ethnic group formed the Kosovo Liberation Army (KLA)?

A Albanians

B Serbs

C Croatians

D Bosnians

Section 3 *(pp. 704–709)*

10. How many nations belonged to the European Union as of 2004?

A 50

B 15

C 12

D 25

11. To what problem did George W. Bush devote most of his attention during his first year as U.S. president?

A War with Iraq

B Terrorism

C Invasion of the Falkland Islands

D The Watergate scandal

Section 4 *(pp. 710–715)*

12. In which year did the United States land a mission on the moon?

A 1969

B 1945

C 1981

D 1979

13. Through what type of art forms can viewers influence the production of the art itself?

A WYSIWYG creations

B Digital jpeg photos

C Interactive productions

D MTV productions

Critical Thinking

Directions: Choose the best answers to the following questions.

Use the following map and your knowledge of world history to answer question 14.

Former Yugoslavia, 1991–1999

14. How many republics were in the former Yugoslavia?

A 5

B 6

C 4

D 8

15. What caused the collapse of communism in the Soviet Union?

A Assassination of Leonid Brezhnev, invasion of Afghanistan

B Efficient central government, strong economy

C Vladimir Putin's reforms, abundant natural resources

D Weak economy, inefficient central government, Gorbachev's reforms, and nationalism

Need Extra Help?							
If You Missed Questions . . .	9	10	11	12	13	14	15
Go to Page . . .	703	704	709	710	713	703	696

16. What resulted from Ronald Reagan's military buildup in the 1980s?

  A A bull market

  B Record budget deficits

  C A record budget surplus

  D The invasion of Iraq

17. Why have the United States, Great Britain, France, and Canada alternated between liberal and conservative leaders from 1970 through today?

  A They wanted to stabilize their economies.

  B They went with the popular, charismatic candidates.

  C They wanted to give bipartisanism a chance.

  D They just could not decide which they liked better.

Analyze the chart and answer the question that follows. Base your answer on the chart and on your knowledge of world history.

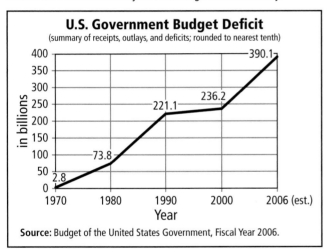

U.S. Government Budget Deficit
(summary of receipts, outlays, and deficits; rounded to nearest tenth)

Source: Budget of the United States Government, Fiscal Year 2006.

18. What can be said about the U.S. budget deficit?

  A Under the Nixon administration, the budget deficit increased to a startling $73.8 billion.

  B The budget deficit remained rather stable under the Reagan and Bush administrations.

  C The 2006 budget deficit is expected to increase even more than it did during the Reagan and Bush administrations.

  D Under the Clinton administration, the budget deficit increased by nearly $150 billion.

Document-Based Questions

Directions: Analyze the document and answer the short-answer questions that follow the document. Base your answers on the document and on your knowledge of world history.

In his 1975 book *Small Is Beautiful,* the British economist E. F. Schumacher wrote:

> *"We must begin to see the possibility of evolving a new lifestyle, with new methods of production and new patterns of consumption: a lifestyle designed for permanence. To give only two examples: in agriculture, we can interest ourselves in the perfection of production methods which are biologically sound and produce health, beauty and permanence. In industry, we can interest ourselves in small-scale technology, 'technology with a human face,' so that people have a chance to enjoy themselves while they are working, instead of working solely for their pay packet and hoping for enjoyment solely during their leisure time."*
>
> —E. F. Schumacher, *Small Is Beautiful,* 1973

19. According to Schumacher, what are the two components of a new lifestyle, one designed for permanence?

20. What do you believe Schumacher meant when he said "technology with a human face"?

Extended Response

21. The European Union established a common European currency, the euro. How would a common global currency, whether the euro or another currency form, affect the global economy?

History ONLINE

For additional test practice, use Self-Check Quizzes—Chapter 21 at **glencoe.com**.

Need Extra Help?						
If You Missed Questions . . .	16	17	18	19	20	21
Go to Page . . .	708	704–709	708	710	710	704

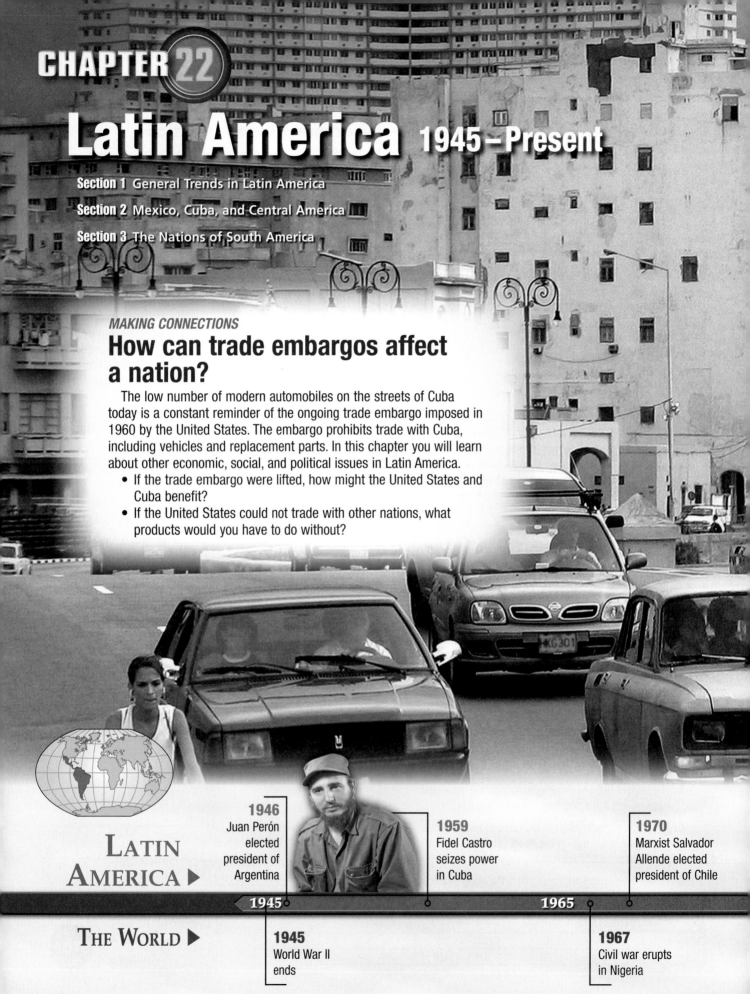

CHAPTER 22

Latin America 1945–Present

Section 1 General Trends in Latin America

Section 2 Mexico, Cuba, and Central America

Section 3 The Nations of South America

MAKING CONNECTIONS

How can trade embargos affect a nation?

The low number of modern automobiles on the streets of Cuba today is a constant reminder of the ongoing trade embargo imposed in 1960 by the United States. The embargo prohibits trade with Cuba, including vehicles and replacement parts. In this chapter you will learn about other economic, social, and political issues in Latin America.

• If the trade embargo were lifted, how might the United States and Cuba benefit?

• If the United States could not trade with other nations, what products would you have to do without?

LATIN AMERICA ▶

1946
Juan Perón elected president of Argentina

1959
Fidel Castro seizes power in Cuba

1970
Marxist Salvador Allende elected president of Chile

1945   1965

THE WORLD ▶

1945
World War II ends

1967
Civil war erupts in Nigeria

1989
U.S. troops
depose Panama's
Manuel Noriega

2007
Daniel Ortega elected
president of
Nicaragua

1985

2005

1991
Boris Yeltsin becomes
president of Russia

FOLDABLES™
Study Organizer

Latin American Country	Economy	Leaders

Summarizing Create
a Folded Table with
three columns. In the
first column, list Latin
American nations. In
the second and third
columns, summarize
information about each nation's economy
and leaders since 1945.

History ONLINE

Chapter Overview—Visit **glencoe.com** to preview Chapter 22.

General Trends in Latin America

GUIDE TO READING

The BIG Idea
Order and Stability Economic instability led some Latin American countries to move toward democracy, while the United States intervened to protect its interests.

Content Vocabulary
- multinational corporations (p. 724)
- megacity (p. 726)
- magic realism (p. 728)

Academic Vocabulary
- consent (p. 725)   • ongoing (p. 725)

People and Places
- Chile (p. 724)   • Bolivia (p. 726)
- Brazil (p. 724)   • Peru (p. 726)
- Argentina (p. 724)   • Colombia (p. 726)
- Organization of American States (OAS) (p. 726)
- Gabriel García Márquez (p. 728)
- Oscar Niemeyer (p. 729)

Reading Strategy
Categorizing Information As you read, use a diagram like the one below to identify social and political challenges in Latin America since 1945.

During the second half of the twentieth century, Latin American countries faced many economic, social, and political challenges. These challenges arose from a rise in population, a large foreign debt, and ongoing foreign military involvement. During this time of instability and change, Latin Americans looked to new artists to reflect the future hopes of the region.

Economic and Political Developments

MAIN IDEA Dependence on foreign imports and investments led to serious economic and political problems in Latin America.

HISTORY & YOU What happens when a nation imports more than it exports? Read to learn about the causes of economic instability in Latin America.

Since the 1800s, Latin Americans had exported raw materials and bought manufactured goods from industrialized countries. The Great Depression caused exports to fall, and revenues to buy manufactured goods declined. In response, Latin Americans developed industries to produce their own goods.

Economic Instability

By the 1960s, however, Latin American countries were still experiencing economic problems. They depended on the United States, Europe, and Japan, especially for the advanced technology needed for modern industries. Also, many Latin American countries had failed to find markets abroad to sell their manufactured products.

These economic failures led to political instability. In the 1960s, repressive military regimes in **Chile, Brazil,** and **Argentina** abolished political parties and returned to export-import economies financed by foreigners. These regimes also encouraged **multinational corporations** (companies with divisions in more than two countries) to come to Latin America. This made these Latin American countries even more dependent on industrialized nations. In the 1970s, Latin American countries tried to maintain their weak economies by borrowing money. Between 1970 and 1982, debt to foreigners grew from $27 billion to $315.3 billion. A number of Latin American economies began to crumble. Wages fell, and unemployment and inflation skyrocketed.

Many people believed that governments had taken control of too many industries. Trying to industrialize too quickly had led to the decline of the economy in the countryside as well. As the economy declined, people continued to move from the countryside into the cities.

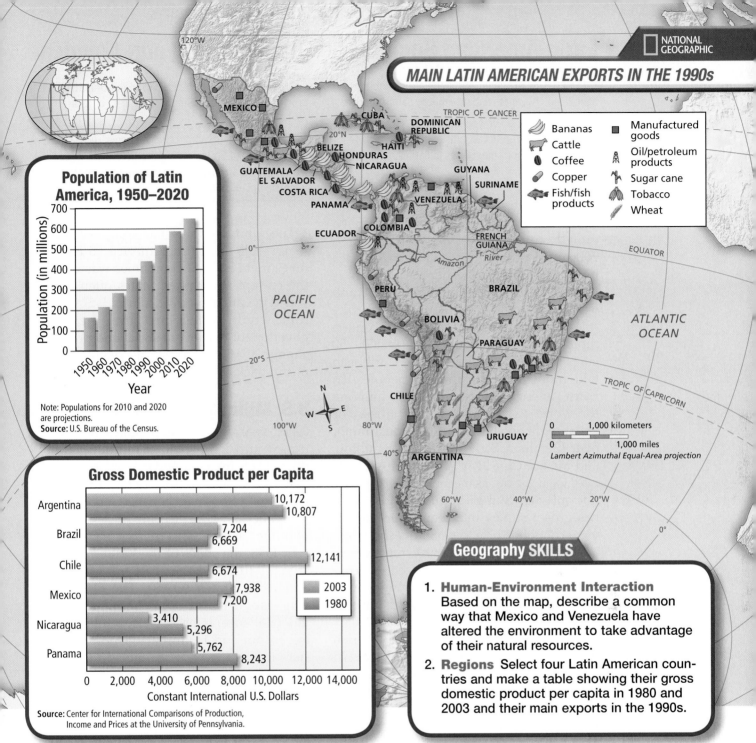

MAIN LATIN AMERICAN EXPORTS IN THE 1990s

Population of Latin America, 1950–2020

Note: Populations for 2010 and 2020 are projections.
Source: U.S. Bureau of the Census.

Legend:
- Bananas
- Cattle
- Coffee
- Copper
- Fish/fish products
- Manufactured goods
- Oil/petroleum products
- Sugar cane
- Tobacco
- Wheat

0 1,000 kilometers
0 1,000 miles
Lambert Azimuthal Equal-Area projection

Gross Domestic Product per Capita

Country	2003	1980
Argentina	10,172	10,807
Brazil	7,204	6,669
Chile	12,141	6,674
Mexico	7,938	7,200
Nicaragua	3,410	5,296
Panama	5,762	8,243

Constant International U.S. Dollars

Source: Center for International Comparisons of Production, Income and Prices at the University of Pennsylvania.

Geography SKILLS

1. **Human-Environment Interaction** Based on the map, describe a common way that Mexico and Venezuela have altered the environment to take advantage of their natural resources.

2. **Regions** Select four Latin American countries and make a table showing their gross domestic product per capita in 1980 and 2003 and their main exports in the 1990s.

A Move Toward Democracy

With the debt crisis in the 1980s came a movement toward democracy. Some military leaders could not deal with their nations' debt problems. At the same time, many realized that military power without popular **consent** could not maintain a strong state. By the mid-1990s, several democratic regimes had been established.

The movement toward democracy was the most noticeable trend of the 1980s and the early 1990s in Latin America. Yet the revival of democracy was fragile. Globalization and the **ongoing** burden of foreign debt stressed several Latin American countries enough that they elected authoritarian figures in the 1990s. In 1992, for example, President Alberto Fujimori returned Peru to an authoritarian system.

✓**Reading Check** **Explaining** Why did the debt crisis of the 1980s create a movement toward democracy?

Latin American Society

MAIN IDEA Economic and population problems have been critical to shaping modern Latin America.

HISTORY & YOU Do you know a city where fast growth has created traffic jams and urban sprawl? Read to learn about megacities in Latin America.

Latin America's economic problems have been made worse by its dramatic growth in population. Between 1950 and 2000, the population in Latin America more than tripled. The population is expected to reach 584 million by 2010 and 643 million by 2020.

With the increase in population came a rapid rise in the size of cities. By 2000, 50 cities in Latin America and the Caribbean had more than one million people. Six Latin American cities are included among the world's 32 most populous cities. For instance, Buenos Aires has a population of over 13 million; São Paulo, over 18 million; and Mexico City, over 19 million. Analysts refer to such cities as megacities. A **megacity** not only has a huge population, but also has grown so fast that regular urban services cannot be provided. Slums and shantytowns are found in many megacities. Crime and corruption from the international drug trade are also found mostly in the larger cities, especially those in **Bolivia, Peru,** and **Colombia.**

The gap between the poor and the rich has remained huge in Latin America. In many Latin American countries, the poor still live in villages. Landholding and urban elites own huge estates and businesses, while peasants and the urban poor struggle to survive. They have little money for consumer goods.

Latin American women's roles have changed. Although the traditional role of homemaker continues, women have also moved into new jobs. In addition to farm labor, women have found jobs in industry and as teachers, professors, doctors, and lawyers.

✓ Reading Check **Describing** What is a megacity? What are living conditions like in megacities?

The U.S. and Latin America

MAIN IDEA During the Cold War, the United States provided aid to anti-Communist regimes in Latin America.

HISTORY & YOU What other countries received aid from the United States during the Cold War? Read to learn how the United States sent troops to protect its interests in Latin America.

The United States has long played a major role in Latin America. Business investment by U.S. companies was one of the reasons the United States often intervened in Latin American affairs. U.S. investors would often pressure the U.S. government to prevent social and political change in Latin America—even if that meant backing dictators.

U.S. Military Involvement

For years, the United States had sent troops into Latin American countries to protect U.S. interests and to bolster friendly dictators. Then in the 1930s, President Franklin D. Roosevelt began a Good Neighbor policy, an effort to end such intervention (see Chapter 18).

In 1948, the states of the Western Hemisphere formed the **Organization of American States (OAS).** The OAS also emphasized the need for Latin American independence. It passed a resolution calling for an end to military action by one state in the affairs of another. The formation of the OAS, however, did not end U.S. involvement in Latin American affairs.

Fighting Communism

Why did American involvement continue? A major reason was the onset of the Cold War. American leaders became more anxious about instability in Latin America. They feared that the poverty in these countries made them ripe for Communist takeover. The Soviet Union, they concluded, would then have more power to threaten U.S. interests around the globe.

Just being accused of having a link to communism meant trouble for some Latin American presidents. For instance, Jacobo Arbenz, president of Guatemala, was overthrown in

1954 with aid from the U.S. Central Intelligence Agency. U.S. business interests had accused Arbenz of being linked to communism. Then when a Communist government took over Cuba in 1959, U.S. anxieties reached a fever pitch (see Section 2).

If it felt that Communist-backed parties were gaining power in South and Central America, the United States used its influence. Even as late as 1981, Jeanne Kirkpatrick, the U.S. ambassador to the United Nations, declared that the Soviet-Cuban Communist "menace" in Central America made it "the most important place in the world for the United States today." To fight communism, the United States provided huge amounts of military aid to support anti-Communist regimes in Latin America.

✓ **Reading Check** **Examining** How did the Cold War impact U.S. policy in Latin America?

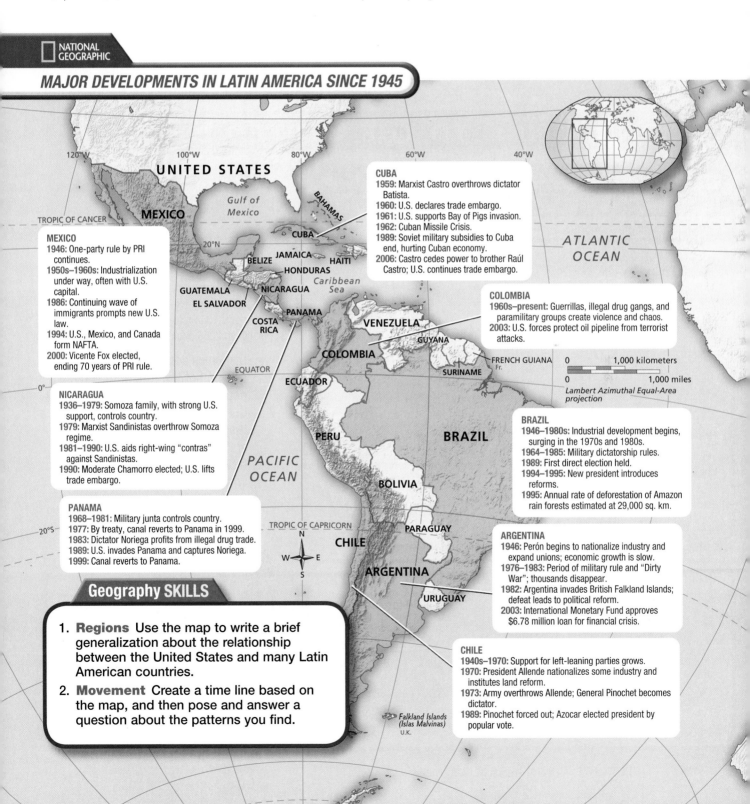

NATIONAL GEOGRAPHIC

MAJOR DEVELOPMENTS IN LATIN AMERICA SINCE 1945

UNITED STATES

Gulf of Mexico

TROPIC OF CANCER

MEXICO

CUBA

JAMAICA   **HAITI**

BELIZE

HONDURAS

GUATEMALA   **NICARAGUA**   Caribbean Sea

EL SALVADOR

COSTA RICA   **PANAMA**

VENEZUELA

GUYANA

COLOMBIA

EQUATOR

ECUADOR

SURINAME

FRENCH GUIANA Fr.

ATLANTIC OCEAN

PERU

BRAZIL

PACIFIC OCEAN

BOLIVIA

TROPIC OF CAPRICORN

PARAGUAY

CHILE

ARGENTINA

URUGUAY

Falkland Islands (Islas Malvinas) U.K.

0   1,000 kilometers
0   1,000 miles
Lambert Azimuthal Equal-Area projection

MEXICO
1946: One-party rule by PRI continues.
1950s–1960s: Industrialization under way, often with U.S. capital.
1986: Continuing wave of immigrants prompts new U.S. law.
1994: U.S., Mexico, and Canada form NAFTA.
2000: Vicente Fox elected, ending 70 years of PRI rule.

CUBA
1959: Marxist Castro overthrows dictator Batista.
1960: U.S. declares trade embargo.
1961: U.S. supports Bay of Pigs invasion.
1962: Cuban Missile Crisis.
1989: Soviet military subsidies to Cuba end, hurting Cuban economy.
2006: Castro cedes power to brother Raúl Castro; U.S. continues trade embargo.

COLOMBIA
1960s–present: Guerrillas, illegal drug gangs, and paramilitary groups create violence and chaos.
2003: U.S. forces protect oil pipeline from terrorist attacks.

NICARAGUA
1936–1979: Somoza family, with strong U.S. support, controls country.
1979: Marxist Sandinistas overthrow Somoza regime.
1981–1990: U.S. aids right-wing "contras" against Sandinistas.
1990: Moderate Chamorro elected; U.S. lifts trade embargo.

BRAZIL
1946–1980s: Industrial development begins, surging in the 1970s and 1980s.
1964–1985: Military dictatorship rules.
1989: First direct election held.
1994–1995: New president introduces reforms.
1995: Annual rate of deforestation of Amazon rain forests estimated at 29,000 sq. km.

PANAMA
1968–1981: Military junta controls country.
1977: By treaty, canal reverts to Panama in 1999.
1983: Dictator Noriega profits from illegal drug trade.
1989: U.S. invades Panama and captures Noriega.
1999: Canal reverts to Panama.

ARGENTINA
1946: Perón begins to nationalize industry and expand unions; economic growth is slow.
1976–1983: Period of military rule and "Dirty War"; thousands disappear.
1982: Argentina invades British Falkland Islands; defeat leads to political reform.
2003: International Monetary Fund approves $6.78 million loan for financial crisis.

CHILE
1940s–1970: Support for left-leaning parties grows.
1970: President Allende nationalizes some industry and institutes land reform.
1973: Army overthrows Allende; General Pinochet becomes dictator.
1989: Pinochet forced out; Azocar elected president by popular vote.

Geography SKILLS

1. **Regions** Use the map to write a brief generalization about the relationship between the United States and many Latin American countries.

2. **Movement** Create a time line based on the map, and then pose and answer a question about the patterns you find.

Latin American Culture

MAIN IDEA Latin American artists and writers are important national figures.

HISTORY & YOU What artists and writers have influenced you? Read to learn about Latin American artists.

Twentieth-century Latin American writers and artists have played important roles in their society. Their work is seen as expressing the hopes of the people. Because of this, artists and writers hold high status in Latin American society.

Literature

In the 1940s, Latin American writers made a significant break from realism and explored other techniques. They developed a unique form of expression called **magic realism.** Magic realism brings together realistic events with dreamlike or fantasy backgrounds. The rules of ordinary life are suspended in order to comment on a national or social situation.

Perhaps the foremost example of magic realism is *One Hundred Years of Solitude,* a novel by **Gabriel García Márquez,** a Colombian writer, who won the Nobel

CONNECTING TO THE UNITED STATES

A GROWING HISPANIC POPULATION

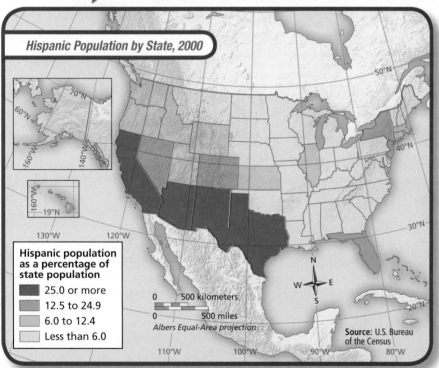

Hispanic Population by State, 2000

Hispanic population as a percentage of state population
- 25.0 or more
- 12.5 to 24.9
- 6.0 to 12.4
- Less than 6.0

0   500 kilometers
0   500 miles
Albers Equal-Area projection

Source: U.S. Bureau of the Census

Political and economic instability in the second half of the twentieth century caused many Latin Americans to immigrate to the United States. Today, Hispanics, also referred to as Latinos, are the largest and fastest-growing minority group in the United States, predicted to make up 24 percent of the population in 2050. Right now:

- Hispanics account for about one-half of the total national population growth.
- California has the largest total Hispanic population of all states, followed by Texas.
- New Mexico is the state in which Hispanics comprise the highest proportion of the total population.

Growing Hispanic Population in the United States, 1990–2050

1990	2005	2050 (projected)
9%	14%	24%

Source: U.S. Bureau of the Census.

CONNECTING TO TODAY

1. **Identifying** Which area of the United States has the largest percentage Hispanic population? Why?
2. **Summarizing** What trends are expected in Hispanic population growth in the United States?

Prize in literature in 1982. In this story of the fictional town of Macondo, the point of view slips back and forth between fact and fantasy. Villagers are not surprised when a local priest rises into the air and floats, for example. Yet when the same villagers are introduced to magnets, telescopes, and magnifying glasses, they are dumbfounded by what they consider to be magic. According to Márquez, fantasy and fact depend on one's point of view.

Whatever styles they use, Latin American writers write about their national reality. Some look back on the past with hatred, rather than with affection. Others, like the Chilean novelist Jorge Edwards, use the theme of the clash of generations to expose the corruption of their country. One writer, the Argentinean novelist Julio Cortázar, uses the element of a game or play that defies societal rules and conventions.

Among Latin American poets, perhaps the best known is Gabriela Mistral from Chile. She began writing poetry as a village schoolteacher and taught school for many years until her poetry made her famous. Lyrical and emotional, her poetry expresses themes of childhood, love, and yearning. In 1945, Mistral became the first Latin American to receive the Nobel Prize in literature.

Art and Architecture

Latin American art and architecture were strongly influenced by international styles after World War II. In painting, abstract styles were more predominant. In architecture, the Bauhaus and Modernist styles were common.

Perhaps the most notable example of modern architecture can be seen in Brasília, the capital of Brazil, which was built in the 1950s and 1960s. The government intended for Brasília to attract development to the interior of Brazil and to lessen the population pressures in coastal Rio de Janeiro.

Brazilian architect **Oscar Niemeyer** was appointed chief architect for the new capital. Niemeyer already had an international reputation as one of the two architects who designed the United Nations building. Niemeyer's outlook is evident in his description of his work in Brasília:

PRIMARY SOURCE

" . . . I did my very best in the structures, trying to make them different with their columns narrow, so narrow that the palaces would seem to barely touch the ground. And I set them apart from the facades, creating an empty space through which, as I bent over my work table, I could see myself walking, imagining their forms and the different resulting points of view they would provoke."

—Oscar Niemeyer

✓ **Reading Check** **Identifying** What novel is the foremost example of magic realism?

Vocabulary
1. **Explain** the significance of: Chile, Brazil, Argentina, multinational corporations, consent, ongoing, megacity, Bolivia, Peru, Colombia, Organization of American States (OAS), magic realism, Gabriel García Márquez, Oscar Niemeyer.

Main Ideas
2. **List** the economic challenges in Latin America since 1945. Use a diagram like the one below to make your list.

3. **Explain** why the formation of the Organization of American States (OAS) did not end U.S. involvement in Latin America.

4. **Name** at least two well-known Latin American writers.

Critical Thinking
5. **The BIG Idea** **Determining Cause and Effect** How did the rapid population growth in many Latin American countries cause problems for their political and economic systems?

6. **Making Connections** How can industrializing too quickly, as in the case of Latin America, lead to an economic decline?

7. **Analyzing Visuals** What is the significance of the colored regions on the map on page 727?

Writing About History
8. **Descriptive Writing** Research further the elements of magic realism and then write a short story using that style.

History ONLINE

For help with the concepts in this section of *Glencoe World History— Modern Times*, go to glencoe.com and click Study Central.

Mexico, Cuba, and Central America

GUIDE TO READING

The BIG Idea
Order and Security Mexico and Central America faced political and economic crises after World War II, making national progress difficult.

Content Vocabulary
- privatization *(p. 730)*
- trade embargo *(p. 733)*
- contras *(p. 735)*

Academic Vocabulary
- regulation *(p. 731)*
- unreliable *(p. 733)*

People and Places
- Institutional Revolutionary Party (PRI) *(p. 730)*
- Vicente Fox *(p. 731)*
- Havana *(p. 732)*
- Nicaragua *(p. 734)*
- Manuel Noriega *(p. 735)*
- Guatemala *(p. 735)*
- Fidel Castro *(p. 732)*
- El Salvador *(p. 733)*
- Panama *(p. 735)*

Reading Strategy
Comparing As you read, use a table like the one below to identify the political and economic challenges faced by El Salvador, Nicaragua, Panama, and Guatemala after 1945.

El Salvador	Nicaragua	Panama	Guatemala

Throughout the twentieth century, Mexico and Central America experienced political turmoil and economic crises. Fidel Castro set up a Marxist government in Cuba, and military or military-dominated dictators ruled most of the Central American countries. The political and economic crises, often ignited by U.S. intervention, hampered national development.

Mexico

MAIN IDEA Political and economic problems have troubled Mexico since the Mexican Revolution.

HISTORY & YOU Do economic issues influence American politics? Read how economic troubles led to political change in Mexico.

The Mexican Revolution in the early 1900s created a political order that remained stable for many years. The official political party of the Mexican Revolution—the **Institutional Revolutionary Party,** or **PRI**—came to dominate Mexico. Every six years, leaders of the PRI chose the party's presidential candidate, who was then elected by the people. During the 1950s and 1960s, steady economic growth led to real gains in wages in Mexico.

Protests

At the end of the 1960s, students began to protest Mexico's one-party government system. On October 2, 1968, university students gathered in Mexico City to protest government policies. Police forces opened fire and killed hundreds. The next two presidents, Luis Echeverría and José López Portillo, made political reforms and new political parties emerged. Greater freedom of debate in the press and universities was allowed.

Debt Crisis

In the late 1970s, vast new reserves of oil were discovered in Mexico. The government became more dependent on revenues from foreign oil sales. Then, when world oil prices dropped in the mid-1980s, Mexico was no longer able to make payments on its foreign debt. The government was forced to adopt new economic policies. One of these policies was **privatization,** the sale of government-owned companies to private firms.

Mexico's debt rose even more after a hurricane caused massive destruction in the Yucatán peninsula in 1988. Damage alone was estimated at $880 million.

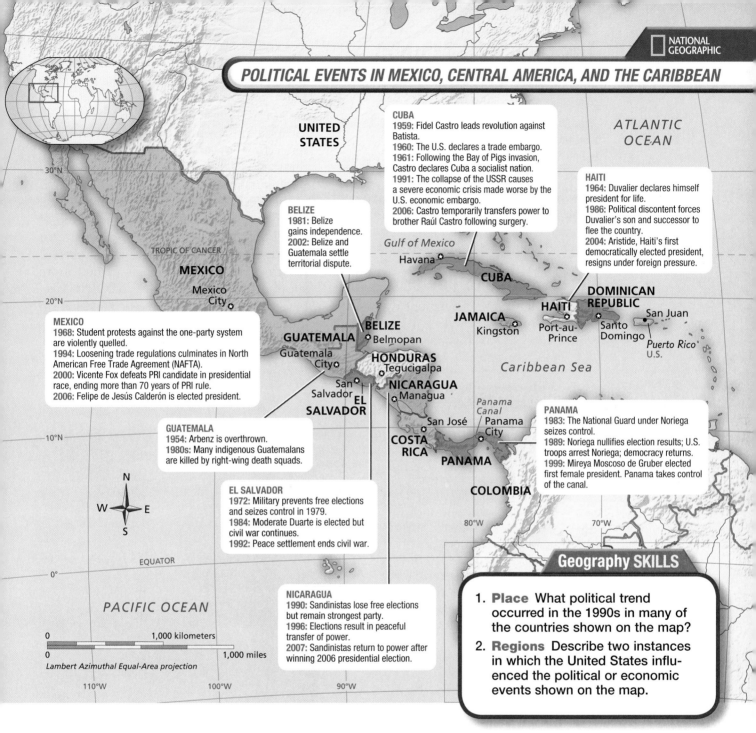

POLITICAL EVENTS IN MEXICO, CENTRAL AMERICA, AND THE CARIBBEAN

UNITED STATES

ATLANTIC OCEAN

30°N

CUBA
1959: Fidel Castro leads revolution against Batista.
1960: The U.S. declares a trade embargo.
1961: Following the Bay of Pigs invasion, Castro declares Cuba a socialist nation.
1991: The collapse of the USSR causes a severe economic crisis made worse by the U.S. economic embargo.
2006: Castro temporarily transfers power to brother Raúl Castro following surgery.

HAITI
1964: Duvalier declares himself president for life.
1986: Political discontent forces Duvalier's son and successor to flee the country.
2004: Aristide, Haiti's first democratically elected president, resigns under foreign pressure.

BELIZE
1981: Belize gains independence.
2002: Belize and Guatemala settle territorial dispute.

Gulf of Mexico

TROPIC OF CANCER

MEXICO

Mexico City

Havana

CUBA

20°N

DOMINICAN REPUBLIC

HAITI
San Juan

JAMAICA
Kingston

Port-au-Prince
Santo Domingo
Puerto Rico U.S.

MEXICO
1968: Student protests against the one-party system are violently quelled.
1994: Loosening trade regulations culminates in North American Free Trade Agreement (NAFTA).
2000: Vicente Fox defeats PRI candidate in presidential race, ending more than 70 years of PRI rule.
2006: Felipe de Jesús Calderón is elected president.

BELIZE
Belmopan

GUATEMALA
Guatemala City

HONDURAS
Tegucigalpa

Caribbean Sea

San Salvador
EL SALVADOR

NICARAGUA
Managua

GUATEMALA
1954: Arbenz is overthrown.
1980s: Many indigenous Guatemalans are killed by right-wing death squads.

10°N

Panama Canal
San José
Panama City

COSTA RICA
PANAMA

PANAMA
1983: The National Guard under Noriega seizes control.
1989: Noriega nullifies election results; U.S. troops arrest Noriega; democracy returns.
1999: Mireya Moscoso de Gruber elected first female president. Panama takes control of the canal.

N
W E
S

EL SALVADOR
1972: Military prevents free elections and seizes control in 1979.
1984: Moderate Duarte is elected but civil war continues.
1992: Peace settlement ends civil war.

COLOMBIA

80°W
70°W

EQUATOR

0°

PACIFIC OCEAN

NICARAGUA
1990: Sandinistas lose free elections but remain strongest party.
1996: Elections result in peaceful transfer of power.
2007: Sandinistas return to power after winning 2006 presidential election.

0   1,000 kilometers
0   1,000 miles
Lambert Azimuthal Equal-Area projection

110°W   100°W   90°W

Geography SKILLS

1. **Place** What political trend occurred in the 1990s in many of the countries shown on the map?
2. **Regions** Describe two instances in which the United States influenced the political or economic events shown on the map.

The next president, Carlos Salinas de Gortari, sped up privatization to relieve the debt crisis. He also changed some restrictive trade **regulations** in order to attract more foreign investors. In 1992, de Gortari began working with the U.S. president and the Canadian prime minister to form the North American Free Trade Agreement (NAFTA). That agreement went into effect in 1994.

NAFTA did not cure Mexico's economic problems, however. The continuing debt crisis, rising unemployment, and corruption scandals increased dissatisfaction with the government. Support for the PRI dropped. In 2000, **Vicente Fox** defeated the PRI candidate for the presidency. Fox's election ended more than seven decades of PRI rule. Fox's successor, Felipe de Jesús Calderón, continued with plans to boost Mexico's economic growth.

✓ Reading Check **Evaluating** How did its oil industry affect Mexico's economy?

The Cuban Revolution

MAIN IDEA The Cuban Revolution established the communist dictatorship of Fidel Castro.

HISTORY & YOU Recall how Lenin led the Russian Revolution. Read to learn about Castro's role in the Cuban Revolution.

In the 1950s, an opposition movement arose in Cuba. It aimed to overthrow the government of the dictator Fulgencio Batista, who had controlled Cuba since 1934.

Castro's Rise to Power

The leader of the movement was a man named **Fidel Castro.** While a law student at the University of Havana, he had become a revolutionary. On July 26, 1953, Castro and his brother Raúl led a band of 165 young people in an attack on the Moncada army camp at Santiago de Cuba. The attack was a disaster. While Fidel and Raúl escaped, they were later captured and sentenced to prison for 15 years. Batista released Fidel and Raúl after 11 months.

After their release, the Castro brothers fled to the Sierra Maestra mountains in Mexico. There they teamed up with a small band of revolutionaries. Castro poured out a stream of propaganda with a small radio station and printing press. As the rebels gained more support, the Batista regime collapsed. Castro's revolutionaries seized **Havana** on January 3, 1959. Many Cubans who disagreed with Castro fled to the United States.

History ONLINE
Student Web Activity—
Visit glencoe.com and complete the activity about Fidel Castro.

INFOGRAPHICS — PRIMARY SOURCE

Fidel Castro's Cuban Revolution

At the time of the Cuban Revolution, U.S. and other foreign investors owned 75 percent of Cuba's fertile land, 90 percent of its public services, and 40 percent of the sugar industry. A corrupt dictator, Fulgencio Batista used open displays of brutality to maintain control, and poverty and unemployment were widespread.

Anti-Batista and anti-American feelings led to support for Fidel Castro and the Cuban Revolution. Castro rose to power in 1959 and has remained Cuba's leader ever since. His Communist regime has brought some social improvements to Cuba, but Cubans still lack freedom.

Fidel Castro and two guerrillas at their mountain hideout during the insurgency against dictator Fulgencio Batista.

CAUSES
- Corrupt dictatorship led by Batista
- Economic dependence on United States

↓

Cuban Revolution

↓

EFFECTS
- Led Cuba to become a Communist state
- Began Fidel Castro's half-century rule in Cuba
- Led to improvements in health care and education
- Led to declining economic conditions in Cuba
- Inspired Communist revolutions elsewhere in the region
- Led to ongoing conflict with the United States, including the Bay of Pigs invasion and a long-standing trade embargo

DOCUMENT-BASED QUESTIONS

1. **Explaining** How did the Cuban Revolution change the relationship between Cuba and the United States?

2. **Determining Cause and Effect** What has been the impact of the Cuban Revolution in Cuba and the rest of the world?

Relations with the United States

Relations between Cuba and the United States quickly deteriorated when Castro's Communist regime began to receive aid from the Soviet Union. Arms from Eastern Europe also began to arrive in Cuba. In October 1960, the United States declared a **trade embargo,** a policy prohibiting trade with Cuba. Just three months later all diplomatic relations with Cuba were broken.

Soon after that, in April 1961, U.S. president John F. Kennedy supported an attempt to overthrow Castro's government. When the invasion at the Bay of Pigs failed, the Soviets made an even greater commitment to Cuba. In December 1961, Castro declared himself a Marxist, drawing even closer to the Soviet Union. The Soviets began placing nuclear missiles in Cuba in 1962, leading to a showdown with the United States.

The Cuban missile crisis made Castro realize that the Soviet Union had been **unreliable.** If the revolutionary movement was to survive, the Cubans would have to start a social revolution in the rest of Latin America. They would do this by starting guerrilla wars and encouraging peasants to overthrow the old regimes. Ernesto Ché Guevara, an Argentinean and an ally of Castro, led such a war in Bolivia. He was killed by the Bolivian army in the fall of 1967. Cuba's strategy failed.

Nevertheless, in Cuba, Castro's Marxist regime continued, but with mixed results. The Cuban people did secure some social gains, such as free medical services for all citizens. With improvements in education, illiteracy was nearly eliminated.

Yet the Cuban economy continued to rely on Soviet aid and the sale of Cuban sugar to Soviet bloc countries. When these Communist regimes collapsed in 1989, Cuba lost their support. As a result, Cuba's economy went into a tailspin. Castro's measures to improve the economy have not entirely succeeded.

✓ Reading Check **Describing** How was Castro's Cuba affected by the collapse of Communist governments in Eastern Europe?

Central America

MAIN IDEA Fearing the spread of communism, the United States intervened in Central American politics during the 1970s and 1980s.

HISTORY & YOU Why might the United States have feared the spread of communism into Central America? Read to learn how the Cold War affected U.S. policy in Central America.

Central America includes seven countries: Costa Rica, Nicaragua, Honduras, El Salvador, Panama, Belize, and Guatemala. Economically, Central America has historically depended on the export of bananas, coffee, and cotton. Prices for these products have varied over time, however, creating economic crises. In addition, a huge gulf between a wealthy elite and poor peasants has created a climate of instability in the region.

The U.S. fear of the spread of communism often led to U.S. support for repressive regimes in Central America. The involvement of the United States was especially evident in the nations of El Salvador, Nicaragua, Panama, and Guatemala.

El Salvador

After World War II, the wealthy elite and the military controlled the government in **El Salvador.** The rise of an urban middle class led to hope for a more democratic government. The army, however, refused to accept the results of free elections that were held in 1972.

World attention focused on El Salvador in the late 1970s and the 1980s, when the country was rocked by a bitter civil war. Marxist-led, leftist guerrillas and right-wing groups battled one another. The Catholic Church became a main target, and a number of priests were killed or tortured, among them Archbishop Oscar Romero. Death squads killed anyone they thought a threat to their interests.

When U.S. president Ronald Reagan claimed evidence of "communist interference in El Salvador," the United States began to provide weapons and training to the Salvadoran army to defeat the guerrillas. The hope was to bring stability to the country, but the killings continued.

TURNING POINT

THE PANAMA CANAL TREATY

Since the failed Bay of Pigs invasion, the U.S. policy in Latin America has been driven more by diplomacy than by military action. In Panama, for example, diplomacy allowed for the peaceful transfer of control of the Panama Canal.

The United States had controlled the Panama Canal since its creation in 1904. As the shortest water passage from the Atlantic to the Pacific Oceans, the canal was extremely important strategically and economically. Yet the desire to end U.S. control had long been an overriding theme in Panamanian politics.

After years of negotiations, U.S. president Jimmy Carter and General Omar Torrijos of Panama finally signed a treaty in 1977. As outlined in the treaty, control of the canal transferred to Panama on December 31, 1999.

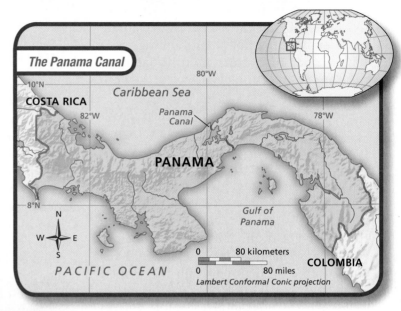

◀ President Carter, Organization of American States secretary general Alejandro Orfila, and General Torrijos at the signing of the Panama Canal Treaty in 1977

CRITICAL THINKING SKILLS

1. **Evaluating** Why is the Panama Canal strategically important?
2. **Contrasting** How did the United States's actions in Cuba differ from its actions in Panama?

In 1984, a moderate, José Duarte, was elected president. The unrest in El Salvador cut short Duarte's efforts at political, social, and economic reforms. Nor could Duarte stop the savage killing. By the early 1990s, at least 75,000 people were dead. A 1992 peace settlement ended the war.

Duarte did not live to see his hope for peace fulfilled. After transferring power to his successor, Duarte said that his government had "laid the foundation for democracy in this country." Duarte died in 1990.

Nicaragua

In **Nicaragua,** the Somoza family seized control of the government in 1937 and maintained control for the next 45 years. It began with Anastasio Somoza Garcia's induction as president, followed by his two sons. Over most of this period, the Somoza regime had the support of the United States. The Somozas enriched themselves at the expense of the Nicaraguan people and used murder and torture to silence opposition.

By 1979, the United States, under President Jimmy Carter, had grown unwilling to support the corrupt regime. In that same year, Marxist guerrilla forces known as the Sandinista National Liberation Front won a number of military victories against government forces and gained control of the country. Soon, a group opposed to the Sandinistas' policies, called the **contras,** began to try to overthrow the new government. Worried by the Sandinistas' alignment with the Soviet Union, the United States supported the contras.

The war waged by the contras undermined support for the Sandinistas. In 1990, the Sandinistas, led by Daniel Ortega, agreed to free elections and lost to a coalition headed by Violeta Barrios de Chamorro, who became Nicaragua's first female president. After 16 years out of power, the Sandinistas won new elections in 2006 and Daniel Ortega became president in January 2007.

Panama and Guatemala

Panama became a nation in 1903 when it broke away from Colombia with help from the United States. In return for this aid, the United States was able to build the Panama Canal and gained influence over the government and economy of Panama. A wealthy oligarchy ruled with U.S. support. After 1968, military leaders of Panama's National Guard were in control. One of these, **Manuel Noriega,** became so involved in the drug trade that President George H. W. Bush sent U.S. troops to Panama in 1989. Noriega was later sent to prison in the United States for drug trafficking.

A major issue for Panamanians was finally settled in 1999 when Panama took control of the Panama Canal. The terms for this change of control had been set in a 1977 treaty with the United States.

In 1954, with support from the United States, Jacobo Arbenz of **Guatemala** was overthrown. A series of military or military-dominated dictators ruled the country for years. Guerrilla forces began forming to oppose the government. Rios Montt, president during the early 1980s, responded by using military action and economic reforms to defeat the guerrillas. As in El Salvador, right-wing death squads began attacking anyone they believed belonged to the opposition.

The indigenous people of Guatemala, the descendants of the ancient Maya, were the main target. The government massacred large numbers of Maya simply because it believed they supported the guerrillas. Entire Maya communities were uprooted, separated, or put under military control. The government killed as many as 200,000 people, mostly unarmed Maya. Many others fled to Mexico as refugees.

✓ Reading Check **Summarizing** What underlying factors led to conflicts in Central America from the 1970s to the 1990s?

Vocabulary
1. **Explain** the significance of: Institutional Revolutionary Party (PRI), privatization, regulation, Vicente Fox, Fidel Castro, Havana, trade embargo, unreliable, El Salvador, Nicaragua, contras, Panama, Manuel Noriega, Guatemala.

Main Ideas
2. **Illustrate** how Mexico has reacted to political and economic crises since World War II. Use a diagram like the one below to make your illustration.

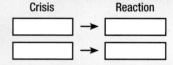

Crisis		Reaction

3. **Explain** why the Cubans attempted to spur revolution in the rest of Latin America.

4. **Name** at least three Central American countries in which the United States has intervened.

Critical Thinking
5. **The BIG Idea** **Making Connections** Were the problems that Mexico and Central America had after 1945 due more to politics or to economics? Explain.

6. **Determining Cause and Effect** Why did Cuba's economy suffer after 1989?

7. **Analyzing Visuals** Examine the photograph of Fidel Castro on page 732. What does the setting of the photograph and Castro's appearance tell you about his struggle?

Writing About History
8. **Persuasive Writing** The United States has increasingly tried in Latin America to negotiate conflicts using economic tools rather than military force. Research the trade embargo imposed upon Cuba. Write a persuasive argument for or against this embargo.

History ONLINE

For help with the concepts in this section of *Glencoe World History—Modern Times*, go to glencoe.com and click Study Central.

The Nations of South America

GUIDE TO READING

The BIG Idea

Self-Determination South American countries have experienced economic, social, and political problems, but democracy has advanced since the late 1980s.

Content Vocabulary
• cooperatives (p. 739)   • cartels (p. 741)

Academic Vocabulary
• task (p. 739)   • fund (p. 741)

People and Places
• Chile (p. 736)
• Salvador Allende (p. 736)
• Augusto Pinochet (p. 736)
• Argentina (p. 737)
• Juan Perón (p. 737)
• Falkland Islands (p. 738)
• Brazil (p. 739)
• Luiz Inácio Lula da Silva (p. 739)
• Peru (p. 739)
• Juan Velasco Alvarado (p. 739)
• Shining Path (p. 740)
• Alberto Fujimori (p. 740)
• Colombia (p. 740)
• Alvaro Uribe (p. 741)
• Venezuela (p. 741)
• Hugo Chávez (p. 741)

Reading Strategy
Determining Cause and Effect As you read, use a table like the one below to list factors leading to the change from military rule to civilian rule.

Argentina	Brazil	Chile	Venezuela

Throughout the twentieth century, most South American countries experienced political unrest and had economic and social problems. Now into the twenty-first century, these countries are largely democratic and have common problems of high inflation, unemployment, and foreign debt. Their focus is now on finding and maintaining economic stability.

Chile and Argentina

MAIN IDEA Ideological battles drove politics in Chile and Argentina in the 1970s and 1980s, but current governments focus on the economy.

HISTORY & YOU Do U.S. voters choose candidates based on how well the economy is doing? Read to learn about transitions in politics in South America.

The history of **Chile** has mirrored the experience of other Latin American countries. However, it took a dramatic step in 1970 when **Salvador Allende** (ah•YEHN•day), a Marxist, became president.

Toward Economic Stability in Chile

Allende tried to create a socialist society through constitutional means. His first steps were to increase wages and to nationalize the largest corporations. Allende's policies were not popular with everyone. Nationalization of the copper industry angered the companies' owners in the United States, as well as the U.S. government. However, Allende gained support in the Chilean congress. Afraid of Allende's growing strength, General **Augusto Pinochet** (PEE•noh•CHEHT) moved to overthrow the government. In September 1973, military forces killed Allende and set up a dictatorship.

The Pinochet regime was one of the most brutal in Chile's history. Thousands of opponents were imprisoned, tortured, or murdered. The regime also outlawed all political parties and did away with the congress. These horrible abuses of human rights led to growing unrest in the mid-1980s. Thousands of Pinochet opponents and other civilians were arrested and were never seen again. Pinochet finally lost in 1989 by free presidential elections.

Chile has since moved toward a more democratic system. Economic conditions have improved, but unemployment remains high. Chile signed trade agreements with the United States, China, and the European Union. The new president, Michelle Bachelet Jeria, is the first woman elected as president of Chile. She heads a country that is moving toward economic stability and growth.

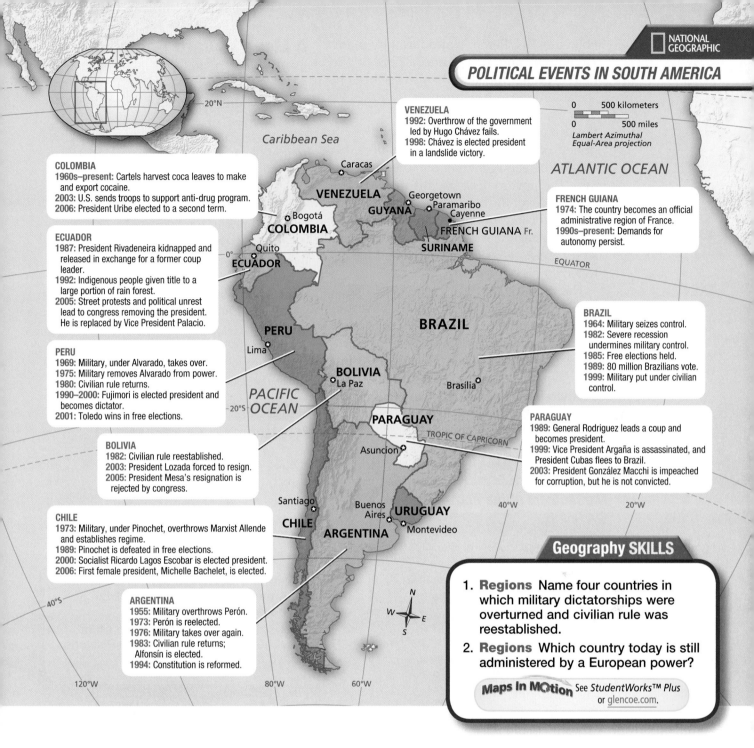

POLITICAL EVENTS IN SOUTH AMERICA

VENEZUELA
1992: Overthrow of the government led by Hugo Chávez fails.
1998: Chávez is elected president in a landslide victory.

0 — 500 kilometers
0 — 500 miles
Lambert Azimuthal Equal-Area projection

Caribbean Sea

ATLANTIC OCEAN

COLOMBIA
1960s–present: Cartels harvest coca leaves to make and export cocaine.
2003: U.S. sends troops to support anti-drug program.
2006: President Uribe elected to a second term.

FRENCH GUIANA
1974: The country becomes an official administrative region of France.
1990s–present: Demands for autonomy persist.

Caracas

VENEZUELA
Georgetown
Paramaribo
GUYANA Cayenne
FRENCH GUIANA Fr.
SURINAME

Bogotá
COLOMBIA

EQUATOR

ECUADOR
1987: President Rivadeneira kidnapped and released in exchange for a former coup leader.
1992: Indigenous people given title to a large portion of rain forest.
2005: Street protests and political unrest lead to congress removing the president. He is replaced by Vice President Palacio.

Quito
ECUADOR

BRAZIL

BRAZIL
1964: Military seizes control.
1982: Severe recession undermines military control.
1985: Free elections held.
1989: 80 million Brazilians vote.
1999: Military put under civilian control.

PERU
1969: Military, under Alvarado, takes over.
1975: Military removes Alvarado from power.
1980: Civilian rule returns.
1990–2000: Fujimori is elected president and becomes dictator.
2001: Toledo wins in free elections.

PERU
Lima

BOLIVIA
La Paz

Brasília

PACIFIC OCEAN

BOLIVIA
1982: Civilian rule reestablished.
2003: President Lozada forced to resign.
2005: President Mesa's resignation is rejected by congress.

PARAGUAY

TROPIC OF CAPRICORN

Asunción

PARAGUAY
1989: General Rodriguez leads a coup and becomes president.
1999: Vice President Argaña is assassinated, and President Cubas flees to Brazil.
2003: President González Macchi is impeached for corruption, but he is not convicted.

CHILE
1973: Military, under Pinochet, overthrows Marxist Allende and establishes regime.
1989: Pinochet is defeated in free elections.
2000: Socialist Ricardo Lagos Escobar is elected president.
2006: First female president, Michelle Bachelet, is elected.

Santiago
CHILE

Buenos Aires
URUGUAY
Montevideo

ARGENTINA

ARGENTINA
1955: Military overthrows Perón.
1973: Perón is reelected.
1976: Military takes over again.
1983: Civilian rule returns; Alfonsín is elected.
1994: Constitution is reformed.

40°W   20°W

Geography SKILLS

1. **Regions** Name four countries in which military dictatorships were overturned and civilian rule was reestablished.
2. **Regions** Which country today is still administered by a European power?

Maps In Motion See *StudentWorks™ Plus* or glencoe.com.

N W E S

120°W   80°W   60°W

A New Strategy in Argentina

Argentina is Latin America's second largest country. For years, it had been ruled by a powerful oligarchy whose wealth was based on growing wheat and raising cattle. Support from the army was crucial to the continuing power of the oligarchy.

In 1943, during World War II, a group of army officers overthrew the oligarchy. The new regime was not sure how to deal with the working classes. **Juan Perón** devised a new strategy. Using his position as labor secretary in the military government, Perón sought to win over the workers, known as the descamisados (the shirtless ones). He encouraged them to join labor unions and increased job benefits.

In 1944, Perón became vice president of the military government. He made sure that people knew he was responsible for the better conditions for workers.

Juan Perón was elected president of Argentina in 1946, with his chief support coming from labor and the urban middle class.

His wife, Eva Perón, was adored by many Argentines and was a major part of the Perón regime. Together the Peróns brought social reforms to Argentina.

To please his supporters, from labor and the urban middle class, Perón followed a policy of increased industrialization. He sought to free Argentina from foreign investors. The government bought the railways and took over the banking, insurance, shipping, and communications industries.

Perón's regime was authoritarian. He created Fascist gangs that used violent means to terrify his opponents.

The military overthrew the Argentinean leader in September 1955. Perón went into exile in Spain. Overwhelmed by problems, military leaders later allowed him to return. He was reelected as president in 1973 but died a year later. In 1976, the military once again took over power. The new regime tolerated no opposition. It is believed that 36,000 people were killed.

A Move Toward Democracy

In April 1982, the military regime invaded the **Falkland Islands,** off the coast of Argentina. Great Britain, which had controlled the islands since the 1800s, sent ships and troops and took the islands back. The loss discredited the military and opened the door to civilian rule in Argentina.

In 1983, Raúl Alfonsín was elected president and worked to restore democratic practices. Nestor Kirchner serves as the current president. While inflation is high, Argentina's economy is becoming more stable, which gives hope that it will continue its democratic path.

✓ Reading Check **Explaining** How did Juan Perón free Argentina from foreign investors?

INFOGRAPHICS **PRIMARY SOURCE**

The Mothers of the Plaza de Mayo

In March 1976, a military junta overthrew the government in Argentina. The junta suspended civil liberties and began a campaign of imprisoning, torturing, and killing government opponents. Many children of the *desaparecidos* ("disappeared ones") were kidnapped.

On April 30, 1977, mothers and grandmothers of *desaparecidos* gathered in the Plaza de Mayo in Buenos Aires risking their own safety. They hoped to locate their children and grandchildren, and to bring those responsible for Argentina's "dirty war" to justice. Although civilian rule returned in 1983, the Mothers of the Plaza de Mayo are still active.

DOCUMENT-BASED QUESTIONS

1. **Explaining** How did the military junta in Argentina attempt to control its opponents?
2. **Speculating** Do you think the silent marches of the Mothers of the Plaza de Mayo have been effective?

The Mothers of the Plaza de Mayo carry banners calling for the return of their missing sons and daughters. Their white scarves represent diapers, in memory of the lost children.

Brazil

MAIN IDEA Brazil's supersized economy has the potential to influence the global economy, but Brazil still struggles to meet the needs of its people.

HISTORY & YOU How did the United States fight poverty in the 1960s? Read to learn how poverty has been a continuing problem in Brazil.

Like other Latin American countries, **Brazil** experienced severe economic problems following World War II. When democratically elected governments proved unable to solve these problems, the military stepped in and seized control in 1964.

An Economic Miracle?

The armed forces remained in direct control of the country for the next 20 years. The military set a new economic direction, reducing government interference in the economy and stressing free-market forces. Beginning in 1968, the new policies seemed to be working. Brazil experienced an "economic miracle" as its economy grew spectacularly.

Ordinary Brazilians benefited little from this economic growth. Furthermore, rapid development led to an inflation rate of 100 percent a year. Overwhelmed, the military leadership retreated and opened the door to a return to democracy in 1985.

Return to Democracy

The new democratic government faced enormous obstacles: massive foreign debt and an inflation rate of 800 percent in 1987. In the 1990s, democratic presidents restored some stability to the economy, but the gap between rich and poor remained wide. Dissatisfaction with this gap helped to elect **Luiz Inácio Lula da Silva**, in 2002. Lula, Brazil's first left-wing president in four decades, has pursued a mission of making Brazil more independent in global trade. His challenges are to generate employment and decrease the foreign debt.

✓ **Reading Check** **Evaluating** What factors led to the return to democracy in Brazil in 1985?

Peru, Colombia, and Venezuela

MAIN IDEA Violence and poverty have challenged Peru, Colombia, and Venezuela.

HISTORY & YOU How does poverty affect a country? Read to learn how poverty contributed to political unrest in Peru, Colombia, and Venezuela.

Other countries of South America have shared in the political, economic, and social problems that plagued Latin America since 1945. Peru, Colombia, and Venezuela have undergone many political changes in response to national problems.

Military and Civilian Rule in Peru

Instability has marked the history of **Peru**. Peru's dependence on the sale of its products abroad has led to extreme ups and downs in the economy. With these ups and downs have come many government changes. A large, poor, and landless peasant population has created an additional source of unrest.

A military takeover in 1968 led to some change. General **Juan Velasco Alvarado** sought to help the peasants. His government seized almost 75 percent of the nation's large landed estates and put ownership of the land into the hands of peasant **cooperatives** (farm organizations owned by and operated for the benefit of peasants). The government also nationalized many foreign-owned companies and froze food prices to help urban workers.

Economic problems continued, however, and Peruvian military leaders removed General Alvarado in 1975. Five years later, unable to cope with Peru's economic problems, the military returned Peru to civilian, democratic rule.

Peru's widespread economic problems made the **task** of the new civilian government even more difficult. Poverty was widespread in 1980, and it took its toll on the people. The life expectancy of Peruvians dropped. An estimated 120 out of every 1,000 infants died, and 60 percent of children under five years of age were malnourished. With unemployment high, there seemed to be no way out of poverty for many Peruvians.

Liberation Theology: A New Role for the Catholic Church

In 1968, the Catholic bishops of Latin America met in Medellín, Colombia. There they spoke out against the "oppression of institutionalized violence" and unjust political structures. They announced that they would urge the clergy to work for the betterment of the poor and victims of social injustice.

The term *liberation theology* was coined soon afterward by Gustavo Gutierrez, a Peruvian priest. It was a form of religion combined with Marxism that made helping the poor the Church's top priority. During the 1970s, at least 850 liberation theology priests and nuns were killed because of their commitment to social justice. Hundreds more have been killed since 1980. Liberation theology continues to be important in Latin America.

Franciscan priest Leonardo Boff preaching in Brazil. The banners behind him emphasize the Church's commitment to helping the poor.

CRITICAL THINKING SKILLS

1. **Defining** What is liberation theology?
2. **Contrasting** How does liberation theology differ from the traditional role of the Catholic Church in Latin America?

In this economic climate, a radical Communist guerrilla group gained support. Known as **Shining Path** the group wanted to create a classless society. Shining Path killed mayors, missionaries, priests, and peasants across Peru.

In 1990, Peruvians chose **Alberto Fujimori** as president. Fujimori, the son of Japanese immigrants, promised to make reforms. However, he later suspended the constitution and congress, became a dictator, and began a campaign against Shining Path guerrillas. Corruption led to Fujimori's removal from power in 2000.

In June 2001, Alejandro Toledo became Peru's first freely elected president of Native American descent. His successor, Alan García Pérez, must create additional jobs and decrease poverty to make Peru more economically stable. The government has prudent fiscal policies and is open to trade and investment.

Colombia: Coffee and Cocaine

Colombia has long had a democratic political system, but a conservative elite led by the owners of coffee plantations has dominated the government. Coffee is an important crop for Colombia, making up about half of the country's legal exports. Yet because the economy relies heavily upon the coffee trade, price fluctuations in either direction can have a negative effect. In 1975, for example, the Brazilian coffee crop was destroyed by frost. Prices for Colombian coffee rose dramatically, causing inflation.

In addition to economic problems, political problems troubled Colombia in the twentieth century. After World War II, Marxist guerrilla groups began to organize Colombian peasants. The government responded violently. More than 200,000 peasants had been killed by the mid-1960s. Violence continued in the 1980s and 1990s.

Peasants who lived in poverty turned to a new cash crop—coca leaves, which are used to make cocaine. As the lucrative drug trade grew, two major **cartels** (groups of drug businesses) formed in Colombia.

The drug cartels used bribes and violence to force government cooperation in the drug traffic and to dominate the market. Colombia became the major supplier of the international drug market. Violence has increased as rebel guerrillas made deals with the drug cartels to oppose the government. The government used an aerial eradication program to try to wipe out cocaine fields, but the program did not have much success. The United States **funded** the antidrug program, and in 2003 sent troops to support it.

Despite the money earned from drug and coffee exports, the Colombian economy remained weak because of high unemployment and the disruption of civil war. **Alvaro Uribe,** elected for a second term in 2006, promised to crack down hard on rebel groups. His economic policies hold promise for Colombia's future.

Chávez Rules Venezuela

A series of military dictators ruled **Venezuela** during the first half of the twentieth century. They promoted the oil industry and allowed for some social reforms.

By 1979, the Venezuelan economy had stalled. Corruption was also widespread. As a result of President Carlos Andrés Pérez's unpopular economic program, people rioted. More than 200 people were killed during the riots. Unrest continued to grow. A group of army lieutenants led by **Hugo Chávez** tried to overthrow the government in 1992. The coup failed and Chávez was put in prison. After Pérez was impeached a year later, Chávez was released.

Many people saw Chávez as a folk hero. When he ran for president in 1998, Chávez won the election in a landslide victory. During 2002 and 2003, Chávez's opposition front staged two national strikes. The military ousted Chávez during the first strike. However, loyal army elements restored him to power two days later. Nor could a national referendum in 2004 remove him. In December 2006, Chávez was reelected president with nearly two-thirds of the votes.

Like most leaders of South American countries, Chávez has many social and economic issues to address. Nearly 80 percent of the population lives in poverty. Real wages are low, and unemployment is high. Likewise, inflation rates remain high as does the foreign debt.

In late 2003, Chávez committed over $1 billion toward new social programs. Funding for this was aided by high oil prices. Venezuela depends on its oil reserves, the sixth largest in the world.

✓ Reading Check **Identifying** On what natural resource does the Venezuelan economy depend?

SECTION 3 REVIEW

Vocabulary
1. **Explain** the significance of: Chile, Salvador Allende, Augusto Pinochet, Argentina, Juan Perón, Falkland Islands, Brazil, Luiz Inácio Lula da Silva, Peru, Juan Velasco Alvarado, cooperatives, task, Shining Path, Alberto Fujimori, Colombia, cartels, fund, Alvaro Uribe, Venezuela, Hugo Chávez.

Main Ideas
2. **Explain** how the invasion of the Falkland Islands affected Argentina.

3. **List** the current leaders of the countries discussed in this section. Use a chart like the one below to make your list.

Country	Leader
Chile	
Argentina	
Brazil	
Peru	
Colombia	
Venezuela	

4. **Identify** some obstacles that current South American governments face.

Critical Thinking
5. **The BIG Idea** **Making Connections** Why is it often easier for the military to seize power than to rule effectively? Which countries discussed in this chapter support this theory?

6. **Organizing** How has democracy advanced in South America since the late 1980s?

7. **Analyzing Visuals** How do the white scarves of the protestors on page 738 make their protest more effective?

Writing About History
8. **Informative Writing** Write an article as if you are an American journalist covering Perón's presidency. Include details about the pros and cons of the Perón regime.

History ONLINE

For help with the concepts in this section of *Glencoe World History— Modern Times*, go to glencoe.com and click Study Central.

Social History

Teenage Life in Argentina

After suffering economic setbacks in the 1980s, Argentina sought to play a more active role in the global marketplace. Cable television and the Internet give Argentine teenagers access to global influences, yet extended families and the living history of festivals preserve the spirit of gaucho life.

Many Argentine teens enjoy traditional festivals. These celebrations often feature horseback events, music, and dancing.

In many areas, the traditional attire of the gaucho, or cowboy, is popular among Argentine youths. The gaucho hat is black, broad, and flat-brimmed.

The baggy gaucho pants are called bombachas. Gauchos tuck them into their boots.

Traditional attire worn by Argentine girls includes long, colorful dresses with full, ruffled skirts.

PROUD TRADITIONS AND FAMILY TIES

Argentina's customs draw upon its European (especially Spanish and Italian) influences, as well as the cultures of native South Americans. These traditions remain a strong influence on many young Argentines, particularly in the countryside. The close bonds of family help make festivals and traditional clothes important. For Argentines, the gaucho (cowboy) is an enduring national symbol of rugged individualism.

Argentina has won two World Cup titles.

Soccer is one of Argentina's most popular sports, in both participation and spectatorship.

Modern urban shopping malls are popular teenage gathering places in Buenos Aires.

Teen fashions are very similar to those in the United States.

FROM GAUCHOS TO GLOBETROTTERS

Young people in Buenos Aires and other cities in Argentina today experience international trends and live in ways very similar to teens in the U.S. Soccer provides Argentina with an athletic connection to its Latin American neighbors. Young Argentines can grow up dreaming of competing in the World Cup, knowing that their nation can watch and cheer them on anywhere on the globe.

ANALYZING VISUALS

1. **Making Generalizations** What types of activities are popular among teenagers in Argentina?

2. **Synthesizing** How do the lifestyles of Argentine teenagers reflect both traditional and global influences?

You can study anywhere, anytime by downloading quizzes and flash cards to your PDA from glencoe.com.

SLUMS IN RIO DE JANEIRO

Shantytowns sprang up in Latin American cities as the inflow of people overwhelmed city services.

Economic, Social, and Political Issues in LATIN AMERICA

- Economic failures in Latin America led to repressive regimes and debt.
- Population and cities grew rapidly, and the gap between rich and poor remains large.
- The United States has long intervened in Latin America to protect its interests.
- Artists and writers hold high status, as their work expresses the hopes of the people.

Economic, Social, and Political Issues in MEXICO, CUBA, and CENTRAL AMERICA

- To help in the relief of its debt crisis, the Mexican government privatized industries.
- The election of Vicente Fox in Mexico ended decades of rule by one party, the PRI.
- The economy of Castro's Cuba declined after the collapse of the Soviet Union, on which Cuba relied.
- Fearing the spread of communism, the United States intervened in Central American politics.

CUBAN REVOLUTIONARIES SEIZE HAVANA, 1959

Fidel Castro led a successful revolution in Cuba and established a Marxist dictatorship there.

VIOLENCE IN CHILE PROTESTING THE BRUTAL RULE OF AUGUSTO PINOCHET

Chile and other South American countries have experienced much political unrest.

Economic, Social, and Political Issues in SOUTH AMERICA

- Ideological battles drove politics in Chile and Argentina; today these governments are more democratic.
- Brazil's economy grew rapidly, but its new democratic government faces inflation and debt.
- Communist guerrillas in Peru and drug cartels in Colombia have troubled these nations.
- Venezuela depends on its huge oil reserves.

STANDARDIZED TEST PRACTICE

TEST-TAKING

When you read a map, pay careful attention to the title and to the map legend. The legend gives information crucial to understanding the map. The information in the legend may also help you eliminate answer choices that are incorrect.

Reviewing Vocabulary

Directions: Choose the word or words that best complete the sentence.

1. Farm organizations that are owned by peasants and operated for their benefit are known as _____.

A cartels

B welfare states

C cooperatives

D communes

2. Mexico City is a _____; its population has grown so fast that in some areas regular urban services cannot be provided.

A megacity

B megatropolis

C minicity

D cooperative

3. The _____ were a group who opposed Sandinista policies in Nicaragua during the 1970s and 1980s.

A contras

B conquistadors

C caudillos

D cartels

4. _____ in Colombia used bribes and violence to force government cooperation in the drug traffic.

A Peasants

B Cartels

C Caudillos

D Contras

Reviewing Main Ideas

Directions: Choose the best answers to the following questions.

Section 1 *(pp. 724–729)*

5. Latin American countries depended on the United States, Europe, and Japan for which of the following?

A Bananas

B Advanced technology

C Coffee imports

D Crude oil

6. Which organization formed in 1948 includes states in the Western Hemisphere?

A North Atlantic Treaty Organization

B North American Free Trade Agreement

C Central American Trade Association

D Organization of American States

7. Who is perhaps the best-known Latin American poet?

A Gabriel García Márquez

B Julio Cortázar

C Gabriela Mistral

D Oscar Niemeyer

Section 2 *(pp. 730–735)*

8. What new economic policy did Mexico follow based on the sale of government-owned businesses to private firms?

A Austerity

B Privatization

C Modernization

D Containment

Need Extra Help?								
If You Missed Questions . . .	1	2	3	4	5	6	7	8
Go to Page . . .	739	726	735	741	724	726	729	730

9. Who led the Cuban Revolution against the Batista regime?

  A Fidel Castro

  B Nikita Khrushchev

  C José Duarte

  D Manuel Noriega

10. What major Panamanian issue was finally settled in 1999?

  A The return of Manuel Noriega

  B Control of the Panama Canal

  C Payment of the lease for the Panama Canal

  D Privatization

Section 3 *(pp. 736–741)*

11. Which group was a main source of support for Juan Perón?

  A Labor and urban middle class

  B Landed gentry

  C Business owners

  D Military

12. Which South American country had an "economic miracle" in the late 1960s and early 1970s?

  A Chile

  B Peru

  C Argentina

  D Brazil

13. About what percent of Venezuela's population lives in poverty?

  A 50

  B 25

  C 80

  D 10

Critical Thinking

Directions: Choose the best answers to the following questions.

Use the following map to answer question 14.

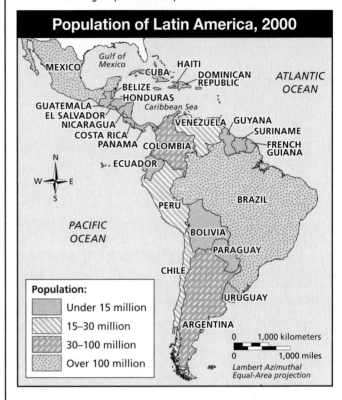

Population of Latin America, 2000

14. Which South American countries have the least population?

  A Brazil, Argentina, Colombia

  B Bolivia, Paraguay, Uruguay

  C Venezuela, Peru, Chile

  D Argentina, Bolivia, Ecuador

15. Why did many military regimes in Latin America fail?

  A They could not cope with debt problems.

  B Their power had popular consent.

  C The countries warred against each other.

  D Their leaders were too weak.

Need Extra Help?							
If You Missed Questions . . .	9	10	11	12	13	14	15
Go to Page . . .	732	735	738	739	741	726	725

16. How did Juan Perón gain support?

A He appealed to the landed elite.

B He had the backing of the United States.

C He maintained loyalty from the military.

D He appealed to the workers and urban middle class.

17. Why do Colombian cartels have so much power?

A They control the coffee market.

B They are backed by the United States.

C They have the support of rebel guerrilla groups.

D Their cocaine fields are resistant to pesticides.

Analyze the bar graph and answer the question that follows based on the graph and on your knowledge of world history.

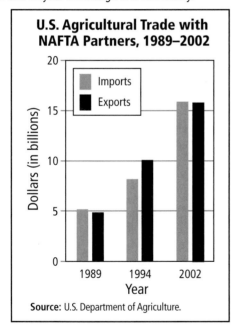

U.S. Agricultural Trade with NAFTA Partners, 1989–2002

Source: U.S. Department of Agriculture.

18. How did NAFTA affect agricultural trade between the United States, Mexico, and Canada?

A Mexico's exports to the United States decreased.

B Canada's exports to Europe increased.

C There was an increase in imports from Mexico and Canada to the United States, as well as exports from the United States to Mexico and Canada.

D Mexico stopped importing agricultural products from the United States.

Document-Based Questions

Directions: Analyze the document and answer the short-answer questions that follow the document. Base your answers on the document and on your knowledge of world history.

One Latin American observer discussed the U.S. invasion of Panama in 1989 in the following words:

> "The first official [U.S.] reason for the invasion of Panama was 'to protect American lives there.' This pretext was not credible, for the cry of 'wolf! wolf!' has been used before in Latin America. . . . The danger to American lives is a hundred times greater every day and night in Washington, D.C., 'the murder capital of the United States,' and in other American cities to which President Bush has hardly applied his policy of protecting North American lives and waging war against drugs (he prefers to wage that war on foreign battlefields)."
>
> —*Latin American Civilization: History and Society, 1492 to the Present*, Benjamin Keen, *1996*

19. To what U.S. action does the observer refer when he talks of the "invasion of Panama"?

20. What does this observer seem to say about U.S. foreign policy?

Extended Response

21. Simply because it believed they supported the guerrilla forces, the Guatemalan government massacred the indigenous people of Guatemala. How does this action compare to the settlers' and government's treatment of Native Americans in the United States during the eighteenth and nineteenth centuries and beyond?

History ONLINE

For additional test practice, use Self-Check Quizzes— Chapter 22 at glencoe.com.

Need Extra Help?

If You Missed Questions . . .	16	17	18	19	20	21
Go to Page . . .	737–738	741	731	735	735	735

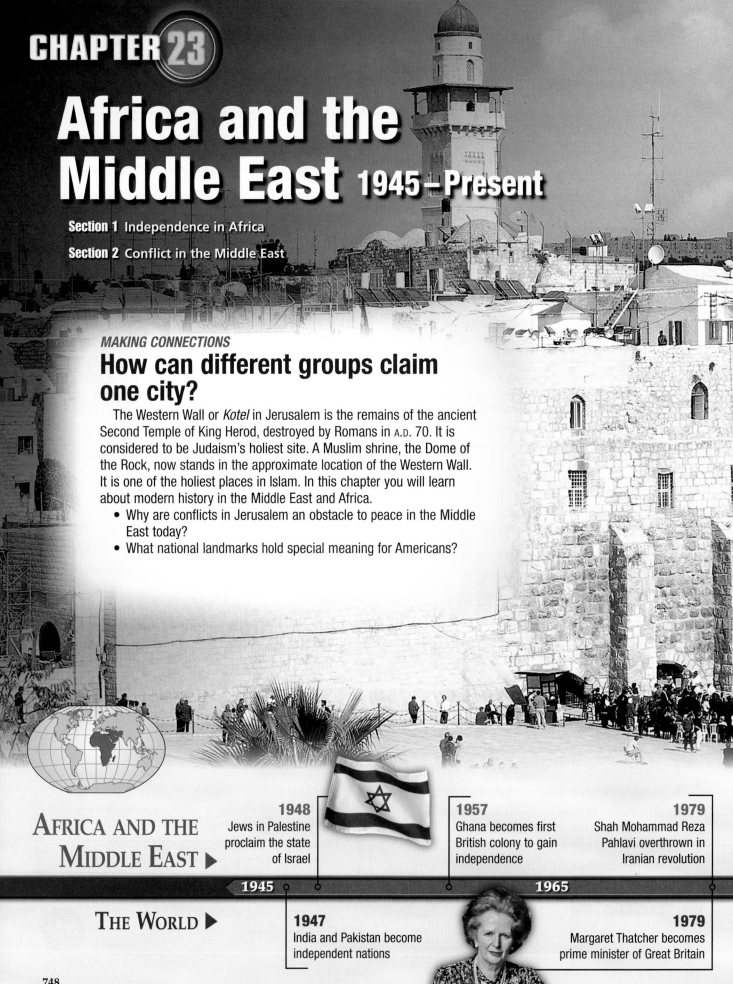

Africa and the Middle East 1945–Present

Section 1 Independence in Africa

Section 2 Conflict in the Middle East

MAKING CONNECTIONS

How can different groups claim one city?

The Western Wall or *Kotel* in Jerusalem is the remains of the ancient Second Temple of King Herod, destroyed by Romans in A.D. 70. It is considered to be Judaism's holiest site. A Muslim shrine, the Dome of the Rock, now stands in the approximate location of the Western Wall. It is one of the holiest places in Islam. In this chapter you will learn about modern history in the Middle East and Africa.

- Why are conflicts in Jerusalem an obstacle to peace in the Middle East today?
- What national landmarks hold special meaning for Americans?

AFRICA AND THE MIDDLE EAST ▶

1948
Jews in Palestine proclaim the state of Israel

1957
Ghana becomes first British colony to gain independence

1979
Shah Mohammad Reza Pahlavi overthrown in Iranian revolution

1945

1965

THE WORLD ▶

1947
India and Pakistan become independent nations

1979
Margaret Thatcher becomes prime minister of Great Britain

1994
Nelson Mandela elected president of South Africa

2004
PLO leader Yasir Arafat dies

1997
Control of Hong Kong is returned to China

1985   2000

FOLDABLES™
Study Organizer

Analyzing Points of View Make a Two-Tab Book to compare Israeli views and political positions during the 1950s to 1980s with those of Palestinians.

Israeli Views and Political Positions

Palestine Views and Political Positions

History ONLINE

Chapter Overview—Visit glencoe.com to preview Chapter 23.

Independence in Africa

GUIDE TO READING

The BIG Idea

Self-Determination After achieving independence from their colonial rulers, many African nations faced political, economic, social, and health challenges.

Content Vocabulary

- apartheid *(p. 751)*
- AIDS *(p. 753)*
- Pan-Africanism *(p. 752)*

Academic Vocabulary

- goal *(p. 750)*
- diverse *(p. 752)*

People and Places

- Ghana *(p. 750)*
- Kwame Nkrumah *(p. 750)*
- South Africa *(p. 750)*
- Jomo Kenyatta *(p. 752)*
- Kenya *(p. 752)*
- Julius Nyerere *(p. 752)*
- Liberia *(p. 753)*
- Nigeria *(p. 753)*
- Rwanda *(p. 754)*
- Democratic Republic of the Congo *(p. 754)*
- Sudan *(p. 754)*
- Nelson Mandela *(p. 754)*
- Desmond Tutu *(p. 754)*
- Chinua Achebe *(p. 757)*
- Noni Jabavu *(p. 757)*

Reading Strategy

Categorizing Information As you read, complete a chart like the one below identifying the problems in Africa during its first stages of independence.

Problems in Africa	
Economic	
Social	
Political	

Africa's road to independence has not been an easy one. Free from colonial rule, many African nations faced serious political, economic, social, and health challenges. Apartheid ended in South Africa, and Nelson Mandela became the country's first black president. Now into the twenty-first century, tension between old and new, native and foreign, still prevails in African society.

Independence and New Nations

MAIN IDEA After gaining their independence, many African states faced political, economic, social, and health challenges.

HISTORY & YOU Has flu ever infected many students in your school at the same time? How did this outbreak affect your school routine? Read to learn how AIDS affects life in Africa.

After World War II, Europeans realized that colonial rule in Africa would have to end. The Charter of the United Nations supported this belief. It stated that all colonial peoples should have the right to self-determination. In the late 1950s and 1960s, most African nations achieved independence.

In 1957 the Gold Coast, renamed **Ghana** and under **Kwame Nkrumah,** was the first British colony to gain independence. Nigeria, the Belgian Congo (renamed Zaire, now the Democratic Republic of the Congo), Kenya, and others soon followed. Seventeen new African nations emerged in 1960. Another 11 nations followed between 1961 and 1965. The Portuguese finally surrendered Mozambique and Angola in the 1970s.

In North Africa, the French granted full independence to Morocco and Tunisia in 1956. Because Algeria was home to a million French settlers, France chose to keep control there. However, Algerian nationalists began a guerrilla war to liberate their homeland. The French leader, Charles de Gaulle, granted Algeria its independence in 1962.

South Africa and Apartheid

In **South Africa,** where whites dominated the political system, the process was more complicated. Blacks began organizing against white rule and formed the African National Congress (ANC) in 1912. Its **goal** was economic and political reform. The ANC's efforts, however, met with little success.

At the same time, by the 1950s, South African whites (descendants of the Dutch, known as Afrikaners) had strengthened the

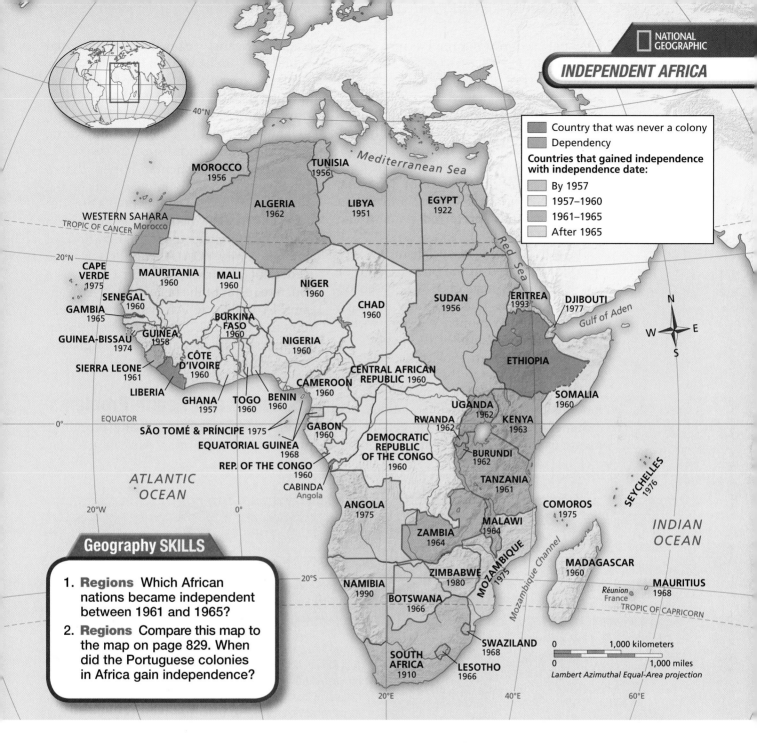

Legend:
- Country that was never a colony
- Dependency
- **Countries that gained independence with independence date:**
  - By 1957
  - 1957–1960
  - 1961–1965
  - After 1965

Mediterranean Sea

MOROCCO 1956
TUNISIA 1956
ALGERIA 1962
LIBYA 1951
EGYPT 1922

WESTERN SAHARA
Morocco
TROPIC OF CANCER

CAPE VERDE 1975
MAURITANIA 1960
MALI 1960
NIGER 1960
CHAD 1960
SUDAN 1956
ERITREA 1993
DJIBOUTI 1977

Red Sea
Gulf of Aden

SENEGAL 1960
GAMBIA 1965
GUINEA-BISSAU 1974
GUINEA 1958
BURKINA FASO 1960
NIGERIA 1960
CENTRAL AFRICAN REPUBLIC 1960

SIERRA LEONE 1961
CÔTE D'IVOIRE 1960
LIBERIA
GHANA 1957
TOGO 1960
BENIN 1960
CAMEROON 1960
ETHIOPIA

SÃO TOMÉ & PRÍNCIPE 1975
GABON 1960
EQUATORIAL GUINEA 1968
REP. OF THE CONGO 1960
CABINDA Angola
DEMOCRATIC REPUBLIC OF THE CONGO 1960
UGANDA 1962
RWANDA 1962
KENYA 1963
BURUNDI 1962
SOMALIA 1960

EQUATOR

ATLANTIC OCEAN

TANZANIA 1961

ANGOLA 1975
ZAMBIA 1964
MALAWI 1964
COMOROS 1975
SEYCHELLES 1976

INDIAN OCEAN

ZIMBABWE 1980
MOZAMBIQUE 1975
MADAGASCAR 1960
Réunion France
MAURITIUS 1968

NAMIBIA 1990
BOTSWANA 1966
TROPIC OF CAPRICORN

SWAZILAND 1968
SOUTH AFRICA 1910
LESOTHO 1966

0 1,000 kilometers
0 1,000 miles
Lambert Azimuthal Equal-Area projection

Geography SKILLS

1. **Regions** Which African nations became independent between 1961 and 1965?

2. **Regions** Compare this map to the map on page 829. When did the Portuguese colonies in Africa gain independence?

laws separating whites and blacks. The result was a system of racial segregation known as **apartheid** ("apartness"). Blacks began demonstrating against these laws.

The white government brutally repressed the demonstrators. In 1960 police opened fire on people who were leading a peaceful march in Sharpeville, killing 69 people, two-thirds of whom were shot in the back. After the arrest of ANC leader Nelson Mandela in 1962, members of the ANC called for armed resistance to the white government.

New Nations and New Leaders

The African states that achieved independence in the 1950s, 1960s, and 1970s still faced many problems. The leaders of these states, as well as their citizens, dreamed of stable governments and economic prosperity. Many of these dreams have yet to be realized.

Most leaders of the newly independent states came from the urban middle class. They had studied in Europe or the United States and knew European languages.

They believed in using the Western democratic model in Africa.

The views of these African leaders on economics were somewhat more **diverse.** Some, such as **Jomo Kenyatta** of **Kenya** and General Mobutu Sese Seko of the present-day Democratic Republic of the Congo, believed in Western-style capitalism. Others, such as **Julius Nyerere** of Tanzania, Kwame Nkrumah of Ghana, and Sékou Touré of Guinea, preferred an "African form of socialism."

The African form of socialism was not like that practiced in the Soviet Union or Eastern Europe. Instead, it was based on African traditions of community in which ownership of the country's wealth would be put into the hands of the people. As Nyerere declared in 1967: "The basis of socialism is a belief in the oneness of man and the common historical destiny of mankind. Its basis . . . is human equality."

Some African leaders believed in the dream of **Pan-Africanism**—the unity of all black Africans, regardless of national boundaries. In the view of Pan-Africanists, all black African peoples shared a common identity. Several of the new African leaders, including Léopold Senghor of Senegal, Kwame Nkrumah, and Jomo Kenyatta, supported Pan-Africanism.

Nkrumah in particular hoped that a Pan-African union would join all of the new countries of the continent in a broader community. His dream never became a reality. However, the Organization of African Unity (OAU), founded by the leaders of 32 African states in 1963, was a concrete result of the belief in Pan-Africanism. In 2002 the African Union (AU) replaced the OAU. This 53-nation group promotes democracy and economic growth in the region.

Economic and Health Problems

Independence did not bring economic prosperity to the new African nations.

PEOPLE *in* HISTORY

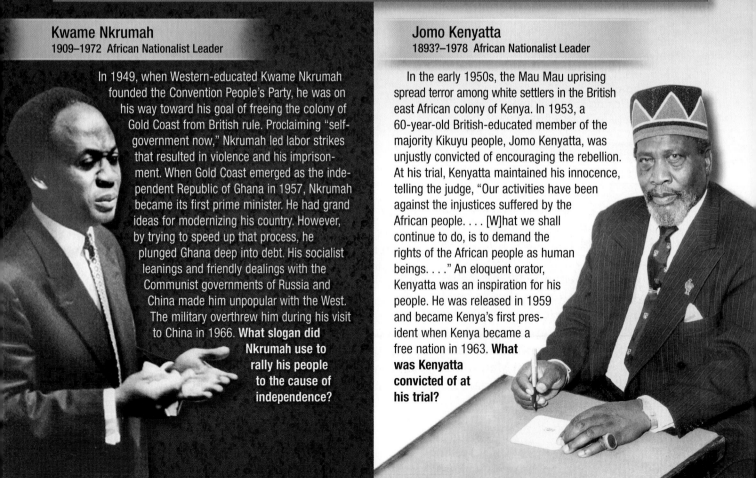

Kwame Nkrumah
1909–1972 African Nationalist Leader

In 1949, when Western-educated Kwame Nkrumah founded the Convention People's Party, he was on his way toward his goal of freeing the colony of Gold Coast from British rule. Proclaiming "self-government now," Nkrumah led labor strikes that resulted in violence and his imprisonment. When Gold Coast emerged as the independent Republic of Ghana in 1957, Nkrumah became its first prime minister. He had grand ideas for modernizing his country. However, by trying to speed up that process, he plunged Ghana deep into debt. His socialist leanings and friendly dealings with the Communist governments of Russia and China made him unpopular with the West. The military overthrew him during his visit to China in 1966. **What slogan did Nkrumah use to rally his people to the cause of independence?**

Jomo Kenyatta
1893?–1978 African Nationalist Leader

In the early 1950s, the Mau Mau uprising spread terror among white settlers in the British east African colony of Kenya. In 1953, a 60-year-old British-educated member of the majority Kikuyu people, Jomo Kenyatta, was unjustly convicted of encouraging the rebellion. At his trial, Kenyatta maintained his innocence, telling the judge, "Our activities have been against the injustices suffered by the African people. . . . [W]hat we shall continue to do, is to demand the rights of the African people as human beings. . . ." An eloquent orator, Kenyatta was an inspiration for his people. He was released in 1959 and became Kenya's first president when Kenya became a free nation in 1963. **What was Kenyatta convicted of at his trial?**

Most still relied on the export of a single crop or natural resource. **Liberia,** for example, depended on the export of rubber; **Nigeria,** on oil. When prices dropped, their economies suffered. To make matters worse, Africa's financial and technical resources were incapable of maintaining economic growth without foreign investment. Most African states imported technology and manufactured goods from the West and depended on foreign financial aid to develop their countries.

The new states also sometimes created their own problems. Scarce national resources were spent on military equipment or expensive consumer goods rather than on building the foundations for an industrial economy. Corruption was common.

African population growth, averaging 3 percent by the 1980s, crippled efforts to build modern economies. Serious droughts were another economic handicap and caused widespread hunger and starvation. Since the 1980s, droughts have recurred in Niger, Mali, Sudan, Somalia, and Ethiopia. Millions fled to other countries looking for food.

As a result of all these problems, poverty is widespread in Africa, especially among the three-fourths of the population still living off the land. Cities have grown tremendously. Surrounding the cities are massive slums populated by rural people who came to the cities looking for employment. The growth of the cities has overwhelmed sanitation and transportation systems. Pollution and perpetual traffic jams are the result.

Millions live without water and electricity in their homes. In the meantime, the fortunate few enjoy lavish lifestyles. The rich in many East African countries are known as the *wabenzi,* or Mercedes-Benz people.

In recent years, the greatest challenge to African progress was the spread of **AIDS,** or acquired immunodeficiency syndrome. AIDS is caused by the virus known as HIV, which is spread through bodily fluids. HIV weakens the immune system so that people with the disease cannot fight other illnesses. AIDS is a worldwide problem, but in Africa it is an epidemic. This crisis led the U.S. Congress in 2003 to authorize $15 billion in funds to treat AIDS in foreign nations, mostly in Africa.

According to the United Nations' 2006 AIDS epidemic update, almost two-thirds of all persons infected with HIV (nearly 40 million worldwide) are living in Africa south of the Sahara. In this area, nearly 3 million people, including children, became infected with HIV, and over 2 million died of AIDS during 2006. In Swaziland, more than 33 percent of the adult population has HIV. Infection levels are also high (20–24 percent) in Botswana, Lesotho, and Namibia.

One of the most striking effects of AIDS in Africa is the impact on children and families. In Africa south of the Sahara, 9 percent of children under the age of 15 have lost at least one parent to AIDS. Many have lost both parents. Very often, other relatives are too poor to take these children into their homes. Many orphans thus become heads of households filled with younger brothers and sisters. For centuries, extended families have been the source of support in difficult times, especially in rural parts of Africa. The AIDS epidemic, however, has overwhelmed this traditional support system.

African nations have taken steps to fight the epidemic. It has proved a tremendous burden, however, because many of these countries do not have the money or health facilities to educate their citizens about the disease and how to protect against it. Nor can they purchase the drugs that would extend the lives of those with HIV.

Uganda mounted an impressive effort to fight AIDS. President Yoweri Museveni involved a wide range of natural leaders in Ugandan society, including religious and tribal leaders, as well as international health and social service agencies. As a result of a major campaign promoting health and sex education, Uganda made significant progress in its fight against AIDS. Overall, Uganda's epidemic has stabilized. However, recent research shows evidence of an increase of HIV infection in rural areas and among older men and women.

Political Challenges

Many people hoped that independence would lead to democracies. They were soon disappointed as democratic governments failed. Between 1957 and 1982, more than 70 leaders were violently overthrown.

In the 1980s, either the military or a single party ruled many major African states. In the 1990s, demand for responsible government grew, but political instability is still a fact of life for many African nations.

Within many African nations, warring ethnic groups undermined the concept of nationhood. This is not surprising since the colonial powers had drawn the boundaries of African nations arbitrarily. Virtually all of these states included widely different ethnic, linguistic, and territorial groups.

For example, during the late 1960s, civil war tore Nigeria apart. Conflicts also broke out among ethnic groups in Zimbabwe. Farther north, in central Africa, fighting between the Hutu and Tutsi created unstable governments in **Rwanda** and Burundi. During the colonial period, Hutu and Tutsi peoples lived together under European control. After independence in 1962, two new countries were created: Rwanda and Burundi. The population in both countries was mixed, but in Rwanda, the Hutu majority ran the government. They resented the position of the Tutsis, who had gotten the best education and jobs under the Belgians. Ethnic fighting was common, and many Tutsis left for neighboring Uganda. They formed a party with the goal of overthrowing the Rwandan government.

In 1994, this tense situation ignited into brutal civil war when a plane carrying the Hutu president was shot down. Hutu militias began a campaign of genocide against Tutsis, killing at least 500,000. Eventually Tutsi rebel soldiers gained control. Hutus, as many as two million, fled the country, many to the **Democratic Republic of the Congo** (DRC). The Tutsis then invaded the DRC. In 1998 a civil war began, and as many as 3.5 million people died as a result.

Ethnic violence has also plagued **Sudan,** Africa's largest nation. In the western province of Darfur, Arab militias attacked African tribal groups with the support of the Arab-led government. Entire villages were burned and tens of thousands of people were killed. An estimated 1.8 million fled to refugee camps. Despite a truce agreement in May 2006, the fighting continues.

✓ **Reading Check** **Explaining** Why was the Organization of African Unity formed?

History ONLINE

Student Web Activity—

Visit glencoe.com and complete the activity on African independence.

Read excerpts from Nelson Mandela's *An Ideal for Which I Am Prepared to Die* on page R55 in the **Primary Sources and Literature Library.**

New Hopes

MAIN IDEA Dictators fell in several African nations, and apartheid ended in South Africa.

HISTORY & YOU Can you name someone in American history who was jailed for political activities? Read to learn about Nelson Mandela.

Not all the news in Africa has been bad. One-party regimes have collapsed and dictators have been ousted in several countries. Apartheid also ended in South Africa.

End of Dictatorships

One dictator ousted was Idi Amin of Uganda. After ruling by terror and brutal repression throughout the 1970s, Amin was deposed in 1979. Dictatorships also came to an end in Ethiopia, Liberia, and Somalia. In these cases, however, bloody civil wars followed the fall of these regimes.

End of Apartheid

One remarkable event was the 1994 election of **Nelson Mandela** to the presidency of the Republic of South Africa. Imprisoned in 1962 for his activities with the African National Congress, Mandela spent almost 26 years in maximum-security prisons in South Africa. For all those years, Mandela never wavered from his resolve to secure the freedom of his country.

Mandela was offered freedom in 1985, with conditions. Yet, he refused to accept a conditional freedom: "Only free men can negotiate; prisoners cannot enter into contracts. Your freedom and mine cannot be separated."

Nobel Peace Prize winner (1984) Bishop **Desmond Tutu** and others worked to free Mandela and to end apartheid. Eventually, worldwide pressure forced the South African government to dismantle apartheid laws. In 1990 Mandela was released from prison. In 1993 the government of F. W. de Klerk agreed to hold democratic national elections—the first in South Africa's history. In 1994 Nelson Mandela became South Africa's first black president.

✓ **Reading Check** **Identifying** Which African countries overthrew dictatorships?

THE END OF APARTHEID — IN SOUTH AFRICA

On the day of South Africa's first democratic election, voters waited in very long lines to cast their ballots.

"During my lifetime I have dedicated myself to this struggle of the African people. I have fought against white domination, and I have fought against black domination. I have cherished the ideal of a democratic and free society in which all persons live together in harmony and with equal opportunities."

— Nelson Mandela, opening statement at the Rivonia Trial, April 20, 1964

CRITICAL THINKING SKILLS

1. **Making Connections** Was Mandela's promise to build "a rainbow nation" consistent with the statement he made 30 years earlier at the Rivonia trial? Explain.

2. **Analyzing** In what ways did the end of apartheid mark a new beginning for South Africa?

Worldwide pressure on the South African government led to the end of apartheid and the election of that country's first black president. Apartheid was the policy of racial separation that became law in 1948 in South Africa.

A series of apartheid laws stripped black South Africans of virtually all civil rights. A decade of peaceful protests against these laws, organized by the African National Congress (ANC), came to an end with the Sharpeville Massacre in 1960.

In 1961 the ANC, by then an outlawed organization, took up arms against the government. In 1963 police arrested the ANC's leaders, including Nelson Mandela. At the Rivonia Trial, Mandela was sentenced to life in prison.

International pressure increased in 1985 when the governments of the United States and Great Britain imposed economic sanctions on South Africa. Finally, in 1990, South African president F. W. de Klerk's government legalized the ANC, freed Mandela, and began to dismantle the apartheid system. Four years later, Mandela became the first democratically elected president of South Africa. In his inaugural address, Mandela promised to build "a rainbow nation at peace with itself and the world."

Society and Culture

MAIN IDEA Tension between old and new, native and foreign, affects African society.

HISTORY & YOU How has e-mail changed how people communicate? Read to learn about the contrast between modern life and tradition in Africa.

Africa is a study in contrasts. Old and new, native and foreign, live side by side. One result is a constant tension between traditional ways and Western culture.

City and Countryside

In general, the impact of the West has been greater in the cities than in the countryside. After all, the colonial presence was first and most firmly established in the cities. Many cities, including Dakar, Lagos, Cape Town, Brazzaville, and Nairobi, are direct products of colonial rule. Most African cities today look like cities elsewhere in the world.

Outside the major cities, where about three-fourths of the inhabitants of Africa live, modern influence has had less of an impact. Millions of people throughout Africa live much as their ancestors did in thatched dwellings without modern plumbing and electricity. They farm, hunt, or raise livestock by traditional methods, wear traditional clothing, and practice traditional beliefs. Conditions such as drought or flooding affect the ability of rural

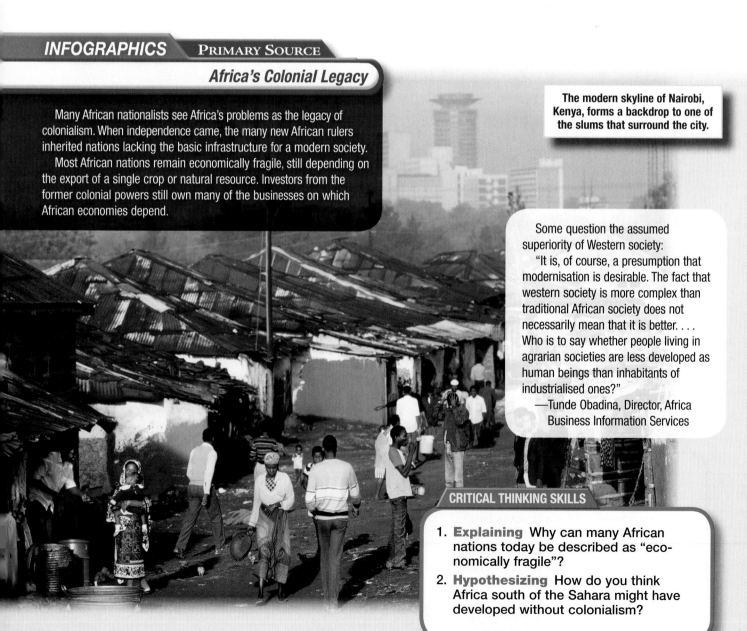

INFOGRAPHICS   PRIMARY SOURCE

Africa's Colonial Legacy

Many African nationalists see Africa's problems as the legacy of colonialism. When independence came, the many new African rulers inherited nations lacking the basic infrastructure for a modern society.

Most African nations remain economically fragile, still depending on the export of a single crop or natural resource. Investors from the former colonial powers still own many of the businesses on which African economies depend.

The modern skyline of Nairobi, Kenya, forms a backdrop to one of the slums that surround the city.

Some question the assumed superiority of Western society:

"It is, of course, a presumption that modernisation is desirable. The fact that western society is more complex than traditional African society does not necessarily mean that it is better. . . . Who is to say whether people living in agrarian societies are less developed as human beings than inhabitants of industrialised ones?"

—Tunde Obadina, Director, Africa Business Information Services

CRITICAL THINKING SKILLS

1. **Explaining** Why can many African nations today be described as "economically fragile"?

2. **Hypothesizing** How do you think Africa south of the Sahara might have developed without colonialism?

Africans to grow crops or tend herds. Migration to the cities for work is one solution. This can be very disruptive to families and villages. Many urban people view rural people as backward. Rural dwellers view the cities as corrupting and destructive to traditional African values and customs.

Women's Roles

In addressing the democratically elected South African parliament in 1994, Nelson Mandela said: "[F]reedom cannot be achieved unless women have been emancipated from all forms of oppression."

Independence from colonial powers changed women's roles in African society. Almost without exception women were allowed to vote and run for political office. However, radical changes have not taken place. Few women hold political offices. While they dominate some professions such as teaching, child care, and clerical work, women do not share in all career opportunities open to men. Most African women are employed in low-paid positions such as farm laborers, factory workers, and servants. Furthermore, in many rural areas, traditional attitudes toward women, including arranged marriages, prevail.

African Culture

Africans have adapted their native artistic traditions to foreign influences. A dilemma for many contemporary African artists is finding a balance between Western techniques and training on the one hand and the rich heritage of traditional African art forms on the other. In some countries, governments make the artists' decisions. Artists are told to depict scenes of traditional African life. These works are designed to serve the tourist industry.

African writers have often addressed the tensions and dilemmas that modern Africans face. The conflicting demands of town versus country and native versus foreign were the themes of most of the best-known works of the 1960s and 1970s.

These themes characterize the works of **Chinua Achebe** and **Noni Jabavu.** A Nigerian novelist who has won international acclaim, Achebe writes about the problems of Africans caught up in the conflict between traditional and Western values. In his novel *Things Fall Apart,* Achebe portrays the simple dignity of traditional African village life. Jabavu, a South African writer, documents the breakdown in African family life due to urbanization in *The Ochre People.* She expresses her impressions of westernization in East Africa and her criticism of traditional notions about "a woman's place" in her book, *Drawn in Color.*

✓ Reading Check **Summarizing** What themes characterize the works of Chinua Achebe and Noni Jabavu?

Vocabulary
1. **Explain** the significance of: Ghana, Kwame Nkrumah, South Africa, goal, apartheid, diverse, Jomo Kenyatta, Kenya, Julius Nyerere, Pan-Africanism, Liberia, Nigeria, AIDS, Rwanda, Democratic Republic of the Congo, Sudan, Nelson Mandela, Desmond Tutu, Chinua Achebe, Noni Jabavu.

Main Ideas
2. **Identify** the country and economic view of each African leader listed below.

Leader	Country	Economic View
Jomo Kenyatta		
Mobutu Sese Seko		
Julius Nyerere		
Kwame Nkrumah		
Sékou Touré		

3. **Describe** factors that contributed to ending apartheid in South Africa.

4. **Explain** why cities in Africa tend to be more modern than the countryside.

Critical Thinking
5. **The BIG Idea** **Determining Cause and Effect** How do you think the political situation in many African nations affects the fight against AIDS?

6. **Analyzing** What are some key reasons why poverty is so widespread in Africa?

7. **Analyzing Visuals** Examine the photograph on page 755. How does this picture reflect the desire of black South Africans to vote?

Writing About History
8. **Descriptive Writing** Assume the role of a journalist who is assigned to cover the conflict in Darfur. Do research and write a short news story describing the living conditions in the refugee camps.

History ONLINE
For help with the concepts in this section of *Glencoe World History—Modern Times,* go to glencoe.com and click Study Central.

Social History

Teenagers in Nigeria

Nigeria's rich oil reserves have attracted Western attention and influence throughout the nation's economy and culture. Across Nigeria, teenagers reflect the tension between Western values and artifacts, and traditional culture. Ethnic traditions, national culture, and Western imports all play off of one another.

Fulani teenage girls often wear tribal tattoos on their face as a symbol of beauty.

Hair braiding is an old tradition in Nigeria. Some teenage girls spend hours at salons having their hair braided into intricate patterns.

Muslim teenage boys in Nigeria wear floor-length robes over baggy cotton, or silk, drawstring pants.

Muslim teenage boys often wear a cloth skullcap, or *kufi*, on their heads.

Traditional attire for Nigerian teenage girls includes a long colorful cloth skirt. Muslim girls may wear dark-colored clothing that covers the entire body, along with a headpiece that can be worn as a veil.

About half of Nigeria's population follows Islam. Studying the Quran is an important part of a Muslim teenager's education.

TRADITIONAL INFLUENCES IN NIGERIA

The Nigerian population contains several different ethnic groups, each with its own language, religious practices, and customs. Many Nigerian groups have adopted Islamic or Christian belief systems. The traditional values of Nigeria's ethnic groups strongly influence teenagers, especially those living in rural areas. Their lifestyles are largely shaped by parents, village leaders, and religious teachers.

Fuji, a musical style based on drums and Islam-influenced vocals is popular in Nigeria.

Despite Nigeria's large oil production, many Nigerian teenagers, both urban and rural, live in poverty.

Many young people wear Western-style tops, pants and sweaters.

Traditional and modern influences often exist side by side in Nigerian households. The father wears a traditional Yoruba outfit while his son wears a Western-style T-shirt.

Teenagers in Nigeria are most likely to attend school in the big cities. Although public school is free, parents must buy school uniforms for their children.

Playing sports such as soccer and listening to Afro-beat or rap music are popular leisure activities for Nigerian teenagers.

GLOBAL INFLUENCES IN NIGERIA

Nigeria has urbanized rapidly in the past quarter century. Its cities receive a steady influx of foreign goods and ideas. The impact of Western culture in urban areas is strong. Many Nigerian teenagers have embraced foreign influences. Nonetheless, traditional culture remains an important influence on most Nigerian teenagers. Their lives reflect a blending of traditional ways and global culture.

ANALYZING VISUALS

1. **Analyzing** What statement does a Nigerian teenager make with the clothes that he or she wears?

2. **Contrasting** How might the daily life of a Nigerian teenager living in the country differ from the daily life of a Nigerian teenager living in the city?

Conflict in the Middle East

GUIDE TO READING

The BIG Idea
Competition Among Countries
Recurring violence and continuing efforts at international mediation have been the norm in the Middle East for decades.

Content Vocabulary
• Pan-Arabism *(p. 762)*   • intifada *(p. 763)*

Academic Vocabulary
• resolution *(p. 760)*   • issue *(p. 760)*

People and Places
• Zionists *(p. 760)*
• Israel *(p. 760)*
• Gamal Abdel Nasser *(p. 761)*
• Sinai Peninsula *(p. 763)*
• West Bank *(p. 763)*
• Anwar el-Sadat *(p. 763)*
• OPEC *(p. 763)*
• Menachem Begin *(p. 763)*
• Yasir Arafat *(p. 763)*
• Iran *(p. 764)*
• Ayatollah Ruhollah Khomeini *(p. 764)*
• Iraq *(p. 765)*
• Saddam Hussein *(p. 765)*
• Kuwait *(p. 765)*
• Persian Gulf *(p. 765)*
• Osama bin Laden *(p. 765)*
• al-Qaeda *(p. 765)*
• Naguib Mahfouz *(p. 767)*

Reading Strategy
Categorizing Information As you read, create a table and fill in the important events in the history of Arab-Israeli conflicts.

Year	Event

Since 1948, Israelis and Arabs have often been in conflict in the Middle East. In Iran, a revolution established an Islamic Republic, while war broke out in Afghanistan. Iraq's quest for territory ultimately led the United States to invade Iraq.

Palestine and the Mideast Crisis

MAIN IDEA Israel was founded as a Jewish state in 1948, but many Palestinian Arabs refused to recognize it.

HISTORY & YOU Do you know someone who holds grudges? Read to learn about the origins of the Israeli-Arab conflict.

In the Middle East, as in Asia and Africa, a number of new nations emerged after World War II. Syria and Lebanon gained their independence just before the end of the war. Jordan achieved complete self-rule soon afterward. These new states were predominantly Muslim.

The Question of Palestine

In the years between the two world wars, many Jews had immigrated to Palestine, believing this area to be their promised land. Tensions between Jews and Arabs had intensified during the 1930s. Great Britain, which governed Palestine under a United Nations (UN) mandate, had limited Jewish immigration into the area and had rejected proposals for an independent Jewish state in Palestine. The Muslim states agreed with this position.

The Zionists who wanted Palestine as a home for Jews were not to be denied, however. Many people had been shocked at the end of World War II when they learned about the Holocaust, the deliberate killing of 6 million European Jews in Nazi death camps. As a result, sympathy for the Jewish cause grew. In 1947, a United Nations resolution declared that Palestine should be divided into a Jewish state and an Arab state. The Jews in Palestine proclaimed the state of Israel on May 14, 1948.

Its Arab neighbors saw the creation of Israel as a betrayal of the Palestinian people, most of whom were Muslim. Outraged, several Arab countries invaded the new Jewish state. The invasion failed, but the Arab states still refused to recognize Israel's right to exist.

As a result of the division of Palestine, hundreds of thousands of Palestinians fled to neighboring Arab countries, where they lived in refugee camps. Other Palestinians came under Israeli rule. Creating a Palestinian state remains an important **issue** in the Middle East today.

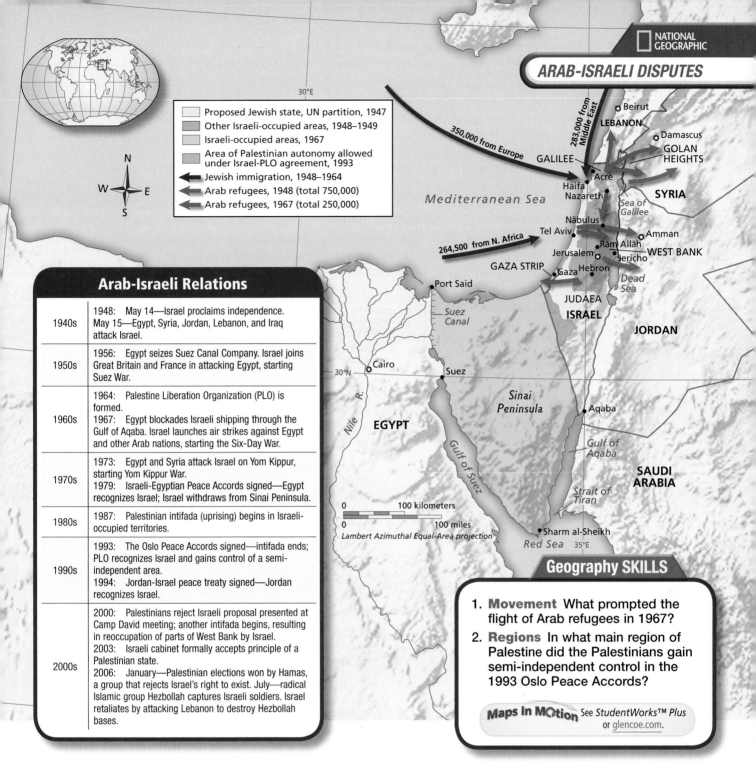

Legend:
- Proposed Jewish state, UN partition, 1947
- Other Israeli-occupied areas, 1948–1949
- Israeli-occupied areas, 1967
- Area of Palestinian autonomy allowed under Israel-PLO agreement, 1993
- Jewish immigration, 1948–1964
- Arab refugees, 1948 (total 750,000)
- Arab refugees, 1967 (total 250,000)

350,000 from Europe

283,000 from Middle East

264,500 from N. Africa

Beirut
LEBANON
Damascus
GOLAN HEIGHTS
GALILEE
Acre
Haifa
Nazareth
SYRIA
Sea of Galilee
Mediterranean Sea
Nābulus
Tel Aviv
Amman
Jerusalem   Rām Allāh   WEST BANK
Jericho
GAZA STRIP
Gaza   Hebron
Dead Sea
JUDAEA
ISRAEL
JORDAN

Port Said
Suez Canal
Cairo
30°N
Suez
EGYPT
Nile R.
Gulf of Suez
Sinai Peninsula
Aqaba
Gulf of Aqaba
SAUDI ARABIA
Strait of Tiran
Sharm al-Sheikh
Red Sea   35°E

30°E

N
W   E
S

0   100 kilometers
0   100 miles
Lambert Azimuthal Equal-Area projection

Arab-Israeli Relations

1940s	**1948:** May 14—Israel proclaims independence. May 15—Egypt, Syria, Jordan, Lebanon, and Iraq attack Israel.
1950s	**1956:** Egypt seizes Suez Canal Company. Israel joins Great Britain and France in attacking Egypt, starting Suez War.
1960s	**1964:** Palestine Liberation Organization (PLO) is formed. **1967:** Egypt blockades Israeli shipping through the Gulf of Aqaba. Israel launches air strikes against Egypt and other Arab nations, starting the Six-Day War.
1970s	**1973:** Egypt and Syria attack Israel on Yom Kippur, starting Yom Kippur War. **1979:** Israeli-Egyptian Peace Accords signed—Egypt recognizes Israel; Israel withdraws from Sinai Peninsula.
1980s	**1987:** Palestinian intifada (uprising) begins in Israeli-occupied territories.
1990s	**1993:** The Oslo Peace Accords signed—intifada ends; PLO recognizes Israel and gains control of a semi-independent area. **1994:** Jordan-Israel peace treaty signed—Jordan recognizes Israel.
2000s	**2000:** Palestinians reject Israeli proposal presented at Camp David meeting; another intifada begins, resulting in reoccupation of parts of West Bank by Israel. **2003:** Israeli cabinet formally accepts principle of a Palestinian state. **2006:** January—Palestinian elections won by Hamas, a group that rejects Israel's right to exist. July—radical Islamic group Hezbollah captures Israeli soldiers. Israel retaliates by attacking Lebanon to destroy Hezbollah bases.

Geography SKILLS

1. **Movement** What prompted the flight of Arab refugees in 1967?
2. **Regions** In what main region of Palestine did the Palestinians gain semi-independent control in the 1993 Oslo Peace Accords?

Maps In Motion See *StudentWorks*™ *Plus* or glencoe.com.

Nasser and Pan-Arabism

In Egypt, a new leader arose who would play an important role in the Arab world. Colonel **Gamal Abdel Nasser** took control of the Egyptian government in the early 1950s. Then on July 26, 1956, Nasser seized the Suez Canal Company, which had been under British and French administration since the 1800s.

Great Britain and France were upset by this threat to their world position. The Suez Canal was an important waterway linking the Mediterranean Sea to Asia. Great Britain and France decided to strike back, and Israel quickly joined them. The three nations launched a joint attack on Egypt, starting the Suez War of 1956.

The United States and the Soviet Union joined in supporting Nasser. Both opposed French and British influence in the Middle East. They forced Britain, France, and Israel to withdraw from Egypt.

Nasser emerged from the conflict as a powerful leader. He began to promote **Pan-Arabism,** or Arab unity. In February 1958, Egypt formally united with Syria in the United Arab Republic (UAR). Nasser was named the first president of the new state. Egypt and Syria hoped that the union would eventually include all Arab states.

Many other Arab leaders were suspicious of Pan-Arabism. Oil-rich Arab states were concerned they would have to share revenues with poorer states in the Middle East. In Nasser's view, Arab unity meant that wealth derived from oil, which currently flowed into a few Arab states or to foreign interests, could be used to improve the standard of living throughout the Middle East. In 1961 Syrian military leaders took over Syria and withdrew the country from its union with Egypt. Nasser continued to work on behalf of Arab interests.

The Arab-Israeli Dispute

During the late 1950s and 1960s, the dispute between Israel and other states in the Middle East became more heated. In 1967 Nasser imposed a blockade against Israeli shipping through the Gulf of Aqaba. He declared: "Now we are ready to confront Israel. We are ready to deal with the entire Palestine question."

Fearing attack, on June 5, 1967, Israel launched air strikes against Egypt and several of its Arab neighbors. Israeli warplanes wiped out most of the Egyptian air force. Israeli armies broke the blockade and

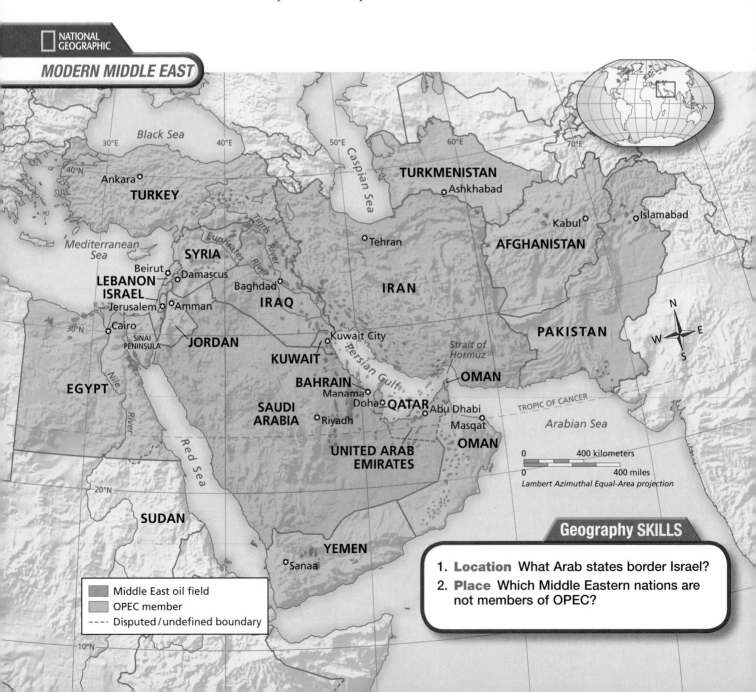

NATIONAL GEOGRAPHIC

MODERN MIDDLE EAST

Black Sea
30°E 40°N 40°E 50°E 60°E 70°E
Ankara○ TURKEY
Caspian Sea
TURKMENISTAN
○Ashkhabad
Kabul○ ○Islamabad
Mediterranean Sea
Tigris River Euphrates River
SYRIA ○Tehran AFGHANISTAN
Beirut○ ○Damascus
LEBANON Baghdad○
ISRAEL IRAQ IRAN PAKISTAN
Jerusalem○ ○Amman
30°N ○Cairo JORDAN Kuwait City○
SINAI PENINSULA KUWAIT Persian Gulf Strait of Hormuz
OMAN
EGYPT BAHRAIN
Manama○ TROPIC OF CANCER
Nile River SAUDI Doha○ QATAR Abu Dhabi○
ARABIA ○Riyadh Masqat○ Arabian Sea
UNITED ARAB OMAN
EMIRATES
Red Sea 0   400 kilometers
0   400 miles
Lambert Azimuthal Equal-Area projection
20°N
SUDAN
YEMEN
○Sanaa
10°N

N
W   E
S

Middle East oil field
OPEC member
---- Disputed / undefined boundary

Geography SKILLS

1. **Location** What Arab states border Israel?
2. **Place** Which Middle Eastern nations are not members of OPEC?

occupied the **Sinai Peninsula.** Israel seized territory on the **West Bank** of the Jordan River, occupied East Jerusalem, and took control of the Golan Heights. During this Six-Day War, Israel tripled the size of territory under its control. As a result, another million Palestinians now lived inside Israel's new border, most of them on the West Bank.

Over the next few years, Arab states continued to demand the return of the occupied territories. Nasser died in 1970, and **Anwar el-Sadat** succeeded him.

On October 6, 1973 (the Jewish holiday of Yom Kippur), Egypt and Syria launched a coordinated surprise attack against Israel. Golda Meir, Israel's prime minister, had little time to mobilize troops. For the first two days of the Yom Kippur War, Israel was on the defensive. Then the tide turned. Israeli forces pushed into Egypt, trapping Egypt's Third Army. A UN-negotiated cease-fire on October 22 saved the Egyptian army from destruction. An agreement in 1974 officially ended this conflict, but the dispute over the occupied territories remained.

Meanwhile, however, the war was having indirect results in Western nations. In 1960, several Arab oil-producing states had formed **OPEC,** the Organization of the Petroleum Exporting Countries, to control the price of oil. During the Yom Kippur War, some OPEC nations announced large increases in the price of oil to foreign countries. The price hikes, coupled with cuts in oil production, led to oil shortages and serious economic problems in the West.

In 1977 U.S. president Jimmy Carter began to press for a compromise peace between Arabs and Israelis. In September 1978 President Carter met with President Sadat of Egypt and Israeli prime minister **Menachem Begin** (BAY•gihn) at Camp David in the United States. The result was the Camp David Accords, an agreement to sign an Israeli-Egyptian peace treaty. The treaty, signed by Sadat and Begin in March 1979, led to a complete Israeli withdrawal from the Sinai Peninsula and ended the state of war between Egypt and Israel. Many Arab countries, however, continued to refuse to recognize Israel.

✓**Reading Check** **Identifying** How did the Yom Kippur War affect the West indirectly?

The Ongoing Crisis

MAIN IDEA The turmoil in the Middle East continues into the twenty-first century.

HISTORY & YOU How did your family think the United States should react to the 9/11 attacks? Read about the U.S. invasion of Iraq.

In 1964 the Egyptians took the lead in forming the Palestine Liberation Organization (PLO) to represent Palestinian interests. The PLO believed that only the Palestinian Arabs should have a state in the Palestine region. At the same time, a guerrilla movement called al-Fatah, headed by the PLO political leader **Yasir Arafat,** began to launch terrorist attacks on Israeli territory. Terrorist attacks continued for decades.

Palestine and Lebanon

During the 1980s, Palestinian Arabs, frustrated by their failure to achieve self-rule, grew more militant. They led an *intifada,* or uprising, in the territories occupied by Israel since the 1967 Arab-Israeli war. Finally, in the Oslo Peace Accords of 1993, Israel and the PLO agreed that the PLO would control a semi-independent area. In return, the PLO recognized the Israeli state.

In 1994 Jordan and Israel signed a peace treaty. This treaty made Jordan the second Arab nation, after Egypt, to recognize Israel.

Even with these changes, little progress was made toward Palestinian statehood. Some Israelis did not want to give up the occupied territories, and some Palestinians did not accept the state of Israel. In the wake of the Palestinian rejection of a proposal offered by Israel at a meeting arranged by President Clinton at Camp David in 2000, a second *intifada* erupted and has continued. Suicide bombings in the heart of Israel led to Israeli reoccupation of significant areas of the West Bank that had been largely controlled by the Palestinian Authority. Nonetheless, a sign of progress emerged in 2003—the Israeli cabinet formally accepted the principle of a Palestinian state.

Yasir Arafat died in 2004. Mahmoud Abbas, a moderate Palestinian, replaced him. Many people were hopeful that real progress might be made at peace talks.

Peacemakers in the Middle East

In October 1994, Israeli prime minister Yitzhak Rabin and King Hussein of Jordan made peace. U.S. president Bill Clinton was on hand to witness the signing of the historic peace treaty (see photo).

The two countries had been in a state of war since 1948, when Jordan and other Arab nations invaded the new state of Israel. However, in 1993, with the signing of the Oslo Accords between Israel and the Palestine Liberation Organization, Jordan became the second Arab nation (after Egypt) to recognize Israel as a nation. The treaty settled territorial disputes and established normal relations between the two nations.

Many Palestinians and right-wing Israelis condemned the treaty. In November 1995, a Jewish extremist assassinated Yitzhak Rabin. At Rabin's funeral, King Hussein paid tribute to him as a brother, friend, and "soldier for peace."

Yitzhak Rabin   Bill Clinton   King Hussein

"This is our gift to our peoples and the generations to come."
—King Hussein of Jordan

CRITICAL THINKING SKILLS

1. **Calculating** How long did a state of war exist between Israel and Jordan?
2. **Making Inferences** Why would some Israelis condemn their own leader for making peace?

However, the January 2006 electoral victory by majority members of Hamas, a Palestinian resistance movement that rejects Israel's right to exist, led to new obstacles to peace.

The conflict between Arabs and Israelis also expanded. Hezbollah, a radical Islamic group that formed in Lebanon in 1982, captured two Israeli soldiers in July 2006. Israel responded with bombing raids and a ground invasion of southern Lebanon to destroy Hezbollah military bases. In return, Hezbollah forces fired rockets into Israel. After much destruction, both sides agreed to a cease-fire in August 2006.

Turmoil in Iran

The conflict between Israel and the Palestinians is one of many challenges in the Middle East. As in other parts of the world, a few people are rich, while many are poor. Some countries prosper because of oil, but others remain in poverty. A response to these problems is the growth of movements based on Islam. Many of these groups believe that Western culture and values have kept Muslim nations poor and weak. They believe that Muslims must return to Islamic culture and values to build prosperous societies. Some of these groups are willing to use violence to bring about an Islamic revolution. Such a revolution took place in **Iran.**

The leadership of Shah Mohammad Reza Pahlavi and revenue from oil made Iran a rich country. Iran was also an ally of the United States in the Middle East in the 1950s and 1960s. But the shah had much opposition in Iran. Many Muslims looked with distaste at the new Iranian society. In their eyes, it was based on materialism, which they identified with American influence.

Leading the opposition to the shah was the **Ayatollah Ruhollah Khomeini** (ko•MAY•nee), a member of the Muslim clergy. By the late 1970s, many Iranians agreed with Khomeini. In 1979, the shah's government collapsed, and an Islamic republic replaced it.

The new government, led by the Ayatollah Khomeini, moved to restore Islamic law. Supporters of the shah were executed or fled the country. Anti-American feelings erupted when militants seized 52 Americans in the United States embassy in Tehran and held them hostage for over a year.

After Khomeini's death in 1989, a more moderate government allowed some civil liberties. Some Iranians were dissatisfied with the government's economic performance. Others, especially young people, pressed for more freedoms and an end to the rule of conservative Muslim clerics. In 1997 a moderate Muslim cleric, Mohammed Khatemi, became president. He pushed for reforms, including more freedom for women and the press. However, conservative clerics soon reversed the new freedoms.

In August 2005, a new president, Mahmoud Ahmadinejad, was elected. An extremist, he called for the destruction of Israel and denied the existence of the Holocaust. Ahmadinejad also defended Iran's nuclear program, which he claimed was peaceful. Other nations, however, feared that Iran was seeking nuclear weapons. A new Middle East crisis was born.

Iraq's Aggression

To the west of Iran was a hostile **Iraq**, led by **Saddam Hussein** since 1979. Iran and Iraq have long had an uneasy relationship. Religious differences have fueled their disputes. Although both are Muslim nations, the Iranians are mostly Shia Muslims. The Iraqi leaders under Saddam Hussein, on the other hand, were mostly Sunni Muslims. Iran and Iraq have fought over territory, too, especially over the Strait of Hormuz. Strategically very important, the strait connects the Persian Gulf and the Gulf of Oman.

In 1980 Saddam Hussein launched a brutal war against Iran. He used children to clear dangerous minefields. He used poison gas against soldiers and civilians, especially the Kurds, an ethnic minority in the north who wanted their own state. In 1988, Iran and Iraq signed a cease-fire without resolving the war's basic issues.

In August 1990, Saddam Hussein sent his troops across the border to seize **Kuwait**, a country at the head of the **Persian Gulf.** The invasion sparked an outcry, and the United States led the international forces that freed Kuwait. Hoping an internal revolt would overthrow Saddam, the allies imposed harsh economic sanctions on Iraq. The overthrow of Saddam Hussein, however, did not happen.

Afghanistan and the Taliban

After World War II, the king of Afghanistan, in search of economic assistance for his country, developed close ties with the Soviet Union. After a full-scale invasion of Afghanistan in 1979, the Soviets occupied the country for 10 years. Eventually anti-Communist forces supported by the United States and Pakistan ousted them. Among these anti-Communist forces were Islamic groups who began to fight for control. One of these, the Taliban, seized the capital city of Kabul in 1996. By the fall of 1998, the Taliban controlled more than two-thirds of the country.

Backed by conservative religious forces in Pakistan, the Taliban provided a base of operations for **Osama bin Laden.** Bin Laden came from a wealthy family in Saudi Arabia and used his wealth to support the Afghan resistance. In 1988 bin Laden founded **al-Qaeda,** or "the Base," which recruited Muslims to drive Westerners out of nations with a largely Muslim population. After the Taliban seized control of much of Afghanistan, bin Laden used bases there to train al-Qaeda recruits.

Osama bin Laden's biggest mission came with the attacks of September 11, 2001, in the United States. After the attacks, a coalition of forces led by the United States launched a war against the Taliban in Afghanistan. By December 2001, the Taliban collapsed and was replaced by a moderate government. Despite U.S. support, the new government has recently had to face a renewal of warfare among various tribal groups and a revival of Taliban forces.

Post-9/11: The War on Iraq

Meanwhile, U.S.-Iraqi tensions increased. In 2002 President George Bush began threatening to remove Saddam Hussein from power. The United States claimed that Saddam had chemical and biological weapons of mass destruction, and was well on the way to developing nuclear weapons. President Bush also argued that Saddam Hussein had close ties to al-Qaeda.

Both of these claims were doubted by many other member states at the United Nations. As a result, the United States was forced to attack Iraq with little support from the world community.

In March 2003 a largely U.S.-led army invaded Iraq. The Iraqi army was quickly defeated, and Saddam Hussein was captured. The war, however, was far from over. No weapons of mass destruction were found. Moreover, for the United States and its partners, rebuilding Iraq was more difficult than defeating the Iraqi army. Saddam Hussein's supporters, foreign terrorists, and Islamic militants all battled the American-led forces.

American efforts since 2003 have focused on training an Iraqi military force capable of defeating rebel forces and establishing order in Iraq. Moreover, the United States moved toward the formation of a temporary Iraqi government that could hold free elections and create a democracy. Establishing a new government was difficult because there were differences among the three major groups in Iraqi society: Shia Muslims, Sunni Muslims, and ethnic Kurds.

Although a new Iraqi government came into being in 2005, it has been unable to establish a unified state. By 2006, Iraq seemed to be descending into a widespread civil war, especially between the Shia, who controlled southern Iraq, and the Sunnis, who controled central Iraq. Saddam Hussein's execution in December 2006 added to the turmoil and incited protests from his followers. In January 2007 President Bush called for an increase of U.S. troops to help end the violence in Iraq.

✓**Reading Check** **Explaining** Why was it difficult to establish a new government in Iraq?

CONNECTING TO THE UNITED STATES

⤷TERRORISM IN THE U.S.

Terrorist acts became more frequent in the later twentieth century. By May 2003, the U.S. State Department had designated 36 groups as Foreign Terrorist Organizations. These groups include urban guerrilla groups in Latin America; militants dedicated to the liberation of Palestine; Islamic militants fighting Western influence in the Middle East; and separatists seeking independent states.

Television has encouraged global terrorism to some extent because terrorists know that newscasts create instant publicity. Television images of American jetliners flying into the World Trade Center in New York City in 2001, for example, created immediate awareness of the goals of the Islamic fundamentalist militants.

- **February 26, 1993: Muslim extremists led by Ramzi Yousef bombed the World Trade Center, killing 6 and wounding 1,000.**

- **September 11, 2001: Muslim extremists in four hijacked airliners attacked landmarks in New York City and Washington, D.C., killing 3,000.**

Terrorist attacks at the World Trade Center, September 11, 2001

CONNECTING TO TODAY

1. **Making Connections** How is the unrest in the Middle East connected to terrorist attacks against the United States?

2. **Comparing and Contrasting** Compare the terrorist attacks of September 11, 2001, with earlier terrorism in the United States.

Society and Culture

MAIN IDEA Islamic fundamentalism has impacted Middle Eastern society, especially women's roles.

HISTORY & YOU Do your parents object to some things you wear? Read about restrictions imposed by Islamic conservatives.

In recent years, conservative religious forces have tried to replace foreign culture and values with Islamic forms of belief and behavior. This movement is called Islamic fundamentalism or Islamic activism. For some Islamic leaders, Western values and culture are based on materialism, greed, and immorality. Extremists want to remove all Western influence in Muslim countries. These extremists give many Westerners an unfavorable impression of Islam.

Islamic fundamentalism began in Iran under Ayatollah Khomeini. There the return to traditional Muslim beliefs reached into clothing styles, social practices, and the legal system. These ideas and practices spread to other Muslim countries. In Egypt, for example, militant Muslims assassinated President Sadat in 1981.

Islamic fundamentalism is a concern in some Middle East countries. In Turkey, the military suspects that "Islamization" is gaining ground in the country. The prime minister has spoken out against restrictions on Islamic-style headscarves and has taken steps to aid religious schools. The military intends to keep Turkey secular and pro-Western.

At the beginning of the twentieth century, women's place in Middle Eastern society had changed little for hundreds of years. Early Muslim women had participated in the political life of society and had extensive legal, political, and social rights. Cultural practices in many countries had overshadowed those rights, however.

In the nineteenth and twentieth centuries, Muslim scholars debated issues surrounding women's roles in society. Many argued for the need to rethink outdated interpretations and cultural practices that prevented women from realizing their potential. Until the 1970s, the general trend in urban areas was toward a greater role for women. Beginning in the 1970s, however, there was a shift toward more traditional roles for women. This trend was especially noticeable in Iran.

The literature of the Middle East since 1945 has reflected a rise in national awareness, which encouraged interest in historical traditions. Writers also began to deal more with secular themes for broader audiences, not just the elite. For example, *Cairo Trilogy* by Egyptian writer **Naguib Mahfouz** tells about a merchant family in Egypt in the 1920s. The changes in the family parallel the changes in Egypt. Mahfouz was the first writer in Arabic to win the Nobel Prize in Literature (in 1988).

✓ Reading Check **Identifying** Who was the first writer in Arabic to win the Nobel Prize in Literature?

Vocabulary

1. **Explain** the significance of: Zionists, resolution, Israel, issue, Gamal Abdel Nasser, Pan-Arabism, Sinai Peninsula, West Bank, Anwar el-Sadat, OPEC, Menachem Begin, Yasir Arafat, *intifada*, Iran, Ayatollah Ruhollah Khomeini, Iraq, Saddam Hussein, Kuwait, Persian Gulf, Osama bin Laden, al-Qaeda, Naguib Mahfouz.

Main Ideas

2. **Explain** how the migration of Jews to Israel has been similar to earlier migrations.

3. **List** the goals of the U.S. involvement in Iraq since 2003 in a chart like the one below.

Goals of U.S. in Iraq Since 2003

4. **Explain** how Muslim extremists view Western values and culture.

Critical Thinking

5. **The BIG Idea** **Analyzing** Why has it proven so difficult to resolve conflict in the Middle East?

6. **Making Connections** Why is the Middle East so important to the global economy?

7. **Analyzing Visuals** Examine the photograph on page 766. What emotions does this image create for you? Why?

Writing About History

8. **Persuasive Writing** Choose the role of either an Arab Palestinian or a Jewish settler. Write a letter to the United Nations, arguing your position on the Palestine issue. What do you think should be done in Palestine and why?

History ONLINE

For help with the concepts in this section of *Glencoe World History— Modern Times*, go to glencoe.com and click Study Central.

What Challenges Did Apartheid Create for South Africans?

How did apartheid affect South Africa? For much of the twentieth century, South Africa's white-run government denied political and economic equality to the country's black majority.

What progress have South Africans made in overcoming the effects of apartheid? Despite facing harsh government repression, South Africans carried on a decades-long campaign against apartheid. The nation finally held free elections in 1994, marking the end of apartheid and the beginning of democracy.

Apartheid in South Africa attracted international attention. Read the excerpts and study the cartoon to learn more about how South Africa faced this challenge.

SOURCE 1

The following passage is from a speech by Desmond Tutu, a black Anglican Archbishop, to the United Nations Security Council on October 23, 1984.

For my beloved country is wracked by division, by alienation, by **animosity**[1], by separation, by injustice, by unavoidable pain and suffering. It is a deeply **fragmented**[2] society, ridden by fear and anxiety . . . and a sense of desperation, split up into hostile, warring factions. . . .

There is little freedom to disagree with the determinations of the authorities. There is large scale unemployment here because of the drought and the recession that has hit most of the world's economy. And it is such a time that the authorities have increased the prices of various foodstuffs and also of rents in black townships—measures designed to hit hardest those least able to afford the additional costs. . . .

The authorities have not stopped stripping blacks of their South African citizenship. . . . The South African government is turning us into aliens in the land of our birth.

White South Africans are . . . scared human beings, many of them; who would not be, if they were outnumbered five to one? Through this lofty body I wish to appeal to my white fellow South Africans to share in building a new society, for blacks are not intent on driving whites into the sea but on claiming only their rightful place in the sun in the land of their birth.

SOURCE 2

African National Congress leader Nelson Mandela discussed South Africa's past and future in a speech he gave after his release from prison in 1990.

Today, the majority of South Africans, black and white, recognize that **apartheid**[3] has no future. It has to be ended by our own decisive mass action in order to build peace and security. The mass campaigns of defiance and other actions of our organizations and people can only **culminate**[4] in the establishment of democracy. The apartheid's destruction on our subcontinent is incalculable. The fabric of family life of millions of my people has been shattered. Millions are homeless and unemployed. Our economy lies in ruins and our people are embroiled in political strife. . . .

We call on our people to seize this moment, so that the process toward democracy is rapid and uninterrupted. . . . We must not allow fear to stand in our way. Universal suffrage on a common voters roll in a united, democratic and non-racial South Africa is the only way to peace and racial harmony. . . .

I have fought against white domination, and I have fought against black domination. I have cherished the ideal of a democratic and free society in which all persons live together in harmony and with equal opportunity. It is an ideal which I hope to live for and to achieve. But, if need be, it is an ideal for which I am prepared to die.

[1] **animosity:** resentment
[2] **fragmented:** broken into pieces

[3] **apartheid:** policy of racial segregation
[4] **culminate:** conclude

ZAPIRO
SOWETAN 15·12·94

FREEDOM

"...after climbing a great hill, one only finds that there are many more hills to climb."
— Nelson Mandela in "The Long Walk to Freedom".

RECONSTRUCTION

ELECTION
KEMPTON PARK
VICTOR VERSTER
POLLSMOOR
THE ISLAND
RIVONIA
ARMED STRUGGLE
TREASON TRIAL
DEFIANCE CAMPA...

▲ This political cartoon by Zapiro, appearing in the newspaper the *Sowetan* in 1994, tracks Mandela's path to freedom.

SOURCE 3

In the 1940s the African National Congress (ANC) formed a Youth League to lead a nonviolent campaign against the apartheid policies of South Africa. In 1960 South African police fired on unarmed demonstrators at Sharpeville, killing 67. A year later the ANC formed an armed wing, Umkhonto we Sizwe, headed by Nelson Mandela to carry out sabotage against government installations.

In 1963 the South African government arrested Mandela and, a year later, sentenced him to life imprisonment. In 1990, amidst growing international and domestic pressure, the government released Mandela. Four years later, he was elected president by voters in South Africa. His **inauguration**[5] marked the end of apartheid.

[5] **inauguration:** ceremonial induction into office

DOCUMENT-BASED QUESTIONS

1. **Explaining** According to Bishop Tutu, what problems did South Africa face in 1984?
2. **Drawing Conclusions** What do you think Mandela hoped to accomplish with his speech?
3. **Assessing** What does the cartoon reveal about the state of the South African nation after Mandela gained his freedom?
4. **Identifying Points of View** How do you think Mandela's experiences influenced the opinions he expressed in his speech?
5. **Synthesizing** What similarities exist between the messages conveyed by all three sources?
6. **Evaluating** What challenges did apartheid create for South Africans? Do you believe that Mandela and Tutu offered effective ideas to deal with these challenges? Why or why not?

STUDY TO GO You can study anywhere, anytime by downloading quizzes and flash cards to your PDA from glencoe.com.

Challenges in AFRICA

- Whites used apartheid laws to maintain power in mostly black South Africa.
- Leaders of newly independent African nations struggled to create stable governments.
- Reliance on the export of a single crop or resource threatened economic prosperity.
- Poverty, hunger, disease, and ethnic conflicts still plague African nations.

THE AIDS EPIDEMIC IN AFRICA

This Zambian cemetery holds mass funerals due to the high number of AIDS victims.

SUICIDE BOMBING IN CENTRAL ISRAEL

Palestinians have launched terrorist attacks on Israel.

Challenges in the MIDDLE EAST

- In 1973, OPEC reduced oil supplies and raised prices, causing economic problems in the West.
- Terrorist attacks on September 11, 2001, led to a war in Afghanistan.
- In 2006, Palestinians chose Hamas to lead them, a group that rejects Israel's right to exist.
- Efforts to establish a stable, democratic government in Iraq continue following the removal of Saddam Hussein from power by a United States-led coalition.

IMPACTS ON SOCIETIES in Africa and the Middle East

- In Africa, constant tension exists between traditional ways and Western culture.
- African women have made political and economic gains, but inequalities remain.
- African artists search for ways to balance Western techniques with traditional art.
- Islamic Fundamentalism has impacted Middle Eastern society, especially women's roles.

CONTRAST BETWEEN OLD AND NEW IN AFRICA

Satellite dishes atop traditional homes in Fès, Morocco, illustrate Africa's transition to the modern world.

STANDARDIZED TEST PRACTICE

TEST-TAKING TIP

Time lines show chronology, or the order in which events happened. You can use your knowledge of chronology to get rid of incorrect answer choices. Think about what events happened during the time and then consider the answer choices.

Reviewing Vocabulary

Directions: Choose the word or words that best complete the sentence.

1. Removing all Western influences in Muslim countries is the goal of _____.

A isolationism

B absolutism

C Islamic radicalism

D Zionism

2. _____, a system of racial segregation, was practiced in South Africa.

A Apartheid

B Achebe

C Pan-Africanism

D Wabenzi

3. _____ is the name Palestinian Arabs give to their uprisings in Israeli-occupied territories.

A Hajj

B Insurgency

C *Hijrah*

D *Intifada*

4. _____ is the belief that all black Africans, regardless of national boundaries, should be united.

A Black power

B Pan-Arabism

C Pan-Africanism

D African imperialism

Reviewing Main Ideas

Directions: Choose the best answers to the following questions.

Section 1 *(pp. 750–757)*

5. Which leader dreamed of a union that would join all African nations in a broader community?

A Nelson Mandela

B Noni Jabavu

C Kwame Nkrumah

D Desmond Tutu

6. Which disease is caused by the HIV virus?

A Influenza

B Hemophilia

C Lupus

D AIDS

7. Who were the intended victims of genocide in Rwanda in 1994?

A Tutsis

B Hutus

C Burundi

D Congo

8. Who was South Africa's first black president?

A Jomo Kenyatta

B F. W. de Klerk

C Julius Nyerere

D Nelson Mandela

Need Extra Help?								
If You Missed Questions . . .	1	2	3	4	5	6	7	8
Go to Page . . .	767	751	763	752	752	753	754	754

Section 2 (pp. 760–767)

9. In what year did the Jews in Palestine proclaim the state of Israel?

A 1962

B 1925

C 1948

D 1945

10. Under whose leadership did Egypt launch the Yom Kippur War against Israel?

A Anwar el-Sadat

B Menachem Begin

C Gamal Abdel Nasser

D Golda Meir

11. After Mohammad Reza Pahlavi's government collapsed in Iran, what new leader moved to restore Islamic law?

A Mahmoud Ahmadinejad

B Ayatollah Ruhollah Khomeini

C Saddam Hussein

D Mohammed Khatemi

12. What ethnic group in northern Iraq did Saddam Hussein attack because they wanted their own state?

A Taliban

B Tutsis

C Hutus

D Kurds

13. Who formed al-Qaeda?

A Saddam Hussein

B Babrak Karmal

C Osama bin Laden

D Ayatollah Ruhollah Khomeini

Critical Thinking

Directions: Choose the best answers to the following questions.

Use the following map to answer question 14.

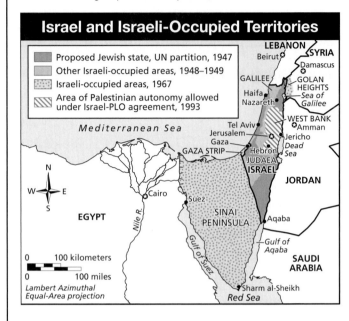

14. Which city is within the West Bank?

A Beirut

B Jerusalem

C Haifa

D Tel Aviv

15. Why do many African nations still depend on former colonial powers?

A They need financial aid to develop their countries.

B They must import oil from the West.

C They need markets for their manufactured goods.

D They have few natural resources on which to base industry.

16. Which of the follow was a result of the Six-Day War?

A Palestine was divided into a Jewish state and an Arab state.

B U.S.-led forces liberated Kuwait from Saddam Hussein.

C Israel occupied the Sinai Peninsula and West Bank.

D U.S.-led forces drove the Taliban out of Afghanistan.

Need Extra Help?								
If You Missed Questions . . .	9	10	11	12	13	14	15	16
Go to Page . . .	760	763	764	765	765	763	753	762

17. Which of the following is a major reason for the growth of movements based on Islam?

A Desire for a homeland

B The Holocaust

C Desire for world domination

D Poverty

Analyze the time line and answer the question that follows. Base your answer on the time line and on your knowledge of world history.

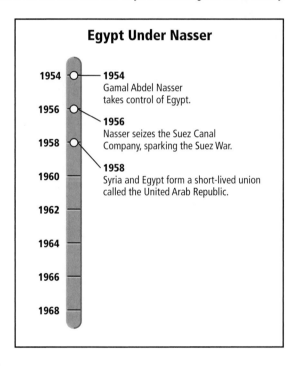

Egypt Under Nasser

1954
Gamal Abdel Nasser takes control of Egypt.

1956
Nasser seizes the Suez Canal Company, sparking the Suez War.

1958
Syria and Egypt form a short-lived union called the United Arab Republic.

18. Which event below logically belongs on this time line?

A Egypt and Israel sign the Camp David Accords.

B Egypt blockades Israeli shipping through the Gulf of Aqaba.

C Egypt invades Israel on Yom Kippur, 1973.

D Militants seize 52 Americans from the U.S. embassy in Tehran.

Document-Based Questions

Directions: Analyze the document and answer the short-answer questions that follow the document. Base your answers on the document and on your knowledge of world history.

On March 21, 1960, Humphrey Taylor, a reporter, described what happened at this peaceful march:

> "We went into Sharpeville the back way, around lunch time last Monday, driving along behind a big grey police car and three armoured cars. As we went through the fringes of the township many people were shouting the Pan-Africanist slogan 'Our Land.' They were grinning and cheerful. . . . Then the shooting started. We heard the chatter of a machine gun, then another, then another. . . . One woman was hit about ten yards from our car. . . . Hundreds of kids were running, too. Some of the children, hardly as tall as the grass, were leaping like rabbits. Some of them were shot, too."
>
> —Humphrey Taylor, as quoted in *The Mammoth Book of Eyewitness History 2000,* Jon E. Lewis

19. Why were these people demonstrating?

20. Based on this account, does the shooting seem justified? Why or why not?

Extended Response

21. The roles of women have changed during the last century. Compare and contrast the roles and rights of women in the Middle East and Africa.

History ONLINE

For additional test practice, use Self-Check Quizzes—Chapter 23 at **glencoe.com**.

Need Extra Help?					
If You Missed Questions . . .	17	18	19	20	21
Go to Page . . .	764	761	751	751	757

STOP

Asia and the Pacific
1945–Present

Section 1 Communist China

Section 2 Independent States in Asia

Section 3 Japan and the Pacific

MAKING CONNECTIONS

How can modernization affect a society?

The rapid modernization of China has created a nation that blends the old with the new. An example can be seen in Hong Kong where traditional Chinese junks can be seen in the harbor of this modern city. In this chapter you will learn how China has emerged into the modern world.

- How has modernization affected the standard of living of the Chinese people?
- Give an example of an aspect of American culture that is a legacy of past traditions.

ASIA AND
THE PACIFIC ▶

THE WORLD ▶

1951
Japan's independence is restored after World War II

1966
Mao Zedong launches Cultural Revolution

1973
President Nixon signs cease-fire agreement with North Vietnam

1945   1965

1957
Ghana gains independence from Britain

1977
Apple II computer is introduced

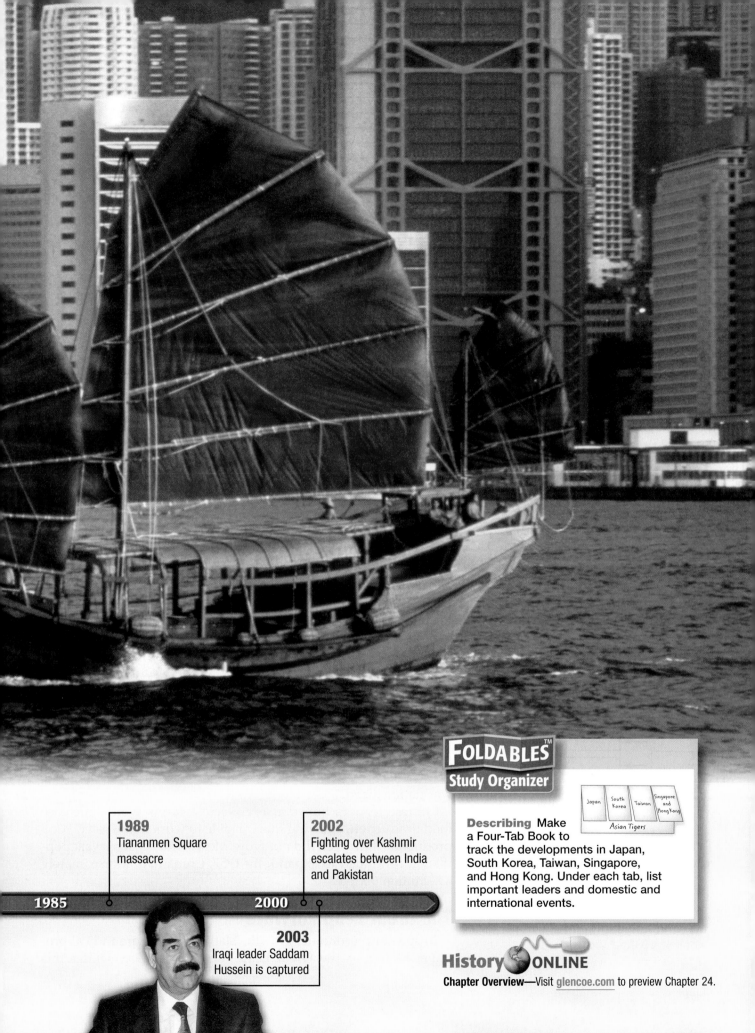

1989
Tiananmen Square
massacre

2002
Fighting over Kashmir
escalates between India
and Pakistan

1985

2000

2003
Iraqi leader Saddam
Hussein is captured

FOLDABLES™
Study Organizer

Japan | South Korea | Taiwan | Singapore and Hong Kong
Asian Tigers

Describing Make
a Four-Tab Book to
track the developments in Japan,
South Korea, Taiwan, Singapore,
and Hong Kong. Under each tab, list
important leaders and domestic and
international events.

History ONLINE

Chapter Overview—Visit glencoe.com to preview Chapter 24.

Communist China

GUIDE TO READING

The BIG Idea
Ideas, Beliefs, and Values The policies of the Chinese Communist government set up in 1949 failed to bring prosperity. Since the 1980s, its economy has moved toward free enterprise, but political freedom is still very limited.

Content Vocabulary
- communes (p. 777)
- permanent revolution (p. 778)
- per capita (p. 778)
- one-child policy (p. 780)

Academic Vocabulary
- final (p. 777)
- source (p. 778)

People, Places, and Events
- Chiang Kai-shek (p. 776)
- Mao Zedong (p. 776)
- Taiwan (p. 776)
- Great Leap Forward (p. 776)
- Great Proletarian Cultural Revolution (p. 778)
- Little Red Book (p. 778)
- Red Guards (p. 778)
- Deng Xiaoping (p. 778)
- Tiananmen Square (p. 779)
- South Korea (p. 781)
- North Korea (p. 781)
- Richard Nixon (p. 781)

Reading Strategy
Determining Cause and Effect As you read, use a chart like the one below to list communism's effects on China's international affairs.

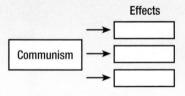

To build his socialist society in China, Mao Zedong launched the Great Leap Forward and the Great Proletarian Cultural Revolution. Neither program was especially successful. In modernizing China, leaders after Mao have built their nation into one of the most powerful countries in Asia.

Mao's China

MAIN IDEA Mao Zedong led the Communists to victory in the civil war, but the human and economic costs of establishing communism were high.

HISTORY & YOU Do you remember what you read earlier about Russia's transformation under Lenin? Read to learn how Mao Zedong transformed China after he took power in 1949.

By 1945, there were two Chinese governments. The Nationalist government of **Chiang Kai-shek,** based in southern and central China, was supported by the United States. The Communist government, led by **Mao Zedong,** had its base in northern China.

Civil War and Its Aftermath

In 1945 a full-scale civil war broke out between the Nationalists and the Communists. In the countryside, promises of land attracted millions of peasants to the Communist Party. Many joined Mao's People's Liberation Army. By the spring of 1949, the People's Liberation Army had defeated the Nationalists. Chiang Kai-shek and two million followers fled to the island of **Taiwan.**

The Communist Party, under the leadership of its chairman, Mao Zedong, now ruled China. In 1955 the Chinese government launched a program to build a socialist society. To win the support of the peasants, lands were taken from wealthy landlords and given to poor peasants. About two-thirds of the peasant households in China received land under the new program. Most private farmland was collectivized, and most industry and commerce was nationalized.

Chinese leaders hoped that collective farms would increase food production, allowing more people to work in industry. Food production, however, did not grow. Meanwhile, China's vast population continued to expand. By 1957, China had approximately 657 million people.

The Great Leap Forward

To speed up economic growth, Mao began a more radical program, known as the **Great Leap Forward,** in 1958. Under this

1949: Communists defeat Nationalists, who flee to Taiwan and establish Republic of China; Mao Zedong proclaims People's Republic of China on the mainland

1960: After millions die from poor planning and poor harvests, the Great Leap Forward ends

1976: Mao Zedong dies; Deng Xiaoping succeeds him

1989: Tiananmen Square protests violently suppressed

1999: China takes control of Macao from Portugal

1945	1955	1965	1975	1985	1995

1945: Civil war between Nationalists and Communists begins

1958: The Great Leap Forward program of reforms begins

1966: Great Proletarian Cultural Revolution begins

1978: Official launch of the Four Modernizations

1997: China regains control of Hong Kong from Great Britain

SOVIET UNION
80°E
40°N
MONGOLIA
100°E
120°E
MANCHURIA
Sea of Japan (East Sea)
JAPAN
XINJIANG
INNER MONGOLIA
Beijing
NORTH KOREA
SOUTH KOREA
140°E
Yellow Sea
PAKISTAN
20°N
TIBET
CHINA
Xi'an
Nanjing
Hefei
Shanghai
NEPAL
SIKKIM
BHUTAN
Wuhan
East China Sea
INDIA
Chongqing
BANGLADESH
Kunming
Taipei
TROPIC OF CANCER
BURMA (MYANMAR)
Guangzhou
Taiwan
Hong Kong
LAOS
Shenzhen
PACIFIC OCEAN
Hainan
THAILAND
VIETNAM
CAMBODIA

0   1000 kilometers
0   1000 miles
Two-Point Equidistant projection

Geography SKILLS

1. **Location** Use the map's scale to determine the approximate distance from Taiwan to mainland China.
2. **Analyzing Visuals** According to the time line, how many years was Mao Zedong China's leader?

○ Pro-democracy student demonstrations, 1986
✹ Site of fighting involving Red Guards, 1966–1969
▢ People's Republic of China (Communist)
▢ Republic of China (Nationalist)
▢ Main areas of Red Guard activity

program, over 700,000 existing collective farms, normally the size of a village, were combined into 26,000 vast **communes.** Each commune contained more than 30,000 people who lived and worked together. Since they had communal child care, more than 500,000 Chinese mothers worked beside their husbands in the fields by mid-1958.

Mao hoped his Great Leap Forward program would enable China to reach the **final** stage of communism—the classless society—before the end of the twentieth century. The government's official slogan promised the following to the Chinese people: "Hard work for a few years, happiness for a thousand."

Despite such slogans, the Great Leap Forward was an economic disaster. Bad weather, which resulted in droughts and floods, and the peasants' hatred of the new system drove food production down. As a result, nearly 15 million people died of starvation. In 1960 the government began to break up the communes and return to collective farms and some private plots.

The Cultural Revolution

Despite opposition within the Communist Party and the commune failure, Mao still dreamed of a classless society. In Mao's eyes, only **permanent revolution**, an atmosphere of constant revolutionary fervor, could enable the Chinese to achieve the final stage of communism.

In 1966 Mao launched the **Great Proletarian Cultural Revolution.** The Chinese name literally meant "great revolution to create a proletarian (working class) culture." A collection of Mao's thoughts, called the *Little Red Book,* became a sort of bible for the Chinese Communists. It was hailed as the most important **source** of knowledge in all areas. The book was in every hotel, in every school, and in factories, communes, and universities. Few people conversed without first referring to the *Little Red Book.*

To further the Cultural Revolution, the **Red Guards** were formed. These were revolutionary groups composed largely of young people. Red Guards set out across the nation to eliminate the "Four Olds"— old ideas, old culture, old customs, and old habits. The Red Guard destroyed temples, books written by foreigners, and foreign music. They tore down street signs and replaced them with ones carrying revolutionary names. The city of Shanghai even ordered that red (the revolutionary color) traffic lights would indicate that traffic could move, not stop.

Vicious attacks were made on individuals who had supposedly deviated from Mao's plan. Intellectuals and artists accused of being pro-Western were especially open to attack. One such person, Nien Cheng, worked for the British-owned Shell Oil Company in Shanghai. She was imprisoned for seven years. She told of her experience in *Life and Death in Shanghai.*

Key groups, however, including Communist Party members and many military officers, did not share Mao's desire for permanent revolution. People, disgusted by the actions of the Red Guards, began to turn against the movement.

✓ **Reading Check** **Explaining** Why was the Great Leap Forward an economic disaster for China?

History ONLINE

Student Web Activity—
Visit glencoe.com to learn to create, modify, and use spreadsheets and complete an activity on China's Four Modernizations.

China After Mao

MAIN IDEA After Mao's death, Deng Xiaoping tried to modernize the nation but faced increased pressures for democratic reform.

HISTORY & YOU If you participated in a protest, would you be risking your life to do so? Read about the risks of public protest in China.

In September 1976, Mao Zedong died at the age of 82. A group of practical-minded reformers, led by **Deng Xiaoping** (DUHNG SHYOW•PIHNG), seized power and brought the Cultural Revolution to an end.

Policies of Deng Xiaoping

Deng Xiaoping called for Four Modernizations—new policies in industry, agriculture, technology, and national defense. For over 20 years, China had been isolated from the technological advances taking place elsewhere in the world. To make up for lost time, the government invited foreign investors to China. The government also sent thousands of students abroad to study science, technology, and modern business techniques.

A new agricultural policy was begun. Collective farms could now lease land to peasant families who paid rent to the collective. Anything produced on the land above the amount of that payment could be sold on the private market. Peasants were also allowed to make goods they could sell to others.

Overall, modernization worked. Industrial output skyrocketed. **Per capita** (per person) income, including farm income, doubled during the 1980s. The standard of living rose for most people. The average Chinese citizen in the early 1980s had barely earned enough to buy a bicycle, radio, or watch. By the 1990s, many were buying refrigerators and color television sets.

Movement for Democracy

Despite these achievements, many people complained that Deng Xiaoping's program had not achieved a fifth modernization— democracy. People could not directly criticize the Communist Party. Those who called for democracy were often sentenced to long terms in prison.

The problem began to intensify in the late 1980s. More Chinese began to study abroad, and they learned more about the West. That information reached more educated people inside the country. As the economy prospered, students and other groups believed that they could ask for better living conditions and greater freedom. Students, in particular, wanted more freedom to choose jobs after they graduated.

In the late 1980s, rising inflation led to growing discontent among salaried workers, especially in the cities. Corruption and special treatment for officials and party members led to increasing criticism as well. In May 1989, student protesters called for an end to the corruption and demanded the resignation of China's aging Communist Party leaders. These demands received widespread support from people in the cities. Discontent led to massive demonstrations in **Tiananmen Square** in Beijing.

Deng Xiaoping believed the protesters were calling for an end to Communist rule. He ordered tanks and troops into the square to crush the demonstrators. Between 500 and 2,000 were killed and many more injured. Democracy remained a dream.

Throughout the 1990s, China's human rights violations and its determination to unify with Taiwan strained its relationship with the West. China's increasing military power has also created international concern. However, China still maintains diplomatic relations with the West.

✓ **Reading Check** **Explaining** Why did farmers produce more under the new agricultural policy?

INFOGRAPHICS PRIMARY SOURCE

Communism Under Deng Xiaoping

Deng Xiaoping's Four Modernizations aimed to move China to a more market-driven economy, but Deng remained committed to a Communist political system. In 1978 the government had briefly allowed people to express their ideas on a wall in Beijing, but when the messages called for more political freedom, the "Democracy Wall" was torn down. Deng said that freedoms like free speech and open debate "had never played a positive role in China."

"The leaders of our nation must be informed that we want to take our destiny into our own hands. We want no more gods or emperors. No more saviors of any kind. We want to be masters of our own country, not modernized tools for the expansionist ambitions of dictators. . . . Democracy, freedom and happiness are the only goals of modernization. Without this fifth modernization, the four others are nothing more than a new-fangled lie."
—Wei Jingsheng, "The Fifth Modernization" (posted on the Democracy Wall, 1978)

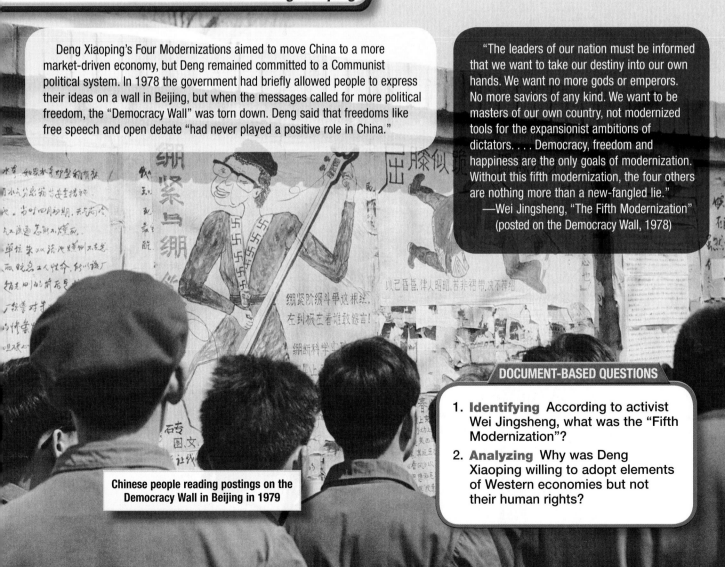

Chinese people reading postings on the Democracy Wall in Beijing in 1979

DOCUMENT-BASED QUESTIONS

1. **Identifying** According to activist Wei Jingsheng, what was the "Fifth Modernization"?

2. **Analyzing** Why was Deng Xiaoping willing to adopt elements of Western economies but not their human rights?

Chinese Society

MAIN IDEA After Mao's death, the state shifted from revolutionary fervor back to family traditions.

HISTORY & YOU Should the government be able to dictate the size of families? Read to learn about family policies in China.

📜 See page R55 to read excerpts from Xiao-huang Yin's *China's Gilded Age* in the **Primary Sources and Literature Library.**

From the start, the Communist Party wanted to create a new kind of citizen, one who would give the utmost for the good of all China. In Mao's words, the people "should be resolute, fear no sacrifice, and surmount every difficulty to win victory."

During the 1950s and 1960s, the Chinese government made some basic changes. Women were now allowed to take part in politics and had equal marital rights—a dramatic shift for the Chinese. Mao feared that loyalty to the family would interfere with loyalty to the state. During the Cultural Revolution, for example, children were encouraged to report negative comments their parents made about the government.

After Mao's death, family traditions returned. People now had more freedom in everyday matters and had better living conditions. Married couples who had been given patriotic names chose more elegant names for their own children. Clothing choices were no longer restricted to a baggy "Mao suit." Today, young Chinese people wear jeans, sneakers, and sweatsuits.

Mao's successors have followed one of his goals to the present day—the effort to control population growth. In 1979 the state began advocating a **one-child policy.** Incentives such as education benefits, child care, and housing were offered to couples who limited their families to one child. Criticized for being oppressive, the policy has been more successful in cities than it has in rural areas.

✓**Reading Check** **Analyzing** How did policies after Mao affect women and families?

NATIONAL GEOGRAPHIC

KOREAN WAR, 1950–1953

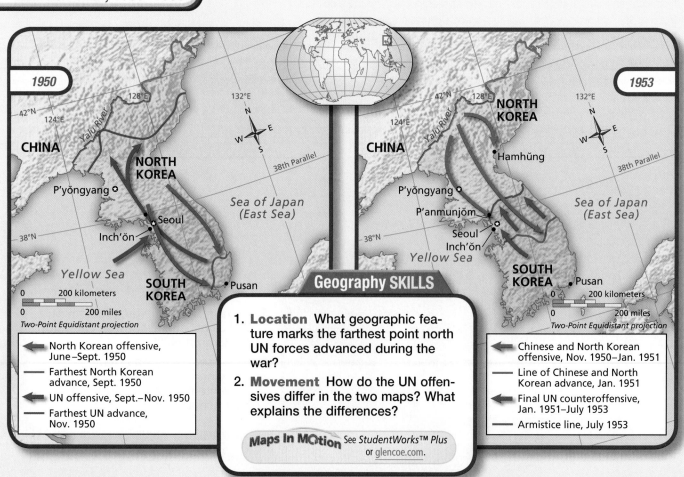

Geography SKILLS

1. **Location** What geographic feature marks the farthest point north UN forces advanced during the war?

2. **Movement** How do the UN offensives differ in the two maps? What explains the differences?

Maps In Motion See *StudentWorks™ Plus* or glencoe.com.

1950

- North Korean offensive, June–Sept. 1950
- Farthest North Korean advance, Sept. 1950
- UN offensive, Sept.–Nov. 1950
- Farthest UN advance, Nov. 1950

0 200 kilometers
0 200 miles
Two-Point Equidistant projection

1953

- Chinese and North Korean offensive, Nov. 1950–Jan. 1951
- Line of Chinese and North Korean advance, Jan. 1951
- Final UN counteroffensive, Jan. 1951–July 1953
- Armistice line, July 1953

0 200 kilometers
0 200 miles
Two-Point Equidistant projection

The Cold War in Asia

MAIN IDEA Cold War tensions between China and the United States led to the Korean War in 1950, but tensions had eased by the 1970s.

HISTORY & YOU Recall that U.S.-Soviet relations improved during the 1970s. Read how U.S-China relations also improved.

In 1950 China signed a pact of friendship and cooperation with the Soviet Union. Some Americans began to worry about a Communist desire for world domination. When war broke out in Korea, the Cold War had arrived in Asia.

The Korean War

Japan controlled Korea until 1945. In August 1945, the Soviet Union and the United States agreed to divide Korea into two zones at the 38th parallel. The plan was to hold elections after World War II to reunify Korea. As American–Soviet relations grew worse, however, two separate governments emerged in Korea—a Communist one in the north and an anti-Communist one in the south.

Tension between the two governments increased. With the approval of Joseph Stalin, North Korean troops invaded **South Korea** on June 25, 1950. President Harry Truman, with the support of the United Nations, sent U.S. troops to repel the invaders. In October 1950, UN forces—mostly Americans—marched across the 38th parallel with the aim of unifying Korea. Greatly alarmed, the Chinese sent hundreds of thousands of troops into **North Korea** and pushed UN forces back across the 38th parallel.

Three more years of fighting led to no final victory. An armistice was finally signed in 1953. The 38th parallel remained, and remains today, the boundary line between North Korea and South Korea.

In 2000 the Korean leaders took part in the first North-South Summit. However, beginning in 2002, fears that North Korea was pursuing nuclear weapons raised tensions.

The Shifting Power Balance

By the late 1950s, relations between China and the Soviet Union began to deteriorate. Faced with a serious security threat from the Soviet Union as well as internal problems, Chinese leaders decided to improve relations with the United States. In 1972 **Richard Nixon** became the first U.S. president to visit Communist China. Diplomatic relations were established in 1979.

By the early 2000s, China was strengthening trade relations around the world. China joined the World Trade Organization in 2001 and normalized trade relations with the United States in 2002.

✓ Reading Check **Examining** Why did China decide to improve relations with the United States?

Vocabulary

1. **Explain** the significance of: Chiang Kai-shek, Mao Zedong, Taiwan, Great Leap Forward, communes, final, permanent revolution, Great Proletarian Cultural Revolution, *Little Red Book,* source, Red Guards, Deng Xiaoping, per capita, Tiananmen Square, one-child policy, South Korea, North Korea, Richard Nixon.

Main Ideas

2. **Identify** the goals of Mao Zedong's Great Leap Forward and Great Proletarian Cultural Revolution.

3. **List** actions of Deng Xiaoping's government that were intended to help modernize China's industry and agriculture. Use a chart like the one below.

Industry	Agriculture

4. **Explain** how the Cold War affected relations between China and the United States.

Critical Thinking

5. **The BIG Idea** **Contrasting** How have China's policies changed since Mao's rule?

6. **Drawing Conclusions** Do you think families in a Western nation would accept a policy like China's one-child policy? Why or why not?

7. **Analyzing Visuals** Examine the photo on page 779. What purpose did the Democracy Wall serve for Chinese activists?

Writing About History

8. **Descriptive Writing** Imagine that you are a foreign-exchange student attending a Beijing university in 1989. You witness the demonstration at Tiananmen Square. Write a letter to a friend at home describing what you saw.

History ONLINE

For help with the concepts in this section of *Glencoe World History— Modern Times,* go to glencoe.com and click Study Central.

Independent States in Asia

Following World War II, many South and Southeast Asian states gained their independence. British India was split into two nations—India and Pakistan. France's reluctance to let go of Vietnam resulted in a long war that involved the United States. While some Southeast Asian countries have moved toward democracy, they have faced some serious obstacles along that path.

GUIDE TO READING

The BIG Idea
Self-Determination British India and colonies throughout Southeast Asia gained independence following World War II, but independence was often followed by continued conflict.

Content Vocabulary
• principle of nonalignment *(p. 782)*
• stalemate *(p. 785)*
• discrimination *(p. 787)*

Academic Vocabulary
• role *(p. 783)*
• transfer *(p. 784)*

People and Places
• Jawaharlal Nehru *(p. 782)*
• Indira Gandhi *(p. 783)*
• Mother Teresa *(p. 783)*
• Sikhs *(p. 783)*
• Punjab *(p. 783)*
• Pakistan *(p. 784)*
• Bangladesh *(p. 784)*
• Aung San Suu Kyi *(p. 785)*
• Ho Chi Minh *(p. 785)*
• Pol Pot *(p. 785)*
• Khmer Rouge *(p. 785)*
• Ferdinand Marcos *(p. 787)*

Reading Strategy
Categorizing Information As you read, use a web diagram like the one below to identify challenges India faced after gaining independence.

India Divided

MAIN IDEA Once it gained independence, British India split into two nations—India and Pakistan—that have faced problems of overpopulation and religious strife.

HISTORY & YOU Do ethnic or religious differences cause problems in your community? Read to learn how differences have led to tensions and sometimes conflict in India and Pakistan.

As British rule ended in India, India's Muslims and Hindus were bitterly divided. India's leaders decided to create two countries: one Hindu (India) and one Muslim (Pakistan). Pakistan would have two regions: West Pakistan and East Pakistan. When India and Pakistan became independent on August 15, 1947, Hindus moved toward India; Muslims, toward Pakistan. More than one million people were killed during the mass migrations. One of the dead was well known. On January 30, 1948, a Hindu militant assassinated Mohandas Gandhi as he was going to morning prayer.

The New India

Having worked closely with Gandhi for Indian independence, **Jawaharlal Nehru** (juh•WAH•huhr•ʟᴀʜʟ NEHR•oo) led the Congress Party, formerly the Indian National Congress. The popular prime minister had strong ideas about India's future. He admired British political institutions and the socialist ideals of the British Labour Party. His goal was parliamentary government and a moderate socialist economy. Under Nehru, the state took ownership of major industries, utilities, and transportation. Private enterprise was permitted at the local level, and farming was left in private hands. Industrial production almost tripled between 1950 and 1965.

Nehru also guided India's foreign policy through the **principle of nonalignment.** Concerned about military conflict between the two superpowers, the United States and the Soviet Union, and about the influence of former colonial powers, Nehru refused to align India with any bloc or alliance.

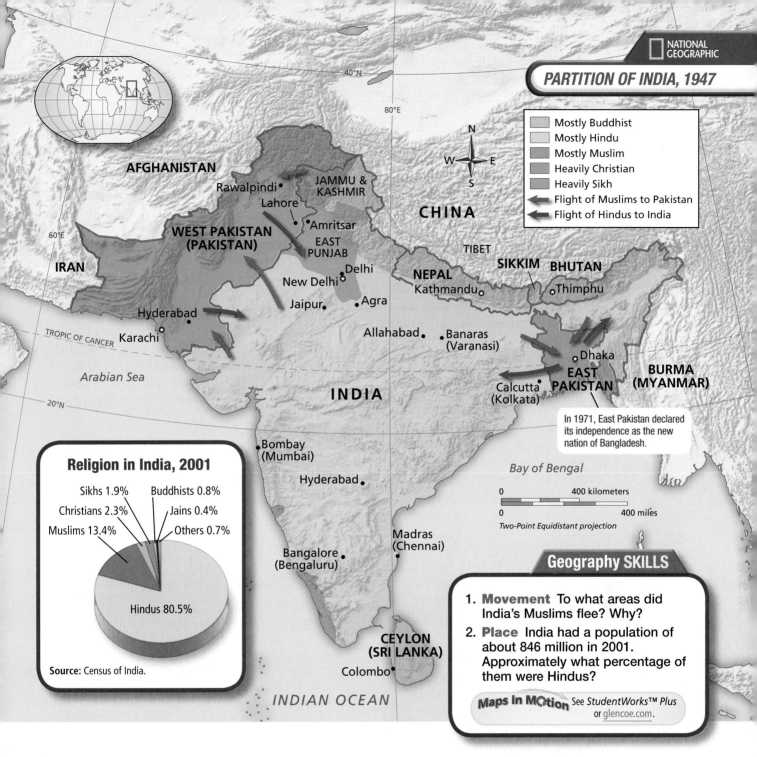

PARTITION OF INDIA, 1947

Legend:
- Mostly Buddhist
- Mostly Hindu
- Mostly Muslim
- Heavily Christian
- Heavily Sikh
- → Flight of Muslims to Pakistan
- → Flight of Hindus to India

40°N

80°E

AFGHANISTAN

Rawalpindi

Lahore

JAMMU & KASHMIR

Amritsar

CHINA

WEST PAKISTAN (PAKISTAN)

EAST PUNJAB

TIBET

IRAN

60°E

Delhi

New Delhi

Jaipur

Agra

NEPAL
Kathmandu

SIKKIM

BHUTAN
Thimphu

Hyderabad

TROPIC OF CANCER

Karachi

Allahabad

Banaras (Varanasi)

Dhaka

Arabian Sea

20°N

INDIA

EAST PAKISTAN

BURMA (MYANMAR)

Calcutta (Kolkata)

In 1971, East Pakistan declared its independence as the new nation of Bangladesh.

Bay of Bengal

Religion in India, 2001

Sikhs 1.9%   Buddhists 0.8%
Christians 2.3%   Jains 0.4%
Muslims 13.4%   Others 0.7%

Hindus 80.5%

Source: Census of India.

Bombay (Mumbai)

Hyderabad

0   400 kilometers
0   400 miles
Two-Point Equidistant projection

Madras (Chennai)

Bangalore (Bengaluru)

Geography SKILLS

1. **Movement** To what areas did India's Muslims flee? Why?
2. **Place** India had a population of about 846 million in 2001. Approximately what percentage of them were Hindus?

Maps In MOtion See *StudentWorks™ Plus* or glencoe.com.

CEYLON (SRI LANKA)

Colombo

INDIAN OCEAN

After Nehru's death, the Congress Party selected his daughter, **Indira Gandhi** (not related to Mohandas Gandhi), as prime minister. She held office for most of the time between 1966 and 1984. In the 1950s and 1960s, India's population grew by 2 percent a year, contributing to widespread poverty. Millions lived in vast city slums. In the slums of Kolkata, **Mother Teresa,** a Catholic nun, helped the poor, sick, and dying.

Indian society grouped people into castes, or social classes. The caste into which people were born largely determined their occupation and **role** in society. The system assured that the lowest castes would remain in poverty. Although caste-based discrimination is illegal in India today, it continues, especially in the countryside.

Growing ethnic and religious strife presented another major problem. One example involved the **Sikhs,** followers of a religion based on both Hindu and Muslim ideas. Many Sikhs lived in the **Punjab,** a northern province, and wanted its independence.

Gandhi refused and in 1984 used her military force against Sikh rebels. More than 450 Sikhs were killed. Seeking revenge, two Sikh members of Gandhi's personal bodyguard assassinated her later that year.

Gandhi's son Rajiv replaced her as prime minister and began new economic policies. He started to encourage private enterprise and to **transfer** state-run industries into private hands. These policies led to a growth in the middle class. Rajiv Gandhi was prime minister from 1984 to 1989. While campaigning for reelection in 1991, he was assassinated. In the following years, the Congress Party lost its leadership position and had to compete with new parties.

Conflict between Hindus and Muslims continued to be a problem in India. Religious differences also fueled a long-term dispute between India and Pakistan over Kashmir, a territory between the two nations. The danger from this conflict escalated in 1998 when both India and Pakistan tested nuclear warheads. Border conflicts in 2002 led to threats of war between these two nuclear powers.

Pakistan

Unlike its neighbor India, **Pakistan** was a completely new nation when it attained independence in 1947. The growing division between East and West Pakistan, separate regions that are very different in nature, caused internal conflicts. West Pakistan is a dry and mountainous area, while East Pakistan has marshy land densely populated with rice farmers. Many people in East Pakistan felt that the government, based in West Pakistan, ignored their needs. In 1971 East Pakistan declared its independence. After a brief civil war, it became the new nation of **Bangladesh.**

Both Bangladesh and Pakistan (as West Pakistan is now known) have had difficulty in establishing stable governments. Military officials have often seized control of the civilian government. Both nations also remain very poor.

✓ **Reading Check** **Summarizing** Why was British India divided into two new nations?

PEOPLE *in* HISTORY

Indira Gandhi
1917–1984 Indian Prime Minister

As the only child of Indian independence leader Jawaharlal Nehru, Indira Nehru Gandhi was swept up in political activism at an early age. At 12 she was a member of the "Monkey Brigade," a group of children who secretly passed information between members of groups opposed to British rule. Once, while riding in a car that contained secret plans for an anti-British protest, she avoided a police search by pleading that doing so would make her late for school. When she became prime minister in 1966, she attempted to modernize India. However, after assuming dictatorial powers and brutally suppressing her opposition, she was voted out in 1977. She returned to office three years later and was assassinated in 1984. **What was the purpose of the "Monkey Brigade"?**

Mother Teresa of Kolkata
1910–1997 Humanitarian

Born as Agnes Gonxha Bojaxhiu in Macedonia, Mother Teresa was of Albanian heritage. She received the name Teresa at Loreto Convent in Ireland, which sent her to Kolkata, India, where she taught at St. Mary's School. Mother Teresa was greatly affected by the suffering and poverty she saw in Kolkata. In 1948 she requested permission to leave St. Mary's School. Without funds, she started a school for poor children. Soon she was joined by volunteers and began to receive financial support. She began the Missionaries of Charity, a group dedicated to caring for suffering people who were ignored by society. In 1979 Mother Teresa was awarded the Nobel Peace Prize. **What caused Mother Teresa to leave St. Mary's School?**

Southeast Asia

MAIN IDEA Colonies in Southeast Asia gained independence, but politics were often unstable; in Vietnam, conflict led to war with the United States.

HISTORY & YOU Do you remember reading about the domino theory of the Cold War? Read how the fear of the spread of communism led the United States into the Vietnam War.

After World War II, most states in Southeast Asia gained independence from their colonial rulers. The Philippines became independent of the United States in 1946. Great Britain also ended its colonial rule in Southeast Asia. In 1948 Burma became independent. Malaya's turn came in 1957. France refused, however, to let go of Indochina. This led to a long war in Vietnam.

Indonesia and Myanmar

In Southeast Asia, the Netherlands was unwilling to give up its colonies and tried to suppress the Indonesian republic proclaimed by Sukarno. When the Indonesian Communist Party attempted to seize power, the United States pressured the Netherlands to grant independence to Sukarno and his non-Communist Nationalist Party. In 1949 the Netherlands recognized the new Republic of Indonesia.

Today, Burma is the independent nation called Myanmar. The people of Myanmar continue to fight for democracy. Leading the struggle is **Aung San Suu Kyi**, the daughter of Aung San, who led the Burma Independence Army in 1947. Educated abroad, Suu Kyi returned to Myanmar in 1988 and became involved in the movement for democracy. Her party won a landslide victory in 1990, but the military rulers refused to hand over power.

Instead, they placed Suu Kyi under house arrest, where she remains. Although the Myanmar government said she was free to leave the country, Suu Kyi knew that if she left, even to be with her husband who was dying of cancer in England in 1999, she would never be allowed to reenter. She stayed to promote democracy. For her efforts, Suu Kyi won the Nobel Peace Prize in 1991.

Vietnam and the Vietnam War

Leading the struggle against French colonial rule was the local Communist Party, led by **Ho Chi Minh.** In August 1945, the Vietminh, an alliance of forces under Communist leadership, seized power throughout most of Vietnam. Ho Chi Minh was elected president of a new republic in Hanoi. Refusing to accept the new government, France seized the southern part of the country.

For years, France fought Ho Chi Minh's Vietminh for control of Vietnam without success. In 1954, after a huge defeat at Dien Bien Phu, France agreed to a peace settlement. Vietnam was divided into two parts. In the north were the Communists, based in Hanoi; in the south, the non-Communists, based in Saigon.

Both sides agreed to hold elections in two years to create a single government. Instead, the conflict continued. The United States, opposed to the spread of communism, aided South Vietnam under nationalist leader Ngo Dinh Diem. In spite of this aid, the Viet Cong, South Vietnamese Communist guerrillas supported by North Vietnam, were on the verge of seizing control of the entire country by early 1965.

In March 1965, President Johnson sent troops to South Vietnam to prevent a total victory for the Communists. North Vietnam responded by sending more forces into the south. By the 1960s, there was a **stalemate**—neither side had made significant gains. With American public opinion divided, President Richard Nixon reached an agreement with North Vietnam in 1973 in the Paris Peace Accords. The United States withdrew. Within two years, Communist armies forcibly reunited Vietnam.

The reunification of Vietnam under Communist rule had an immediate impact on the region. By the end of 1975, both Laos and Cambodia had Communist governments. In Cambodia, **Pol Pot,** leader of the **Khmer Rouge** (kuh•MEHR ROOZH), massacred more than a million Cambodians. However, the Communist triumph in Indochina did not lead to the "falling dominoes" that many U.S. policy makers had feared (see Chapter 27).

✓ Reading Check **Identifying** Give reasons for U.S. entry into and withdrawal from the Vietnam War.

After World War II, most Southeast Asian nations gained independence from their colonial rulers. France's refusal to let go of Indochina led to a long war in Vietnam that involved the United States and Communist China. The Vietnam War was a turning point because it intensified Cold War tensions and the American commitment to the policy of containment.

In 1954 France and Vietnam had signed the Geneva Peace Accords. Because of the Korean War, China and the Soviet Union wanted to avoid another conflict with the United States. They pressured Vietnam to agree to a temporary partition of Vietnam. This was meant to save French pride and satisfy the Americans. Vietnam was to be reunified in 1956 after national elections were held to determine the government.

The United States believed that the Geneva Accords gave too much to the Communists and began efforts to build up the anti-Communist government in South Vietnam led by Ngo Dinh Diem. Diem's regime was repressive, however, and led to more people joining the Communist National Liberation Front (NLF).

American involvement expanded significantly in 1964 with the Gulf of Tonkin Resolution, which gave President Lyndon Johnson broad war powers. In 1965 U.S. bombing missions began, and the first large commitments of U.S. combat troops were sent to Vietnam.

NATIONAL GEOGRAPHIC
VIETNAM WAR, 1968–1975

* Major Viet Cong assault during Tet Offensive, 1968
← Ho Chi Minh Trail
← U.S. and S. Vietnamese offensives
● Major U.S. base
☀ Areas in neutral countries bombed by U.S.

Lao Cai
Red River
Pingxiang CHINA
Dien Bien Phu
U.S. bombs Hanoi, Dec. 1972
Hanoi
Haiphong
20°N
110°E
U.S. mines Haiphong Harbor, 1972
LAOS
NORTH VIETNAM
Gulf of Tonkin
Vientiane
S. Vietnamese invade Laos, Feb.–Mar. 1971
DMZ (Demilitarized Zone)
17th Parallel
Hue
Da Nang
Mekong River
Quang Ngai
THAILAND
Kon Tum
U.S. invades Cambodia, April–June 1970
Qui Nhon
CAMBODIA
SOUTH VIETNAM
Tonle Sap
Da Lat
Nha Trang
Phnom Penh
Tay Ninh
Bien Hoa
South Vietnam surrenders, April 1975
Saigon
10°N
Can Tho
Mekong Delta
Gulf of Thailand
South China Sea
0   200 kilometers
0   200 miles
Two-Point Equidistant projection

American troops of the Airborne Infantry in South Vietnam, 1966

DOCUMENT-BASED QUESTIONS

1. **Analyzing Visuals** What evidence on the map suggests that the war widened in the early 1970s?

2. **Making Connections** How did Cold War fears help lead to the partition of Vietnam?

Maps In Motion See StudentWorks™ Plus or glencoe.com.

Democracy in Southeast Asia

MAIN IDEA In recent years, some nations in Southeast Asia have moved toward democracy.

HISTORY & YOU Can you think of any scandals involving U.S. politicians? Read to learn why some leaders in Southeast Asia were forced to step down.

At first, many new leaders in Southeast Asia hoped to set up democratic states. By the end of the 1950s, however, hopes for rapid economic growth had failed. This failure and internal disputes led to military or one-party regimes.

In recent years, some Southeast Asian societies have once again moved toward democracy. However, serious obstacles remain for these peoples.

The Philippines and Indonesia

In the Philippines, two presidents have been forced out of office in recent years. In 1986 a public uprising forced **Ferdinand Marcos** to flee the country on charges of corruption and involvement in the killing of a popular opposition leader, Benigno Aquino. Corazon Aquino, wife of the murdered leader, became president in 1986.

Charges of corruption led to the ousting of another Filipino leader in 2001. The new leader, Gloria Arroyo, promised greater integrity in government. She faced an economy weakened by a global economic crisis. Terrorism remains a challenge for the Philippines. Muslim rebels on the island of Mindanao, for example, have used terror to promote their demands for independence.

In Indonesia, widespread rioting in 1998 forced General Suharto, a long-term authoritarian, to step down. Since then the government has struggled to improve the economy, which has suffered from slow growth and high unemployment. The tsunami of December 2004 and an earthquake in 2005 have caused the current president, Susilo Bambang Yudhoyono, further economic woes. Ethnic and religious conflicts continue to trouble the nation.

Women in South and Southeast Asia

Across the region, the rights and roles of women have changed. In India, women's rights expanded after independence. Its constitution of 1950 forbade **discrimination,** or prejudicial treatment, based on gender and called for equal pay for equal work. Child marriage was also outlawed. Women were encouraged to attend school and to enter the labor market. Virtually all women in Southeast Asian nations were granted full legal and political rights. In rural areas, however, old customs and attitudes survive.

✓ Reading Check **Identifying** List the challenges to democracy that nations in Southeast Asia face.

SECTION 2 REVIEW

Vocabulary
1. **Explain** the significance of: Jawaharlal Nehru, principle of nonalignment, Indira Gandhi, Mother Teresa, role, Sikhs, Punjab, transfer, Pakistan, Bangladesh, Aung San Suu Kyi, Ho Chi Minh, stalemate, Pol Pot, Khmer Rouge, Ferdinand Marcos, discrimination.

Main Ideas
2. **Identify** groups involved in tensions in India and the reasons for those tensions.

3. **List** the Southeast Asian countries discussed in this section that gained their independence. Use a chart like the one below to make your list.

Country	Year of Independence

4. **Describe** how the rights and roles of women in South and Southeast Asia have changed since 1950.

Critical Thinking
5. **The BIG Idea** **Evaluating** To what extent can the Vietnam War be seen as an anti-imperialist revolt?

6. **Evaluating** Do you think the division of British India into two countries had some benefits? Explain.

7. **Analyzing Visuals** Examine the map on page 786. Where did most of the fighting occur during the Vietnam War?

Writing About History
8. **Persuasive Writing** Do you believe that removing U.S. troops from Vietnam was the right thing to do? In one page or less, defend your position.

History ONLINE

For help with the concepts in this section of *Glencoe World History—Modern Times,* go to glencoe.com and click Study Central.

Japan and the Pacific

GUIDE TO READING

The BIG Idea
Ideas, Beliefs, and Values Since 1945, Japan and the four "Asian tigers" have become economic powerhouses, while Australia and New Zealand remain linked culturally to Europe.

Content Vocabulary
• occupied *(p. 788)*
• state capitalism *(p. 790)*

Academic Vocabulary
• maintain *(p. 788)*   • dramatic *(p. 788)*

People and Places
• Douglas MacArthur *(p. 788)*
• Kim Il Sung *(p. 791)*
• Syngman Rhee *(p. 791)*
• Taipei *(p. 792)*
• Singapore *(p.793)*
• Hong Kong *(p. 793)*
• Australia *(p. 793)*
• New Zealand *(p. 793)*

Reading Strategy
Categorizing Information As you read, use a table like the one below to list the key areas of industrial development in South Korea, Taiwan, and Singapore.

South Korea	Taiwan	Singapore

Japan made a dramatic recovery, transforming itself from ruins of war to a world power within 50 years. The "Asian tigers" imitated Japan's success and became industrial powerhouses. While Australia and New Zealand now have closer ties to their Asian neighbors, they remain strongly European.

The Transformation of Japan

MAIN IDEA After the Allied occupation following World War II, Japan became a world industrial power by the end of the twentieth century.

HISTORY & YOU Have you ever experienced a setback but rebounded stronger than before? Read about Japan's economic success after the war.

In August 1945, Japan was in ruins, and a foreign army occupied its land. A mere 50 years later, Japan had emerged as the second greatest industrial power in the world.

The Allied Occupation of Japan

From 1945 to 1952, Japan was an **occupied** country—its lands were held and controlled by Allied military forces. An Allied administration under the command of U.S. general **Douglas MacArthur** governed Japan. As commander of the occupation administration, MacArthur was responsible for destroying the Japanese war machine, trying Japanese civilian and military officials charged with war crimes, and laying the foundations of postwar Japanese society.

Under MacArthur's firm direction, Japanese society was remodeled along Western lines. A new constitution renounced war as a national policy. Japan agreed to **maintain** armed forces at levels that were only sufficient for self-defense. The constitution established a parliamentary system and reduced the power of the emperor (who was forced to announce that he was not a god). The constitution also guaranteed basic civil and political rights and gave women the right to vote.

On September 8, 1951, the United States and other former World War II allies (but not the Soviet Union) signed a peace treaty restoring Japanese independence. On the same day, Japan and the United States signed a defensive alliance in which the Japanese agreed that the United States could maintain military bases in Japan.

Since regaining its independence, Japan has emerged as an economic giant. The country's **dramatic** recovery from the war has been described as the "Japanese miracle." How did the miracle occur? The causes were not only economic but also political and

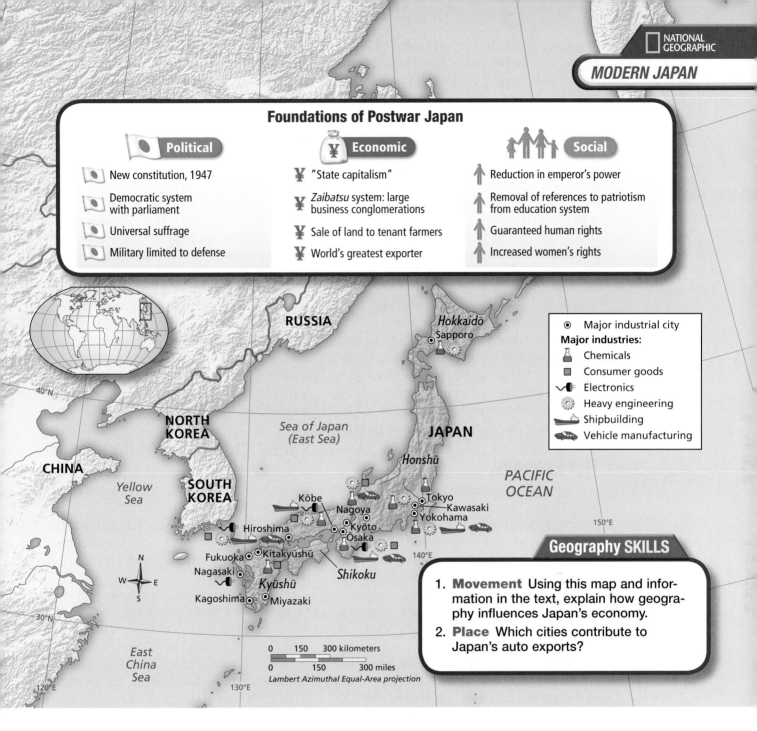

Foundations of Postwar Japan

Political

- New constitution, 1947
- Democratic system with parliament
- Universal suffrage
- Military limited to defense

¥ Economic

- "State capitalism"
- *Zaibatsu* system: large business conglomerations
- Sale of land to tenant farmers
- World's greatest exporter

Social

- Reduction in emperor's power
- Removal of references to patriotism from education system
- Guaranteed human rights
- Increased women's rights

Major industrial city

Major industries:
- Chemicals
- Consumer goods
- Electronics
- Heavy engineering
- Shipbuilding
- Vehicle manufacturing

RUSSIA

Hokkaidō
Sapporo

NORTH KOREA

Sea of Japan (East Sea)

JAPAN

Honshū

CHINA

Yellow Sea

SOUTH KOREA

Kōbe
Nagoya
Hiroshima
Kyōto
Osaka
Tokyo
Kawasaki
Yokohama

PACIFIC OCEAN

150°E

140°E

Fukuoka Kitakyūshū
Nagasaki
Kyūshū
Kagoshima Miyazaki

Shikoku

East China Sea

120°E
130°E

30°N

40°N

0   150   300 kilometers
0   150   300 miles
Lambert Azimuthal Equal-Area projection

Geography SKILLS

1. **Movement** Using this map and information in the text, explain how geography influences Japan's economy.
2. **Place** Which cities contribute to Japan's auto exports?

social. The political causes will be examined first, followed by a review of social and cultural aspects of Japanese society.

Politics and Government

Modeled on the U.S. Constitution, Japan's new constitution called for universal suffrage and a balance of power among the executive, legislative, and judicial branches of government. These principles have held firm. Japan today is a stable democratic society. At the same time, the current Japanese political system retains some of Japan's nineteenth-century political system under the Meiji. An example involves the distribution of political power. Japan has a multi-party system with two major parties—the Liberal Democrats and the Socialists. In practice, however, the Liberal Democrats have dominated the government. At one point, they remained in office for 30 years. A few party leaders would decide key issues such as who should be the prime minister.

Today, the central government plays an active role in the economy. It establishes price and wage policies and subsidizes vital industries. This government role in the economy is widely accepted in Japan. Indeed, it is often cited as a key reason for the efficiency of Japanese industry and the emergence of Japan as an industrial giant. Japan's economic system has been described as **state capitalism.**

In recent decades, Japan has experienced problems with its political leadership. Two prime ministers were forced to resign over improper business dealings, but economic factors were at work, too. After three decades of spectacular growth, the Japanese economy went into a slump.

Since 2001, the two prime ministers have both been Liberal Democrats who have worked to reduce government debt and to privatize some government programs. Some progress has been made, but the outlook for the economy today is for moderate growth.

The Economy

During their occupation of Japan, Allied officials had planned to dismantle the large business conglomerations known as the *zaibatsu*. With the rise of the Cold War, however, the policy was scaled back. Only the 19 largest companies were affected. In addition, the new policy did not keep Japanese companies from forming loose ties with each other, which basically gave rise to another *zaibatsu* system.

The occupation administration had more success with its land-reform program. Half of the population lived on farms, and half of all farmers were tenants of large landowners. Under the reform program, lands were sold on easy credit terms to the tenants. The reform program created a strong class of independent farmers.

At the end of the Allied occupation in 1952, the Japanese gross national product was one-third that of Great Britain or France. Today, it is larger than both put together and well over half that of the United States. Japan is one of the largest exporting nations in the world and a leading producer of cars and consumer electronics. Its per capita income equals or surpasses that of most Western states.

What explains the Japanese success? Some analysts point to cultural factors. The Japanese are group-oriented and find it easy to cooperate with one another. The labor force is highly skilled. Japanese people also share common values and respond in similar ways to the challenges of the modern world.

Other analysts have cited more practical reasons for the Japanese economic success. For example, because its industries were destroyed in World War II, Japan was forced to build entirely new, modern factories. Japanese workers also spend a substantially longer period of time at their jobs than do workers in other advanced societies. Corporations reward innovation and maintain good management-labor relations. Finally, some experts contend that Japan uses unfair trade practices—that it dumps goods at prices below cost to break into a foreign market and restricts imports from other countries.

Social Changes and Culture

During the occupation, Allied planners wanted to eliminate the aggressiveness that had been part of Japanese behavior before and during the war. A new educational system removed all references to patriotism and loyalty to the emperor. It also stressed individualism.

Efforts to remake Japanese behavior through laws were only partly successful. Many of the characteristics of traditional Japanese society have persisted into the present day, although in altered form. Emphasis on the work ethic, for example, remains strong. The tradition of hard work is stressed in the educational system.

Women's roles are another example of the difficulty of social change. After the war, women gained the vote and were encouraged to enter politics. However, the subordinate role of women in Japanese society has not been entirely eliminated. Women are legally protected against discrimination in employment, yet very few have reached senior levels in business, education, or politics. Women now make up more than 40 percent of the workforce, but most are in retail or service occupations. Their average salary is only about 60 percent that of males.

Japanese writers reflected their changing culture. Many writers who had been active before the war resurfaced, but their writing turned more sober. This "lost generation" described its piercing despair. For them, fear of losing their culture to the Americanization of postwar Japan made defeat harder to bear.

Increasing wealth and a high literacy rate led to a massive outpouring of books. Current Japanese authors were raised in the crowded cities of postwar Japan, where they soaked up movies, television, and rock music. These writers speak the universal language of today's world.

Haruki Murakami is one of Japan's most popular authors today. He was one of the first to discard the somber style of the earlier postwar period and to speak the contemporary language. *A Wild Sheep Chase,* published in 1982, is an excellent example of Murakami's gripping, yet humorous, writing.

✓ **Reading Check** **Explaining** How is the Japanese government involved in Japan's economy?

The "Asian Tigers," Australia, and New Zealand

MAIN IDEA The "Asian tigers" are successful industrial societies.

HISTORY & YOU Do you own any products from an "Asian tigers" country? Read about the economic success of the "Asian tigers."

Sometimes called the "Asian tigers," South Korea, Taiwan, Singapore, and Hong Kong have imitated Japan in creating successful industrial societies. Australia and New Zealand, to the south and east of Asia, now have closer trade relations with their Asian neighbors.

South Korea

In 1953 the People's Republic of Korea (North Korea) was under the rule of the Communist leader **Kim Il Sung**. The Republic of Korea (South Korea), was under the dictatorial president **Syngman Rhee**.

CONNECTING TO THE UNITED STATES

JAPANESE ANIME IN THE U.S.

- The first Japanese anime program shown on U.S. television was "Atom Boy" in 1964. It became the highest-rated syndicated show on television.
- Most anime now being produced is usually higher in quality than television anime but not as rich as theatrical anime.
- Anime is most popular with U.S. high school and college students, but, as in Japan, its appeal has no age limits.

Japanese animation, or anime, was originally inspired by American and European animators. It has its roots in manga, or Japanese comics, which by the early twentieth century had become a very popular form of literature for most of Japanese society. Manga had developed from traditional woodblock prints with captions, which eventually were collected in books that told stories.

Unlike Western cartoons, which are aimed primarily at children, anime appeals to all age groups. Artists don't "talk down" to their audiences. Plots are not predictable—heroes make mistakes, major characters can die, and there may not be a happy ending. Plots often feature strong female characters. Stylistically, anime is more cinematic than Western cartoons.

1. **Summarizing** What were the two biggest influences on anime?
2. **Making Inferences** Why does anime appeal to all age groups?

The Continuing Role of the United Nations in Korea

When the Korean War broke out in June 1950, the United Nations intervened by sending troops to repel North Korean aggression. It was the first undertaking of its kind in the history of the UN. In spite of a 1953 armistice, a state of war still exists between North Korea and South Korea. The armistice created a demilitarized zone, or DMZ, between North and South Korea. It is the world's most heavily fortified border, and a constant reminder of tensions between the two Koreas.

In recent years, there have been negotiations to improve relations between the two Koreas. In October 2000, the UN General Assembly adopted a resolution entitled "Peace, Security and Unification on the Korean Peninsula," encouraging the peace process. It was cosponsored by 157 nations, including both Koreas. In October 2006, however, North Korea conducted an underground nuclear test in spite of a warning from the UN Security Council that such a test "would represent a clear threat to international peace and security."

U.S. and South Korean soldiers with the UN flag

CRITICAL THINKING SKILLS

1. **Describing** What role did the United Nations play in Korea in the early 1950s, and what role does it play today?
2. **Analyzing** What possibility is there for the reunification of Korea?

Rhee ruled harshly. Demonstrations broke out in the capital city of Seoul in the spring of 1960. Rhee was forced to retire. A coup d'etat in 1961 put General Park Chung Hee in power. Two years later, Park was elected president and began to strengthen the South Korean economy.

South Korea gradually emerged as a major industrial power in East Asia. The key areas for industrial development were chemicals, textiles, shipbuilding, and automobile production.

Like many other countries in the region, South Korea was slow to develop democratic principles. Park ruled by autocratic means and suppressed protest. However, opposition to military rule began to develop. Democracy finally came in the 1990s. Elections held during an economic crisis in 1997 brought the reformer Kim Tae-jung to the presidency. Roh Moo-hyun now serves as president.

Taiwan: The Other China

Defeated by the Communists, Chiang Kai-shek and his followers established their capital at **Taipei** on Taiwan. Chiang Kai-shek maintained that the Republic of China was the legitimate government of all Chinese people. Of course, the Communist government on the mainland claimed to rule all of China, including Taiwan. With protection of American military forces, Chiang Kai-shek's new regime concentrated on economic growth with no worries about a Communist invasion.

Making good use of foreign aid and the efforts of its own people, the Republic of China built a modern industrialized society. A land-reform program, which put farmland in the hands of peasants, doubled food production. Local manufacturing and commerce also expanded. By 2000, over three-fourths of the population lived in urban areas. By 2004, Taiwan's economy was growing at a 6 percent rate.

Prosperity, however, did not at first lead to democracy. Chiang Kai-shek ruled by decree and refused to allow new political parties to form. After Chiang's death in 1975, the Republic of China slowly moved toward a more representative form of government. By 2002, free elections had enabled opposition parties to win control.

A major issue for Taiwan is whether it will become an independent state or will be unified with mainland China. The United States supports self-determination by Taiwan's people. The People's Republic of China on the mainland remains committed to unification.

Singapore and Hong Kong

Singapore, once a British colony and briefly a part of the state of Malaysia, is now an independent state. Under the leadership of Prime Minister Lee Hsien Loong, Singapore is a highly developed and successful free-market economy based on banking, shipbuilding, oil refineries, and electronics. Its port is one of the world's busiest in terms of tonnage handled. The authoritarian political system has created a stable environment for economic growth. Its citizens, however, are beginning to demand more political freedoms.

Like Singapore, **Hong Kong** became an industrial powerhouse with standards of living well above the levels of its neighbors. Having ruled Hong Kong for over 150 years, Great Britain returned control of Hong Kong to mainland China in 1997. China, in turn, promised that, for the next 50 years, Hong Kong would enjoy a high degree of economic freedom under a capitalist system.

Australia and New Zealand

Both **Australia** and **New Zealand** have identified themselves culturally and politically with Europe rather than with their Asian neighbors. Their political institutions and values are derived from European models, and their economies resemble those of the industrialized countries in the world. Both are members of the British Commonwealth. Both are also part of the United States–led ANZUS defensive alliance (Australia, New Zealand, and the United States).

In recent years, however, trends have been drawing both states closer to Asia. First, immigration from East Asia and Southeast Asia has increased rapidly. More than one-half of current immigrants into Australia come from East Asia. Second, trade relations with Asia are increasing rapidly. About 60 percent of Australia's export markets today are in East Asia. Asian trade with New Zealand is also on the increase.

✓ Reading Check **Identifying** What is the relationship between Taiwan and mainland China?

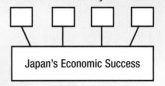

SECTION **3** REVIEW

Vocabulary
1. **Explain** the significance of: occupied, Douglas MacArthur, maintain, dramatic, state capitalism, Kim Il Sung, Syngman Rhee, Taipei, Singapore, Hong Kong, Australia, New Zealand.

Main Ideas
2. **Illustrate** the factors that contributed to the "Japanese miracle." Use a diagram like the one below to make your illustration.

Japan's Economic Success

3. **Explain** how Taiwan's land reform program affected its economic growth.

4. **List** the ways in which Australia and New Zealand are similar to European nations.

Critical Thinking
5. **The BIG Idea** **Predicting** What further impact do you think the return of Hong Kong to China will have on either country?

6. **Analyzing** How are women's roles in Japan an example of the difficulty of social change?

7. **Analyzing Visuals** Examine the illustration of anime on page 791. How is anime similar to and different from comic books popular in the mid-1900s, such as "Superman"?

Writing About History
8. **Informative Writing** Do additional research on Japan and the "Asian tigers" and explain in an essay why these states have been so successful.

History ONLINE

For help with the concepts in this section of *Glencoe World History— Modern Times*, go to glencoe.com and click Study Central.

Teenagers in Tokyo Today

Much of Japan lay in ruins at the end of World War II. The Japanese restored factories, developed new industries, and expanded trade. Today, Japan has the second largest economy in the world. It is a leader in high-technology products. Tokyo teens are influenced by both Japanese traditions and cultural trends from around the world.

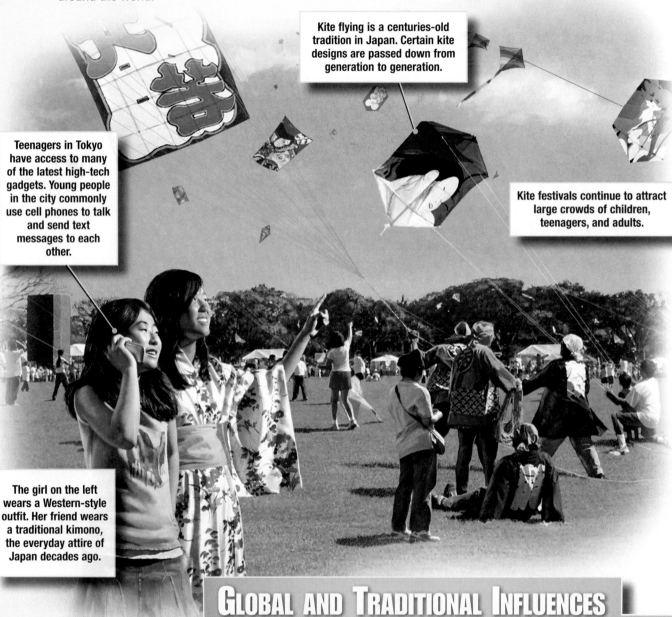

Kite flying is a centuries-old tradition in Japan. Certain kite designs are passed down from generation to generation.

Teenagers in Tokyo have access to many of the latest high-tech gadgets. Young people in the city commonly use cell phones to talk and send text messages to each other.

Kite festivals continue to attract large crowds of children, teenagers, and adults.

The girl on the left wears a Western-style outfit. Her friend wears a traditional kimono, the everyday attire of Japan decades ago.

GLOBAL AND TRADITIONAL INFLUENCES

Teenagers around the world worry about their appearance, and Tokyo teens are exposed to a variety of global influences and fads. Many have adopted the fashions and lifestyles common among teens in the West. Traditional Japanese attire remains an important part of the Tokyo teenager's wardrobe, though. Both boys and girls wear kimonos for ceremonial occasions such as graduations, weddings, funerals, and shrine rituals.

Shopping is a popular activity among Tokyo teens. Many of them work to earn money for clothes, DVDs, and CDs.

Students must pass difficult exams to advance into high school and then into college. Because there is great competition to get into the best colleges, many teens are under major stress.

Riding bicycles is a popular leisure activity among Tokyo teenagers. In a congested city plagued by traffic jams up to 50 miles long, the bicycle provides a quick and efficient mode of transportation.

Uniforms are an important part of daily life in Japan for both adults and children.

Baseball is one of Japan's most popular sports.

Japan's best Little Leaguers go on to play in the country's professional ranks.

WHAT DO TOKYO TEENAGERS DO?

Tokyo teenagers lead active lives filled with school, sports, part-time jobs, musical instruments, and video games. Their pursuits reflect both global and traditional influences. A teen may spend an afternoon watching a Hollywood movie on DVD or flying a kite at a traditional Japanese festival. A Tokyo youth might attend a rock 'n' roll concert or a sumo match. Meals may be fast food or traditional sukiyaki dishes.

ANALYZING VISUALS

1. **Drawing Conclusions** Why do you think Western culture exerts such a strong influence on Tokyo teenagers?

2. **Comparing and Contrasting** How do you think your life is similar to and different from that of a teenager living in Tokyo?

795

STUDY TO GO You can study anywhere, anytime by downloading quizzes and flash cards to your PDA from glencoe.com.

RED GUARDS PARADE IN BEIJING DURING THE CULTURAL REVOLUTION, 1971

These marchers are holding Mao's *Little Red Book*.

CHINA After World War II

- Mao Zedong's Communists won the civil war, and the Nationalists fled to Taiwan.
- In 1950 China entered the Korean War on the side of North Korea.
- Deng Xiaoping modernized China and faced increasing pressures for reform.
- China moved from a revolutionary culture back to a focus on family traditions.

SOUTH AND SOUTHEAST ASIA After World War II

- After independence, British India split into India (Hindu) and Pakistan (Muslim).
- India and Pakistan struggled with poverty and ethnic strife.
- Southeast Asian colonies gained independence; internal disputes led to military or one-party regimes.
- Conflict between South Vietnam and Communist North Vietnam led the United States into war.

MASS MIGRATION TO INDIA AND PAKISTAN, 1947

The division of British India set off a mass migration of Hindus to India and Muslims to Pakistan. More than a million people died in the resulting violence.

A FACTORY IN MIYAZAKI, JAPAN

Although women have legal protections against discrimination in Japan, few have reached senior levels in business, education, or politics.

JAPAN AND THE PACIFIC After World War II

- Japan overcame defeat in World War II and emerged as an industrial power.
- South Korea, Taiwan, Singapore, and Hong Kong became economic powerhouses.
- Mainland China's claims on Taiwan contribute to Taiwan's uncertain future.
- Australia and New Zealand identify culturally with Europe, but immigration and trade pull them toward Asia.

STANDARDIZED TEST PRACTICE

TEST-TAKING TIP

Even if you believe you know the correct answer immediately, read all of the answer choices and eliminate those you know are wrong. Doing so will help you confirm that the answer choice you think is correct is indeed correct.

Reviewing Vocabulary

Directions: Choose the word or words that best complete the sentence.

1. When the Allied forces held and controlled its lands, Japan was _____ country.

A an imperialist

B an occupied

C a satellite

D a subordinate

2. Under Mao Zedong's Great Leap Forward, collective farms were combined into vast _____.

A manors

B commonwealths

C protectorates

D communes

3. India's 1950 constitution forbade _____, or prejudicial treatment, based on gender.

A antifeminism

B segregation

C discrimination

D glass ceilings

4. Japan's economic system is called _____ because the government plays an active role in setting prices and wage policies and in subsidizing industries.

A state capitalism

B market driven

C free enterprise

D socialism

Reviewing Main Ideas

Directions: Choose the best answers to the following questions.

Section 1 *(pp. 776–781)*

5. Who were the Red Guards?

A Communist youth groups under Mao Zedong

B Soviet troops fighting China for control of Manchuria

C Communist Chinese forces fighting Chiang Kai-shek

D Japanese troops fighting in China during World War II

6. Deng Xiaoping's Four Modernizations included new policies in what four areas?

A Industry, agriculture, technology, and democracy

B National defense, industry, democracy, and technology

C Agriculture, national defense, industry, and technology

D Industry, banking, technology, and agriculture

7. In 1979 what policy did the Chinese government put in place to try to control population growth?

A Family-planning policy

B Late-marriage policy

C Pro-abortion policy

D One-child policy

Section 2 *(pp. 782–787)*

8. Who guided India's foreign policy using the principle of nonalignment?

A Mohandas Gandhi

B Jawaharlal Nehru

C Indira Gandhi

D Mother Teresa

Need Extra Help?								
If You Missed Questions . . .	1	2	3	4	5	6	7	8
Go to Page . . .	788	777	787	790	778	778	780	782

9. What group wanted independence for the Punjab province of India, where they lived?

   A Sikhs

   B Muslims

   C Hindus

   D Kurds

10. Who led the Communist Party in French-ruled Vietnam?

    A Pol Pot

    B Ferdinand Marcos

    C Ho Chi Minh

    D Sukarno

Section 3 (pp. 788–793)

11. Who commanded Allied forces governing Japan after World War II?

    A Richard Nixon

    B Douglas MacArthur

    C Winston Churchill

    D Hideki Tojo

12. What characteristic of South Korea, Taiwan, Singapore, and Hong Kong led to their nickname of the "Asian tigers"?

    A Military strength

    B Imperialist ambitions

    C Ruthless battle tactics

    D Economic strength

13. What nation claims to be the legitimate government of all of China?

    A Taiwan

    B South Korea

    C Singapore

    D Hong Kong

Critical Thinking

Directions: Choose the best answers to the following questions.

Use the following map to answer question 14.

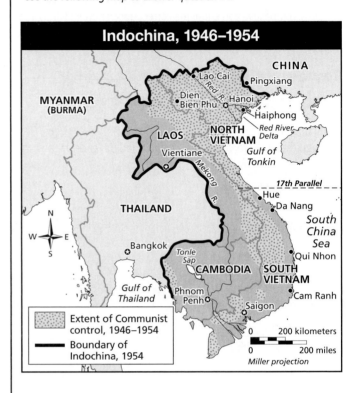

Indochina, 1946–1954

14. Approximately how much of Vietnam did the Communists control between 1946 and 1954?

    A 10 percent

    B 25 percent

    C 50 percent

    D 75 percent

15. Between 1966 and 1976, the destruction of temples, the seizure of books, and the imprisonment of artists and intellectuals were closely related to which movement in China?

    A Great Leap Forward

    B Long March

    C Tai Ping Rebellion

    D Cultural Revolution

Need Extra Help?							
If You Missed Questions . . .	9	10	11	12	13	14	15
Go to Page . . .	783	785	788	791	792	785	778

GO ON

16. Why does conflict between India and Pakistan over Kashmir cause global concern?

    A Because Pakistan is much smaller than India

    B Because both nations have nuclear weapons

    C Because communism may spread as a result

    D Because the conflict could interrupt world oil supplies

17. How did the Vietnam War affect politics of the region?

    A Vietnam had a Communist government, but Laos and Cambodia remained democratic.

    B Vietnam and Laos had Communist governments, but Cambodia remained democratic.

    C Laos, Cambodia, and Vietnam had Communist governments.

    D Communism continued to spread from Indochina to neighboring nations.

Analyze the chart and answer the question that follows. Base your answer on the chart.

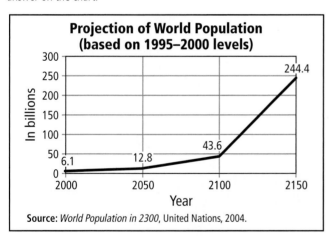

Projection of World Population (based on 1995–2000 levels)

In billions — 6.1 (2000), 12.8 (2050), 43.6 (2100), 244.4 (2150)

Source: *World Population in 2300*, United Nations, 2004.

18. According to the chart, how will world population change between 2000 and 2150?

    A Rise at a constant rate

    B Decline slowly and then begin a rapid rise in 2100

    C Rise at a decreasing rate

    D Rise at an increasing rate

Document-Based Questions

Directions: Analyze the document and answer the short-answer questions that follow the document. Base your answers on the document and on your knowledge of world history.

Read the following excerpt from the book *Japanese Women,* published in 1955:

> "A quick glance at educational statistics reveals a higher percentage of female as compared to male high school graduates entering colleges and universities. The overwhelming majority of female college and university graduates, over 80 percent, are taking up employment and doing so in a wider range of fields than in the past. Better education and the availability of more job opportunities have increasingly made it possible for women to look upon marriage as an option rather than a prescribed lifestyle. . . ."
>
> —*Japanese Women,* 1955

19. What does this passage reveal about the role of women in Japan after World War II?

20. What challenges do modern Japanese women—and women worldwide—face in the workplace?

Extended Response

21. The population in many South Asian and Southeast Asian countries has rapidly increased. What strategies can these nations take to overcome the adverse effects of overpopulation?

History ONLINE

For additional test practice, use Self-Check Quizzes—Chapter 24 at glencoe.com.

Need Extra Help?

If You Missed Questions . . .	16	17	18	19	20	21
Go to Page . . .	784	785	799	790	790	784

STOP

CHAPTER 25

Changing Global Patterns

Section 1 Challenges of a New Century

Section 2 New Global Communities

MAKING CONNECTIONS

Who is affected by civil war?

Conflicts throughout the world have forced millions of people from their homes. Violent conflicts over border disputes in places like Ethiopia and Eritrea have forced thousands of people into refugee camps like the one shown in this photo. Refugees depend upon assistance from the international community in order to survive. In this chapter you will learn about efforts to solve global problems.

- What is the United Nations doing to resolve and prevent conflicts around the world?
- Give an example of a problem in another nation and explain how it affects the United States.

THE WORLD ▶

1962
Scientist Rachel Carson warns of pesticide dangers

1984
Widespread famine begins in western Africa

1990
World Wide Web created

1960

1980

1969
U.S. moon landing

1986
Nuclear accident at Chernobyl

2001
Terrorists attack
U.S. World Trade Center
and Pentagon

2006
North Korea
performs its first
nuclear test

2000

2006
World population
passes 6.5 billion mark

FOLDABLES™
Study Organizer

World Challenges			
Environment	Social	Economic	Political

Identifying Identify
environmental, social,
economic, and politi-
cal challenges in the
world today and
record them on a
Folded Chart. Under
each entry, briefly summarize
the challenge.

History ONLINE

Chapter Overview—Visit glencoe.com to preview Chapter 25.

Challenges of a New Century

GUIDE TO READING

The BIG Idea
New Technologies Today's societies face many challenges, and they must balance the costs and benefits of the technological revolution.

Content Vocabulary
- bioterrorism *(p. 804)*
- ecology *(p. 806)*
- deforestation *(p. 806)*
- desertification *(p. 806)*
- greenhouse effect *(p. 806)*
- sustainable development *(p. 806)*
- global economy *(p. 807)*

Academic Vocabulary
- function *(p. 803)*
- environment *(p. 805)*

People and Events
- Neil Armstrong *(p. 804)*
- Green Revolution *(p. 805)*
- Rachel Carson *(p. 806)*
- Kyoto Protocol *(p. 806)*
- Universal Declaration of Human Rights *(p. 809)*
- Patriot Act *(p. 811)*

Reading Strategy
Determining Cause and Effect As you read, complete a table like the one below to determine the cause and effect of global concerns.

Concern	Cause	Effect
Deforestation		
Greenhouse effect		
Weapons		
Hunger		

In the twenty-first century, science and technology continue to build a global community connected by the Internet. Scientific advances have brought benefits in medicine and agriculture, but also new weapons of war. Development is creating great wealth, but it also damages the planet. The uneven distribution of our global wealth may be one factor contributing to a new challenge—terrorism.

Technological Revolution

MAIN IDEA The benefits of the technological revolution must be balanced against its costs.

HISTORY & YOU Do you eat organic foods? Read to learn about organic farming and the Green Revolution.

Since World War II, but especially since the 1970s, a stunning array of changes has created a technological revolution. Like the first and second Industrial Revolutions, this revolution is also having a profound effect on people's daily lives and on entire societies.

Communication, Transportation, and Space

Global transportation and communication systems are transforming the world community. People are connected and "online" throughout the world as they have never been before. Space exploration and orbiting satellites have increased our understanding of our world and of solar systems beyond our world.

Since the 1970s, jumbo jet airlines have moved millions of people around the world each year. A flight between London and New York took half a day in 1945. Now, that trip takes only five or six hours. The Internet—the world's largest computer network—provides quick access to vast quantities of information. The World Wide Web, developed in the 1990s, has made the Internet even more accessible to people everywhere. Satellites, cable television, facsimile (fax) machines, cellular telephones, and computers enable people to communicate with one another practically everywhere in the world. Communication and transportation systems have made the world a truly global village.

The computer may be the most revolutionary of all technological inventions of the twentieth century. The first computer was really a product of World War II. British mathematician Alan Turing designed the first electronic computer to crack enemy codes. Turing's machine did calculations faster than any human. IBM of the

SCIENCE, TECHNOLOGY, & SOCIETY

Satellite Communications

The communications satellite Syncom-IV was launched by space shuttle Discovery.

Today, hundreds of satellites orbit Earth. Some are used to predict the weather, and others help navigate ships, aircraft, and cars. Communications satellites are used to relay radio, television, and telephone signals.

Communication satellites are part of everyday life. Television stations transmit their programs to a satellite as radio waves. The satellite amplifies the signal and transmits it to your cable or dish provider to forward to your television. Satellite phones receive signals via satellite relay. They are much more costly than cell phones, so they are not commonly used. In an emergency, satellite phones may offer the only means of communication. When a hurricane destroyed Florida's cell towers, rescue workers could still communicate by satellite phone.

CRITICAL THINKING SKILLS

1. **Comparing and Contrasting** What are the advantages and disadvantages of satellite phones and cell phones?
2. **Finding the Main Idea** What role do satellites play in the transmission of a television broadcast?

Television signals travel in a straight line. To receive the signal, an antenna must have a "clear line of sight" to the source. Since Earth is curved, its surface obstructs the line of sight. Satellites solve this problem by allowing signals to travel high above Earth giving them an unobstructed line to homes.

United States made the first computer with stored memory in 1948. The IBM 1401, marketed in 1959, was the first computer used in large numbers in business and industry. These early computers used thousands of vacuum tubes to **function.** These machines took up considerable space. The development of the transistor and the silicon chip produced a revolutionary new approach to computers.

Then, in 1971, the microprocessor was invented and paved the way for the personal computer. Both small and powerful, the personal computer became a regular fixture in businesses, schools, and homes by the 1990s. The computer made many routine tasks easier and became important in nearly every area of modern life. Other tools and machines depend on computers to function. For example, a computer makes many of the decisions used in flying an airplane.

Through their personal computers, people can go on the Internet, a huge web of linked computer networks. The Internet was introduced to the public for the first time in 1972. That same year, electronic mail, or e-mail, was introduced.

The system mushroomed, and by the early 1990s, a new way of sending Internet information called hypertext transfer protocol (http) had been developed. This, combined with the invention of Web browsers, made it easier for people to use the Internet. By early 2007, there were more than 1 billion Internet users worldwide.

Technological developments have also improved our ability to explore space. Ever since **Neil Armstrong** and Buzz Aldrin landed on the moon in 1969, the exploration of space has continued. Space probes have increased our understanding of distant planets. Satellites in orbit provide information about weather on Earth. Other satellites transmit communication signals for radio, television, and telephone.

Launched in 1990, the Hubble Space Telescope (HST), a large astronomical observatory, orbits about 375 miles above Earth's surface. This enables the HST to avoid the distorting effects of the Earth's atmosphere and to provide incredibly clear views of our own solar system and distant galaxies. The National Aeronautics and Space Administration (NASA) sent two rovers, called *Spirit* and *Opportunity*, to the planet Mars. They arrived in 2004. Based on the minerals that the rovers found in Mars's rocks, NASA scientists determined that the now-barren planet once had abundant supplies of water. NASA plans additional missions to Mars to prepare for the eventual landing of humans on the planet.

Weapons of Mass Destruction

The technological revolution has also led to frightening methods of destruction, such as nuclear, biological, and chemical weapons. The end of the Cold War reduced the risk of major nuclear conflict, but regional nuclear conflicts are still possible. There are also fears that terrorists will obtain and use nuclear materials.

Anthrax-filled letters were used to kill U.S. citizens in 2001. Since then, there has been an increased awareness of the threat from biological and chemical weapons. Biowarfare, the use of disease and poison against civilians and soldiers in wartime, is not new. In Europe in the 1300s, plague-infested corpses were thrown over city walls during a siege to infect those inside. Chemical weapons were used extensively in World War I and during the Iran-Iraq war in the 1980s.

Governments have made agreements to limit the research, production, and use of biological and chemical weapons. In 1972, the United States and the Soviet Union agreed to permit work only on defensive biological weapons. However, these measures have not prevented terrorists from practicing **bioterrorism,** the use of biological and chemical weapons in terrorist attacks. In 1995, for example, members of the Japanese religious sect Aum Shinrikyo released a chemical agent, sarin gas, in a Tokyo subway. Thousands were injured and 12 were killed.

Health Care and Health Crises

In the field of health, new medicines enable doctors to treat both physical and mental illnesses. New technologies, including computer-aided imaging, have enabled doctors to perform "miracle" operations. Mechanical valves and pumps for the heart as well as organ transplants have allowed people to live longer and more productive lives.

Some technological changes have led to a new field called bioethics. This deals with moral choices in medical research. For example, genetic engineering alters the genetic information of cells to produce new variations. Some scientists question whether genetic engineering might accidentally create new strains of deadly bacteria that could not be controlled. The overuse of antibiotics has already created "supergerms" that do not respond to antibiotic treatment. Stem-cell research (using stem cells from human embryos to research cures for such diseases as Alzheimer's and Parkinson's) has caused much heated discussion. Also, human cloning and implanting a fertile egg into a human surrogate mother have generated intense debate in many countries around the world.

Concern about the side effects of modern medicines has also led to a dramatic growth in the holistic health-care movement that employs natural methods of healing such as herbal remedies, massage therapy, and acupuncture.

Certain infectious diseases have raised global concerns in recent decades. One devastating disease is AIDS or "acquired immune deficiency disease." (See Chapter 23.) AIDS is a global issue of great seriousness. Nearly 3 million people died of AIDS in 2006 and millions live with HIV. The World Health Organization and the UN continue to sponsor initiatives to educate the public about the disease, provide treatment to those already infected, and search for a cure.

Agriculture

In agriculture, the **Green Revolution** has promised immense returns. The Green Revolution refers to the development of new strains of rice, corn, and other grains that have greater yields. Promoted as the technological solution to feeding the world's population, huge quantities of chemical fertilizers are needed to grow the new strains. Many farmers cannot afford the fertilizers. In addition, the new crops have been subject to insects. The pesticides used to control the insects create environmental problems.

The growing concern with chemical pesticides in food has led to a dramatic increase in the practice of organic farming. Organic farming rejects the use of chemical fertilizers and pesticides, growth hormones, and livestock feed additives. Its goal is to maintain a healthy and sustainable **environment.**

✓ **Reading Check** **Identifying** Why was the development of the World Wide Web significant?

INFOGRAPHICS

The Global AIDS Epidemic

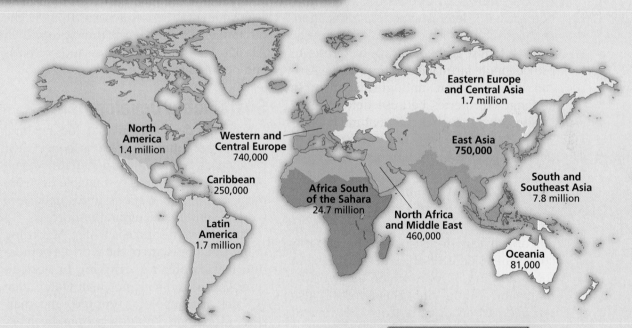

Eastern Europe and Central Asia
1.7 million

North America
1.4 million

Western and Central Europe
740,000

East Asia
750,000

Caribbean
250,000

Africa South of the Sahara
24.7 million

South and Southeast Asia
7.8 million

North Africa and Middle East
460,000

Latin America
1.7 million

Oceania
81,000

AIDS first appeared in the 1980s. HIV, the virus that causes AIDS, spreads through the exchange of body fluids. It can spread through sexual activity, blood transfusions, and even from infected mothers to their babies.

New drugs are helping people with HIV live longer. A major challenge today is paying for the expensive drugs for the millions who need them, especially in poor countries.

CRITICAL THINKING SKILLS

The map is an estimate of the world population living with AIDS in 2006.

1. **Identifying** How many people living in Eastern Europe or Central Asia are infected with AIDS?

2. **Analyzing** What is the main obstacle to making HIV drugs widely available?

Environmental Crisis

MAIN IDEA Environmental damage endangers the world's sustainable development.

HISTORY & YOU Does your family drive a hybrid vehicle? Read to learn about environmental challenges in today's world.

In *Silent Spring*, published in 1962, **Rachel Carson**, an American scientist, argued that the buildup of pesticides—chemicals sprayed on crops to kill insects—was having unforeseen results. Insects were dying, but so too were birds, fish, and other wild animals. Also, the pesticide residue on food harmed humans.

Carson's warnings alarmed many scientists and gave rise to the new science of **ecology**, the study of the relationship between living things and their environment. Since then, scientific research studies have shown that dangers to the environment have many sources.

Three sources are by-products of population growth: deforestation, desertification, and destruction of the tropical rain forests. **Deforestation** is the clearing of forests to provide more farmland and timber. The African lion, elephant, and gorilla are now endangered species because deforestation has destroyed much of their natural habitat. **Desertification** is the formation of degraded soil, turning semi-arid lands into nonproductive deserts. Overgrazing, poor cultivation practices, and destruction of vegetation in semi-arid lands destroy the soil's productivity.

Tropical rain forests near the equator cover only 6 percent of Earth's surface, but they support 50 percent of the world's plant and animal life. These forests also remove carbon dioxide from the air and return oxygen to it. They are crucial to our survival, yet logging, road-building, and clearing for agriculture are destroying tropical forests at an alarming rate.

Chemical Wastes and Disasters

Chemical wastes pose another danger to the environment. The release of chlorofluorocarbons—gases used in aerosol cans, refrigerators, and air conditioners—destroys the ozone layer. This is the thin layer in the upper atmosphere that shields Earth from the sun's ultraviolet rays.

Acid rain results when sulfur spewed out by factories mixes with moisture in the air. Acid rain is responsible for killing forests in North America and Europe.

Global warming has the potential to create a global crisis. The **greenhouse effect,** the warming of the Earth because of the buildup of carbon dioxide in the atmosphere, contributes to the melting of the polar ice caps, rising sea levels, and devastating droughts and storms.

A conference on global warming was held in Kyoto, Japan. To reduce emissions, more than 150 nations signed the **Kyoto Protocol.** The European Union and Japan ratified the treaty in 2002. The United States did not.

Ecological disasters have also harmed our environment. A chemical plant at Bhopal, India, released toxic fumes into the air in 1984. A nuclear accident at Chernobyl in 1986 released radiation. Hundreds died, and there were long-lasting health and environmental consequences. In 1989 the oil tanker *Exxon Valdez* ran aground in Alaska. The spill killed thousands of birds and polluted fishing areas.

Sustainable Development

Economic development that does not limit the ability of future generations to meet their basic needs is known as **sustainable development.** In promoting sustainable development, the United Nations urges nations to work to conserve all natural resources.

One natural resource is water. According to the UN, one-sixth of the world's population lacks water for drinking or agriculture. Those who have no clean water often get sick with cholera, typhoid, and diarrhea. More than 5 million people die every year from the lack of water or from drinking untreated water.

Many nations have enacted recycling and water conservation programs. They have also curbed the dumping of toxic materials. This may help achieve sustainable development.

✓ Reading Check **Defining** What makes development "sustainable"?

Poverty and Civil Strife

MAIN IDEA Poverty, hunger, and civil strife continue to plague many developing nations.

HISTORY & YOU Do you have enough to eat each day? Read to learn about food shortages and world hunger.

After World War II, especially since the 1970s, the world developed a global economy. In a **global economy,** the production, distribution, and sale of goods are done on a worldwide scale. Almost 40 percent of the profits of U.S. businesses come from the sale of goods abroad or investments in foreign nations.

Gap Between Rich and Poor

One feature of the global economy is the wide gap between rich and poor nations. Rich nations are developed. They are mainly in the Northern Hemisphere and include countries such as the United States, Canada, Germany, and Japan. Developed nations have well-organized industrial and agricultural systems, make use of advanced technologies, and have strong educational systems. The poor nations, or developing nations, are located mainly in the Southern Hemisphere. They include many nations in Africa, Asia, and Latin America. Developing nations are primarily farming nations with little technology.

A serious problem in developing nations is an explosive population growth. According to UN projections, the world's population could double by 2050, reaching over 12 billion. Much of that rapid growth will take place in developing nations, which can least afford it. Some developing nations have taken steps to decrease population growth. China advocated a one-child policy (see Chapter 24), and India encouraged a national family welfare program to reduce its population growth rate. However, neither measure has been very successful.

World Hunger

Growing enough food for more and more people creates a severe problem in many developing countries. An estimated 1 billion people worldwide today suffer from hunger.

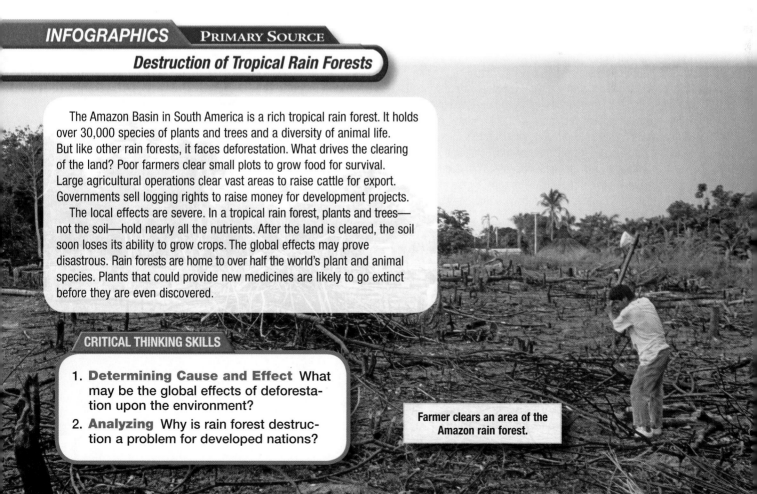

INFOGRAPHICS PRIMARY SOURCE
Destruction of Tropical Rain Forests

The Amazon Basin in South America is a rich tropical rain forest. It holds over 30,000 species of plants and trees and a diversity of animal life. But like other rain forests, it faces deforestation. What drives the clearing of the land? Poor farmers clear small plots to grow food for survival. Large agricultural operations clear vast areas to raise cattle for export. Governments sell logging rights to raise money for development projects.

The local effects are severe. In a tropical rain forest, plants and trees—not the soil—hold nearly all the nutrients. After the land is cleared, the soil soon loses its ability to grow crops. The global effects may prove disastrous. Rain forests are home to over half the world's plant and animal species. Plants that could provide new medicines are likely to go extinct before they are even discovered.

CRITICAL THINKING SKILLS

1. **Determining Cause and Effect** What may be the global effects of deforestation upon the environment?
2. **Analyzing** Why is rain forest destruction a problem for developed nations?

Farmer clears an area of the Amazon rain forest.

Every year, more than 8 million people die of hunger, many of them young children. Poor soil, increasing populations, and natural catastrophes contribute to world hunger.

Economic factors also contribute to widespread hunger. Growing crops for export, for example, might lead to big profits for large landowners. However, it leaves many small farmers with little land on which to grow food.

Civil War and Ethnic Conflict

Civil wars have also created food shortages. War not only disrupts normal farming, but warring groups try to limit access to food to destroy their enemies. In Sudan, 1.3 million people starved when combatants of a civil war in the 1980s prevented food from reaching them. As unrest continued during the early 2000s in Darfur (see Chapter 23), families were forced to leave their farms. As a result, an estimated 70,000 people had starved by mid-2004.

The Darfur situation has awakened the world to the practice of genocide. Many observers believed that the Sudanese regime conducted a systematic campaign to kill ethnic African peoples. The Serbian policy of ethnic cleansing of Bosnian Muslims in the 1990s also revived memories of Nazi atrocities.

Ethnic and religious conflicts have also caused tension in Asian and Southeast Asian countries. Tibet seeks independence from the Chinese government that has suppressed dissent among ethnic minorities. Tibet's Dalai Lama has been in exile in India since 1959. In 1999, violence between Christians and Muslims broke out in East Timor (in the Moluccas Islands). Nearly 10,000 people died due to the conflict. A pact in 2002 supposedly ended the fighting, though clashes have continued.

✓ **Reading Check** **Explaining** What steps have India and China taken to help control population?

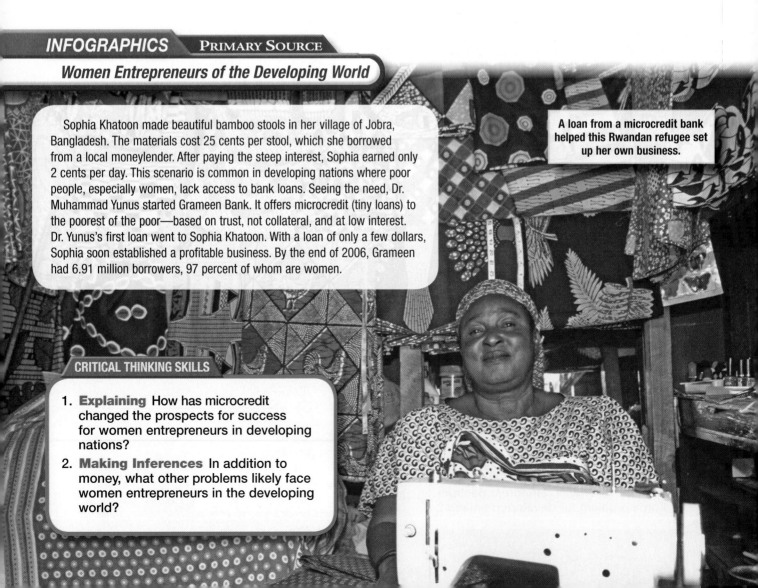

INFOGRAPHICS PRIMARY SOURCE

Women Entrepreneurs of the Developing World

Sophia Khatoon made beautiful bamboo stools in her village of Jobra, Bangladesh. The materials cost 25 cents per stool, which she borrowed from a local moneylender. After paying the steep interest, Sophia earned only 2 cents per day. This scenario is common in developing nations where poor people, especially women, lack access to bank loans. Seeing the need, Dr. Muhammad Yunus started Grameen Bank. It offers microcredit (tiny loans) to the poorest of the poor—based on trust, not collateral, and at low interest. Dr. Yunus's first loan went to Sophia Khatoon. With a loan of only a few dollars, Sophia soon established a profitable business. By the end of 2006, Grameen had 6.91 million borrowers, 97 percent of whom are women.

A loan from a microcredit bank helped this Rwandan refugee set up her own business.

CRITICAL THINKING SKILLS

1. **Explaining** How has microcredit changed the prospects for success for women entrepreneurs in developing nations?

2. **Making Inferences** In addition to money, what other problems likely face women entrepreneurs in the developing world?

Political and Social Challenges

MAIN IDEA Not all nations guarantee their people basic human rights and equality.

HISTORY & YOU To what rights are you entitled? Read to learn about the Universal Declaration of Human Rights.

Many political and social changes have taken place as a result of World War II. As democracy spread, many countries affirmed and extended rights to their people, both male and female.

Human Rights

The United Nations took the lead in affirming the basic human rights of all people. On December 10, 1948, the UN's General Assembly adopted the **Universal Declaration of Human Rights.** According to the declaration:

PRIMARY SOURCE

"All human beings are born free and equal in dignity and rights. . . . Everyone is entitled to all the rights and freedoms set forth in this Declaration, without distinction of any kind, such as race, color, sex, language, religion, political or other opinion, national or social origin, property, birth or other status. . . . Everyone has the right to life, liberty, and security of person. . . . Everyone has the right to freedom of movement. . . . Everyone has the right to freedom of opinion and expression."

—*Universal Declaration of Human Rights,* 1948

Since the adoption of the UN declaration, the human rights movement has achieved much success in freeing political prisoners and bringing economic and political change around the world. Nevertheless, human rights violations still occur worldwide.

Governments themselves often carry on the violence. Dictators and military regimes often punish people who disagree with their views. In Cuba, Chile, Myanmar, Iraq, Iran, and other countries, people have been persecuted for opposing repressive governments. In other countries, such as Bosnia and Rwanda, ethnic, religious, and racial hatreds have led to the mass murder of hundreds of thousands of people.

New Democracies

After World War II, African and Asian leaders wanted democratic governments. Within a decade, however, military dictatorships or one-party governments replaced democratic systems in Africa, Asia, and Latin America. In recent years, however, interest in democracy has rekindled. For instance, South Korea, Taiwan, and the Philippines hold free elections. Similar developments have taken place in a number of African countries and throughout Latin America.

Unfortunately, conflict due to regional, ethnic, and religious differences creates discord around the world. Ethnic divisions in Yugoslavia, unrest in the Middle East, and conflicts among ethnic groups in Africa all remain to be resolved.

Equality for Women

In the social and economic spheres of the Western world, the gap that once separated men and women has been steadily narrowing. More and more women are joining the workforce, and they make up half of university graduates in Western countries. Many countries have laws that require equal pay for women and men doing the same work, and some laws prohibit promotions based on gender. Nevertheless, women in many Western countries still do not hold many top positions in business or government.

Bound to their homes and families and subordinate to men, women in developing nations face considerable difficulties. They often are unable to obtain education, property rights, or decent jobs. Domitila Barrios de Chungara, a miner's wife from Bolivia, said in a 1981 interview:

PRIMARY SOURCE

"But women like us, housewives, who get organized to better our people, well they beat us up and persecute us. . . . [People do not know] what it's like to get up at four in the morning and go to bed at eleven or twelve at night, just to be able to get all the housework done, because of the lousy conditions we live in."

—*Domitila Barrios de Chungara,* 1981

✓ **Reading Check** **Identifying** Which organization developed the Universal Declaration of Human Rights?

Challenge of Terrorism

MAIN IDEA Acts of terrorism, now a part of modern society, have a worldwide effect.

HISTORY & YOU Have you heard details about new security at American airports? Read to learn how terrorism challenges the world.

Acts of terror have become a regular feature of modern society. Terrorists often kill civilians and take hostages to achieve their political goals.

Modern Terrorism

During the late 1970s and 1980s, many countries placed their concern about terrorism at the top of foreign policy agendas. Terrorist acts have received considerable media attention. When Palestinian terrorists kidnapped and killed 11 Israeli athletes at the Munich Olympic Games in 1972, hundreds of millions of people watched the drama unfold on television. Indeed, some observers believe that television newscasts contribute to the spread of terrorism.

Some terrorists are militant nationalists who want separatist states. The Irish Republican Army (IRA), for example, wants to unite Northern Ireland, governed by Great Britain, with the Irish Republic. (See Chapter 21.) Since the early 1970s, violence has rocked the country. IRA leaders now seem more willing to open normal relations with the Northern Ireland police. This is a big step toward achieving the goal of the Good Friday Peace Pact of 1998: a Protestant-Catholic governing coalition.

Sometimes terrorism is state-sponsored. Militant governments in Iraq, Syria, Cuba, and North Korea have provided sanctuary and support to numerous terrorist organizations.

The Impact of 9/11

One of the most destructive acts of terrorism occurred on September 11, 2001, in the United States. (See Chapter 21.) Following the horrific attacks on the World Trade Center and the Pentagon, President George W. Bush vowed to wage war on terrorism. This process began with military

CONNECTING TO THE UNITED STATES

HOMELAND SECURITY

The mission of the Department of Homeland Security (DHS) is to lead national efforts to prevent, prepare for, and respond to terrorist attacks and natural disasters. The DHS coordinates a vast network of state and local emergency management and law enforcement agencies. It plans responses to worst-case scenarios even as its agencies work to prevent them.

DHS Strategic Goals
- Identify potential terrorist threats and likely targets
- Detect and prevent attacks
- Coordinate the national response to terrorist acts and natural disasters
- Lead recovery efforts after terrorist acts and natural disasters

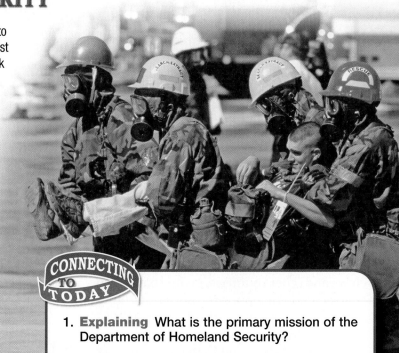

A terrorism response ▶ exercise in Los Angeles

CONNECTING TO TODAY

1. **Explaining** What is the primary mission of the Department of Homeland Security?

2. **Making Connections** How are school safety drills similar to the exercise in the photo?

action by the United States and its allies against Afghanistan in October 2001.

At home, President Bush asked Congress to pass legislation to help track down terrorist suspects. An antiterrorist bill known as the **Patriot Act** was passed in October 2001. The Patriot Act allowed secret searches to avoid tipping off terrorism suspects. The law made it easier to wiretap suspects and to track e-mail, seize voice mail, and monitor library records. These sweeping and controversial measures led some Americans to debate how far constitutional rights should be restricted to protect them against terrorist attacks. In 2002 Congress established the Department of Homeland Security to coordinate efforts against terrorism at home.

Worldwide, one of the most noticeable changes in public policies since September 11, 2001, has been increased security at airports. Many European and Asian governments have also begun working more closely together in their intelligence and police activities to track down terrorists.

Islamic Militants

The causes of recent world terrorism are complex. Some analysts say this terrorism is rooted in the clash of Western and Islamic cultures. They argue that the Christians and Muslims have viewed each other with hostility since at least the time of the Crusades. Others suggest that poverty and ignorance lie at the root of the problem. Extremists find it easy to stir up resentment against wealthy Western societies. Finally, some say terrorism would be rare if the Israeli-Palestinian conflict could be solved.

One reason Middle Eastern terrorists have targeted Westerners can be traced to Western investment in the Middle East oil industry, which began in the 1920s. This industry brought wealth to ruling families in some Middle Eastern kingdoms, but most citizens remained very poor. They often blamed the West, especially the United States, for supporting the ruling families.

The oil business increased Middle Eastern contact with the West. Some Muslims feared that this contact would weaken their religion and their way of life. Some Muslims began organizing movements to overthrow their pro-Western governments. Muslims who support these movements are called fundamentalist militants. They promote their own vision of what a pure Islamic society should be. Most Muslims around the world do not share this vision, nor do they agree with the use of terrorism.

The movement for a conservative Islamic society was first seen in 1979 in Iran. (See Chapter 23.) After the revolution of 1979, the legal system, clothing styles, and social practices were regulated by a strict interpretation of Islam. These practices have spread to other Muslim countries.

✓ Reading Check **Explaining** How does the Patriot Act help law enforcement detect terrorist plots?

Vocabulary
1. **Explain** the significance of: function, Neil Armstrong, bioterrorism, Green Revolution, environment, Rachel Carson, ecology, deforestation, desertification, greenhouse effect, Kyoto Protocol, sustainable development, global economy, Universal Declaration of Human Rights, Patriot Act.

Main Ideas
2. **Summarize** the technological advances made and the drawback or cost of each in the areas listed below.

Technological Advances	Drawback or Cost
Communications	
Transportation	
Space Exploration	
Health Care	
Agriculture	
Weaponry	

3. **Explain** how desertification endangers sustainable development.

4. **List** the rights mentioned in the Universal Declaration of Human Rights.

Critical Thinking
5. **The BIG Idea** **Identifying Central Issues** How can societies balance their desire for economic development with the pressures such development places on the environment?

6. **Evaluating** Why must ethics be part of technological advances?

7. **Analyzing Visuals** Describe the type of business owned by the woman in the image on page 808. What products does she produce? What tools does she use?

Writing About History
8. **Expository Writing** In an essay, describe why some leaders disagree about the best solutions to global environmental problems.

History ONLINE

For help with the concepts in this section of *Glencoe World History—Modern Times*, go to glencoe.com and click Study Central.

New Global Communities

The BIG Idea
Order and Security The global economy and new global threats have prompted organizations and individuals to work on global problems.

Content Vocabulary
- peacekeeping forces (p. 812)
- nuclear proliferation (p. 813)
- globalization (p. 815)
- multinational corporation (p. 815)
- grassroots level (p. 817)
- nongovernmental organizations (NGOs) (p. 817)
- disarmament groups (p. 817)

Academic Vocabulary
- migration (p. 814)
- projection (p. 814)

People and Events
- Franklin Delano Roosevelt (p. 812)
- World Bank (p. 815)
- International Monetary Fund (IMF) (p. 815)
- World Trade Organization (WTO) (p. 816)
- Hazel Henderson (p. 817)
- Elise Boulding (p. 817)

Reading Strategy
Organizing Information As you read, create a pyramid like the one below to depict how the United Nations is organized.

Security Council

In today's world, nations and communities are more closely connected than ever. This has meant that problems in one part of the world can affect people all over the globe. In the words of British Prime Minister Tony Blair, "Today conflicts rarely stay within national boundaries." Increasingly, the world's nations must unite to create lasting solutions to the contemporary problems of poverty, nuclear proliferation, global warming, and terrorism.

The United Nations

MAIN IDEA The United Nations focuses on international problems.

HISTORY & YOU Do you recall from Section 1 the Universal Declaration of Human Rights of the United Nations? Read to learn about the UN's structure and activities.

In recent decades, many nations have become more convinced that there are significant problems that can only be solved by working with other nations. Today, the United Nations (UN) is one of the most visible symbols of the new globalism.

The UN was founded in 1945 at the end of World War II. U.S. president **Franklin Delano Roosevelt** was especially eager to create an organization to work for peace. One of the UN's two chief goals is peace. The other goal is human dignity. These goals were clearly stated in the UN's charter. Members pledged "to save succeeding generations from the scourge of war . . . to reaffirm faith in fundamental human rights . . . and to promote social progress and better standards of life in larger freedom."

The General Assembly of the United Nations is made up of representatives from all member nations. It has the power to discuss any important question and to recommend action. The Security Council advises the General Assembly and passes resolutions that require the organization to act. Five nations have permanent seats on the Security Council: the United States, Russia, Great Britain, France, and China. Ten other members are chosen by the General Assembly and serve for limited terms. Because each permanent member can veto a decision, deliberations can often end in a stalemate. The head administrator of the United Nations is the secretary-general.

Specialized agencies function under the UN's direction. These agencies address economic and social problems and organize conferences on important issues such as population growth and the environment. The UN has also provided **peacekeeping forces**—military forces from neutral member states that settle conflicts and supervise truces in "hot spots" around the globe.

UNESCO and World Literacy

Today, about 770 million adults—one-fifth of the world's adult population—lack basic reading and writing skills. This statistic represents a shocking waste of human potential. To combat this problem, the United Nations Education, Scientific and Cultural Organization (UNESCO) coordinates the efforts of many organizations participating in its Education for All program. The program's goal is to increase global literacy by 50 percent by 2015.

The United Nations sees literacy as essential to ending poverty, slowing population growth, achieving gender equality, and ensuring economic development. Literacy provides access to education, which contributes to a more productive workforce and to fuller participation in today's world.

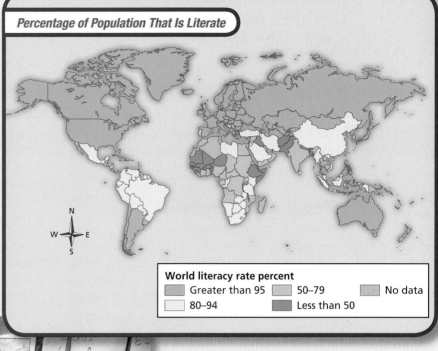

Percentage of Population That Is Literate

World literacy rate percent
- Greater than 95
- 80–94
- 50–79
- Less than 50
- No data

An adult literacy class in Bolivia

CRITICAL THINKING SKILLS

1. **Making Connections** Based on the map and what you know about developing nations, how is literacy related to development?

2. **Analyzing** Why is literacy important to education?

The UN established the International Atomic Energy Agency (IAEA) in 1957. This agency operates a safeguards system against **nuclear proliferation**—the spread of nuclear weapons production technology and knowledge to nations without that capability. The greatest risk comes from countries that have not joined or have violated the Nuclear Nonproliferation Treaty (NPT). India, Pakistan, Israel, North Korea, and Iran fall within these categories. In 1998, India and Pakistan exploded nuclear devices underground. North Korea performed its first nuclear test in October 2006, and Iran refused to shelve its nuclear enrichment program.

As the IAEA director said, "The threat of nuclear terrorism is real and current. . . . the existence of a nuclear threat anywhere is a threat everywhere, and as a global community, we will win or lose this battle together."

✓ Reading Check **Identifying** What is one goal of the International Atomic Energy Agency?

History ONLINE
Student Web Activity—
Visit glencoe.com to learn how to create and modify a database and to learn more about the United Nations.

Population and Migration

MAIN IDEA The ever-increasing world population affects the world economy.

HISTORY & YOU Has your family ever moved to a new community? Read to learn why some people have migrated.

The growth of new global communities depends on population and **migration** trends. Population patterns and global migrations are affecting the type of communities in which people will live.

Population Trends

A July 2006 estimate put the current world population at over 6.5 billion people, only 18 years after passing the 5-billion mark. At its current rate of growth, the world population could reach 12.8 billion by 2050, according to the UN's long-range population projections. The UN's more conservative **projection** puts that number at 8.9 billion. Even with the more conservative figure, the world population is expected to increase nearly 37 percent over the next four decades.

Soon, the most populous nations in the world will be developing countries, especially India and China. By 2050, India will have surpassed China in population and will likely remain the most populous country in the world thereafter.

In wealthy regions such as Western Europe, though, population is declining and "graying"—a larger percentage of the population is reaching retirement. In 2000, European nations had the oldest population of any region in the world: 15 percent of the population was 65 or older. By 2050, 28 percent are expected to be in this age group. In fact, by 2050, the United States is expected to be the only wealthy nation with a growing population.

Life expectancy is projected to increase worldwide after 2050. In all projection scenarios, the age distribution will shift toward older people. Due to longer life expectancies and lower birth rates in the future, the number of people 80 and over and those who live beyond 100 might rise. Just 1.1 percent of the population was 80 and over in 2000; by 2300, that percentage will increase to 17. An older population places a demand on the economy because the taxes of workers must be stretched further to cover care of the elderly.

Developing countries will face a different kind of problem. Between 2000 and 2050, the less-developed countries are expected to experience a 61 percent increase in population. This number of people might mean increased migrations as well as increased urbanization. Since many cities lack the infrastructure to support the larger populations, concerns are rising about future international health and environment problems.

Global Migrations

Since 1945, tens of millions of people have migrated from one part of the world to another. There are many reasons for these migrations. Persecution for political reasons caused many people from Pakistan, Bangladesh, Sri Lanka, Eastern Europe, and East Germany to seek refuge in Western European countries. Brutal civil wars in Asia, Africa, the Middle East, and Europe led millions of refugees to seek safety in neighboring countries. A devastating famine in Africa in 1984–1985 caused hundreds of thousands of Africans to move to relief camps throughout the continent to find food.

Most people who have migrated, however, have done so to find jobs. Latin Americans seeking a better life have migrated to the United States. Guest workers from Turkey, southern and eastern Europe, North Africa, India, and Pakistan have entered more prosperous Western European lands. In the 1980s, about 15 million guest workers worked and lived in Europe.

Many host countries allowed guest workers to stay for several years. In the 1980s and 1990s, however, foreign workers often became scapegoats when countries faced economic problems. Political parties in France and Norway, for example, called for the removal of blacks and Arabs in order to protect the ethnic purity of their nations. In Asian countries, there is often a backlash against other Asian ethnic groups.

✓ Reading Check **Summarizing** Give four reasons why people migrate.

Globalization

MAIN IDEA International organizations and citizen groups work to solve global problems.

HISTORY & YOU Do you recall how the American Red Cross started? Read to learn how many kinds of groups work on world problems.

The technology revolution has tied people and nations closely together and contributed to globalization. **Globalization** is the process by which people and nations have become more interdependent. Economically, globalization has taken the form of a global economy. Politically and socially, globalization has led to the emergence of citizen groups and other transnational organizations that work across national boundaries to bring solutions to problems that are common to all humans.

Global Economic Organizations

The global economy began to develop after World War II and gained momentum in the 1980s and 1990s. After World War II, the United States and other nations set up the **World Bank** and the **International Monetary Fund (IMF).** The World Bank is actually a group of five international organizations, largely controlled by developed countries. It provides grants, loans, and advice for economic development in developing countries. The World Bank's stated goal is "a world free of poverty."

The IMF, founded in 1945, is now an "organization of 184 countries." Its goal is to oversee the global financial system. To achieve its goal, the IMF watches exchange rates and offers financial and technical assistance to developing nations. Both the World Bank and the IMF have been criticized for forcing inappropriate Western economic practices on non-Western nations. Critics also argue that World Bank and IMF policies only aggravate the poverty and debt of developing nations.

Another reflection of the global economy is the **multinational corporation** (a company that has divisions in more than two countries).

INFOGRAPHICS

Economic Interdependence

Resources are spread unevenly around the world. No nation has all the resources it needs to prosper. To get what they need, nations trade. The exchange generally benefits both nations. For example, Japan has few mineral resources; however, it can buy minerals from other countries and sell its manufactured products all over the world.

Business people now think globally when making economic decisions. A business might locate its factories in developing nations where wages are low. Activities that require advanced technology or highly educated workers might be located in developed nations. Markets are also global. Businesses design products to appeal to the diverse tastes of consumers around the world. Economic interdependence creates global problems as well. For example, an economic downturn in one nation can spread to other nations. Industrial pollution can also spread across national boundaries.

These container ships in the Port of Los Angeles, California, transport goods all over the world.

CRITICAL THINKING SKILLS

1. **Explaining** What is one reason that nations trade with one another?
2. **Analyzing** How have businesses become more global in their economic decisions?

The UN Millennium Development Goals

Kofi Annan

At the United Nations Millennium Summit in 2000, world leaders agreed to work together to achieve eight development goals by 2015. Developing countries are enacting reforms, and developed countries are supporting them with aid and expertise. The United Nations coordinates these efforts and tracks progress with country report cards. The 2006 report shows some progress, but the world still has a long way to go.

DEVELOPMENT GOALS

1. Eradicate extreme poverty and hunger
2. Achieve universal primary education
3. Promote gender equality and empower women
4. Reduce child mortality
5. Improve maternal health
6. Combat HIV/AIDS, malaria and other diseases
7. Ensure environmental sustainability
8. Develop a global partnership for development

"We will have time to reach the Millennium Development Goals . . . but only if we break with business as usual. . . . Success will require sustained action . . . . It takes time to train the teachers, nurses and engineers; to build the roads, schools and hospitals; to grow the small and large businesses able to create the jobs and income needed. So we must start now. And we must more than double global development assistance over the next few years. Nothing less will help to achieve the Goals."

—Kofi Annan
UN Secretary-General
from 1997 to 2006

DOCUMENT-BASED QUESTIONS

1. **Summarizing** According to Kofi Annan, how can the goals be achieved?
2. **Assessing** What role does the UN play in achieving these goals, and why is this role important?

Prominent examples of multinational corporations include Siemens, IBM, Toyota, and the Sony Corporation. The growing number of multinational corporations that do business around the world increasingly tie one country to another in a global economy. For example, an economic downturn in the United States can create stagnant conditions in Europe and Asia. We live in an interdependent world.

Global trade is another important component of the global economy. Over the years, many nations joined in talks to make trade between countries free and easy. These talks led to General Agreement on Trade and Tariffs (GATT). In 1995, the nations that had signed the GATT treaties agreed to create the **World Trade Organization (WTO).** Made up of more than 140 member nations, the WTO arranges trade

agreements and settles trade disputes. The WTO has been criticized for ignoring environmental and health concerns and for leaving out small and developing countries. Still, it is the only global organization that deals with rules of trade among nations.

Groups of nations have joined together to form trading blocs. By 2004, the European Union included 25 member states and is the world's largest single trading entity. The EU has a single internal market and a common currency (the euro).

Elsewhere, the North American Free Trade Agreement (NAFTA) created a free-trade area for Canada, the United States, and Mexico. The Asia Pacific Economic Cooperation (APEC) agreement has tried to do the same among nations that border the Pacific Ocean.

Transnational Organizations

Global awareness has led to new social movements that involve ordinary citizens and focus on problems that nations share. Problem areas include threats to the environment, women's and men's liberation, child labor, appropriate use of technology, and promotion of peace.

Some organizations, such as the Red Cross, draw their membership from people in many different countries. Some individuals act at the **grassroots level**—that is, in their own community. A favorite slogan of grassroots groups is "Think globally, act locally." **Hazel Henderson,** a British-born economist, believes that these individuals can be powerful agents for change.

PRIMARY SOURCE

"These aroused citizens are by no means all mindless young radicals. Well-dressed, clean-shaven, middle-class businessmen and their suburban wives comprise the major forces in California fighting against nuclear power. Hundreds of thousands of middle-class mothers are bringing massive pressure to ban commercials and violent programs from children's television."

—Hazel Henderson, *Creating Alternative Futures*

Another movement that addresses world problems is the growth of **nongovernmental organizations (NGOs).** NGOs are often represented at the United Nations. They include professional, business, and cooperative organizations, as well as foundations. Also included are religious, peace, and **disarmament groups** that work to limit the size of military forces and weapons stocks. Other NGOs protect the welfare of women and children and include environmental and human rights groups.

American educator **Elise Boulding** promotes NGOs. She believes they can educate people to consider problems globally. She says that all NGOs are expected "to define problems in global terms, to take account of human interests and needs as they are found in all parts of the planet." The number of international NGOs increased from 176 in 1910 to nearly 37,000 in 2000.

Global solutions to global problems have been hindered by political and ethnic disputes. Even as the world becomes more global and interdependent, disruptive forces work against efforts to enhance our human destiny.

Many lessons can be learned from the study of world history. One is especially clear: a lack of involvement in the affairs of one's society can lead to a sense of powerlessness. An understanding of our world heritage and its lessons might well give us the opportunity to make wise choices in a crisis-laden and often chaotic age. We are all creators of history. The choices we make in our everyday lives will affect the future of world civilization.

✓ **Reading Check** **Explaining** What is the European Union?

Vocabulary

1. **Explain** the significance of: Franklin Delano Roosevelt, peacekeeping forces, nuclear proliferation, migration, projection, globalization, World Bank, International Monetary Fund (IMF), multinational corporation, World Trade Organization (WTO), grassroots level, Hazel Henderson, nongovernmental organizations (NGOs), disarmament groups, Elise Boulding.

Main Ideas

2. **List** the nations that have permanent seats on the UN Security Council. Use a chart like the one below to make your list.

Nations That Have Permanent Seats on the UN Security Council
1.
2.

3. **Explain** why the age distribution in the world's population will shift toward older people after 2050.

4. **Name** three international organizations that were established to help solve global economic problems.

Critical Thinking

5. **The BIG Idea** **Making Connections** Why is the United Nations so important in today's world?

6. **Evaluating** Why is nuclear proliferation a global concern?

7. **Analyzing Visuals** Examine the map on page 813. Is there an area or country with a literacy rate that surprised you? Explain why or why not.

Writing About History

8. **Descriptive Writing** Choose one NGO to research. Write an essay about the organization's mission, goals, accomplishments, and failures.

History ONLINE

For help with the concepts in this section of *Glencoe World History—Modern Times*, go to glencoe.com and click Study Central.

You can study anywhere, anytime by downloading quizzes and flash cards to your PDA from glencoe.com.

THE TECHNOLOGICAL REVOLUTION

- Advanced communication and transportation systems are linking the world's people.
- New technologies for exploring space have increased our understanding of the universe.
- Weapons of mass destruction, or WMDs, are a grim result of the technological revolution.
- Breakthroughs in medicine and agriculture save lives, but some raise ethical questions.

REPAIRING THE HUBBLE SPACE TELESCOPE

The Hubble Space Telescope provides images of our solar system and other galaxies.

CAR BOMB DESTROYS NIGHTCLUB IN BALI, INDONESIA

All nations must face the challenge of terrorism.

GLOBAL CHALLENGES

- Deforestation, chemical wastes, oil spills, and nuclear accidents threaten the environment.
- Nations must conserve natural resources to achieve sustainable development.
- Poverty, hunger, and civil unrest plague many developing countries.
- Human rights violations occur worldwide.
- Terrorism has become part of modern society.

RED CROSS HELPS FAMINE VICTIMS IN SUDAN

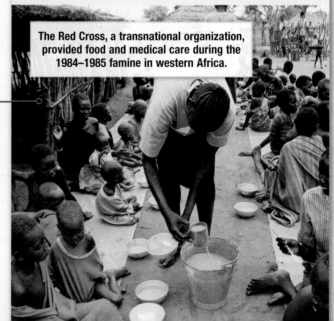

The Red Cross, a transnational organization, provided food and medical care during the 1984–1985 famine in western Africa.

GLOBAL SOLUTIONS

- The United Nations works for world peace and human dignity.
- Nongovernmental organizations focus on issues such as disarmament, child welfare, and human rights.
- Economic interdependence has given rise to international organizations to address issues affecting the global economy.

STANDARDIZED TEST PRACTICE

TEST-TAKING TIP

If you do not know the answer to a question, eliminate any answer choices that you know are incorrect. Then choose the best answer from the remaining choices.

Reviewing Vocabulary

Directions: Choose the word or words that best complete the sentence.

1. The _____ has produced new strains of rice, corn, and other grains that have greater yields.

  A greenhouse effect

  B global economy

  C Neolithic Revolution

  D Green Revolution

2. North Korea's recent test of its first nuclear weapon is an example of nuclear _____.

  A disarmament

  B proliferation

  C bioterrorism

  D globalism

3. Overgrazing and poor cultivation practices in semi-arid lands are creating _____, or a decline in the soil's productivity.

  A desertification

  B organic evolution

  C deforestation

  D conservation

4. The technology revolution has contributed to _____, or the process by which people and nations have become more interdependent.

  A secularization

  B sustainable development

  C bioterrorism

  D globalization

Reviewing Main Ideas

Directions: Choose the best answers to the following questions.

Section 1 *(pp. 802–811)*

5. What invention in 1971 made small personal computers possible?

  A The vacuum tube

  B The World Wide Web

  C The microprocessor

  D Hypertext transfer protocol

6. What new field deals with moral issues involved in technological advances, such as stem-cell research?

  A Bioethics

  B Genetic engineering

  C Ethnic cleansing

  D Ecology

7. Which of the following is the main cause of global warming?

  A Rising sea levels

  B Increase in solar radiation

  C Release of chlorofluorocarbons into the atmosphere

  D Buildup of carbon dioxide in the atmosphere

8. The world's developing nations are mostly located in which hemisphere?

  A Northern

  B Southern

  C Eastern

  D Western

Need Extra Help?								
If You Missed Questions . . .	1	2	3	4	5	6	7	8
Go to Page . . .	805	813	806	815	803	804	806	807

9. What is the main goal of the Irish Republican Army?

  A To help Great Britain in time of war

  B To form a Protestant-Catholic coalition

  C To unite Northern Ireland with the Irish Republic

  D To make Southern Ireland an independent state

Section 2 *(pp. 812–817)*

10. What are the two main bodies of the United Nations?

  A General Assembly and National Council

  B Security Council and National Assembly

  C National Council and National Assembly

  D Security Council and General Assembly

11. Which country is expected to be the most populous in the world by 2050?

  A United States

  B India

  C China

  D Sudan

12. For what reason have most people migrated?

  A To find jobs

  B To escape persecution

  C To find food

  D To escape civil war

13. Which organization oversees the global financial system?

  A World Bank

  B World Trade Organization

  C International Monetary Fund

  D United Nations

Critical Thinking

Directions: Choose the best answers to the following questions.

Use the following map to answer question 14.

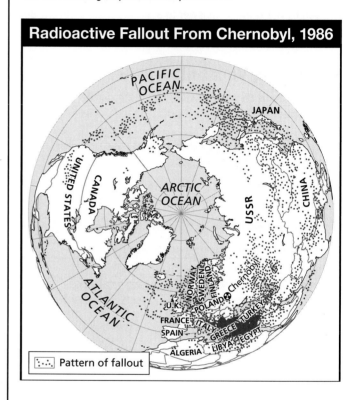

Radioactive Fallout From Chernobyl, 1986

:···: Pattern of fallout

14. Which of the following is a true statement about the global effects of the nuclear accident at Chernobyl?

  A Fallout covered more than half of the Southern Hemisphere.

  B Fallout extended as far as eastern Canada.

  C Fallout covered about two-thirds of the Northern Hemisphere.

  D The heaviest fallout occurred in the Soviet Union.

15. What would be a global economic effect should a war or revolution occur in the Middle East?

  A A devaluation of the euro

  B A big increase in the price of oil

  C A recession or a depression

  D A drop in the market price of grains

Need Extra Help?							
If You Missed Questions . . .	9	10	11	12	13	14	15
Go to Page . . .	810	812	814	814	815	806	816

16. Which of the following is a true statement about world population between now and 2050?

  A The greatest population growth will occur in wealthy nations.

  B Migrations and urbanization in developing countries will increase.

  C The population's average age will become increasingly younger.

  D Disease and starvation will reduce life expectancy worldwide.

17. Which argument below might come from an opponent of stem-cell research?

  A The research might produce deadly "supergerms" that cannot be controlled.

  B The research might make it possible to create a human being in a laboratory.

  C The research uses cells from human embryos.

  D The research alters the genetic makeup of an organism.

Analyze the cartoon and answer the question that follows. Base your answer on the cartoon and on your knowledge of world history.

18. Which problem is the subject of this cartoon?

  A World hunger

  B Population growth

  C Global warming

  D Deforestation

Document-Based Questions

Directions: Analyze the document and answer the short-answer questions that follow the document. Base your answers on the document and on your knowledge of world history.

Rachel Carson cautioned about the dangers of harmful chemicals in her book, *Silent Spring*:

> *"It is not my contention that chemical pesticides must never be used. I do contend that we have put poisons and biologically potent chemicals into the hands of persons largely or wholly ignorant of their potentials for harm. . . . Future generations are unlikely to condone our lack of prudent concern for the integrity of the natural world that supports all life."*
>
> —Rachel Carson, *Silent Spring*, 1962

19. Summarize the argument that Carson is presenting in this quotation.

20. In Carson's opinion, who will question the lack of concern shown for the natural world?

Extended Response

21. Terrorism has become part of modern life. What are some possible causes of global terrorism?

History ONLINE

For additional test practice, use Self-Check Quizzes—Chapter 25 at **glencoe.com**.

Need Extra Help?						
If You Missed Questions . . .	16	17	18	19	20	21
Go to Page . . .	807	804	806	806	806	811

World Wide Wonder

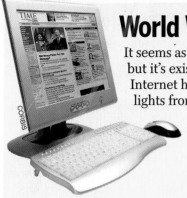

It seems as if the Internet has been around forever, but it's existed only since 1969. Over the years, the Internet has grown in importance. Here are highlights from its history.

1969 A U.S. Defense Department agency called the Advanced Research Project Agency (ARPA) connects four universities in a communications network. It is called ARPANET. This primitive network is the start of the Internet era.

1972 The first electronic mail (e-mail) is sent.

1982 The word Internet is used for the first time.

1984 The Domain Name System (DNS) is put in place. Extensions such as .com, .org, and .edu are used to identify network addresses.

1990 Englishman Tim Berners-Lee invents the World Wide Web while working in a Swiss physics laboratory.

1993 Mosaic, the first web browser to use graphics, becomes available.

1994 Companies begin to sell items on the Internet. The term spam, meaning unsolicited e-mail, is first introduced.

1999 College student Shawn Fanning introduces Napster, a program that lets Internet users swap music for free. Calling it a violation of copyright, the music industry gets Napster declared illegal. Eventually, Napster becomes a pay service.

Shawn Fanning

2004 The worm MyDoom infects Internet servers, affecting about one-twelfth of all e-mail messages.

2006 Users of the Internet worldwide number more than one billion.

REUTERS/LOU DEMATTEIS

VERBATIM

❝ I do not know how the Third World War will be fought, but I can tell you what they will use in the Fourth—rocks. ❞

ALBERT EINSTEIN,
declaring that an atomic war would end world civilization

❝ There can be no liberty unless there is economic liberty. ❞

MARGARET THATCHER,
prime minister of Great Britain, a firm believer in free-market capitalism

❝ It's a very humbling occasion. Kenyans have given me a challenge. ❞

MWAI KIBAKI,
elected democratic president of Kenya, on succeeding in 2003 the repressive party that ruled the country for 39 years

❝ Women suddenly have more value in this society. ❞

LULUA ABDULLAH AL-OMARI,
Kuwaiti mother of four, on efforts to encourage female voters in Kuwait's first elections since women won the right to vote in 2005

❝ Everything has changed, but nothing is better. ❞

FAY WELDON,
English author, on the impact of feminism on women's lives

MELTDOWN!

These satellite photos show the Arctic ice cap in 1979 and 2005. An area twice the size of Texas, normally covered by ice, is now open water. Scientists fear the ice cap, as well as Earth's glaciers, are melting because of global warming. Polluting gases produced by burning coal, oil, and other fossil fuels are a major cause of global warming. These "greenhouse" gases trap the heat from sunlight, raising Earth's temperature. Most of the world's countries have signed the 1997 Kyoto Protocol, a treaty that requires them to reduce their greenhouse emissions. But as the pictures show, efforts to turn down the heat haven't yet succeeded.

1979

2005

NASA

What's in a Name?

Africa has the most countries of any continent. Since the 1960s, many of those nations have gained independence—and changed their names. Can you match the current name of the African country (1–10) to its previous name, or names (a–j)?

1. Democratic Republic of the Congo
2. Lesotho
3. Djibouti
4. Burkina Faso
5. Malawi
6. Mali
7. Zimbabwe
8. Benin
9. Tanzania
10. Zambia

a. Upper Volta
b. Southern Rhodesia
c. Sudanese Republic
d. The countries of Tanganyika and Zanzibar
e. Dahomey
f. Zaire
g. French Territory of the Afars and the Issas
h. Northern Rhodesia
i. Basutoland
j. Nyasaland

Answers: (1. f; 2. i; 3. g; 4. a; 5. j; 6. c; 7. b; 8. e; 9. d; 10. h)

MILESTONES

DEBUTS. THE EURO, the official currency of the member countries of the European Union. The euro replaces the French franc and 12 other European currencies. The nations will use common bills and coins, making it easier to do business.

CLONED. DOLLY, a Finn Dorset lamb. She is the first mammal cloned from an adult cell. A six-year-old female sheep gave birth to Dolly on July 5, 1996. This feat by Scottish scientists raises ethical issues.

DIED. PABLO NERUDA, Chilean poet and winner of the 1971 Nobel Prize in Literature. Neruda was appointed ambassador to France by his friend, Salvador Allende, Chile's socialist president. Neruda

died shortly after military officers removed Allende from office in 1973. Protests against the dictatorship took place at his funeral.

KILLED. An estimated **800,000 RWANDANS** in 100 days, beginning in April 1994. The victims, members of a minority ethnic group called the Tutsis, were killed by the majority Hutus. The two groups have been at odds for many years. The immediate cause of the violence was the death of the president of Rwanda, a Hutu, whose plane had been shot down.

OPENED. QINGHAI-TIBET RAILWAY, a 709-mile engineering marvel connecting the Tibetan capital to the rest of China; in Lhasa, in 2006. Critics of the project say it threatens Tibet's environment and will erode Buddhist culture by bringing in ethnic Chinese immigrants. Reaching an altitude of 16,404 feet, the railway is the world's highest.

AP PHOTO/PAUL CLEMENTS

Dolly the sheep

BY THE NUMBERS

1 million Deaths each year from malaria, which is spread by the anopheles mosquito and kills mostly children in Africa

44% Portion of athletes at the 2004 Summer Olympics who are women, up from 38% at the 2000 Games

8.7 million Number of millionaires on the planet, according to a recent study

17 Number of No. 1 hits by the Beatles, tied with Elvis for the most No. 1 hits by any single act

98 Number of minutes it took *Sputnik*, the first artificial satellite, to orbit Earth

MICHAEL ROUGIER/TIME & LIFE PICTURES/GETTY IMAGES

Sputnik

1,888 The estimated number of languages spoken in Africa

5 The number of current Communist states (China, Vietnam, Laos, Cuba, and North Korea)

CRITICAL THINKING

1. **Finding the Main Idea** What are the supporting details the writer uses in "Meltdown!" to get across the point that global warming is taking place?

2. **Inferring** Based on the information in the "Milestone" about Pablo Neruda, where do you think the poet stood politically?

REFERENCE PAGES

Contents

Mini Almanac	R1
Foldables	R6
Skills Handbook	R12
Primary Sources & Literature Library	R32
English/Spanish Glossary	R58
Index	R83
Acknowledgements and Photo Credits	R104

MINI ALMANAC

*A*n almanac is a book or table that contains a variety of statistical, tabular, or general information. The most common almanacs in history have been those that kept astronomical data or that gave weather predictions and related advice to farmers. In agricultural societies it was important to keep accounts of natural phenomena so that farmers would have an idea of when to plant and harvest their crops. Ancient Egyptians carved their almanacs on sticks of wood and called them "fingers of the sun." The first printed almanac was prepared in Europe in 1457. *The Old Farmer's Almanac* has been published continuously since 1792. Because almanacs are compact and concise, they are a popular way of presenting a wide variety of information.

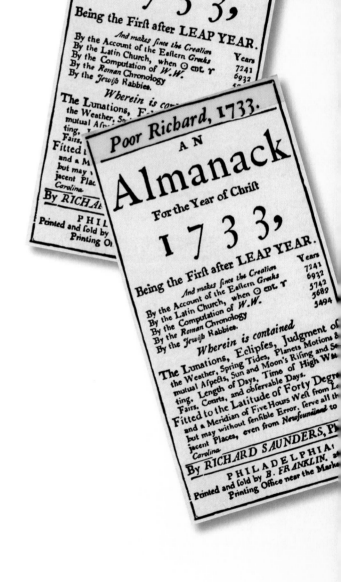

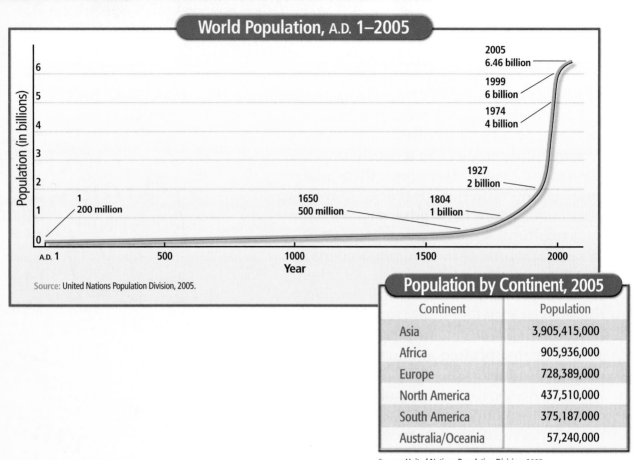

World Population, A.D. 1–2005

Population (in billions)

1 / 200 million

1650 / 500 million

1804 / 1 billion

1927 / 2 billion

1974 / 4 billion

1999 / 6 billion

2005 / 6.46 billion

Year

Source: United Nations Population Division, 2005.

Population by Continent, 2005

Continent	Population
Asia	3,905,415,000
Africa	905,936,000
Europe	728,389,000
North America	437,510,000
South America	375,187,000
Australia/Oceania	57,240,000

Source: United Nations Population Division, 2005.
Note: Populations are estimates.

Life Expectancy

Country	Years
Andorra	83.51
Japan	81.25
France	79.73
Israel	79.46
New Zealand	78.81
United Kingdom	78.54
United States	77.85
Chile	76.77
China	72.58
Egypt	71.29
Brazil	71.97
Russia	67.08
India	64.71
South Africa	42.73
Mozambique	39.82

Source: *The World Factbook,* 2007.

Infant Mortality

Country	Infant Deaths per 1,000 Live Births
South Africa	61
India	55
Egypt	31
Brazil	29
China	23
Russia	15
Chile	9
United States	6
South Korea	6
United Kingdom	5
Canada	5
France	4
Germany	4
Japan	3

Source: *The World Factbook,* 2007.

Most Populous Countries

Country	Population
China	1,311,000,000
India	1,122,000,000
United States	299,000,000
Indonesia	225,000,000
Brazil	187,000,000
Pakistan	166,000,000
Bangladesh	147,000,000
Russia	142,000,000
Nigeria	135,000,000
Japan	128,000,000

Source: *World Population Data Sheet,* 2006.

World's Richest Countries

Country	Gross National Income per Capita (in U.S. dollars)
Luxembourg	65,630
Norway	59,590
Switzerland	54,930
Denmark	47,390
Iceland	46,320

Source: World Development Indicators, 2005, World Bank.

World's Poorest Countries

Country	Gross National Income per Capita (in U.S. dollars)
Congo, Democratic Republic of	120
Liberia	130
Ethiopia	160
Malawi	160
Guinea-Bissau	180

Source: World Development Indicators, 2005, World Bank.

Highest Inflation Rates

Country	Rate of Inflation (percent)
Zimbabwe	976.4
Iraq	50
Guinea	27
Myanmar (Burma)	21.4
Afghanistan	16.3
Venezuela	15.8
Iran	15.8
Serbia	15.5
Malawi	15.1
São Tomé and Príncipe	15

Source: *The World Factbook,* 2007.

Lowest Inflation Rates

Country	Rate of Inflation (percent)
Nauru	−3.6
San Marino	−1.7
Vanuatu	−1.6
Northern Marianas	−0.8
New Caledonia	−0.6
Barbados	−0.5
Dominica	−0.1
Niger	0.2
Japan	0.4
Kiribati	0.5

Source: *The World Factbook,* 2007.

World's Ten Largest Companies, 2006

Rank	Company	Revenue (in millions of U.S. dollars)
1.	Exxon Mobil (United States)	339,938.0
2.	Wal-Mart Stores (United States)	315,654.0
3.	Royal Dutch Shell (Netherlands)	306,731.0
4.	BP (United Kingdom)	267,600.0
5.	General Motors (United States)	192,604.0
6.	Chevron (United States)	189,481.0
7.	DaimlerChrysler (Germany)	186,106.3
8.	Toyota Motor (Japan)	185,805.0
9.	Ford Motor (United States)	177,210.0
10.	ConocoPhillips (United States)	166,683.0

Source: *Fortune 500,* 2006.

Most Livable Countries

Rank	Country	Rank	Country	Rank	Country
1.	Norway	10.	Switzerland	19.	Spain
2.	Iceland	11.	Finland	20.	New Zealand
3.	Australia	12.	Luxembourg	21.	Germany
4.	Ireland	13.	Belgium	22.	Hong Kong (SAR)*
5.	Sweden	14.	Austria	23.	Israel
6.	Canada	15.	Denmark	24.	Greece
7.	Japan	16.	France	25.	Singapore
8.	United States	17.	United Kingdom		
9.	Netherlands	18.	Italy		

Source: United Nations Human Development Index, 2006.
Note: The criteria includes life expectancy, adult literacy, school enrollment, educational attainment, and per capita gross domestic product (GDP).
*Special Administrative Region of China

Highest Adult Literacy Rates

Country	Rate of Literacy (percent)
Andorra	100
Finland	100
Georgia	100
Greenland	100
Liechtenstein	100
Luxembourg	100
Norway	100
Estonia	99.8
Latvia	99.8
Poland	99.8

Source: The World Factbook, 2007.
Note: Literacy is defined by each country.

Lowest Adult Literacy Rates

Country	Rate of Literacy (percent)
Niger	17.6
Burkina Faso	26.6
Sierra Leone	29.6
Benin	33.6
Guinea	35.9
Afghanistan	36
Somalia	37.8
The Gambia	40.1
Senegal	40.2
Iraq	40.4

Source: The World Factbook, 2007.
Note: Literacy is defined by each country.

World Adult Illiteracy by Gender

Source: United Nations, 2004.

Years, by Country, in Which Women Gained the Right to Vote

Year	Country	Year	Country
1893	New Zealand	1945	Italy
1902	Australia	1945	Japan
1913	Norway	1947	Argentina
1918	United Kingdom	1947	Mexico
1918	Canada	1950	India
1919	Germany	1952	Greece
1920	United States	1956	Egypt
1930	South Africa	1963	Kenya
1934	Brazil	1971	Switzerland
1944	France	1980	Iraq

Highest Military Expenditures

Country	Billions of U.S. Dollars per Year	Percentage of Gross Domestic Product (GDP)
United States	518.1	4.1
China	81.5	4.3
France	45.0	2.6
Japan	44.3	1.0
United Kingdom	42.8	2.4
Germany	35.1	1.5
Italy	28.2	1.8
Korea, South	21.1	2.6
India	19.0	2.5
Saudi Arabia	18.0	10.0

Source: *The World Factbook*, 2007.

Nuclear Weapons Capability

Country	Date of First Test
United States	1945
Russia (Soviet Union)	1949
United Kingdom	1952
France	1960
China	1964
India	1974
Pakistan	1998

Source: U.S. Department of State and *TIME* magazine.

Communication Around the World

Country	Daily Newspaper Circulation per 1,000 Persons	Radios per 1,000 Persons	Televisions per 1,000 Persons	Telephone Main Lines per 1,000 Persons	Cellular Phone Subscribers per 1,000 Persons	Estimated Personal Computers per 1,000 Persons
Canada	159	1,047	691	658	417	487
China	23	339	350	209	214	28
Cuba	114	185	242	51	1.6	32
France	201	950	628	566	696	347
Germany	305	948	661	658	785	435
Italy	104	878	494	453	1,018	231
Japan	578	956	785	558	680	383
Mexico	98	330	283	147	254	83
Russia	105	418	421	242	120	89
South Africa	32	338	177	107	364	73
United Kingdom	329	1,432	652	591	841	406
United States	198	2,118	854	621	543	659

Source: *Encyclopædia Britannica Almanac*, 2006.

FOLDABLES™ are three-dimensional, interactive, graphic organizers used to help organize and retain information. Every chapter in your text uses a Foldable to help you identify and learn about the Big Ideas discussed in the chapter. The following pages provide complete folding instructions for the nine different Foldables used throughout your Student Edition text.

Table of Contents

Folded Table or Chart R7

Four-Tab Book R7

Four-Door Book R8

Layered-Look Book R8

Shutter Fold R9

Three-Pocket Book R9

Three-Tab Book R10

Trifold Book R11

Two-Tab Book R11

Basic Foldable Shapes

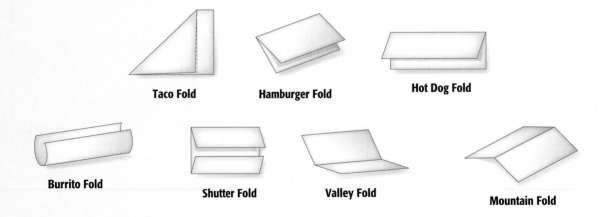

Taco Fold Hamburger Fold Hot Dog Fold

Burrito Fold Shutter Fold Valley Fold Mountain Fold

FOLDABLES

FOLDED TABLE OR CHART

1. Fold the number of vertical columns needed to make the table or chart.
2. Fold the horizontal rows needed to make the table or chart.
3. Label the rows and columns.

Remember: Tables are organized along vertical and horizontal axes, while charts are organized along one axis, either horizontal or vertical.

Table   **Chart**

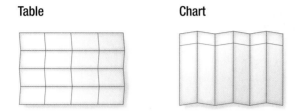

FOUR-TAB BOOK

1. Fold a sheet of paper (8½" × 11") in half like a *hot dog.*
2. Fold this long rectangle in half like a *hamburger.*
3. Fold both ends back to touch the *mountain top* or fold it like an *accordion.*
4. On the side with two *valleys* and one *mountain top,* make vertical cuts through one thickness of paper, forming four tabs.

Use this book for data occurring in fours.

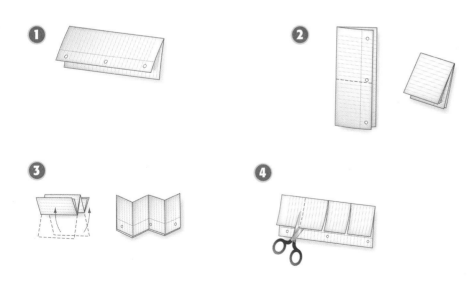

FOUR-DOOR BOOK

1. Make a *shutter fold* using 11" × 17" or 12" × 18" paper.

2. Fold the *shutter fold* in half like a *hamburger.* Crease well.

3. Open the project and cut along the two inside *valley folds.*

4. These cuts will form four doors on the inside of the project.

Use this fold for data occurring in fours. When folded in half like a *hamburger,* a finished *four-door book* can be glued inside a large (11" × 17") *shutter fold* as part of a larger project.

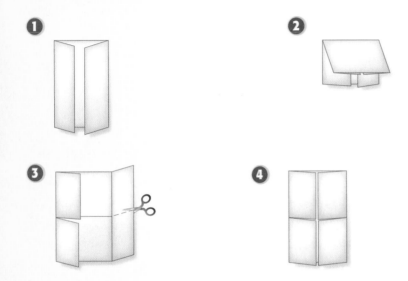

LAYERED-LOOK BOOK

1. Stack two sheets of paper (8½" × 11") so that the back sheet is one inch higher than the front sheet.

2. Bring the bottom of both sheets upward and align the edges so that all of the layers or tabs are the same distance apart.

3. When all tabs are an equal distance apart, fold the papers and crease well.

4. Open the papers and glue them together along the *valley,* or inner center fold, or staple them along the *mountain.*

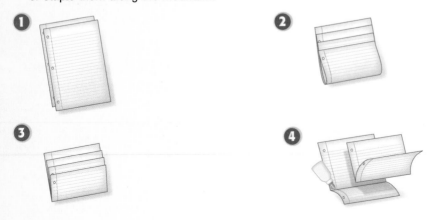

SHUTTER FOLD

1. Begin as if you were going to make a *hamburger* but instead of creasing the paper, pinch it to show the midpoint.

2. Fold the outer edges of the paper to meet at the pinch, or midpoint, forming a *shutter fold.*

Use this book for data occurring in twos. Or, make this fold using 11" × 17" paper and smaller books—such as the half-book, journal, and two-tab book— that can be glued inside to create a large project full of student work.

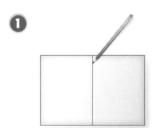

THREE-POCKET BOOK

1. Fold a horizontal sheet of paper (11" × 17") into thirds.

2. Fold the bottom edge up two inches and crease well. Glue the outer edges of the two-inch tab to create three pockets.

3. Label each pocket. Use to hold notes taken on index cards or quarter sheets of paper.

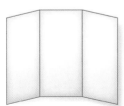
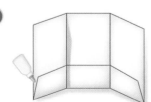

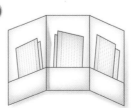

FOLDABLES

FOLDABLES

THREE-TAB BOOK

1. Fold a sheet of paper like a *hot dog.*

2. With the paper horizontal, and the fold of the *hot dog* up, fold the right side toward the center, trying to cover one half of the paper.

Note: If you fold the right edge over first, the final graphic organizer will open and close like a book.

3. Fold the left side over the right side to make a book with three folds.

4. Open the folded book. Place your hands between the two thicknesses of paper and cut up the two *valleys* on one side only. This will form three tabs.

Use this book for data occurring in threes, and for two-part Venn diagrams.

Variation A:
Draw overlapping circles on the three tabs to make a Venn diagram.

Variation B:
Cut each of the three tabs in half to make a six-tab book.

1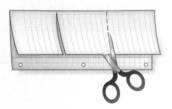

2

3

4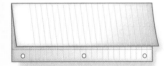

TRIFOLD BOOK

1. Fold a sheet of paper (8½" × 11") into thirds.
2. Use this book as is, or cut into shapes. If the trifold is cut, leave plenty of fold on both sides of the designed shape, so the book will open and close in three sections.

Use this book to make charts with three columns or rows, large Venn diagrams, and reports on data occurring in threes.

  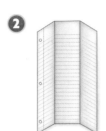

TWO-TAB BOOK

1. Take a *folded book* and cut up the *valley* of the inside fold toward the *mountain top.* This cut forms two large tabs that can be used front and back for writing and illustrations.
2. The book can be expanded by making several of these folds and gluing them side-by-side.

Use this book with data occurring in twos. For example, use it for comparing and contrasting, determining cause and effect, finding similarities and differences, and more.

SKILLS HANDBOOK

TABLE OF CONTENTS

Critical Thinking Skills

Identifying the Main Idea	R13
Determining Cause and Effect	R14
Making Generalizations	R15
Distinguishing Fact from Opinion	R16
Formulating Questions	R17
Analyzing Information	R18
Evaluating Information	R19
Making Inferences	R20
Comparing and Contrasting	R21
Detecting Bias	R22
Synthesizing Information	R23
Drawing Conclusions	R24
Predicting	R25
Problems and Solutions	R26

Social Studies Skills

Reading a Map	R27
Interpreting Graphs	R28
Sequencing Events	R29
Interpreting Political Cartoons	R30
Analyzing Primary Sources	R31

Identifying the Main Idea

Why Learn This Skill?

Finding the main idea in a reading passage will help you see the "big picture" by organizing information and assessing the most important concepts to remember.

Learning the Skill

Follow these steps to learn how to identify the main idea. Then answer the questions below.

1. Determine the setting of the passage.

2. As you read the material, ask: What is the purpose of this passage?

3. Skim the material to identify its general subject. Look at the headings and subheadings.

Evidence indicates that all the victims were ritually killed to consecrate successive stages of the [Pyramid of the Moon's] construction. . . . A wounded foreigner, most likely a prisoner of war, was apparently buried alive with his hands tied behind him. Animals representing mythical powers and military might surrounded him—pumas, a wolf, eagles, a falcon, an owl, and rattlesnakes. . . . Finely crafted offerings included weapons of obsidian and a figurine of solid greenstone, perhaps a war goddess to whom the burial was dedicated. Each subsequent burial was different, but all had the same aim: "Human sacrifice was important to control the people," says Sugiyanga, "to convince them to do what their rulers wanted."

—A. R. Williams, "Pyramid of Death," *National Geographic*, October 2006

4. Identify any details that support a larger idea or issue.

5. Identify the central issue. Ask: What part of the selection conveys the main idea?

Pyramid of the Moon, Mexico ▶

Practicing the Skill

1. Where did this article appear?
2. What is the main idea of the passage?
3. What details support the main idea?

APPLYING THE SKILL

Find an article about the city of Teotihuacán and bring it to class. On a slip of paper, write the main idea of the article and explain why it is important. Display the article and the slip of paper on a bulletin board.

DETERMINING CAUSE AND EFFECT

Why Learn This Skill?

Determining cause and effect involves considering *why* an event occurred. A *cause* is the action or situation that produces an event. What happens as a result of the cause is an effect.

SKILLS HANDBOOK

Learning the Skill

Follow these steps to learn how to identify cause-and-effect relationships. Then answer the questions below.

2. Decide whether one event caused the other. Look for "clue words" such as *because, led to, due to, brought about, produced, as a result of, so that, since,* and *therefore.*

4. Identify the outcomes of events. Remember that some effects have more than one cause, and some causes lead to more than one effect. Also, an effect can become the cause of yet another effect.

Since the aftermath of the 1991 gulf war, nearly four million Kurds have enjoyed complete autonomy in the region of Iraqi Kurdistan—protected from Saddam under a "no-fly zone" north of the 36th parallel and behind the defensive wall of the Kurds' highly disciplined army, the peshmerga. They have held region-wide elections, formed a legislature, and chosen a president, establishing a world entirely apart from Baghdad—a de facto independent state. For the first time in their long history, Kurds are wielding significant political power, successfully negotiating for control over their own military forces and authority over new oil discoveries in their own terrain. Under the federated Iraq being called for by the international community, they would have powers of autonomy that match—or even exceed—what they now enjoy.

—Frank Viviano, "The Kurds in Control," *National Geographic,* January 2006

3. Look for logical relationships between events, such as "She overslept, and then she missed her bus."

1. Identify two or more events or developments.

An Iraqi Kurd ▶

Practicing the Skill

1. Based on the reading, why have the Kurds in Iraq begun to enjoy complete autonomy?
2. What is the cause for this recent autonomy?
3. What is the cause-and-effect chain that could lead to an even greater autonomy and international recognition of this autonomy?

APPLYING THE SKILL

Use library or Internet sources to research Kurdish culture under the rule of Saddam Hussein. Then explain the causes and effects of his dictatorship in a chart like the following:

Causes➞	Kurdish culture➞	Effects

MAKING GENERALIZATIONS

Why Learn This Skill?

Generalizations are judgments that are usually true, based on the facts at hand. If you say, "We have a great soccer team," you are making a generalization. If you also say that your team is undefeated, you are providing evidence to support your generalization.

Learning the Skill

Follow these steps to learn how to make a valid generalization. Then answer the questions below.

1. Identify the subject matter.

Berbers live throughout North Africa, but nowhere has denial of their identity been more systematic than in Morocco, ethnically the most Berber of the region's countries. Although 60 percent of its population claim Berber descent and nearly 40 percent speak one of three Berber languages, Morocco's constitution declares the country part of Arab North Africa, proclaims Arabic as its official language, and makes no mention of the Berbers. This is a legacy of the Arab nationalism that sparked colonial-era independence movements in the region and, in the name of unity, ignored or even suppressed the cultures and languages of non-Arab peoples.

—Jeffrey Taylor, "Among the Berbers," *National Geographic*, January 2005

2. Collect factual information and examples relevant to the topic.

3. Identify similarities among these facts.

4. Use these similarities to form some general ideas about the subject.

Practicing the Skill

1. Based on the facts above, what generalization can you make about the status of Berbers in Morocco?
2. What evidence supports your generalization?

APPLYING THE SKILL

Use library or Internet resources to research the status of Berbers in another country in North Africa. Write a generalization based on what you found. Provide details to support your generalization.

DISTINGUISHING FACT FROM OPINION

Why Learn This Skill?

Distinguishing fact from opinion can help you make reasonable judgments about what others say and write. Facts can be proved by evidence such as records, documents, or historical sources. Opinions are based on people's differing values and beliefs.

SKILLS HANDBOOK

Learning the Skill

Follow these steps to learn how to identify facts and opinions. Then answer the questions below.

After decades of economic progress, Puerto Rico is struggling, and the mainland has both missed this horrific economic slide and contributed to it through benign neglect.

Poverty on the island is rampant. The per capita income is just about half that of the poorest state in the United States. Nearly one-third of the population was unemployed in 2000. And a good quarter of all employment is in government jobs . . .

The bleak picture is set out in a long-overdue, exhaustive study . . . from the Center for the New Economy, a nonpartisan Puerto Rican research group, and the Brookings Institution.

Much of the blame can be put on Washington, which has been tone deaf to the island's needs and has miscalculated where help was needed. . . .

—New York Times, "Puerto Rico, an Island in Distress," October 23, 2006

1. Identify the facts. Ask: Can these statements be proved? Where would I find information to verify them?

2. If a statement can be proved by information from a reliable source, it is factual.

3. Identify opinions by looking for statements of feelings or beliefs. They may contain words like *should, would, could, best, greatest, all, every,* or *always.*

◀ A street vendor, Puerto Rico

Practicing the Skill

1. What are two factual statements in the editorial?
2. Which statements are opinions?

APPLYING THE SKILL

Find a news article and an editorial about the same issue. Identify two facts and two opinions from these sources.

FORMULATING QUESTIONS

Why Learn This Skill?
Asking questions helps you to process information and understand what you read.

Learning the Skill
Follow these steps to learn how to formulate questions.
Then answer the questions below.

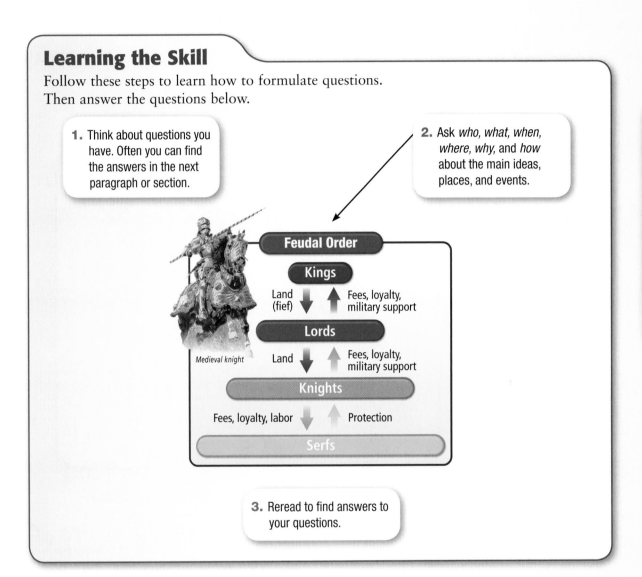

1. Think about questions you have. Often you can find the answers in the next paragraph or section.

2. Ask *who, what, when, where, why,* and *how* about the main ideas, places, and events.

Feudal Order

Kings

Land (fief) ⬇️ ⬆️ Fees, loyalty, military support

Lords

Medieval knight Land ⬇️ ⬆️ Fees, loyalty, military support

Knights

Fees, loyalty, labor ⬇️ ⬆️ Protection

Serfs

3. Reread to find answers to your questions.

Practicing the Skill
1. What is the topic of the chart?
2. Select the parts of the chart you would like to understand better.
3. Formulate two questions about these parts.
4. Where might you find answers to your questions?

APPLYING THE SKILL
Formulate two more questions about the information on this page. Then use Internet sources to find answers to your questions.

ANALYZING INFORMATION

Why Learn This Skill?

The ability to analyze information is important in deciding what you think about a subject. Analysis requires a critical study of what an author or artist is trying to get across.

Learning the Skill

Follow these steps to learn how to analyze information. Then answer the questions below.

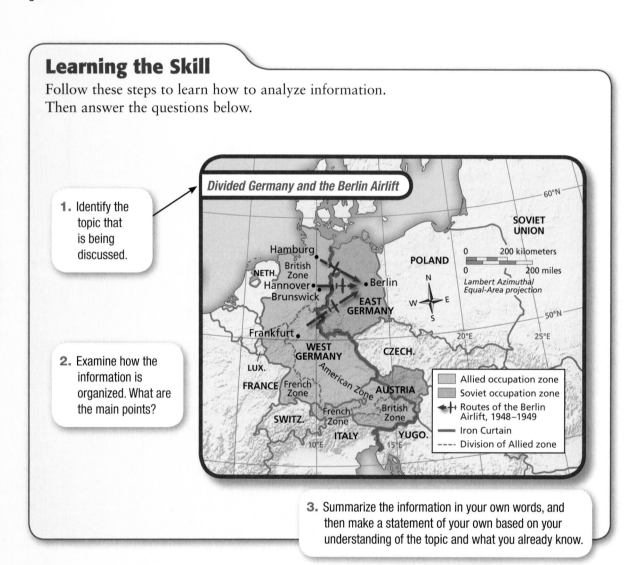

1. Identify the topic that is being discussed.

Divided Germany and the Berlin Airlift

2. Examine how the information is organized. What are the main points?

3. Summarize the information in your own words, and then make a statement of your own based on your understanding of the topic and what you already know.

Practicing the Skill

1. Based on the title, what does the information on the map represent?
2. How is the information organized? What are the main points?
3. Summarize the information from the map, and then provide your analysis based on the information and what you know about the Berlin Airlift.

APPLYING THE SKILL

Find a news story about another airlift operation in history. Analyze the story and use your analysis to summarize the similarities and differences between this airlift and the Berlin Airlift.

EVALUATING INFORMATION

Why Learn This Skill?

We live in an information age. The amount of information available can be overwhelming, and it is sometimes difficult to know when information is true and useful. You need to evaluate what you read and hear to determine the reliability of the information presented.

Learning the Skill

When evaluating information to determine its reliability, ask yourself the following questions as you read:

- Is there bias? In other words, does the source unfairly present just one point of view, ignoring any arguments against it?
- Is the information published in a credible, reliable publication?
- Is the author or speaker identified? Is he or she an authority on the subject?
- Is the information up-to-date?
- Is the information backed up by facts and other sources? Does it seem to be accurate?
- Is it well-written and well-edited? Writing that has errors in spelling, grammar, and punctuation is likely to be careless in other ways as well.

Source A

Oil prices are so high, becuz big oil companys are trying to goug us. Greedy oil executives, are driven up prices to get richer.

—published on an individual's Internet blog

Source B

It's certainly clear that high oil prices aren't dulling demand for energy products. According to the Energy Dept.'s Energy Information Administration (EIA), U.S. demand for gasoline in June was 9.5 million barrels a day, a record.

—*BusinessWeek*, July 7, 2006

Source C

The single biggest factor in the inflation rate last year was from one cause: the skyrocketing prices of OPEC oil. We must take whatever actions are necessary to reduce our dependence on foreign oil—and at the same time reduce inflation.

—President Jimmy Carter, January 23, 1980

Practicing the Skill

Look at the above statements about oil prices. Rank them in order of most reliable to least reliable, and then explain why you ranked them as you did.

APPLYING THE SKILL

Find an advertisement that contains text and bring it to class. In a brief oral presentation, tell the class whether the information in the advertisement is reliable or unreliable and why.

MAKING INFERENCES

Why Learn This Skill?

To *infer* means to evaluate information and arrive at a conclusion. When you make inferences, you "read between the lines," or use clues to figure something out that is not stated directly in the text.

SKILLS HANDBOOK

Learning the Skill

Follow these steps to learn how to make inferences.
Then answer the questions below.

1. Read carefully for stated facts and ideas.

In Bamako I live in a guest house called the Centre d'Acceuil, run by Spanish nuns. The rooms are cheap—a bed, mosquito netting. The bad thing about the Centre d'Acceuil is that although there are ten rooms for rent, there is only one shower. Moreover, it is constantly occupied these days by a young Norwegian, who came here not realizing how hot it gets in Bamako. The African interior is always white-hot. It is a plateau relentlessly bombarded by the rays of the sun, which appears to be suspended directly above the earth here: make one careless gesture, it seems, try leaving the shade, and you will go up in flames….The Norwegian, after several suffocating, sweltering days, decided to leave everything and return home. But he had to wait for the plane. And the only way he could survive until then, he concluded, was by never coming out from under the shower.

—Ryszard Kapuściński, *The Shadow of the Sun*

2. Summarize the information and list important facts.

3. Apply related information that you may already know.

4. Use your knowledge and insight to develop some logical conclusions.

Practicing the Skill

1. What facts are presented in the passage?
2. What can you infer from the presence of mosquito netting?
3. What can you infer about the availability of air transportation in Bamako?

APPLYING THE SKILL

Make inferences based on pictures of Africa you find on the Internet, and write questions based on your inferences. Exchange your pictures and questions with another student and answer each other's questions.

COMPARING AND CONTRASTING

Why Learn This Skill?

When you make comparisons, you determine similarities among ideas, objects, or events. When you contrast, you are noting differences between ideas, objects, or events. Comparing and contrasting are important skills because they help you choose among several possible alternatives.

Learning the Skill

Follow these steps to learn how to compare and contrast. Then answer the questions below.

2. To compare, determine a common area or areas in which comparisons can be drawn. Look for similarities within these areas.

1. Identify or decide what two or more items will be compared and/or contrasted.

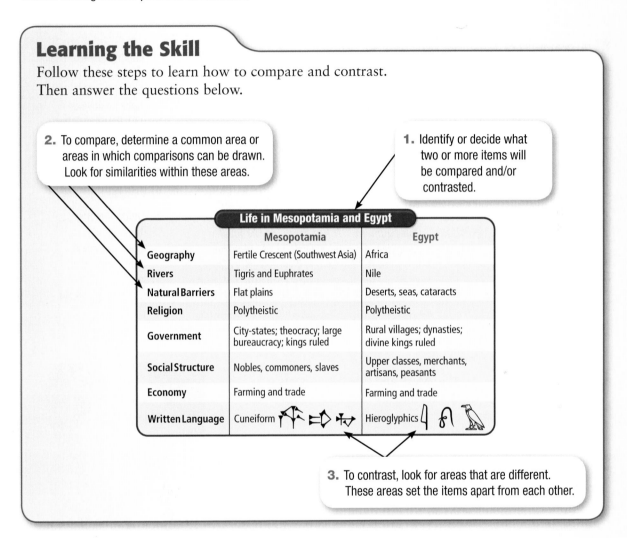

Life in Mesopotamia and Egypt

	Mesopotamia	Egypt
Geography	Fertile Crescent (Southwest Asia)	Africa
Rivers	Tigris and Euphrates	Nile
Natural Barriers	Flat plains	Deserts, seas, cataracts
Religion	Polytheistic	Polytheistic
Government	City-states; theocracy; large bureaucracy; kings ruled	Rural villages; dynasties; divine kings ruled
Social Structure	Nobles, commoners, slaves	Upper classes, merchants, artisans, peasants
Economy	Farming and trade	Farming and trade
Written Language	Cuneiform	Hieroglyphics

3. To contrast, look for areas that are different. These areas set the items apart from each other.

Practicing the Skill

1. What characteristics does the table use to compare and contrast life in Mesopotamia and Egypt?
2. How was life in Mesopotamia similar to life in Egypt?
3. How was life in Mesopotamia different from life in Egypt?

APPLYING THE SKILL

With a partner, research life in the other three early culture hearths—the Indus Valley, the Huang He Valley, and Middle America. Use your information to create a table like the one above. Develop three questions based on your table. Exchange your work with another pair of students and answer the questions based on their table.

DETECTING BIAS

Why Learn This Skill?

Most people have a point of view, or bias. This bias influences the way they interpret and write about events. Recognizing bias helps you judge the accuracy of what you hear or read.

SKILLS HANDBOOK

Learning the Skill

Follow these steps to learn how to detect bias. Then answer the questions below.

3. Determine the author's point of view.

2. Identify statements of fact.

The bourgeoisie . . . has put an end to all feudal, patriarchal, idyllic relations. It has pitilessly torn asunder the motley feudal ties that bound man to his "natural superiors," and has left remaining no other nexus between man and man than naked self-interest, than callous "cash payment." It has drowned the most heavenly ecstasies of religious fervour, of chivalrous enthusiasm . . . in the icy water of egotistical calculation. It has resolved personal worth into exchange value. And in place of the numberless and feasible chartered freedoms, has set up that single, unconscionable freedom—Free Trade. In one word, for exploitation, veiled by religious and political illusions, naked, shameless, direct, brutal exploitation.

—Karl Marx and Friedrich Engels,
The Manifesto of the Communist Party

4. Identify any expression of opinion or emotion. Look for words that have positive or negative overtones for clues about the author's feelings on the topic.

5. Determine how the author's point of view is reflected in the work.

1. Examine the author's identity, especially his or her views and particular interests.

Karl Marx ▶

Practicing the Skill

1. Are there any statements of fact presented in this passage? If so, what are they?
2. What opinions are stated?
3. What evidence of bias do you find? Do the authors think it is a good thing or a bad thing that the bourgeoisie have put an end to feudal ties?

APPLYING THE SKILL

Find written material about a topic of interest to you. Possible sources include editorials, letters to the editor, and political pamphlets. Apply the steps for recognizing bias to the material. Write a paragraph summarizing your findings.

SYNTHESIZING INFORMATION

Why Learn This Skill?

Synthesizing information involves combining information from two or more sources. Information gained from one source often sheds new light upon other information.

Learning the Skill

Follow these steps to learn how to synthesize information.
Then answer the questions that follow.

Source A

"Rome has been rising for 3,000 years," says Darius Arya, an archaeologist and director of the American Institute for Roman Culture. Much of Rome is situated in a floodplain, including the modern city center, known in antiquity as Campus Martius, at a bend of the Tiber River. Although the Romans put up levees, the city still flooded periodically, so they built upward, laying new structures and streets on earlier ones. "It was cost-effective, and it worked," Arya says. "We see the Romans jacking their city up two meters at a time, raising themselves above the water but also burying their past."

—Paul Bennett, "In Rome's Basement," *National Geographic*, July 2006

> **1.** Analyze each source separately to understand its meaning.

> **2.** Determine what information each source adds to the subject.

Source B

Of all the old saws about the Eternal City, at least one remains simply true: dig a deep hole almost anywhere here, and you'll unearth an archaeological artifact or two.

Yet a wave of public and private building projects is suddenly focusing unusual attention on Rome's rich subterranean world as one treasure after another emerges at a steady clip.

"We're walking on the world's largest untapped underground museum," said Maria Antonietta Tomei, a government official responsible for coordinating archaeological digs in Rome.

During the last week reports surfaced that 800 coins from the fourth and fifth centuries BC had been unearthed during the reconstruction of a movie theater near the Trevi Fountain.

—"Treasures galore still emerging from underneath Rome," *Taipei Times (online)*, December 27, 2006

> **3.** Identify points of agreement and disagreement between the sources. Ask: Can Source A give me new information or new ways of thinking about Source B?

> **4.** Find relationships between the information in the sources.

Practicing the Skill

1. What is the main subject of each passage?
2. What does Source A say about the subject?
3. What information does Source B add?
4. Sum up what you have learned from both sources.

APPLYING THE SKILL

Find two sources of information on a topic dealing with archaeological excavations in Rome. What are the main ideas in each? How does each add to your understanding of the topic?

DRAWING CONCLUSIONS

Why Learn This Skill?

A conclusion is a logical understanding that you reach based on details or facts that you read or hear. When you draw conclusions, you use stated information to figure out ideas that are unstated.

Learning the Skill

Follow these steps to draw conclusions. Then answer the questions below.

1. Read carefully for stated facts and ideas.

2. Summarize the information and list important facts.

DARFUR FACTS

1.8 million people currently live in camps or makeshift settlements in Darfur.	Political infighting prevents 250,000 Darfur refugees from receiving humanitarian aid.
215,000 Sudanese have fled to Chad because of continuing violence.	300,000 people in Darfur have been killed or died as a result of the conflict.
The Sudanese government spent $18 million on weapons in 2003.	Between 2000 and 2003, arms and ammunition exports to Sudan from China increased by a factor of 30.
China, Russia, and France are major suppliers of arms to Sudan and permanent members of the UN Security Council.	The UN Security Council agreed to extend an existing arms embargo to the Sudanese government in March 2005.

Source: Amnesty International, Fall 2006.

3. Apply related information that you may already know.

4. Use your knowledge and insight to develop some logical conclusions.

Practicing the Skill

1. Which facts from the table support the conclusion that "the Sudanese government is trying to drive out the people of Darfur"?
2. What conclusion might you draw about why the UN Security Council waited so many years before extending an existing arms embargo to Sudan?

APPLYING THE SKILL

Find an article describing a current conflict in Africa. Use the steps on this page to draw conclusions about the causes of the conflict. Summarize your conclusions in a paragraph.

PREDICTING

Why Learn This Skill?

Predicting future events can be difficult and sometimes risky. The more information you have, however, the more accurate your predictions will be. Making good predictions will help you understand what you read.

Learning the Skill

Follow these steps to learn how to make a prediction.
Then answer the questions below.

1. Gather information about the decision or action.

2. Use your knowledge about history and human behavior to identify what consequences could result.

There is little freedom to disagree with the determinations of the authorities [in South Africa]. There is large scale unemployment here because of the drought and the recession that has hit most of the world's economy. And it is such a time that the authorities have increased the prices of various foodstuffs and also of rents in black townships—measures designed to hit hardest those least able to afford the additional costs. . . .

The authorities have not stopped stripping blacks of their South African citizenship. . . . The South African government is turning us into aliens in the land of our birth.

White South Africans are. . . .scared human beings, many of them; who would not be, if they were outnumbered five to one? Through this lofty body I wish to appeal to my white fellow South Africans to share in building a new society, for blacks are not intent on driving whites into the sea but on claiming only their rightful place in the sun in the land of their birth.

—Bishop Desmond Tutu, speech on apartheid to the United Nations Security Council, October 23, 1984

3. Analyze each consequence by asking: How likely is this to occur?

Practicing the Skill

1. What events do the passage describe?
2. Do you think what the author described changed after his speech?
3. On what do you base this prediction?
4. What occurrences might have an effect on changing these events?
5. What are the possible outcomes for all involved, of the appeal proposed by the author?

APPLYING THE SKILL

Find a newspaper or magazine article that describes the current state of politics, economy, or society in South Africa. Analyze the article, and describe how the people of South Africa are trying to solve the problem. Predict three consequences of the actions described. On what do you base your prediction?

PROBLEMS AND SOLUTIONS

Why Learn This Skill?

Suppose you are not doing well in basketball. You wonder why you cannot do better since you always go to practice, try your best, and pay attention to the coach's instructions. In order to improve a situation such as this one, you need to identify a specific problem and then take actions to solve it.

SKILLS HANDBOOK

Learning the Skill

Follow these steps to help you through the problem-solving process. Then answer the questions below.

1. Identify the problem.

2. Gather information.

3. List possible solutions.

In just two decades . . . China's Northeast has gone from dynamo to dinosaur, tracing virtually the opposite trajectory of the country's thriving southern coastal regions. . . . The region's industrial production has sagged to less than 9 percent of national output, while its heavy reliance on state-owned enterprises—once a blessing, now a curse—has made market-oriented reforms seem like all shock and no therapy. The landscape left behind is . . . [t]housands of obsolete state-run factories, millions of laid-off workers, a growing gap between rich and poor, rampant corruption, deadly human and environmental disasters. . . .

Hoping to reverse this dangerous slide, Beijing has so far spent 7.5 billion dollars to rehabilitate the region, closing or privatizing old state-owned factories while retraining workers for industries more suited to the 21st century. . . . The real key, however, will be foreign investment. The region that once symbolized China's drive for self-sufficiency is now unabashedly courting foreign investors. . . . It is too early to tell whether the rust belt can truly be revitalized.

—Brook Larmer, "The Manchurian Mandate," *National Geographic*, September 2006

4. Consider the advantages and disadvantages of each solution.

5. Choose the best solution to your problem and carry it out.

6. Evaluate the effectiveness of the solution.

Practicing the Skill

1. What problem does the writer present in this selection?
2. What options are available to solve this problem? Can you think of any other options?
3. Explain the solutions implemented according to the selection. Were they successful? How do you determine this?

APPLYING THE SKILL

Select a current political problem that needs to be solved. The problem can be anything from the conflict between Israel and Palestine to the agreement on a constitution by all members of the European Union. Create a presentation in which you identify the problem, list options with their advantages and disadvantages, choose a solution, and evaluate the chosen solution.

READING A MAP

Why Learn This Skill?

Maps can direct you down the street, across the county, or around the world. An ordinary map holds all kinds of information. Learn the map's code, and you can read it like a book.

Learning the Skill

Follow these steps to learn how to read a map. Then answer the questions below.

5. Determine the relationship between map measurements and actual distances on Earth by using the scale bar.

1. Look at the title of the map—it tells you what kind of information the map shows.

2. Study the map key to determine the meaning of the symbols, colors, and lines used on the map.

6. Use lines of latitude and longitude to determine the absolute location of places on the map.

3. Read the labels on the map to learn where things such as cities, groups of people, and physical features are located.

4. Find the compass rose to learn the orientation of the map.

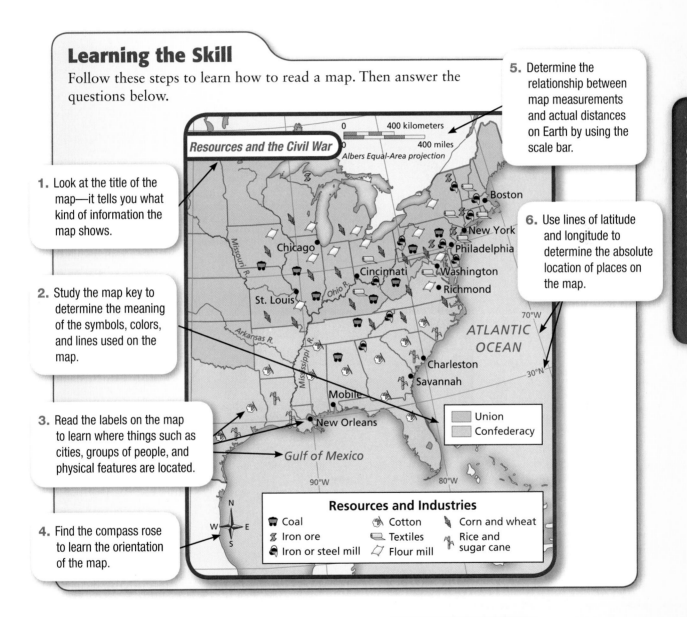

Resources and the Civil War
Albers Equal-Area projection

| | Union |
| | Confederacy |

Resources and Industries

- 🪨 Coal
- ⚒ Iron ore
- ⚙ Iron or steel mill
- 🌱 Cotton
- 📦 Textiles
- 🌾 Flour mill
- 🌿 Corn and wheat
- 🌾 Rice and sugar cane

Practicing the Skill

1. What kinds of resources enabled the North to triumph over the South?
2. Where are most cities located? Why?

APPLYING THE SKILL

Choose a map from your world history text and work with a partner to write three questions that can be answered by reading the map. Then exchange questions with another pair and answer each other's questions.

INTERPRETING GRAPHS

Why Learn This Skill?

Graphs are visual representations of statistical data. Large amounts of information can be condensed when presented in a graph. Studying graphs allows readers to see relationships clearly. **Bar graphs** use bars of different lengths to compare different quantities. **Circle graphs** show the relationship of parts to a whole as percentages.

Learning the Skill

Follow these steps to learn how to interpret graphs. Then answer the questions that follow.

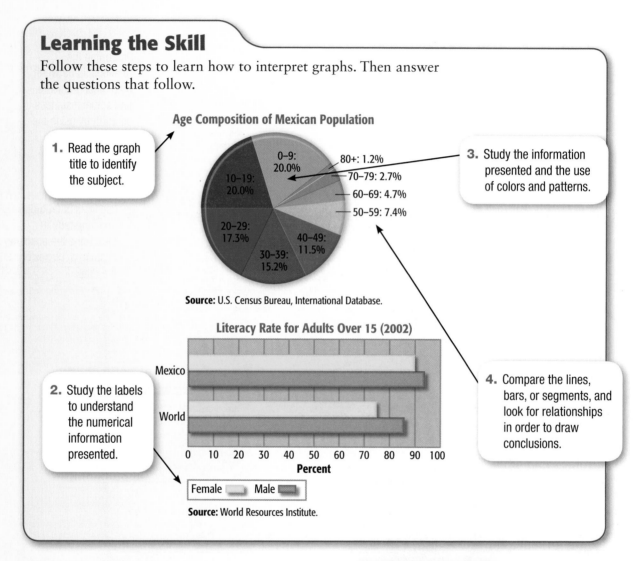

1. Read the graph title to identify the subject.

Age Composition of Mexican Population

0–9: 20.0%
10–19: 20.0%
20–29: 17.3%
30–39: 15.2%
40–49: 11.5%
50–59: 7.4%
60–69: 4.7%
70–79: 2.7%
80+: 1.2%

Source: U.S. Census Bureau, International Database.

3. Study the information presented and the use of colors and patterns.

2. Study the labels to understand the numerical information presented.

Literacy Rate for Adults Over 15 (2002)

Mexico

World

0   10   20   30   40   50   60   70   80   90   100
Percent

Female   Male

Source: World Resources Institute.

4. Compare the lines, bars, or segments, and look for relationships in order to draw conclusions.

Practicing the Skill

1. How does the literacy rate in Mexico compare to literacy in the rest of the world?
2. What percentage of the Mexican people are under 20 years of age?
3. What general population trends in Mexico do these two graphs show?

APPLYING THE SKILL

Poll your classmates about countries they would like to visit. Use the data to design and draw a line, bar, or circle graph.

SEQUENCING EVENTS

Why Learn This Skill?

Sequencing involves placing facts in the order in which they occurred. Sequencing helps you deal with large quantities of information in an understandable way. In studying history, sequencing can help you understand cause-and-effect relationships among events. This in turn helps analysts to predict outcomes of various events or policies.

Learning the Skill

Follow these steps to sequence events.
Then answer the questions below.

When the new moon of the month Shawwal appeared in the same year [1st September 1326], the Hijaz caravan left Damascus and I set off along with it. At Bosra the caravans usually halt for four days so that any who have been detained at Damascus by business affairs may make up on them. Thence they go to the Pool of Ziza, where they stop for a day, and then through al-Lajjun to the Castle of Karak. Karak, which is also called "The Castle of the Raven," is one of the most marvellous, impregnable, and celebrated of fortresses. . . . The caravan stopped for four days at a place called ath-Thaniya outside Karak, where preparations were made for entering the desert.

—Ibn Battuta, *Travels in Asia and Africa 1325–1354*

1. Look for dates or clue words such as *in 1920, later that year, first, then,* and *in the late eighteenth century.*

2. Arrange facts in the order in which they occurred.

3. Consider using an organizational tool such as a time line, which makes it easy to see the chronology, as well as any cause-and-effect relationships, between events.

Practicing the Skill

1. What dates or clue words in this selection can help determine the sequence of events being described?
2. Fill in a time line like the one below to show the sequence of events as described in the selection.

First Event   Final Event

APPLYING THE SKILL

Find a newspaper or magazine article about a world event. Sequence the information presented in the article in a time line or chart.

INTERPRETING POLITICAL CARTOONS

Why Learn This Skill?

Political cartoonists use art to express opinions. Their work appears in newspapers, magazines, books, and on the Internet. Political cartoons usually focus on public figures, political events, or economic or social conditions. They can give you a summary of an event or circumstance and the artist's opinion in a quick, entertaining manner.

Learning the Skill

To interpret a political cartoon, follow these steps.
Then answer the questions below.

2. Identify the characters or people shown. They may be caricatures, or unrealistic drawings that exaggerate the characters' physical features.

1. Read the title, caption, or conversation balloons. They help you identify the subject of the cartoon.

3. Identify any symbols shown. Symbols are things that stand for something else. Commonly recognized symbols may not be labeled. Unusual symbolism will be labeled.

5. Identify the cartoonist's purpose. What statement or idea is he or she trying to get across? Decide if the cartoonist wants to persuade, criticize, or just make people think.

4. Examine the actions in the cartoon—what is happening and why?

"...after climbing a great hill, one only finds that there are many more hills to climb."
—Nelson Mandela in "The Long Walk to Freedom"

Practicing the Skill

1. Who is depicted in the cartoon? What is he doing?
2. What do the stones along the path represent?
3. What overall message do you think the cartoonist is trying to send?

APPLYING THE SKILL

Bring a newspaper or news magazine to class. With a partner, analyze the message in each political cartoon that you find.

ANALYZING PRIMARY SOURCES

Why Learn This Skill?

An eyewitness account of a place or event is a primary source. The advantage of a primary source is that it contains firsthand knowledge. Primary sources may include diaries, letters, memoirs, interviews with eyewitnesses, photographs, news articles, and legal documents. Often they provide detailed accounts of events, but reflect only one perspective. For this reason, you must examine as many sources as possible before drawing any conclusions.

Learning the Skill

Follow these steps to learn how to analyze a primary source. Then answer the questions below.

The festivals generally conclude with an amusement unknown in Europe—a combat between two elephants. . . .

A wall of earth is raised three or four feet wide and five or six high. The two ponderous beasts meet one another face to face, on opposite sides of the wall, each having a couple of riders. . . . The riders animate the elephants either by soothing words, or by chiding them as cowards, and urge them on with their heels, until the poor creatures approach the wall and are brought to the attack. The shock is tremendous, and it appears surprising that they ever survive the dreadful wounds . . . inflicted with their teeth, their heads, and their trunks. . . .

The fight of these noble creatures is attended with much cruelty. . . . [S]ome of the riders are trodden underfoot; and killed on the spot. . . [T]his amusement . . . does not always end with the death of a rider: . . . some spectators are knocked down and trampled upon. . . .

—François Bernier, *Travels in the Mogul Empire 1656–1668*

1. Identify the author of the source. Note any biases or opinions expressed by the author or creator of the source.

2. Identify when and where the document was written.

3. Read the document for its content and try to answer the five "W" questions: Who is it about? What is it about? When did it happen? Where did it happen? Why did it happen?

4. Determine what kind of information may be missing from the primary source.

Practicing the Skill

1. How can you tell the source contains firsthand knowledge of the elephant fight?
2. Who has the author's sympathy? How can you tell?
3. What information from the source did you find valuable? What about the topic of elephant fights would you still like to learn?

APPLYING THE SKILL

Find a firsthand account of a recent event or a historical event. Evaluate its validity and usefulness as a primary source.

PRIMARY SOURCES & LITERATURE LIBRARY

CONTENTS

An Egyptian Father's Advice to His Son	R34
The Burning of Books	R35
Plague in Athens	R35
From the *Iliad*	R36
Muhammad's Wife Remembers the Prophet	R38
A Woman May Need to Have the Heart of a Man	R39
The Buddha's Sermon	R39
Five Poems	R40
A Reformation Debate	R42
The Silk Industry in China	R43
Declaration of the Rights of Woman and the Female Citizen	R43
From *Candide*	R44

Imperial Decree to Free the Serfs	R46
The Unfortunate Situation of Working Women	R47
The Impact of British Rule in India	R47
From *Shooting an Elephant*	R48
Over the Top—World War I	R50
Gandhi Takes the Path of Civil Disobedience	R51
The Holocaust—The Camp Victims	R51
From *A Room of One's Own*	R52
Progress Never Stops	R54
An Ideal for Which I Am Prepared to Die	R55
China's Gilded Age	R55
Civil Peace, from *Girls at War and Other Stories*	R56

LIBRARY

What Is It and How Do I Use It?

The primary sources as defined here are written testimony or documents from a particular era in history or about an important development. The source may be the writings of a noted historian or political leader, or it may be from the diary of someone who lived at the time and recorded the events of the day.

Reading primary sources is an excellent way to understand how and why people believed and acted as they did in the past. While many people might have written down their stories or beliefs, the sources chosen here are from witnesses who were close to events or especially sensitive to them.

Checking Your Sources

When you read primary or secondary sources, you should analyze them to determine if they are dependable or reliable. Historians usually prefer primary sources to secondary sources, but both can be reliable or unreliable, depending on the following factors.

Time Span

With primary sources, it is important to consider how much time passed from the date the event occurred to the date that the primary source was written. Generally, the longer the time span between the event and the account, the less reliable the account is. As time passes, people often forget details and fill in gaps with events that never took place. Although we like to think we remember things exactly as they happened, the fact is, we often remember them very differently than they occurred.

Reliability

Another factor to consider when evaluating a primary source is the writer's background and reliability. When reading a historical document, try to determine if the statements and information can be proved. If the information can be verified as true by independent sources, then it probably is fact.

Opinions

When evaluating a primary source, you should also decide whether or not the account has been influenced by emotion, opinion, or exaggeration. Writers sometimes distort the truth to suit their personal purposes. Ask yourself: Why did the person write the account? Do any words or expressions reveal the author's emotions or opinions? Again, you may wish to compare the account with another primary source document about the same event. If the two accounts differ, ask yourself why they differ and then conduct your own outside research to determine which account can be verified by other authoritative sources.

Interpreting Primary Sources

To help you analyze a primary source, use the following steps:

- *Examine the origins of the document.*
  You need to determine if it is indeed a primary source.

- *Find the main ideas.*
  Read the document and summarize the main ideas in your own words.

- *Reread the document.*
  Difficult ideas and historical documents are not always easily understood on the first reading.

- *Use a variety of resources.*
  Use a dictionary, an encyclopedia, and maps to further your understanding of the topic. These resources are tools to help you discover new ideas and knowledge and check the validity of sources.

▲ Prussian soldiers

LIBRARY

▲ Polish children at Auschwitz

The First Civilizations and Empires

Prehistory–A.D. 500

PRIMARY SOURCES

LIBRARY

Reader's Dictionary

fraud: deception

imperial: relating to the empire or the emperor

archives: official documents that are preserved for historical or public use

discourse: discussion

decree: an order that has the force of law

calamity: distress or misery

AN EGYPTIAN FATHER'S ADVICE TO HIS SON

Upper-class Egyptians enjoyed compiling collections of wise sayings to provide guidance for leading an upright and successful life. This excerpt from The Instruction of the Vizier Ptah-hotep dates from around 2450 B.C.

Then he said to his son:

If you are a leader commanding the affairs of the many, seek out for yourself every good deed, until it may be that your own affairs are without wrong. Justice is great, and it is lasting; it has been disturbed since the time of him who made it, whereas there is punishment for him who passes over its laws. Wrongdoing has never brought its undertaking into port. It may be that it is **fraud** that gains riches, but the strength of justice is that it lasts . . . .

If you are a man of standing who is pleasing to god, if he is correct and inclines toward your ways and listens to your instruction, while his manners in your house are fitting, and if he takes care of your property as it should be, seek out for him every useful action. He is your son, . . . you should not cut your heart off from him.

If he [the son] goes astray and does not carry out your instruction, so that his manners in your household are wretched, and he rebels against all that you say, while his mouth runs on in the most wretched talk, quite apart from his experience, while he possesses nothing, you should cast him off: he is not your son at all. He was not really born to you . . . He is one whom god has condemned in the very womb.

◄This rendition of an Egyptian father teaching his son is on the wall of the Tomb of Sennedjem.

THE BURNING OF BOOKS

L i Su was a chief minister of the first Qin emperor. A follower of Legalism, he hoped to eliminate all rival theories of government.

Your servant suggests that all books in the **imperial archives,** save the memoirs of Qin, be burned. All persons in the empire, except members of the Academy of Learned Scholars, in possession of the Book of Odes, the Book of History, and **discourses** of the hundred philosophers [including Confucius] should take them to the local governors and have them burned. Those who dare to talk to each other about the Book of Odes and the Book of History should be executed and their bodies exposed in the market place. Anyone referring to the past to criticize the present should, together with all members of his family, be put to death. Officials who fail to report cases that have come under their attention are equally guilty. After thirty days from the time of issuing the **decree,** those who have not destroyed their books are to be branded and sent to build the Great Wall. Books not to be destroyed will be those on medicine and pharmacy, agriculture and arboriculture [the cultivation of trees and shrubs]. People wishing to pursue learning should take the officials as their teachers.

◀ Chinese scroll

PLAGUE IN ATHENS

T hucydides (471–c. 400 B.C.) is regarded as the first scientific historian. In his account of the plague that broke out in Athens in 430 B.C., Thucydides simply presents the facts, describing the disease's symptoms and impact on the city itself.

. . . Externally, the body was not so very warm to the touch; it was not pale, but reddish, livid, and breaking out in small blisters and ulcers. But internally it was consumed by such a heat that the patients could not bear to have on them the lightest coverings or linen sheets. . . .

The Athenians suffered further hardships owing to the crowding into the city of the people from the country districts; and this affected the new arrivals especially. For since no houses were available for them and they had to live in huts that were stifling in the hot season, they perished in wild disorder. Bodies of dying men lay one upon another, and half-dead people rolled about in the streets and, in their longing for water, near all the fountains. . . . The **calamity** which weighed upon them was so overpowering that men became careless of all law, sacred as well as profane. And the customs which they had hitherto observed regarding burial were all thrown into confusion, and they buried their dead each one as he could. . . .

LIBRARY

DOCUMENT-BASED QUESTIONS

1. **Evaluating** Does any part of the Egyptian father's advice have value today for sons or daughters? Be specific and support your answer.
2. **Drawing Conclusions** Why did Li Su think that burning books would eliminate all rival theories of government?
3. **Listing** What hardships did newcomers to Athens face during the time of the plague?

The First Civilizations and Empires

Prehistory–A.D. 500

WORLD LITERATURE

LIBRARY

Homer ▶

About the Author

Homer is probably one of the best known figures to have emerged from Greek antiquity. Writing in the eighth century B.C., Homer's most famous works are the *Iliad* and the *Odyssey*. These works mark the beginnings of Greek literature and are used as models even in contemporary work. The *Iliad* is the story of the Trojan War, and the *Odyssey* recounts the challenges of one Greek hero, Odysseus (also known as "Ulysses"), in returning to his homeland.

Reader's Dictionary

covenant: a binding agreement or promise
spoil: to plunder from an enemy in war

FROM THE ILIAD

By Homer, translated by Samuel Butler

*I*n the Iliad, *Hektor was the Trojans' hero and son of King Priam. Achilles, the Greeks' hero, was the son of Peleus. Hektor killed Achilles' friend Patroklos, and Achilles was determined to avenge the death.*

Hektor was first to speak. "I will no longer flee you, son of Peleus," said he, "as I have been doing hitherto. . . .[Let] me either slay or be slain, for I am in the mind to face you. Let us, then, give pledges to one another by our gods; . . . [that if] I take your life, I am not to treat your dead body in any unseemly fashion, but when I have stripped you of your armor, I am to give up your body to the Achaeans, And do you likewise."

Achilles glared at him and answered, "Fool . . . [there] can be no **covenants** between men and lions, wolves and lambs can never be of one mind, but hate each other out and out. . . . Therefore there can be no understanding between you and me . . . till one or other shall fall. . . . You have no more chance, and Pallas Athena will forthwith vanquish you by my spear: you shall now pay me in full for the grief you have caused me on account of my comrades whom you have killed in battle."

He poised his spear as he spoke and hurled it. Hektor saw it coming and avoided it; he watched it and crouched down so that it flew over his head and stuck in the ground beyond; Athena then snatched it up and gave it back to Achilles without Hektor's seeing her; Hektor thereon said . . . "You have missed your aim, Achilles. . . . [And] now for your own part avoid my spear if you can—would that you might receive the whole of it into

◀ Athena

your body; if you were once dead the Trojans would find the war an easier matter, for it is you who have harmed them most."

He poised his spear as he spoke and hurled it. His aim was sure for he hit the middle of Achilles' shield, but the spear rebounded from it, and did not pierce it. Hektor was angry when he saw that the weapon had sped from his hand in vain, and stood there in dismay for he had no second spear. . . . [Then] he said to himself, "Alas! The gods have lured me on to my destruction. . . . [Death] is now indeed exceedingly near at hand and there is no way out of it. . . . My doom has come upon me; let me not then die ingloriously and without a struggle, but let me first do some great thing that shall be told among men hereafter."

As he spoke he drew the keen blade that hung so great and strong by his side, and gathering himself together he sprang on Achilles . . . . Achilles mad with rage darted towards him. . . . He eyed [Hektor's] fair flesh over and over to see where he could best wound it, but all was protected by the goodly armor of which Hektor had **spoiled** Patroklos after he had slain him, save only the throat where the collar-bones divide the neck from the shoulders, and this is the quickest place for the life-breath to escape: here then did Achilles strike him as he was coming on towards him, and the point of his spear went right through the fleshy part of the neck, but it did not sever his windpipe so that he could still speak. Hektor fell headlong, and Achilles vaunted over him saying, "Hektor, you deemed that you should come off scatheless when you were spoiling Patroklos. . . . Fool that you were: for I, his comrade, mightier far than he, was still left behind him at the ships, and now I have laid you low. The Achaeans shall give him all due funeral rites, while dogs and vultures shall work their will upon yourself."

Then Hektor said, as the life-breath ebbed out of him, "I pray you . . . , let not dogs devour me at the ships of the Achaeans, but accept the rich treasure of gold and bronze which my father and mother will offer you, and send my body home, that the Trojans and their wives may give me my dues of fire when I am dead."

Achilles glared at him and answered, "Dog . . . [though] Priam . . . should bid them offer me your weight in gold, even so your mother shall never lay you out and make lament over the son she bore, but dogs and vultures shall eat you utterly up."

Hektor with his dying breath then said, "I know you what you are, and was sure that I should not move you, for your heart is hard as iron. . . ."

When he had thus said the shrouds of death's final outcome enfolded him, whereon his life-breath went out of him and flew down to the house of Hades, lamenting its sad fate that it should enjoy youth and strength no longer.

LIBRARY

DOCUMENT-BASED QUESTIONS

1. **Describing** How does Achilles plan to avenge his friend Patroklos' death beyond killing Hektor?
2. **Explaining** Explain Achilles' concern with Hektor's armor.
3. **Interpreting** What does Hektor's last request reveal about Greek attitudes towards death?

Applications Activity
Outline a story for a modern epic. Who would be your hero and why?

New Patterns of Civilization

A.D. 400–1500

PRIMARY SOURCES

Reader's Dictionary

cobble: repair shoes

accrue: to happen as a direct result of some other action

err: make mistakes

remonstrate: to scold or reproach

lamentation: an expression of mourning

LIBRARY

▲ Woman playing a lute

MUHAMMAD'S WIFE REMEMBERS THE PROPHET

What kind of man was Muhammad that he could achieve such profound changes in Arab civilization? This description comes from his wife, Ayesha, the daughter of Abu Bakr.

When Ayesha was questioned about Muhammad she used to say:

He was a man just such as yourselves. He laughed often and smiled much. He would mend his clothes and **cobble** his shoes. He used to help me in my household duties; but what he did oftenest was to sew. If he had the choice between two matters, he would choose the easiest, so long as no sin could **accrue** therefrom. He never took revenge excepting where the honor of God was concerned. When angry with anyone, he would say, "What hath taken such a one that he should soil his forehead in the mud."

His humility was shown by his accepting the invitation even of slaves. . . . He would say: "I sit at meals as a servant does and I eat like a servant. For I really am a servant."

Muhammad hated nothing more than lying. Whenever he knew that any of his followers had **erred** in this respect, he would hold himself aloof from them until he was assured of their repentance.

He did not speak rapidly, running the words into one another, but enunciated each syllable distinctly, so that what he said was imprinted in the memory of everyone who heard him.

He used to stand for such a long time at his prayers that his legs would swell. When **remonstrated,** he said: "What! Shall I not behave as a thankful servant should?"

He refused to accept presents that had been offered as alms. Neither would he allow anyone in his family to use what had been brought as alms. "For," said he, "alms are the impurity of mankind."

A WOMAN MAY NEED TO HAVE THE HEART OF A MAN

Christine de Pizan was widowed at age 25. She supported her three children by copying manuscripts, compiling a manual of instructions for knights, and writing books. The following is from her 1405 work, The Treasure of the City of Ladies.

It is the responsibility of every baron to spend the least possible time at his manors and his own estate, for his duties are to bear arms, to attend the court of his prince and to travel. Now, his lady stays behind and must take his place. . . . Her men should be able to rely on her for all kinds of protection in the absence of their lord. . . . She ought to know how to use weapons and be familiar with everything that pertains to them, so that she may be ready to command her men if the need arises. She should know how to launch an attack or to defend against one.

In addition she will do well to be a very good manager of the estate. . . . She will busy herself around the house; she will find plenty of orders to give. She will have the animals brought in at the right time [and] take care how the shepherd looks after them. . . .

In the winter-time, she will have her men cut her willow groves and make vine props to sell in the season. She will never let them be idle. . . . She will employ her women . . . to attend to the livestock, . . . [and] to weed the courtyards. . . . There is a great need to run an estate well, and the one who is most diligent and careful about it is more than wise and ought to be highly praised.

◀ A wandering Buddhist sage

THE BUDDHA'S SERMON

Siddhartha Gautama, the Buddha, gave sermons in India, which were written down after 250 B.C. An excerpt from one of these follows.

1. Now this, O monks, is the noble truth of pain: birth is painful, old age is painful, sickness is painful, death is painful, sorrow, **lamentation,** dejection, and despair are painful. Contact with unpleasant things is painful, not getting what one wishes is painful. In short the five khandhas of grasping are painful.
2. Now this, O monks, is the noble truth of the cause of pain: that craving which leads to rebirth, combined with pleasure and lust, finding pleasure here and there, namely, the craving for passion, the craving for existence, the craving for non-existence.
3. Now this, O monks, is the noble truth of the cessation of pain: the cessation without a remainder of that craving, abandonment, forsaking, release, non-attachment.
4. Now this, O monks, is the noble truth of the way that leads to the cessation of pain: this is the noble Eightfold Path. . . .

DOCUMENT-BASED QUESTIONS

1. **Describing** According to Ayesha, what kind of man was Muhammad? Did he behave like a ruler?
2. **Identifying** What are some of the duties and responsibilities of the medieval gentlewoman, according to Christine de Pizan's account?
3. **Summarizing** According to the Buddha, what is the cause of pain?

New Patterns of Civilization

A.D. 400–1500

WORLD LITERATURE

◀ Li Bo

About the Author

Li Bo was born in A.D. 701 in western China. People began praising his beautiful poems even before he reached adulthood. Throughout his life he traveled extensively in China, amazing people with his ability to compose insightful, touching poems. He wrote about the world around him, the people he met, and the emotions he felt. By the time of his death in A.D. 762, he was regarded as one of China's greatest poets, a distinction he still holds today.

Reader's Dictionary

sparse: few and scattered

thrush: a type of small to medium sized bird that is an excellent singer

brooklet: a small brook or creek

FIVE POEMS

By Li Bo

In the following poems, Li Bo interprets parting from a friend, life as a journey, and his experience with his homeland.

Taking Leave of a Friend

Blue mountains to the north of the walls,
  White river winding about them;
Here we must make separation
And go out through a thousand miles of
  dead grass.

Mind like a floating wide cloud,
Sunset like the parting of old acquaintances
Who bow over their clasped hands at a
  distance.
Our horses neigh to each other as we are
  departing.

Clearing at Dawn

The fields are chill, the **sparse** rain has
  stopped;
The colours of Spring teem on every side.
With leaping fish the blue pond is full;
With singing **thrushes** the green boughs
  droop.
The flowers of the field have dabbled their
  powdered cheeks;
The mountain grasses are bent level at the
  waist.
        By the bamboo stream the
          last fragment of cloud
        Blown by the wind
          slowly scatters away.

◀ This painting is titled *Spring Dawn Over Elixir Terrace.*

LIBRARY

Hard Is the Journey

Gold vessels of fine wines,
thousands a gallon,
Jade dishes of rare meats,
costing more thousands,
I lay my chopsticks down,
no more can banquet,
And draw my sword and stare
wildly about me:

Ice bars my way to cross
the Yellow River,
Snows from dark skies to climb
the T'ai-hang Mountains!

At peace I drop a hook
into a **brooklet,**
At once I'm in a boat
but sailing sunward . . .

(Hard is the Journey,
Hard is the Journey,
So many turnings,
And now where am I?)

So when a breeze breaks waves,
bringing fair weather,
I set a cloud for sails,
cross the blue oceans!

Listening to a Flute in Yellow Crane Pavilion

I came here a wanderer
thinking of home
remembering my far away Ch'ang-an.
And then, from deep in Yellow Crane
     Pavilion,
I heard a beautiful bamboo flute
play "Falling Plum Blossoms."
It was late spring in a city by the river.

▲ *Landscape of the Four Seasons*
by Shen shih-Ch'ung

In the Mountains on a Summer Day

Gently I stir a white feather fan,
With open shirt sitting in a green wood.
I take off my cap and hang it on a jutting
     stone;
A wind from the pine-tree trickles on my
     bare head.

DOCUMENT-BASED QUESTIONS

1. **Identifying** What detail in *Taking Leave of a Friend* reveals a custom in Li Bo's times?

2. **Interpreting** What is the meaning of the last line of *Listening to a Flute in Yellow Crane Pavilion?*

3. **Drawing Conclusions** Li Bo describes beauty and peace and luxury in *Hard Is the Journey*. Why does he call the journey "hard"?

Applications Activity
Write a poem describing your hometown. Make sure to include a description of something unique to that area.

The Early Modern World

1400–1800

PRIMARY SOURCES

Reader's Dictionary

contention: point made in an argument
Scripture: passage from the Bible
revered: honored or respected
hemp: a fiber from the mulberry bush
imprescriptible: cannot be taken away by law

▲ Martin Luther

Ulrich Zwingli ▼

In 1529 Martin Luther and Ulrich Zwingli debated over the sacrament of the Lord's Supper, or Communion.

LUTHER: Although I have no intention of changing my mind, which is firmly made up, I will nevertheless present the grounds of my belief and show where the others are in error. . . .Your basic **contentions** are these: In the last analysis you wish to prove that a body cannot be in two places at once, and you produce arguments about the unlimited body which are based on natural reason. I do not question how Christ can be God and man and how the two natures can be joined. For God is more powerful than all our ideas, and we must submit to his word.

Prove that Christ's body is not there where the **Scripture** says, "This is my body!" God is beyond all mathematics and the words of God are to be **revered** and carried out in awe. It is God who commands, "Take, eat, this is my body." I request, therefore, valid scriptural proof to the contrary.

ZWINGLI: I insist that the words of the Lord's Supper must be figurative. This is ever apparent, and even required by the article of faith; "taken up into heaven, seated at the right hand of the Father." Otherwise, it would be absurd to look for him in the Lord's Supper at the same time that Christ is telling us that he is in heaven. One and the same body cannot possibly be in different places. . . .

LUTHER: I call upon you as before: your basic contentions are shaky. Give way, and give glory to God!

ZWINGLI: And we call upon you to give glory to God and to quit begging the question! The issue at stake is this: Where is the proof of your position?

LUTHER: It is your point that must be proved, not mine. But let us stop this sort of thing. It serves no purpose.

ZWINGLI: It certainly does! It is for you to prove that the passage in John 6 speaks of a physical meal.

LUTHER: You express yourself poorly. . . . You're going nowhere.

THE SILK INDUSTRY IN CHINA

During the 1600s Sung Ying-Hsing wrote a book on Chinese industry called T'ien-kung K'ai-wu (Chinese Technology in the Seventeenth Century), *which included sections on the production of silk.*

. . . Members of the aristocracy are clothed in flowing robes decorated with patterns of magnificent mountain dragons, and they are rulers of the country. Those of lowly stations would be dressed in **hempen** jackets and cotton garments to protect themselves from the cold winter and cover their nakedness in summer, in order to distinguish themselves from the birds and beasts. Therefore nature has provided the materials for clothing. Of these, the vegetable [plant] ones are cotton, hemp, *meng* hemp, and creeper hemp; those derived from birds, animals, and insects are furs, woolens, silk, and spun silk. . . .

But, although silk looms are to be found in all parts of the country, how many persons have actually seen the remarkable functioning of the draw-loom: Such words as "orderly government" [*chih,* i.e., the word used in silk reeling], "chaos" [*luan,* i.e., when the fibers are entangled], "knowledge or good policy" [*ching-lun,* i.e., the warp thread and the woven pattern] are known by every schoolboy, but is it not regrettable that he should never see the actual things that gave rise to these words?

▲ Emperor's robe, Qing dynasty

DECLARATION OF THE RIGHTS OF WOMAN AND THE FEMALE CITIZEN

Olympe de Gouges composed her own Declaration of the Rights of Woman and the Female Citizen *in 1791. Following are excerpts.*

1. Woman is born free and lives as equal to man in her rights. Social distinctions can be based only on the common utility.
2. The purpose of any political association is the conservation of the natural and **imprescriptible** rights of woman and man; these rights are liberty, property, security, and especially resistance to oppression. . . .
4. Liberty and justice consist of restoring all that belongs to others; thus, the only limits on the exercise of the natural rights of woman are perpetual male tyranny; these limits are to be reformed by the laws of nature and reason. . . .
6. The law must be . . . the same for all: male and female citizens. . . .
7. No woman is an exception; she is accused, arrested, and detained in cases determined by law. Women, like men, obey this rigorous law. . . .
11. The free communication of thoughts and opinions is one of the most precious rights of woman, since that liberty assured the recognition of children by their fathers. . . .

DOCUMENT-BASED QUESTIONS

1. **Drawing Conclusions** Was a conclusion reached in the debate presented between Luther and Zwingli?
2. **Listing** According to Sung Ying-Hsing, from what two sources was all clothing made?
3. **Defending** Olympe de Gouges states that free communication of thoughts is one of the most precious rights of women. Do you agree or disagree?

The Early Modern World

1400–1800

WORLD LITERATURE

LIBRARY

◀ Voltaire

About the Author

Voltaire was born François-Marie Arouet on November 21, 1694. He assumed the pen name "Voltaire" in 1718. Voltaire was a critical and satiric writer who used his wit to attack both church and state. *Candide* is one of Voltaire's most brilliant and most well-known works.

Reader's Dictionary

bulwark: strong support or protection
summarily: done without delay or formality

FROM CANDIDE

By Voltaire

Candide has been taught that "everything is for the best." However, his adventures usually prove the opposite. Here, he has just been cast out of a castle. The "men in blue" he meets are army recruiters for Frederick the Great, king of Prussia, who was at war with the French when Voltaire wrote Candide.

Candide . . . dragged himself into the neighboring village, which was called Waldberghofftrarbkdikdorff; he was penniless, famished, and exhausted. At the door of a tavern he paused forlornly. Two men dressed in blue [Prussian soldiers] took note of him:

—Look, chum, said one of them, there's a likely young fellow of just about the right size.

They approached Candide and invited him very politely to dine with them.

—Gentlemen, Candide replied with charming modesty, I'm honored by your invitation, but I really don't have enough money to pay my share.

—My dear sir, said one of the blues, people of your appearance and your merit don't have to pay; aren't you five feet five inches tall?

—Yes, gentlemen, that is indeed my stature, said he, making a bow.

—Then, sire, you must be seated at once; not only will we pay your bill this time, we will never allow a man like you to be short of money; for men were made only to render one another mutual aid.

—You are quite right, said Candide; it is just as Dr. Pangloss always told me, and I see clearly that everything is for the best.

They beg him to accept a couple of crowns, he takes them, and offers an I.O.U.; they won't hear of it, and all sit down at table together.

—Don't you love dearly . . .?

—I do indeed, says he, I dearly love Miss Cunégonde.

—No, no, says one of the gentlemen, we are asking if you don't love dearly the King of the Bulgars [Frederick the Great].

—Not in the least, says he, I never laid eyes on him.

—What's that you say? He's the most charming of kings, and we must drink his health.

—Oh, gladly, gentlemen; and he drinks.

—That will do, they tell him; you are now the **bulwark,** the support, the defender, the hero of the Bulgars; your fortune is made and your future assured.

Promptly they slip irons on his legs and lead him to the regiment. There they cause him to right face, left face, present arms, order arms, aim, fire, doubletime, and they give him thirty strokes of the rod. Next day he does the drill a little less awkwardly and gets only twenty strokes; the third day, they give him only ten, and he is regarded by his comrades as a prodigy.

Candide, quite thunderstruck, did not yet understand very clearly how he was a hero. One fine spring morning he took it into his head to go for a walk, stepping straight out as if it were a privilege of the human race, as of animals in general, to use his legs as he chose. He had scarcely covered two leagues when four other heroes [Prussian soldiers], each six feet tall, overtook him, bound him, and threw him into a dungeon. At the court-martial they asked which he preferred, to be flogged thirty-six times by the entire regiment or to receive **summarily** a dozen bullets in the brain. In vain did he argue that the human will is free and insist that he preferred neither alternative; he had to choose; by virtue of the divine gift called "liberty" he decided to run the gauntlet thirty-six times, and actually endured two floggings. The regiment was composed of two thousand men. That made four thousand strokes. As they were prepar-

▲ Frederick the Great, king of Prussia

ing for the third beating, Candide, who could endure no more, begged as a special favor that they would have the goodness to smash his head. His plea was granted; they bandaged his eyes and made him kneel down. The King of the Bulgars [Frederick the Great], passing by at this moment, was told of the culprit's crime; and as this king had a rare genius, he understood, from everything they told him of Candide, that this was a young metaphysician, extremely ignorant of the ways of the world, so he granted his royal pardon, with a generosity which will be praised in every newspaper in every age. A worthy surgeon cured Candide in three weeks with the ointments described by Dioscorides. He already had a bit of skin back and was able to walk when the King of the Bulgars went to war with the King of the Abares.

Nothing could have been so fine, so brisk, so brilliant, so well-drilled as the two armies. The trumpets, the fifes, the oboes, the drums, and the cannon produced such a harmony as was never heard in hell. First the cannons battered down about six thousand men on each side; then volleys of musket fire removed from the best of worlds about nine or ten thousand rascals who were cluttering up its surface.

DOCUMENT-BASED QUESTIONS

1. **Explaining** Explain the irony of the soldiers' statement, "your fortune is made and your future assured."

2. **Making Connections** Why is Candide punished? How does this relate to the philosophy of the Enlightenment?

3. **Analyzing** What is Voltaire's attitude toward the "King of the Bulgars"?

Applications Activity

Write a satirical piece criticizing something about a television show or movie. Remember that a satire does not directly attack but criticizes by showing how ridiculous something is.

LIBRARY

An Era of European Imperialism

1800–1914

PRIMARY SOURCES

Reader's Dictionary

autocrat: a monarch who rules with unlimited authority

close: an enclosed area of land

abject: existing in a low state or condition

infanticide: killing an infant

resuscitation: restoration or renewal

▲ Czar Alexander II

LIBRARY

IMPERIAL DECREE TO FREE THE SERFS

In 1861 the Russian czar Alexander II issued the Emancipation Manifesto, *an imperial decree to free his country's serfs.*

By the grace of God, we, Alexander II, Emperor and **Autocrat** of all the Russias, King of Poland, Grand Duke of Finland, etc., to all our faithful subjects, make known:

Examining the condition of classes and professions comprising the state, we became convinced that the present state legislation favors the upper and middle classes, . . . but does not equally favor the serfs. . . . These facts had already attracted the attention of our predecessors, and they had adopted measures aimed at improving the conditions of the peasants. But decrees on free farmers and serfs have been carried out on a limited scale only.

We thus came to the conviction that the work of a serious improvement of the condition of the peasants was a sacred inheritance bequeathed to us by our ancestors, a mission which, in the course of events Divine Providence called upon us to fulfill. . . .

In virtue of the new dispositions above mentioned, the peasants attached to the soil will be invested within a term fixed by the law with all the rights of free cultivators. . . .

At the same time, they are granted the right of purchasing their **close,** and, with the consent of the proprietors, they may acquire in full property the arable lands and other appurtenances [rights of way] which are allotted to them as a permanent holding. By the acquisition in full property of the quantity of land fixed, the peasants are free from their obligations towards the proprietors for land thus purchased, and they enter definitely into the condition of free peasants-landholders.

THE UNFORTUNATE SITUATION OF WORKING WOMEN

This article was published in L'Atelier, *a Parisian workingman's newspaper, in 1842.*

Although women's work is less productive for society than that of men, it does, nevertheless, have a certain value, and, moreover, there are professions that only women can practice. For these, women are indispensable. . . . It is these very workers in all these necessary trades who earn the least and who are subject to the longest layoffs. Since for so much work they earn only barely enough to live from day to day, it happens that during times of unemployment they sink into **abject** poverty.

Who has not heard of the women silkworkers' dirty, unhealthy, and badly paid work; of the women in the spinning and weaving factories working fourteen to sixteen hours (except for one hour for both meals); always standing, without a single minute for repose, putting forth an enormous amount of effort. And many of them have to walk a league or more, morning and evening, to get home. Nor should we neglect to mention the danger that exists merely from working in these large factories, surrounded by wheels, gears, enormous leather belts that always threaten to seize you and pound you to pieces.

The existence of women who work as day laborers, and are obliged to abandon . . . the care of their children to indifferent neighbors is no better. . . . We believe that the condition of women will never really improve until workingmen can earn enough to support their families, which is only fair. Woman is so closely linked to man that the position of the one cannot be improved without reference to the position of the other.

THE IMPACT OF BRITISH RULE IN INDIA

In 1871 Dadabhai Naoroji commented on the benefits and the problems of British rule in India.

Benefits of British Rule:
In the Cause of Humanity: Abolition of suttee and **infanticide.** *Civilization:* Education, both male and female. . . . **Resuscitation** of India's own noble literature. *Politically:* Peace and order. Freedom of speech and liberty of the press. . . . Improvement of government in the native states. Security of life and property. Freedom from oppression. . . . *Materially:* Loans for railways and irrigation. Development of a few valuable products, such as indigo, tea, coffee, silk, etc. Increase of exports. Telegraphs.

The Detriments of British Rule:
In the Cause of Humanity: Nothing. *Civilization:* [T]here has been a failure to do as much as might have been done. *Politically:* Repeated breach of pledges to give the natives a fair and reasonable share in the higher administration of their own country, . . . an utter disregard of the feelings and views of the natives. *Financially:* [N]ew modes of taxation, without any adequate effort to increase the means of the people to pay.

Summary: British rule has been: morally, a great blessing; politically, peace and order on one hand, blunders on the other; materially, impoverishment. . . . Our great misfortune is that you do not know our wants. When you will know our real wishes, I have not the least doubt that you would do justice. The genius and spirit of the British people is fair play and justice.

LIBRARY

DOCUMENT-BASED QUESTIONS

1. **Explaining** Why does Czar Alexander II free the serfs?
2. **Identifying Points of View** What is the attitude of the *L'Atelier* writer toward women and women's work? Is the author of the article likely to be a woman or a man? What makes you think so?
3. **Summarizing** Summarize the benefits and problems of British rule in India.

An Era of European Imperialism

1800–1914

WORLD LITERATURE

▲George Orwell

About the Author

George Orwell was the pen name of English author Eric Arthur Blair, who was born in Motihari, India, on June 25, 1903. Although born in India, he was educated in England. He lived for 46 years, and during that time, he wrote many influential essays, novels, and newspaper articles. His two most famous works are 1984 and Animal Farm, both of which are commentaries against totalitarianism.

Reader's Dictionary

mahout: a keeper and driver of an elephant
dominion: rule, control
sahib: title meaning "sir" or "master"

By George Orwell

George Orwell served for several years as an assistant superintendent in the Indian Imperial Police but resigned due to his distaste of imperialism. In Shooting an Elephant, *he describes an incident that happened to him, and he satirizes the problems of colonial rule.*

I had halted on the road. As soon as I saw the elephant I knew with perfect certainty that I ought not to shoot him. It is a serious matter to shoot a working elephant—it is comparable to destroying a huge and costly piece of machinery—and obviously one ought not to do it if it can possibly be avoided. And at that distance, peacefully eating, the elephant looked no more dangerous than a cow. I thought then and I think now that his attack of "must" was already passing off; in which case he would merely wander harmlessly about until the **mahout** came back and caught him. Moreover, I did not in the least want to shoot him. I decided that I would watch him for a little while to make sure that he did not turn savage again, and then go home.

But at that moment I glanced round at the crowd that had followed me. It was an immense crowd, two thousand at the least and growing every minute. It blocked the road for a long distance on either side. I looked at the sea of yellow faces above the garish clothes—faces all happy and excited over this bit of fun, all certain that the elephant was going to be shot. They were watching me as they would watch a conjurer about to perform a trick. They

Colonial hunter ▶

LIBRARY

did not like me, but with the magical rifle in my hands I was momentarily worth watching. And suddenly I realized that I should have to shoot the elephant after all. The people expected it of me and I had got to do it; I could feel their two thousand wills pressing me forward irresistibly. And it was at this moment, as I stood there with the rifle in my hands, that I first grasped the hollowness, the futility of the white man's **dominion** in the East. Here was I, the white man with his gun, standing in front of the unarmed native crowd—seemingly the leading actor of the piece; but in reality I was only an absurd puppet pushed to and fro by the will of those yellow faces behind. I perceived in this moment that when the white man turns tyrant it is his own freedom that he destroys. He becomes a sort of hollow, posing dummy, the conventionalized figure of a **sahib.** For it is the condition of his rule that he shall spend his life in trying to impress the "natives," and so in every crisis he has got to do what the "natives" expect of him. He wears a mask, and his face grows to fit it. I had got to shoot the elephant. I had committed myself to doing it when I sent for the rifle. A sahib has got to act like a sahib; he has got to appear resolute, to know his own mind and do definite things. To come all that way, rifle in hand, with two thousand people marching at my heels, and then to trail feebly away, having done nothing—no, that was impossible. The crowd would laugh at me. And my whole life, every white man's life in the East, was one long struggle not to be laughed at.

▼ Working elephants, 1890s

. . . But I did not want to shoot the elephant. . . . The sole thought in my mind was that if anything went wrong those two thousand Burmese would see me trampled on, and reduced to a grinning corpse. And if that happened it was quite probable that some of them would laugh. That would never do. There was only one alternative. I shoved the cartridges into the magazine and lay down on the road to get a better aim.

The crowd grew very still, and a deep, low, happy sigh, as of people who see the theater curtain go up at last, breathed from innumerable throats. They were going to have their bit of fun after all.

. . . When I pulled the trigger I did not hear the bang or feel the kick—one never does when a shot goes home—but I heard the devilish roar of glee that went up from the crowd. . . . You could see the agony of it jolt [the elephant's] whole body and knock the last remnant of strength from his legs.

. . . In the end I could not stand it any longer and went away. I heard later that it took him half an hour to die. . . .

. . . I often wondered whether any of the others grasped that I had done it solely to avoid looking a fool.

DOCUMENT-BASED QUESTIONS

1. **Drawing Conclusions** Why does the narrator ultimately decide that he must shoot the elephant?

2. **Recognizing Bias** What does this story reveal about Orwell's attitudes about imperialism? How can you tell?

3. **Explaining** According to Orwell in this piece, who held the power in colonial India?

Applications Activity

Write a narrative account of an incident when you felt people were pushing you to act in opposition to your original intentions.

LIBRARY

The Twentieth Century Crisis

1914–1945

PRIMARY SOURCES

Reader's Dictionary

parapet: wall of earth piled on top of a trench

snipers: people who shoot at exposed individuals from a concealed location

civil disobedience: refusal to obey governmental demands

exploitation: unfair use for one's own advantage

disarmament: reducing or eliminating weapons

▲Battle of the Somme

AN AMERICAN SOLDIER REMEMBERS WORLD WAR I

Arthur Guy Empey reflects upon his experiences during World War I in the trenches in France.

Suddenly, the earth seemed to shake and a thunderclap burst in my ears. I opened my eyes,—I was splashed all over with sticky mud, and men were picking themselves up from the bottom of the trench. The parapet on my left had toppled into the trench, completely blocking it with a wall of tossed-up earth. The man on my left lay still. . . . A German "Minnie" (trench mortar) had exploded in the [trench]. . . . Stretcher-bearers came up the trench on the double. After a few minutes of digging, three still, muddy forms on stretchers were carried down the communication trench to the rear. Soon they would be resting "somewhere in France," with a little wooden cross over their heads. They had done their bit for King and Country, had died without firing a shot. . . . I was dazed and motionless. Suddenly a shovel was pushed into my hands, and a rough but kindly voice said: "Here, my lad, lend a hand clearing the trench, but keep your head down, and look out for snipers. . . ."

Lying on my belly on the bottom of the trench, I filled sandbags with the sticky mud. . . . The harder I worked, the better I felt.

Occasionally a bullet would crack overhead, and a machine gun would kick up the mud on the bashed-in parapet. At each crack I would duck and shield my face with my arm. One of the older men noticed this action of mine, and whispered: "Don't duck at the crack of a bullet, Yank; the danger has passed,—you never hear the one that wings you. Always remember that if you are going to get it, you'll get it, so never worry." . . . [Days later] we received the cheerful news that at four in the morning we were to go over the top and take the German frontline trench. My heart turned to lead.

GANDHI TAKES THE PATH OF CIVIL DISOBEDIENCE

Mohandas Gandhi explains why British rule in India must end.

▲ Mohandas Gandhi

Before embarking on civil disobedience and taking the risk I have dreaded to take all these years, I would fain approach you and find a way out.

My personal faith is absolutely clear. I cannot intentionally hurt anything that lives, much less fellow human beings, even though they may do the greatest wrong to me and mine. Whilst, therefore, I hold the British rule to be a curse, I do not intend harm to a single Englishman or to any legitimate interest he may have in India.

I must not be misunderstood. Though I hold the British rule in India to be a curse, I do not, therefore, consider Englishmen in general to be worse than any other people on earth. I have the privilege of claiming many Englishmen as dearest friends. Indeed much that I have learned of the evil of British rule is due to the writings of frank and courageous Englishmen who have not hesitated to tell the truth about that rule.

And why do I regard British rule as a curse? It has impoverished the ignorant millions by a system of progressive exploitation and by a ruinously expensive military and civil administration which the country can never afford.

It has reduced us politically to serfdom. It has sapped the foundations of our culture. And, by the policy of cruel disarmament, it has degraded us spiritually. Lacking the inward strength, we have been reduced . . . to a state bordering on cowardly helplessness. . . .

THE HOLOCAUST— THE CAMP VICTIMS

A French doctor describes the victims of one of the gas chambers at Auschwitz-Birkenau during the Holocaust.

It is mid-day, when a long line of women, children, and old people enter the yard. The senior official in charge . . . climbs on a bench to tell them that they are going to have a bath and that afterwards they will get a drink of hot coffee. They all undress in the yard. . . . The doors are opened and an indescribable jostling begins. The first people to enter the gas chamber begin to draw back. They sense the death which awaits them. The SS men put an end to the pushing and shoving with blows from their rifle butts beating the heads of the horrified women who are desperately hugging their children. The massive oak double doors are shut. For two endless minutes one can hear banging on the walls and screams which are no longer human. And then—not a sound. Five minutes later the doors are opened. The corpses, squashed together and distorted, fall out like a waterfall. The bodies which are still warm pass through the hands of the hairdresser who cuts their hair and the dentist who pulls out their gold teeth. . . .

DOCUMENT-BASED QUESTIONS

1. **Describing** How did Arthur Empey feel and act during his time in the trenches of World War I?

2. **Analyzing** Why do you think Gandhi believed that nonviolent civil disobedience would encourage the British to free India?

3. **Identifying Points of View** What is the French doctor's point of view about the events he describes at the Auschwitz-Birkenau death camp?

LIBRARY

The Twentieth Century Crisis

1914–1945

WORLD LITERATURE

Reader's Dictionary

agog: full of intense interest or excitement
moon: to dream

◀ Virginia Woolf

About the Author

Virginia Woolf was born in 1882 in London. Her work changed the ways many modern novels were written. She used an experimental narrative technique known as stream of consciousness, in which characters are portrayed through their inner lives and thoughts without explanation from the writer. She is also known for her feminist writings. One of the most famous of these is *A Room of One's Own.* Its title reflects her belief that a woman "must have money and a room of her own" in order to write.

FROM A ROOM OF ONE'S OWN

by Virginia Woolf

Virginia Woolf was a fervent supporter of women's rights. In A Room of One's Own, *she responds to those who would question the capabilities of women because there was no "female Shakespeare."*

. . . Let me imagine, since facts are so hard to come by, what would have happened had Shakespeare had a wonderfully gifted sister, called Judith, let us say. Shakespeare himself went, very probably—his mother was an heiress—to the grammar school, where he may have learnt Latin—Ovid, Virgil and Horace—and the elements of grammar and logic. He was, it is well known, a wild boy who poached rabbits, perhaps shot a deer, and had, rather sooner than he should have done, to marry a woman in the neighbourhood, who bore him a child rather quicker than was right. That escapade sent him to seek his fortune in London. He had, it seemed, a taste for the theatre; he began by holding horses at the stage door. Very soon he got work in the theatre, became a successful actor, and lived at the hub of the universe, meeting everybody, knowing everybody, practising his art on the boards, exercising his wits in the street, and even getting access to the palace of the queen. Meanwhile his extraordinarily gifted sister, let us suppose, remained at home. She was as adventurous, as imaginative, as **agog** to see the world as he was. But she was not sent to school. She had no chance of learning grammar and logic, let alone of reading Horace and Virgil. She picked up a book now and then, one of her brother's perhaps, and read a few pages. But then her parents came in and told her to mend the stockings or mind the stew and not **moon** about with books and papers. They would have spoken sharply but kindly, for they were substantial people who knew the conditions of life for a woman and loved their daughter—indeed, more likely than not she was the apple of her father's eye. Perhaps she scribbled some pages up in an apple loft on the sly, but was careful to hide them or set fire to them. Soon, however, before she was out of her teens, she was to be betrothed to the son of a neighbouring wool-stapler. She cried out that marriage was hateful to her, and for that she was severely beaten by her father. Then he ceased to scold her. He begged her instead not to hurt him, not to shame him in this matter of her marriage. He would give her a chain of beads or a fine petticoat, he said; and there were tears in his eyes. How could she disobey him? How could she break his heart? The force of her own gift alone drove her to it. She made up a small parcel of her belongings, let herself down by a rope one summer's night and took the road to London. She was not seventeen. The birds that sang in the hedge were not more musical than she was. She had the quickest fancy, a gift like her brother's, for the tune of words. Like him, she had a taste for the theatre. She stood at the stage door; she wanted to act, she said. Men laughed in her face. The manager—a fat, loose-lipped man—guffawed. He bellowed something about poodles dancing and women acting—no woman, he said could possibly be an actress. He hinted—you can imagine what. She could get no training in her craft. Could she even seek her dinner

in a tavern or roam the streets at midnight? Yet her genius was for fiction. . . . At last—for she was very young, oddly like Shakespeare the poet in her face, with the same grey eyes and rounded brows—at last Nick Greene the actor-manager took pity on her; [but] she . . . killed herself one winter's night and lies buried at some cross-roads where the omnibuses now stop outside the Elephant and Castle. That, more or less, is how the story would run, I think, if a woman in Shakespeare's day should have had Shakespeare's genius.

▲ Many of William Shakespeare's plays were performed at the Globe Theatre in London.

▼ William Shakespeare

DOCUMENT-BASED QUESTIONS

1. **Describing** What were "the conditions of life for a woman" that made Judith's parents scold her for attempting to read and write?

2. **Drawing Conclusions** What is Woolf's conclusion about the possibility of a woman becoming Shakespeare?

3. **Analyzing** Why does Virginia Woolf have Shakespeare marry, but Shakespeare's sister run away from marriage?

Applications Activity
What does a person today need to succeed as a writer or artist? Write a descriptive account to illustrate your argument.

Toward a Global Civilization

1945–Present

PRIMARY SOURCES

Reader's Dictionary

reserve: a reservation; land set aside for use by a particular group

squatters: those who settle on public land without rights or permission

perturbation: major change or disturbance

▲ John Glenn

LIBRARY

PROGRESS NEVER STOPS

In 1962 John J. Glenn, Jr., was commander of the first U.S. crewed spacecraft to orbit the earth. Glenn spoke to a joint meeting of Congress six days after he returned from orbit.

What did we learn from the flight? . . . The Mercury spacecraft and systems design concepts are sound and have now been verified during manned flight. We also proved that man can operate intelligently in space and can adapt rapidly to this new environment.

Zero G or weightlessness appears to be no problem. As a matter of fact, lack of gravity is a rather fascinating thing. Objects within the cockpit can be parked in midair. For example, at one time during the flight, I was using a hand-held camera. Another system needed attention; so it seemed quite natural to let go of the camera, take care of the other chore, then reach out, grasp the camera, and go back about my business.

There seemed to be little sensation of speed although the craft was traveling at about five miles per second—a speed that I too find difficult to comprehend.

The view from that altitude defies description. The horizon colors are brilliant and sunsets are spectacular. It is hard to beat a day in which you are permitted the luxury of seeing four sunsets. . . .

Our efforts today and what we have done so far are but small building blocks in a huge pyramid to come.

But questions are sometimes raised regarding the immediate payoffs from our efforts. Explorations and the pursuit of knowledge have always paid dividends in the long run— usually far greater than anything expected at the outset. Experimenters with common, green mold, little dreamed what effect their discovery of penicillin would have.

We are just probing the surface of the greatest advancements in man's knowledge of his surroundings that has ever been made. . . . Knowledge begets knowledge. Progress never stops.

AN IDEAL FOR WHICH I AM PREPARED TO DIE

Nelson Mandela gave this speech during his trial in South Africa in 1964. Following the trial, he was sentenced to life in prison.

The whites enjoy what may well be the highest standard of living in the world, whilst Africans live in poverty and misery. Forty percent of the Africans live in hopelessly overcrowded and, in some cases, drought-stricken **reserves,** where soil erosion and the overworking of the soil make it impossible for them to live properly off the land. Thirty percent are labourers, labour tenants, and **squatters** on white farms. The other thirty percent live in towns where they have developed economic and social habits which bring them closer, in many respects, to white standards. Yet forty-six percent of all African families in Johannesburg do not earn enough to keep them going.

The complaint of Africans, however, is not only that they are poor and whites are rich, but that the laws which are made by the whites are designed to preserve this situation. . . .

During my lifetime I have dedicated my life to this struggle of the African people. I have fought against white domination, and I have fought against black domination. I have cherished the ideal of a democratic and free society in which all persons live together in harmony with equal opportunities. It is an ideal which I hope to live for, and to see realized. But my lord, if needs be, it is an ideal for which I am prepared to die.

CHINA'S GILDED AGE

Xiao-huang Yin recounts his trip through China in 1994.

Recently I took a six-week journey across China. It was my first trip back since . . . 1985. In the course of my visit I saw—I felt—the **perturbations** of profound and chaotic social change. China's stunning hurtle from a centrally planned economy to a free market has set off an economic explosion and generated tremendous prosperity. Its economic growth was 13 percent in 1993, and average personal income in urban areas had doubled since 1985. With the state-owned sector accounting for less than 30 percent of total economic output, the socialist system is becoming an empty shell. Across China the lines between the state and private economies are blurring. At the largest national department store in Shanghai, a symbol of Chinese socialist business, customers now bargain for better prices. The counters within the store have been contracted out to shop clerks, who decide the prices. Dual ownership has in essence turned this state enterprise into a private business. . . .

Not everyone gets rich quick, but the economic boom has brought most urban Chinese a huge improvement in their standard of living. Color TV sets, refrigerators, and VCRs, considered luxuries when I lived in China, can be found in almost every working-class urban household—at least in the prosperous coastal cities.

LIBRARY

DOCUMENT-BASED QUESTIONS

1. **Identifying Central Issues** What are the immediate and long-term "payoffs" of John Glenn's 1962 space mission, according to his report to Congress?

2. **Explaining** What ideal does Nelson Mandela discuss?

3. **Evaluating** Why does Xiao-huang Yin believe that socialism is becoming an "empty shell" in China?

Toward a Global Civilization

1945–Present

WORLD LITERATURE

LIBRARY

▲ Chinua Achebe

About the Author

Chinua Achebe was born in Nigeria and was christened Albert Chinualamogu. He rejected his British name while studying at the University College of Ibadan. Many of his works deal with the impact of Western values and culture on African society. He has done more than almost any other author to spread the understanding and influence of African literature worldwide.

Reader's Dictionary

commandeer: to seize for military purposes
Biro: a British term for a ballpoint pen
raffia: fiber of a type of palm tree

CIVIL PEACE FROM GIRLS AT WAR AND OTHER STORIES

By Chinua Achebe

"*Civil Peace*" is one of the stories from *Girls at War and Other Stories* in which Achebe responds to the Nigerian civil war. The story takes place in the forests of Nigeria in 1970, just after the war has ended.

Jonathan Iwegbu counted himself extraordinarily lucky. "Happy survival!" meant so much more to him than just a current fashion of greeting old friends in the first hazy days of peace. It went deep to his heart. He had come out of the war with five inestimable blessings—his head, his wife Maria's head and the heads of three out of their four children. As a bonus he also had his old bicycle—a miracle too but naturally not to be compared to the safety of five human heads.

The bicycle had a little history of its own. One day at the height of the war it was **commandeered** "for urgent military action." Hard as its loss would have been to him he would still have let it go without a thought had he not had some doubts about the genuineness of the officer. It wasn't his disreputable rags, nor the toes peeping out of one blue and one brown canvas shoes, nor yet the two stars of his rank done obviously in a hurry in **Biro,** that troubled Jonathan; many good and heroic soldiers looked the same or worse. It was

rather a certain lack of grip and firmness in his manner. So Jonathan, suspecting he might be amenable to influence, rummaged in his **raffia** bag and produced the two pounds with which he had been going to buy firewood which his wife, Maria, retailed to camp officials for extra stock-fish and corn meal, and got his bicycle back. That night he buried it in the little clearing in the bush where the dead of the camp, including his own youngest son, were buried. When he dug it up again a year later after the surrender all it needed was a little palm-oil greasing. "Nothing puzzles God," he said in wonder.

He put it to immediate use as a taxi and accumulated a small pile of Biafran money ferrying camp officials and their families across the four-mile stretch to the nearest tarred road. His standard charge per trip was six pounds and those who had the money were only glad to be rid of some of it in this way. At the end of a fortnight he had made a small fortune of one hundred and fifteen pounds.

Then he made the journey to Enugu and found another miracle waiting for him. It was unbelievable. He rubbed his eyes and looked again and it was still standing there before him. But, needless to say, even that monumental blessing must be accounted also totally inferior to the five heads in the family. This newest miracle was his little house in Ogui Overside. Indeed nothing puzzles God! Only two houses away a huge concrete edifice some wealthy contractor had put up just before the war was a mountain of rubble. And here was Jonathan's little zinc house of no regrets built with mud blocks quite intact! Of course the doors and windows were missing and five sheets off the roof. But what was that? And anyhow he had returned to Enugu early enough to pick up bits of old zinc and wood and soggy sheets of cardboard lying around the neighborhood before thousands more came out of their forest holes looking for the same

things. He got a destitute carpenter with one old hammer, a blunt plane and a few bent and rusty nails in his tool bag to turn this assortment of wood, paper and metal into door and window shutters for five Nigerian shillings or fifty Biafran pounds. He paid the pounds, and moved in with his overjoyed family carrying five heads on their shoulders.

▲ *Children Dancing*, c. 1948, by Robert Gwathmey

DOCUMENT-BASED QUESTIONS

1. **Drawing Conclusions** What does Jonathan's encounter with the false officer reveal about the conditions of the war?

2. **Identifying** Biafra lost the civil war. What clues in the text indicate this outcome?

3. **Evaluating** Do you think it is effective for Achebe to discuss the war through an individual account rather than as a direct discussion of the devastation created? Why or why not?

Applications Activity
Choose a contemporary problem and describe it through the effect it has on an individual or family.

GLOSSARY/ GLOSARIO

- Content vocabulary terms in this glossary are words that relate to world history content. They are **highlighted** yellow in your text.
- Los términos del vocabulario de contenido de este glosario son palabras relacionadas con el contenido de historia mundial. Están resaltadas en **amarillo** en tu libro de texto.
- Words below that have an asterisk (*) are academic vocabulary terms. They help you understand your school subjects and are **boldfaced** in your text.
- Las palabras que tienen un asterisco (*) son términos del vocabulario académico. Ellas te ayudarán a comprender los temas escolares y están en **negritas** en tu libro de texto.

ENGLISH	ESPAÑOL

a

abolitionism: a movement to end slavery (p. 401)

abolicionismo: movimiento para terminar con la esclavitud (pág. 401)

absolutism: a political system in which a ruler holds total power (p. 228)

absolutismo: sistema político en el que el gobernante mantiene un poder total (pág. 228)

*abstract: a style of art, emerging around 1910, that spoke directly to the soul and avoided visual reality by using only lines and color (p. 440)

*abstracto: estilo de arte, surgido alrededor de 1910, que habla directamente al alma y evita la realidad visual al utilizar solamente líneas y colores (pág. 440)

acropolis: in early Greek city-states, a fortified gathering place at the top of a hill that was sometimes the site of temples and public buildings (p. 40)

acrópolis: en las ciudades-estado de la antigua Grecia, lugar fortificado de reuniones en la cima de una montaña, donde en ocasiones había templos y edificios públicos (pág. 40)

*administrator: one who manages the affairs of a government or a business (p. 258)

*administrador: el que dirige los asuntos de un gobierno o negocio (pág. 258)

*advocate: support; speak in favor of (p. 426)

*abogar: apoyar; hablar en favor de (pág. 426)

*aid: assistance such as money or supplies (p. 540)

*ayuda: asistencia, ya sea en dinero o insumos (pág. 540)

AIDS: acquired immunodeficiency syndrome; caused by the HIV virus that is spread through bodily fluids and weakens the body's immune system; AIDS is a worldwide problem (p. 753)

sida: síndrome de inmunodeficiencia adquirida; causado por el virus de inmunodeficiencia humana (VIH), que se transmite a través de los fluidos corporales y debilita el sistema inmunitario del organismo; el sida es un problema mundial (pág. 753)

*amendment: an alteration proposed or effected by parliamentary or constitutional procedure (p. 333)

*enmienda: alteración propuesta o realizada por el parlamento o un procedimiento constitucional (pág. 333)

anarchy: political disorder; lawlessness (p. 258)

anarquía: desorden político; sin leyes (pág. 258)

annexed: incorporated territory into an existing political unit, such as a city or country (p. 456)

anexado: territorio incorporado a una unidad política existente, como una ciudad o un país (pág. 456)

*annual: yearly (p. 555)

*anual: en un año, cada año (pág. 555)

annul: declare invalid (p. 184)

anular: declarar no válido (pág. 184)

apartheid: "apartness," the system of racial segregation in South Africa from the 1950s until 1991 (p. 751)

apartheid: "separación", sistema de segregación racial in Sudáfrica desde la década de 1950 hasta 1991 (pág. 751)

appeasement: satisfying reasonable demands of dissatisfied powers in an effort to maintain peace and stability (p. 621)

apaciguamiento: satisfacer demandas razonables de potencias insatisfechas en un esfuerzo por mantener la paz y la estabilidad (pág. 621)

*approach: the way or method one examines or studies an issue or a concept (p. 405)

*enfoque: la manera o el método en que uno examina o estudia un asunto o un concepto (pág. 405)

*arbitrary: at one's discretion; random (p. 315)

*arbitrario: a la discreción de uno; aleatorio (pág. 315)

armada: a fleet of warships (p. 220)

armada: flota de barcos de guerra (pág. 220)

armistice: a truce or agreement to end fighting (p. 544)

armisticio: tregua o acuerdo para finalizar una guerra (pág. 544)

arms race: building up armies and stores of weapons to keep up with an enemy (p. 667)

carrera armamentista: aumento de los ejércitos y almacenamiento de armas para igualar al enemigo (pág. 667)

Aryan: a term used to identify people speaking Indo-European languages; Nazis misused the term, treating it as a racial designation and identifying the Aryans with the ancient Greeks and Romans and twentieth-century Germans and Scandinavians (p. 570)

ario: término utilizado para identificar a las personas que hablan lenguas indo-europeas; los nazis abusaron de este término, tomándolo como una designación racial e identificando a los arios con los antiguos griegos y romanos y con los alemanes y escandinavos del siglo XX (pág. 570)

*assembly: the fitting together of parts to make a complete product (p. 577)

*ensamblaje: la unión de piezas para armar un producto completo (pág. 577)

assembly line: pioneered by Henry Ford in 1913, a manufacturing method that allowed much more efficient mass production of goods (p. 419)

línea de ensamblaje: método de producción, introducido por Henry Ford en 1913, que permitía producir artículos masivamente con mucha mayor eficiencia (pág. 419)

*attain: to gain or achieve (p. 172)

*lograr: ganar o alcanzar (pág. 172)

*authority: power; person in command (p. 228)

*autoridad: poder; persona a cargo (pág. 228)

autonomous: self-governing (p. 703)

autónomo: con gobierno propio (pág. 703)

balance of trade: the difference in value beween what a nation imports and what it exports over time (p. 204)

balanza comercial: la diferencia en valor entre lo que una nación importa y lo que exporta en un período de tiempo (pág. 204)

banners: in Qing China, separate military units made up of Manchus; the empire's chief fighting force (p. 277)

estandartes: en la China de los Qing, unidad militar independiente constituida por manchúes y la principal fuerza de combate de ese imperio (pág. 277)

Bantu: a family of languages spoken in central and southern Africa; a member of any group of the African peoples who speak the language (p. 101)

bantú: una familia de idiomas hablados en el centro y sur de Africa; un miembro de cualquier grupo de los pueblos africanos que hablan dicho idioma (pág. 101)

baroque: an artistic style of the seventeenth century characterized by complex forms, bold ornamentation, and contrasting elements (p. 237)

barroco: estilo artístico del siglo XVII caracterizado por formas complejas, ornamentación audaz y elementos contrastantes (pág. 237)

*benefit: to be useful or profitable to (p. 281)

*benéfico: ser útil o dar beneficios (pág. 281)

bioterrorism: the use of biological and chemical weapons in terrorist attacks (p. 804)

bioterrorismo: uso de armas biológicas o químicas en ataques terroristas (pág. 804)

blitz: the British term for the German air raids on British cities and towns during World War II (p. 648)

blitz: término británico para referirse a los ataques aéreos alemanes a ciudades y pueblos británicos durante la Segunda Guerra Mundial (pág. 648)

GLOSSARY

blitzkrieg: German for "lightning war," a swift and sudden military attack; used by the Germans during World War II (p. 628)

blitzkrieg: término alemán para "guerra relámpago", una táctica utilizada por los alemanes durante la Segunda Guerra Mundial (pág. 628)

bloc: a group of nations with a common purpose (p. 681)

bloque: grupo de naciones con un objetivo común (pág. 681)

bourgeoisie: the middle class, including merchants, industrialists, and professional people (pp. 342, 420)

burguesía: clase media, incluye a los comerciantes, industriales y profesionales (pp. 342, 420)

boyar: a Russian noble (p. 232)

boyar: noble ruso (pág. 232)

Buddhism: a religious doctrine introduced in northern India in the sixth century B.C. by Siddhārtha Gautama, known as the Buddha, or "Enlightened One" (p. 24)

budismo: doctrina religiosa introducida en el norte de la India en el siglo VI a.C. por Siddhartha Gautama, conocido como Buda (o "el Iluminado") (pág. 24)

budget deficit: the state that exists when a government spends more than it collects in revenues (p. 708)

déficit presupuestario: el estado que existe cuando un gobierno gasta más de los ingresos que recibe (pág. 708)

bureaucracy: an administrative organization that relies on nonelective officials and regular procedures (p. 292)

burocracia: organización administrativa basada en funcionarios no elegidos y procedimientos habituales (pág. 292)

Bushido: "the way of the warrior," the strict code by which Japanese samurai were supposed to live (p. 110)

bushido: "código del guerrero", estricto código según el cual debían vivir los samuráis japoneses (pág. 110)

caliph: a successor of Muhammad as spiritual and temporal leader of the Muslims (p. 92)

califa: sucesor de Mahoma como líder espiritual y temporal de los musulmanes (pág. 92)

***capable:** having or showing ability (p. 363)

***capaz:** que tiene o demuestra habilidad (pág. 363)

capital: money available for investment (p. 378)

capital: dinero disponible para invertir (pág. 378)

cartels: groups of drug businesses (p. 741)

cártel: grupo de negociantes de drogas (pág. 741)

cash crop: a crop that is grown for sale rather than for personal use (p. 476)

cultivos para vender: cultivo destinado para la venta y no para su consumo personal (pág. 476)

caste system: a set of rigid categories in ancient India that determined a person's occupation and economic potential, as well as his or her position in society, based partly on skin color (p. 23)

sistema de castas: conjunto de categorías rígidas en la antigua India que determinaba la ocupación de una persona y su potencial económico, así como su posición en la sociedad, parcialmente sobre la base del color de la piel (pág. 23)

caudillo: in post-revolutionary Latin America, a strong leader who ruled chiefly by military force, usually with the support of the landed elite (p. 475)

caudillo: en la América Latina post revolucionaria, líder poderoso que gobernaba principalmente mediante la fuerza militar, a menudo con el respaldo de la elite hacendada (pág. 475)

***cease:** to come to an end (p. 600)

***cesar:** llegar al fin (pág. 600)

***chemical:** produced by chemicals (p. 710)

***químico:** producido mediante reactivos químicos (pág. 710)

Christian humanism: a movement that developed in northern Europe during the Renaissance combining classical learning (humanism) with the goal of reforming the Catholic Church (p. 176)

humanismo cristiano: movimiento que se desarrolló en el norte de Europa durante el Renacimiento que combinaba las enseñanzas clásicas (humanismo) con la meta de reformar la Iglesia católica (pág. 176)

Christianity: monotheistic religion that emerged during the first century A.D. (p. 56)

cristianismo: religión monoteísta que surgió en el siglo primero D.C. (pág. 56)

city-state: a state with political and economic control over the surrounding countryside (p. 10)

ciudad-estado: ciudad con control político y económico sobre los campos que la rodean (pág. 10)

GLOSSARY

*civil: involving the general public or civic affairs (p. 468)

civil disobedience: refusal to obey laws that are considered to be unjust (p. 596)

civilization: a complex culture in which large numbers of people share a number of common elements such as social structure, religion, and art (p. 7)

civil rights movement: began in 1954 when the U.S. Supreme Court ruled that the practice of racial segregation (separation) was illegal; led to passage of Civil Rights Act of 1964 (which created the means to end segregation and discrimination in the workplace and all public places) and the Voting Rights Act (which made it easier for African Americans to vote in southern states) (p. 682)

clan: a group of related families (p. 281)

*classical: authoritative, traditional; relating to the literature, art, architecture, or ideals of the ancient Greek and Roman world (p. 43)

Cold War: the period of political tension following World War II and ending with the fall of Communism in the Soviet Union at the end of the 1980s (p. 650)

collaborator: a person who assists the enemy (p. 641)

*collapse: to break down completely; to suddenly lose force or effectiveness (p. 174)

collective bargaining: the right of unions to negotiate with employers over wages and hours (p. 558)

collectivization: a system in which private farms are eliminated and peasants work land owned by the government (p. 564)

colony: a settlement of people living in a new territory, linked with the parent country by trade and direct government control (p. 204)

Columbian Exchange: the extensive exchange of plants and animals between the Old and New Worlds, especially during the sixteenth and seventeenth centuries (p. 200)

commercial capitalism: economic system in which people invest in trade or goods to make profits (p. 134)

commodity: a marketable product (p. 499)

commonwealth: a republic (p. 225)

commune: in China during the 1950s, a group of collective farms, which contained more than 30,000 people who lived and worked together (p. 777)

---

*civil: relacionado con asuntos generales públicos o civiles (pág. 468)

desobediencia civil: rechazo a obedecer leyes que son consideradas injustas (pág. 596)

civilización: compleja cultura en la que un gran número de personas comparte ciertos elementos, como la estructura social, la religión y el arte (pág. 7)

movimiento por los derechos civiles: comenzó en 1954 cuando la Corte Suprema de los EE.UU. estableció que la práctica de la segregación (separación) racial era ilegal; provocó la aprobación de la Ley de los Derechos Civiles de 1964 y de la Ley del Derecho al Voto, la primera permitió poner fin a la segregación y discriminación en los centros de trabajo y lugares públicos, y la segunda facilitó el voto a los afronorteamericanos en los estados sureños (pág. 682)

clan: grupo de familias relacionadas (pág. 281)

*clásico: documentado, tradicional; relacionado con la literatura, el arte, la arquitectura o los ideales del mundo antiguo griego y romano (pág. 43)

Guerra Fría: período de tensión política que siguió a la Segunda Guerra Mundial y que culminó con la caída del comunismo en la Unión Soviética a fines de la década de 1980 (pág. 650)

colaborador: persona que ayuda al enemigo (pág. 641)

*colapsar: desplomarse completamente; perder súbitamente la fuerza o efectividad (pág. 174)

convenio colectivo: derecho de los sindicatos a negociar con los empleadores acerca de remuneraciones y horarios (pág. 558)

colectivización: sistema en el cual se eliminan las granjas privadas y los campesinos trabajan la tierra perteneciente al gobierno (pág. 564)

colonia: asentamiento de personas que están viviendo en un nuevo territorio enlazado a la madre patria por el comercio y el control directo del gobierno (pág. 204)

Intercambio Colombino: extenso intercambio de plantas y animales entre el Nuevo Mundo y el Viejo, especialmente durante los siglos XVI y XVII (pág. 200)

capitalismo comercial: sistema económico en el cual la gente invierte en el comercio y en bienes con el fin de obtener ganancias (pág. 134)

artículo de consumo: producto que se puede comercializar (pág. 499)

mancomunidad: una república (pág. 225)

comuna: grupo de granjas colectivas de China durante la década de 1950, cada una de las cuales contenía más de 30,000 personas que vivían y trabajaban juntas (pág. 777)

GLOSSARY

GLOSSARY

*community: a group of people with common interests and characteristics living together within a larger society (p. 286)

*compensation: payment (p. 593)

*complex: having many intricate parts (p. 523)

*complexity: the state of being complex or of having many intricate parts (p. 107)

concentration camp: a camp where prisoners of war, political prisoners, or members of minority groups are confined, typically under harsh conditions (p. 570)

concession: a political compromise (p. 502)

*conflict: opposition; a fight, battle, or war (p. 218)

Confucianism: the system of political and ethical ideas formulated by the Chinese philosopher Confucius toward the end of the Zhou dynasty; it was intended to help restore order to a society that was in a state of confusion (p. 31)

conquistador: a Spanish conqueror of the Americas (p. 198)

conscription: military draft (p. 523)

*consent: approval (p. 725)

conservatism: a political philosophy based on tradition and social stability, favoring obedience to political authority and organized religion (p. 388)

*constitution: the basic principles and laws of a nation, state, or social group that determine the powers and duties of the government and guarantee certain rights to the people in it (p. 390)

consulate: government established in France after the overthrow of the Directory in 1799, with Napoleon as first consul in control of the entire government (p. 362)

*consumer: relating to one who consumes or uses economic goods (p. 341)

consumer society: a society preoccupied with buying goods (p. 684)

*context: the circumstances surrounding a situation or event (p. 507)

contras: rebels financed by the United States who began a guerrilla war against the Sandinista government in Nicaragua (p. 735)

*controversy: a dispute or quarrel (p. 437)

*conversion: the change from one belief or form to another (p. 26)

*comunidad: grupo de personas con intereses y características comunes que viven juntas en una sociedad mayor (pág. 286)

*compensación: pago (pág. 593)

*complejo: que tiene muchas partes complicadas (pág. 523)

*complejidad: estado de ser complejo o de tener muchas partes complicadas (pág. 107)

campo de concentración: campamento donde se confina a prisioneros de guerra, prisioneros políticos o miembros de grupos minoritarios, por lo general bajo severas condiciones (pág. 570)

concesión: compromiso político (pág. 502)

*conflicto: oposición; pelea, batalla o guerra (pág. 218)

confucianismo: sistema de ideas políticas y éticas formuladas por el filósofo chino Confucio hacia fines de la dinastía Zhou; fue concebido para restaurar el orden en una sociedad que estaba en estado de confusión (pág. 31)

conquistador: se refiere a los conquistadores españoles de las Américas (pág. 198)

conscripción: llamado obligatorio al servicio militar (pág. 523)

*consentimiento: aprobación (pág. 725)

conservadurismo: filosofía política basada en la tradición y estabilidad social sobre la base de la obediencia a la autoridad política y a la religión organizada (pág. 388)

*constitución: principios básicos y leyes de una nación, estado o grupo social, que determina los poderes y los deberes del gobierno y garantiza ciertos derechos al pueblo (pág. 390)

consulado: gobierno establecido en Francia después del derrocamiento del Directorio en 1799, con Napoleón como primer cónsul y en control de todo el gobierno (pág. 362)

*consumidor: relativo al que consume o usa un bien (pág. 341)

sociedad de consumo: sociedad preocupada en comprar bienes (pág. 684)

*contexto: circunstancias que rodean una situación o evento (pág. 507)

contras: rebeldes financiados por los Estados Unidos que entablaron una guerra guerrillera contra el gobierno sandinista en Nicaragua (pág. 735)

*controversia: disputa o querella (pág. 437)

*conversión: cambio de una creencia o forma a otra (pág. 26)

*convert: to change over from one belief to another (p. 226)

*cooperation: common effort (p. 544)

cooperative: a farm organization owned by and operated for the benefit of the farmers (p. 739)

*corporation: form of business organization that has a separate legal entity with all the rights and responsibilities of an individual, including the right to buy and sell property, enter into legal contracts, and sue and be sued (p. 139)

cottage industry: a method of production in which tasks are done by individuals in their rural homes (p. 379)

coup d'état: a sudden overthrow of the government (p. 357)

*creative: imaginative (p. 239)

creole: a person of European descent born in the New World and living there permanently (pp. 208, 472)

Crusades: military expeditions carried out by European Christians in the Middle Ages to regain the Holy Land from the Muslims (p. 125)

cultural imperialism: referring to Western nations' control of other world cultures similar to how they had controlled colonial governments (p. 713)

culture: the way of life a people follows (p. 99)

*currency: coins, for example, that are in circulation and used as a medium of exchange (p. 704)

*cycle: a series of events that recur regularly and usually lead back to the starting point (p. 27)

czar: Russian for "caesar," the title used by Russian emperors (p. 232)

*convertir: cambiar de una fe a otra (pág. 226)

*cooperación: esfuerzo común (pág. 544)

cooperativa: sociedad agrícola perteneciente a agricultores y administrada para su beneficio (pág. 739)

*corporación: forma de organizar los negocios que tiene una entidad legal independiente con todos los derechos y responsabilidades de un individuo, incluso el derecho a comprar y vender la propiedad, establecer contratos legales y demandar o ser demandados judicialmente (pág. 139)

industria casera: método de producción en el que las tareas las realizan las personas en sus hogares (pág. 379)

golpe de estado: súbito derrocamiento del gobierno (pág. 357)

*creativo: imaginativo (pág. 239)

criollo: descendiente de europeos nacido en el Nuevo Mundo y que vive permanentemente allí (pp. 208, 472)

Cruzadas: expediciones militares llevadas a cabo por cristianos europeos en la Edad Media para reconquistar la Tierra Santa de manos de los musulmanes (pág. 125)

imperialismo cultural: se refiere al control ejercido por los países occidentales sobre otras culturas del mundo, similar a como controlaban los gobiernos coloniales (pág. 713)

cultura: forma de vida que siguen las personas (pág. 99)

*moneda: dinero, por ejemplo, el que se encuentra en circulación y se usa como medio de intercambio (pág. 704)

*ciclo: serie de eventos que se repiten regularmente y que por lo general llevan al punto de partida (pág. 27)

zar: "césar" en ruso; título adoptado por los emperadores rusos (pág. 232)

d

Dao: "Way," the key to proper behavior under Confucianism (p. 27)

*decline: a change to a lower state or level (p. 162)

deficit spending: when a government pays out more money than it takes in through taxation and other revenues, thus going into debt (p. 559)

deforestation: the clearing of forests (p. 806)

deism: an eighteenth-century religious philosophy based on reason and natural law (p. 312)

demilitarized: elimination or prohibition of weapons, fortifications, and other military installations (p. 621)

tao: "Camino", la clave para la conducta apropiada bajo el confucianismo (pág. 27)

*declinar: cambio a un estado o nivel más bajo (pág. 162)

gastos deficitarios: gastos gubernamentales que exceden a lo que se recibe a través de los impuestos y otros ingresos, por lo que se endeuda (pág. 559)

deforestación: tala de bosques (pág. 806)

deísmo: filosofía religiosa del siglo XVIII basada en la razón y en la ley natural (pág. 312)

desmilitarizar: eliminar o prohibir las armas, fortificaciones y otras instalaciones militares (pág. 621)

GLOSSARY

GLOSSARY

democracy: "the rule of the many," government by the people, either directly or through their elected representatives (p. 41)

democracia: "gobierno de la mayoría", gobierno por personas elegidas directamente o a través de sus representantes elegidos (pág. 41)

*demonstration: a public display of group feeling toward a person or a cause (p. 700)

*demostración: muestra pública de los sentimientos colectivos hacia una persona o causa (pág. 700)

depression: a period of low economic activity and rising unemployment (p. 556)

depresión: período de baja actividad económica y aumento del desempleo (pág. 556)

*derived: process of obtaining a product from a parent substance (p. 380)

*derivado: proceso de obtención de un producto a partir de una sustancia progenitora (pág. 380)

desertification: formation of degraded soil, turning semi-arid lands into nonproductive deserts (p. 806)

desertificación: formación de suelos degradados, que convierte los terrenos semiáridos en desiertos improductivos (pág. 806)

de-Stalinization: the process of eliminating Stalin's more ruthless policies (p. 675)

desestalinización: proceso de eliminación de las políticas más crueles de Stalin (pág. 675)

détente: a phase of relaxed tensions and improved relations between two adversaries (p. 694)

détente: fase de relajamiento de las tensiones y mejoramiento de las relaciones entre dos adversarios (pág. 694)

deterrence: during the Cold War, the U.S. and Soviet policies of holding huge arsenals of nuclear weapons to prevent war; each nation believed that neither would launch a nuclear attack since both knew that the other side could strike back with devastating power (p. 669)

disuasión: durante la Guerra Fría, las políticas de los EE.UU. y de los soviéticos de mantener enormes arsenales de armas nucleares para evitar la guerra; cada país creía que ninguno lanzaría un ataque nuclear ya que ambos sabían que la otra parte podía responder con un ataque devastador (pág. 669)

dictatorship: a form of government in which a person or small group has absolute power (p. 420)

dictadura: forma de gobierno en el que una persona o un pequeño grupo tiene el poder absoluto (pág. 420)

direct democracy: a system of government in which the people participate directly in government decision making through mass meetings (p. 43)

democracia directa: sistema de gobierno en el que las personas participan directamente en las decisiones del gobierno mediante asambleas masivas (pág. 43)

direct rule: colonial government in which local elites are removed from power and replaced by a new set of officials brought from the mother country (p. 454)

gobierno directo: gobierno colonial en el que se le retira el poder a la elite local y se lo dan a nuevos funcionarios traídos de la metrópoli (pág. 454)

disarmament group: a nongovernmental group that works to limit the size of military forces and weapons stocks (p. 817)

grupo de desarme: grupo no gubernamental que trabaja para limitar el tamaño de las fuerzas armadas y de las reservas de armamentos (pág. 817)

discrimination: prejudicial treatment usually based on race, religion, class, sex, or age (p. 787)

discriminación: tratamiento prejuiciado, generalmente por la raza, la religión, la clase social, el género o la edad (pág. 787)

dissident: a person who speaks out against the regime in power (p. 694)

disidente: persona que critica abiertamente al régimen que tiene el poder (pág. 694)

*diverse: varied and not alike (p. 752)

*diverso: variado o que no se parece (pág. 752)

divine right of kings: the belief that kings receive their power from God and are responsible only to God (p. 225)

derecho divino de los reyes: creencia de que los reyes reciben su poder de Dios y de que responden sólo ante Dios (pág. 225)

*document: an original or official paper that gives proof of or support to (p. 121)

*documento: papel original u oficial que prueba o apoya algo (pág. 121)

*domain: where one has absolute ownership of land or other property (p. 250)

*dominio: donde alguien tiene la propiedad absoluta de la tierra u otro bien (pág. 250)

*domestic: relating to or originating within one's country (p. 352)

*doméstico: relativo al país de uno u originado en él (pág. 352)

*dominate: influence or control (p. 620)

*dominar: influir o controlar (pág. 620)

domino theory: idea that if one country falls to communism, neighboring countries will also fall (p. 671)

teoría del domino: idea de que si un país cae ante el comunismo, los países colindantes también lo harán (pág. 671)

dowry: a gift of money or property paid at the time of marriage, either by the bride's parents to her husband or, in Islamic societies, by a husband to his wife (p. 167)

dote: dinero o bienes pagados en el momento del matrimonio por los padres de la novia a su esposo, o en sociedades islámicas, por el marido a su esposa (pág. 167)

*draft: to select for some purpose; to conscript (p. 210)

*reclutar: seleccionar para algún propósito; alistar (pág. 210)

*drama: a composition that tells a story usually involving conflicts and emotions through action and dialogue and typically designed for the theater (p. 238)

*drama: composición que cuenta una historia, por lo general implicada con conflictos y emociones, a través de la acción y el diálogo, diseñada habitualmente para el teatro (pág. 238)

*dramatic: remarkable; notable; amazing (p. 788)

*dramático: considerable; notable; sorprendente (pág. 788)

Duma: the Russian legislative assembly (p. 434)

Duma: la asamblea legislativa rusa (pág. 434)

dynasty: a family of rulers whose right to rule is passed on within the family (p. 14)

dinastía: familia de gobernantes cuyo derecho a gobernar se transmite dentro de la familia (pág. 14)

ecology: the study of the relationships between living things and their environment (p. 806)

ecología: estudio de las relaciones entre los seres vivos y su ambiente (pág. 806)

encomienda: a system of labor the Spanish used in the Americas; Spanish landowners had the right, as granted by Queen Isabella, to use Native Americans as laborers (p. 199)

encomienda: sistema de trabajo empleado por los españoles en las Américas; los terratenientes españoles tenían el derecho, otorgado por la reina Isabel, a emplear a los nativoamericanos como peones (pág. 199)

elector: an individual qualified to vote in an election (p. 357)

elector: persona calificada para votar en una elección (pág. 357)

*element: a distinct group within a larger group (p. 588)

*elemento: un grupo particular dentro de un grupo mayor (pág. 588)

emancipation: the act of setting free (p. 400)

emancipación: acción de dejar en libertad (pág. 400)

empire: a large political unit or state, usually under a single leader, that controls many peoples or territories (p. 12)

imperio: gran unidad política, comúnmente bajo un solo líder, que controla a muchos pueblos o territorios (pág. 12)

enclosure movement: in Great Britain during the 1700s, the Parliamentary decree that allowed fencing off of common lands, forcing many peasants to move to town (p. 378)

movimiento de cerramiento: durante los años 1700, un decreto del parlamento británico autorizó a cercar terrenos públicos, lo que obligó a muchos campesinos a marcharse a las ciudades (pág. 378)

*enhanced: improved (p. 674)

*mejorado: perfeccionado (pág. 674)

enlightened absolutism: a system in which rulers tried to govern by Enlightenment principles while maintaining their full royal powers (p. 318)

absolutismo ilustrado: sistema en el cual los gobernantes trataban de gobernar por medio de principios de la Ilustración mientras mantenían todos sus poderes reales (pág. 318)

entrepreneur: a person interested in finding new business opportunities and new ways to make profits (p. 378)

empresario: persona interesada en hallar nuevas oportunidades de negocios y nuevas formas de obtener ganancias (pág. 378)

*environment: the complex factors—climate, soil, and living things—that act upon an ecological community and determine its form and survival (p. 805)

*medioambiente: complejos factores—clima, suelo y seres vivientes— que actúan sobre una comunidad ecológica y determinan su forma y supervivencia (pág. 805)

epic poem: a long poem that tells the deeds of a great hero, such as the Iliad and the Odyssey of Homer (p. 39)

*establish: to set up permanently; to found (p. 611)

estate: one of the three classes into which French society was divided before the revolution: the clergy (first estate), the nobles (second estate), and the townspeople (third estate) (p. 340); a landed property usually with a large house on it (p. 471)

eta: Japan's outcast class, whose way of life was strictly regulated by the Tokugawa (p. 287)

*ethics: moral principles; generally recognized rules of conduct (p. 45)

*ethnic: relating to people who have common racial, religious, or cultural origins (p. 638)

ethnic cleansing: a policy of killing or forcibly removing an ethnic group from its lands; used by the Serbs against the Muslim minority in Bosnia (pp. 588, 703)

*eventually: in the end (p. 601)

*exclusion: barred from inclusion or participation in (p. 345)

*exclusive: limited to a single individual or group (p. 493)

*expand: to enlarge or to spread (p. 248)

*exploit: to make use of meanly or unfairly for one's own advantage (p. 454)

*export: to send a product or service for sale to another country (p. 454)

*external: relating to dealings or relationships with foreign countries (p. 352)

extraterritoriality: living in a section of a country set aside for foreigners but not subject to the host country's laws (p. 490)

poema épico: extenso poema que cuenta las hazañas de un gran héroe, como la Iliada y la Odisea, de Homero (pág. 39)

*establecer: fijar permanentemente; fundar (pág. 611)

estado: cada una de las tres clases en las que se dividía la sociedad francesa medieval: el clero (primer estado), los nobles (segundo estado) y la plebe (tercer estado) (pág. 340)

eta: la clase más baja de la sociedad japonesa, cuya forma de vida era estrictamente regulada por el Tokugawa (pág. 287)

*ética: principios morales; reglas de conducta generalmente aceptadas (pág. 45)

*étnico: relativo a las personas que tienen el mismo origen racial, religioso o cultural (pág. 638)

limpieza étnica: política de matar o expulsar por la fuerza a un grupo étnico de sus territorios; usada por los serbios contra las minorías musulmanas en Bosnia (pp. 588, 703)

*finalmente: al final (pág. 601)

*excluir: impedir incluirse o participar en algo (pág. 345)

*exclusivo: limitado a un sólo individuo o grupo (pág. 493)

*expandir: ampliar o extender (pág. 248)

*explotar: utilizar cruel o injustamente para provecho propio (pág. 454)

*exportar: enviar en venta un producto o servicio a otro país (pág. 454)

*externo: relativo a tratos o relaciones con países extranjeros (pág. 352)

extraterritorialidad: vivir en una sección de un país apartada para extranjeros, pero no sujeta a las leyes del país anfitrión (pág. 490)

f

faction: a dissenting group (p. 351)

fascism: a political philosophy that glorifies the state above the individual by emphasizing the need for a strong central government led by a dictatorial ruler (p. 561)

federal system: a form of government in which power is shared between the national government and state governments (p. 333)

feminism: the movement for women's rights (p. 426)

facción: grupo de disidentes (pág. 351)

fascismo: filosofía política que glorifica al estado por sobre el individuo y enfatiza la necesidad de tener un gobierno central fuerte encabezado por un gobernante dictatorial (pág. 561)

sistema federal: forma de gobierno en la cual el poder es compartido entre el gobierno nacional y los gobiernos estatales (pág. 333)

feminismo: movimiento a favor de los derechos de las mujeres (pág. 426)

GLOSSARY

feudalism: political and social system that developed during the Middle Ages when royal governments were no longer able to defend their subjects; nobles offered protection and land in return for service (p. 120)

feudalismo: sistema político y social que se desarrolló durante la Edad Media cuando los gobiernos reales ya no podían defender a sus pueblos; los nobles ofrecían protección y tierras a cambio de servicios (pág. 120)

***final:** the last in a series, process, or progress (p. 777)

***final:** el último de una serie, proceso o progreso (pág. 777)

***financier:** one who deals with finance and investment on a large scale; one who specializes in raising and expending public monies (p. 416)

***financista:** persona que maneja las finanzas e inversiones a gran escala; persona especializada en colectar y gastar los fondos públicos (pág. 416)

fresco: a painting done on fresh, wet plaster with water-based paints (p. 173)

fresco: pintura hecha en yeso fresco y húmedo con pinturas a base de agua (pág. 173)

***function:** operate (p. 803)

***funcionar:** operar (pág. 803)

***fund:** to provide money for (p. 741)

***financiar:** aportar dinero para algo (pág. 741)

gender parity: a policy by which women have to make up either a certain number of the candidates in an election or a certain number of those elected (p. 712)

paridad de género: política mediante la cual las mujeres deben contar con un determinado número de candidatos en las elecciones o con un determinado número entre los elegidos (pág. 712)

gender stereotyping: restricting what a person could do just because of the person's gender (p. 712)

estereotipia de género: la restricción en el juicio de lo que una persona puede hacer, basándose sólo en su género (pág. 712)

***generation:** a group of individuals born and living at the same time (p. 312)

***generación:** grupo de individuos que nacen y viven en una misma época (pág. 312)

genocide: the deliberate mass murder or physical extinction of a particular racial, political, or cultural group (pp. 588, 640)

genocidio: matanza masiva deliberada o extinción física de un grupo racial, político o cultural en particular (pp. 588, 640)

geocentric: literally, earth-centered; a system of planetary motion that places Earth at the center of the universe, with the sun, moon, and other planets revolving around it (p. 304)

geocéntrico: literalmente, centrado en la Tierra; sistema de movimiento planetario que ubica a la Tierra como el centro del universo, con el Sol, la Luna y los otros planetas girando en torno a ella (pág. 304)

global economy: an economy in which the production, distribution, and sale of goods take place on a worldwide scale, as in a multinational corporation (p. 807)

economía global: economía en la cual la producción, distribución y venta de bienes se realiza a escala mundial, como en una corporación multinacional (pág. 807)

globalization: the movement toward a more integrated and interdependent world economy (pp. 713, 815)

globalización: movimiento hacia una economía mundial más integrada e independiente (pp. 713, 815)

***goal:** an aim or a purpose (p. 750)

***meta:** objetivo o propósito (pág. 750)

grand vizier: the Ottoman sultan's chief minister who carried the main burdens of the state and who led the council meetings (p. 251)

gran visir: ministro principal de los sultanes otomanos, que se ocupa de los principales problemas del estado y encabezaba las reuniones del consejo (pág. 251)

grassroots level: community level (p. 817)

nivel de base: nivel comunitario (pág. 817)

greenhouse effect: global warming caused by the buildup of carbon dioxide in the atmosphere (p. 806)

efecto invernadero: calentamiento global causado por la acumulación de dióxido de carbono en la atmósfera (pág. 806)

***guaranteed:** assured the fulfillment of a condition (p. 333)

***garantizado:** que asegura el cumplimiento de una condición (pág. 333)

guerrilla tactics: the use of unexpected maneuvers like sabotage and subterfuge to fight an enemy (p. 602)

tácticas de guerrilla: uso de maniobras inesperadas, como sabotajes y subterfugios para luchar contra un enemigo (pág. 602)

gunpowder empire: an empire formed by outside conquerors who unified the regions that they conquered through their mastery of firearms (p. 250)

imperio de pólvora: imperio formado por conquistadores extranjeros que unificaron regiones conquistadas gracias a su habilidad con las armas de fuego (pág. 250)

hans: approximately 250 domains into which Japan was divided under the Tokugawa (p. 286)

han: cada uno de los aproximadamente 250 dominios en los que se dividió Japón bajo los Tokugawa (pág. 286)

harem: "sacred place," the private domain of an Ottoman sultan, where he and his wives resided (p. 250)

harén: "lugar sagrado", dominio privado del sultán otomano, donde residían él y sus esposas (pág. 250)

heavy industry: the manufacture of machines and equipment for factories and mines (p. 674)

industria pesada: manufactura de máquinas y equipo destinadas a fábricas y minas (pág. 674)

heliocentric: literally, sun-centered; the system of the universe proposed in 1543 by Nicholas Copernicus, who argued that the earth and planets revolve around the sun (p. 304)

heliocéntrico: literalmente, centrado en el Sol; sistema del universo propuesto en 1543 por Nicolás Copérnico, quien sostuvo que la Tierra y los planetas giraban en torno al Sol (pág. 304)

*highlighted: centered attention on (p. 489)

*resaltar: centrar la atención en algo (pág. 489)

Hinduism: the major Indian religious system, which had its origins in the religious beliefs of the Aryans who settled India after 1500 B.C. (p. 24)

hinduismo: principal sistema religioso de la India, que tuvo sus orígenes en las creencias religiosas de los arios que se establecieron en la India después del año 1500 a.C. (pág. 24)

hominid: humans and other humanlike creatures that walk upright (p. 4)

homínido: humanos y otras criaturas similares a los humanos que caminaban erectos (pág. 4)

hostage system: a system used by the shogunate to control the daimyo in Tokugawa Japan; the family of a daimyo lord was forced to stay at their residence in the capital whenever the lord was absent from it (p. 286)

sistema de rehén: sistema utilizado por el shogunado para controlar al daimyo en el Japón de los Tokugawa; la familia de un daimyo estaba obligada a permanecer en su residencia en la capital mientras él se encontrara ausente (pág. 286)

humanism: an intellectual movement of the Renaissance based on the study of the humanities, which included grammar, rhetoric, poetry, moral philosophy, and history (p. 170)

humanismo: movimiento intelectual del Renacimiento basado en el estudio de las humanidades, que incluía gramática, retórica, poesía, filosofía moral e historia (pág. 170)

*hypothetical: assumed but not known (p. 385)

*hipotético: supuesto, pero no comprobado (pág. 385)

*ideological: based on a set of beliefs (p. 650)

*ideológico: basado en un conjunto de convicciones (pág. 650)

*ignorant: unaware; lacking knowledge of (p. 178)

*ignorante: desinformado; falto de conocimientos sobre algo (pág. 178)

imperator: commander in chief; the Latin origin of the word *emperor* (p. 50)

emperador: comandante en jefe; el origen latino de la palabra es *"imperator"* (pág. 50)

imperialism: the extension of a nation's power over other lands (p. 450)

imperialismo: extensión del poder de una nación hacia otras tierras (pág. 450)

*impose: to establish or apply (p. 293)

*imponer: establecer o aplicar (pág. 293)

*incentive: something that motivates (p. 282)

*incentivo: algo que motiva (pág. 282)

GLOSSARY

indemnity: payment for damages (p. 495)

indigenous: native to a region (p. 460)

indirect rule: colonial government in which local rulers are allowed to maintain their positions of authority and status (p. 454)

***individuality:** a total character that distinguishes an individual from others (p. 402)

inductive reasoning: the doctrine that scientists should proceed from the particular to the general by making systematic observations and carefully organized experiments to test hypotheses or theories, a process that will lead to correct general principles (p. 309)

indulgence: a release from all or part of punishment for sin by the Catholic Church, reducing time in purgatory after death (p. 178)

industrial capitalism: an economic system based on industrial production or manufacturing (p. 384)

inflation: a rapid increase in prices (p. 222)

***innovation:** a new idea, method, or device (p. 13)

Inquisition: a court established by the Catholic Church to discover and try heretics; also called the Holy Office (p. 136)

***insecure:** uncertain, shaky; not adequately covered or sustained (p. 435)

***instability:** not steady; wavering (p. 162)

***intelligent:** having a high degree of understanding and mental capacity (p. 262)

***intensity:** extreme degree of strength, force, energy, or feeling (p. 443)

***intervention:** involvement in a situation to alter the outcome (p. 475)

intifada: "uprising," militant movement that arose during the 1980s among supporters of the Palestine Liberation Organization living in Israel (p. 763)

***investor:** a person or entity that commits money to earn a financial return (p. 608)

***involvement:** a commitment or a connection to (p. 630)

Islam: monotheistic religion that emerged in the Arabian Peninsula during the seventh century A.D. (p. 91)

isolationism: a policy of national isolation by abstention from alliances and other international political and economic relations (p. 630)

***issue:** a vital or unsettled matter (p. 760)

indemnización: pago por daños (pág. 495)

indígena: nativo de una región (pág. 460)

dominio indirecto: gobierno colonial en el que los gobernantes locales pueden mantener sus posiciones de autoridad y estatus (pág. 454)

***individualidad:** conjunto total de caracteres que distinguen a un individuo de los otros (pág. 402)

razonamiento inductivo: doctrina de que los científicos debían proceder de lo particular a lo general, mediante observaciones sistemáticas y experimentos cuidadosamente organizados para probar las hipótesis o teorías, proceso que conduciría a principios generales correctos (pág. 309)

indulgencia: perdón de todo o parte de un castigo por pecar otorgado por la Iglesia católica, reduciendo el tiempo en el purgatorio tras la muerte (pág. 178)

capitalismo industrial: sistema económico basado en la producción industrial o la manufactura (pág. 384)

inflación: rápido aumento de los precios (pág. 222)

***innovación:** idea, método o dispositivo nuevos (pág. 13)

Inquisición: un tribunal establecido por la Iglesia Católica para descubrir y someter a juicio a los herejes; ll amado además el Santo Oficio (pág. 136)

***inseguro:** que no es cierto, convulsivo; que no está cubierto o sostenido adecuadamente (pág. 435)

***inestabilidad:** que no está estático; que se balancea (pág. 162)

***inteligente:** que tiene una alto grado de comprensión y capacidad mental (pág. 262)

***intensidad:** grado de fortaleza, fuerza, energía o sentimiento (pág. 443)

***intervención:** involucrarse en una situación para alterar el resultado (pág. 475)

intifada: "levantamiento", movimiento militante surgido en la década de 1980 entre quienes respaldaban a la Organización para la Liberación de Palestina y vivían en Israel (pág. 763)

***inversor:** persona o entidad que compromete su dinero para obtener una ganancia económica (pág. 608)

***implicación:** compromiso o conexión con algo (pág. 630)

islam: religión monoteísta que surgió en la Península Arábiga en el siglo VII d.C. (pág. 91)

aislacionismo: política de aislamiento nacional mediante la abstención de establecer alianzas y relaciones políticas y económicas internacionales (pág. 630)

***asunto:** cuestión vital o no acordada (pág. 760)

GLOSSARY

janissary: a soldier in the elite guard of the Ottoman Turks (p. 248)

jenízaro: soldado de la guardia elite de los turcos otomanos (pág. 248)

jihad: "struggle in the way of God" (p. 192)

jihad: "lucha en el camino de Dios" (pág. 192)

journeyman: a worker who has learned a trade and works for wages for other masters (p. 341)

jornalero: trabajador que ha aprendido un oficio y trabaja por un salario para un patrón (pág. 341)

Judaism: monotheistic religion developed among the Israelites (p. 17)

Judaísmo: religión monoteísta desarrollada por los israelitas (pág. 17)

*justification: the process of being justified, or deemed worthy of salvation, by God (p. 183)

*justificación: proceso de ser justificado o juzgado digno de la salvación por Dios (pág. 183)

kaiser: German for "caesar," the title of the emperors of the Second German Empire (p. 397)

káiser: término alemán para "césar", título de los emperadores del Segundo Imperio Alemán (pág. 397)

kamikaze: Japanese for "divine wind", a suicide mission in which young Japanese pilots intentionally flew their airplanes into U.S. fighting ships at sea (p. 647)

kamikaze: término japonés para "viento divino", misión suicida en la que jóvenes pilotos japoneses intencionalmente estrellaban sus aviones contra los buques de guerra de los EE.UU. (pág. 647)

*labor: people with all their abilities and efforts (p. 248)

*mano de obra: personas con todas sus habilidades y esfuerzo (pág. 248)

laissez-faire: literally, "let [people] do [what they want]"; the concept that the state should not impose government regulations but should leave the economy alone (p. 314)

laissez-faire: literalmente, "dejar [a las personas] hacer [lo que quieran]"; el concepto de que el estado no debe imponer regulaciones gubernamentales, sino que debe dejar la economía andar sola (pág. 314)

*legislature: an organized body that makes laws (p. 586)

*legislatura: cuerpo organizado que hace las leyes (pág. 586)

*liberal: broad-minded; associated with ideals of the individual, especially economic freedom and greater participation in government (p. 365)

*liberal: de mente amplia; asociado con los ideales del individuo, especialmente la libertad económica y una mayor participación en el gobierno (pág. 365)

liberalism: a political philosophy originally based largely on Enlightenment principles, holding that people should be as free as possible from government restraint and that civil liberties—the basic rights of all people—should be protected (p. 390)

liberalismo: filosofía política originalmente basada en gran medida en los principios de la Ilustración, que sostenía que las personas deben estar lo más libres posible de las restricciones gubernamentales y que las libertades civiles—los derechos básicos de las personas—deben protegerse (pág. 390)

*liberated: freed (p. 664)

*liberado: independizado (pág. 664)

lineage group: an extended family unit that has combined into a larger community (p. 103)

grupo de linaje: unidad extendida de una familia que se ha mezclado en una comunidad mayor (pág. 103)

literacy: the ability to read (p. 429)

alfabetización: capacidad de leer y escribir (pág. 429)

Lutheranism: the religious doctrine that Martin Luther developed; it differed from Catholicism in the doctrine of salvation, which Luther believed could be achieved by faith alone, not by good works; Lutheranism was the first Protestant faith (p. 180)

luteranismo: doctrina religiosa que desarrolló Martín Lutero; difiere del catolicismo en cuanto a la doctrina de salvación, que Lutero consideraba que podía alcanzarse mediante la fe sola, no por buenas acciones; el luteranismo fue la primera fe protestante (pág. 180)

GLOSSARY

magic realism: a form of expression unique to Latin American literature; it combines realistic events with dreamlike or fantasy backgrounds (p. 728)

realismo mágico: singular forma de expresión de la literatura latinoamericana; combina elementos realistas sobre un fondo de sueños o fantasía (pág. 728)

Magna Carta: the "Great Charter" of rights, which King John was forced to sign by the English nobles at Runnymeade in 1215 (p. 121)

Carta Magna: "Gran Carta Real" de derechos que el rey Juan Sin Tierra fue obligado a firmar por los nobles ingleses en Runnymede en 1215 (pág. 121)

mainland states: part of a continent, as distinguished from peninsulas or offshore islands (p. 293)

territorio continental: parte de un continente, a diferencia de las penínsulas o las islas (pág. 293)

*maintain: to keep in an existing state of repair or efficiency (p. 788)

*mantener: conservar un estado existente de compostura o eficiencia (pág. 788)

*major: great; significant in size or importance (p. 144)

*principal: significativo en tamaño o importancia (pág. 144)

mandate: a nation governed by another nation on behalf of the League of Nations (p. 547)

mandato: nación gobernada por otra en nombre de la Liga de Naciones (pág. 547)

Mandate of Heaven: claim by Chinese kings of the Zhou dynasty that they had direct authority from heaven to rule and to keep order in the universe (p. 27)

Mandato del Cielo: reivindicación de los reyes de la dinastía Zhou de China de que ellos recibieron directamente del cielo la autoridad para gobernar y mantener en orden el universo (pág. 27)

Mannerism: an artistic movement that emerged in Italy in the 1520s and 1530s; it marked the end of the Renaissance by breaking down the principles of balance, harmony, and moderation (p. 236)

manierismo: movimiento artístico surgido en Italia en las décadas de 1520 y 1530; marcó el fin del Renacimiento al romper los principios de balance, armonía y moderación (pág. 236)

manor: in medieval Europe, an agricultural estate that a lord ran and peasants worked (p. 133)

feudo: en la Europa medieval, propiedad agrícola administrada por un señor y trabajada por campesinos (pág. 133)

mass production: production of goods in quantity usually by machinery (p. 419)

producción masiva: producción de bienes en grandes cantidades, generalmente con el empleo de máquinas (pág. 419)

*media: channels or systems of communication (p. 563)

*medios: canales o sistemas de comunicación (pág. 563)

megacity: a city that has grown so fast in population that it cannot provide regular urban services (p. 726)

megaciudad: ciudad cuya población ha crecido tan rápidamente que no puede garantizar los servicios urbanos habituales (pág. 726)

mercantilism: a set of principles that dominated economic thought in the seventeenth century; it held that the prosperity of a nation depended on a large supply of gold and silver (p. 204)

mercantilismo: conjunto de principios que dominaban el pensamiento económico en el siglo XVII; sostenía que la prosperidad de una nación dependía de tener grandes cantidades de oro y plata (pág. 204)

mercenary: a soldier who sells his services to the highest bidder (p. 164)

mercenario: soldado que vende sus servicios al mejor postor (pág. 164)

mestizo: a person of mixed European and native American Indian descent (pp. 208, 473)

mestizo: persona que desciende de un progenitor europeo y uno nativoamericano (pp. 208, 473)

Middle Passage: the journey of enslaved persons from Africa to the Americas, so called because it was the middle portion of the triangular trade route (p. 206)

Paso Central: viaje de los africanos esclavizados a las Américas, llamado así porque era la porción intermedia de la ruta del comercio triangular (pág. 206)

*migration: the movement of people from one country, place, or locality to another (p. 814)

*migración: flujo de personas de un país, lugar o localidad a otra (pág. 814)

militant: combative (p. 218)

militante: persona combativa (pág. 218)

militarism: reliance on military strength (p. 396)

militarismo: dependencia de la fuerza militar (pág. 396)

GLOSSARY

GLOSSARY

*military: relating to the armed forces or to soldiers, arms, or war (pp. 101, 523)

*militar: relativo a las fuerzas armadas o a los soldados, las armas o la guerra (pp. 101, 523)

*minimal: barely adequate (p. 680)

*mínimo: escasamente adecuado (pág. 680)

ministerial responsibility: the idea that the prime minister is responsible to the popularly elected legislative body and not to the king or president (p. 432)

responsabilidad ministerial: concepto de que el primer ministro es responsable ante el poder legislativo electo por el pueblo y no ante el rey o el presidente (pág. 432)

mita: a labor system that the Spanish administrators in Peru used to draft native people to work in the Spanish landowners' silver mines (p. 210)

mita: sistema de trabajo usado por los funcionarios españoles en Perú para reclutar nativos para trabajar en las minas de plata de los terratenientes españoles (pág. 210)

mobilization: the process of assembling troops and supplies and making them ready for war (pp. 525, 664)

movilización: proceso de agrupar tropas y suministros y prepararlos para la guerra (pp. 525, 664)

modernism: a movement in which writers and artists between 1870 and 1914 rebelled against the traditional literary and artistic styles that had dominated European cultural life since the Renaissance (p. 438)

modernismo: movimiento en el que escritores y artistas se rebelaron entre 1870 y 1914 en contra de los estilos literarios y artísticos tradicionales que habían dominado la vida cultural europea desde el Renacimiento (pág. 438)

money economy: an economic system based on money rather than barter (p. 134)

economía monetaria: sistema económico basado en el dinero y no en el trueque (pág. 134)

monotheistic: having one god (p. 19)

monoteísta: que tienen un solo dios (pág. 19)

*motive: a reason to take action (p. 499)

*motivo: razón para una acción (pág. 499)

mulatto: a person of mixed African and European descent (p. 208)

mulato: persona descendiente de un progenitor europeo y otro africano (pág. 208)

multinational corporation: a company with divisions in more than two countries (pp. 724, 815)

corporación multinacional: compañía con divisiones en más de dos países (pp. 724, 815)

multinational state: a state in which people of many nationalities live (p. 393)

estado multinacional: estado en el que viven personas de diversas nacionalidades (pág. 393)

nationalism: the unique cultural identity of a people based on common language, religion, and national symbols (p. 366)

nacionalismo: singular identidad cultural de un pueblo basada en un idioma, una religión y símbolos nacionales en común (pág. 366)

natural rights: rights with which all humans are born, including the rights to life, liberty, and property (p. 241)

derechos naturales: derechos con los que todos los humanos nacen, entre ellos el derecho a la vida, la libertad y la propiedad (pág. 241)

natural selection: the principle set forth by Charles Darwin that some organisms are more adaptable to the environment than others; in popular terms, "survival of the fittest" (p. 406)

selección natural: principio establecido por Charles Darwin de que algunos organismos son más adaptables al medio que otros; en términos populares, "supervivencia de los más aptos" (pág. 406)

Nazi: shortened form of the German *Nazional,* or the National Socialist German Workers' Party; a member of such party (p. 568)

nazi: forma abreviada de la palabra alemana *Nazional* o Partido Nacionalsocialista Alemán del Trabajo; miembro de ese partido (pág. 568)

Neolithic Revolution: the shift from hunting of animals and gathering of food to the keeping of animals and the growing of food on a regular basis that occurred around 8000 B.C. (p. 7)

Revolución Neolítica: el cambio desde la caza de animales y recolección de alimentos hasta el mantenimiento de animales y el cultivo de alimentos de manera habitual que ocurrió alrededor del 8000 a.C. (pág. 7)

*network: an interrelated or interconnected group or system (p. 290)

*red: grupo o sistema interrelacionado o interconectado (pág. 290)

neutrality: refusal to take sides or become involved in wars between other nations (p. 630)

neutralidad: rechazo a tomar parte o involucrarse en guerras entre otras naciones (pág. 630)

new monarchy: in the fifteenth century, government in which power had been centralized under a king or queen, i.e., France, England, and Spain (p. 141)

nueva monarquía: en el siglo XV, gobierno en el que el poder se había centralizado bajo un rey o reina, como en Francia, Inglaterra y España (pág. 141)

nongovernmental organization: an organization that has no government ties and works to address world problems (p. 817)

organización no gubernamental: organización que no tiene lazos con el gobierno y trabaja en la solución de problemas mundiales (pág. 817)

*nuclear: being a weapon whose destructive power comes from a nuclear reaction (p. 667)

*nuclear: arma cuyo poder destructivo proviene de una reacción nuclear (pág. 667)

nuclear proliferation: the spread of nuclear weapons production technology and knowledge to nations without that capability (p. 813)

proliferación nuclear: extensión de la tecnología y el conocimiento para la producción de armas nucleares a países que no tienen esa capacidad (pág. 813)

*occupation: the military force occupying a country or the policies carried out by it (p. 639)

*ocupación: fuerza militar que ocupa un país o las políticas llevadas a cabo por ella (pág. 639)

occupied: held by a foreign power (p. 788)

ocupado: poseído por un poder extranjero (pág. 788)

oligarchy: "the rule of the few", a form of government in which a select group of people exercises controls (pp. 41, 611)

oligarquía: literalmente, "gobierno de pocos", forma de gobierno en el que un grupo selecto de personas ejerce el control (pp. 41, 611)

one-child policy: China's effort, beginning in 1979, to control population growth; incentives such as education benefits, child care, and housing are offered to couples who limit their families to one child (p. 780)

política de un solo hijo: esfuerzo realizado por China a partir de 1979 para controlar el crecimiento de su población; se ofrecen beneficios, como la educación, guarderías y viviendas a las parejas que tengan solo un hijo (pág. 780)

*ongoing: continuing (p. 725)

*en curso: que continúa (pág. 725)

Open Door policy: a policy, proposed by U.S. secretary of state John Hay in 1899, that stated all powers with spheres of influence in China would respect equal trading opportunities with China and not set tariffs giving an unfair advantage to the citizens of their own country (p. 495)

política de puertas abiertas: política propuesta por el secretario de estado de los EE.UU. John Hay en 1899, que establecía que todas las potencias con esferas de influencia en China respetarían las oportunidades comerciales equitativas con China y no establecerían tarifas que dieran ventajas injustas a los ciudadanos de sus países (pág. 495)

organic evolution: the principle set forth by Charles Darwin that every plant or animal has evolved, or changed, over a long period of time from earlier, simpler forms of life to more complex forms (p. 406)

evolución orgánica: principio establecido por Charles Darwin de que cada planta o animal ha evolucionado, o cambiado, durante un largo periodo, de formas más primitivas y simples de vida a formas más complejas (pág. 406)

orthodoxy: traditional beliefs, especially in religion (p. 258)

ortodoxia: creencia tradicional, especialmente en religión (pág. 258)

*overseas: movement or transport over the sea; land beyond the sea (p. 194)

*ultramar: movimiento o transportación por mar; tierras allende los mares (pág. 194)

Pan-Africanism: the unity of all black Africans, regardless of national boundaries (pp. 594, 752)

panafricanismo: movimiento unitario de toda el África negra, independientemente de las fronteras nacionales (pp. 594, 752)

Pan-Arabism: Arab unity, regardless of national boundaries (p. 762)

panarabismo: unidad árabe, independientemente de las fronteras nacionales (pág. 762)

GLOSSARY

GLOSSARY

*participation: having a part in or sharing in something (p. 695)

*participación: tener una parte en algo o compartir algo (pág. 695)

partisan: a resistance fighter in World War II (p. 635)

partisano: luchador de la resistencia en la Segunda Guerra Mundial (pág. 635)

pasha: an appointed official in the Ottoman Empire who collected taxes, maintained law and order, and was directly responsible to the sultan's court (p. 250)

pachá: oficial designado en el Imperio otomano que cobraba impuestos, mantenía la ley y el orden y era directamente responsable ante la corte del sultán (pág. 250)

*passive: not active (p. 429)

*pasivo: no activo (pág. 429)

patrician: wealthy, powerful landowners, they formed the ruling class in the Roman Republic (p. 49)

patricio: rico y poderoso terrateniente; formaban la clase dominante en la República Romana (pág. 49)

peacekeeping forces: military forces drawn from neutral members of the United Nations to settle conflicts and supervise truces (p. 812)

fuerzas de paz: fuerza militar formada por miembros neutrales de las Naciones Unidas para resolver conflictos y supervisar treguas (pág. 812)

peninsulare: a person born on the Iberian Peninsula; typically, a Spanish or Portuguese official who resided temporarily in Latin America for political and economic gain and then returned to Europe (pp. 208, 472)

peninsular: persona nacida en la Península Ibérica; por lo general, un funcionario español o portugués que residía temporalmente en América Latina para obtener ganancia política y económica y luego regresar a Europa (pp. 208, 472)

per capita: per person (p. 778)

per cápita: por persona (pág. 778)

*percent: a part of a whole divided into 100 parts (p. 196)

*porcentaje: parte de un todo dividido en 100 partes (pág. 196)

perestroika: fundamental restructuring of the Soviet economy; policy introduced by Gorbachev (p. 696)

perestroika: reestructuración fundamental de la economía soviética; política introducida por Gorbachov (pág. 696)

permanent revolution: an atmosphere of constant revolutionary fervor favored by Mao Zedong to enable China to overcome the past and achieve the final stage of communism (p. 778)

revolución permanente: atmósfera constante de fervor revolucionario apoyada por Mao Zedong para permitir a China vencer su pasado y lograr la etapa final del comunismo (pág. 778)

*perspective: viewpoint (p. 276)

*perspectiva: punto de vista (pág. 276)

*phase: a part in the development cycle (p. 497)

*fase: parte de un ciclo de desarrollo (pág. 497)

philosophe: French for "philosopher"; applied to all intellectuals—i.e., writers, professors, journalists, economists, and social reformers—during the Enlightenment (p. 312)

philosophe: término francés para "filósofo", se aplicaba a todos los intelectuales—escritores, periodistas, economistas y reformadores sociales—durante la Ilustración (pág. 312)

*philosopher: a person who seeks wisdom or enlightenment; a scholar or a thinker (p. 302)

*filósofo: persona que busca la sabiduría o la iluminación; estudioso o pensador (pág. 302)

photomontage: a picture made of a combination of photographs (p. 578)

fotomontaje: imagen compuesta de una combinación de fotografías (pág. 578)

planned economies: economic systems directed by government agencies (p. 531)

economía planificada: sistema económico dirigido por agencias gubernamentales (pág. 531)

plantation: a large agricultural estate (p. 205)

plantación: propiedad agrícola grande (pág. 205)

plebeian: in the Roman Republic, a social class made up of minor landholders, craftspeople, merchants, and small farmers (p. 49)

plebeyos: en la República Romana, clase social compuesta de terratenientes menores, artesanos, mercaderes y pequeños granjeros (pág. 49)

plebiscite: a popular vote (p. 399)

plebiscito: voto popular (pág. 399)

pogrom: organized persecution or massacre of a minority group, especially Jews (p. 443)

pogromo: persecución organizada o masacre de un grupo minoritario, especialmente judíos (pág. 443)

*policy: an overall plan embracing the general goals and acceptable procedures of a governmental body (p. 219)

*política: plan global que comprende las metas generales y los procedimientos aceptables de un cuerpo gubernamental (pág. 219)

policy of containment: a plan to keep something, such as communism, within its existing geographical boundaries and prevent further aggressive moves (p. 666)

política de contención: plan para mantener algo, como por ejemplo el comunismo, dentro de sus fronteras geográficas existentes e impedir posteriores acciones agresivas (pág. 666)

polis: the early Greek city-state, consisting of a city or town and its surrounding countryside (p. 40)

polis: ciudad-estado de la antigua Grecia, que consistía en una ciudad o pueblo y los campos circundantes (pág. 40)

popular culture: entertainment created for a profit and for a mass audience (p. 713)

cultura popular: entretenimiento creado para obtener una ganancia y para un público de masas (pág. 713)

porcelain: a ceramic made of fine clay baked at very high temperatures (p. 283)

porcelana: cerámica hecha de arcilla fina horneada a temperaturas muy altas (pág. 283)

postmodernism: an artistic movement that emerged in the 1980s; its artists do not expect rationality in the world and are comfortable with many "truths" (p. 713)

postmodernismo: movimiento artístico que surgió en la década de 1980; los artistas no esperan que el mundo sea razonable y aceptan muchas "verdades" (pág. 713)

*precise: exact or sharply defined (p. 177)

*preciso: exacto o bien definido (pág. 177)

predestination: the belief that God has determined in advance who will be saved (the elect) and who will be damned (the reprobate) (p. 183)

predestinación: creencia de que Dios ha determinado anticipadamente quién se salvará (el elegido) y quien se condenará (el réprobo) (pág. 183)

prefecture: in the Japanese Meiji Restoration, a territory governed by its former daimyo lord (p. 504)

prefectura: en la Restauración Meiji japonesa, territorio gobernado por el anterior daimyo (pág. 504)

*primary: most important (p. 205)

*primordial: de la mayor importancia (pág. 205)

*principle: a fundamental law or idea; when said of people (e.g., someone is highly principled), it means a devotion to high codes or rules of conduct (p. 265)

*principio: ley o idea fundamental; dicho de una persona (por ejemplo, alguien de elevados principios), significa su devoción a elevados códigos o reglas de conducta (pág. 265)

principle of intervention: idea that great powers have the right to send armies into countries where there are revolutions to restore legitimate governments (p. 389)

principio de intervención: idea de que las grandes potencias tienen el derecho de enviar ejércitos a países donde existen revoluciones a fin de restaurar los gobiernos legítimos (pág. 389)

principle of nonalignment: Jawaharlal Nehru's refusal to align India with any bloc or alliance (p. 782)

principio de no alineamiento: rechazo de Jawaharlal Nehru de alinear a la India en algún bloque o alianza (pág. 782)

privatization: the sale of government-owned companies to private firms (p. 730)

privatización: venta de compañías del estado a firmas privadas (pág. 730)

*process: a series of actions or operations necessary to meet a specified end (p. 284)

*proceso: serie de acciones u operaciones necesarias para lograr un fin dado (pág. 284)

*prohibit: to prevent or to forbid (p. 573)

*prohibir: impedir o proscribir (pág. 573)

*projection: an estimate or a calculation (p. 814)

*proyección: estimación o cálculo (pág. 814)

proletariat: the working class (p. 420)

proletariado: clase trabajadora (pág. 420)

propaganda: ideas spread to influence public opinion for or against a cause (p. 526)

propaganda: ideas que se difunden para influir en la opinión pública a favor o en contra de una causa (pág. 526)

GLOSSARY

protectorate: a political unit that depends on another government for its protection (p. 452)

protectorado: unidad política que depende de otro gobierno para su protección (pág. 452)

provincial: local; of or relating to a province (p. 496)

provincial: local; de una provincia o relativo a ella (pág. 496)

psychoanalysis: a method by which a therapist and patient probe deeply into the patient's memory; by making the patient's conscious mind aware of repressed thoughts, healing can take place (p. 441)

psicoanálisis: método mediante el cual un terapeuta y un paciente indagan profundamente en la memoria del paciente; al hacer que la mente consciente del paciente tome consciencia de pensamientos reprimidos se puede llegar a la cura (pág. 441)

*psychological: mental; directed toward the will or mind (p. 542)

*psicológico: mental; dirigido hacia la voluntad o la mente (pág. 542)

*published: printed for distribution (p. 182)

*publicado: impreso para su distribución (pág. 182)

puddling: process in which coke derived from coal is used to burn away impurities in crude iron to produce high quality iron (p. 380)

pudelación: proceso en el cual se utiliza coque derivado del carbón para extraer impurezas del hierro bruto mediante el fuego y producir un hierro de alta calidad (pág. 380)

queue: the braided pigtail that was traditionally worn by Chinese males (p. 277)

coleta: cola de pelo trenzado usada tradicionalmente por los hombres en China (pág. 277)

quipu: a system of knotted strings used by the Inca people for keeping records (p. 149)

quipu: sistema de cuerdas con nudos usado por los incas para mantener sus registros (pág. 149)

racism: the belief that race determines a person's traits and capabilities (p. 451)

racismo: creencia de que la raza determina los rasgos y la capacidad de las personas (pág. 451)

*radical: relating to a political group associated with views, practices, and policies of extreme change (p. 392)

*radical: relativo a grupos políticos asociados con puntos de vista, prácticas y políticas de cambios extremos (pág. 392)

*ratio: proportion (p. 556)

*relación: proporción (pág. 556)

rationalism: a system of thought expounded by René Descartes based on the belief that reason is the chief source of knowledge (p. 309)

racionalismo: sistema del pensamiento, expuesto por René Descartes, basado en la creencia de que la razón es la fuente principal del conocimiento (pág. 309)

realism: mid-nineteenth century movement that rejected romanticism and sought to portray lower- and middle-class life as it actually was (p. 407)

realismo: movimiento de mediados del siglo XIX, que rechazaba al romanticismo y buscaba retratar la vida de las clases media y baja tal como eran (pág. 407)

real wages: the actual purchasing power of income (p. 681)

salario real: poder adquisitivo real de los ingresos (pág. 681)

*recovery: an upturn (p. 678)

*recuperación: mejoría (pág. 678)

*redistribution: alteration in the distribution of; reallocation (p. 476)

*redistribución: alteración en la distribución de algo; reasignación (pág. 476)

redistribution of wealth: the shifting of wealth from a rich minority to a poor majority (p. 605)

redistribución de las riquezas: cambio de las riquezas de las manos de una minoría rica a las de una mayoría pobre p. 605)

regime: the government in power (p. 399)

régimen: gobierno en el poder (pág. 399)

*region: a broad geographic area distinguished by similar features (p. 146)

*región: amplia área geográfica distinguida por características similares (pág. 146)

GLOSSARY

*regulation: a governmental rule or order that controls activities (p. 731)

*regulación: pauta u orden gubernamental que controla las actividades (pág. 731)

reparation: a payment made to the victor by the vanquished to cover the costs of a war (p. 545)

reparación: pago hecho a los victoriosos por los derrotados para cubrir los costos de una guerra (pág. 545)

republic: a form of government in which the leader is not a king and certain citizens have the right to vote (p. 49)

república: forma de gobierno en la cual el líder no es un rey y ciertos ciudadanos tienen derecho a votar (pág. 49)

*require: to demand as being necessary (p. 573)

*requerir: demandar por necesidad (pág. 573)

*resolution: an expression of opinion or intent (p. 760)

*resolución: expresión de opinión o intento (pág. 760)

*resolve: determination; a fixed purpose (p. 630)

*decisión: determinación; propósito establecido (pág. 630)

*responsive: quick to respond or react to (p. 696)

*sensible: que responde o reacciona rápidamente a algo (pág. 696)

*restoration: a bringing back to a former position or condition (p. 226)

*restauración: restablecer algo a una posición o condición anterior (pág. 226)

*revelations: divine truths (p. 90)

*revelaciones: verdades divinas (pág. 90)

*revenue: the yield of sources of income that a nation or state collects and deposits into its treasury for public use (p. 122)

*renta: producto de las fuentes de ingreso que un país o estado recibe y deposita en su tesorería para uso público (pág. 122)

revisionist: a Marxist who rejected the revolutionary approach, believing instead in evolution by democratic means to achieve the goal of socialism (p. 421)

revisionista: marxista que rechazó el enfoque revolucionario y cree en cambio en una evolución por medios democráticos para lograr los objetivos del socialismo (pág. 421)

*revolution: a sudden, complete change; an overthrow of government (p. 7)

*revolución: cambio completo y brusco; derrocamiento de un gobierno (p. 7)

*rigid: inflexible, unyielding (p. 320)

*rígido: inflexible, inquebrantable (pág. 320)

rococo: an artistic style that replaced baroque in the 1730s; it was highly secular, emphasizing grace, charm, and gentle action (p. 326)

rococó: estilo artístico que sustituyó al barroco en la década de 1730; era muy secular, hacía énfasis en la gracia, el encanto y las acciones nobles (pág. 326)

*role: a socially expected behavior pattern (p. 783)

*papel a desempeñar: patrón de comportamiento esperado por la sociedad (pág. 783)

romanticism: an intellectual movement that emerged at the end of the eighteenth century in reaction to the ideas of the Enlightenment; it stressed feelings, emotion, and imagination as sources of knowing (p. 402)

romanticismo: movimiento intelectual que surgió a finales del siglo XVIII como respuesta a las ideas de la Ilustración; hacía énfasis en los sentimientos, la emoción y la imaginación como fuentes del conocimiento (pág. 402)

salon: the elegant drawing rooms of great urban houses where, in the eighteenth century, writers, artists, aristocrats, government officials, and wealthy middle-class people gathered to discuss the ideas of the philosophes, helping to spread the ideas of the Enlightenment (p. 316)

salón: elegantes salas de las grandes casas urbanas donde, en el siglo XVIII, escritores, artistas, aristócratas, funcionarios gubernamentales y personas acomodadas de la clase media se reunían para discutir las ideas de los *philosophes,* con lo que ayudaban a divulgar las ideas de la Ilustración (pág. 316)

salvation: the state of being saved (that is, going to heaven) through faith alone or through faith and good works (p. 178)

salvación: estado de ser salvado (es decir, ir al cielo) a través de la fe sola o de la fe y buenas obras (pág. 178)

samurai: "those who serve", Japanese warriors similar to the knights of medieval Europe (p. 110)

samuráis: "aquellos que sirven", guerreros japoneses similares a los caballeros de la Europa medieval (pág. 110)

GLOSSARY

sanctions: restrictions intended to enforce international law (p. 625)

sans-culottes: "without breeches", members of the Paris Commune who considered themselves ordinary patriots (in other words, they wore long trousers instead of fine knee-length breeches of the nobles) (p. 347)

satellite state: a country that is economically and politically dependent on another country (p. 666)

scientific method: a systematic procedure for collecting and analyzing evidence that was crucial to the evolution of science in the modern world (p. 309)

secede: withdraw (p. 401)

secular: worldly (p. 162)

secularization: indifference to or rejection of religion or religious consideration (p. 405)

self-strengthening: a policy promoted by reformers toward the end of the Qing dynasty under which China would adopt Western technology while keeping its Confucian values and institutions (p. 492)

separation of powers: a form of government in which the executive, legislative, and judicial branches limit and control each other through a system of checks and balances (p. 312)

sepoy: an Indian soldier hired by the British East India Company to protect the company's interests in the region (p. 466)

serf: in medieval Europe, a peasant legally bound to the land who had to provide labor services, pay rents, and be subject to the lord's control (p. 133)

***series:** a group of related things or events (p. 275)

shah: king (used in Persia and Iran) (p. 256)

***shift:** a change in direction or attitude (p. 704)

Shinto: "the Sacred Way" or "the way of the Gods", the Japanese state religion; among its doctrines are the divinity of the emperor and the sacredness of the Japanese nation (p. 112)

shogun: "general", a powerful military leader in Japan (p. 110)

social contract: the concept proposed by Rousseau that an entire society agrees to be governed by its general will, and all individuals should be forced to abide by the general will since it represents what is best for the entire community (p. 315)

Social Darwinism: theory used by Western nations in the late nineteenth century to justify their dominance; it was based on Charles Darwin's theory of natural selection, "the survival of the fittest", and applied to modern human societies (p. 442)

sanciones: restricciones impuestas para obligar a cumplir la ley internacional (pág. 625)

sans-culottes: "sin pantalones", miembros de la Comuna de París que se consideraban patriotas ordinarios (en otras palabras, usaban calzones largos en vez de finos pantalones hasta la rodilla) (pág. 347)

estado satélite: país que depende económica y políticamente de otro (pág. 666)

método científico: procedimiento sistemático para recolectar y analizar evidencias, fue crucial para la evolución de la ciencia en el mundo moderno (pág. 309)

secesión: separación (pág. 401)

secular: mundano (pág. 162)

secularización: indiferencia o rechazo a la religión o la consideración religiosa (pág. 405)

autofortalecimiento: política promovida por reformadores hacia fines de la dinastía Qing, bajo la cual China adoptaría la tecnología occidental, aunque mantendría sus valores e instituciones confucianos (pág. 492)

separación de poderes: forma de gobierno en la cual las ramas ejecutiva, legislativa y judicial se limitan y controlan entre sí a través de un sistema de controles y balances (pág. 312)

cipayo: soldado indio contratado por la Compañía Británica de la India Oriental para proteger los intereses de esa compañía en la región (pág. 466)

siervo: en la Europa medieval, campesino confinado legalmente a la tierra y que tenía que proporcionar servicios, pagar rentas y estar sujeto al control del señor (pág. 133)

***serie:** grupo de cosas o eventos relacionados entre sí (pág. 275)

sha: rey (se usaba en Persia e Irán) (pág. 256)

***cambio:** variación en la dirección o la actitud (pág. 704)

sintoísmo: "el Camino Sagrado" o "el Camino de los Dioses", religión de estado en Japón; entre sus doctrinas están la divinidad del emperador y la santidad de la nación japonesa (pág. 112)

shogun: "general", poderoso líder militar de Japón (pág. 110)

contrato social: concepto propuesto por Rousseau de que una sociedad completa accede a ser gobernada por su voluntad general y que todos los individuos deben ser forzados a someterse al deseo general, ya que representa lo mejor para la comunidad completa (pág. 315)

darwinismo social: teoría utilizada en las naciones occidentales a finales del siglo XIX para justificar su dominio; se basaba en la teoría de la selección natural de Charles Darwin, "la supervivencia de los más aptos", aplicada a las sociedades humanas modernas (pág. 442)

socialism: a system in which society, usually in the form of the government, owns and controls the means of production (p. 385)

***sole:** being the only one (p. 674)

***source:** a document or primary reference book that gives information (p. 778)

soviets: Russian councils composed of representatives from the workers and soldiers (p. 538)

***sphere:** any of the concentric, revolving, spherical transparent shells in which, according to ancient astronomy, the stars, sun, planets, and moon are set (p. 304)

spheres of influence: areas in which foreign powers have been granted exclusive rights and privileges, such as trading rights and mining privileges (p. 493)

***stability:** the state of being stable; strong enough to endure (p. 228)

stalemate: the condition that exists when neither of two opposing sides is able to make significant gains (p. 785)

state capitalism: an economic system in which the central government plays an active role in the economy, establishing price and wage policies and subsidizing vital industries (p. 790)

***style:** having a distinctive quality or form (p. 173)

submission: act of submitting to the control or authority of another (p. 91)

***subsidy:** government payment to encourage or protect a certain economic activity (pp. 204, 505)

***successor:** one that follows, especially one who succeeds to a throne or an office (p. 258)

suffrage: the right to vote (p. 427)

sultan: "holder of power", the military and political head of state under the Seljuk Turks and the Ottomans (pp. 94, 250)

surrealism: artistic movement that seeks to depict the world of the unconscious (p. 579)

***survive:** to remain alive or in existence (p. 5)

sustainable development: economic development that does not limit the ability of future generations to meet their basic needs (p. 806)

suttee: the Hindu custom of cremating a widow on her husband's funeral pyre (p. 265)

***symbol:** something that stands for something else by way of association; a visible sign of something invisible (p. 702)

systematic agriculture: the keeping of animals and the growing of food on a regular basis (p. 7)

socialismo: sistema en el cual la sociedad, por lo general en la forma de un gobierno, posee y controla los medios de producción (pág. 385)

***solo:** ser el único (pág. 674)

***fuente:** documento o libro de referencia primaria que ofrece información (pág. 778)

soviet: consejo ruso, compuesto de representantes de los trabajadores y los soldados (pág. 538)

***esfera:** cualquiera de las capas esféricas, transparentes, concéntricas y giratorias en las que, según la astronomía antigua, estaban las estrellas, el Sol, los planetas y la Luna (pág. 304)

esferas de influencia: áreas en las que a una potencia extranjera se le han garantizado derechos y privilegios exclusivos, como derechos comerciales y privilegios de minería (pág. 493)

***estabilidad:** propiedad de estable; suficientemente fuerte como para resistir (pág. 228)

estancamiento: condición que existe cuando ninguno de las dos partes opuestas puede obtener ventajas significativas (pág. 785)

capitalismo de estado: sistema económico en el cual el gobierno central desempeña una función activa en la economía, mediante políticas de precios y salarios y el subsidio de industrias vitales (pág. 790)

***estilo:** tener una cualidad o forma distintiva (pág. 173)

sometimiento: acto de someterse al control o autoridad de otro (pág. 91)

***subsidio:** pago gubernamental para estimular o proteger cierta actividad económica (pp. 204, 505)

***sucesor:** el que sigue, especialmente el que sigue en el trono o en un cargo (pág. 258)

sufragio: derecho a votar (pág. 427)

sultán: "poseedor del poder", líder militar y político del estado bajo el gobierno de los turcos seléucidas y otomanos (pp. 94, 250)

surrealismo: movimiento artístico que trata de representar la vida del inconsciente (pág. 579)

***sobrevivir:** mantenerse vivo o en existencia (pág. 5)

desarrollo sostenible: desarrollo económico que no limita la capacidad de generaciones futuras de satisfacer sus necesidades básicas (pág. 806)

suttee: costumbre hindú de incinerar a la viuda en la pira funeraria de su esposo (pág. 265)

***símbolo:** algo que sustituye a algo más por asociación; signo visible de algo invisible (pág. 702)

agricultura sistemática: el mantenimiento de animales y la siembra de alimento de modo regular (pág. 7)

Glossary   **R79**

taille: an annual direct tax, usually on land or property, that provided a regular source of income for the French monarchy (p. 340)

taille: impuesto directo anual, por lo general sobre la tierra o la propiedad, que generaba una fuente regular de ingresos para la monarquía francesa (pág. 340)

*target: something or someone marked for attack (p. 529)

*blanco: algo o alguien marcado para ser atacado (pág. 529)

*task: a duty or function (p. 739)

*tarea: deber o función (pág. 739)

*technology: the science or study of the practical or industrial arts; applied sciences (p. 132)

*tecnología: ciencia o estudio de las artes prácticas o industriales; ciencia aplicada (pág. 132)

Thatcherism: the economic policy of British Prime Minister Margaret Thatcher, which limited social welfare and restricted union power (p. 707)

thatcherismo: política económica de la primera ministra británica Margaret Thatcher, que limitaba el bienestar social y restringía el poder de los sindicatos (pág. 707)

totalitarian state: a government that aims to control the political, economic, social, intellectual, and cultural lives of its citizens (p. 560)

estado totalitario: gobierno que aspira a controlar la vida política, económica, social, intelectual y cultural de sus ciudadanos (pág. 560)

total war: a war that involves the complete mobilization of resources and people, affecting the lives of all citizens in the warring countries, even those remote from the battlefields (p. 531)

guerra total: guerra que implica la movilización completa de recursos y personas, afecta a las vidas de todos los ciudadanos en los países en guerra, incluso de aquellos alejados de los campos de batalla (pág. 531)

trade embargo: a policy prohibiting trade with a particular country (p. 733)

embargo comercial: política que prohíbe el comercio con un país en particular (pág. 733)

*traditional: established; customary (p.109)

*tradicional: establecido; habitual (pág. 109)

*traditions: established customs of a people (p. 462)

*tradiciones: costumbres establecidas de un pueblo (pág. 462)

*transfer: to take over the control of (p. 784)

*transferir: transmitir el control de algo (pág. 784)

*transformation: conversion; change in character or condition (p. 55)

*transformación: conversión; cambio en el carácter o condición (pág. 55)

*transition: changeover; the move toward one form, stage, or style to another (p. 419)

*transición: conversión; el cambio de una forma, estado o estilo a otro (pág. 419)

*transport: the moving of goods or people (p. 13)

*transportar: trasladar bienes o personas (pág. 13)

*transportation: means of travel from one place to another (p. 204)

*transporte: medio de viajar de un lugar a otro (pág. 204)

trench warfare: fighting from ditches protected by barbed wire, as in World War I (p. 527)

guerra de trincheras: combate desde trincheras protegidas por alambres de púa, como en la Primera Guerra Mundial (pág. 527)

*trend: a pattern or general tendency (p. 578)

*tendencia: patrón o inclinación general (pág. 578)

triangular trade: a pattern of trade that connected Europe, Africa and Asia, and the American continents; typically, manufactured goods from Europe were sent to Africa, where they were exchanged for enslaved persons, who were sent to the Americas, where they were exchanged for raw materials that were then sent to Europe (p. 206)

comercio triangular: patrón comercial que conectaba a Europa, África y Asia con las Américas, por lo general se enviaban manufacturas de Europa a África, donde las intercambiaban por esclavos que enviaban a las Américas y donde los cambiaban por materias primas que enviaban a Europa (pág. 206)

tribute: goods or money paid by conquered peoples to their conquerors (p. 147)

tributo: bienes o dinero pagado por pueblos conquistados a sus conquistadores (pág. 147)

GLOSSARY

ulema: a group of religious advisers to the Ottoman sultan; this group administered the legal system and schools for educating Muslims (p. 251)

ulema: grupo de consejeros religiosos del sultán otomano; este grupo administraba el sistema legal y las escuelas para educar a los musulmanes (pág. 251)

uncertainty principle: the idea put forth by Heisenberg in 1927 that the behavior of subatomic particles is uncertain, suggesting that all of the physical laws governing the universe are based on uncertainty (p. 579)

principio de incertidumbre: idea establecida por Heisenberg en 1927 de que el comportamiento de las partículas subatómicas es incierto, lo que sugiere que todas las leyes físicas que rigen el universo se basan en la incertidumbre (pág. 579)

*uncharted: not mapped; unknown (p. 459)

*ignoto: que no aparece en el mapa; desconocido (pág. 459)

*unification: the act, process, or result of making into a coherent or coordinated whole; the state of being unified (p. 395)

*unificación: acción, proceso o resultado de convertir algo en un entero coherente o coordinado; estado de estar unificado (pág. 395)

*unique: distinctive; unequaled (p. 326)

*único: distintivo; sin igual (pág. 326)

universal law of gravitation: one of the three rules of motion governing the planetary bodies set forth by Sir Isaac Newton in his *Principia;* it explains that planetary bodies do not go off in straight lines but instead continue in elliptical orbits about the sun because every object in the universe is attracted to every other object by a force called gravity (p. 305)

ley de la gravitación universal: una de las tres reglas del movimiento que rigen los cuerpos planetarios establecida por sir Isaac Newton en su *Principia;* explica que los cuerpos planetarios no se mueven en línea recta, sino que continúan en órbitas elípticas alrededor del Sol, porque cada objeto en el universo es atraído hacia todos los otros objetos por una fuerza llamada gravedad (pág. 305)

universal male suffrage: the right of all males to vote in elections (p. 392)

sufragio universal masculino: el derecho de todos los hombres a votar en elecciones (pág. 392)

*unprecedented: having nothing that has been done or said in the past to compare to (p. 560)

*sin precedentes: que no se ha hecho o dicho algo similar en el pasado (pág. 560)

*unreliable: not dependable (p. 733)

*desconfiar: que no se puede confiar (pág. 733)

*unrestricted: having no restrictions or bounds (p. 531)

*irrestricto: que no tiene restricciones ni límites (pág. 531)

urban society: a system in which cities are the center of political, economic, and social life (p. 162)

sociedad urbana: sistema social en el cual las ciudades son el centro de la vida política, económica y social (pág. 162)

varna: the name given by Aryans in ancient India to a group of people in what was believed to be an ideal social structure of four groups (p. 23)

varna: el nombre que los arios de la antigua India le dieron a un grupo social del cual se creía que era una estructura social ideal de cuatro grupos (pág. 23)

vassal: under feudalism, a man who served a lord in a military capacity (p. 120)

vasallo: en el feudalismo, hombre que servía a un señor en calidad de militar (pág. 120)

vernacular: the language of everyday speech in a particular region (p. 171)

vernácula: lengua que se habla cotidianamente en una región particular (pág. 171)

viceroy: a governor who ruled as a representative of a monarch (p. 468)

virrey: gobernador que regía como representante de un monarca (pág. 468)

*violation: a disregard of rules or agreements (p. 620)

*violación: desacato de las reglas o acuerdos (pág. 620)

*virtually: almost entirely; nearly (p. 48)

*virtualmente: casi enteramente; aproximadamente (pág. 48)

GLOSSARY

*volunteer: one who enters the military voluntarily (p. 592)

*voluntario: quien entra voluntariamente al ejército (pág. 592)

war communism: in World War I Russia, government control of banks and most industries, the seizing of grain from peasants, and the centralization of state administration under Communist control (p. 541)

comunismo de guerra: en la Rusia de la Primera Guerra Mundial, el control gubernamental de los bancos y la mayoría de las industrias, la confiscación de granos a los campesinos y la centralización de la administración estatal bajo el control comunista (pág. 541)

war of attrition: a war based on wearing the other side down by constant attacks and heavy losses, such as World War I (p. 529)

guerra de desgaste: guerra que se basa en desgastar al otro bando con constantes ataques y grandes pérdidas, como en la Primera Guerra Mundial (pág. 529)

welfare state: a state in which the government takes responsibility for providing citizens with services such as health care (p. 680)

estado de bienestar: estado en el que el gobierno asume la responsabilidad de proveer a los ciudadanos de servicios como la atención sanitaria (pág. 680)

*widespread: widely extended or spread out (p. 644)

*generalizado: ampliamente extendido o diseminado (pág. 644)

women's liberation movement: the renewed feminist movement of the late 1960s, which demanded political and economic equality with men (p. 685)

movimiento de liberación de la mujer: movimiento feminista renovado de finales de la década de 1960, que exigía la igualdad política y económica con los hombres (pág. 685)

zaibatsu: in the Japanese economy, a large financial and industrial corporation (p. 598)

zaibatsu: en la economía japonesa, gran corporación financiera e industrial (pág. 598)

zamindar: a local official in Mogul India who received a plot of farmland for temporary use in return for collecting taxes for the central government (p. 263)

zamindar: oficial local en la India de los mogoles, que recibía un lote de terreno para su uso temporal a cambio de cobrar impuestos para el gobierno central (pág. 263)

Zionism: an international movement originally for the establishment of a Jewish national or religious community in Palestine and later for the support of modern Israel (p. 443)

sionismo: movimiento internacional que originalmente abogaba por el establecimiento de una comunidad nacional o religiosa judía en Palestina y después por el apoyo al Israel moderno (pág. 443)

GLOSSARY

The following abbreviations are used in the index: m = map;
f = feature (photograph, picture, painting, cartoon, chart); t = table; q = quote

Abbas, Mahmoud, 763
Abbasid Empire, 93
'Abbās (shāh of Safavid Empire), 258, 268
'Abd ar-Rahmān, 95f
Abdulhamid II (Ottoman ruler), 586
abolitionism, 401
Aborigines, 5
Abraham, 18, 90
absolutism, 228; in Central and Eastern Europe, 231–233; and crisis in Europe, 216–245; enlightened, 318–322, 319m; Louis XIV and, 229f, 242; response to crises, 228–233, 242
abstract painting, 440
Abū al-'Abbās (caliph of Abbasid Empire), 93
Abū Bakr (caliph of Arab Empire), 92–93
Achebe, Chinua, 757
Acheson, Dean, 666q
Achilles, 39
acid rain, 806
acquired immunodeficiency syndrome (AIDS), 753, 805, 805f
Acropolis, 40f
Act of Supremacy: of 1534, 185
Adenauer, Konrad, 679–680, 680f
***Adoration of the Magi* (Dürer),** 175
Adrianople, 59
Aegean Sea, 56
Aegospotami, 43
***Aeneid* (Virgil),** 53
Aeschylus, 44
Afghanistan, 695, 709; invasion by Soviet Union, 695; Soviet occupation of, 765; Taliban in, 765; U.S. invasion of, 765, 811
Afonso I (king of the Congo), 206, 206f, 206q
Africa, 4. *See also* Central Africa; East Africa; *individual states*; North Africa; West Africa; Atlantic slave trade, 204–207; Bantu spread ironworking across, 88; centers of trade in, 99t; changing names of nations, 823f; colonial legacy in, 754, 756, 756f; David Livingstone arrives in, 452; dictatorships ended in, 754; economic problems of, 752–753, 756f; emergence of civilizations, 98–99; on the eve of colonialism, 464–465m; expansion of Ottoman Empire in,

249–250; Great Britain annexes west coastal states of, 452; health problems of, 752–753; imperialism in, 450, 456–463, 457m, 593m; independent nations of, 750, 751m; infection of cattle, 517f; influenced by nationalism, 614; leaders of independent states, 751–752; malaria outbreak, 823f; nationalism in, 462–463, 592–594, 593m, 610f; new imperialism and, 482; number of Africans who fought in World War II, 659f; number of languages spoken in, 823f; percentage of Africa controlled by colonial powers, 517f; political challenges in, 753–754, 809; scramble for, 465f; society and culture of, 103, 756–757; sources of enslaved Africans, 206; women's roles in, 757
African Americans: civil rights movement, 346f, 682; enslaved, 401; as part of the military during World War II, 646; post-Civil War, 435; relocation to northern cities during World War II, 646; segregation becomes illegal in U.S. public schools, 688f
African National Congress (ANC), 750–751, 754, 755f
African Union (AU), 752
Afrikaners (Boers), 457m, 460–461, 750
Agamemnon (king of Mycenae), 39, 44
Agra, 265
agriculture. *See also* farming; systematic agriculture: during the Columbian Exchange, 200; in Early Middle Ages, 132; Green Revolution, 805; improvements in during High Middle Ages, 132–133; plantations, 205–206; systematic, 2, 7
Aguinaldo, Emilio, 453
Ahmadinejad, Mahmoud, 765
Ahuizotl (Aztec king), 150–151f
AIDS (acquired immunodeficiency syndrome), 753, 805, 805f
airplane: advances in, 802; computers used in, 803; first flight of, 418
Aix-la-Chapelle, Treaty of, 322
Aiyar, G. S., 471
Akbar (shāh of India), 264f, 264q, 268, 373f; expansion of Mogul rule in India, 216; reign of, 262–264

Akhenaten (pharaoh of Egypt), 15f, 16
Akkadian Empire, 11
Albania, 676; transition from communism, 701m
Albany Congress, 325f
Alberti, Leon Battista, 162
Albert (Prince of Great Britain), 409q
Aldrin, Buzz, 804
Alexander II (czar of Russia), 400
Alexander III (czar of Russia), 400
Alexander the Great (king of Macedonia), 46–47. *See also* Hellenistic Era; conquest of Egyptian Empire, 16; death of, 36; empire of, 46m; Hellenistic Era and, 45–47; invasion of Persian Empire, 21, 46
Alexandra (empress of Russia), 536
Alexandria, Egypt, 47
Alexius I (Byzantine emperor), 125
al-Fatah, 763
Alfonsin, Raúl, 738
Algeria: French colony in, 458; independence of, 750
Allah, 90
Allende, Salvador, 736
Allied Powers: division of Germany into four zones, 666; help to Communists' enemies during Russian Revolution, 541; U.S. as arsenal of, 645; in World War I, 530
Allied Reparations Commission, 555
al-Mutawakkil (caliph of Abbasid Empire), 96f
Al-Omari, Lulua Abdullah, 822q
al-Qaeda, 708f, 709, 765
Alvarado, Juan Velasco, 739
American Civil War, 401, 427, 435
American Red Cross, 400f
American Revolution, 330–332, 334; land claims after, 331m; surrender of British at Yorktown, 334f
Amin, Idi, 754
Amritsar massacre, 596
Anabaptist(s), 183m, 185; persecution of an, 188f
anarchy, 258
Anasazi, 144
Angkor Thom, 114
Angkor Wat Temple, 114
Anglican Church (Church of England), 183m, 184–185, 186f
Angola, 750

Anime, 791f
Annam, 452
Annan, Kofi, 816f
annexed, 456
annul, 184
***Antigone* (Sophocles),** 44
anti-Semitism. *See also* Holocaust; Jews; Nazi Germany: of Hitler, 568, 569f; *Kristallnacht,* 572f, 573; of Nazi Germany, 570, 571f, 572f, 573, 580f, 654f; Nuremberg laws, 573; Reformation and, 186; roots of, 443; Zionism and, 442f, 443
Antoninus Pius (Roman emperor), 51
Antony, Marc, 50
ANZUS defensive alliance, 793
apartheid, 750–751, 754, 755f
APEC (Asia Pacific Economic Cooperation), 816
Appian Way, 53
Aquino, Benigno, 787
Aquino, Corazon, 787
Arab Empire, 92–93; conquest of Persian Empire, 93; defeat of Byzantine army, 92
Arabia: independence of, 587
Arab-Israeli conflict, 704
Arab-Israeli disputes, 760, 761m, 762–764
Arab nationalism, 590–591
Arafat, Yasir, 763
Aramco, 591
Arandora Star, 642
Arbenz, Jacobo, 735
Arc de Triomphe, 338
archaeology: discovery of King Tut's tomb, 658f
Archimedes, 302
archipelago, 114
architecture: ancient Egyptian, 17; ancient Greek, 43; the baroque period, 237–238; basilica style, 137; Bauhaus, 658f; in early Japan, 112; of Enlightenment, 325–326; functionalism in, 440; Gothic, 138, 138f; Inca, 149; Islamic, 97; Latin American, 729; during Middle Ages, 137–138; modernism in, 440; neo-Gothic style, 402; in the Ottoman Empire, 252; Palace of Versailles, 234–235f; Renaissance, 173–174; Roman, 53; Romanesque, 137; romanticism in, 402; what significance a building can convey, 452–453
Ardennes Forest, 628
Argentina, 724, 737; authoritarian rule in, 611; caudillos and, 476; export economy of, 479,

INDEX

608; Great Depression in, 609*f*, 610; independence of, 474, 475; major developments in, 727*f*; move toward democracy, 738; nationalism in, 610*f*; new strategy in, 737–738; political events in, 737*m*; teenage life in, 742–743*f*
Aristotle, 41, 45, 302, 304
armada, 220
Armenian genocide, 587–588, 588*f*
armistice, 544
arms race, 667
Armstrong, Neil, 804
Arroyo, Gloria, 787
Articles of Confederation, 333
art(s). *See also* architecture; drama; literature; music; painting; poetry; sculpture; theater: African, 757; after the Renaissance, 236–238; baroque period, 237–238; Chinese, 283; classical Greek, 43–44; dadaism, 578; Dark Age of ancient Greece, 39*f*; early African, 103; of Enlightenment, 325–327; golden age in China, 109; the golden age of literature, 238–240; Islamic, 97; Japanese theater, 288; Latin American, 729; Mannerism, 236; of Nazi Germany, 579; Northern Renaissance, 175; in the Ottoman Empire, 252; photomontage, 578; postmodernism, 713; realism in, 406*f*, 407; Renaissance, 173–175; Rococo style, 326, 326*f*; in Roman Empire, 53; romanticism in, 402–403, 403*f*; surrealism, 578–579; in the Tokugawa Era in Japan, 287–288; trends in after World War II, 713
Aryans, 22; Nazi German view of, 442–443, 569*f*, 570, 571, 571*f*, 573
Ashurbanipal (king of Assyrian Empire), 20
Asia, 98. *See also* South Asia; Southeast Asia; Western Asia; Asian theater during World War II, 633, 635; the Asian world, 106–115; Cold War in, 781; ethnic and religious conflicts in, 808; imperialism in, 450; nationalism in, 595, 610*f*, 614; New Order in, 643; political challenges in, 809; trade networks from East Africa to, 105*f*; women in, 787; World War II in, 1705-1709, 632*m*
Asian tigers, 791–793
Asia Pacific Economic Cooperation (APEC), 816
Aśoka (king of Mauryan Empire), 26
assembly line, 419, 577

***Assertio Septem Sacramentorum* (Henry VIII),** 184*f*
Assyrian Empire, 20–21
astrolabe, 97, 197*f*
astronomy: Scientific Revolution and, 304–305, 306*f*
Atatürk (Mustafa Kemal), 588–589, 610*f*
Athens, city-state of, 40, 41
Atlantic slave trade, 204–207
atman, 24
atoms, 440, 579
Attlee, Clement, 680
Augsburg, Peace of, 178*m*, 181, 182
Augustan Age, 53
Augustus (Roman emperor) (Gaius Octavius), 50, 51*f*, 55; Age of, 50, 53; becomes emperor, 37; population of Rome during reign, 53
Aum Shinrikyo, 804
Aung San Suu Kyi, 785
Aurangzeb (shāh of India), 265
Auschwitz, 640; the Final Solution at, 641*f*
Australia, 796; recent years, 793
Australopithecus, 4
Austria, 231; Austrian Empire, 231–232; Austro-Prussian War, 396; authoritarian rule in, 566–567; Congress of Vienna, 388–389; Crimean War, 395; expansion of, 231*m*; German unification and, 396, 622; Italian unification and, 395–396; right to vote for women, 684; Seven Years' War, 322–323; succession of Maria Theresa in, 322; war with France, 347
Austria-Hungary: anti-Semitism in, 443; Balkans and, 437; creation of, 399; end of Austro-Hungarian Empire, 544; government of, 434; industrialization in, 419; nationalities in, 392*m*, 393; as part of Central Powers in World War I, 530; response to assassination of Archduke Ferdinand, 524; Triple Alliance, 436, 522, 527, 528, 532, 544
Austrian Empire: 319–321; nationalism in, 399; nationalities in, 392*m*, 393; revolutions of 1848 and, 393
Austrian Succession, War of, 322
Austro-Prussian War, 396
authoritarian governments, 580
authoritarian states, 566; Eastern Europe, 566–567; Spain, 567
autonomous, 703
***Autumn* (Ba Jin),** 501
Avignon, 140

Axis Powers, 633, 654, 664
Axum, Kingdom of, 99
Ayacucho, Battle of, 475
Ayutthaya, 114
Azerbaijan, 256; independence from Soviet Union, 696
Azikiwe, Nnamdi, 594
the Aztec, 147; destruction of civilization, 198–199; practice of human sacrifice, 147; role of religion in Aztec society, 150–151*f*

Bābur (shāh of India), 262
Babylon, 11; capture by Persians, 21; Hammurabi comes to power in, 3
Bacciochi, Elisa, 364*f*
Bach, Johann Sebastian, 327
Bacon, Francis, 303*m*, 308*q*, 309
Bagehot, Walter, 398*f*
Baines, Edward, 387*f*
Ba Jin, 501, 501*q*
balance of power: Congress of Vienna and, 388–389
balance of trade, 204
Balfour, Arthur James, 590*f*, 591
Balfour Declaration, 590*f*, 591
Balkans: Crimean War, 394–395; crises in, 437, 524; expansion into by Ottomans, 268; first war of the, 444*f*
Bande Mataram, 471
Bangladesh, 112; creation of, 784
Bantu(s), 101; migration of, 102*m*; spread of ironworking across Africa, 88, 102*m*, 130
baroque period, 237–238
baroque style, 326, 327
barrel vault, 137
Barrios de Chungara, Domitila, 809*q*
Barton, Clara, 400*f*, 427
Baseball Player at Bat, 428*f*
Basescu, Traian, 702
Basho, Matsuo, 288
Batista, Fulgencio, 732, 732*f*
Battle of Ayacucho, 475
Battle of Britain, 630–631
Battle of Hastings, 120
Battle of Ivry, 242*f*
Battle of Masurian Lakes, 527
Battle of Midway Island, 633
Battle of Mohacs, 250
Battle of Plassey, 266*m*, 268
Battle of the Coral Sea, 633
Battle of Tours, 95*f*
Bauhaus School, 658*f*
Bay of Naples, 52
Bay of Pigs, 669–670, 732*f*
Beccaria, Cesare, 314
Beer Hall Putsch, 568

Beethoven, Ludwig van, 403–404
Begin, Menachem, 763
Beijing, China, 108, 274, 491, 495, 779, 779*f*; Red Guards parade in, 796*f*
Belarus: independence from Soviet Union, 696
Belgian Congo, 750
Belgium, 134; artistic Renaissance in, 175; Hitler's victory against, 628; imperialism by, 457*m*, 459, 593*m*; independence of, 391; industrialization in, 383, 419
Bell, Alexander Graham, 417
Bellarmine (Cardinal), 305*q*
Benedictine order, 119
Benin, 103, 279
Berbers, 93, 100
Berlin Airlift, 667*f*
Berlin Conference, 459, 465*f*
Berlin Wall, 669, 672–673*f*, 688*f*; destruction of, 718*f*; fall of, 702*f*
Berners-Lee, Tim, 822*f*
Bernhardi, Friedrich von, 442
Bernini, Gian Lorenzo, 237
Beslan, 699
Beveridge, Albert, 453*q*
Bhopal chemical disaster, 806
Bible: comparison of views on, 186*f*; Gutenberg's, 166*f*; Hebrew, 18; New Testament, 56; Old Testament, 18
Bill of Rights: American, 332*f*, 333, 390; English, 217, 227
bin Laden, Osama, 708–709, 708*f*, 765
bioethics, 804
biological weapons, 804
bioterrorism, 804
biowarfare, 804
birth control, 426
Birth of a Nation, 576
Bismarck, Otto von, 396–397, 397*f*, 434, 436, 436*f*, 459; at Berlin Conference, 465*f*; William II fires, 414
Black Death, 139–140, 142–143*f*
Black Dragon Society, 599
Blackfriars, 238
***The Black Man's Burden* (Morel),** 462*f*
Blackshirts, 580*f*
Blair, Tony, 707
Blake, William, 405
blitz, 648, 658*f*; London's finest hour, 652–653*f*
blitzkrieg, 628
bloc, 681
Bloody Mary, 185
"Bloody Sunday", 434, 536, 715; in St. Petersburg, Russia, 415
Blucher, 381

Blue Mosque: in İstanbul, 158–159*f*
bodhi, 25
The Body of Civil Law **(Justinian Code),** 123*f*
Boers (Afrikaners), 457*m,* 460–461
Boff, Leonardo, 740*f*
Bohemia, 181, 224, 393
Boleyn, Anne, 184, 185
Bolívar, Simón, 474–475, 474*f*
Bolivia, 475, 608, 726; political events in, 737*m*
Bolsheviks, 538, 548, 564; Lenin and the, 538–539; Old, 565; seize power in Russia, 539–540
Bonaparte, Jerome, 364*f*
Bonaparte, Joseph, 364*f*
Bonaparte, Louis, 364*f*
Bonaparte, Napoleon. *See* Napoleon Bonaparte (emperor of France)
Boniface VIII (pope), 140
Bonivard, François, 403*f*
Borghese, Pauline, 364*f*
Bosnia, 524, 718; annexation of, 437; wars in, 703
Bosnia-Herzegovina, 703
Bosnian War, 588
Bossuet, Jacques-Benigne, 229*q*
Botswana, 753
Boulding, Elise, 817
Bourbon dynasty, 396
bourgeoisie (burghers), 342, 384, 420
Boxer Rebellion, 495, 497*m,* 498*f*
Boxers, 495
boyars, 232
Boyle, Robert, 303*m,* 306
Boyle's Law, 306
Brahman, 24
Brahma the Creator, 24
Brahmins, 23
Brandt, Willy, 680, 705
Brazil, 208, 724, 739, 744; authoritarian rule in, 611; "economic miracle", 739; export economy of, 476, 479, 608; Great Depression in, 609*f,* 610, 611; harvesting coffee in, 482*f;* independence of, 475; major developments in, 727*f;* nationalism in, 610*f;* as part of Portuguese Empire, 199, 211; political events in, 737*m;* return to democracy, 739; silver mines in, 212*f*
Brazzaville, 756
Brezhnev, Leonid, 694
Brezhnev Doctrine, 694
Briand, Aristide, 556
British East India Company, 267, 466, 467, 490
British India. *See also* India
Brittany, 715; Fest Noz, 715

Brunelleschi, Filippo, 165*f,* 173–174
Brussels, 237
bubonic plague, 139, 142–143*f*
Buddhism, 24–25; stupas show spread of, 25*f*
budget deficits, 707
Bulgaria, 437, 566–567; transition from communism, 701*m*
bureaucracy, 292
burghers, 167
Burma (modern Myanmar): British control of, 452, 454, 493; independence of, 785; resistance to colonial rule in, 454*f,* 455
Burundi, 754
Bush, George, 707, 735
Bush, George W., 707, 765, 766, 810–811; 9/11, 707–708; war on terror, 708*f*
Bushido, 110
Byzantine Empire, 249; conquered by the Ottomans, 268; Crusades and, 123–125; Europe and, 118–125
Byzantium, 58

Cabot, John, 197
Caesar, Julius (Roman emperor), 50, 51*f*
Cairo Trilogy **(Mahfouz),** 767
Calderón, Felipe de Jesús, 731
Calvin, John, 182–184, 186, 221
Calvinism, 182–184, 183*m,* 186*f,* 188, 224
Cambodia, 452, 785
Cambyses (king of Persia), 21
Cameroon, 456
Camp David Accords, 763
Canada, 664–666, 709; American-Canadian relations, 683; NAFTA and, 816; Official Languages Act, 709; Quebec secession issue, 709; Seven Years' War and, 324–325, 330; U.S. and, 707–709
Canning, Charles, 467*f*
The Canterbury Tales **(Chaucer),** 171
Can Vuong, 455
Cao Xuein: *The Dream of the Red Chamber,* 283
Cape Colony, 460, 460*f,* 461
Cape Horn, 144
Cape Town, South Africa, 460, 756
capital, 378
capitalism: commercial, 280; industrial, 384
Caravaggio, 238
caravanserai: Safavid, 260–261*f*
caravel, 197*f*

Cardenas, Lázaro, 610*f,* 611–612
Caribbean, 206; economic dependence of, 476; export economy of, 608; political events in, 731*m;* U.S. role in, 609
Carolingian Empire, 120
Carson, Rachel, 806
Carter, Howard, 658*q*
Carter, Jimmy, 695, 707, 735, 763
Carthage, 48–49
Cartwright, Edmund, 380
cash crops, 476
Caspian Sea, 256
caste system, 23–24, 783
Castiglione, Baldassare, 166, 166*q*
Castle of Chillon, 403*f*
Castro, Fidel, 669, 732*f,* 744*f*
Castro, Raúl, 732
Çatalhüyük, Turkey, 8*f*
Catherine II (Catherine the Great) (Russian ruler), 319*m,* 321–322, 321*f,* 322, 334*f*
Catherine of Aragon, 184, 185
Catholic Church. *See also* Catholicism: Anglican Church and, 184–185; beliefs of, 186*f;* decline of power, 140–141; in Europe, 1600, 183*m;* in fascist Italy, 563; French Revolution and, 340, 341*f,* 345; Galileo versus, 304–305, 305*f;* Great Schism, 140; liberation theology, 740*f;* Martin Luther versus, 179–180; Napoleon Bonaparte and, 363; papal monarchy, 135–136; Papal States, 135; Peace of Augsburg and, 181; reformation of, 176–178, 187; role of the in medieval Europe, 118; state and Church in colonial Latin America, 210–211
Catholicism. *See also* Catholic Church: Spain's militant, 218
Catholic Reformation, 187
Cavendish, Margaret, 303*m,* 307, 307*q*
Cavour, Camillo di, 395–396
Ceauşescu, Nicolae, 702
Central Africa: Hutu versus Tutsi in, 754; imperialism in, 459
Central America, 733–735. *See also individual states;* economic dependence of, 476; export economy of, 479, 608; independence of, 475; as part of Spanish Empire, 199; political events in, 731*m;* U.S. role in, 609
Central Europe, 122. *See also individual states;* absolutism in, 231–233; governments of, 434; literacy and, 429; revolutions of 1848 in, 393
Central Powers: in World War I, 530

Central Treaty Organization (CENTO), 669
Cervantes, Miguel de, 239
Cezanne, Paul, 439
Chacabuco, Battle of, 475
Chaeronea, Battle of, 45
Chaldeans, 19, 20; King Nebuchadnezzar, 21
Chamberlain, Houston Stewart, 442–443
Chamorro, Violeta Barrios de, 735
Charlemagne (Charles the Great) (king of the Franks), 120
Charles I (king of England), 225, 226*f;* execution of, 242*f*
Charles I (king of Spain), 164, 181
Charles II (king of England), 226
Charles V (Holy Roman emperor), 179, 181
Charles V (king of Spain), 150–151*f*
Charles VII (king of France), 140*f*
Charles VIII (king of France), 164
Charles X (king of France), 391
Chaucer, Geoffrey, 171
Chauvet, Jean-Marie, 5*f*
Chavez, Hugo, 741
Chechnya, 698*f,* 698–699
checks and balances, 312, 333
Cheka, 541
chemical wastes, 806
chemical weapons, 804
chemistry: classification of elements, 405; Scientific Revolution and, 306
Chernobyl nuclear accident, 806
Chiang Kai-shek, 606*f;* attempt to build a republic, 614; versus Communists, 601*m,* 601–603, 776; flight to Taiwan, 776; as leader of China, 603–605; as leader of Republic of China (Taiwan), 792–793; losing control of China, 667; New Life Movement of, 604*f,* 605; seeks to appease Japan, 624–625
Chichén Itzá: El Caracol at, 130–131*f*
children: in China, 780; labor performed by, 380, 381*f,* 383, 385; in Renaissance Italy, 167; in World War II, 641–642
"Children of Israel", 18–19
Chile, 724, 736; art of, 613; export economy of, 608; Great Depression in, 610; independence of, 474–475; major developments in, 727*f;* number of governments

INDEX

between 1931 and 1932, 659*f*; political events in, 737*m*; protest of brutal rule of Augusto Pinochet, 744*f*; toward economic stability in, 736

China, 27, 296. *See also* People's Republic of China; Boxer Rebellion, 495; Chinese society and culture, 280–282; civil war in, 499, 776; cultural changes in, 499–501, 500*f*; democracy movement in, 778–779, 779*f*; early dynasties of, 28*t*; economic changes in, 281*f*; economy of, 499–500; Europeans in, 279; family in ancient, 30–31; first contacts with the West, 276; Four Modernizations, 779*f*; goes to war with Japan, 414; golden age in arts, 109; Han dynasty, 28; imperialism in, 492–495, 500, 512; influenced by nationalism and revolution, 614; isolation of, 278*f*; at its height, 274–279; Korean War, 781; Long March, 602*f*, 603; under the Ming and Qing dynasties, 1368–1911, 275*m*; the Ming dynasty, 274–276; New Life Movement, 605; Northern Expedition, 601*m*; one-child policy, 807; Open Door Policy, 494–495, 494*f*, 599; Opium War, 490, 491*f*; population growth, 281*t*, 780, 807, 814; Qin dynasty, 27–28; Qing dynasty, 277–279; Red Guards, 778; reunification of, 106–109; revolution and transition in, 512; revolution of 1911, 496–499; rural in the 1930s, 607*f*; sale of British goods in, 512*f*; Shang dynasty, 27; Shanghai Massacre, 601; Song dynasty, 106; spheres of influence in, 489*m*, 512; Tai Ping Rebellion, 490–491; Taiwan, claims on, 793; Tang dynasty, 106; urban in the 1930s, 606*f*; war with Japan, 493, 507, 624–625; Zhou dynasty, 27

chinampas, 147

Chinese Communist Party (CCP), 600, 602*f*, 607*f*; is formed, 453

Chirac, Jacques, 705

chlorofluorocarbons, 806

Choshu, Japan, 503

Christian Democratic Union (CDU), 679; in West Germany, 706

Christian humanism, 176–178, 178*f*

Christianity. *See also* Catholic Church: adoption by Roman Empire, 56–57; medieval, 135–137; Rome and the rise of, 48–59; spread of in Roman Empire, 56, 57*f*; teachings of Jesus, 55–56

Chulalongkorn (king of Thailand), 452

Churchill, Winston, 634, 651, 652–653*f*

Church of England (Anglican Church), 183*m*, 184–185, 186*f*, 188

Cicero, 170

citizen, 358*f*

citizenship: views of, in revolutionary France, 358–359*f*; who should be a citizen, 358–359*f*

city(ies): African, 756–757; bombing of during World War II, 648–649; public health and sanitation in, 422–423

city-states, 10. *See also* polis; Greek, 40

Civil Code (Napoleonic Code), 363

Civil Constitution of the Clergy, 345

civil disobedience, 596; Gandhi and, 470, 470*f*, 596, 597*f*

civilization, 7; change comes to India's, 23*f*; early American, 144–149; early Chinese, 27–31; early Greek, 38–41; early Indian, 22–26; in early Mesoamerica, 144–147; early South American, 148–149; emergence of African, 98–99; in Europe after fall of Western Roman Empire, 118–122; Harappan, 22; height of Mycenaean civilization, 36; Indus River valley, 22–24; the Maya and the Toltec, 144–147; the Olmec, 144; in Southeast Asia, 114–115; Sumerian, 10–13; toward a global, 660–823

Civil Rights Act of 1964, 425*f*, 682, 683*f*

civil rights movement, 346*f*, 682, 688; 1960s and, U.S., 682

civil service: exam under Emperor Jen-Tsung, 30*f*; rule of merit, 30*f*

Civil War: in the U.S., 207, 452

civil wars: as ongoing challenge, 808

Ci Xi (Chinese empress dowager), 492*f*, 493, 496, 498*f*

clan(s), 281

classical music, 327

classless society, 420, 420*f*

Clay, Lucius, 667*f*

Cleisthenes (Athenian reformer), 41

Clemenceau, Georges, 545, 545*f*

Clement VII (pope), 181

Cleopatra VII (Egyptian pharaoh), 16

Clermont, 383

Clinton, Bill, 707, 763, 764*f*

Clive, Sir Robert, 266*f*, 267

cloning, 804, 823*f*

clothing: of France, 348–349*f*

Clovis (king of the Franks), 118

coal industry, 380, 384–385

Code of Hammurabi, 12–13

coke, 380

Colbert, Jean-Baptiste, 230

Cold War, 650, 713; arms race, 667–668; in Asia, 781; Berlin Wall, 669; confrontation of the superpowers, 664–666; Cuban Missile Crisis, 669–671; development of, 664–671, 668*t*; division of Germany, 666; intensifies, 695; Marshall Plan, 666; military alliances, 668–669; political division and conflict during, 688; in Southeast Asia, 786*f*; Soviet Union and Eastern Europe during, 688; spread of, 667–671, 668*f*; Truman Doctrine, 665–666; Vietnam and the domino theory, 671; Western Europe and North America during, 688

collaborators, 641

collective bargaining, 421, 558

collectivization, 564–565, 776–777

Colombia, 726, 740; coffee and cocaine, 740–741; drug cartels in, 744; independence movement in, 474, 475; independence of Panama, 735; major developments in, 727*f*; political events in, 737*m*; U.S. intervention in, 477

colonial rule. *See* imperialism

colony, 204

Colosseum, 60–61*f*

Columbian Exchange, 199–200, 202–203*f*

Columbus, Christopher, 196, 200*f*; arriving in the Americas, 131, 212*f*, 373*f*

Comintern (Communist International), 595, 600

command economy, 675*f*, 675*t*

commercial capitalism, 280

Committee of Public Safety, 352, 353, 354*f*, 357

Committee of Union and Progress (CUP), 588*f*

commodities, 499

common law, 120

commonwealth, 225

communes, 777

communism, 419; in art, 612*f*, 613; in Asia, 595, 595*f*; in China, 600–603, 776–781; in Europe, 1694s, 561*m*; Great Depression and, 557; in North Korea, 781; revolts against, 677; in Russia, 540*f*; in Southeast Asia, 595, 595*f*, 785, 786*f*; in Soviet Union, 563–565; transition of Eastern Europe from, 701*m*; U.S. fighting spread of in Latin America, 726–727; U.S. intervention in Central American politics, 744

Communist China. *See* People's Republic of China

Communist International. *See* Comintern

***The Communist Manifesto* (Marx),** 419, 420*f*

Communist National Liberation Front (NLF), 786*f*

Communist People's Liberation Army, 664

Communist(s), 539; celebrations in Moscow, 614*f*; in China, 614; complacent and corrupt in Soviet Union, 694; in Czechoslovakia, 676, 677; fear of infiltration in the U.S., 681–682; in Hungary, 677; number of current Communist states, 823*t*; patterns of control in Eastern Europe, 676–677; in Poland, 677; Red Terror, 541; triumph in Russia, 541

Compromise of 1867, 399

computer-aided imaging, 804

computers, 802–804

concentration camps, 570

Concert of Europe, 389; breakdown of, 394–395

concessions, 502

***The Conditions of the Working-Class in England in 1844* (Engels),** 386*f*

Coney Island, 428*f*

Confederate States of America, 401

Confederation of the Rhine, 365

Confucianism, 31, 604*f*

Confucius, 30*f*, 31, 32*f*

Congo: Belgian colonies in, 459; Democratic Republic of, 750, 752, 754

Congress of Vienna, 388–389; Europe after, 389*m*

Congress Party, 782, 784

conquistadors, 198; seizing of land ruled by Aztec and Inca, 212

conscription, 523

conservatism, 388–389

Conservative Party, 432, 559; of Great Britain, 707

Constantine (Roman emperor), 57, 58–59, 254*f*; conversion to Christianity, 57*f*; his contributions to the spread of Christianity, 57*t*; legalizes Christianity, 37

Constantinople, 58, 123, 255*m*; fall of, 255*f*; Muslim attack of, 93; "New Rome", 58

Constitution: American, 333, 401, 425*f*, 435; Austrian, 434; French, of 1791, 346; French, of 1795, 357; French, of 1875, 432–433; German, 434; Japanese, 788, 789; Meiji, 504; Mexican, of 1917, 478*f*, 479; Turkish, 586

Constitutional Convention, 333

INDEX

consulate, 362
consuls, 50
consumer society, 684
Continental Army, 332
Continental Congress, 331–332
Continental System, 365, 366
contras, 735
Convention People's Party, 752*f*
Conwy Castle in Wales, 126*f*
cooperatives, 739
Copernicus, Nicolaus, 303, 303*m*, 304, 306*f*, 334*f*
Corday, Charlotte, 352*f*
Córdoba. *See also* Fatimid dynasty
Cornwallis (General), 332
Cort, Henry, 380
Cortázar, Julio, 729
Cortés, Hernán, 150–151*f*, 195, 198–199, 200*f*
Costa Rica, 475
cottage industry, 379, 381*f*, 387*f*
cotton industry, 379–380, 384, 385, 401
Council for Mutual Economic Assistance (COMECON), 666
council of the plebs, 50
Council of Trent, 187
coup d'état, 357
Courbet, Gustave, 406*f*, 407
Cranmer, Thomas, 184
***The Creation* (Haydn),** 327
creoles, 208, 212, 472, 474
Crimean War, 394–395, 400*f*, 410, 427
***On Crimes and Punishments* (Beccaria),** 314
Croatia, 703
Croats, 392*m*, 393
Cromwell, Oliver, 225, 226, 226*f*
crops: cash, 476; rotation of, 133
Cruikshank, George, 356*f*
Crusades, 123, 124*m*, 125
Cuba, 196, 669; Cuban Revolution, 732–733; decline of Cuban economy, 744; economic dependence of, 476; Great Depression in, 609*f*; major developments in, 727*f*; political events in, 731*m*; as protectorate of U.S., 477; relations with the U.S., 733
Cuban Missile Crisis, 669–671, 670*f*, 688, 733
Cuban Revolution, 732–733; Cuban revolutionaries seize Havana, 744*f*; Fidel Castro's, 732*f*
cubism, 440
cultural imperialism, 713
Cultural Revolution (China), 778; Red Guards parade in Beijing, 796*f*

culture: Chinese, 280–283; distinctive Korean, 289; early African, 103; in early Japan, 111–112; of early Mesoamerica, 145*m*; early South American, 148; identity and, 713–715; Islamic, 96–97; Latin American, 728–729; mass, 576–577, 578*f*; medieval, 137–139; popular, 713; regional identity in Western Europe, 714*m*; in Southeast Asia, 114; spread and transformation of Western, 718; Western culture and society, 710–715; world of European, 236–241
culture of modernity, 438–440
cuneiform, 13, 32*f*
Curie, Marie, 440, 444; Nobel Prize for Chemistry, 517f
currency. *See* euro; Ṣafavid use of coins, 260–261*f*
Cuzco, 149
Cyrus (Cyrus the Great) (king of Persia), 21
czar, 232
Czechoslovakia, 546, 677, 700–701; Communist control of, 676; democracy in, 567; Dubček's "socialism with a human face", 677; Hitler's destruction of, 622; invasion by Soviet Union, 677; Nazi invasion of, 518–519*f*; right to vote for women, 684; split into Czech Republic and Slovakia, 701; transition from communism, 701*m*
Czech Republic, 698, 701
Czechs: in Austrian Empire, 392*m*, 393, 434

dadaism, 578
d'Aelders, Etta Palm: citizenship for women, 358*q*
da Feltre, Vittorino, 173*q*
da Gama, Vasco, 196; lands in Calicut, 272
Dai Vet, 114
Dakar, 756
Dalai Lama, 808
d'Albuquerque, Alfonso, 196
Dalí, Salvador, 579
Damascus, Syria, 93
dancing cabinet, 507
d'Anglas, Boissy, 359*f*
Dante Alighieri, 171, 171*f*
Danton, Georges, 350, 352
Dao, 27, 31
Darfur, Sudan, 754, 808
Darius I (king of Persia), 21
Dark Age: of ancient Greece, 39–40, 39*f*
Darwin, Charles, 405–406
da Silva, Luiz Inácio Lula, 739
David, Jacques-Louis, 342*f*, 352*f*, 361*f*

***David Copperfield* (Dickens),** 407
da Vinci, Leonardo, 162, 174, 174*f*, 373*f*
Dawes Plan, 556
D-Day, 634, 634*f*, 636, 636*f*, 637*m*
death camps, 571, 640; Auschwitz, 640, 641*f*
***The Death of Marat* (David),** 352*f*
de Beauharnais, Eugène, 364*f*
de Beauharnais, Hortense de, 364*f*
de Beauvoir, Simone, 684*f*, 685
De Beers mining company, 460*f*
de Cervantes, Miguel, 239
de Chamorro, Violeta Barrios, 735
Declaration of Independence, 332; U.S., 240*f*
Declaration of the Rights of Man and the Citizen, 345, 353, 358*f*
***Declaration of the Rights of the Negro Peoples of the World* (Garvey),** 594
***Declaration of the Rights of Woman and the Female Citizen* (Gouges),** 345*q*
Defender of the Faith, 184*f*
deficit spending, 559
de Firmont, Henry, 352*q*
deforestation, 806, 807*f*, 818
Degas, Edgar, 506*f*
de Gaulle, Charles, 678, 679, 750
de Geoffrin, Marie-Thérèse, 316–317
de Gortari, Carlos Salinas, 731
de Gouges, Olympe, 345, 345*q*, 353; writes declaration of rights for women, 273
de Guzmán, Dominic, 136
Deir el-Bahri, 16
de Klerk, F. W., 754, 755*f*
Delacroix, Eugène, 403, 403*f*
de la Cruz, Sor Juana Inés, 211
de las Casas, Bartolome, 210*q*
de Lesseps, Ferdinand, 457
Delhi, India, 262; the siege of, 482*f*
demand-side economics, 558*f*
demilitarized, 621
demilitarized zone (DMZ), 792*f*
democracy, 41; Argentina's move toward, 738; Brazil's return to, 739; Chinese movement for, 777*m*, 778–779, 779*f*; comparing

Athenian to modern U.S., 42*t*; direct, 43; in Europe, 1930s, 561*m*; Latin America's move toward, 725; mass society and, 414–443; ministerial responsibility and, 432; Pericles expands Athenian, 42*f*; in Southeast Asia, 787; in Western Europe, 432–433
Democracy Wall, 779*f*
Democratic Republic of Congo, 750, 752, 754
Deng Xiaoping (emperor of China), 778, 796
Denmark: adoption of gender parity policies, 712; Latin American colonies of, 473*m*
de Pizan, Christine, 172, 172*q*
depression, 556
de Sautuola, Marcelino Sanz, 5*f*
Descartes, René, 303*m*, 308–309, 308*q*
***The Descent of Man* (Darwin),** 406
desertification, 806
de Staël, Anne-Louise-Germaine, 363
de-Stalinization, 675
détente, 694
deterrence, 669
de Vega, Lope, 240
developed nations, 807
developing nations, 807; population trends in, 814; women entrepreneurs in, 808*f*
development: sustainable, 806; United Nations goals for, 816*f*
Dewey, Commodore George, 452
Díaz, Porfirio, 478
Dickens, Charles, 407
dictatorship, 420
Diderot, Denis, 313, 321, 321*f*, 334*f*
Diem, Ngo Dinh, 785, 786*f*
Dien Bien Phu, Vietnam, 785
Diocletian (Roman emperor), 58–59
direct democracy, 43
the Directory, 357
direct rule, 454, 462
disarmament groups, 817
***Discourse on Method* (Descartes),** 308
***Discourse on the Origins of the Inequality of Mankind* (Rousseau),** 315
discrimination, 787
Disraeli, Benjamin, 398*f*
dissidents, 694
***Divine Comedy* (Dante),** 171, 171*f*
divine right of kings, 225
documentaries, 577, 577*f*
Doge, 164
domestication, 7

INDEX

Dominican Republic, 477, 477*f*

Dominican(s): missionaries in the Spanish Empire, 211

domino theory, 671; Vietnam and, 671

Donatello, 165*f*, 173

Don Giovanni **(Mozart),** 327

Don Quixote **(Cervantes),** 239

dowry, 167

drama: ancient Greek, 44; Kabuki, 294–295*f*

Dravidians, 23

Drawn in Color **(Jabavu),** 757

The Dream of the Red Chamber **(Xuein),** 283

Dreyfus, Alfred, 442*f*, 443

Dreyfus Affair, 442*f*, 443

Duarte, José, 734

Dubček, Alexander, 677

Du Bois, W.E.B., 594

Duke of Wellington, 367

Duma, 434, 538

Dun, Mao, 501

Dürer, Albrecht, 175

Dutch, 293

Dutch East India Company, 454

Dutch East Indies, 452, 454; Japanese invasion of, 631

Dutch Republic: American Revolution, 332; Belgium annexed by, 391

dynasty, 14

Early Middle Ages: agriculture in, 132; population, 132

East Africa: imperialism in, 459; societies in, 101; trade networks from East Africa to Asia, 105*f*

East Asia: East Asian world, 272–299

Eastern Europe, 122, 676–677, 700–703. *See also individual states;* absolutism in, 231–233; after World War I, 547; authoritarian states in, 566–567; during the Cold War, 688; Communist patterns of control, 676–677; conflict of superpowers over, 664; economic and political change in, 718; Gorbachev stops giving Soviet military support to, 696; governments of, 434; revolutions in, 700–702; Soviet Union and, 674–677; ten countries join the European Union, 704; transition from communism, 701*m*

Eastern Front: World War I, 527–528

Eastern Orthodox Church, 183*m*

Eastern Roman Empire. *See* Byzantine Empire

East Germany, 705–706; Berlin Wall, 669; creation of, 666

Eastman, George, 439

East Timor, 808

Ebert, Friedrich, 544

Echeverría, Luis, 730

ecological disasters, 806

ecology, 806

economic imperialism in Latin America, 476

economic interdependence, 815*f*, 816

economics: laissez-faire, 313*f*, 314, 314*f*; Smith on, 313–314; supply-side versus demand-side, 558*f*

economy(ies): colonial, 454; consumer, 675*t*; global, 419, 807, 815–816, 815*f*; *keiretsu,* 598*f*; money, 134; market, 675*t*; planned, 531; *zaibatsu,* 598, 598*f*, 790

Ecuador, 148, 474; political events in, 737*m*

Eden, Fanny, 516*q*

Edict of Milan, 57

Edict of Nantes, 221

Edict of Worms, 179

Edison, Thomas, 414, 416–417

education: Elizabethan, 372*f*; humanist, 172–173; in Japan, 506; literacy and, 429; Second Industrial Revolution and, 428–429; universal, 428–429; universities in the High Middle Ages, 139

Edward I (king of England), 121

Edward VI (king of England), 185

Edwards, Jorge, 729

Egypt: Camp David Accords, 763; imperialism in, 457; independence of, 456–457; Islamic revivalism and, 767; literature in, 767; Napoleon's plans for, 361; Palestinian Liberation Organization and, 763; Pan-Arabism in, 762; Six-Day War, 761*f*, 762–763; Suez Canal, 457–458, 458*f*; Suez War, 761, 761*f*; in United Arab Republic, 762; Yom Kippur War, 761*f*, 763

Egypt, ancient, 14–17; discovery of King Tut's tomb, 658*f*; geography of, 15*m*; Great Sphinx, 14; Middle Kingdom, 15; mummification, 14; New Kingdom, 15–16; Old Kingdom, 14; pyramids of, 14; society of, 16

Einsatzgruppen, 640

Einstein, Albert, 305, 440–441, 444, 579, 658*f*, 822*q*

Eisenhower, Dwight D., 634, 681*q*

electors, 357

electricity, 405, 416–418

El Greco, 236

elite class, 424

Elizabeth I (queen of England), 185, 219, 225

El Salvador, 475, 731*m*, 733, 733–734, 735

Elvis, 823*f*

e-mail, 803–804

emancipation, 400

Emancipation Proclamation, 401

Embarkation for Cythera **(Watteau),** 326

Émile **(Rousseau),** 315

empire(s): 11; Abbasid, 93; Akkadian, 11; Arab, 92–93; Assyrian, 20–21; Carolingian, 120; early Indian, 26; Egyptian, 14–17; Gupta, 26; Holy Roman, 122; Islamic, 92–95; Macedonian, 45–47; Mauryan, 26; Mogul, 262–267; Mongol, 94; Ottoman, 248–253; Persian, 21; Roman, 52–59; Safavid, 256–259; Umayyad, 93

Enabling Act, 570

enclosure movement, 378

encomienda, 199; system, 210*f*

Encyclopedia, or Classified Dictionary of the Sciences, Arts, and Trades **(Diderot),** 313, 321*f*

Engels, Friedrich, 386*q*, 419, 420*f*

England, 120. *See also* Great Britain; Bill of Rights, 227; British control of India, 266*f*; city population of, 422; civil war and commonwealth, 225; defeat of the Spanish Armada, 216, 220*m*; Elizabethan education, 372*f*; English explorers and settlements, 201; establishment of the English Parliament, 121; Glorious Revolution, 227; population of, 1750–1851, 379*f*; Protestantism in, 219; the Restoration, 226–227; revolutions in, 225–227; Shakespeare's, 238; the Stuarts and divine right, 225; surrender of British to Americans at Yorktown, 334*f*; United Kingdom formed with Scotland, 330

The English Constitution **(Bagehot),** 398*f*

English Reformation, 184–185

enlightened absolutism, 318–322, 319*m*

Enlightenment, 334; absolutism and, 318–322, 319*m*; arts of, 325–327; Europe in age of, 311*m*; French Revolution and, 342, 345; influence of Locke and Newton on, 310–311; liberalism and, 390; philosophes of, 312–313, 315; reading in, 316; religion in, 317; romanticism and, 403; salons in, 316–317; Scientific Revolution

and, 306*f*, 310; social contract of, 315; social sciences of, 313–314; women's rights and, 315, 426

entrepreneurs, 378

environmental crisis, 806, 807*f*

ephors, 41

The Epic of Gilgamesh, 13

epic poem(s): of ancient Greece, 39; *The Epic of Gilgamesh,* 13; *Iliad,* 39; *Odyssey,* 39

Equal Pay Act of 1963, 425*f*, 712

Erasmus, Desiderius, 176–178, 178*f*, 188

Erhard, Ludwig, 680

Eridu, 10

Eşfahān, 257; center of Şafavid economic power, 260–261*f*

Esmā'īl (shāh of Şafavid Empire), 256, 268

Essay Concerning Human Understanding **(Locke),** 310

estates, 340–342, 348–349*f*

Estates-General, 342–344

Estonia: independence from Soviet Union, 696

Ethiopia, 461, 753, 754; defeat of Italy by, 458; Mussolini's invasion of, 622

ethnic cleansing, 588, 703; in Bosnia, 588, 808

Etruscans: Arch of Constantine in Rome, 62*f*; defeated by Rome, 48; influence on early development of Rome, 48

Euphrates River, 10

euro, 704, 816; debut of, 823*f*

Europe. *See also* Central Europe; Eastern Europe; *individual states;* Western Europe: in 1871, 433*m*; in 1687, 555*m*; in 1694s, 561*m*; after Peace of Augsburg, 178*m*; after Peace of Westphalia, 224*m*; after World War I, 543*m*; after World War II, 650*m*; alliances in, 1678, 523*m*; anti-Semitism in, 443; arrival of Europeans in Southeast Asia, 292–293; and the Byzantine Empire, 118–125; Congress of Vienna, 388–389, 389*m*; crisis and absolutism in, 216–245; domination of world economy by early 1900s, 444; education in, 428–429; era of European imperialism, 374–515; Europeans in China, 279; Europeans in Japan, 284–286; European theater during World War II, 633, 634; European voyages of discovery, 195*m*; European rivals during Age of Exploration, 201; feudalism, 286*f*; imperialism of. *See* imperialism; Industrial Revolution in, 382–385; Jewish population in Europe before and after World War II, 639*f*; kingdoms and feudalism, 118–122; leisure in, 429; liberalism

INDEX

and, 390; in the Middle Ages, 132–141; migration in, 706f; Napoleonic, 364m; nationalism in, 390, 398–400; national unification in, 394–397; the New Order in, 638–639; new social structure, 683–685; North America and, 704–709; population growth of, 423m; population trends in, 814; reform in, 398–400; religious conflicts in, 242; revival of trade in medieval, 134; revolutions in, 390–393; rivalry of superpowers during Cold War, 664; road to World War I, 444, 522–525; Seven Years' War in, 323, 323m; social structure of, 424; Thirty Years' War, 224; urban environment of, 422–423; the Wars of Religion, 218–221; witchcraft trials, 222–223; women in, 425–427, 684–685; world of European culture, 236–241; World War II and, 628–631, 629m; World War I in, 527m

European Community (EC), 704

European Economic Community (EEC), 704; 1721, 679m; move toward unity, 681

European Recovery Program. See Marshall Plan

European Union (EU), 704, 718; euro, 704; euro as currency of, 816; expansion of, 1721-2007, 705m; as trading bloc, 816

Evening News (London), 429

evolution: organic, 406

Exploration, Age of, 194–211; Atlantic slave trade, 204–207; early exploration of West Africa, India, and the Americas, 212; European rivals, 201; European voyages of discovery, 195m; motives and means to explore, 194–195; new lands to explore, 197; Portuguese explorers, 196; race for riches, 196–197; Spanish Empire, 198–200; Spanish explorers, 196–197; technology and exploration, 197f

extraterritoriality, 490

Exxon Valdez oil spill, 806

Ezānā (king of Axum), 99

Facing Mount Kenya **(Kenyatta),** 594q

factions, 351

Factory Act of 1833, 385

Falkland Islands, 738

family: in ancient China, 30–31; changes in the Western culture, 711; in early African society, 103; lineage groups, 103; in nineteenth century, 426; in Renaissance Italy, 167

Family (Ba Jin), 501

Famous Places on the Tokaido: a Record of the Process of Reform **(Hiroshige III),** 506f

Fanning, Shawn, 822f

Faraday, Michael, 405

farming: during Aztec Empire, 147; debates over organic, 710; decline in 1950s Europe, 684; in early Japan, 111; in Early Roman Empire, 52; Neolithic farming villages, 6f; organic, 805; spread of, 6m

Fascio di Combattimento, 561

fascism, 561; in Europe, 1930s, 561m; in Italy, 560–563, 562f

Fatimid dynasty, 93

Faucher-Gudin, 351f

Federalists, 401

Federal Republic of Germany, 666

federal system, 333

Female Association for the Care of the Poor and Sick, 427

feminism, 426

Ferdinand, Archduke Francis, 524, 524f, 548f

Fertile Crescent, 8f, 10

Fest Noz, 715

feudalism, 120; comparing Japanese and European, 286t; European, 118–122

fief, 120

Fielding, Henry, 327

Fifteenth Amendment, 435

Fifth Modernization, 778, 779f

filial piety, 30

Fillmore, Millard, 502

film. See movies

Final Solution. See Holocaust

Finland, 546; women's suffrage in, 427

Firmont, Henry de, 352q

First Battle of the Marne, 526

First Continental Congress, 331

First International, 421

First Republic of France, 350–351

First War of Independence in India, 466–467, 467f

Five Pillars of Islam, 92f

Five Women Who Loved Love **(Saikaku),** 287

Five Year Plans, 564

Flanders, 201

Flaubert, Gustave, 407

Florence, Italy, 163, 164, 165f, 171f, 173, 174, 174f, 188

flying buttress, 138, 138f

flying shuttle, 379

footbinding, 282

Forbidden City. See Imperial City

Ford, Gerald, 707

Ford, Henry, 418f, 419

Formosa. See Taiwan (Formosa)

Four Modernizations, 778, 779f

Four Olds, 778

"Fourteen Points": Woodrow Wilson's proposal, 544

Fourteen Saints, Church of the, 326

Fourteenth Amendment, 435

Fox, Vicente, 731, 744

Fragonard, Alexandre, 359f

France: American Revolution, 332; anti-Semitism in, 443; bans wearing of headscarves by Muslims, 706q; Boxer Rebellion and, 495; city population of, 422; Congress of Vienna, 388, 389; Crimean War, 394; declares war on Germany, 623; de Gaulle and, 678–679; democracy in, 432–433; Franco-Prussian War, 396, 397; French explorers and settlements, 195m, 201, 209m; French Wars of Religion, 221; German unification and, 396–397; Great Depression and, 558; Hitler's victory against, 628–630; imperialism by. See France, colonial interests of; impressionism and postimpressionism in, 438–439; industrialization in, 383, 419; Italian unification and, 396; Italian wars, 164; Laos occupied by, 493; under Louis XIV, 228–230; National Assembly, 704; Ottoman territories controlled by, 590; Popular Front government in, 558; reparation demands by, 554–555; response to German expansion, 620, 622; right to vote for women, 684; Ruhr Valley occupation by, 555, 555m; Second Empire of, 399; Seven Years' War, 322–325; spheres of influence in China, 493; Suez War, 761; Third Republic of, 432–433; three estates of, 340–342, 341f; Triple Entente, 436, 522; uncertainties in, 704–705; Vichy France, 630; vying for trade in India, 267; war with Austria, 347

France, colonial interests of: in Africa, 456–458, 457m, 459, 462, 592, 593m, 750; in Latin America, 472–473, 473m; in Middle East, 587m, 588, 590; in Southeast Asia, 451m, 452, 480–481f, 595, 595f, 785, 786f

France, First Republic of, 350–351

France, revolutionary: army of, 355; the Directory, 357; radicalization of, 350–352; Reign of Terror, 338, 349f, 353–354, 356, 356f; revolution of 1848 in, 391–392

France, Second Republic of, 392

Franciscan(s): missionaries in the Spanish Empire, 211

Francis I (king of France), 181

Francis Joseph (ruler of Austria-Hungary), 399, 434

Franco, Francisco, 567, 567q

Franco-Prussian War, 396, 397

Frankenstein, Victor, 516q

Frankenstein (Shelley), 404, 404f, 405

Frankfurt, Germany, 423

Frankfurt Assembly, 392

Franklin, Benjamin, 313f, 325f

Frederick I (king of Holy Roman Empire), 122

Frederick I (king of Prussia), 231

Frederick II (Frederick the Great) (king of Prussia), 319, 319m, 320, 320f, 322, 323

Frederick II (king of Holy Roman Empire), 122

Frederick the Wise (elector of Saxony), 178, 179

Frederick William I (king of Prussia), 319

Frederick William IV (king of Prussia), 392

Frederick William the Great Elector, 231, 242

French and Indian War, 324m, 324f

French Empire, 365

French Guiana, 737m

French Indochina, 452, 454, 480–481f, 595, 595f, 785, 786f

French New Deal, 558

French Republic: Fifth, 678; Fourth, 678

French Revolution: background to, 340–342; beginning of, 338, 340–347; causes of the, 368; clothing of, 349f; long-term effects of, 368; Napoleon and ideals of, 362–363, 364f, 365; radicalization of, 350–352; short-term effects of, 368; spread of ideals of, 364f, 365

French Wars of Religion, 221; Battle of Ivry, 242f; beginning of, 216

French West Africa, 456

fresco, 173, 175, 326

Freud, Sigmund, 438, 441, 441f, 444, 579

Friend of the People (Marat), 350

Fuhlrott, Johann, 5f

Führer, 570

fuji, 759f

Fujimori, Alberto, 740

Fulton, Robert, 383

functionalism, 440

fundamentalist militants, 811

Fuyo, 598f

INDEX

Gabriel, 90
Gaelic, 715
Galen, 306
Galilee, 55
Galileo, 303, 303*m*, 306*f*, 373*f*;
Catholic Church versus, 304–305,
305*q*; Church condemns teachings
of, 273
Gallipoli, 530
Gandhi, Indira, 782–784, 784*f*
**Gandhi, Mohandas
(Mahatma),** 470, 470*f*, 482,
596, 597*f*, 610*f*, 614, 782; revives
India's movement for independence,
453; Salt Walk, 659*f*
Gandhi, Rajiv, 784
Garcia, Anastasio Somoza,
734
Garibaldi, Giuseppe, 396, 397*f*
Garvey, Marcus, 594
Gasparovic, Ivan, 701
**GATT (General Agreement on
Trade and Tariffs),** 816
gender parity, 712
gender stereotyping, 712
**General Agreement on Trade
and Tariffs (GATT),** 816
*General Theory of
Employment, Interest, and
Money* **(Keynes),** 558*f*, 559
General War Commissariat,
242
genetic engineering, 804
Geneva, Switzerland,
183–184
Geneva Peace Accords, 786*f*
Genghis Khan, 94; life in his
army, 116–117*f*
genocide, 588, 640, 642*f*. *See
also* ethnic cleansing; Holocaust;
Armenian, 587–588, 588*f*; in
Darfur, 808; in Rwanda, 754
Gentileschi, Artemisia, 238
gentlemen's agreement, 508
geocentric, 304
geography: how it influences
civilization, 2
George, David Lloyd, 545
George I (king of England),
330
Georgia: independence from
Soviet Union, 696
German Communist Party,
544
German Confederation, 392;
North, 396, 397
**German Democratic
Republic,** 666
German East Africa, 456
German Reformation, 181
**German Social Democratic
Party,** 420*f*, 421
German Southwest Africa,
456

German Workers' Party, 568
Germany, 4. *See also* East
Germany; Nazi Germany; West
Germany; 1950–1961, 672–673*m*;
anti-Semitism in, 443; Bauhaus
architecture, 658*f*; Bosnian Crisis
and, 437; Boxer Rebellion and, 495;
collapse and armistice, World War I,
543–544; divided Germany and the
Berlin Airlift, 667*m*; division of, 651,
666; German offensive during World
War I, 542–543; Great Depression
and, 556–557, 557*f*, 558, 569;
industrialization in, 419; inflation in,
555–556, 558; old order in, 434;
political change in postwar, 680*f*;
provisions of Treaty of Versailles,
546, 554–555; racism in,
442–443; religious warfare in, 181;
reparations for World War I, 545,
555, 556; results of peace treaties
after World War I, 548*f*; reunification
of, 696, 702; reunification woes,
705–706; revolutionary forces
in, 544; right to vote for women,
684; sinking of the *Lusitania*, 531;
Spanish Civil War and, 566*f*, 567;
spheres of influence in China, 493;
transition from communism, 701*m*;
Treaty of Brest-Litovsk with Russia,
540; Triple Alliance, 436, 522;
unification of, 395*m*, 396–397;
Weimar Republic, 558
**Germany, colonial interests
of:** in Africa, 456, 457*m*, 459, 592,
593*m*; in China, 494; in Southeast
Asia, 451*m*
Gerzso, Gunther, 613, 613*q*
Ghana, Kingdom of, 100;
independence of, 750, 752*f*;
Nkrumah's leadership in, 752, 752*f*
Ghanza (Ghazni), 113
ghettos: Jewish, 443
Gill, Irving, 658*f*
*Giovanni Arnolfini and His
Bride* **(van Eyck),** 175
Girondins, 351, 352
global economy, 807, 815–
816; economic interdependence,
815*f*, 818; Second Industrial
Revolution and, 419
globalization, 713, 815;
economic, 815–816, 815*f*; global
challenges, 818; global solutions,
818; political and social, 817
global warming, 711*f*, 806,
822*f*
Glorious Revolution: England,
227
Goebbels, Joseph, 576–577
Gold Coast, 456, 750
Gómez, Juan Vicente, 609
Gomułka, Władysław, 677
Good Friday Peace Pact, 809
Good Neighbor policy, 609,
612, 726

Gorbachev, Mikhail, 696, 697*f*,
698, 700, 718
Gordon, Charles, 458
**Gordon, George (Lord
Byron),** 403*f*; death of, 517*f*
Gothic architecture, 138, 138*f*
Gothic literature, 404
Government of India Act,
596, 610*f*
governments: absolutism, 228;
autonomous, 703; democracy, 41;
direct democracy, 43; socialist, 385;
theocracy, 11; totalitarian, 580
Gozzoli, Benozzo, 165*f*
Grameen Bank, 808*f*
Gran Colombia, 474*f*
Grand Alliance: World War II,
632, 654
Grand Army of Napoleon,
365–367
Great Britain. *See also* England:
abolishment of slavery in British
Empire, 517*f*; alliance with Japan,
493; American Revolution, 330–
332; annexes west coastal states
of Africa, 452; Balfour Declaration,
590*f*, 591; Battle of Britain,
630–631; the blitz, 652–653*f*,
658*f*; Boer War, 461; bombing of
cities during World War II, 648;
Boxer Rebellion and, 495; China
and, 489–490; conflict in Falkland
Islands, 738; Congress of Vienna,
388–389; Crimean War, 394;
declares war on Germany, 623;
decline of, 680–681; democracy
in, 432; explorers, 195*m*; fight
for control in Greece, 664; Great
Depression and, 557, 559; Indian
words into English language, 517*f*;
Industrial Revolution in, 378–382,
386–387*f*, 419; industry in by
1850, 379*m*; Irish nationalism in,
398; London Paddington station,
374–375*f*; Napoleon and, 365;
Opium War, 490, 491*f*; Ottoman
territories controlled by, 590;
Parliament of, 330; as part of the
Grand Alliance, World War II, 633;
political reform in, 398, 398*f*;
reacts to Hitler's aggression, 621,
622; right to vote for women, 684;
Royal African Company, 373*f*; Salt
Acts, 596, 597*f*; siege of Delhi,
482*f*; Seven Years' War, 322–325;
spheres of influence in China, 493;
Suez War, 761; Tehran Conference,
650; Thatcherism and, 707; trade
unions in, 421; Triple Entente, 436,
522; War of 1812, 401; women's
rights in, 426–427, 427*f*; Yalta
Conference, 650
**Great Britain, colonial
interests of:** in Africa, 456–462,
457*m*, 592–594, 593*m*, 750; in
Hong Kong, 490, 793; in India,
466–471, 469*m*, 596, 597*f*, 610*f*;

in Latin America, 473*m*, 475, 476,
608; in Middle East, 586–587,
587*m*, 588, 590, 591, 760; in
Southeast Asia, 451*m*, 452, 785
Great Depression, 556,
557–559, 557*f*; "Hoover Village",
580*f*; impact of global depression,
580; in Latin America, 609–610,
609*f*, 611; responses to, 556–557;
unemployment during, 557*f*
**Greater East Asia Co-
Prosperity Sphere,** 631
Great Leap Forward, 776–777
Great Mosque of Sãmarrã,
96*f*, 97, 130
Great Peloponnesian War, 43
**Great Proletarian Cultural
Revolution,** 778
Great Pyramid at Giza, 14
Great Rebellion in India,
466–467, 467*f*
Great Retreat of Napoleon,
367
Great Schism, 140
Great Sphinx, 14
Great Wall of China, 28; history
and legend of, 29*f*
Great War for Empire,
323–325
Great Zimbabwe, 101, 104*f*
Greece: civil war in, 664; classical,
43–45; failure of Mussolini's
invasion of, 631; independence of,
437, 586; invasion of Turkey, 588;
the Truman Doctrine, 665
Greece, ancient: classical,
36, 43–45; classical Greek arts,
43–44; Dark Age of, 36, 39–40;
defeat of the Persians, 43; Great
Peloponnesian War, 43; Mycenae
as first Greek state, 38–39; polis as
center of Greek life, 40–41
Greek tragedies, 44
greenhouse effect, 806
Green Revolution, 805
Gregory VII (pope), 135
Gregory XI (pope), 140
Gropius, Walter, 658*f*
**Group of United Officers
(GOU),** 610*f*, 611
Guam, 435
**Guang Xu (Chinese
emperor),** 492*f*, 493, 498*f*
Guatemala, 475, 477, 613, 735;
massacre of indigenous people,
735; political events in, 731*m*
Guernica, Spain, 566*f*, 567
Guernica **(Picasso),** 566*f*, 567
guerrilla tactics, 602
Guevara, Ernesto Ché, 733
guilds, 135
guillotine, 352
Guinea, 752
Gulf of Aqaba, 762
Gulf of Mexico, 144
Gulf of Tonkin Resolution,
786*f*

INDEX

gunpowder: Chinese invention, 108

gunpowder empire, 250

Gupta Empire, 26; India after, 112–113

Gutenberg, Johannes: press, 166*f*

Gutenberg's press, 166*f*

Gutierrez, Gustavo, 740*f*

Guzmán, Dominic de, 146

The Habits of Good Society, 424

Hadrian (Roman emperor), 51

Haiti, 473, 477, 609; first independent state in Latin America, 452; political events in, 731*m*

Hamas, 761*f*, 764

Hamburg, Germany, 427

Hammurabi (king of Babylon), 11; Code of, 12–13; comes to power in Babylon, 3, 11

Handel, George Frideric, 327

Han dynasty, 28; ends, 3

Hangul: Korean writing system, 289

Hangzhou, 106, 108

Hannibal (Carthaginian general), 49, 49*f*

Hanoi, Vietnam, 785

Hanoverians, 330

hans, 286

Hapsburg dynasty, 181, 393, 399

Harappa, India, 22

harem, 250

Hargreaves, James, 379

Harris, Betty, 386*q*

Harris, Townsend, 502

Harvey, William, 303*m*, 306, 373*f*

Hastings, Battle of, 120

Hatshepsut (Egyptian pharaoh), 16

Havana, 732; Cuban revolutionaries seize, 744*f*

Havel, Václav, 701

Hawaiian Islands, 435, 435*f*

Hay, John, 494, 494*f*

Haydn, Franz Joseph, 327

health care: advances in, 804–805

Heavenly Kingdom of Great Peace, 490

heavy industry, 674

Hebrew Bible, 18

Heian period (in Japan), 110

Heisenberg, Werner, 579

Helen of Troy, 39

heliocentric, 304

heliocentric system, 334

Hellenistic Era: Alexander the Great and the, 45–47; cultural

accomplishments of, 47; sculpture, 62*f*

Henderson, Hazel, 817, 817*q*

Henry II (king of England), 120

Henry IV (king of France) (Henry of Navarre), 221, 242

Henry IV (king of Germany), 135

Henry VIII (king of England), 184–185, 184*f*, 188

Henry Pu Yi (emperor of China), 624

heresy, 136

hermit kingdom: Korea, 289

Herzegovina: annexation of, 437

Herzl, Theodor, 442*f*, 443

Hesse, Hermann, 579

Heydrich, Reinhard, 572*q*, 640

Hezbollah, 761*f*, 764

Hidalgo, Miguel, 339, 473, 473*q*

hieroglyphics, 16, 17*f*; Maya, 145

High Middle Ages: Church's role in, 136; improvements in agriculture, 132–133; population growth during, 132; universities in, 139

High Renaissance, 174

Hijrah, 91

Hildegard of Bingen, 136, 137*f*

Himmler, Heinrich, 571, 571*f*, 638, 640

Hindenburg, Paul von, 570

Hinduism, 24

Hindu Kush, 22

Hindus: Indian National Congress and, 469; migration to India of, 782, 783*m*; rivalry with Muslims in India, 467, 469–470, 596, 782, 784; Sepoy Mutiny and, 466–467

Hiroshige III, 506*f*

Hiroshima, 635, 648, 649*m*, 649*f*

Hispanic Americans: growing population in U.S., 728*f*

Hispaniola, 472–473

History of the Cotton Manufacture in Great Britain (Baines), 387*f*

The History of Tom Jones, a Foundling (Fielding), 327

Hitler, Adolf, 557*f*, 563, 568, 570*q*, 620, 623*f*, 633*q*. *See also* Nazi Germany; annexes Austria, 622; attacks the Soviet Union, 631; demands the Sudetenland, 622; early victories in World War II, 628–630; economic policies of, 572; forms alliance with Mussolini, 621–622; German path to war and, 620–623; Hitler Youth, 574–575*f*; invades Poland, 623; propaganda of, 576, 577*f*; resettlement plans for Slavic peoples, 638; rises to power, 569–570; signs Nazi-Soviet

Nonaggression Pact, 622–623; Spanish Civil War and, 566*f*, 567; SS and, 571; suicide of, 635; Third Reich, 620; views of, 568, 573; violates Treaty of Versailles, 620–621

HIV, 753, 805, 805*f*

Hobbes, Thomas, 240–241

Höch, Hannah, 578

Ho Chi Minh, 595, 595*f*, 785

Holocaust, 640–642, 641, 654. *See also* Final Solution; death camps, 640; death toll, 640–641; *Einsatzgruppen,* 640; Jewish population in Europe before and after World War II, 639*f*; New Order and the, 638–643; U.S. Holocaust Memorial Museum, 642*f*

Holstein, 396

Holtzendorf, Admiral, 531

Holy Land, 125

Holy Roman Empire, 122, 181, 224, 319*m*

Homeland Security, Department of, 810*f*, 811

Homer, 39, 53; Dark Age of ancient Greece and, 39–40

hominid, 4

Homo erectus, 4

Homo sapiens, 4

Homo sapiens sapiens, 4–5

Honduras, 475, 477

Honecker, Erich, 702

Hong Kong: British control of, 490; returned to Chinese control, 793

Hong Xiuquan, 490

"Hoover Village", 580*f*

hostage system, 286

House of the Ladies, 467

housing: early, 8*f*

Huayna Inca (Incan ruler), 148

Hubble Space Telescope, 804; repairing the, 818*f*

Hugh Capet (king of France), 122

Huguenots, 221

Huitzilopochtli (Aztec god), 147, 150–151*f*

Hülegü Khan, 94

humanism, 170, 188; Christian, 176–178; development of, 170; in education, 172–173; vernacular literature and, 171–172, 171*f*

human rights movement, 809

humans: evidence of early, 5*m*; first, 4–7

human sacrifice, 145, 147, 150–151*f*

Hume, David, 313*f*

Hundred Years' War, 140*m*, 141; English capture of Joan of Arc during, 131

Hungarians, 393, 399

Hungary, 181, 546, 677, 698; authoritarian rule in, 566–567;

Hungarian uprising of 1720, 688*f*; nationalism in, 399; right to vote for women, 684; Soviet Union attack on Budapest, 677; transition from communism, 701*m*

hunger, world, 807–808

Huns, 59

Hurricane Katrina, 709

Husák, Gustav, 677

Hussein, Saddam, 708*f*, 765–766

Hussein (king of Jordan), 764*f*

Hutu, 754

hydrogen bomb, 674

Hyksos, 15–16

hypertext transport protocol (http), 804

Ibn-Rushd, 97

Ibn Sa'ūd, 590–591, 610*f*

Ibn Sīnā, 97

Ibsen, Henrik, 438

Ife, 103

Ignatius of Loyola, 187

Ile-de-France. *See* Paris, France

Iliad (Homer), 39

Imperial City, 272–273*f*, 274–275, 283

Imperialism, 450;: in Africa, 456–463, 750; in China, 492–495, 600; cultural, 713; economic, in Latin America, 476; effects of, in Africa, 461–463; era of European, 374–515; height of, 452–481; in India, 466–471; by Japan, 503*m*, 507–508, 508*f*, 599; in Latin America, 472–475, 473*m*; motives for, 450–451; new, 450–451, 453*f*, 462*f*; resistance to, 455; in Southeast Asia, 452–455; trade and imperialism in Japan, 512

imperialism, new, 450-451, 453*f*, 462*f*, 482

Imperial Rule Assistance Association, 599

impressionism, 438, 439*f*, 506*f*

Impression Sunrise (Monet), 439*f*

the Inca, 148–149; army of, 149; conquest of the, 199; Pachacuti builds empire in South America, 272; Pachacuti launches campaign of conquest, 131

India: after the Guptas, 112–113; British colonial rule in, 468, 469*m*; British gain control of, 266*f*; caste system in, 783; culture of, 470–471; early civilization in, 22–26; early empires in, 26; Europeans come to, 267; Gandhi revives the movement for independence, 453; incorporation of Indian words into English language, 517*f*; independence of, 596, 597*f*; Islam

INDEX

and Indian society, 113; migrations to, 782, 783*m*, 796*f*; nationalism in, 469–470, 596, 597*f*, 610*f*; new imperialism and, 482; nuclear test by, 813; number of people who died of famine between 1800 and 1900, 517*f*; partition of, 782–784, 783*m*; population growth in, 783, 807, 814; religions of, 783*f*; Sepoy Mutiny in, 466–467, 467*f*; Seven Years' War in, 323*m*, 323–324, 330; split of British India, 796; Victoria Memorial, 452–453

Indian National Congress (INC), 469, 596, 597*f*, 782; forms, 414

Indian Ocean, 98; crossing the, 105*f*; trade, 104*m*

indigenous, 460; massacre of indigenous Maya people in Guatemala, 735

indirect rule, 454, 461

Indochinese Communist Party, 595*f*

Indonesia: independence of, 785; recent years, 787

inductive reasoning, 309

indulgence, 178

Indus River, 22, 46

Indus River valley: change comes to India's civilization, 23*f*; cities built in, 2

industrial capitalism, 384

Industrial Revolution: cities and, 383–384; coal industry and, 380; cotton production and, 379–380; cultural movement arising from the, 410; electricity and, 416–418; an English factory worker tells all, 516*f*; in Europe, 383–385, 417*m*; factories and, 380; in Great Britain, 378–382, 379*m*; ideologies arising from the, 410; iron industry and, 380; population growth and, 383; railroads and, 381–382; reform and, 419; romanticism as response to, 404*f*, 405; Second. *See* Industrial Revolution, Second; a showcase for industry and progress, 408–409*f*; social classes of, 384–385; socialism and, 385, 419–421; spread of, 382–383; steam engine and, 380; steel industry and, 416; workers' lives during, 386–387*f*

Industrial Revolution, Second, 416; economic causes and effects, 444; education and, 428–429; improvements for London's working class, 430*f*; leisure and, 428*f*, 429; London's industrial owners, 431*f*; new patterns of, 418–419; new products of, 416–418; reform and, 419; social effects of, 444; socialism and, 419–421; social structure of, 419, 424; trade unions and, 419, 421; urban environment of,

422–423; women and, 425–427; World's Fair in Paris, 414–415

industrial working class, 383, 384–385, 419–421

inflation, 222; in Weimar Germany, 555–556, 558

influenza: epidemic of 1918, 532*f*

Innocent III (pope), 135

Inquisition, 136

***Institutes of the Christian Religion* (Calvin),** 183

Institutional Revolutionary Party (PRI), 611, 730

International Atomic Energy Agency (IAEA), 813

International Monetary Fund (IMF), 815

Internet, 802, 803–804, 822*f*

***The Interpretation of Dreams* (Freud),** 441

intervention: principle of, 389

intifada, 761*f*, 763

Inuit, 144

Iran. *See also* Persia: conflicts with Iraq, 765; Islamic society in, 764–765, 811; nuclear program of, 765, 813; oil in, 589, 764; Persia becomes, 589–590, 610*f*; women in, 767

Iraq: British control of, 590; conflicts with Iran, 765; invasion of Kuwait, 765; U.S. invasion of, 765–766

Iraq War, 707, 708*f*

Ireland, 220

Irigoyen, Hipólito, 611

Irish nationalism, 398

Irish potato famine, 383, 384*f*

Irish Republican Army (IRA), 384*f*, 809

iron, 380, 435; Bantu spread ironworking across Africa, 88

Iroquois, 144

Ishmael (son of Abraham), 90

Islam, 91; in Afghanistan, 765; as challenge to Eastern Roman Empire, 124; in Europe, 1364, 183*m*; Five Pillars of, 92*f*; in Iran, 764–765; Islamic culture, 96–97; Islamic empires, 92–95; Islamic philosophy, 96–97; Islamic science, 96–97; Islamic society, 96; Islamic trade network, 290; movements based on, 764, 767, 811; Muslims in the U.S., 258*f*; rise of, 90–92; spread of, 94*m*; world of, 90–97

Islamic militants, 811

Israel, 442*f*, 443; Arab-Israeli disputes, 760, 761*m*, 762–764; Balfour Declaration, 590*f*, 591; Camp David Accords, 763; "Children of", 18–19; creation of, 760, 761*f*; Lebanon invasion by, 761*f*, 764; Oslo Accords, 761*f*, 763; religion in, 19; Six-Day War,

761*f*, 762–763; Yom Kippur War, 761*f*, 763

Israel, Kingdom of, 19. *See also* Israel

Israelites, 18–21

İstanbul, Turkey, 249; Blue Mosque, 158–159*f*; Topkapi Palace, 251*f*

Italian Renaissance. *See* Renaissance, Italian

Italian wars, 164

Italy. *See also* Renaissance, Italian: alliance with Germany, 621–622; city-states of, 163–164; democracy in, 433; fascism in, 560–563, 562*f*; Great Depression and, 557*f*; imperialism by, 457*m*, 458, 593*m*, 594, 610*f*; industrialization in, 419; Italian expansion, 1935–1939, 621*m*; Napoleon's campaigns in, 361; as one of the Allies during World War I, 545; Renaissance, 163*m*; revolts of 1830 in, 391; revolts of 1848 in, 393; right to vote for women, 684; Spanish Civil War and, 567; Triple Alliance, 436, 522; unification of, 395*m*, 395–396

Ito Hirobumi (ruler of Japan), 504

Iturbide, Agustín de, 474

Itzamna (Maya god), 145

***Ivanhoe* (Scott),** 404

Ivan III (czar of Russia), 141

Ivan IV (czar of Russia), 232

Jabavu, Noni, 757

Jacobins, 351, 356

Jahāngīr (shāh of India), 264

Jahān (shāh of India), 264–265; building of Taj Mahal, 265–266, 372*f*

James I (king of England), 225

James II (king of England), 226

Japan, 296. *See also* Japan, postwar; after World War II, 796; alliance with Britain, 493; anime of, 791*f*; bioterrorism in, 804; bombing of cities, 635, 648; colonial policies of, 643; conquest of Manchuria, 623–624; cooperation with Nazi Germany, 625; economics of Meiji, 504–505; emergence of, 110–112; feudalism, 286*f*; foreign trade by, 503*f*, 505*f*; fortunes fading during World War II, 633; goes to war with China, 414; Greater East Asia Co-Prosperity Sphere, 631; great unifiers of, 284; imperialism by, 503*m*, 507–508, 508*f*, 599; invasion of China, 627*f*; invasion of Korea, 289; isolation ends in, 502–503; Japanese expansion, 624*m*; Japanese isolation, 111*f*;

Japanese path to war, 623–625; Japanese war policy in Asian areas, 643; Kabuki performances, 294–295*f*; *keiretsu* economy of, 598*f*; and Korea, 285*m*, 508, 781; launches attack, 625; life and culture in early, 111–112; Manchuria and, 599; martial arts, 288*f*; Meiji Restoration, 503, 504–507; militarism in, 599; mobilization during World War II, 647; Nara and Heian periods, 110; new Asian order, 625; new "community", 631; plan to seize Soviet Siberia, 625; political changes in, 284–286; politics of Meiji, 504; Sat-Cho alliance, 503; spheres of influence in China, 493; sumo as national sport, 510–511*f*; Tokugawa, 284–288, 502; trade and imperialism in, 512; U.S. relations with, 508; war with China, 493, 624–625; war with Russia, 507–508, 508*f*; Westernization of, 506*f*; World War II and, 631–632; *zaibatsu* economy of, 598, 598*f*

Japan, postwar, 789*m*; Allied occupation of, 788–789, 790; economy of, 789*f*, 790; politics and government of, 789–790, 789*f*; society and culture of, 789*f*, 790–791; teenagers in, 794–795*f*; Toyota factory in Miyazaki, 796*f*; *zaibatsu* economy of, 790

Japanese Americans: internment in the United States, 646*f*

jati, 24

Jayavarman, 114

Jefferson, Thomas, 332, 362*f*

Jeria, Michelle Bachelet, 736

Jerusalem, 18, 56, 125, 249, 763

Jesuits (Society of Jesus), 187; missionaries in the Spanish Empire, 211; mission states in Latin America, 209*m*

Jesus, 90, 137; teachings of, 55–56

***The Jewish State* (Herzl),** 443

Jews. *See also* anti-Semitism; Holocaust; Judaism; Nazi Germany; Zionism: hostility toward. *See* anti-Semitism; immigration to Palestine, 443, 760; immigration to U.S., 443; Jewish population in Europe before and after World War II, 639*f*; Jewish traditions, 18*f*

Joan of Arc, 140*f*, 141; English capture of, 131

Joao (king of Portugal), 206*f*

John (king of England): signs Magna Carta, 89

John Paul II (pope), 700

Johnson, Lyndon B., 671, 681, 682, 785, 786*f*

INDEX

Jordan: British control of, 590; independence of, 760; Israel recognized by, 761f, 763, 764f
Joseph II (ruler of Austria), 319m, 320–321, 322
Joyce, James, 579
Juárez, Benito, 476
Judaea, 55
Judah, Kingdom of, 19
Judaism, 18; in Europe, 1364, 183m; Jewish traditions, 18f
Julius Caesar (Roman ruler), 50, 51f
Julius II (pope), 174f, 178
Justinian (Byzantine emperor), 123, 123f, 252
Justinian Code, 123f

Kaaba, 90, 91f
Kabul, Afghanistan, 765
Kaczynski, Lech, 700
kaiser, 397
Kajinosuke, Tanikaze, 510–511f
Kamakura shogunate, 110–111; Minamoto Yoritomo establishes, 89
kami, 111
kamikaze, 111f, 647
Kanagawa, Treaty of, 502
Kandinsky, Wassily, 440
Kangxi (emperor of China): reign of, 278–279
Kanpur (Cawnpore), India, 467
Kashmir, 784
Katsav, Moshe, 680f
Kellogg-Briand Pact, 556
Kemal, Mustafa (Atatürk), 588–589, 610f
Kennan, George, 666
Kennedy, John F., 681, 682, 710; Bay of Pigs, 733; Cuban Missile Crisis, 669–671
Kent State University: student protest, 682
Kenya: independence of, 750; Kenyatta's leadership in, 752, 752f; nationalism in, 593–594, 610f
Kenyatta, Jomo, 594, 594q, 610f, 752, 752f
Kepler, Johannes, 303, 303m, 304, 306f
Kepler's First Law, 304
Kerensky, Aleksandr, 538
Kesari (Tilak), 471
Keynes, John Maynard, 558f, 559
Khafre (Egyptian pharaoh), 14
Khajuraho: Hindu temple at, 112f
khanates, 108
Khatemi, Mohammed, 765
Khatoon, Sophia, 808f
Khmer, 290

Khmer Rouge, 785
Khomeini, Ayatollah Ruhollah, 707, 764–765, 767, 811
Khrushchev, Nikita, 669, 670q, 676f, 677, 688, 694; the Khrushchev Era, 675–676
Khufu (Egyptian pharaoh), 14
Kibaki, Mwai, 822q
Kiebknecht, Karl, 544
Kiel, 544
Kiev, 122
Kikuyu Association, 593–594
Kilwa, 101; Great Mosque of, 104f
Kim Il Sung, 791
kimono, 794f
King, Martin Luther, Jr. (Dr.), 346f, 682, 683f
The King and I, 452
King John (king of England), 120
Kipling, Rudyard, 462q
Kirch, Gottfried, 307, 307q
Kirchner, Nestor, 738
Kirkpatrick, Jeanne, 727
Kisaburo, Onogawa, 510–511f
Kitty Hawk, North Carolina, 418
Klaus, Václav, 701
Kodak, 439
Kohl, Helmut, 702f, 706
Kolkata (Calcutta), India, 267, 469, 783, 784f
Korea, 296. See also North Korea; South Korea; distinctive culture of, 289; division of, 781; hermit kingdom, 289; independence of, 507; Japan and, 1324-1364, 285m; Japanese annexation of, 508; Japanese influence in, 493, 507; Korean War, 780m, 781; martial arts, 288f; Russian designs on, 492–493, 507; United Nations' role in, 792f
Korean War, 669, 780m, 781, 792f, 796
Kosovo, 703, 718
Kosovo, 703, 718; wars in, 703
Kosovo Liberation Army (KLA), 703
Kosygin, Alexei, 694
Kovác, Michal, 701
Kowloon Peninsula, China, 491
Kraft durch Freude (Strength Through Joy), 577
Kremlim, 697f
Kristallnacht, 572f, 573
Kshatriyas, 23
Kublai Khan (emperor of China), 94, 108, 110, 194; establishment of the Yuan dynasty, 131
Kurds, 765, 766
Kush, Kingdom of, 98
Kuwait, 765

Kwasniewski, Aleksander, 700
Kyōto, Japan, 110, 284, 503, 504, 806
Kyōto Protocol, 711f, 806, 822f

labor union. See trade unions
Labour Party, 432, 559; of Great Britain, 680, 707
La Fête Champêtre (Watteau), 326f
Lagos, 756
Lagos Weekly Record (Macaulay), 593
laissez-faire, 313f, 314, 314f
Lake Baikal, 493
Lake Tanganyika, 459
Lake Texcoco, 147
language(s): Indo-European, 48
Laos: communism in, 785; French control of, 452, 493
Late Middle Ages, 139–141
Latin America. See also Central America; individual states; South America: in 1939, 609m; authoritarian rule in, 610–612; colonial, 208–211, 209m, 212; culture of, 612f, 613, 728–729; economic and political developments, 724–725; economic imperialism in, 476; economic instability, 724; economies of, 479, 608; Great Depression in, 609–610, 609f; gross domestic product per capita, 725f; Haiti, 452; inequality in, 476; influenced by nationalism, 614; main exports in the 1990s, 725m; major developments in, 727m; move toward democracy, 725; nationalism in, 472–475, 608–613, 610f; nation building in, 475–476; new imperialism and, 482; political challenges in, 809; population, 725f, 726; social classes in, 208–209; society, 726; state and church, 210–211; U.S. and, 726–727; U.S. role in, 477, 477f, 608–609
Latin language, 171f; classical, 170, 171
Latvia, 546; independence from Soviet Union, 696
Lavoisier, Antoine, 303m, 306
Law of Nations, 55
Law of 22 Prairial, 355f, 356
Lawrence, T. E., 586
Lawrence of Arabia, 530
Leading the People (Delacroix), 403
League of Combat, 561
League of Nations, 545, 627f; African territories supervised by, 592, 593m; European territories supervised by, 555m; Germany joins, 556; Ottoman territories

supervised by, 590; weakness of, 554
Lebanon: French control of, 590; independence of, 760; Israeli invasion of, 761f, 764
lebensraum, 568
Legislative Assembly (French), 346, 350
legitimacy, principle of, 388
leisure, 428f, 429, 577
Lenin, V. I., 536, 538, 539q, 540q; Bolsheviks and, 538–539; Comintern created by, 595; Diego Rivera's portrait of, 613; embalming of, 658f; Ho Chi Minh influenced by, 595f; New Economic Policy of, 563–564; Soviet Union created by, 563
Leningrad, 644
Leopold II (king of Belgium), 459
Leo X (pope), 179, 184f
Lesotho, 753
Lesseps, Ferdinand de, 457
Leviathan (Thomas Hobbes), 240
Liaodong Peninsula, 493, 507, 508
liberalism, 390
Liberal Party, 432
liberal studies, 172–173
liberation theology: new role for the Catholic Church, 740f
Liberia, 461, 753–754
Li Bo, 109
Libya: Italian control of, 458; nationalism in, 594, 610f
Liebknecht, Karl, 544
Life and Death in Shanghai (Nien Cheng), 778
life expectancy, 814
light bulb: invention of, 416
"lightning war", 628
Liliuokalani (queen of the Hawaiian Islands), 435, 435f
Lima, Peru, 199, 475
Lincoln, Abraham, 401
lineage groups, 103
Lin Zexu, 490q, 491f
The Lion Hunt (Delacroix), 403
Lisbon, Portugal, 200f
literacy: Enlightenment and, 316; public education and, 429; rates of, 813m; United Nations programs for, 813f
literature, 280–283; African, 757; of the Augustan Age, 53; Chinese, 283; of Enlightenment, 327; the golden age of, 238–240; Gothic, 404; Islamic, 97; Latin American, 728–729; Middle Eastern, 767; modernism in, 438; romanticism in, 404–405; Spanish, 238–240; stream of consciousness in, 579; symbolist writers, 438;

INDEX

of Tokugawa Era, 287–288; vernacular, 139, 171–172, 171*f*
Lithuania, 546; independence from Soviet Union, 696
***Little Red Book* (Mao Zedong),** 778, 796*f*
Livingstone, David, 459; arrives in Africa, 452
Livy, 53
Li Zicheng, 276
Lobengula (southern African king), 463*q*
Locarno, Treaty of, 556
Locke, John, 240*f*, 241, 310–311, 310*q*, 313*f*; writes *Two Treatises of Government,* 217
Lombardy, 393, 396
London, England, 648; the blitz, 652–653*f*; newspapers in, 316, 429; population of, 383, 422
longbow(s), 141
Long Count, 145
Long March, 601*m*, 602*f*, 603
loom: water-powered, 380
Loong, Lee Hsien, 793
Lord Chamberlain's Men, 238
Lord of the Rings, 713
Lord Tokitaka, 285, 285*q*
Lorraine, 397, 546
Louisiana Purchase, 338, 362*f*
Louis-Napoleon (Napoleon III, emperor of France), 392, 395, 399
Louis Philippe (king of France), 391, 391*f*, 392
Louis XIV (king of France), 228, 229*q*; and absolutism, 229*f*; begins absolute rule of France, 217; comes to power, 229–230; France under, 228–230; legacy of, 230; Palace of Versailles, 216–217*f*, 234–235*f*; signing of Treaty of Nijmegen, 242*f*
Louis XV (king of France): statute of replaced by guillotine then by obelisk, 368*f*
Louis XVI (king of France), 342, 350; concession of, 344*f*, 345; Estates-General and, 342–343; execution of, 338, 351–352, 351*f*, 354*f*; fall of Bastille and, 344; flight of, 346
Louis XVIII (king of France), 367
Low Countries, 181; artistic Renaissance in, 175
Lower Egypt, 14
Ludendorff, Erich, 542, 543*q*
Luftwaffe, 630–631
Lusitania: the sinking of, 530*f*
Luther, Martin, 176, 178*f*, 179–181, 182, 184*f*, 372*q*; on Jews, 186; Ninety-five Theses of, 179, 180*f*; on role of women, 186
Lutheranism, 180–181, 183*m*, 186*f*, 188
Luxemburg, Rosa, 544

Lydia, 21
Lyon, France, Reign of Terror in, 353, 354*f*

MacArthur, Douglas, 633, 788
Macartney, Lord George, 278*f*, 279; leads British trade mission to China, 273
Macaulay, Herbert, 593
Macaulay, Lord Thomas, 468*q*
Macedonian Empire, 45–47: of Alexander the Great, 46*m*
Machiavelli, Niccolò, 165, 174*f*, 188, 372*q*
machine guns, 528*f*
Machu Picchu, 149, 152*f*
***Madame Bovary* (Flaubert),** 407, 410
Madero, Francisco, 478–479
Madinah (Medina), 91, 250, 591
Madras (Chennai), India, 322, 323, 469
Madrid, Spain, 237, 567
Magellan, Ferdinand, 196–197
***The Magic Flute* (Mozart),** 327
magic realism, 728
Maginot Line, 628–629
Magna Carta, 121, 121*f*; King John signs the, 89, 121*f*
Magyars, 392*m*, 393
Mahfouz, Naguib, 767
Maḥmūd of Ghanza, 113
Major, John, 707
Makkah (Mecca), 90, 249, 591
Malaya, 785
Malay Peninsula, 114, 292
Malaysia, 793
Mali, 753
Mali, kingdom of, 100–101
***Malleus Maleficarum* (Witch Hammer),** 223*f*
Manchester, England, 381
Manchukuo, 624
Manchuria, 276; Japanese control of, 599, 623–624, 627*f*; Russian control of, 492–493
Manchus, 276. *See* Qing dynasty of China
Mandate of Heaven, 27; dynastic cycles and the, 28*f*
mandates, 547
Mandela, Nelson, 750, 754, 755*f*, 757
manga, 791*f*
Mannerism, 236
manor, 133
manorial system, 133–134
Mansa Mūsā (king of Mali), 101
Mao Zedong, 602, 658*q*, 667, 796; Cultural Revolution, 778; death

of, 778; forms People's Republic of China, 667; Great Leap Forward, 776–777; *Little Red Book,* 778; Long March, 601*m*, 602*f*, 603, 614*f*; rise to power, 776; society under, 780
Marat, Jean-Paul, 350, 352*f*
Marconi, Guglielmo, 417, 417*q*, 576
Marco Polo, 194, 276
Marcos, Ferdinand, 787
Marcus Aurelius (Roman emperor), 51, 58
Maria Theresa (ruler of Austrian Empire), 320, 320*f*, 322
Marie Antoinette (queen of France), 342, 353
Marc Antony, 50
market economy, 675*f*, 675*t*
Marlborough, Duke of, 424
Marne: First Battle of, 526; Second Battle of, 542
Márquez, Gabriel García, 728
marriage: in nineteenth century, 426; in Renaissance Italy, 167
***The Marriage of Figaro* (Mozart),** 327
Mars exploration, 804
Marshall, George C., 666
Marshall Plan, 666, 678; aid, 1948–1951, 679*f*
Martel, Charles (Charles the Hammer), 95*f*; defeats Arab forces at Battle of Tours, 88
Marx, Karl, 385, 419–421, 420*f*, 595, 612*f*
Marxism, 386*f*, 419–421; in China, 600; Great Depression and, 557, 557*f*; spread of, 595
Marxist Social Democratic Party, 434
Mary (queen of England), 184, 185
Masaccio, 173
Massachusetts Bay Colony, 201; founding by English, 216
The Massacre of the Armenians, 588*f*
mass culture, 576–577, 578*f*
***Mass in B Minor* (Bach),** 327
mass media, 429, 562
mass production, 419, 577
mass society: education in, 428–429; emergence of, 422; leisure in, 428*f*, 429, 577; movies in, 576–577; radio in, 576; social structure of, 424; urban environment of, 422–423; women in, 425–427
Masurian Lakes, Battle of, 527
***Mathematical Principles of Natural Philosophy* (Newton),** 305
Matsuhito (emperor of Japan), 504

Matta, Roberto, 613
Mau Mau uprising, 752*f*
Mauryan Empire, 26
the Maya, 144–146; calendars, 146; civilization begins to flourish, 130; massacre of in Guatemala, 735; practice of human sacrifice, 145
Mazarin, Cardinal, 229
mbaqanga, 713
McCarthy, Joseph R., 681–682
McCay, Winsor, 627*f*
McKinley, William, 452, 453
Medes, 20
Medici, Cosimo de', 164, 165*f*
Medici, Lorenzo de', 164, 165*f*
Medici, Piero de', 165*f*
Medici family: patronage of, 165*f*
medicine: germ theory of disease, 405; Scientific Revolution and, 306; women in, 427
Mediterranean: Rome's conquest of, 48–49
Mediterranean Sea, 10, 14, 134
Meerut, India, 466
megacity, 726
Mehmed II (sultan of Ottoman Empire), 249, 255*f*
Meiji Restoration, 503, 512; economics of, 504–505; education of, 506; military of, 506; politics of, 504; social structure of, 506–507
Mei-ling Soong, 604*f*
***Mein Kampf* (Hitler),** 568
Meir, Golda, 763
Melaka, 196
Mellaart, James, 5*f*
Mendeleyev, Dmitry, 405
Menelik (emperor of Ethiopia), 465*f*
Menses (king of Egypt), 14
mercantilism, 204; laissez-faire versus, 314*f*; trade, colonies, and, 204–206
mercenaries, 164
Merida, Carlos, 613
merit. *See also* civil service; civil service: rule of, 30*f*
Merkel, Angela, 706
Mesoamerica, 144; cultures of early, 145*m*; early civilizations in, 144–147
Mesopotamia, 10, 22, 26, 27; ancient, 10–13, 11*m*
***Messiah* (Handel),** 327
mestizos, 208, 212, 472, 473
Methodism, 317
Metternich, Klemens von, 388, 393
Mexican Revolution, 478–479, 478*f*, 611, 730
Mexican War, 475–476
Mexico, 730–731; art of, 612*f*, 613; authoritarian rule in, 611–612;

caudillos, role of, 475–476; Constitution of 1917, 478*f*, 479; debt crisis, 730–731; Great Depression in, 609*f*, 610; Hidalgo's revolt in, 473–474; Independence Day in, 474; inequality in, 476; Institutional Revolutionary Party (PRI), 611, 730; Laws of Reform, 476; major developments in, 727*f*; Mexican Revolution, 730; NAFTA and, 816; nationalism in, 473–474, 610*f*; oil industry in, 608, 610, 610*f*, 612, 614*f*; as part of Spanish Empire, 199; political events in, 731*m*; protests in, 730; revolution in, 478–479, 478*f*, U.S. intervention in, 477; war with U.S., 475–476

Mexico Today and Tomorrow (Rivera), 612*f*

Michelangelo Buonarroti, 165*f*, 174, 174*f*, Sistine Chapel, 188*f*

Middle Ages, 118. *See also* Early Middle Ages; feudalism; High Middle Ages; Late Middle Ages; Europe in, 132–141; growth of cities during, 135; noble men and women, 168*f*; peasants and the middle class, 169*f*; revival of trade during, 134; vernacular literature, 139

middle class(es): in China of the 1930s, 606*f*, industrial, 383, 384; mass society and, 424; in Middle Ages, 169*f*

Middle East. *See also individual states:* of 1919–1935, 587*m*; after World War I, 543*m*; Arab-Israeli disputes, 760, 761*m*, 762–764; influenced by nationalism and revolution, 614; modern, 762*m*; nationalism in, 586–590, 610*f*; society and culture of, 767; women in, 767

Middle Kingdom (Egypt), 15

Middle Passage, 206

Midnight (Dun), 501

migration(s): of Bantus, 102*m*; diversity and, 198*f*, in Europe, 706*f*; global, 814; mass migration to India and Pakistan, 796*f*; Yugoslavians into Germany, 706

Milan, Italy, 163, 164, 181, 188

militant, 218

militarism, 396, 523; in Japan, 599

Milošević, Slobodan, 703

Minamoto Yoritomo, 110; establishes Kamakura shogunate, 89

Ming dynasty, 108, 274–276; China under, 275*m*; fall of the, 276; overthrow of, 273

Ming Hong Wu (emperor of China), 274

Mir Jaffier: Battle of Plassey, 266*f*

Missionaries of Charity, 784*f*

Mistral, Gabriela, 729

mita, 210

Mitsui, 598, 598*f*

Mitterrand, François, 704–705

mobilization, 525, 644; of workforce during World War II, 645*f*

Modena, 396

Modern Devotion, 178

modernism, 438; in architecture, 440; in literature, 438; in music, 440; in painting, 438–440

Mogadishu, 101

Mogul Empire: expansion of, 1530–1707, 263*m*; life in Mogul India, 265–266; the Mogul dynasty, 262–265

Moguls. *See also* Mogul Empire: decline of the, 264–265; grandeur of the, 262–267; history and culture, 268; rise of the, 262

Mohammad Reza Pahlavi (shāh of Iran), 590, 764

Mohammed Ali Jinnah, 596

Mohammed Khatemi, 765

Moldavia, 394; independence from Soviet Union, 696

Moluccas (Spice Islands), 293. *See also* spice trade; spice trade in the, 296*f*

Mombasa, 101

monarchies: new, 141

Monet, Claude, 438, 439*f*, 506*f*

money economy, 134

Mongkut (king of Thailand), 452

Mongol Empire, 94, 108, 109*m*; campaigns of, 111*m*; religion in, 108

Mongolia, 108, 492

Mongols: army meals, 116–117*f*, on the move, 116–117*f*

Monk, George, 226

Monkey Brigade, 784*f*

monotheistic, 19

Monroe, James, 475, 477*f*

Monroe Doctrine, 475, 477*f*

Montcalm (General), 325

Montenegro, 437, 703

Montesquieu, baron de, 312, 333

Montezuma (Aztec ruler), 198, 200*f*

Montt, Rios, 735

Moo-hyun, Roh, 792

Moon landing, 710; U.S. astronauts first to walk on the Moon, 718*f*

Moors, 141

More, Sir Thomas, 184*f*, 185, 385

Morel, Edward, 462*q*

Morgan, J. P., 417

Morisot, Berthe, 438

Morocco: French protectorate in, 458; independence of, 750

Moses, 18, 19, 90, 92

Mothers of the Plaza de Mayo, 738*f*

Mother Teresa, 783, 784*f*

Mound Builders, 144

the Mountain, 351–352

Mount Sinai, 19

Mozambique, 459, 750

Mozart, Wolfgang Amadeus, 327

Muʿāwiyah (caliph of Umayyad Empire), 93

muezzin, 96*f*

Muhammad, 90; life of, 90–91; returns to Makkah, 88; Southwest Asia in his time, 91*m*; teachings of, 92

Muhammad Ahmad (the Mahdi), 458

Muhammad Ali, 457

Muhammad Ture (king of Songhai), 101

Mukhtar, Omar, 594, 610*f*

mulattoes, 212

Mulroney, Brian, 709

multinational corporation(s), 724, 815–816

multinational state, 393

mummification, 14

Munich, Germany, 568, 713; 1972 Olympic Games, 713

Munich Conference, 622

Munich Olympic Games: terrorism at, 809

"Munken incident", 623

Murakami, Haruki, 791

Murat, Caroline, 364*f*

Murat, Joachim, 364*f*

Murrow, Edward R., 658*f*

Museveni, Yoweri, 753

Muslim League, 469–470, 596

Muslims: in France, 715; France bans wearing of headscarves by, 706*f*; migration to Pakistan of, 782, 783*m*; rivalry with Hindus in India, 467, 469–470, 596, 782, 784; Sepoy Mutiny and, 466–467; Shia, 765, 766; Sunni, 765, 766; teenagers in Nigeria, 758–759*f*

Mussolini, Benito (Il Duce), 557*f*, 561–563, 562*f*, 580, 622, 631, 635

Myanmar, 785. *See also* Burma (modern Myanmar)

Mycenae, 38; first Greek state, 38–39; height of Mycenaean civilization, 36

Nanjing, Treaty of, 490, 491*f*

Nantes, France, Reign of Terror in, 353

Napier, John, 303

Naples, Italy, 164, 181, 393, 396

Napoleon Bonaparte (emperor of France), 368; Arc de Triomphe and, 338; coronation of, 361*f*, coup d'état by, 338, 357, 362; defeat at Waterloo, 339, 367; domestic policies of, 362–363; empire of, 365–366; fall of, 366–367; family of, 364*f*, on Frederick the Great, 320*f*, invasion of Russia by, 339, 366*m*, 366–367, 452; Louisiana Purchase and, 362*f*, revolutionary ideals spread by, 364*f*, 365; rise of, 360–362

Napoleonic Code (Civil Code), 363

Napoleonic Wars: number of people killed, 373*f*

Napoleon II, 399

Napoleon III. *See* Louis-Napoleon

Nara period (Japan), 110

Nasser, Gamal Abdel, 761–762, 762, 763

National Aeronautics and Space Administration (NASA), 804

National Assembly, 343–345, 350; of France, 704

National Convention, 350, 352, 354, 357

nationalism, 366; in Africa, 462–463, 592–594, 593*m*, 610*f*; Africa and Asia influenced by, 614; and alliances of World War I, 522; Arab, 590–591; in Argentina, 610*f*; Armenian, 587–588; in Asia, 595, 610*f*; in Brazil, 610*f*; in China, 496–499, 600–603; in Europe, 390, 398–400; extreme, 442–443; fascism and, 562; Hitler and, 568; in India, 469–470, 596, 597*f*, 610*f*; in Iran (Persia), 589–590, 610*f*; Irish, 398; Jewish, 590*f*, 591; in Kenya, 593–594, 610*f*, in Latin America, 472–475, 608–613, 610*f*, 614; in Libya, 594, 610*f*, in Mexico, 473–474, 610*f*, in Middle East, 586–590, 610*f*; Middle East and China influenced by, 614; Napoleon and, 366; in Saudi Arabia, 591, 610*f*, in Southeast Asia, 455; in Turkey, 586–589, 610*f*, in the U.S., 401; in Vietnam, 455, 480–481*f*, 595

Nationalist Party (Guomindang), 497, 499, 600–603, 776

National Socialist German Workers' Party (NSDAP). *See* Nazi Party

NAFTA (North American Free Trade Agreement), 816

Nagasaki, Japan, 502, 507, 635, 648, 649*m*, 649*f*

Nagy, Imre, 677

Nairobi, Kenya, 756, 756*f*

Namibia, 753

Nanjing, China, 490–491, 601

national unification: of Germany, 395*m*, 396–397; of Italy, 395*m*, 395–396

Native Americans: death from European diseases, 212*f*; effect of the missionaries on, 211; *encomienda* system, 199, 210*f*; in French and Indian War, 324; as labor source in Latin America, 209–210; in Mexican revolt, 473–474; mita system and, 210; population, 209*m*; Queen Isabella's rules regarding, 199; working silver mines in Brazil, 212*f*

Nazi, 568

Nazi Germany. *See also* Germany; Hitler, Adolf: of 1933–1939, 570–573; alliance with Italy, 621–622, 621–622; anti-Semitism of, 570, 571*f*, 572*f*, 573; attacks Denmark and Norway, 622; attacks the Netherlands, Belgium, and France, 622; bombing of cities during World War II, 648; breaks through British defenses in Egypt, 631; changing attitudes toward women's roles, 647; demands for the Sudetenland, 622; economic policies of, 572; Enabling Act, 570; Final Solution, 640; German expansion, 1935–1939, 621*m*; German path to World War II, 620–623; Hitler Youth members, 642; Holocaust, 640–642; invades Bohemia, Moravia, and Slovakia, 622; invades Poland, 623; invades the Soviet Union, 631; invasion of Czechoslovakia, 518–519*f*; launches the Battle of Britain, 630–631; leisure in, 577; liberates Mussolini, 631; major Nazi death camps, 639*m*; mobilization during World War II, 647; Nazi-Soviet Nonaggression Pact, 623–623; propaganda in, 576–577, 577*f*; resettlement of Poland, 638; rise of, 580; Schlieffen Plan, 525; slave labor in, 639; spectacles used by, 572; terror used in, 571, 571*f*; union with Austria, 622; women in, 573

Nazi Party, 580

Nazism. *See also* Nazi Germany: message of, 569*f*; origin of, 568; rise of, 569–570

Nazi-Soviet Nonaggression Pact, 622–623, 623*f*

Neanderthals, 4

Nebuchadnezzar (king of Chaldeans), 21

Nefertari (queen of Egypt), 17*f*

Nehru, Jawaharlal, 596, 614, 782

Nehru, Motilal, 596

Neolithic Age, 7

Neolithic Revolution, 6*f*, 7

neo-Nazis, 706

Nero (Roman emperor), 54, 56

Neruda, Pablo, 823*f*

Nerva (Roman emperor), 51

the Netherlands, 134, 218; artistic Renaissance in, 175; the Dutch at Batavia, 292*f*; Dutch colonies in Latin America, 209*m*; Dutch explorers and settlements, 201; explorers, 195*m*; Hitler's victory against, 628; imperialism by. *See* the Netherlands, colonial interests of; industrialization in, 419; as a power in Southeast Asia, 293; resistance during Wars of Religion, 218–219

the Netherlands, colonial interests of: in Cape Town, 460; in Latin America, 473*m*; in Southeast Asia, 451*m*, 785

Neumann, Balthasar, 326

Neutra, Richard, 658*f*

Nevsky, Alexander (prince of Novgorod), 122

New Deal, 559

New Economic Policy (NEP), 563–564

New Granada (Colombia), 474

New Kingdom (Egypt), 15–16

New Life Movement, 604*f*, 605

new monarchies, 141

New Order: Japan's, 625

New State, 610*f*, 611

New Stone Age. *See* Neolithic Revolution

New Testament, 56

Newton, Sir Isaac, 303, 303*m*, 305, 306*f*, 311, 313*f*, 372*q*, 440

New Zealand, 796; recent years, 793

NGOs (nongovernmental organizations), 817. *See* nongovernmental organizations (NGOs)

Nicaragua, 734, 734–735; independence of, 475; major developments in, 727*f*; political events in, 731*m*; U.S. intervention in, 477

Nicholas II (czar of Russia), 434, 525, 536; death of, 541

Niemeyer, Oscar, 729

Nien Cheng, 778

Niépce, Joseph, 517*f*

Niger, 753

Nigeria: British control of, 456; civil war in, 754; independence of, 750; nationalism in, 593, 594; oil in, 753; teenagers in, 758–759*f*, 758–759*f*

Nightingale, Florence, 400*f*, 427

Nile River, 14, 15

Ninety-five Theses (Luther), 179, 180*f*

nirvana, 25

Nixon, Richard M., 671, 682, 707, 718; Chinese relations and, 781; Vietnam War and, 785; Watergate scandal, 707

Nkrumah, Kwame, 750, 752, 752*f*

nobility: in France, 340, 341*f*; of Italian Renaissance, 166–167

nomads, 5; temporary settlements of, 8*f*

nonalignment, principle of, 782

nongovernmental organizations (NGOs), 817. *See* NGOs (nongovernmental organizations)

nonviolence. *See* civil disobedience

Noriega, Manuel, 735

Normandy, 634; Allied troops land at, 654*f*; invasion of, 636–637*m*, 637*f*

North Africa: imperialism in, 456–458; World War II in Europe and, 1939–1941, 629*m*

North America: during the Cold War, 688; different cultures in early, 144; Europe and, 704–709; imperialism in, 450; Industrial Revolution spread to, 383; Seven Years' War in, 324–325, 324*f*; Western Europe and, 678–685

North American Free Trade Agreement (NAFTA), 709, 816

North Atlantic Treaty Organization (NATO), 664, 668, 681, 688; member nations, 1713, 665*m*; nations joining as of 1955, 665*m*

Northern Expedition, 600, 601*m*

Northern Ireland, 715; "Bloody Sunday", 715; conflict in, 707; Good Friday Agreement, 715; Protestants and Catholics clash in, 718*f*

Northern Renaissance art, 175

North German Confederation, 396, 397

North Korea. *See also* Korea: communist rule in, 791; creation of, 781; Korean War, 780*m*, 781; nuclear test by, 792*f*, 813

North Vietnam, 785, 796

Norway: adoption of gender parity policies, 712; women's suffrage in, 427

Notre Dame cathedral, 354

Nubia, 98

Nuclear Nonproliferation Treaty, 813

nuclear proliferation, 765, 781, 784, 792*f*, 804, 813

Nuremberg laws, 573

Nuremberg rallies, 569*f*, 572, 577*f*

Nyerere, Julius, 752

The Oath of the Tennis Court June 20th 1553 (David), 342–343*f*

Obadina, Tunde, 756*f*

Observations Upon Experimental Philosophy (Cavendish), 307

The Ochre People (Jabavu), 757

Octavian. *See* Augustus (Roman emperor) (Gaius Octavius)

Oda Nobunaga, 284; seize of Kyōto, Japan, 216

Odysseus, 39

Odyssey (Homer), 39

Official Languages Act: Canada, 709

oil: in Argentina, 610; in Iran, 589, 764; in Mexico, 608, 610, 610*f*, 612; in Middle East, 762, 763, 811; in Nigeria, 753; in Saudi Arabia, 591

Old Kingdom (Egypt), 14

Old Stone Age. *See* Paleolithic Age

Old Testament, 18

Oleg (Viking leader), 122

oligarchy, 41, 611

Oliver Twist (Dickens), 407

the Olmec, 144

Olson, Culbert, 646*q*

Olympic games: number of athletes competing in first modern, 517*f*

Omar Khayyám, 97

one-child policy, 780

One Day in the Life of Ivan Denisovich (Solzhenitsyn), 675–676

One Hundred Days of Reform, 493

One Hundred Years of Solitude (Márquez), 728

Open Door Policy, 494–495, 494*f*, 599

Opium War, 490, 491*f*

Orange Free State, 460

Oresteia (Aeschylus), 44

Organization of African Unity (OAU), 752

Organization of American States (OAS), 726

Organization of Petroleum Exporting Countries (OPEC), 763

On the Origin of Species by Means of Natural Selection (Darwin), 405–406

Ortega, Daniel, 735

Ōsaka, 284

Oslo Accords, 761*f*, 763, 764*f*

Ostia, 52

INDEX

Otto I (king of Germany), 122
Ottoman Empire, 248–253, 587m. *See also* Ottoman Turks; in the 1450s, 254–255f; advance against Ṣafavids, 256, 257t; Armenian genocide, 587–588, 588f; break up of the, 547; Crimean War and, 394; destruction of, 530; division of, 590; Egypt and, 456–457; end of, 614; expansion into Europe, 249–250; expansion into Western Asia and Africa, 249–250; expansion of, 248, 249m; fall of, 586–588; imperial sultans, 250–251; nature of Ottoman rule, 250; Palestine and, 443; problems in the, 253; society and the role of women, 252; Topkapi Palace, 251f; World War I impact on, 586–587
Ottoman Turks: control of Western Asia and Africa, 249–250; expansion into Europe, 250; rise of the, 248–250; siege of Constantinople, 249
OVRA, 562
Owen, Robert, 385

Pachacuti (Inca ruler), 148; builds empire in South America, 272; launches campaign of conquest, 131
Pacific: after World War II, 796; World War II in, 1941–1945, 632m
painting: abstract, 440; Arch of Constantine in Rome, 62f; Chinese landscape, 109; cubism in, 440; of Enlightenment, 326; fresco, 173, 326; of High Renaissance, 174; impressionism in, 438, 439f; Latin American, 729; Mannerism, 236; modernism in, 438–440; of Northern Renaissance, 175; oil, 175; postimpressionism in, 439, 439f; realism in, 406f, 407; of Renaissance, 173; Rococo style, 326, 326f; romanticism in, 402–403, 403f; surrealism in, 578–579
Pakistan, 112; Afghanistan and, 765; Bangladesh separates from, 784; creation of, 596, 782; migrations to, 782, 783m, 796f; nuclear test by, 813; split of British India, 796
Palace of Versailles, 234–235f
Paleolithic Age, 5
Palestine: British control of, 590; conflict in, 760, 761m, 762–764; Jewish immigration to, 443, 591; Lebanon and, 764; nationalism of Arabs and Jews in, 591; Oslo Accords, 763

Palestine Liberation Organization (PLO), 761f, 763, 764f
Palestinian Authority, 763
Pan-Africanism, 594, 752
Panama, 735; break from Colombia, 735; independence of, 477; major developments in, 727f; U.S. intervention in, 477
Panama Canal, 477; opens, 415; Panama's control of, 735; Treaty, 734m
Pan-Arabism, 762
Pankhurst, Emmeline, 427, 427f
papacy: reform of, 178–178, 187
Papal States, 135, 178, 393
Paraguay, 475, 609f; political events in, 737m
Paris, Treaty of: of 1763, 324, 325; of 1783, 332; of 1856, 394
Paris Commune, 347, 350, 352
Paris Peace Accords, 785
Paris Peace Conference, 545
Paris (prince of Troy), 39
Park, Chung Hee, 792
Parma, 396
Parthenon, 40f, 43
Pasha, Enver, 588q
pashas, 250
Pasteur, Louis, 405
patriarchal, 13
patricians, 49
Patriot Act, 811
Paul (apostle), 56
Paul III (pope), 178f, 187, 188
Pax Romana, 51
peacekeeping forces, 812–813
Peace of Augsburg, 178m, 181, 182, 188
Peace of Westphalia, 224; Europe after, 224m
Pearl Harbor: Japanese attack of, 632, 654
Pearson, Lester, 683
peasant(s): in France, 341, 341f, 344, 352; of Italian Renaissance, 167; in Russia, 400
Peloponnesian War, Great, 43
PEMEX, 610f, 612
peninsulares, 208, 212, 472, 474
Pentagon: terrorist attack on, 709, 810
People's Liberation Army (PLA), 602f, 603, 776
People's Republic of China: after World War II, 796; Cultural Revolution, 778; democracy movement in, 777m; Deng Xiaoping, 778–779; enters Korean War, 780m, 796; Four Modernizations, 778; Great Leap Forward, 776–777; Hong Kong returned to, 793; Long March, 601m; Mao Zedong. *See* Mao

Zedong; Nationalist-Communist alliance in, 600–601; New Life Movement, 604f; Northern Expedition, 600; one-child policy, 780; population growth in, 776; Red Guards, 777m; resumption of relations with U.S., 671; Taiwan, claims on, 792; Tibet conflict, 808; U.S. relations with, 781; Vietnam War, 786f; World Trade Organization membership, 781
People's Republic of Korea. *See* North Korea
per capita, 778
perestroika, 696
Perez, Alan Garcia, 740
Pérez, Carlos Andrés, 741
Pergamum, Kingdom of, 47
Pericles, 42q, 43; age of, 43; expands Athenian democracy, 42f
Perón, Evita, 738
Perón, Isabel, 738f
Perón, Juan, 611, 737–738, 738f
Perry, Matthew, 502, 508f; arrives in Japan, 512f
Persia. *See also* Iran; Iran develops from, 589–590; nationalism in, 589–590, 610f; oil discovered in, 589; Qājār dynasty, 589
Persian carpets, 268f
Persian Empire, 20m, 21; Darius I begins expanding, 3; invasion of Egypt, 21
Persian Gulf, 101, 765
Peru, 726, 739; Communist guerrillas in, 744; export economy of, 479; independence of, 475; military and civilian rule in, 739–740; political events in, 737m; U.S. role in, 608
Pétain, Marshal Henri, 630
Peter III (czar of Russia), 321, 321f, 323
Peter the Great (czar of Russia), 217, 232–233, 233, 242
Petrarch, 170
Philip II Augustus (king of France), 122
Philip II (king of Macedonia), 45
Philip II (king of Spain), 218, 242; height of Spanish power under, 219m
Philip IV (king of France), 140
Philippines, 291; acquisition by U.S., 435, 452–453; democracy in, 809; independence gained by, 785; independence movement by, 453; recent years, 787; Spanish, 452
philosophes, 312–313, 315
philosophy: Greek, 44–45; Islamic, 96–97; Socratic method, 44
Physiocrats, 313

Picasso, Pablo, 439–440, 566f, 567
Piedmont, Kingdom of, 393, 395–396
Pincevent site, 8f
Pinel, Philipe, 351q
Pinochet, Augusto, 736; protest of his brutal rule of Chile, 744f
Pitt, William (the Elder), 324, 330
Pizarro, Francisco, 199
Plato, 44, 45f, 302; establishment of Academy, 44
Plaza de Mayo: mothers of, 738f
plebeians, 49
plebiscite, 399
PLO (Palestine Liberation Organization), 761f, 763, 764f
Poe, Edgar Allen, 405
poetry: Chinese, 109
pogroms, 443
Poland, 546, 638, 677, 698, 700; authoritarian rule in, 566–567; German invasion of, 623, 654f; nation-state, 546; revolution crushed in, 391; right to vote for women, 684; transition from communism, 701m
Poles: in Austrian Empire, 392m, 393, 434
policy of containment, 666
polis, 40, 40f; as center of ancient Greek life, 40
Politburo, 564
Politics (Aristotle), 45
Pol Pot, 785
Pompey, 50
Pontius Pilate, 56
Pope, Alexander, 313f
popes, 119. *See* papacy
popular culture, 713. *See also* youth culture; global exchange of popular music, 717f; rock and roll around the world, 716–717f; U.S. in the 1950s and 1960s, 686–697f
Popular Front government in France, 558
population: of Africa, 753; of China, 776, 780; city, 422, 435; current trends, 814; in developing nations, 807; environmental effects of growth, 806; in Europe, 423m; of India, 783; industrialization and, 383; of Japan, 598; world, 807, 814
porcelain, 283; Ming, 282f
Port Arthur, Manchuria, 507, 508f
Portillo, José López, 730
Portugal, 196; arrival in China, 276; imperialism by. *See* Portugal, colonial interests of; industrialization in, 419; Portuguese colonies in Latin America, 209m; Portuguese explorers, 195m, 196; takes control

INDEX

of trade with Asia, 105*f*; trading with Japan, 284–285
Portugal, colonial interests of: in Africa, 457*m*, 459, 593*m*, 750; in Latin America, 472, 473*m*, 475, 476; in Southeast Asia, 451*m*
postimpressionism, 439, 439*f*
postmodernism, 713
Potsdam Conference, 651
praetors, 50
"Prague Spring", 677
The Praise of Folly **(Erasmus),** 178, 178*f*
PRI (Institutional Revolutionary Party), 611
The Prince **(Machiavelli),** 165
The Princess **(Tennyson),** 426
Princip, Gavrilo, 524
Principia **(Newton),** 305
principle of intervention, 389
principle of legitimacy, 388
principle of nonalignment, 782
printing: Gutenberg's press, 166*f*; invention of in China, 109; Scientific Revolution and, 302
The Prisoner of Chillon **(Byron),** 403*f*
Prisoner of Chillon **(Delacroix),** 403*f*
privatization, 730
proletariat, 420
propaganda, 526; in Fascist Italy, 562, 562*f*; in Nazi Germany, 576–577, 577*f*
protectorate, 452
Protestantism. *See also* Protestant Reformation: Anabaptists, 185; Anglicans, 184–185; Calvinism, 182–184; in England, 219; Lutheranism as start of, 180, 180*f*; society and, 186; Zwinglians, 182
Protestant Reformation, 176. *See also* Protestantism; beginning of, 188; in England, 184–185; in Germany, 181; Martin Luther and, 176, 178*f*, 179–180, 180*f*; reasons for, 176–178; spreading of, 188
Prussia, 231; army in, 319–320; Austro-Prussian War, 396; bureaucracy in, 319–320; city population of, 422; Congress of Vienna, 388–389; the emergence of, 231; enlightened absolutism, 319*m*, 319–320; expansion of, 231*m*; Franco-Prussian War, 396, 397; German unification and, 396–397; Seven Years' War, 322–323
psychoanalysis, 441, 441*f*
Ptolemaic system, 304
Ptolemy, 302, 304
Ptolemy (Egyptian pharaoh), 47
Pueblo Bonito, 32*f*
Puerto Rico, 435, 477

Pugachov, Yemelyan, 321
Punic Wars, 49*m*
Puritans, 225
Puteoli, 51
Putin, Vladimir, 698; Chechnya policy, 699; Russia under, 698–699
Pu Yi, Henry (infant emperor of China), 498
Pyramid of Kukulcan, 146*f*
pyramids: of ancient Egypt, 14; Great Pyramid at Giza, 14

Qājār dynasty of Persia, 589
Qianlong (emperor of China), 278*q*, 279
Qin dynasty, 27–28
Qing, 276. *See also* Qing dynasty of China
Qing dynasty of China, 277–279, 512; begins, 273; China under, 275*m*; decline of, 488–495; empire of 1911, 497*m*; fall of, 496–499; imperialism in China and, 492–495; Opium War, 490, 491*f*; pressures on, 488–489; Qing adaptations, 277; reform efforts of, 491–492, 496; Revolution of 1911 brings an end to the, 512*f*; Tai Ping Rebellion, 490–491
Qin Shihuangdi (emperor of China), 27
Quebec: secession issue, 709, 718
queues, 277, 500*f*
"Quiet Night Thoughts" (Li Bo), 109
quipu, 149
Quo Vadis, 576
Quran, 92*f*

Rabin, Yitzhak, 680*f*, 764*f*
racism: in Germany, 442–443; of Hitler, 568; imperialism and, 451
Radical Party, 611
Radical's Arms **(Cruikshank),** 356*f*
Raffles, Sir Thomas Stamford, 452
Ramadan, 92
Raphael, 174
Rasputin, Grigory, 536–537
rationalism, 308–309
Reagan, Ronald, 695, 707, 733
Reagan Revolution, 707
realism, 407, 410; in art, 406*f*, 407; in literature, 407
realpolitik, 396
Red Army, 536, 541
Red Cross, 817; helps famine victims in Sudan, 818*f*
Red Guards, 777*m*, 778; parade in Beijing, 796*f*
"Red Scare", 681–682, 688

Red Sea, 15, 99
Red Shirts, 396
Red Square, 697*f*
Red Terror, 541
Reform Act of 1832, 398*f*, 427*f*
Reform Act of 1867, 398*f*, 432
Reform Act of 1884, 432
Reformation. *See* Protestant Reformation
regional identity: nationalism and, 715; in Western Europe, 714*m*
Reichstag, 569, 570
Reign of Terror, 353–354, 354–355*f*, 368; beginning of, 338; clothing during, 348–349*f*; clothing worn during, 349*f*; decapitation of Feraud, 359*f*; end of, 356; victims, by class, 356*f*
reincarnation, 24
relativity, theory of, 440–441
religion(s). *See also individual religions:* Aztec, 147, 150–151*f*; Buddhism, 24–25; Calvinism, 224; in early African society, 103; Enlightenment and, 317; in Europe, 1364, 183*m*; French Revolution and, 354; Hinduism, 24; of India, 783*f*; in Israel, 19; Judaism, 18; in Mongol Empire, 108; monotheistic, 19; in Ottoman world, 251; religious trends, 714; rise of Islam, 90–92; Shinto, 112; in Southeast Asia, 291; Sumerian, 10; trends in Western culture, 714–715
religious orders: Benedictine, 119; Cistercian, 136; Dominicans, 136; Franciscans, 136; new orders during Middle Ages, 136
Renaissance, Italian, 162–163, 163*m*; art after the, 236–238; art of, 173–175; education of, 172–173; High Renaissance, 174; humanism of, 170–172; Italian city-states of, 163*m*, 163–164; Italian wars of, 164; in Italy and Northern Europe, 188; in northern Europe, 175; popes of, 178–178; Scientific Revolution and, 302; society, 166–167, 168–169*f*
Renoir, Pierre-Auguste, 438
reparations, 545, 555, 556
Republicans, 401
Republic of China. *See* Taiwan (Formosa)
Republic of Korea. *See* South Korea
Republic of Virtue, 353–354, 356
The Republic **(Plato),** 44
Restoration, 226–227
Revive China Society, 496
Revolutionary Alliance, 497
Revolution of 1911, 498–499
On the Revolutions of the Heavenly Spheres **(Copernicus),** 304
Revolutions of 1830, 390–391

Revolutions of 1848, 391–393
Reza Khan (Reza Shāh Pahlavi), 589–590
Reza Shāh Pahlavi (shāh of Iran), 589–590, 610*f*
Rhee, Syngman, 792
Rhineland, 621
Rhodes, Cecil, 460*f*, 461
Rhodesia, 461
Richelieu, Cardinal, 228
Riefenstahl, Leni, 577*f*
Rio de Janeiro, 744*f*
Riou, Edouard, 458*f*
The Rite of Spring **(Stravinsky),** 440
Rivera, Diego, 612*f*, 613
River Arno, 174*f*
Riza-i-Abbasi, 259
Robespierre, Maximilien, 352, 352*f*, 353*q*, 354, 355*f*, 356, 358*q*; citizenship, 358*q*
Rockefeller, Nelson, 613
Rocket, 381–382, 382*f*
Rococo style, 326, 326*f*
Rodriguez, Simon, 474*f*
Roe v. Wade, 712
Roma, 641
Roman Catholic Church. *See* Catholic Church
Roman Confederation, 48
Roman Empire, 52–55, 93. *See also* Rome, ancient; coronation of Charlemagne, 120; decline of, 58–59; Early, 51–52; end of the, 58–59; fall of the Western, 37, 59; involvement with Cleopatra VII, 16; Late, 58; *Pax Romana,* 51; from Republic to Empire, 50; Roman law, 54*f*
Romania, 702; authoritarian rule in, 566–567; independence of, 437; transition from communism, 701*m*
Romanians, 392*m*, 393
Roman law, 55; Law of Nations, 55; Twelve Tables, 54*f*, 55
Romanov, Michael (czar of Russia), 232
Roman Republic, 49–50. *See also* Rome, ancient; council of the plebs, 50; from Republic to Empire, 50; Roman Senate, 50; start of, 36
Romansch, 392*m*
Roman Senate, 50
romanticism, 402, 410; in art and music, 402–404; in literature, 404–405
Rome, ancient, 48, 137. *See also* Roman Empire; Roman Republic; Colosseum, 60–61*f*; conquest of the Mediterranean, 48–49; games of death in, 60–61*f*; life in, 52*f*, 53–55; Punic Wars, 49*m*; rise of, 48–52; rise of Christianity and, 48–59; sack of, 164; sack of by Vandals, 59; sack

INDEX

of by Visigoths, 59; slavery in, 53; Twelve Tables, 54f
Rome, Italy, 396; Sistine Chapel in, 174, 174f
Romero, Oscar (Archbishop), 733
Rommel, Erwin, 633
Romulus Augustulus (Roman emperor), 59
Roosevelt, Franklin Delano, 630; Executive Order 6706, 646f; Good Neighbor policy, 609, 612, 726; New Deal, 559, 681; United Nations supported by, 812; Yalta Conference, 650
Roosevelt, Theodore, 477, 477f, 508
Roosevelt Corollary, 477f
Rosetta Stone, 372f
Rosie the Riveter, 645f
Rothschild, Lord, 590f
Rothwell, Richard, 404f
Roundheads, 225
Rousseau, Jean-Jacques, 315
Royal Road, 21
Rubens, Peter Paul, 238
Ruhr Valley, 555, 555m
Runnymeade, 120
Russia, 561. See also Soviet Union; Balkans and, 437; Boxer Rebellion and, 495; city population of, 422; civil war in, 537m, 540–541; communism in, 539, 540f; Congress of Vienna, 388–389; Crimean War, 394–395; energy wealth, 699; enlightened absolutism, 319m, 321–322; expansion of, 1505–1725, 232m; government of, 434; independence from Soviet Union, 696; industrialization in, 419; the March Revolution, 537–538; mobilization of, 525; Napoleon's invasion of, 339, 366m, 366–367, 452; the new, 698–699, 698f; New Economic Policy in, 563–564; Peter the Great, 232–233; under Putin, 698–699; reform in, 399–400; the Russian Revolution, 536–541; Seven Years' War, 323; spheres of influence in China, 492–493; Triple Entente, 436, 522; using supplies of oil and gas as political lever, 699; war with Japan, 507–508, 508f; under Yeltsin, 698
Russian Revolution, 536–541, 539f, 548; background to, 536–538; beginnings of, 536–537; Bolsheviks seize power, 539–540; civil war, 537m, 540–541; from czars to communists, 538–541; Lenin and the Bolsheviks, 538–539; the March Revolution, 537–538; provisional government, 538; triumph of the Communists, 541

Russo-Japanese War, 507–508, 508f
Ruthenians, 392m, 393
Rutherford, Ernest, 579
Rwanda, 754; number of Rwandans killed during Tutsi-Hutu conflict in 1994, 823f

Sadat, Anwar el-, 763, 767
Ṣafavid dynasty of Persia, 256–257. See also Ṣafavid Empire; Ṣafavids; at the crossroads of trade and of history, 260–261f; life under, 259; rule of the, 256–259
Ṣafavid Empire. See also Ṣafavid dynasty of Persia; Ṣafavids: 1501–1722, 257m; advance against Ottoman Turks, 256; compared to Ottoman Empire, 257t; glory and decline, 258
Ṣafavids, 256–257. See also Ṣafavid dynasty of Persia; Ṣafavid Empire; history and culture, 268
Ṣafi od-Dīn (Turkish leader), 256
Saikaku, Ihara, 287
Saint Benedict, 119
Saint Bernard of Clarvaux, 136
Saint Domingue, Hispaniola, 472
Saint Francis of Assisi, 136, 137f
Saint Nicholas (Santa Claus), 137
Saint Peter's Basilica, Rome, 180f, 237f
Sakhalin Island, 508
Salt March, 596, 597f; number of miles walked, 659f
Samoan Islands, 435
samurai, 110, 111f
San, Aung, 785
Sánchez Navarro family, 476
Sandinistas, 735
Sanjo Palace in Kyoto, 126f
San Martin, José de, 474–475, 474f
sans-culottes, 347, 349f
Sanskrit, 23f
Santa Anna, Antonio López de, 475–476
Santiago de Compostela, 137
Santo Domingo, 477f
Sarajevo: assassination of Archduke Ferdinand in, 524
Sardinia, 395
Sargon (king of Akkadians), 11
SA (Storm Troops) (Brownshirts), 568
Sat-Cho alliance, 503, 504
satrapies, 21
Satsuma, Japan, 503

Saudi Arabia: creation of, 591, 610f; nationalism in, 591, 610f; oil discovered in, 591
Savonarola, Girolamo, 164
Saya San, 454f, 455
Say's Law, 558f
Schindler, Oscar, 658q
Schleswig, 396
Schlieffen Plan, 525, 527m
Schliemann, Heinrich, 38
School of Athens **(Raphael),** 174
Schröder, Gerhard, 680f
Schutzstaffeln. See SS
science: in ancient Egypt, 17; Islamic, 96–97; junk, 442; nineteenth century, 405–406, 440–441; technology and science in Western culture, 710
scientific method, 308f, 309, 310
Scientific Revolution, 306f, 334; astronomy and, 304–305, 306f; causes of, 302–303; chemistry and, 306; intellectuals of, 303m; medicine and, 306; rationalism and, 308–309; women's contributions to, 307
Scotland, 220; United Kingdom formed with England, 330
Scott, Sir Walter, 404
scribe, 13
sculpture: ancient Greek, 44; Benin, 103; during Hellenistic Era, 47, 62f; of Michelangelo, 174f; modernism in, 439; Renaissance, 173–174; Roman, 53; Yorubas produce terra-cotta, 89
Sea of Marmara, 248
The Seasons **(Haydn),** 327
Secondat, Charles-Louis de. See Montesquieu, baron de
Second Battle of the Marne, 542
Second Continental Congress, 332
Second Empire of France, 399
Second German Empire, 397
Second International, 421
Second Republic of France, 392
The Second Sex **(de Beauvoir),** 684f, 685
Seko, Mobutu Sese, 752
Selim I (sultan of Ottoman Empire), 249
Selim II (sultan of Ottoman Empire), 253
Seljuk Turks, 93–94, 125, 126f
Senegal, 594, 752
Senghor, Leopold, 594, 752
separation of powers, 312, 333
Sepoy Mutiny (Great Rebellion) (First War of

Independence), 466–467, 467f, 482
September 11, 2001, 765, 766f, 810–811
Serbia, 524, 703; Bosnian Crisis and, 437
Serbs: in Austrian Empire, 392m, 393
serfs, 133; in Russia, 400
Seven Years' War, 322–325, 323m, 324m, 324–325f
Sforza, Francesco, 164
shāh, 256; role of the, 259
Shaka Zulu, 460f, 461
Shakespeare, William, 238, 239q
Shandong Peninsula, 493
Shang dynasty, 27
Shanghai Massacre, 601
Sharpeville Massacre, 750, 755f
Shelley, Mary, 404, 404q, 405
Shia Muslims, 765, 766
Shining Path, 740
Shinto, 112
Shiva the Destroyer, 24
shogun, 110
Shōtoku Taishi (Japanese ruler), 110
Siberia, 492, 540, 565, 675–676
Sicily, Kingdom of, 393, 396
Siddhārtha Gautama (Gautama Buddha), 24
Siddhārtha **(Hesse),** 579
Sieveking, Amalie, 427
sikhara, 112f
Sikhs, 783, 783m
Sikkim, 493
Silent Spring **(Carson),** 806
Silesia, 322, 323
Silk Road, 26, 107; trade flourishes on, 88; travel begins on, 3
Silva, Luiz Inácio Lula da, 739
Simon, Paul, 713
Simon Peter (apostle), 56
Sinai Peninsula, 763
Sinan, 252
Singapore, 796; colony of, 452; recent years, 793
Sistine Chapel, 174, 174f
Six-Day War, 761f, 762–763
slavery: abolishment in British Empire, 517f; Dutch merchants' charge for one enslaved African, 373f; enslaved Africans working on a sugarcane plantation, 212f; slave trade, 205–206; sources of enslaved Africans, 206; in the U.S., 401, 435
slave trade, 205–206; African slave trade of Europe, Asia, and the Americas, 212; Atlantic, 204–207, 205m; effects of, 207; growth of, 206; Middle Passage, 206; the Royal African Company, 373f;

triangular trade, 206, 212; in West Africa, 456

Slavs: in Austrian Empire, 434

Slovakia, 701

Slovaks, 392*m*, 393

Slovenes, 392*m*, 393

Slovenia, 703

Smith, Adam, 313–314, 313*f*, 314*f*

The Social Contract **(Rousseau),** 315

Social Darwinism, 442, 442*f*, 451, 568

Social Democratic Party: emergence of German, 414

Social Democrats: in West Germany, 705–706

socialism, 385; African, 752; early, 385; industrialization and, 419–421; utopian, 184*f*, 385

socialist parties, 419, 421, 434

Socialists: in France, 704

social sciences: of the Enlightenment, 313–314

Social Security Act, 559

Society for Revolutionary Republican Women, 354

society(ies): ancient Egyptian, 16; Chinese, 280–283; classless, 420, 420*f*, consumer, 684; early African, 103; in East and South Africa, 101; Inca, 149; Industrial Revolution impact on, 383–385; Islam and Indian society, 113; Islamic, 96; Latin America, 726; mass, 422–429; in Ottoman Empire, 252; patriarchal, 13; in Song dynasty, 107–108; in Southeast Asia, 114; urban, 162; Western, 710–715

Society of Friends: condemnation of slavery, 207

Society of Harmonious Fists (Boxers), 495

Society of Jesus (Jesuits), 187

Socrates, 44, 45*f*

Sokoto, 461

Solomon (king of Israelites), 18

Solon (Athenian reformer), 41

Solzhenitsyn, Aleksandr, 675

Somalia, 753, 754

Song dynasty, 106; role of women in, 107*f*

Songhai, Kingdom of, 101

Songs of Experience **(Blake),** 405

Songs of Innocence **(Blake),** 405

Sophocles, 44

South Africa: apartheid in, 750–751, 754, 755*f*, democratic elections in, 754, 755*f*, imperialism in, 460–461; societies in, 101

South African Republic (Transvaal), 460

South America: cultures of early, 144, 148*m*; early civilizations, 148–149; imperialism in, 450; nationalist revolts in, 474–475; nations of, 736–741; number of countries under colonial power, 517*f*; as part of Spanish Empire, 199; political events in, 737*m*

Southeast Asia, 114*m*, 289; after independence, 785; after World War II, 796; civilization in, 114–115; conflicts in, 290; democracy in, 787; ethnic and religious conflicts in, 808; formation of states in, 114–115; imperialism in, 451*m*, 452–455; Japanese colonial policies, 643; most under Western rule, 453; nationalism in, 455, 643; new imperialism and, 482; religions and cultures of, 291*m*; religious and political systems, 291–292; society and culture, 114; during the spice trade, 290–293, 296; women in, 787

Southeast Asia Treaty Organization (SEATO), 669

South Korea, 796. *See also* Korea; creation of, 781; democracy in, 809; Korean War, 780*m*, 781; recent years, 791–792, 792

South Vietnam, 785, 796

Soviet Union, 674. *See also* Russia; by 1939, 565*m*; Afghanistan occupation by, 765; aid to Cuba, 733; attack on Budapest, 677; Battle of Kursk, World War II, 635; biological weapon agreement, 804; blockade of West Berlin, 666; breakup of, 695*m*, 697*f*; China and, 600, 781; during the Cold War, 664–671, 688; collectivization in, 564–565; creation of, 563; decline of, 694–699; decline of Cuban economy, 744; Eastern Europe and, 674–677; economic and political change in, 718; explodes its first atomic bomb, 667; Five Year Plans of, 564; former Soviet republics, 697*t*; German-Soviet war, 644; Hitler and the Soviets, 622–623, 631; industrialization in, 564, 565*m*; installation of hotline communications system, 671; invasion of Czechoslovakia, 677; Korea and, 781; mobilization during World War II, 644–645; Nazi-Soviet Nonaggression Pact, 622–623; as part of the Grand Alliance, 633; policy of deterrence, 669; postwar Soviet leaders, 674–676; refusal to participate in 1984 Los Angeles Olympic Games, 713; remains in Eastern Europe, 664; role of women in the war effort, 645; Spanish Civil War and, 567; Stalin, 564–565;

under stress, 694–695; Suez War, 761; Tehran Conference, 650; Yalta Conference, 650

space race, 710; U.S. astronauts first to walk on the Moon, 718*f*; U.S. landing on moon, 710

Spain: American Revolution, 332; as an Arab state, 93; authoritarian rule in, 567; conflicts during Wars of Religion, 218–220; conquest of the Inca, 199; defeat of the Spanish Armada, 220*m*; destruction of Aztec civilization, 198–199; height of Spanish power under Philip II, 219*m*; imperialism by. *See* Spain, colonial interests of; industrialization in, 419; Italian wars, 164; Second Republic of, 567; Seven Years' War, 325; Spanish-American War, 435, 452; Spanish Civil War, 566*f*, 567; Spanish colonies in Latin America, 209*m*; Spanish Empire, 198–200; Spanish explorers, 195*m*, 196–197

Spain, colonial interests of: in Africa, 457*m*, 593*m*; in Latin America, 472–475, 473*m*, 476

Spanish-American War, 435, 452, 477

Spanish Armada: defeat of the, 216, 220, 220*m*

Spanish Civil War, 566*f*, 567

Spanish Empire, 198–200

Sparta, city-state of, 41; ephors, 41

Spartacus, 53

Speer, Albert, 647

Spencer, Herbert, 442, 442*f*

spheres of influence, 489*m*

Spice Islands, 296. *See also* Moluccas (Spice Islands); spice trade

spice trade: arrival of Europeans, 292–293; the Dutch at Batavia, 292*f*; impact on the mainland, 293; Islamic trade network, 290; in the Moluccas, 296*f*; Southeast Asia during the, 290–293

Spirit, Mars rover, 804

The Spirit of the Laws **(Montesquieu),** 312

Spring **(Ba Jin),** 501

Sputnik I, 669, 674, 710, 823*f*

SS (*Schutzstaffeln***),** 571, 571*f*

Stalin, Joseph, 580, 622, 623*f*, 676, 688; creating a new industrial base in the Soviet Union, 674; death of, 675; effects of, on Soviet Union, 565; fear of capitalist West, 664; Five Year Plans of, 564; Korean War and, 781; Potsdam Conference, 651; reign of, 674–675; rise of, 564; Yalta Conference, 650

Stamp Act, 331

Stanley, Henry, 459, 464*f*

The Starry Messenger **(Galileo),** 304

The Starry Night **(van Gogh),** 439*f*

steam engine, 380, 382*f*

steam locomotive, 381, 382*f*

steel industry, 416, 435

stem-cell research, 804

Stephenson, George, 381

Steppenwolf **(Hesse),** 579

Stevin, Simon, 303

Stockton & Darlington, 381

Stonebreakers **(Courbet),** 406*f*

Storm Troops (SA) (Brownshirts), 568

Stravinsky, Igor, 440

Stresemann, Gustav, 556

student revolts, 685; Kent State University, 682; in Mexico, 730

Sudan: British control of, 458; Darfur conflict, 754, 808; drought in, 753; Red Cross helps famine victims in, 818*f*

Sudentenland, 622

Sudras, 23

Suez Canal, 457, 458, 458*f*, 464*f*, 761; inauguration of the, 482*f*

Suez Canal Company, 761, 761*f*

Suez War, 761, 761*f*

suffrage, 427; African American, 435; universal male, 392, 432, 433

suffrage movement, women's, 425*f*

Suharto, General, 787

Sukarno, Achmed, 785

sukiyaki, 795*f*

Süleyman I (Süleyman the Magnificent) (sultan of Ottoman Empire), 250, 252*f*, 268

Sullivan, Louis H., 440

Sumerian(s), 10; creativity of, 13

Sumitomo, 598

sumo: ceremony of, 510–511*f*; wrestlers, 510–511*f*

Sumptuary Laws: clothing and, 348–349*f*

Sundiata Keita (king of Mali), 100

Sun Fo, 605*q*

Sunni Ali (king of Songhai), 101

Sunni Muslims, 268, 765, 766

Sun Yat-sen (Chinese nationalist), 496–499, 497*q*, 498*f*, 512, 516*q*, 600–601, 603*q*

supply-side economics, 558*f*

surrealism, 578–579

Susa, 21

Suu Kyi, Aung San, 785

Swadeshamitram **(Aiyar),** 471

Swahili: traders, 105*f*

Swan, Joseph, 416

Swaziland, 753

Sweden: right to vote for women, 684

INDEX

Swift, Jonathan, 313*f*
Switzerland: Calvinism in, 182–184; voting rights in, 558; Zwinglian Reformation in, 182
Syncom-IV satellite, 803*f*
Syria: French control of, 590; independence of, 760; in United Arab Republic, 762; Yom Kippur War, 761*f*, 763
systematic agriculture, 6*f*, 7; develops, 2

Tabrīz, 256
Tae-jung, Kim, 792
Tagore, Rabindranath, 470*f*, 471, 471*q*
Taipei, Taiwan, 792
Tai Ping Rebellion, 490–491
Taiwan (Formosa), 277, 796; democracy in, 809; Japanese control of, 493, 507, 599; Nationalist Chinese settle on, 776, 792; recent years, 792–793
Taj Mahal, 265–266, 268*f*, 372*f*, 452, 468
Taliban, 708*f*, 709, 765
Tang dynasty, 106; role of women in, 107*f*
Tannenberg, Battle of, 527
Tanzania, 752
technology: environment and, 711*f*; exploration and, 197*f*; and horror of war, 534–535*f*; impact on industrialization, 410; of Industrial Revolution, 379–382; Scientific Revolution and, 302–303; of Second Industrial Revolution, 416–419; since the 1970s, 802–805; spread and transformation of Western, 718; Sumerian, 13; during Tang and Song dynasties, 107–108; technological revolution, 818; and trench life define total war, 534–535*f*; Western culture, 710; of World War I, 528*f*
Tehran Conference, 650
telephone: cell, 803*f*; invention of, 417; satellite, 803*f*
television: satellites and, 803*f*; terrorism and, 766*f*, 809
Tellem, 88
Temüjin, 108. *See* Genghis Khan
Ten Commandments, 19
Tennis Court Oath, 342–*343f*, 343–344
Tennyson, Lord, 426*m*
Tenochtitlán, 147
Teotihuacán: collapse of, 130
terrorism, 818; in Afghanistan, 765; car bomb, 818*f*; in Iraq, 766; Islamic militants and, 811; modern, 809; nuclear, 813; in Philippines, 787; in the U.S., 765, 766*f*, 810–811, 810*f*; weapons of mass destruction, 804

Tetzel, Johann, 179, 180*f*
Thackeray, William Makepeace, 408*q*
Thailand (Siam): independence maintained by, 452
Thatcher, Margaret, 707, 822*q*
theater: Japanese Kabuki, 288, 294–295*f*; Shakespearean, 238
Thebes, 43, 45
Theodosius I (Roman emperor), 57, 57*f*
theory of relativity, 440–441, 659*f*
Theravada Buddhism. *See* Buddhism
***Things Fall Apart* (Achebe),** 757
Third Reich, 569*f*, 570
Third Republic of France, 432–433
***Third Symphony* (Beethoven),** 404
Thirteenth Amendment, 435
Thirty Years' War, 224, 242; start of the, 216
Three People's Principles, 498
***Throne of Saint Peter* (Bernini),** 238
Thuku, Harry, 594, 594*q*, 610*f*
Tiananmen Square, 779, 779*f*
Tianjin, Treaty of, 491
Tibet, 106, 493, 808
Tientsin, 512*f*
Tiepolo, Giovanni Battista, 326
Tigris River, 10
Tikal, 145
Tilak, Balwantrao Gangadhar, 471
Timur Lenk (Tamerlane) Empire, 113, 256
Title IX Education Amendment, 425*f*
Title VII of Civil Rights Act of 1728, 425*f*
Tito (Josip Broz), 676
Togo, 456
Tojo, Hideki, 647
Tokitaka, Lord, 285, 285*q*
Tokugawa Era, 287–288, 294–295*f*, 296. *See also* Japan
Tokugawa Ieyasu, 284; takes title of shogun in Japan, 272
Tokugawa shogunate, 502
Toledo, Alejandro, 740
the Toltec, 146–147
Tonkin, 452
Topa Inca (Incan ruler), 148
Topkapi Palace, 251*f*
total war, 531; the impact of, 531–533; and women, 533
Toudouze, Georges, 530*f*
Tourè, Sékou, 752
Tours, Battle of, 93, 94, 95*f*; Charles Martel defeats Arab forces at, 88

Toussaint-Louverture, François-Dominique, 472–473
Toyotomi Hideyoshi, 284, 372*q*
trade: under Abbasid Empire, 93; Atlantic slave, 204–207, 205*m*; balance of, 204; colonies and mercantilism, 204–206; Columbian Exchange and international trade, 200*f*; Commodore Perry and Japan, 512*f*; in early Japan, 111; in Early Roman Empire, 51–52; effects of the slave, 207; global, 816; imperialism and trade in Japan, 512; Indian Ocean, 104*m*; Islamic trade network, 290; medieval routes, 134*m*; merchants in a covered market in the 1400s, 152*f*; path of Black Death, 139–140; routes of the ancient world, 26*m*; Safavid, 260–261*f*; sale of British goods in China, 512*f*; travel on Silk Road begins, 3; triangular trade, 206; two centers of trade in Africa (Kush and Axum), 99*t*; in West Africa, 100*m*
Trafalgar, Battle of, 365
Trajan (Roman emperor), 51
Trans-Siberian railway, 493
Transvaal (later South African Republic), 460
***Treatise on Toleration* (Voltaire),** 312
Treaty of Kanagawa, 512
Treaty of Locarno, 556
Treaty of Nanjing, 490, 491*f*
Treaty of Nijmegen: signing of, 242*f*
Treaty of Paris: of 1763, 224, 325; of 1783, 332; of 1856, 394
Treaty of Tianjin, 491
Treaty of Tordesillas, 197, 373*f*
Treaty of Versailles, 546*f*, 548; French demands for enforcement of, 554–555
trench warfare, 527, 528*f*, 548; tactics of, 529; during World War I, 534–535*f*
Trevithick, Richard, 381
triangular trade, 206, 212
Triple Alliance, 436, 444, 522; Tenochtitlán and other city-states, 147
Triple Entente, 436, 444, 522
Triplicane Literary Society, 471
Tripoli: Italian control of, 458
***Triumph of the Will* (Riefenstahl),** 577*f*
Trojan War, 39, 44
tropical rain forest destruction, 806, 807*f*
Trotsky, Leon, 539, 541, 563, 564
Trudeau, Pierre, 709

Truman, Harry S., 635, 648, 681; Korean War and, 781; Potsdam Conference, 651; Truman Doctrine, 665–666
Truman Doctrine, 665–666
Tula, 146
Tunisia: French protectorate in, 458; independence of, 750
Turing, Alan, 802
Turkey: Islamic revivalism and, 767; modernization of, 589; nationalism in, 586–589, 610*f*; Republic of, 588, 610*f*; the Truman Doctrine, 665; Young Turks, 586, 588*f*
Turkish Republic, 588, 610*f*
Tut (king of Egypt), 659*f*
Tutsi, 754
Tutu, Desmond, 754
Twelve Tables, 54*f*
Two Sicilies, Kingdom of, 393, 396
***Two Treatises on Government* (Locke),** 241; John Locke writes, 217

Uganda, 753, 754
Uighurs, 106
Ukraine, 540; independence from Soviet Union, 696
Ukrainians, 393
ulema, 251
Ulyanov, Vladimir Ilyich. *See* Lenin, V. I.
***Ulysses* (Joyce),** 579
Umayyad Empire, 93
UNESCO (United Nations Education, Scientific and Cultural Organization), 813*f*
Union of French Indochina, 452, 454
Union of South Africa, 461
Union of Soviet Socialist Republics (USSR). *See* Soviet Union
United Arab Republic (UAR), 762
United Fruit Company, 608
United Kingdom of Great Britain. *See also* Great Britain: creation of, 330
United Nations, 818; AIDS initiatives of, 805; creation of, 812; General Assembly of, 812; Iraq war and, 766; Israeli statehood and, 760; in Korea, 780*m*, 792*f*; Korean War, 781, 792*f*; literacy programs of, 813*f*; Millennium Development Goals of, 816*f*; NGOs and, 817; nuclear proliferation and, 813; peacekeeping role of, 812–813; plans for establishing at the Yalta Conference, 651; Security Council of, 812; sustainable development promoted by, 806; Universal

INDEX

Declaration of Human Rights, 809; view of colonialism, 750; Yom Kippur War and, 763

United Nations Education, Scientific and Cultural Organization (UNESCO), 813*f*

United States: 1960s and civil rights, 682; Afghanistan invasion by, 765, 811; after World War II, 681–683; agreement with Gorbachev about nuclear weapons, 696; American-Canadian relations, 683, 707–709; architecture in, 440; Articles of Confederation, 333; Bill of Rights, 332*f*, 333, 390; biological weapon agreement, 804; Boxer Rebellion and, 495; Camp David Accords, 763; China and, 490, 781; civil rights movement in, 346*f*; Civil War, 207, 401, 410, 427, 435, 452; Cold War and, 664–671; Constitution, 333; control of Panama Canal, 735; economy of, 435; entry into World War I, 531; entry into World War II, 632; fear of communism, 664; Good Neighbor policy, 609, 612; Great Depression and, 559; growing Hispanic American population, 728*f*; Guam and, 435; Hawaiian Islands and, 435, 435*f*; Homeland Security, Department of, 810*f*, 811; imperialism by, 435, 451*m*, 452, 453*f*, 494–495; Industrial Revolution spread to, 383; installation of hotline communications system, 671; intervention in Central American politics, 744; Iran hostage crisis, 764–765; Iraq invasion by, 765–766; Iraq invasion of Kuwait and, 765; "island hopping" to Japan in World War II, 633; Japanese anime and, 791*f*; Japanese expansion and, 599; Japanese isolation and, 502–503; Japanese products in, 505*f*, 598*f*; Japanese relations with, 508; Korean War, 780*m*, 781, 792*f*; Kyōto Protocol and, 711*f*; Latin America and, 475, 476, 477, 477*f*, 608–609, 726–727; League of Nations and, 554; Louisiana Purchase, 338, 362*f*; mass culture of, 578*f*; Mexican War, 475–476; Mexico and, 612; mobilization during World War II, 645–646; Monroe Doctrine, 475, 477*f*; NAFTA and, 816; nationalism in, 401; new social structure, 683–685; Open Door Policy, 494–495, 494*f*, 599; as part of the Grand Alliance, 633; Philippines and, 435, 452–453, 785; policy of deterrence, 669; population trend in, 814; Puerto Rico and, 435, 477; revolution, 330–332; right to vote for women, 684; sanctions on Japan, 625;

slavery in, 207, 401, 435; social upheaval, 682; Samoan Islands and, 435; Spanish-American War, 435, 452, 477; stock market crash in, 556; Suez War, 761; Tehran Conference, 650; terrorism in, 765, 766*f*, 810–811, 810*f*; U.S. astronauts first to walk on the Moon, 718*f*; Vietnam War, 785, 786*f*; War of 1812, 401; war on terror, 708*f*; wind farms, 711*f*; women in the postwar world, 684–685; women's rights in, 425*f*, 426; Yalta Conference, 650

Universal Declaration of Human Rights, 809

universal law of gravitation, 305

universal male suffrage, 392, 432, 433

University of Bologna: founding of, 130

University of Paris, 139

Untouchables, 24

Upper Egypt, 14

Ur, 10, 11*m*; Standard of, 12*f*

Uribe, Alvaro, 741

Uruguay, 475

Uruk, 10

Utopia (More), 184*f*, 385

utopian socialists, 184*f*, 385

Uzbekistan: independence from Soviet Union, 696

Vaisyas, 23

Vandals, 59; sack of Rome, 59

Vanderbilt, Consuelo, 424

van Eyck, Jan, 175

van Gogh, Vincent, 439, 439*f*

Vargas, Getúlio, 610*f*, 611

varnas, 23

Vatican City, 563

Venetia, 393, 396

Venezuela, 734*m*, 741; Chávez rules in, 741; dependence on oil reserves, 744; independence of, 474, 475; political events in, 737*m*; U.S. role in, 609

Venice, Italy, 134, 163, 164, 188

Verdun, France, 529

vernacular literature, 139, 171–172, 171*f*

Versailles: Palace of Louis XIV, 216–217*f*

Versailles, Treaty of: French demands for enforcement of, 554–555

Vesalius, Andreas, 303*m*, 306

Vespucci, Amerigo, 197, 197*f*

Vichy France, 630

Victor Emmanuel II (king of Piedmont), 395, 396

Victor Emmanuel III (king of Italy), 562, 563, 634

Victoria Memorial, 452–453

Victorian Age, 398

Victoria (queen of England), 398, 463, 467, 490, 491*f*

Viet Cong, 785

Viète, François, 302–303

Vietminh, 785

Vietnam, 30, 114. *See also* North Vietnam; South Vietnam; communism in, 595, 595*f*; domino theory and, 671; French control of, 452, 480–481*f*; nationalism in, 455, 480–481*f*, 595; Vietnam War, 785, 786*f*

Vietnam War, 682, 685, 785, 786*f*

Villa, Pancho, 478*f*, 479

A Vindication of the Rights of Women (Wollstonecraft), 315

Virgil, 53, 170, 171*f*

Visconti family, 164

Vishnu the Preserver, 24

Visigoths, 59; sack of Rome, 59

Volga River, 122, 540, 633

Voltaire, 312, 313*f*, 320

von Richthofen, Manfred (the Red Baron), 529*f*

von Schlieffen, Alfred, 525

von Wegerer, Alfred, 546*q*

Voting Rights Act of 1729, 682, 683*f*

wabenzi, 753

Wagner, Richard, 577*f*

Walachia, 394

Walesa, Lech, 700

Walpole, Robert, 330

war of attrition, 529

War of Austrian Succession, 322

War of 1812, 401

Warren, Earl, 682

Warsaw Pact, 664, 668, 688; members as of 1719, 665*m*

Wars of Religion. *See* French Wars of Religion

Washington, George, 324*f*, 332, 338

Watergate, 707, 718

Waterloo, Battle of, 339, 367

Watt, James, 380

Watteau, Antoine, 326, 326*f*

Watts riots, 682

The Wealth of Nations (Smith), 314, 314*f*

weapons of mass destruction, 804, 818

Wei Jingsheng, 779*q*

Weimar Republic, 558

Weldon, Fay, 822*q*

Wellington, Duke of, 367

Wells, H. G., 528*q*

Wesley, John, 317

West Africa: imperialism in, 456; kingdoms in, 100–101; trade in, 100*m*

The West African Pilot (Azikiwe), 594

West Bank, 763

Western Asia: ancient, 10–13; expansion of Ottoman Empire in, 249–250

Western Europe: during the Cold War, 688; democracy and, 432–433; new unity, 678–681; North America and, 678–685; regional identity in, 714*m*; winds of change in, 704–707

Western Front: World War I, 526–527

Western Roman Empire, 59

West Germany, 679, 680*f*, 705–706; Berlin Airlift, 667*f*; Berlin Wall, 669; creation of, 666; its economic miracle, 679–680

The White Man's Burden (Kipling), 462*f*

Wilberforce, William, 372*q*

A Wild Sheet Chase (Murakami), 791

William I (emperor of Germany), 410*f*

William I (king of Prussia), 396, 397

William II (emperor of Germany), 414, 434, 436, 436*f*, 437, 495*q*, 524, 544

William of Normandy, 120

William the Silent (prince of Orange), 219, 227

Wilson, Woodrow, 532, 544, 554, 558, 595*f*, 627*f*; "Fourteen Points", 544; League of Nations, 545

Winkelmann, Maria, 303*m*, 307

witchcraft, 222; hysteria, 223*f*; trials, 222–223

Wittenberg, Germany, 179, 180*f*

Wolfe (General), 325

Wollstonecraft, Mary, 315

women, 529. *See also* women, rights of; in Africa, 757; in China, 31, 107*f*, 281–282, 780; in ancient Egyptian society, 16; in Aztec Empire, 147; changes in women's lives in Western culture, 711; Civil Code and, 363; in colonial Latin America, 211; contributions to the Nazi war effort, 647; Enlightenment and rights of, 315; as entrepreneurs in developing world, 808*f*; equality challenges today, 809; as factory workers, 383, 385; family and, 426; in fascist Italy, 563; in French Revolution, 353–354; in Japan, 506–507, 647, 790–791, 796*f*; jobs and, 425–426; in manorial societies, 134; marriage and, 426;

in Mesopotamian society, 13; in Middle Eastern society, 767; in Mogul India, 265; Nazism and, 573; opportunities during Second Industrial Revolution, 425–427, 444; in Ottoman Empire, 252; portion of athletes at 2004 Summer Olympics, 823*f*; in the postwar world, 684–685; Quran and, 96; Reformation and, 186; religious orders and, 136; in Renaissance, 173; salon hosting by, 316–317, 329*f*; Scientific Revolution and, 307; in South and Southeast Asia, 787; in Soviet Union during the war effort, 645; in Tokugawa Japan, 287; total war and, 533; in Turkey, 589

women, rights of: American movement, 684*f*; citizenship for, Etta Palm d'Aelders, 358*q*; Equal Pay Act of 1963, 712; movement for, 425*f*, 426–427, 427*f*; right to vote, 558, 684; *Roe v. Wade*, 712; women's movement, 712; in the workforce, 712*f*

Women's Social and Political Union, 427, 427*f*

Wordsworth, William, 356*q*, 405, 405*q*

working class(es): industrial, 383, 384–385; in London, 1654, 430*f*; mass society and, 424; Second Industrial Revolution and, 419–421

Works Progress Administration (WPA), 559

World Bank, 815

World Health Organization, 805

World's Fair: in Paris, 414–415

World Trade Center: 9/11 attack, 709; terrorist attacks on, 766*f*, 810

World Trade Organization (WTO), 816; China joins, 781

World War I, 526–533; aftermath of, 580; alliances in Europe, 523*m*; Balkans and, 437; begins, 415; causes of, 522–523, 548; Eastern Front, 527–528; end of, 542–547, 548; entry of U.S. in, 531; in Europe, 527*m*; German offensive, 542–543; the great slaughter, 528–529; illusions and stalemate, 526–528; impact of total war, 531–533; international rivalries set the stage for war, 444; last year of the war, 542–544; legacies of the war, 546–547; manipulation of public opinion, 532; new technology of, 528*f*; number killed (combined with World War II figures), 659*f*; Ottoman Empire and, 586–587; outbreak of war, 524–525; peace settlements, 544–547; road to, 522–525; total war and women, 533; trench warfare, 659*f*; war in the air, 529; Western Front, 526–527; widening of the war, 530–531

World War II: advance of the Allies, 632–633; Allied troops land at Normandy, 654*f*; in Asia and the Pacific, 632*m*; Asian theater, 633; balance of power after, 665*m*; Battle of Britain, 630–631; beginning of, 654; blitz of Great Britain, 652–653*f*, 658*f*; bombing of cities, 648–649; bombing of Hiroshima and Nagasaki, 635; causes of, 626–627*f*; children in the war, 641–642; course of, 628–635; D-Day, 634; in Europe and North Africa, 1703-1705, 629*m*; European theater, 633, 634; Europe at war, 628–631; German path to war, 620–623; Grand Alliance, 632; Hitler's attack on the Soviet Union, 631; Hitler's early victories, 628–630; home front and aftermath of war, 644–651, 645*f*; Japan at war, 631–632;

Japanese path to war, 623–625; Jewish population in Europe before and after World War II, 639*f*; last years of the war, 634–635; lives affected by war, 654; Nazi invasion of Czechoslovakia, 518–519*f*; Normandy invasion, 636–637*f*; number killed (combined with World War I figures), 659*f*; number of Africans who fought in, 659*f*; paths to war, 620–625; peace and a new war, 650–651; Tehran Conference, 650; turning of the tide, 633; U.S. after, 681–683; Yalta Conference, 650

Worms, Edict of, 179

Wright, Frank Lloyd, 440

Wright, Orville, 418

Wright, Wilbur, 418

writing: cuneiform, 13, 32*f*; Hangul, 289; hieratic script, 16; hieroglyphics, 16; Sanskrit, 23*f*

Wuhan, China, 500, 600

Würzburg: palace of, 326

Wu Zhao (empress of China), 107*f*

Yadong, Tibet, 493

Yahweh, 19

Yalta Conference, 650–651

Yangtze River. *See* Chang Jiang

Yasuda, 598

Yekaterinburg, Russia, 541

Yellow River. *See* Huang He

Yeltsin, Boris, 696, 698, 698*f*, 698*q*; Russia under, 698

Yi Sŏng-gye (emperor of Korea), 289

Yokahama: earthquake of 1687, 659*f*

Yom Kippur War, 761*f*, 763

Yong Le (emperor of China), 274, 283

Yorktown, Battle of, 332

Yorubas: production of metal and terra-cotta sculptures, 89

Young Kikuyu Association, 594, 610*f*

Young Turks, 586, 588*f*

Yousef, Ramzi, 766*f*

Yuan dynasty, 108. *See also* Kublai Khan

Yuan Shigai (ruler of China), 498–499, 498*f*

Yucatán Peninsula, 144

Yudhoyono, Susilo Bambang, 787

Yugoslavia, 676; authoritarian rule in, 566–567; conflicts in Bosnia and Kosovo, 703, 718; disintegration of, 703; ethnic conflict in, 809; migrants in Germany, 706; split into Serbia and Montenegro, 703; transition from communism, 701*m*

Yunus, Muhammad, 808*f*

zaibatsu **economy of Japan,** 598, 598*f*, 790

Zaire, 750

zamidars, 263

Zapata, Emiliano, 478*f*, 479, 516*q*

Zhang Zhidong, 488*q*

Zheng He, 274; the voyages of, 274–276, 277*m*

Zhou dynasty, 27

Zhu Yuanzhang (emperor of China), 108

Zimbabwe, 101, 754

Zionism, 442*f*, 443, 590*f*, 591, 760

Zola, Émile, 438

Zulu, 460–461, 460*f*

Zunyi, China, 602*f*

Zürich, Switzerland, 182

Zwingli, Ulrich, 182

Zwinglian Reformation, 182

INDEX

Acknowledgments

Glencoe would like to acknowledge the artists and agencies that participated in illustrating this program: American Artists Reps Inc.; Deborah Wolfe Ltd/illustrationOnLine.com; GeoNova LLC; Mendola Artist Representatives.

Photo Credits

Cover (tl)Kress Collection, Washington D.C./Bridgeman Art Library, (tcl)Kieran Doherty/Reuters/CORBIS, (tcr)AFP/Getty Images, (tr)Private Collection, Archives Charmet/Bridgeman Art Library, (c)Rene Burri/Magnum Photos, (b)Tibor Bognar/CORBIS; **endsheet** (b)photolibrary.com/Index Open, (bkgd)Getty Images; **iv** Erich Lessing/Art Resource, NY; **v** Art Archive/Russian Historical Museum, Moscow/Dagli Orti; **vii** Carlos Carrion/Sygma/CORBIS; **viii** Science Museum/SSPL/The Image Works; **xvii** Comstock/PictureQuest; **xix** Stockbyte/Punchstock; **xx** Getty Images; **A28** (t to b)Michael Von Ruber/Imagestate, (2)David S. Boyer/Getty Images, (3)John Lamb/Getty Images, (4)Panoramic Images/Getty Images; **GH2** BananaStock/PictureQuest; **GH13** Copyright © 2008 by David W. Boles. All Rights Reserved.; **GH14-1** age fotostock/SuperStock; **2** (t)Topham/The Image Works, (b)Charles & Josette Lenars/CORBIS; **2–3** David S. Boyer/Getty Images; **3** Roger Wood/CORBIS; **12** British Museum, London/Bridgeman Art Library; **15** Art Archive/Luxor Museum, Egypt/Dagli Orti; **17** (l)Roger Wood/CORBIS, (r)Werner Forman/CORBIS; **18** Kathleen Voege/Getty Images; **23** (inset)Eames Collection/Newberry Library, (bkgd)Topham/The Image Works; **29** (inset)Liu Liqun/ChinaStock, (bkgd)Paul Souders/CORBIS; **30** (l)Reuters/CORBIS, (r)Art Archive/Bibliothèque Nationale Paris; **32** (t)Art Archive/Musée du Louvre Paris/Dagli Orti, (b)akg-images; **36** Art Archive/Eton College/Dagli Orti; **36–37** Images Etc Ltd/Alamy Images; **37** (t)Araldo de Luca/CORBIS, (b)Bridgeman Art Library/Getty Images; **39** (l)Visual Arts Library (London)/Alamy Images, (c)Erich Lessing/Art Resource, NY, (r)The British Museum/Imagestate; **40** Alinari Archives/The Image Works; **42** Time & Life Pictures/Getty Images; **45** (l)The British Museum/Topham-HIP/The Image Works, (r)SEF/Art Resource, NY; **49** Art Archive/Museo Capitolino Rome/Dagli Orti; **51** (l)Prisma/Ancient Art & Architecture Collection, (r)Bridgeman Art Library/Getty Images; **52** (inset)Erich Lessing/Art Resource, NY, (bkgd)C. M.Dixon/Ancient Art & Architecture Collection Ltd; **54** Mary Evans Picture Library/The Image Works; **57** Scala/Art Resource, NY; **62** (t)Art Archive/Musée du Louvre, Paris/Dagli Orti, (b)Yoshio Tomii/SuperStock; **70** (t)Will & Deni McIntyre/CORBIS, (b)David Samuel Robbins/CORBIS; **71** (t)Robert Nickelsberg/Getty Images, (b)ML Sinibaldi/CORBIS; **72** (t)CORBIS, (b)Ace Stock Limited/Alamy Images; **73** (t)Atlantide Phototravel/CORBIS, (b)Denis Sinyakov/AFP/Getty Images; **74** (t)Michel Setboun/CORBIS, (bl)Bettmann/CORBIS, (br)Blank Archives/Getty Images; **75** (t)STR/AFP/Getty Images, (b)Jack Hollingsworth/Getty Images; **76** (t)Ted Streshinsky/CORBIS, (b)CORBIS; **77** (t)Deshakalyan Chwodhury/AFP/Getty Images, (b)Sebastian D'Souza/AFP/Getty Images; **78** Aaron Horowitz/CORBIS, (c)Kenneth Garrett/Getty Images, (b)CORBIS; **79** (t)Muhannad Fala'ah/Getty Images, (b)Madaree Tohlala/AFP/Getty Images; **80** (t)Hardy/zefa/CORBIS, (bl)CORBIS, (br)Comstock Images/Alamy Images; **81** (t)Quique Kierszenbaum/Getty Images, (b)Ted Spiegel/CORBIS; **82** (t)Ashley Cooper/CORBIS, (c)Chip Somodevilla/Getty Images, (b)ArkReligion.com/Alamy Images; **83** (t)Maynard Owen Williams/National Geographic/Getty Images, (b)Don MacKinnon/Getty Images; **84** (t)Beth Wald/Aurora/Getty Images, (bl)Ralph A. Clevenger/CORBIS, (br)Martin Harvey/Alamy Images; **85** (t)Nicholas DeVore/Getty Images, (cl)CORBIS, (cr)Paul Chesley/Getty Images, (b)Penny Tweedie/Wildlight; **86** (t)Pete Saloutos/CORBIS, (c)David Ball/CORBIS, (b)age fotostock/SuperStock; **88** Werner Forman/Art Resource, NY; **88–89** age fotostock/SuperStock; **89** (l)Heini Schneebeli/Bridgeman Art Library, (r)National Museum, Tokyo/SuperStock; **91** Peter Sanders/HAGA/The Image Works; **95** Chateau de Versailles, France/Bridgeman Art Library; **96** Topham/The Image Works; **104** (l)Werner Forman/Art Resource, NY, (r)Chris Howes/Wild Places Photography/Alamy Images; **105** (t)Sonia Halliday Photographs, (b)Private Collection/Bridgeman Art Library; **107** Musee Guimet, Paris/Bridgeman Art Library; **111** AAAC/Topham/The Image Works; **112** Robert Preston/Alamy Images; **121** Bettmann/CORBIS; **123** Christel Gerstenberg/CORBIS; **124** Art Resource, NY; **126** (t)Art Archive/Turkish and Islamic Art Museum, Istanbul/Dagli Orti, (c)age fotostock/SuperStock, (b)Werner Forman/Art Resource, NY; **130** (t)Jose Fuste Raga/CORBIS, (b)Topham/The Image Works; **130–131** Panoramic Images/Getty Images; **131** Stapleton Collection/CORBIS; **137** (l)Michael Teller/akg-images, (r)akg-images; **138** (inset)Andrea Pistolesi/Getty Images, (bkgd)Art Kowalsky/Alamy Images; **140** akg-images; **146** Richard A. Cooke/CORBIS; **151** Snark/Art Resource, NY; **152** (t)Historical Picture Archive/CORBIS, (b)Topham/The Image Works; **155** Giraudon/Art Resource, NY; **158–159** Danny Lehman/CORBIS; **160** Scala/Art Resource, NY; **160–161** Paul Hardy/CORBIS; **161** (t)HIP/Art Resource, NY, (b)Bildarchiv Preussischer Kulturbesitz/Art Resource, NY; **165 166** Erich Lessing/Art Resource, NY; **171** Scala/Art Resource, NY; **172** (l)Francis G. Mayer/CORBIS, (r)Art Archive/Galleria Brera Milan/Dagli Orti; **174** (l)Biblioteca Reale, Turin/Bridgeman Art Library, (r)akg-images; **178** (l)Private Collection/Bridgeman Art Library, (r)Bettmann/CORBIS; **180** Foto Marburg/Art Resource, NY; **184** (l)Francis G. Mayer/CORBIS, (r)Art Archive/Musée Granet Aix-en-Provence/Dagli Orti; **188** (t)Scala/Art Resource, NY, (c b)Bettmann/CORBIS; **192** The Granger Collection, New York; **192–193** Elk Photography; **193** Scala/Art Resource, NY; **197** (l)Art Archive/Marine Museum, Lisbon/Dagli Orti, (r)Bettmann/CORBIS; **198** Shannon Stapleton/Reuters/CORBIS; **200** (t)Art Archive/Musée de la Marine, Paris/Dagli Orti, (b)The Granger Collection, New York; **202** (cw from top)Punchstock, (2)Alamy Images, (3)Getty Images, (4)C Squared Studios/Getty Images, (5)Punchstock, (6)PhotoAlto/Getty Images; **202–203** Art Archive/Bibliothèque des Arts Décoratifs Paris; **203** (cw from top)Alan and Sandy Carey/Getty Images, (2)CORBIS, (3)Artville/Getty Images, (4)Brand X Pictures/Punchstock, (5)Artville/Getty Images, (6)Punchstock; **206** Mary Evans Picture Library; **210** The Granger Collection, New York; **212** (t)Charles Walker/Topham/The Image Works, (c)Bildarchiv Preussischer Kulturbesitz/Art Resource, NY, (b)North Wind Picture Archives/Alamy Images; **216** (l)Charles Dixon (1924)/Mary Evans Picture Library, (r)Private Collection/Dinodia/Bridgeman Art Library; **216–217** Gail Mooney/Masterfile; **217** Stock Montage/Hulton Archive/Getty Images; **223** Giraudon/Bridgeman Art Library; **226** (l)Private Collection/Christie's Images/Bridgeman Art Library, (r)Topham/The Image Works; **229** (l)Art Archive/Dagli Orti, (r)Giraudon/Bridgeman Art Library; **234** (t)Archivo Iconografico, S.A./CORBIS, (b)Gian Berto Vanni/CORBIS; **235** (t)Author's Image/Alamy Images, (b)Tony Craddock/Getty Images; **237** (t)Alinari Archives/CORBIS, (b)Joseph Martin/Bridgeman Art Library; **239** Victoria & Albert Museum, London/Art Resource, NY; **240** Bob Daemmrich/PhotoEdit; **242** (t)Scala/Art Resource, NY, (c)Private Collection/Bridgeman Art Library, (b)Erich Lessing/Art Resource, NY; **246** (l)Erich Lessing/Art Resource, NY, (r)Bridgeman Art Library; **246–247** Manish Swarup/AP Images; **247** National Portrait Gallery, Smithsonian Institution/Art Resource, NY; **251** (inset)age fotostock/SuperStock, (bkgd)Arthus-Bertrand/CORBIS; **252** Ali Meyer/CORBIS; **254** Araldo de Luca/CORBIS; **255** (t)HIP/Art Resource, NY, (b)Erich Lessing/Art Resource, NY; **257** age fotostock/SuperStock; **258** Ed Kashi/CORBIS; **264** (l)Private Collection/Dinodia/Bridgeman Art Library, (r)Stapleton Collection/Victoria & Albert Museum, London/Bridgeman Art Library; **266** National Portrait Gallery, London; **268** (t)Stapleton Collection, UK/Bridgeman Art Library, (c)The Metropolitan Museum of Art/Art Resource, NY, (b)David Ball/Spectrum Colour Library/Imagestate; **272** (l)Collection of the New York Historical Society/Bridgeman Art Library, (r)National Museum of Ancient Art, Lisbon, Portugal/Bridgeman Art Library; **272–273** Yann Layma/The Image Bank/Getty Images; **273** Erich Lessing/Art Resource, NY; **278** Visual Arts Library, London/Alamy Images; **281** Free Library, Philadelphia/Bridgeman Art Library; **282** Museum of East Asian Art/HIP/The Image Works; **286** (l)Bridgeman Art Library/Getty Images, (r)Christie's Images/SuperStock; **288** Chris Ware/The Image Works; **292** The British Library/Heritage Images/Imagestate; **296** (t)Historical Picture

PHOTO CREDTIS

Archive/CORBIS, (c)Réunion des Musées Nationaux/Art Resource, NY, (b)Bridgeman Art Library; **300** Galleria Palatina, Palazzo Pitti, Florence/Bridgeman Art Library; **300–301** Scott Gilchrist/Masterfile; **301** (t)Joseph Sohm/Jupiter Images, (b)Hu Weibiao/Panorama/The Image Works; **305** (l)Scala/Art Resource, NY, (r)Galleria Palatina, Palazzo Pitti, Florence/Bridgeman Art Library; **306** Johann Brandst/akg-images; **313** (l)Musee de la Ville de Paris, Musee Carnavalet, Paris/Lauros/Giraudon/Bridgeman Art Library, (r)Bettmann/CORBIS; **314** Bettmann/CORBIS; **316** Art Archive/City Temple, London/Eileen Tweedy; **320** (l)Kurpfalzisches Museum, Heidelberg, Germany/Lauros/Giraudon/Bridgeman Art Library, (r)Art Archive/Museum der Stadt, Vienna/Dagli Orti; **321** (l)Art Archive/Russian Historical Museum, Moscow/Dagli Orti, (r)Louvre, Paris/Giraudon/Bridgeman Art Library; **325** CORBIS; **326** Erich Lessing/Private Collection/Art Resource, NY; **328 329** Réunion des Musées Nationaux/Art Resource, NY; **332** Joel Page/AP Images; **334** (t b)North Wind Picture Archives/Alamy Images, (c)Bettmann/CORBIS; **338** Bridgeman-Giraudon/Art Resource, NY; **338–339** John Lamb/Getty Images; **339** (l)Art Archive/Antochiw Collection, Mexico/Mireille Vautier, (r)Art Archive/Musée de L'Armée, Paris/Dagli Orti; **341** Erich Lessing/Art Resource, NY; **342–343** akg-images; **344** Giraudon/Art Resource, NY; **346** Bob Adelman/Magnum Photos; **351** Mary Evans Picture Library; **352** (l)Erich Lessing/Art Resource, NY, (r)Explorer/E.S. Collection/Mary Evans Picture Library; **354** (l)Musée Carnavalet, Paris/Giraudon/Bridgeman Art Library, (r)Mary Evans Picture Library; **355** (l)Private Collection/Bridgeman Art Library, (r)Archivo Iconografico, S.A./CORBIS; **356** George Cruikshank, The Radical's Arms, November 13, 1819. Etching with hand coloring. Published by George Humphrey, London, England. Collection of the Grunwald Center for the Graphic Arts, Hammer Museum, UCLA. Richard Vogler Cruikshank Collection; **359** Erich Lessing/Art Resource, NY; **361** Art Archive/Dagli Orti; **362** Kress Collection, Washington, D.C./Bridgeman Art Library; **368** (t)Musée des Beaux-Arts, France/Giraudon/Art Resource, NY, (c)Erich Lessing/Art Resource, NY, (b)Giraudon/Art Resource, NY; **371** The Granger Collection, New York; **374–375** Adoc-photos/Art Resource, NY; **376** Erich Lessing/Art Resource, NY; **376–377** Keith Levitt/Index Stock Imagery; **377** (t)Private Collection/Bridgeman Art Library, (b)Archives Charmet, Bibliotheque des Arts Decoratifs, Paris, France/Bridgeman Art Library; **381** Mary Evans Picture Library; **382** Science Museum/SSPL/The Image Works; **384** Mary Evans Picture Library; **387** Bettmann/CORBIS; **391** Bibliotheque Nationale, Paris/Bridgeman Art Library; **397** (l)SuperStock, (r)Art Archive/Museo Civico Cremona/Dagli Orti; **398** HIP-Archive/Topham/The Image Works; **400** Private Collection/Bridgeman Art Library; **403** Giraudon/Art Resource, NY; **404** (t)SuperStock, (b)MEPL/The Image Works; **406** Galerie Neue Meister, Dresden, Germany/Staatliche Kunstsammlungen Dresden/Bridgeman Art Library; **408–409** Time & Life Pictures/Getty Images; **410** (t)Yale Center for British Art, Paul Mellon Collection/Bridgeman Art Library, (c)Archives Charmet, Musee de la Ville de Paris, Musee Carnavalet, Paris/Bridgeman Art Library, (b)Musee des Beaux-Arts, Rouen, France/Bridgeman Art Library; **414** Bettmann/CORBIS; **414–415** ND/Roger Viollet/Getty Images; **415** (t)Swim Ink 2/CORBIS, (b)Mary Evans Picture Library/The Image Works; **418** AFP/Getty Images; **420** Bildarchiv Preussischer Kulturbesitz/Art Resource, NY; **425** Michelle D. Bridwell/PhotoEdit; **427** Hulton-Deutsch Collection/CORBIS; **428** (inset)Bettmann/CORBIS, (bkgd)Lake County Museum/CORBIS; **435 436** Bettmann/CORBIS; **439** (l)Digital Image © The Museum of Modern Art/Licensed by SCALA/Art Resource, NY, (r)Réunion des Musées Nationaux/Art Resource, NY; **441** Bettmann/CORBIS; **442** (l)Michael Nicholson/CORBIS, (r)Imagno/Getty Images; **444** (t)Imperial Cadett School/Scherl/SV-Bilderdienst/The Image Works, (c b)Roger-Viollet/The Image Works; **447** CORBIS; **448** (l)Private Collection/Bridgeman Art Library, (r)Chicago Historical Museum/Bridgeman Art Library; **448–449** Robert Harding World Imagery/Getty Images; **449** Hulton-Deutsch Collection/CORBIS; **453** Library of Congress, LC-USZ62-52583; **454 458** Mary Evans Picture Library; **460** (l)Topham/The Image Works, (r)The British Library/HIP/The Image Works; **462** (l)Hulton-Deutsch Collection/CORBIS, (r)Library of Congress, Prints & Photographs Division, NYWT&S Collection, LC-USZ62-130451; **464** Mary Evans Picture Library; **465** (t)akg-images, (b)Alinari Archives/The Image Works; **467** Hulton-Deutsch Collection/CORBIS; **470** (l)Time & Life Pictures/Getty Images, (r)DPA/The Image Works; **474** (l)Bettmann/CORBIS, (r)Private Collection/Archives Charmet/Bridgeman Art Library; **477** Bettmann/CORBIS; **478** Underwood & Underwood/CORBIS; **482** (t)Art Archive/Museo Civico Revoltella Trieste/Dagli Orti, (c)British Library, London/Bridgeman Art Library, (b)Royal Geographical Society, London/Bridgeman Art Library; **486** (t)Topham/The Image Works, (b)Bettmann/CORBIS; **486–487** GP Bowater/Alamy Images; **487** rochaphoto/Alamy Images; **491** Art Archive/Eileen Tweedy; **492** (l)Mary Evans Picture Library/The Image Works, (r)Hu Weibiao/Panorama/The Image Works; **494 498** Bettmann/CORBIS; **500** Mary Evans Picture Library/The Image Works; **505** Twphoto/CORBIS; **506** Asian Art & Archaeology/CORBIS; **508** Bettmann/CORBIS; **512** (t)Ann Ronan Picture Library/HIP/The Image Works, (c)Hulton Archive/Getty Images, (b)Private Collection/Bridgeman Art Library; **515** Bettmann/CORBIS; **518–519** Three Lions/Getty Images; **520** Bettmann/CORBIS; **520–521** Topham/The Image Works; **521** (l)Bettmann/CORBIS, (r)CORBIS; **524** Bettmann/CORBIS; **528** Hulton-Deutsch Collection/CORBIS; **529** (l)Bettmann/CORBIS, (r)Hulton-Deutsch Collection/CORBIS; **530** (l)Bettmann/CORBIS, (r)Mary Evans Picture Library; **532** Underwood & Underwood/CORBIS; **539** RIA Novosti/Tretyakov Gallery, Moscow/Bridgeman Art Library; **540** Snark/Art Resource, NY; **545** Lebrecht Music & Arts/The Image Works; **546** Imperial War Museum/akg-images; **548** (t)Private Collection/Bridgeman Art Library, (c)Delaware Art Museum/Bridgeman Art Library, (b)Albert Harlingue/Roger-Viollet/The Image Works; **552** Ann Ronan Picture Library/Heritage-Images/The Image Works; **552–553** Bettmann/CORBIS; **553** (l)Mary Evans Picture Library, (r)Bettmann/CORBIS; **557** (t)akg-images, (b)Art Archive/Imperial War Museum; **558** Bettmann/CORBIS; **562** (l)akg-images, (r)Underwood & Underwood/CORBIS; **566** (t)Art Archive/Reina Sofia Museum, Madrid, (b)akg-images; **569 571** Mary Evans Picture Library/The Image Works; **572** (t)Mary Evans Picture Library/The Image Works, (b)Bettmann/CORBIS; **574** Stapleton Collection/CORBIS; **575** CORBIS; **577** (l)CORBIS, (r)Bettmann/CORBIS; **578** Najlah Feanny/CORBIS; **580** (t)Bettmann/CORBIS, (c)Mary Evans Picture Library/The Image Works, (b)Hulton-Deutsch Collection/CORBIS; **583** CORBIS; **584** Mary Evans Picture Library/The Image Works; **584–585** Bettmann/CORBIS; **585** Mary Evans Picture Library/The Image Works; **588** Private Collection/Bridgeman Art Library; **595** (l)Tim Page/CORBIS, (r)Hulton-Deutsch Collection/CORBIS; **597** (t)Bettmann/CORBIS, (b)Margaret Bourke-White/Time & Life Pictures/Getty Images; **598** Myrleen Ferguson Cate/PhotoEdit; **602** Private Collection/Bridgeman Art Library; **604** Time Inc./Time & Life Pictures/Getty Images; **612** Schalkwijk/Art Resource, NY; **614** (t)S.M./SV-Bilderdienst/The Image Works, (c)State Russian Museum, St. Petersburg/Bridgeman Art Library, (b)SSPL/The Image Works; **617** Bettmann/CORBIS; **618** (t)David J. & Janice L. Frent Collection/CORBIS, (b)Bettmann/CORBIS; **618–619** CORBIS; **619** Bettmann/CORBIS; **623** CORBIS; **627** Bettmann/CORBIS; **629** Fox Photos/Getty Images; **634** Bettmann/CORBIS; **636** (l)AP Images, (r)Hulton Deutsch Collection/CORBIS; **637** (t)Three Lions/Getty Images, (b)Peter J. Carroll/AP Images; **641** dpa/CORBIS; **642** Evan Vucci/AP Images; **645** (l)CORBIS, (r)Laski Diffusion/Getty Images; **646** CORBIS; **649** (t)Bettmann/CORBIS, (b)Peace Memorial Museum/epa/CORBIS; **652** (l)Bettmann/CORBIS, (r)Fox Photos/Getty Images; **653** (t)Hulton Archive/Getty Images, (b)NRM/SSPL/The Image Works; **654** (t)Bettmann/CORBIS, (c)Jeffrey Markowitz/CORBIS, (b)Hulton-Deutsch Collection/CORBIS; **660–661** Patrick Robert/CORBIS SYGMA; **662** Science Museum/SSPL/The Image Works; **662–663** Bettmann/CORBIS; **663** (t)Bettmann/CORBIS, (b)Walter Dhladhla/AFP/Getty Images; **667** Bettmann/CORBIS; **668** AP Images; **670** Library of Congress, LC-USZ62-130423; **672 673** AP Images; **675** akg-images; **676** Bettmann/CORBIS; **680** Johannes Eisele/AFP/Getty Images; **683** Francis Miller/Time & Life Pictures/Getty Images; **684** NASA/Roger Ressmeyer/CORBIS; **686** Michael Ochs Archive/CORBIS; **687** Harry Diltz/CORBIS; **688** (t)Bettmann/CORBIS, (c)Look and Learn/Bridgeman Art Library, (b)Bettmann/CORBIS; **692** Bettmann/CORBIS; **692–693** Tom Stoddart/Getty Images; **693** Digital Vision/Getty Images; **697** Peter Turnley/CORBIS; **698** (t)Patrick Chauvel/Sygma/CORBIS, (b)Steve Raymer/CORBIS; **702** Lynne Fernandes/The Image Works; **706** Philip Wolmuth/Alamy Images; **708** Ali Al-Saadi/AFP/Getty Images;

711 (inset)Matthias Rietschel/AP Images, (bkgd)Marco Cristofori/ CORBIS; 712 Shepard Sherbell/CORBIS; 716 (l)Getty Images, (r)Michael Ochs Archives/CORBIS; 717 (t)Pictorial Press Ltd/Alamy Images, (b)Robert Grossman/Africaphotos.com; 718 (t)Tom Stoddart/Getty Images, (c)Alan Lewis/CORBIS SYGMA, (b)Bettmann/ CORBIS; 722 Lester Cole/CORBIS; 722–723 Alejandro Ernesto/ epa/CORBIS; 723 (t)Susana Gonzalez/Bloomberg News/Landov, (b)Boris Yurchenko/AP Images; 732 734 CORBIS; 738 Carlos Carrion/Sygma/CORBIS; 740 Bernard Bisson/CORBIS SYGMA; 744 (t)Rika/dpa/CORBIS, (c)Bettmann/CORBIS, (b)Diego Goldberg/ Sygma/CORBIS; 748 (t)Rick Barrentine/CORBIS, (b)Adam Woolfitt/ CORBIS; 748–749 CORBIS; 749 Martin H. Simon/CORBIS; 752 (l)Al Fenn/Time & Life Pictures/Getty Images, (r)PA/Topham/The Image Works; 755 Peter Turnley/CORBIS; 756 David Turnley/CORBIS; 764 David Brauchli/CORBIS SYGMA; 766 Chao Soi Cheong/AP Images; 769 Jonathan Shapiro; 770 (t)Gideon Mendel/CORBIS, (c)Reuters/CORBIS, (b)Charles O. Cecil/The Image Works; 774 Bettmann/CORBIS; 774–775 Michael Von Ruber/Imagestate; 775 Francoise Demulder/CORBIS; 779 Bettmann/CORBIS; 784 (l)Henri Bureau/Sygma/CORBIS, (r)Bettmann/CORBIS; 786 Christian Simonpietri/Sygma/CORBIS; 791 Steve & Ghy Sampson/Getty Images; 792 Kim Kyung-Hoon/Reuters/CORBIS; 796 (t)Hulton Archive/Getty Images, (c)Bettmann/CORBIS, (b)Michael S. Yamashita/CORBIS; 800 (l)Alfred Eisenstaedt/Time & Life Pictures/ Getty Images, (r)Caroline Penn/CORBIS; 800–801 Jorgen Schytte/ Peter Arnold, Inc.; 801 Reuters/CORBIS; 803 Bettmann/CORBIS; 807 Mark Edwards/Peter Arnold, Inc.; 808 Phillipe Lissac/Godong/ CORBIS; 810 Kim Kulish/CORBIS; 813 Ron Giling/Peter Arnold, Inc.;

815 Reed Saxon/AP Images; 816 Chip East/Reuters/CORBIS; 818 (t)CORBIS, (c)Radar Bali/AP Images, (b)Viviane Moos/CORBIS; 821 Kjell Nilsson-Maki/CartoonStock; R1 (l)Francis G. Mayer/ CORBIS, (r)Bettmann/CORBIS; R12 Chad Baker-Ryan McVay/Getty Images; R13 Richard I'Anson/Lonely Planet Images; R14 Thomas Dworzak/Magnum Photos; R16 Robert Frerck/Odyssey Productions; R17 SuperStock; R22 Imagno/Getty Images; R30 Jonathan Shapiro; R32 Réunion des Musées Nationaux/Art Resource, NY; R33 (t)CORBIS, (b)Main Commission for the Investigation of Nazi War Crimes, courtesy of the United States Holocaust Memorial Museum; R34 Art Archive/Dagli Orti; R35 (l)Réunion des Musées Nationaux/Art Resource, NY, (r)Scala/ Art Resource, NY; R36 (t)Erich Lessing/Art Resource, NY, (b)Alinari/ Art Resource, NY; R37 Hervé Lewandowski/Réunion des Musées Nationaux/Art Resource, NY; R38 Scala/Art Resource, NY; R39 Peter Willi/Superstock; R40 (t)Mary Evans Picture Library, (b)The Metropolitan Museum of Art, Edward Elliott Family Collection. Purchase, The Dillon Fund Gift, 1982. 1982.2.2; R41 Burstein Collection/CORBIS; R42 (t)Stock Montage, (b)Art Archive/University Library Geneva/Dagli Orti; R43 Lowe Art Museum/Superstock; R44 Bridgeman-Giraudon/Art Resource, NY; R45 Art Archive/Musée du Chateau de Versailles/Dagli Orti; R46 R48 Hulton Archive/Getty Images; R49 Mary Evans Picture Library; R50 Bridgeman Art Library; R51 Hulton-Deutsch Collection/CORBIS; R52 Bettmann/CORBIS; R53 (l)Bettmann/ CORBIS, (r)Private Collection/Bridgeman Art Library; R54 Bettmann/CORBIS; R56 (l)Ho/Suhrkamp/AP Images, (r)Greg Stott/Masterfile; R57 The Butler Institute of American Art.